http://www.porsche.com – Dr. Ing.h.c.F. Porsche AG
http://www.ford.com – Ford Motor Company
http://www.marketfacts.com – Market Facts, Inc.
http://www.jwtworks.com – J. Walter Thompson
http://www.jdpower.com – J.D. Power and Associates
http://www.acnielsen.com – ACNielsen Corporation
http://www.namelab.com – NameLab Inc.
http://www.ama.org – American Marketing Association
http://www.mra-net.org – Marketing Research Association
http://www.ftc.gov – Federal Trade Commission
http://www.hertz.com – The Hertz Corporation
http://www.avis.com – Avis Rent A Car System, Inc.
http://www.aol.com – America Online
http://www.yahoo.com – Yahoo! Inc.
http://www.lycos.com – Lycos, Inc.
http://www.eff.org – Electronic Frontier Foundation
http://www.privacyalliance.org – Online Privacy Alliance
http://www.gallup.com – The Gallup Organization
http://www.npd.com – NPD, Inc.
http://www.careerpath.com – CareerPath.com
http://www.marketresearch.org.uk – United Kingdom's Market Research Society
http://www.aapor.org – American Association for Public Opinion Research
http://www.worldopinion.com – WorldOpinion
http://www.epicurious.com – Epicurious Food

Chapter 5
http://www.rjrt.com – R.J. Reynolds Tobacco Company
http://www.coke.com – The Coca-Cola Company
http://www.pepsico.com – PepsiCo, Inc.
http://www.tm.com – The Times Mirror Company
http://www.irs.gov – Internal Revenue Service

Chapter 6
http://www.galoob.com – Galoob Toys, Inc.
http://www.keebler.com – Keebler Company
http://www.pg.com – Proctor & Gamble
http://www.tgifridays.com – T.G.I. Friday's Inc.
http://www.carnationmilk.com – Nestlè Carnation
http://www.rubbermaid.com – Rubbermaid Inc.
http://www.cdc.gov – Centers for Disease Control and Prevention
http://www.mcdonalds.com – McDonald's Corporation
http://www.jackinthebox.com – Foodmaker, Inc.
http://www.burgerking.com – Burger King Corp.
http://www.wendys.com – Wendy's International, Inc.
http://www.nick.com – Viacom International Inc.
http://www.mercedes-benz.com – DaimlerChrysler
http://www.nescafe.com.au – Nestlè Australia Ltd.

Chapter 7

http://www.ngf.org –
http://www.nsga.org – National Sporting Goods Association
http://www.cmr.com – Competitive Media Reporting
http://www.taylormadegolf.com – Taylor Made Golf
http://www.callawaygolf.com – Callaway Golf
http://www.cobragolf.com – Cobra Golf, Inc.
http://www.titleist.com – Titleist and FootJoy
http://www.arbitron.com – The Arbitron Company
http://www.npd.com – The NPD Group
http://www.acnielsen.com – ACNielsen Corporation
http://www.brunswickbowling.com – Brunswick
http://www.dowjones.com – Dow Jones News
http://www.odci.gov – Central Intelligence Agency
http://www.claritas.com – Claritas Inc.
http://www.microsoft.com – Microsoft Corporation
http://www.wal-mart.com – Wal-Mart Stores, Inc.
http://www.datamindcorp.com – DataMind Corporation
http://www.ibm.com – IBM Corporation
http://www.oracle.com – Oracle Corporation
http://www.ibi.com – Information Builders Inc.
http://www.acxiom.com – Acxiom RTC Inc.
http://www.marriott.com – Marriott International
http://www.libraryspot.com – StartSpot Mediaworks, Inc.
http://www.hoovers.com – Hoover's Company Information
http://www.stat.usa.gov/inqsamle.html – STAT-USA/Internet World Wide Web
http://www.yahoo.com – Yahoo! Inc.
http://www.nabspace.co.nz – National Advertising Bureau
http://www.infoscan.com – Infoscan, Inc.
http://www.yankelovich.com – Yankelovich Partners Inc.
http://www.harrisinteractive.com – Harris Interactive
http://www.natdecsys.com – National decisions Systems
http://www.mediamark.com – MRI Cable Report – Mediamark Research Inc.
http://www.doc.gov – U.S. Department of Commerce
http://www.brint.com – BRINT
http://www.census.gov – U.S. Census Bureau
http://www.sbaonline.sba.gov – Small Business Administration
http://www.findsvp.com – FIND/SVP
http://www.ssb.no – Statistics Norway
http://www.statcan.ca/start.html – Statistics Canada

Chapter 8
http://www.nexis.com – LEXIS-NEXIS a division of Reed Elsevier Inc.
http://www.jdpower.com – J.D. Power and Associates
http://www.toyota.com – Toyota

DON'T FORGET
TO SUBSCRIBE TODAY!

In order to start receiving issues of *AMERICAN DEMOGRAPHICS*, complete the card and return today. It's that easy to subscribe!

EXPLORING MARKETING RESEARCH
SEVENTH EDITION

EXPLORING MARKETING RESEARCH
SEVENTH EDITION

WILLIAM G. ZIKMUND
Oklahoma State University

THE DRYDEN PRESS
HARCOURT COLLEGE PUBLISHERS

Fort Worth   Philadelphia   San Diego   New York   Orlando   Austin   San Antonio
Toronto   Montreal   London   Sydney   Tokyo

Publisher	MIKE ROCHE
Acquisitions Editor	BILL SCHOOF
Market Strategist	LISÉ JOHNSON
Developmental Editor	JANA PITTS
Project Editor	COLBY ALEXANDER
Art Director	BURT SLOAN
Production Manager	CINDY YOUNG
Cover Artist	HUMBERTO CALZADA

Address for Domestic Orders:
The Dryden Press, 6277 Sea Harbor Drive, Orlando, FL 32887-6777

Address for International Orders:
International Customer Service
The Dryden Press, 6277 Sea Harbor Drive, Orlando, FL 32887-6777
407-345-3800
(fax) 407-345-4060
(e-mail) hbintl@harcourtbrace.com

Address for Editorial Correspondence:
The Dryden Press, 301 Commerce Street, Suite 3700, Fort Worth, TX 76102

Web Site Address:
http://www.harcourtcollege.com
THE DRYDEN PRESS, DRYDEN, and the DP LOGO are registered trademarks of Harcourt Brace & Company.

ISBN: 0-03-026218-6
Library of Congress Catalog Card Number: 99-64502

Printed in the United States of America

9 0 1 2 3 4 5 6 7 8 048 9 8 7 6 5 4 3 2 1

The Dryden Press
Harcourt College Publishers

To Sybil

The Dryden Press Series in Marketing

Assael
Marketing

Avila, Williams, Ingram, and LaForge
The Professional Selling Skills Workbook

Bateson
Managing Services Marketing: Text and Readings
Third Edition

Blackwell, Blackwell, and Talarzyk
Contemporary Cases in Consumer Behavior
Fourth Edition

Boone and Kurtz
Contemporary Marketing WIRED
Ninth Edition

Boone and Kurtz
Contemporary Marketing 1999

Churchill
Basic Marketing Research
Third Edition

Churchill
Marketing Research: Methodological Foundations
Seventh Edition

Czinkota and Ronkainen
Global Marketing

Czinkota and Ronkainen
International Marketing
Fifth Edition

Czinkota and Ronkainen
International Marketing Strategy: Environmental Assessment and Entry Strategies

Dickson
Marketing Management
Second Edition

Dunne and Lusch
Retailing
Third Edition

Engel, Blackwell, and Miniard
Consumer Behavior
Eighth Edition

Ferrell, Hartline, Lucas, Luck
Marketing Strategy

Futrell
Sales Management: Teamwork, Leadership, and Technology
Fifth Edition

Grover
Theory & Simulation of Market-Focused Management

Ghosh
Retail Management
Second Edition

Hoffman
Marketing: Best Practices

Hoffman/Bateson
Essentials of Services Marketing
Fourth Edition

Hutt and Speh
Business Marketing Management: A Strategic View of Industrial and Organizational Markets
Sixth Edition

Ingram
Selling

Ingram, LaForge, and Schwepker
Sales Management: Analysis and Decision Making
Fourth Edition

Lindgren and Shimp
Marketing: An Interactive Learning System

Krugman, Reid, Dunn, and Barban
Advertising: Its Role in Modern Marketing
Eighth Edition

Oberhaus, Ratliffe, and Stauble
Professional Selling: A Relationship Process
Second Edition

Parente
Advertising Campaign Strategy: A Guide to Marketing Communication Plans
Second Edition

Reedy
Electronic Marketing

Rosenbloom
Marketing Channels: A Management View
Sixth Edition

Sandburg
Discovering Your Marketing Career CD-ROM

Schaffer
Applying Marketing Principles Software

Schaffer
The Marketing Game

Schellinck and Maddox
Marketing Research: A Computer-Assisted Approach

Schnaars
MICROSIM

Schuster and Copeland
Global Business: Planning for Sales and Negotiations

Sheth, Mittal, and Newman
Customer Behavior: Consumer Behavior and Beyond

Shimp
Advertising and Promotions: Supplemental Aspects of Integrated Marketing Communications
Fifth Edition

Stauble
Marketing Strategy: A Global Perspective

Talarzyk
Cases and Exercises in Marketing

Terpstra and Sarathy
International Marketing
Eighth Edition

Watson
Electronic Commerce

Weitz and Wensley
Readings in Strategic Marketing Analysis, Planning, and Implementation

Zikmund
Exploring Marketing Research
Seventh Edition

Zikmund
Essentials of Marketing Research

Harcourt Brace College Outline Series

Peterson
Principles of Marketing

PRINCIPLES OF MARKETING

NEW FOR 2000! Czimkota, Dickson, Dunne, Griffin, Hoffman, Hutt, Lindgren, Lusch, Ronkainen, Rosenbloom, Sheth, Shimp, Siguaw, Simpson, Speh, & Urbany, *Marketing: Best Practices* 0-03-021109-3
The Dryden Press has brought together sixteen of the best and brightest authors in marketing to create the most cutting-edge text to hit the principles market in years. The premise behind Marketing: Best Practices was to combine the expertise of leading marketers into a principles text that offers the best of the best in every chapter. Each chapter is penned by an authority from that particular field of marketing, many of whom are widely renowned inside the classroom and the boardroom for their marketing acumen. This revolutionary new text combines the best practices from every area of marketing—from advertising to services, consumer behavior to retailing, international to technology.

Assael, *Marketing* (1998) 0-03-024811-6 (Chapters 1-10) or 0-15-560772-3 (Chapters 1-23)
Offering complete classroom flexibility, this innovative new edition enables instructors to custom design a principles of marketing text to meet their students' particular needs. Written by a renowned marketing authority, the text includes 10 "core" chapters focusing on the "4 P's" as well as a choice of 13 "optional" chapters, enabling instructors to choose the topics they teach and incorporate outside materials into the classroom.

Boone and Kurtz, *Contemporary Marketing 1999* (1999) 0-03-022313-X
Best-selling authors Boone and Kurtz continue to lead the market with their innovative, up-to-the-minute, student-friendly texts. This 1999 paperback edition is a completely updated version of the best-selling 1998 *Contemporary Marketing Wired* text at a reduced price.

Boone and Kurtz, Contemporary Marketing WIRED (1998) 0-03-018597-1
Nine editions of continuous improvement have led to the most exciting introductory marketing text and package in classroom history, and this edition continues to set new standards as the market leader.

Lindgren and Shimp, *Marketing: An Interactive Learning System* (1996) 0-03-017479-1
This new CD-ROM learning system is available as a "runtime" package to instructors and students, bringing a 21st century dimension to exploring the world of marketing in the classroom.

Sandburg, *Discovering Your Marketing Career CD-ROM* 0-03-19157-2
Discovering Your Marketing Career helps students assess their compatibility with careers in marketing and land the job of their choice. In one multi-media CD-ROM program, students receive broad guidance and practical advice on everything from clarifying their interest in a particular marketing career to preparing and implementing an effective job search strategy.

CONSUMER BEHAVIOR

Engel, Blackwell, and Miniard, *Consumer Behavior, Eighth Edition* (1995) 0-03-098464-5
Diverse and balanced coverage of consumer behavior research in theory and application, from some of the pioneering authors in this field.

Sheth, Mittal, and Newman, *Customer Behavior: Consumer Behavior and Beyond* (1999) 0-03-098016-X
Customer behavior seeks to make a connection between customer behavior principles and the elements of marketing strategy. This anxiously anticipated text goes beyond traditional consumer behavior books by focusing not only on the behavior of "buyers," but also on the behavior of users and payers.

ADVERTISING AND PROMOTION

NEW FOR 2000! Parente, *Advertising Campaign Strategy: A Guide to Marketing Communication Plans, Second Edition* 0-03-021114-X
This leading text not only illustrates what effective advertising campaigns are, but it also illustrates how to successfully execute them. A comprehensive and detailed campaign guide is outlined to take students step-by-step through the advertising process. Nine out of the top!) advertising and journalism schools in the US use Parente's Advertising Campaign Strategy.

NEW FOR 2000: Shimp, *Advertising, Promotion, and Supplemental Aspects of Integrated Marketing Communications, Fifth Edition* 0-03-021113-1
The fifth edition of Terence Shimp's market-leading *Advertising, Promotion and Supplemental Aspects of Integrated Marketing Communications* fully integrates all aspects of marketing communication, providing a more complete treatment of sales promotion, point-of-purchase communications, and advertising media selection than any text on the market.

SALES MANAGEMENT

NEW FOR 2000! Ingram, LaForge, & Schwepker, *Sales Management, Fourth Edition* 0-03-026699-8
This leading text continues to set the standard in sales management texts with its up-to-the-minute coverage of the trends and issues in the dynamics sales field, equipping students with a strong sales foundation and the innovative skills needed for 21st century selling.

Futrell, Sales Management: *Teamwork, Leadership, and Technology, Fifth Edition* (1998) 0-03-010629-X
Completely revised and updated for 21st century selling, this popular text has been renamed and revamped to reflect issues affecting salespeople today and well beyond.

PERSONAL/PROFESSIONAL SELLING

NEW FOR 2000: Ingram, LaForge, Avila, Schwepker, & Williams, *Selling* 0-03-026701-3
Selling's professional selling chapters can be mixed and matched with sales management chapters from Ingram's Sales Management, Fourth Edition to create an outstanding customized sales course.

Oberhaus, Ratliffe, and Stauble, *Professional Selling: A Relationship Process* (1995) 0-03-000639-2
This leading edge text is designed to be the conceptual core for the competency-based learning system. It links the firm's marketing philosophy with a relational selling approach using sales communication skills.

INTERNATIONAL MARKETING

NEW FOR 2000! Terpstra and Sarathy, *International Marketing, Eighth Edition* 0-03-02112-3
The Eighth Edition of this popular text has been completely revised, reflecting current developments in the field. Drawing on the extensive and unparalleled international marketing experience of its authors, *International Marketing* takes a comprehensive look at the environment, problems, and practices of today's international marketing arena.

Czinkota and Ronkainen, *Global Marketing* (1996) 0-03-010649-4
This text covers managerial issues in marketing from a truly global perspective, looking at management concepts from the view of a firm that operates worldwide. Government issues are also addressed and analyzed from a viewpoint not limited to the US.

Czinkota and Ronkainen, *International Marketing, Fifth Edition* (1998) 0-03-024401-3
The market leading text which is best known for its extremely current coverage, unique chapter coverage, and prestigious author team who have consulted all of the world.

Czinkota and Ronkainen, *Readings in International Marketing Strategy: Environmental Assessment and Entry Strategies* (1995) 0-03-098373-8
This reader deals with the environment, external and internal strategic dimensions

and implementation considerations from the viewpoint of the new entrant into the international market.

Hassan, *Global Marketing: Perspectives & Cases* (1994) 0-03-098107-7
This book delivers current, innovative, and thought-provoking methods on how to identify intermarket opportunities in a globally competitive environment, thereby providing international marketing students with the tools and framework necessary to profile intermarket segments.

Schuster and Copeland, *Global Business: Planning for Sales and Negotiations* (1996) 0-03-010519-6
Written for undergraduates, graduate students, and executives in training, *Global Business* is a useful tool for anyone involved in business or government transactions with someone from another country.

For a complimentary examination copy, please call 1.800.237.2665. And don't forget to visit us online at www.dryden.com!

MARKETING RESEARCH

NEW FOR 2000! Zikmund, *Exploring Marketing Research, Seventh Edition* 0-03-026218-6
This comprehensive, practical, and extremely student-friendly market leader offers the most up-to-date coverage of the current marketing research issues available. Intended primarily for undergraduates, this best-seller emphasizes such important issues as total quality management and global marketing research, integrating both topics throughout the text.

Churchill, *Basic Marketing Research, Third Edition* (1996) 0-03-098367-3
This leading introductory text breaks the complex maze of marketing research down into seven straightforward stages. A managerial emphasis, new photo essays, profiles of marketing research professionals, and real research studies provide excellent views of modern practices in the field.

Churchill, Marketing Research: Methodological Foundations, Seventh Edition (1999) 0-03-023816-1
This market leader has established itself as a classic by presenting its material from both a quantitative and qualitative perspective, and allowing students to develop an appreciation for the six stages of the research process. *Marketing Research* is the market leader at the graduate level.

Zikmund, *Essentials of Marketing Research* (1999) 0-03-024356-4
In response to market feedback, Zikmund and The Dryden Press have developed this new abridged version of the best selling *Exploring Marketing Research*. This new text was designed specifically for marketing research classes where a more concise introduction to marketing research topics is desired.

MARKETING MANAGEMENT & MARKETING STRATEGY

NEW FOR 2000! Stauble, *Marketing Strategy: A Global Perspective* 0-03-026216-X
Marketing Strategy: A Global Perspective introduces strategic applications, global strategy, and emerging perspectives in an approach that captures the challenges of marketing strategy. It is designed to help students integrate the "4 Ps" of marketing in a broader framework with a strategic application in addressing global strategy.

Ferrell, Hartline, Lucas and Luck, *Marketing Strategy* 0-03-024801-9
Marketing Strategy is presented from a perspective that guides strategic marketing management in the social, economic, and technological arenas in which businesses function today. This text helps students develop a customer-oriented market strategy and market plan.

Dickson, *Marketing Management, Second Edition* (1997) 0-03-017742-1
This text presents cutting-edge marketing management concepts in a traditional format, supplemented by the market's most innovative teaching tools.

Lewison, *Marketing Management: An Overview* (1996) 0-03-098153-0
This text provides an alternative to the traditional marketing management texts in the market by offering a concise overview for the advanced level marketing course, enabling instructors to incorporate other materials, such as cases, into the course.

RETAILING/RETAIL MANAGEMENT

Dunne and Lusch, *Retailing, Third Edition* (1999) 0-03-024758-6
The third edition of *Retailing*, like much of retailing itself, has undergone significant changes from prior editions. Given the impact of the Internet and the "global village," there has never been a more exciting time to study retailing—and this text addresses just those issues in great depth.

MARKETING SERVICES

Bateson, *Managing Services Marketing: Text and Readings, Fourth Edition* (1999) 0-03-022519-1
Bateson's latest edition of this market leading text combines coverage of key topics in services marketing with a variety of articles selected from such areas as marketing, organizational behavior, operations management, and strategy literature. The increased emphasis on services in the marketing field has led us to develop the current balance of text and readings. In addition to the marketing departments, services courses may also be found in areas such as hotel/hospitality management.

Hoffman and Bateson, *Essentials of Marketing of Services* (1997) 0-03-015217-8
Designed especially for the undergraduate, this unique text goes beyond the "common sense" approach to customer service and concentrates on 15 core topics (in 15 chapters), giving students a solid understanding of the complex relationships existing between employees, the organization and the customer as they relate to service issues.

MARKETING CHANNELS

Rosenbloom, *Marketing Channels: A Management View, Sixth Edition* (1999) 0-03-024482-X
This market-leading text brings the field of marketing channels to life and contributes to the making of each marketing channels course with its classic managerial framework. Rosenbloom continues to set the standard as the premier text in the field by examining channel management, relationship marketing and the role of technology as marketing channels move into the 21st century.

INDUSTRIAL MARKETING

Hutt and Speh, *Business Marketing Management: A Strategic View of Industrial and Organizational Markets , Sixth Edition* (1998) 0-03-020633-2
Providing the most current and complete treatment of business-to-business marketing, this comprehensive market leader captures and integrates the latest developments in market analysis, relationship management, supply chain management, and marketing strategy development.

INTERNET MARKETING

NEW FOR 2000! Reedy, Schullo, & Zimmerman, Electronic Marketing Integrating Electronic Resources into the Marketing Process, First Edition 0-03-021107-7
This innovative and exciting new first edition combines the traditional proven marketing process of situation analysis, marketing planning, and marketing implementation to introduce the enhanced speed, accuracy, and targetability of electronic marketing resources.

ELECTRONIC COMMERCE

NEW FOR 2000! Watson, Berthon, Pitt, & Zinkhan, *Electronic Commerce*, First Edition 0-03-026533-9
This exciting new text from The Dryden Press provides a strategic marketing and managerial perspective of electronic commerce. The research of the four highly-qualified authors provides the basis for the book, allowing for first-hand experience, varied viewpoints, and relevance.

FOR A COMPLIMENTARY EXAMINATION COPY, PLEASE CALL
1.800.237.2665. AND DON'T FORGET TO VISIT US ONLINE AT
WWW.DRYDEN.COM!

Preface

The Seventh Edition of Exploring Marketing Research is copyrighted for the year 2000. This makes it a book for the new millennium. The years between the previous edition of Exploring Marketing Research and this new millennium edition have given rise to e-commerce and an information revolution. It is quite clear that new information technologies and research methodologies that are currently emerging have dramatically changed the nature of marketing research. The Internet's World Wide Web, with its great potential for instantaneous and interactive access to information from around the globe, has brought about one of the most dramatic changes ever to occur in the discipline. However, its future impact will be even more profound. This Seventh Edition of Exploring Marketing Research reflects the astonishing changes in information technology that have taken place in the last few years. I have worked diligently and carefully to make this edition a book that reflects the practice of marketing research in our new digital age.

Although the Seventh Edition is quite different from past editions, it retains the distinguishing attributes previous editions.

ORGANIZATION OF THE BOOK

The organization of the Seventh Edition of Exploring Marketing Research follows the logic of the marketing research process. The book is organized into eight parts. Each part presents the basic research concepts for one of the stages in the research process and discusses how these concepts relate to decisions about conducting specific projects.

- Part 1: *Introduction* discusses the scope of marketing research, provides an overview of the entire marketing research process, and explains the nature of global information systems. It also discusses organizational and ethical issues in marketing research.

- Part 2: *Beginning Stages of the Research Process* covers problem definition, research proposals, exploratory research, and secondary data.

- Part 3: *Research Designs for Collecting Primary Data* examines the concepts and issues related to designing and using surveys, observation studies, and experiments.

- Part 4: *Measurement Concepts* discusses the logic of measurement and the practical issues involved in attitude measurement and questionnaire design.

- Part 5: *Sampling and Fieldwork* explains why sampling is required, how to design samples, how to conduct fieldwork, and how to determine sample size. A review of basic statistical concepts appears in this part of the book.

- Part 6: *Data Analysis and Presentation* covers editing and coding, descriptive data analysis and inferential statistical analysis, and communication of research results. It ends with a final note on the use of marketing research.

- Part 7: *Comprehensive Cases with Computerized Databases* provides materials that challenge students to apply and integrate the concepts they have learned.

- Part 8 provides several video research projects.

NEW TO THE SEVENTH EDITION

Chapter 1 places a new emphasis on relationship marketing so its impact on marketing research can be better illustrated in subsequent chapters.

Each passing year the use of global information systems in business and not-for-profit organizations grows more important. This edition focuses on the latest technological means for instantaneous and interactive access to information from around the globe.

Chapter 2: Information Systems and Knowledge Management has been substantially revised to reflect this focus. This chapter, placed early in the book, sets the stage for a book-long discussion of the Internet and other new technologies influencing marketing research. It begins by making a distinction between *data, information,* and *knowledge* and shows how knowledge management enhances the organization's intellectual capital. The Internet's role in our global, e-commerce economy is introduced in this chapter to serve as a framework for a variety of discussions throughout the book. Specific technical details about secondary data searchers on the Internet are reserved for Chapter 7.

Chapter 4: The Human Side of Marketing Research reflects the growing use of cross-functional teams in marketing research. It provides an early introduction to ethical issues. Concerns about privacy have caught the attention of the public and marketing research world. The impact of new technology on privacy is discussed in depth. Critical thinking questions at the end of the chapter about ethics appear in every chapter following Chapter 4. A special icon ♟ designates these questions.

Chapter 7: Secondary Data in a Digital Age has been substantially revised. The technology is rapidly changing and this new edition is at the cutting edge. This chapter now incorporates discussions of data mining and other new methodologies that are modifying the way marketing researchers view secondary data investigations.

Chapter 8: Survey Research: An Overview and *Chapter 9: Survey Research: Basic Methods of Communication with Respondents* have been updated to reflect the role new technologies, such as answering machines, new caller ID systems, and the Internet.

Chapter 9 expands its coverage of computerized surveys using electronic interactive media, such as the Internet.

Chapter 14: Questionnaire Design now discusses writing questions and formatting Web pages for Internet surveys.

Chapter 15: Sampling Designs and Sampling Procedures now incorporates a new section on sampling problems associated with surveys conducted on the Internet.

To the Point is a new pedagogical feature that provides meaty quotes with valuable insights about research issues.

Various new cases have been added to this new edition. Several of these are new video cases or cases with computerized databases.

Internet sites can add considerable value for students of marketing research. A serious effort has been made to provide current URLs for numerous worthwhile Internet links. These appear in the end of chapter feature called *Exploring the Internet* and through the text itself. These are not just a bunch of shallow links to trivial places, but educational sites where a professor will want his or her students to go to learn more about a concept.

FEATURES STUDENTS WILL LIKE

More than other marketing textbooks, *Exploring Marketing Research*, Seventh Edition, addresses students' need to comprehend the field literally. To achieve these objectives, the text emphasizes the following elements:

- *Numerous, real, easy-to-understand examples* stimulate students to search for additional information about marketing research. The "What Went Wrong?" and "What Went Right?" boxes portray failures and successes in specific marketing research situations.

- *A straightforward prose style* presents a balanced coverage of marketing research as it is actually practiced. This is a comprehensive coverage rather than a superficial treatment of topics. Considerable effort has been directed toward explaining topics with examples that clarify rather than mystify.

- *The text explains statistical concepts* in a simple, straightforward manner. This is a managerially oriented marketing research textbook, not a statistics monograph. The statistical and quantitative aspects of the text were written for those who need a book that provides an understanding of basic concepts. Too many students approach the prospect of statistical material with a great deal of unnecessary trepidation. The text devotes an entire section to a review of statistics. Even students with rusty statistical skills will benefit from a quick review of the basic statistical concepts. "Statistical Tutor" boxes aid in the learning process by visually reflecting statistical concepts.

- *Each chapter begins with a clear statement of learning objectives* to provide students with an expectation of what is to come. Students can also use the objectives to determine whether they understand the major points of the chapter.

- *An opening vignette* describing an actual situation relevant to the chapter focuses students' attention on the pragmatic aspects of each chapter.

- To enhance students' understanding of conceptual materials, *Exploring Marketing Research* includes many exhibits that indicate and *visually highlight ideas* and relationships among variables. A full-color format enhances the imagery and appeal of the artwork and photographs.

- *Learning the vocabulary* of marketing research is essential to understanding the topic. *Exploring Marketing Research* facilitates this in three ways. First, key concepts are boldfaced and completely defined when they first appear in the textbook. Second, all key terms and concepts are listed at the end of each chapter, and many terms are highlighted in a marginal glossary. Third, a glossary summarizing all key terms and definitions appears at the end of the book for handy reference. A glossary of frequently used symbols is also included.

- *End-of-chapter materials* were carefully designed to promote student involvement in the classroom. The end-of-chapter questions for review and critical thinking stimulate thinking about topics beyond the text's coverage. Review materials enhance students' understanding of key concepts.

- *The end-of-chapter cases present interesting, real-life research situations* that require students to make thoughtful decisions. They offer the opportunity for active participation in a decision-making process, one of the most effective forms of learning.

- "Exploring the Internet" exercises appear at the end of every chapter. This feature helps students navigate the Internet. These activities range from going to the Census Bureau's Population Clock to being participants in Internet surveys.

- Several *video research projects* appear in Part 8. A video research project, presented in several segments, is an innovative pedagogical tool that represents an actual research situation. Each segment allows students to think about various decisions and uses a video dramatization to provide an in-depth look at marketing research.

- *Real world video cases* illustrate marketing research in practice. The cases portray actual research activities and companies, such as Fossil, Paradigm Entertainment, and Hard Candy, that conduct marketing research around the world.

- *A Web site* that provides numerous links to other relevant Web sites with marketing research content.

FEATURES THE PROFESSOR WILL LIKE

Materials to supplement the content of the textbook are available to help instructors perform their vital teaching function. The extensive learning package provided with Exploring Marketing Research includes a test bank, a computerized test bank, an instructor's manual, PowerPoint presentation slides, transparency masters, videocassettes containing case materials, a floppy disk containing databases for several cases, a marketing research Web site on the Internet (http://www.dryden.com/marketing/research.html), and other ancillary materials.

- *PowerPoint* is a state-of-the-art presentation graphics program for IBM compatible computers. This integrated program allows instructors to retrieve and edit any of the preloaded transparencies that accompany the book. Images can easily be edited, added, or deleted.

- All chapters that follow Chapter 4: The Human Side of Marketing Research: Organizational and Ethical Issues, include end-of-chapter questions dealing with ethical issues. These questions are marked with a symbol.

- *Video cases with questions for homework assignments or classroom discussion* are included in the text and the *Instructor's Manual*. These cases allow classroom discussions of case solutions to be integrated with video materials. Teaching notes are provided for these video cases as well as for all other cases in the text.

- *Five comprehensive cases appear at the end of the book.* Each case discusses an entire research project and includes a database useful for assignments dealing with statistical analysis.

- All comprehensive cases and several other cases are marked with a symbol to indicate the data set in the case is stored on a floppy disk that is available to instructors.

- A CD-ROM containing the data sets and the student version of SPSS software is available for the students, which allows them to fully develop their computer skills.

- *Video Research Projects* allows professors to involve students and show that marketing research involves various decisions on many projects. Thorndike Sports Equipment uses video dramatization to provide an in-depth look at one organization's use of marketing research. This innovative educational drama consists of five video units especially created for this textbook. Each unit focuses on a particular aspect of a racquetball racquet manufacturer's need for and utilization of marketing research and data analysis. Each unit provides a springboard for classroom discussions.

● A new marketing research *Web site on the Internet* (http://dryden.com/marketing/research.html) enhances the way marketing research can be taught. The Web site will provide the latest information about "what's new" and "what's cool" in marketing research. Links to other research-related sites, tips about using the supplemental video library, and much more are planned for the site.

This book and its supplements are for the undergraduate student who must meet the future challenge of marketing management. The professor should find Exploring Marketing Research a useful aid in facilitating student achievement.

The Dryden Press will provide complimentary supplements or supplement packages to those adopters qualified under its adoption policy. Please contact your local sales representative to learn how you may qualify. If as an adopter or potential user you receive supplements you do not need, please return them to your sales representative or send them to: Attn: Returns Department, Troy Warehouse, 465 South Lincoln Drive, Troy, MO 63379.

ACKNOWLEDGMENTS

The author would like to acknowledge the help of the market researching muse, who came to him at odd times with no understanding of the requirements of family life. The time required to sequester oneself to write a textbook must be paid for by family and friends.

I am deeply indebted to Dr. Don Sciglimpaglia, San Diego State University, who offered encouragement as the book was being conceptualized and read the entire manuscript through several drafts. His many insightful suggestions were adopted with gratitude. John Bush greatly enhanced the book by making numerous suggestions and by providing the first draft of Chapter 25.

I appreciate Guan Kheng "Adam" Low's punctuality, computer skills, and his sincere effort to please. His assistance is greatly appreciated.

Many colleagues contributed ideas for this book. They recommended many suggestions that greatly enhanced this book. For their insightful reviews of the manuscript of the Seventh Edition or reviews of previous editions of Exploring Marketing Research, I would like to thank:

Gerald Albaum, *University of Oregon*
William Bearden, *University of South Carolina*
Joseph A. Bellizzi, *Arizona State University-West*
James A. Brunner, *University of Toledo*
F. Anthony Bushman, *San Francisco State University*
Thomas Buzas, *Eastern Michigan University*
Roy F. Cabaniss, *Western Kentucky University*
Michael d'Amico, *University of Akron*
Ron Eggers, *Barton College*
H. Harry Friedman, *City University of New York–Brooklyn*
Ron Goldsmith, *Florida State University*
Larry Goldstein, *Iona College*
David Gourley, *Arizona State University*
Jim Grimm, *Illinois State University*
Al Gross, *Robert Morris College*
Don Heinz, *University of Wisconsin*
Craig Hollingshead, *Marshall University*
Victor Howe, *University of Kentucky*
Roy Howell, *Texas Tech University*

Rhea Ingram, *University of Kentucky*
P.K. Kannan, *University of Maryland*
Susan Kleine, *Arizona State University*
David B. Klenosky, *Purdue University*
C.S. Kohli, *California State University-Fullerton*
Jerome L. Langer, *Assumption College*
James H. Leigh, *Texas A&M University*
Larry Lowe, *Bryant College*
Karl Mann, *Tennessee Technological University*
Charles R. Martin, *Wichita State University*
Tom K. Massey, *University of Missouri-Kansas City*
Sanjay Mishra, *University of Kansas*
G.M. Naidu, *Universithy of Wisconsin-Whitewater*
Charles Prohaska, *Central Connecticut State University*
Alan Sawyer, *University of Florida*
Robert Schaffer, *California State University-Pomona*
Leon G. Schiffman, *City University of New York-Baruch*
K. Sivakumar, *University of Illinois at Chicago*
Mark Speece, *Central Washington University*
Harlan Spotts, *University of Wisconsin-Parkside*
Wilbur W. Stanton, *Old Dominion University*
Bruce L. Stern, *Portland State University*
James L. Taylor, *University of Alabama*
Gail Tom, *California State University-Sacramento*
Deborah Utter, *Boston College*
David Wheeler, *Suffolk University*
Richard Wilcox, *Carthage College*
Margaret Wright, *University of Colorado*
Clifford E. Young, *University of Colorado-Denver*
William Lee Ziegler, *Bethune Cookman College*

Designer Burl Sloan created an attractive design for this book. Humberto Calzada graciously allowed us to reproduce his painting, "Gate to an Imaginary Future," for the cover. I hope the artwork brings as much joy to others.

There are many people to thank at the Dryden Press. Bill Schoof Jr. is an editor who understands the new media and technologies required for education in the new millennium. I appreciate his enthusiasm and strong support for this book. Jana Pitts joined the project in midstream to perform the necessary developmental efforts during a crucial stage of the book. I am in her debt for making my work easier. The diligent work of Linda Blundell on permissions is greatly appreciated. Colby Alexander and Cindy Young organized the production tasks. I appreciate that they were always responsive to my requests. Lisé Johnson's creative thinking is especially appreciated. She is a person with an ever-present smile and it is a joy to work with her. I appreciate working with such fine professionals.

For debts extending over a longer period and less directly, I wish to thank Leo Aspinwall, Philip Cateora, Charles Hinsderman, Jerome Scott, and William Stanton.

William G. Zikmund
August 1999

About the Author

A native of the Chicago area, William G. Zikmund now lives in Tulsa, Oklahoma. He is a professor of marketing at Oklahoma State University. He received a bachelor of science in marketing from the University of Colorado, a master of science in marketing from Southern Illinois University, and a Ph.D. in business administration with a concentration in marketing from the University of Colorado.

Before beginning his academic career, Professor Zikmund worked in marketing research for Conway/Millikin Company (a marketing research supplier) and Remington Arms Company (an extensive user of marketing research). Professor Zikmund also has served as a marketing research consultant to several business and nonprofit organizations. His applied marketing research experiences range from interviewing and coding to designing, supervising, and analyzing entire research programs.

During his academic career, Professor Zikmund has published dozens of articles and papers in a diverse group of scholarly journals ranging from the Journal of Marketing to the Accounting Review to the Journal of Applied Psychology. In addition to Exploring Marketing Research, Professor Zikmund has written Essentials of Market Research, Business Research Methods, Marketing, Effective Marketing, and a work of fiction, A Corporate Bestiary.

Professor Zikmund is a member of professional organizations such as the American Marketing Association, the Academy of Marketing Science, the Association for Consumer Research, the Society for Marketing Advancement, and the Southwest Marketing Association. He has served on the editorial review boards of the Journal of Marketing Education, Marketing Education Review, Journal of the Academy of Marketing Science, and the Journal of Business Research.

Brief Contents

Detailed Contents

EXPLORING MARKETING RESEARCH

SEVENTH EDITION

Chapter 1

The Role of Marketing Research

M ARKETING RESEARCH INDICATES A MAJOR SHIFT IN AMERICANS' eating behavior, which is connected to consumers' scarcity of free time. For instance, an increasing number of Americans are eating their meals away from home.[1] A whole new culture of "dashboard dining" has developed as the car has become a popular place where people eat. In addition, when families dine at home, they often seek the convenience of ready-made or hassle-free entrees provided by restaurants, supermarkets, or packaged-food marketers. The drive for greater convenience has been sparked by both an increase in the number of women in the workforce (leaving latchkey kids to prepare their own meals) and the move away from three square meals a day. A survey by the Roper Organization shows that only 24 percent of consumers eat three meals a day, and 61 percent eat either two or three meals augmented by snacks. And, although some 70 percent of meals are still made at home, the way the meals are prepared has changed. People would love to cook if they could find the time, but they don't. They want "something you boil in water two minutes and it's done."

Sara Lee Bakery, maker of frozen cheesecakes and other frozen sweet goods, experienced sales declines during 1997 and 1998. One reason was Sara Lee's failure to recognize these changing consumer attitudes toward meals at home.[2] When the company conducted marketing research to investigate its problem, managers learned Sara Lee had a great deal of brand equity. Consumers had warm, positive feelings toward the brand; however, they did not find Sara Lee's image relevant in terms of how they live today. The research indicated grabbing a dessert to eat in front of the TV at 9 p.m. was more likely than sitting down to eat cheesecake after dinner. After research uncovered this "nobody eats dessert as a family anymore" lifestyle, Sara Lee created "Add some delicious to your life" as an advertising slogan. The aim of this research-based campaign is to offer consumers a reason to indulge themselves and to celebrate small occasions. To that end, the ads show people interacting with one another through food. At Sara Lee and at thousands of other organizations in the United States and around the globe, marketing research is an important management tool.

What you will learn in this chapter

To understand the importance of marketing research as a management decision-making tool.

To recognize that the essence of marketing research is to fulfill the marketing manager's need for knowledge of the market.

To define marketing research.

To understand the difference between basic and applied marketing research.

To explain that marketing research is a means for implementing the marketing concept and total quality management programs.

To discuss the various categories of marketing research activities.

To understand the managerial value of marketing research and its role in the development and implementation of marketing strategy.

To understand when marketing research is needed and when it should not be conducted.

The following examples demonstrate how marketing research can lead to new products, improvements in existing goods and services, and changes in marketing strategy. As you read these examples, imagine that you are a marketing manager and consider the importance of marketing research in providing information that is essential for good decision making.

Clairol's Park Avenue offices includes a test salon at which the company tries out various hair-care items on women volunteers. Researchers watch through a two-way mirror as the volunteers shampoo, condition, or color their hair with test products from Clairol or competitors. The volunteers receive free hair styling for their help. In return, the company gets to observe how they react to products and to learn whether they understand and correctly follow label directions. Sometimes "verbatims," or favorable comments, from the volunteers are recorded and later used in advertising.

A survey conducted by the J. Paul Getty Museum uncovered the fact that only 7 percent of its visitors brought children to the museum located in Malibu, California. This figure was substantially lower than the 15 to 20 percent reported by other museums. The museum initiated a family program on weekends and provided toys for children to play with while visiting as direct consequences of the survey findings.[3]

Jelly Belly brand sells 40 varieties of jelly beans, with the numbers growing every year. Some of the flavors under development have come from suggestions from visitors to Jelly Belly's Internet Web site. In return for filling out an interactive questionnaire, visitors who participate in an interactive survey get samples sent to them. One question the company asks is for input on new flavors. Jelly Belly gets a great response on this and marketers take all the suggestions seriously. Researchers categorize them and group them by similar flavors. Some of the ideas are put back on the Web for people to vote for their favorites. The company has received some really off-the-wall flavor ideas. Among the strangest are flavors such as Dill Pickle, Tacos, Persimmon Pudding, Blackened Plantain, and Cream of Wheat.[4]

Campbell Soup Company's IntelligentQuisine brand of frozen meals designed to combat high blood pressure, high cholesterol, and diabetes, despite its $30 million commitment in resources from its Center for Nutrition and Wellness, never made it to national distribution. Tests in limited markets indicated that demand was not great enough to warrant national marketing.[5] On the other hand, Pepsi's Storm set records for test market sales in the lemon-lime drink category.[6]

Consumption of regular and instant coffee is on the decline. However, sales of specialty or gourmet coffee, such as amaretto-flavored coffee or coffee made from arabica beans, are growing rapidly. Sales of ground specialty and gourmet coffees reached an estimated $1.6 billion in 1998 to command about 30 percent of the total coffee market.[7] The typical American consumer drinks 1.87 six-ounce cups per day. However, 10 percent of Americans drink ten or more cups a day.[8] The Specialty Coffee Association of America forecasts there will be more than 10,000 specialty coffee cafés in the United States at the turn of the century. Starbucks, Barnie's Coffee and Teas, and other retailers that have taken advantage of this trend toward fresher, better quality coffee find statistics from the Specialty Coffee Association of America, the federal government, and industry analysts to be very useful.

The European advertising agency for Free Spirit, a product line extension of Impulse body spray, did psychological testing with teenage girls in the United Kingdom, Italy, and Germany. The research revealed deficiencies in Impulse's long-running advertising concept of a man impulsively giving flowers to a pretty woman. In Europe the idea of a man being attracted to a woman solely because of her looks, ignoring her personality and dynamism, was outdated and not appealing. This research finding was used to develop a television commercial showing a Free Spirit woman who dives into the sea fully clothed. Attracted by her "free spirit," a man entices her out of the sea with flowers.[9]

Each of these examples illustrates a different aspect of a marketing research problem. The Sara Lee cheesecake study and the J. Paul Getty Museum survey show how research findings can be directly translated into product and service offerings. The Clairol example points out the value of observation and product-usage analysis to understand consumer behavior. The Jelly Belly example suggests that new technologies are changing the nature of marketing research. The other examples illustrate how researchers use techniques other than surveys. Internal records, government and trade association statistics, experiments, and test marketing also provide valuable tools for marketing research. The examples presented here illustrate only a few applications of marketing research. This chapter introduces the student to the nature of marketing research and its role in marketing decision making.

The Nature of Marketing Research

Marketing research covers a wide range of phenomena. In essence, it fulfills the marketing manager's need for knowledge of the market. The manager of a food company may ask, "Will a package change improve my brand image?" A competitor may ask, "How can I monitor my sales and retail trade activities?" A marketing manager in the industrial tools market may ask, "To whom am I losing sales? From whom am I taking sales?" All of these marketing questions, as well as other concerning most other marketing decisions, require information about how customers, distributors, and competitors will respond to marketing decisions. Marketing research is one of the principal tools for answering questions such as these because it links the consumer, the customer, and the public to the marketer through the information used to identify and define marketing opportunities and problems; to generate, refine, and evaluate marketing actions; to monitor marketing performance; and to improve the understanding of marketing as a process.[10] The task of marketing research is to help specify and supply accurate information to reduce the uncertainty in decision making. Although marketing research provides information about consumers and the marketplace for developing and implementing marketing plans and strategies, it is not the only source of information. Every day marketing managers translate their experiences with marketing phenomena into marketing strategies. Information from a manager's experiences frequently is used in an intuitive manner because of the time pressures of business decisions or because the problem does not warrant more formal methods. However, the primary task of marketing management is effective decision making. Flying-by-the-seat-of-the-pants decision making—decision making without systematic inquiry—is like betting on a long shot at the racetrack because the horse's name is appealing. Occasionally there are successes, but in the long run intuition without research can lead to disappointment. Marketing research helps decision makers shift from intuitive information gathering to systematic and objective investigating.

Marketing Research Defined

Marketing research is defined as the systematic and objective process of generating information to aid in making marketing decisions. This process includes specifying what information is required, designing the method for collecting information, managing and implementing the collection of data, analyzing the results, and communicating the findings and their implications.[11]

marketing research
The systematic and objective process of generating information to aid in making marketing decisions.

This definition suggests first that research information is not intuitive or haphazardly gathered. Literally, research (re-search) means "to search again." The term connotes patient study and scientific investigation where in the researcher takes another, more careful look at the data to discover all that is known about the subject.

Second, if the information generated, or data collected, and analyzed, is to be accurate, the marketing researcher must be objective. The need for objectivity was cleverly stated by the nineteenth-century American humorist Artemus Ward: "It ain't the things we don't know that gets us in trouble. It's the things we know ain't so." The researcher should be detached and impersonal rather than biased and attempting to support his or her preconceived ideas. If bias enters into the research process, its value is considerably reduced.

As an example, a developer owned a large area of land and wished to build a high-prestige shopping center. He wanted a research report to demonstrate to prospective retailers that there was a large market potential for such a center. He conducted his survey exclusively in an elite neighborhood. Not surprisingly, the findings showed that a large percentage of the respondents wanted a high-prestige shopping center. Results of this kind are misleading and should be disregarded. In this example had the prospective retailers discovered how the results had been obtained, the developer would have lost credibility. Had the retailers been ignorant of the bias in design and unaware that the researchers were not impartial, the decision may have had more adverse consequences than one made strictly on intuition. The importance of striving for objectivity cannot be overemphasized: without objectivity, research is valueless.

This definition of marketing research also points out an objective to facilitate the managerial decision-making process for all aspects of the firm's marketing mix: pricing, promotion, distribution, and product decisions. The definition is not restricted to any one aspect of the marketing mix. By providing the necessary information on which to base decisions, marketing research can reduce the uncertainty of a decision and thereby decrease the risk of making the wrong decision. However, research should be an aid to managerial judgment and not a substitute for it.

Management is more than conducting marketing research: applying the research remains a managerial art. For example, a few years ago research indicated that women who bought frozen dinners tended to lead hectic lives and had trouble coping with everyday problems. Using this information, an advertising agency developed an ad for Swanson showing a run-down woman flopping into a chair just before her family was to arrive home for dinner. Suddenly realizing that she had a problem, the woman got the bright idea of cooking a frozen dinner. The beginning of the ad turned out to be a terrible mistake. The company quickly found out that the last thing women wanted to be reminded of was how tired they were. Research can suggest directions for changes in the marketing mix, but it cannot ensure correct marketing execution.

Finally, this definition of marketing research is limited by one's definition of marketing. Although research in the marketing area of a for-profit corporation is marketing research, a broader definition of marketing research includes non-profit organizations such as the American Heart Association, the San Diego Zoo, and the Boston Pops Orchestra. Each of these organizations exists to satisfy social needs, and each requires marketing skills to produce and distribute the products and services that people want. Hence, marketing research may be conducted by organizations that are not business organizations. The federal government, for example, performs many functions that are similar, if not identical, to those of business organizations. Federal managers may use research techniques for evaluative purposes in much the same way as managers at DuPont or Ford. In this book the term *marketing research* applies to all types of organizations and institutions that engage in some form of marketing activity.

Partnership for a Drug Free America is a nonprofit organization that conducts applied research. In 1997, its research indicated that the organization should target younger children. As a result, it created a public service announcement called "Big 'Ol Bug" to appeal to children ages 6 to 8. The rock music lyrics include the line, "I'd rather be a big 'ol bug than ever try a stupid drug." The research also led to another public service announcement called "Brain Damaged" to appeal to preteen children. Talking in the first person, a funny, likable brain talks and explains that drugs make a brain slow, confused, and barely able to think.

Basic Research and Applied Research

One purpose of conducting marketing research is to develop and evaluate concepts and theories. **Basic** or **pure research** attempts to expand the limits of knowledge. It does not directly involve the solution to a particular pragmatic problem. It has been said that there is nothing so practical as a good theory. Although this is true in the long run, basic marketing research findings generally cannot be immediately implemented by a marketing executive. Basic research is conducted to verify the acceptability of a given theory or to learn more about a certain concept. **Applied research** is conducted when a decision must be made about a specific real-life problem. Our focus is on applied research—those studies that are undertaken to answer questions about specific problems or to make decisions about particular courses of action or policies.

Applied research is emphasized in this discussion because most students will be oriented toward the day-to-day practice of marketing management. This discussion is aimed at students and researchers who will be exposed to short-term, problem-solving research conducted for businesses or nonprofit organizations. However, the procedures and techniques used by applied and basic researchers do not differ substantially; both employ the scientific method to answer the question at hand. Broadly defined, the term **scientific method** refers to the techniques and procedures used to recognize and understand marketing phenomena. In the scientific method, empirical evidence (facts from observation or experimentation) is analyzed and interpreted to confirm or disprove prior conceptions. In basic research, testing these prior conceptions or hypotheses and then making inferences and conclusions about the phenomena lead to the establishment of general laws about the phenomena. Use of the scientific method in applied research ensures objectivity in gathering facts and testing creative ideas for alternative marketing strategies. The essence of research, whether basic or applied, lies in the scientific method. Much of this book deals with scientific methodology. Thus, the techniques of basic and applied research differ largely in degree rather than substance.

basic (pure) research
Research conducted to expand the limits of knowledge to verify the acceptability of a given theory, or to learn more about a certain concept.

applied research
Research conducted when a decision must be made about a real-life problem.

scientific method
The techniques and procedures used to recognize and understand marketing phenomena.

The Marketing Concept

Although our concern focuses on marketing research, marketing managers should understand how marketing research fits into the broader scope of marketing. Research is one of the primary tools that enables firms to implement the

marketing concept
The most central idea in marketing thinking, which calls on managers to be consumer oriented, to stress long-run profitability rather than sales volume, and to adopt a cross-functional perspective.

philosophical idea of the marketing concept.[12] The **marketing concept** is the most central idea in marketing thinking. It has evolved over time as production- and engineering-oriented firms have responded to changes in the economic environment to become marketing-oriented firms. The marketing concept is a threefold conceptualization concerned with

1. to be consumer oriented
2. to stress long-run profitability rather than sales volume
3. to adopt a cross-functional perspective for the integration and coordination of marketing and other corporate functions

Consumer Orientation

According to the marketing concept, the consumer is at the center of the operation, the pivot point about which the business moves to achieve the balanced best interests of all concerned. According to this philosophy, the firm creates products and services with consumers' needs in mind. Many marketing theorists and operating marketing managers believe that the satisfaction of consumers' wants is the justification for a firm's existence.

TO THE POINT

The aim of marketing is to know your customer so well that when your prospects are confronted with your product, it fits them so exactly that it sells itself.

PETER DRUCKER

Crisco Savory Seasonings, a new line of flavored vegetable oils patterned after more expensive gourmet cooking oils, is a good example of consumer orientation. The oils come in four all-natural flavors: Roasted Garlic, Hot & Spicy, Classic Herb, and Lemon Butter.[13] The oils fill a consumer need for quick and easy preparation. The flavored oils can be used in a wide range of cooking methods—stir-frying, sautéing, pan-frying, marinades, and dressings—either as an ingredient or a cooking medium. Savory Seasonings can be thought of as a "speed-scratch product" that helps consumers cut down on meal preparation time, yet satisfies their desire for giving meals a homemade touch. Procter & Gamble's research showed 72 percent of households still prepare dinner at home nightly and 32 percentof households prepare the meal in less than 30 minutes. Armed with this information, Procter & Gamble leveraged the strong brand equity of Crisco to make an affordable, convenient product for everyday use. Procter & Gamble realized that knowledge of consumers' needs, coupled with product research and development, leads to successful marketing strategies and that industry leadership—indeed, corporate survival—depends on satisfying consumers.

Profit Orientation

Consumer orientation does not mean slavery to consumers' every fleeting whim. Implicit in the marketing concept is the assumption of the continuity of the firm, and the firm must make a profit to survive in the long run. Most consumers would prefer to have a Porsche priced under $15,000. However, the production costs of this car exceed that figure, and the firm surely would fail if it attempted to satisfy this desire.

The second aspect of the marketing concept argues against profitless volume, or sales volume for the sake of volume alone. Marketing cost analysis has taught

Colgate-Palmolive's introduction of Ultra Palmolive or Pots and Pans was a direct result of being consumer oriented. Colgate-Palmolive's customer research showed 71 percent of consumers use liquid dish soap to wash pots and pans at least four times a week. In addition, consumers considered pots and pans the most bothersome items. Nevertheless, they will wash them even if they have a dishwasher. While its competitors were focusing on promoting liquid dishwashing soap as gentle to hands, a better grease cutter, or effective in killing bacteria, company executives used marketing research to help solve a real customer problem.[14]

numerous firms that 20 percent of their customers have been responsible for 80 percent of their profits and that salespeople have spent too much time on unprofitable accounts. The marketing concept suggests that these firms should reevaluate their efforts to sell to small, unprofitable accounts.

A Cross-Functional Effort

Marketing personnel do not work in a vacuum, isolated from other company activities. The actions of people in areas such as production, credit, and research and development may affect an organization's marketing efforts. Similarly, the work of marketers will affect activities in other departments. Problems are almost certain to arise from lack of an integrated, companywide effort. The marketing concept stresses a cross-functional perspective to achieve consumer orientation and long-term profitability.

Problems occur when focusing on consumer needs is viewed as the sole responsibility of the marketing department. Indeed, other functional areas' goals may conflict with customer satisfaction or long-term profitability. For instance the engineering department may want long lead times for product design, with simplicity and economy as a major design goal. Marketing, however, may prefer short lead times and more complex designs with custom components and optional features for multiple models. The finance department may want fixed budgets, strict spending justifications, and prices that cover costs, whereas the marketing department may seek flexible budgets, liberal spending rationales, and below-cost prices to develop markets quickly.

Similar differences in outlook may occur with the other functional areas of the organization, and these may be sources of serious conflicts. Exhibit 1.1 illustrates what happens when a company fails to integrate its marketing efforts.

Exhibit 1.1   A Failure to Communicate

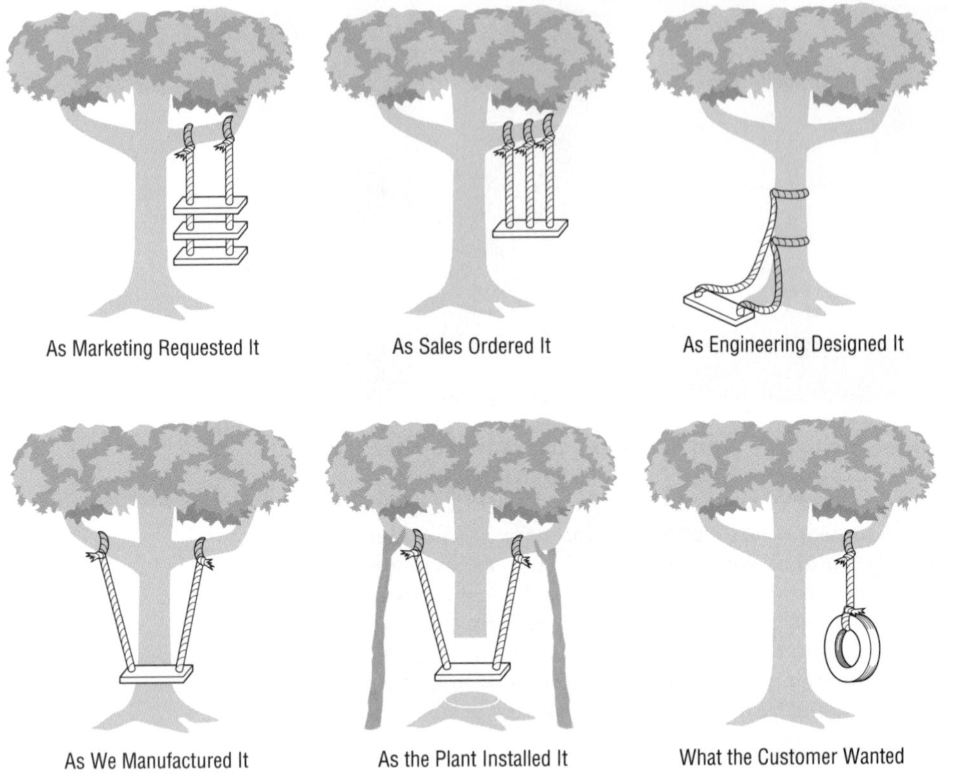

As Marketing Requested It

As Sales Ordered It

As Engineering Designed It

As We Manufactured It

As the Plant Installed It

What the Customer Wanted

When a firm lacks organizational procedures for communicating marketing information and coordinating marketing efforts, the effectiveness of its marketing programs will suffer. Marketing research findings produce some of the most crucial marketing information; thus, such research is management's key tool for finding out what customers want and how best to satisfy their needs. It is vital, then, that management conduct marketing research, that researchers produce valid and reliable results, and that those results be communicated to decision makers so that they can help shape the firm's marketing strategy.

Keeping Customers and Building Relationships

relationship marketing
Communicates the idea that a major goal of marketing is for a company to build long-term relationships with the parties that contribute to its success.

So far, we have talked about getting customers, but keeping customers is equally important. Marketers want customers for life. Effective marketers work to build long-term relationships with their customers. The term **relationship marketing** is used to communicate the idea that a major goal of marketing is to build long-term relationships with the parties that contribute to the company's success.

Once an exchange is made, effective marketing stresses managing the relationships that will bring about additional exchanges. Effective marketers view making a sale not as the end of a process but as the start of the organization's relationship with a customer. Satisfied customers will return to a company that has treated them well if they need to repurchase the same product in the future. If they need a related item, satisfied customers know the first place to look.

Relationship marketing often involves rewarding loyal customers. Burger King used marketing research in its fast-food restaurants in Long Island, Florida, to investigate the impact of Mondex smart cards for purchasing food items. The trial smart card program offers the convenience of not having to use cash and allows participating consumers to earn bonus points to be exchanged for free meals.

Total Quality Management

Total quality management is a business philosophy that has much in common with the marketing concept.[15] It embodies the belief that the management process must focus on integrating customer-driven quality throughout the organization. Total quality management stresses continuous improvement of product quality and service. Managers improve durability and enhance features as the product ages. They strive to improve delivery and other services to keep their brands competitive.

The philosophy underlying the implementation of total quality management was clearly articulated by a Burger King executive: "The customer is the vital key to our success. We are now looking at our business through the customers' eyes and measuring our performance against their expectations, not ours."[16] A company that employs a quality strategy must evaluate itself through the eyes of the customer.

Obviously, the marketing concept and total quality management are closely intertwined. In a company that practices total quality management, manufacturing's orientation toward lowest-cost productivity should harmonize with marketing's commitment to quality products at acceptable prices. For example, if Ford Motor Company advertises that "Quality Is Job One," the production department must make sure that every automobile that comes off the assembly line will meet consumers' quality specifications. The notion that quality improvement is every employee's job must be integrated throughout the organization so that marketing and production will be in harmony. If this conflicts with manufacturing's desire to allow for variations from quality standards, the firm must implement statistical quality controls and other improve-

total quality management
A business philosophy that focuses on integrating customer-driven quality throughout an organization with continuous improvement of product quality and service.

Marketing research is a means to bridge the information gap between marketing executives and consumers. Bareback Jeans come without back pockets because women indicated they wanted a slim fit and a button front, but, unlike male jeans consumers, had no need for back pockets.

ments in the manufacturing operation to improve its systems and increase productivity.

Thus, total quality management extends beyond production operations to involve every employee in the organization. In other words, every employee's job is linked to producing and marketing high-quality, low-cost products that satisfy customers. Companies that adopt the total quality philosophy view employees as internal customers. They visualize a chain of customers within the production/delivery system.[17] An accountant who prepares a report for a sales manager should view the manager as a customer who will use the information to make decisions that will benefit external customers who buy the company's products. Every employee should contribute to quality improvement and the satisfaction of consumers' needs.

Implementing a total quality management program requires considerable measurement. It involves routinely asking customers to rate a company against its competitors. It involves measuring employee attitudes. It involves monitoring company performance against benchmark standards. These activities use marketing research extensively, so marketing research with external customers and with employees in the organization (internal customers) contributes much to a total quality management program.

Chapter 8 discusses the measurement of quality and customer satisfaction in detail. Throughout this book, however, we will explain how marketing research can help to achieve customer-driven quality.

Marketing Research: A Means for Implementing the Marketing Concept

Satisfying the consumer is a major goal of marketing. One purpose of marketing research is to obtain information that identifies consumers' problems and needs, bridging the information gap between marketing executives and consumers. Researching consumer needs in this way enables firms to fulfill the marketing concept.

Rubbermaid's new-product development process epitomizes this function.[18] Every new Rubbermaid product starts with research that asks one simple question: What's wrong with existing products? No consumer problem is considered too small, no concern too finicky. In research about children's lunch boxes, parents indicated they often worried about where to put milk money, allergy medicines, keys, and other small things their kids needed to bring to school. When Rubbermaid came out with its backpack lunch box, which was designed to slip easily into a backpack, it built in a change holder.

Another company marketing backpacks to teenagers wanted to get feedback on a new pocket. Teenage subjects immediately pointed out it was too small for a Walkman. The new pocket did not satisfy its customers' needs so the company changed the backpack design.

Measuring consumer satisfaction is another means of determining how well a company is fulfilling the marketing concept. Customer satisfaction research can ascertain whether an organization's total quality management program is meeting customer expectations and management objectives. General Electric's major-appliance division sent the questionnaire, shown in Exhibit 1.2, to customers after repair calls to determine how well the company was accomplishing its objective of consumer satisfaction. The questionnaire asked whether the appointment was scheduled promptly, whether the repair person showed up on time and was polite, and if the customer was satisfied with the service. Customer satisfaction surveys such as this tend to be standardized and ongoing so that performance can be compared against previously established standards. These measures lead to the evaluation of managers according to consumers' perceptions of quality in addition to the evaluation of actual operational quality. Customer satisfaction research plays a major role in customer retention efforts because it provides information about the likelihood that the organization will keep its existing customers.

Marketing research can also help eliminate commercialization of products that are not consumer oriented. Sometimes ideas that look like technological breakthroughs in the laboratory fall flat when presented to consumers. For example, a powdered pain reliever was supposed to be a soothing remedy because it was to be mixed with milk. It did not soothe customers, however. Research showed that the public thought this great step forward was actually a step backward in convenience of usage. The form was there, but someone forgot the consumer benefit.

By improving efficiency, research also facilitates profitability. For instance, during the introduction or a new product, accurate forecasting of the product's potential sales volume is an essential basis for estimating its profitability. A firm considering the introduction of a cat snack that contains hairball medicine might rely on a test market experiment to determine the optimal price for this new concept. Extensive testing should be done to ensure that the marketing program is fine-tuned to maximize the firm's profitability while satisfying the consumer.

Analysis of data may also be a form of marketing research that can increase efficiency. Marketing representatives from Exxon Chemical Company used laptop computers to run a complex set of calculations to show sales prospects the advantage of Exxon products over competitors' products. Such analysis of research data improves the salesperson's batting average and the firm's efficiency.

Exhibit 1.2   Marketing Research May Measure Consumer Satisfaction

---

QUALITY OF SERVICE SURVEY

Please rate the service you recently received from GE Factory Service (product and date shown on the reverse side). Consider all service calls required for this particular problem. Indicate your answers by checking the appropriate box for each question.

1. When you called for service were you able to get through on the first call without getting a busy signal? — YES ☐   NO ☐

2. When you called, were you placed on hold? — YES ☐   NO ☐

3. Did the person you talked with on the phone give you the feeling that he/she really cared about your problem? — YES ☐   NO ☐

4. What day was your appointment scheduled for? — SAME DAY ☐   NEXT DAY ☐   3RD DAY ☐   4TH DAY ☐   LATER ☐

5. Was this the day you most preferred? — YES ☐   NO ☐

6. If not, what day would you have most preferred? — SAME DAY ☐   NEXT DAY ☐   3RD DAY ☐   4TH DAY ☐   LATER ☐

7. When was the technician scheduled to arrive? — AM 8-12 ☐   PM 12-5 ☐   EVENING AFTER 5 ☐   ALL DAY 8-5 ☐

8. Was this time of day you most preferred? — YES ☐   NO ☐

9. Did the technician come on the scheduled day? — YES ☐   NO ☐

10. Did the technician arrive during the scheduled time period? — YES ☐   NO ☐

11. Did the technician give you the feeling he/she really cared about your problem? — YES ☐   NO ☐

12. Did the technician seem to be knowledgeable and competent about your product? — YES ☐   NO ☐

13. Did the technician explain what was done to fix your problem? — YES ☐   NO ☐

14. Were the charges on the invoice explained to you? — YES ☐   NO ☐

15. Considering the service you received, how would you rate the charges for:

	NO CHARGE INVOLVED	VERY REASONABLE	REASONABLE	UNREASONABLE	VERY UNREASONABLE
LABOR (incl. home call)	☐	☐	☐	☐	☐
PARTS	☐	☐	☐	☐	☐
TOTAL CHARGE	☐	☐	☐	☐	☐

16. How many trips were required to complete the repair? — 1 ☐   2 ☐   3 ☐   4 ☐   MORE THAN 4 ☐

17. Overall, how would you rate our technician? — EXCELLENT ☐   GOOD ☐   FAIR ☐   POOR ☐

18. If a part was needed to complete the repair, was the part: — AVAILABLE ON SERVICE TRUCK ☐   MAILED TO YOU ☐   BROUGHT BACK LATER BY A TECHNICIAN ☐   NO PART NEEDED ☐

19. If a part was ordered, how many days did it take for you to get the part? — NO PART ORDERED ☐   SAME DAY ☐   1-4 DAYS ☐   5-9 DAYS ☐   MORE THAN 9 DAYS ☐

20. Considering all these questions, how satisfied are you with the overall service you received? — VERY SATISFIED ☐   SATISFIED ☐   NEITHER SATISFIED/DISSATISFIED ☐   DISSATISFIED ☐   VERY DISSATISFIED ☐

21. If you needed to replace the product you had repaired, how likely would you be to buy the General Electric or Hotpoint brand? — DEFINITELY WOULD BUY GE/HOTPOINT ☐   PROBABLY WOULD BUY GE/HOTPOINT ☐   MIGHT OR MIGHT NOT BUY GE/HOTPOINT ☐   PROBABLY WOULD NOT BUY GE/HOTPOINT ☐   DEFINITELY WOULD NOT BUY GE/HOTPOINT ☐

22. Please add any comments you have about the service you received.

_____

_____

_____

_____

Because of the need for integrating company efforts, a marketing researcher must be knowledgeable not only about marketing research but about the entire spectrum of marketing activities as well.

The Managerial Value of Marketing Research for Strategic Decision Making

Effective marketing management requires research. Primestar, the direct-broadcast satellite TV service, uses marketing research to determine which kinds of programming to add to its lineup of channels. A company executive says, "Research has driven every aspect of our business decisions."[19] At Ford Motor Company research is so fundamental that the company hardly makes any significant decision without the benefit of some kind of marketing research. The prime managerial value of marketing research comes from reduced uncertainty through information that facilitates decision making about marketing strategies and tactics to achieve an organization's strategic goals.

TO THE POINT

The secret of success is to know something nobody else knows.

ARISTOTLE ONASSIS

Developing and implementing a marketing strategy involves four stages:

1. identifying and evaluating opportunities
2. analyzing market segments and selecting target markets
3. planning and implementing a marketing mix that will satisfy customers' needs and meet the objectives of the organization
4. analyzing marketing performance.[20]

Identifying and Evaluating Opportunities

Before developing a marketing strategy, an organization must determine where it wants to go and how to get there. Marketing research can help answer these questions by investigating potential opportunities to identify attractive areas for company action.

Marketing research may provide diagnostic information about what is occurring in the environment. A mere description of some social or economic activity, such as trends in consumer purchasing behavior, may help managers recognize problems and identify opportunities for enriching marketing efforts.

One reason for Mattel Toys' success in the rapidly changing toy market is the company's commitment to consumer research. Much of its success may be traced to the way it goes about identifying opportunities for its new products. For example, marketing research showed that instead of military, spy, or sports heroes, young boys preferred fantasy figures. Boys spend much time fantasizing about good versus evil. Research showed that timeless fantasy figures, both ancient and futuristic, were visually exciting, and because they were timeless, boys could do more with them. Several lines of action figures, including American Gladiators toys, were a result of this research. Video games by Nintendo and Sega also reflect an awareness of this research finding.

In a research study on running shoes the purpose was to investigate the occasions or situations associated with product use, that is, when individuals wore their running shoes. The researchers found that most owners of running shoes wore the shoes while walking, not running. Also, most of this walking was part of a normal daily activity like shopping or commuting to work rather than for exercise. Many of the people who wore running shoes for routine activities considered them an alternative to other casual shoes. This research ultimately led to the development of the walking shoe designed for comfortable, everyday walking.[21]

Market opportunities may be evaluated using many performance criteria. In many cases marketing research supplies the information to determine which opportunities are best for the organization. For example, when market demand is the performance criterion, this information typically is estimated using marketing research techniques.

Estimates of market potential or predictions about future environmental conditions allow managers to evaluate opportunities. Accurate sales forecasts are among the most useful pieces of planning information a marketing manager can have. Complete accuracy in forecasting the future is not possible because change is constantly occurring in the marketing environment. Nevertheless, objective forecasts of demand or changing environments may be the foundations on which marketing strategies are built.

Analyzing and Selecting Target Markets

The second stage of marketing strategy development is to analyze market segments and select target markets. The American Marketing Association found that more than 90 percent of the organizations it surveyed engaged in research to determine market characteristics and trends.[22] Marketing research is a major source of information for determining which market segments' characteristics distinguish them from the overall market.

Market segmentation studies at Harley-Davidson provide a good example of this essential activity. Marketing research depicts the Harley-Davidson motorcycle purchaser as a 38-year-old male (80 percent) with some college (44 percent). He is likely to be married (72 percent) and without children (55 percent). The average Harley owner has a household income in excess of $50,000.[23]

Planning and Implementing a Marketing Mix

Using the information obtained in the two previous stages, marketing managers plan and execute a marketing mix strategy. However, marketing research may be needed to support specific decisions about virtually any aspect of the marketing mix. Often the research is conducted to evaluate an alternative course of action. For example, advertising research investigated whether Raquel Welch would make a good spokesperson for a specific brand of hair coloring. She was filmed in some test commercials to endorse the brand, but the commercials were never aired because, although viewers recognize her as an outstanding personality in the test commercials, they did not perceive her as a user of home hair coloring kits or as an authority on such products. Subsequent research indicated that Ms. Welch would make a good spokesperson for a fitness center.

Managers face many diverse decisions about marketing mixes. The following examples highlight selected types of research that might be conducted for each element of the marketing mix.

Product Research. Product research takes many forms and includes studies designed to evaluate and develop new products and to learn how to adapt existing product lines. Concept testing exposes potential customers to new-product ideas to judge the concepts' acceptance and feasibility. Product testing determines a product prototype's strengths and weaknesses or whether a finished product performs better than competing brands or according to expectations. Brand-name evaluation studies investigate whether a name is appropriate for a product. Package

British Airways' marketing research revealed that many travelers find air travel a frustrating experience—from the office to the airport to a hotel or a meeting and back again. Air travelers want to know they're being cared for. With these findings in mind, executives at British Airways made a decision to alter its service. The airline relaunched its Club Europe business-class services to smooth business travelers' paths, providing them more time and space and, above all, eliminating the hassle. The new Club Europe service, whose cost exceeded 70 million British pounds, includes new seats, more business lounges, telephone check-in, limousines at taxi rates, and speedier service through security and customs at Heathrow's Terminal One.[24]

testing assesses size, color, shape, ease of use, and other attributes of a package. Product research encompasses all applications of marketing research that seek to develop product attributes that will add value for consumers.

Recently, Chee-tos became the first major brand of snack food to be made and marketed in China.[25] Product taste tests revealed traditional cheese-flavored corn puffs Chee-tos did not appeal to Chinese consumers. So the company conducted consumer research with 600 different flavors to learn which flavors would be most appealing. Among the flavors tested and disliked by Chinese consumers were ranch dressing, nacho, Italian pizza, Hawaiian barbecue, peanut satay, North Sea crab, chili prawn, coconut milk curry, smoked octopus, caramel, and cuttlefish. Research did show that consumers liked some flavors. So, when Chee-tos were introduced in China, they came in two flavors: savory American cream and zesty Japanese steak.

The initial concept for Pretty Feet portrayed the brand as a rough-skin remover for women's feet. After a period of disappointing sales volume, the company conducted product positioning research. The research showed that although most women used Pretty Feet primarily on their feet, many prospects in the target market were not especially concerned about rough skin on their feet because their shoes often hid their feet. Furthermore, many potential product users expressed interest in removing rough skin from other parts of their bodies, especially their hands. When the brand was renamed Pretty Feet & Hands and the product repositioned as a rough-skin remover for *both* feet and hands, sales quadrupled.

Pricing Research. Most organizations conduct pricing research. A competitive pricing study is a typical marketing research project in this area. However, research designed to learn the ideal price level or determine if consumers will pay a price high enough to cover cost is not uncommon. For example, a Bausch & Lomb survey of 5,000 contact lens wearers showed that more than 60 percent of contact lens wearers would be interested in one-day disposable lenses if the price came down to about a dollar a day. This led to the introduction of its Softlens brand, which proclaimed a significant price advantage over competitors. Pricing research may also investigate when discounts or coupons should be offered, explore if there are critical product attributes that determine how consumers perceive value, or determine if a product category, such as soft drinks, has price gaps among national brands, regional brands, and private labels.[26]

Ford Motor Company tested a leasing program that limited the mileage a customer can drive annually in return for monthly savings.[27] In Florida, marketing research evaluated consumers' reactions to a special 10,000-mile-a-year lease that would cut monthly payments by $25. In Ohio, a lease that limited drivers to

WHAT WENT RIGHT?

Ameritech Test Towns

TELECOMMUNICATION COMPANY AMERITECH'S STRATEGY involves providing innovative, user-friendly telephone and communication services. Before it introduces a new service, it selects a small midwestern town and gets the cooperation of its residents to try some futuristic telecommunications application.[28]

The approach assures that even the most innovative equipment or service is easy for consumers to use. Ameritech knows that with sophisticated equipment, the ability of consumers to take advantage of the technology is very important. If products are designed to do useful things for customers, the company has found that small changes in design make for very big differences in the success of the product.

Take, for example, a voice-recognition system Ameritech tested for automated collect-call acceptance. Fresh out of development, a recorded prompt asked callers for the answer to what should have been a yes-or-no question, and those were the only answers the system was able to recognize. "But real-life customers used words like 'sure' and 'OK'" and the system failed on more than 20 percent of calls.

After an adjustment, the prompt specified "yes" or "no" as the only appropriate aswers, avoiding nonstandard responses and the ensuing consumer frustration. By taking advantage of the fact that people adapt their vocabulary, Ameritech could change the prompt and virtually eliminate the problem. The company's marketing researchers know that involving the consumer is really the secret to these kinds of breakthroughs.

12,000 miles for a $15 reduction was investigated. Existing research had already uncovered that larger number of car leasors, especially the elderly, are willing to make the mileage-for-money trade. However, the company believes an extended research project is necessary to learn if customers who go over the limit will become upset. If customers do become irritated, the new pricing strategy may not be worth it to Ford.

Campbell Soup Company provides another example of how price research can keep a company from making a marketing mistake. Campbell Soup Company pulled its Soup du Jour, a single-serving, microwaveable soup, out of the Seattle and Portland markets when price researchers found that consumers considered the retail price too high. Campbell went back to the laboratory to reformulate the product so it could be marketed at a more attractive price. Research may answer many questions about price. Is there a need for seasonal or quantity discounts? Are coupons more effective than price reductions? Is a brand price elastic or price inelastic? How much of a price difference is optimal to differentiate items in the product line?

Distribution Research. Manufacturers, wholesalers, and retailers often cooperate to conduct research about the distribution process. Frito-Lay, for example, has developed research expertise in supermarket space management. The snack food company conducts research to help Pathmark, Safeway, and other supermarkets improve consumer traffic flows and increase snack food purchases. Williams-Sonoma, Sears, and KB Toys are among the many major retailers that have researched home shopping services via the Internet. New interactive media and home delivery as a means of distribution have the potential to revolutionize channel-of-distribution systems, and millions of dollars are being spent to research their impact. Although most distribution research will not have the dramatic impact of the research on Internet shopping systems, such research is important to many organizations. A typical study in the distribution area may be conducted to select retail sites or warehouse locations. A survey of retailers or wholesalers may be of other channel members. Distribution research often is needed to gain knowledge about retailers' and wholesalers' operations and to learn their reactions to a manufacturer's marketing policies.

The 3M Corporation surveys its industrial distributors to determine, anonymously, how they feel about doing business with each of their suppliers, including 3M. The purpose of the research is to investigate distributors' attitude about relationships with sales representatives, ordering procedures, on-time delivery, training of distributor personnel, product quality, and many other activities that help build long-term relationships.

Promotion Research. Research that investigates the effectiveness of premiums, coupons, sampling deals, and other sales promotions is classified as promotion research. However, more time, money, and effort are spent on advertising research. Promotion research includes buyer motivation studies to generate ideas for copy development, media research, and studies of advertising effectiveness.

The marketing research findings of Zale's, a large retailer of jewelry, helped create advertising with large, one-word headlines that simply asked, "Confused?" "Nervous?" or "Lost?" The advertisements overtly acknowledged the considerable emotional and financial risks that consumers faced in jewelry purchases. Research had shown that typical consumers felt unable to determine the relative quality of various jewelry items, believed jewelry purchases were expensive, and needed reassurance about their purchases, especially because they often purchased jewelry for someone else.

The development of Smilk's cartoon spokesperson advertising campaign provides an example of how advertising research is a valuable tool in developing effective advertisements. Smilk is a low-fat, flavored milk drink for kids.[29] Smilk's cartoon spokesperson, Smilkster, is a hip cow who has spots of many different colors and wears shades and sneakers. Smilkster was originally depicted as a traditional cow on all fours, complete with an udder because she was female. However, marketing research found this female conceptualization of the cartoon spokesperson was popular only with very young children and was particularly disliked by older boys. Subsequent research uncovered that boys would be more receptive to a male cow character and advertising using a trendy Smilkster was created.

Media research helps advertisers decide whether television, newspapers, magazines, or other media alternatives are best-suited to convey the advertiser's message. Choices among media alternatives may be based on research that shows how many people in the target audience each advertising vehicle can reach.

The Integrated Marketing Mix. The individual elements of the marketing mix do not work independently of the other elements. Hence, many research studies investigate various combinations of marketing ingredients to gather information to suggest the best possible marketing program.

Analyzing Marketing Performance

After a marketing strategy has been implemented, marketing research may serve to inform managers whether planned activities were properly executed and are accomplishing what they were expected to achieve. In other words, marketing research may be conducted to obtain feedback for evaluation and control of marketing programs. This aspect of marketing research is especially important for successful total quality management.

performance-monitoring research
Research that regularly provides feedback for evaluation and control of marketing activity.

Performance-monitoring research refers to research that regularly, sometimes routinely, provides feedback for evaluation and control of marketing activity. For example, most firms continuously monitor wholesale and retail activity to ensure early detection of sales declines and other anomalies. In the grocery and drug industries, sales research may use Universal Product Codes on packages read by electronic cash registers and computerized checkout counts to provide valuable market share information to store and brand managers interested in the retail sales volumes of their products. Market share analysis and sales analysis are the most common forms of performance-monitoring research. Almost every organization compares its current sales with previous sales and competitors' sales. However, analyzing marketing performance is not limited to the investigation of sales figures.

United Airline's Omnibus in-flight surveys provide a good example of performance-monitoring research for quality management. United routinely selects sample flights and administers questionnaires concerning in-flight service, food, and so forth. The Omnibus survey is conducted quarterly to determine who is flying and for what reason. It enables United to track demographic changes and monitor customer ratings of its services on a continuing basis, allowing the company to gather vast amounts of information at low cost. The information regarding customer reaction to services can be compared over time. For example, suppose United decided to change its menu for in-flight meals. The results of the Omnibus survey might indicate that shortly after a menu change, customers' ratings of food and meals declined. Such information would be extremely valuable because it would allow management to quickly spot similar trends among passengers in areas such as airport lobbies, gate-line waits, or cabin cleanliness. Thus, management could react rapidly to improve deficiencies.

When analysis of marketing performance indicates things are not going as planned, marketing research may be required to explain why something went wrong. Detailed information about specific mistakes or failures is frequently sought. If a general problem area is identified, breaking down industry sales volume and a firm's sales volume into different geographical areas may explain specific problems. Exploring problems in greater depth may indicate which managerial judgments were erroneous.

When Is Marketing Research Needed?

A marketing manager confronted with two or more alternative courses of action faces the initial decision of whether or not to conduct marketing research. The determination of the need for marketing research centers on (1) time constraints, (2) the availability of data, (3) the nature of the decision to be made, and (4) the value of the research information in relation to costs.

Time Constraints

Systematic research takes time. In many instances management will believe that a decision must be made immediately, allowing no time for research. Decisions sometimes are made without adequate information or thorough understanding of market situations. Although not ideal, sometimes the urgency of a situation precludes the use of research.

WHAT WENT WRONG?

Inspector Clouseau of the Crusty French Loaf?

ADVERTISING IS A HECTIC BUSINESS WITH TIGHT deadlines and rush jobs.

When the Leo Burnett Advertising Agency suggested using an Inspector Clouseau look-alike for Pillsbury's new crusty French loaf, the idea was enthusiastically supported. What could be more perfect for a French bread product than using a spokesperson impersonating the French detective character in the humorous Pink Panther movies? Normally, Pillsbury's researchers test consumer reactions to a rough production version of the commercial featuring either a series of still photographs or live-action videotapes simulating viewing situations of the story. This time, however, the timetable was tight, and Pillsbury decided to forgo research with a rough comercial and instead prepare a finished commercial. When marketing research ultimately tested reactions to the final commercial, the researchers uncovered a problem: too much character recognition. The researchers discovered that the Clouseau character was so successful that he overshadowed the product. The viewers tended to register high levels of recognition of Clouseau and forget about the product. Although the Clouseau character connected very well with French bread, eliminating the research on a rough commercial had caused a problem. However, because the finished commercial was tested after production, the research results allowed the advertiser to revise it by giving the product more time and exposure during the commercial.[30]

Availability of Data

Often managers already possess enough information to make sound decisions with no marketing research. When they lack adequate information, however, research must be considered. Managers must ask themselves if the research will provide the information needed to answer the basic questions about a decision. Furthermore, if a potential source of data exists, managers will want to know how much it will cost to obtain the data.

If the data cannot be made available, research cannot be conducted. For example, prior to 1980 the People's Republic of China had never conducted a population census in mainland China. Rwanda never has. Organizations engaged in international business often find that data about business activity or population characteristics found in abundance when investigating the United States are nonexistent or sparse when the geographic area of interest is a developing country. Imagine the problems facing marketing researchers who wish to investigate market potential in places like the Czech Republic, Yugoslavian Macedonia, and other emerging countries.

Nature of the Decision

The value of marketing research will depend on the nature of the managerial decision to be made. A routine tactical decision that does not require a substantial investment may not seem to warrant a substantial expenditure for marketing research. For example, a computer company must update its operator's instruction manual when it makes minor product modifications. The research cost of determining the proper wording for updating the manual is likely to be too high for such a minor decision. The nature of the decision is not totally independent of the next issue to be considered: the benefits versus the costs of the research. In general, however, the more strategically or tactically important the decision, the more likely research will be conducted.

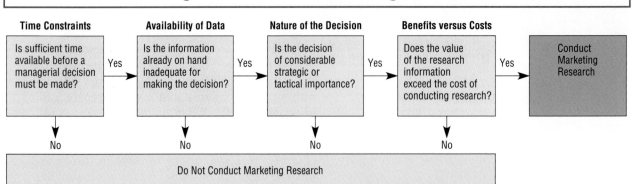

Exhibit 1.3 **Determining When to Conduct Marketing Research**

Benefits versus Costs

Earlier we discussed some of the managerial benefits of marketing research. Of course, conducting research to obtain these benefits requires an expenditure. There are both costs and benefits to conducting marketing research. In any decision-making situation managers must identify alternative courses of action and then weigh the value of each alternative against its cost. Marketing research can be thought of as an investment alternative. When deciding whether to make a decision without research or to postpone the decision in order to conduct research, managers should ask three questions: (1) Will the payoff or rate of return be worth the investment? (2) Will the information gained by marketing research improve the quality of the marketing decision enough to warrant the expenditure? (3) Is the proposed research expenditure the best use of the available funds?

For example, *TV-Cable Week* was not test marketed before its launch. Although the magazine had articles and stories about TV personalities and events, its main feature was program listings, channel by channel, showing the exact programs that a particular subscriber could receive. To produce a custom magazine for each individual cable TV system in the country required developing a costly computer system. Because the development necessitated a substantial expenditure, one that could not be scaled down for research, conducting research was judged to be an improper investment. The value of the research information was not positive because the cost of information exceeded its benefits. Unfortunately, pricing and distribution problems became so compelling after the magazine was launched that the product was a marketing failure. Nevertheless, without the luxury of hindsight, managers made a reasonable decision not to conduct research. They analyzed the cost of the information (that is, the cost of test marketing) relative to the potential benefits of the information. Exhibit 1.3 outlines the criteria for determining when to conduct marketing research.

Marketing Research Is a Global Activity

Marketing research, like all business activity today, has become increasingly global. Some companies have extensive international marketing research operations. Upjohn conducts marketing research in 160 different countries.

The world economy has become global, and corporations market products in many countries. People think of their home culture as the normal way of life, but consumers in other cultures may have different values, beliefs, and behaviors. Marketing research helps marketers understand cultural differences. Colgate-Palmolive is a progressive company that conducts marketing research around the world. Colgate-Palmolive used marketing research when it introduced Axion dishwashing gel in Colombia, where it is sold in outside markets such as this one in Cali.

Companies that conduct business in foreign lands must understand the nature of these particular markets and judge whether these markets require customized marketing strategies. For example, although the 15 nations of the European Union now share a single formal market, marketing research shows they do not share identical tastes for many consumer products. Marketing researchers have found no such thing as a typical European consumer; language, religion, climate, and centuries of tradition divide the nations of the European Union. Scantel Research, a British firm that advises companies on color preferences, found inexplicable differences in the ways Europeans take their medicine. The French prefer to pop purple pills, but the English and Dutch favor white ones. Consumers in all three countries dislike bright red capsules, which are big sellers in the United States. This example illustrates that companies that do business in Europe must judge whether they need to adapt to local customs and buying habits.[31]

Nielsen/IMS International, which includes A.C. Nielsen, with its television ratings, is the world's largest marketing research company. More than 70 percent of its business comes from outside the United States.[32] Although the nature of marketing research can change around the globe, the need for marketing research is universal.

Throughout this book, we will discuss the practical problems involved in conducting marketing research in Europe, Asia, Latin America, the Middle East, and elsewhere.

Summary

Marketing research is a tool that companies use to discover consumers' wants and needs so that they can satisfy those wants and needs with their product offerings. Marketing research is the marketing manager's source of information about market conditions. It covers topics ranging from long-range planning to near-term tactical decisions.

Marketing research is the systematic and objective process of generating information—gathering, recording, and analyzing data—to aid marketing decision making. The research must be conducted systematically, not haphazardly. It must be objective to avoid the distorting effects of personal bias. Applied marketing research seeks to facilitate managerial decision making. Basic or pure research seeks to increase the knowledge of theories and concepts.

Marketing research is a means of implementing the marketing concept, the most central idea in marketing. The marketing concept says that a firm must be oriented toward both consumer satisfaction and long-run profitability (rather than short-run sales volume). Organizations need to focus on both creating and keeping customers. Furthermore, cross-functional activities need to be integrated to achieve these goals.

Marketing research can help implement the marketing concept by identifying consumers' problems and needs, improving efficiency, and evaluating the effectiveness of marketing strategies and tactics.

Total quality management is a business philosophy that has much in common with the marketing concept. Companies that have adopted the total quality philosophy view employees as internal customers. Implementing a total quality management program requires considerable marketing research with external customers and with employees in the organization (internal customers).

The development and implementation of a marketing strategy involves four stages: (1) identifying and evaluating opportunities, (2) analyzing market segments and selecting target markets, (3) planning and implementing a marketing mix that will satisfy customers' needs and meet the objectives of the organization, and (4) analyzing marketing performance. Marketing research helps in each stage by providing information for strategic decision making.

Managers use marketing research to define problems, identify opportunities, and clarify alternatives. They also use it to determine what went wrong with past marketing efforts, describe current events in the marketplace, or forecast future conditions.

Marketing managers determine whether marketing research should be conducted based on (1) time constraints, (2) availability of data, (3) the nature of the decision to be made, and (4) the benefit of the research information versus its costs.

Key Terms and Concepts

Marketing research
Basic (pure) research
Applied research

Scientific method
Marketing concept
Relationship marketing

Total quality management
Performance-monitoring research

Questions for Review and Critical Thinking

1. Is it possible to make sound marketing decisions without marketing research? What advantages does research offer to the decision maker over seat-of-the-pants decision making?
2. An advertising agency's slogan is "People listen to us because we listen to them." Has this firm integrated the marketing research function with the marketing concept?
3. Name some products that logically might have been developed with the help of marketing research.
4. In your own words define marketing research and describe its task.
5. Which of the following organizations are likely to use marketing research? Why? How?
   a. Manufacturer of breakfast cereals
   b. Manufacturer of nuts, bolts, and other fasteners
   c. Federal Trade Commissiond. Hospital
   e. Computer software publisher
6. An automobile manufacturer is attempting to predict the type of car consumers will desire in the year 2020. Is this basic or applied research? Explain.
7. The owner of 22 restaurants was asked how he does marketing research. He answered that he does it after midnight driving around in a pickup truck: "I stay up late. If it's midnight and I don't have anything else to do, I drive around town and look at the lines in front of places. I'll look at the trash and see if a guy's doing business. If he's got a real clean bunch of trash cans and an empty dumpster, he's not doing any business. I find out a lot by talking to my vendors. I ask the bread guy how many boxes of buns the drive-in down the street is buying. Very few restaurateurs do that. But that's the way I research my market." Is this marketing research?

8. Comment on the following statements:
   a. Marketing managers are paid to take chances with decisions. Marketing researchers are paid to reduce the risk of making those decisions.
   b. A marketing strategy can be no better than the information on which it is formulated.
   c. The purpose of research is to solve marketing problems.

9. In what specific ways can marketing research influence the development and implementation of marketing strategy?
10. What is the relationship between marketing research and a total quality management program?

 Exploring the Internet: What is Ahead?

The Internet is a worldwide network of computers that allows an individual access to information and documents from distant sources. In essence, the Internet is combination of worldwide-communication systems and the world's largest public library for a seemingly endless range of information. The Internet is discussed in depth in Chapter 2 and Chapter 7. An "Exploring the Internet" exercise is included in each of the remaining chapters. The home page for this textbook is located at

   http://www.dryden.com/mktg/zikmund

The author's home page is located at

   http://www.bus.okstate.edu/zikmund

This feature gives you an opportunity to use the Internet to gain additional insights about marketing research.

Video-Case 1.1 **Hard Candy** [33]

WHEN DINEH MOHAJER DECIDED TO PAINT HER TOE-nails baby blue with a polish she custom-blended in her bathroom, she didn't know she was about to become a fashion icon. She didn't know she would become the creative force behind a multimillion-dollar company. And she didn't know she'd spark a frenzied copycat craze in the fiercely competitive cosmetics industry. She just knew she wanted baby blue nail polish. When she couldn't find it, she made it herself. When the saleswomen at a trendy Los Angeles shoe salon admired her pastel toes, Mohajer's sister Pooneh said, "We should go into business. This is crazy. Everyone's dying for this product." The sisters became partners, each investing $200. They brought in Dineh's boyfriend, Ben Einstein, as a third partner, and Hard Candy was born.

Hard Candy's first sale came as a surprise during a presentation of the polishes at Los Angeles Fred Segal. A young girl spotted the samples and begged her mother to buy all four bottles. The store immediately ordered 200 more bottles of Sky, Sunshine, Lime, and Violet. Family and friends worked day and night to fill the orders. Hard Candy took off.

Hard Candy's main advantage in the marketplace is its ability to serve a niche in the cosmetics market. "We have developed a direct line to the consumer," explains Einstein, vice president and cofounder. "We know exactly what's happening because we are young. I guess we have our ears to the street and we know when something is changing. I don't think if you're 60 years old, living in New York City, and you're on the 58th floor you're going to have your fingers on anything. It's not the same thing as just seeing the trends on Melrose or Beverly Hills. We know as fast as they come. That's our advantage."

Hard Candy understands that every product has an intrinsic value that sets it apart from competitors. Mohajer contends that her products have a value that is futuristic. But the company has set its sights on the global market as well as the future. It has been particularly successful in the United States, Japan, and London, plans to expand to South America, and will increase its distribution in Japan and Asia.

Although Hard Candy is still a young company, social responsibility is an important issue. "One hundred percent of the profits from our new color, Love, will be donated to the American Foundation for AIDS Research (AMFAR)," says Mohajer. "I think Hard Candy has been blessed in a way, so it's only right that we do something that's charitable—something that we believe helps our customers." Hard Candy strongly believes that it is important to raise awareness about AIDS, particularly among young people.

Hard Candy's innovation propelled the start-up company to overnight success, but it left its founder with little time to deal with many of the nuts and bolts issues of organizing a business. Einstein contacted the consulting firm of Ernst & Young for help, and with a $50,000 loan from Dineh Mohajer's parents, Hard Candy retained the firm. "Ernst & Young provides an entrepreneurial support division that specializes in taking young companies—like Hard Candy—helping them grow, and establishing a nurturing relationship," explains Mohajer.

Ernst & Young also conducted a search to find an ad hoc CEO to help the company organize and implement business systems. "It was basically a temporary thing," says Dineh Mohajer. "For a given term, a CEO comes in and helps companies that need short-term direction and integration of systems—basically cleaning house and setting up of procedures." A new executive in charge of financial information inventory systems was brought on board, as well as a vice president of sales. "Some of the first steps we took in strategic planning were hiring departments heads. We hired marketing, production, and sales managers throughout the country and overseas," says Geannie Chavez, vice president of sales. "Hard Candy started to grow so quickly that if it didn't have some kind of formal structure implemented in the organization, the company wouldn't be able to take its success to the next level. Hard Candy needed the guidance that the seasoned CEO brought to the company."

"When you're in the middle of running and putting out fires left and right, it's like crisis management," says Pooneh Mohajer. "It's very difficult to take a step back, take a deep breath, and say, 'Okay, what's our strategy here?' With the expertise of the new CEO, we were able to implement accounting systems, inventory tracking systems, and basically put together a management team, a controller, which are all crucial management positions that Hard Candy needed to take the company to the next level."

Although Hard Candy is growing at an astonishing rate, its fairly loose structure has kept the corporate grind at bay. "We are doing better about conducting meetings and making sure we accomplish goals on a regular basis," admits Einstein. Because Hard Candy is still a small business, making decisions is still relatively easy. In the near future, the firm plans to expand its sales, marketing, public relations, and other department, including accounting and operations.

With more than three years under their belts and some business systems in place, the three founders are confident enough to run the business themselves. The temporary CEO is gone. "Collectively the three owners are the CEOs," explains Dinah Mohajer, "but individually, we don't have the track record as being CEOs." Remarkably, this team approach has fueled Hard Candy's success. Although the company's structure may be as unconventional as its product colors and names, it works. Today Hard Candy offers seasonal cosmetic lines, and plans to expand its distribution into South America and Asia and introduce a line of Hard Candy clothing and accessories. There are still issues and challenges that can't be glossed over, but as Dineh Mohajer explains, "I am a business owner; my heart is in the business."

QUESTIONS

1. Dineh Mohajar is the same age as Hard Candy's target market. So are many key employees. If the owner of a company is a member of its target market, are the owner's insights about her product requirements enough or does the company need marketing research?

2. Hard Candy has a toll-free telephone hotline. Callers' names are recorded in a database. What implications could this have for marketing research surveys?

3. Hard Candy is expanding into new product categories and into new countries. How do the information needs of an entrepreneurial company change as it grows from a small start-up to a large international business?

Case 1.2 **Texas Department of Highways**

THE POPULATION OF TEXAS HAD BEEN GROWING AT A rapid rate for decades. With the population growth, the state's highways and cities' streets faced a growing problem with litter. The careless disposal of beverage containers had become a particular problem. It was estimated that the cost of picking up litter along the state's highways amounted to more than $20 million.

The Texas Department of Highways and Public Transportation determined that a marketing effort to educate the people of Texas concerning the detrimental effects of littering was in order. It believed that every citizen needed to be reminded or persuaded not to litter. A few years ago, the Texas Department of Highways decided it needed to research the litter problem.

QUESTIONS

1. Should a state agency such as the Texas Department of Highways use marketing research? Why or why not?

2. If yes, what form should the marketing research take?

Case 1.3 **The Atlanta Braves**[34]

A VISIT TO TURNER FIELD, THE ATLANTA BRAVES' $242.5 million, state-of-the-art ballpark, feels like a trip back to the future.

BellSouth, one of the team's corporate sponsors, describes the stadium as "20th century tradition meets 21st century technology."

The Braves marketing campaign reflects the charm and nostalgia of baseball's past but it has a futuristic slogan, "Turner Field: Not just baseball. A baseball theme park."

Sure, baseball purists will love the fact they're closer to the action at Turner Field than at any other major league ballpark. It's only 45 feet from first to third bases to the dugouts. On top of that, there's a Braves Museum and Hall of Fame with more than 200 artifacts. Cybernauts will find Turner  Field exciting because it's a ballpark that makes them a part of the action. At the stadium, built for the 1998 summer Olympics and converted for baseball use since the games, are interactive games to test fans' hitting and pitching skills, as well as their knowledge of baseball trivia; electronic kiosks with touch screens and data banks filled with scouting reports on 300 past and present Braves, along with the Braves' Internet home page; a dozen 27-inch television monitors mounted above the Braves' Clubhouse Store, broadcasting all the other major league games in progress, and a video ticker-tape screen underneath, spitting out up-to-the-minute scores and stats.

A sophisticated BellSouth communications system, with four miles of fiber-optic cable underneath the playing field will allow for World Series games to be simulcast around the globe, as well as special black boxes placed throughout the stadium will allow for as many as 5,500 cellular phone calls an hour.

Welcome to the future of baseball. The idea behind the marketing of Turner Field is that for many fans it is not enough to simply provide nine innings of baseball.

Turner Field's theme-park concept was the brainchild of Braves President Stan Kasten. In the early 1990s, as the Braves grew into one of the best teams in baseball, Kasten increasingly became frustrated while watching fans flock to Atlanta-Fulton County Stadium a few hours before games with little to do but eat overcooked hot dogs and watch batting practice.

As Kasten saw it, they spent too much time milling on the club-level concourse and too little time spending money. What if he could find a way for families to make an outing of it, bring the amenities of the city to Hank Aaron Drive, and create a neighborhood feel in a main plaza at the ballpark? "I wanted to broaden fans' experience at the ballpark and broaden our fan base," Kasten says. "People have no problem spending money when they're getting value. We have one of the highest payrolls in baseball, and I needed to find new ways to sustain our revenues."

Turner Field's main entry plaza opens three hours before games—compared to two hours for the rest of the ballpark—and will stay open about two hours after games. On weekends, there'll be live music.

Everyone's invited—$1 "skyline seats" are available for each game—and that buck gets you anywhere, from the open-air porch at the Chop House restaurant, which specializes in barbecue, bison dogs, Moon Pies, and Tomahawk lager, to the grassy roof at Coke's Sky Field, where fans can keep cool under a mist machine.

Interactive games in Scouts Alley range from $1 to $4, and the chroma-key studios in the East and West Pavilions, where fans can have their picture inserted into a baseball card or a great moment in Braves history, cost $10 to $20. The Museum is $2. And it should come as no surprise that there are seven ATMs located throughout the ballpark.

One of the Braves' key marketing objectives is to help build a new generation of baseball fans. Its new stadium was planned so fans will find something to be loved and learned at every turn. The minute a fan's ticket is torn, he or she becomes part of the happening Turner Field.[33]

QUESTIONS

1. What are the key elements of the Turner Field marketing mix?

2. What aspects of the Atlanta Braves marketing mix might have been influenced by or developed based on marketing research?

3. What role should marketing research play in a sporting organization such as the Atlanta Braves

Chapter 2

Information Systems and Knowledge Management

F ROM HIS OFFICE WINDOW OVERLOOKING THE MAIN FLOOR OF the Harvard Cooperative Society, CEO Jerry Murphy can glance down and see customers shopping. They make their way through the narrow aisles of the crowded department store, picking up a sweatshirt here, trying on a baseball cap there, checking out the endless array of merchandise that bears the Harvard University insignia.

Watching Murphy, you can well imagine the Coop's founders, who started the store in 1882, peering through the tiny windowpanes to keep an eye on the shop floor. Was the Harvard Square store attracting steady traffic? Were the college students buying enough books and supplies for the Coop to make a profit? Back then, it was tough to answer those questions precisely. The owners had to watch and wait, relying only on their gut feelings to know how things were going from minute to minute.

Now, more than a hundred years later, Murphy can tell you, down to the last stockkeeping unit, how he's doing at any given moment. His window on the business is the Packard Bell PC that sits on his desk. All day long it delivers up-to-the-minute, easy-to-read electronic reports on what's selling and what's not, which items are running low in inventory and which have fallen short of forecast. In a matter of seconds the computer can report gross margins for any product or supplier, and Murphy can decide whether the margins are fat enough to justify keeping the supplier or product on board. "We were in the 1800s, and we had to move ahead," he says of the $55 million business.

To do so, Murphy installed a computerized decision support system. A decision support system is a sophisticated software program that analyzes the data an executive deems critical to his or her business and delivers the analyses to a computer screen as easy-to-read graphics and text reports. A decision support system can, for instance, spot a potential cash flow problem before it happens, enabling a CEO to avert a crisis.

Or it can show that seasonal inventory is not moving as fast as it was last year, which might prompt a company president to reduce prices to avoid getting stuck with extra goods. Its ultimate purpose is to give executives the detailed information they need to assess the state of their company and make informed decisions.

Decision support systems are not new: Large corporations have been using them for years. What's changed is how much more available they are to small and growing businesses. Cheaper, easier-to-use desktop computers and software have brought the price of entry—including hardware, software, and technical help—down from an average of about $100,000 to about $20,000. Most of the costs come not from the hardware or software but from the labor needed to organize the information so the software can read and analyze it.[1]

The Harvard Cooperative Society's use of a computerized decision support system illustrates how the management of information has changed in recent years. This chapter discusses the nature of decision support systems within the context of knowledge management and global information systems. It goes on to discuss the nature of decision support systems within the context of global information systems. It goes on to discuss the dramatic implications of the Internet on marketing research.

Information versus Data

data
Facts or recorded measures of certain phenomena.

information
Any body of facts in a format suitable for decision making or in a context that defines the relationship between two pieces of data.

Marketing managers must distinguish between data and information. **Data** are simply facts or recorded measures of certain phenomena; **information** is a body of facts in a format suitable to support decision making or to define the relationship between two pieces of data. To illustrate the difference between data and information, consider that Toys "Я" Us records thousands of unsummarized facts. A store clerk feeds data into the computer system each time he or she enters a transaction into a cash register. Simultaneously the data are also entered into a computerized inventory system. These data lack any meaning, however, until managers request the information system to translate the data into product sales totals by store, by county, or by state when they request forecasts for future time periods.

Zoos around the world increasingly use decision support systems and databases such as the Animal Records Keeping System to tap into information about their animal collections. The information ranges from how inbred an animal is to how much it costs and the number of times it has been on loan. Zoos are not just tracking animals; they keep customer databases as well. For example, if 10,000 people attended the zoo on the first Saturday of June in 1998 but only 6,000 attended the first Saturday of June in 1999, the zookeeper can see whether it was raining, whether there was another community event, or what else may have caused the drop.

The Characteristics of Valuable Information

Not all information is valuable to decision makers. Marketing information is useful if it helps a marketing manager make a decision. Information can be evaluated using four characteristics: relevance, quality, timeliness, and completeness.

Relevance

Information is relevant if it suits the needs of the marketer. The decision maker gets exactly what he or she wants from relevant information. Relevant information applies to the situation if it clarifies the questions that face the decision maker. It is meaningful because it is organized to meet the decision maker's requirements.

Quality

High-quality information is accurate, valid, and reliable. High-quality data present a good picture of reality. Information quality depends on the degree to which the information represents the true situation. This is a critical issue in marketing research, and it will be discussed throughout this textbook.

The author regularly receives two catalogs from Bloomingdales, one addressed to Mr. Zikmund and one to Mr. Vikmund. Bloomie's mailing list has problems with its information quality.

This is a critical issue in marketing research, and it will be discussed throughout this textbook.

Timeliness

Marketing is a dynamic field in which out-of-date information can lead to poor decisions. Marketing information must be timely, that is, provided at the right time.

Computerized information systems can record events and dispense relevant information soon after a transaction takes place. A great deal of marketing information becomes available almost at the moment that a transaction occurs.

Computer technology has redefined standards for timely information. For example, if a marketing manager at Kmart wishes to know the sales volume of any store worldwide, detailed information about any of thousands of products can be instantly determined. At Kmart a point-of-sale checkout system uses UPC scanners and satellite communications to link individual stores to the headquarters' computer system from which managers can retrieve and analyze up-to-the-minute sales data on all merchandise in each of 2,100 stores.

Completeness

Information completeness refers to having the right quantity of information. Marketing managers must have sufficient information about all aspects of their decisions. For example, a researcher investigating eastern European markets may plan to analyze four former Soviet-bloc countries. Population information may be available on all four countries along with each country's inflation rate. However, information about disposable personal income may be available only for three of the countries. If information about disposable personal income or another economic characteristics cannot be obtained, the information is incomplete. Often incomplete information leads decision makers to conduct marketing research.

As the twenty-first century begins, countries' borders are blurring to facilitate international marketing. The 15-nation European Union is becoming a single market, and companies that are marketing in Europe have a high demand for electronic data interchange systems and multilingual software for global information systems.

Knowledge Management

Effective organizations make a concerted effort to capture, organize, and share what the organization and its employees know.[2] They create knowledge, which is broader, deeper, and richer than data or information.[3] Knowledge can be defined many ways. However, for our purposes, **knowledge** is a blend of information, experience, and insights that provide a framework that can be thoughtfully applied when assessing new information or evaluating relevant situations.

Knowledge management is a process to create an inclusive, comprehensive, easily accessible organizational memory, which is often called the organization's intellectual capital.[4]

The purpose of knowledge management is to organize the intellectual capital of an organization in a formally structured way for easy use. Knowledge is presented in a way that helps employees comprehend and act on that information.[5]

New information technologies and new ways of thinking about data, information, and knowledge lie at the heart of knowledge management. Effective organizations systematically manage activities from information acquisition to the distribution of knowledge. Tools for preserving and sharing data, information, and knowledge involve global information systems, decision support systems, the Internet and intranets, as well as other communication vehicles as basic as newsletters.

knowledge
A blend of information, experience, and insights that provides a framework that can be thoughtfully applied when assessing new information or evaluating relevant situations.

knowledge management
A process to create an inclusive, comprehensive, easily accessible organizational memory, which is often called the organization's intellectual capital.

Global Information Systems

The well-being of a multinational corporation, indeed, the health of any business organization that plans to prosper in the twenty-first century will depend on information about the world economy and global competition. Contemporary marketers require timely and accurate information from countless sources to maintain competitive advantages.

Increased global competition and technological advances in interactive media have given rise to global information systems. A **global information system** is an organized collection of computer hardware, software, data, and personnel designed to capture, store, update, manipulate, analyze, and immediately display information about worldwide business activities.[6] A global information system is a tool for providing past, present, and projected information on internal operations and external activity. It organizes and integrates data from production, operations, marketing, finance, accounting, and other business functions. It organizes and integrates data from production, operations, marketing, finance, accounting, and other business functions. Using satellite communications, high-speed microcomputers, electronic data interchanges, fiber optics, CD-ROM data storage, fax machines, and other technological advances in interactive media, global information systems are changing the nature of business.

Consider a simple example. At any moment, United Parcel Service (UPS) can track the status of any shipment around the world. UPS drivers use hand-held electronic clipboards called delivery information acquisition devices (DIADs) to record appropriate data about each pickup or delivery. The data are then entered into the company's main computer for record keeping and analysis. A satellite telecommunications system allows UPS to track any shipment for a customer.

With so much diverse information available in a global information system, organizations have found it necessary to determine what data, information, and knowledge are most useful to particular business units.

global information system
An organized collection of computer hardware, software, data, and personnel designed to capture, store, update, manipulate, analyze, and immediately display information about worldwide business activity.

TO THE POINT

An immense and ever-increasing wealth of knowledge is scattered about the world today; knowledge that would probably suffice to solve all the mighty difficulties of our age, but it is dispersed and unorganized. We need a sort of mental clearing house for the mind: a depot where knowledge and ideas are received, sorted, summarized, digested, clarified and compared.[7]

H. G. WELLS

Decision Support Systems

An organization may have several, even many, decision support systems that are components of its larger global information system. A marketing **decision support system** is a computer-based system that helps decision makers confront problems through direct interaction with databases and analytical software programs. The purpose of a decision support system is to store data and transform them into organized information that is easily accessible to marketing managers. If executives at Motorola must price their cellular phones for European markets, they can get immediate information about international exchange rates without leaving their desks. An advertising agency can find out the next day how many urban viewers remember its Nike commercial aired during the Super Bowl.

Decision support systems serve specific business units within a company, operating within the context of the global information system. It should be understood that a single decision support system is not independent from the more comprehensive global information system.

decision support system
A computer based system that helps decision makers confront problems through direct interaction with databases and analytical software programs.

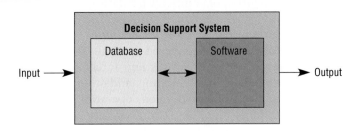

Exhibit 2.1 **Decision Support System**

Exhibit 2.1 illustrates a decision support system. Raw, unsummarized data are input to the decision support system. Data collected in marketing research projects are a major source of this input, but the data input may be purchased or collected by accountants, sales managers, production managers, or company employees other than marketing researchers. Effective marketers spend a great deal of time and effort collecting information for input into the decision support system. Useful information is the output of a decision support system. A decision support system requires both databases and software.

Databases and Data Warehousing

database

A collection of raw data arranged logically and organized in a form that can be stored and processed by a computer.

A **database** is a collection of raw data arranged logically and organized in a form that can be stored and processed by a computer. A customer mailing list is one type of database. Population characteristics may be recorded by state, county, and city in another database. Databases often exist in computer storage devices such as hard-disk drives, but other types of databases may exist in a vendor company's computers.

Because most companies compile and store many different databases, they often develop data warehousing systems. *Data warehousing* is a term that managers of information technology use to refer to the process that allows important data collected from day-to-day computer systems (often called operating systems) to be stored and organized into separate systems designed for simplified access.[8] The concept of a *data warehouse* implies a comprehensive collection of all data that characterize the operations of an organization. More specifically, a data warehouse is the multitiered computer storage of current and historical data and the mechanics of selecting and using information that is relevant to decision-making tasks. Data warehouse management requires that the detailed data from operational systems be extracted, transformed, and stored (warehoused) so that the various database files (commonly referred to as *tables)* are consistent. Organizations with data warehousing may integrate databases from both inside and outside the company.[9]

The development of data warehouses requires database management software to provide easy access to the data. It also allows for sophisticated analysis, such as data mining as discussed in Chapter 7.

Software

software

Consists of various types of programs that tell computers, printers, and other hardware what to do.

The **software** portion of a decision support system consists of various types of programs that tell computers, printers, and other hardware what to do. Advances in spreadsheet and statistical software have revolutionized the analysis of marketing data. A decision support system's software allows managers to combine and restructure databases, diagnose relationships, estimate variables, and otherwise analyze the various databases.

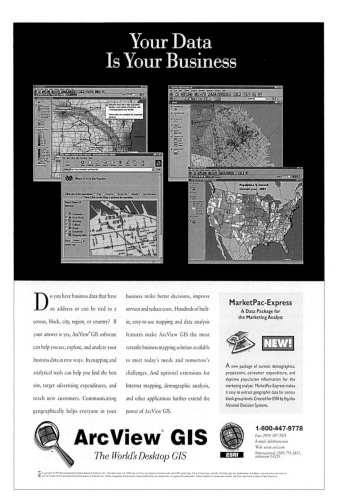

ESRI's ArcView databases and computer software for colorful maps allow researchers to exhibit marketing data by geographical area such as zip code, census track, or sales territory. ArcView integrates visualization and data management tools so customization of maps is an easy pint-and-click task.

Depending on the software, computer-based reporting systems provide a wealth of information related to costs, shipments, sales, and so on. The database of internal records can generate a number of periodic reports to help managers improve performance. Often accounting information can be transformed, using an electronic spreadsheet, to provide marketing information. A product manager might ask the computer for sales by product line, inventory reports, back-order reports, and so forth every month or every week (in some cases, every day).

Decision support systems have advanced internal reporting in many ways. Desktop computer terminals with graphics software now convert endless

Exhibit 2.2 **Four Major Sources of Marketing Input for Decision Support Systems**

SOURCE	EXAMPLES
Internal records	Orders, goods-in-process inventory, product-line sales histories
Proprietary marketing research	Survey findings, test market results
Marketing intelligence	Competition price changes, new industry technology
Outside vendors and external distributors	Industry sales trends, competitors' market shares, demographic trends

---

columns of numbers to color charts, graphs, and maps. For example, members of PepsiCo's business planning group can generate on demand hundreds of charts and graphs that compare sales and earnings for each division with past performance and corporate projections.

Most of today's software is so user-friendly that it is easy for nonexperts to maintain direct control over a computer's tasks and outcomes. A manager can sit at a computer terminal and instantaneously retrieve data files and request special, creative analyses to refine, modify, or generate information in a tailor-made format suited specifically for evaluating particular consequences or alternatives.

Input Management

The discussion to this point has focused on the organization and accessibility of computerized information. We have not described the nature of the input function in detail.

Inputs include all the numerical, text, voice, and image data that enter the decision support system. Systematic accumulation of pertinent, timely, and accurate data is essential to the success of a decision support system. Clearly, the input function must be managed.

Decision support system managers, systems analysts, and programmers are responsible for the system as a whole, but many functions within an organization provide input data. Marketing researchers, accountants, corporate librarians, sales personnel, production managers, and many others within the organization help to collect data and provide input for the decision support system.

Input data can come from both internal and external sources. Exhibit 2.2 shows four major sources of input for marketing data: internal records, proprietary marketing research, marketing intelligence, and outside vendors and external distributors of data. Each source can provide valuable input.

Internal records, such as accounting reports of sales and inventory figures, provide considerable data that may become useful information for marketing managers. An effective data collection system establishes orderly procedures to ensure that data about costs, shipments, inventory, sales, and other aspects of regular operations are routinely collected and entered into the computer.

Marketing research has already been defined as a broad set of procedures and methods. To clarify the decision support system concept, consider a narrower view of marketing research. **Proprietary marketing research** emphasizes the company's gathering of new data. Few proprietary marketing research procedures and methods are conducted regularly or continuously. Instead, research projects conducted to study specific company problems generate data; this is proprietary marketing research. Most of this book deals with this kind of marketing research. Providing managers with nonroutine data that

proprietary marketing research
A data collection system that gathers new data to investigate specific problems.

WHAT WENT WRONG?

Special K[10]

SPECIAL K, THE FAT-FREE, TOASTED RICE CEREAL, HAVing made its debut in 1955, is the grandmother of diet foods.

A recent television commercial showed a thin and beautiful woman expressing her happiness with Special K. She was shown in front of her bedroom mirror taking pride in the fact that she looks great in a skin-tight dress. What could go wrong with television commercials showing attractive models squeezing their drop-dead perfect bodies into clingy dresses and attributing it to Special K as part of their diets?

Plenty, as it turned out. In letters written to the company, women indicated they were alien-ated by the ads. They told Kellogg they really couldn't relate to advertising techniques that used unrealistic body images. This was especially strong among baby boomers viewing the message. One woman's comment about the Special K commercial said it all. "When she was in that little dress saying, 'I'm hot, I'm great,' it really bothered me. Because I could never be like that."

Based on such marketing intelligence information (and subsequent research to confirm the findings), Kellogg dropped the ad campaign and started a new one that suggested healthy, even chunky, can be beautiful. In place of thin women tugging at their clothes, one commercial shows men at a bar. It pokes fun at women's complaints about their bodies. "I have my mother's thighs. I have to accept that," one man says. "Do these make my butt look big?" another asks. The message: "Men don't obsess about these things. Why do women?"

otherwise would not be available is a major function of proprietary marketing research.

The term *marketing intelligence* has been defined in a variety of ways. A restrictive and specialized definition works best: A marketing intelligence system consists of a network of sources and regular procedures by which marketing executives obtain everyday information about nonrecurrent developments in the external marketing environment.For example, Procter & Gamble discovered a need to change its slogan for Puritan Oil, "Make it his oil for life," through marketing intelligence. Ongoing investigations of consumer complaints registered via the company's toll-free telephone number indicated that the slogan was considered sexist. Consumers didn't like the new theme, even though it was only slightly changed from the earlier "Make it your oil for life." Toll-free numbers and consumer correspondence are two of many sources of intelligence about external environments.

Sales forces work in firms' external environments so they commonly provide essential marketing intelligence. Sales representatives' call reports frequently alert managers to changes in competitors' prices and new-product offerings.

Outside vendors and external distributors market information as their products. Many organizations specialize in the collection and publication of high-quality information. One outside vendor, the A. C. Nielsen Company, provides television program ratings, audience counts, and information about the demographic composition of television viewer groups. Other vendors specialize in the distribution of information. Public libraries have always purchased information, traditionally in the form of books, and they have served as distributors of this information.

Media representatives often provide useful data about their audiences' characteristics and purchasing behavior. *Advertising Age, The Wall Street Journal, Sales and Marketing Management,* and other trade and business-oriented publications are important sources of information. These publications keep managers

RESEARCH INSIGHT

We Are Resetting Our Clocks to Real Time[11]

IMAGINE A WORLD IN WHICH TIME SEEMS TO VANISH and space seems completely malleable. Where the gap between need or desire and fulfillment collapses to zero. Where distance equals a microsecond in lapsed connection time. A virtual world created at your command. Imagine a world in which everything you do, from work to education, is clothed as an entertainment-like experience, veiled by technology so subtle and transparent that you have no idea it is there at all. Habits, attitudes, opinions, preferences, expectations, demands, perceptions, and needs all adapt unwittingly to an environment in which immediacy rules.

All of this may sound like material for a science fiction thriller. But it is very nearly the world we are living in today.

Technology is transforming our existence in profound ways, and the pace of change is speeding up, not slowing down. Almost all technology today is focused on compressing to zero the amount of time it takes to acquire and use information, to learn, to make decisions, to initiate action, to deploy resources, to innovate. When action and response are simultaneous, we are in *real time*.

Real time is what Regis McKenna calls our sense of ultracompressed time and foreshortened horizons in these years of the millennial countdown. The change in our consciousness of time is the creation of ubiquitous programmable technology producing results at the click of a mouse or the touch of a button or key. Real time occurs when time and distance vanish, when action and response are simultaneous.

up-to-date about the economy, competitors' activities, and other aspects of the marketing environment.

Companies called data specialists record and store certain marketing information. Computer technology has changed the way many of these organizations supply data, favoring the development of computerized databases.

Computerized Data Archives

Historically, collections of organized and readily retrievable data were available in published form at libraries. The *Statistical Abstract of the United States,* which is filled with tables of statistical facts, provides a characteristic example. Printed copies of this book can be found in most public and corporate libraries. In recent years, the *Statistical Abstract* has also become available in a digital format on CD-ROM, and certain portions are available on the Internet. The entire 1990 census is also available in print, on CD-ROM, and on certain databases that can be accessed on the Internet. As the twenty-first century progresses, even more data will be stored in digitized form in computerized data archives.

Today, businesspeople can use personal computers and modems to access on-line information services, such as Nexis/Lexis, or Dow-Jones News Retrieval, without leaving their offices. The amount of data accessible by computer is extensive.

Commercial Database Search Systems

Numerous database search and retrieval systems are available as subscription services or in libraries. Modern library patrons command a computer to search databases from a range of vendors. A researcher can query the library computer to learn whether the library owns a particular book and whether that book is on the shelf or checked out.

Computerized database searches offer the most efficient and exhaustive way to find published information. Major wholesalers or on-line vendors of bibliographic databases include BRS (BRS Information Technologies), INFOTRAC, DIALOG (Dialog Information Services, Inc.), NEXIS (Mead Data Central, Inc.), and Dow Jones News/Retrieval Services. These services provide access to computer-readable databases for business executives and scholars.

DIALOG, for example, maintains more than 350 databases. A typical database may have a million or more records, each consisting of a one- or two-paragraph abstract that summarizes the major points of a published article along with bibliographic information. One of the DIALOG's databases, ABI/INFORM, abstracts significant articles in more than 800 current business and management journals.

The discussion thus far has focused on bibliographic databases, but many computerized archives provide more than abstracts of published articles and journals. *The New York Times* database and the Dow Jones/Text-Search Services are full-text databases that allow the retrieval of an entire article or document. ABI/INFORM offers full-text versions of the articles on CD-ROM.

Several types of databases from outside vendors and external distributors are so fundamental to decision support systems that they deserve further explanation.

Statistical Databases.
Statistical databases contain numerical data for market analysis and forecasting. Statistical databases are exemplified by geographical information systems and scanner databases.

Geographic Databases.
A geographic information system is a decision support system that maps geographic areas by demographic, sales, and other relevant marketing variables. For various purpose and in various ways, these systems use powerful software to prepare computer maps using databases of relevant variables. Companies such as Claritas, Urban Decision Systems, and CACI all offer geographic/demographic databases that are widely used in industry.

Scanner Databases.
Optical scanners in supermarkets and other retail outlets provide a wealth of product and brand sales information collectively known as scanner data or single-source data. (The term *single-source data* refers to the ability of these systems to gather several types of interrelated data, such as purchase, sales promotion, or advertising frequency data, from a single source in a format that will facilitate integration, comparison, and analysis.) As the number of scanner-equipped stores continues to increase, scanner systems are replacing mechanical systems for in-store auditing. Substituting mechanized record keeping for human record keeping results in greater accuracy and rapid feedback about store activity.

One disadvantage of single-source scanner data is that the largest stores, such as supermarkets, mass merchandisers, and warehouse retailers, are most likely to have scanner systems, causing the sample of stores to be less than perfectly representative. However, things are changing. A.C. Nielsen and the National Housewares Manufacturers Association formed a partnership to provide data generated by the Universal Product Codes scanned at housewares retailers' checkouts. Nevertheless, if a large percentage of a product category's sales occur in small stores or in vending machines (for example, candy), which tend not to have scanners, the marketer should be aware that the scanner data may not be representative.

The Universal Product Code (UPC) contains information on the category of goods (differentiating grocery and drug items, for example), the manufacturer, and product identification based on size, flavor, color, and so on. As the laser beam at the checkout counters reads the code, a computer-assisted sales receipt is printed with price and other descriptive information, and the computer records this in its memory for inventory management and analytical purposes.

Financial Databases. Competitors' and customers' financial data, such as income statements and balance sheets, may interest marketing managers. These are easy to access in financial databases. CompuStat publishes a financial database of extensive financial data about thousands of companies broken down by industry and other criteria. To illustrate the depth of this pool of information, CompuStat's Global Advantage offers extensive data on 6,650 companies in more than 30 countries in Europe, the Pacific Basin, and North America.

Image and Video Databases. As the twenty-first century progresses, video databases of digitally stored photographs and films will be commonplace. Today the Library of Congress maintains an extensive image database of historical photographs. The Fine Art Museum of San Francisco maintains digital images of its collection in its ImageBase. The Cartoon Bank (www.cartoonbank.com) archives more than 85,000 cartoons from *The New Yorker Magazine*. Web portals, such as Excite.com and Snap.com, offer up-to-the-minute forecasts and hourly updated satellite photographs for the weather in any city in the United States.

Video databases will have a major impact on the marketing of many goods and services. For example, movie studios provide clips of upcoming films on the Internet. Marketing of health care will radically change, especially in rural areas, when computerized patient records, including X-rays and other medical images, are instantly available to any hospital or faraway medical specialist.[12] Just imagine the value of video databases to advertising agencies' decision support systems.

Exhibit 2.3 describes the most popular on-line information services. For a more extensive listing, see the *Gale Directory of Databases*.[13]

Networks and Electronic Data Interchange

Although personal computers work independently, they can connect through networks to other computers. Networking involves linking two or more computers to share data and software.

electronic data interchange (EDI)
Occurs when one company's computer system is integrated with another company's system

Electronic data interchange (EDI) systems integrate one company's computer system directly with another company's system. Today much input to a company's decision support system comes through networks from other companies' computers. Companies such as Computer Technology Corporation and Microelectronics market data services that allow corporations to exchange business information with suppliers or customers. For example, every evening Wal-Mart transmits millions of characters of data about the day's sales to its apparel suppliers. Wrangler, a supplier of blue jeans, for instance, shares the data and a model that interprets the data. It also shares software applications that act to replenish stocks in Wal-Mart stores. This decision support system

Exhibit 2.3 Selected On-Line Information Services and Examples of Their Databases

INFORMATION ON-LINE SERVICE	SELECTED SAMPLE DATABASES	TYPE OF DATA
BRS (BRS Information Technologies)	ABI/INFORM*	Abstracts of significant articles in over 800 business and management journals
	Disclosure Database	Financial data on over 12,500 publicly held companies that file reports with the Securities and Exchange Commission
	PTS PROMPT	Abstracts of articles on industries, companies, products, markets, and similar topics in leading business/trade journals, with some full-text records
Infotrac	General BusinessFile	Full-text articles and abstracts on finance, acquisitions and mergers, international trade, money management, new technologies and products, local and regional business trends and investments and banking.
	General Reference Center (Magazine Index)	A general interest database to search magazines, reference books, and newspapers for information on current evens, popular culture, the arts and sciences, sports, and more.
Books In Print		Describes books in and out of print. Almost 2 million titles retrievable by title, author, subject, publisher, publication date, ISBN, and more.
LegalTrac		Case studies, government regulations, practice of law, statutes, taxation and international law. Articles from law reviews and law and bar association journals.
Predicasts PROMT	See above description	
DIALOG (Dialog Information Services, Inc.)	ABI/INFORM*	See description under BRS
	ASI (American Statistics Index)	Abstracts and indexes of federal government statistical publications
	Business Dateline*	Full texts of articles in U.S. and Canadian regional business publications
	CENDATA	Current economic and demographic statistics and facts from U.S. census data
	Disclosure Database	See description under BRS
	Investext*	Full texts of reports on companies and industries prepared by investment analysts in investment banking and other financial research organizations
	PTS Marketing & Advertising Reference Service (MARS)	Abstracts of articles on marketing and advertising for consumer goods and services, including advertising as a function and market strategies
	PTS PROMT	See description under BRS
	Trade and Industry Index	Index of over 300 trade, industry, and commercial journals, with selected coverage of many more, plus local and regional publications
NEXIS (Mead Data Central, Inc.)	ABI/INFORM*	See description under BRS
	Advertising Age	Full text of articles in this basic advertising weekly
	Business Dateline	See description under DIALOG
	New York Times	Full text for articles in this newspaper
	Value Line Datafile*	Financial facts about some 1,800 companies in over 80 industries
Dow Jones News/Retrieval (Dow Jones & Company)	*Advertising Age*	See description under NEXIS
	Business Dateline	See description under NEXIS
	Disclosure Database	See description under BRS
	Dow Jones Enhanced Current Quotes	Current price quotations for stocks, bonds, options, mutual funds, Treasury issues. Related databases cover current and historical price quotations for stocks, bonds, futures, and indexes.
	Dow Jones Text-Search Services	Six files, which include full text in *The Wall Street Journal, Washington Post, Barron's Business Week* and other business periodicals

*These databases are also on CD-ROM.

determines when to send specific quantities of specific sizes and colors of jeans to specific stores from specific warehouses. The result is a learning loop that lowers inventory costs and leads to fewer stockouts.

What Is the Internet?

Internet
A worldwide network of computers that allows users access to information and documents from distant success.

e-mail
Electronic mail a user can send to communicate with other users over the internet.

The **Internet** is a worldwide network of computers that allows users access to information and documents from distant sources. Because it is a combination of a worldwide communication system and the world's largest public library for a seemingly endless range of information, many people believe the Internet is the most important communications medium since television.

The Internet has changed the way millions of people think about getting and distributing information. It is estimated that more than 150 million users are linked across the Internet.[14] The number of users doubled annually in the 1990s, making it the fastest-growing communications medium in history.[15]

Computer communication and resource discovery are two central functions of the Internet. Electronic mail and messaging is the most widespread communication function. For example, users send messages on the Internet by **e-mail** (electronic mail) to ask questions of experts or, in other ways, communicate with individuals who share similar interests. Just as a letter delivered by a postal worker requires an address, so does e-mail. An e-mail address consists of two parts, separated by the *at* symbol (@). The name of the user's mailbox is on the left-hand side. The name of the system on which the mailbox resides is on the right-hand side. System, or domain, names have two or more fields, separated by dots and can follow many different naming schemes, such as by country (.us, .jp) or by type of activity (.com, .org).

The domain is typically a company name, institutional name, or organizational name associated with the host computer. For example, *Forbes* magazine Internet edition is located at forbes.com. The "com" indicates this domain is a commercial site. Educational sites end in "edu," government sites end in "gov," and other types of organizations end in "org."

The Internet allows instantaneous and effortless access to a great deal of information. Noncommercial and commercial organizations make a wealth of data and other resources available on the Internet. For example, the U.S. Library of Congress provides full text of all versions of House and Senate legislation and full

If you discover an Internet term you do not understand, chances are that you will find its definition at NetLingo: The Internet Language Dictionary (http://www.netlingo.com).

text of the Congressional Record. The Internal Revenue Service, as well, makes it possible to download an income tax form. Harcourt Brace College Publishers (http://www.hbcollege.com) and its Dryden Press division (http://www.dryden. com) have on-line directories that allow college professors to access information about the company and its textbooks.

The Internet began in 1969 as an experimental hookup between computers at Stanford University, the University of California at Santa Barbara, the University of California at Los Angeles, and the University of Utah in conjunction with the Department of Defense.[16] The Defense Department was involved because it wanted a research and development communications network that could survive nuclear war. The Internet gradually grew into a nationwide network of connected computers and now is a worldwide network often referred to as the "information superhighway." The Internet has no central computer, instead each message sent bears an address code that lets the sender forward a message to a desired destination from any computer linked to the Net.[17] Many benefits of the Internet arise because the Internet is a collection of thousands of small networks, both domestic and overseas, rather than a single computer operation. These many small networks contain millions of databases that are accessible to Internet users, mostly without fees.

TO THE POINT

The Net is 10.5 on the Richter scale of economic change.

NICHOLAS NEGROPONTE

The Internet consists of host computers that access what are called servers to reach data.[18] A **host** is a computer that performs user services, either client or server, such as sending and receiving e-mail and navigating the World Wide Web. A client machine is the requestor of activity that mediates between the end user and a remote server. So the client machine asks for work, but **servers,** computers that provide services on the Internet, do the actual work. The same machine can do double duty as client and server. A personal computer usually is only a client; however, a campus mainframe can be a server for local users and a client allowing access to machines elsewhere on the Internet.

There are several types of servers. A file server contains documents and programs that can be accessed and downloaded via the host to a user's own personal computer. A list server permits subscribers to use a mailing list to communicate with others around the globe. A user discussion server permits multiple users to communicate in real time with others. Note that the same university mainframe that provides access for the faculty may also act as a server, providing the faculty and other Internet users with a collection of publicly accessible files.

In the following pages we discuss the World Wide Web and how to use the Internet for research. However, you must first be cautioned that the Internet is constantly changing. The description of the Internet, especially home page addresses, may be out of date by the time this book is published. *Be aware that the Internet of today will not be the Internet of tomorrow.*

host
A computer that one or more persons can use directly by logging on to a personal computer connected to it in order to access network services.

server
A computer that provides services on the Internet.

Navigating the Internet

Anyone with a computer and a modem can access the Internet by subscribing to a gateway company, such as America Online, AT&T WorldNet, Earthlink, or WorldCom, known as an Internet Service Provider (ISP). In addition, many college and university campus networks also offer Internet access either in common user laboratories or through off-campus dial-up services.

WHAT WENT RIGHT?

Action Man

ACTION MAN IS THE EUROPEAN COUNTERPART TO G.I. Joe, and he has his very own Web site, courtesy of Hasbro Europe, the U.K.-based division of toymaker Hasbro International.[19] After a design team created the site, graphics services manager Julian Jones decided he needed to find out how people were using it. To do so, he installed Market Focus, a site-analysis tool on the company's server. The first thing Jones learned from the Market Focus reports was that fully 40 percent of Action Man's visitors never even crossed the threshold. From that information, he deduced that they were literally being blown away by the time it took to load the site's snazzy graphics. "We thought people would wait," says Jones, "but we were wrong."

By making the opening image smaller, the team reduced the number of visitors who bailed before entering to 25 percent. Also in response to the data, Jones rearranged links to take visitors deeper into the site on the first click. As a result,

the duration of the average visit has increased by almost 50 percent to 11 minutes.

Jones could have tried tracking site usage himself, but analyzing the data produced by a log server is tedious, time-consuming, and often produces errors. Fortunately, the Internet industry has never been shy about offering solutions, and there now exists a whole category of tools that address the tracking problem. These products use different means, but they have in mind the same end: to tally, slice, and present log data so that they yield valuable visitor information.

The companies that offer site-tracking services collect data from clients' server logs and provide regular reports. Depending on the company and the customer, these services can take readings once a day or as often as every half-hour. (Not surprisingly, frequent readings of server logs can exact a price in performance, but some site owners prefer that to the possibility of receiving outdated reports.) Once they are collected, the data can be amassed in a variety of ways, enabling users to answer questions such as: How many visitors came from Japan? How many visitors went straight from the home page to our order form? Or even, how many visitors from Japan went straight from the home page to our order form?

World Wide Web
A graphical interface system of thousands of interconnected pages or documents.

content provider
Party that furnishes information on the World Wide Web.

web site
One or more Web pages with related information about a particular topic.

home page
The introductory page or opening screen of a web site.

hyperlinks
Connections from one Web page to other Web pages, which may be on any computer connected to the Internet.

The **World Wide Web (WWW)** refers to that portion of the Internet servers that support a retrieval system that organizes information into "documents" called Web pages. These World Wide Web documents, which may include graphic images, video clips, and sound clips, are formatted in a special programming language called HTML (hypertext markup language) that allows for the linking and sharing of information. Hypertext refers to a graphical interface system that allows related resources to be linked together. HTTP (Hypertext Transfer Protocol) is the traditional method for transferring and displaying HTML information on the Internet.

Over the past few years, many universities, government agencies, academic associations, newspapers, TV networks, libraries, and corporations have decided to provide information on the Internet. Parties that furnish information on the World Wide Web are called **content providers.** Content providers maintain Web sites. A **Web site** consists of one or more Web pages with related information about a particular topic, such as a university Web site with pages about its mission, courses, and faculty. The introductory page or opening screen is called the **home page** because it provides basic information about the purpose of the document along with a menu of selections or links that lead to other screens with more specific information. Thus, each page can have connections or **hyperlinks** to other pages, which may be on any computer connected to the Internet. People using the World Wide Web may be viewing information on their host computer or on a machine halfway around the world. The World Wide Web allows users to point and click where they want to go and to call up video, sound bytes, and graphics from different participating computer networks around the world.

To access the World Wide Web, the typical home user needs a Web **browser,** which is a software program with a graphical user interface that enables the user to display Web pages as well as navigate the Internet.[20] Popular Web browsers, such as Netscape Navigator and Microsoft Explorer, make it easy to move from server to server on the World Wide Web (often called navigating the Net, navigation, or surfing). With these Web browsers even a novice on the Internet can search for information by simply using point-and-click graphics that resemble the familiar Windows or Macintosh interface. The links to other documents are usually highlighted by appearing in another color, by being underlined, or by having a unique icon. Often the user may be linked to a series of expanded menus or navigation buttons containing descriptions of the contents of various Web pages around the Internet. The user moves the cursor to highlighted words or colorful icons and then clicks the mouse button to immediately go to the file, regardless of what server it may be stored on. At this point the user can either read or download the material. By clicking on "U.S. Government Information" in one electronic document, for example, a Netscape user might connect to a computer with more information in Washington, DC. A few more clicks, and the user could be perusing files from the U.S. Census Bureau or the Small Business Administration.

Most web browsers also allow the user to enter a **Uniform Resource Locator** (**URL**) into the Web program. The URL is really just a Web site address that Web browsers recognize. A Web site is any computer host acting as a location that can be accessed with the browser software. Many Web sites allow any user or visitor to access its Web pages without previous approval. However, many commercial sites require that the user have a valid account and password before access is granted.

A researcher who finds a particular site or document on the Internet or is just looking for a resource list on a particular subject can use one of the many Internet search engines. A **search engine** is a computerized directory that allows anyone to search the World Wide Web for information in a particular way. Some search titles or headers of documents, others search words in the documents themselves, and still others search other indexes or directories. Yahoo (http://www.yahoo.com) and Excite (http://www/excite.com) offer such a broad array of resources and services that they are also called portals. A person using Yahoo will find lists of broad categories on topics such as art, business, entertainment, and government. Clicking on one of these topics leads to other subdirectories or home pages. An alternative way to use a search engine is to type keywords and phrases associated with the search and wait for a list of Web sites to be displayed. (See Exhibit 2.4).

Some of the most comprehensive and accurate search engines are:

Yahoo	http://www.yahoo.com
Snap	http://www.snap.com
Gobble	http://www.gobble.com
Hotbot	http://www.hotbot.com
Go network	http://www.go.com
Excite	http://www.excite.com
Lycos	http://www.lycos.com
Alta Vista	http://www.altavista.com
WebCrawler	http://www.webcrawler.com

Some specialized search engines provide unique services tailor-made for a

browser
A software program with a graphical user interface that enables the user to display Web pages as well as navigate the Internet.

Uniform Resource Locator (URL)
A Web site address that Web browsers recognize.

search engine
A computerized directory that allows anyone to search the World Wide Web for information in a particular way.

Doing a Category Search

As each menu comes up, the useer selects from it. The search progressively narrows until a specific web site is reached.

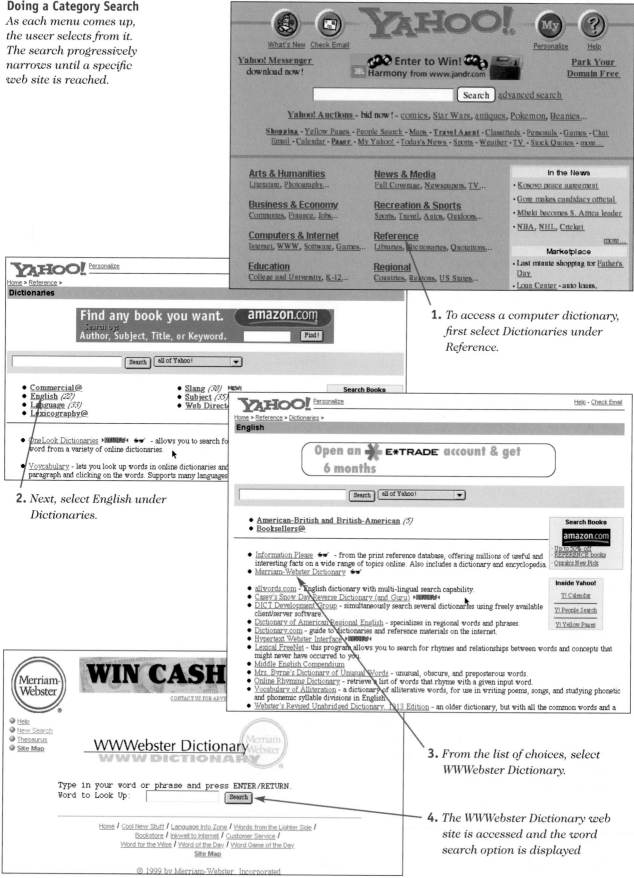

1. *To access a computer dictionary, first select Dictionaries under Reference.*

2. *Next, select English under Dictionaries.*

3. *From the list of choices, select WWWebster Dictionary.*

4. *The WWWebster Dictionary web site is accessed and the word search option is displayed*

© 1999 by Merriam-Webster, Incorporated

Doing a Search

A string search lets the user type in a keyword or phrase that relates to the topic.

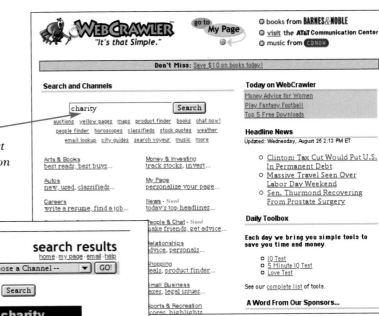

1. *First, move the cursor to the text box preceeding the Search button and enter a word.*

2. *After the Search button is selected, a list of documents will appear.*

3. *By selecting a document from the list, you access Web sites associated with the document.*

particular industry or for a specific task. For example, Excalibur Image Surfer at http://isurf.interpix.com, http://www.interpix.com, or http://www.isurf.yahoo.com provides a means for finding images available on the Internet.

Interactive Media and Environmental Scanning

interactive medium
A medium a person can use to communicate with and interact with other users, as well as with the Internet.

environmental scanning
Entails all information gathering that is designed to detect indications of environmental changes in their initial stages of development.

People who use the Internet interact with their computers. It is an **interactive medium** because a user clicks a command, and the computer responds in sophisticated ways so the user and equipment can have a continuing conversation. Two or more individuals who communicate via one-to-one e-mail on a service such as America Online are also using interactive media. So are those individuals who communicate with many senders and receivers via bulletin boards. Because of its vastness, the Internet is an especially useful source for scanning many types of changes in the environment. **Environmental scanning** entails all information gathering that is designed to detect indications of environmental changes in their initial stages of development.

In 1999 Ford Motor Company initiated an ambitious Internet-based relationship marketing program called "The Connection" that, among other things, helps the automobile marketer scan its environment using the Internet.[21] A Dealer connection creates a centralized communication service linking its dealers via an Internet connection. Its Buyer connection allows prospective buyers to get price quotes and financial information via Ford's Web site. The Owner connection allows an owner who registers and supplies pertinent vehicle information to get free e-mail and other ownership perks. A perk might be a free Hertz upgrade or an autographed photo of one of the Ford-sponsored NASCAR drivers. In return Ford collects data at all levels, which allows it to scan for trends and apply its learning at a local level.

Push Technology

push technology
Delivers content to the viewer's desktop using computer software known as smart agents to find information without the user having to do the searching.

smart agent software
Capable of learning an Internet user's preferences and automatically searching out information in selected Web sites and then distributing it.

Push technology delivers content to the viewer's desktop, using computer software known as smart agents or intelligent agents to find information without the user having to do the searching, or stores entire Web sites complete with images and links on a user's computer for later viewing.[22] **Smart agent software** is capable of learning an Internet user's preferences and automatically searching out information in selected Web sites and then distributing the information.

The PointCast Network provides an example. The company is a pioneer in the development of personalized Web pages through push technology. PointCast's software "surfs the Web," and automatically sends personalized information to an individual's computer. Users get stock quotes, news, sports, weather, and other information. Users can customize the sections of the service they want delivered. Push technology continuously updates the information and displays it at the user's request. With PointCast, advertising messages for products, which coincide with the computer user's interests, appear in the upper right-hand corner of each screen.

cookies
Small computer files that a content provider can save onto the computer of someone who visits its Web site.

Push technology may employ surveys of customer preferences or they may use cookies. **Cookies** or "magic cookies" are small computer files that a content provider can save onto the computer of someone who visits its Web site. The cookies allow a computer connected to the Internet to track other Web sites visited by the user and store these Web sites into a file that uses the cookie in place of the person's name, which in most cases the company never knows. If a person looks up a weather report by keying in a zip code using Time-Warner's Pathfinder, the computer notes that. This is a clue that tells where the person lives or maybe where he or she wished they lived. The computer notes whether a

It has been said, "Computing is not about computers anymore. It is about living."[24] Certainly, this holds true for researchers investigating secondary data. Seemingly overnight, marketplace data have become digital. The PointCast Network is a personalized information service that allows the user to select what types of information services will automatically be sent to his or her computer. For those who are "wired," the Internet is currently the research medium of choice. In the twenty-first century every marketing researcher will understand how to access and use the Internet.

user looks up stock quotes (though Time-Warner does not capture the symbols of the specific stock the person follows). If the person visits the Netly News, Pathfinder will record the person's interest in technology. Then the next time the person visits Pathfinder might serve up an ad for a modem, an on-line brokerage firm, or a restaurant in Mountain View, California, depending on what the computer's managed to learn.[23]

Push technology is having a major impact on the nature of marketing research. We will explore this topic in several places throughout this textbook.

Intranets

An **intranet** is a company's private data network that uses Internet standards and technology.[25] The information on an intranet—data, graphics, even video and voice—is available only inside the organization. Thus, a key difference between the Internet and an intranet is that firewalls or security software programs are installed to limit access to only those employees authorized to enter the system.[26]

A company's intranet uses Internet features, such as electronic mail, Web pages, and browsers, to build a communications and data resource at a specific company.[27] Company information is accessible using the same point-and-click technology found on the Internet. Managers and employees use links to get complete up-to-date information. An intranet lets authorized personnel—some of whom previously were isolated on departmental local area networks—look at product drawings, employee newsletters, sales and other kinds of company information. Whether the information comes from a spreadsheet or word processing document is not an issue to the user of an intranet. Managers and employees do not have to worry about the format of the information. Groupware such as Lotus Notes and Microsoft Exchange and other technology can facilitate the transfer of data, information, and knowledge.[28]

intranet
A company's private data network that uses Internet standards and technology.

Knowledge from Experts—Experience and Expertise Databases

In organizations that practice knowledge, management, intranets function to make the knowledge of company experts more accessible throughout their organizations.[29] There is a well-organized and purposeful effort to retain, analyze, and organize employee expertise so that it is easily obtainable anytime from anywhere. Extracting knowledge from experts and putting it into document databases may not be easy because experts often are unassuming, busy, and otherwise uncooperative. To collect and organize expert knowledge many companies have hired journalists, librarians, and business researchers to work with their experts. These knowledge workers interview the experts, write relevant documents, update experience and expertise databases, and make sure white papers, reports, and related databases are put in a database that is accessible across the organization.

Internet2

As we mentioned earlier, information technology changes rapidly. As sophisticated as the Internet and intranets are today, new technologies, such as Internet2, will dramatically enhance researchers' ability to answer marketing problems in the future.

Internet2 (http://www.internet2.edu/) is a collaborative effort involving over 100 universities, industrial organizations, and governmental affiliates in the United States. The goal of Internet2 is to build and operate a research network with greater than 100 times the bandwidth typical of the current Internet.

Summary

Increased global competition and technological advances in interactive media have spurred development of global information systems. A global information system is an organized collection of computer hardware, software, data, and personnel designed to capture, store, update, manipulate, analyze, and immediately display information about worldwide business activity.

Marketing managers distinguish between data and information. Data are simply facts or recorded measures of certain phenomena, but information refers to a body of facts in a format suitable for decision making or in a context that defines relationships between two pieces of data.

Information can be evaluated based on four characteristics: relevance, quality, timeliness, and completeness. Relevant information provides the information a marketer needs. High-quality information is accurate, valid, and reliable; it presents a good picture of reality. Timely information is obtained at the right time. Computerized information systems can record events and present information soon after a transaction takes place, improving timeliness. Complete information presents the right quantity of information. Marketing managers must have sufficient information to relate all aspects of their decisions together.

A computer-based marketing decision support system helps decision makers confront problems through direct interactions with databases and analytical models. A decision support system stores data and transforms them into organized information that it makes easily accessible to marketing managers.

A database is a collection of raw data arranged logically and organized in a form that can be stored and processed by a computer. Marketing data come from four major sources: internal records, proprietary marketing research, marketing intelligence, and outside vendors and external distributors. Each source can provide valuable input. Because most companies compile and store many different databases, they often develop data warehousing systems. A data warehouse is a comprehensive collection of data that describes the extensive operations of an organization. Data warehouse management requires that the detailed data from operational systems be extracted, transformed, and stored (warehoused) so that the various database tables from both inside and outside the company are consistent.

Numerous database search and retrieval systems are available by subscription or in libraries. Computer-assisted database searching has made the collection of external data faster and easier. Marketers refer to many different types of databases.

Although personal computers work independently, they can connect to other computers in networks to share data and software. Electronic data interchange (EDI) allows one company's computer systems to join directly to another company's system.

The Internet is a worldwide network of computers that allows users access to information and documents from distant sources. It is a combination of a worldwide communication system and the world's largest public library. Because of the creation of a system of thousands of interconnected pages, or documents, called the World Wide Web (WWW), the Web can be easily accessed with Web browsers and search engines.

An intranet is a company's private data network that uses Internet standards and technology.[30] The information on an intranet—data, graphics, even video and voice—is available only inside the organization. Thus, a key difference between the Internet and an intranet is that firewalls or security software programs are installed to limit access to only those employees authorized to enter the system.[31]

A company's intranet uses Internet features to build a communications and data resource at a specific company. Groupware such as Lotus Notes and Microsoft Exchange and other technology can facilitate the transfer of data, information, and knowledge. In organizations that practice knowledge management, intranets function to make the knowledge of company experts more accessible throughout their organizations.

Key Terms and Concepts

Data	Internet	Uniform Resource Locator (URL)
Information	e-mail	Interactive medium
Knowledge	Host	intranet
Knowledge management	Server	Links
Decision support system	World Wide Web (WWW)	Hyperlinks
Database	Content provider	Environmental scanning
Software	Web site	Push technology
Proprietary marketing research	Home page	Smart agent software
Electronic data interchange	Search engine	Cookies

Questions for Review and Critical Thinking

1. What is the difference between data and information? Provide examples.
2. What are the characteristics of useful information?
3. Discuss how the components or subsystems of a decision support system interrelate.
4. What type of databases might be found in the following organizations?
   a. Holiday Inn
   b. A Las Vegas gambling casino
   c. Anheuser-Busch
5. If a manufacturer sells directly to retailers, what type of marketing intelligence information would you expect to find in the company's decision support system?
6. What type of questions could a brand manager of a packaged goods firm expect to answer with the company's decision support system?
7. What makes a decision support system successful?
8. What are the four major sources of input for a decision support system?
9. Go to your college's or university's library. Provide three examples of computerized databases that are available.
10. In your own words, describe the Internet. What is its purpose?
11. How can an intranet help manage knowledge?

Exploring the Internet

1. Go to your school's computer center to learn how to obtain an e-mail address and how to establish an account that allows you to access the Internet. Get instructions explaining how you can get on (and off) the Internet using your local computer system.

2. The Spider's Apprentice is a Web site that provides many useful tips about using search engines. Go to http://www.monash.com then click on "The Spiders' Apprentice" to learn the ins and outs of search engines.

3. CopperSky Writing and Research's Web site host the Official Netscape Guide to Internet Research at http://www.coppersky.com/ongir/index.html. Users can navigate on the site directly to an excerpt from the book that offers ten friendly tips for Internet research. At the time of this writing the URL was http://www.coppersky.com/ongir/excerpts/10friendly.htm.

4. Use a web browser to visit Yahoo at http://www.yahoo.com. You will see a list of the major search categories. Click on Business and Economics. What additional search categories become available to you?

5. CEO Express (http://www.ceoexpress.com), a Business Researcher's Interest (http://www.brint.com/interest.html), and WorldOpinion (http://www.worldopinion.com) provide information about research topics and links to other Web pages. These pages will be extremely useful in your study of many marketing research topics. Visit these sites often during your study of marketing research.

6. For a useful business and personal tool, go to http://www.mapblast.com. Describe the site.

7. To learn more about data warehousing, to to http://www.knowledgecenters.org/ and http://www.datawarehousing.org.

8. Use the Internet to see if you can find information to answer the following questions.
   a. What is today's weather like in Denver?
   b. What restaurants are in the French Quarter in New Orleans?
   c. Is there much information about Brazil and its population demographics?

Case 2.1 Bank of Montreal

IMAGINE SECURING APPROVAL FOR A HOME MORTGAGE loan in about the time it takes to get a pepperoni pizza. That's the goal of Lending On Pathway, a decision support system application that is part of a multimillion-dollar client/server initiative at $41 billion (U.S.) Bank of Montreal.[32]

This object-oriented application is intended to compress the mortgage loan approval process from the current 24 hours to about 12 minutes. The idea for the service is that when a customer calls in, the loan officer takes the application, and by the time the conversation is finished, they'd have an approval. Lending On Pathway does this by automating many of the decisions now made by human underwriters. In the traditional loan process, a person looks over a combination of paper-based applications and on-line credit bureau files to establish an applicant's creditworthiness. The new system simultaneously analyzes the financial data from applicants, on-line information from credit bureaus, and customer data from a data warehouse. The system analyzes this information and weighs it against predefined lending criteria. It lets users perform what-if analyzes, such as manipulating terms and loan amounts to determine what best suits a customer's needs.

In a four-month pilot test, the average time it took the system to issue a decision once all data were piped into the system was 30 to 45 seconds. During the pilot, more than 350 mortgages were processed and the bank's booking ratio increased by 20 percent. Now the bank is deploying the program to its 1,200 branches.

The bank intends to tap much of the same data warehouse and decision support technology that is used in the Lending On Pathway application to push other kinds of loans and services. The bank hopes to do much more sophisticated predictive modeling. It hopes to be able to look at customers' activities and learn what they reveal about their needs.

Human need still apply. Most large lenders are using or developing automated underwriting capabilities, but none see technology as a replacement for human underwriters. Instead, the systems function more as workflow engines, which automatically approve clear-cut applications while routing only the more complex cases to human beings.

When a customer calls in for the Bank of Montreal's streamlined home mortgage loan, bank staff at workstations input the applicant's data in English on a series of graphically oriented screens developed in Smalltalk. Unlike the previous and more rigid forms-based interface, the Smalltalk screens can be easily negotiated in any order. During the application interview, the system is so easy that the employee can be using it and still converse with a client. This may seem like a minor point, but a conversational tone gives customers a warm-and-fuzzy feeling about the bank and that can translate into more business.

QUESTIONS

1. What databases would you expect to find in the Bank of Montreal's global information system?

2. Briefly explain or outline your opinion of the components of the Bank of Montreal's decision support system.

3. Should information on income, credit, and loans outstanding be considered personal information?

Video-Case 2.1 **Fossil**[33]

WHEN FOSSIL RECENTLY OPENED THE DOORS ON ITS chain of specialty stores, it created the perfect place to showcase its ever-growing product line. "This is "Fossil in a box. Really, for us to be able to communicate the essence of the brand, we had to be in a retail setting where it was all together in one place—where you could walk into this environment and it's very readily communicated what our brand image was from a product perspective," says vice president of image Tim Hale.

At the retail store surrounded by Fossil's trademark salute to 1950s' nostalgia, shoppers can choose from hundreds of different Fossil products. Although Fossil is best known for its fashion-savvy watches, the company's trendy eye wear, leather goods, sports caps, and even boxer shorts are becoming hot fashion accessories around the world. While the majority of its products are manufactured in Hong Kong, Fossil designs its products at its corporate headquarters in Richardson, Texas.

Stephane Thatcher, director of marketing, says, "For each product division that we have—watches, sunglasses, leather goods—we have a design team. That design team spends a lot of time overseas researching trends and seeing what's new and happening. Spending a lot of time in Europe and in Hong Kong, and really finding out what's going on in those markets and then adapting them to our market and to our customers."

Whether it's a Fossil kiosk in Hong Kong or the flagship Fossil store in Dallas, Fossil employs a universal product strategy. "We have a business system that works, and that system is that you buy at least 85 percent of your product from a core assortment that we have identified as our best-selling product. We still do realize that there are some cultural differences. Some parts of the world like a little more gold than silver, some areas sell more blue dials than yellow dials, and we allow a 15 percent tweak factor for regional differences in taste levels," says Gary Bolinger, senior vice president of international sales and marketing.

QUESTIONS

1. How might a company like Fossil use a global information system?

2. Fossil believes its Retro Americana image, in general, works worldwide. However it believes distributors in different geographical areas need to "tweak" its product mix. What role might decision support systems (databases and software) play in the adjustment of product assortments?

Chapter 3

The Marketing Research Process

S UPPOSE YOU ARE ASSIGNED TO TAKE CHARGE OF THE MAR-keting research effort when R. J. Reynolds Tobacco Company is developing an almost smokeless cigarette. You are told that the smokeless cigarette does not burn tobacco and greatly reduces the production of harmful substances linked to health concerns. R. J. Reynolds' executives believe it will be the world's cleanest cigarette. The new cigarette is lit like a normal cigarette, then a carbon heat source at its tip generates warm air that passes through tobacco extract, flavorings, and glycerine to form smoke that tastes like cigarette smoke. The cigarette includes carbon monoxide and nicotine at levels similar to low-tar brands now on the market. However, because tobacco does not burn, most of the combustion products linked to cancer and other health concerns are eliminated or greatly reduced. The new cigarette produces almost no sidestream smoke, and after the first few puffs there is no ash and no odor. Furthermore, the smoke exhaled dissipates quickly. The cigarette does not burn down. It remains lit for as long as a king-size cigarette and extinguishes itself.

Will a smokeless cigarette appeal to smokers? Will nonsmokers be more tolerant of a smokeless cigarette? In what situations will a smokeless cigarette be preferred to a regular cigarette? The research process can help answer questions such as these, but what form should the research take? Should a laboratory taste test be conducted? Should a survey of nonsmokers be part of the research strategy?

What you will learn in this chapter

To classify marketing research as either exploratory research, descriptive research, or causal research.

To list the stages in the marketing research process.

To identify and briefly discuss the various decision alternatives available to the researcher during each stage of the research process.

To explain the difference between a research project and a research program.

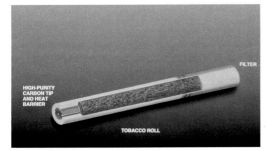

This chapter discusses how managers make decisions about planning research strategies and tactics. It also overviews the types of research designs and briefly discusses the stages in the research process.

Decision Making

decision making
The process used to resolve a problem or to choose from alternative opportunities.

Formally defined, **decision making** is the process of resolving a problem or choosing from alternative opportunities. A decision maker must recognize the nature of the problem or opportunity, identify how much information is available, and determine what information is needed. Every marketing problem or decision-making situation can be classified on a continuum ranging from complete certainty to absolute ambiguity. To facilitate discussion, the scale of Exhibit 3.1 has three categories: certainty, uncertainty, and ambiguity.[1]

Certainty

Complete certainty means that all the information the decision maker needs is available; the decision maker knows the exact nature of the marketing problem or opportunity. For example, an advertising agency may need to know the demographic characteristics of subscribers to magazines in which it may place a client's advertisements. The agency knows exactly what information it needs and where to find the information. If a manager is completely certain about both the problem or opportunity and future outcomes, then research may not be needed at all. However, perfect certainty, especially about the future, is rare.

Uncertainty

Uncertainty means that the manager grasps the general nature of desired objectives, but the information about alternatives is incomplete. Predictions about forces that shape future events are educated guesses. Under conditions of uncertainty, effective managers recognize that spending additional time to gather information to clarify the nature of a decision can be valuable.

Ambiguity

Ambiguity means that the nature of the problem to be solved is unclear. Objectives are vague and decision alternatives are difficult to define. This is by far the most difficult decision situation.

Exhibit 3.1 **Continuum of Decision Making**

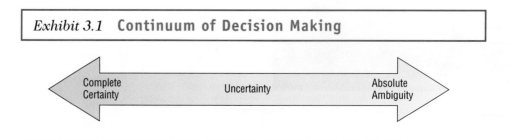

Complete Certainty — Uncertainty — Absolute Ambiguity

Marketing managers face a variety of problems and decisions. Complete certainty and predictable future outcomes may make marketing research a waste of time. However, under conditions of uncertainty or ambiguity, marketing research becomes more attractive to the decision maker. As the situation moves along the scale toward ambiguity, the more likely it is that additional time must be spent on marketing research.

Types of Marketing Research

Marketing research provides information to reduce uncertainty. It helps focus decision making. Sometimes marketing researchers know exactly what their marketing problems are and design careful studies to test specific hypotheses. For example, a soft drink company introducing a new clear cola might want to know whether a gold or silver label would make the packaging more effective. This problem is fully defined and an experiment may be designed to answer the marketing question with little preliminary investigation.

In more ambiguous circumstances management may be totally unaware of a marketing problem. For example, McDonald's may notice that Mo's Burgers, a competitor in the Japanese market, introduced Mo's Roast Katsu Burger, a roast pork cutlet drenched in traditional Japanese katsu sauce and topped with shredded cabbage. The managers may not understand much about Japanese consumers' feelings about this menu item. Ordinarily, some exploratory research is necessary to gain insights into the nature of such a problem. To understand the variety of research activity, it is beneficial to categorize types of marketing research.

Marketing research can be classified on the basis of either technique or function. Experiments, surveys, and observational studies are just a few common research techniques. Classifying research by its purpose or function shows how the nature of the marketing problem influences the choice of methods. The nature of the problem will determine whether the research is (1) exploratory, (2) descriptive, or (3) causal.

Exploratory Research

Exploratory research is conducted to clarify the nature of ambiguous problems. Management may have discovered a general problem, but it may need research to gain a better understanding of the dimensions of the problem and to aid analysis. Exploratory research is *not* intended to provide conclusive evidence from which to determine a particular course of action. Usually exploratory research is conducted with the expectation that subsequent research will be required to provide such conclusive evidence. Rushing into detailed surveys before less expensive and more readily available sources of information have been exhausted can lead to serious mistakes.

For example, suppose a Chinese fast-food restaurant chain is considering expanding its hours and product line with a breakfast menu. Exploratory research with a small number of current customers might find a strong negative reaction to eating a spicy vegetable breakfast at a Chinese fast-food outlet. Thus, exploratory research might help crystallize a problem and identify information needed for future research.

exploratory research
Initial research conducted to clarify and define the nature of a problem.

A 1997 study by the American Academy of Pediatrics found only 22 percent of children are potty trained by age 2¹/₂. This compares to 90 percent in 1961. The study found no relationship between attendance at day care, moms working outside the home, or the presence of siblings and when children toilet train.² Descriptive research such as this can be very helpful when planning marketing strategy.

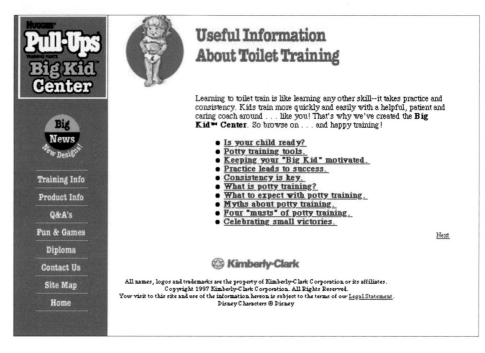

Descriptive Research

descriptive research
Research designed to describe characteristics of a population or phenomenon.

The major purpose of **descriptive research**, as the name implies, is to describe characteristics of a population. Marketing managers frequently need to determine who purchases a product, portray the size of the market, identify competitors' actions, and so on. Descriptive research seeks to determine the answers to *who, what, when, where,* and *how* questions.

Infiniti learned from descriptive research that Americans generally start to shop for a car by considering six models. They then narrow the field and usually visit three showrooms before they settle on a model. This takes an average of two weeks. However, buyers of luxury cars typically take twice as long to complete the decision and make a purchase. These descriptive findings, combined with knowledge that they faced competition from dozens of luxury models on the market, influenced Infiniti to encourage dealers to emphasize the quality of the consumer's shopping experience. The company made sizable investments in dramatic architecture for showrooms and elegant furnishings such as fountains and indoor bridges. Some Infiniti showrooms have contemplation zones—designated areas where customers can sit without harassment to consider car purchases in Zen-like silence.³

Magazines typically conduct descriptive surveys to identify the characteristics of their audience. For years *Teen* magazine managers sensed that 12- to 15-year-old girls cared a lot about fragrances, lipstick, and mascara, but they lacked any quantitative evidence. Their descriptive research found that 94.1 percent of 12- to 15-year-old girls use cream rinse/conditioner, 86.4 percent use fragrance, and 84.9 percent use lip gloss. Of the girls using fragrance, 77 percent preferred using their own brand, 17 percent shared their brand, and 6 percent used someone else's brand. Results showed that most girls use cosmetics, brand loyalty begins early, and 12- to 15-year-olds prefer using and choosing their own brands.⁴

Accuracy is of paramount importance in descriptive research. While they cannot completely eliminate errors, good researchers strive for descriptive precision. Suppose a study seeks to describe the market potential for portable digital music

EXPLORING RESEARCH ETHICS

Poetry and Research: An Odd Couple?

I keep six honest serving men,
(they taught me all I knew),
their names are What, and Why, and When,
and How, and Where, and Who.

Rudyard Kipling

KIPLING'S WORDS CAN BE HELPFUL TO THE MARKETING researcher. Those who ask the questions *what, why,* *when, how, where,* and *who* will start on the right road to solving their marketing research problems.

players for MP 3 formats. If the study does not precisely measure sales volume, it will mislead the managers who are making production scheduling, budgeting, and other decisions based on it.

Unlike exploratory research, descriptive studies are based on some previous understanding of the nature of the research problem. Although the researcher may have a general understanding of the situation, the conclusive evidence that answers questions of fact necessary to determine a course of action has yet to be collected. Many circumstances require descriptive research to identify the reasons consumers give to explain the nature of things. In other words, a *diagnostic analysis* is performed when consumers answer questions such as "Why do you feel that way?" Although they may describe why consumers feel a certain way, the findings of a descriptive study such as this, sometimes called *diagnostics*, do not provide causal evidence. Frequently, descriptive research attempts to determine the extent of differences in needs, attitudes, and opinions among subgroups.

Causal Research

The main goal of **causal research** is to identify cause-and-effect relationships between variables. Exploratory and descriptive research normally precedes cause-and-effect relationship studies. In causal studies researchers typically have an expectation about the relationship to be explained, such as predicting the influence of price, packaging, advertising, and the like on sales. Thus, researchers must be quite knowledgeable about the subject. Ideally the manager wants to establish that one event (say, new package) is the means for producing another event (an increase in sales). Causal research attempts to establish that when we do one thing, another thing will follow. The word *cause* is common in everyday conversation, but from a scientific research perspective, a true causal relationship is impossible to prove. Nevertheless, researchers seek certain types of evidence to help them understand and predict relationships.

A typical causal study has management change one variable (for example, advertising) and then observe the effect on another variable (such as sales). Some evidence for causality comes from the fact that the cause precedes the effect. In other words, having an *appropriate causal order of events*, or temporal sequence, is one criterion for causality that must be met to be able to measure a relationship. If a consumer behavior theorist wishes to show that an attitude change causes a behavior change, one criterion that must be established is that attitude change must precede the behavior change in time.

causal research
Research conducted to identify cause-and-effect relationships among variables.

concomitant variation
The way in which two phenomena or events vary together.

In the preceding example, some evidence of concomitant variation exists because advertising and sales appear to be associated. **Concomitant variation** occurs when two phenomena or events vary together. When the criterion of concomitant variation is not met—that is, when there is no association between the variables—reasoning suggests that no causal relationship exists. If two events vary together, one event may be the cause; however, this by itself is not sufficient evidence for causality because the two events may have a common cause; that is, both may be influenced by a third variable. For instance, a large number of ice cream cones were sold one morning at Atlantic City's beach. That afternoon, a large number of drownings occurred. Most of us would not conclude that eating ice cream causes drownings; more likely, on that day the beach was crowded and the number of people probably influenced both ice cream sales and drownings. The effect could have been produced in other ways. Thus, causation requires more than concomitant variation and a proper time sequence between the occurrence of two events. There may be plausible alternative explanations for the observed relationship. A plurality of causes is possible.

Consider a presidential candidate who reduces advertising expenditures near the end of the primary campaign race and wins many more delegates in the remaining primaries. To infer causality—that reducing advertising increased the number of delegates—might be inappropriate because the presumed cause of the increase in delegates may not have been the real cause. It is more likely that near the end of the race, marginal candidates withdrew. The real cause probably was unrelated to advertising.

In these examples the third variable that is the source of the spurious association is a very salient factor readily identifiable as the true influence of change. However, within the complex environment in which managers operate, identifying alternative or complex causal facts can be difficult.

In summary, research to infer causality should:

1. Establish the appropriate causal order or sequence of events
2. Measure the concomitant variation between the presumed cause and the presumed effect
3. Recognize the presence or absence of alternative plausible explanations or causal factors[5]

Even when these three criteria for causation are present, the researcher can never be certain that the causal explanation is adequate.

Most basic scientific studies in marketing (for example, the development of consumer behavior theory) ultimately seek to identify cause-and-effect relationships. One often associates science with experiments. To predict a relationship between, say, price and perceived quality of a product, causal studies often create statistical experiments with controls that establish contrast groups. A number of marketing experiments are conducted by both theory developers and pragmatic businesspeople. More will be said about experiments and causal research in Chapters 11 and 12.

Uncertainty Influences the Type of Research

The uncertainty of the research problem is related to the type of research project. Exhibit 3.2 illustrates that exploratory research is conducted during the early stages of decision making, when the decision situation is ambiguous and management is very uncertain about the nature of the problem. When management is aware of the problem but lacks some knowledge, descriptive research usually results. Causal research requires sharply defined problems but uncertainty about future outcomes.

Exhibit 3.2   Types of Marketing Research

DEGREE OF PROBLEM DEFINITION	EXPLORATORY RESEARCH (AMBIGUOUS PROBLEM)	DESCRIPTIVE RESEARCH (AWARE OF PROBLEM)	CAUSAL RESEARCH (PROBLEM CLEARLY DEFINED)
Possible situation	"Our sales are declining and we don't know why."	"What kind of people are buying our product? Who buys our competitor's product?"	"Will buyers purchase more of our product in a new package?"
	"Would people be interested in our new-product idea?"	"What features do buyers prefer in our product?"	"Which of two advertising campaigns is more effective?"

Note: The degree of uncertainty of the research problem determines the research methodology.

Stages in the Research Process

As previously noted, marketing research can take many forms, but systematic inquiry is a common thread. Systematic inquiry requires careful planning in an orderly investigation. Marketing research, like other forms of scientific inquiry, involves a sequence of highly interrelated activities. The stages of the research process overlap continuously, and it is somewhat of an oversimplification to state that every research project follows a neat, ordered sequence of activities. Nevertheless, marketing research often follows a generalized pattern. The stages are: (1) defining the problem, (2) planning a research design, (3) planning a sample, (4) collecting the data, (5) analyzing the data, and (6) formulating the conclusions and preparing the report.

Exhibit 3.3 portrays these six stages as a cyclical process. The circular flow concept is used because the conclusions from research studies usually generate new ideas and problems that need to be investigated. In practice the stages overlap chronologically and are functionally interrelated; sometimes the later stages are completed before the earlier ones. The terms *forward linkage* and *backward linkage* are associated with the interrelationships of the various stages. **Forward linkage** implies that the earlier stages of research influence the design of the later stages. Thus, the objectives of the research outlined in the problem definition will have an impact on the selection of the sample and how the data will be collected. The decision concerning who will be sampled will affect the wording of questionnaire items. For example, if the research concentrates on respondents with low educational levels, the wording of the questionnaire will be simpler than the language used when the respondents are college graduates. **Backward linkage** implies that the later steps influence the earlier stages of the research process. If it is known that the data will be analyzed by computer, then computer coding requirements will be included in the questionnaire design. Perhaps the most important backward linkage is the knowledge that the executive who will read the research report needs certain information. The professional researcher anticipates executives' needs for information in the planning process and considers these needs during the analysis and tabulation stages.

forward linkage
A term implying that the early stages of the research process influence the design of the later stages.

backward linkage
A term implying that the later stages of the research process influence the early stages.

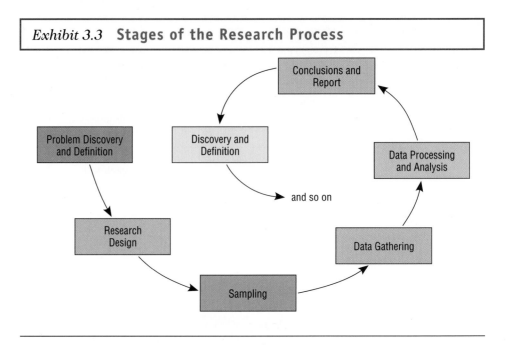

Exhibit 3.3 **Stages of the Research Process**

Alternatives in the Research Process

The researcher must choose among a number of alternatives during each stage of the research process. The research process can be compared to a map. On a map some paths are better charted than others; some are difficult to travel and some are more interesting and beautiful than others. Rewarding experiences may be gained during the journey. One must remember that there is no right or best path for all journeys. The road one takes depends on where one wants to go and the resources (money, time, labor, and so on) available for the trip. The map analogy is useful for the marketing researcher because in each stage of the research process there are several paths to follow. In some instances, the quickest path will lead to appropriate research because of time constraints. In other circumstances, when money and human resources are plentiful, the appropriate path may be quite different. Exploration of the various paths of marketing research decisions is the primary purpose.

The following sections briefly describe the six stages of the research process.[6] Exhibit 3.4 shows the decisions that researchers must make in each stage. Discussion of the research process begins with problem discovery and definition because most research projects are initiated to remedy managers' uncertainty about some aspect of the firm's marketing program.

Problem Discovery and Definition

Exhibit 3.4 shows that the research process begins with *problem discovery*. Identifying the problem is the first step toward its solution. In general usage the word *problem* suggests that something has gone wrong. Actually, the research task may be to clarify a problem, define an opportunity, or monitor and evaluate current operations. The concept of problem discovery and definition must encompass a broader context that includes analysis of opportunities. It should be noted that the initial stage is problem *discovery* rather than *definition*. The researcher may not have a clear-cut statement of the problem at the outset of the research process; often only symptoms of the problem are apparent at that point. Sales may be declining, but management may not know the exact nature of the

Exhibit 3.4 Flowchart of the Marketing Research Process

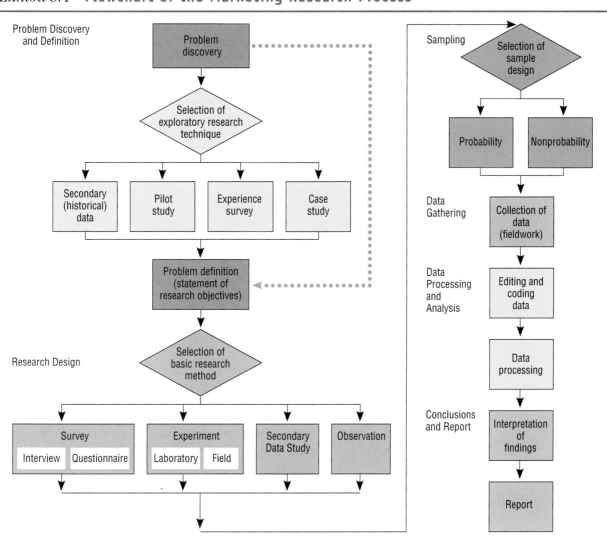

Note: Diamond-shaped boxes indicate stages in the research process in which a choice of one or more techniques must be made. The dotted line indicates an alternative path that skips exploratory research.

problem. Thus, the problem statement often is made only in general terms; what is to be investigated is not yet specifically identified.

Albert Einstein noted that "the formulation of a problem is often more essential than its solution."[7] This is good advice for marketing managers as well. Too often they concentrate on finding the right answer rather than asking the right question. Many managers do not realize that defining a problem may be more difficult than solving it. In marketing research if the data are collected before the nature of the marketing problem is carefully thought out, they probably will not help solve the problem.

Defining the Problem. In marketing research the adage "a problem well defined is a problem half solved" is worth remembering. This emphasizes that an orderly definition of the research problem lends a sense of direction to the inves-

problem definition stage
The stage in which management seeks to identify a clear-cut statement of the problem or opportunity.

tigation. Careful attention to the **problem definition stage** allows the researcher to set the proper research objectives. If the purpose of the research is clear, the chances of collecting necessary and relevant information and omitting surplus information will be much greater.

To be efficient, marketing research must have clear objectives and definite designs. Unfortunately, little or no planning goes into the formulation of many research problems. Consider the case of the Ha-Psu-Shu-Tse brand of Indian fried bread mix (from the Pawnee Indian word for red corn). The owner of the company, Mr. Ha-Psu-Shu-Tse, thought that his product, one of the few Native American food products available in the United States, was not selling because it was not widely advertised. He wanted a management consulting group to conduct some research concerning advertising themes. However, the management consultants pointed out to the Ha-Psu-Shu-Tse family that using the family name on the bread mix might be a foremost source of concern. They suggested consumer behavior research to investigate the brand image rather than advertising copy research might be a better initial starting point. Family management agreed.

It should be emphasized that the word *problem* refers to the managerial problem (which may be a lack of knowledge about consumers or advertising effectiveness) and the information need to help *solve* the problem. This must precede determination of the purpose of the research. Frequently the marketing researcher will not be involved until line management has discovered that some information about a particular aspect of the marketing mix is needed. Even at this point the exact nature of the problem may be poorly defined. Once a problem area has been discovered, the marketing researcher can begin the process of precisely defining it.

Although the problem definition stage of the research process probably is the most important one, it frequently is a neglected area of marketing research. Too many researchers forget that the best place to begin a research project is at the end. Knowing what is to be accomplished determines the research process. A problem definition error or omission is likely to be a costly mistake that cannot be corrected in later stages of the process. Chapter 5 discusses problem definition in greater detail.

Exploratory Research.

Exploratory research usually is conducted during the initial stage of the research process. The preliminary activities undertaken to refine the problem into researchable form need not be formal or precise. The purpose of the exploratory research process is to progressively narrow the scope of the research topic and transform ambiguous problems into well-defined ones that incorporate specific research objectives. By investigating any existing studies on the subject, talking with knowledgeable individuals, and informally investigating the situation, the researcher can progressively sharpen the concepts. After such exploration, the researcher should know exactly which data to collect during the formal phases of the project and how to conduct the project. Exhibit 3.4 indicates that a decision must be made regarding the selection of one or more exploratory research techniques. The exhibit presents the exploratory research stage in yellow to indicate that this stage is optional.

The marketing researcher can employ techniques from four basic categories to obtain insights and gain a clearer idea of the problem: secondary data analysis, pilot studies, case studies, and experience surveys. These are discussed in detail in Chapter 6. This section will briefly discuss secondary data and focus group interviews, the most popular type of pilot study.

Secondary Data *Secondary* or *historical data* are data previously collected and assembled for some project other than the one at hand. (*Primary data* are data gathered and assembled specifically for the project at hand.) Secondary data

A typical focus group session brings together six to ten people to explore consumer opinions and behaviors. Focus groups, like other pilot studies, use sampling but do not apply rigorous standards.

often can be found inside the company, at a public or university library, or on the Internet. In addition some firms specialize in providing types of information, such as economic forecasts, that are useful to many organizations. The researcher who gathers data from the *Census of Population* or *The Survey of Current Business* is using secondary sources.

A literature survey of published articles and books that discusses theories and past empirical studies about a topic is an almost universal first step in academic research projects. A literature survey also is common in many applied research studies. Students who have written term papers should be familiar with using computer search systems, indexes to published literature, and other library sources to compile bibliographies that portray past research.

Suppose, for example, that a bank is interested in determining the best site for additional automated teller machines. A logical first step would be to investigate the factors that bankers in other parts of the country consider important. By reading articles in banking journals, management might quickly discover that the best locations are inside supermarkets located in residential areas where people are young, highly educated, and earning higher-than-average incomes. These data might lead the bank to investigate census information to determine where in the city such people live. Reviewing and building on the work already compiled by others is an economical starting point for most research.

Secondary data can almost always be gathered more quickly and at lower cost than primary data. However, secondary data may be outdated, and they may not meet researchers' needs exactly because they were collected for another purpose. Nevertheless, secondary sources often prove to be very valuable in exploratory research. Investigating such sources has saved many a researcher from reinventing the wheel in primary data collection.

Pilot Studies The term **pilot study** covers a number of diverse research techniques. Pilot studies collect data from the ultimate consumers or the actual subjects of the research project to serve as a guide for the larger study. When the term *pilot study* is used within the context of exploratory research, the data collection methods are informal and the findings may lack precision.[8] For instance, a downtown association concerned with revitalization of the central business district conducted to a very flexible survey using open-ended questions. The interviewers were given considerable latitude to identify changes needed in the shopping area. The results of this survey suggested possible topics for formal investigation.

The focus group interview is a more elaborate kind of exploratory pilot study that has become increasingly popular in recent years. The focus group session brings together six to ten people in a loosely structured format based on the assumption that individuals are more willing to share their ideas as they share in the ideas of others. Information obtained in these studies is qualitative and serves to guide subsequent quantitative study.

pilot study
A collective term for any small-scale exploratory research technique that uses sampling but does not apply rigorous standards.

For example, the Philadelphia Museum used focus groups to investigate how well its exhibits and shows were catering to the public. A local resident who had never visited the museum mentioned that he was not aware of any important artwork at the museum. Another participant in the same focus group assumed the museum would be filled with "pictures I would not understand....I've seen art where it looked like kids splashed paint." These findings (confirmed by other research) influenced the museum to reinstate an image of van Gogh's *Sunflowers* on the cover of its brochures.[9]

Four basic methods of exploratory research have been identified, but such research does not have to follow a standard design. Because the purpose of exploratory research is to gain insights and discover new ideas, researchers may use considerable creativity and flexibility. Data generally are collected using several exploratory techniques. Exhausting these sources usually is worth the effort because the expense is relatively low. Furthermore, insights into how and how not to conduct research may be gained from activities during the problem definition stage. If the conclusions made during this stage suggest marketing opportunities, the researcher is in a position to begin planning a formal, quantitative research project.

Statement of Research Objectives. A researcher must initially decide precisely what to research. After identifying and clarifying the problem, with or without exploratory research, the researcher should make a formal statement of the problem and the *research objectives*. This delineates the type of information that should be collected and provides a framework for the scope of the study.

A typical research objective might seek to answer a question such as, "To what extend did the new pricing program achieve its objectives?" In this sense the statement of the problem is a research question.

Design and style are important ways to differentiate a product from its competition. This Red Devil Ergo 2000 wall scraper is ergonomically designed with soft, oversized handles contoured to fit a palm, thumb, and fingers. The design was based on research findings that showed people found conventional putty knives and scrapers too short, hard, and squared-off, which resulted in slamming their thumbs against the side of the blade while scraping. Simplicity of the functional design is reinforced by the aesthetic design, which evokes comfort.

The best expression of a research objective is a well-formed, testable research hypothesis. A *hypothesis* is a statement that can be refuted or supported by empirical data. For example, an exploratory study might lead to the hypothesis that a market share decline recognized by management is occurring predominantly among households in which the head of the household is 45 to 65 years old with an income of $35,000 per year or less. Another hypothesis might be that concentrating advertising efforts in monthly waves (rather than conducting continuous advertising) will cause an increase in sales and profits. Once the hypothesis has been developed, the researcher is ready to select a research design.

Planning the Research Design

After the researcher has formulated the research problem, he or she must develop the research design as part of the **research design stage**. A **research design** is a master plan that specifies the methods and procedures for collecting and analyzing the needed information; it is a framework for the research plan of action. The objectives of the study determined during the early stages of the research are included in the design to ensure that the information collected is appropriate for solving the problem. The researcher also must determine the sources of information, the design technique (survey or experiment, for example), the sampling methodology, and the schedule and cost of the research.

research design stage
The stage in which the researcher determines a framework for the research plan of action by selecting a basic research method.

research design
A master plan that specifies the methods and procedures for collecting and analyzing needed information.

Selection of the Basic Research Method.
Here again, the researcher must make a decision. Exhibit 3.4 shows the four basic design techniques for descriptive and causal research: surveys, experiments, secondary data, and observation. The objectives of the study, the available data sources, the urgency of the decision, and the cost of obtaining the data will determine which design technique should be chosen. The managerial aspects of selecting the research design will be considered later.

Survey research is often used by movie marketers. Gauging audiences' responses to three or four versions of trailers and television commercials is a typical research project designed to bring more people in on opening night. Audience previews have been responsible for the decisions about the final version of many films.

WHAT WENT WRONG?

Obstacles of Consumer Research[10]

MANY MANAGERS VIEW CONSUMER RESEARCH AS a necessary precursor to product introduction. Unfortunately, innovative products that lack much in common with existing products often prove this attitude wrong. Hair styling mousse is now a massive hit, yet its initial U.S. market tests flopped. People said it was "goopy and gunky," and they did not like its feel when it "mooshed" through their hair. Similarly, when the telephone answering machine was consumer tested, it faced an almost universally negative reaction since most individuals felt that using a mechanical device to answer a phone was rude and disrespectful. Today, of course, many people regard their answering machines as indispensable and would dread scheduling daily activities without them. In the same vein, the computer mouse flunked its initial testing. Surveys indicated that potential customers found it awkward and unnecessary.

Surveys about new food products face terrible problems. For one, a person's desire for food is powerfully influenced by the ambiance of the meal, dining companions, and what foods were eaten recently, all of which confound and confuse the results of survey research. Even more erratic results come from studies of children's food, like a new cereal or snack. The responses of kids are strongly swayed by how well they like the people doing the test and the playthings available. Worse, kids quickly change their minds, and in a taste test of several foods a child can judge one food the best but an hour later proclaim the same food as "icky."

Marketing researchers must be aware of the potential problems when deciding exactly what research design will best solve their research problems.

Surveys The most common method of generating primary data is the survey. Most people have seen the results of political surveys by Gallup or Harris, and some have been respondents (members of a sample who supply answers) to marketing research questionnaires. A *survey* is a research technique in which information is gathered from a sample of people through a questionnaire. The task of writing a questionnaire, determining the list of questions, and designing the format of the printed or written questionnaire is an essential aspect of the development of a survey research design.

Research investigators may choose to contact respondents by telephone, mail, or in person. An advertiser spending $1,300,000 for 30 seconds of commercial time during the Super Bowl may telephone people to quickly gather information concerning their responses to the advertising. A forklift truck manufacturer trying to determine a cause for low sales in the wholesale grocery industry might choose a mail questionnaire because the appropriate executives are hard to reach by telephone. A manufacturer of a birth control device for men might determine the need for a versatile survey method wherein an interviewer can ask a variety of personal questions in a flexible format. While personal interviews are expensive, they are valuable because investigators can use visual aids and supplement the interviews with personal observations. Each of these survey methods has advantages and disadvantages. A researcher's task is to find the most appropriate way to collect the needed information.

Experiments Marketing *experiments* hold the greatest potential for establishing cause-and-effect relationships. Experimentation allows investigation of changes in one variable, such as sales, while manipulating one or two other variables, perhaps price or advertising, under controlled conditions. Ideally experimental control provides a basis for isolating causal factors by eliminating outside, or exogeneous, influences.

Test marketing is a frequently used form of marketing experimentation. The example of Chelsea, Anheuser-Busch's "not-so-soft soft drink," illustrates the usefulness of marketing experiments. Anheuser-Busch first introduced Chelsea as a drink with a slight alcoholic content—about 0.4 percent—that was a socially acceptable alternative to beer for adults who did not want to get intoxicated. During an experiment to test market the "not-so-soft soft drink" and the "not-so-sweet" concept, a Virginia nurses' association and some religious groups strongly criticized the company and the new product. These critics suggested that Anheuser-Busch had introduced a product that might encourage children to become beer drinkers. They contended that Chelsea was packaged like beer and looked, foamed, and poured like it. The criticism led the brewery to suspend production, advertising, and promotion of the drink. Later it reintroduced the product as a soft drink with only "a trace of alcohol" as a "natural alternative" to soft drinks with not-so-sweet and stylish attributes. Similar problems occurred in the second experiment. This experiment pointed out to Anheuser-Busch that the variable—alcohol level—caused an inadvertent miscommunication: Consumers confused the original Chelsea with beer.

An experiment controls conditions so that one or more variable can be manipulated in order to test a hypothesis. In the Chelsea situation there was a trial of a proposed course of action and an observation of the effect on sales. This case illustrates that extraneous variables are difficult to control and can influence results. It also portrays a field experiment that involved a deliberate modification of the marketing system. Other experiments—laboratory experiments, for example—are deliberate modifications of an environment created for the research itself. One example of a laboratory experiment is a toy company showing alternate versions of a proposed TV commercial to groups of children and observing which one keeps their attention longest.

Secondary Data Like exploratory research studies, descriptive and causal studies use previously collected data. Although the terms *secondary* and *historical* are interchangeable, we will use the term *secondary data* here. An example of a secondary data study is the use of a mathematical model to predict sales on the

Summer 1999

Beat the heat with our classic summer coolers!

AIRY MESH
Our famous Polo
now $2 less than
last year.

SPLASHY SWIMSUITS
Fifteen pages of 'em,
all with our famous
flattering fit.

BEST "T" DEAL EVER
It's softer, it's heftier,
it's Super-T –
now only $12.

1999 price rollbacks continue on 18 all-time best-sellers!

Direct marketers often conduct experiments to determine how to increase response to pamphlets, catalogs, or Internet offerings. Experiments have shown that the wording of headline copy and prices can greatly influence the success of direct marketing.

WHAT WENT RIGHT?

Rolling Rock

FOR MANY YEARS ROLLING ROCK BEER WAS A REGIONAL brand in western Pennsylvania.[11] Its signature package was a longneck green bottle with a white painted label featuring icons such as a horsehead, a steeplechase, and the number "33" that allude to a legend about the beer being brought to you "from the glass-lined tanks of Old Latrobe." The brand, now marketed by Labatt USA, expanded nationally during the 1980s by focusing on core consumers who purchased specialty beers for on-premise consumption and who were willing to pay higher prices than for national brands such as Budweiser.

As years went by, packaging options expanded to include bottles with mystique-less paper labels for take-home consumption, often packaged in 12-packs. In the mid-1990s, in response to a competitive explosion from microbrews, Rolling Rock offered a number of line extensions, such as Rock Bock and amber Rock Ice. They failed. Sales stagnated. In New York and other crucial markets price reductions to the level of Budweiser and Miller became inhibiting aspects of its marketing program. Marketing executives held the view that the longneck painted bottle was the heart of the brand. However, earlier efforts to develop cheaper imitations of the painted-label look had not achieved success.

Rolling Rock executives decided to conduct a massive consumer study, recruiting consumers at shopping malls and other venues to view "live" shelf sets of beer, not just specialty beer but beer at every price range from subpremiums and up. Consumers given money to spend in the form of chips were exposed to "old-bundle" packages (the old graphics, and the paper-label stubbies) and "new-bundle" packages (two new graphics approaches, including the one ultimately selected, and painted-label longnecks), at a variety of price points, and asked to allocate their next 10 purchases. Some were even invited to take the "new-bundle" packages home with them for follow-up research.

As the marketing executives had hoped, the results did not leave any room for interpretation: Not only did the new packages meet with consumers' strong approval, but consumers consistently indicated that they would be willing to pay more for the brand in those packages. In fact, they were not only *willing* to pay more, the *expected* to pay more, particularly those already in the Rock franchise. In three regions, the Northeast, Southeast, and West, purchase intent among users increased dramatically both at prices 20 cents higher per 6-pack and at prices 40 cents higher. The increase in purchase intent was milder in the Midwest, but Rock there already commanded a solid premium over Bud and other premium beers. The sole exception to that trend was in the brand's core markets in Pennsylvania and Ohio, where Rock has never entirely escaped its shot-and-a-beer origins, and even there, purchase intent declined by only 2 percent at each of the higher prices.

---

basis of past sales or a correlation with related variables. Manufacturers of digital cameras may find that sales are highly correlated with discretionary personal income. To predict future market potential, projections of disposable personal income from the government or a university may be acquired. This information can be used mathematically to forecast sales. Formal secondary data studies have benefits and limitations similar to those of exploratory studies that use secondary data, but generally the quantitative analysis of secondary data is more sophisticated.

Observation The objective of many research projects is merely to record what can be observed, for example, the number of automobiles that pass by a proposed site for a gasoline station. This can be mechanically recorded or observed by humans. Research personnel known as *mystery shoppers* may act as customers to observe actions of sales personnel or do comparative shopping to learn prices at comparative shopping to learn prices at competing outlets.

The main advantage of the observation technique is that it records behavior without relying on reports from respondents. Observation methods often are nonreactive because date are collected unobtrusively and passively without a respondent's direct participation. For instance, the A. C. Nielsen Company uses a "people meter" attached to television sets to record the programs being watched by each household member. This eliminates the possible bias of respondents stating that they watched the president's State of the Union address rather than a situation comedy on another station.

Observation is more complex than mere "nose counting," and the task is more difficult than the inexperienced researcher would imagine. Several things of interest, such as attitudes, opinions, motivations, and other intangible states of mind, simply cannot be observed.

TO THE POINT

You cannot put the same shoe on every foot.

SYRUS

The "Best" Research Design. It is argued that there is no one best research design and there are no hard-and-fast rules for good marketing research. This does not mean, however, that the researcher faces chaos and confusion. It means that the researcher can choose among many alternative methods for solving a problem. Consider the researcher who must forecast sales for the upcoming year. Some commonly used forecasting methods are executive opinion, sales force composite opinions, user expectations, projection of trends, and analysis of market factors.

The ability to select the most appropriate research design develops with experience. Inexperienced researchers often jump to the conclusion that the survey method is the best design because they are most familiar with this method. When Chicago's Museum of Science and Industry wanted to determine the relative popularity of its exhibits, it could have conducted a survey. Instead, a creative researcher familiar with other research designs suggested a far less expensive alternative: an unobtrusive observation technique. The researcher suggested that the museum merely keep track of the frequency with which the floor tiles in front of the various exhibits had to be replaced, indicating where the heaviest traffic occurred. When this was done, the museum found that the chick-hatching exhibit was the most popular. This method provided the same results as a survey but at a much lower cost.

After determining the proper design, the researcher moves on to the next stage—planning the sample.

Sampling

Although the sampling plan is included in the research design, the **sampling stage** is a distinct phase of the research process. For convenience, however, we will treat the sample planning and the actual sample generation processes together in this section.

If you take your fist bite of a steak and conclude that it needs salt, you have just conducted a sample. *Sampling* involves any procedure that uses a small number of items or parts of the population to make a conclusion regarding the whole population. In other words, a sample is a subset from a larger population. If

sampling stage
The stage in which the researcher determines who is to be sampled, how large a sample is needed, and how sampling units will be selected.

Surveys should be representative. In 1936 telephone and Literary Digest *subscribers were disproportionately Republicans who did not support Roosevelt.*

certain statistical procedures are followed, a researcher need not select every item in a population because the results of a good sample should have the same characteristics as the population as a whole. Of course, when errors are made, samples do not give reliable estimates of the population. A famous example of error due to sampling is the 1936 *Literary Digest* fiasco. The magazine conducted a survey and predicted that Alf Landon would win over Franklin D. Roosevelt by a landslide. The magazine made an error in sample selection. The postmortems showed that *Literary Digest* had sampled telephone and magazine subscribers. In 1936 these people were not a representative cross-section of voters because a disproportionate number of them were Republicans.

This famous example suggests that the first sampling question to ask is "Who is to be sampled?" The answer to this primary question requires the identification of a *target population*. Defining this population and determining the sampling units may not be so easy. If, for example, a savings and loan association surveys people who already have accounts for answers to image questions, the selected sampling units will not represent *potential* customers. Specifying the target population is a crucial aspect of the sampling plan.

The next sampling issue concerns *sample size*. How big should the sample be? Although management may wish to examine every potential buyer of a product or service, doing so may be unnecessary as well as unrealistic. Typically larger samples are more precise than smaller ones, but proper probability sampling can allow a small proportion of the total population to give a reliable measure of the whole. A later discussion will explain how large a sample must be in order to be truly representative of the universe or population.

The final sampling decision concerns choosing how to select the sampling units. Students who have taken a statistics course generally understand simple random sampling in which every unit in the population has an equal and known chance of being selected. However, this is only one type of sampling. For example, a cluster sampling procedure may reduce costs and make data gathering procedures more efficient. If members of the population are found in close geographical clusters, a sampling procedure that selects area clusters rather than individual units in the population will reduce costs. Rather than selecting 1,000 individuals throughout the United States, it may be more economical to first select 25 counties and then sample within those counties. This will substantially reduce travel, hiring, and training costs. In determining the appropriate sampling plan, the researcher will have to select the most appropriate sampling procedure for meeting the established study objectives.

There are two basic sampling techniques: probability and nonprobability sampling. A *probability sample* is a sample in which every member of the population has a known, nonzero probability of selection. If sample units are selected on the basis of personal judgment (for example, a test market city is selected because it appears to be typical), the sample method is a *nonprobability sample*. In reality, the sampling decision is not a simple choice between two methods. Simple random samples, stratified samples, quota samples, cluster samples, and judgmental samples are some of the many methods for drawing a sample. A full discussion of these techniques must be postponed to a later chapter.

Data Gathering

Once the research design (including the sampling plan) has been formalized, the process of gathering or collecting information, the **data gathering stage**, may begin. Data may be gathered by humans or recorded by machines. Scanner data illustrate electronic data collection by machine.

data gathering stage
The stage in which the researcher collects the data.

Obviously, the many research techniques involve many methods of *data gathering*. The survey method requires some form of direct participation by the respondent. The respondent may participate by filling out a questionnaire or by interacting with an interviewer. If an unobtrusive method of data gathering is used, the subjects do not actively participate. For instance, a simple count of motorists driving past a proposed franchising location is one kind of data gathering method. However the data are collected, it is important to minimize errors in the process. For example, the data gathering should be consistent in all geographical areas. If an interviewer phrases questions incorrectly or records a respondent's statements inaccurately (not verbatim), major data collection errors will result.

Often there are two phases to the process of gathering data: pretesting and the main study. A *pretesting phase* using a small subsample may determine whether the data gathering plan for the *main study* is an appropriate procedure. Thus, a small-scale pretest study provides an advance opportunity for an investigator to check the data collection form to minimize errors due to improper design elements, such as a poor question wording or sequence. A researcher may also benefit by discovering confusing interviewing instructions, learning if the questionnaire is too long or too short, and uncovering other such field errors. Tabulation of data from the pretests provides the researcher with a format of the knowledge that may be gained from the actual study. If the tabulation of the data and statistical results does not answer the researcher's questions, the investigator may need to redesign the study.

Data Processing and Analysis

Editing and Coding. After the fieldwork has been completed, the data must be converted into a format that will answer the marketing manager's questions. This is part of the **data processing and analysis stage**. Data processing generally begins with editing and coding the data. *Editing* involves checking the data collection forms for omissions, legibility, and consistency in classification. The editing process corrects problems such as interviewer errors (an answer recorded on the wrong portion of a questionnaire, for example) before the data are transferred to the computer.

data processing and analysis stage
The stage in which the researcher performs several interrelated procedures to convert the data into a format that will answer management's questions.

Before data can be tabulated, meaningful categories and character symbols must be established for groups of responses. The rules for interpreting, categorizing, recording, and transferring the data to the data storage media are called *codes*. This coding process facilitates computer or hand tabulation. If computer analysis is to be used, the data are entered into the computer and verified.

Computer-assisted (on-line) interviewing is a recent development that illustrates the impact of technological change on the research process. Telephone interviewers, seated at a computer terminal, read survey questions displayed on the monitor. The interviewer asks the questions and then types the respondents' answers on the keyboard. Thus, answers are collected and processed into the computer at the same time, eliminating intermediate steps that could introduce errors.

Analysis. *Analysis* is the application of reasoning to understand the data that have been gathered about a subject. In its simplest form analysis may involve determining consistent patterns and summarizing the relevant details revealed in the investigation. The appropriate analytical technique for data analysis will be determined by management's information requirements, the characteristics of the research design, and the nature of the data gathered. Statistical analysis may range from portraying a simple frequency distribution to very complex multivariate analysis, such as multiple regression. Later chapters will discuss statistical analysis under three general categories: univariate analysis, bivariate analysis, and multivariate analysis.

Conclusions and Report Preparation. As mentioned earlier, most marketing research is applied research with the purpose of making a marketing decision. An important but often overlooked aspect of the marketing researcher's job is to look at the analysis of the information collected and ask, "What does this mean to management?" The final stage in the research process, the **conclusions and report preparation stage**, consists of interpreting the information and making *conclusions* for managerial decisions.

conclusions and report preparation stage
The stage in which the researcher interprets information and draws conclusions so they can be communicated to the decision makers.

The research *report* should effectively communicate the research findings. All too many reports are complicated statements of technical aspects and sophisticated research methods. Frequently management is not interested in detailed reporting of the research design and statistical findings, but wishes only a summary of the findings. If the findings of the research remain unread on the marketing manager's desk, the study will have been useless. The importance of effective communication cannot be overemphasized. Research is only as good as its applications.

Marketing researchers must communicate their findings to a managerial audience. The written report serves another purpose as well: It is a means of providing historical documents that will be a source of record for later use, such as repeating the survey or providing a basis for building on the survey findings.

Now that we have outlined the research process, note that the order of this textbook follows the flowchart of the research process presented in Exhibit 3.4. Keep this flowchart in mind while reading later chapters.

The Research Program Strategy

Our discussion of the marketing research process began with the assumption that the researcher wished to gather information to achieve a specific marketing objective. We have emphasized the researcher's need to select specific techniques for solving one-dimensional problems such as identifying market segments, selecting the best packaging design, or test marketing a new product.

However, when we think about a firm's marketing mix activity in a given period of time (such as a year), we realize that marketing research is not a one-shot activity—it is a continuous process. An exploratory research study may be followed by a survey, or a researcher may conduct a specific research project for each aspect of the marketing mix. If a new product is being developed, the different types of research might include (1) market potential studies to identify the size and characteristics of the market, (2) product usage testing to record consumers' reactions to prototype products, (3) brand name and packaging research to determine the product's symbolic connotations, and (4) test marketing the new product. Because research is a continuous process, management should view marketing research at a strategic planning level. The **program strategy** refers to a firm's overall plan to use marketing research. It is a planning activity that places a series of marketing research projects in the context of the company's marketing plan.

The marketing research program strategy can be likened to a term insurance policy. Conducting marketing research minimizes risk and increases certainty. Each research project can be seen as a series of term insurance policies that makes the marketing manager's job a bit safer.

program strategy
The overall plan to conduct a series of marketing research projects; a planning activity that places each marketing project in the context of the company's marketing plan.

Summary

Decision making is the process by which managers resolve problems or choose among alternative opportunities. Decision makers must recognize the nature of the problem or opportunity, identify how much information is available, and recognize what information they need. Every marketing decision can be classified on a continuum ranging from complete certainty to absolute ambiguity.

Exploratory, descriptive, and causal research are three major types of marketing research projects. The clarity with which the research problem is defined determines whether exploratory, descriptive, or causal research is appropriate. Exploratory research is appropriate when management knows only the general nature of a problem; it is used not to provide conclusive evidence but to clarify problems. Descriptive research is conducted when there is some understanding of the nature of the problem to provide an accurate description of the characteristics of a population. Causal research identifies cause-and-effect relationships when the research problem has been narrowly defined.

Research proceeds in a series of six interrelated phases. The first is problem definition, which may include exploratory research using secondary data, experience surveys, or pilot studies. Once the problem is defined, the researcher selects a research design. The major designs are surveys, experiments, secondary data analysis, and observation. Creative research design can minimize the cost of obtaining reliable results. After the design has been selected, a sampling plan is chosen, using a probability sample, a nonprobability sample, or a combination of the two.

The design is put into action in the data-gathering phase. This phase may involve a small pretest before the main study is undertaken. In the analysis stage the data are edited and coded, then processed, usually by computer. The results are interpreted in light of the decisions that management must make. Finally, the analysis is presented to decision makers in a written or oral report. This last step is crucial because even an excellent project will not lead to proper action if the results are poorly communicated.

Quite often research projects are conducted together as parts of a research program. Such programs can involve successive projects that monitor an established product or a group of projects undertaken for a proposed new product to determine the optimal form of various parts of the marketing mix.

A major problem faces students of marketing research who must consider each stage in the research process separately. However, without concentrated emphasis on the total research process, understanding the individual stages is difficult. Thus, learning marketing research is like walking a tightrope between too broad and too narrow a focus.

Key Terms and Concepts

Decision making
Exploratory research
Descriptive research
Causal research
Concomitant variation
Forward linkage

Backward linkage
Problem definition stage
Pilot study
Research design stage
Research design
Sampling stage

Data gathering stage
Data processing and analysis stage
Conclusions and report preparation stage
Program strategy

Questions for Review and Critical Thinking

1. For each of the following situations, decide whether the research should be exploratory, descriptive, or causal:
   a. Establishing the functional relationship between advertising and sales
   b. Investigating consumer reactions to the *idea* of a new laundry detergent that prevents shrinkage in hot water
   c. identifying target market demographics for a shopping center
   d. Estimating sales potential for concrete vibrators in a northwestern sales territory
2. Describe a research situation that allows one to infer causality.
3. A researcher is interested in knowing the answer to a why question, but does not know beforehand what sort of answer will satisfy. Will answering this question involve exploratory, descriptive, or causal research? Explain.
4. Do the stages in the research process follow the scientific method?
5. Why is the problem definition stage of the research process probably the most important stage?
6. The Treasury Department is conducting technological research into the feasibility of creating a plasticlike

substance on which currency notes can be printed. Currency printed on this substance would increase the circulation life of lower-value currency notes and enhance their utility in vending-type equipment. What type of consumer research should be conducted?

7. Which research design seems appropriate for the following studies?
   a. The manufacturer and marketer of flight simulators and other pilot training equipment wish to forecast sales volume for the next 5 years.
   b. A local chapter of the American Lung Association wishes to identify the demographic characteristics of individuals who donate more than $500 per year.
   c. A major petroleum company is concerned with the increased costs of marketing regular leaded gasoline and is considering dropping this product.
   d. A food company researcher wishes to know what types of food are carried in brown-bag lunches to learn if the company can capitalize on this phenomenon.
8. Should the marketing research program strategy be viewed as a strategic planning activity?

 ## Exploring the Internet

1. Use a Web browser to go to the Gallup Organization's home page at http://www.gallup.com. The Gallup home page changes on a regular basis. However, there should be an opportunity to read the results of a political poll. Select the "Gallup Poll" option and then view the results of a research study by selecting the special option. On a sheet of paper, list the various stages of the research process and how they were followed in Gallup's special project.

2. Use a Web browser to access Lycos (http://www.lycos.com). What keyword topics can be investigated? How might the information you find help you design a research project?
3. Use your Web browser to view the Advertising Research Foundation's home page at http://www.arfsite.org. The Advertising Media Internet Center will show an icon for "Research Monitor." Click on "Research Monitor." What research information can be accessed?

Video-Case 3.1 **Paradigm Entertainment**

IN 1990, THREE OUT-OF-WORK SOFTWARE ENGINEERS took their expertise in 3-D military computer simulations and found success offering it to a broad range of companies outside the defense industry.[12] Their company Paradigm Simulation formed a strategic alliance with Silicon Graphics and provided services for clients such as BMW, NASA, Chrysler, and Boeing. After Paradigm Simulation created an innovative 3-D video game called Pilot Wings for Nintendo, the Japanese gaming giant, the company took a new direction and created a division called Paradigm Entertainment, which focused on software for creating video games. Its executives try to build a strong relationship with its primary customers, companies such as Nintendo and Sega that market video games. It tries to understand game players who buy games as its secondary customers. However, the company realizes that learning what game players (primarily young

boys) want in a game is vital, and this task is not secondary. Marketing research plays an important part in determining the features video games should have.

QUESTIONS

1. Suppose a video game company approached Paradigm with an idea for a new video game. Using the flowchart in Exhibit 3.4, outline the steps in the research process that you would recommend that Paradigm take.

2. If Paradigm becomes partners with video game marketers, what type of research information might these companies have at their disposal?

Case 3.2 **Hudson Coffee Company**

HARRISON HUDSON, PRESIDENT AND FOUNDER OF HUDson Coffee Company, sat in a new-product meeting with his marketing staff. F. Marvin Schwartz, marketing manager, was discussing the need to develop a marketing plan for Columbian Coffee Cooler, the proposed brand name for a new-product line of iced-coffee drinks. The lines was to include five flavors: standard coffee, Swiss chocolate, mocha, espresso, and amaretto. Schwartz explained that the marketing of the canned iced-coffee line was designed to be similar to the marketing strategies used by most soft drink marketers.

As Hudson listened to the presentation of some plans that he already had discussed with Schwartz, he remembered that five years ago he had returned to his alma mater for a football weekend. He had been appalled that Sunday morning in the Notre Dame student union to see students ordering doughnuts and Coke or Dr Pepper rather than coffee for their breakfast drink. It was a tremendous shock. That weekend had a major impact on Hudson's thinking. The importer and blender of exclusive coffees, manufacturer of coffee pots, and Notre Dame alumnus began to think that the growth era for coffee was over.

Schwartz indicated that soft drink consumption now exceeded 30 gallons per person a person a year

and was substantially more for preteen and teenage children. He estimated that soft drink consumption now made up 30 percent of the beverage market. He pointed out, however, that the public was not consciously aware of this extremely large volume.

Hudson saw canned iced coffee as an opportunity to compete in the soft drink market. He thought it was a product that would bring Hudson Coffee into the soft drink age. However, he was unsure whether there was adequate demand for the product line.

QUESTIONS

1. If you were a marketing research staff member attending this meeting, how would you define the research problem? Write a detailed statement of the research objectives for the Columbian Coffee Cooler project.

2. What type of information might be acquired using primary data sources? Using secondary data sources?

3. Outline a program strategy.

Note: The names used in this case are fictitious to ensure confidentiality.

Case 3.3 Frito-Lay

HISPANICS DON'T MUNCH ON POTATO CHIPS AS often as average consumers. In fact, they are 52 percent less likely to eat "salty snacks" then the general market. How could Frito-Lay appeal to this growing segment of the population?

Initial focus groups by the Market Segment Group found that Hispanic teens and young adults thought Frito-Lay products tasted too mild. And they weren't impressed with low-fat or unflavored tortilla chips; they wanted bolder, spicier flavors. Latino consumers also said they were unaware of most Frito-Lay advertising, and often bought individual bags of snacks, rather than family-sized products.

Next, Burke Marketing Research and Market Segment conducted door-to-door interviews. They found that Hispanics tended to buy snacks at small local grocery stores, not the 21-aisle supermarkets down the road. The study also indicated that, if presented with the right products, these consumers might buy more Frito-Lay snacks, perhaps in larger sizes.

Meanwhile, teams from Strategy Research Corporation were cruising Hispanic neighborhoods in Los Angeles, San Antonio, and Miami, in traveling test kitchens: giant RVs. Their mission: get Hispanic women to sample 43 salty snacks and assess the ones they liked. Why women? Because they buy most of the groceries. Why the RVs? Because Hispanics are less likely to shop at malls, where taste tests are commonly performed. The research led to the development of four products: Doritos Salsa Verde, Lay's Adobaditas, Frito's Flamin' Hot Sabrositos, and Frito's Lime 'n Chile Sabrositos.

A second round of focus groups gathered Hispanic male teens and young adults, a demographic group that consumes a lot of chips. They liked one tagline in particular: "Sabor a Todo Volumen" (the loudest taste). At first, Frito-Lay execs questioned the use of Spanish, but researchers were confident. While kids spoke English at school, many turned to Spanish at home. And previous focus groups had

shown that most Latinos weren't aware of the company's English-language ads. If the company truly wanted to tap the Hispanic market, it had to talk the talk.

Doritos Salsa Verde became the focus of the Hispanic advertising strategy–the Doritos brand sold well among teens so it made sense to capitalize on that popularity and target Hispanic male teens and young adults who speak Spanish. They were bicultural and embraced certain aspects of life in America but still felt close to their roots. Dieste & Partners developed several ads and showed them to kids in focus groups. One spot featured a hip, young woman singing Spanish rock music, a growing movement in Hispanic youth culture. The kids loved it.

Another key element in the campaign was the "Happy Face" logo, an icon of Frito-Lay's sister company in Mexico. In focus groups, Mexican Americans said the logo reminded them of snack foods from home. Given that Mexican Americans comprise 63 percent of all Hispanics in the United States, Frito-Lay knew it had to act on this finding. The "Happy Face" appears in all packaging and advertising.

In 1997, Frito-Lay launched its Hispanic products in San Antonio. IRI tracked sales in stores that served a majority of Hispanic shoppers. Sales of the Doritos brand jumped 32 percent after the rollout; the Salsa Verde flavor represented 15 percent of all sales. last year, Frito-Lay expanded the line into other locations in the United States with large Hispanic populations. Sales topped $100 million and Doritos Salsa Verde accounted for nearly 50 percent.

QUESTIONS

1. Outline Frito-Lay's research program strategy.
2. How did the early research projects influence the subsequent research projects?

A RESEARCH MANAGER AND A SALES MANAGER HAD TO CROSS A swiftly flowing river. The sales manager immediately flung off his clothes, dove in, and, with many furious strokes and the help of a strong downstream current, finally managed to cross the river. With much loud huffing and puffing, he emerged, pounded his chest, and proudly told everyone of his exploit. The research manager, in the meantime, carefully calculated the speed of the current, observed the location of shallow water and sandy bottom, the height of the banks and other factors, determined the best starting point, and quietly waded across. Upon arriving on the other side, he didn't say anything to anyone.[1]

While this story undoubtedly stereotypes sales managers and marketing researchers, it should be remembered that most jokes originate as some form of complaint. The story makes some salient points about the difference between line and staff marketing managers.

This chapter investigates the human side of marketing research. Most of this text deals with research methodology and the research process. However, several organizational, managerial, and ethical issues need to be discussed.

The chapter first explores researchers' human side by discussing the place of research in the organization, then it considers some sources of the conflicts between marketing researchers and managers and some ways to reduce these conflicts. It also discusses the role of the research suppliers and contractors.

Society expects marketing researchers to maintain certain standards of conduct and do what is morally right. This chapter ends with a discussion of a variety of ethical issues that face managers and marketing researchers.

What you will learn in this chapter

To recognize the degree of marketing research sophistication in various organizations.

To discuss the organizational structure of marketing research in various organizations.

To identify the various individual job titles within the marketing research industry.

To discuss the often conflicting relationship between marketing management and researchers.

To understand the role that research suppliers and research contractors play in the marketing research industry.

To identify the criteria for determining when outside research suppliers are needed.

To explain why ethical questions are philosophical questions.

To define societal norms.

To describe the three parties involved in most research situations and how interaction among them may identify ethical questions.

To discuss the rights and obligations of the respondent.

To discuss the rights and obligations of the researcher.

To discuss the rights and obligations of the client sponsor.

To take each of the three parties' perspectives and discuss selected issues such as deception, privacy, and advocacy research.

To discuss the role of codes of ethics in marketing research.

The Mission of the Research Department

A mission statement identifies the marketing research department's purpose within the organization. It explains what the department hopes to accomplish.

Exhibit 4.1 details the mission statement of General Foods' marketing research department. It shows the importance of a complete program of research that meets the needs of decision makers. It also suggests that the mission of the research department is a key factor in the success of a research function within an organization.

An executive at a major packaged goods company has stressed that the research mission should be integrated with other units in the organization:

> The most successful research departments are those whose mission is directly linked to the decision makers' needs. In most cases this means the research department must be valued, integrated, and an active part of the company's marketing process.
>
> Conversely those research departments that have not been successful seem to be independent of the decision makers' needs. Such departments tend to be isolated and operate within a vacuum. Their output may be technically precise but it is rarely put to use because research is independent of the decision makers.[2]

TO THE POINT

To manage a business is to manage its future; and to manage the future is to manage information.

MARION HARPER

Exhibit 4.1 General Foods' Research Department Mission/Roles

The research mission is to:

Support General Foods' best food company strategy by providing the highest quality marketing intelligence upon which strategic and tactical decisions are based.

The Department will accomplish its mission by:

- Providing ad hoc marketing information which is relevant to the issues, appropriate (in terms of accuracy, timeliness, and risk), and commensurate with the true needs of the marketing decision maker.
- Integrating market/marketing information in a total intelligence to facilitate the identification, development, and execution of significant, long-term strategic planning.
- Exercising leadership in accumulating GF marketing experience and utilizing it to develop a knowledge base about marketing and the marketing process.
- Exercising leadership in the development of research methods which will significantly improve marketing decision making.
- Maintaining a high degree of consistency of methodology to facilitate decision making across GF's many businesses.
- Maintaining assurance of objectivity in the collection, analysis, interpretation, and use of marketing information.

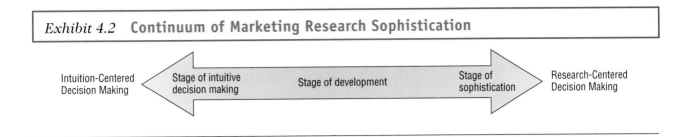

Exhibit 4.2 **Continuum of Marketing Research Sophistication**

Degree of Marketing Research Sophistication

As businesspeople have come to recognize that marketing research is a useful decision-making tool, its use has become more widespread. An organization's willingness to use research generally parallels its acceptance of the marketing concept. Just as some firms remain in the production-oriented stage, some ignore or are ignorant of marketing research. The use of marketing research has evolved from a stage in which managers make decisions intuitively to a stage of **research sophistication** in which managers have considerable experience in the proper use of research techniques. Marketing management's attitudes toward research methodology can range along a continuum from ignorance of research and intuition-centered decision making to sophisticated, research-centered decision making. See Exhibit 4.2. For purposes of discussion, three levels of marketing research sophistication can be identified.

research sophistication
A stage in which managers have considerable experience in the proper use of research techniques.

Stage of Intuitive Decision Making

Marketing managers in this stage may be ignorant about marketing research or they may believe that research methodology is appropriately confined to the ivory tower of academia or, at best, to technical research conducted elsewhere in the organization. These managers depend heavily on intuition and experience, and obtain their information informally.

Stage of Sophistication

In this stage marketing research has become a proactive force to identify decision makers' information needs. Marketing managers in this final stage recognize the potential of research to improve the decision-making process. They recognize that a fortune teller is probably a better bargain than poor research. They also recognize that while good research does not completely eliminate uncertainty, it can be an economically warranted means of at least reducing that uncertainty.

Stage of Development

Most companies are neither completely ignorant nor completely informed about what marketing research can and cannot do. Companies may use marketing research for the first few times on blind faith. Marketing managers in this stage naively believe that the result of the application of research methodology is the decision itself, rather than the information on which to base a good decision.

They fail to see that good research can only reduce uncertainty; it cannot eliminate it. Managers developing a knowledge of research seem most impressed with complex research they are not capable of evaluating. Some statistical analysis in a research report impresses these managers. Show them the same analysis on a computer graphic and they are awestruck.

Over time managers gain experience and become increasingly familiar with marketing research. They begin to use research more often and to recognize occasions when it should be applied.

Sometimes, marketing managers become disillusioned as they develop more research sophistication, perhaps even feeling betrayed by marketing research. These managers become very cynical because they have made costly mistakes in research-based decisions. This vulnerability arises from failure to distinguish good from bad research or from assuming that good research effectively makes a management decision.

This is a learning stage. Companies employ marketing research, but they do not exploit its full potential. Gradually, they increase their research sophistication.

Organizational Structure Of Marketing Research

A survey of companies that belonged to the American Marketing Association found that 76 percent of them reported having formal marketing research departments. Formal research departments are most common among consumer products, manufacturers and retailers.[3] Larger companies are more likely to have marketing research departments.

The place of marketing research in an organization and the structure of the research department will vary substantially depending on the firm's acceptance of the marketing concept and its stage of marketing research sophistication. Improper placement of the marketing research department can isolate it.

At General Motors the marketing research department's goal is to provide cost-effective market understanding that allows General Motors to beat competitors to opportunities for existing and new products. The marketing research department's primary mission is to provide relevant, accurate, useable, and timely market information. The director of research says, "our added value is found when we participate as an active and equal member of the decision-making team. This active role must be accomplished by being perceived as coming to the team without a personal point-of-view as that perception could negatively affect the credibility of our primary mission."[5]

Researchers may lack a voice in executive committees when they have no continuous relationship with marketing management. Sometimes the research department is positioned at an inappropriately low level.

Given that research and the decision makers are linked together, the best organization structure is to report as high up in the senior management ranks as possible—at least to the senior marketing vice president and preferably higher. The research department should also be able to have as broad a perspective across the company as possible. This is because of the information flow which the research department manages, interprets, and communicates.[4]

Marketing Research as a Staff Function

Research departments that perform a staff function must wait for management to request assistance. Often the term **client** is used by the research department to refer to line management for whom services are being performed.

The research department responds to clients' requests and is responsible for the design and execution of all research. It should function like an internal consulting organization that develops action-oriented, data-based recommendations.

In a small firm the vice president of marketing may be in charge of marketing research. This officer generally will have the sales manager collect and analyze sales histories, trade association statistics, and other internal data. If a survey needs to be conducted, an advertising agency or a firm that specializes in marketing research will be contracted to do the job. At the other extreme, a large company like Procter & Gamble may staff its research departments with more than 100 people.

In a medium-sized firm the research department might be organized as shown in Exhibit 4.3. The director of marketing research, chief information office, or **director of marketing information systems** provides leadership and integrates staff-level activities. (This position will be discussed in greater detail in the next section.) The **research analyst** is responsible for client contact, project design, preparation of proposals, selection of research suppliers, and supervision of data collection, analysis, and reporting activities.[6] Normally the research analyst is responsible for projects for all or several of a medium-sized firm's products. He

client
Term often used by the research department to refer to line management for whom services are being performed.

director of marketing information systems
Provides leadership and integrates staff-level activities. (Also called director of marketing research and chief information officer.

research analyst
Responsible for client contact, project design, preparation of proposals, selection of research suppliers, and supervision of data collection, analysis, and reporting activities.

Exhibit 4.3 **Structure of a Medium-Sized Research Department**

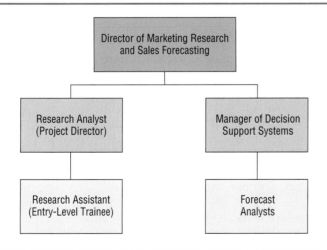

Exhibit 4.4   Organization of the Marketing Research Department in a Large Firm

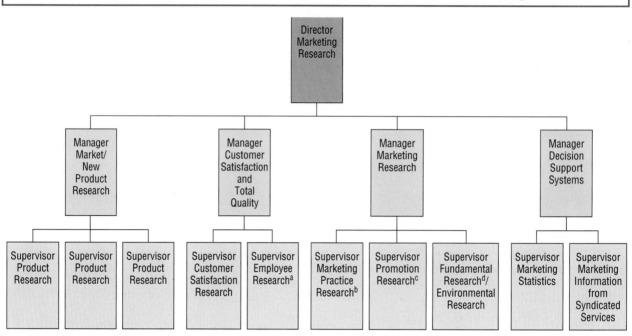

(by product groupings)

[a]Conducts research to improve total quality management in production.
[b]Conducts research that cuts across product lines or involves competitive marketing practices or characteristics of customer groups.
[c]Conducts research to measure the effectiveness of promotional activities and cut across product lines.
[d]Conducts research aimed at gaining a basic understanding of various elements of the marketing process.

research assistant
Provides technical assistance with questionnaire design, analysis of data, and so on.

manager of decision support systems
Supervises the collection and analysis of sales, inventory, and other periodic data.

forecast analyst
Provides technical assistance such as running computer programs and manipulating data to forecast sales.

manager of customer quality research
Specializes in conducting surveys to measure consumers' satisfaction with product quality.

or she works with product or division management and makes recommendations based on analysis of collected data. A junior analyst, or **research assistant** (associate), provides technical assistance with questionnaire design, analysis of data, and so on. The **manager of decision support systems** supervises the collection and analysis of sales, inventory, and other periodic data. Sales forecasts for product lines usually are developed using analytical and quantitative techniques. Sales information is provided to satisfy the planning, analysis, and control needs of decision makers. The manager of decision support systems may be assisted by a **forecast analyst,** who provides technical assistance such as running computer programs and manipulating data to forecast sales.

Personnel within a planning department may perform the marketing research function in a medium-sized firm. These individuals may plan or design research studies and then contract with outside firms that supply research services such as interviewing or data processing.

As marketing research departments grow, they tend to specialize by product or strategic business unit. For example, Marriott Corporation has a director of marketing research for lodging (for example, Marriott Hotels and Resorts, Courtyard by Marriott, and Fairfield Inn) and it has a director of marketing research for contract services and restaurants (e.g., Roy Rogers, Big Boy, and Senior Living Services). Each business unit's research director reports to the vice president of corporate marketing services. Many large organizations have **managers of customer quality research** who specialize in conducting surveys to measure consumers' satisfaction with product quality.

Exhibit 4.4 illustrates the organization of the marketing research department of a major firm. Within this organization, the centralized marketing research department conducts research for all of the division's product groups. This is typical of a large research department that conducts much of its own research, including fieldwork. The director of marketing research reports to the vice president of marketing.

The department in Exhibit 4.4 does not use outside marketing research contractors. To some extent this is rare; nevertheless, the full-service department example facilitates discussion of marketing research's interfaces with other departments.

TO THE POINT

The longer the title, the less important the job.

GEORGE MCGOVERN

The Director of Marketing Research as a Manager

The **director of marketing research** plans, executes, and controls the marketing research function. This person typically serves on executive committees that identify competitive opportunities and formulate marketing strategies for the organization. The director's responsibility is to provide the research point of view on these strategic issues.

Directors of marketing research must remember that they are managers rather than researchers. Marketing research directors tend to face several typical problems:

1. Skilled professionals find greater allure in conducting research than in managing people. They pride themselves on being hands-on researchers.

2. Operating managers perceive managers as chief project directors and expect them to do the work themselves. The research management role is not recognized.

3. Many able practitioners have trouble delegating responsibility. They may secretly fear the loss of control, or they may genuinely feel "I can do it better myself." Some may be loath to surrender the plaudits that often go to those who actually work on the project.

4. Some research managers view their staffs as mere extensions of their own capabilities, as extra arms and legs. Because managers cannot possibly do everything well themselves, this practice is bound to create problems. They may produce shoddy work, or they will be unable to attract or retain able staff.

5. Finally, research is often seen as a hodgepodge of techniques available to answer individual, unrelated questions. The view of a research operation, therefore, encompasses an array of more or less equal projects, each handled by a project director. Hence, a full-time leader seems unnecessary.[6]

Many organizations have an infrequent rather than a constant need for marketing research. They may conduct little research "in-house." Rather, their marketing research manages may rely heavily on outside research suppliers or consultants when the need for a study arises. In these organizations, the marketing research manager's primary responsibilities involve communicating research needs to outside research suppliers and evaluating research proposals. The role of marketing research suppliers is discussed later in this chapter. Chapter 5 discusses problem definition and research proposals.

director of marketing research
Plans, executes, and controls the marketing research function.

WHAT WENT WRONG?

Getting the Job Done

MANY YEARS AGO, I DISCOVERED WHAT MY ROLE WAS when I was just learning how to run a market research department. I was in a company where the chief executive officer took it upon himself to get to know his young managers. Periodically he would invite me to have lunch with him. Conversation ranged from topics that were on his mind to questions about what we were learning in market research that would help the company grow.

As a shrewd man, he'd learned the value of developing alternate channels of communication about what was going on in the organization and about pros and cons of decisions that would sooner or later reach his desk. He was also a very shrewd and demanding motivator of people.

At lunch once he asked me. "How many people do we have in this market research department now?" I mumbled something to the effect that we were overworked and didn't have enough people. He continued and asked me, "About how much money do we spend on market research totally—both the people and the project costs?"

I'd tell him and then explain that we weren't spending as much per sales dollar as our principal competitors and that we had very rigid controls on costs and on project approvals. He'd nod and explain to me how many dollars' worth of merchandise a salesperson had to sell in a year simply to pay the expense of my department.

After catching my attention, he'd proceed with the topic that was on his mind. Some major marketing-oriented project had failed—I can't remember now whether it was a new product, a new advertising campaign, a new promotion, or just what it was. In any case the failure was clear and visible in the organization.

Then he asked me, "With all these people and all this money we spend in market research, how come we didn't have the marketing intelligence to tell us that this project wasn't going to succeed?" I said that the research we had done had raised serious questions about whether the project should go ahead. His response was, "Well, if we had reason to believe that this project wasn't going to succeed, why did we go ahead?"

My reply was, "Well, we tried to tell the brand group that it wasn't going to succeed, but they really believed in the project and they wanted to go ahead and so they ignored us and went ahead."

Then followed a long, deathly silence. Then he looked me straight in the eye, smiled and said, "Well, you didn't get your job done, did you?" And that's how I learned what the role of market research should be in a corporation.

Sources of Conflict Between Marketing Management and Marketing Research

In principle the functions of marketing research should merge harmoniously with the objectives of marketing management for the benefit of both parties. In practice the relationship between the marketing research department and the users of marketing research frequently is characterized by misunderstanding and conflict.

Research that Implies Criticism

A product manager who requests a survey of dealer loyalty will not be happy if the survey finds that the dealers are extremely critical of him or her. Similarly, a sales manager who informally projects a 5 percent increase in sales will not like hearing from the research department that the market potential indicates sales volume should be up by 20 percent. In each of these situations marketing research presents information that implies criticism of a line executive's decision. In personal life a sure way to lose a friend is to be openly critical of him or her. In business there is little difference.

Money

Research budgets are a source of conflict between management and researchers. Many managers see research as an expenditure rather than an investment. Managers who have had little experience with marketing research do not understand the valuable contributions of good research. Most marketing researchers contend that research is only as good as the budget allocated for it. A researcher can become frustrated knowing that a project initially had laudable goals, but became focused instead on how to save money.

Time: Emergency Research

If research programs are not systematically planned, marketing researchers will encounter emergency requests. Too often researchers are asked to begin a study after something goes wrong rather than at an earlier stage, when the research could have aided in effective decision making. Studies conducted after trouble occurs often produce unfavorable data that disparage the decision makers, making managers leery of all research projects.

When something goes wrong, managers want the research results immediately. Researchers believe, however, that good research takes time. Marketing researchers suffer occasional lapses from good practice because of the urgency of a project. Sometimes a marketing researcher will have to submit to the time pressure and do a quick-and-dirty study. A few sudden events do require acquiring data quickly, but most rush jobs could be avoided with proper planning of the research program. If it is necessary to conduct a study with severe time limitations, the researcher should be sure to point this out to management. Overuse of such precautions, on the other hand, can cause managers to see researchers as unnecessarily cautious and to mistrust their conclusions.

Intuitive Decision Making

So far the discussion has implied that managers are decision oriented and researchers generally are not. Many line marketing managers regard marketing as an art. "They enjoy flying by the seat of their pants—though you will never get them to admit it. They revel in chaos, abhor facts, and fear research." They may see research as taking the fun out of their jobs. They are action-oriented. "Some executives have a self-image as people of action. They pride themselves on their ability to reach decisions quickly, and in a crisp, authoritative manner. Thirsting for action, they become impatient with what seems to them the plodding tempo of research." Some managers may complacently believe that intuitive decisions have brought them to their present positions, so why waste time waiting for research?[7]

DeLorean Motor Company's decision to market an expensive sports car illustrates this phenomenon. Porsche and Datsun provided competing alternatives, and few people could afford cars in this class. Yet John Z. DeLorean overestimated demand for the DMC-12 because in his mind there was nothing quite like it on the road. DeLorean's confidence and sense that he could not fail became a major problem. His own marketing research showed that perhaps 12,000 DMC-12s at most could be sold in a year, yet production was scheduled at the equivalent of

20,000 cars per year. Today, except for its role as a "time machine" in the Back to the Future movies, the DeLorean is barely remembered.

If managers do use research, they often request simple projects that will provide concrete results with certainty. Researchers tend to see problems as complex questions that can be answered only within probability ranges. One aspect of this conflict is the belief that a research report provides findings, but cannot make decisions. Decision-oriented executives may unrealistically expect research to make decisions for them or provide some type of guarantee that the correct action will be taken. While research provides information for decision making, it does not always solve all the uncertainties of complex decisions. Certain alternatives may be eliminated, but the research may reveal new aspects of a problem. Although research is a valuable decision-making tool, it does not relieve the executive of the decision-making task.

Presentation of the right facts can be extremely useful. However, decision makers often believe that researchers collect the wrong facts. Many researchers view themselves as technicians who generate numbers using sophisticated mathematical and statistical techniques; they may spend more time on technical details than on satisfying managerial needs. Each person who has a narrow perspective of another's job is a partial cause of problem of generating limited or useless information.

A typical example is a researcher who disagrees with a marketing executive's simplified conception that all research is survey research. Without a careful definition of the problem, the executive might request that the researcher conduct a telephone survey to measure advertising effectiveness. The researcher, who sees the measurement of advertising effectiveness as a complex and expensive task, may feel pressured to deliver more than the survey promises. The researcher knows the technique is inadequate for the request and therefore may focus on more elaborate techniques.

A comparison has been made between weather reporters and marketing researchers. The average person watching a TV weather report wants to know whether he or she needs to take an umbrella to work the next day. The weather reporter provides enormous amounts of information: It's snowing in Washington, sunny in San Diego, and raining in Texas. Maps full of lines showing fronts, high- and low-pressure areas, and other weather facts are extraneous information to the person who simply does not want to risk getting wet. Fortunately, most weather reporters eventually let us know if rain is forecasted. In a similar vein, the marketing researcher may be overly technical with clients.

Future Decisions Based on Past Experience

Managers wish to predict the future, but researchers measure only current or past events. In 1957 Ford introduced the Edsel, one of the classic marketing failures of all time. One reason for the Edsel's failure was that the marketing research conducted several years before the car's introduction indicated a strong demand for a medium-priced car for the "man on his way up." By the time the car was introduced, however, consumer preference had shifted to two cars, one being a small import for the suburban wife. Not all research information is so dated, but all is based on what people have done in the past rather than what they will do in the future.

Pseudo-Research and Organizational Politics

A product manager once demanded a market test for a new product. The marketing researcher had reason to suspect that the product manager was really interested in a nationwide introduction of the product but needed a confidence booster to takes this step. The exchange between them went something like this:

RESEARCHER:	What if the test results are favorable?
PRODUCT MANAGER:	Why, we'll launch the product nationally, of course.
RESEARCHER:	And if the results are unfavorable?
PRODUCT MANAGER:	They won't be. I'm sure of that.
RESEARCHER:	But just suppose they are.
PRODUCT MANAGER:	I don't think we should throw out a good product just because of one little market test.
RESEARCHER:	Then why test?
PRODUCT MANAGER:	Listen, Smith, this is a major product introduction. It's got to have some research behind it.[7]

The product manager was really telling the marketing researcher to justify a decision that already had been made. If the test market's results had contradicted the decision, the product manager would have disregarded the research. This is **pseudo-research** because it is conducted not to gather information for marketing decisions but to bolster a point of view and satisfy other needs.

pseudo-research
Activities that appear to be research but are conducted for the purposes of organizational politics rather than objective gathering of information.

The most common type of pseudo-research is performed to justify a decision that has already been made. Management is already committed, but research is still requested. For example, a media buyer who has been wined and dined regularly at the most fashionable New York restaurants may feel compelled to present management with some hard facts from a research study to justify the purchase of advertising space. Another example is a young manager in the new-product development groups who is highly enthusiastic about a new freeze-dried vegetable product. She knows that top management is carefully watching her progress in the firm and that this is her big opportunity. She asks the marketing research department to select a test market with a vigorous local sales effort and a strong distributor who likes to promote new products heavily because this will make her pet product look like a winner. By the time the product goes national, she will have been promoted to another job.

Occasionally marketing research is used to pass on blame for failure to another area. A product manager may deliberately request a research study with no intention of paying attention to the findings and recommendations. The manager knows that the particular program is in trouble but plays the standard game to cover up for the mismanagement of the program. If the project fails, marketing research will become the scapegoat.

An ambitious subordinate or an administrator who wants to hide the source of criticism may use marketing research to disparage someone. Such misuse causes executives to view marketing research as a threat. Line executives may fear that research will undermine their authority or cast doubt on their abilities.

Politicians have concocted a particular type of pseudo-research as a means to damage opposing candidates' reputations. A *push poll* is political telemarketing under the guise of a political poll. Its name derives from the fact that the purpose of the poll is to push voters away from a candidate. Politicians running for office call thousands of potential voters, tell them they are conducting a survey, and than ask loaded questions that put a negative spin on an opponent's behavior. For example, in a recent Colorado election the following question was asked:

> Please tell me if you would be more likely or less likely to vote for Roy Romer if you knew that Governor Romer appoints a parole board which has granted early release to an average of four convicted felons per day every day since Romer took office.[8]

Pseudo-research does exist, but such projects clearly are in the minority. Nevertheless, students should know about these tactics, none of which is recommended. This book assumes that marketing research will be conducted by competent professionals who have no ulterior motives. The last part of this chapter provides a complete discussion of ethics in marketing research.

Other Areas of Conflict

The conflicts between managers and researchers are aggravated by the gap between what management demands and what research offers. Exhibit 4.5 illustrates the differences between marketing researchers and managers and details many sources of conflict between them.

Reducing the Conflict Between Management and Research

A solution to the conflict revolves around better communication between managers and researchers so that each will grow to understand the other's activities and needs. Over the years there has been a gradual process of education by marketing researchers to apprise management of the limitations of research as well as its strengths.

Just as users need education on the benefits of research, researchers need an understanding of and some experience in the areas they are researching. Better communications makes both parties more competent.

Marketing managers need to better assess their information needs and work with researchers to plan the research activities that will supply this information. Managers must become involved with projects during the beginning stages. Early involvement increases the likelihood that managers will accept and act on the results. Researchers' responsibility should be made explicit by a formal job description. Better planning and an annual statement of the research program for the upcoming year will help minimize emergency assignments, which usually waste resources and demoralize personnel.

Marketing researchers must understand management's perspective. They must realize that they are businesspeople first and technicians second. Researchers must try to enhance companies' profits by their contributions. Perhaps the best way for them to do this is to orient themselves toward decision making. They should realize that information is sometimes needed urgently. They should strive to develop cost-saving research alternatives, and occasionally they may still have to do a quick-and-dirty study that may not satisfy all professional standards, but will provide usable and timely information. In other words, they should focus on results. Perhaps the most important factor is more effective communication of the research findings and research designs. The researchers must understand the interests and needs of the user of the research. If researchers are sensitive to the decision-making orientation of management and can translate research performance into management language, much organizational conflict will diminish.

Exhibit 4.5 Probable Areas of Top Management–Marketing Research Conflict

TOP MANAGEMENT POSITION	AREA	MARKETING RESEARCH POSITION
MR[a] lacks sense of accountability. Sole MR function is as an information provider.	Research responsibility	Responsibility should be explicitly defined and consistently followed. Desire decision-making involvement with TM.[b]
Generally poor communicators. Lack enthusiasm, skills, and imagination.	Research personnel	TM is anti-intellectual. Researchers should be hired, judged, and compensated on research capabilities.
Research costs too much. Since MR contribution is difficult to measure, budget cuts are relatively defensible.	Budget	"You get what you pay for." Research needs continuing, long-range TM commitment.
Tend to be overengineered. Not executed with proper sense of urgency. Exhibit ritualized, staid approach.	Assignments	Too many nonresearchable or emergency requests. Insufficient time and money allocated.
MR best equipped to do this. General direction sufficient. MR must appreciate and respond. Can't help changing circumstances.	Problem definition	TM generally unsympathetic to this widespread problem. Not given all the relevant facts. Changed after research is under way.
Characterized as dull with too much jargon and too many qualifiers. Not decision oriented. Too often reported after the fact.	Research reporting	TM treats superficially. Good research demands thorough reporting and documentation. Insufficient lead time given.
Free to use as it pleases. MR shouldn't question. Changes in need and timing of research are sometimes unavoidable. MR deceived by not knowing all the facts.	Use of research	TM use to support a predetermined position represents misuse. Isn't used after requested and conducted—wasteful. Used to confirm or excuse past decisions.

[a]MR = marketing researcher.
[b]TM = top manager.

A **research generalist** can effectively serve as a link between management and the research specialist. The research generalist acts as a problem definer, an educator, a liaison, a communicator, and a friendly ear. This intermediary could work with specialists who understand management's needs and demands. The student of marketing research who has a business degree seems most suited for this coordinating function.

Several strategies for reducing the conflict between management and research are possible. Managers generally should plan the role of research better, and researchers should become more decision oriented and improve their communication skills (see Exhibit 4.6).[9]

In many organizations reduction of conflict is accomplished with the establishment of cross-functional teams.

research generalist
The person who saves effectively as a communication link between management and the research specialist because he or she understands the needs of both parties.

Cross-Functional Teams

As more companies awaken to the challenge of the global information age and the need to act quickly, old forms of organization structures are fading fast. Today everyone in a progressive organization from accountants to engineers engages in a unified effort to consider all issues related to the development, production, or marketing of new products.

EXPLORING RESEARCH ISSUES

Star Trek: The Way Decisions Really Are

THE STAR TREK TELEVISION PROGRAM AND MOVIES have been popular for years. Why this fascination? The major reason seems to revolve around the decision making that we all face. Each show is based on a decision that Captain Kirk must make, which involves uncertainty, turbulence, and either too little or too much data. Captain Kirk always seems to make the right decision but in different ways.

Star Trek provides a useful and practical model for decision making. Captain Kirk has two aides to his problem solving. One is represented by Science Officer Spock, who is unemotional, logical, and precise; he deals with the ship's computer. The other is represented by Lt. Commander McCoy, who is emotional and concerned about humans and their relationships.

Spock represents data gathering, alternative generation, and implementation. McCoy represents communication, human relationships, and the gamut of human emotions. Captain Kirk must make decisions that balance the analytical and human relationships. Both the Mr. Spock and Dr. McCoy roles are needed by all managers to make effective decisions. Captain Kirk also plays a key role. Neither Mr. Spock nor Dr. McCoy would make the best decision. Kirk is needed to balance their inputs appropriately to make the best decision.

If we personified the typical marketing research manager and the typical line marketing manager as *Star Trek* characters, who would be Mr. Spock and who would be Dr. McCoy? Top managers must make decisions like Captain Kirk, weighing the relevant inputs from all resources.

---

cross-functional teams
Teams composed of individuals from various organizational departments such as engineering, production, finance, and marketing who share a common purpose.

Cross-functional teams are composed of individuals from various organizational departments such as engineering, production, finance, and marketing who share a common purpose. Current management thinking suggests that cross-functional teams help organizations focus on a core business process, such as customer service or new-product development. Working in teams reduces the tendency for employees to focus single-mindedly on an isolated functional activity. The use of cross-functional teams to help employees to improve product quality and increase customer value is a major trend in business today.

At trend-setting organizations many marketing research directors are members of cross-functional teams. New-product development, for example, may be done by a cross-functional team of engineers, finance executives, production personnel, marketing managers, and marketing researchers who take an integrated approach to solve problem or exploit opportunities. In the old days, marketing research may not have been involved in developing new products until long after many key decisions about product specifications and manufacturing had been made. Now marketing researchers' input is part of an integrative team effort. Researchers act as both business consultants and as providers of technical services. Researchers working in teams are more likely to understand the broad purpose of their research and less likely to focus exclusively on research methodology.

The effective cross-functional team is a good illustration of the marketing concept in action. It reflects an effort to satisfy customers by using all the organization's resources. Cross-functional teams are having a dramatic impact on how the role of marketing research is viewed within the organization.

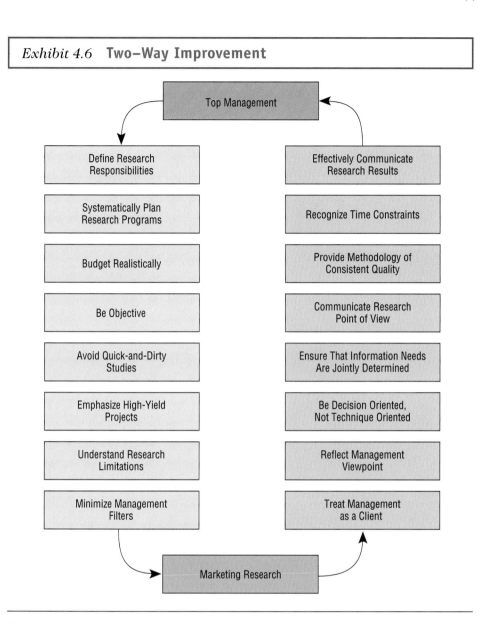

Exhibit 4.6 **Two–Way Improvement**

Top Management

Define Research Responsibilities

Systematically Plan Research Programs

Budget Realistically

Be Objective

Avoid Quick-and-Dirty Studies

Emphasize High-Yield Projects

Understand Research Limitations

Minimize Management Filters

Effectively Communicate Research Results

Recognize Time Constraints

Provide Methodology of Consistent Quality

Communicate Research Point of View

Ensure That Information Needs Are Jointly Determined

Be Decision Oriented, Not Technique Oriented

Reflect Management Viewpoint

Treat Management as a Client

Marketing Research

Research Suppliers and Contractors

The marketing research manager (in smaller firms, the marketing manager) must also interact with **research suppliers,** or commercial marketing research services. Although much marketing research activity is conducted in private companies' marketing research departments, much of it occurs in firms that may be variously classified as marketing research consulting companies (for example, Market Facts, Inc.), advertising agencies (such as J. Walter Thompson), suppliers of syndicated research services (such as Starch INRA Hooper), interviewing agencies, universities, and government agencies.

And, with the growth of global business and the trend to be a "right-sized organization" focusing on core competencies, there is more emphasis on working with research suppliers as "partners."

research supplier
A commercial marketing research service that conducts marketing research activity for clients. The marketing research supplier may be thought of as a marketing research consulting company.

A. C. Nielsen is one of the world's largest research suppliers. This advertisement indicates they understood how cultural factors and local situations influence research methods.

Who you do **BUSINESS** with makes a world of **DIFFERENCE.**

Products and ideas are now flowing across international borders as quickly as they once moved across town. You need an information partner who is right there beside you. Region by region. Country by country.

You need ACNielsen.

Our information network extends across more than 90 countries and covers 4.7 billion people.

But just as important is the scope of our services. From tracking daily information at store 52 in Peoria, Illinois, to monitoring product introductions and expansions across four continents, ACNielsen gives you real solutions to your business needs.

When you want to identify emerging concepts from around the world, we can help. We know what new ideas are succeeding. Where they are succeeding. And why.

If you're penetrating new markets, our international household panels in fifteen countries give you the consumer insight you need to succeed. No other information company comes close to this capability.

Let ACNielsen make a world of difference to your business. Call 1-800-988-4226.

ONLY ACNielsen has the **ANSWER.**

ACNielsen

ACNielsen is a copyright of ACNielsen Company
©1996 ACNielsen. All rights reserved.

---

syndicated service
A marketing research supplier that provides standardized information for many clients.

standardized research service
A research organization that has developed a unique methodology for investigating a specialty area, such as advertising effectiveness.

No matter how large a firm's marketing research department, some projects are too expensive to perform in-house. A **syndicated service** is a marketing research supplier that provides standardized information for many clients. For example, J. D. Power and Associates sells research about customers' ratings for automobile quality and reasons for satisfaction. Most automobile manufacturers and their advertising agencies subscribe to this syndicated service because the company provides important industrywide information it gathers from a national sample of thousands of car buyers. By specializing in this type of customer satisfaction research, J. D. Power gains certain economies of scale.

Syndicated services can provide expensive information economically to numerous clients because its value is not specific to one client but interests many. Such suppliers offer standardized information to measure media audiences, wholesale and retail distribution data, and other forms of data gathering.

A number of organizations supply **standardized research services** at the request of individual clients. Typically the research organization has developed a unique methodology for investigating a specialty area, such as advertising effectiveness or brand-name evaluation. These research suppliers will conduct studies for individual clients using the same methods they use for other clients. For example, BASES/Burke Institute's Day After Recall (DAR) is an organization that tests advertising recognition/recall and supplies wholesale and retail distribution data so a client can compare its scores with the average score for a product category.

Even when a firm could perform the research task in-house, research suppliers may be able to conduct the project at a lower cost, faster, and from a completely objective perspective. A company that wishes to quickly evaluate a new advertising strategy may find the research department at an ad agency able to provide technical expertise on copy development research that is not available within the company itself.

Limited-service research suppliers specialize in particular research activities, such as syndicated service, field interviewing, or data processing. Full-service research suppliers contract for entire ad hoc marketing research projects. The client usually controls these marketing research agencies or management consulting firms, but the research supplier handles most of the operating details of these **custom research** projects, tailoring them to the client's unique needs. A custom research supplier may employ individuals with titles such as *account executive, account group manager,* and other titles that imply relationships with clients, as well as functional specialists such as *statistician, librarian, director of field services, director of tabulation and data processing,* and *interviewer.*

Exhibit 4.7 lists the top 25 global research suppliers and their 1998 revenues.[10] Most of these firms provide a variety of services ranging from design activities to

custom research
A marketing research study designed for an individual client and tailored to the client's unique needs.

Exhibit 4.7 **Top 20 U.S. Research Organizations**

Rank 1998	Organization	Headquarters	Total research revenues[a] (millions)	Percent and revenues from outside U.S. ($ in millions)	
1	ACNielsen Corp.	Stamford, Conn.	$1,425.4	72.6%	$1,305.0
2	IMS Health Inc.	Westport, Conn.	1,084.0	62.0	672.5
3	Information Resources Inc.	Chicago	511.3	22.4	114.3
4	Nielsen Media Research Inc.	New York	401.9	2.6	10.4
5	NFO Worldwide Inc.	Greenwich, Conn.	275.4	39.9	110.0
6	Westat Inc.	Rockville, Md.	205.4		
7	The Arbitron Co.	New York	194.5	3.9	7.6
8	Maritz Marketing Research Inc.	St. Louis	169.1	25.0	42.3
9	The Kantar Group Ltd.	London	150.6	19.3	29.1
10	The NYPD Group Inc.	Port Washington, N.Y.	138.5	16.0	22.2
11	Market Facts Inc.	Arlington Heights, Ill.	136.5	14.9	20.3
12	Taylor Nelson Sofress Intersearch	Horsham, Pa.	68.9	18.5	12.7
13	J. D. Power and Associates	Agoura Hills, Calif.	64.8	10.5	6.8
14	United Information Group	New York	59.0		00
15	Audits & Surveys Worldwide Inc.	New York	58.3[b]	33.3[b]	00
16	Opinion Research Corp. International	Princeton, N.J.	58.2	31.0	00
17	Burke Inc.	Cincinnati	52.4	20.2	00
18	Roper Starch Worldwide Inc.	Harrison, N.Y.	51.3	20.7	00
19	Macro International Inc.	Calveton, Md.	48.7	39.0	00
20	Abt Associates Inc.	Cambridge, Mass.	45.8	30.0	00

fieldwork. Their services are not covered in detail here because they are discussed throughout the book, especially in the sections on fieldwork. However, some managerial and human aspects of dealing with research suppliers should be briefly mentioned at this point.

In many cases, the marketing research manager's job is primarily administrative: hiring interviewing services, data processing services, and so on. When it is necessary to hire outside research suppliers or contractors, the marketing researcher must be able to evaluate such specialized services. An analogy is the make-or-buy decision in the factory: The researcher can hire a research service to conduct the project or conduct the project with internal personnel.

Considerations for Hiring Outside Suppliers

Expertise acquired from experience in similar situations may be a major reason for hiring outside suppliers. This consideration is important not only for the purchase of syndicated services but also for hiring an organization for a custom study. For example, Name Lab has considerable methodological expertise to help a marketer evaluate a brand name for a new product or service. Outside researchers may be experts in the latest statistical procedures or other complex techniques with which someone within the organization may be unfamiliar. On the other side of the coin, especially for marketers of technically complex industrial products, research suppliers often lack sufficient familiarity with a product or its customers to do an adequate job. The urgency of the decision and personnel resources influence the decision to use outside suppliers. When there are time pressures and the internal staff is busy with other projects, managers may decide to buy rather than make research. Of course, obtaining data quickly may be costly; economic factors are always important. The need for objectivity is another consideration. Outside consultants may be able to look objectively at a problem without concern for internal politics. If two internal interest groups espouse different solutions to a particular problem, the research consultant may provide answers without fear of reprisal from within the organization. The consultant is able to look at a problem with a fresh perspective rather than in the stereotypic manner of an internal employee.

A dramatic, innovative change in an organization's marketing plan may require secrecy. Hence, if confidentiality is a prime consideration, it may be best to have internal personnel conduct the research. The need for quality control is still another consideration that may influence the make-or-buy decision.

A major problem with research suppliers is the high variability of their performances. Suppliers may range from highly qualified, full-service agencies to hustlers, charlatans, and thieves. On rare occasions, an unethical or unqualified researcher will even misrepresent findings. Identifying unqualified research suppliers before the contract is signed is not always easy. Managers should be wary of contractors who offer research at unusually low prices. The technical specifications of study (such as sample size and data collection procedure) should be carefully scrutinized and the reputation of the firm thoroughly checked. Many marketing research books depict the researcher as a knight in shining armor who exposes the truth. The low-cost research agency that skips some of the details of research may be more like the dragon than the knight. However, most marketing researchers are highly competent professionals. Most students of marketing research will become managers who must evaluate researchers. The following chapters provide information that will enable managers to make selection decisions that bypass or eliminate the inept or unethical marketing research suppliers from serious consideration.

Ethical Issues in Marketing Research

As in all human interactions, there are ethical issues in marketing research. Our earlier discussion of organizational politics and the use of pseudo-research to bolster one's position within the organization illustrates a situation where ethics come into play. Throughout this book selected ethical issues will arise concerning fair business dealings, proper research techniques, and appropriate use of research results. The remainder of this chapter addresses society's and managers' concerns about the ethical implications of marketing research.

Ethical Questions Are Philosophical Questions

Ethical questions are philosophical questions. There is no general agreement among philosophers about the answers to such questions. However, the rights and obligations of individuals generally are dictated by the norms of society. **Societal norms** are codes of behavior adopted by a group; they suggest what a member of a group ought to do under given circumstances. This chapter reflects the author's perceptions of the norms of our society (and undoubtedly his own values to some extent).[11]

societal norms
Codes of behavior adopted by a group that suggest what a member of a group ought to do under given circumstances.

General Rights and Obligations of Concerned Parties

Most research situations involve three parties: the researcher, the sponsoring client (user), and the respondent (or subject). The interaction of each party with one or both of the other two parties identifies a series of ethical questions.

Exhibit 4.8 **Interaction of Rights and Obligations**

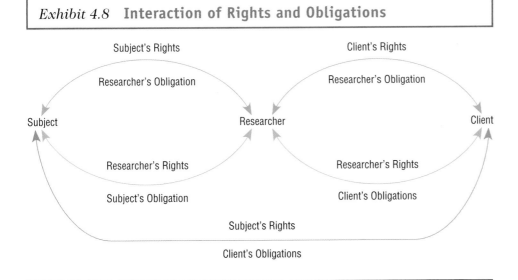

Consciously, each party expects certain rights and feels certain obligations toward the other parties. Exhibit 4.8 diagrams this relationship. Any society imposes a set of normatively prescribed expectations of behavior (including rights and obligations) associated with a social role, such as researcher, and another, reciprocal role, such as respondent. Certain ethical behaviors may be expected only in specific situations, while other expectations may be more generalized. Conflicting perspectives about behavioral expectations may create ethical problems. For instance, several ethical issues concern the researcher's expected rights versus those of the respondent/subject. A number of questions arise because researchers believe they have the right to seek information, but subjects believe they have a right to privacy. A respondent who says, "I don't care to answer your question about my income" believes that he or she has the right to refuse to participate. Yet some researchers will persist in trying to get that information. In general, a field-worker is expected not to overstep the boundary society places on consumer privacy.

For each of the subject's rights there is a corresponding obligation on the part of the researcher. For example, the individual's right to privacy dictates that the researcher has an obligation to protect the anonymity of the respondent. When that respondent discloses information about personal matters, it is assumed that such information will be guarded from all people other than the researcher.

Rights and Obligations of the Respondent

The ethical issues vary somewhat depending on whether the participant has given willing and informed consent. The notion of **informed consent** suggests the individual understands the reason for the research and waives his or her right to privacy when he or she agrees to participate in the research study. In an unobtrusive observation study the participant's rights differ from a survey respondent's rights because he or she has not willingly consented to be a subject of the research.

The Obligation to Be Truthful. When a subject provides willing consent to participate, it is generally expected that he or she will provide truthful answers. Honest cooperation is the main obligation of the respondent or subject. In return for being truthful, the subject has the right to expect confidentiality and anonymity. Privacy is a profound ethical issue in marketing research.

Privacy. Americans relish their privacy. Hence, the right to privacy is an important issue in marketing research. This issue involves the subject's freedom to choose whether or not to comply with the investigator's request. Traditionally researchers have assumed that individuals make an informed choice. However, critics have argued that the old, the poor, the poorly educated, and other underprivileged individuals may be unaware of their right to choose. They have further argued that the interview may begin with some vague explanation of its purpose, initially ask questions that are relatively innocuous, and then move to questions of a highly personal nature. It has been suggested that subjects be informed of their right to be left alone or to break off the interview at any time. Researchers should not follow the tendency to "hold on" to busy respondents. However, this view definitely is not universally accepted in the research community.

Another aspect of the privacy issue is illustrated by this question: Is a telephone call that interrupts someone's favorite television program an invasion of privacy? The answer to this issue—and to most privacy questions—lies in the

informed consent

Notion that suggests the individual understands the reason for the research and waives his or her right to privacy when he or she agrees to participate in the research study.

dilemma of where the rights of the individual end and the needs of society for better scientific information on consumer preference take over. Generally certain standards of common courtesy have been set by interviewing firms, for example, not to interview late in the evening and at other inconvenient times. However, several critics may never be appeased. The computerized interview (sometimes called a *junk phone call*) has stimulated increased debate over this aspect of the privacy issue. As a practical matter, respondents may feel more relaxed about privacy issues if they know who is conducting the survey. Thus, it is generally recommended that field interviewers indicate that they are legitimate researchers by passing out business cards, wearing name tags, or in other ways identifying the names of their companies.

In an observation study the major ethical issues concern whether the observed behavior is public or private. Generally it is believed that unobtrusive observation of public behavior in places such as stores, airports, and museums is not a serious invasion of privacy. However, recording private behavior with hidden cameras and the like represents a violation of this right. For example, in a survey almost all research directors and line marketing executives disapproved of the practice of observing women putting on brassieres through a one-way mirror.

Deception. In a number of situations the researcher creates a false impression by disguising the purpose of the research. The researcher, at least at the outset of the research, is not open and honest. Bluntly stated, to avoid biased reactions, the researchers lie to the subject. Deception or concealment results from the researcher's failure to observe or straightforwardly ask about the phenomena of interest, and hold all other factors constant, without partially deceiving the respondent. Generally, such deception is justified under two conditions: (1) The researcher assumes that no physical danger or psychological harm will result from the deception, and (2) the researcher takes personal responsibility for informing the respondent of the concealment or deception after the research project ends. This issue is interrelated with a the subject's right to be informed.

The issue of deception concerns the means-to-an-end philosophical issue. The primary question is: Does a minor deception substantially increase the value of the research? Suppose a survey research project involves contacting busy executives. Pretending to be calling long distance might improve the response rate, but is this a justifiable means to this end?

A distinction has been made between deception and discreet silence. The ethical question concerning the manifest content of a questionnaire versus the true purpose of the research has been cleverly stated as follows:

> Must we really explain, when we ask the respondent to agree or disagree with the statement, "prison is too good for sex criminals; they should be publicly whipped or worse," it is really the authoritarianism of his personality we are investigating, and not the public opinion on crime and punishment?[12]

The Right to Be Informed. It has been argued that subjects have a right to be informed of all aspects of the research. This includes information about its purpose and sponsorship. The argument for the researcher's obligation to protect this right is based on the academic tradition of informing and enlightening the public.

A pragmatic argument for providing respondents with information about the nature of the study concerns the long-run ability of researchers to gain cooperation from respondents. If the public understands why survey or experimental information has been collected and that the researchers may be trusted with private information, it may be easier in the long run to conduct research. Several research suppliers have suggested that public relations work is needed to convince consumers of the integrity of the research industry.

Rights and Obligations of the Researcher.

General business ethics should be a standard for marketing research firms and marketing research departments. Our concern is not with issues such as bribery or the welfare and safety of one's employees, but with ethical issues that are specifically germane to marketing research practices.

More has been written about the ethics of researchers than about those of the other two parties because this group's purpose is clearly identifiable. Researchers have obligations to both subjects and clients as well as corresponding rights. A number of professional associations have developed standards and operating procedures for ethical practices by researchers. Exhibits 4.9 and 4.10 present the **codes of ethics** for two professional associations, the American Marketing Association and the Marketing Research Association. These codes show that there are several opinions about the nature of ethical practices. Several major issues invite further exploration.

code of ethics
A set of guidelines that states the standards and operating procedures for ethical practices by researchers.

The Purpose of Research Is Research.

Businesspeople are expected not to misrepresent a sales tactic as marketing research. The Federal Trade Commission has indicated that it is illegal to use any plan, scheme, or ruse that misrepresents the true status of the person making the call as a door opener to gain admission to a prospect's home, office, or other establishment. This sales ploy is considered unethical as well as illegal. No research firm should engage in any practice other than scientific investigation.

Objectivity.

Throughout this book the text stresses the need for objective scientific investigation to ensure accuracy. Researchers should maintain high standards to ensure that their data are accurate. Furthermore, they must not intentionally try to prove a particular point for political purposes.

Avoid Misrepresenting Research.

Research companies (and clients) should not misrepresent the statistical accuracy of their data, nor should they overstate the significance of the results by altering the findings. Basically the researcher has the obligation to both the client and the subjects to honestly analyze the data and correctly report the actual data collection methods. For example, the failure to report a variation from a technically correct probability sampling procedure is ethically questionable. Likewise, any major error that has occurred during the course of the study should not be kept secret from management or the sponsor. Hiding errors or variations from the proper procedures tends to distort or shade the results. A more blatant breach of the researcher's responsibilities would be the outright distortion of data.

Protect the Right to Confidentiality of Both Subjects and Clients.

A number of clients might desire a list of favorable industrial sales prospects generated from a research survey. It is the researcher's responsibility to ensure that the privacy and anonymity of the respondents are preserved. If the respondent's name and address are known, this information should not be forwarded to the sponsoring organization under any circumstances.

Information that a research supplier obtains about a client's general business affairs should not be disseminated to other clients or third parties. The client or user of marketing research has a number of rights and obligations. The primary right is to expect objective and accurate data from the research supplier. This party should also expect respect for any instructions of confidentiality.

Exhibit 4.9 Code of Ethics of the American Marketing Association

The American Marketing Association, in furtherance of its central objective of the advancement of science in marketing and in recognition of its obligations to the public, has established these principles of ethical practice of marketing research for the guidance of its members.

In an increasingly complex society, marketing research is more and more dependent upon marketing information intelligently and systematically obtained. The consumer is the source of much of this information. Seeking the cooperation of the consumer in the development of information, marketing management must acknowledge its obligation to protect the public from misrepresentation and exploitation under the guise of research.

Similarly the research practitioner has an obligation to the discipline he practices and to those who provide support for his practice—an obligation to adhere to basic and commonly accepted standards of scientific investigation as they apply to the domain of marketing research.

It is the intent of this code to define ethical standards required of marketing research in satisfying these obligations.

Adherence to this code will assure the user of marketing research that the research was done in accordance with acceptable ethical practices. Those engaged in research will find in this code an affirmation of sound and honest basic principles which have developed over the years as the profession has grown. The field interviewers who are the point of contact between the profession and the consumer will also find guidance in fulfilling their vitally important role.

For Research Users, Practitioners and Interviewers

1. No individual or organization will undertake any activity which is directly or indirectly represented to be marketing research, but which has as its real purpose the attempted sale of merchandise or services to some or all of the respondents interviewed in the course of the research.
2. If a respondent has been led to believe, directly or indirectly, that he is participating in a marketing research survey and that his anonymity will be protected, his name shall not be made known to anyone outside the research organization or research department, or used for other than research purposes.

For Research Practitioners

1. There will be no intentional or deliberate misrepresentation of research methods or results. An adequate description of methods employed will be made available upon request to the sponsor of the research. Evidence that fieldwork has been completed according to specifications will, upon request, be made available to buyers of research.
2. The identity of the survey sponsor and/or the ultimate client for whom a survey is being done will be held in confidence at all times, unless this identity is to be revealed as part of the research design. Research information shall be held in confidence by the research organization or department and not used for personal gain or made available to any outside party unless the client specifically authorizes such release.
3. A research organization shall not undertake studies for competitive clients when such studies would jeopardize the confidential nature of client-agency relationships.

For Users of Marketing Research

1. A user of research shall not knowingly disseminate conclusions from a given research project or service that are inconsistent with or not warranted by the data.
2. To the extent that there is involved in a research project a unique design involving techniques, approaches or concepts not commonly available to research practitioners, the prospective user of research shall not solicit such a design from one practitioner and deliver it to another for execution without the approval of the design originator.

For Field Interviewers

1. Research assignments and materials received, as well as information obtained from respondents, shall be held in confidence by the interviewer and revealed to no one except the research organization conducting the marketing study.
2. No information gained through a marketing research activity shall be used, directly or indirectly, for the personal gain or advantage of the interviewer.
3. Interviews shall be conducted in strict accordance with specifications and instructions received.
4. An interviewer shall not carry out two or more interviewing assignments simultaneously unless authorized by all contractors or employers concerned.

Members of the American Marketing Association will be expected to conduct themselves in accordance with provisions of this code in all of their marketing research activities.

Exhibit 4.10 Code of Ethics of the Marketing Research Association

CODE of ETHICS

The Code of Professional Ethics and Practices of the

MARKETING RESEARCH ASSOCIATION, INC.

is subscribed to as follows:

1. To maintain high standards of competence and integrity in marketing and survey research.

2. To exercise all reasonable care and to observe the best standards of objectivity and accuracy in the development, collection, processing and reporting of marketing and survey research information.

3. To protect the anonymity of respondents and hold all information concerning an individual respondent privileged, such that this information is used only within the context of the particular study.

4. To thoroughly instruct and supervise all persons for whose work I am responsible in accordance with study specifications and general research techniques.

5. To observe the rights of ownership of all materials received from and/or developed for clients, and to keep in confidence all research techniques, data and other information considered confidential by their owners.

6. To make available to clients such details on the research methods and techniques of an assignment as may be reasonably required for proper interpretation of the data, providing this reporting does not violate the confidence of respondents or clients.

7. To promote the trust of the public for marketing and survey research activities and to avoid any procedure which misrepresents the activities of a respondent, the rewards of cooperation or the uses of the data.

8. To refrain from referring to membership in this organization as proof of competence, since the organization does not so certify any person or organization.

9. To encourage the observance of the principles of this code among all people engaged in marketing and survey research.

Avoid Dissemination of Faulty Conclusions. The American Marketing Association's marketing research code of ethics states that "a user of research shall not knowingly disseminate conclusions from a given research project or service that are inconsistent with or not warranted by the data."

A dramatic example of a violation of this principle occurred in an advertisement of a cigarette smoker study. The advertisement compared two brands and stated that "Of those expressing a preference, over 65 percent preferred" the advertised brand to a competing brand. The misleading portion of this reported result was that most of the respondents did not express a preference; they indicated that both brands tasted about the same. Thus, only a very small percentage of those studied actually revealed a preference, and the results were somewhat misleading. Such shading of results violates the obligation to report accurate findings.

Competitive Research Proposals. Consider a client who has solicited several bids for a marketing research project. The client requests the research supplier that wins the bid to appropriate ideas from the proposal of a competing research supplier and include them in the research study. This generally is regarded as unethical.

TO THE POINT
_____

He uses statistics as a drunken man uses a lampost–for support rather than illumination.

ANDREW LANG

Rights and Obligations of the Client Sponsor (User)

Ethical Behavior Between Buyer and Seller. The general business ethics expected between a purchasing agent and a sales representative should hold in the marketing research situation. For example, if the purchasing agent has already decided to purchase a product (or research proposal) from a friend, it would be unethical for that person to solicit competitive bids that have no chance of being accepted just to fulfill a corporate purchasing policy stating that a bid must be put out to some number of competitors. The typical business and other commitments unrelated to a specific marketing research situation are ethical questions with which we will not deal here.

An Open Relationship with Research Suppliers. The client sponsor has the obligation to encourage the research supplier to objectively seek out the truth. To encourage this objectivity, a full and open statement of the problem, *explication* of constraints in time and money, and any other insights that may help the supplier anticipate costs and problems should be provided. In other words, the research sponsor should encourage efforts to reduce bias and to listen to the voice of the public.

An Open Relationship with Interested Parties. Conclusions should be based on the data. A user of research should not knowingly disseminate conclusions from a research project or service that are inconsistent with or not warranted by the data. Violation of this principle is perhaps the greatest transgression that a client can commit. Justifying a self-serving or political position that is not warranted from the data poses serious ethical questions. Indicating that the data show something to make a sale is also a serious matter.

Advocacy research—research undertaken to support a specific claim in a legal action—puts the client in a unique situation. Advocacy research, such as a survey conducted to show that a brand name is not a generic name, differs from research that traditionally has been intended for internal use only. The conventional factors, such as sample size, people to be interviewed, and questions to be asked, are weighed against cost when making an internal decision. In advocacy

advocacy research
Research undertaken to support a specific claim in a legal action.

WHAT WENT WRONG?

Hertz Was Not Amused

A FEW YEARS AGO, A MAGAZINE CALLED *Corporate Travel* published the results of a consumer survey of the travel industry. In the category of rental cars, the magazine declared Avis the winner of what was to be its first annual Alfred Award, named for Alfred Kahn, former chairman of the Civil Aviation Board. Avis, not surprisingly, quickly launched an advertising campaign touting its standing in the poll.

Joseph Russo, vice president for government and public affairs at Avis's archrival, Hertz, was not amused. He called the magazine's editor and asked if he could see a press release and any other material that might explain the survey's results and methodology. "We've won virtually every other poll that's ever been done," said Russo. (Indeed, surveys like these are popularity contests that tend to favor bigger competitors over smaller ones; and they are almost impossible to duplicate or verify.) "So we wanted to see if we were missing the beat." But Russo said he could not get much information about the survey. "I said, How many people voted in this, was it bigger than a bread basket?"

It turned out that the survey responses had disappeared under mysterious circumstances. The magazine's marketing manager, who had overseen the poll, had left the magazine. "A search of their files has also failed to turn up any statistical tabulation or record of the responses for any category," wrote the president of Corporate Travel's parent to Hertz. Meanwhile, said Russo, "We had corporate accounts saying, I see you guys came in after Avis."

Eventually Hertz filed suit against the publisher of the magazine and Avis, charging false advertising. "We said if we allow this to go on, anyone will be able to do anything on the basis of a survey." Russo said. The parties settled, with Avis agreeing to stop calling itself the car rental company of choice among business travelers.

---

research the court's opinion of the value of the research may be based exclusively on sampling design or some methodological issue. Thus, the slightest variation from technically correct sampling procedures may be magnified by an attorney until a standard marketing research project no longer appears adequate in the judge's eye. How open should the client be in the courtroom?

The ethics of advocacy research present a number of serious questions. Consider the following quote:

> Almost never do you see a researcher who appears as an independent witness, quite unbiased. You almost always see a witness appearing either for the FTC or for the industry. You can almost predict what is going to be concluded by the witness for the FTC. And you can almost predict what will be concluded by the witness for industry. That says that research in this setting is not after full truth and it is not dispassionate in nature. And for those of us who consider ourselves to be researchers, that is a serious quandary.[13]

Advocacy researchers do not necessarily bias results intentionally. However, attorneys rarely submit advocacy research evidence that does not support their clients' positions.

The question surrounding advocacy research is one of objectivity: Can the researcher seek out the truth when the legal client wishes to support its position

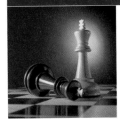

WHAT WENT WRONG?

Privacy Flap Sinks AmEx Database Deal

AMERICAN EXPRESS KILLED A PARTNERSHIP WITH A database marketing firm two months after the deal outraged privacy advocates. [17]

The move was a dramatic illustration of how consumer concern about privacy has the attention of Corporate America. AmEx is only the latest consumer giant to terminate a program after privacy protests. AmEx, however, claims the partnership was killed because it did not appear to be profitable.

Privacy experts and regulators were surprised at AmEx's partnership with KnowledgeBase

Marketing because AmEx had been regarded as a leader on privacy issues. It does not sell information on specific customer transactions. But under the partnership, KnowledgeBase's data on 175 million Americans would have been made available to any merchant who accepts AmEx cards. While KnowledgeBase would have filled the individual merchant's request for information—people who work within a mile of a restaurant that wants to increase its lunch business, for instance—AmEx would have gotten a cut from each deal.

"Companies like American Express are finally seeing the errors of their greedy ways," says privacy advocate Rep. Jerry Kleczka, D-Wis. "But," he cautions, "There will be someone else doing it tomorrow."

The privacy issue isn't going away," adds John Featherman, editor of *Privacy Newsletter*. "It will only get bigger."

at a trial? The ethical question stems from a conflict between legal ethics and research ethics. Although the courts have set judicial standards for marketing research methodology, perhaps only the client and individual researcher can resolve this question. [14]

Privacy

People believe the collection and distribution of personal information without their knowledge is a serious violation of their privacy. The privacy rights of subjects create a privacy obligation on the part of the client. Suppose a database marketing company is offering a mailing list compiled by screening millions of households to obtain brand usage information. The information would be extremely valuable to your firm, but you suspect those individuals who filled out the information forms were misled into thinking they were participating in a survey. Would it be ethical to purchase the mailing list? If respondents have been deceived about the purpose of a survey and their names subsequently are sold as part of a user mailing list, this practice is certainly unethical. The client and the research supplier have the obligation to maintain respondents' privacy.

Consider another example. Sales managers know that a marketing research survey of their business-to-business customers' buying intentions includes a means to identify the customer's name with each questionnaire. This confidential information could be of benefit to a sales representative calling on a specific customer. A client wishing to be ethical must resist the temptation to identify those accounts (that is, those respondents) who are the hottest prospects.

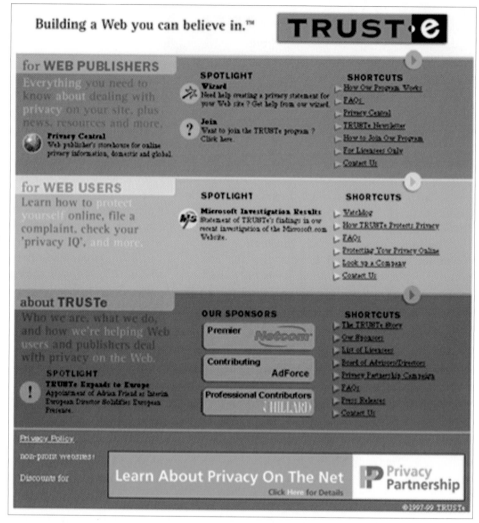

TrustE (*http://www.Truste.org*) is a third-party organization that evaluates sites'
privacy policies, certifies web sites and issues a seal of trust to organizations that meet
its privacy standards.[18] TrustE classifies sites into three categories: "no exchange,"
where no personal user data are collected, "one-to-one exchange," where the sites
collect user data for their own purposes but do not share them with third parties; and
"third-party exchange," where sites share the information with others. "One-to-one
exchange" sites would be permitted to share user data—such as credit card numbers,
names, and addresses—with business partners in order to complete transactions as
long as the business partners agree not to collect the user data themselves.[19]

Privacy on the Internet

Privacy on the Internet is a controversial issue. A number of groups question
whether Web site questionnaires, registration forms, and other means of collecting personal information are legitimate. Many marketers argue that their organizations don't need to know who the user is because the individual's name is not
important for their purposes. However, they do want to know certain information
(such as demographic characteristics or product usage) associated with an

anonymous profile. For instance, a Web advertiser could reach a targeted audience without having access to identifying information. Of course, unethical companies may ignore this guideline.

In July 1998, America Online (AOL) established a new privacy policy. AOL will not read customers' e-mail, collect any information about Web site visits, or give key data to other organizations without authorization. AOL will seek parents' written approval to get data from children at sites targeting kids.[15] Research shows that people are more willing to disclose sensitive information if they know the Web site's privacy policy.[16]

For this reason, many high-traffic Web sites such as Yahoo and Lycos have privacy statements that visitors can easily access. Organizations such as the Electronic Frontier Foundation and Online Privacy Alliance are involved in developing privacy guidelines.

Commitment to Research. Some potential clients have been known to request research proposals from research suppliers when there is a low probability that the research will be conducted. For example, obtaining an outsider's opinion of a company problem via a research proposal provides an inexpensive consultation. If the information supports a given manager's position in an intracompany debate, it could be used politically rather than as a basis for research. A research consultant's opinion may be solicited even though management is not really planning research and funds have not been allocated for the project. Most research practitioners believe that because the research supplier must spend considerable effort planning a custom-designed study, the client has the obligation to solicit proposals only for seriously considered projects.

Pseudo-Pilot Studies. Clients should be open about the marketing problem to be investigated. However, there is a special case of this problem that should be explained. Sometimes a client suggests that a more comprehensive study is in the planning stages and the proposal the research supplier is bidding on is a pilot study. The research consultant is told that if he or she does a good job during the pilot study stages, there will be an additional major contract down the line. Too often such pilot studies lead to nothing more; the comprehensive study never materializes, and the consultant must absorb a loss.

A Final Note on Ethics

There are certainly unethical researchers in the world and a number of shady dealings do occur. The marketing researchers's honesty is no different from any other aspect of business ethics, or of personal morality, for that matter. One may occasionally run across a researcher who produces a report on fabricated findings. Likewise, interviewers occasionally cheat by filling out the questionnaires themselves. In pre-Castro Cuba there was at least one firm that, for a fee, would provide a handsomely engraved certificate attesting that the Court of Public Opinion held the client or his products in whatever kind of high esteem might be desired (with no extra charge for percentages). Under some circumstances even honest researchers take shortcuts, some of which may be ethically questionable. However, researchers, like most businesspeople, generally are ethical people. The answer to the question "What is ethical?" is not easy—only one's conscience can prevent any questionable practice.

Summary

Different firms have varying degrees of marketing research sophistication. In the first stage of such sophistication, firms ignore research and rely on intuition. In the second stage, they are naively impressed with marketing research and expect it to remove all risk from marketing decisions. During this development stage managers may become disillusioned with research because they have made costly mistakes based on its findings (including poor research). In the last stage the firm has a realistic appreciation for marketing research and uses it as a tool to reduce risk rather than as a way to foretell the future.

A marketing research function may be organized in any number of ways depending on its firm's size, business, and stage of research sophistication. Marketing research managers must remember they are managers, not just researchers.

There are various individual job titles in the marketing research industry. Some of the most common include director of marketing research, research analyst, research assistant, manager of sales research, forecast analyst, and manager of customer quality research.

The are several sources of conflict between marketing managers and marketing researchers. Managers may be unhappy if research shows they are doing a poor job, or they may use research to pass the buck when they encounter difficulty. Managers with narrow conceptions of research may expect it to deliver sophisticated results with overly simplified procedures. In addition managers may resent attempts to reduce intuitive decision making, or they may commission pseudo-research for political reasons rather than for discovering facts. Finally, unrealistic time and money constraints may preclude effective research.

There are many ways to reduce the conflict between researchers and managers. Mutual education, improved planning, emphasis on effective communication, and use of research generalists as go-betweens are some of the methods.

Research suppliers and contractors can augment the research staff of a small firm, or they can provide services impossible for even large firms to handle internally. However, some of these firms are unreliable, do a sloppy job, or even falsify results. Managers need to exercise care in using such services, especially when they offer research at unrealistically low prices.

There is no general agreement about the answers to ethical questions that surround marketing research. However, societal norms suggest the codes of conduct that are appropriate in given circumstances. There are three concerned parties in marketing research situations: the researcher, the sponsoring client (user), and the respondent (subject). Each party has certain rights and obligations. The respondent's rights include privacy and being informed about all aspects of the research; the subject's main obligation is to give honest answers to research questions. The researcher is expected to adhere to the purpose of the research; maintain objectivity; avoid misrepresenting research findings; protect subjects' and clients' right to confidentiality; and avoid shading research conclusions. The client is obligated to observe general business ethics when dealing with research suppliers; avoid misusing the research findings to support its aims; respect research respondents' privacy; and be open about its intentions to conduct research and the marketing problem to be investigated. A potential transgression occurs when advocacy research—research conducted to support a specific legal claim—is undertaken.

Key Terms and Concepts

Research sophistication
Client
Director of marketing information systems
Research analyst
Research assistant
Manager of decision support systems

Forecast analyst
Manager of customer quality
Director of marketing research
Pseudo-research
Research generalist
Cross-functioned teams
Research supplier

Syndicated service
Standardized research service
Custom research
Societal norms
Informed consent
Code of ethics
Advocacy research

Questions for Review and Critical Thinking

1. What are the stages of marketing research sophistication? Name some companies that you think are in each stage.
2. What might the organizational structure of the research department be like for the following organizations?
   a. a large advertising agency
   b. a founder-owned company that operates a 20-unit restaurant chain
   c. your university
   d. an industrial marketer with four product divisions
   e. a large consumer products company
3. What problems do marketing research directors face in their roles as managers?
4. What are some of the basic causes of conflict between top management and marketing research?
5. Comment on the following situation. A product manager asks the research department to forecast costs for some basic ingredients (raw materials) for a new product. The researcher comments that this is not a research job; it is a production forecast.
6. What is the difference between research and pseudo-research? Cite several examples of each.
7. How can a marketing researcher help top management better understand the functions and limitations of research?
8. To whom should marketing research be accountable?
9. What do you think would be the best way to find work in marketing research?
10. Identify a research supplier in your area, and determine what syndicated services and other functions are available to clients.
11. Go to the library to learn the job titles and responsibilities for the various types of marketing research jobs. (*Hint:* One of the best sources is Thomas Kinnear and Ann Root, eds., *1994 Survey of Marketing Research* [Chicago: American Marketing Association, 1995].)
12. Name some marketing research practices that may be ethically questionable.
13. What actions might the marketing research industry take to convince the public that marketing research is a legitimate activity and that firms that misrepresent their intentions and distort findings to achieve their aims are not "true" marketing research companies?
14. Page through your local newspaper to find some articles derived from survey research results. Was the study's methodology indicated for this news item? Could this research have been considered advocacy research?
15. Comment on the ethics of the following situations:
   a. A food warehouse club advertises "savings up to 30 percent" after a survey showed a range of savings from 2 to 30 percent below average prices for selected items.
   b. A radio station broadcasts the following message during a syndicated rating service's rating period: "Please fill out your diary."
   c. A sewing machine retailer advertises a market test and indicates that the regular price will be cut to one-half for three days only.
   d. A researcher tells a potential respondent that the interview will last 10 minutes rather than the 30 minutes he or she actually anticipates.
   e. A respondent tells an interviewer that she wishes to cooperate with the survey, but her time is valuable and, therefore, she expects to be paid for the interview.
   f. When you visit your favorite sports team's home page on the Internet, it asks you to fill out a registration questionnaire before you enter the site. The team then sells your information (team allegiance, age, address, and so on) to a company that markets sports memorabilia via catalog and direct mail.
16. Comment on the following interview:

INTERVIEWER: Good afternoon, sir. My name is Mrs. Johnson with Counseling Services. We are conducting a survey concerning Memorial Park. Do you own a funeral plot? Please answer yes or no.

RESPONDENT: (pauses)

INTERVIEWER: You do not own a funeral plot, do you?

RESPONDENT: No.

INTERVIEWER: Would you mind if I sent you a letter concerning Memorial Park? Please answer yes or no.

RESPONDENT: No.

INTERVIEWER: Would you please give me your address?

Exploring the Internet

1. Use a Web browser to go to the Gallup Organization's home page at http://www.gallup.com. Select the "About Gallup" option. What are the key aspects of this research company's mission?

2. Use a Web browser to go to the NPD, Inc. home page at http://www.npd.com. Select the "career opportunities" option. They select "Getting started at NPD" and "Building a Career" options. What would a career in marketing research be like at NPD?

3. There are many Internet sites that list job opportunities and information that is useful for job applicants. Use your Web browser and search for marketing management and marketing research jobs at the following URL addresses:

   http://www.jobs.hotjobs.com
   http://www.careerpath.com
   http://www.monster.org

4. One of the United Kingdom's Market Research Society's purposes is to set and enforce the ethical standards to be observed by research practitioners. Go to its Web site at http://www.marketresearch.org.uk to view its code of conduct and evaluate it in light of the AMA's code.

5. The American Association for Public Opinion Research (AAPOR) and the World Association for Public Opinion Research (WAPOR) are professional societies of individuals engaged in public opinion research, market research, and social research. Links to commercial organizations, government agencies, academic institutions, and nonprofit organizations conducting marketing research can be found in its bluebook at http://www.aapor.org/bluebook/. Another source, WorldOpinion (http://www.worldopinion.com), profiles and provides links for top research firms in the United States, as well as major international organizations.

Case 4.1 Barton Boomer's Diary

BARTON BOOMER, DIRECTOR OF MARKETING RESEARCH FOR a large consumer packaged goods corporation, has a B.S. in marketing from Michigan State University. He joined the firm nine years ago after a one-year stint as a marketing research trainee in the corporate headquarters of a western packing corporation. Four years ago, he received this MBA in the night program at a local university. Bart has a wife and two children. He earns $100,000 a year and owns a home in the suburbs. He is typical of a marketing research director except that he keeps a diary. At the end of every working day, he faithfully records the events that took place. Several entries that describe his interactions with his firm's product and marketing managers are excerpted here.

January 7
Ross York, the brand manager for the cereal group, appeared to be under considerable pressure to get out a new product this year. He told me that the in-house usage tests were going to be the most important factor in the go/no-go decision for "his baby." He mentioned that the six-week test period was too long, and he wanted to shorten it to three weeks by placing the product with heavy users.

January 9
I presented Ted with the negative results from our advertising copy testing. Just like a brand manager, he said to me, "You research guys are just like doctors. Every once in awhile you make the wrong diagnosis and lose the patient. Bart, eight out of ten products fail even with good research. You and I know it's hard to measure a truly creative advertising campaign before it has been run for several months in the marketplace. Charlie down at the agency and I think this is one of our best ideas. We jointly came up with it. I would like you to think about how to test this ad after we produce it and run it in the marketplace for several months."

January 30
Woodie Woodmark came into my office all flustered. People in sales had come up with a forecast that looked substantially different from his. He wanted me to come up with a sales forecast that confirmed his forecasts. He needed the information in two weeks. He had to cover himself with the vice president of marketing.

January 31
Joan Mendez, my top young research analyst, resigned today. She said she was taking a position at an advertising agency where working conditions were a little bit better.

February 12
The president called and said that the shaving lotion research study was extremely interesting. She said she was surprised that marketing research could gather so many facts in such a short period of time.

February 14
I called Quality Field Service Enterprises. I told them I had a rush job for 300 door-to-door interviews. Margaret said she was too busy with a home placement study and she couldn't do the job for several weeks. I called Midwest Interviewing and made a deal with Shirley. I told her I owed her one.

March 9
The executive vice president of marketing said he liked my presentation of the results from the distributor survey. He said that we should do a distributor survey on a regular basis to keep Ralph down in sales on his toes.

March 18
Bob Brown, the assistant brand manager for shampoo products, came to me and said he had been working on an idea in his spare time. He said that he would like me to do some exploratory research, but that he didn't want his boss to know until the results looked favorable.

March 20
A headhunter from an executive personnel service called and said that a top ad agency was looking for a marketing research manager. I told him I would think about it.

March 21
Love Fridays! Hank Coolidge from Metro Data Processing took me out to lunch.

March 26

Ross said he had a frozen-hamburger survey that showed exactly what he wanted to present to management. He asked me to present an executive summary in "just about 10 minutes. Then I take over. Remember, I don't want to have comments about statistical significance—whatever that means." He indicated he thought my report was great—"long and hard to read, but great." It made my day.

March 29

In our new-product meeting the sales manager reported that sales volume in our western test market for product X had slowed down considerably. He explained that he thought the regional sales manager may have been too enthusiastic about the product. He thought that the western sales force may have persuaded the distributors to buy a four-month supply. Nevertheless, the overstocking problem would take care of itself as soon as the product got off the ground. It's too bad I had to follow that act. The product manager blew his stack when I told him about the results at the consumer level. Everything I came up with indicated that the trial rate was low and the repurchase rate was extremely low. The meeting ended when we decided to revise our mar-

keting strategy quickly, before the introductory period of the test market was completed.

April 1

I had a meeting with the shampoo product manager today. She said that we were having some budget problems. She had to cut either advertising or marketing research. She said that she thought we could cut the focus group interviews with teenagers. "Just do the interviews with adults and we will eliminate some of our budget problems," she said.

April 2

I tried to meet with the executive vice president of marketing today. I wanted to discuss the upcoming test market. He told me he was too busy. Told me to check with the assistant brand manager for the product group about the reformulation taste test.

April 3

I called the headhunter today.

QUESTION

What organizational and human relations problems are indicated in the diary?

Case 4.2 Epicurious Food: Private Policy

EPICURIOUS FOOD IS A GOURMET FOOD ORIENTED WEB site (http//www.epicurious.com). Its privacy policy follows:

> Epicurious Food is committed to bringing you information that's tailored to your individual needs and, at the same time. to protecting your privacy. The following is a summary of the various ways we treat the information you provide us while using Epicurious Food.
>
> Epicurious Food does not collect personally identifying information except with your specific knowledge and consent. And we do not share such information with any outside party, so there's no need for you to "opt out" to get off mailing lists.
>
> Sometimes you will provide us with data that don't reveal your personal identity—what type of recipe you're seeking, for example. We use this sort of information for editorial purposes, and occasionally for other internal purposes (maybe we'll show chicken-eaters a certain ad, for example) but we don't connect it to any name, address

> or other identifying information. This way we can give you customized information without compromising your privacy.
>
> In a few cases—if you e-mail a question or some feedback to us, for example—we may request your name, e-mail address or other information so that we can, for example, e-mail you with a personal reply. If you choose to supply this information we will use it only for the specific purpose for which you supply it—unless we tell you otherwise at the time of collection, in which case you'll have an option to forbid other uses by us.
>
> In other cases, we may require certain personal information:
>
> When using the "Send recipe to a friend" function, for example, you must enter your return e-mail address. Again, we will use such information only for the specific purpose for which you supply it—unless we tell you otherwise at the

time of collection, in which case you'll have an option to forbid other uses by us.

We will never share any of your personally identifying data with any other party without your explicit permission, nor use it for unapproved commercial purposes.

A few special cases are worth noting. From time to time we may run competitions or request material we can publish to participate, you must usually supply us with your identity, which you agree to have publicly associated with your submission. The exact rules vary from case to case, and will be noted clearly on the relevant pages. Your participation will always be voluntary and knowing.

We may offer to send you information or updates from Epicurious Food via e-mail or otherwise; obviously, signing up will put you on a specific mailing list. We will not put you on any other mailing lists, from us or anyone else, without your permission.

In addition, your postings to our forums, chat and any other public discussion areas are not private. These postings are governed by User Agreement, which is accessible at any time from the bottom of any page on Epicurious Food.

You should be aware that any information you post in our public areas may be seen, collected and used by others, and may result in unsolicited messages from other posters or parties. Alas, we can't control this; you post at your own risk.

You may have read about "cookies," nuggets of information that are placed by a Web site in a storage place on your own computer. Epicurious Food uses cookies only to control the display of ads—to ensure that you don't see the same ad too many times in a single session, for example. Our cookies do not contain any personally identifying information.

While using Epicurious Food you may notice that our advertisers occasionally serve you cookies, either directly or when you link to their sites. We cannot directly control what our advertisers or these cookies do, but it's our policy that advertisers on Epicurious Food should use cookies the same way we do.

If you don't like cookies, your Web browser likely includes an option that allows you not to accept them. We don't recommend using this option, though: It makes browsing our site a less enjoyable experience.

Finally, while your individual information is protected as outlined above, we reserve the right to use aggregated, anonymous data about our users as a group. For instance, we might report to potential advertisers that a certain percentage of our users appear to be vegetarians, based on their recipe requests.

KIDS: Be sure to ask your parents for permission before you send any information about yourself—like your name, address or e-mail address—over the Internet, to us or to anyone else. Never buy anything online without permission. Oh, and tell your parents to read this page, too!

PARENTS: We encourage you to get involved with your kids' online usage so you can be aware of what they're doing. If Epicurious Food knowingly collects personally identifying data from children, we use it for internal purposes only—we don't post it, publish it or provide it to any third parties. Of course, we treat your personally identifying data the same way.

As mentioned above, for certain purposes we may use anonymous, aggregated data about our users. Kids' information may be included in this—but anonymously.

If your kids disclose information about themselves in our public discussion areas, they may get unsolicited messages from other parties. Accordingly, you should tell them not to do so.

If you're worried about your kids' activities or their privacy on Epicurious Food, we encourage you to e-mail us.

This Privacy Policy may be modified from time to time; notice of changes will appear on this page, so check back often. Any such changes will be prospective, never retroactive.

If you have concerns or questions about any aspect of this policy, please send us e-mail. We welcome your feedback. You can also send us regular mail at the following address:

Privacy Policy Coordinator
Epicurious Food
CondéNet Inc.
140 East 45th Street, 37th Floor
New York, NY 10017, USA

EXERCISE

Evaluate this privacy statement.

Chapter 5

Beginning Stages of the Research Process

O NCE UPON A TIME, A SEA HORSE GATHERED UP HIS SEVEN pieces of eight and cantered out to find his fortune. Before he had traveled very far he met an Eel, who said,

"Psst. Hey, bud. Where ya goin'?"

"I'm going out to find my fortune," replied the Sea Horse proudly.

"You're in luck," said the Eel. "For four pieces of eight you can have this speedy flipper, and then you'll be able to get there a lot faster."

"Gee, that's swell," said the Sea Horse, and paid the money and put on the flipper, and slithered off at twice the speed. Soon he came upon a Sponge, who said,

"Psst. Hey. bud. Where ya goin'?" "I'm going out to find my fortune," replied the Sea Horse.

"You're in luck," said the Sponge. "For a small fee I will let you have this jet-propelled scooter so that you will be able to travel a lot faster."

So the Sea Horse bought the scooter with his remaining money and went zooming through the sea five times as fast. Soon he came upon a Shark, who said.

"Psst. Hey, bud. Where you goin'?"

"I'm going out to find my fortune," replied the Sea Horse.

"You're in luck. If you'll take this shortcut," said the Shark, pointing to his open mouth, "you'll save yourself a lot of time."

"Gee, thanks," said the Sea Horse, and zoomed off into the interior of the Shark, there to be devoured.

The moral of this fable is that if you're not sure where you're going, you're liable to end up someplace else—and not even know it.[1]

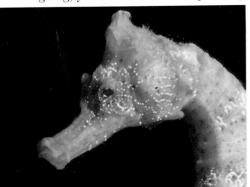

The lesson contained in the fable about the sea horse's journey should be kept in mind by all researchers during the beginning stages of the marketing research process. Marketing research is conducted to solve managerial problems. Before a research design is chosen, managers and researchers need a sense of direction for the investigation. An adage reminds that if you do not know where you are going, any road will take you there. This suggests some good advice to managers and researchers: Defining the marketing problem carefully is extremely important because it determines the purpose of the research and, ultimately, the research design. This chapter explains how to define a marketing problem and how to prepare a research proposal.

The Nature of Marketing Problems

Chapter 3 indicated that a decision maker's degree of uncertainty influences decisions about the type of research that will be conducted. In this chapter we elaborate on the conditions under which decision making occurs and the process by which managers clearly define marketing problems and opportunities.

Remember that a marketing manager may be completely certain about a business situation. For example, a retail store that has been recording and analyzing optical scanner data for years knows exactly what information its scanners need to record every day. Routine research techniques regularly investigate routine problems. The problem has already been defined.

At the other extreme, a manager or researcher may describe an absolutely ambiguous decision-making situation. The nature of the problem to be solved is unclear. The objectives are vague and the alternatives are difficult to define. This is by far the most difficult decision situation.

Most marketing decision situations fall between these two extremes. Managers usually grasp the general nature of the objectives they wish to achieve, but they often remain uncertain about the full details of the problem. Important information is missing. Ambiguity or uncertainty needs to be cleared up before making a formal statement of the marketing problem.

EXPLORING RESEARCH ISSUES

The Rest Is Arithmetic

THE LATE BOB KEITH, THEN PRESIDENT OF THE PILLSbury Company, was once persuaded by Pillsbury's researchers to review one of his major marketing decisions using a sophisticated, mathematical technique that required some input from him. He agreed to the outcomes, their values, and their probabilities, and chose the decision rule he felt most appropriate. The computer then calculated the expectations, compared them, and reported the alternative that should be chosen according to that rule. Mr. Keith disagreed, noting that another alternative was obviously the only correct choice—indeed, it was the choice that had been made not long before. "How can that be?" the researchers asked. "You accepted all the values and probabilities and chose the decision rule yourself. The rest is arithmetic." "That's fine," Keith replied, "but you forgot to ask me about a few other things that were more important."[2]

The Importance of Proper Problem Definition

The formal quantitative research process should not begin until the problem has been clearly defined, but properly and completely defining a marketing problem is easier to say than to do. When a problem or opportunity is discovered, managers may have only vague insights about a complex situation. Market share may be declining on the West Coast and management does not know the reason. If quantitative research begins before the manager learns exactly what is important, the investigation may yield false conclusions. The right answer to the wrong question may be absolutely worthless—indeed, it may even be harmful.

A few years ago, R. J. Reynolds Company believed in marketing research indicating that Real cigarettes could not fail. The company's research showed consumers were shifting to natural products of all kinds. Executives interpreted the marketing research to mean that smokers did not want flavorings or additives in cigarettes. This led to advertising themes that stressed benefits like "nothing artificial added" and "all natural." Unfortunately, although methodologically sound, the research missed a crucial point: smokers really did not care about flavorings and additives until they were asked. The research was based on a fundamental misconception that was not uncovered in the problem definition stage of the research. The real marketing problem was to find a way to appeal to smokers who actually were interested in low-tar cigarettes.

Consider what happened when Coca-Cola made the decision to change its Coke formula. Management's definition of the problem focused on a need to improve Coke's taste because its competitor's "Pepsi Challenge" advertising campaign touted Pepsi's superior taste. The research question was to investigate the ultimate consumer reaction to the taste of reformulated Coke. The results of the taste test led to the introduction of "new" Coke and the market withdrawal of regular Coke. As soon as consumers learned the company's original formula was no longer available, there were emotional protests from Coca-Cola loyalists. The consumer protests were so passionate and determined that the original formula was quickly brought back as Coca-Cola Classic. We have since learned that the consumer protests associated with dropping the original formula for Coke indicated a larger problem: Coke's marketing research was too narrow in scope and the problem was inadequately defined. The company carried out a series of taste tests in shopping malls. No take-home taste tests were conducted, nor were consumers asked if the new Coke should replace the original. The marketing research failed to identify consumers' emotional attachment and loyalty to the brand as a problem for investigation. The Coca-Cola mistake teaches a valuable lesson: Do not ignore investigating the emotional aspects of buying behavior.

The Process of Defining the Problem

problem definition
The indication of a specific marketing decision area that will be clarified by answering some research questions.

Just because a problem has been discovered or an opportunity recognized does not mean that the problem has been defined. A **problem definition** indicates a specific marketing decision that will be clarified by answering some research questions.

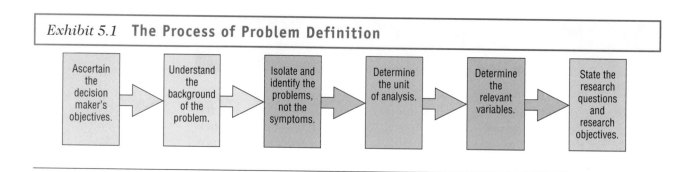

Exhibit 5.1 **The Process of Problem Definition**

The process of defining the problem involves several interrelated steps, as shown in Exhibit 5.1:

1. Ascertain the decision maker's objectives.
2. Understand the background of the problem.
3. Isolate and identify the problem, not the symptoms.
4. Determine the unit of analysis.
5. Determine the relevant variables.
6. State the research questions (hypotheses) and research objectives.

Ascertain the Decision Makers' Objectives

**decision makers'
objectives**
*Managerial goals
expressed in
measurable terms.*

As a staff person, the research investigator must attempt to satisfy the **decision makers' objectives**—those of the brand manager, sales manager, and others who requested the project. Management and organizational theorists suggest that the decision maker should express goals to the researcher in measurable terms. Unfortunately, this viewpoint is overly optimistic:

> Despite a popular misconception to the contrary, objectives are seldom clearly articulated and given to the researcher. The decision maker seldom formulates his objectives accurately. He is likely to state his objectives in the form of platitudes which have no operational significance. Consequently, objectives usually have to be extracted by the researcher. In so doing, the researcher may well be performing his most useful service to the decision maker.[3]

Researchers who must conduct investigations when the marketing manager wants the information "yesterday" usually get little assistance when they ask, "What are your objectives for this study?" Nevertheless, even decision makers who have only a gut feeling that marketing research might be a good idea benefit greatly if they work with the marketing researcher to articulate precise research objectives.[4] Both parties should attempt to gain a clear understanding of the purpose for undertaking the research.

One effective technique for uncovering elusive research objectives consists of presenting the marketing manager with each possible solution to a problem and asking whether he or she would follow that course of action. A no answer can prompt further questioning to determine why the course of action is inappropriate; this usually will help formulate objectives. By illuminating the nature of the marketing opportunity or problem, exploratory research also helps managers clarify their research objectives.

Exhibit 5.2   The Iceberg Principle

The Iceberg Principle

Why do so many marketing research projects begin without clear objectives or adequate problem definitions? Marketing managers are logical people, and it seems logical that definition of the problem is the starting point for any enterprise. Frequently, however, marketing researchers and managers cannot discover actual problems because they lack sufficiently detailed information. The **iceberg principle** serves as a useful analogy (see Exhibit 5.2). A sailor on the open sea notices only the 10 percent of an iceberg that extends above the surface of the water, while 90 percent is submerged. The dangerous part of many marketing problems, like the submerged portion of the iceberg, is neither visible to nor understood by marketing managers. If the submerged portions of the problem are omitted from the problem definition (and subsequently from the research design), the decisions based on the research may be less than optimal. The example of New Coke is a case in point. Omission of important information or faulty assumptions about the situation can be extremely costly.

iceberg principle
The principle indicating that the dangerous part of many marketing problems is neither visible to nor understood by marketing managers.

TO THE POINT

The real voyage of discovery consists not in seeking new landscapes, but in having new eyes.

MARCEL PROUST

Understand the Background of the Problem

Although no textbook outline for identifying the marketing problem exists, the iceberg principle illustrates that understanding the background of the problem is vital. Often experienced managers know a great deal about a situation and can provide the researcher with considerable background information about previous events and why they happened. Under these circumstances, when the decision maker's objectives are clear, the problem may be diagnosed exclusively by exercising managerial judgment. On other occasions, when information about what has happened before is inadequate or when managers have trouble identifying the problem, a situation analysis is the logical first step in defining the problem. A **situation analysis** involves the informal gathering of background information to familiarize researchers or managers with the decision area. Gaining an awareness of marketplace conditions and an appreciation of the situation often requires exploratory research. The many exploratory research techniques developed to help formulate clear definitions of the problem are covered in Chapter 6.

situation analysis
The informal gathering of background information to familiarize researchers or managers with the decision area.

Exhibit 5.3 **Symptoms Can Be Confusing**

ORGANIZATION	SYMPTOMS	PROBLEM DEFINITION BASED ON SYMPTOM	TRUE PROBLEM
Twenty-year-old neighborhood swimming association in a major city	Membership has been declining for years. New water park with wave pool and water slides moved into town a few years ago.	Neighborhood residents prefer the expensive water park and have negative image of swimming pool.	Demographic changes: Children in this 20-year-old neighborhood have grown up. Older residents no longer swim.
Cellular phone manufacturer	Distributors complain prices are too high.	Investigate industrial user to learn how much prices need to be reduced.	Sales management: Distributors do not have adequate product knowledge to communicate product's value.
Microbrewery	Consumers prefer the taste of competitor's brand.	What type of reformulated taste is needed?	Package: Old-fashioned package influences taste perception.

Isolate and Identify the Problem, Not the Symptoms

Anticipating the many influences and dimensions of a problem is impossible for any researcher or executive. For instance, a firm may have a problem with its advertising effectiveness. The possible causes of this problem may be low brand awareness, the wrong brand image, the wrong media, or perhaps too small a budget. Management's job is to isolate and identify the most likely causes. Certain occurrences that appear to be the problem may be only symptoms of a deeper problem. Exhibit 5.3 illustrates how symptoms may cause confusion about the nature of the true problem.

Other problems may be identified only after gathering background information and conducting exploratory research. How does one ensure that the fundamental problem has been identified rather than its symptoms? There is no easy answer to this question. Executive judgment and creativity must be exercised. The archeological puzzle in Exhibit 5.4 shows that good researchers must be creative in developing problem definitions by investigating situations in new ways.

Determine the Unit of Analysis

Defining the problem requires that the researcher determine the unit of analysis for the study. The researcher must specify whether the investigation will collect data about individuals, households, organizations, departments, geographical areas, or objects. In studies of home buying, for example, the husband–wife dyad typically is the unit of analysis rather than the individual because many purchase decisions are jointly made by husband and wife.

Researchers who think carefully and creatively about situations often discover that a problem may be investigated at more than one level of analysis. Determining the unit of analysis, although relatively straightforward in most projects, should not be overlooked during the problem definition stage of the research. It is a fundamental aspect of problem definition.

Determine the Relevant Variables

variable

Anything that may assume different numerical values.

Another aspect of problem definition is identification of key variables. The term *variable* is important in research. A **variable** is anything that varies or changes in value. Because a variable represents a quality that can exhibit differences in value, usually in magnitude or strength, it may be said that a variable generally is anything that may assume different numerical or categorical values.

Attitudes toward airlines may be a variable ranging from positive to negative. Each attribute of airlines' services, such as safety, seat comfort, and baggage handling, is a variable.

In statistical analysis, a variable is identified by a symbol, such as X. Categories or numerical values may then be associated with this symbol. The variable gender may be categorized as male of female; gender is a **categorical** or **classificatory variable,** since it has a limited number of distinct values. On the other hand, sales volume may encompass an infinite range of numbers; if is a **continuous variable,** one that can have in infinite number of values.

In causal research, the terms *dependent variable* and *independent variable* are frequently encountered. A **dependent variable** is a criterion or variable that is to be predicted or explained. An **independent variable** is a variable that is expected to influence the dependent variable. For example, average sales compensation may be a dependent variable that is influenced or predicted by an independent variable such as number of years of experience. These terms are discussed in greater detail in the chapters on experimentation and data analysis.

Managers and researchers must be careful to include all relevant variables necessary to define the managerial problem. Likewise, variables that are superfluous (not directly relevant to the problem) should not be included.

The process of identifying the relevant variables overlaps with the process of determining the research objectives. Typically each research objective will mention a variable or variables that need to be measured or analyzed.

categorical (classificatory) variable
A variable that has a limited number of distinct values.

continuous variable
A variable that has an infinite number of values.

dependent variable
A criterion or variable expected to be predicted or explained.

independent variable
A variable that is expected to influence a dependent variable.

State the Research Questions and Research Objectives

Both managers and researchers expect problem-solving efforts to result in statements of research questions and research objectives. At the end of the problem definition stage, the researcher should prepare a written statement that clarifies any ambiguity about what the research hopes to accomplish.

Exhibit 5.4 **A Puzzle**

What language is written on this stone found by archaeologists?

Answer (turn book upside down):

The language is English: TO/TIE/MULES/TO. A great deal of time and effort is spent looking at familiar problems. Managers often do not look at these problems in a new light, however. Too often they see what they want to see or what they want to expect. They give stereotyped answers to problems. A good researcher creatively develops a hypothesis by looking at problems in a new way.

Clarity in Research Questions and Hypotheses

Formulating a series of research questions and hypotheses adds clarity to the statement of the marketing problem. A personal computer company made the following statement about an advertising problem:

- In the broadest sense, the marketing problem is to determine the best ways [name of the company] can communicate with potential purchasers of laptop computers.
- How familiar are consumers with the various brands of computers?
- What attitudes do consumers have toward these brands?
- How important are the various factors for evaluating the purchase of a laptop computer?
- How effective are the communications efforts of the various competitive marketers in terms of message recognition?

Research questions make it easier to understand what is perplexing managers and to indicate what issues have to be resolved. A research question is the researcher's translation of the marketing problem into a specific inquiry.

A research question can be too vague and general if stated in terms such as: Is advertising copy X better than advertising copy Y? Advertising effectiveness can be variously measured by sales, recall of sales message, brand awareness, intention to buy, and so on. Asking a more specific research questions (e.g., Which advertisement has a higher day-after recall score?) helps the researcher design a study that will produce pertinent information. The answer to the research question should be a criterion that can be used as a standard for selecting alternatives. The stage of the research obviously is related to problem definition. The goal of defining the problem is to state the research questions clearly and to develop well-formulated hypotheses.

Defining the unit of analysis is an important aspect of the problem definition process. In many marketing research studies, the family rather than the individual is the appropriate unit of analysis.

A **hypothesis** is an unproven proposition or possible solution to a problem. Hypothetical statements assert probable answers to research questions. A hypothesis is a statement about the nature of the world; in its simplest form it is a guess. A sales manager may hypothesize that salespeople who show the highest job satisfaction will be the most productive. An advertising manager may believe that if consumers' attitudes toward a product are changed in a positive direction, consumption of the product will increase. Problem statements and hypotheses are similar. Both state relationships, but problem statements are interrogative while hypotheses are declarative. Sometimes the two types of statements are almost identical in substance. An important difference, however, is that hypotheses usually are more specific than problem statements; typically they are closer to the actual research operations and testing. Hypotheses are statements that can be empirically tested.

A formal statement of a hypothesis has considerable practical value in planning and designing research. It forces researchers to be clear about what they expect to find through the study, and it raises crucial questions about the data that will be required in the analysis stage. When evaluating a hypothesis, researchers should ensure that the information collected will be useful in decision making. Notice how the following hypotheses express expected relationships between variables:

hypothesis
An unproven proposition or supposition that tentatively explains certain facts or phenomena; a probable answer to a research question.

- There is a positive relationship between buying on the Internet and the presence of younger children in the home.

- Sales are lower for salespersons in regions that receive less advertising support.

- Consumers will experience cognitive dissonance after the decision to purchase a fax machine.

- Opinion leaders are more affected by mass media communication sources than nonleaders.

- Among nonexporters, the degree of perceived importance of overcoming barriers to exporting is related positively to general interest in exporting (export intentions).[4]

TO THE POINT

I don't know the key to success, but the key to failure is trying to please everybody.

BILL COSBY

WHAT WENT WRONG?

"The Slacks Don't Fit!"

A MAJOR CATALOG RETAILER WAS EXPERIENCING A large number of returns for its boys' slacks. Mothers were indicating on the return forms that they were returning the slacks because they didn't fit properly. Management thus defined the research problem as determining how to redesign the catalog's diagrams and rewrite the instructions to help consumers place their mail orders for slacks. However, when interviewers from Oxtoby-Smith, a survey research company, brought the catalogs with the diagrams and instructions to consumers' homes, they found out that the boys' slacks actually fit perfectly. They also learned the mothers

had ordered several pairs of slacks for their teenage sons in the hope that the teenagers would find at least one pair they would be willing to wear; then they returned the other pairs of slacks. The mothers felt uncomfortable with this buying situation, but did not wish to reveal the true reasons for returning the slacks. It was less trouble to provide the explanation of poor fit. The diagrams were not the problem. The instructions were not the problem.

The researcher at Oxtoby-Smith stated, "The lesson I learned from this discovery was that sometimes assumptions about the nature of the problem can be mistaken. That's okay if the research we do to investigate the problem we think we have enables us to identify the real problem. Very often, a major job of the researchers is to find out what the problem is. Frankly, sometimes that means not assuming that the client knows what the problem is."[5]

Decision-Oriented Research Objectives

research objective

The researcher's version of the marketing problem; it explains the purpose of the research in measurable terms and defines standards for what the research should accomplish.

The **research objective** is the researcher's version of the marketing problem. After the research questions or hypotheses have been stated, the research project objectives are derived from the problem definition. They explain the purpose of the research in measurable terms and define standards for what the research should accomplish. In addition to explaining the reasons for conducting the project, research objectives help ensure that the research project will be manageable in size.

Exhibit 5.5 illustrates how the marketing problem of a nationwide retail chain store—whether it should offer an in-home shopping service using Internet computerized ordering—is translated into research objectives.

In some instances marketing problems and the project's research objectives are identical. However, the objectives must specify the information needed to make a decision. Identifying the needed information may require that managers or researchers be extremely specific, perhaps even listing the exact wording of the question in a survey or explaining exactly what behavior might be observed or recorded in an experiment. Statements about the required precision of the information or the source of information may be required to clearly communicate exactly what information is needed. Many product buying decisions, for example, are made by both husband and wife. If this is the case, the husband–wife decision-making unit is the unit of analysis. The objective of obtaining X information about research questions from this unit should be specifically stated.

Exhibit 5.5 Marketing Problem Translated into Research Objectives

MARKETING MANAGEMENT PROBLEM/QUESTIONS	RESEARCH QUESTIONS	RESEARCH OBJECTIVES
Should the retail chain store offer in-home shopping via the Internet?	Are consumers aware of Internet home shopping systems? What are consumers' reactions to Internet shopping?	To determine consumer awareness with aided recall To measure consumer attitudes and beliefs about home shopping systems
In which of several possible forms should the service be offered?	How do consumers react to service from A? B? C? What are the perceived benefits of each form of service?	To obtain ratings and rankings of each form of service To identify perceived benefits of and perceived objections to the system
What market segment should be the target market?	Will consumers use the service? How often? Do the answers to the above questions differ from demographic group? Who are the best prospects?	To measure purchase intentions; to estimate likelihood of usage To compare—using cross-tabulations—levels of awareness, evaluations, purchasing intentions, etc., of men versus women, high-income versus low-income groups, young consumers versus older consumers, etc.
What pricing strategy should we follow?	How much do prospective customers think the service will cost? Do prospective customers think this product will be priced higher or lower than competitive offerings? Is the product perceived as a good value?	To ascertain consumers' knowledge and expectations about prices To learn how the price of this service is perceived relative to competitors' pricing To determine the perceived value of the service

Note: For simplicity, hypotheses are omitted from the exhibit.

The search objective is useful if it is a **managerial action standard** that specifies the performance criterion to be used. If the criterion to be measured (for example, sales or attitude changes) turns out to be X, management will do A; if it is Y, management will do B.[6] This type of objective leaves no uncertainty about the decision to be made once the research is finished.

The research objectives should be limited to a manageable number. Fewer study objectives make it easier to ensure that each will be addressed fully.

Exhibit 5.6 shows how the statement of the marketing problem influences the research objectives. The specific objectives, in turn, become the basis for the research design.

Exhibit 5.5 translated the broad research objective—to determine consumers' perceived need for a home shopping service—into specific objectives, namely to determine consumer awareness, obtain ranked preferences for alternative forms of the service, compare the needs of various market segments, and so on. The specific objectives influence decisions about the research design, because they indicate the type of information needed.

Exhibit 5.6 also shows how exploratory research can help managers in the overall definition of the marketing problem. However, in routine situations or when managers are quite familiar with the background information, it is quite likely that the problem definition will be based exclusively on the decision maker's objectives.

Once the research has been conducted, the results may show an unanticipated aspect of the problem and suggest a need for additional research to satisfy the main objective. Many researchers who have uncovered additional aspects of a marketing problem after finishing fieldwork recommend designing studies to include questions designed to reveal the unexpected.

managerial action standard
A performance criterion or objective that expresses specific actions that will be taken if it is achieved.

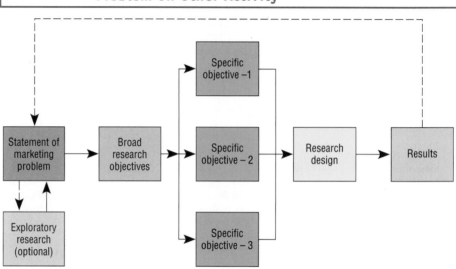

Exhibit 5.6   Influence of the Statement of the Marketing Problem on Other Activity

---

How Much Time Should Be Spent Defining the Problem?

Budget constraints usually influence the amount of effort that will be spent defining the problem. Most marketing situations are complex, and numerous variables may have some influence. Searching for every conceivable cause and minor influence is impractical. The importance of the recognized problem will dictate a reasonable amount of time and money to spend determining which possible explanations are most likely. Marketing managers, being responsible for decision making, may wish the problem definition process to proceed quickly. Researchers who take long periods of time to carefully define problems may frustrate managers. However, the time taken to identify the correct problem is time well spent.

The Research Proposal

research proposal
A written statement of the research design that includes a statement explaining the purpose of the study and a detailed, systematic outline of procedures associated with a particular research methodology.

The **research proposal** is a written statement of the research design. It always includes a statement explaining the purpose of the study (research objectives) or a definition of the problem. It systematically outlines the particular research methodology and details the procedures that will be followed during each stage of the research process. Normally a schedule of costs and deadlines will be included in the research proposal. Exhibit 5.7 illustrates a short research proposal for the Internal Revenue Service that explored public attitudes toward a variety of tax-related issues.

Exhibit 5.7   An Abbreviated Version of a Research Proposal for the IRS[7]

Purpose of the Research

The general purpose of the study is to determine the taxpaying public's perceptions of the IRS's role in administering the tax laws. In defining the limits of this study the IRS identified the study areas to be addressed. A careful review of those areas led to the identification of the following specific research objectives:

1. To identify the extent to which taxpayers cheat on their returns, their reasons for doing so, and approaches that can be taken to deter this kind of behavior

2. To determine taxpayers' experience and level of satisfaction with various IRS services

3. To determine what services taxpayers need

4. To develop an accurate profile of taxpayers' behavior relative to the preparation of their income tax returns

5. To assess taxpayers' knowledge and opinions about various tax laws and procedures

Research Design

The survey research method will be the basic research design. Each respondent will be interviewed in his or her home. The personal interviews are generally expected to last between 35 and 45 minutes, although the length will vary depending on the previous tax-related experiences of the respondent. For example, if a respondent has never been audited, questions on audit experience will not be addressed. Or, if a respondent has never contacted the IRS for assistance, certain questions concerning reactions to IRS services will be skipped.

Some sample questions that will be asked are:

Did you (or your spouse) prepare your federal tax return for (year)?

☐ Self
☐ Spouse
☐ Someone else

Did the federal income tax package you received in the mail contain all the forms necessary for you to fill out your return?

☐ Yes
☐ No
☐ Didn't receive one in the mail
☐ Don't know

If you were calling the IRS for assistance and someone were not able to help you immediately, would you rather get a busy signal or be asked to wait on hold?

☐ Busy signal
☐ Wait on hold
☐ Neither
☐ Don't know

During the interview a self-administered questionnaire will be given to the taxpayer to ask certain sensitive questions such as:

Have you ever claimed a dependent on your tax return that you weren't really entitled to?

☐ Yes
☐ No

Sample Design

A survey of approximately 5,000 individuals located in 50 counties throughout the country will provide the data base for this study. The sample will be selected on a probability basis from all households in the continental United States.

Eligible respondents will be adults, over the age of 18. Within each household an effort will be made to interview the individual who was most familiar with completing the federal tax forms. When there is more than one taxpayer in the household, a random process will be used to select the taxpayer to be interviewed.

Data Gathering

The field-workers of a consulting organization will be utilized to conduct the interview.

Data Processing and Analysis

Standard editing and coding procedures will be utilized. Simple tabulation and cross-tabulations will be utilized to analyze the data.

Report Preparation

A written report will be prepared, and an oral presentation of the findings will be made by the research analyst at IRS convenience.

Budget and Time Schedule

Any complete research proposal should include a schedule of how long it will take to conduct each stage of the research and a statement of itemized costs.

Preparation of a research proposal forces the researcher to critically think through each stage of the research process. Vague plans, abstract ideas, and sweeping generalizations about problems or procedures must become concrete and precise statements about specific events. Information to be obtained and research procedures to be implemented have to be clearly specified so others may understand their exact implications. All ambiguities about why and how the research will be conducted must be clarified before the proposal is complete.

Because the proposal is a clearly outlined plan submitted to management for acceptance or rejection, it initially performs a communication function; it serves as a mechanism that allows managers to evaluate the details of the proposed research design and determine if alterations are necessary. The proposal helps managers decide if the proper information will be obtained and if the proposed research will accomplish what is desired. If the marketing problem has not been adequately translated into a set of specific research objectives and a research design, the client's assessment of the proposal will help ensure that the researchers revise the proposal to meet the client's information needs.

The proposal must communicate exactly what information will be obtained, where it will be obtained, and how it will be obtained. For this reason, it must be explicit about sample selection, measurement, fieldwork, and so on. For instance, most survey proposals will include a copy of the proposed questionnaire, at a bare minimum some sample questions, to ensure that managers and researchers agree on the information to be obtained and on the wording of questions.

The format for the IRS research proposal in Exhibit 5.7 follows the six stages in the research process outlined in Exhibit 3.4. Each stage implies that one or more questions must be answered before selecting one of the various alternatives facing the marketing researcher. For example, before a proposal can be completed, one has to ask what is to be measured. A simple statement like "market share" may not be enough; market share may be measured by auditing retailers' or wholesalers' sales, using trade association data, or asking consumers what brands they buy. What is to be measured is just one of many important questions that need to be answered before setting the research process into motion. This issue will be addressed in greater detail in Chapter 13; for now, an overview of issues for each stage of the research process will suffice. Exhibit 5.8 outlines some of the basic questions that managers and researchers typically must answer when planning a research design.

Review the IRS research proposal in Exhibit 5.7 to see how some of these issues were answered in a specific situation.[8] However, you will have to read the entire textbook before you can fully understand these issues.

In business one often hears the adage "Don't say it, write it." This is wise advice for the researcher who is proposing a research project to management. Misstatements and faulty communication may occur if the parties rely only on each individual's memory of what occurred at a planning meeting. Writing the research design in a proposal format, specifying exactly what will be done, creates a record to which everyone can refer and eliminates many problems that might arise after the research has been conducted. Finding out after completion of the research that information related to a particular variable was omitted or that the sample size was too small for a particular subgroup is less likely to occur with written proposals. Furthermore as a statement of agreement between the marketing executives and researchers, the formal proposal will reduce the tendency for someone reading the results to say, "Shouldn't we have had a larger sample?" or "Why didn't you do it this way?" As a record of the researcher's obligation, the proposal also provides a standard for determining whether the actual research was conducted as originally planned.

Exhibit 5.8 **Basic Questions Typically Asked When Planning a Research Design**	

DECISIONS TO MAKE IN THE RESEARCH PROCESS	BASIC QUESTIONS
Problem definition	What is the purpose of the study? How much is already known? Is additional background information necessary? What is to be measured? How? Can the data be made available? Should research be conducted? Can a hypothesis be formulated?
Selection of basic research design	What types of questions need to be answered? Are descriptive or causal findings required? What is the source of the data? Can objective answers be obtained by asking people? How quickly is the information needed? How should survey questions be worded? How should experimental manipulations be made?
Selection of sample	Who or what is the source of the data? Can the target population be identified? Is a sample necessary? How accurate must the sample be? Is a probability sample necessary? Is a national sample necessary? How large a sample is necessary? How will the sample be selected?
Data gathering	Who will gather the data? How long will data gathering take? How much supervision is needed? What operational procedures need to be followed?
Data analysis and evaluation	Will standardized editing and coding procedures be used? How will the data be categorized? Will computer or hand tabulation be used? What is the nature of the data? What questions need to be answered? How many variables are to be investigated simultaneously? What are the criteria for evaluation of performance?
Type of report	Who will read the report? Are managerial recommendations requested? How many presentations are required? What will be the format of the written report?
Overall evaluation	How much will the study cost? Is the time frame acceptable? Is outside help needed? Will this research design attain the stated research objectives? When should the research be scheduled to begin?

When the research will be conducted by a consultant or an outside research supplier, the written proposal serves as a company's bid to offer a specific service. Typically a client will solicit several competitive proposals, and these written offers will help management judge the relative quality of alternative research suppliers.

One final comment needs to be made about the nature of research proposals: Not all proposals follow the same format. The researcher must adapt his or her proposal to the target audience. An extremely brief proposed submitted by an organization's internal marketing research department to its own marketing executives bears little resemblance to a complex proposal submitted by a university professor to federal government agency to test a basic consumer research issue.

Anticipating Outcomes

The data processing and analysis section in Exhibit 5.7 is extremely brief because we will not discuss this topic until Chapter 20. However, at this stage some advice about data analysis is needed.

dummy tables

Representations of the actual tables that will be in the findings section of the final report; used to gain a better understanding of what the actual outcomes of the research will be.

On aspect of problem definition often lacking in research proposals is anticipating the outcomes—that is, the statistical findings—of the study. The use of a dummy table in the research proposal often helps the manager gain a better understanding of what the actual outcome of the research will be. **Dummy tables** are representations of the actual tables that will be in the findings section of the final report. They get the name because the researcher fills in or "dummies up" the tables with likely but fictitious data. In other words, the researcher anticipates what the final research report will contain (table by table) before the project begins. A research analyst can present dummy tables to the decision maker and ask, "Given these findings, will you be able to make a decision to solve your managerial problem?" If the decision maker says yes, the proposal may be accepted. However, if the decision maker cannot glean enough information from the dummy tables to make a decision about what the company would do with the hypothetical outcome they suggest, he or she must rethink what outcomes and data analyses are necessary to solve the problem. In other words, the marketing problem is clarified by deciding on action standards or performance criteria and recognizing the types of research findings necessary to make specific decisions.

Summary

The first step in any marketing research project is to define the problem or opportunity. Decision makers must express their objectives to researchers to avoid getting the right answer to the wrong question. Defining the problem often is complicated in the portions of the problem may be hidden from view. The research must help management isolate and identify the problem to ensure that the real problem, rather than a symptom, is investigated.

A variable is anything that changes in value. Variables may be categorical or continuous. One aspect of problem definition is the identification of the key dependent variables and key independent variables.

Research questions and hypotheses are translations of the marketing problem into marketing research terms. A hypothesis is an unproven proposition or a possible solution to the problem. Hypotheses state relationships between variables that can be empirically tested. Research objectives specify information needs. For the research project to be successful, the research problem must be stated in terms of clear and precise research objectives.

The research proposal is a written statement of the research design that makes the research process operative for the specific problem. The research proposal allows managers to evaluate the details of the proposed research and determine if alterations are needed. Most research proposals will include the following sections: purpose of the research, research design, sample design, data gathering and/or field-work techniques, data processing and analysis, budget, and time schedule.

Key Terms and Concepts

Problem definition
Decision makers' objectives
Iceberg principle
Situation analysis
Variable

Categorical (classificatory) variable
Continuous variable
Dependent variable
Independent variable
Hypothesis

Research objective
Managerial action standard
Research proposal
Dummy tables

Questions for Review and Critical Thinking

1. In its broadest context, what is the task of problem definition?
2. In the following nine-dot square, connect all nine dots using no more than four straight lines and without lifting the pencil from the paper. What does the solution of this problem infer about the solutions of problem definition situations?

    •   •   •
    •   •   •
    •   •   •

3. What is the iceberg principle?
4. State a problem in your field of interest and list some variables that might be investigated to solve this problem.
5. Go the library, find business journals, and record and evaluate some hypotheses that have been investigated in recent years. Identify the key independent and dependent variables.
6. Evaluate the following statement of marketing problems:
    a. A farm implement manufacturer: Our objective is to learn the most effective form of advertising so we can maximize product line profits.
    b. An employees' credit union: Our problem is to determine the reasons why employees join the credit union, determine members' awareness of credit union services, and measure attitudes and beliefs about how effectively the credit union is operated.
    c. The producer of a television show: We have a marketing problem. The program's ratings are low. We need to learn how we can improve our ratings.
    d. A soft-drink manufacturer: The marketing problem is that we do not know if our bottlers are more satisfied with us than our competitors' bottlers are with them.

    e. A women's magazine: Our problem is to document the demographic changes that have occurred in recent decades in the lives of women and to put them in historical perspective; to examine several generations of American women through most of this century, tracking their roles as students, workers, wives, and mothers and noting the changes in timing, sequence, and duration of these roles; to examine at what age and for how long a woman enters various stages of her life: school, work, marriage, childbearing, divorce. This will be accomplished by analyzing demographic data over several generations from this perspective.
    f. A manufacturer of fishing boats: The problem is to determine sales trends over the past five years by product category and to determine the seasonality of unit boat sales by quarters by region of the country.
    g. The marketer of a new spreadsheet software package: The purpose of this research is (1) to identify the market potential for the product, (2) to identify what desirable features the product should possess, and (3) to determine possible advertising strategies/channel strategies for the product.
7. What purpose does the research proposal serve?
8. What role should managers play in the development of the research proposal?
9. Comment on the following statements:
    a. "The best marketing researchers are prepared to rethink and rewrite their proposals."
    b. "The *client's* signature is an essential element of the research proposal."

10. You have been hired by a group of hotel owners, restaurant owners, and other businesspeople engaged in businesses that benefit from tourism on South Padre Island, Texas. They wish to learn how they can attract a large number of college students to their town during spring break. Define the marketing research problem. (You may substitute a beach town in Florida or California if you prefer.)

11. You have been hired by a local Big Brothers and Big Sisters organization to learn how they can increase the number of males who volunteer to become Big Brothers to fatherless boys. Define your research objectives.

12. You have solicited research proposals from several firms. The lowest bidder has the best questionnaire and proposal. However, there is one feature from a firm that will not receive the bid that you particularly like. How should you handle this situation?

Exploring the Internet

1. How could the Internet help define a marketing problem that needs to be researched?

2. Could e-mail be used to solicit research proposals from marketing research suppliers? What would the advantages and disadvantages of using this method of distribution be?

Case 5.1 EZPass[9]

IN THE 1990S, A TASK FORCE WAS FORMED AMONG EXECUTIVES of seven regional transportation agencies in the New York–New Jersey area. The mission of the task force was to investigate the feasibility and desirability of adopting electronic toll collection (ETC) for the interregional roadways of the area. Electronic toll collection consists of providing commuters with small transceiver (tags) that emit a tuned radio signal. Receivers placed at toll booths are able to receive the radio signal and identify the commuter associated with the particular signal. Commuters establish ETC accounts that are debited for each use of a toll-based roadway or facility, thus eliminating the need for the commuter to pay by cash or token. Because the radio signal can be read from a car in motion, ETC can reduce traffic jams at toll plazas by allowing tag holders to pass through at moderate speeds.

At the time the New York/New Jersey agencies were studying the service, electronic toll collection was already being successfully used in Texas and Louisiana. Even though several of the agencies had individually considered implementing ETC they recognized that independent adoption would fall far short of the potential benefits achievable with an integrated interregional system.

The task force was most interested in identifying the ideal configuration of service attributes for each agency's commuters, and determining how similar or different these configurations might be across agencies. The task force identified a lengthy list of attributes that was ultimately culled to seven questions:

- How many accounts are necessary and what statements will be received?
- How and where does one pay for EZPass?
- What lanes are available for use and how they are controlled?
- Is the tag transferable to other vehicles?
- What is the price of the tag and possible service charge?
- What are other possible uses for the EZPass tag (airport parking, gasoline purchases)?

From a marketing researcher's perspective, it also seemed important to assess commuter demand for the service. However, the task force was not convinced that it needed a projection of demand because it was committed to implementing ETC regardless of initial commuter acceptance. The task force considered its principal role to be investigating commuters' preferences for how the service should be configured *ideally*.

QUESTIONS

1. Evaluate the problem definition. Has the problem been defined adequately?

2. What type of research design would you recommend for this project?

Case 5.2 The Norlin Group

THE NORLIN GROUP IS AN ADVERTISING AGENCY WITH approximately $2 million in billings. One of its largest clients, a manufacturer and marketer of air guns, was contacted by an inventor who wished to sell the company on the idea for a new product that could convert traditional pistols, rifles, and other firearms into air guns. The client, who used the ad agency's research department for all of its consumer research, requested a proposal from the Norlin Group. Case Exhibit 5.1-1 shows the research project description that the agency's research department gave to its client.

QUESTIONS

1. Evaluate the problem definition.

2. If this research proposal were submitted to you, how would you react?

*Note: The name of this organization is fictitious so that participants can remain anonymous.

Case Exhibit 5.1-1 Research Project Description

Product: TURNS ANY CENTER-FIRE FIREARM INTO AN AIR GUN. USES PNEUMATIC CARTRIDGE WITH SPECIALLY DESIGNED bullet that is sized precisely to match firearm ammo. Special handheld pump (sold with shells) pumps air into cartridge up to 3,000 psi. Prices unknown.

Foreseen Application: Legislation has placed severe restrictions on where gun owners can shoot their firearms. Indoor ranges are even being closed. Legal locations to practice with a firearm are becoming more and more difficult to find. Furthermore, cost of ammo has increased, making practice expensive. This product, due to lower velocities, will enable the firearm owners to use their own guns indoors, in backyards, or in other residential locations. Accuracy over shorter ranges is high. Also, cost should be one-half to one-third the cost of conventional ammo.

Marketing Issue: To acquire the technology to produce this product, our client must acquire the entire company at a substantial cost. This research should identify whether the market potential for the product will justify the capital expenditure.

Research Objectives:
A. Among gun-owning consumers, determine:
    (1) Basic reactions to product concept
    (2) Foreseen applications by consumers
    (3) Validity of clients's foreseen application
    (4) Price sensitivity/expectations
    (5) Willingness to buy
    (6) Frequency of foreseen use

B. Among police/military training units, determine:
    (1) Basic reactions to product concept
    (2) Foreseen applications
    (3) Appropriateness for training
    (4) Reaction to cost/price sensitivity
    (5) Willingness to buy/use

Research Audience (to include both urban and nonurban samples):
A. Civilian consumers
    (1) Avid gun enthusiasts
    (2) "Average" gun owner
    (3) "Weekend" gun user

B. Police departments
    (1) Training personnel
    (2) Range operators
C. Military
    (1) Training instructors
    (2) Purchasing agents

Case 5.3 The Skool

THE SKOOL WAS A SINGLES BAR IN CHICAGO'S RUSH STREET area. This area, located on Chicago's Near North Side by the Gold Coast, is approximately seven blocks long and three blocks wide and is popular for evening entertainment.

The Skool once was one of the most popular spots on Rush Street. There had always been wall-to-wall people on Friday afternoons, but lately the crowds had begun to go elsewhere.

A marketing research consultant who patronized The Skool because it was two blocks from his home knew the manager, Ray Schalk, well.

After some discussions with her, the consultant sent a letter proposing that The Skool conduct some marketing research. (See Case Exhibit 5.1-2.)

QUESTIONS

1. Has the research problem been adequately defined?

2. Evaluate the research proposal.

Case Exhibit 5.1-2 The Skool's Marketing Research Proposal

DEAR RAY:

Here is a brief outline of what I believe The Skool must consider if it is to regain its popularity on Rush Street. As you know, The Skool's management has changed the decor and exterior of The Skool, hired exceptional bands, and used various other promotions to improve business. In spite of this, a decline in The Skool's popularity has been evidenced. As these efforts have not brought back the crowd The Skool once had, I suggest The Skool undertake a marketing research investigation of consumer behavior and consumer opinions among Rush Street patrons.

I recommend this project because The Skool once had what it takes to be a popular bar on Rush Street and should still have the potential to regain this status. Most likely, the lack of patronage at The Skool is caused by one or both of the following factors:

1. A change in the people or type of people who patronize Rush Street bars

2. A change in the opinions of The Skool held by people who patronize Rush Street bars

The problem for The Skool's management is to determine the specifics of the change either in the people or in the opinions of the regular patrons of Rush Street and The Skool.

Determining what type of information is desired by The Skool's management depends on some underlying facts about the popularity of the bars on Rush Street. An assumption must be made concerning this question: Does the crowd (weekend and Wednesday patrons) go where the regulars go, or do the regulars go where the crowd goes? If you believe that the regulars follow the crowd, a general investigation should be conducted to test why the masses go to the popular bars. If the assumption is made that a bar is popular because there are always people (regulars) there, the best method to increase business is to get a regular following who will attract the crowd.

Of course, the optimal position is to appeal to both the regulars and the crowd. Thus, there are numerous areas for investigation:

- Who visits Rush Street bars? What are the group characteristics?
- What motivates these people to go to the various bars and thus makes them popular? For example, to what extent does the number of stag girls in the bars bring about more patrons? (Note: Remember that The Skool, Rush-up, Filling Station, and Barnaby's had female waitresses at the start of their popularity. Could this have been a factor in their appeal?) How important is bartender rapport with the patrons?
- What do drinkers like and dislike about The Skool?
- What is the awareness among beer drinkers of Watney's quality? Do they like it? How does having Bud on tap affect a bar's popularity?

- What image does The Skool project? Is it favorable or unfavorable? Has it lost the image it once had because it is trying to be the Store Annex, Barnaby's, Rush-up, and The Skool combined? Is the decor consistent? How can a favorable image be put back into Rush Street drinkers' minds? You might think The Skool can appear to all Rush Street people, but you can't be all things to all people. A specialization of image and customers may bring back the crowd for The Skool.

- How important is it to be first with a new promotion? For example, did Barnaby's idea of starting a wine and chicken feast make it the place to go to, at least in the short run? If a food promotion would go over, what should The Skool try?

There are many ways in which The Skool would benefit if it conducted a marketing research survey. Of course, the above suggestions for investigation are not all-inclusive, as I have not had a chance to talk with you to determine which areas are the most important. If you would like to have me submit a formal research proposal to determine how The Skool can improve its business, I will be happy to talk with you any evening.

Sincerely yours,
Bill Jerpe

Chapter 6

Exploratory Research and Qualitative Analysis

O N A GRAY AND GUSTY DAY IN JUNE, 35 GIRLS BETWEEN the ages of 5 and 9 were gathered in a conference room near the San Francisco Airport, looking at prototypes of toys they'd never seen before.[1] Lewis Galoob Toys had convened a series of focus groups to watch real live kids interact with a doll being developed for 1995. The name of the doll was Sky Dancer.

Deborah Rivers, the research consultant who led the groups, would have preferred a less sterile environment to put the girls at their ease, but this windowless room would have to do. On one wall were pictures of military airplanes. Directly across was a one-way mirror, so that the precise reactions of the participants could be videotaped and analyzed later.

The grainy tapes show bunches of girls—some scruffy, some bright-eyed, some with bows in their hair. Rivers begins by making a "pinkie promise" with each girl to ensure that everything said between these walls will be the truth. The children are happy to swear on their honor. They have a good idea that, just around the bend, there will be a reward for their consultations. So they like everything, agree to everything.

"You know," Rivers says dubiously to the kids, "some people say that flying toys are only for boys. Is that true?" The response is immediate: "No!" The notion that anything could be "only for boys" is summarily rejected. Then Rivers's tone changes. She has the girls close their eyes and then reads a brief set piece from her clipboard: "I'd like to welcome you to the enchanted world of Sky Dancers! Each beautiful Sky Dancer unfolds her elegant wings and flies with the wind...." She goes on to evoke ocean waves and shimmering moons—cue words to let the Sky Dancer whammy take effect.

The girls open their eyes. By now Rivers has brought out a bevy of dolls—winged ballerinas, from the look of them. They are garish and plastic, with pink-and-lavender nylon hair. The girls blink a few times at the dolls. Many love them at first sight; others praise faintly, hoping they won't blow their chance to

What you will learn in this chapter

To understand the differences between qualitative research and quantitative research.

To explain the purposes of exploratory research.

To identify the four general categories of exploratory research.

To explain the advantages and disadvantages of experience surveys, case study methods, focus group interviews, projective techniques, depth interviews, and other exploratory research techniques.

To understand when exploratory techniques are appropriate and to understand their limitations.

To understand how technology is changing the nature of exploratory research.

get the money they've been promised. Two of the 35 girls react to the doll with open disdain. "Well," says a girl named Kate, who's missing a front tooth, "she's not the best thing in the world."

But Rivers isn't discouraged; this doll's got a gimmick. She picks up her prototype by its flowery base—or, more accurately, its pistol-grip launcher—and tugs at a string. The doll starts to twirl; its wings lift, by virtue of aerodynamic design, until all at once the Sky Dancer has risen free of its base and whizzed straight up in the air, winged arms whirring like a helicopter blade. The girls respond in a hushed chorus: "Cooool!"

Postflight, Rivers elicits comments on the doll and asks the girls how they like it. One claims she wants a Sky Dancer "more than the whole universe." At a certain point, Rivers leaves the room. Behind the mirror are a few Galoob employees, including Scott Masline, the firm's vice president of marketing and a driving force in the doll's development. Rivers wants to check with Masline to see if he'd like any departures from the script. It's also an ideal chance to observe the girls at their most candid.

In one group, Rivers's exit is greeted with silence. Finally, Emily, a blond girl with a ponytail, speaks: "She's probably going to get the money," she says quietly.

"How much are you guys getting?" ask a waif from across the table.

"We're all getting $25," Emily replies.

Behind the glass, Scott Masline is ignoring the girls' discussion. He's pleased. It seems that girls don't need an elaborate story line to understand his product; "flying doll" is clear to them. Best of all, he has heard the elongated syllable "Cooool" uttered eight out of eight times.

Focus group research serves as a source for developing new toys that are then subjected to further research investigation. At Galoob, research helps reduce some of the risks in the volatile toy industry.

This chapter discusses the various exploratory research techniques used in marketing research.

Exploratory Research: What It Is and What It Is Not

When a researcher has a limited amount of experience with or knowledge about a research issue, exploratory research is a useful preliminary step. It helps ensure that a more rigorous, conclusive future study will not begin with an inadequate understanding of the nature of the marketing problem. The findings of the Sky Dancer exploratory research, for instance, would lead the researchers to emphasize learning more about girl's preferences in subsequent conclusive studies.

Conclusive research answers questions of fact necessary to determine a course of action. Exploratory research, on the other hand, never has this purpose. Most, but certainly not all, exploratory research designs provide *qualitative* data. Usually exploratory research provides greater understanding of a concept or crystallizes a problem rather than providing precise measurement or *quantification*. The focus of qualitative research is not on numbers but on words and observations: stories, visual portrayals, meaningful characterizations, interpretations, and other expressive descriptions. A researcher may search for numbers to indicate economic trends but does not perform a rigorous mathematical analysis. Any source of information

Exploratory researchers can be creative in their search for ideas. Researchers who conduct beeper studies provide consumers or business subjects with a questionnaire and instruct them to record their actions, interactions, moods, and stress levels every time the beeper goes off. Asking subjects to use disposable cameras, video cameras, and tape recorders is a variation of the beeper study.[2]

may be informally investigated to clarify which qualities or characteristics are associated with an object, situation, or issue.

Alternatively, the purpose of quantitative research is to determine the quantity or extent of some phenomenon in the form of numbers. Most exploratory research is not quantitative. This chapter discusses exploratory research under the assumption that its purpose is qualitative. **Exploratory research** may be a single investigation or a series of informal studies to provide background information. Researchers must be creative in the choice of information sources to be investigated. They must be flexible enough to investigate all inexpensive sources that may possibly provide information to help managers understand a problem. This flexibility does not mean that researchers need not be careful and systematic when designing exploratory research studies. Most of the techniques discussed in this chapter have limitations. Researchers should be keenly aware of the proper and improper uses of the various techniques.

exploratory research
Initial research conducted to clarify and define the nature of a problem.

Why Conduct Exploratory Research?

The purpose of exploratory research is intertwined with the need for a clear and precise statement of the recognized problem. Researchers conduct exploratory research for three interrelated purposes: (1) diagnosing a situation, (2) screening alternatives, and (3) discovering new ideas.

Diagnosing a Situation

Much already has been said about the need or situation analysis to clarify a problem's nature. Exploratory research helps diagnose the dimensions of problems so that successive research projects will be on target; it helps set priorities for research. In some cases exploratory research helps orient management by gathering information on an unfamiliar topic. A research project may not yet be planned, but information about an issue will be needed before the marketing strategy can be developed.

For example, when an advertising agency got an account for a new coffee containing chicory, the firm began the research process with exploratory research to diagnose the situation. The researchers learned that almost nobody had heard of chicory. It wasn't being used and nobody seemed to know how to use it. This led to the hypothesis that the advertising could portray the chicory ingredient any way the client wanted.

Screening Alternatives

When several opportunities arise, such as numerous new product ideas, and budgets don't allow trying all possible options, exploratory research may be used to determine the best alternatives. Many good products are not on the market because a company chose to market something better. Some new product ideas are found to be unworkable, or an exploratory look at market data (size, number, and so on) may depict a product alternative as not feasible because the market of buyers is too small. This aspect of exploratory research is not a substitute for conclusive research; however, certain evaluative information can be gained from such studies.

Concept testing is a frequent reason for conducting exploratory research. **Concept testing** is a general term for many different research procedures, all of which have the same purpose: to test some sort of stimulus as a proxy for a new, revised, or repositioned product or service. Typically consumers are presented with a written statement or filmed representation of an idea and asked if they would use it, whether they like it, and so on. Concept testing is a means of evaluating ideas by providing a feel for their merits prior to the commitment of any research and development, manufacturing, or other company resources.

Keebler's Sweet Spots, combination of shortbread cookie and chocolate drop, was more than a cookie, almost a candy.[3] When Keebler researched the positioning concept for Sweet Spots, it considered two alternative concepts: (1) an upscale product for the indulgent cookie eater, and (2) a lunchbox filler for children.

Researchers look for trouble signals in consumer evaluations of concepts to reduce the number of concepts under consideration or improve them to avoid future problems. Concept testing portrays the functions, uses, and possible applications for the proposed good or service. For example, marketers scrapped a concept for a men's shampoo that claimed to offer a special benefit to hair damaged by overexposure to the sun, heat from a hair dryer, or heavy perspiration after exploratory research showed that consumers thought the product was a good idea for someone with an outdoor lifestyle, but not for themselves.[4] Early research indicated that although the product was seen as unique, the likelihood of persuading men that it matched their self-images was low.

concept testing

Any exploratory research procedure that tests some sort of stimulus as a proxy for an idea about a new, revised, or repositioned product, service, or strategy.

TO THE POINT

The cure for boredom is curiosity. There is no cure for curiosity.

DOROTHY PARKER

If a concept is flawed, but the product has not been evaluated negatively, researchers may learn that the product concept needs to be refined or repositioned. For example, Procter & Gamble marketed Enviro-Paks—soft plastic refill pouches of detergents, fabric softeners, and other cleaning products—in Europe and Canada before concept testing them in the United States. Concept testing

---

Exhibit 6.1 Concept Statements for Two Seafood Products

SQUID CONCEPT ALTERNATIVE 1: CALAMARIOS	SQUID CONCEPT ALTERNATIVE 2: SCLAM CHOWDER

CALAMARIOS[a] are a new and different seafood product made from tender, boneless North Atlantic squid. The smooth white body (mantle) of the squid is thoroughly cleaned, cut into thin, bite-sized rings, then frozen to seal in their flavor. To cook CALAMARIOS, simply remove them from the package and boil them for only eight minutes. They are then ready to be used in a variety of recipes.

For example, CALAMARIOS can be combined with noodles, cheese, tomatoes, and onions to make "Baked CALAMARIOS Cacciatore." Or CALAMARIOS can be marinated in olive oil, lemon juice, mint, and garlic and served as a tasty squid salad. CALAMARIOS also are the prime ingredient for "Calamari en Casserole" and "Squid Italienne." You may simply want to steam CALAMARIOS, lightly season them with garlic, and serve dipped in melted butter. This dish brings out the fine flavor of squid. A complete CALAMARIOS recipe book will be available free of charge at your supermarket.

CALAMARIOS are both nutritious and economical. Squid, like other seafoods, is an excellent source of protein. CALAMARIOS can be found at your supermarket priced at $3.50 per pound. Each pound you buy is completely cleaned and waste-free.

Because of their convenient versatility, ample nutrition, and competitive price, we hope you will want to make CALAMARIOS a regular item on your shopping list.

SCLAM CHOWDER is a delicious new seafood soup made from choice New England clams and tasty, young, boneless North Atlantic squid. Small pieces of clam are combined with bite-sized strips of squid and boiled in salted water until they are soft and tender. Sautéed onions, carrots, and celery are then added together with thick, wholesome cream, a dash of white pepper, and a sprinkling of fresh parsley. The entire mixture is then cooked to perfection, bringing out a fine, natural taste that will make this chowder a favorite in your household.

SCLAM CHOWDER is available canned in your supermarket. To prepare, simply combine SCLAM CHOWDER with 1-1/2 cups of milk in a saucepan, and bring to a boil over a hot stove. After the chowder has reached a boil, simmer for 5 minutes and then serve. One can makes 2–3 servings of this hearty, robust seafood treat. Considering its ample nutrition and delicious taste, SCLAM CHOWDER is quite a bargain at $2.89 per can.

Both clams and squid are high in protein, so high in fact that SCLAM CHOWDER makes a healthy meal in itself, perfect for lunches as well as with dinner. Instead of adding milk, some will want to add a cup of sour cream and use liquid chowder as an exquisite sauce to be served on rice, topped with grated Parmesan cheese.

However you choose to serve it, you are sure to find SCLAM CHOWDER a tasty, nutritious, and economical seafood dish.

[a]CALAMARIO is the Italian word for squid. Prices adjusted for inflation.

---

with American consumers indicated that Americans preferred refill packaging that was different from what was available overseas—packaging that would be more convenient to use.

Exhibit 6.1 shows excellent concept statements for two seafood products made from squid. Portraying the intangibles (brand image, product appearance, name, and price) and a description of the product stimulates reality. The idea is clearly conveyed to the subject.

Discovering New Ideas

Marketers often conduct exploratory research to generate ideas for new products, advertising copy, and so on. For example, automobile marketers have consumers

Researchers conducting concept testing ask consumers to react to a stimulus and indicate what they like and dislike. Automobile marketers have consumers design their dream cars on video screens using computerized design systems adapted from those used by automotive designers.

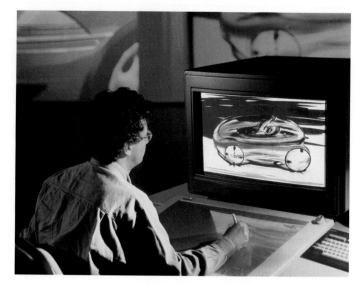

design their dream cars on video screens using computerized design systems adapted from those used by automotive designers. This exploratory research generates ideas that would never have occurred to the firms' own designers.[5]

Uncovering consumer needs is a great potential source of product ideas. One goal for exploratory research is to first determine what problems consumers have with a product category. When research has to determine what kinds of products people will buy, there is a difference between asking people about what they want or need and asking them about their problems. When you ask a customer what he or she wants in a dog food, the reply likely will be "Something that is good for the dog." If you ask what the problems with dog food are, you may learn that "The dog food smells bad when it is put into the refrigerator."[6] Once problems have been identified through research, the marketing job is to find how to solve them.

Categories of Exploratory Research

There are many techniques for investigating undefined research problems. Several of the most popular qualitative techniques are discussed in the next section. However, the *purpose,* rather than the *technique,* determines whether a study is exploratory, descriptive, or causal. For example, telephone surveys (discussed in Chapter 9) are sometimes used for exploratory purposes, although they are used mainly for descriptive research. The versatile qualitative techniques discussed in this chapter tend to be used primarily—but not exclusively—for exploratory purposes.

A manager may choose from four general categories of exploratory research methods: (1) experience surveys, (2) secondary data analysis, (3) case studies, and (4) pilot studies. Each category provides various alternative ways to gather information.

A chain saw manufacturer received from its Japanese distributor a recommendation to modify its product with a drilling attachment on the sprocket (replacing the chain and guide bar) for use as a mushroom-planting device. The distributor indicated that many such units had been sold in Japan. However, an experience survey with only one individual, the president of the Mushroom Growers Association, indicated that the product was not feasible in the United States. Most Americans favor a white, cultured mushroom grown in enclosed areas or caves rather than the variety of mushrooms grown on wood in Japan. The mushroom expert indicated that Americans believe too many superstitious tales about poisonous mushrooms and would not change their eating habits to include the Japanese variety.

Experience Surveys

If management decides that an idea is worthwhile, the decision maker may personally spend some time analyzing the situation. In attempting to gain insight into the problems at hand, researchers may discuss the concepts with top executives and knowledgeable individuals, both inside and outside the company, who have had personal experience in the field. This constitutes an informal **experience survey.** People who are knowledgeable about the area to be investigated often are willing to share their experiences with others (competitors excluded, of course). For example, a firm that is ready to launch a new product may discuss the general nature of the product with some of its key retailers and wholesalers. Members of the company's sales force also may be a valuable source of information. The purpose of such discussions is to exhaust the information available from relatively inexpensive sources before gathering expensive primary data. While the interviews with knowledgeable individuals may reveal nothing conclusive, they may help define the problem more formally.

Exploratory research during situation analysis may be quite informal. Input from knowledgeable people both inside and outside the company may come from little more than informal conversations. Just to get ideas about the problem, the marketing manager, rather than the research department, may conduct an experience survey. An experience survey may constitute a small number of interviews with some carefully selected people. Some formal questions may be asked, but the respondents generally will be allowed to discuss the questions with few constraints. Knowledgeable people should be selected because they are articulate individuals on a particular subject rather than taking a representative probability sample. The purpose is to help formulate the problem and clarify concepts rather than to develop a conclusive evidence.

experience survey
An exploratory research technique in which individuals who are knowledgeable about a particular research problem are questioned.

Secondary Data Analysis

Another economical and quick source of background information is trade literature in the public library or on the Internet. Searching through such material is exploratory research with *secondary data.* Basic theoretical research rarely is conducted without extensive reviews of the literature in the field or reviews of similar research reports. Using secondary data may be equally important in applied research.

Suppose the brand manager of a company that manufactures dental hygiene products is contacted by an inventor of a tongue cleaner. The inventor states that her stainless steel device cleans the tongue deposits that cause bad breath. Shortly thereafter, the brand manager finds information in the library that explains the practice of tongue cleaning: it began centuries ago and is common practice among certain Asian people. If the problem had concerned an existing product, the manager's situational analysis might have begun with an analysis of sales records by region, customer, or some other source of internal data.

Investigating data that have been compiled for some purpose other than the project at hand, such as accounting records or trade association data, are the most frequent forms of exploratory research. Because this is also a technique for conclusive research (both descriptive and causal research), a separate chapter (Chapter 7) is devoted to the investigation of secondary sources.

Marketing managers often conduct situation analysis using experience surveys and secondary data studies without a need for assistance from marketing research specialists. Informal situation analysis can indicate projects that still need clarification and may warrant further exploratory investigation. At this point, the marketing research specialist is called in to design a more elaborate exploratory study.

Case Studies

case study method

The exploratory research technique that intensively investigates one or a few situations similar to the problem situation.

The purpose of the **case study method** is to obtain information from one or a few situations that are similar to the researcher's problem situation. For example, a bank in Montana may intensively investigate the marketing activities of an innovative bank in California. A shirt manufacturer interested in surveying retailers may first look at a few retail stores to identify the nature of any problems or topics that a larger study should investigate.

A marketing research manager for Schwinn bicycles used observation techniques to conduct an exploratory case study analysis. Here is a description of the case situation in his own words:

> We had a very successful dealer on the West Coast. He sold a lot of bicycles. So it occurred to me that we'd go out and find out how he's doing it. We'll use a tape recorder and get in the back room where we'll hear these magic words that he says to people to make them buy bicycles. We'll take that tape back to the factory. We'll have it all typed out. We'll print it in the *Reporter* [a dealer newsletter]. We'll send it to all the other dealers and everybody can say the same words. And, boy, we'll need another factory! Right? So we go out. The guy's got a nice store out in Van Nuys. We sit in the back room and we listen. The first customers come in, a man and a woman with a boy about nine or ten years old. The dad says, "Which one is it?" The son says, "This one over here." Dad looks at it. He says to the clerk, "How much is it?" The clerk says, "$179.95." The father says, "Okay we'll take it." It blew the whole bit. So we stand there and we listen to some of these conversations going on like this. Suddenly it dawned on us that it was not what they say, it's the atmosphere of the store. Here, it was not Joe's old, dirty bike shop, but here was beautiful store on the main street. A big sign was in front, "Valley Cyclery" inside

WHAT WENT RIGHT?

TGI Friday's

BECAUSE TGI FRIDAY'S THOUGHT THE NAVY WAS AN extremely efficient food handler, perhaps more efficient than for-profit companies, the restaurant wanted to understand the sources of that efficiency. Friday's executives concluded that successful imitation of the Navy's food-handling operations might help the firm gain some expertise and lead to increased proficiency in performing its service. This matter was of particular interest to Friday's because the firm's strategy calls for building smaller restaurants with almost the same number of seats as were included in the older designs (5,700 square feet with 210 seats compared to 9,200 square feet with 240 seats). These smaller designs place a premium on handling food product efficiently.

To study the Navy's food-based work processes, Friday's CEO spent a day aboard the nuclear submarine USS *West Virginia*. His visit occurred when a crew of 155 was engaged in a 70-day voyage.

Because the submarine had a crew of duty 24 hours per day, the Navy served four meals daily in an extremely confined space. A quick calculation shows that four daily meals, for 70 days, for 155 people, is more than 43,000 meals.

The Navy was pleased to let Friday's use its operations as a case study. According to one Navy official, "These aren't things we want to keep secret. All of our food service research and development is funded by American tax dollars."

As with all exploratory research, the results from case analyses should be seen as tentative. Generalizing from a few cases can be dangerous because most situations are atypical in some sense. The bank in Montana may not be in a market comparable to the one in California. Even if the situations are not directly comparable, however, a number of insights can be gained and hypotheses suggested for future research. Obtaining information about competitors may be very difficult because they generally like to keep the secrets of their success to themselves. The exact formula of Coca-Cola, for example, is known by only a few top executives in the firm; they feel that confidentiality is a definite competitive edge in their product strategy. Thus, the researchers may have limited access to information available from other firms.

[were] fluorescent lights, carpeting on the floor, stereo music, air-conditioning, a beautiful display of bicycles. It was like a magnet. People came in. So, maybe this is the catch. We tried to introduce that idea to other dealers. Put a bigger investment into your store and see what happens. Some of them did, and it happened.[6]

This observation study serendipitously led to a discovery that would change Schwinn's entire channel of distribution strategy. The opportunity was a direct result of being open-minded in the problem discovery stage of marketing research.

The primary advantage of the case study is that an entire organization or entity can be investigated in depth with meticulous attention to detail. This highly focused attention enables the researcher to carefully study the order of events as they occur or to concentrate on identifying the relationships among functions, individuals, or entities. A fast-food restaurant may test a new menu item or a new store design in a single location before launching the change throughout the chain to learn about potential operating problems that could hinder service quality.

Conducting a case study often requires the cooperation of the party whose history is being studied. A successful franchisee may be willing to allow the franchisor access to records and reports. Intensive interviews or long discussions with the franchisee and his or her employees may provide an understanding of the situation. The researcher has no standard procedures to follow; he or she must be flexible and attempt to glean information and insights wherever they appear. This freedom to search for whatever data an investigator deems important makes the success of any case study highly dependent on the alertness, creativity, intelligence, and motivation of the individual performing the case analysis.

TO THE POINT

I never predict. I just look out the window and see what is visible—but not yet seen.

PETER DRUCKER

Pilot Studies

pilot study
A collective term for any small-scale exploratory research technique that uses sampling, but does not apply rigorous standards.

The term **pilot study** covers a number of diverse research techniques. Within the context of exploratory research, the term *pilot study* indicates that some aspect of the research (for example, fieldwork) will be on a small scale. Thus, a pilot study is a research project that involves sampling, but it relaxes the rigorous standards used to obtain precise, quantitative estimates from large, representative samples.

In one kind of pilot study researchers or managers try to experience what consumers experience to gain inexpensive and valuable insight. Without indicating their real positions with the company, researchers/managers may wait on customers, ride in repair trucks, and answer telephones. For example, the chairperson of Avis occasionally gets on line with airport customers waiting for cars or works behind the counter to get customer reactions. This form of pilot study may yield true comprehension of the situation to be investigated.

A pilot study generates primary data but usually for qualitative analysis. This characteristic distinguishes pilot studies from research that gathers background information using secondary data. Some researchers refer to pilot studies that generate qualitative information as *qualitative research*. The primary data usually come from consumers or other subjects of ultimate concern rather than from knowledgeable experts or case situations. This distinguishes pilot studies from experience surveys and case studies. Major categories of pilot studies include focus group interviews, projective techniques, and depth interviews.

Focus Group Interviews

focus group interview
An unstructured, free-flowing interview with a small group of people.

Marketing executives have been hearing a lot about focus group interviews lately. Focus group interviews, such as the one for Sky Dancer described at the beginning of this chapter, are so popular that many advertising and research agencies consider them the *only* qualitative research tool. As noted in Chapter 3, a **focus group interview** is an unstructured, free-flowing interview with a small group of people. It is not a rigidly constructed question-and-answer session but a flexible format discussion of a brand, advertisement, or new-product concept. The group meets at a central location at the predesignated time; typically it consists of an interviewer or moderator and six to ten participants, although larger groups are sometimes used. The participants may range from consumers talking about hair coloring, petroleum engineers talking about problems in the oil patch, or children talking about toys. The moderator introduces the topic and encourages group

When the Cole, Henderson, and Drake advertising agency conducted focus groups with serious tennis players, they learned that, however pleasant they were off the court, those who played two or three times per week were concerned with only one thing on the court—winning. These players, both men and women, were enthusiastic about any product that gave them a competitive edge. One focus group member said, "I want a weapon when I buy a tennis racquet. A menacing racquet with lots of power is very important."[7]

members to discuss the subject among themselves. Ideally, the discussion topics emerge at the group's initiative. Focus groups allow people to discuss their true feelings, anxieties, and frustrations, as well as the depth of their convictions, in their own words. The primary advantages of focus group interviews are that they are relatively fast, easy to execute, and inexpensive. In an emergency situation three or four group sessions can be conducted, analyzed, and reported in less than a week at a cost substantially lower than that of other attitude measurement techniques. It must be remembered, however, that a small group of people will not be a representative sample no matter how carefully they are recruited. Focus group interviews cannot take the place of quantitative studies.

The flexibility of group interviews has some advantages especially when compared with the rigid format of a survey. Numerous topics can be discussed and many insights gained, particularly with regard to the contingencies of consumer behavior. Responses such as the following, which would be unlikely to emerge in a survey, often come out in group interviews: "*If* it is one of the three brands I sometimes use and *if* it is on sale, I buy it; *otherwise*, I buy my regular brand" or "*If* the day is hot and I have to serve the whole neighborhood, I make Kool-Aid, *otherwise* I give them soda or Coke."[8] If a researcher is investigating a target group to determine who consumes a particular beverage or why a consumer purchases a certain brand, situational factors must be taken into account. If the researcher does not realize the impact of the occasion on which the particular beverage is consumed, the results of the research may be general rather than portraying the consumer's actual thought process. A focus group elicits situationally specific responses—on a hot day the whole neighborhood gets Kool-Aid; but if there are just a few kids, they get soda or Coke.

The Carnation Company provides an interesting example of the type of information focus group interviews can provide.[8] Past research had revealed that many people did not drink powdered milk because of a perceived taste deficiency compared with fluid milk. Carnation decided to reposition the brand to make it more appealing. First, Carnation sought answers to the following questions:

Why do the majority of consumers who drink milk shun powdered milk?

What would get them to drink it?

In contrast, why do present powdered-milk drinkers find the product acceptable?

These research questions suggested the need to develop hypotheses through the focus group technique. Separate sessions with users and nonusers were conducted. Discussions with nonusers confirmed that taste was a major barrier

Synergy among focus group participants can trigger a chain of responses that help diagnose situations. During a focus group of people who had never visited the J. Paul Getty Museum, a middle-aged man said, "I've been told there's heavy, very classical type of art, somewhat stuffy and standoffish. It's the kind of place you wouldn't want to take your kids and let them run around." An older woman agreed: "I get the impression it's a little stuffy and has old art." A younger man put in his two cents' worth: "I was driving up past Malibu and I saw the sign, I'd never heard of it before. I thought it was a place where they were going to show you how to refine oil or something."[10]

to use. Sessions with users revealed that a large percentage solved the taste problem by mixing powdered milk half and half with fluid whole milk, producing a cheaper, better-tasting, low-fat milk. Carnation hypothesized that nonusers would be more likely to convert if the company repositioned its product as a milk extender. Quantitative research confirmed this hypothesis, and Carnation executed the strategy with an advertising and promotion campaign that told the milk extender story.

Focus groups often are used for concept screening and concept refinement. The concept may be continually modified, refined, and retested until management believes it is acceptable. The specific advantages of focus group interviews have been categorized as follow:[9]

Synergy: The combined effort of the group will produce a wider range of information, insights, and ideas than will the cumulation of separately secured responses from a number of individuals.

Snowballing: A bandwagon effect often operates in a group interview situation. A comment by one individual often triggers a chain of responses from the other participants. Brainstorming of ideas frequently is encouraged in focus group sessions.

Serendipity: It is more often the case in a group than in an individual interview that some idea drops out of the blue. The group also affords a greater opportunity to develop an idea to its full potential.

Stimulation: Usually, after a brief introductory period, the respondents want to express their ideas and expose their feelings as the general level of excitement over the topic increases.

Security: In a well-structured group the individual usually can find some comfort in the fact that his or her feelings are similar to those of others in the group and that each participant can expose an idea without being obliged to defend it or follow through and elaborate on it. One is more likely to be candid because the focus is on the group rather than on the individual; the participant soon realizes that the things said are not necessarily being identified with him or her.

Spontaneity: Because no individual is required to answer any given question in a group interview, the individual's responses can be more spontaneous and less conventional. They should provide a more accurate picture of the person's position on some issue. In the group interview people speak

WHAT WENT RIGHT?

Are Brooms and Mops Only "Women's Tools"?

SOMETIMES THE BEST IDEAS POP INTO PEOPLE'S MINDS just as they're drifting off to sleep. Five years ago, about an hour into on of Rubbermaid Inc.'s drowsier focus groups on housewares, a woman frustrated by the pace shattered the calm by accusing the industry of sexism.

"Why do companies continue to treat brooms and mops like they were 'women's tools'?" she complained. "They're poorly designed and second-class to hammers and saws, which are balanced and molded to fit men's hands. Brooms and mops make housework more miserable, not easier."

The outburst sent Rubbermaid executives scrambling for notepads. The company didn't make cleaning products at the time, but it was more than willing to listen to reasons why it should. The woman's remarks not only made sense but eventually convinced the company to enter a product category it had avoided for so long.

After five years of research and development, Rubbermaid's housewares products division introduced a line of about 50 cleaning products and brushes. They ranged for a $1.29 sink brush to a $15.99 push broom, and while you can't saw wood or hammer a nail with them, each has been specially designed to make cleaning easier. Handles are supposed to fit comfortably in consumers' hands, and bristles are angled to reach tight spaces. Focus groups helped Rubbermaid identify areas of the house that need cleaning, right down to the spaces between banister supports. The company identified what people use to clean those spaces (most people use a dust rag for banisters). Rubbermaid employees also called consumers at home and asked them what cleaning products they owned and what they expected to pay for them. The company even researched the product line's color. All of the products are blue because consumers associate blue most closely with freshness and cleanliness.

---

only when they have definite feelings about a subject, not because a question requires a response.

Specialization: The group interview allows the use of a more highly trained interviewer (moderator) because certain economies of scale exist when a number of individuals are interviewed simultaneously.

Structure: The group interview affords more control than the individual interview with regard to the topics covered and the depth in which they are treated. The moderator often is one of the participants and, therefore, has the opportunity to reopen topics that received too shallow a discussion when initially presented.

Speed: The group interview permits securing a given number of interviews more quickly than does interviewing individual respondents.

Scientific scrutiny: The group interview allows closer scrutiny in several ways. First, the session can be observed by several people; this affords some check on the consistency of the interpretations. Second, the session can be tape recorded or even videotaped. Later, detailed examination of the recorded session can offer additional insight and help clear up disagreements about what happened.

Group Composition. The ideal size of the focus group is six to ten relatively homogeneous people. If the group is too small, one or two members may intimidate the others. Groups that are too large may not allow for adequate participation by each group member. Homogeneous groups seem to work best. This allows for concentrating on consumers with similar lifestyles, experiences, and communication skills. The session does not become rife with too many arguments and different viewpoints stemming from diverse backgrounds.

When the Centers for Disease Control and Prevention tested public service announcements about AIDS through focus groups, it discovered that single-race groups and multicultural groups reacted differently.[11] By conducting separate focus groups, the organization was able to gain important insights about which creative strategies were most appropriate for targeted versus broad audiences.

Typically, in a homogeneous group, married, full-time homemakers with children at home would be separated from unmarried, working women. Having first-time mothers in a group with women who have three or four children reduces the new mothers' participation; they look to the more experienced mothers for advice. Although they may differ in their opinions, they defer to the more experienced mothers.

Researchers who wish to collect information from different types of people should conduct several focus groups; for example, one focus group might consist only of men and another only of women. Thus, a diverse sample may be obtained even though each group is homogeneous. Most focus group experts believe that four focus group sessions (often in different cities) can satisfy the needs of exploratory research.

Environmental Conditions.

The group session may take place at the research agency, the advertising agency, a hotel, or one of the subjects' homes. Research suppliers that specialize in conducting focus groups operate from commercial facilities that have videotape cameras in observation rooms behind one-way mirrors and microphone systems connected to tape recorders and speakers to allow observation by others who aren't in the room. Some researchers suggest that a coffee klatsch or bull session atmosphere be established in the commercial research facility to ensure that the mood of the sessions will be as relaxed and natural as possible. They expect more open and intimate reports of personal experiences and sentiments to be obtained under these conditions.

The Moderator.

moderator
The person who leads a focus group discussion.

Exhibit 6.2 is a partial transcript of a focus group interview. Notice how the **moderator** ensures that everyone gets a chance to speak and how he or she contributes to the discussion.

The moderator's job is to develop a rapport with the group and to promote interaction among its members. The moderator should be someone who is really interested in people, carefully listens to what others have to say, and can readily establish rapport and gain people's confidence and make them feel relaxed and eager to talk. Careful listening is especially important because the group interview's purpose is to stimulate spontaneous responses. The moderator's role is also to focus the discussion on the areas of concern. When a topic is no longer generating fresh ideas, the effective moderator changes the flow of discussion. The moderator does not give the group total control of the discussion, but normally has prepared questions on topics that concern management. However, the timing of these questions in the discussion and the manner in which they are raised are left to the moderator's discretion. The term *focus group* thus stems from the moderator's task: He or she starts out by asking for a general discussion but usually *focuses* in on specific topics during the session.

Planning the Focus Group Outline.

discussion guide
A document prepared by the focus group moderator that contains remarks about the nature of the group and outlines the topics or questions to be addressed.

Effective focus group moderators prepare discussion guides to help ensure that the groups cover all topics of interest. The **discussion guide** begins with a written statement of the prefatory remarks to inform

---

Exhibit 6.2   What Happens in a Focus Group?

"My company is interested in finding out how people feel about different products and services," the moderator tells the semicircle of women. "In this group situation, what we're doing is exploring how you feel. Today we're interested in talking about restaurants and eating out."

The women have been told that someone "from a market research company" is listening to them, but they don't know which franchiser is the sponsor.

When the moderator displays the first card on the easel beside her, a card reading "McDonald's, Jack in the Box, Carl's Jr., Burger King, Wendy's," she asks, "What do you think of these restaurants?"

"The only one I really enjoy going to is Carl's Jr.," says Anne, a bright-faced woman in her early twenties who wears athletic shorts and thongs. "I don't know what Burger King does to their hamburgers, but I always get indigestion."

"You get indigestion at Burger King?" the moderator asks solicitously.

Anne nods. "It looks great when they bring it to you, but as soon as I start eating it, and especially when I finish, I get this awful feeling...."

"I think it looks great on TV," says Nancy, whose hair has been frosted two colors for a total of three. "The lettuce is so crispy, you know—"

"Oh yeah, and it's these huge hamburgers," says Laura.

"But then you get it and it's all crushed together," Anne says ruefully.

"I think the worst is Jack in the Box," says Victoria, a very thin woman who lives in Reseda, near a block that she contends houses one of every food franchise in the world. "The meat doesn't taste like meat. It tastes...low-grade. Fatty. The last time I ate there—I had a coupon for it and we were close by and this friend of mine hadn't tried it—" she explains quickly, "it was terrible. I've heard that Wendy's—I haven't been there yet, but everybody who goes there thinks it's terrific."

"Really?" Nancy looks a little funny at Victoria. "Wendy's?"

"I've been there," Anne says. "It's terrible."

"Is it terrible?" Victoria asks sheepishly, retreating from the group's conclusion that she's been taking restaurant advice from a pack of cretins out there in Reseda.

"Oh, my daughter is the hamburger addict of the world, and she couldn't finish it," Nancy says. "It ran all down—it was so greasy—"

"I like Burger King," says Marlene, who has had nine children in the 25-year marriage, "and I like Carl's Jr." She smiles nicely, relishing the impending heresy: "McDonald's I could vomit from." The women giggle. "I like Jack in the Box Super Tacos."

---

the group about the nature of the focus group, then it outlines topics or questions to be addressed in the group session.

A cancer center that wanted to warn the public about the effects of the sun used the discussion guide in Exhibit 6.3. The marketing researchers had several objectives for this question guide:[12]

- The first question, asking participants to describe their feelings about being out in the sun, was intended to elicit the range of views present in the group, given that some individuals might view being out in the sun as a healthful practice while others would view it as dangerous. It seemed important to have group members see the extent to which others held views different from their own. Furthermore, this was the only question asked of every participant in turn. As no one could fail to be able to answer, it gave each individual a nonthreatening chance to talk and thus broke the ice.

- The second question, asking whether participants could think of any reason to be warned about exposure to the sun, was simply designed to introduce in question form the idea of a warning.

- Succeeding questions were asked, first on an open-ended bases, about possible formats of warnings of danger from the sun. Respondents were

---

Exhibit 6.3 **Discussion Guide from a Cancer Center**

Thank you very much for agreeing to help out with this research. We call this a focus group; let me explain how it works, and then please let me know if something isn't clear.

This is a discussion, as though you were sitting around just talking. You can disagree with each other, or just comment. We do ask that just one person talks at a time, because we tape-record the session to save me from having to take notes. Nothing you say will be associated with you or your church—this is just an easy way for us to get some people together.

The subject is health risk warnings. Some of you may remember seeing a chart in a newspaper that gives you a pollen count or a pollution count. And you've heard on the radio sometimes a hurricane watch or warning. You've seen warnings on cigarette packages or cigarette advertising, even if you don't smoke. And today we're going to talk about warnings about the sun. Before we start, does anybody have a question?

1. OK, let's go around and talk about how often you spend time in the sun, and what you're likely to be doing. (FOR PARENTS): What about your kids—do you like them to be out in the sun?

2. OK, can you think of any reason that somebody would give you a warning about exposure to the sun?

(PROBE: IS ANY SUN EXPOSURE BAD, OR ONLY A CERTAIN DEGREE OF EXPOSURE, AND IF SO, WHAT IS IT? OR IS THE SUN GOOD FOR YOU?)

3. What if we had a way to measure the rays of the sun that are associated with skin problems, so that you could find out which times of the day or which days are especially dangerous? How could, say, a radio station tell you that information in a way that would be useful?

4. Now let me ask you about specific ways to measure danger. Suppose somebody said, "We monitored the sun's rays at noon, and a typical fair-skinned person with unprotected skin will burn after 40 minutes of direct exposure." What would you think?

5. Now let me ask you about another way to say the same kind of thing. Suppose somebody said, "The sun's rays at noon today measured 10 times the 8 a.m. baseline level of danger." What would you think?

6. OK, now suppose that you heard the same degree of danger expressed this way: "The sun's rays at noon today measured 8 on a sun danger scale that ranges from 1 to 10." What would you think?

7. What if the danger scale wasn't numbers, but it was words. Suppose you heard, "The sun's rays at noon showed a moderate danger reading," or "The sun's rays showed a high danger reading." What would you think?

8. And here's another possibility—what if you heard: "Here's the sun danger reading at noon today—the unprotected skin of a typical fair-skinned person will age the equivalent of one hour in a ten-minute period."

9. OK, what if somebody said today is a day to wear long sleeves and a hat, or today is a day you need sunscreen and long sleeves. What would you think?

10. OK, here's my last question. There are really three things you can do about sun danger—you can spend less time in the sun, you can go out at less dangerous times of day like before 10 in the morning or after 4 in the afternoon, and you can cover your skin by wearing a hat, or long sleeves, or using protective sunscreen lotion. Thinking about yourself listening to the radio, what kind of announcement would make you likely to do one or more of those things? (PARENTS: WHAT WOULD MAKE YOU BE SURE THAT YOUR CHILD WAS PROTECTED?)

11. And what would you be most likely to do to protect yourself? (YOUR CHILD?)

12. Before we break up, is there anything else you think would be useful for M. D. Anderson's people to know?

OK, thank you *very* much for your help.

asked to react to any formats that participants suggested on an open-ended basis, then to react to formats the cancer center personnel had in mind.

- Finally, the bottom line question asked which format would be most likely to induce participants to take protective measures, and then a catch-all question asked for any comments they wanted to pass along to the sponsor, which was revealed as the Houston-based cancer center.

Notice that the researchers who planned the outline established certain objectives for each part of the focus group. The initial effort was to break the ice and establish a rapport within the group. The logical flow of the group session then moved from general discussion about sunbathing to more focused discussion of types of warnings about danger from sun exposure.

Focus Groups as Diagnostic Tools.
Researchers predominately use focus groups as a means of conducting exploratory research. Focus groups can be helpful in later stages of a research project, but the findings from surveys or other quantitative techniques raise more questions than they answer. Managers who are puzzled about the meaning of survey research results may use focus groups to better understand what consumer surveys indicate. In such a situation the focus group supplies diagnostic help after quantitative research has been conducted.

Focus Groups That Use Videoconferencing.
The videoconferencing industry has improved in quality and grown dramatically in recent years. And, as the ability to communicate via telecommunications and videoconferencing links has improved, the number of companies using these systems to conduct focus groups has increased. With traditional focus groups, marketing managers and creative personnel often watch the moderator lead the group from behind one-way mirrors. If the focus group is being conducted out of town, the marketing personnel usually have to spend more time in airplanes, hotels, and taxis than they do watching the group session. With videoconferenced focus groups, the marketing personnel can stay home.

Focus Vision Network of New York is a marketing research company that provides videoconferencing equipment and services for clients. The Focus Vision system is modular, which allows it to be wheeled around so close-ups of each group member can be captured. The system operates via a remote keypad that allows observers in a far-off location to pan the focus group room or zoom in on a particular participant. The system allows marketing managers at remote locations to send messages in to the moderator. For example, while testing new product names in one focus group, an observing manager had an idea and contacted the moderator, who tested the new name on the spot.[13]

Shortcomings.
The shortcomings of focus groups are similar to those of most qualitative research techniques, as discussed under the head "A Warning about Exploratory Research" later in this chapter. However, two specific shortcomings of focus groups should be pointed out. First, they require sensitive and effective moderators; self-appointed participants may dominate these sessions giving somewhat misleading results. If participants react negatively toward the dominant member, a halo effect on attitudes toward the concept or topic of discussion may occur. This situation should be carefully avoided. Second, some unique sampling problems arise in focus groups. Researchers often select focus groups participants because they have similar backgrounds and experiences or because screening indicates that the participants are more articulate or gregarious than

EXPLORING RESEARCH ISSUES

Typical Consumers or Professional Respondents?

CLIENTS THAT LACK PHYSICAL FACILITIES FOR CONDUCTing focus groups regularly hire research suppliers that specialize in focus group research. What is a research supplier's responsibility when recruiting individuals to participate in a focus group? Should respondents be recruited because they will make the session go well or because they are typical consumers?

A disturbing example of a lack of objectivity in research occurred when managers of a client organization observed a focus group interview being conducted by a research supplier that had previously worked for the client on other projects. They noticed that some of the respondents looked familiar. A review of the video recordings of the session found that, to make the session go smoothly, the focus group moderators had solicited subjects who in the past had been found to be very articulate and cooperative. It is questionable whether such "professional respondents" can avoid playing the role of expert.

the typical consumer. These participants may not be representative of the entire target market. (The Exploring Research box on page 152 also addresses this issue.)

TO THE POINT

Necessity, mother of invention.

WILLIAM WYCHERLEY

Interactive Media and On-Line Research

The use of the Internet for qualitative exploratory research is growing rapidly. For example, Nickelodeon now uses an on-line group of viewers to learn about a variety of subjects.[14] These kids use personal computers and the Internet to talk with each other and with network researchers about pets, parents, peeves, and pleasures. Kids post notes on the computer bulletin board whenever they want to. Three times a week they log on for scheduled electronic conferences during which Nickelodeon researchers lead discussions on topics such as "is this a good scoring methodology for a game show?" or "Do kids understand if we show a sequence of program titles and air times?" On one occasion, the kids told researchers they were confused by the various locations shown in a segment of *The Tomorrow People*, a futuristic series with events occurring around the world. Realizing that the sight of a double-decker bus wasn't enough for a modern kid to identify London, the producers wrote the name of the city on the screen.

Research companies often set up a private chat room on their company Web sites for focus group interviews. Participants in these chat rooms feel their anonymity is very secure. Often they will make statements or ask questions they would never address under other circumstances.[15] This can be a major advantage for a company investigating sensitive or embarrassing issues. A disadvantage of on-line focus groups is that the researcher cannot see how people are reacting.[16]

Projective Techniques

There is an old story about asking a man why he purchased a Mercedes. When asked directly why he purchased a Mercedes, he responds that the car holds its value and does not depreciate much, that it gets better gas mileage than you'd expect, or that it has a comfortable ride. If you ask the same person why a neighbor purchased a Mercedes, he may well answer, "Oh, that status seeker!" This story illustrates that individuals may be more likely to give true answers (consciously or unconsciously) to disguised questions. Projective techniques seek to discover an individual's true attitudes, motivations, defensive reactions, and characteristic ways of responding.

The underlying assumption behind these methods lies in Oscar Wilde's phrase "A man is least himself when he talks in his own person; when he is given a mask he will tell the truth." In other words advocates of projective techniques assume that when directly questioned, respondents may not express their true feelings because they are embarrassed about answers that reflect negatively on their self-concept; they wish to please the interviewer with the right answer or they cannot reveal unconscious feelings of which they are unaware. However, if respondents are presented with unstructured, ambiguous stimuli, such as cartoons or inkblots, and are allowed considerable freedom to respond, they will express their true feelings.

A **projective technique** is an indirect means of questioning that enables respondents to project beliefs and feelings onto a third party, onto an inanimate object, or into a task situation. Respondents are not required to provide answers in any structured format. They are encouraged to describe a situation in their own words with little prompting by the interviewer. Individuals are expected to interpret the situation within the context of their own experiences, attitudes, and personalities and to express opinions and emotions that may be hidden from others and possibly themselves. The most common projective techniques in marketing research are word association tests, sentence completion methods, third-person techniques, and thematic apperception tests.

projective technique
An indirect means of questioning that enables a respondent to project beliefs and feelings onto a third party, onto an inanimate object, or into a task situation.

Word Association Tests.

During a **word association test**, the subject is presented with a list of words, one at a time, and asked to respond with the first word that comes to his or her mind. Both verbal and nonverbal responses (such as hesitation in responding) are recorded. For example, a researcher who reads a list of job tasks to sales employees expects that the word association technique will reveal each individual's true feelings about the job task. A sales representative's first thought presumably is a spontaneous answer because the subject does not have enough time to think about and avoid making admission that reflect poorly on himself or herself.

word association test
A projective technique in which the subject is presented with a list of words, one at a time, and asked to respond with the first word that comes to mind.

Word association frequently is used to test potential brand names. For example, a liquor manufacturer attempting to market a clear-colored light whiskey tested the brand names *Frost, Verve, Ultra,* and *Master's Choice. Frost* was seen as upbeat, modern, clean, and psychologically right; *Verve* was too modern, *Ultra* was too common, and *Master's Choice* was not upbeat enough.

Interpreting word association tests is difficult, and the marketing researcher should make sure to avoid subjective interpretations. When there is considerable agreement in the free-association process, the researcher assumes that the test has revealed the consumer's inner feelings about the subject. Word association tests are also analyzed by the amount of elapsed time. For example, if the researcher is investigating alternative advertising appeals for a method of birth

EXPLORING RESEARCH ISSUES

Cigarette Smoking— Are Smokers Being Honest with Themselves?

CIGARETTE SMOKING IN PUBLIC SPACES IS AN emotionally charged and hotly debated issue. Direct, undisguised questioning may not be the best alternative because cigarette smoking seems to trigger ego defense mechanisms. Marketing researchers directly questioned why 179 smokers who believed cigarettes to be a health hazard continued to smoke. The majority answered, "Pleasure is more important than health," "Moderation is OK," "I like to smoke." Such responses suggest that smokers are not dissatisfied with their habit. However, in another portion of the study, researchers used the sentence completion method. Respondents were asked to give the first thing that came to mind after hearing the sentence "People who never smoke are _____."

The answers were "better off," "happier," "smarter," "wiser," "more informed." To "Teenagers who smoke are_____," smokers responded with "foolish," "crazy," "uninformed," "stupid," "showing off," "immature," "wrong." The sentence completion test indicated that smokers are anxious, uncomfortable, dissonant, and dissatisfied with their habit. The sentence completion test elicited responses that the subjects would not have given otherwise.

---

control, a hesitation in responding may indicate that the response was delayed because the subject is emotionally involved in the word (possibly seeking an acceptable response). The analysis of projective technique results takes into account not only what consumers say, but also what they do not say.

Word association tests can also be used to pretest words or ideas for questionnaires. This enables the researcher to know beforehand whether and to what degree the meaning of a word is understood in the context of a survey.

sentence completion method

A projective technique in which respondents are required to complete a number of partial sentences with the first word or phrase that comes to mind.

Sentence Completion Method.

The **sentence completion method** is also based on the principle of free association. Respondents are required to complete a number of partial sentences with the first word or phrase that comes to mind. For example:

People who drink beer are _____.

A man who drinks a clear beer is _____.

Imported beer is most liked by _____.

The woman in the commercial _____.

Answers to sentence completion questions tend to be more extensive than responses to word association tests. The intent of sentence completion questions is more apparent, however.

third-person technique

A projective technique in which the respondent is asked why a third person does what he or she does or what a third person thinks about a product. The respondent is expected to transfer his or her attitudes to the third person.

Third-Person Technique and Role Playing.

The Iowa Poll asked, Will you wind up in heaven or hell? Nearly all Iowans believed they would be saved, but one-third described a neighbor as a "sure bet" for hell.[17]

Almost literally, providing a mask is the basic idea behind the **third-person technique.** Respondents are asked why a third person (for example, a neighbor) does what he or she does or what he or she thinks about a product. For example, male homeowners might be told:

We are talking to a number of homeowners like yourself about this new type of lawn mower. Some men like it the way it is; others believe that it should be improved. Please think of some of your friends or neighbors, and tell us what it is they might find fault with on this new type of lawn mower.

Respondents can transfer their attitudes to neighbors, friends, or coworkers. They are free to agree or disagree with an unknown third party.

The best-known and certainly a classic example of a study that used this indirect technique was conducted in 1950, when Nescafe Instant Coffee was new to the market. Two shopping lists, identical except for the brand of coffee, were given to two groups of women:

Pound and a half of hamburger

2 loaves of Wonder bread

Bunch of carrots

1 can of Rumford's Baking Powder

(Nescafé Instant Coffee) (Maxwell House Coffee, drip grind)

2 cans Del Monte peaches

5 pounds potatoes

The instructions were:

Read the shopping list below. Try to project yourself into the situation as far as possible until you can more or less characterize the woman who bought the groceries. Then write a brief description of her personality and character. Whenever possible indicate what factors influenced your judgment.

Forty-eight percent of the housewives given the Nescafé list described the Nescafé user as lazy and a poor planner. Other responses implied that the instant coffee user was not a good wife and spent money carelessly. The Maxwell House user, however, was thought to be practical, frugal, and a good cook.[17]

Role playing is a dynamic reenactment of the third-person technique in a given situation. The **role-playing technique** requires the subject to act out someone else's behavior in a particular setting. The photo on this page shows a child in a role-playing situation. She projects herself into a mother role using a pretend telephone and describes the new cookie she has just seen advertised. Child Research Service believes this projective play technique can be used to determine a child's true feelings about a product, package, or commercial. "When they [children] do speak, youngsters frequently have their own meaning for many words. A seemingly positive word such as 'good,' for example, can be a child's unflattering description of the teacher's pet in his class. In a role-playing game, the child can show exactly what 'good' means to him."[19]

role-playing technique
A projective technique that requires the subject to act out someone else's behavior in a particular setting.

A child placed in a role-playing situation may be better able to express her true feelings. A child may be told to pretend she is a parent talking to a friend about toys, food, or clothing. Thus the child does not feel pressure to directly express her opinions and feelings.

Role playing is particularly useful in investigating situations in which interpersonal relationships are the subject of the research, for example, salesperson–customer, husband–wife, or wholesaler–retailer relationships.

thematic apperception test (TAT)

A projective technique that presents a series of pictures to research subjects and asks them to provide a description of or a story about the pictures.

Thematic Apperception Test (TAT). A **thematic apperception test (TAT)** presents subjects with a series of pictures in which consumers and products are the center of attention. The investigator asks the subject to tell what is happening in the pictures and what the people might do next. Hence, themes (thematic) are elicited on the basis of the perceptual-interpretive (apperception) use of the pictures. The researcher then analyzes the contents of the stories that the subjects relate.

The picture or cartoon stimulus must be sufficiently interesting to encourage discussion but ambiguous enough not to disclose the nature of the research project. Clues should not be given to the character's positive or negative predisposition. A pretest of a TAT investigating why men might purchase chain saws used a picture of a man looking at a very large tree. The subjects of the research were homeowners and weekend woodcutters. When confronted with the picture of the imposing tree, they almost unanimously said that they would get professional help from a tree surgeon. Thus, early in the pretesting process the researchers found out that the picture was not sufficiently ambiguous for the subjects to identify with the man in the picture. If subjects are to project their own views into the situation, the environmental setting should be a well-defined, familiar problem, but the solution should be ambiguous.

Frequently a series of pictures with some continuity is presented so that stories may be constructed in a variety of settings. The first picture might portray two women discussing a product in a supermarket; in the second picture, a

---

Exhibit 6.4   Picture Frustration Version of TAT

Exhibit 6.5 **Excerpts from a Depth Interview**

An interviewer (I) talks with Marsha (M) about furniture purchases. Marsha indirectly indicates she delegates the buying responsibility to a trusted antique dealer. She has already said that she and her husband would write the dealer telling him the piece they wanted (e.g., bureau, table). The dealer would then locate a piece that he considered appropriate and would ship it to Marsha from his shop in another state.

M: ...We never actually shopped for furniture since we state what we want and (the antique dealer) picks it out and sends it to us. So we never have to go looking through stores and shops and things.

I: You depend on his (the antique dealer's) judgment?

M: Um, hum. And, uh, he happens to have the sort of taste that we like and he knows what our taste is and always finds something that we're happy with.

I: You'd rather do that than do the shopping?

M: Oh, much rather, because it saves so much time and it would be so confusing for me to go through stores and stores looking for things, looking for furniture. This is so easy that I just am very fortunate.

I: Do you feel that he's a better judge than...

M: Much better.

I: Than you are?

M: Yes, and that way I feel confident that what I have is, is very, very nice because he picked it out and I would be doubtful if I picked it out. I have confidence in him, (the antique dealer) knows everything about antiques, I think. If he tells me something, why I know it's true—no matter what I think. I know he is the one that's right.

This excerpt is most revealing of the way in which Marsha could increase her feeling of confidence by relying on the judgment of another person, particularly a person she trusted. Marsha tells us quite plainly that she would be doubtful (i.e., uncertain) about her own judgment, but she "knows" (i.e., is certain) that the antique dealer is a good judge, "no matter what I think." The dealer once sent a chair that, on first inspection, did not appeal to Marsha. She decided, however, that she must be wrong, and the dealer right, and grew to like the chair very much.

---

person might be preparing the product in the kitchen; the final picture might show the product being served at the dinner table.

Cartoon Tests. The **picture frustration** version of the TAT uses a cartoon drawing in which the respondent suggests a dialogue in which the characters might engage. Exhibit 6.4 is a purposely ambiguous illustration of an everyday occurrence. The two office workers are placed in a situation and the respondent is asked what the woman might be talking about. This setting could be used for discussions about products, packaging, the display of merchandise, store personnel, and so on.

> **picture frustration**
> *A version of the TAT uses a cartoon drawing in which the respondent suggests dialog in which the characters might engage.*

Depth Interviews

Motivational researchers who want to discover reasons for consumer behavior may use relatively unstructured, extensive interviews during the primary stages of the research process. The **depth interview** is similar to the client interview of a clinical psychologist or psychiatrist. The researcher asks many questions and probes for additional elaboration after the subject answers. Unlike projective techniques, the subject matter is generally undisguised. The interviewer's role is extremely important in the depth interview. He or she must be a highly skilled individual who can encourage the respondent to talk freely without influencing the direction of the

> **depth interview**
> *A relatively unstructured, extensive interview in which the interviewer asks many questions and probes for in-depth answers.*

conversion. Probing statements such as "Can you give me an example of that?" and "Why do you say that?" stimulate the respondent to elaborate on the topic. An excerpt from a depth interview is given in Exhibit 6.5

International marketing researchers find that in certain cultures depth interviews work far better than focus groups. They provide a quick means to assess buyer behavior in foreign lands.

The depth interview may last more than an hour and requires an extremely skilled interviewer; hence, it is expensive. In addition, the area for discussion is largely at the discretion of the interviewer, so the success of the research depends on the interviewer's skill—and, as is so often the case, good people are hard to find. A third major problem stems from the necessity of recording both surface reactions and subconscious motivations of the respondent. Analysis and interpretation of such data are highly subjective, and it is difficult to settle on a true interpretation.

An example of conflicting claims is illustrated by a study of prunes done by two organizations. One study used projective techniques to show that people considered prunes shriveled, tasteless, and unattractive; symbolic of old age and parental authority (thus disliked); and associated with hospitals, boarding houses, peculiar people, and the army. The other study stated that the principal reason why people did not like prunes was the fruit's laxative property.

Finally, alternative techniques, such as focus groups, can provide much of the same information as depth interviews.

A Warning About Exploratory Research

Exploratory research cannot take the place of conclusive, quantitative research. Nevertheless, a number of firms use what should be exploratory studies as the final, conclusive research project. This has led to incorrect decisions. The most important thing to remember about exploratory research techniques is that they have limitations. Most of them are qualitative, and interpretation of the findings typically is judgmental. For example, the findings from projective techniques can be vague. Projective techniques and depth interviews were frequently used in the 1950s by practitioners who categorized themselves as motivational researchers. They produced some interesting and occasionally bizarre hypotheses about what was inside the buyer's mind, such as:

> A woman is very serious when she bakes a cake because unconsciously she is going through the symbolic act of giving birth.

> A man buys a convertible as a substitute mistress.

> Men who wear suspenders are reacting to an unresolved castration complex.[18]

Unfortunately, bizarre hypotheses cannot be relegated to history as long past events. Several years ago researchers at the McCann-Erickson advertising agency interviewed low-income women about their attitudes toward insecticides. The women indicated that they strongly believed a new brand of roach killer sold in little plastic trays was far more effective and less messy than traditional bug sprays. Rather than purchase the new brand, however, they remained stubbornly loyal to their old bug sprays. Baffled by this finding, the researchers did extensive qualitative research with female consumers. They concluded from the women's drawings and in-depth descriptions of roaches that women subconsciously identified roaches with men who had abandoned them. Spraying the roaches and watching them squirm and die was enjoyable. The women thus gained control over the roaches and vented their hostility toward men.[19] Conclusions based on qualitative research may be subject to considerable interpreter bias.

Findings from focus group interviews likewise may be ambiguous. How is a facial expression or nod of the head interpreted? Have subjects fully grasped the idea or concept behind a nonexistent product? Have respondents overstated their interest because they tend to like all new products? Because of such problems in interpretation, exploratory findings should be considered preliminary.

Another problem with exploratory studies deals with the ability to make projections from the findings. Most exploratory techniques use small samples, which may not be representative because they have been selected on a probability basis. Case studies, for example, may have been selected because they represent extremely good or extremely bad examples of a situation rather than the average situation.

Before making a scientific decision the researcher should conduct a quantitative study with an adequate sample to ensure that measurement will be precise. This is not to say that exploratory research lacks value; it simply means that such research cannot deliver what it does not promise. *The major benefit of exploratory research is that it generates insights and clarifies the marketing problems for hypothesis testing in future research.* One cannot determine the most important attributes of a product until one has identified those attributes. Thus, exploratory research is extremely useful, but it should be used with caution.

However, occasions do arise where the research process should stop at the exploratory stage. If a cheese producer conducts a focus group interview to get a feel for consumers' reactions to a crispy snack food made from whey (what is left over from cheese making) and exploratory findings show an extremely negative reaction by almost all participants, the cheese manufacturer may no longer wish to continue the project.

Some researchers suggest that the greatest danger in using exploratory research to evaluate alternative advertising copy, new-product concepts, and so on is not that a poor idea will be marketed, because successive steps of research will prevent that. The real danger is that a good idea with promise may be rejected because of findings at the exploratory stage. On the other hand, when everything looks positive in the exploratory stage, the temptation is to market the product without further research. Instead, after conducting exploratory research, marketing management should determine whether the benefits of the additional information would be worth the cost of further research. In most cases when a major commitment of resources is at stake, conducting the quantitative study is well worth the effort. Many times good marketing research only documents the obvious. However, the purpose of business is to make a profit, and decision makers want to be confident that they have made the correct choice.

Summary

Qualitative research is subjective in nature. Much of the measurement depends on evaluation by the researcher rather than vigorous mathematical analysis. Quantitative research determines the quantity or extent of an outcome in numbers. It provides an exact approach to measurement.

This chapter focused on qualitative exploratory research. Exploratory research may be conducted to diagnose a situation, screen alternatives, or discover new ideas. It may take the form of gathering background information by investigating secondary data, conducting experience surveys, scrutinizing case studies, or utilizing pilot studies. The purpose of the research, rather than the technique, determines whether a study is exploratory, descriptive, or causal. Thus, the techniques discussed in this chapter are primarily but not exclusively used for exploratory studies.

The case study method involves intensive investigation into one particular situation that is similar to the problem under investigation.

Focus group interviews are unstructured, free-flowing, group dynamics sessions that allow individuals to initiate the topics of discussion. Interaction among respondents is synergistic and spontaneous, characteristics that have been found to be highly advantageous.

As the ability to communicate via the Internet, telecommunications and video-conferencing links improve, a number of companies begin to use the new media to conduct focus group research.

Projective techniques are an indirect means of questioning respondents. Some examples are word association tests, sentence completion tests, the third person technique, the role-playing technique, and thematic apperception tests.

Depth interviews are unstructured, extensive interviews that encourage a respondent to talk freely and in depth about an undisguised topic.

Although exploratory research has many advantages, it also has several shortcomings and should not take the place of conclusive, quantitative research.

Knowing where and how to use exploratory research is important. Many firms make the mistake of using exploratory studies as final, conclusive research projects. This could lead to decisions based on incorrect assumptions. Exploratory research techniques have limitations: The interpretation of the findings is based on judgment, samples are not representative, they rarely provide precise quantitative measurement, and the ability to generalize the quantitative results is limited.

Key Terms and Concepts

Exploratory research	Moderator	Role-playing technique
Concept testing	Discussion guide	Thematic apperception test (TAT)
Experience survey	Projective technique	Picture frustration
Case study method	Word association test	Depth interview
Pilot study	Sentence completion method	
Focus group interview	Third-person technique	

Questions for Review and Critical Thinking

1. Comment on the following remark by a marketing consultant: "Qualitative exploration is a tool of marketing research and a stimulant to thinking. In and by itself, however, it does not constitute market research."

2. What type of exploratory research would you suggest in the following situations?
   a. A product manager suggests development of a non-tobacco cigarette blended from wheat, cocoa, and citrus.
   b. A research project has the purpose of evaluating potential brand names for a new insecticide.
   c. A manager must determine the best site for a convenience store in an urban area.
   d. An advertiser wishes to identify the symbolism associated with cigar smoking.

3. A concept statement for a new frozen food product follows. Evaluate the adequacy of the concept statement.
   INTRODUCING CHICKEN MARINADE MEALS FROM CREATE-A-MEAL!
   Now you can quickly and easily make delicious, marinated chicken and serve the perfect side dish too, with new Chicken Marinade Meals from Create-A-Meal! It comes with both a highly flavored marinade for your chicken and a pasta/vegetable medley to complete the meal—a delicious traditional dinner has never been easier. Simply add your chicken to the special two-minute marinade and broil. Cook the combination of flavored pasta or potatoes and crisp, colorful Green Giant vegetables, and serve with the chicken for a delicious home-cooked meal.
   Varieties:
   • Roasted Garlic Herb with Pasta Primavera
   • Teriyaki with Oriental Pasta/Vegetable Medley

- Mesquite Chicken with Roasted Potatoes and Vegetables
- Lemon Pepper Chicken with White Cheddar Rotini and Broccoli
- Honey Mustard Chicken with Garden Herb Pasta and Vegetables
- Red Wine Chicken with Roasted Potateos and Vegetables

Found in your grocer's freezer case
Suggested Retail Price, $3.09
Servings: 4
Size: 21 oz. bag

4. What benefits can be gained from case studies? What dangers, if any, do they present? In what situations are they most useful?

5. What is the function of a focus group? What are its advantages and disadvantages?

6. If a researcher wanted to conduct a focus group with teenagers, what special considerations might be necessary?

7. A focus group moderator plans to administer a questionnaire before starting the group discussion about several new product concepts. Is this a good idea? Explain.

8. Discuss the advantages and disadvantages of the following focus group techniques:
   a. A videoconferencing system that allows marketers to conduct focus groups in two different locations with participants who interact with each other.
   b. A system that uses telephone conference calls to hold group sessions.

9. A packaged goods manufacturer receives many thousands of customer letters a year. Some are complaints. Some are compliments. They cover a broad range of topics. Are these letters a possible source for exploratory research? Why or why not?

10. How might exploratory research be used to screen various ideas for advertising copy in television commercials?

11. Most projective techniques attempt to assess a respondent's true feelings by asking indirect questions rather than using direct questions that could give the respondent a good idea about the researcher's true motives. Is this deception?

Exploring the Internet

1. How might the following organizations use a usernet bulletin board for exploratory research?
   a. zoo
   b. computer software manufacturer
   c. video game manufacturer

2. Connect with a special interest bulletin board such as one for college students. Conduct an electronic focus group exploring what factors are used as a criteria to choose destinations for spring break.

Case 6.1 Hamilton Power Tools Corporation (A)

On July 13, 1997, Mr. Campagna, the marketing manager for Hamilton Power Tools, was anxiously awaiting his meeting with the marketing research firm. He felt the findings from the marketing research would change Hamilton from a sales-oriented company to a firm that would adopt the consumer-oriented philosophy of the marketing concept.

For more than 45 years Hamilton Power Tools had been marketing industrial products by catering to the construction and industrial tool markets. Its construction product lines included power trowels, concrete vibrators, generators, and power-actuated tools. Its industrial products were primarily pneumatic tools: drills, screwdrivers, and so on. One of its products, the gasoline-powered chain saw, was somewhat different from traditional construction and industrial tools. The chain saw line had been added in 1949 when John Hamilton Sr. had the opportunity to acquire a small chain saw manufacturer. Hamilton believed that construction workers would have a need for gasoline-powered chain saws. He acquired the business to diversify the company into other markets.

During the 1990s the chain saw market was rapidly changing and Hamilton Power Tool executives began to realize they needed some expert marketing advice. Mr. Campagna felt that a major change in the company's direction was on the horizon. Campagna had been in the chain saw business for 15 years. Reports from trade publications, statistics from the Chain Saw Manufacturers' Association, and personal experience had led him to believe that the recent chain saw industry was composed of roughly the following markets: professionals (lumberjacks), farmers, institutions, and casual users (home or estate owners with may trees on their lots). The casual user segment was considered to be the future growth market. Campagna wished to ensure that Hamilton would not make any mistakes in marketing its product to this segment of weekend woodcutters who once or twice a year used a chain saw to cut firewood or prune trees in the backyard.

In March 1997 when chain saw sales began to slow down because of the seasonal nature of the business, Campagna and Ray Johnson, the chain saw sales manager, had a meeting with John Hamilton Sr. Although Hamilton believed they had been doing well enough in chain saw sales over the past decade, Campagna and Johnson were able to persuade the aging executive that some consumer research was necessary. After talking with several marketing research firms, Hamilton Power Tools hired Consumer Metrics of Chicago to perform two research projects. The first was a thematic apperception test (TAT).

The TAT research was completed the first week of July. Campagna arranged for a meeting with the marketing research firm the following week. As Dale Conway and Frank Baggins made their presentation of the results of the survey of chain saw users, Campagna thought back to the day Consumer Metrics had originally suggested the idea of a TAT to John Hamilton. Conway had sold him on the idea with his argument that motivational research was widely used in consumer studies to uncover people's buying motives. Conway had mentioned that Consumer Metrics had recently hired a young, bright MBA. This MBA—Baggins, as it turned out—had specialized in consumer psychology and marketing research at a major state university. Conway had thought that Baggins was one of the best-qualified people to work on this type of project. Since Hamilton Power Tools had had no experience in consumer research, Campagna had been eager to proceed with the in-depth TAT.

Conway told Campagna, Hamilton, and Johnson that in the TAT respondents are shown a series of pictures and are asked to tell their feelings concerning the people in the photographs. He told Campagna that although the present study was exploratory, it could be used to gain insights into the reasons people make certain purchases. He also suggested that the test would be a means for gaining the flavor of the language people use in talking about chain saws, and it could be a source of new ideas for copywriting.

Campagna remembered that at one time he had thought this project wouldn't be very worthwhile; however, he also realized he did not know that much about the consumer market. During the initial meeting with the research firm, it had been proposed that an exploratory research project be conducted within the states of Illinois and Wisconsin to obtain some indication of the attitudes of potential casual users toward chain saws. The researcher had suggested a TAT. Campagna had not known much about this type of research and needed time to think. After a week's deliberation, he called Conway and told the researchers to go ahead with the project. Case Exhibit 6.1-1 shows the TAT used by the researchers.

At the meeting, Conway and Baggins carefully presented the research results. They pointed out that in the TAT study several screening questions were asked at the beginning of the interview. The findings of this study were based on those respondents who either planned to purchase a chain saw in the next 12 months, already owned a chain saw, or had used a chain saw in the past. The presentation closely followed the written report submitted to Campagna. The findings were as follows:

The first photograph (Exhibit A of Case Exhibit 6.1-1) shown to the respondent pictured a man standing looking at a tree. The interviewer asked the respondent the following question.

I have a problem which you may find interesting. Here's a picture of a man who is thinking about the purchase of a chain saw. Suppose that such a man is your neighbor. What do you suppose he is thinking about?

After the respondent's initial answer, the following probing question was asked:

Now, if he came to you for advice and you really wanted to help him, what would you tell him to do? Why do you think this would be the best thing for him to do?

Initial responses seemed to center around what the man would do with the tree. Many respondents expressed an interest in the tree and were concerned with preservation. It seemed that pride in having a tree that beautified the owner's property was important to some respondents. Some of the typical responses given are as follows:

He's thinking about cutting the tree down.

Why cut a whole tree when you can save part of it?

He could trim out part of those trees and save some of them.

We lose trees due to disease and storm damage.

Trees beautify property and make it more valuable.

I don't like to destroy trees.

Considering the alternatives to buying a chain saw was the next step many of the respondents took. Basically the ultimate consumer sees the alternatives to the purchase of a chain saw as.

1. Using a hand saw
2. Hiring a tree surgeon
3. Renting or borrowing a chain saw

These alternatives were in the respondents' minds partly because they were concerned about the cost of doing the job. They seemed to be worried about the investment in a chain saw, about whether it paid to buy one for a small, single-application job. (Another reason for the alternatives came out in responses to a later picture.) Some quotations illustrating these points are as follows:

He's thinking how to go about it. He will use his hand saw.

He doesn't have to invest in a chain saw for only one tree.

He's thinking about how to get the tree down—the cost of doing it himself versus having someone else do it. Have him cut it down himself, it's not too big a tree. He'll save the cost.

He's thinking whether it pays for a couple of trees.

If it would be worth it. How much longer with an axe.

He's thinking whether he should do it himself or get someone else do it for him. Get someone who knows what he is doing.

He's thinking he'll rent a chain saw for a small area and would buy one for a large area.

The best way to get a job done. Chain saw is faster, but a hand saw is cheaper. Depends on how much work he has to do.

An interesting comment made by two respondents was "He's thinking about Dutch elm disease." The area had recently been hit by that disease. The respondents were projecting their situations into the TAT pictures.

Other statements were made concerning the ease and speed of using a chain saw. Some questions regarding the characteristic performance of a chain

---

Case Exhibit 6.1-1 **Hamilton TAT Study**

| **Exhibit A** | **Exhibit B** | **Exhibit C** | **Exhibit D** |

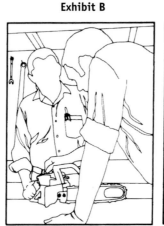  

---

saw were raised in response to this question; however, Exhibit B covered this area more adequately. This picture showed two men standing in a chain saw store looking at a chain saw. The question asked went as follows:

> *Here is a picture of the same man in a chain saw store. Suppose he's a friend of yours—your next-door neighbor, perhaps. Tell me what you think he will talk about with the chain saw clerk.*

The issue most frequently raised was how the chain saw worked. An equal number of respondents wanted to know first how much it cost. Weight (lightness) was the next most frequently raised issue. Horsepower was of concern among many of the respondents. Other subjects they thought the man would talk about with the clerk were maintenance and availability of repair, performance (what size tree the chain saw would cut), durability and expected life, safety (what safety features the chain saw had), and ease of starting the chain saw. In relation to price, comments were made such as:

> *Well, price is the most important, of course.*

> *He's wondering how he will pay for it.*

One respondent said, "He's not considering price; price means nothing in regard to safety." One individual was concerned whether the chain would come off the "blade" (respondents referred to the guide bar as a "blade" rather than a "guide bar").

Various other issues were raised by respondents. These are as follows:

> *Ease of handling*

> *Length of blade*
>
> *Which was the best brand?*
>
> *Whether it had direct drive*
>
> *Whether it had a gas protector*
>
> *Self-lubrication*
>
> *The warranty (guarantee)*
>
> *Ease of controls*
>
> *Specifications*
>
> *Availability of credit*
>
> *Possibility of mixing oil and gas*

The third picture (Exhibit C) showed a man cutting a felled tree with the chain saw. The question asked was as follows:

> *The man in the picture is the same man as in the last picture. He purchased the chain saw he was looking at. Knowing that he purchased the chain saw, what can you tell me about him? Can you tell me anything about the character and personality of this man?*

A follow-up question was:

> *What do you suppose this man is thinking about while he's using his chain saw?*

A common response was that the man was satisfied. Typical responses were: "He's pleased," "He's happy he bought the chain saw," "Lots of time saved," and "He's happy with the chain saw, he made the right decision." Many favorable overtones to using a chain saw were given, for example,

> *Sure beats bucking with an axe.*

He's thinking about speed of getting through, time saved.

How much easier it is to cut a tree down with a chain saw than a hand saw.

He seems to be saying "Why didn't I buy a chain saw sooner?"

Respondents in general seemed to think the man was using the chain saw for the first time.

Very prominent in many respondents' answers was the fear of using a chain saw—it seemed to be a major reason why people would not purchase one. Some typical comments were:

He's a little frightened. He doesn't know how to go about it, but he's willing to learn.

If he gets caught in that blade…

He's watching what he's doing—he could lose a limb.

He might be somewhat apprehensive about the use of it.

He looks scared of it.

He better think safety.

In general the test, as it is designed to do, made the respondents project their own personalities and backgrounds onto the character of the man. A wide variety of responses was given describing the man. He was described as a blue-collar worker, an office worker laboring after hours and on weekends, a somewhat wealthy man able to afford a chain saw, and a homeowner. A number of responses indicated that he was a do-it-yourselfer, a man who liked to "do his own thing." "Farmer" was another more than scattered response. Associations, with an outdoorsman, a man who liked to keep in shape, were also indicated. One quotation seems to sum it all up:

This seems to be his first job. He seems to be happy about it. He seems to think the chain saw will lighten his workload. He looks like he has not owned many power tools. He looks excited. He seems like he will be able to do a lot of cleanup work that he would not have been able to do without the chain saw. The chain saw is sure an improvement over the hand saw. It's faster, easier to use.

The fourth picture (Exhibit D) showed a man and woman seated before a fireplace. The question read,

Here's a picture of the same man (as) in the previous pictures, sitting and talking with a woman; what do you suppose they're talking about?

An analysis of the fourth picture in the projec-

tion test showed that respondents felt the man and woman in the picture were happy, content, cozy, and enjoying the fireplace. The man was "enjoying the fruits of his labor." It came out very strongly that a man who uses a chain saw is proud of himself after he cuts the wood; he thinks his cutting of wood with a chain saw is a job well done. Some typical comments concerning this were:

He's very happy to cut is own wood for his fireplace—real proud of himself.

He's telling her how much he saved by cutting it himself.

They're talking about the logs, how pleased he is with himself.

He's thinking about the beauty of the fire, fire logs he himself sawed from their property.

The people projecting onto the picture seemed to think that because the job was well done, purchasing a chain saw was worthwhile:

The man in the picture is saying, "The chain saw pays for itself. There's a $300 job, and you will be able to use the chain saw afterwards."

Work's done, and there's enough for winter, and he has trees for winters to come.

What a good buy that chain saw was. Cut wood costs, save money.

The woman in the picture was also very happy; she was satisfied and probably thinking about the future. But most of all she was very proud of her husband. This came out very strongly. For example,

The woman is looking to the enjoyment of the fireside and of the money saved because they cut their own wood. She might have questioned the investment before this, before sitting in front of the fireplace.

She is proud of her husband.

She is pleased the tree is down.

The woman is probably proud of the fireplace and starting the fire. He's probably thinking about the wood he sawed.

The man and woman are congratulating each other on finally getting around to buying a chain saw and cutting firewood.

She is complimenting him on his ability and on how handy it is to have a man around the house.

She is also thinking that possibly it was easier for her husband to use a chain saw.

The woman didn't care about the chain saw, but she was satisfied. The husband's concern over his wife's approval of this investment was also brought out by this picture—evidently men were worried that their wives would not see the value of a chain saw purchase. Also, there were implications that the man should be tired after using the chain saw—"and he had to work hard in the afternoon to get the logs for the fireplace."

After the presentation, Campagna was reasonably impressed. He asked Hamilton what his opinion was. Hamilton said, "This is all very interesting, but I don't see how it can lead to greater profits in our chain saw division.

QUESTIONS

1. How should Conway and Baggins respond to Hamilton's question?

2. Is Hamilton investigating the casual user market segment correctly?

3. What conclusions would you draw from the thematic apperception test? Do you feel this is a valid and reliable test?

4. What specific recommendations would you make to Campagna concerning the casual user chain saw market?

Case 6.2 Today's Man[20]

DAVID FELD, FOUNDER OF TODAY'S MAN, A $204 MILLION retailer based in Moorestown, New Jersey, guessed that many men equated buying clothes with going to the dentist, but he didn't know why. Feld paid for focus groups to uncover the truth, but he never met a focus group he trusted.

Finally, Feld's advertising agency recommended he talk to a company of professional hypnotists based in New York. Feld was skeptical, but he was desperate and curious enough to commission a study focused on why men feel uncomfortable in clothing stores. "The results really shook us up," Feld reports. The comments the men made under hypnosis had the ring of authenticity for which he had been searching.

Hypnotized men revealed that they often hated  the way their clothes fit but didn't know how to complain. "One guy told us that the last time he bought a suit, it didn't fit right—but he didn't say anything," Feld says. "He then told the hypnotist how insecure and dopey he felt when he wore that suit." Furthermore, some of the groggy men admitted to a sense of powerlessness—they felt ganged up on by both their wives and pushy salespeople. "We had never gotten that answer before," Feld says.

QUESTION

Evaluate the research methods used by Today's Man.

Video -Case 6.3 **Upjohn's Rogaine**[21]

THE UPJOHN COMPANY, BASED IN KALAMAZOO, MICHIGAN, manufactures and markets pharmaceuticals and health-related products. With over 19,000 employees and distribution in over 30 countries, from Australia to Zaire, its annual sales top $1 billion. Upjohn is constantly developing and marketing new products. One recent example is Rogaine.

Originally developed as an antihypertension drug, Rogaine was shown in clinical tests to encourage moderate hair growth on some balding male volunteers. Thereafter, Upjohn quickly applied to the U.S. Food & Drug Administration (FDA) for the right to market the drug as a hair-growth product in the United States.

QUESTIONS

1. Define Rogaine's marketing problem from a marketing research perspective.
2. What type of exploratory marketing research should Rogaine conduct?

Video-Case 6.4 **Trading Cards Focus Group**

A MANUFACTURER OF BASEBALL CARDS, FOOTBALL CARDS, and other sport and novelty cards had never conducted business research with its customers. The president of the company decided that they needed to learn more about their customers. He instructed his business research department to conduct a focus group with some boys in the fourth grade.

QUESTIONS

1. Outline what you would like to learn in the focus group.
2. What particular problems might be involved when conducting a focus group with children?

Chapter 7

Secondary Data Research in a Digital Age

T HE TYPICAL GOLFER IS NO LONGER THE WHITE MALE COUNTRY club member with above-average household income and a penchant for knickers.[1] In recent years golf equipment manufacturers using secondary data to track trends have recognized that changes in the demographics of their customer base have begun to affect marketing strategy in the $6.4 billion equipment and apparel retail markets. Fastest growth among golfers' ranks: juniors (ages 12 to 17), younger adults (ages 18 to 29), women, and those in lower income brackets (with household income less than $30,000).

The National Golf Foundation claims that 26.5 million Americans played golf in 1997, which was up 7 percent from 1996. Nearly one in five of those are avid golfers who play more than 25 rounds per year. More than one in five golfers is between 18 and 29 years old, and their numbers grew by 10 percent in 1997. But the largest percentage increase of any age group was among juniors, an increase of 34 percent in 1997, according to the NGF.

The Zandi Group, a New York City-based research company that tracks the habits of young consumers, reports that golf's stock is rising among the twenty-something set. In a recent survey, the 20-to-29-year-olds ranked golf first, ahead of such trendy sports as mountain biking, snowboarding and major league soccer. Zandi attributes golf's dramatic gains in popularity to the success of Tiger Woods and male and female twenty-somethings who've been tearing up the pro tours. Women are also starting to make an impact on the links. While the total number of men playing golf rose 6 percent in 1997, the number of women grew 10 percent. And in the last ten years, the number of women who have taken up the sport grew 23.9 percent, to 5.7 million. Today, women

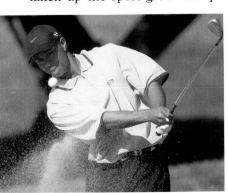

spend about $3 billion a year on equipment, apparel and greens fees, which accounts for about 20 percent of total golf expenditures.

Once considered a sport for the elite, golf has been growing in popularity among people in lower-income households. The NGF says

What you will learn in this chapter

To discuss the advantages and disadvantages of secondary data.

To give typical examples of secondary data analysis conducted by marketing managers.

To understand the nature of model building with secondary data.

To discuss the various internal and proprietary sources of secondary data and give examples.

To discuss the channels of distribution for external sources of secondary data.

To identify various external sources of secondary data and give examples.

the number of golfers who live in households with incomes under $30,000 rose 16 percent in 1997. Meanwhile, their wealthier compatriots, those whose incomes are between $30,000 and $50,000, declined in number by 5 percent, and those in the $50,000 to $75,000 bracket dropped by 7 percent. Golf's upper crust has seen a noticeable surge, however.

The number of golfers with incomes over $75,000 rose 32 percent in 1997. Whether it's Tiger Woods or some other force that's boosting the sport's popularity, equipment and apparel sales are on the up and up. Total golf equipment sales rose nearly 10 percent, to an estimated $3.92 billion in 1997, according to the National Sporting Goods Association. Apparel and shoe sales rose 2.7 percent to an estimated $1.89 billion in 1997.

Even as young duffers flock in droves to the golf course, matures and seniors still make up about 25 percent of total golfers. The average age of avid male golfers is 50 years old, and among avid female golfers, the average age is even higher—55.4 years old. The number of golfers over age 50 is expected to explode in the coming years, as maturing "baby boomers" continue to seek healthful, active interests that put less wear and tear on the body.

The shift in demographics is already affecting product development. Club makers are developing lighter-weight clubs for seniors, for example, as well as specialty woods, which can replace long irons and are easier to use.

Most of the manufacturers spend the majority of their ad dollars in television and magazines, according to Competitive Media Reporting. Taylor Made golf clubs spent an estimated $17.3 million on advertising in 1997, the largest amount for any one product. Callaway golf clubs ranked second at $16.5 million, and Cobra golf clubs were third at $12.2 million. Among golf ball manufacturers, Titleist spent $12.2 million to advertise its line. Fourteen of the top 20 golf advertisers spent the majority of their advertising on television versus print, but twelve of the top 20 spent at least 40 percent of their ad budgets on magazines, according to CMR data.

These facts about the golf market illustrate the richness and value of secondary data. They also illustrate that analysis and interpretation are important activities, because secondary data may not be extensive enough to answer all of the researcher's questions.

This chapter discusses how to conduct research with secondary data in a digital age. It examines many of the diverse sources for secondary data. It also includes two appendices: Selected Sources for Secondary Data Retrieving with Computers.

Secondary Data Research Advantages

secondary data
Data that have been previously collected for a project other than the one at hand

Secondary data are gathered and recorded by someone else prior to (and for purposes other than) the current project. Secondary data usually are historical and already assembled. They require no access to respondents or subjects.

Advantages

The primary advantage of secondary data comes from availability. Obtaining them is almost always faster and less expensive than acquiring primary data. This is particularly true when electronic retrieval is used to access digitally stored data. In many situations, collecting secondary data is instantaneous.

Consider the money and time saved by researchers who obtained updated population estimates for a town during the interim between the 1990 and 2000 censuses. Instead of doing the fieldwork themselves, researchers could acquire estimates from a firm dealing in demographic information or from sources such as *Sales and Marketing Management's Survey of Buying Power*. Many of the activities normally associated with primary data collection (for example, sampling and data processing) are eliminated.

In some instances data cannot be obtained using primary data collection procedures. For example, a manufacturer of farm implements could not duplicate the information in the *Census of Agriculture* because much of the information there (for example, taxes paid) might not be accessible to a private firm.

TO THE POINT

If I have seen farther than others, it is because I have stood on the shoulders of giants.

ISAAC NEWTON

Disadvantages

An inherent disadvantage of secondary data is that they were not designed specifically to meet the researchers' needs. Thus, researchers must ask how pertinent the data are to their particular project. To evaluate secondary data, researchers should ask questions such as these:

- Is the subject matter consistent with our problem definition?
- Do the data apply to the population of interest?
- Do the data apply to the time period of interest?
- Do the secondary data appear in the correct units of measurement?
- Do the data cover the subject of interest in adequate detail?

Consider the following typical situations:

- A researcher interested in forklift trucks finds that the secondary data on the subject are included in a broader, less pertinent category encompassing all industrial trucks and tractors. Furthermore, the data were collected five years earlier.
- An investigator who wishes to study individuals earning more than $100,000 per year finds the top category in a secondary study reported at $75,000 or more per year.
- A brewery that wishes to compare its per-barrel advertising expenditures with those of competitors finds that the units of measurement differ because some report point-of-purchase expenditures with advertising whereas others do not.
- Data from a previous warranty card study show where consumers prefer to purchase the product but provide no reasons.

Each of these situations shows that, even when secondary information is available, it can be inadequate. The most common reasons why secondary data do not adequately satisfy research needs are (1) outdated information, (2) variation in definition of terms, (3) different units of measurement, and (4) lack of information to verify the data's accuracy.

Information quickly becomes outdated in our rapidly changing environment. Because the purpose of most studies is to predict the future, secondary data must be timely to be useful.

Every primary researcher has the right to define the terms or concepts under investigation to satisfy the purpose of his or her primary investigation. This is little solace, however, to the investigator of the African American market who finds secondary data reported as "—percent nonwhite." Variances in terms or variable classifications should be scrutinized to determine if differences are important. The populations of interest must be described in comparable terms. Researchers frequently encounter secondary data that report on a population of interest that is similar but not directly comparable to their population of interest. For example, Arbitron reports its television audience estimates by geographical areas known as ADI (Areas of Dominant Influence). An ADI is a geographic area consisting of all counties in which the home market commercial television stations receive a preponderance of total viewing hours. This unique population of interest is used exclusively to report television audiences. The geographic areas used in the census of population, such as Metropolitan Statistical Areas, are not comparable to ADIs.

Units of measurement may cause problems if they do not conform exactly to a researcher's needs. For example, lumber shipments in millions of board-feet is quite different from billions of ton-miles of lumber shipped on freight cars. Head-of-household income is not the same unit of measure as total family income. Often the objective of the original primary study may dictate that the data are summarized, rounded, or reported such that, although the original units of measurement were comparable, aggregated or adjusted units of measurement are not suitable in the secondary study.

When secondary data are reported in a format that does not exactly meet the researcher's needs, data conversion may be necessary. **Data conversion** (also called data transformation) is the process of changing the original form of the data to a format suitable to achieve the research objective. For example, sales for food products may be reported in pounds, cases, or dollars. An estimate of dollars per pound may be used to convert dollar volume data to pounds or another suitable format.

Another disadvantage of secondary data is that the user has no control over their accuracy. Although timely and pertinent secondary data may fit the researcher's requirements, the data could be inaccurate. Research conducted by other persons may be biased to support the vested interest of the source. For example, media often publish data from surveys to identify the characteristics of their subscribers or viewers, but they will most likely exclude derogatory data from their reports. If the possibility of bias exists, the secondary data should not be used.

Investigators are naturally more prone to accept data from reliable sources such as the U.S. government. Nevertheless, the researcher must assess the reputation of the organization that gathers the data and critically assess the research design to determine whether the research was correctly implemented. Unfortunately, such evaluation may not be possible if the manager lacks information that explains how the original research was conducted.

Researchers should verify the accuracy of the data whenever possible. **Cross-checks** of data from multiple sources—that is, comparison of the data from one source with data from another—should be made to determine the similarity of independent projects. When the data are not consistent, researchers should

data conversion
The process of changing the original form of the data to a format suitable to achieve the research objective. Also called data transformation.

cross-checks
The comparison of the data from one source with data from another source to determine the similarity of independent projects.

Exhibit 7.1   Evaluating Secondary Data

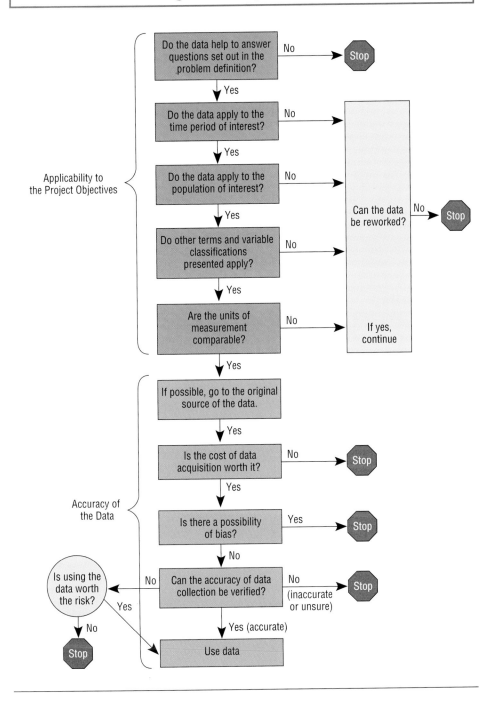

attempt to identify reasons for the differences or to determine which data are most likely to be correct. If the accuracy of the data cannot be established, the researcher must determine whether using the data is worth the risk. Exhibit 7.1 illustrates a series of questions that should be asked to evaluate secondary data before use.[2]

Typical Objectives for Secondary Data Research Designs

It would be impossible to identify all possible purposes of marketing research using secondary data. However, it is useful to illustrate some common marketing problems that can be addressed with secondary research designs. Exhibit 7.2 shows three general categories of research objectives: fact-finding, model building, and database marketing.

Fact-Finding

The simplest form of secondary data research is fact-finding. A marketer of frozen food might be interested in knowing how often frozen pizza is consumed in the United States. Secondary data available from National Eating Trends, a service of the NPD group, Inc., shows U.S. households serve frozen pizza an average of 11 times per year, most often for dinner (59 percent, followed by lunch (32 percent). And Nielsen Marketing Research data indicate that the deluxe/combination is the best-selling type of frozen pizza in the country, at 34 percent. Next is pepperoni, at 25 percent; and cheese, at 21 percent; followed by sausage, beef/hamburger, and Canadian bacon. According to the Nielsen data, frozen pizza tastes tend to be regional. More than half the frozen pizzas sold in the New York area are plain cheese. In Dallas, frozen pepperoni pizza outsells frozen sausage pizza three to one, whereas in Chicago, sausage is twice as popular as pepperoni. Canadian bacon has its largest share in Minneapolis.[3] These simple facts would interest a researcher who was investigating the frozen foods market. Fact-finding can serve more complex purposes as well.

Exhibit 7.2 Common Research Objectives for Secondary Data Studies

Broad Objective	Specific Research Example
Fact-finding	Identifying consumption patterns Tracking trends
Model building	Estimating market potential Forecasting sales Selecting trade areas and sites
Database marketing	Enhancement of customer databases Development of prospect lists

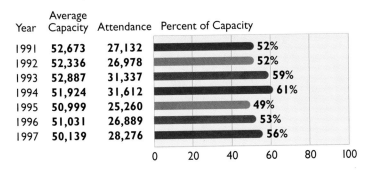

	Average		Major League Baseball attendance/capacity						
Year	Capacity	Attendance	Percent of Capacity						
1991	**52,673**	**27,132**					52%		
1992	**52,336**	**26,978**					52%		
1993	**52,887**	**31,337**					59%		
1994	**51,924**	**31,612**					61%		
1995	**50,999**	**25,260**					49%		
1996	**51,031**	**26,889**					53%		
1997	**50,139**	**28,276**					56%		

Exhibit 7.3   Major League Baseball Attendance/Capacity

Identify Consumer Behavior for a Product Category.

A typical objective for a secondary research study might be to uncover all available information about consumption patterns for a particular product category or to identify demographic trends that affect an industry. For example, this chapter began with a description of the golf market in the United States. This example illustrates the wealth of factual information about consumption and behavior patterns that can be obtained by carefully collecting and analyzing secondary data.

Trend Analysis.

Marketers watch for trends in the marketplace and the environment. **Market tracking** refers to the observation and analysis of trends in industry volume and brand share over time. Scanner research services and other organizations provide facts about sales volume to support this work.

Almost every large consumer goods company routinely investigates brand and product category sales volume using secondary data. This type of analysis typically involves comparisons with competitors or the company's own sales in comparable time periods. It also involves industry comparisons among different geographic areas. Exhibit 7.3 shows trends in attendance at major league baseball games and how they relate to stadium capacity.

Environmental Scanning.

In many instances, the purpose of fact-finding is simply to study the environment to identify trends. **Environmental scanning** entails information gathering and fact-finding designed to detect indications of environmental changes in their initial stages of development. As mentioned in Chapter 2, the Internet can be used for environmental scanning; however, there are other less recurrent means such as periodic review of contemporary publications and reports. For example, in the late-1990s environmental scanning for information about members of the millennium generation (also called Generation Y)[6] showed them to be enthusiastic about activities that their parents or grandparents enjoyed during their leisure time, especially if the older Generation-X cohort sneered at it. In particular, it showed that today's teens find certain activities appealing, such as bowling and swing dancing. As a result of scanning the environment, Brunswick began promoting Cosmic Bowling, a darkened bowling alley lit only by glow-in-the-dark alleys, pins, balls, and flashing laser lights.[4]

market tracking
The observation and analysis of trends in industry volume and brand share over time.

environmental scanning
Information gathering and fact-finding that is designed to detect indications of environmental changes in their initial stages of development.

The director of MIT's Media Lab, Nicholas Negroponte, thinks of a smart agent "as a computerized English butler. An agent builds a model of you, which can be likened to the process of human-to-human acquaintanceship. The longer you know somebody, the better you can guess what they mean (versus say), what they want (versus ask for) and what they do (versus say they do). So, too, with agents.

One type of agent looks at millions of bits go zooming past and tries to pick out the ones that are of interest to you. Like catching fly balls.

Another type of agent works in the network. They go searching and sifting through stacks of libraries, reading daily newspapers, and joining electronic chat groups, to find answers to specific questions or topics that may interest you.[6]

push technology
A term referring to an Internet information technology that automatically delivers content to the researcher's or manager's desktop.

A number of on-line information services, such as Dow-Jones News Retrieval, allow for routine collection of news stories about industries, product lines, and other topics of interest that have been specified by the researcher. As we mentioned in Chapter 2, **push technology** is an Internet information technology that automatically delivers content to the researcher's or manager's desktop.[7] Push technology uses "electronic smart agents" to find information without the researcher having to do the searching. The smart agent, which is a custom software program, filters, sorts, prioritizes, and stores information for later viewing.[8] This frees the researcher from doing the searching. The true value of push technology is that the researcher who is scanning the environment can customize the nature of the news and information he or she wants, have it PC delivered quickly, and view it at leisure.

Model Building

model building
Involves using secondary data to help specify relationships among two or more variables. Model building can involve the development of descriptive or predictive equations.

The second general objective for secondary research, model building, is more complicated than simple fact finding. **Model building** involves specifying relationships between two or more variables, perhaps extending to the development of descriptive or predictive equations. Models need not include complicated mathematics, though. In fact, decision makers often prefer simple models that everyone can readily understand over complex models that are difficult to comprehend. For example, market share is company sales divided by industry sales. Although some may not think of this simple calculation as a model, it represents a mathematical model of a basic relationship.

Exhibit 7.4 Market Potential for Crackers in Europe

COUNTRY	(1) POPULATIONS PROJECTION FOR 2005 (THOUSANDS)	(2) ANNUAL PER CAPITA CRACKER CONSUMPTION (U.S. $)	(3) MARKET ESTIMATE POTENTIAL ($000)
United States	58,408	9.48	553,708
Germany	82,399	1.91	157,382
Italy	56,264	4.33	243,623
France	59,612	3.56	212,219
Spain	39,225	0.62	24,320

Model building will be illustrated by discussing three common objectives that can be satisfied with secondary research: estimating market potential, forecasting sales, and selecting sites.

Estimating Market Potential for Geographic Areas. Marketers often estimate market potential using secondary data. In many cases exact figures may be published by a trade association or another source. However, when the desired information is unavailable, the researcher may estimate market potential by transforming secondary data from two or more sources. For example, managers may find secondary data about market potential for a country or other large geographic area, but this information may not be broken down into smaller geographical areas, such as by metropolitan area, or in terms unique to the company, such as sales territory. In this type of situation, researchers often need to make projections for the geographic area of interest.

An extended example will help explain how secondary data can be used to calculate market potential. A marketer of crackers is contemplating building a processing plant in Europe. Managers wish to estimate market potential for the United Kingdom, Germany, Spain, Italy, and France. Secondary research uncovered data for per capita cracker consumption and population projections for the year 2005. The data for the United States and the five European countries, appear in Exhibit 7.4. (The per capita cracker consumption were obtained from A. C. Nielsen Company.[9] The population estimates are based on information from the *CIA Factbook* database.)

To calculate market potential for Italy in the year 2005, multiply that country's population in the year 2000 by its per capita cracker consumption:

$$56,264 \times 4.33 = 243,623$$

In Italy the market potential for crackers is $243,623 thousand or $243,623,000. As seen in Exhibit 7.4, although Germany's population is much higher, it has a much lower market potential.

Of course, the calculated market potential for each country in Exhibit 7.4 is a simple estimate. The marketer might recognize that dollar sales volume will be influenced by each country's inflation rate and other variables. Past inflation rates, also found in secondary data sources, could be added to the calculation to improve the estimate.

WHAT WENT WRONG?

California School Enrollment

IN THE EARLY 1980S, CALIFORNIA USED A STANDARD demographic projection method, based on birth and death rates, to predict a decline in the number of children statewide.[10] Forecasts made in 1980 showed that the California population had fairly stabilized. Schools closed around the state.

Eighteen years later, the opening of new classrooms throughout California became a regular occurrence. Planners in the state's education department did not foresee the huge wave of immigration from Asia and Latin America that began in the mid-1980s. They did not consider that the immigrants included many young women from countries with high fertility rates, or that female baby boomers would delay childbearing until later in life. Forecasters drew a straight line and predicted that everything would stem from the way things were in the past and the present. It was the equivalent of saying if General Motors is now the largest corporation, it will always remain the largest corporation.

Forecasting Sales. Marketing managers need information about the future.[10] They need to know what company sales will be next year and in future time periods. Sales forecasting is the process of predicting sales totals over a specific time period.

Accurate sales forecasts, especially for products in mature, stable markets, frequently come from secondary data research that identifies trends and extrapolates past performance into the future. Marketing researchers often use internal company sales records to project sales. A rudimentary model would multiply past sales volume by an expected growth rate. A researcher might investigate a secondary source and find that industry sales are expected to grow by 10 percent; multiplying company sales volume by 10 percent would give a basic sales forecast.

Exhibit 7.5 illustrates trend projection using a moving average projection of growth rates. Average daily room rates (prices) in hotels located in the United States are secondary data from Coopers and Lybrand Lodging Research (www.lodgingrearch.com).[12] The moving average sums growth rates for the latest three years and divides by 3 (number of years) to forecast the increase in room rates.

Using the three-year average growth rate for the 1996, 1997, and 1998 sales periods of 6.0 percent, the forecast for 1999 is calculated as $78.47 \times $78.47 \ 0.06 = $83.19.

Moving average forecasting best suits a static competitive environment. More dynamic situations make other sales forecasting techniques more appropriate.

Statistical trend analysis using secondary data can be much more advanced than in our preceding simple example. Many statistical techniques build forecasting models using secondary data. This chapter emphasizes secondary data research rather than statistical analysis. Chapter 23, "Bivariate Statistical Analysis: Measures of Association," and Chapter 24, "Multivariate Statistical Analysis," explain more sophisticated statistical model building techniques for forecasting sales.

site analysis techniques
Involves use of secondary data to select the best location for retail or wholesale operations.

Analysis of Trade Areas and Sites

Marketing managers examine trade areas and use **site analysis techniques** to select the best locations for retail or wholesale operations. Secondary data research helps managers make this site selection decisions. Some organizations, especially

---

Exhibit 7.5   Sales Forecast Using Secondary Data and the Moving Average Method

YEAR (DECLINE)	AVERAGE DAILY HOTEL ROOM RATE ($)	RATE OF GROWTH (DECLINE) FROM PREVIOUS YEAR	THREE-YEAR MOVING AVERAGE RATE RATE OF GROWTH (DECLINE)
1990	$58.01	–	–
1991	58.14	+0.2	–
1992	58.96	+1.4	–
1993	60.54	+2.7	1.4
1994	62.90	+3.9	2.7
1995	65.89	+4.8	3.8
1996	70.00	+6.2	5.0
1997	74.29	+6.1	5.7
1998	78.47	+5.6	6.0

Forecast for 1999: $78.47 \times $78.47 0.06 = $83.19

---

franchisers, have developed special computer software based on analytical models to select sites for retail outlets. The researcher must obtain the appropriate secondary data for analysis with the computer software.

The **index of retail saturation** offers one way to investigate retail sites and to describe the relationship between retail demand and supply.[11] It is easy to calculate once the appropriate secondary data are obtained:

index of retail saturation
A calculation that describes the relationship between retail demand and supply.

$$\text{Index of retail saturation} = \frac{\text{Local market potential (demand)}}{\text{Local market retailing space}}$$

Exhibit 7.6 shows the relevant secondary data for shoe store sales in a five-mile ring surrounding a Florida shopping center. These types of data can be purchased from vendors of market information such as Urban Decision Systems.

First, local market potential (demand) is estimated by multiplying population times annual per capita shoe sales. The index of retail saturation is:

Index of retail saturation = $14,249,000/41 = 152

Exhibit 7.6   Secondary Data for the Calculation of an Index of Retail Saturation[12]

1. Population	261,785
2. Annual per capita shoe sales	$54.43
3. Local market potential (line 1 line 2)	$14,249,000
4. Square feet of retail space used to sell shoes	94,000 sq. ft.
5. Index of retail saturation (line 3/line 4)	152

This index figure can be compared with those of other areas to determine which sites have the greatest market potential with the least amount of retail competition. An index value above 200 is considered to indicate exceptional opportunities.

Database Marketing

database marketing
The practice of maintaining customer databases with customers' names, addresses, phone numbers, past purchases, responses to past promotional offers, and other relevant data such as demographic and financial data.

As we have already mentioned, a database is a collection of data arranged in a logical manner and organized in a form that can be stored and processed by a computer. **Database marketing** is the practice of maintaining customer databases with customers' names, addresses, phone numbers, past purchases, responses to past promotional offers, and other relevant data such as demographic and financial data. It also means organizations use their databases to develop one-to-one relationships and highly targeted promotional efforts with their individual customers. For example, a fruit catalog company maintains a database of previous customers including what purchases they made during the Christmas holidays. The following year the company sends last year's gift list to customers to help them send the same gifts to their friends and relatives.[13]

Because database marketing requires vast amounts of data compiled from numerous sources, much secondary data are acquired with the exclusive purpose of developing or enhancing a customer database. The transaction record, which often provides the item purchased, its value, customer name, address, and zip code, is the building block for many databases. This may be supplemented with data customers provide directly, such as data on a warranty card, and by secondary data purchased from third parties. For example, credit services may sell databases about applications for loans, credit card payment history, and other financial data. Several other companies, such as Donnelley (Cluster Plus) and Claritas (PRIZM), collect primary data and then sell demographic data that can be related to small geographic areas such as zip code. (It should be remembered that when the vendor collects the data, they are primary data, but when the database marketer incorporates the data into his or her database, they are secondary data.)

Now that some of the purposes of secondary data analysis have been addressed, it is appropriate to discuss sources of secondary data.

Sources of Secondary Data

Chapter 2 classified secondary data as either internal to the organization or external. Modern information technology makes this seem somewhat simplistic. Some accounting documents are indisputably internal records of the organization. Researchers in another organization cannot have access to them. Clearly, a book published by the federal government and located at the public library is external to the company. However, in today's world of electronic data interchange the data that appear in a book published by the federal government may also be purchased from an on-line information vendor for instantaneous access and subsequently stored in a company's decision support system.

internal and proprietary data
Secondary data that originate inside the organization.

Internal data should be defined as data that originated in the organization, or data created, recorded, or generated by the organization. **Internal and proprietary data** is perhaps a more descriptive term.

Internal and Proprietary Data Sources

Most organizations routinely gather, record, and store internal data to help them solve future problems. The accounting system can usually provide a wealth of in-

WHAT WENT RIGHT?

Insight from Microsoft[16]

ONE OF THE FIRST WAYS MICROSOFT BEGAN USING information tools internally was by phasing out printed computer reports. In many companies, when you go into a top executive's office you see books of bound computer printouts with monthly financial numbers, dutifully filed away on a shelf. At Microsoft, those numbers are made available only on a computer screen. When someone wants more detail, he or she can examine it by time pe-riod, locale, or almost any other way. When we first put the financial reporting system on-line, people started looking at the numbers in new ways. For example, they began analyzing why our market share in one geographic area as different from our share somewhere else. As we all started working with the information, we discovered er-rors. Our data-processing group apologized. "We're very sorry about these mistakes," they said, "but we've been compiling and distributing these numbers once a month for five years and these same problems were there all along and no one mentioned them." People hadn't really been using the print information enough to discover the mistakes.

formation. Routine documents such as sales invoices allow external financial re-porting, which in turn can be a source of data for further analysis. If the data are properly coded into a modular database in the accounting system, the researcher may be able to conduct more detailed analysis using the decision support system. Sales information can be broken down by account or by product and region; in-formation related to orders received, back orders, and unfilled orders can be identified; sales can be forecast on the basis of past data.

Researchers frequently aggregate or disaggregate internal data. Other useful sources of internal data include salespeoples' call reports, customer complaints, service records, warranty card returns, and other records. For example, a com-puter service firm used internal secondary data to analyze sales over the previous three years, categorizing business by industry, product, purchase level, and so on. The company discovered that 60 percent of its customers represented only 2 percent of its business and that nearly all of these customers came through tele-phone directory advertising. This simple investigation of internal records showed that, in effect, the firm was paying to attract customers it did not want.

Data Mining

Large corporations' decision support systems often contain millions or even hun-dreds of millions of records of data. These complex data volumes are too large to be understood by managers. Consider, for example, a credit card company col-lecting data on customer purchases. Each customer might make on average of ten transactions in a month, or 120 per year. With 3 million customers and five years of data, it's easy to see how record counts quickly grow beyond the comfort zone for most humans.[14]

Two points need to be made about data volume. First, relevant marketing data are often in independent and unrelated files. Second, the number of distinct pieces of information each data record might contain is often large. When the number of distinct pieces of information contained in each data record and data

Information including entire Web sites complete with images and links on a company computer, can be gathered according to the researcher's specifications and delivered by e-mail or continuously through an Internet connection. For example, BackWeb (http://www.backweb.com) empowers companies to adapt quickly to changing market conditions through direct interaction with their employees, partners, and customers. BackWeb's Internet software allows businesses to efficiently gather, target and deliver sizable digital data of any format—audio, video, software files, html, and others—to user desktops across their extended enterprise. Users browse the information on their PC whenever time is available.

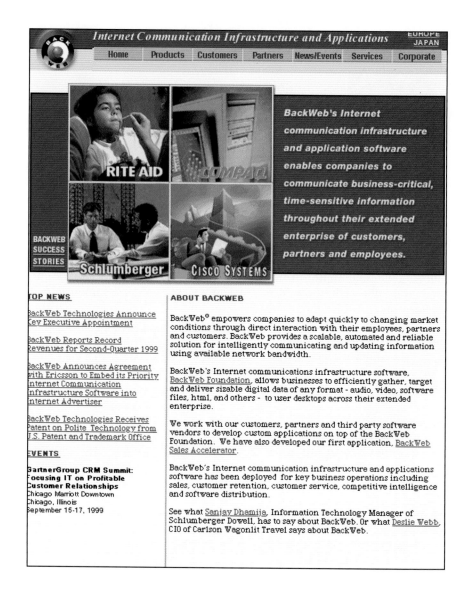

data mining
The use of massively parallel computers to dig through volumes of data to discover patterns about an organization's customers and products. It is a broad term that applies to many different forms of analysis

neural networks
A form of artificial intelligence in which a computer is programmed to mimic the way that human brains process information.

volume grow too large, end users don't have the capacity to make sense of it all. Data mining helps understand the underlying meaning of the data.

The term **data mining** refers to the use of powerful computers to dig through volumes of data to discover patterns about an organization's customers and products. It is a broad term that applies to many different forms of analysis. For example, **neural networks** are a data-mining form of artificial intelligence in which a computer is programmed to mimic the way that human brains process information. One computer expert put it this way:

A neural network learns pretty much the way a human being does. Suppose you say "big" and show a child an elephant, and then you say "small" and show her a poodle. You repeat this process with a house and a giraffe as examples of "big" and then a grain of sand and an ant as examples of "small." Pretty soon she will figure it out and tell you that a truck is "big" and a needle is "small." Neural networks can similarly generalize by looking at examples.[15]

Wal-Mart uses data mining. Wal-Mart's information system, with more than 7 terabytes of data, houses data on point of sale, inventory, products in transit, market statistics, customer demographics, finance, product returns, and supplier performance. The data are mined to develop "personality traits" for each of Wal-

Mart's 3,000 or so outlets, which Wal-Mart managers use to determine product mix and presentation for each store. Wal-Mart's data-mining software looks at individual items for individual stores to decide the seasonal sales profile of each item. The data-mining system keeps a year's worth of data on the sales of 100,000 products and predicts which items will be needed in each store.[16]

Market basket analysis is a form of data mining that analyzes anonymous point-of-sale transaction databases to identify coinciding purchases or relationships between products purchased and other retail shopping information.[17] Consider this example about patterns in customer purchases. Grocery chains that have mined their databases provided by checkout scanners have found that when men go to a supermarket to buy diapers in the evening between 6:00 P.M. and 8:00 P.M., they sometimes walk out with a six-pack of beer as well. Knowing this behavioral pattern, it's possible for a supermarket chain to lay out its stores so that these items are closer together.[18]

Revisiting the example of a credit card company with large volumes of data allows us to illustrate a *customer discovery* data-mining application. The credit card company will probably track information about each customer: age, gender, number of children, job status, income level, past credit history, and so on. Very often the data about these factors will be mined to find the patterns that make a particular individual a good or bad credit risk.[19]

When the identify of the customer who makes repeated purchases from the same organization is known, an analysis can be made of sequences of purchases. *Sequence discovery,* the use of data mining to detect sequence patterns, is a popular application among direct marketers, such as catalog retailers. A catalog merchant has information for each customer, revealing the sets of products that the customer buys in every purchase order. A sequence discovery function can then be used to discover the set of purchases that frequently precedes the purchase of a microwave oven. As another example, sequence discovery used on a set of insurance claims could lead to the identification of frequently occurring medical procedures performed on patients, which in turn could be used to detect cases of medical fraud.

Data mining requires sophisticated computer resources and it is expensive. That's why companies like DataMind, IBM, Oracle, Information Builders, and Acxiom Corporation offer data-mining services. Customers send the databases they want analyzed and let the data-mining company do the "number crunching."

External Data: The Distribution System

external data
Data created, recorded, or generated by an entity other than the researcher's organization.

External data are created, recorded, or generated by an entity other than the researcher's organization. The government, newspapers and journals, trade associ-

This advertisement's copy says "To our data mining system, they're twins. Because both order milk with their hamburgers." It illustrates an example of market basket analysis.[20]

WHAT WENT RIGHT?

Marriott Vacation Club International

OVER THE PAST THREE YEARS MARRIOTT VACATION Club International, the nation's largest seller of vacation time-share condos, has slashed the amount of junk mail it has to send out to get a response. How? With a computer, a database, and some help from Acxiom Corporation, which specializes in data processing of secondary for marketers.

What Marriott is doing is called data mining. This is the science of combing through digitized customer files to detect patterns. Marriott starts with names, mostly of hotel guests. Digging into a trove of motor vehicle records, property records, warranty cards, and lists of people who have bought by mail, Acxiom enriches the prospect list. It adds such facts as the customers' ages, estimated incomes, what cars they drive, and if they golf. Then Marriott uses complex computer programs (neural networks) to figure out who is most likely to respond to a mailed flyer.

Using these clues, Marriott is able to cast its net a little more narrowly and catch more fish. Data mining has increased the response rate to Marriott's direct-mail, time-share pitches to certain hotel guests from 0.75 percent to 1 percent. That seems like a slim gain, but it makes a big difference to a company that sent out 3 million glossy solicitations at a cost of up to $1.50 each last year.

ations, and other organizations create or produce information. Traditionally this information has been in published form, perhaps available from a public library, trade association, or government agency. Today, however, computerized data archives and electronic data interchange make external data as accessible as internal data. Exhibit 7.7 illustrates some traditional ways of distributing information and some modern ways of distributing information.

Information as a Product and Its Distribution Channels.

Because secondary data have value, they can be bought and sold in the same way as other products. Just as bottles of perfume or plumbers' wrenches may be distributed in many ways, secondary data also flow through various channels of distribution.[21] Many users, such as the Fortune 500 corporations, purchase documents and computerized census data directly from the government. However, many small companies get census data from a library or another intermediary or vendor of secondary information.

Libraries.

Traditionally libraries' vast storehouses of information have served as a bridge between users and producers of secondary data. The library staff deals directly with the creators of information, such as the federal government, and intermediate distributors of information, such as abstracting and indexing services. The user needs only to locate the appropriate secondary data on the library shelves. Libraries provide collections of books, journals, newspapers, and so on for reading and reference. They also stock many bibliographies, abstracts, guides, directories, and indexes, as well as offering access to basic databases.

The word *library* typically connotes a public or university facility. However, many major corporations and government agencies also have libraries. A corporate librarian's advice on sources of industry information or the United Nations librarian's help in finding statistics about international markets can be invaluable.

Exhibit 7.7 Information as a Product and Its Distribution Channels

Traditional Distribution of Secondary Data

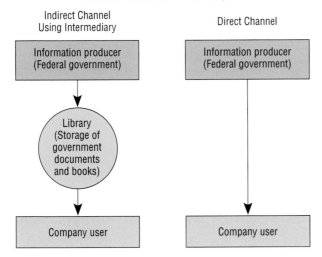

Modern Distribution of Secondary Data

Indirect Computerized Distribution Using an Intermediary

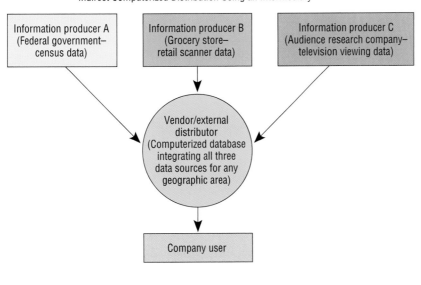

Direct, Computerized Distribution

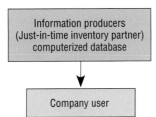

Exhibit 7.8   **Popular Internet Addresses**

NAME	DESCRIPTION	WEB ADDRESS
Yahoo	Portal that serves as a gateway to all kinds of places on the Web.	http://www.yahoo.com
CEOexpress	The 80/20 rule applied to the Internet. A series of links designed by a busy executive for busy executives.	http://www.ceoexpress.com
The New York Public Library Home Page	Library resources and links available on-line.	http://www.nypl.org
Census Bureau	Demographic information from the U.S. Census Bureau.	http://www.census.gov
Statistical Abstract	Highlights from the primary reference book for government statistics.	http://census.gov/stat_abstract
STAT-USA/Internet	A comprehensive source of U.S. government information that focuses on economic, financial, and trade data.	http://www.stat-usa.gov/inqsample.html
Advertising Age	*Advertising Age* magazine provides marketing media, advertising, and public relations content.	http://www.adage.com
Inc. Online	*Inc.* magazine's resources for growing a small business.	http://www.inc.com
Wall Street Journal Interactive	Provides a continually updated view of business news around the world.	http://www.wsj.com
CNN Financial News	Provides business news, information on managing a business, information on managing money, and other business data.	http://www.cnnfn.com
NAICS—North American Industry Classification System	Describes the new classification system that will replace the old SIC system.	http://www.census.gov/epcd/www/naics.html
MapQuest	Allows users to enter an address and zip code and see a map on desktop.	http://www.mapquest.com
Business Europe	Provides links to obtain information about European countries.	http://businesseurope.com

The Internet.   The Internet is, of course, a new source of distribution of much secondary data. Its creation has added an international dimension to the acquisition of secondary data.[22] For example, http://www.libraryspot.com provides links to libraries on-line, including law libraries, medical libraries, and music libraries. Its reference desk feature links to calendars, dictionaries, encyclopedias, maps, and other sources typically found at a traditional library's reference desk.

In Chapter 2 we discussed how to access and use the Internet. At this point, it is useful, however, to point to Exhibit 7.8, which shows some of the more common Internet addresses where secondary data may be found.

Vendors. The information age offers many channels besides libraries through which to access data. Many external producers make secondary data valuable directly from the organizations that produce the data or through intermediaries, which are often called *vendors*. In recent years the growth of on-line vendor services has allowed managers to access external databases via desktop computers with telecommunications capabilities. Vendors, such as the Dow Jones News Retrieval Service, now allow managers to access thousands of external databases via desktop computers and telecommunications systems. Hoovers (www.hoovers.com), specializes in providing information about thousands of companies' financial situations and operations.

Producers. Classifying external secondary data by the nature of the producer of information yields five basic sources: books and periodicals, government sources, media sources, trade association sources, and commercial sources. The following section discusses each type of secondary data source.

Books and Periodicals. Books and periodicals found in a library often are considered the quintessential secondary data source. A researcher who finds books on a topic of interest obviously is off to a good start.

Professional journals, such as the *Journal of Marketing, Journal of Marketing Research, Journal of the Academy of Marketing Science, Marketing Research: A Magazine of Management and Application,* and *The Public Opinion Quarterly,* as well as commercial business periodicals such as *The Wall Street Journal, Fortune,* and *Business Week,* contain much useful material. *Sales and Marketing Management's Survey of Buying Power* is a particularly useful source for information about markets. To locate data in periodicals, indexing services such as the *ABI/INFORM and Business Periodicals Index* and *The Wall Street Journal Index* are very useful. Guides to data sources also are helpful. For example, *American Statistical Index and Business Information Sources* is a very valuable source. See Appendix 7A to this chapter for a description of these and other reference guides.

TO THE POINT

The man who does not read good books has no advantage over the man who cannot read them.

MARK TWAIN

Government Sources. Government agencies produce data prolifically. Most of the data published by the federal government can be counted on for accuracy and quality of investigation. Most students are familiar with the U.S. *Census of Population,* which provides a wealth of data.

The *Census of Population* is only one of many resources that the government provides. Banks and savings and loans rely heavily on the *Federal Reserve Bulletin* and the *Economic Report of the President* for data relating to research on financial and economic conditions. Builders and contractors use the information in the *Current Housing Report and Annual Housing Survey* for their research. The *Statistical Abstract of the United States* is an extremely valuable source of information about the social, political, and economic organizations of the United States. It abstracts data available in hundreds of other government publications and serves as a convenient reference to more specific statistical data. Appendix 7A at the end of the chapter provides an annotated list of some of these important government documents. Visit the home page for this book (http://www.dryden.com/mktng/zikmund) for links to many of these important documents.

The federal government is a leader in making secondary data available on the Internet. STAT-USA/Internet is an authoritative and comprehensive source of U.S. government information that focuses on economic, financial, and trade data. It contains:

- More than 18,000 market research reports on individual countries an markets compiled by foreign experts at U.S. embassies.

- Economic data series, current and historical, such as gross domestic product, balance of payment, and merchandise trade.

- Standard reference works, such as the *Economic Report of the President,* the *Budget of the United States Federal Government,* and the *World Fact Book.*

- Worldwide listings of businesses interested in buying U.S. products.

STAT-USA/Internet World Wide Web server address is http//www.stat.usa.gov/inqsamle.html. However, only subscribers who pay a fee have access to this service.

State, county, and local government agencies can also be useful sources of information. Many state governments publish state economic models and forecasts, and many cities have metropolitan planning agencies that provide data about the population, economy, transportation system, and so on. These are similar to the federal government data but are more current and structured to suit local needs.

Many cities and states publish information on the Internet. Many search engines have directory entries that allow easy navigation to a particular state. A researcher using Yahoo, for example, needs only to click "regional information" to find numerous paths to information about states. Yahoo address on the World Wide Web is http://www.yahoo.com.

Media Sources.

Information on a broad range of subjects is available from broadcast and print media. *CNNfn* and *Business Week* are valuable sources for information on the economy and many industries. Information about special-interest topics may also be available. For example, *Money* magazine commissioned a research study about all aspects of Americans' financial affairs, and the report of this survey is available free to potential advertisers. Data about the readers of magazines and the audiences for broadcast media typically are profiled in media kits and advertisement.

American Woodworker magazine reports there are nearly 19.6 million woodworkers: 17.2 million of these are amateurs, whereas 2.4 million are professionals. *American Woodworker* also provides the demographic characteristics of woodworking households: 84 percent are male, 78 percent are married, the average age is 45, and the average household income is $48,000.[23]

Data such as these are plentiful because the media like to show that their vehicles are viewed or heard by advertisers' target markets. These types of data should be given careful evaluation, however, because often they cover only limited aspects of a topic. Nevertheless, they can be quite valuable for research, and they are generally free of charge.

Trade Association Sources.

Trade associations, such as the Food Marketing Institute or the American Petroleum Institute, serve the information needs of a particular industry. The trade association collects data on a number of topics of specific interest to firms, especially market size and market trends. Association members have a source of information that is particularly germane to their industry questions. For example, the Newspaper Advertising Bureau (NAB) has catalogued and listed in its computer the specialized sections that are currently popular in newspapers. The NAB has surveyed all daily, Sunday, and weekend newspapers in the United States and Canada on their editorial content and has stored this information, along with data on rates, circulation, and mechanical requirements, in its computer for advertisers' use.

Commercial Sources. Numerous firms specialize in selling and/or publishing information. For example, the R. L. Polk Company publishes information on the automotive field, such as average car values and new-car purchase rates by zip code. Many of these organizations offer information in published formats and as on-line or CD-ROM databases. The following discussion of several of these firms provides a sampling of the diverse data that are available.

Market Share Data. A number of syndicated services supply either wholesale or retail sales volume data based on product movement. A. C. Nielsen Company, the world's largest marketing research service, performs a wide range of marketing research activities.

Although it is best known for its television rating operations, its National Scan Track and Nielsen Retail Index Service combine to offer a major market tracking service. Scanner data and in-store audits measure consumer response at the point of sale. Using a carefully selected sample of stores, Nielsen Retail Index Service tracks volume at the retail level in nonscanner stores. Nielsen auditors visit the stores at regular intervals to track sales to customers, retail inventories, brand distribution, out-of-stock conditions, prices, and the like for competing brands as well as the client's own brand.

Information Resources, Inc. surveys a national sample of supermarkets with optical scanning checkouts for its INFOSCAN, a syndicated service that provides on-line or weekly data about product item movement and brand share as well as other aggregate product sales information. Organizations such as this allow researchers to monitor sales data before, during, and after changes in advertising frequency, price, distribution of free samples, and similar marketing tactics. Many primary data investigations use scanner data to measure the results of experimental manipulations such as altering advertising copy. Chapter 12 provides additional detail about data from scanning systems combined with consumer panels and electronic test markets.

Systems based on UPC bar code technology have been implemented in factories, warehouses, and transportation companies to research inventory levels, shipments, and the like.

Demographic and Census Updates. A number of firms, such as CACI/Instant Demographics and Urban Decision Systems, offer computerized U.S. census files and updates of these data by small geographic areas, such as zip codes (see Exhibit 7.9). Impact Resources provides in-depth information on minority customers and other market segments through its MART Consumer Intelligence System.

Consumer Attitude and Public Opinion Research. Many research firms offer specialized syndicated services that report findings from attitude research and opinion polls. For example, Yankelovich provides custom research—tailored for specific projects—and several syndicated services. Its public opinion research studies, such as the voter and public attitude surveys that appear in *Time,* are a source of secondary data. One of the more interesting of these services is the *Yankelovich Monitor,* a cost-shared annual census of changing social values and how they can affect consumer marketing. The *Monitor* charts the

---

Exhibit 7.9 Many Firms Specialize in Computerized Census and Demographic Data

---

growth and spread of new social values, the types of customers who support the new values and those who continue to support traditional values, and the ways in which people's values affect purchasing behavior.

Louis Harris Company is another public opinion research firm that provides syndicated and custom research for business. One of its services is its ABC News/Harris survey. This survey is released three times per week and monitors the pulse of the American public on topics such as inflation, unemployment, energy, attitudes toward the president, elections, and so on.

Consumption and Purchase Behavior Data. The National CREST Report (Consumer Report on Eating Share Trends) is a syndicated source of data about the types of meals people eat and how people consume food. The data, called diary panel data, are based on records of meals and diaries kept by a group of households that have agreed to record their consumption behavior over an extended period of time.

National Family Opinion (NFO), Marketing Research Corporation of America (MRCA), and many other syndicated sources sell diary panel data about consumption and purchase behavior. Since the advent of scanner data, purchase panels are more commonly used to record purchases of apparel, hardware, home furnishings, jewelry, and other durable goods than of nondurable consumer packaged goods.

**Exhibit 7.10 Starch Readership Service Measures the
Impact of Advertising**

Advertising Research. Readership and audience data are supplied by a number of firms. W. R. Simmons and Associates measures magazine audiences; Arbitron measures radio audiences; the Nielsen Television Index measures television audiences. By specializing in collecting and selling audience information on a continuing basis, these commercial sources provide a valuable service to their subscribers.

Assistance in measuring advertising effectiveness is another syndicated service. For example, Starch INRA Hooper measures the impact of advertising in magazines. Readership information, such as that illustrated in Exhibit 7.10, is obtained for competitors' ads or the client's own ads. Respondents are classified as noted readers, associated readers, or read-most readers.

Burke Marketing Research provides a service that measures the extent to which respondents recall television commercials aired the night before. It provides product category norms, or average DAR (day-after recall) scores, and DAR scores for other products.

An individual advertiser would be unable to monitor every minute of every television program before deciding on the appropriate ones in which to place advertising. However, the Nielson Television Index service is sold to numerous clients, agencies, television networks, and advertisers at relatively inexpensive rates.

Exhibit 7.11   Examples of Single-Source Databases

National Decision Systems http://www.natdecsys.com	Integrates geodemographic data with many syndicated databases to provide data about product purchase behavior, media usage, demographic characteristics, lifestyle variables, and business activity by many geographical breakdowns.
PRIZM by Claritas Corporation http://www.claritas.com	PRIZM, which stands for Potential Rating Index for Zip Markets, is based on the birds-of-a-feather assumption that people live near others who are like themselves. PRIZM combines census data, consumer surveys about shopping and lifestyle, and purchase data to identify market segments. Colorful names such as Young Suburbia and Shot Guns and Pickups describe 40 segments that can be identified by ZIP Code. Claritas also has a lifestyle census in the United Kingdom (www.claritas.co.uk).
MRI Cable Report—Mediamark Research Inc. http://www.mediamark.com	Integrates information on cable television viewing, including pay cable channels (HBO, Disney Channel, etc.), with demographic and product usage information.

Single-Source, Data-Integrated Information

A. C. Nielsen Company offers data from both its television meters and scanner operations. The integration of these two types of data helps marketers investigate the impact of television advertising on retail sales. In other ways as well users of data find merging two or more diverse types of data into a single database to offer many advantages.

National Decision Systems, PRIZM by Claritas Corporation, ClusterPlus by SMI, Mediamark Research Inc., and many other syndicated databases report product purchase behavior, media usage, demographic characteristics, lifestyle variables, and business activity by geographic area such as zip code. Although data are often called geodemographic, they cover such a broad range of phenomena that no one name is a good description.

These data use small geographic areas such as zip codes as the unit of analysis. Thus, although the average income of a zip code is given, it does not necessarily reflect the income of every individual in that zip code.

The marketing research industry uses the term *single-source data* for diverse types of data offered by a single company. Exhibit 7.11 identifies several major marketers of single-source data.

single-source data
Diverse types of data offered by a single company. The data are usually integrated by a common variable such as geographic area or store.

Sources for Global Research

As business has become more global, so has the secondary data industry. The Japan Management Association Research Institute (JMAR), Japan's largest provider of secondary research data to government and industry, recently opened an office in San Diego. JMAR's goal is to help U.S. firms access its enormous store of data about Japan to develop and plan their business there. The office at San Diego will translate and act as an intermediary between Japanese researchers and U.S. clients.

Secondary data compiled outside the United States have the same limitations as domestic secondary data. However, international researchers should watch for certain pitfalls that frequently are associated with foreign data and cross-cultural research. First, data may simply be unavailable in certain countries. Second, the accuracy of some data may be called into question. This is especially likely with official statistics that may be adjusted for the political purposes of foreign governments. Finally, although economic terminology may be standardized, various countries use different definitions and accounting and recording practices for many economic concepts. For example, different countries may measure disposable personal income in radically different ways. International researchers should take extra care to investigate the comparability of data among countries.

The U.S. government and other organizations compile databases that may aid international marketers. For example, the *Arthur Andersen European Community Sourcebook* is a comprehensive reference guide that provides information about suppliers, sources of funding, laws and regulations, and detailed profiles of each European Union member state. Arthur Andersen also publishes a *European Review* newsletter that reports on current activity in the European Union. The appendix to this chapter lists many secondary data sources, including some that offer information about countries around the world.

The U.S. federal government offers a wealth of data about foreign countries. *The CIA Fact Book* and the *National Trade Data Bank* are especially useful. Both can be accessed using the Internet. This section describes the National Trade Data Bank (NTDB), the U.S. government's most comprehensive source of world trade data, to illustrate what is available.

The National Trade Data Bank was established by the Omnibus Trade and Competitiveness Act of 1988.[24] Its purpose was to provide ". . . reasonable public access, including electronic access . . ." to an export promotion data system that was centralized, inexpensive, and easy to use.

The U.S. Department of Commerce has the responsibility for operating and maintaining the NTDB, and works with federal agencies that collect and distribute trade information to keep the NTDB up-to-date. The NTDB has been published monthly on CD-ROM since 1990. Over 1,000 public and university libraries offer public access to the NTDB through the Federal Depository Library system.

The National Trade Data Bank consists of 133 separate trade- and business-related programs (databases). By using it, small- and medium-sized companies get immediate access to information that until now only Fortune 500 companies could afford.

Topics on the NTDB include export opportunities by industry, country, and product; foreign companies or importers looking for specific products; how-to market guides; demographic, political, and socioeconomic conditions in hundreds of countries; and much more. NTDB offers one-stop shopping for trade information from more than 20 federal sources. You no longer need to know which federal agency produces the information: All you need to know is NTDB.

Some of the specific information that can be obtained from the NTDB are shown in Exhibit 7.12.

Exhibit 7.12 **Examples of Information Contained in the NTDB**

Agricultural commodity production and trade
Basic export information
Calendars of trade fairs and exhibitions
Capital markets and export financing
Country reports on economic and social policies and trade practices
Energy production, supply, and inventories
Exchange rates
Export licensing information
Guides to doing business in foreign countries
International trade terms directory
How-to guides
International trade regulations/agreements
International trade agreements
Labor, employment and productivity
Maritime and shipping information
Market research reports
Overseas contacts
Overseas and domestic industry information
Price indexes
Small business information
State exports
State trade contacts
Trade opportunities
U.S. export regulations
U.S. import and export statistics by country and commodity
U.S. international transactions
World Fact Book
World minerals production

Summary

Secondary data are data that have been gathered and recorded previously by someone else for purposes other than those of the current researcher. Secondary data usually are historical, are already assembled, and do not require access to respondents or subjects. Primary data are data gathered for the specific purpose of the current researcher.

The chief advantage of secondary data is that they are almost always less expensive to obtain than primary data. Generally they can be obtained rapidly and may include information not otherwise available to the researcher. The disadvantage of secondary data is that they were intended specifically to meet the researcher's needs. The researcher must examine secondary data for accuracy, bias, and soundness. One way to do this is to cross-check various available sources.

Secondary research designs address many common marketing problems. There are three general categories of secondary research objectives: fact-finding, model building, and database marketing. A typical fact-finding study might seek to uncover all available information about consumption patterns for a particular product category or to identify business trends that affect an industry. Model building is more complicated; it involves specifying relationships between two or more variables. Model building need not involve a complicated mathematical process, but it can help marketers to estimate market potential, forecast sales, select sites, and accomplish many other objectives. The practice of database marketing, which involves maintaining customer databases with customers' names, addresses, phone numbers, past purchases, responses to past promotional offers, and other relevant data such as demographic and financial data, is increasingly being supported by marketing research efforts.

Managers often get data from internal proprietary sources such as accounting records. On the other hand, external data are created, recorded, or generated by another entity. The government, newspapers and journals, trade associations, and other organizations create or produce information. Traditionally this information has been distributed in published form, either directly from producer to researcher, or indirectly through intermediaries such as public libraries.

Modern computerized data archives; electronic data interchange; and the Internet have changed the distribution of external data, making them almost as accessible as internal data. *Push technology* is a term referring to an Internet information technology that automatically delivers content to the researcher's or manager's desktop. This helps in environmental scanning.

Data mining is use of massively parallel computers to dig through volumes of data to discover patterns about an organization's customers and products. It is a broad term that applies to many different forms of analysis.

The marketing of multiple types of related data by single-source suppliers has radically changed the nature of secondary data research.

As business has become more global, so has the secondary data industry. International researchers should watch for certain pitfalls that can be associated with foreign data and cross-cultural research.

Key Terms and Concepts

Secondary data	Push technology	Site analysis techniques
Data conversion	Data mining	Index of retail saturation
Cross-checks	Neural networks	Internal and proprietary data
Environmental scanning	Market tracking	External data
Database marketing	Model building	Single-source data

Questions for Review and Critical Thinking

1. Secondary data have been called the first line of attack for marketing researchers. Discuss this description.
2. Suppose you wish to learn about the size of the soft-drink market, particularly root beer sales, growth patterns, and market shares. Indicate probable sources for these secondary data.
3. Over the past five years, a manager has noted a steady growth in sales and profits for her division's product line. Does she need to use any secondary data to further evaluate her division's condition?
4. Identify some typical research objectives for secondary data studies.
5. How might a retailer, such as Victoria's Secret, use data mining?
6. If you went to the library, what would be the best source for the following data?
   a. State population, state income, and state employment for Illinois and Indiana
   b. Maps of U.S. counties and cities
   c. Trends on automobile ownership
   d. Divorce trends in the United States
   e. Median weekly earnings of full-time, salaried workers for the previous five years
   f. Annual sales of the top ten fast-food companies
   g. Brands of beer recently introduced in the United States
   h. Attendance at professional sports contests

7. Suppose you are a marketing research consultant. A client comes to your office and says, "Within the next 24 hours, I must have the latest information on the supply and demand of Maine potatoes." What would you do?

8. Find the following data in the *Survey of Current Business* for May 1998:

   a. U.S. gross domestic product for the first quarter of 1998

   b. Fixed investment for residential structures for the first quarter of 1998

   c. Exports of goods and services for the first quarter of 1998

9. Use the most recent *Sales and Marketing Management Survey of Buying Power* to find the total population, median age, and total retail sales for (a) your home town (county) and (b) the town (county) in which your school is located.

10. A newspaper reporter reads a study that surveyed children. The reporter writes that a high percentage of children recognize Joe Camel, cigarette spokescartoon, but fails to report that the study also found that a much higher percentage of children indicated very negative attitudes toward smoking. Is this a proper use of secondary data?

Exploring the Internet

1. The home page for BRINT Research Initiative: Business Research, Management Research & Information Technology Research is http://www.brint.com/. It contains links to hundreds of information base Web sites. Visit this site and report what interesting sources you can go to.

2. PopClocks estimate the U.S. and world populations. Go to the Census Bureau home page, navigate to the population section, and then find today's estimate of the U.S. and world populations.

3. Use a Web browser to visit the Small Business Administration's home page at http://www.sbaonline.sba.gov. What type of information can be accessed?

4. Use the Internet to learn what you can about Indonesia.

   a. Use your Web browser to go to http://www.asiadragons.com/indonesia

   b. Use Yahoo to visit the *CIA Fact Book*.

   c. Go to Infoseek or Open Text Index and use Indonesia as a search word. How much information is available?

5. FIND/SVP is a company that provides information about many different industries. Go to the FIND/SVP home page at http://www.findsvp.com. Select an industry. What industry information is available?

6. Go to Statistics Norway at http://www.ssb.no/. What data, if any, can you obtain in English?

   a. What languages can be used to search this Web site?

   b. What databases might be of interest to the business researcher?

7. Go to Statistics Canada at http://www.statcan.ca

   a. What languages can be used to search this Web site?

   b. What databases might be of interest to the business researcher?

8. Use the Internet to see if you can find information to answer the following questions:

   a. What is today's weather like in Denver?

   b. Is there information about Brazil and its population demographics?

   c. How do you get a passport?

9. Martindale's Health Science Guide; Martindale's "The Reference Desk" & Martindale's Graduate & Undergraduate Center are hosted by the University of California, Irvine Libraries http://www.lib.uci.edu/. Martindale's "The Reference Desk" http://www sci.lib.uci.edu/HSG/Ref.html provides hyperlinks to a vast amount of information. The CALCULATORS ON-LINE CENTER site http://www.sci.lib.uci.edu/HSG/RefCalculators.html and the Part IIA: Statistics http://www-sci.lib.uci.edu/HSG/RefCalculators.html site are extremely valuable for researchers interested in statistical methods. Visit the site and report what you find.

10. The University of Michigan library's Statistical Resources on the Web (http://www.lib.umich.edu/libhome/Documents.center/stats.html) provides links to secondary data for Agriculture, Business and Industry, Demographics, Economics, Education, Energy, Environment, Finance, Foreign Government Data Sources and many other subjects. Visit the site and report what you find.

Case 7.1 Porter and Gentry Advertising, Inc.

PORTER AND GENTRY, INC. IS A MEDIUM-SIZED ADVERTISING agency known for its creative marketing planning. A client, Joseph S. Yarbrough Brewing Company, has been extremely pleased with its long-standing relationship with the agency.

One Friday during a business lunch with the client at which the client's product was conscientiously consumed by the agency's principals, Porter, the agency's president, suggested to Yarbrough that the brewery was not advertising to a major market segment. Porter explained that the Asian American market was the fastest-growing minority market in the country and was projected to become a major market segment by 2010. He indicated that there were more than 3 million Asian-Americans in California alone.

The client seemed more interested in performing quality control on his product than in what Porter was saying. The agency president wisely allowed the conversation to drift for a while.

Later, Gentry again brought up the subject of the Asian American market. Yarbrough said, "Right now,

I've got other priorities. And to be quite honest with you, I think that most Asian-Americans are mainstream. They watch network TV. They read the same stuff as the average working person. But I'll tell you something: If you can come up with some hard data to show me that this market really deserves serious consideration, I'll give it a try."

QUESTIONS

1. What secondary sources might Porter and Gentry use to determine the exact size of the Asian American market?

2. What characteristics are peculiar to the Asian American market? List and discuss some of these characteristics.

3. Prepare a research presentation for Yarbrough.

Case 7.2 Middlemist Precision Tool Company (A)

DENNIS MIDDLEMIST WAS A WEEKEND DO-IT-YOUR-selfer. A hobby he particularly enjoyed was custom building furniture for his own home. After many years of frustrations with trial-and-error adjustment of his radial arm saw using a T-square and trial cuts, Middlemist decided that he needed to invent an alignment device.

Before long, Middlemist had designed a solution. A custom prototype was built at a local engineering job shop. When Middlemist tested the device, it seemed to work perfectly for his needs. The proud inventor sought out an attorney to patent the device, and it looked as if a patent would be available. At this point, Middlemist started to dream about the possibility of the Middlemist Precision Tool Company and the vast empire he would leave to his children. In reality, however, he knew little about marketing and wondered what market information he would need, such as what the market potential would be, before getting serious about manufacturing the device. He

thought the best place to start would be to determine the number of radial arm saws in the United States and the number of prospective customers for his invention.

QUESTIONS

1. If you were a research consultant called in to help Dennis Middlemist define his marketing problem, what information do you think would be most important to him?

2. Middlemist has decided to see what information about the radial arm saw market can be found in secondary data sources. Go to your library and find what you can about radial arm saws and/or any related information that might be of value to Middlemist.

Selected Sources for Secondary Data

Major Indexes

ABI/INFORM database. Accessible on CD-ROM as *ABI/INFORM* Ondisc. A much-used database abstracting significant articles by subject that are published in more than 900 business and management journals.

Applied Science & Technology Index (New York: H. W. Wilson Company; monthly except July, with periodic cumulations). Accessible online as *WILSONLINE* and on CD-ROM as *WILSONDISC.* Indexes more them 300 journals in applied sciences such as geology and oceanography; technological fields such as petroleum and gas, physics, and plastics; and engineering disciplines, including telecommunications and environmental engineering.

Business Periodicals Index (New York: H. W. Wilson Company; monthly except July, with periodic cumulations). Accessible online as *WILSONLINE* and on CD-ROM as *WILSONDISC.* This is a much-used index of more than 300 U.S. and a foreign business/management periodicals, including both scholarly and popular journals. At the end of each issue is an index of business book reviews appearing in the periodicals covered.

PAIS International in Print (New York: Public Affairs Information Service; monthly with periodic cumulations). Accessible online as *PAIS International Online* and on CD-ROM as PAIS on CD-ROM. A subject index to public policy literature. Business topics covered emphasize economic factors, industry surveys, and business-societal interactions rather than details of business operations. Besides selectively indexing articles written in English and in five other languages, it covers some books, government publications, and pamphlets.

Reader's Guide to Periodical Literature (New York: H. W. Wilson Company; published partly monthly and partly semimonthly, with periodic cumulations). Accessible online as *WILSONLINE* and on CD-ROM as *WILSONDISC.* Indexes nearly 200 general-interest U.S. and Canadian magazines by subject and author. Does not cover business, academic, or other scholarly magazines and, thus, is of greater interest to general audiences.

The Wall Street Journal Index (Ann Arbor, MI: University Microfilms International; monthly with annual cumulations). Indexes, articles, and news in *The Wall Street Journal*'s eastern edition by subject and by company. Articles from the *Journal* can be found on-line in full text by using the database *Dow Jones News/Retrieval.*

Reference Guides

American Statistics Index (Bethesda, MD: Congressional Information Service; monthly in two parts, with annual cumulations). Accessible on-line and on CD-ROM as *Statistical Masterfile*. CIS publishes three companion guides that describe in detail published statistics from a wide variety of sources. This one indexes and abstracts the statistical publications of the federal government, congressional committees, and other federal programs. The tables are indexed by detailed subject and category, commodity or industry, geographic area, title, and report number.

The companion guides are *Statistical Reference Index* (described later) and *Index to International Statistics* (described in last section). Yet another monthly index/abstract is *CIS Index,* which is used to identify, evaluate, and obtain information contained in the working papers of the U.S. Congress. It covers hearings, prints, documents, reports, and special publications.

Business Information Sources, by Lorna M. Daniells, 3rd ed. (Berkeley, CA: University of California Press, 1993). An annotated bibliography of books, periodicals, and reference sources in all important areas of business. Of its 21 chapters, three focus on business/economic statistical sources, one on investment sources and one on marketing (including marketing research, product development, selling, advertising, retailing, and service industries).

Encyclopedia of Business Information Sources (Detroit: Gale Research, Inc.; biennial with interim supplement). Identifies sources of information on approximately 1,000 business subjects or industries. For each topic, it lists pertinent abstracts and indexes, bibliographies, directories, on-line databases, periodicals, statistical sources, trade and other organizations.

Encyclopedia of Geographic Information Sources: U.S. Volume, 4th ed. (Detroit: Gale Research, Inc., 1987.) Lists useful information sources for over 300 U.S. cities and for states and regions. A companion volume is *Encyclopedia of Geographic Information Sources: International Volume* (1988) covering sources on 75 nations and 80 major foreign industrial cities.

Monthly Catalog of United States Government Publications (Washington, DC: U.S. Government Printing Office; monthly, with semiannual index). Accessible on-line as *GPO Monthly Catalog;* also on CD-ROM. Describes publications of the U.S. government, arranged by publication number (which is also by issuing agency). Includes subject and title indexes.

Standard Industrial Classification Manual (Washington, DC: U.S. Office of Management and Budget, 1987). Explains the coding scheme developed by the federal government to make it easier to collect and tabulate statistics on products, industries, or services, especially in the various economic censuses. Commonly called the *SIC Code,* it (or expanded versions of it) is now also used by many commercial sources such as publishers of directories or indexing/abstracting services, because it offers a logical means of classifying industry data and is so well-known. Especially useful for locating industry number statistics on a specific product.

Statistical Reference Index (Bethesda, MD: Congressional Information Service, monthly in two parts, with annual cumulations). Accessible on CD-ROM as *Statistical Masterfile.* SRI is a companion service to *American Statistics Index,* covering U.S. statistical publications published by non-government sources, including trade and professional associations, institutes, commercial publishers, businesses, independent research organizations, state governments, and university research centers. This could be especially useful for identifying statistical publications of trade associations covering a specific industry or annual statistical issues of trade journals. Its format is similar to *ASI.*

Statistics Sources (Detroit: Gale Research, Inc.; 2 volumes, annual). A subject guide to statistics on over 20,000 topics, including many business and economic subjects. Arranged alphabetically by very specific subject or geographic location and indicates where statistics can be found. A companion volume is *State and Local Statistics Sources,* 1994/95, for sources of key data on the state, city, and local levels. For the names of several reference guides to international information, see the last section on "Selected International Sources."

Census Data

Census statistics can be of great value to market researchers because the figures are quoted in such detail, both by subject and by geographic location. The data can be used as a starting point even when they are somewhat out-of-date. The censuses of population and housing are taken every 10 years in the year ending in 0; the other censuses are taken every 5 years in the years ending with 2 and 7. The economic censuses covering manufacturing, retail, wholesale, and services industries are perhaps the most important for statistics on business establishments. These consist of series of reports in an "Industry Series," a "Geographic Area Series" by state, and a specialized "Subject Series." Following are descriptions of all the periodic censuses except the transportation and government censuses. For a note about on-line accessibility of all census reports, see the bibliography at the end of this listing.

Census of Agriculture

Includes data by state and county of the number, types, and sizes of farms, land use, irrigation, agricultural products, and value of products. More recent *Agricultural Statistics* are published by the U.S. Department of Agriculture, whereas some agricultural commodity statistics are in the *CRB Commodity Year Book.*

Census of Construction Industries

For building and heavy construction contractors, special trade contractors, and land subdividers and developers, this gives detailed statistics on number of construction establishments, number of employees, payroll, hours, value of construction work, cost of materials, rental costs, and capital expenditures.

Census of Housing

Detailed tabulations of housing conditions and occupancy statistics for states, counties, MSAs, and places with over 1,000 inhabitants. Volumes published in the 1990 census include:

- *General Housing Characteristics* (Series 1990 CH-1), with detailed statistics for each state on units in structure, value and rent, number of rooms, tenure, and vacancy characteristics for states, counties, places of 1,000 inhabitants or more. Separate reports will be produced for American Indian and Alaska Native areas (CH-1-1A), (Metropolitan Statistical Areas) (CH-1-1B), and for urbanized areas (CH-1-1C).
- *Detailed Housing Characteristics* (Series 1990 CH-2), which focuses on housing subjects collected on a sample basis. It also has separate reports similar in coverage to those for CH-1.
- *Housing Subject Reports* (Series 1990 CH-3), 10 special reports on such subjects as space utilization and structural characteristics.

Census of Manufactures

Useful statistics on each of about 450 manufacturing industries, with reports for specific industries and reports for each state. Figures include number of establishments, inventories, payrolls, production hours worked, value added by manufacture, capital expenditures, and more. *Annual Survey of Manufactures and Current Industrial Reports* update some of the statistics between censuses.

Census of Mineral Industries

This specialized census covers statistics (in industry reports and geographic area reports) on establishments for over 30 industries in metal and coal mining, oil and gas extraction, and mining and quarrying of nonmetallic minerals.

Census of Population

Presents population characteristics of states, counties, MSAs, and places of 1,000 or more inhabitants. The reports from the 1990 census are:

- *General Population Characteristics* (Series 1990 CP-1), consisting of separate reports by state, each with detailed statistics on age, sex, race, Hispanic origin, marital status, and household relationship characteristics for states, counties, and places of 1,000 or more inhabitants. Separate reports will be produced for American Indian and Alaska Native areas (CP-1-1A), or MSAs (CP-1-1B), and for urbanized areas (CD-1-1C).
- *Social and Economic Characteristics* (Series 1990 CP-2), focusing on population subjects collected on a sample basis. It also will have separate reports similar to those in CP-1.
- *Population Subject Reports* (CP-3), including 30 reports on particular subjects such as migration, income, and the older population.

Current Population Reports

Include several useful continuing reports covering statistics on such topics as population characteristics (Series P-20), population estimates and projections

(Series P-25), and consumer income (Series P-60). The last contains statistics on socioeconomic characteristics of persons, families, and households.

Census of Population and Housing

The volumes in the 1990 census include:

- *Summary Population and Housing Characteristics* (Series 1990 CPH-1), providing population and housing unit counts as well as summary statistics on age, sex, race, Hispanic origin, household relationship, units in structure, value and rent, number of rooms, tenure, and vacancy characteristics for local government, including American Indian and Alaska Native areas.

- *Population and Housing Unit Counts* (Series 1990 CPH-2), with total population and housing unit counts for 1990 and previous censuses, and data shown for states, counties, minor civil divisions, and places.

- *Population and Housing Characteristics for Census Tracts and Block Numbering Areas* (Series 1990 CPH-3), especially useful for population and housing statistics for census tracts and blocks within MSAs.

- *Population and Housing Characteristics for Congressional Districts of the 103rd Congress* (Series 1990 PHC-4).

- *Summary Social, Economic, and Housing Characteristics* (Series 1990 PHC-5), with sample data for local governments.

Census of Retail Trade

Presents statistics on states, MSAs, Primary Metropolitan Statistical Areas (PMSAs), Consolidated Metropolitan Statistical Areas (CMSAs), counties, and places. Data include sales, payroll, employees, number of establishments, sales by merchandise lines, and so forth, arranged by Standard Industrial Classification (SIC) code number. Some current statistics based on a sample survey are in *Revised Monthly Retail Trade: Sales and Inventories*, which has an annual summary.

Census of Service Industries

Gives statistics on retail service organizations such as hotels, beauty parlors, and laundries on receipts, employment, number of units, payrolls, and the like for states, MSAs, counties, and cities. Does not include information on the professions, insurance, or real estate. Current sample survey statistics are in *Service Annual Survey*.

Census of Wholesale Trade

Wholesaler statistics for states, MSAs, and counties on sales, number of establishments, payrolls, warehouse space, expenses, and so forth, arranged by SIC code number. Some current data are in *Revised Monthly Wholesale Trade: Sales and Inventories*, which also has an annual summary.

Bibliography of Census Data

Census Catalog & Guide (Washington, DC: U.S. Bureau of the Census; annual.) A descriptive guide to census statistics and reports arranged by broad census subjects such as agriculture and population. Symbols with each item note which are available on computer tapes. CD-ROM, diskettes, and microfiche. Much of the on-line data are accessible via the Internet.

Statistical Data

Business Statistics (Washington, DC: U.S. Bureau of Economic Analysis; biennial). This biennial statistical supplement to the *Survey of Current Business* contains extensive historical tables (annually for 29 years and monthly for the most recent four years) for about 1,900 series contained in the monthly *Survey*. An explanatory note for each series describes the series and indicates original sources of data.

County and City Data Book (Washington, DC: U.S. Bureau of the Census; published irregularly, although at least every five years). Accessible on-line and on DC-ROM. Provides breakdowns by city and county for income, population, education, housing, banking, manufacturing, capital expenditures, mineral and agricultural production, retail and wholesale sales, voting records, and other categories. Data are taken from censuses and other government publications and are published as a supplement to the *Statistical Abstract*. The Census Bureau also publishes a *State and Metropolitan Area Data Book* (triennial) with much of the same statistics for metropolitan areas.

In 1992 a commercial publisher began publishing *County and City Extra: Annual Metro, City and County Data Book* (Lanham, PA: Bernan Press) as a means of making available the most up-to-date statistical information for every U.S. state, county, metropolitan area, and place. This is accessible on-line, and on CD-ROM as County and City Plus CD-ROM.

County Business Patterns (Washington, DC: U.S. Bureau of the Census: annual series of report). Accessible on-line and on CD-ROM. For every four-digit SIC industry, this gives statistics on number of establishments, employees, and payroll by employment size class, for every U.S. state and county. Includes data on financial, insurance, and real estate industries not found in the censuses of retail trade or service industries.

CRB Community Year Book (New York: Commodity Research Bureau). Presents statistics on prices, production, exports, stocks, and so forth for about 100 commodities, and a few financial futures.

Economic Indicators (Washington, DC: Council of Economic Advisors; monthly). Current statistics and some charts on prices, wages, money, credit, gross domestic product, federal finance, production, and other series that indicate the country's economic condition.

Economic Report of the President (Washington, DC: U.S. Government Printing Office; annual) Reviews economic conditions of the United States and economic policy of the administration, taken from the president's yearly address to Congress on the country's economic outlook. Much of this consists of the *Annual Report* of the Council of Economic Advisors, including statistics relating to income, employment, and production.

Federal Reserve Bulletin (Washington, DC: Board of Governors of the Federal Reserve System; monthly). Current financial and economic statistics, including money, stock, and bank credit, banking institutions, financial markets (including interest rates), federal finance, securities markets and corporate finance, funds flow, economic indicators such as industrial production, and some international statistics.

Historical Statistics of the United States: Colonial Times to 1970 (Washington, DC: U.S. Bureaus of the Census, 1975, 2 volumes). A supplement to the *Statistical Abstract* (noted later), this useful book provides long-term historical trends for basic U.S. statistics. It is arranged in 24 subject sections, and each section contains a short discussion of the sources used to find these statistics.

Industry Norms & Key Business Ratios, desk-top edition (New York: Dun & Bradstreet Information Services: annual). Useful for its financial and operating ratios on over 800 lines of business, arranged by industry (four-digit SIC). An alternate source is Robert Morris Associates *Annual Statement Studies* (Philadelphia), with ratios for some 360 lines of business, also arranged by four-digit SIC.

Monthly Labor Review (Washington, DC: U.S. Bureau of Labor Statistics). Contains articles on nationwide labor conditions and trends. Statistics in each issue include labor force data (employment, unemployment, hours), labor compensation and collective bargaining, price data (consumer and producer price indexes), productivity, injury, and illness.

Predicasts Basebook (Cleveland: Predicasts, Inc.; annual). Available on-line as *PTS U.S. Time Series.* A comprehensive loose-leaf statistical service providing approximately 27,700 time series for very specific products/industries and for basic economic indicators, arranged by expanded seven-digit SIC numbers. Each record contains about 10 years of data, calculated growth rate, and the source from which the figures were taken.

Predicasts Forecasts (Cleveland: Predicasts, Inc.; quarterly with annual cumulations). Available also on-line as *PTS U.S. Forecasts.* Contains both short- and long-range statistical forecasts for products/industries and for the U.S. economy, arranged by an expanded seven-digit SIC number, taken from journal articles, newspapers, government publications, and other sources. For each topic it often has projections for shipments, production, sales, consumption, exports, and so on. Includes the source for each figure.

An expensive companion service, covering forecasts for products/industries in foreign countries, is *Worldcasts* (eight volumes, four of which are for *World-Product-Casts* and four for *World-Regional-Casts*). On-line counterpart is *PTS International Forecasts.*

Standard & Poor's Statistical Service (New York: Standard & Poor's Corporation; one loose-leaf volume with monthly supplements). Contains useful historical and current business/economic statistics, arranged in the following sections: banking and finance; production indexes and labor statistics; price indexes (commodities, producer and consumer price indexes, cost of living); income and trade; building and building materials; energy, electric power, and fuels; metals; transportation; textiles, chemicals, paper; agricultural products; Security Price Index Record (the last section contains long-term trends for S&P's stock price index and Dow Jones averages).

Statistical Abstract of the United States (Washington, DC: U.S. Bureau of the Census; annual). Available also on-line. One of the most valuable statistical reference books, consisting of many social, political, and economic statistical tables each taken from original government reports. It also serves as a reference for more detailed information because it gives the source at the foot of each table and also includes guides to statistics, state statistical abstracts, and some foreign statistics at the end.

Statistics of Income (Washington, DC: Internal Revenue Service of Treasury Department; annual). Income statistics collected by the IRS in two volumes: one based on individual tax returns and the other corporations. Data for the latter include tables by industry and by asset size. Because publication of these data may be slow, the quarterly *SOI Bulletin* is useful for preliminary statistics on individual and corporate income as well as those for partnerships and sole proprietorships.

Survey of Current Business (Washington, DC: U.S. Bureau of Economic Analysis; monthly). An important source for current business statistics. Especially noted for its figures on national income, gross domestic product, and personal consumption expenditures which are in each issue and also in more detail in its annual "National Income and Product Accounts" issue (July). Certain issues also contain data on international transactions and foreign direct investments in the United States. Blue pages in each issue cover statistics for general business indicators, commodity prices, construction and real estate, labor/employment/earnings, domestic trade, finance, foreign trade, transportation and communication, and 13 major manufacturing industries. Yellow pages give "Business Cycle Indicators," monthly estimates for over 250 business cycles, both in table and chart format. For a biennial providing historical statistics from the *Survey,* consult the entry for *Business Statistics.*

Market Data

The Lifestyle Market Analyst (Wilmette, IL: Standard Rate & Data Service; annual). A new reference guide for consumer market analysis at the local, regional, or national level. Section 1 analyzes each ADI (Area of Dominant Influence) market in terms of demographic characteristics, and over 50 lifestyle interests. Sections 2 and 3 provide the same data by specific lifestyle activity and by demographic data.

Market Guide (New York: Editor & Publisher; annual). Provides market facts on U.S. and Canadian daily newspaper cities, including population, number of households, transportation, climate, retail outlets, principal industries, banks, and automobiles. It also contains tables somewhat similar to those in the *Survey of Buying Power* covering population, disposable personal income, households, and retail sales (for each of nine retail store groups) by county, newspaper city, and Metropolitan Statistical Area. Ranked tables are at front.

Rand McNally Commercial Atlas & Marketing Guide (Chicago; annual). Contains marketing data such as figures from the *Survey of Buying Power,* population for Ranally metropolitan areas, maps of trading areas, MSAs, and ZIP codes as well as state and large-city maps.

Sourcebook of Zip Code Demographics (Fairfax, VA: CACI; annual). For researchers needing marketing statistics arranged by U.S. Zip Code, this annual contains census statistics and other proprietary marketing estimates for population and housing (including number of households, and a housing profile), demographic figures (percentage by age distribution, race, and median age), socioeconomic statistics (percentage distribution of households by income, education, employment profile), and a purchasing potential index for 13 types of products/services.

Survey of Buying Power (New York: *Sales & Marketing Management;* extra August issue of S&MM).
- *Sales & Marketing Management* publishes three useful extra issues each year, and this is the most important one for researchers interested in geographical variations of population, income, and retail sales. Section C contains current statistical estimates for population (by age groups), households, effective buying income (EBI), and retail sales for six store groups—all for U.S. states, counties, MSAs and some cities, Section B gives regional and state summaries and metro rankings for the same data.

- Earlier volumes of the *Survey* included statistics for Canadian provinces, counties, and cities; now Canadian tables are prepared separately as *Survey of Buying Power: Canadian Data,* and subscribers to *S&MM* must request it each year from the publisher.

- The October issue is a "Survey of Media Markets." This contains media market projection tables showing percentage changes over five years for population, EBI, and total retail sales for each metro area. It also has "Media Market Profiles" for each Arbitron ADI market, and a section ranking metro areas for each of 10 retail merchandise lines.

- A third extra issue (in June each year) is a "Sales Manager's Budget Planner," intended more for sales managers than for market researchers.

For several international market data sources, see "Selected International Sources" at the end of this bibliography.

Marketing Reference Guides

Market Share Reporter (Detroit: Gale Research, Inc.; annual). An annual compilation of reported market share data on companies, products, and services that appeared in periodicals and brokerage reports. It is arranged by two-digit SIC categories and within each chapter by four-digit SIC, and it covers not only brand market share data but also corporate market shares, institutional shares (shares for countries, regions, etc.), and product/commodity/service, and facility shares. Data for each usually include brief information on the entry, list of products or companies with number of units sold an percentage of group, and name of source. Many entries are taken from the database *Investext.*

PTS Marketing and Advertising Reference Service database. This MARS database abstracts articles on marketing and advertising of consumer products and services. It covers not only specific consumer products/services but also articles on new products, marketing and advertising strategies, market size/market share information, advertising and promotion campaigns, articles on producer organizations, ad agencies, public relations firms, and much more. Over 140 key publications are scanned for pertinent articles, and many are now reproduced in full.

Industry Data

Industry Surveys (New York: Standard & Poor's Corporation; annual with three updates). Separate "Basic Analysis" surveys for about 20 major U.S. industries, each including comparative statistics for leading companies in that industry. Supplemented by a short "Current Analysis" with some more recent data (usually two per year).

U.S. Industrial Outlook (Washington, DC: International Trade Administration of the Department of Commerce; annual). A much used source for short discussions of recent trends on each of approximately 350 specific manufacturing and service industries with prospects over the coming five years. There are many other possible sources for information on industries, several of which are listed elsewhere in this appendix. The census, for instance, contains statistics on four-digit industries, as does the annual *County Business Patterns*. Predicasts publications give industry statistics on an expanded seven-digit SIC number. Dun's *Industry Norms & Key Business Ratios* has ratios by four-digit industries. The *Encyclopedia of Business Information Sources* is a good place to start if you do not know which statistics, abstracts, directories, periodicals, and so on are available on any one industry/subject. The monthly *Statistical Reference Index* offers one way to locate statistical volumes compiled by various trade associations as well as annual statistical issues sometimes appearing in trade journals such as the *Oil & Gas Journal*. Using a directory of national associations, such as the annual *Encyclopedia of Associations, Volume 1: National Organizations of the U.S.* (Gale Research, Inc.), is another way to identify trade associations that may have useful industry statistics or other suggestions for industry information.

Two of the guides noted later offer a means of finding current articles on industries, some of which may be annual statistical issues of articles giving market share or a short-range outlook for the coming year. Researchers who want lists of the major U.S. trade journals in any one industry can consult one of several directories such as the annual *Standard Periodical Directory* or the lesser known (but perhaps more useful for this purpose) *Standard Rate & Data Service: Business Publication Rates and Data* (Wilmette, IL: monthly). It lists trade journals by industry group and gives subscription and advertising rate information.

Industry Reference Guides

Findex (Bethesda, MD: Cambridge Scientific Abstracts; annual, with midyear supplement). Available on-line. A descriptive directory of approximately 13,000 market research reports, studies, and surveys on specific products or industries available from over 500 U.S. and foreign research publishers. They are arranged by subject categories, and for each there is a brief description, publisher, date, paging, and price. Selected company reports are described at the end.

Predicasts F&S Index United States (Cleveland: Predicasts, Inc.: weekly, with monthly, quarterly, and annual cumulations). On-line counterpart is *PST F&S Indexes*. Useful for identifying current information on products, industries, and companies reported in more than 750 trade and business magazines, newspapers, and special reports. The industry/products section is arranged by an expanded seven-digit SIC number, and for many industries the data are arranged by subheadings covering topics such as market information, sales, and consumption. The company section lists articles containing recent news and financial and marketing information about each company.

Companion indexes covering Europe and other foreign countries are *Predicasts F&S Index Europe* and *Predicasts F&S Index International* (both are monthly, with quarterly and annual cumulations). These are on-line in *PTS F&S Indexes.*

PTS PROMPT database. Available on DC-ROM. PROMPT is an acronym for "Predicasts Overview of Market and Technology." This database provides quick access to abstracts (and some full text) on industries, companies, products, markets, and applied technology from a wide range of worldwide journals and other sources, such as investment analysts' reports, research studies, and government publications. It can be useful for identifying articles on such subjects as competitive activities, new products and technologies, market size and share, financial trends, mergers and acquisitions, contracts, joint ventures, and new facilities. There is a print version called *PROMPT* (Cleveland: Predicasts, Inc., monthly, with quarterly and annual cumulations).

Trade and Industry Index database. Complete abstracting of some 300 trade, industry, and commerce journals, with selective abstracting of business/industry articles in about 1,200 additional publications. Covers also about 85 local and regional business publications.

Corporate Directories

Dun's Market Identifiers (a database produced by Dun & Bradstreet Information Services). Contains directory information about both public and private U.S. companies with five or more employees or with $1 million or more in sales. The database covers all types of commercial and industrial establishments as well as all product areas. Data on more than 7 million businesses have been gathered via interviews.

Million Dollar Directory: Leading Public and Private Companies (Parsippany, NJ: Dun & Bradstreet Information Services; 5 volumes, annual). Available on-line, and on CD-ROM as *Dun's Million Dollar Disc.* This is a good directory to start when seeking brief facts about any of some 160,000 leading U.S. public and private businesses. The first three volumes usually give officers/directors, approximate sales, employees, stock exchange, ticker symbol, SIC numbers, and more, for each company. Two other volumes index the companies by geographic location and by SIC industry. Some libraries may subscribe to just one volume containing facts on the *Top 50,000 Companies.*

An alternative directory is *Standard & Poor's Register of Corporations, Directors, and Executives* (New York: Standard & Poor's Corporation; 1 volume of 3, annual, with cumulated supplements). Accessible on-line as

Standard & Poor's Register—Corporate, and on CD-ROM. The other two volumes contain a list of directors and executives, with brief facts about each and the indexes.

Standard Directory of Advertisers (Wilmette, IL: National Register Publishing Company; 2 volumes; annual, with supplements). Volume 1 is a classified directory of some 25,000 U.S. companies that advertise nationally, giving for each not only the usual basic facts but also names of marketing and sales personnel, advertising agencies, sometimes advertising appropriations, and advertising media used. Volume 2 contains indexes, including one for trade names. There is a separate "Geographic Index."

Two companion volumes are *Standard Directory of International Advertisers & Agencies* (annual) covering foreign companies that advertise and foreign advertising agencies; and *Standard Directory of Advertising Agencies* (3 per year, with supplements), which contains approximate annual billings and names of accounts for each U.S. agency listed.

Thomas Register of American Manufacturers (New York: Thomas Publishing Company; 26 volumes, annual). Accessible on-line as *Thomas Register On-line,* and on CD-ROM. Probably the best directory for identifying a U.S. manufacturing company or locating the manufacturer of a particular brand. It lists over 145,000 companies by very specific product, alphabetically and by brand name. For each company it usually gives the address, products made, and asset range. Volumes 17 and 18 list the companies alphabetically, with vol. 18 including a trade name index; volumes 19 to 26 are a "Catalog File."

The Fortune 500 (annual, in *Fortune,* April issue). Each year *Fortune* publishes four ranked lists of largest companies. This one ranks the largest U.S. industrial corporations by sales, assets, profits, and so forth, and also by industry. Fortune's other ranked lists are:

- "The Fortune Service 500" (first June) with separate rankings for the 100 largest diversified service companies, 100 commercial banks, diversified financial companies, 50 largest (each) savings institutions, life insurance companies, retailing companies, transportation companies, and utilities.

- "The Fortune Global 500" (first July), ranking the largest industrial companies in the world, and the largest banks.

- "The Fortune Global 500" (last July), with separate rankings of worldwide service companies in the same categories as in the U.S. ranked list.

There are many other sources for ranked lists of top companies. See Daniells's *Business Information Sources* (3rd ed., 1993), or use *Business Rankings Annual* (Detroit: Gale Research, Inc.).

Greenbook: International Directory of Marketing Research Companies and Services (New York Chapter, American Marketing Association; annual). A descriptive list of marketing research companies, arranged alphabetically with four indexes, including one by geographic location.

To identify the numerous published business and industrial directories, buyer's guides, and rosters (both U.S. and foreign), consult a guide such as *Directories in Print* (Detroit: Gale Research, Inc.; annual with supplements) and its companion guide, *City & State Directories in Print.*

Selected International Sources

Statistics

Demographic Yearbook (New York: United nations). Also accessible on-line. Presents detailed demographic characteristics of the population in over 200 countries, including births, deaths, life expectancy, marriages, and divorces.

European Marketing Data and Statistics and International Marketing Data and Statistics (London: Euromonitor; annuals). Comparative country statistics for basic economic indicators and marketing topics for 33 countries (in the European volume) and over 150 (in the volume covering other foreign countries). The economic data sections deal with population, households, consumer expenditures, consumer prices, and transportation; the marketing sections contain data for retail sales by type, advertising patterns, and media access (including number of radios and TVs in use), and for consumption of various consumer products. Key sources are described at the front of both volumes.

Statistical Yearbook (New York: United Nations). This is the basic U.N. statistical yearbook. For each U.N. country, it gives statistics on population and labor force, employment and wages, finance, education, statistics on each of many basic economic activities, foreign trade, transportation, communication, and tourism. Because it is slow in being published, check the U.N. *Monthly Bulletin of Statistics* for useful current statistics.

The United Nations publishes other, more specialized yearbooks, including *Industrial Statistics Yearbook* (2 volumes), which gives general industrial and commodity production statistics; *International Trade Statistics Yearbook* (2 volumes), which provides import/export statistics by individual country and by commodity by country; and *National Accounts Statistics* (3 unnumbered volumes, published annually), which contains national income figures, including gross domestic product, and consumer expenditure statistics for over 160 countries.

Statistical Yearbook (Paris: United Nations Educational, Scientific and Cultural Organization). UNESCO's statistical annual covers statistical tables, by country, for education (including educational expenditures); science and technology; culture and communication (including libraries, book production, newspapers and other periodicals, museums, film and cinema, and radio/TV broadcasting).

Reference Guides

Europa World Year Book (London: Europa Publications; 2 volumes). Important source for brief information about countries, such as recent history, economic statistics, government, political organizations, and holidays; also lists important newspapers, periodicals, radio and TV stations, banks, insurance companies, trade associations, railroads, and much more. Some data on international organizations are at the front of volume 1.

European Directory of Marketing Information Sources (biennial) and *International Directory of Marketing Information Sources* (London: Euromonitor Plc; biennial). These two guides describe the following types of information available for each foreign country: official sources and publications (including statistical publications); libraries and information sources; leading market research companies; information databases; abstracts and indexes; major business and marketing journals; leading business and marketing associations; and European business contracts (such as embassies and chambers of commerce).

Index to International Statistics (Bethesda, MD.: Congressional Information Service; monthly, in two parts, with annual cumulations). A companion service to *American Statistics Index,* this abstracts and indexes the statistical publications (in English) published by major international government organizations (IGOs) such as the United Nations and the Organization for Economic Cooperation and Development. It identifies statistics on individual countries but does not cover statistical publications for each country. Some of these latter publications may be found in the previous source.

Corporate Directories and Investment Data

Disclosure/Worldscope: Industrial Company Profiles and Disclosure/Worldscope: Financial & Service Company Profiles (Bridgeport, CT: D/W Partners; 8 unnumbered volumes; annual). Available on-line and on CD-ROM. There are five volumes in the first title. Four volumes contain concise (one-page) statistical profiles for more than 3,000 leading industrial companies in 24 countries and 18 industries. Statistics, usually for a 6-year period, cover financial statement data, financial ratios and growth rate, per-share data, and more. The fifth volume is a "User's Guide." Two of three volumes of the second title give similar data for over 1,000 major financial, transportation, and utilities companies in 24 countries. The third volume is a "User's Guide."

Moody's International Manual (New York: Moody's Investors Service; 2 volumes, annual, with supplements). Accessible on CD-ROM as *Moody's International Plus.* A financial manual covering major corporations in some 100 countries and arranged by county. Data given for each country usually include a brief financial history, a description of business and property, officers, financial statement figures, among others. Center blue pages contain comparative international statistics.

Primary International Businesses (New York: Dun & Bradstreet Information Services; annual). Directory-type information for approximately 50,000 leading companies in 140 countries; arranged by country, with indexes by SIC industries and by company.

Standard Directory of International Advertisers & Agencies (Wilmette, IL: National Register Publishing Company; annual). Describes both large foreign companies that advertise and foreign advertising agencies. Besides the usual directory information for each company, this often gives names of sales personnel, the name of the ad agency, advertising appropriations, and media used. Noted elsewhere in this appendix are two indexes that are good sources for locating current articles and news about foreign companies and industries: *Predicasts F&S Index Europe* and *Predicasts F&S Index International.* Both are accessible on-line as *PTS F&S Indexes.*

Database Searching and Retrieving with Computers

Recent developments in information technology have had a major impact on the retrieval and use of published data. Many manual retrieval methods are being replaced by computerized database retrieval systems.

A large organization might subscribe to the Lexis system, for example. A business executive could use the computer retrieval system to search for articles related to new laws pertaining to the Internal Revenue Service policy for the office at home deduction. If the executive needed a broader search to look for material not found in Lexis, the computer may be asked to search all the databases offered by an on-line vendor such as the Dow Jones News Retrieval Service. Searching three or more databases is possible, but of course this increases the cost of the research.

A Step-by-Step Search for a Computerized Bibliography

To illustrate the database searching process, consider an example. ProQuest is found in many public and university libraries. ProQuest Direct allows the user to create a computerized bibliography efficiently by collecting information stored in commercial databases. Three examples follow:

Periodical Abstracts Research II access over 1,800 publications covering general reference, health, social sciences, humanities, education, general business, communications, law, general sciences, and medicine. Full text is available for over 800 titles.

ABI/INFORM Global accesses nearly 1,500 publications covering accounting, finance, marketing, management, international business, real estate, taxation, investment and banking, business trends, and new technologies and products. Full text is available for over 800 titles. **National Newspapers** accesses national newspapers, such as the *New York Times, Washington Post,* and *USA Today,* and regional newspapers. Full text is available for most titles.

The typical search begins at the ProQuest search by word screen illustrated in Exhibit 7B.1 and progresses through title of articles screens. (Before coming to the search by word screen, several simple menu options may have to be turned on or off. However, because the system is menu driven, advancing to this screen

Exhibit 7B.1 The ProQuest® Search Screen

Search by word—basic

Enter a word or phrase.

| e-mail surveys |

BASIC | ADVANCED

Search

◉ Current (1997 - Present)
○ Backfile

Search Wizard
Subject List

Exhibit 7B.2 Sample Results from a Computerized Search for Articles
on "E-mail Surveys"

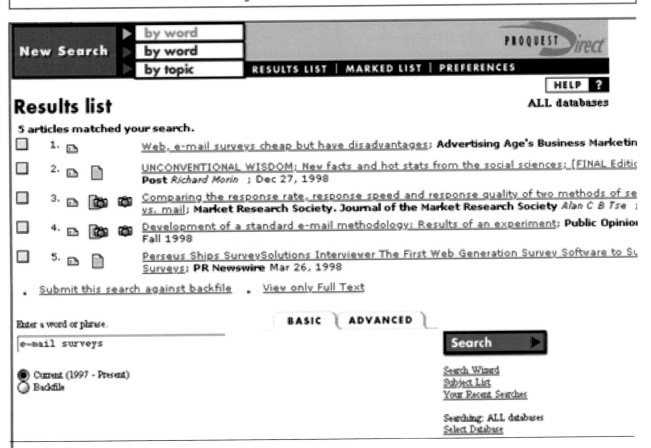

is very simple.) Database searching requires that the researcher initiate either a controlled vocabulary search by indicating specific descriptive terms or names, such as a company name, or a subject list search.

An article can be available in any or all of the following five formats.

- *Citation* format displays bibliographic information, such as author, title, source, and date.

- *Abstract* format displays the citation plus a brief summary of the article.

Exhibit 7B.3 **Sample Results of an Abstract from a Computerized Search for Articles "E-mail Surveys"**

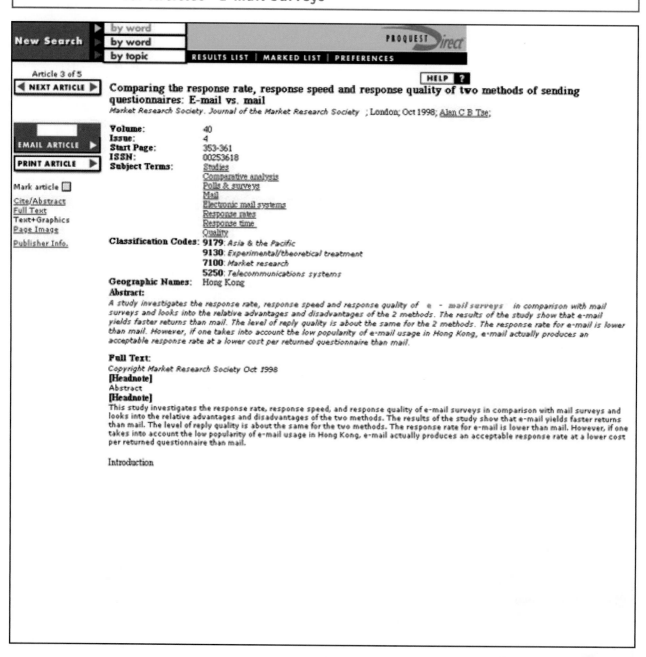

New Search — by word / by word / by topic   PROQUEST *Direct*

RESULTS LIST | MARKED LIST | PREFERENCES

Article 3 of 5   ◀ NEXT ARTICLE ▶   HELP ?

Comparing the response rate, response speed and response quality of two methods of sending questionnaires: E-mail vs. mail
Market Research Society. Journal of the Market Research Society ; London; Oct 1998; Alan C B Tse;

EMAIL ARTICLE ▶
PRINT ARTICLE ▶

Mark article ☐
Cite/Abstract
Full Text
Text+Graphics
Page Image
Publisher Info.

Volume:	40
Issue:	4
Start Page:	353-361
ISSN:	00253618
Subject Terms:	Studies
	Comparative analysis
	Polls & surveys
	Mail
	Electronic mail systems
	Response rates
	Response time
	Quality

Classification Codes: 9179: *Asia & the Pacific*
9130: *Experimental/theoretical treatment*
7100: *Market research*
5250: *Telecommunications systems*

Geographic Names: Hong Kong

Abstract:
A study investigates the response rate, response speed and response quality of e - mail surveys in comparison with mail surveys and looks into the relative advantages and disadvantages of the 2 methods. The results of the study show that e-mail yields faster returns than mail. The level of reply quality is about the same for the 2 methods. The response rate for e-mail is lower than mail. However, if one takes into account the low popularity of e-mail usage in Hong Kong, e-mail actually produces an acceptable response rate at a lower cost per returned questionnaire than mail.

Full Text:
Copyright Market Research Society Oct 1998
[Headnote]
Abstract
[Headnote]
This study investigates the response rate, response speed, and response quality of e-mail surveys in comparison with mail surveys and looks into the relative advantages and disadvantages of the two methods. The results of the study show that e-mail yields faster returns than mail. The level of reply quality is about the same for the two methods. The response rate for e-mail is lower than mail. However, if one takes into account the low popularity of e-mail usage in Hong Kong, e-mail actually produces an acceptable response rate at a lower cost per returned questionnaire than mail.

Introduction

- *Full Text* format displays the citation, abstract, and the complete text of the article in ASCII format.

- *Text + Graphics* format displays the citation, abstract, and the complete text of the article in ASCII format, plus originally published images in thumbnail size adjustable for size.

- *Page Image* format displays scanned images of the article as it was originally published. Adobe Acrobat Reader is needed to display Page Image format. It can be downloaded for free from the PQD host site.

An on-screen icon indicates the available formats for each article.

Exhibit 7B.2 shows the ProQuest® Screen for a search on "e-mail surveys."

Exhibit 7B.3 shows an abstract obtained in a ProQuest/ABI/Inform search for articles on "e-mail surveys."

A controlled vocabulary search relies on standard search terms (specific descriptors or vocabulary code names) in the search list whereas a free text search finds matches for user-specified keywords. Standard search terms provide a common language for describing key topics in articles. In Exhibit 7B.2, "e-mail surveys" is a standard search term (vocabulary code) that indicates the primary focus of the article. A free text search identifies articles on the basis of words in the abstract. Articles that mention e-mail surveys but do not have it as a primary focus may be found in this way.

Perhaps the major advantage of computerization is the computer's ability to merge or delete references to obtain precisely what is needed. A researcher interested in e-mail surveys may also use the descriptor "market research," which would restrict the search to articles that discuss e-mail surveys used in market research, with a simple change of options in the menu. Most systems offer several search options, such as an *and* option to merge two descriptive search terms or a *not* option to eliminate certain references. For example, a researcher studying survey research may wish to exclude *political polls.* The *not* option allows for this. If a search does not retrieve enough abstracted articles, the *or* option can broaden the search, so instead of the limited search terms *cars,* a researcher might enter *cars* or *automobiles.* You will have to study the individual search and retrieval system to investigate all the options it offers.

Compact Disk—Read Only Memory (CD-ROM) systems provide an alternative technology for storing data and database searching. Large amounts of data (the equivalent of 275,000 printed pages or 1,500 floppy diskettes) can be stored on a single compact disc. Many libraries have CDs that contain bibliographic indexes and databases. The CD-ROM can be inserted into the microcomputer workstation at the library or wherever the microcomputer is located.

CD-ROM systems are also widely used for the storage of financial, statistical, and market databases. For example, *Lotus One Source—CD/Corporate: U.S. Public Companies* is a CD-ROM system that allows access to a wealth of data. *U.S. Public Companies* includes basic business and financial information from *Moody's U.S. Companies* database plus relevant data from *Moody's Investors Service, Predicasts, Thomson Financial Networks, UMI/Data Courier, Marquis Who's Who in Finance and Industry, Dow Jones News Retrieval Service, Market Guide,* and *Muller Data Corporation.*

Chapter 8

Survey Research: An Overview

T O THE LIST OF SUCH AUTOMOTIVE PIONEERS AS HENRY FORD, father of the moving assembly line, Charles Kettering, inventor of the self-starter, and Harold Sperlich, developer of the minivan, add J. David Power III, popularizer of customer satisfaction.

You don't think Power belongs in the same league with these guys? Consider this: Since Power published his first Customer Satisfaction Index (CSI) in 1967, keeping customers happy has become a major goal not only for automakers and dealers but also for a good-sized chunk of U.S. business. He has helped make *customer satisfaction* part of the language. A search of Nexis, the publications and wire service database, shows nearly 10,000 references to the term since Power's first study appeared.

In the automobile business scoring high in the Power rankings has become a preoccupation, celebrated in national advertising and rewarded with higher profits. For four years Honda's Acura dealers festooned the windows of the Integra and Legend with decals reading "J. D. Power & Associates No. 1 Customer Satisfaction Index"—and stood back to watch sales accelerate. Nissan declares that customer satisfaction "is at the heart of everything we do." When it launched its luxury Infiniti division, it made customer satisfaction an explicit aim—above sales, profits, and market share. That Infiniti succeeded in only tying for first place with another new Japanese entry, Toyota's Lexus, dampened its ardor not at all.

Says George Borst, vice president of strategic and product planning for Toyota's U.S. sales operation: "Power discovered a niche in the industry many years ago, when it wasn't the top-line issue that it is today, and quantified it. Whether he caused it or caught the wave isn't important." William Pochiluk, who runs the Autofacts consulting firm in West Chester, Pennsylvania, is even more emphatic. Says he: "I think Power has changed the auto business forever. There was a time when he was the only

guy in the business making these kinds of pronouncements, and he grabbed the attention of consumers."

In the United States there are twelve Power studies that measure the performance of automakers and their dealers. Power also launched the first Canadian CSI and the first Japanese CSI rating luxury cars, produced as part of a joint venture with Japan's Research & Development Inc. Similar ventures have been established in Europe and Korea.

J. D. Power and Associates conducts its surveys by mail with a list of registered automobile owners purchased from R. L. Polk Company. A typical questionnaire sent to 70,000 car owners may contain as many as 90 questions and take more than 30 minutes to complete. Power needs about 150 completed questionnaires per model to get statistically significant results. The firm mails a dollar bill with each questionnaire as an incentive for car owners to respond. The response rate averages 38 percent and sometimes reaches 50 percent. Power attributes the high response rate to the company's reputation and the American public's seriousness about the cars they buy. The J. D. Power research organization's success depends on the quality of its surveys.[1]

The purpose of survey research is to collect primary data—data gathered and assembled specifically for the project at hand. This chapter is the first of two on survey research and defines the subject. It also discusses typical research objectives that may be accomplished with surveys and various advantages of the survey method. It explains many potential errors that researchers must be careful to avoid. Finally, it classifies the various survey research methods.

The Nature of Surveys

respondent
The person who verbally answers an interviewer's questions or provides answers to written questions.

survey
A method of primary data collection in which information is gathered by communicating with a representative sample of people.

Surveys require asking people—called **respondents**—for information using either verbal or written questioning. Questionnaires or interviews collect data through the mail, on the telephone, or face-to-face. The more formal term, **sample survey,** emphasizes that the purpose of contacting respondents is to obtain a representative sample of the target population. Thus, a **survey** is defined as a method of primary data collection based on communication with a representative sample of individuals.

Survey Objectives: Type of Information Gathered

The type of information gathered in a survey varies considerably depending on its objectives. Typically, surveys attempt to describe what is happening or to learn the reasons for a particular marketing activity.

Identifying characteristics of target markets, measuring consumer attitudes, and describing consumer purchasing patterns are common survey objectives. Most marketing surveys have multiple objectives; few gather only a single type of factual information. For example, a snowmobile manufacturer might conduct a survey to determine whether consumers are aware of the brand name and learn what purchasers like and dislike about various product features. Demographic information and media exposure might also be included in the survey to help plan a market segmentation strategy. Although consumer surveys are a common form of marketing research, not all survey research is conducted with the ultimate consumer. Frequently studies focus on wholesalers, retailers, or industrial buyers.

Because most survey research is descriptive research, the term *survey* is most often associated with quantitative findings. Although it is true that most

Surveys are taken because consumers' opinions count. Data collection is based on a representative sample of individuals.

surveys are conducted to quantify certain factual information, some aspects of surveys may also be qualitative.

In new-product development, a survey often has a qualitative objective of testing and refining new-product concepts. Stylistic, aesthetic, or functional changes may be welcome suggestions. The qualitative nature of advertising may also be an objective of survey research, as the following account of a test of a rough commercial for AT&T shows:

"It was an earlier commercial we did for A.T.&T.," he says. "We called it 'Fishing Camp.' The idea was this: These guys go off to a fishing camp in the north woods, somewhere far away, where they're going to have a terrific time together and do all this great fishing, only what happens is that it rains all the time and the fishing is a bust. Mind you, this was a humorous ad. The emphasis was on the humor. Anyway, the big moment occurs when the fishing guys are talking on the phone to their jealous friends back home—who naturally want to know how great the fishing is—and what you see are the fishing guys, huddled in this cabin, with the rain pouring down outside, and one of the guys is staring at a frying pan full of hamburgers sizzling on the stove while he says into the phone, 'Boy, you should see the great trout we've got cooking here.' O.K., so we made a photomatic of the commercial and we decided we'd test it. Our test audience generally gave the first part very positive responses, but when it came to the question 'What was cooking in the frying pan?' just about every person answering said 'Trout.' I mean it was definitely and unmistakably hamburger in the frying pan, but the guy in the ad had said, 'Boy, you should see the great trout we've got cooking here,' so the test audience all said 'Trout.' I have to tell you, we were very discouraged. Some of our guys were even talking of junking the commercial, which was a good one, with a nice humorous flow to it. Well, we ended up making it, but what we had to do was, when we came to that segment, we put the camera almost *inside* the frying pan, and in the frying pan we put huge, crude chunks of hamburger that were so raw they were almost red. I mean, just about all you could see was raw meat. This time, when we took it to the audience, it tested O.K. That is, most of the test audience—though, in fact, still not everybody—finally said 'Hamburger.' But the experience taught me an important lesson. It taught me not to worry about being too obvious visually, and that a lot of things can go wrong in thirty seconds."[2]

Although most marketing surveys are descriptive, they can also be designed to provide insights about causal explanations or to explore ideas.

Advantages of Surveys

Surveys provide a quick, inexpensive, efficient, and accurate means of assessing information about a population. The examples given earlier in the chapter illustrate that surveys are quite flexible and, when properly conducted, extremely valuable to the manager.

As we discussed in Chapter 1, marketing research has proliferated since the general adoption of the marketing concept. The growth of survey research is related to the simple idea that to find out what consumers think, one should ask them.[3]

Over the last 50 years, particularly during the last two decades, survey research techniques and standards have become quite scientific and accurate. When properly conducted, surveys offer managers many advantages. However, they can also be used poorly.

It may be no exaggeration to say that the greater number of surveys conducted today are a waste of time and money. Many are simply bad surveys.

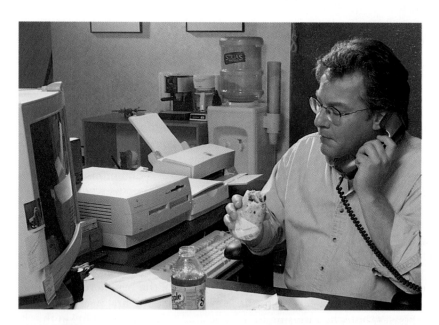

Survey research reveals that the lunch hour isn't what it used to be. Nearly 40 percent of U.S. workers won't break for lunch.[4] Furthermore, the survey by an office furniture manufacturer showed that even those who do take a break are not doing much more than quickly refueling. The study showed the lunch "hour" averages 36 minutes at or near the employee's regular place of work. The survey revealed even more. Pressed for time in their personal lives, more than half of the workers who take a lunch break don't eat anything at all—they run errands. About 28 percent make personal phone calls, 27 percent go shopping, 6 percent check on their kids in day care, and 1 percent are out looking for another job. About 37 percent read a book or newspaper and 14 percent jog or work out at a fitness center.

Marketing managers at Marriott Corporation know that people want a hotel room to feel residential because they see a hotel room as a home away from home. Customers prefer a clearly marked place to sit down, straight furniture legs, light walls, big bathrooms, spacious desk areas, and a long telephone cord. How did Marriott Corporation, the largest operator of hotels in the country, learn about its customers' preferences? Simple! Marketing researchers have built an assortment of fake hotel rooms modeled on the competition and conducted surveys to test consumers' reactions. Customers walk through and rate the rooms.

Samples are biased; questions are poorly phrased; interviewers are not properly instructed and supervised; and results are misinterpreted. Such surveys are worse than none at all because the sponsor may be misled into a costly area. Even well-planned and neatly executed surveys may be useless if, as often happens, the results come too late to be of value or converted into a bulky report which no one has time to read.[5]

The disadvantages of surveys are best described in specific sections for each form of data collection (personal interview, telephone, mail, and other self-administered formats). However, errors are common to all forms of surveys, so it is appropriate to describe them generally.

Errors in Survey Research

A manager who is evaluating the quality of a survey must estimate its accuracy. Exhibit 8.1 outlines the various forms of survey error. The two major sources of survey error are random sampling error and systematic error.

Random Sampling Error

Most surveys try to portray a representative cross section of a particular target population. Even with technically proper random probability samples, however, statistical errors will occur because of chance variation. Without increasing sample size, these statistical problems are unavoidable. However, **random sampling errors** can be estimated; Chapters 16 and 17 will discuss these in greater detail.

random sampling error
A statistical fluctuation that occurs because of chance variations in the elements selected for a sample.

Exhibit 8.1 **Categories of Survey Errors**

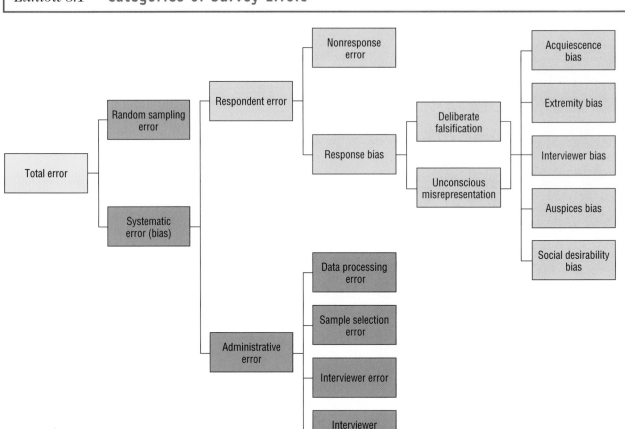

Systematic Error

Systematic error results from some imperfect aspect of the research design or from a mistake in the execution of the research. Because all sources of error rather than those introduced by the random sampling procedure are included, these errors or biases are also called nonsampling errors. A **sample bias** exists when the results of a sample show a persistent tendency to deviate in one direction from the true value of the population parameter. The many sources of error that in some way systematically influence answers can be divided into two general categories: respondent error and administrative error. These are discussed in the following sections.

Respondent Error

Surveys ask people for answers. If people cooperate and give truthful answers, the survey will likely accomplish its goal. If these conditions are not met, nonresponse error or response bias, the two major categories of **respondent error,** may cause a sample bias.

Nonresponse Error

Few surveys have 100 percent response rates. A researcher who obtains an 11 percent response to a five-page questionnaire concerning various brands of spark plugs may face a serious problem. To use the results, the researcher must be sure that those who did respond to the questionnaire were representative of those who did not.

The statistical differences between a survey that includes only those who responded and a survey that also includes those who failed to respond are referred to as a **nonresponse error.** This problem is especially acute in mail surveys, but it also threatens telephone and face-to-face interviews.

People who are not contacted or who refuse to cooperate are called **nonrespondents.** A nonresponse occurs if someone is not at home and a subsequent callback also finds the subject not at home. (The number of **not-at-homes** is increasing with the proportion of married women in the labor force—now about 70 percent.) A parent who must juggle the telephone and a half-diapered child and refuses to participate in the survey because he or she is too busy is also a nonresponse. **Refusals** occur when people are unwilling to participate in the research. Not-at-homes and refusals can seriously bias survey data.

Self-selection bias is a problem that frequently plagues self-administered questionnaires. In a restaurant, for example, a customer on whom a waiter spilled soup, a person who was treated to a surprise dinner, or others who feel strongly about the service are more likely to respond to self-administered questionnaires left at the table than individuals who are indifferent about the restaurant. Self-selection biases distort surveys because they overrepresent extreme positions while underrepresenting responses from those who are indifferent.

Arbitron, a research firm, had problems getting people to record their radio-listening habits in diaries every day; in one period only 28 percent of a sample filled in the diary. Arbitron conducted a survey to find differences between people who were willing and unwilling to keep diaries. The diary keepers were found to favor middle-of-the-road, "beautiful" music and news/talk stations; nonrespondents favored contemporary and rap stations. Comparing the demographics of the sample with the demographics of the target population is one means of inspecting for possible biases in response patterns. If a particular group, such as older citizens, is underrepresented or if any potential biases appear in a response

nonresponse error
The statistical differences between a survey that includes only those who responded and a perfect survey that would also include those who failed to respond.

nonrespondent
A person who is not contacted or who refuses to cooperate in the research.

not-at-home
A person who is not at home on the first or second contact.

refusal
A person who is unwilling to participate in the research.

self-selection bias
A bias that occurs because people who feel strongly about a subject are more likely to respond than people who feel indifferent about it.

Nonresponse error can be high when conducting international marketing research. Many cultures do not share the same values about providing information. In Mexico citizens are reluctant to provide information over the phone to strangers. In many Middle Eastern countries many women would refuse to be interviewed by a male interviewer.

EXPLORING RESEARCH ISSUES

You Are What You Eat?

SURVEY RESPONDENTS SAYING ONE THING AND DOING another is a response bias problem. As part of its ongoing survey of eating habits, MRCA Information Services, a Chicago market research firm, asked 4,700 people from 2,000 households nationwide if they agreed with this statement: "Adults should eliminate meat from their diets. True or false?"[9] About 25 percent said it was true, about 50 percent said it was false, and the remainder said they didn't know.

The firm also asked respondents about their meat consumption. Only 1 percent didn't eat meat at all. But the most revealing finding was that another 2 percent of respondents who considered themselves vegetarians ate meat, as did the 5 percent who called themselves "meat avoiders." In fact, both groups ate only about an ounce less meat a day than self-reported meat eaters. And the self-reported "vegetarians" were consuming only about six fewer grams of fat per day than the meat eaters.

A dietitian and consultant to the National Livestock and Meat Board interpreted the data to mean that "People are reporting their intentions as opposed to their actions."

pattern, additional efforts should be made to obtain data from the underrepresented segments of the population. For example, personal interviews may be used instead of telephone interviews for the underrepresented segments.

After a refusal, an interviewer can do nothing other than be polite. The respondent who is not at home when called or visited should be scheduled for contact at a different time of day or on a different day of the week.

In a mail survey the researcher never really knows whether a nonrespondent has refused to participate or is just indifferent. Researchers know that those who are most involved in an issue are more likely to respond to a mail survey. Several techniques will be discussed later for encouraging respondents to reply to mail surveys.

Response Bias

response bias
A bias that occurs when respondents tend to answer questions with a certain slant that consciously or unconsciously misrepresents the truth.

A **response bias** occurs when respondents tend to answer questions with a certain slant. People may consciously or unconsciously misrepresent the truth. If a distortion of measurement occurs because respondents' answers are falsified or misrepresented, either intentionally or inadvertently, the resulting sample bias will be a *response bias*.

Consider this modern version of the *Literary Digest* study.[6] In a New York City mayoral election, all the polls showed David Dinkins, a black candidate, leading Rudolph Giuliani, a white candidate, by 12 to 16 percentage points, but Dinkins won by just 2 percentage points. On the same day Douglas Wilder, a black candidate in a Virginia gubernatorial election, was 9 to 11 percentage points ahead of the white candidate in the polls but won the Virginia governorship by only 0.3 percentage points. After these elections, research experts explained that whites who say they are undecided in a black–white race nevertheless usually vote overwhelmingly for the white candidate. People who plan to vote against a black candidate, for whatever reason, seem reluctant to admit their true intentions. Perhaps they fear being labeled racists or wish to have the interviewer think they are socially progressive. But the end result is that in elections with racially mixed candidates, the survey results are likely to have response bias. Thus, to estimate the true vote, the poll should include a corrective measure to allow for this response bias.

Deliberate Falsification. Occasionally people deliberately give false answers. It is difficult to assess why people knowingly misrepresent answers. A response bias may occur when people misrepresent answers to appear intelligent, conceal personal information, avoid embarrassment, and so on. For example, respondents may be able to remember the total amount of money spent grocery shopping, but they may forget the exact prices of individual items that they purchased. Rather than appear ignorant or unconcerned about prices, they may provide their best estimate and not tell the truth, namely that they cannot remember. Sometimes respondents become bored with the interview and provide answers just to get rid of the interviewer. At other times respondents provide the answers they think are expected of them to appear well informed. On still other occasions, they give answers simply to please the interviewer.

One explanation for conscious and deliberate misrepresentation of facts is the so-called average man hypothesis. Individuals may prefer to be *viewed* as average and alter their reports of the truth to conform more closely to their *perception* of the average person. Average man effects have been found to exist in responses to questions regarding savings account balances, car prices, voting behavior, and hospital stays.

Unconscious Misrepresentation. Even when a respondent is consciously trying to be truthful and cooperative, response bias can arise from the question format, the question content, or some other stimulus. For example, bias can be introduced by the situation in which the survey is administered. The results of two in-flight surveys concerning aircraft preference illustrate this point. Passengers flying on B-747s preferred B-747s to L-1011s (74 percent versus 19 percent), while passengers flying on L-1011s preferred L-1011s to B-747s (56 percent versus 38 percent). The reversal in preference between the B-747 and the L-1011 appears to have been largely a function of the aircraft the respondent was flying on when the survey was conducted, although sample differences may have been a factor. A likely influence was the respondent's satisfaction with the plane on which he or she was flying when surveyed. In other words, in the absence of any strong preference, the respondent may simply have been trying to identify the aircraft traveled on and indicated that as his or her preference.[7]

Respondents who misunderstand questions may unconsciously provide bi-

The National Restaurant Association research shows that when it comes to diet there is considerable response bias. In response to survey questions, Americans say they intend to be virtuous in their eating (fresh fruit and bran muffins), but what they actually eat (many hamburgers) is quite different.

WHAT WENT WRONG?

Burger Favorites: A Failure to Communicate

SOMETIMES IT IS JUST A MATTER OF HOW YOU ASK THE question. When Burger King sent a survey company into the field to query fast-food fanciers on which they preferred, flame-broiled or fried hamburgers, they found a three-to-one preference for the open flame, or flame-broiled method—Burger King's own. The company and its agency immediately incorporated that finding into a comparative advertising campaign.

But when Leo Shapiro, president of a marketing research company, conducted his own survey, he rephrased the question and came up with distinctively different answers. "If you have two methods of cooking and it's a verbal survey, the choice of words could influence the outcome," Shapiro said in explaining why he decided to conduct his own survey of 308 fast-food customers. An interviewer asked: "Do you prefer a hamburger that is grilled on a hot stainless-steel grill or cooked by passing the raw meat through an open gas flame?" Shapiro's researchers found that 53 percent preferred their burgers from a stainless-steel grill. This means they opted for McDonald's fried over Burger King's open flame. The interviewer then added another dimension:

The chain that grills on a hot stainless-steel griddle serves its cooked hamburgers at the proper temperature without having to use a microwave oven. And the chain that uses the flame puts the hamburgers after they are cooked into a microwave oven before serving them. Just knowing this, from which of these two chains would you prefer to buy a hamburger?

McDonald's hot stainless-steel griddles and microwaveless restaurants won again. This time they pulled in a 5-1/2-to-1 margin over Burger King. The Burger King hamburgers do come off one at a time, so in rush periods the microwave is used to preserve the serving temperature and to melt the cheese. Burger King refuses to provide details on its survey beyond saying it was national, done by a nationally known public opinion company, that the question asked was "Do you prefer your hamburgers flame-broiled or fried?" and that they are completely satisfied with the survey.

"We found the word 'fried' was unappetizing," Shapiro said. "You don't eat fried foods. The word 'cooked' is neutral, and 'open-gas' is more precise but less appetizing [than Burger King's "flame-broiled" description]." Shapiro stated that the most significant finding of this survey is how important the methods of cooking and serving were to the hamburger consumer.

---

ased answers. They may be willing to answer but unable to do so because they have forgotten the exact details. Asking "When was the last time you attended a concert?" may result in a best-guess estimate because the respondent has forgotten the exact date.

A bias may also occur when a respondent has not thought about an unexpected question. Many respondents will answer questions even though they have given them little thought. For example, in most investigations of consumers' intentions, the predictability of the intention scales depends on how close the subject is to making a purchase. The intentions of subjects who have little knowledge of the brand or the store alternatives being surveyed and the intentions of subjects who have not yet made any purchase plans cannot be expected to accurately predict purchase behavior.

Asking respondents how spicy they like their chili is unlikely to produce well-articulated answers. In many cases consumers cannot adequately express their feelings in words; there is an unconscious communication breakdown. An international marketing research survey provides a classic example of a communications breakdown. A survey in the Philippines found that despite seemingly high toothpaste usage only a tiny percentage of people responded positively when asked, "Do you use toothpaste?" As it turned out, the brand name *Colgate* is a generic name for toothpaste in the Philippines. When researchers returned and asked, "Do you use Colgate?" the positive response soared.

As the time between a purchasing or shopping event and the survey contact increases, the tendency for underreporting information about that event increases. Time lapse influences ability to precisely remember and communicate specific factors. Unconscious misrepresentation bias sometimes occurs because consumers unconsciously avoid facing the realities of a future buying situation. Housing surveys record that Americans overwhelmingly continue to aspire to owning detached, single-family dwellings (preferably single-level, ranch-type structures that require two to five times the amount of land per unit required for attached homes). However, builders know that *attached* housing purchases by first buyers is higher than respondents expect.

Types of Response Bias.

There are five specific categories of response bias: acquiescence bias, extremity bias, interviewer bias, auspices bias, and social desirability bias. These categories overlap and are not mutually exclusive. A single biased answer may be distorted for many complex reasons, some reasons being deliberate and some being unconscious misrepresentations.

Acquiescence.

Some respondents are very agreeable; these yea-sayers accept all statements they are asked about. This tendency to agree with all or most questions is particularly prominent in new product research. Questions about a new-product idea generally elicit some **acquiescence bias** because respondents give positive connotations to most new ideas. For example, Spaulding, Rawlings, and Mizuno found that consumers responded favorably when they were asked about pump baseball gloves (with a mechanism similar to those in pump basketball shoes). However, when these expensive gloves hit the market, they sat on the shelves. When conducting new-product research, researchers should recognize the high likelihood of acquiescence bias.

acquiescence bias
A category of response bias that results because some individuals tend to agree with all questions or to concur with a particular position.

Another form of acquiescence is evident in some people's tendency to disagree with all questions. Thus, acquiescence bias is a response bias due to the respondents' tendency to concur with a particular position.

Extremity Bias.

Some individuals tend to use extremes when responding to questions; others always avoid extreme positions and tend to respond more neutrally.

Asian values about survey research differ from those in American culture. Asians have less patience with the abstract and rational question wording commonly used in the United States. Researchers must be alert for culture-bound sources of response bias in international marketing research. For example, the Japanese do not wish to contradict others, leading to a bias toward acquiescence and yea-saying.

extremity bias
A category of response bias that results because response styles vary from person to person; some individuals tend to use extremes when responding to questions.

interviewer bias
A response bias that occurs because the presence of the interviewer influences answers.

Response styles vary from person to person, and they may cause an **extremity bias** in the data. This issue is dealt with in Chapter 14 on attitude research.

Interviewer Bias. Response bias may arise from interplay between interviewer and respondent. If the interviewer's presence influences respondents to give untrue or modified answers, the survey will have **interviewer bias.** Many homemakers and retired people welcome the interviewer's visit as a break in routine activities. Respondents may give answers they believe will please the interviewer rather than the truthful responses. Respondents may wish to appear intelligent and wealthy—of course they read *Scientific American* rather than *Playboy.*

Quite often respondents give socially acceptable rather than truthful responses to save face in the presence of an interviewer. The interviewer's age, sex, style of dress, tone of voice, facial expressions, or other nonverbal characteristics may have some influence on a respondent's answer. If an interviewer smiles and makes a positive statement after a respondent's answer, the respondent will be more likely to give similar responses. In a research study on sexual harassment against saleswomen, male interviewers might not yield as candid responses as female interviewers would.

Many interviewers, contrary to instructions, will shorten or rephrase a question to suit their needs. This potential source of influenced responses can be avoided to some extent if interviewers receive training and supervision that emphasize the necessity for them to appear neutral.

If interviews go on too long, respondents may feel that time is being wasted. They may answer as abruptly as possible with little forethought.

Auspices Bias. Suppose the National Rifle Association is conducting a study on gun control. The answers to the survey may be deliberately or subconsciously misrepresented because respondents are influenced by the organization conducting the study. If a national committee on gun control conducted the same study, respondents' answers might vary. This would constitute an **auspices bias.**

auspices bias
Bias in the responses of subjects caused by the respondents being influenced by the organization conducting the study.

social desirability bias
Bias in responses caused by respondents' desire, either conscious or unconscious, to gain prestige or appears in a different social role.

Social Desirability. A **social desirability bias** may affect a response either consciously or unconsciously because the respondent wishes to create a favorable impression. Answering that one's income is only $35,000 a year might be difficult for someone whose self-concept is that of an upper-middle-class person, "about to make it big." Incomes may be inflated, education overstated, or perceived respectable answers given to gain prestige. In contrast answers to questions that seek factual information or matters of public knowledge (zip code, number of children, and so on) usually are quite accurate. An interviewer's presence may increase a respondent's tendency toward an inaccurate answer to sensitive questions such as "Did you vote in the last election?" "Do you have termites or roaches in your home?" or "Do you color your hair?"

Administrative Error

administrative error
An error caused by the improper administration or execution of the research task.

The results of improper administration or execution of the research task are **administrative errors.** An error is caused by the improper administration or execution of the research task. They are inadvertently (or stupidly) caused by confusion, neglect, omission, or some other blunder. Four types of administrative errors are data processing error, sample selection error, interviewer error, and interviewer cheating.

Data Processing Error

The accuracy of data processed by computer, as with any arithmetic or procedural process, is subject to error because data must be edited, coded, and entered into the computer by people. The accuracy of data processed by computer depends on correct data entry and programming. **Data processing errors** can be minimized by establishing careful procedures for verifying each step in the data processing stage.

Sample Selection Error

Sample selection error is systematic error that results in an unrepresentative sample because of an error in either the sample design or the execution of the sampling procedure. Executing a sampling plan free of procedural error is difficult. A firm that selects its sample from the phone book will have some systematic error, because unlisted numbers are not included. Stopping female respondents during daytime hours in shopping centers excludes working women who shop by mail or telephone. In other cases, the wrong person may be interviewed. Consider a political pollster who uses random digit dialing to select a sample rather than a list of registered voters. Unregistered 17-year-olds may be willing to give their opinions, but they are the wrong people to ask because they cannot vote.

Interviewer Error

Interviewers' abilities vary considerably. When interviewers record answers, they may check the wrong response or may be unable to write fast enough to record answers verbatim. Selective perception may cause **interviewer error** by influencing the way interviewers record data that do not support their own attitudes and opinions.

data processing error
A category of administrative error that occurs because of incorrect data entry, computer programming, or other procedural errors during the analysis stage.

sample selection error
An administrative error caused by improper sample design or sampling procedure execution.

interviewer error
Mistakes made by interviewers when performing their tasks.

Look at you walk, Timmy Baldwin. To make it easy, Luvs made a special diaper just for you. New Luvs Walker for Boys. Its padding is narrower between your legs than ordinary diapers. For easy walking, it also has super absorbency for your large wettings, plus Luvs LeakGuard up front where boys like you need it. And best of all, since you love anything with wheels, your diaper has lots of cars and trains. In a new, small Walker 1, cause you're a little guy to be walking. And as you grow, Timmy, there's Walker 2 and 3. So now, for every boy and girl at every stage of development, Newborn to Walker, Luvs is custom making a special new diaper. **Introducing new Luvs Phases.**

Luvs Phases

Custom made for outstanding leakage protection.

When Pampers introduced Luvs for Girls and Luvs for Boys, a competitor's survey research showed that gender-specific diapers were not important to consumers. However, this research suffered from response bias. When asked in surveys, parents gave a socially desirable answer when they said they did want to stereotype their children in male or female roles. However, the American cultural value—blue for boys and pink for girls—in fact could not be overcome. Analysis of sales and subsequent research shows parents will not put pink diapers on boys.[8]

Interviewer Cheating

interviewer cheating
The practice of filling in fake answers or falsifying interviewers by field-workers.

Interviewer cheating occurs when an interviewer falsifies entire questionnaires or fills in answers to questions that have been intentionally skipped. Some interviewers cheat to finish an interview as quickly as possible or to avoid questions about sensitive topics.

If interviewers are suspected of faking questionnaires, they should be told that a small percentage of respondents will be called back to confirm whether the initial interview was actually conducted. This will discourage interviewers from cheating.

Rule-of-Thumb Estimates for Systematic Error

Sampling error due to random or chance fluctuations may be estimated by calculating confidence intervals with the statistical tools presented in Chapters 17, 20, 21, and 23.

The methods for estimating systematic, or nonsampling, error are less precise. Many researchers have established conservative rules of thumb based on experience to estimate systematic error. They have found it useful to have some benchmark figures or standard of comparison to understand how much error can be expected. For example, according to some researchers in the consumer packaged-goods field, approximately one-half of those who say they "*definitely* will buy" or "*probably* will buy" within the next three months actually do make a purchase.[9] For consumer durables, however, the figures are considerably lower; only about one-third of those who say they definitely will buy a certain durable within the next three months will actually do so. Among those who say they *probably* will buy, the number who actually purchase durables is so much lower that it is scarcely worth including it in the early purchase estimates for new durables. Thus, researchers often present actual survey findings *and* their interpretations of estimated purchase response based on estimates of nonsampling error. For example, one pay-per-view cable TV company surveys geographic areas it plans to enter and estimates the number of people who indicate they will subscribe to its service. The company knocks down the percentage by a "ballpark 10 percent" because experience in other geographic areas has indicated that there is a systematic upward bias of 10 percent on this intentions question.

What Can Be Done to Reduce Survey Error?

Now that we have examined the sources of error in surveys, you may have lost some of your optimism about survey research. Don't be discouraged! The discussion emphasized the bad news because it is important for marketing managers to realize that surveys are not a panacea. There are, however, ways to handle and reduce survey errors. For example, Chapter 15 on questionnaire design discusses the reduction of response bias; Chapter 16 and 17 discuss the reduction of sample selection and random sampling error. Indeed, much of the remainder of this book discusses various techniques for reducing bias in marketing research. The good news lies ahead!

Classifying Survey Research Methods

Now that we have discussed the various advantages and disadvantages of surveys in general, it is appropriate to classify surveys according to several criteria. Surveys may be classified based on the method of communication, the degrees of structure and disguise in the questionnaire, and the time frame in which the data are gathered (temporal classification).

Method of Communication

Chapter 9 classifies surveys according to method of communicating with the respondent, covering topics such as personal interviews, telephone interviews, and mail surveys. The classifications based on structure and disguise and on time frame will be discussed in the remainder of this chapter.

Structured and Disguised Questions

In designing a questionnaire (or interview schedule), the investigator must decide how much structure or standardization is needed.[10] A **structured question** limits the number of allowable responses. For example, the respondent may be instructed to choose one alternative response such as "under 18," "18–35," or "over 35" to indicate his or her age. **Unstructured questions** do not restrict the respondent's answers. An open-ended, unstructured question such as "Why do you shop at Safeway?" allows the respondent considerable freedom in answering.

The researcher must also decide whether to use **undisguised** or **disguised questions**. A straightforward, or undisguised question such as "Do you have dandruff problems?" assumes that the respondent is willing to reveal the information. However, researchers know that some questions are threatening to a person's ego, prestige, or self-concept. Therefore, they have designed a number of indirect techniques of questioning to disguise the purpose of the study.

Questionnaires can be categorized by their degree of structure and degree of disguise. For example, interviews in exploratory research might use *unstructured-disguised* questionnaires. The projective techniques discussed in Chapter 6 fall into this category. Other classifications typically are *structured-undisguised, unstructured-undisguised,* and *structured-disguised.* These classifications have two limitations. First, the degree of structure and the degree of disguise vary; they are not clear-cut categories. Second, most surveys are hybrids, asking both structured and unstructured questions. Recognizing the degrees of structure and disguise necessary to meet survey objectives will help in the selection of the appropriate communication medium for conducting the survey.

structured question
A question that imposes a limit on the number of allowable responses.

unstructured question
A question that does not restrict the respondents' answers.

undisguised question
A straightforward question that assumes the respondent is willing to answer.

disguised question
An indirect question that assumes the purpose of the study must be hidden from the respondent.

WHAT WENT RIGHT?

Scotchgard[12]

3M CHEMICAL'S SCOTCHGARD PROTECTION WILL, FOR the first time, appeal directly to consumers with a product-labeling system and ads that communicate applications and differentiated benefits for categories such as apparel, carpeting, and home furnishings.

The labels appear on carpeting and home furnishings, such as Ikea couches, and apparel hang-tags. Each calls out relevant claims for garments in key Scotchgard categories such as outerwear, kids' clothing, and uniforms. Whereas a booklet designed for outerwear plays up water resistance, one for children's apparel addresses resistance to stains such as juice.

Initiatives stemmed from research with a cross section of the population that showed while 95 percent of consumers were aware of Scotchgard, only 26 percent knew what it does. Marketers learned the brand was invisible to the consumer.

Temporal Classification

Although most surveys are individual projects conducted only once over a short time period, other projects require multiple surveys over a long period. Thus, surveys can be classified on a temporal basis.

Cross-Sectional Studies. A nationwide survey was taken to examine the different attitudes of cross sections of the American public toward the arts. One aspect of the survey dealt with museums. In general the public's attitudes toward museums were very positive. Museum preferences varied by demographics or cross sections of the population: People in towns and rural areas showed greater interest in historical museums, whereas city and suburban residents leaned more heavily than others toward art museums. The young (16- to 20-year-olds) were more interested than others in art museums and less interested in historical museums.[11] Such a study is a **cross-sectional study** because it collected the data at a single point in time. Such a study samples various segments of the population to investigate relationships among variables by cross-tabulation. Most marketing research surveys fall into this category, particularly those that deal with market segmentation. The typical method of analysis in the cross-sectional survey is to divide the sample into appropriate subgroups. For example, if a winery expects income levels to influence attitudes toward wines, the data are analyzed to similarities or differences among the income subgroups.

cross-sectional study
A study in which various segments of a population are sampled and data are collected at a single moment in time.

TO THE POINT

A man's feet should be planted in his country, but his eyes should survey the world.

GEORGE SANTAYANA

longitudinal study
A survey of respondents at different times, thus allowing analysis of changes over time.

Longitudinal Studies. In a **longitudinal study** respondents are questioned at two or more different times. The purpose of longitudinal surveys is to examine continuity of responses and to observe changes that occur over time. Many syndicated polling services, such as the Gallup Poll, are conducted on a regular basis. The Gallup survey asked Americans to indicate how often they get the news on-line. The

Consumer panels provide longitudinal data. NFO has a separate Hispanic panel consisting of 16,000 households.

longitudinal results reveal that the percentage of Americans who occasionally get their news on-line grew from 12 percent in 1995 to 17 percent in 1998 to 23 percent in 1999.[13] The Yankelovich Monitor has been tracking American values and attitudes for more than 30 years. It illustrates a longitudinal study with successive samples because researchers survey several different samples at different times. Longitudinal studies of this type are sometimes called *cohort* studies, because similar groups of people who share a certain experience during the same time interval (cohorts) are expected to be included in each sample. Exhibit 8.2 shows changes in consumers' satisfaction with several industries. The steepest declines in approval are in the health-care industry.

In applied marketing research, typical longitudinal studies that use successive samples are called **tracking studies** because successive waves are designed to compare trends and identify changes in variables such as consumer satisfaction, brand image, or advertising awareness. These studies are useful for assessing aggregate trends but do not allow for tracking changes in individuals over time.

Conducting surveys in waves with two or more sample groups avoids the problem of response bias resulting from a prior interview. A respondent who was interviewed in an earlier survey about a certain brand may become more aware of the brand or pay more attention to its advertising after being interviewed. Using different samples eliminates this problem. However, one can never be sure whether the changes in the variable being measured are due to a different sample or to an actual change in the variable over time.

tracking study
A type of longitudinal study that uses successive samples to compare trends and identify changes in variables such as consumer satisfaction, brand image, or advertising awareness.

TO THE POINT

Time is but the stream I go a-fishing in.

HENRY DAVID THOREAU

Exhibit 8.2 Longitudinal Research from the Harris Poll

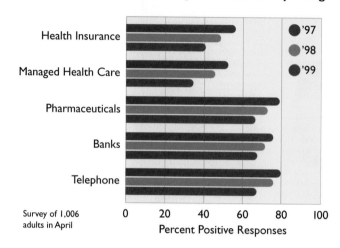

How Good a Job Is This Industry Doing?

Survey of 1,006 adults in April

Percent Positive Responses

Consumer Panel. A longitudinal study that gathers data from the same sample of individuals or households over time is called a **consumer panel.** Consider the packaged-goods marketer that wishes to learn about brand-switching behavior. A consumer panel that consists of a group of people who record their purchasing habits in a diary over time will provide the manager with a continuous stream of information about the brand and product class. Diary data that are recorded regularly over an extended period enable the investigator to track repeat-purchase behavior and changes in purchasing habits along with changes in price, special promotions, or other aspects of marketing strategy.

Panel members may be contacted by telephone, in a personal interview, or by mail questionnaire. Typically media exposure and purchase diaries are completed by respondents and mailed back to the organization. If the panel members have agreed to field test new products, personal or telephone interviews may be required. The nature of the problem dictates which communication method to use.

Because panels generally are expensive to conduct, they often are managed by contractors who offer their services to many organizations. A number of commercial firms, such as National Family Opinion (NFO), Inc., Market Research Corporation of America, and Consumer Mail Panels, Inc., specialize in maintaining consumer panels. Because clients of these firms need to share the expenses with other clients to acquire longitudinal data at a reasonable cost, panel studies ask questions about a number of product classes.

The typical first questionnaire sent to panel members asks about ownership, product usage, pets, family members, and demographic data. The purpose of such a questionnaire is to gather the behavioral and demographic data that will be used in conjunction with future surveys to identify heavy buyers, difficult-to-reach customers, and so on. Individuals selected as members of consumer panels usually are compensated with cash or attractive gifts.

Marketers with products purchased by few households find panels an economical means of reaching respondents who own their products. A two-stage process typically is used. A panel composed of around 15,000 households can be screened with a one-question statement attached to another project. For example, a question in an NFO questionnaire screens for ownership of certain uncommon products, such as snowmobiles and motorcycles. This information is stored in a database. Then households with the unusual item can be sampled again with a longer questionnaire.

Total Quality Management and Customer Satisfaction Surveys

As Chapter 1 described, a **total quality management** strategy emphasizes market-driven quality as a top priority. Total quality management involves implementing and adjusting the firm's business strategy to assure customers' satisfaction with the quality of goods and services.

For many years U. S. corporations failed to keep pace with the product quality strategies of a number of overseas competitors.[14] For example, Xerox Corporation lost a substantial portion of its market share to Ricoh, Canon, and other Japanese copier makers because the Japanese offered both lower prices and higher quality. Xerox scrutinized its product and production strategies and discovered it was destroying itself with sloppiness and inefficiency. The conclusion of its internal audit was that Xerox, like many other U. S. businesses, had lost sight of "an axiom as old as business itself...focusing on quality that meets the customer's requirements."[15]

Today, however, Xerox and many other U. S. organizations recognize the need for total quality management programs. Executives and production workers are sometimes too far removed from the customer. The company needs a means to bridge this gap with feedback about quality of goods and services. This means marketing research. Of course, these programs are not the exclusive domain of marketing researchers. However, in an organization driven by the quality concept, marketing research plays an important role in the management of total product quality.

total quality management
A business philosophy that emphasizes market-driven quality as a top organizational priority.

What Is Quality?

Organizations used to define quality by engineering standards. Most companies no longer see quality that way. Some managers say that having a quality product or service means that the good or service conforms to the consumers' requirements, that the product is acceptable. Effective executives who subscribe to a total quality management philosophy, however, believe that the product's quality must go beyond acceptability for a given price range. Rather than having consumers relieved that nothing went wrong, consumers should experience some delightful surprises or reap some unexpected benefits. In other words, quality assurance is more than just meeting minimum standards. The level of quality is the degree to which a good or service corresponds to buyers' expectations.

Obviously, a Jaguar S-type does not compete with a Nissan Altima. Buyers of these automobiles are in different market segments, and their expectations of quality differ widely. Nevertheless, managers at Jaguar and Nissan try to establish what quality level their target market expect, and then to produce and market goods and services that continually surpass expectations.

Internal and External Customers

Organizations such as Arbor, Inc, which have adopted the total quality management philosophy, believe that a focus on customers must include more than external customers. They believe that everyone in the organization has customers:

> Every person, in every department, and at every level, has a customer. The customer is anyone to whom an individual provides service, information, support, or product. The customer may be another employee or department (internal) or outside the company (external).[16]

Total quality management programs work most effectively when every employee knows exactly who his or her customers are and what output internal and external customers expect. Also, it is important to know how customers perceive suppliers to be meeting their needs. All too often differences between perceptions and reality are not understood.

Implementing Total Quality Management

This chapter began by describing J. D. Power & Associates. The firm's success is due in part to its ability to satisfy companies' needs to measure quality.

Implementing a total quality management program requires considerable survey research. A firm must routinely ask customers to rate it against its competitors. It must periodically measure employee knowledge, attitudes, and expectations. It must monitor company performance against benchmark standards. It must determine whether customers found any delightful surprises or major disappointments. In other words, a total quality management strategy expresses the conviction that to improve quality an organization must regularly conduct surveys to evaluate quality improvement.

Exhibit 8.3 illustrates the total quality management process. Overall, the exhibit shows that tracking quality improvement requires longitudinal research. The process begins with a *commitment and exploration stage* during which management makes a commitment to total quality assurance and marketing researchers explore external and internal customers' needs and beliefs. The research must discover what product features customers value, what problems customers are having with the product, what aspects of product operation or customer service have disappointed customers, what the company is doing right, and what the company may be doing wrong.

After identifying internal and external customers' problems and desires, comes the *benchmarking stage.* Research must establish quantitative measures that can serve as benchmarks or points of comparison against which to evaluate future efforts. The surveys must establish initial measures of overall satisfaction, of the frequency of customer problems, and of quality ratings for specific attributes. It is essential to identify the company's or brand's position relative to competitors' quality positions.

The *initial quality improvement stage* establishes a quality improvement process within the organization. Management and employees must translate quality issues into the internal vocabulary of the organization. The company must establish performance standards and expectations for improvement.

For example, at Bank One Corporation in Columbus, Ohio, the organization translates customer requirements into specifications and policies. Management specifies quality standards and sets procedures and objectives in terms of these standards. Bank One believes it is important that all employees know what is expected of them to achieve consistent quality. To accomplish company goals, managers and employees must be motivated and trained. Bank One insists that every manager is a customer champion who leads by example. Every service employee must know the quality standards for his or her job because employee awareness of the need for service quality is a major means to achieve customer satisfaction.

Employees can face roadblocks that obstruct progress toward meeting customer needs. To clear these obstructions, Bank One managers create teams of employees to develop quality improvement projects because some problems defy

---

Exhibit 8.3 Longitudinal Research for Total Quality Management

Time	Marketing Research Activity with External Consumers (Customers)	Marketing Management Activity	Marketing Research Activity with Internal Consumers (Employees)
Time 1 — Commitment and exploration stage	Exploratory study to determine the quality the customer wants, discover customer problems, and identify the importance of specific product attributes.	Establish marketing objective that the customer should define quality.	Exploratory study to determine (1) whether internal customers, such as service employees, are aware of the need for service quality as a major means to achieve customer satisfaction and (2) whether they know the quality standards for their jobs. Establish whether employees are motivated and trained. Identify road blocks that prevent employees from meeting customer needs.
Time 2 — Benchmarking stage	Benchmarking study to measure overall satisfaction and quality ratings of specific attributes.	Identify brand's position relative to competitors' satisfaction and quality rating; establish standards for customer satisfaction.	Benchmarking to measure employees' actual performance and perceptions about performance.
Time 3 — Initial quality improvement stage	Tracking wave 1 to measure trends in satisfaction and quality ratings.	Improve quality; reward performance.	Tracking wave 1 to measure and compare what is actually happening with what should be happening. Establish whether the company is conforming to its quality standards.
Time 4 — Continuous quality improvement	Tracking wave 2 to measure trends in satisfaction and quality ratings.	Improve quality; reward performance.	Tracking wave 2 to measure trends in quality improvement.

individual efforts. The creation of employee teams to analyze and investigate problems and then to develop and implement solutions can make significant strides toward improvement of service quality.[17]

After managers and employees have set quality objectives and implemented procedures and standards, the firm continues to track satisfaction and quality ratings in successive waves. The purpose of tracking wave 1 in Exhibit 8.3 is to measure trends in satisfaction and quality ratings. Marketing researchers determine whether the organization is meeting customer needs as specified by quantitative standards.

The next stage, *continuous quality improvement* consists of many consecutive waves with the same purpose—to improve over the previous period. Continuous quality improvement requires that management allow employees to initiate problem solving without a lot of red tape. Employees should be able to initiate proactive communications with consumers. In tracking wave 2 management compares results with those of earlier stages. Quality improvement management continues.

Management must reward performance. At Bank One managers reward performance by recognizing individuals and groups that work diligently toward achieving established standards. Bank One gives We Care awards to individuals who exceed the requirements of duty. The firm gives Best of the Best awards to teams and branches with the best performance. The best bank in the Bank One system receives the Chairman's Quality Award for Customer Service.[18]

Exhibit 8.3 shows that total quality management programs measure performance against customers' standards, not against standards determined by quality engineers within the company. All changes within the organization are oriented toward improvement of customers' perceptions of quality. The exhibit indicates the necessary integration of establishing consumer requirements, quantifying benchmark measures, setting objectives, conducting marketing research studies, and making adjustments in the organization to improve quality. Continuous quality improvement is an ongoing process.

The process expressed in Exhibit 8.3 works for marketers of both goods and services. However, service products and customer services offered along with goods have some distinctive aspects. We will first discuss the quality of goods and then consider the quality of services.

In general marketers of consumer and industrial goods track customer satisfaction to investigate customer perceptions of product quality by measuring perceptions of the eight product characteristics listed in Exhibit 8.4.[19] These studies measure whether a firm's perceptions about product characteristics conform to customers' expectations and how these perceptions change over time. For example, any customer satisfaction survey will investigate a good's performance by asking, "How well does the product perform its core function?" To determine the quality of a recycling lawn mower, a researcher might ask, "How well does the mower cut grass and eliminate the need for bagging clippings?" The researcher may ask questions to determine whether the product's quality of performance was a delightful surprise, something well beyond expected performance. Similar questions will cover the other major product characteristics.

Time after time, studies have shown differences between what customers expected and what the service front-line, contact personnel delivered. Marketers who stress service quality strategies focus on the service encounter because service quality depends on what takes place during the service encounter.

Measuring service quality involves comparing expectations with performance. Consumers who perceive high service quality believe service providers matched their expectations.

Exhibit 8.4 Quality Dimensions for Goods and Services

DETERMINANTS OF THE QUALITY OF GOODS

Performance: How well does the product perform its core function? How well does a razor shave a beard?

Features: Does the product have adequate auxiliary dimensions that provide secondary benefits? Does a motor oil have a convenient package?

Conformance with specifications: What is the incidence of defects? Does a vineyard sell spoiled wine?

Reliability: Does the product ever fail to work? Does the product perform with consistency? Will the lawn mower work properly each time it is used?

Durability: What is the economic life of the product? How long will a motorcycle last?

Serviceability: Is the service system efficient, competent, and convenient? Does a computer software manufacturer have a toll-free number and a technical staff to quickly answer questions?

Aesthetic design: Does the product's design look and feel like a quality product?
Is a snowmobile aerodynamic?

DETERMINANTS OF SERVICE QUALITY

Access: Is contact with service personnel easy? Does a visit to the dentist require a long delay in the waiting room?

Communication: Is the customer informed? Does he or she understand the service and how much it will cost? Does a computer repair technician explain needed repairs in understandable language?

Competence: Has the service provider mastered the required skill, and is he or she proficient in managing support personnel? Does a tax account have a CPA designation?

Courtesy: Are personnel polite and friendly? Do all bank tellers smile and greet customers warmly?

Reliability: Does the service consistently meet standards? Are the personnel dependable?

Credibility: Do the service providers have integrity? Is the doctor who performs a heart operation trustworthy and believable?

In organizations that wish to improve service quality, managers must identify and analyze customer service needs and then establish specifications for the level of service. They must then train front-line personnel and given them the responsibility for quality service. Front-line personnel need to be motivated and encouraged to deliver the service according to these specifications. Finally, regular surveys with both external customers and internal employees measure results against standards.

Marketers investigate service quality to measure customer satisfaction and perceived quality in terms of the six service attributes given in Exhibit 8.4. Specific considerations concerning the actual measurement of quality of goods and service delivery are further addressed in Chapters 13, 14, and 15.

Summary

Survey research is a common tool for asking respondents questions. Surveys can provide quick, inexpensive, and accurate information for a variety of objectives. The typical survey is a descriptive research study with the objective of measuring awareness, product knowledge, brand usage behavior, opinions, and so on. The term *sample survey* is often used because a survey is expected to obtain a representative sample of the target population.

Two major forms of error are common in survey research. The first random sampling error is caused by chance variation and results in a sample that is not absolutely representative of the target population. Such errors are inevitable, but they can be predicted using the statistical methods discussed in later chapters on sampling. The second major category of error, systematic error, takes several forms. Nonresponse error is caused by people who are sampled but do not respond and by those whose answers may differ from those of respondents in some significant way. This type of error can be reduced by comparing the demographics of the sample population with those of the target population and making a special effort to contact underrepresented groups.

Response bias occurs when a response to a questionnaire is falsified or misrepresented, either intentionally or inadvertently. There are five specific categories of response bias: acquiescence bias, extremity bias, interviewer bias, auspices bias, and social desirability bias. An additional source of survey error comes from administrative problems such as inconsistencies in interviewers' abilities, cheating, coding mistakes, and so forth. Surveys may be classified according to methods of communication, the degrees of structure and disguise in the questionnaires, and on a temporal basis. Questionnaires may be structured, with limited choices of responses, or unstructured, with open-ended responses. Disguised questions may be used to probe sensitive subjects.

Surveys may consider the population at a given moment or follow trends over a period of time. The first approach, the cross-sectional study, usually is intended to separate the population into meaningful subgroups. The second type of study, the longitudinal study, can reveal important population changes over time. Longitudinal studies may involve contacting different sets of respondents or the same ones repeatedly. One form of longitudinal study is the consumer panel. Such studies are expensive to conduct, so firms often hire contractors who provide their services to many other companies, thus spreading costs over many products.

Total quality management involves implementing and adjusting a firm's business strategy to assure customers' satisfaction with the quality of goods and services. The level of quality is the degree to which a good or service corresponds to buyers' expectations. Marketing research provides companies the means to provide feedback about quality goods and services.

Implementing a total quality management program requires considerable survey research conducted in waves. A firm routinely asks customers to rate it against its competitors. It also measures employee attitudes and monitors company performance against benchmark standards. After identifying customer problems and desires, the firm tracks satisfaction and quality ratings in successive waves. Total quality management research is an ongoing process for continuous quality improvement. Total quality management works for marketers of both goods and services.

Key Terms and Concepts

Respondent
Sample survey
Survey
Random sampling error
Systematic error
Sample bias
Respondent error
Nonresponse error
Nonrespondent
Not-at-home
Refusal

Self-selection bias
Response bias
Acquiescence bias
Extremity bias
Interviewer bias
Auspices bias
Social desirability bias
Administrative error
Data processing error
Sample selection error
Interviewer error

Interviewer cheating
Structured question
Unstructured question
Undisguised question
Disguised question
Cross-sectional study
Longitudinal study
Tracking study
Consumer panel
Total quality management

Questions for Review and Critical Thinking

1. Name several nonbusiness applications of survey research.
2. A major petroleum corporation marketed its gasoline through a franchise dealer organization under a national brand name. The corporation was considering building a number of company-owned stations with a new brand name to market a low-priced gasoline product to compete with independent dealers. Would survey research have been useful? Is so, how?
3. What survey research objectives might Ford Motor Company develop to learn about car buyers?
4. Give an example of each type of error listed in Exhibit 8.1.
5. In a survey, chief executive officers (CEOs) indicated that they would prefer to relocate their businesses in Atlanta (first choice), San Diego, Tampa, Los Angeles, or Boston. The CEOs who said they were going to build the required office space in the following year were asked where they were going to build. They indicated they were going to build in New York, Los Angeles, San Francisco, or Chicago. Explain the difference.
6. What potential sources of error might be associated with the following situations:
   a. In a survey of frequent flyers aged 50 and older, researchers concluded that price does not play a significant role in airline travel because only 25 percent of the respondents check off price as the most important consideration in determining where and how they traveled, while 35 percent rate price as being unimportant.
   b. A survey of voters finds that most respondents do not like negative political ads, that is, advertising by one political candidate that criticizes or exposes secrets about the opponent's "dirty laundry."
   c. Researchers who must conduct a 45-minute personal interview decide to offer $10 to each respondent because they believe that people who will sell their opinions are more typical than someone who will talk to a stranger for 45 minutes.
   d. A company's sales representatives are asked what percentage of the time they spend making presentations to prospects, traveling, talking on the telephone, participating in meetings, working on the computer, and engaging in other on-the-job activities. What potential sources of error might be associated with asking such a question?
7. What topics about consumer behavior might be extremely sensitive issues about which to directly question respondents?
8. A survey conducted by the National Endowment for the Arts asked, "Have you read a book within the last year?" What response bias might be possible with this question?
9. In what ways might survey results for buying intentions be adjusted for consumer optimism?
10. Name some common objectives of cross-sectional surveys.
11. Give an example of a political situation in which longitudinal research might be useful. Name some common objectives for a longitudinal study in a business situation.
12. What are the advantages and disadvantages of using consumer panels?
13. Page through your local newspaper to find some stories derived from survey research results. Was the study's methodology appropriate for this news item? Could the research have been termed *advocacy research*?
14. Suppose you are the marketing research director for your state's tourism bureau. Assess the state's information needs, and identify the information you will collect in a survey of tourists who visit your state.
15. A researcher sends out 200 questionnaires, but 50 are returned because the addresses are inaccurate. Of the 150 delivered questionnaires, 50 were completed and mailed back. However, 10 of these respondents wrote that they did not want to participate in the survey. The researcher indicates the response rate was 33.3 percent. Is this the right thing to do?

Exploring the Internet

1. Located at the University of Connecticut, the Roper Center is the largest library of public opinion data in the world. The methodology and findings of many surveys may be found at http://www.ropercenter.uconn.edu. Surf to the center report on a study of your choice.
2. Go to ASI Research Web site (http://www.asiresearch.com) to learn what type of survey research services the firm offers. What hot links about other survey research services can be accessed through ASI's Web site?
3. Look up *Journal of Empirical Generalizations in Marketing Science,* an electronic journal established at the University of South Australia

(http://msc.city.unisa.edu.au/msc/JEMS_INTRO.html), or go to the Marketing Science Centre home page (http://msc.unisa.edu.au) and click on Marketing Research on-line. Navigate from there. Browse an article and see if you can find a research paper that uses survey research as the method for collecting data. Go to the magazine home page.

4. The National Longitudinal Surveys (NLS) provide data on the labor force experience (current labor force and employment status, work history, and characteristics of current or last job) of five groups of the U.S. population. Go to http://www.bls.gov/opub/hom/homtoc.htm to learn about the objectives and methodology for this study.

Case 8.1   The Greeting Card Study

SELECTED ADULT MEMBERS OF A CONSUMER PANEL WERE sent the following cover letter and a questionnaire referred to as a purchase diary (the green purchase diary form is not shown here).

We are presently conducting a study for a greeting card manufacturer who, in order to be able to provide the "right card for the right person," would like to know the type of cards being purchased now and to whom they are being sent. We are asking our members to participate in this project by keeping a record of the greeting cards they purchase and receive during the *next month*.

As a participant, here is what we would like you to do.

1. Please record all purchases of greeting cards made by your and members of your household in the green purchase diary form provided for July. It is most important for this study that we have the information for *all* cards purchased by *everyone* in your household. Please make it known that as soon as someone in your household purchases a greeting card, he or she should either show you the card, or give you the appropriate information so you can make the diary entry as soon after the purchase as possible.

    Section 1 is for entries of individual greeting cards; Section 2 is to record the purchases of boxes or packages of cards.

2. Here is the very unusual part of this study. Please save all of the greeting cards you and other members of your household receive during the month of July and follow "Instructions for Cards Received" (blue page).

    Accurate reporting is very important, so please read the instruction page for each form carefully. Your report will be for the month of July, so on July 31 or as soon after as possible, please return the appropriate materials. (We've enclosed a postage-paid envelope for your convenience.)

    Your cooperation is deeply appreciated. We are sending you a dollar bill, as a token of our sincere thanks for your time and effort. Thank you very much!

QUESTIONS

1. Evaluate the cover letter. What type of appeal is used? Does the format of the cover letter follow the pattern indicated in the textbook?

2. In your opinion will the respondents comply with the researcher's request? Why or why not?

3. What sources of survey error are most likely in a study of this type?

Video-Case 8.2   **The Walker Group**

THE WALKER GROUP IS ONE OF THE 15 LARGEST marketing research companies in the world. The Walker Group's total revenue tops that of such well-known names as J. D. Power and Associates, Roper, and Yankelovich Partners. Walker's clients include many Fortune 500 and Blue Chip industry leaders such as Cummins Engine Company, Lenscrafters, Continental Cablevision, Florida Power and Light, Oglethorpe Power Corporation, and Energy.

The Indianapolis-based company was founded in 1939 as a field interviewing service by Tommie Walker, mother of Frank Walker, the current chairperson and chief executive officer of the organization. In the 1920s Tommie Walker's late husband worked for a bank that was considering sponsoring an Indianapolis radio show featuring classical music. The bank wanted to know who was listening to this show. Tommie was hired to do the interviewing, and she threw herself into the work. After that, referrals brought her more interviewing work for surveys. During an interview with a woman whose husband was a district sales manager for the A&P grocery chain, she learned that A&P was looking for a surveyor in the Midwest. A&P's sales manager liked Tommie, but wouldn't hire anyone without a formal company, a field staff, and insurance. Tommie founded Walker Marketing Research on October 20, 1939, and her business with A&P lasted 17 years.

Today, the Walker Group specializes in business, health care, and consumer research, as well as database marketing. The company is organized into six strategic business units.

Walker Market Research and Analysis conducts traditional market research services that range from questionnaire design and data collection to advanced analysis and consultation. Walker has expertise in helping companies measure how their actions are perceived by the audiences most important to them, and how this affects their image, reputation, corporate citizenship, recruiting, sales, and more.

Data Source is a business unit that primarily is concerned with data collection and processing data. They specialize in telephone data collection.

Customer Satisfaction Measurement (CSM), as

the name implies, specializes in measuring customer satisfaction and in helping clients improve their relationship with customers.

CSM Worldwide Network spans more than 50 countries. It is the first international network of professional research and consulting businesses dedicated to customer satisfaction measurement and management. The CSM Worldwide Network assures that multicountry customer satisfaction research is consistent by taking into account local conditions and cultural norms. Network members are trained to use consistent methods that allow standardization and comparability of information from country to country.

Walker Direct designs, develops databases, and implements direct-marketing programs that help generate leads for businesses and raise funds for nonprofit organizations.

Walker Clinical is a health-care product use research company. Walker helps pharmaceutical, medical-device, and consumer-product manufacturers test how well new products work and how customers like them.

QUESTIONS

1. What type of custom survey research projects might Walker Market Research and Analysis conduct for its clients?

2. What stages are involved in conducting a survey? For which stages might a client company hire a research supplier like Walker Marketing Research and Analysis? Data Source?

3. What is the purpose of customer satisfaction measurement?

4. What measures, other than findings from surveys, might a company use to evaluate the effectiveness of a total quality management program?

Case 8.3   Turner's Department Store

TURNER'S HAD BEEN IN BUSINESS FOR 47 YEARS. THE FIRST store was located downtown, but the organization had been expanding over the years. The local department store chain operates ten department stores and junior department stores, ranging in size from 10,000 to 60,000 square feet. All stores were located in a single metropolitan area with a population of approximately 600,000 people. The firm's volume strength was in soft goods, although it also handled housewares and small appliances in all stores as well as major appliances in some stores. Price savings on name brands were the primary emphasis of Turner's merchandising strategy.

Turner's was considering its first major venture into survey research. Mr. Clay Turner, executive vice president, had indicated that "we want to find out what customers and noncustomers think about us and to learn what directions we may take to gain a bigger share of the market." He sent a list of research needs (see Case Exhibit 8.3-1) to several marketing research consultants.

QUESTIONS

1. Has the marketing research problem been adequately defined?
2. What type of survey would you recommend?
3. What sources of survey error are most likely in this project?
4. Prepare a brief research proposal for this project.

Note: Names are fictitious to ensure confidentiality.

Case Exhibit 8.3-1   Research Needs for Turner's Department Stores

We're not looking for praise or compliments but as honest an appraisal as possible. The questions contained here are merely suggestions and may be amplified, condensed, or changed as need be to arrive at a summary that can be acted on.

What Turner's wants to know is "How do people look upon Turner's, and what should we do to merit more of their patronage?" We will appreciate having from you:

1. Your suggested questionnaire
2. Sampling size or sizes
3. Degree of expected accuracy
4. Costs or costs
5. Time frame in which the study may be completed
6. Type of summary or summaries to be presented on completion
7. Recommendations for action

Perhaps the study should encompass all or part of the following:

1. A sampling sufficient to give an overall picture
2. The Sampling to be divided as equally as possible among people who shop frequently and those who shop at Turner's occasionally, seldom, or never
3. The sampling to be done a various income levels, as equitably as possible in relationship of the specific income levels to the total, perhaps
     $8,000–$15,000
     $15,000–$35,000
     $35,000–$55,000
     $55,000–$75,000
     Over $75,000
5. The sampling to be done by age level breakdown: under 25, 25–35, 35–44, over 44
6. The sampling to include family composition: ages of children, if any, and number of boys and girls

7. Of those who shop often or occasionally at Turner's, what departments they depend on. Examples: men's apparel; women's apparel; women's sportswear; women's hosiery; women's accessories; cosmetics and fragrances; men's, women's, and children's shoes; costume jewelry; fabrics, linens, sheets, towels, bedspreads, draperies, etc.; small appliances; major appliances; housewares; giftware; china; glassware; lamps; radios and televisions; boys' wear; girls' wear; infants' needs.

8. Some idea of readership of Turner's newspaper advertising, preferably among various income levels.

9. How people perceive us in relation to other local retail firms (Sears, Macy's, Penney's, Kmart, Bloomingdale's);

   Turner's merchandise is most like: _____

   Turner's fashions are most like: _____

   Turner's prices are most like: _____

   Turner's stores look most like: _____

   Turner's advertising is most like: _____

   Turner's prices are as low or lower than: _____

10. Turner's salespeople are: helpful _____ courteous _____ discourteous _____ not helpful _____

11. Of those who do not shop at Turner's: "I would shop more at Turner's if _____."

12. Turner's advertising is: informative ____ not informative ____ sometimes honest ____ not accurate____

13. Do you think Turner's carries a large number of well-known brands?

14. Among those who shop often at Turner's: Do you shop most at the nearest Turner's store? Or do you go to another Turner's? Which one?

15. When you go to Turner's with a specific purchase in mind, do you usually find it in stock? (This applies particularly to everyday items such as hosiery, underwear, jeans, housewares, small appliances, etc.)

16. If the interviewer has a Turner's charge account: Is charge authorization prompt?

17. When did you last shop at Turner's? (A week ago, a month ago, three months ago)

18. If the interviewee has previously shopped at Turner's, but no longer does so, is it because of a bad experience? Credit? Exchange, refund, or adjustment of a merchandise purchase?

19. Turner's values are: _____ excellent _____ good _____ fair _____ poor

20. Turner's carries: some irregulars and seconds ____ many irregulars and seconds ____ all first quality

21. I believe seconds and irregulars offer excellent value: yes _____ no _____

Chapter 9

Survey Research:
Basic Methods of Communication with Respondents

FORD MOTOR COMPANY CONDUCTS STYLE RESEARCH CLINICS TO appraise consumer reactions to exterior and interior styling of new automotive designs. First, fiberglass prototypes or mockups of proposed models are made. Then respondent are recruited, usually after short telephone interviews, brought to a showroom, and exposed to a test car mockup so it can be compared with competing models from the world market. Personal interviewers ask about every detail of the car as the prospects pore over it. Ultimately the results are fed back to designers in Detroit. Millions were spent on surveys about the Ford Taurus and Mercury Sable as well as Ford's new Jaguar S-type.

Chrysler also conducts research to learn consumers' reactions to its cars both on and off the road. Chrysler researchers give each survey participant a device called a Gridpad to improve the accuracy and speed of data collection. The Gridpad looks a little bit like an Etch-a-Sketch, but it is a rather sophisticated, flat, 8-by-10-inch box with a penlike wand. While the survey respondent inspects new car models, multiple-choice questions are displayed on a screen. To respond, the individual simply touches the appropriate box on the Gridpad with the wand.

When all the questions have been answered, the information is downloaded into a desktop computer. Previously, survey participants used pencils to fill out the questionnaires, which then had to be sorted, boxed, and shipped to processing centers. The manager of business planning/research for Chrysler estimates that using the Gridpad saves about 100,000 sheets of paper on each research project.

What you will learn in this chapter

To understand when personal interview, telephone, or self-administered surveys should be concluded.

To discuss the advantages and disadvantages of personal interviews.

To explain when door-to-door personal interviews should be used instead of mall intercept interviews.

To discuss the advantages and disadvantages of telephone surveys.

To discuss random digit dialing and other methods of selecting telephone numbers for surveys.

To discuss the advantages and disadvantages of mail, Internet, and other self-administered questionnaires.

To increase response rates to mail surveys.

To select the appropriate survey research design.

To provide examples of the influence of modern technology on survey research.

To discuss the importance of pretesting questionnaires.

Media Used to Communicate with Respondents

During most of the twentieth century, survey data were obtained when individuals responded to questions asked by human interviewers (interviews) or to questions they read (questionnaires). Interviewers communicated with respondents face-to-face or over the telephone or respondents filled out a self-administered paper questionnaire, which was typically distributed by mail. These media for conducting surveys remain popular with marketing researchers.

However, as we mentioned in Chapters 2 and 7, digital technology is having a profound impact on society in general and marketing research in particular. It's greatest impact is in the creation of new forms of communications media.

Human Interactive Media and Electronic Interactive Media

When two people engage in a conversation, human interaction takes place. Human interactive media are a personal form of communication. The messages are directed at a particular individual (or a small group) who has the opportunity to interact with another human being. When we think of the traditional role of interviewing, most people envision two people engaged in a face-to-face dialogue or a conversation on the telephone. Electronic interactive media allow marketers to reach a large audience, to personalize individual messages, and to provide the opportunity for interaction by using digital technology. To a large extent electronic interactive media are controlled by the users themselves. No other human need be present. In the context of surveys, respondents are not passive audience members. They are actively involved in a two-way communication when electronic interactive media are utilized.

The Internet, a medium that is radically altering many organizations' research strategies, provides a prominent example of the new electronic interactive media. Consumers determine the information to which they will be exposed, and for how long they will view or hear it. Electronic interactive media also include CD-ROM and DVD materials, Touch-Tone telephone systems, interactive kiosks in stores, and other forms of digital technology.

Noninteractive Media

The traditional questionnaire received by mail and completed by the respondent does not allow a dialogue or an exchange of information providing immediate feedback. Hence, from our perspective, we will classify self-administered questionnaires printed on paper as noninteractive. This does not mean they are without merit. It only means this type of survey is not as flexible as surveys using interactive communication media.

Each technique for conducting surveys has its merits and shortcomings. The purpose of this chapter is to explain when different types of surveys should be used. This chapter begins with a discussion of surveys that use live interviews. It then discusses noninteractive, self-administered questionnaires. Finally, it explains how digital technology can be used in survey research.

Using Interviews to Communicate with Respondents

Interviews can be categorized based on the medium through which the researcher communicates with individuals and records data. For example, interviews may be conducted door-to-door, in shopping malls, or on the telephone. Traditionally interview results have been recorded using paper and pencil, but computers are increasingly supporting survey research.

The discussion on interviews begins by examining the general characteristics of personal interviews, which are conducted face-to-face. It proceeds to look at the unique characteristics of door-to-door personal interviews, personal interviews conducted in shopping malls, and telephone interviews.

Personal Interviews

Although the history of marketing research is sketchy, the gathering of information through face-to-face contact with individuals has a long history. Periodic censuses were used to set tax rates and aid military conscription in the ancient empires of Egypt and Rome.[1] During the Middle Ages, the merchant families of Fugger and Rothschild prospered in part because their far-flung organizations enabled them to get information before their competitors did.[2] Today it is common to hear something similar to the following at doorstep throughout the United States:

Good afternoon, my name is _____ **. I am with** _____

Marketing Research Company and we are conducting a survey on _____ **.**

Personal interviews are direct communications between businesses and consumers in which interviewers ask respondents questions face-to-face. This versatile and flexible method is a two-way conversation between interviewer and respondent.

personal interview
Face-to-face communication in which an interviewer asks a respondent to answer questions.

The Advantages of Personal Interviews

Marketing researchers find that personal interviews offer many unique advantages. One of the most important is the opportunity for feedback.

The Opportunity for Feedback. Personal interviews provide the opportunity for feedback to the respondent. For example, in a personal interview a consumer who is reluctant to provide sensitive information may be reassured

EXPLORING RESEARCH ISSUES

Do You Cheat on Your Income Tax? How the IRS Asks Sensitive Questions

During the course of a personal interview concerning taxpayers' opinions of the Internal Revenue Service, respondents were requested to provide information on income tax cheating behavior. Needless to say, these were highly sensitive questions. The IRS used the lock box technique to ask about tax cheating.

The Lock box technique combines two methods of ensuring confidentiality. First, the questionnaire is self-administered. This frees the respondent to reply in a truthful manner without concern about the interviewer's reaction. Second, upon completion of the instrument, the respondent rolls it up, secures it with a rubber band, and places it in a sealed box (similar to a ballot box). The box is translucent, approximately the size of a shoe box, and is designed to

hold five to six questionnaires. At all times there is at least one other instrument in the box to further reassure the respondent that his or her responses will remain confidential. Once the box is full, the instruments are removed and the box resealed.

Respondents were given the following instructions for answering ten questions:

At this point we would like to ask you some specific questions about how you handle your taxes. Because the questions are more personal, and we want you to answer honestly, we are going to let you fill out this part of the questionnaire privately. Once you are finished, you will drop the questionnaire into this box.

As you can see, the box is sealed so your questionnaire will not be removed until it is sent to our central office in Virginia. I will never see the questionnaire. There is no identifying information on this questionnaire (show respondent questionnaire), so your answers will never be identified by name. In fact, we are not interested in individual persons, but in different kinds of people.

Questionnaire

1. Have you ever failed to file a tax return which you think you should have?
    Yes . . . 1
    No . . . 2

2. Have you ever purposely listed more deductions than you were entitled to?
    Yes (*GO TO Q. 3*) . . . 1
    No (*GO TO Q. 4*) . . . 2

3. About how much was the largest amount?
    Amount:_____

4. Have you ever purposely failed to report some income on your tax return—even just a minor amount?
    Yes (*GO TO Q. 5*) . . . 1
    No (*GO TO Q. 6*) . . . 2

5. About how much was the largest amount of income you have reported?
    Amount:_____

6. How honest do you think you were on filling out your tax return for [year]? Circle the answer that best describes how honest you think you were.

Absolutely honest	Pretty honest	Somewhat honest	Not at all honest

7. Have you ever claimed a dependent on your tax return that you weren't really entitled to?
    Yes . . . 1
    No . . . 2

8. Some people pay fewer taxes than are required by the tax code. Below is a list of ways people have avoided paying all their taxes. For each of the ways, show on the scale how often you use each of these methods by circling the appropriate point.

A. Failing to report some income.

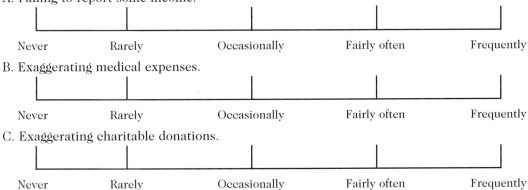

| Never | Rarely | Occasionally | Fairly often | Frequently |

B. Exaggerating medical expenses.

| Never | Rarely | Occasionally | Fairly often | Frequently |

C. Exaggerating charitable donations.

| Never | Rarely | Occasionally | Fairly often | Frequently |

9. The following questions ask you about things some people do when filing their tax return. For each one, show on the scale whether your conscience would bother you if you did it. Circle one of the 5 numbers on the line to show whether your conscience would be bothered.

A. Not filing a return on purpose.

| 1 | 2 | 3 | 4 | 5 |
| Not at all | | Some | | A lot |

B. Understating your income.

| 1 | 2 | 3 | 4 | 5 |
| Not at all | | Some | | A lot |

C. Overstating your medical expenses.

| 1 | 2 | 3 | 4 | 5 |
| Not at all | | Some | | A lot |

D. Claiming an extra dependent.

| 1 | 2 | 3 | 4 | 5 |
| Not at all | | Some | | A lot |

E. Padding business travel expenses.

| 1 | 2 | 3 | 4 | 5 |
| Not at all | | Some | | A lot |

F. Not declaring large gambling earnings.

| 1 | 2 | 3 | 4 | 5 |
| Not at all | | Some | | A lot |

G. Understanding your income.

| 1 | 2 | 3 | 4 | 5 |
| Not at all | | Some | | A lot |

10. Did you stretch the truth a little in order to pay fewer taxes for [year]?

Yes . . . 1
No . . . 2

When visitors enter Remington Park race track, it is likely they will participate in a survey. Interviewers ask only one question: "What is your zip code?" As simple as this survey may seem, it provides valuable information about the race track's geographic market segments.

that his or her answers will be strictly confidential. Personal interviews offer the lowest chance of misinterpretation of questions because the interviewer can clarify any questions respondents have about the instruction or questions. After the interview has been terminated, circumstances may dictate that the respondent be given additional information concerning the purpose of the study. This is easily accomplished with the personal interview.

Probing Complex Answers.

probing
A method used in personal interviews in which the interviewer asks the respondent for clarification of answers to standardized questions.

An important characteristic of personal interviews is the opportunity to probe. If a respondent's answer is too brief or unclear, the researcher may *probe* for a more comprehensive or clearer explanation. In **probing** the interviewer asks for clarification of answers to standardized questions, such as "Can you tell me more about what you had in mind?" (See Chapter 18 on fieldwork for an expanded discussion of probing.) Although interviewers are expected to ask questions exactly as they appear on the questionnaire, probing allows them some flexibility. Depending on the research purpose, personal interviews vary in the degree to which questions are structured and in the amount of probing required. The personal interview is especially useful for obtaining unstructured information. Skilled interviewers can handle complex questions that cannot easily be asked in telephone or mail surveys.

Length of Interview.

If the research objective requires an extremely lengthy questionnaire, personal interviews may be the only option. Generally telephone interviews last less than 10 minutes, whereas a personal interview can be much longer, perhaps 1-1/2 hours. A general rule of thumb on mail surveys is that they should not exceed six pages.

Completeness of Questionnaire.

item nonresponse
Failure of a respondent to provide an answer to a survey question.

The social interaction between a well-trained interviewer and a respondent in a personal interview increases the likelihood that the respondent will answer all the items on the questionnaire. The respondent who grows bored with a telephone interview may terminate the interview at his or her discretion simply by hanging up the phone. Self-administration of a mail questionnaire, however, requires more effort by the respondent. Rather than write lengthy responses, however, the respondent may fail to complete some of the questions. **Item nonresponse**—failure to provide an answer to a question—is least likely to occur when an experienced interviewer asks questions directly.

Props and Visual Aids. Interviewing respondents face to face allows the investigator to show them new-product samples, sketches of proposed advertising, or other visual aids. In a survey to determine whether a superlightweight chain saw should be manufactured, visual props were necessary because the concept of weight is difficult to imagine. Two small chain saws currently on the market and a third, wooden prototype disguised and weighted to look and feel like the proposed model were put in the back of a station wagon. Respondents were asked to go to the car, pick up each chain saw, and compare them. This research could not have been done in a telephone interview or mail survey.

Marketing research that uses visual aids has become increasingly popular with researchers who investigate film concepts, advertising problems, and moviegoers' awareness of performers. Research for movies often begins by showing respondents videotapes of the prospective cast. After the movie has been produced, film clips are shown and interviews conducted to evaluate the movie's appeal, especially which scenes to emphasize in advertisements.

High Participation. Although some people are reluctant to participate in a survey, the presence of an interviewer generally increases the percentage of people willing to compete the interview. Respondents typically are required to do no reading or writing—all they have to do is talk. Many people enjoy sharing information and insights with friendly and sympathetic interviewers.

Disadvantages of Personal Interviews

Personal interviews also have some disadvantages. Respondents are not anonymous and therefore may be reluctant to provide confidential information to another person. Suppose a survey asked top executives, "Do you see any major internal instabilities or threats (people, money, material, and so on.) to the achievement of your marketing objectives?" Many managers may be reluctant to answer this sensitive question honestly in a personal interview in which their identities are known.

Interviewer Influence. Some evidence suggests that demographic characteristics of the interviewer influence respondents' answers. For example, one research study revealed the male interviewers produced larger amounts of interviewer variance than females in a survey in which 85 percent of the respondents were female. Older interviewers who interviewed older respondents produced more variance than other age combinations, whereas younger interviewers who interviewed younger respondents produced the least.

Differential interviewer techniques may be a source of bias. The rephrasing of a question, the interviewer's tone of voice, and the interviewer's appearance may influence the respondent's answer. Consider the interviewer who has conducted 100 personal interviews. During the next one, he or she may selectively perceive or anticipate the respondent's answer. The interpretation of the response may differ somewhat from the intended response. Our image of the person who does marketing research typically is that of the dedicated scientist. Unfortunately, some interviewers do not fit that ideal. Considerable interviewer variability exists. Cheating is possible; interviewers may cut corners to save time and energy, faking parts of their reports by dummying up part or all of the questionnaire. Control over interviewers is important to ensure that difficult, embarrassing, or time-consuming questions are handled in the proper manner.

Anonymity of Respondent. In a personal interview, the respondent is not anonymous and may be reluctant to provide confidential information to another person. Researchers often spend considerable time and effort to phrase sensitive questions to avoid social desirability bias. For example, the interviewer may show the respondent a card that lists possible answers and ask the respondent to read a category number rather than be required to verbalize sensitive answers.

Cost. Personal interviews are expensive, generally substantially more costly than mail or telephone interviews. The geographic proximity of respondents, the length and complexity of the questionnaire, and the number of people who are nonrespondents because they could not be contacted (not-at-homes) will all influence the cost of the personal interview.

Door-to-Door Interviews and Shopping Mall Intercepts

Personal interviews may be conducted at the respondents' homes or offices, or in many other places. Increasingly personal interviews are being conducted in shopping malls. Mall intercept interviews allow many interviews to be conducted quickly. Often respondents are intercepted in public areas of shopping malls and then asked to come to a permanent research facility to taste new food items or to view advertisements. The locale for the interview generally influences the participation rate and, thus, the degree to which the sample represents the general population.

door-to-door interview
A method of administering questionnaires at respondents' doorsteps that increases the participation rate in the survey.

Door-to-Door Interviews. The presence of an interviewer at one's door generally increases the likelihood that one will be willing to complete the interview. Because **door-to-door interviews** increase the participation rate, they provide a more representative sample of the population than mail questionnaires. For example, response rates to mail surveys are substantially lower among Hispanics whether the questionnaire is printed in English or Spanish.[3] People who do not have telephones, have unlisted telephone numbers, or are otherwise diffi-

EXPLORING RESEARCH ISSUES

Exit Polls: The Networks Versus the West Coast

SURVEY RESEARCHERS HIRED BY TELEVISION NETworks often interview voters at the voters exist polling places. These exit polls often terminate as much as an hour before the voting ends be-cause the news director wants the results ready in time to project the winner as soon as the local polls close. A number of West Coast residents believe that such early projections about presidential races by national television news networks before their local polls close influence their voting behavior, especially voter turnout. The networks argue that they should not with-hold the news of the results once they are known. Are early election projections an ethical practice? Take a stand.

cult to contact may be reached using door-to-door interviews. Such interviews can help solve the problem of nonresponse; however, they may underrepresent some groups and overrepresent others.

Door-to-door interviews may exclude individuals who live in multiple-dwelling units with security systems, such as high-rise apartment dwellers or executives who are too busy to grant personal interviews during business hours. Telephoning an individual in one of these subgroups to make an appointment may make the total sample more representative; however, obtaining a representative sample of this security-conscious subgroup based on a listing in the telephone directory may be difficult.

People who are at home and willing to participate, especially if interviewing is conducted in the daytime, are somewhat more likely to be over 65 years of age, homemakers, or retired people. These and other variables related to respondents' tendencies to stay at home may affect participation.

Callbacks. When a person selected to be in the sample cannot be contacted on the first visit, a systematic procedure normally is initiated to call back at another time. **Callbacks,** or attempts to recontact individuals selected for the sample, are the major means of reducing nonresponse error. The cost per interview of an interviewer calling back on a sampling unit is higher because subjects who initially were not at home generally are more widely dispersed geographically than the original sample units. Callbacks in door-to-door interviews are important because not-at-home individuals (for example, working parents) may systematically vary from those who *are* at home (nonworking parents, retired people, and the like).

callback
An attempt to recontact individuals selected for a sample who were not available initially.

Mall Intercept Interviews. Personal interviews conducted in shopping malls are referred to as **mall intercept interviews,** or shopping center sampling. Interviewers typically intercept shoppers at a central point within or at an entrance to the mall. The main reason mall intercept interviews are conducted is because their costs are lower. No travel is required to the respondent's home; instead, the respondent comes to the interviewer, and many interviews can be conducted quickly in this way.

mall intercept interview
Personal interview conducted in shopping malls.

A major problem with mall intercept interviews is that individuals usually are in a hurry to shop so the incidence of a refusal is high—typically around 50 percent. Nevertheless, the commercial marketing research industry conducts more personal interviews in shopping malls than it conducts door-to-door.

In such an interview, the researcher must recognize that he or she should not be looking for a representative sample of the total population. Each mall will have its own target market's characteristics, and there is likely to be a larger bias than with careful household probability sampling. However, personal interviews in shopping malls are appropriate when the target group is a special market segment such as the parents of children of bike-riding age. If the respondent indicates that he or she has a child of this age, the parent can then be brought into a rented space and shown several bikes. In this way the mall intercept interview allows the researcher to show large, heavy, or immobile visual materials, such as a television commercial, or give an individual a product to take home to use and be recontacted later by telephone. Mall intercept interviews are also valuable when the cooking and tasting of products must be closely coordinated and timed to follow each other. They may also be appropriate when a consumer durable product must be demonstrated. For example, when videocassette recorders and DVD players were innovations in the prototype stage, the extensive space required to set up and properly display these units ruled out in-home testing.

TO THE POINT

A man's feet should be planted in his country, but his eyes should survey the world.

GEORGE SANTAYANA

Global Considerations. Willingness to participate in a personal interview varies dramatically around the world. For example, in many Middle-Eastern countries women would never consent to be interviewed by a man. And in many countries the idea of discussing grooming behavior and personal-care products with a stranger would be highly offensive. Few people would consent to be interviewed on such topics.

The norms about appropriate business conduct also influence businesspeople's willingness to provide information to interviewers. For example, conducting business-to-business interviews in Japan during business hours is difficult because managers, strongly loyal to their employer, believe they owe absolute commitment to their employees while on the job. In some cultures when a businessperson is reluctant to be interviewed, it may be possible to get a reputable third party to intervene so an interview may take place.

Telephone Interviews

Good evening, I'm with a nationwide marketing research company. Are you watching television tonight?

A: Yes.

Did you see the made-for-television movie on CBS?

EXPLORING RESEARCH ISSUES

Ameritech's Privacy Manager

AMERITECH'S NEW PHONE SERVICE CALLED PRIVACY Manager is intended to screen annoying sales calls for telemarketers.[7] However, it is also sure to have an impact on researchers using telephone surveys.

Ameritech's chief executive says that in product usage tests with 200 customers, reaction to Privacy Manager was off the charts. "We have never had a product test this good," says the CEO, including voice mail and caller ID. "It satisfied a need that consumers have just been pleading to have resolved."

Here's how it works: A customer needs to have a caller ID display box first, and the Privacy Manager service costs $3.95 a month. Calls normally shown on the ID screen with a name and number go right through. But any calls made from phone numbers classified as "private," "blocked," "out of area," "unavailable," or "unknown" are intercepted. A recording comes on and asks outside callers to reveal their identity by speaking their name.

Anyone who doesn't leave a name is automatically disconnected. If callers leave a name, the person they attempted to call hears the phone ring, and a recorded message says: "This is Privacy Manager. You have a call from..." and then the name of the caller. The customer is given three choices: accept the call, reject it, or play a message that says: "We don't accept telemarketing calls. Please add me to your do-not-call list."

For the past two decades, **telephone interviews** have been the primary method of commercial survey research. The quality of data obtained by telephone may be comparable to the quality of the data collected in personal interview. Respondents are more willing to provide detailed and reliable information on a variety of personal topics over the telephone than with personal interviews. Telephone surveys can provide representative samples of the general population in the United States but may be a problem in less developed countries.

telephone interview
The primary method of commercial survey research.

The Characteristics of Telephone Interviews

Telephone interviews have several distinctive characteristics that set them apart from other survey techniques. The advantages and disadvantages of these characteristics are discussed in the section.

Speed. One advantage of telephone interviewing is the speed of data collection. Rather than taking several weeks for data collection by mail or personal interviews, hundreds of telephone interviews can be conducted literally overnight. When the interviewer enters the respondents' answers directly into a computerized system, the data processing speeds up even more.

Cost. As the cost of personal interviews continues to increase, telephone interviews are becoming relatively inexpensive. It is estimated that telephone interviews cost less than 25 percent of the cost of door-to-door personal interviews.[4] Travel time and costs of travel are eliminated.

Absence of Face-to-Face Contact. Telephone interviews are more impersonal than face-to-face interviews. Respondents may answer embarrassing or confidential questions more willingly in a telephone interview than in a personal interview. However, a mail survey, although not perfect, is the best medium for gathering extremely sensitive information because it is anonymous. There is some evidence that people provide income and other financial information only reluctantly even with telephone interviews. Such questions may be personally threatening for a variety of reasons, and high refusal rates for this type of question occur in each form of survey research.

Although telephone calls may be less threatening because no interviewer is present, the absence of face-to-face contact can also be a liability. The respondent cannot see that the interviewer is still writing down the previous comment and may continue to elaborate on an answer. If the respondent pauses to think about an answer, the interviewer may not realize this and go on to the next question. Hence, there is a greater tendency to record no answers and incomplete answers in telephone interviewing than in personal interviewing.

Cooperation.

In some neighborhoods, people are reluctant to allow a stranger to come inside the house or even stop on the doorstep. The same individual, however, may be perfectly willing to cooperate with a telephone survey request. Likewise, interviewers may be somewhat reluctant to conduct face-to-face interviews in certain neighborhoods, especially during the evening hours. Some individuals will refuse to participate, and the researcher should be aware of potential nonresponse bias. Some evidence exists that the likelihood of an unanswered call and not-at-home respondent varies by the time of day, the day of the week, and the month of the year.

The number of people who own telephone answering machines is growing. Although their effect has not been studied extensively, it is clear that many individuals will not return a call to help someone conduct a survey. Some researchers argue that leaving the proper message on an answering machine will produce return calls. The message left on the machine should explicitly state the purpose of the call is not sales related.[5] Others believe no message should be left because respondents will be reached if the researchers call back. The logic is based on the fact that answering machines are not turned on 100 percent of the time. Thus, if enough callbacks are made at different times and on different days, most respondents are reachable.[6] Caller ID services can have a similar impact if respondents do not pick up the phone when unfamiliar numbers appear on the display.

Refusal to cooperate with interviews is directly related to interview length. A major study of survey research found that interviews of 5 minutes or less had a refusal rate of 21 percent; interviews of between 6 and 12 minutes had 41 percent refusal rates; and interviews of 13 minutes or more had 47 percent rates.[8] In unusual cases a few highly interested respondents will put up with longer interviews. A good rule of thumb is to keep telephone interviews approximately 10 to 15 minutes long. In general 30 minutes is the maximum amount of time most respondents will spend unless they are highly interested in the survey subject. Evidence suggests that over the last few years the percentage of Americans cooperating with telephone surveys is declining.[9]

Representative Samples.

Practical difficulties complicate obtaining representative samples based on listings in the telephone book. Slightly more than 96 percent of households in the United States have telephones. People without phones are more likely to be poor, aged, rural, or living in the South. They may be a minor segment of the market, but unlisted phone numbers and numbers too recent to be printed in the directory are a greater problem. Unlisted numbers fall into two groups: those unlisted because of mobility and those unlisted by choice. Individuals with unlisted numbers because of a household move differ slightly from those with published numbers. The unlisted group tends to be younger, more urban, and less likely to own a single-family dwelling. When a telephone number is unlisted by choice, the household tends to have higher incomes. However a number of low-income households are unlisted by circumstance. Researchers conducting surveys in areas where the proportion of unlisted phone numbers is high, such as in California (Sacramento, 68.3 percent; Los Angeles/Long Beach, 66.7 percent; and Oakland, 67.3 percent), should pay special attention to making accurate estimates of these numbers.[10] In other markets such as New Haven/Waterbury, where fewer than 25 percent of phone numbers are unlisted, this may not be a major problem. Nationally slightly less than 30 percent of phone numbers are unlisted.

The problem with unlisted phone numbers can be partially resolved through the use of random digit dialing. **Random digit dialing** eliminates the counting of names in a list (for example, calling every fiftieth name in a column) and subjectively determining whether a directory listing is a business, institution, or legitimate household. In its simplest form random digit dialing begins with telephone exchanges (prefixes) for the geographic areas in the sample. Using a table of random numbers, the last four digits to complete the telephone number are selected. Telephone directories can be ignored entirely or used in combination with the assignment of one or several random digits. Random digit dialing also helps overcome the problem of new listings and recent changes in numbers being absent from directories. Unfortunately, the refusal rate in commercial random digit dialing studies (approximately 40 percent) is higher than the 25 percent refusal rate when surveying uses only listed telephone numbers.

random digit dialing
Using telephone exchanges and a table of random numbers, respondents with unlisted phone numbers may be contacted.

Callbacks. An unanswered call, a busy signal, or a not-at-home respondent requires a callback. Telephone callbacks are much easier to make than callbacks in personal interviews. However, as mentioned, the ownership of telephone answering machines is growing, and their effects on callbacks need to be studied.

Limited Duration. Respondents who run out of patience with the interview can merely hang up. To encourage participation, interviews should be relatively short. The length of the telephone interview is definitely limited.

Lack of Visual Medium Because visual aids cannot be used in telephone interviews, packaging research, television and print advertising copy testing, and concept tests that require visual materials cannot be conducted by phone. Certain attitude scales and measuring instruments, such as the semantic differential (see Chapter 14), cannot be used easily because they require the respondent to see a graphic scale.

Central Location Interviewing

Research agencies or interviewing services typically conduct all telephone interviews from a central location. They contract for WATS (wide-area telecommunications service) lines from long-distance telephone services at fixed charges so that they can make unlimited telephone calls throughout the entire country or within specific geographic areas. Such **central location interviewing** allows firms to hire a staff of professional interviewers and to supervise and control the quality of interviewing more effectively. When telephone interviews are centralized and computerized, additional cost economies are realized.

central location interviewing
Telephone interviews conducted from a central location using WATS lines at fixed charges.

Phone cards have been used as a means to obtain cooperation with computerized voice-activated telephone interviews. An organization may provide customers with a prepaid phone card as a sales promotion. When the card user dials a specified number to activate the phone card, a recorded message offers additional minutes if the caller will respond to an interactive voice-response survey.

Computer-Assisted Telephone Interviewing

computer-assisted telephone interview (CATI)
Technology that allows answers to telephone interviews to be directly entered into a computer for processing.

Advances in computer technology allow telephone interviews to be directly entered into the computer through the on-line **computer-assisted telephone interviewing** (CATI) process. Telephone interviewers are seated at computer terminals. Monitors display the questionnaires, one question at a time, along with precoded possible responses to the question. The interviewer reads each question as it appears on the screen. When the respondent answers, the interviewer enters the response directly into the computer, and it is automatically transcribed into the computer's memory. The computer then displays the next question on the screen. This type of computer-assisted telephone interviewing requires that answers to the questionnaire be highly structured. If a respondent gives an unacceptable answer, that is, one not precoded and programmed, the computer will reject it.

Computer-assisted telephone interviewing systems include telephone management systems to handle phone number selection and perform automatic dialing, and other labor-saving functions. These systems can automatically control sample selection by randomly generating names or fulfilling a sample quota. A computer can generate an automatic callback schedule. A typical call management system might schedule recontact attempts to recall no answers after two hours, recall busy numbers after ten minutes, and allow the interviewer to enter a more favorable time slot (day and hour) when a respondent indicates that he or she is too busy to be interviewed. Software systems also allow researchers to request daily status reports on the number of completed interviews relative to quotas.

Computerized Voice-Activated Telephone Interview. Technological advances have combined computerized telephone dialing and voice-activated computer messages to allow researchers to conduct telephone interviews without human interviewers. However, researchers have found computerized voice-activated telephone interviewing works best with very short, simple questionnaires. One system includes a voice-synthesized module controlled by a microprocessor. With it the sponsor is able to register a caller's single response such as "true/false," "yes/no," "like/dislike," or "for/against." This type of system has been used by television and radio stations to register callers' responses to certain issues. One system, Telsol, begins with an announcement that the respondents are listening to a recorded message. Many people are intrigued with the idea of talking to a robot or a computer, so they stay on the line. The computer then asks questions, leaving blank tape in between to record the answers. If respondents do not answer the first two questions, the computer disconnects and goes to the next call.

Global Considerations

Different cultures often have different norms about proper telephone behavior. For example, Latin American business-to-business researchers have learned that businesspeople will not open up to strangers on the telephone. Hence, survey respondents usually find personal interviews more suitable than telephone surveys. In Japan, because the language does not lend itself to long telephone interviews, respondents consider it ill-mannered if interviews go beyond 20 minutes.

Self-Administered Questionnaires

Many surveys do not require an interviewer's presence. Marketing researchers distribute questionnaires to consumers through the mail and in many other ways. They insert questionnaires in packages and magazines. They may locate questionnaires at the points of purchase or in high-traffic locations. They may even fax questionnaires to individuals. Questionnaires are usually printed on paper, but they may be programmed into computers. No matter how the **self-administered questionnaires** are distributed to the members of the sample, they are different from interviews because the respondent takes responsibility for reading and answering the questions.

Self-administered questionnaires present a challenge to the marketing researcher because they rely on the efficiency of the written word rather than the skills of the interviewer. The nature of self-administered questionnaires is best illustrated by explaining the nature of mail questionnaires.

self-administered questionnaire
Survey in which the respondent takes the responsibility for reading and answering the questions.

Mail Questionnaires

A **mail survey** is a self-administered questionnaire sent to respondents through the mail. This paper-and-pencil method presents several advantages and disadvantages.

mail survey
A self-administered questionnaire sent to respondents through the mail.

Geographic Flexibility. Mail questionnaires can reach a geographically dispersed sample simultaneously because interviewers are not required. Respondents (such as farmers) who are located in isolated areas or those (such as executives) who are otherwise difficult to reach can easily be contacted by mail. For example, a pharmaceutical firm may find that doctors are inaccessible to personal or telephone interviews. A mail survey can reach both rural and urban doctors who practice in widely dispersed geographic areas.

Cost. Mail questionnaires are relatively low in cost compared with personal interviews and telephone surveys, though they are not cheap. Most include follow-up mailings, which require additional postage and printing costs. Questionnaires photocopied on poor-grade paper have a greater likelihood of being thrown in the wastebasket than more expensive, high-quality printing jobs.

Respondent Convenience. Mail and other self-administered questionnaires can be filled out when the respondents have time; thus, there is a better chance that respondents will take time to think about their replies. In some situations, particularly in business-to-business marketing research, mail questionnaires allow respondents to collect facts, such as sales statistics, that they may not recall accurately. Checking information by verifying records or, in household surveys, by consulting with other family members should provide more valid, factual information than either personal or telephone interviews would allow. A catalog retailer may use mail surveys to estimate sales volume for catalog items by sending a mock catalog as part of the questionnaire. Respondents would be asked to indicate how likely they would be to order selected items. Using the mail allows respondents to consult other family members and to make their decisions within normal time spans. Many hard-to-reach respondents are best contacted by mail because they place a high value on their own convenience.

Anonymity of Respondent. In the cover letter that accompanies a mail or self-administered questionnaire, marketing researchers almost always state that the respondents' answers will be confidential. Respondents are more likely to provide sensitive or embarrassing information when they can remain anonymous.

For example, the question "Have you borrowed money at a regular bank?" was asked in a personal interview and a mail survey conducted simultaneously. The results were a 17 percent response in personal interviews and a 42 percent response in mail survey. Although random sampling error may have accounted for part of this difference, the results suggest that for personal and sensitive financial issues mail surveys are more confidential than personal interviews.

Anonymity can also reduce social desirability bias. People are more likely to agree with controversial issues, such as extreme political candidates, when given self-administered ballots than when speaking to interviewers on the phone or at their doorsteps.

Absence of Interviewer. Although the absence of an interviewer can induce respondents to reveal sensitive or socially undesirable information, it can also be a disadvantage. Once the respondent receives the questionnaire, the questioning process is beyond the researcher's control. Although the printed stimulus is the same, each respondent will attach a different personal meaning to each question. Selective perception operates in research as well as in advertising. The respondent does not have the opportunity to question the interviewer. Problems that might be clarified in a personal or telephone interview remain misunderstandings in a mail survey. There is no interviewer to probe for additional information or clarification of an answer, and the recorded answers may be assumed to be complete.

Respondents have the opportunity to read the entire questionnaire before they answer individual questions. Often the text of a later question will provide information that affects responses to earlier questions.

Standardized Questions. Mail questionnaires typically are highly standardized, and the questions are quite structured. Questions and instructions must be clear-cut and straightforward; if they are difficult to comprehend, the respondents must use their own interpretations, which may be wrong. Interviewing allows for feedback from the interviewer regarding the respondent's comprehension of the questionnaire. An interviewer who notices that the first 50 respondents are having some difficulty understanding a question can report this to the research analyst so revisions can be made. With a mail survey, however, once the questionnaires are mailed, it is difficult to change the format or the questions.

Time Is Money. If time is a factor in management's interest in the research results or if attitudes are rapidly changing (for example, toward a political event), mail surveys may not be the best communication medium. A minimum of two to three weeks is necessary for receiving the majority of the responses. Follow-up mailings, which usually are sent when the returns begin to trickle in, require an additional two or three weeks. The lapsed time between the first mailing the cut-off date (when questionnaires will no longer be accepted) normally is six to eight weeks. In a regional or local study, personal interviews can be conducted more quickly. However, conducting a national study by mail might be substantially faster than conducting personal interviews across the nation.

Length of Mail Questionnaire. Mail questionnaires vary considerably in length, ranging from extremely short, postcard questionnaires to lengthy, multi-page booklets that require respondents to fill in thousands of answers. A general rule of thumb is that a mail questionnaire should not exceed six pages in length. When a questionnaire requires a respondent to expend a great deal of effort, an incentive is generally required to induce the respondent to return the questionnaire. The following sections discuss several ways to obtain high response rates even when questionnaires are longer than average.

Response Rates

Surveys that are boring, unclear, or too complex get thrown in the wastebasket. A poorly designed survey may be returned by only 15 percent of those sampled; thus, it will have a 15 percent response rate. The basic calculation for obtaining a **response rate** is to count the number of questionnaires returned or completed, then divide the total by the number of eligible people who were contacted or requested to participate in the survey. Typically, the number in the denominator will be adjusted for faulty addresses and similar problems that reduce the number of eligible participants.[12]

response rate
Calculated by counting the number of questionnaires returned or completed divided by the number of eligible people who were contacted to participate in the survey.

The major limitations of mail questionnaires relate to response problems. Respondents who complete the questionnaire may not be typical of all people in the sample. Individuals with a special interest in the topic are more likely to respond to a mail survey than those who are indifferent.

A researcher has no assurance that the intended subject will be the person who fills out the questionnaire. The wrong person answering the questions may be a problem when surveying corporate executives, physicians, and other professionals, who may pass questionnaires on to subordinates to complete.

There is some evidence that cooperation and response rates rise as home value increases.[13] Also, if the sample has a high proportion of retired and well-off householders, response rates will be lower. Mail survey respondents tend to be better educated than nonrespondents. Poorly educated respondents who cannot read and write well may skip open-ended questions to which they are required to write out their answers—if they return the questionnaire at all. Rarely will a mail survey have the 80 to 90 percent response rate that can be achieved with personal interviews. However, the use of follow-up mailings and other techniques may increase the response rate to an acceptable percentage. If a mail survey has a low response rate, it should not be considered reliable unless it demonstrates with some form of verification that nonrespondents are similar to respondents.

Increasing Response Rates for Mail Surveys

Nonresponse error is always a potential problem for mail surveys. Individuals who are interested in the general subject of the survey are more likely to respond than those with less interest or experience. Thus, people who hold extreme positions on an issue are more likely to respond than individuals who are largely indifferent to the topic. To minimize this bias, researchers have developed a number of techniques to increase the response rate among sampling units. For example, almost all surveys include prepaid-postage return envelopes. Forcing respondents to pay their own postage can substantially reduce the response rate.

Exhibit 9.1   Example of Cover Letter for Household Survey

Official letterhead	WASHINGTON STATE UNIVERSITY PULLMAN, WASHINGTON 99968 DEPARTMENT OF RURAL SOCIOLOGY ROOM 23, Wilman Hall
Date mailed	April 19, 19XX
Inside address in matching type	Oliver Jones 2190 Fontane Road Spokane, Washington 99467
What study is about; its social usefulness	Bills have been introduced in Congress and our State Legislature to encourage the growth of rural and small town areas and slow down that of large cities. These bills could greatly affect the quality of life provided in both rural and urban places. However, no one really knows in what kinds of communities people like you want to live or what is thought about these proposed programs.
Why recipient is important (and, if needed, who should complete the questionnaire)	Your household is one of a small number in which people are being asked to give their opinion on these matters. It was drawn in a random sample of the entire state. In order that the results will truly represent the thinking of the people of Washington, it is important that each questionnaire be completed an returned. It is also important that we have about the same number of men and women participating in this study. Thus, we would like the questionnaire for your household to be completed by an adult female. If none is present, then it should be completed by an adult male.
Promise of confidentiality; explanation of identification number	You may be assured of complete confidentiality. The questionnaire has an identification number for mailing purposes only. This is so that we may check your name off of the mailing list when your questionnaire is returned. Your name will never be placed on the questionnaire.
Usefulness of study *"Token" reward for participation*	The results of this research will be made available to officials and representatives in our state's government, members of Congress, and all interested citizens. You may receive a summary of results by writing "copy of results requested" on the back of the returns envelope, and printing your name and address below it. Please do not put this information on your questionnaire itself.
What to do if questions arise	I would be most happy to answer any questions you might have. Please write or call. The telephone number is (509) 335-8623.
Appreciation	Thank you for your assistance.
	Sincerely,
Pressed blue ballpoint signature	
Title	Don A. Dillman Project Director

Designing and formatting attractive questionnaires and wording questions so they are easy to understand also help ensure a good response rate. However, special efforts may be required even with a sound questionnaire. Several of these are discussed in the following subsections.

cover letter

Letter that accompanies a questionnaire to induce the reader to complete and return the questionnaire.

Cover Letter.   The **cover letter** that accompanies the questionnaire or is printed on the first page of the questionnaire booklet is an important means of inducing the reader to complete and return the questionnaire. Exhibit 9.1 illustrates a cover letter and some of the points considered by a marketing research professional to be important in gaining respondents' attention and cooperation. The first paragraph of the letter explains why the study is important. The basic appeal is one of social usefulness. Two other frequently used appeals are to ask the respondent to help the sponsor—"Will you do us a favor?"—and the egotistical appeal "Your opinions are important! Cover letters ensure confidentiality, indicate a postage-paid reply envelope, describe the incentive as a reward for participation, explain that answering the questionnaire will not

Exhibit 9.2 **Plots of Actual Response Patterns for Two Commercial Surveys**

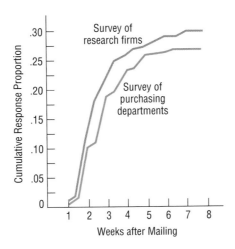

be difficult and will take only a short time, and describe how the person was scientifically selected for participation.

Money Helps. The respondent's motivation for returning a questionnaire may be increased by offering monetary incentives or premiums. Although pens, trading stamps, lottery tickets, and a variety of premiums have been used, monetary incentives appear to be the most effective and least biasing incentive. Although money may be useful to all respondents, its primary advantage may be as a way to attract attention and create a sense of obligation. It is perhaps for this reason that monetary incentives work for all income categories. Often cover letters try to boost response rates with messages such as "We know that the attached dollar [or coin] cannot compensate you for your time. It is just a token of our appreciation." Response rates have increased dramatically when the monetary incentive was to be sent to a charity of the respondent's choice rather than directly to me respondent.

Interesting Questions. The topic of the research cannot be manipulated without changing the definition of the marketing problem. However, certain interesting questions can be added to the questionnaire, perhaps at the beginning, to stimulate respondents' interest and to induce cooperation. Questions of little concern to the researchers, but which the respondents want to answer, may provide respondents who are indifferent to the major portion of the questionnaire with a reason for responding.[14]

Follow-ups. Exhibit 9.2 shows graphic plots of cumulative response rates for two mail surveys. The curves are typical of most mail surveys: The response rates start relatively high for the first two weeks, then gradually taper off.

After responses from the first wave of mailings begin to trickle in, most studies use follow-up letter or postcard reminders. These request that the questionnaires be returned because a 100 percent return rate is important. A follow-up may include a duplicate questionnaire or merely serve as a reminder to return the original questionnaire.

PepsiCo Foods International, marketer of Lay's potato chips, is unifying its current market-leading potato chip brands worldwide with Walkers Crisps in the U. K., Papas Sabritas in Mexico, and Matutano chips in Spain using the Lay's name and a new global package design highlighted by a bold new icon called the Banner Sun. [15]

This initiative followed the most comprehensive market research program in food products history. Over 100,000 consumers in 30 countries were interviewed to describe, understand, and develop the worldwide potato chip market. PepsiCo learned that potato chips are "the cola of snacks." In country after country, potato chips are consumers' favorite snack. The company's new international marketing approach enables Lay's to communicate and enchance the concept of potato chips as a timeless, simple pleasure to consumers around the world.

Both of the studies in Exhibit 9.2 used follow-ups. Notice how the cumulative response rates picked up around week four.

Advance Notification.

Advance notification, by either letter or telephone, has been successful in some situations. For example, A. C. Nielsen has used this technique to ensure a high cooperation rate in filling out diaries of television watching. Advance notices that go out closer to the questionnaire mailing time produce better results than those sent too far in advance. The optimal lead time for advance notification is three days before the mail survey is to arrive.

Survey Sponsorship.

Auspices bias may result from the sponsorship of a survey. One business-to-business marketer wished to conduct a survey of its wholesalers to learn their stocking policies and their attitudes concerning competing manufacturers. A mail questionnaire sent under the corporate letterhead very likely would have received a much lower response rate than the questionnaire actually sent, which used a commercial marketing research firm's letterhead. The sponsorship of well-known and prestigious organizations such as universities or government agencies may also significantly influence response rates.

A mail survey sent to members of a consumer panel will receive an exceptionally high response rate because panel members have already agreed to cooperate with surveys.

Other Techniques.

Numerous other devices have been used for increasing response rates. For example, the type of postage (commemorative versus regular stamp), degree of personalization of the cover letter (letters individually typed versus printed), color of the questionnaire paper, and many other factors have been used for increasing response rates. Each has had at least limited success in certain situations. Unfortunately, under other conditions they fail to increase response rates significantly. The researcher should consider his or her particular situation. For example, the researcher who is investigating consumers faces one situation; the researcher who is surveying corporate executives faces quite another.

Keying Mail Questionnaires with Codes.

A marketing researcher planning a follow-up should not disturb respondents who already have returned the questionnaires. The expense of mailing questionnaires to those who already

Samsonite inserts this product registration questionnaire into all luggage and business case products. The chance to win a "sweepstakes" prize encourages consumers to respond to the questionnaire. The results of the questionnaire become a key element of Samsonite's consumer database and its direct-marketing programs.

have responded is usually avoidable. One device for eliminating those who have already responded from the mailing list for follow-up mailings is to mark the questionnaires so that they may be keyed to identify members of the sampling frame who are nonrespondents. Blind keying of questionnaires on a return envelope (systematically varying the job number or room number of the marketing research department, for example) or use of visible code numbers on the questionnaire has been used for this purpose. Visible keying is indicated with statements such as "The sole purpose of the number on the last pages is to avoid sending a second questionnaire to people who complete and return the first one." Ethical researchers key questionnaires strictly to increase response rates, thereby preserving respondents' anonymity.

Global Considerations.

Researchers conducting surveys in more that one country must recognize that postal services and cultural circumstances differ around the world. For example, Backer Spielvogel & Bates Worldwide advertising agency conducts its Global Scan survey in 18 countries. In the United States the questionnaire is mailed to individuals selected for the sample, but mail is not used in several other countries. The questionnaire may be personally delivered to respondents because of a fear of letter bombs, unreliable delivery service, or low literacy rates in a particular country.[16]

Printed, Self-Administered Questionnaires that Use Other Forms of Distribution

Many forms of self-administered questionnaires are very similar to mail questionnaires. Airlines frequently pass out questionnaires to passengers during flights. Restaurants, hotels, and other service establishments frequently print short questionnaires on cards so that customers can evaluate the service. *Tennis Magazines, Advertising Age, Wired,* and many other publications have inserted questionnaires to inexpensively survey current readers and often to provide the source for a magazine article. Many manufacturers use their warranty or owner registration cards to collect demographic information and data about where and why products were purchased.

Using owner registration cards is an extremely economical technique for tracing trends in consumer habits. Again, problems may arise because people who fill out self-administered questionnaires differ from those who do not.

Extremely long questionnaires may be dropped off by an interviewer and then picked up at a later time. The **drop-off method** sacrifices some cost savings because it requires travel to each respondent's location.

drop-off method
Requires the interviewer to travel to the respondent's location to drop off questionnaires that will be picked up later.

fax survey
Uses fax machines as a way for respondents to receive and return questionnaires.

Fax Surveys

Fax surveys use fax machines as a way for respondents to return questionnaires and as a means to deliver questionnaires.[17] A questionnaire inserted in a magazine may instruct the respondent to clip out the questionnaire and fax it to a certain phone number. In a mail survey, a prepaid-postage envelope places little burden on the respondent. Faxing a questionnaire to a long-distance number requires that the respondent pay for the transmission of the fax. Thus, a disadvantage of fax surveys is that only respondents with fax machines who are willing to exert the "extra" effort return questionnaires. It is likely that people with extreme opinions will be more likely to respond.

Questionnaires can also be distributed via fax machines. These fax surveys replace the sender's printing and postage costs are and delivered and/or returned faster than traditional mail surveys. Questionnaires distributed via fax can deal with timely issues. Although most households do not have fax machines, when the sample consists of organizations that are likely to have fax machines, the sample coverage may be adequate.

The accompanying story about fax machines and a Joe Camel survey illustrate a situation in which using a fax method of return caused serious problems.

E-Mail Surveys

e-mail survey
Distribution of surveys through electronic mail.

Questionnaires are beginning to be distributed via e-mail, or electronic mail. E-mail is a relatively new method of communication, and many individuals cannot be accessed by it. However, certain circumstances lend themselves to **e-mail** surveys, such as internal surveys of employees or surveys of retail buyers who regularly deal with the organization via e-mail. The benefits of this method include cheaper distribution and processing fees, faster turnaround time, more flexibility, and less paper chasing. Not much academic research has been conducted on e-mail surveys. However, it has been argued that many respondents feel they can be more candid on e-mail than on personal or telephone surveys for the same reasons they are candid on other self-administered questionnaires. Researchers

Technological innovation can change more than the way business is done in an industry—it can change entire cultures. The mechanical clock made regular working hours possible.[20] The invention of railroads and the mass production of automobiles changed the way people thought about distance.[21] Television changed the way we think about news and entertainment.[22] And, because the Internet is the most important communication medium since the introduction of television, it is having a profound impact on marketing research. Self-administered polls will increasingly become person–machine electronic transactions.

at Socratic Technologies and American Research claim that when people are contacted to take part in electronic research they are more likely to participate than in identical investigations using written materials.[18] It has been suggested that e-mail questionnaires are successful for two reasons: They arouse curiosity because they are novel and they reach respondents when they are opening their e-mail, which is when they are prepared to interact.

Computerized Questionnaires Using Interactive Media

Electronic interactive media allow marketers to reach a large audience, to personalize individual messages, and to provide the opportunity for interaction by using digital technology. Surveys conducted on the Internet, at interactive kiosks, or by sending disks by mail can be interactive.[19] Many of these interactive surveys can utilize color, sound, and animation, which help to increase participant cooperation and willingness to spend more time answering the questionnaires.

Computer-interactive surveys are programmed in much the same way as computer-assisted telephone interviewing surveys. That is, software is available to allow questioning to branch off into two or more different lines depending on each respondent's answer to filtered questions. The difference is that there is no interviewer. The respondent interacts directly with software on an Internet Web site or an on-site computer. In other words, the respondent self-administers a computer program that asks questions in a sequence determined by his or her previous answers. The questions appear on the computer screen, and answers are recorded by simply pressing a key or clicking an icon, thus immediately entering the data into the computer's memory. Of course, these methods avoid labor costs associated with data collection and processing of paper-and-pencil questionnaires.

computer-interactive survey
Survey in which the respondent self-administers a computer program that asks questions in a sequence determined by the respondent's previous answers.

Greenfield Online is located at http://www.greenfieldonline.com This advertisement shows it offers a variety of Internet survey options.

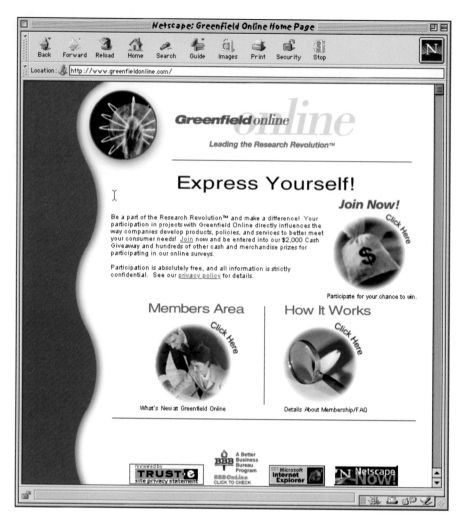

One major advantage of computer-assisted surveys is the computer's ability to sequence questions based on previous responses. The computer can be programmed to skip from question 6 to question 9 if the answer to question 6 is no. Furthermore, responses to previous questions can lead to questions that can be personalized for individual respondents. (For example, "When you cannot buy your favorite brand, Revlon, what brand of lipstick do you prefer?") However, the questionnaire is designed for the research problem, and computerization should not compromise this. Often the respondent's name personalizes the questionnaire.

A major disadvantage of computer-interactive surveys is that open-ended response questions require that respondents have both the skill and the willingness to type lengthy answers into the computer.

Internet survey
Survey in which a computer user navigates to a particular Web site where questions are displayed.

Internet Surveys

The typical **Internet survey** appears when a computer user intentionally navigates to a particular Web site where questions are displayed. (In some cases, a research company sends an e-mail requesting a user visit a certain URL.) The respondent provides an answer by highlighting a phrase or by clicking an icon. In

Java Cookie Demonstration

This document demonstrates web browser client access to cookies from a java applet. Special thanks to Tom Vrankar for this script, for more information about additional scripts please visit Tom Vrankar's Java Collection.

Cookies represent user state information stored in a web browser client, and are usually silently manipulated by the web server. They enable a web feature similar to the Washington D.C. subway system of tracking riders by means of paper slips with magnetic ink containing information (e.g. station entry and exit names, timestamps, and remaining fare). The cookie is this metaphorical paper slip.

This applet will work with Netscape Navigator 3.0 and above; hopefully it will eventually work with Microsoft Internet Explorer 3.0. In any case, java execution must be available and enabled. The complete package including the java source code, and this page is available for download in zip format.

In the applet below there are two text components. In the first, you may enter any string to set into your browser as a cookie. The details of the Set-cookie: protocol are followed. In general, cookies are of the form name=value. You may set more than one cookie, but only one with a given name as they will overwrite.

The second text component displays all cookies visible to the applet. It's updated whenever you hit <Enter> or <Return> in the first.

Set-cookie :

Available Cookies :

Marketers with a presence on the World Wide Web find that their Web sites are emerging as a source of customer data. Researchers can combine a variety of technologies to learn who is visiting their sites. For example, "cookies," which observe and track a Web surfer's movements from page to page, and interactive surveys can be combined to provide consumer profiles of people who are attracted to advertising banners.

some instances, the visitor cannot venture beyond the survey page without providing information for the organization's "registration" questionnaire. When cooperation is voluntary, response rates are low. And, as with other questionnaires that rely on voluntary self-selection, participants tend to be more deeply involved with the subject of the research than the average person.

However, the Internet also provides a new, convenient way for organizations to confidentially survey employees, suppliers, and distributors. For example, employees are instructed to navigate to a particular Web site at a convenient time. When an individual logs on to the Web site, an interactive questionnaire may ask questions about sensitive issues such as a supervisor's effectiveness. In many circumstances, a research supplier specializing as a host for Internet surveys, such as SurveyOnline (http://www.surveyonline.com), is used to secure confidential answers in a simple, quick, and very cost-effective manner.

Other Electronically Interactive Surveys

A computer may be installed in a kiosk at a trade show, at a professional conference, in an airport, or other high-traffic location to administer an interactive survey. Because the respondent chooses to interact directly with an on-site computer, self-selection often is a problem in this type of survey. Computer-literate individuals are most likely to complete these interactive questionnaires. At temporary locations, such as a convention, these surveys often require a fieldworker to be at the on-site location to explain how to use the computer system. This is an obvious disadvantage.

Survey Research that Mixes Modes

Many survey research objectives dictate the use of a combination of telephone, mail, Internet, or personal interview surveys. For example, the researcher may conduct a short telephone screening interview to determine whether respondents are eligible for recontact in a more extensive personal interview. Such a **mixed-mode survey** combines the ad-

mixed-mode survey
Study that employs any combination of survey methods.

Exhibit 9.3 Typical Advantages and Disadvantages of the Traditional Survey Methods

	DOOR-TO-DOOR PERSONAL INTERVIEW	MAIL INTERCEPT PERSONAL INTERVIEW	TELEPHONE	MAIL	INTERNET
Speed of data collection	Moderate to fast	Fast	Very fast	Researcher has no control over return of questionnaire; slow	Instantaneous
Geographic flexibility	Limited to moderate	Confined, urban bias	High	High	Worldwide
Respondent cooperation	Excellent	Moderate to low	Good	Moderate—poorly designed questionnaire will have low response rate	Varies depending on Web site
Versatility of questioning	Quite versatile	Extremely versatile	Moderate	Highly standardized format	Extremely versatile
Questionnaire length	Long	Moderate to long	Moderate	Varies depending on incentive	Modest
Item non-response	Low	Medium	Medium	High	Sotfware can assure none
Possibility for respondent misunder-standing	Lowest	Lowest	Average	Highest—no interviewer present for clarification	High
Degree of Inter-viewer influence of answers	High	High	Moderate	None—interviewer absent	None
Supervision of Interviewers	Moderate	Moderate to high	High, especially with central location WATS interviewing	Not applicable	Not applicable
Anonymity of respondent	Low	Low	Moderate	High	Respondent can be anonymous or known
Ease of call-back or follow-up	Difficult	Difficult	Easy	Easy, but takes time	Moderate
Cost	Highest	Moderate to high	Low to moderate	Lowest	Low
Special features	Visual materials may be shown or demonstrated; extended probing possible	Taste tests, viewing of TV commercials possible	Fieldwork and supervision of data collection are simplified; quite adaptable to computer technology	Respondent may answer questions at own convenience; has time to reflect on answers	Stream media may provide graphics and ani-mation

Note: The emphasis is on _typical_ surveys. For example, an elaborate mail survey may be far more expensive than a short personal interview, but this generally is not the case.

vantages of the telephone survey (such as fast screening) and those of the personal interview. A mixed-mode study can employ any combination of survey methods. Conducting a mixed-mode study in two waves, however, creates the possibility that some respondents will not cooperate or will be unavailable in the second wave of the survey.

Several variations of survey research use cable television channels. For example, a telephone interviewer calls a cable subscriber and asks him or her to tune in to a particular channel at a future time. An appointment is made to interview the respondent shortly after the program or visual material is displayed. NBC uses this type of mixed-mode research to concept test many of its proposed new programs.

Selecting the Appropriate Survey Research Design

Earlier discussions of research design and problem definition emphasized that many research tasks may lead to similar decision-making information. There is no best form of survey; each has advantages and disadvantages. A researcher who must ask highly confidential questions may use a mail survey, thus sacrificing speed of data collection to avoid interviewer bias. If a researcher must have considerable control over question phrasing, central location telephone interviewing may be appropriate.

To determine the appropriate technique, the researcher must ask several questions: Is the assistance of an interviewer necessary? Are respondents interested in the issues being investigated? Will cooperation be easily attained? How quickly is the information needed? Will the study require a long and complex questionnaire? How large is the budget? The criteria—cost, speed, anonymity, and so forth—may differ for each project.

Exhibit 9.3 summarizes the major advantages and disadvantages of typical mall intercept, door-to-door, mail, telephone, and Internet surveys. It emphasizes the typical types of surveys. For example, a creative researcher might be able to design highly versatile and flexible questionnaires, but most researchers use standardized questions. An elaborate mail survey may be far more expensive than a short personal interview, but generally this is not the case.

Pretesting

After the questionnaires have been completed or returned, an investigator who is surveying 3,000 consumers does not want to find that most respondents misunderstood a particular question, skipped a series of questions, or misinterpreted the instructions for filling out the questionnaire. To avoid problems such as these, screening procedures, or *pretests*, are often used. **Pretesting** involves a trial run with a group of respondents to iron out fundamental problems in the instructions of survey design. Here the researcher looks for such things as the point at which respondent fatigue sets in, whether there are any particular places in the questionnaire where respondents tend to terminate, and other considerations. Unfortunately, this stage of research may be eliminated due to costs or time pressures.

pretesting
Screening procedure that involves a trial run with a group of respondents to iron out fundamental problems in the survey design.

Broadly speaking, there are three basic ways to pretest. The first two involve screening the questionnaire with other research professionals, and the third—most often called pretesting—is a trial run with a group of respondents. When screening the questionnaire with other research professionals, the investigator asks them to look for such things as difficulties with question wording, problems with leading questions, and bias due to question order. An alternate type of screening might involve a client or the research manager who ordered the research. Often managers ask for information but, when they see the questionnaire, find that it does not really meet their needs. Only by checking with the individual who has requested the questionnaire does the researcher know for sure that the information needed will be provided. Once the researcher has decided on the final questionnaire, data should be collected with a small number of respondents (perhaps 100) to determine whether the questionnaire needs refinement.

TO THE POINT

Practice is the best of all instructors

PUBLILIUS SYRUS

Ethical Issues in Survey Research

Chapter 4 mentioned that the American Marketing Association's code of ethics expresses researchers' obligation to protect the public from misrepresentation and exploitation under the guise of marketing research. Many more ethical issues apply as well, such as the respondents' right to privacy, the use of deception, the respondents' right to be informed about the purpose of the research, the need for confidentiality, the need for honesty in collecting data, and the need for objectivity in reporting data. You may wish to reexamine these issues now that various survey research techniques have been discussed.[23]

Summary

Interviews and self-administered questionnaires are used to collect survey data. Interviews can be categorized based on the medium used to communicate with respondents. Interviews may be conducted door-to-door, in shopping malls, or on the telephone. Traditionally, interviews have been recorded using paper and pencil, but computers are increasingly being used by survey researchers.

Personal interviews are a flexible method that allows researchers to use visual aids and various kinds of props. Door-to-door personal interviews get high response rates, but they are also more costly to administer than other types of surveys. The presence of an interviewer may also influence subjects' responses.

When a sample need not represent the entire United States, mall intercept interviews may reduce costs.

Telephone interviewing has the advantage of speed in data collection and lower costs per interview. However, not all households have telephones, and not all telephone numbers are listed in directories. This causes problems in obtaining a representative sampling frame. Absence of face-to-face contact and inability to use visual materials also limit telephone interviewing. However, computer-assisted telephone interviewing from central locations is improving the quality of telephone surveys.

Traditionally self-administered questionnaires have been delivered via the mail. Today, however, self-administered questionnaires may be dropped off, administered at central locations, or administered via computer. Mail questionnaires generally are less expensive than telephone or personal interviews, but they also introduce a much larger chance of nonresponse error. Several methods can be used to encourage higher response rates. Mail questionnaires must be more structured than other types of surveys and cannot be changed if problems are discovered in the course of data collection. The Internet and other new interactive media provide new, convenient ways for organizations to conduct surveys. Pretesting a questionnaire on a small sample of respondents is a useful way to discover problems while they can still be corrected.

Key Terms and Concepts

Personal interview
Probing
Item nonresponse
Door-to-door interview
Callback
Mall intercept interview
Telephone interview
Random digit dialing

Central location interviewing
Computer-assisted telephone interview (CATI)
Self-administered questionnaire
Mail survey
Response rate
Cover letter
Follow-up

Drop-off method
Computer-interactive survey
Fax survey
Internet survey
E-mail survey
Mixed-mode survey
Pretesting

Questions for Review and Critical Thinking

1. What type of survey (classified by communications medium) would you use in the following situations? Why?
   a. Survey of the buying motives of industrial engineers
   b. Survey of the satisfaction levels of rental-car users
   c. Survey of television commercial advertising awareness
   d. Survey of top corporate executives

2. A publisher offers college professors one of four best-selling mass-market books as an incentive for filling out a ten-page mail questionnaire about a new textbook. What advantages and disadvantages does this incentive offer?

3. "Individuals are less willing to cooperate with surveys today than they were 15 years ago." Comment on this statement.

4. What do you think should be the maximum length of a self-administered questionnaire?

5. Do most surveys use a single communication mode (for example, the telephone) as most textbooks suggest?

6. A survey researcher reports, "205 usable questionnaires out of 942 questionnaires delivered in our mail survey converts to a 21.7 percent response rate." What are the subtle implications of this statement?

7. Evaluate the following survey designs:
   a. A researcher suggests mailing a small safe (a metal file box with a built-in lock) without the lock combination to respondents with a note explaining that respondents will be called in a few days for a telephone interview. During the telephone interview, the combination is given and the safe may be opened.
   b. A shopping center that wishes to evaluate its image places packets including a questionnaire, cover letter, and stamped return envelope in the mall where customers can pick them up if they wish.
   c. A questionnaire is programmed on a floppy disk and then mailed to individuals who own computers. Respondents insert the disk into their computers, answer the questions, and mail the disk back to the research company in a special mailer. Each respondent is guaranteed a monetary incentive but has the option to increase it by playing a slot-machine game programmed onto the floppy disk.
   d. A mall intercept interviewing service is located in a regional shopping center. The facility contains a small room for television and movie presentations. Shoppers are used as sampling units, However, mall intercept interviewers recruit additional subjects for television commercial experiments by offering them several complimentary tickets for special sneak previews. Individuals contacted at the mall are allowed to bring up to five guests. In some cases the complimentary tickets are offered through ads in a local newspaper.
   e. *Time* selects a mail survey rather than a telephone survey for a study conducted to determine the demographic characteristics and purchasing behavior of its subscribers.

8. What type of research studies lend themselves to the use of e-mail as a method of survey research? What are the advantages and disadvantages of survey communications using e-mail?

9. Comment on the ethics of the following situations:
   a. A research plans to use invisible ink to code questionnaires to identify respondents in a distributor survey.
   b. A political action committee conducts a survey about its cause. At the end of the questionnaire, it includes a request for a donation.
   c. A telephone interviewer calls at 1 p.m. on Sunday and asks to conduct an interview.
   d. An industrial marketer wishes to survey its own distributors. It invents the name "Mountain States Marketing Research" and sends out a mail questionnaire under this name.
   e. A questionnaire is printed on the back of a warranty card included inside the package of a food processor. The questionnaire includes a number of questions about shopping behavior, demographics, and customer life styles. At the bottom of the warranty card is a short note in small print that says, "Thank you for completing this questionnaire. Your answers will be used for marketing studies and to help us serve you better in the future. You will also benefit by receiving important mailings and special offers from a number of organizations whose products and services relate directly to the activities, interests, and hobbies in which you enjoy participating on a regular basis. Please indicate if there is some reason you would prefer not to receive this information."

10. How might the marketing research industry take action to ensure that the public believes that telephone surveys and door-to-door interviews are legitimate activities and that firms that misrepresent and deceive the public using marketing research as a sales ploy are not true marketing researchers?

11. A research company in The Netherlands offers a free computer to a sample of citizens who agree that in exchange for the computer they will answer questions downloaded every week.

12. The American Testing Institute (also known as the U.S. Testing Authority) mails respondents what it calls a television survey. A questionnaire is sent to a respondent, who is asked to complete it and mail it back along with a check for $14.80. In return for answering eight questions on viewing habits, the institute promises to send the respondent one of 20 prizes ranging from $200 to $2,000 in value. These prizes include video recorders, diamond watches, a lifetime supply of camera film, color televisions, and two nights of hotel accommodations at a land development resort community. The institute lists the odds of winning as one in 150,000 on all prizes except the hotel stay, for which the odds are 149,981 out of 150,000. During a three-month period, the institute sends out 200,000 questionnaires. What are the ethical issues in this situation?

Exploring the Internet

1. Go to the Car Talk Opinion Poll at http://cartalk.com/Poll. Participate in the survey. What were the first three questions on the survey?

2. Go to ASI Research Web site (http://www.asiresearch.com) to learn what type of survey research services the firm offers. What hot links about other surveys and survey research services can be accessed through ASI's Web site?

3. Go to NPD Group (http://www.npd.com) and click on the company overview. What type of custom and syndicated survey research services does it offer? Search "What's New" and report any information you find about the company's PC-Meter service.

4. Use a search engine, such as Yahoo, Excite, or Infoseek, to see what you will find if you enter "telephone survey" as keywords.

5. Survey Online is located at http://www.surveyonline.com/#Welcome to surveyOnline. What unique service does this company offer?

6. To learn more about customer satisfaction surveys go to CustomerSat.com at http://www.customersat.com/hrquetions1.htm.

7. Walker Information services provides numerous white papers on marketing research reports and issues, such as "A Brief History of Telephone Sampling," at http://www.walkerinfo.com/resources/.

Case 9.1 Behavioral Science Research of Coral Gables, Florida

LAWYERS USE FOCUS GROUPS AND SURVEYS TO FIND OUT what wins in the courtroom. Their research shows that demographics and values affect the way juries see evidence. It also shows that trial arguments, like advertising copy, often succeed or fail on the turn of a phrase. Jury research gives lawyers an edge when the case is close, the facts are controversial, and the jury pool is diverse.[24]

"We know that various demographic groups and people with various types of jobs will respond differently to the same facts," says Robert Ladner, president of Behavioral Science Research in Coral Gables, Florida. "A high school teacher has different responses to arguments than an elementary school teacher or a college professor does."

Ladner has developed PercepTrac, a juror database that operates like the databases used by television researchers. PercepTrac has a handheld device that mock jurors use to gauge their positive or negative responses to facts presented in a trial. During the attorneys' opening statements, for example, mock jurors twist a knob on the device to register the degree of positive or negative feelings about each statement. Ladner typically shows the trial to 30 "jurors" equipped with the device, just as an advertising agency would run a campaign past a focus group.

"I can track the responses of those 30 people according to their age, income, and psychographic profile. I can track those responses, minute by minute, for everything that goes on in the mock trial," Ladner says. Watching the resulting data "is like looking at an electrocardiogram."

Ladner was recently hired by a Florida city that had to condemn some land for a new road. "We had to evaluate two elements: the perception that the damages paid were not sufficient," he says.

Ladner first conducted a survey to find out the "core attitudes" of people in the jury pool. His goal was to learn who was most likely to be sympathetic to the government and who was most likely to favor the property owner. He found that non-Hispanic whites were the ethnic group most sympathetic to the Department of Transportation's need to widen roads, but they were also more sympathetic to property owners than were blacks or Hispanics. A majority of blacks (56 percent) felt that the DOT was unfair in taking the property, compared with 23 percent of whites; and 78 percent of blacks felt that property owners are greedy, compared with 41 percent of whites.

Next, the city's attorney presented his case to a mock jury equipped with PercepTrac. He lost the mock trial, but the device showed a small point that had alienated the jury and eroded the credibility of the municipality's case. That small point was a legal term used in condemnation proceedings: *a taking*.

"To Joe Lunchbucket on the jury, the word *taking* has enormous negative connotations," says Ladner. In the actual trial, the city's attorney described his case in everyday language and won.

Mock juries also show how nonfactual things, such as mannerisms, may alienate or attract jurors. "For years, this was considered voodoo litigation," Ladner says. "But not only does it work, it also gives trial attorneys a sense of confidence in their preparation. They know what to look for, and they can prepare targeted arguments rather than guess which ones are going to work."

The effectiveness of jury research is easy to test, and Ladner says that PercepTrac juries predict the actual verdict 80 percent of the time. "Your stuff has to be bulletproof," Ladner says. "You have to know these people as if you are living inside their bodies and brains and are seeing with their eyes."

QUESTIONS

1. Does this survey fall into the traditional categories of surveys discussed in the textbook? What are the advantages of this type of survey?
2. What sources of survey error are most likely to occur in a study of this type?
3. Is this type of research ethical?

Case 9.2 Royal Bee Electric Fishing Reel

ROYAL BARTON STARTED THINKING ABOUT AN ELECTRIC fishing reel some 14 years earlier when his father had a stroke and lost the use of an arm. To see that happen to his dad, who had taught him the joys of fishing and hunting, made Barton realize what a chunk a physical handicap could take out of a sports enthusiast's life. Being able to cast and retrieve a lure or experience the thrill of a big bass trying to take your rig away from you were among the joys of life that would be denied Barton's father forever.

Barton was determined to do something about it, if not for his father, then at least for others who had suffered a similar fate. So, after tremendous personal expense and years of research and development, Barton has perfected what is sure to be the standard bearer for all future freshwater electric reels. Forget those saltwater jobs, which Barton refers to as "winches." He has developed something that is small, compact, and has incredible applications.

He calls it the Royal Bee. The first word is obviously his first name. The second word refers to the low buzzing sound the reel makes when in use.

The Royal Bee system looks simple enough and probably is if you understand the mechanical workings of a reel. A system of gears ties into the gears of the existing spool, and a motor switch in the back drives the gears attached to the triggering system.

All gearing of the electrical system is disengaged so that you can cast normally. But when you push the button for retrieve, it engages two gears. After the gears are engaged, the trigger travels far enough to touch the switch that tightens the drive belt, and there is no slipping. You cannot hit the switch until the gears are properly engaged. This means that you cast manually, just as you would normally fish, then you reengage the reel for the levelwind to work. And you can do all that with one hand!

The system works on a 6-volt battery that you can attach to your belt or hang around your neck if you are wade fishing. If you have a boat with a 6-volt battery systems, the reel can actually work off of it. There is a small connector that plugs into the reel, so you could easily use more than one of the reels off the same battery. For instance, if have two or three outfits equipped with different lures, you just switch the connector from reel to reel as you use it. A reel with the Royal Bee system can be used in a conventional manner. You do not have to use it as an electric reel unless you choose to do so.

Barton believes the Royal Bee may not be just for handicapped fishermen. Ken Cook, one of the leading professional anglers in the country, is sold on the Royal Bee. After he suffered a broken arm, he had to withdraw from some tournaments because fishing with one hand was difficult. By the time his arm healed, he was hooked on the Royal Bee because it increased bassing efficiency. As Cook explains, "The electric reel has increased my efficiency in two ways. One is for flipping, where I use it all the time. The other is for fishing topwater when I have to make a long cast. When I'm flipping, the electric reel gives me instant control over slack line. I can keep both hands on the rod. I never have to remove them to take up slack. I flip, engage the reel, and then all I have to do is push the lever with my thumb to take up slack instantly."

Cook's reel (a Ryobi 4000) is one of several that can be converted to the electric retrieve. For flipping, he loads his reel with 20-pound test line. He uses a similar reel with lighter line when fishing a surface lure. "What you can do with the electric reel is eliminate unproductive reeling time," Cook says.

A few extra seconds may not mean much if you are out on a neighborhood pond just fishing on the weekend. But it can mean a bunch if you are in tournament competition where one extra cast might make the difference in going home with $50,000 tucked in your pocket. "Look at it this way," Cook explains. "Let's suppose we're in clear water and it's necessary to make a long cast to the cover we want to fish with a topwater lure. There's a whole lot of unproductive water between us and the cover. With the electric reel, I make my long cast and fish the cover. Then, when I'm ready to reel in, I just press the retrieve lever so the battery engages the necessary gears, and I've got my lure back ready to make another cast while you're still cranking."

When Royal Barton retired from his veterinary supply business, he began enjoying his favorite pastimes: hunting, fishing, and developing the Royal Bee system. He realized he needed help in marketing his product, so he sought professional assistance to learn how to reach the broadest possible market for the Royal Bee system.

QUESTIONS

1. What is the marketing problem? What are Barton's information needs? Outline some survey research objectives for a research project on the Royal Bee system.
2. What type of survey—personal interview, telephone interview, or mail survey—should be selected?
3. What sources of survey error are most likely to occur in a study of this type?
4. What means should be used to obtain a high response rate?

Case 9.3   PC Ratings

THE HOME TESTING INSTITUTE MAINTAINS A CONSUMER panel. The following cover letter was sent to members of the panel who indicated they used a computer at their workplace.

Dear HTI Panel Member,

The computer arena is extremely competitive and hot! The software industry, on-line services, computer retailers—everyone in the computer industry and everyone affected by the industry (that means all of us) needs accurate, credible research on what consumers really want and need.

Because of this intense interest, HTI has been flooded with requests for information on computer (PC) use. We've been doing surveys and asking questions about computer usage. Recently, you filled out a survey in which you informed us that a member of your household uses a computer at their workplace. This makes your household the perfect candidate for our new and exciting market research project—PC Ratings. We're inviting everyone in your household that uses a computer at work to become the world's first PC Raters.

Make Your Opinions Count
Here's your chance to voice your opinions to the computer industry. As participants, you and your household members will be representing thousands of other US households and individuals in this cutting-edge market research program.

To qualify for our PC Ratings "At Work" Panel, all that's needed is an IBM or compatible computer that runs Windows and has access to the World Wide Web, either through a direct connection or a modem connection to an on-line service. We need ALL TYPES of people to be representative of all Americans.

What is PC Ratings?
PC Ratings is breakthrough market research from HTI. It's like TV ratings for the PC! And it's your chance to show decision makers in the computer industry which software and on-line services people really like and use.

Participation is East and Absolutely FREE. There is never any cost to you. We pay for everything—telephone calls, disks, postage. And we send you FREE THANK YOU GIFTS for participating.

What Do You Have To Do?

The best part of participating in PC Ratings is that you can make a huge impact on the future of computer technology—earning free gifts in the process—and it only takes a couple of minutes each month! Here's exactly how it works.

After you are selected for membership on our PC Ratings panel, we send you the free, patented PC Ratings software for you and your household members to install on the computers they use at work. The installation process only takes a couple of minutes and only has to be done once.

Once installed, the PC Ratings software runs quietly in the background tracking where you go on the Web as well as any on-line applications you use. You'll hardly know it's there!

Each month you then receive a "data retrieval" disk from us. It takes just a few minutes to retrieve the tracking information stored by the ratings software. Then you just mail us the disk in the postage-paid envelope that we provide. That's it. That's all there is to it! It's amazing when you think of the wealth of information that you can help generate with virtually zero effort—all the while receiving free gifts and entry in a monthly sweepstakes!

Confidentiality and Privacy Guaranteed!

As with all research conducted by HTI, the information you provide is strictly confidential. HTI combines the data you provide with that from thousands of other panelists to create ratings—your computer usage is never linked to your name. Additionally, be assured PC Ratings software does not record any information you enter or use on your computer. All PC Ratings does is track what applications or on-line services you use and for how long.

And There Are Special Benefits for PC Ratings Members!

As an active PC Ratings panelist, you'll regularly get:

- Entry in a monthly sweepstakes with prizes like TVs and camcorders

- PC Ratings Report, the exclusive monthly panelist newsletter filled with inside market research news and much more. It arrives each month via your monthly retrieval disk.

- Surprise "thank you" gifts mailed to you periodically

- PC Ratings Help Desk—Our specially trained team of computer experts are available to you 24 hours a day, 7 days a week. They're ready to answer any questions about your computer and PC Ratings. They're a great resource and will answer any question you have about PC Ratings and its interaction with specific software or hardware, with Windows or with going on-line.

Any Questions?

Please take a look at the enclosed Question and Answer brochure. You'll find answers to the most frequently asked questions we've received about PC Ratings. And if you have a question we haven't answered, don't hesitate to call 1-800-XXX-XXXX.

What's Next?

Please take a couple of minutes to fill out the enclosed survey and drop it in the mail. As soon as we receive your completed survey, we'll mail you the patented PC Ratings Installation software to install on the PCs that you use.

That's it. That's all there is to it.
Start making a difference! Return your completed survey today. Let the computer industry know what you and your household members think is important. Influence the future of technology and earn free gifts in the process. This invitation is a once in a lifetime opportunity. I truly believe PC Ratings will be as historic and important as TV Ratings.

Sincerely,

Janet Hall

Director of Research

QUESTIONS

1. What are the strengths and weaknesses of this cover letter?
2. What level of cooperation do you expect HTI will obtain?
3. What are the possible sources of error that might be associated with this survey?

Case 9.4   Mazda

Mazda's 929 model, a Japanese automobile, was introduced to the American market in 1992. To assure customer satisfaction, buyers of the 929 are called approximately a week after purchase. The telephone interview that follows is a transcript of one of Mazda's customer satisfaction interviews:

Customer: Hello

Interviewer: Yes, (customer's name). We have some questions here on the delivery of your new car.

Customer: Okay.

Interviewer: At the time of delivery, were you pleased with the delivery of the 929?

Customer: Oh.

Interviewer: When you picked it up from the dealer.

Customer: Well, it had a dent in the hood, and it wasn't perfect.

Interviewer: Are you saying no then? I need a "yes" or "no."

Customer: Okay—no.

Interviewer: Okay. And now can you tell us why you weren't pleased with it?

Customer: Okay, because there was a dent in the hood.

Interviewer: It has a dent in the hood. Now did they take care of it for you?

Customer: It couldn't be corrected, they said.

Interviewer: Oh—okay.

Customer: They said that they would try to get it out with that process of pulling it out. I don't know. They put hot things under it, but it didn't work.

Interviewer: Were the features and operating controls explained to your satisfaction?

Customer: Yes.

Interviewer: Were the terms of the warranty explained to your satisfaction?

Customer: Yes.

Interviewer: Was the maintenance schedule explained to your satisfaction?

Customer: Yes.

Interviewer: Would you recommend that dealer to a friend?

Customer: Yes.

Interviewer: Okay. We do want to thank you for your cooperation and you will be receiving a follow-up call from us within a couple of weeks.

Customer: Thank you. The day after the survey the local dealership called the car buyer. The salesperson said he had done his best, and the buyer was going to get him in trouble with his boss. Later in the day the sales manager called and said to bring the car in and they would switch hoods with another Mazda 929 of the same color.

About a week later an interviewer called and asked if the problem has been resolved to the customer's satisfaction. The customer said "yes."

QUESTIONS

1. What are the survey research objectives for a customer satisfaction program? Is the use of customer satisfaction surveys a good idea?
2. Why did Mazda choose a telephone survey rather than communication by mail or personal interview?
3. The results of the survey were communicated to the local dealership. Is this ethical?

Chapter 10

Observation

One day, Sherlock Holmes asked Dr. Watson how many steps led up to the Baker Street apartment. Watson responded that he did not know. Holmes replied, "Ah, Watson, you see but you do not *observe*."

Although we like Dr. Watson, are constantly looking around in our daily lives, we often do not observe in a scientific sense. Holmes, however, trained himself to see what others overlook by systematically observing the environment. This chapter discusses the observation method of data gathering in marketing research.

What you will learn in this chapter

To distinguish between scientific observation and casual observation.

To discuss what can and cannot be observed.

To understand when observation research is the appropriate research design.

To discuss the characteristics of observation research.

To give examples of nonverbal behavior that can be observed.

To discuss the various situations in which direct observation studies may take place.

To define response latency.

To discuss scientifically contrived observation.

To discuss some ethical issues in observation studies.

To define physical-trace evidence.

To recognize that content analysis obtains data by observing and analyzing the content of messages.

To explain the purposes of content analysis.

To describe the various types of mechanical observation and methods for measuring physiological reactions.

To discuss the UPC system and the place of scanner data in observation research.

When Is Observation Scientific?

Observation becomes a tool for scientific inquiry when it

1. Serves a formulated research purpose
2. Is planned systematically
3. Is recorded systematically and related to more general propositions rather than simply reflecting a set of interesting curiosities
4. Is subjected to checks or controls on validity and reliability[1]

observation

The systematic process of recording the behavioral patterns of people, objects, and occurrences without questioning or otherwise communicating with them.

In marketing research **observation** is the systematic process of recording the behavioral patterns of people, objects, and occurrences without questioning or otherwise communicating with them. The researcher who uses the observation method of data collection witnesses and records information as events occur or compiles evidence from records of past events.

TO THE POINT

Where observation is concerned, chance favors only the prepared mind.

LOUIS PASTEUR

What Can Be Observed?

A wide variety of information about the behavior of people and objects can be observed. Exhibit 10.1 outlines seven kinds of observable content: physical actions, such as shopping patterns or television viewing; verbal behavior, such as sales conversations; expressive behavior, such as tone of voice or facial expressions; spatial relations and locations, such as traffic counts; temporal patterns, such as amount of time spent shopping or driving; physical objects, such as the amount of newspapers recycled; and verbal and pictorial records, such as the content of advertisements.

Domain Stores, a fast-growing $50 million chain of 23 furniture stores headquartered in Norwood, Massachusetts, hired Grid II, a market research firm, to videotape consumers in one of the furniture stores. Analysis of the videotapes revealed that people shop for furniture in twos. Of the 1,034 customers who entered the store, 954 came in pairs.

In addition, facial expressions and other nonverbal behavior indicated that many male customers were visibly ill at ease amid fluffed pillows and floral duvets. "The typical customer needs to be in the store at least nine minutes to feel comfortable enough to buy," says the company's CEO. "But if the spouse or boyfriend pulls her away too soon, we lose out on the sale." As a result of the observation research, the company remodeled its 23 stores with entertainment centers where sports fans can watch live events via cable.[2]

Exhibit 10.1 **What Can Be Observed**

PHENOMENON	EXAMPLE
Physical action	Shopper's movement pattern in a store
Verbal behavior	Statements made by airline travelers while waiting in line
Expressive behavior	Facial expressions, tones of voices, and other forms of body language
Spatial relations and locations	How close visitors at an art museum stand to paintings
Temporal patterns	How long fast-food customers wait for their orders to be served
Physical objects	What brand-name items are stored in consumers' pantries
Verbal and pictorial records	Bar codes on product packages

(Although investigation of secondary data uses observation—see Chapter 7—it is not extensively discussed in this chapter.)

The observation method may be used to describe a wide variety of behavior, but cognitive phenomena such as attitudes, motivations, and preferences cannot be observed. Thus, observation research cannot provide an explanation of why a behavior occurred or what actions were intended. Another limitation is that the observed behavior generally is of short duration. Behavior patterns that occur over a period of several days or weeks generally are either too costly or impossible to observe.

The Nature of Observation Studies

Marketing researchers can observe people, objects, events, or other phenomena using either human observers or machines designed for specific observation tasks. Human observation best suits a situation or behavior that is not easily predictable in advance of the research. Mechanical observation, as performed by supermarket scanners or traffic counters, can very accurately record situations or types of behavior that are routine, repetitive, or programmatic.

Human or mechanical observation may be *unobtrusive;* that is, it may not require communication with a respondent. For example, rather than asking customers how much time they spend shopping in his or her store, a supermarket manager might observe and record the intervals between when shoppers enter and leave the store. The unobtrusive or nonreactive nature of the observation method often generates data without a subject's knowledge. Situations in which an observer's presence is known to the subject involve **visible observation**; situations in which a subject is unaware that observation is taking place involve **hidden observation**. Hidden, unobtrusive observation minimizes respondent error. Asking subjects to participate in the research is not required when they are unaware that they are being observed.

The major advantage of observation studies over surveys, which obtain self-reported data from respondents, is that the data do not have distortions, inaccuracies, or other response biases due to memory error, social desirability bias, and so on. The data are recorded when the actual behavior takes place.

visible observation
A situation in which the observer's presence is known to the subject.

hidden observation
A situation in which the subject is unaware that observation is taking place.

WHAT WENT RIGHT?

Envirosell

PACO UNDERHILL RUNS ENVIROSELL, A NEW YORK consumer research company that conducts observation research. He became interested in using cameras to analyze the flow of human traffic through public places after hearing a lecture by urban geographer William Whyte. Envirosell's clients now include companies such as Quaker Foods, Bloomingdale's, Revlon, and Hallmark Cards. The following is one reporter's account of what he learned about the value of observation research.

Underhill's research in retail settings led him to develop a body of observations he calls *aisle theory.* Among his seminal findings is something we'll call the derriere-brush factor, although he calls it by another name. At his offices in New York, he showed me a film clip shot with a time-lapse camera aimed at a tie display in a narrow, heavily traveled aisle of the Bloomingdale's department store in Manhattan. Such aisles,

meant to carry shoppers from store entrances onward into the store, are known in the retail industry as "driveways" or "power aisles."

Shoppers entered and dispersed; most zipped right by a tie display. Underhill stopped the projector.

"Stand up," he commanded.

I stood.

"OK, you are standing at a counter. You are looking at ties. One of the most sensitive parts of your anatomy is your tail."

He began brushing my tail with his hand. Derriere-brush factor, he told me, "is simply the idea that the more likely you are to be brushed from the rear while you shop, the less likely you'll be converted from browser to buyer." In retail-speak the "conversion ratio" of that display or counter will be low.

Underhill's stop-action film showed how few people stopped to examine the ties in the rack. Traffic swept past the few browsers in disconcerting volume.

When Bloomingdale's chairman saw the video, he called the clerk in charge of that department and had him move the tie rack out of the driveway. Later, a Bloomingdale's vice president called Underhill and told him the chairman had

Observation of Human Behavior

Surveys emphasize verbal responses while observation studies emphasize and allow for the systematic recording of nonverbal behavior. Toy manufacturers such as Fisher Price use the observation technique because children often cannot express their reactions to products. By observing children at play with a proposed toy, doll, or game, marketing researchers can identify the elements of a potentially successful product. Toy marketing researchers might observe play to answer the following questions: How long does the child's attention stay with the product? Does the child put it down after 2 minutes or 20 minutes? Are the child's peers equally interested in the toy?

Behavioral scientists have recognized that nonverbal behavior can be a communication process by which meanings are exchanged among individuals. Head nods, smiles, raised eyebrows, and other facial expressions or body movements have been recognized as communication symbols. Observation of nonverbal communication may hold considerable promise for the marketing researcher.

personally had the sales tracked from that lone tie rack and discovered that within 6 weeks the increase had paid for Underhill's services. "That told me two things," Underhill said. "One, I wasn't charging enough, and two, the markup on ties was even more obscene than I thought."

"He picks up common sense things," said Judith Owens, vice president, marketing, of the National Retail Federation in New York, who periodically invites Underhill to show his stop-action films to the federation's many members. She watched one film of an audio store that drew mostly teenage clientele, yet placed its racks of CDs so high the kids couldn't reach them. "You watch that happen, then you hear Paco say if you drop your display by 18 inches you'll increase your productivity. Everybody says, my God, I never thought of that."

He showed AT&T that almost 20 percent of the people who came into its Phone Center stores were under 10 years old, and how salespeople spent a lot of their time simply protecting expensive phone systems displayed too close to the ground. His films showed how most people who entered a Revco drugstore failed to pick up a shopping basket and thus were automatically limited to buying only what they could carry.

Early in 1991 the Woolworth Corporation asked Underhill to study several of its Champs Sports stores to help figure out which layouts and designs worked best. Woolworth was planning a huge national expansion of the chain. It knew that sales from the rear section of each store—the hard goods section displaying such items as weights and basketballs—lagged far behind sales from other sections, but it didn't know why.

John Shanley, director of research for Woolworth, remembers how Underhill's stop-action film instantly solved the mystery. During peak sales periods a line of customers would form from the cash register to the opposite wall of the store. "It literally prevented people from going from the front to the back," Shanley recalls. "They walked up to this line, turned and walked away." As a result, all of Champs' 500 stores now feature a checkout area (known in the industry as the "cash-wrap") designed so that lines form along an axis from front to back. "All of a sudden the sales in the back of the store picked up," Shanley recalled.

But, I asked, shouldn't that barrier effect have been obvious without Underhill's help? "The obvious," Shanley answered, "isn't always that apparent."

Focus groups observed behind one-way mirrors are often videotaped. The ability to replay video records allows researchers to perform detailed analysis of physical actions.

Exhibit 10.2 Nonverbal Communication: Status and Power Gestures

BEHAVIOR	BETWEEN STATUS EQUALS		BETWEEN STATUS NONEQUALS		BETWEEN MEN AND WOMEN	
	INTIMATE	NONINTIMATE	USED BY SUPERIOR	USED BY SUBORDINATE	USED BY MEN	USED BY WOMEN
Posture	Relaxed	Tense (less relaxed)	Relaxed	Tense	Relaxed	Tense
Personal space	Closeness	Distance	Closeness (optional)	Distance	Closeness	Distance
Touching	Touch	Don't touch	Touch (optional)	Don't touch	Touch	Don't touch
Eye gaze	Establish	Avoid	Stare, ignore	Avert eyes, watch	Stare, ignore	Avert eyes
Demeanor	Informal	Circumspect	Informal	Circumspect	Informal	Circumspect
Emotional expression	Show	Hide	Hide	Show	Hide	Show
Facial expression	Smile[a]	Don't smile[a]	Don't smile	Smile	Don't smile	Smile

[a]Behavior not known.

For example, in customer–salesperson interactions it has been hypothesized that in low-importance transactions wherein potential customers are plentiful and easily replaced (for example, a shoe store), the salesperson may show definite nonverbal signs of higher status than the customer. When customers are scarce, as in big-ticket purchase situations (for example, real estate sales), the opposite should be true: Many nonverbal indicators of deference might be emitted by the salesperson. An observation study using the nonverbal communication measures shown in Exhibit 10.2 could test this hypothesis.

Of course, verbal behavior is not ignored—indeed, in certain observation studies it is very important.

Complementary Evidence

The results of observation studies may amplify the results of other forms of research by providing *complementary evidence* concerning individuals' true feelings. Focus group interviews often are conducted behind one-way mirrors from which marketing executives observe as well as listen to what is occurring. This allows for interpretation of nonverbal behavior such as facial expressions or head nods to supplement information from interviews.

One focus group session concerning hand lotion recorded that all the women's hands were above the table while they were casually waiting for the session to begin. Seconds after the women were told that the topic was to be hand lotion, all hands were placed out of sight. This observation, along with the group discussion, revealed the women's anger, guilt, and shame about the condition of their hands. Although they felt they were expected to have soft, pretty hands, their housework obligations required them to wash dishes, clean floors, and do other chores that were detrimental to their hands.

When focus group behavior is videotaped, observation of the nonverbal communication symbols can add even more to marketers' knowledge of the situation.

At IBM direct observation is facilitated by television cameras and videotape equipment to help develop easy-to-use computers.

Direct Observation

Direct observation can produce a detailed record of events that occur or what people actually do. The observer plays a passive role; that is, there is no attempt to control or manipulate a situation—the observer merely records what occurs. Many types of data can be obtained more accurately through direct observation than by questioning. For example, recording traffic counts and/or observing the direction of traffic flows within a supermarket can help managers design store layouts that will maximize the exposure of departments that sell impulse goods. A manufacturer can determine the number of facings, shelf locations, display maintenance, and other factors regarding store conditions. If directly questioned in a survey, most shoppers would be unable to accurately portray the time they spent in each department. The observation method could, however, accomplish this task without difficulty.

In the direct observation method the data consist of records of events made as they occur. An observation form often helps keep the observations consistent and ensures that all relevant information is recorded. A respondent is not required to recall—perhaps inaccurately—an event after it has occurred; instead, the observation is instantaneous.

In many cases, direct observation is the only or the most straightforward form of data collection. The produce manager at a Jewel grocery store may periodically gather competitive price information at the Safeway and IGA stores in the neighborhood. In other situations observation is the most economical technique. In a common observation study, a shopping center manager may observe the license plate (tag) numbers on cars in its parking lot. These data, along with automobile registration information, provide an inexpensive means of determining where customers live.

Certain data may be more quickly or easily obtained using direct observation than by other methods. Sex, race, and other respondent characteristics often are simply observed. Researchers investigating a diet product may use observation when selecting respondents in a shopping mall. Overweight people may be prescreened by observing pedestrians, thus eliminating a number of screening interviews.

direct observation
A straightforward attempt to observe and record what naturally occurs; the investigator does not create an artificial situation.

WHAT   WENT   WRONG?

*Doctors
Should Examine
Their Watches*

WHEN QUESTIONED IN A SURVEY, DOCTORS ANSWERED that they spent about nine times more time informing patients than they actually did. The physicians who were directly questioned answered that they spent about 12 minutes giving information to the average patient, but videotapes of the doctor/patient encounters indicated that the doctors spent only 1.3 minutes giving information. Furthermore, the doctors underestimated how much the patients wanted to know about their illnesses. When doctors' answers were compared with patients' answers about how much patients wanted to know, doctors underestimated the amount of information two out of three times.

In a quality-of-life survey, respondents were asked a series of questions that were compiled into an index of well-being. Direct observation was also used by the interviewers because the researchers wanted to investigate the effect of weather conditions on people's answers. The researchers quickly and easily observed and recorded outside weather conditions on the day of the interviews, as well as the temperature and humidity in the building in which the interviews were taken.[4]

Recording the decision time necessary to make a choice between two alternatives is a relatively simple, unobtrusive task that can be done through direct observation. The term **response latency** refers to the recording of choice time as a measure of the strength of the preference between alternatives. It is hypothesized that the longer a decision maker takes to choose between two alternatives, the closer the two alternatives are in terms of preference. However a quick decision is assumed to indicate that the psychological distance between alternatives is considerable. The response latency measure is gaining popularity now that computer-assisted data collection methods are becoming more common (because the computer can record decision times).

response latency
The amount of time necessary to make a choice between two alternatives; used as a measure of the strength of preference.

Errors Associated with Direct Observation

Although no interaction with the respondent occurs in direct observation, the method is not error free; the observer may record events subjectively. The same visual cues that may influence the interplay between interviewer and respondent (e.g., the subject's age or sex) may come into play in some types of direct observation settings. For example, the observer may subjectively attribute a particular economic status or education background to the subject. A distortion of measurement resulting from the cognitive behavior or actions of the witnessing observer is called **observer bias**. A research project using observers to evaluate whether sales clerks are rude or courteous illustrates how field-workers may be required to rely on their own interpretations of people or situations during the observation process.

If the observer does not record every detail that describes the persons, objects, and events in a given situation, accuracy may suffer. As a general guideline, the observer should record as much detail as possible. However, the pace of

observer bias
A distortion of measurement resulting from the cognitive behavior or actions of the witnessing observer.

events, the observer's memory, the observer's writing speed, and other factors will limit the amount of detail that can be recorded.

Interpretation of observation data is another major problem. Facial expressions and other nonverbal communication may have several meanings. Does a smile always mean happiness? Because someone is standing or seated in close proximity to the president of a company, does that necessarily portray a direct indication of that person's status?

Scientifically Contrived Observation

Most observation takes place in a natural setting. Intervention by the investigator to create an artificial environment to test a hypothesis is called **contrived observation**. This increases the frequency of occurrence of certain behavior patterns. For example, an airline passenger complaining about a meal or service from the flight attendant may actually be a researcher recording that person's reactions. If the situation were not contrived, the research time spent waiting and observing situation would expand considerably. A number of retailers use observers called *mystery shoppers* to come into a store and pretend to be interested in a particular product or service; after leaving the store, the "shopper" evaluates the salesperson's performance.

contrived observation
Observation in which the investigator creates an artificial environment in order to test a hypothesis.

Ethical Issues in the Observation of Humans

Observation methods introduce a number of ethical issues. Hidden observation raises the issue of the respondent's right to privacy. For example, a firm interested in acquiring information about how women put on their brassieres might persuade some retailers to place one-way mirrors in dressing rooms so that this behavior may be observed unobtrusively. Obviously, there is a moral question to be resolved in such situations. Other observation methods, especially contrived observation, raise the possibility of deception of subjects.

Some people might see contrived observation as entrapment. To entrap means to deceive or trick into difficulty, which clearly is an abusive action. The difficulty is one of balancing values. If the researcher obtains permission, the subject may not act in a typical manner. Thus, the researcher must determine his or her own view of the ethics involved and decide whether the usefulness of the information is worth telling a white lie.

Observation of Physical Objects

Physical phenomena may be the subject of observation study. Physical-trace evidence is a visible mark of some past event or occurrence. For example, the wear on a library book indirectly indicates which books are actually read (handled most often) when checked out. A classic example of physical-trace evidence in a nonprofit setting investigates erosion traces: The floor tiles around the hatching-chick exhibit at Chicago's Museum of Science and Industry must be replaced every six weeks. Tiles in other parts of the museum need not be replaced for years. The selective erosion of tiles, indexed by the replacement rate, is a measure of the relative popularity of exhibits.

This research design indicates that a creative marketing researcher has many options available for determining the solution to a problem. The story about Curtis Publishing Company and Charles Coolidge Parlin, generally recognized as one of the founders of commercial marketing research, counting garbage cans at the turn of the twentieth century illustrates another study of physical traces.

> Parlin designed an observation study to persuade Campbell's Soup Company to advertise in the *Saturday Evening Post*. Campbell's was reluctant to advertise because they believed that the *Post* was read primarily by working people who would prefer to make soup from scratch, peeling the potatoes and scraping the carrots, rather than paying 10¢ for a can of soup. To demonstrate that rich people weren't the target market, Parlin selected a sample of Philadelphia garbage routes. Garbage from each specific area of the city that was selected was dumped on the floor of a local National Guard Armory. Parlin had the number of Campbell's soup cans in each pile counted. The results indicated that the garbage from the rich people's didn't contain many cans of Campbell's soup. Although they didn't make soup from scratch themselves, their servants did. The garbage piles from the blue-collar area showed a large number of Campbell's soup cans. This observation study was enough evidence for Campbell's. They advertised in the *Saturday Evening Post*.[3]

The method used in this study is now used in a scientific project at the University of Arizona in which aspiring archaeologists sift through modern garbage; they examine soggy cigarette butts, empty milk cartons, and half-eaten Big Macs. Investigation of Arizona household garbage has revealed many interesting findings. For example, in Hispanic households the most popular baby food is squash.[4] It accounts for 38 percent of the baby food vegetables Hispanic babies consume. By contrast, in Anglo households peas account for 29 percent of all baby vegetables; squash ranks above only spinach, which is last. (Squash has been a dietary staple in Mexico and Central America for more than 9,000 years.)

TO THE POINT

What would you rather believe? What I say, or what you saw with your own eyes?

GROUCHO MARX

Sorting through fast-food restaurants' garbage reveals that wasted food from chicken restaurants (not counting bones) accounts for 35 percent of all food bought. This is substantially greater than the 7 percent of wasted food at fast-food hamburger restaurants.

What is most interesting about the garbage project is the comparison between the results of surveys about food consumption with the contents of respondents' garbage—garbage does not lie.[5] The University of Arizona project indicates that people consistently underreport the quantity of junk food they eat and overreport the amount of fruit and diet soda they consume. Most dramatically, however, studies show that alcohol consumption is underreported by 40 to 60 percent.

Garbage is even more revealing in Buenos Aires, Argentina. The research company Garbage Data Dynamics analyzes discarded containers, newspapers, and other garbage in that city. Because garbage is collected daily in Buenos Aires and people typically dispose of garbage in small bags with grocery store names printed on them, certain types of data that cannot be collected in the United States can be obtained. The results are so specific that they can show what brand of soft drink was consumed with a certain meal.

Counting an recording physical inventories by retail or wholesale audits allows researchers to investigate brand sales on regional and national levels, market shares, seasonal purchasing patterns, and so on. Marketing research suppliers offer audit data at both the retail and wholesale levels.

An observer can record physical-trace data to discover things that a respondent could not recall accurately. For example, actually measuring the number of ounces of a liquid bleach used during a test provides a precise physical-trace answer without relying on the respondent's memory. The accuracy of respondents' memories is not a problem for the firm that conducts a pantry audit. The pantry audit requires an inventory of the brands, quantities, and package sizes in a consumer's home rather than responses from individuals. The problem of untruthfulness or some other form of response bias is avoided. For example, the pantry audit prevents the possible problem of respondents erroneously claiming to have prestige brands in the cabinet. However, gaining permission to physically check consumers' pantries is not easy, and the fieldwork is expensive. Furthermore, the brand in the pantry may not reflect the brand purchased most often if it was substituted because of a cents-off coupon, an out-of-stock condition, or another reason.

Content Analysis

Content analysis obtains data by observing and analyzing the contents or messages of advertisements, newspaper articles, television programs, letters, and the like. It involves analysis as well as observation, systematically analyzing people's communications to identify the specific information contents and other characteristics of their messages. Content analysis studies the message itself; it involves the design of a systematic observation and recording procedure for quantitative description of the manifest content of communication. This technique measures the extent of emphasis or omission of a given analytical category. For example, the content of advertisements might be investigated to evaluate their use of words, themes, characters, or space and time relationships. The frequency of appearance of blacks, women, or other minorities in mass media has been a topic of content analysis.

A content analysis may ask questions such as whether some advertisers use certain types of themes, appeals, claims, or deceptive practices more than others or whether recent consumer-oriented actions by the Federal Trade Commission have influenced the contents of advertising. A cable television programmer might do a content analysis of network programming to evaluate its competition. For example, every year researchers analyze the Super Bowl to see how much of the visual material is live-action play and how much is replay, or how many shots focus on the cheerleaders and how many on spectators. The information content of television commercials directed at children can be investigated, as can company images portrayed in advertising, and numerous other topics.

content analysis
The systematic observation and quantitative description of the manifest content of communication.

Study of the content of communications is more sophisticated than simply counting the items; it requires a system of analysis to secure relevant data. In an employee role-playing session involving leaders and subordinates, videotapes were analyzed to identify categories for verbal behaviors (e.g., positive reward statements, positive comparison statements, and self-evaluation requests). Trained coders, using a set of specific instructions, then recorded and coded the leaders' behavior into specific verbal categories.

The Naisbitt Group provides a syndicated service that illustrates the use of content analysis in marketing research. John Naisbitt is a researcher who uses newspaper content analysis to project social trends. The Naisbitt Group monitors local events throughout the United States based on monthly content analysis of 6,000 local newspapers. It publishes the results quarterly in the *Trend Report.* The *Trend Report* has used content analysis to predict: a trend among companies toward downsizing and more democratic, equalitarian, and spontaneous actions (the organization person is giving way to the entrepreneur, and individuals are less constrained by layers of management).

Mechanical Observation

In many situations the primary—and sometimes the only—means of observation is mechanical rather than human. Videotape cameras, traffic counters, and other machines help observe and record behavior. Some unusual observation studies have used motion picture cameras and time-lapse photography. An early application of this observation technique photographed train passengers and determined their levels of comfort by observing how they sat and moved in their seats. Another time-lapse study filmed traffic flows in an urban square and resulted in a redesign of the streets. Similar techniques may help managers design store layouts and resolve problems dealing with people or objects moving through spaces over time.

When Steelcase, an office furniture manufacturer, decided there was an opportunity for a new product specifically designed for work teams, researchers believed that observation was the best research method. Steelcase placed video cameras at various companies so its staff could observe firsthand how teams operate. After the recording period ended, the researchers exhaustively analyzed the tapes, looking for the patterns of behavior and motion that workers don't even notice themselves. The main observation was that people in teams function best if they can do some work collaboratively and some privately. These findings were utilized to design the Personal Harbor brand of modular office units. The units are similar in shape and size to a phone booth and can be arranged around a common space where a team works, fostering synergy but also allowing a person to work alone when necessary.[6]

Television Monitoring

Perhaps the best-known marketing research project involving mechanical observation and computerized data collection is the A. C. Nielsen Television Index (NTI), the system for estimating national television audiences. The NTI uses a consumer panel and mechanical observation to obtain ratings for television programs. More than 4,000 households, scientifically selected to be representative of the U.S. population, have agreed to become members of the panel and have meters placed in their homes. For years the A. C. Nielsen Company was criticized because its audiometer passively recorded only which shows were playing on TV sets. Because it indicated only whether a set was on a particular channel or turned off, advertisers did not know whether the entire family or just one individual (or perhaps no one) was watching. The diary system, in which family members logged in their viewing habits, was used to supplement the passive meter. However, the diary system had problems, too. It worked well during the network-only television era, but recording viewing activity in a diary became increasingly complex in an age of cable television systems with dozens of channels.

Many experts also believe that diaries exhibit a so-called *halo bias*. When viewers fill out diaries two or three days after watching television, they tend to remember only their favorite shows and forget others. As a result, top-rated programs such as "Star Trek: Voyager" could receive disproportionately high audience estimates.

Nielsen set out to make improvements. After spending years developing and testing, Nielsen developed a system that promised to be an improvement because information about who was watching which programs would be built into the measuring system.

The People Meter, a microwave-based, computerized television rating system, was designed to use state-of-the-art electronic measuring to replace passive meters and the 30-year-old diary system. When the panel household's television set is turned on, a question mark appears on the screen to remind viewers to indicate who is watching. The viewer then uses a handheld electronic device that resembles a television remote control to record who is watching. A device attached to the television automatically sends the viewer's age and sex and what programs are being watched over telephone lines to the Nielsen's computers. People Meters measure a show's ratings and provide demographic profiles overnight.

Critics of the People Meter argue that subjects in Nielsen's panel grow bored over time and do not always record when they begin or stop watching television. Nielsen Media Research is now working an a unique technology that will allow its people meters to scan the room, recognize each family member by his or her facial characteristics, and record when they enter or leave the room.

Internet Monitoring

Media Metrics is a marketing research company that tracks the popularity of sites on the World Wide Web and proprietary on-line services such as America On-line. The company installs a special tracking program on the personal computers of a sample of computer users who volunteer to participate in the research effort. Many organizations with Web sites consisting of multiple pages track how may users visit each page on the Web site. They also use "cookies" (see Chapter 2) to track the paths or sequence of pages that visitors follow.

Scanner-Based Research

Lasers performing optical character recognition and bar-code technology like the universal product code (UPC) have accelerated the use of mechanical observa-

television monitoring
Computerized mechanical observation used to obtain television ratings.

tion in marketing research. Chapter 7 noted that a number of syndicated services offer secondary data about product category movement generated from retail stores using scanner technology.

This technology now allows researchers to investigate more demographically or promotionally specific questions. For example, scanner research has investigated the different ways consumers respond to price promotions and how those differences affect a promotion's profitability. One of the primary means of implementing this type of research is through the establishment of a **scanner-based consumer panel** to replace consumer purchase diaries.

In a typical scanner panel each household is assigned a bar-coded card that members present to the clerk at the register. The household's code number is coupled with the purchase information recorded by the last scanner. Furthermore, as with other consumer panels, background information about the household obtained through answers to a battery of demographic and psychographic survey questions can also be coupled with the household code number.

Aggregate data, such as actual store movement as measured by scanners, will also be available. These data parallel the results of a standard mail diary panel, with some important improvements:

1. The data measure observed (actual) purchase behavior versus reported behavior (recorded later in a diary).

2. Substituting mechanical for human record-keeping improves accuracy.

3. Measures are unobtrusive, eliminating interviewing and possible respondents' (social desirability) bias as in a mail diary.

4. More extensive purchase data can be collected because all UPC categories are measured. In a mail diary respondents could not possibly reliably record all items they purchased. Because all UPC-coded items are measured in the panel, users can investigate many product categories to determine loyalty, switching rates, and so on for their own brands as well as for other companies' products and to locate product categories for possible market entry.

5. The data collected from computerized checkout scanners can be combined with data about advertising, price changes, and sales promotions. Researchers can scrutinize them with powerful analytical software provided by the scanner data providers.

Scanner data an show a marketer week by week how a product is doing, even in a single store, and track sales against local ads or promotions. Furthermore, several organizations, such as Information Resources Inc. Behavior Scan System, have developed scanner panels and expanded them into electronic test market systems. These are discussed in greater detail in Chapter 12.

Advances in bar-code technology have led to **at-home scanning systems** that use hand held wands to read UPC symbols. Consumer panelists perform their own scanning *after* they have taken home the products. This advance makes it possible to investigate purchases made at toy stores, department stores, drugstores, and other retailers that do not have in-store scanning equipment.

Measuring Physiological Reactions

Marketing researchers have used a number of other mechanical devices to evaluate consumers' physical and physiological reactions to advertising copy, packaging, and other stimuli. Researchers use such means when they believe that consumers are unaware of their actual reactions to stimuli such as advertising, or that consumers

---

scanner-based consumer panel

A type of consumer panel in which the participants' purchasing habits are recorded with a laser scanner rather than a purchase diary.

at-home scanning system

A system whereby consumer panelists perform their own scanning after taking home the products using hand-held wands that read UPC symbols.

will not provide honest responses. There are four major categories of mechanical devices used to measure physiological reactions: (1) eye-tracking monitors, (2) pupilometers, (3) psychogalvanometers, and (4) voice pitch analyzers.

A magazine or newspaper advertiser may wish to grab readers' attention with a visual scene and then direct it to a package or coupon. Eye-tracking equipment records how the subject reads the ad or views a TV commercial and how much time is spent looking at various parts of the stimulus.

In physiological terms the gaze movement of a viewer's eye are measured with an **eye-tracking monitor**, which measures unconscious eye movements. Originally developed to measure astronauts' eye fatigue, these devices track eye movements through invisible infrared light beams that lock into a subject's eyes. The light reflects off the eye, and eye-movement data are recorded while another tiny video camera monitors which magazine page is being perused. The data are analyzed by computer to determine which components in an ad (or other stimuli) were seen and which were overlooked.

Modern eye-tracking systems need not keep a viewer's head in a stationary position. Measuring rough television commercials, especially animations, with the eye-tracking systems helps advertisers emphasize selling points.

The remaining physiological observation techniques are based on a common principle:

> Physiological research depends on the fact that adrenalin is produced when the body is aroused. When adrenalin goes to work, the heart beats faster and more strongly, and even enlarges.

> Blood flows to the extremities and increases capillary dilation at the fingertips and earlobes. Skin temperature increases, hair follicles stand up, skin pores emit perspiration, and the electrical conductivity of skin surfaces is affected. Eye pupils dilate, electrical waves in the brain increase in frequency, breathing is faster and deeper, and the chemical composition of expired air is altered. This process offers a choice of about 50 different measures—the question of which measure to use is to some extent irrelevant since they are all measuring arousal.[7]

The **pupilometer** observes and records changes in the diameter of a subject's pupils. A subject is instructed to look at a screen on which an advertisement or other stimulus is projected. Holding constant the brightness and distance of the stimulus from the subject's eyes, changes in pupil size may be interpreted as changes in cognitive activity that result from the stimulus rather than eye dilation and constriction from light intensity, distance from the object, or other physiological reactions to the conditions of observation. This method of research is based on the assumption that increased pupil size reflects positive attitudes toward and interest in advertisements.

The **psychogalvanometer** measures galvanic skin response (GSR), a measure of involuntary changes in the electrical resistance of the skin. This device uses the assumption that physiological changes, such as increased perspiration, accompany emotional reactions to advertisements, packages, and slogans. Excitement increases the body's perspiration rate, which increases the electrical resistance of the skin. The test is an indicator of emotional arousal or tension.

Voice pitch analysis is a relatively new physiological measurement technique. Emotional reactions are measured through physiological changes in a person's voice. Abnormal frequencies in the voice, caused by changes in the autonomic nervous system, are measured with sophisticated, audio-adapted comput-

eye-tracking monitor
A mechanical device used to observe eye movements. Some eye monitors use infrared light beams to measure unconscious eye movements.

pupilometer
A mechanical device used to observe and record changes in the diameter of a subject's pupils.

psychogalvanometer
A device that measures galvanic skin response, a measure of involuntary changes in the electrical resistance of the skin.

voice pitch analysis
A physiological measurement technique that records abnormal frequencies in the voice that are supposed to reflect emotional reactions to various stimuli.

Examination of this Toyota Tercel ad with an eye-tracking monitor shows that only 24 percent of consumer viewing time was given to the Tercel message and that 76 percent of the time was spent examining the top of the ad. According to the president of Perception Research Services, the 24 percent figure is far lower than the PRS "quality" time norm of 63 percent. Quality time is the time spent by the viewer on the communications elements in an ad that are directly product related.[8]

er equipment. Computerized analysis compares the respondent's voice pitch during warm-up conversations (normal range) with verbal response to questions about his or her evaluative reaction to television commercials or other stimuli. This technique, unlike other physiological devices, does not require the researcher to surround subjects with mazes of wires or equipment.

All of these devices assume that physiological reactions are associated with persuasiveness or predict some cognitive response. This has not yet been clearly demonstrated, however. There is no strong theoretical evidence to support the argument that a physiological change is a valid measure of future sales, attitude change, or emotional response. Another major problem with physiological research is the *calibration,* or sensitivity, of measuring devices. Identifying arousal is one thing, but precisely measuring *levels* of arousal is another. In addition, most of these devices are expensive. However, as a prominent researcher points out, physiological measurement is coincidental: "Physiological measurement isn't an exit interview. It's not dependent on what was remembered later on. It's a live blood, sweat, and tears, moment-by-moment response, synchronous with the stimulus."[9]

Each of these mechanical devices has another limitation in that the subjects are usually placed in artificial settings (watching television in the laboratory rather than at home) and they know that they are being observed.[10]

Summary

Observation is a powerful tool for the marketing researcher. Scientific observation is the systematic process of recording the behavioral patterns of people, objects, and occurrences without questioning or otherwise communicating with them. A wide variety of information about the behavior of people and objects can be observed. Seven kinds of content are observable: physical actions, verbal behavior, expressive behavior, spatial relations and locations, temporal patterns, physical objects, and verbal and pictorial records. Thus, both verbal and non-verbal messages may be observed.

A major disadvantage of the observation technique is that cognitive phenomena such as attitudes, motivations, expectations, intentions, and preferences are not observable. Furthermore, only overt behavior of short duration can be observed. Nevertheless, many types of data can be obtained more accurately through direct observation than by questioning respondents. Observation is the only or most direct method for collecting certain data.

Marketing researchers employ both human observers and machines designed for specific observation tasks. Human observation is commonly used when the situation or behavior to be recorded is not easily predictable in advance of the research. Mechanical observation can be used when the situation or behavior to be recorded is routine, repetitive, or programmatic. Human or mechanical observation may be unobtrusive. Human observation brings the possibility of subjective error even though the observer does not interact with the respondent.

Observation can sometimes be contrived by creating the situations to be observed. This can reduce the time and expense of obtaining reactions to certain circumstances. Contrived observation, hidden observation, and other observation research designs that might use deception often raise ethical concerns about subjects' right to privacy and right to be informed.

Physical-trace evidence serves as a visible record of past events. Content analysis obtains data by observing and analyzing the contents of the messages in written and/or spoken communications. Content analysis can determine the information content of phenomena. Mechanical observation uses a variety of devices to record behavior directly. Mechanical observation takes many forms. National television audience ratings are based on mechanical observation and computerized data collection. Scanner-based research is growing in popularity because of increased use of laser scanners in retail stores. Many syndicated services offer secondary data collected through scanner systems. Physiological reactions, such as arousal or eye movement patterns, may be observed using a number of mechanical devices.

Key Terms and Concepts

Observation
Physical actions
Verbal behavior
Expressive behavior
Spatial relations and locations
Temporal patterns
Physical objects
Verbal and pictorial records

Visible observation
Hidden observation
Direct observation
Response latency
Observer bias
Contrived observation
Content analysis

Television monitoring
Scanner-based consumer panel
At-home scanning system
Eye-tracking monitor
Pupilometer
Psychogalvanometer
Voice pitch analysis

Questions for Review and Critical Thinking

1. Yogi Berra, former New York Yankee catcher, said, "You can observe a lot just by watching." How does this fit in with the definition of scientific observation?

2. What are the advantages and disadvantages of observation studies relative to surveys?

3. Under what conditions are observation studies most appropriate?

4. Suggest some new uses for observation studies. Be creative.

5. A multinational fast-food corporation plans to locate a restaurant in La Paz, Bolivia. Secondary data for this city are outdated. How might you determine the best location using observation?

6. Discuss how an observation study might be combined with a personal interview.

7. The lost-letter technique has been used to predict voting behavior. Letters addressed to various political groups are spread throughout a city. The "respondent" finds an envelope, reads the address of a group supporting (or opposing) a candidate, and mails back (or throws away) the envelope. It is assumed that this indicates a favorable (or unfavorable) attitude toward the organization. Would this technique be appropriate in marketing research?

8. Outline a research design using observation for each of the following situations:

   a. A bank wishes to collect data on the number of customer services and the frequency of customer use of these services.

   b. A state government wishes to determine the driving public's use of seat belts.

   c. A researcher wishes to know how many women have been featured on *Time* covers over the years.

   d. A fast-food franchise wishes to determine how long a customer entering a store has to wait for his or her order.

   e. A magazine publisher wishes to determine exactly what people see and what they pass over while reading one of its magazines.

   f. A food manufacturer wishes to determine how people use snack foods in their homes.

   g. An overnight package delivery service wishes to observe delivery workers beginning at the point where they stop the truck, continuing to the point where they deliver the package, and finally at the point where they return to the truck.

9. Watch the nightly news on a major network for one week. Observe how much time reporters spend on national news, commercials, and other activity. (*Hint:* Think carefully about how you will record the contents of the programs.)

10. Comment on the ethics of the following situations:

    a. During the course of telephone calls to investors, a stockbroker records respondents' voices when they are answering sensitive investment questions and then conducts a voice pitch analysis. The respondents do not know their voices are being recorded.

   b. A researcher plans to invite consumers to be test users in a simulated kitchen located in a shopping mall and to videotape their reactions to a new microwave dinner from behind a one-way mirror.

   c. A marketing researcher arranges to purchase the trash from the headquarters of a major competitor. The purpose is to sift through discarded documents to determine the company's strategic plans.

Exploring the Internet

The University of Arizona Department of Anthropology houses the Bureau of Applied Research in Anthropology. The garbage project is one of the bureau's research activities. Use a search engine to find the University of Arizona's home page and then navigate to the garbage project. What information is available?

Case 10.1 Texas Instruments and E-Lab

E-Lab LLC is a business research and design firm in Chicago that specializes in observing people, identifying patterns in behavior and developing an understanding of why these patterns exist.[11] The company then uses the knowledge that it gains as a framework in the product development process. Texas Instruments (TI) used E-Lab to investigate the mobility, connectivity, and communications needs of law enforcement officers, which led to ideas for a set of computing and communications products. As part of its product development research, TI's Advanced Integrated Systems Department and E-Lab researchers spent 320 hours shadowing police officers in three Texas police departments. Shadowing involves asking questions while observing. They walked foot patrols, rode in patrol cars, and pedaled with bike patrols. They spent time with crowd control, narcotics, homicide, dispatch, and juvenile teams. They recorded their observations and interviews on paper, digital camera, and video.

A number of interesting findings emerged from all this research. First, police officers are very social so it was important that any product TI developed should enhance socialization rather than detract

from it. For example, an in-car computing and communications device should be able to access a database that lists names and numbers of experts on the force so officers can call or e-mail the experts directly. Second, police officers are not driven by procedure. That told TI that the procedures for an investigation should reside in the device and that the device should prompt the officer at each step in the process. And third, officers rely on informal information about people and activities on their beats. This information may be kept on scraps of paper, on a spreadsheet back in the office, or in the police officer's head. Business researchers concluded that any device that TI develops should have a place to compile and share informal information.

QUESTIONS

1. Identify the research design used by E-Lab.

2. Compare this research design with a survey research design. What advantages, if any, did this research design have over a survey?

Case 10.2 Pretesting Company[12]

Basically it looks like a desk lamp with a chunky smoked-glass body. In fact, it is Lee Weinblatt's People Reader, a device designed to surreptitiously monitor the way people react to magazine advertising. Behind the smoked glass are two tiny, remote-controlled video cameras, one that tracks eye movements and another that monitors which page is being perused. In a nearby office, technicians measure each dismissive glance and longing gaze.

Will a high school senior unconsciously dwell on an Air Force recruitment ad featuring computer screens that look like video games? Will a middle-aged man linger over an automobile ad featuring leggy female models? The People Reader was intended to answer questions like these for companies that spend millions of dollars on advertising and, in the past, have had to depend on the accuracy of a test subject's memory.

Mr. Weinblatt, 43 years old, is founder of the Pretesting Company, a 5-year-old concern in Englewood, N.J., that has become the leader in sleight-of-hand advertising research. He has developed an extensive bag of tricks, some of them incorporating technology originally developed for espionage. The People Reader is one; another is a mock car radio that plays prerecorded material and measures the speed with which a driver silences a commercial. There is also a television system that measures the tendency of viewers armed with remote-control devices to "zap" a particular commercial and a computer-simulated supermarket to measure the allure of a new package. Mr. Weinblatt has hidden video cameras in a fake bar of Ivory soap, a box of cereal ("old hat," he says now) and in a ceiling sprinkler.

The unifying theme of Mr. Weinblatt's technology [is] eliciting responses consumers may not be aware of. Typically, people being tested are given only a limited idea—and often the wrong one—about what is actually being measured.

Since starting his company in 1985, Mr. Weinblatt has acquired an impressive list of clients, including Ralston Purina, RJR Nabisco's Planter's peanuts, S. C. Johnson's Raid insecticide, *Sports Illustrated,* and the *New Yorker.* Although Pretesting remains small, with revenues of $5.5 million, clients say Mr. Weinblatt offers them insights unlike those generated by any other advertising researchers. "I've recommended his tests many times," said Sue Le Barron, a project manager for pet food marketing research at Ralston Purina.

Traditionally, advertising research has been based on fairly overt approaches. To test a proposed television ad, for example, companies arrange to transmit the commercials to television sets of test subjects during normal programming and then interview them the next day on their ability to remember the ad and on their reactions. Similarly, the traditional method of pretesting a new package or design is to expose it to a focus group of consumers who examine and react to it. Mr. Weinblatt argues that such techniques provide at best a murky picture, often failing to measure the impact of subliminal messages or, in the case of focus groups, prompting judgments in situations that don't mirror real life.

"Diagnostical research can be very useful not understanding what the problem is with a product, but it can never tell you what people are going to do in the real world," said Mr. Weinblatt. "Do people read *Newsweek* from the front or the back? How do you time the sequence of television ads? How does print stack up against TV? The questions have been piling up."

Mr. Weinblatt has been tinkering with attention-measuring devices since 1971. Armed with a master's degree in industrial psychology (and, later, in photography), he started out with the research subsidiary of the Interpublic Group of Companies Inc., which owns several major advertising agencies.

At the time, many advertising researchers were experimenting with "pupilmetrics," the measurement of pupil dilation, by filming people who were strapped into chairs and whose heads were anchored into wax molds. Mr. Weinblatt designed equipment that was less intrusive. His first assignment came from Philip Morris, which he said wanted to find the least noticeable place to mount warning labels required by the Surgeon General on a pack of cigarettes. "We found that it didn't make any difference," said Mr. Weinblatt. "Smokers don't want to see."

In 1976, Mr. Weinblatt started Telcom Research, a manufacturer of portable eye movement recorders, which he sold in 1982, just before it was about to go bankrupt. But he continued inventing increasingly unobtrusive measurement devices, and founded the Pretesting Company in 1985. Today he holds 28 patents.

To measure the chances that consumers will be attracted to a new package on crowded supermarket shelves, Mr. Weinblatt developed a computer-simulated shopping spree. Researchers evaluating a new line of dog food, for example, begin by recreating a supermarket rack in the dog food section that contains the new package. They then photograph the shelf as a whole and take close-ups of each quadrant of the shelf. This material is mixed in with similar sequences depicting the store entrance and several other supermarket sections.

People being tested are then told to "walk" through the store by reviewing slides of these images on a screen. Pressing buttons on a controller, they can move forward or backward between shelves and move in for closeups. At each section they are asked to pick up out what, if anything, they would like to buy. Their answers, however, constitute only a small part of the test. The key measurements, according to Mr. Weinblatt, are based on the way they move through the slides. Unknown to the customers, a computer linked to the controller logs the amount of time spent at each picture and provides an instant tabulation of how long a person lingered at the dog food rack and at a particular part of it containing the new product. That data, in turn, can be compared with data for the rest of the supermarket and for competing products.

Mr. Weinblatt concedes there have been instances in which he incorrectly predicted that a commercial would fail. Nevertheless, he argues, his measurements offer crucial information in a world of cluttered store shelves, where nine out of ten new products fail. "The typical person spends 22 minutes shopping in a supermarket that contains 18,000 products," said Mr. Weinblatt. "What we're saying is, before you bet all that money on a new product, let's do the ideal and see if people are even going to notice it."

QUESTION

1. Evaluate each observation technique used by the Pretesting Company. What possible applications might each technique have?

Case 10.3 Tulsa's Central Business District (A)

THE METROPOLITAN TULSA CHAMBER OF COMMERCE recognized that there was a critical gap between the availability of timely information about the central business district (CBD) and the need for this information for investment decision making, commercial marketing efforts, and the continued pursuit of the goal of downtown revitalization. The Chamber of Commerce undertook four separate research projects to gather information about the CBD. One project was a physical inventory of the existing downtown commercial base. The objectives of the study were to determine what types of establishments were operating in the CBD and the number of vacancies there and to generally profile the commercial geography of the CBD. The researchers found that the central business district was based on the U.S. Bureau of the Census classification scheme. The CBD was identified as the area encompassed by the inner dispersal loop (a system of expressways), which corresponded identically with census tract 25 (see Case Exhibit 10.3-1 below).

A team of ten pedestrian field-workers covered each block in the inner dispersal loop. The field-work-

ers used the observation form in Case Exhibit 10.3-2 on page 306 to record the company name, address, primary business activity, estimate frontage, and other relevant information about each building site or office. Standard Industrial Classification (SIC) codes for retailers were recorded by the field-workers. SIC codes for all other establishments were recorded by research assistants after the data were collected. All the data were identified by census block.

QUESTIONS

1. Evaluate this research design.
2. What changes, if any, would you make in the observation form?
3. What problems would you expect in the data collection stage?
4. What techniques would you use to analyze the data?

Case Exhibit 10.3-1 Census Blocks in Census Track 25

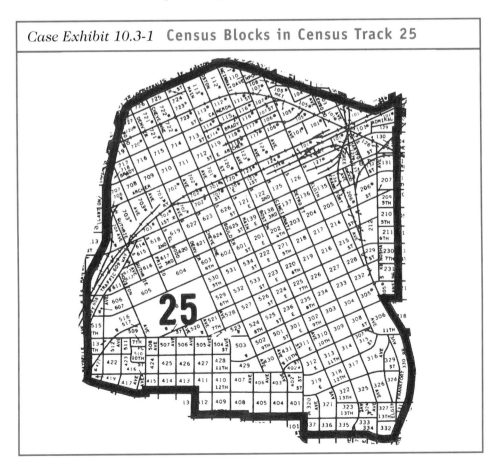

Exhibit 10.3-2 **Observation Study Recording Form**

Company Name _____

_____

Address: _____

Tulsa, Oklahoma

Activities: __ 1 Vacant   __ 2 Retail __ 3 Wholesale __ 4 Manufacturing

__ 5 Service   __ 6 Other (Specify) _____

Retail SIC: __52 __53 __54 __55 __56 __57 __58 __59 __60

Other Activities (describe): _____

_____

Is the Building: __1 For Sale? __2 For Rent?

Leasable Space: _____

Realtor's Name: _____

Realtor's Phone: _____

Rent (per sq. foot) _____

Is the Building Being: __1 Restored? __2 Remodeled?

Estimated Frontage (Feet): _____

Estimated Number of Stories: _____

Comments: _____

_____

_____

Chapter 11

Experimental Research

An Overview

DOES THE SIZE OF A PACKAGE INFLUENCE A PERSON TO INCREASE or decrease consumption? A series of tightly controlled laboratory experiments found evidence that larger packages encourage consumers to increase the amount of the product they use.

The hypothesis for one of the experiments was that the larger a package's size, the more of it one will use on a given occasion.[1] The experiment required altering package size while holding the total supply of the product constant. The procedure went as follows:

The researchers recruited 98 adult women through local Parent-Teacher Associations (PTA), and $6 was donated to the respective organization for each participant. Two different products (Crisco Oil and Creamette Spaghetti) in two different sizes were selected for the study. In both cases, the larger package held twice as much of the product as the smaller package. The supply for each brand was held constant by leaving the smaller package full and by only using half of the larger package. The volume of each product was determined by the package sizes in which each was sold.

Each subject was randomly assigned to use either a relatively small or a relatively large package, each holding identical volumes of the product. Two products were used for generalizability, and the pattern of results was expected to be similar for both parties.

In individual meetings each subject was told that researchers were collecting some basic "home economics–related" information about two different types of products. The subject was then led to one of four isolated cubicles in which there was a large or small package of one of the two products. The research assistant assigned to each cubicle did not know the purpose of the study. When the subject arrived, the research assistant read a scenario involving the use of the

product (for Crisco Oil, "You are frying a chicken dinner for yourself and another adult" and for Creamette Spaghetti, "You are making spaghetti for yourself and another adult.") The subject was asked to show how much of the product she would use in this situation and how much money that use of the product would entail. After the subject left the cubicle, a researcher measured the amount the subject intended to use. The procedure was repeated for all subjects.

The dependent measure was the volume of the product each subject indicated she would use. Subjects indicated their use of oil by pouring it into a frying pan; they indicated their use of spaghetti by placing it in a large (dry) pot. The volume of oil they used was measured by pouring the liquid into a narrow beaker. The volume of spaghetti was measured by holding the strands together and measuring the circumference with a finely graduated tape measure; this was later translated to an approximation of an individual count.

As was hypothesized, manipulating the package size while holding the supply of each product constant indicates that increases in a package's size are associated with increases in product usage.

Related experiments also show that consumers will use more from a full container than from a half-empty one. Even when a package recommends an amount to use, as household cleaners do, research shows consumers ignore such instructions 70 percent of the time.[2]

This chapter explores the nature of experimentation in marketing.

The Nature of Experiments

Most students are familiar with the concept of experimentation in the physical sciences. When the term *experiment* is mentioned, we typically conjure up an image of a chemist surrounded by bubbling test tubes and Bunsen burners. Behavioral and physical scientists have been far ahead of marketing researchers in the use of experimentation. Nevertheless, the purpose of experimental research is the same.

Experimental research allows the investigator to control the research situation so that *causal* relationships among variables may be evaluated. The marketing experimenter manipulates a single variable in an investigation and holds constant all other relevant, extraneous variables. Events may be controlled in an experiment to a degree not possible in a survey.

The researcher's goal in conducting an experiment is to determine whether the experimental treatment is the cause of the effect being measured. If a new marketing strategy (for example, new advertising) is used in a test market and sales subsequently increase in that market, but not in markets where the new strategy is not employed, the experimenter can feel confident that the new strategy caused the increase in sales.

Experiments differ from other research methods in degree of control over the research situation. In an **experiment** one variable (the *independent variable*) is manipulated and its effect on another variable (the *dependent variable*) is measured, while all other variables that may confound the relationship are eliminated or controlled. The experimenter either creates an artificial situation or deliberately manipulates the given situation.

For example, a famous marketing experiment investigated the influence of brand name identification on consumers' taste perceptions. The experimenter manipulated whether consumers tasted beer in labeled or unlabeled bottles. One

experiment
A research investigation in which conditions are controlled so that an independent variable(s) can be manipulated to test a hypothesis about a dependent variable. Allows evaluation of causal relationships among variables while all other variables are eliminated or controlled.

week respondents were given a six-pack containing bottles labeled with tags bearing only letters. The following week, respondents received another six-pack with brand labels. Thus, actual purchase from a store never occurred, but respondents drank the beer at home at their leisure. The experimenter measured reactions to the beers after each tasting The beer itself was the same in each case, so differences in taste perception were attributed to label (brand) influence. This example illustrates that once an experimenter manipulates the independent variable, changes in the dependent variable are measured. The essence of an experiment is to do something to an individual and observe the reaction under conditions that allow his or her performance to be measured against a known baseline.

An Illustration: A Unit Pricing Experiment

The concept of experimentation is best illustrated with an extended example concerning unit pricing. Whether consumers actually use unit price information is an issue of considerable controversy.[3] Unit pricing allows shoppers to avoid any confusion due to price calculations, especially among packages of different sizes. Some evidence shows that unit pricing has failed to change consumers' purchasing habits. However, much of the research on it depends on interviewing techniques, phrasing of questions, and store promotion of unit pricing. Suppose a researcher argues that unit price information must be presented in a usable display format or the consumers will not use the information. The current form of unit price display is a separate shell tag for each item. However, this type of information may not facilitate price comparisons. Exhibit 11.1 shows unit prices organized into a single list.

Exhibit 11.1   **List of Unit Prices**

LISTED IN ORDER OF INCREASING PRICE PER QUART/PINT

Par, 48 oz.	$1.08	$0.72 per quart	36.0¢ per pint
Par, 32 oz.	$0.76	$0.76 per quart	38.0¢ per pint
Sweetheart, 32 oz.	$1.10	$1.10 per quart	55.0¢ per pint
Brocade, 48 oz.	$1.70	$1.13 per quart	55.0¢ per pint
Sweetheart, 22 oz.	$0.78	$1.13 per quart	56.5¢ per pint
Super 6, 32 oz.	$1.18	$1.18 per quart	59.0¢ per pint
White Magic, 32 oz.	$1.18	$1.18 per quart	59.0¢ per pint
Brocade, 32 oz.	$1.26	$1.26 per quart	63.0¢ per pint
Brocade, 22 oz.	$0.90	$1.31 per quart	65.5¢ per pint
Super 6, 22 oz.	$0.90	$1.31 per quart	65.5¢ per pint
White Magic, 22 oz.	$0.90	$1.31 per quart	65.5¢ per pint
Brocade, 12 oz.	$0.54	$1.44 per quart	72.0¢ per pint
Super 6, 12 oz.	$0.58	$1.55 per quart	77.5¢ per pint
Ivory, 32 oz.	$1.60	$1.60 per quart	80.0¢ per pint
Dove, 22 oz.	$1.12	$1.63 per quart	81.5¢ per pint
Ivory, 22 oz.	$1.12	$1.63 per quart	81.5¢ per pint
Lux, 22 oz.	$1.12	$1.63 per quart	81.5¢ per pint
Palmolive, 32 oz.	$1.70	$1.70 per quart	85.0¢ per pint
Ivory, 12 oz.	$0.64	$1.71 per quart	85.5¢ per pint
Palmolive, 22 oz.	$1.20	$1.75 per quart	87.5¢ per pint
Palmolive, 12 oz.	$0.68	$1.81 per quart	90.5¢ per pint

Exhibit 11.2   The Design of the Unit Price Experiment

	FIRST 5 WEEKS	SECOND 5 WEEKS
Store 1	Record sales	Shelf tag format, record sales
Store 2	Record sales	Shelf tag format, record sales
Store 3	Record sales	List format, record sales
Store 4	Record sales	List format, record sales

A survey asking respondents if they use the traditional format of unit pricing or have any problems understanding traditional unit pricing might not yield the true responses. It may not be socially desirable for respondents to admit they have problems understanding the traditional format. Or they may be unwilling to provide true responses because they are embarrassed that they do not use a procedure that might reduce their grocery bills. Many of the other limitations of surveys, such as interviewer bias and misunderstanding the question, might also cause errors.

In the simplest form of experiment, the researcher's purpose might be to compare the effectiveness of the *typical shelf tag display* and the *list format,* measuring changes toward less expensive brands or sizes. The hypothesis would be that a single list of brands' sizes and their unit prices is an effective arrangement of unit price information. A shift toward the purchase of less expensive items can be measured by average price paid per unit—the dependent variable.

Let us assume that marketing researchers will be conducting the research in a supermarket chain in a midwestern city. The supermarket chain has four stores in this city, and none of the stores has previously used unit price information. For a period of five weeks, brand purchases for five product categories may be recorded in every story to indicate sales over a given period. During the next five weeks, two stores may be assigned unit prices on separate shelf tags, and the remaining two stores will displace unit price information in the list format (see Exhibit 11.2). This manipulation will concern an independent or experimental treatment variable.

Table 11.1 shows that the average price paid per unit purchased for dishwashing detergent was 65.0¢ for all stores before the experiment. After the manipulation of the unit price information, the average price paid per unit in the shelf tag stores was 61.6¢, and in the list format stores the average price was 60.0¢. Here the results indicated that unit price information was effective in shifting purchases toward less expensive items in both the shelf tag condition and the list condition as opposed to no display of unit price information before the ex-

---

Table 11.1   Results of Unit Price Experiment for Dishwashing Detergent

	AVERAGE PRICE PAID PER UNIT	
TREATMENT	FIVE WEEKS BEFORE EXPERIMENT	DURING EXPERIMENT
Shelf tag treatment (stores 1 and 2)	65.0¢	61.6¢
List format treatment (stores 3 and 4)	65.0¢	60.0¢
Total all stores	65.0¢	61.0¢

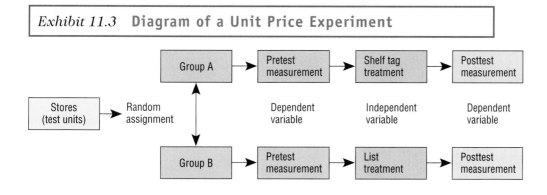

Exhibit 11.3 Diagram of a Unit Price Experiment

periment. Furthermore, the average price paid per unit was lower in the list for-mat condition than in the shelf tag condition, suggesting that the list format was more effective.

Some of the influence of shifts in purchases may have been due to differences in the stores (for example, shoppers in the stores with the lists of unit prices may have been more sophisticated than those in other stores). To eliminate or mini-mize this problem, the researchers could have randomly assigned the experimen-tal condition of the unit pricing format to the stores. The randomization would have minimized the possibility that the changes in the variable under study would have been due to forces other than the unit price format. In our example, this randomization process resulted in both the shelf tag and list format stores having equal average prices per unit (65.0¢) before the experiment began.

Our experiment has shown that a change in the presentation of unit price in-formation (the independent variable) caused a change in the average unit price paid (the dependent variable) when other variables were controlled for possible causal effects. For example, store image was held *constant* because the experi-ment occurred only in stores with the same retailer name. We know the store image may have affected sales, but we controlled for this variable by using only one type of store in one city. We also assumed invariance for certain variables; that is, we did not expect them to vary appreciably. For example, the tempera-ture in the store may have affected the amount of time shoppers spent in the store, but we were assuming (without checking on or controlling this assump-tion) that all stores were the same on this variable. In other cases, we assumed that some variables were irrelevant; for example, the color of the store managers' eyes may have varied, but we assumed that this had no effect on the purchase of products. This was a simple experiment intended to introduce some of the con-cepts of marketing experimentation. The remainder of this chapter explores these and other aspects of experimental designs.

Exhibit 11.3 diagrams the unit price experiment. This can be helpful in the definition of pertinent terminology presented in the next section.

Basic Issues in Experimental Design

Decisions must be made about several basic element of an experiment. These is-sues are (1) manipulation of the independent variable, (2) selection and mea-surement of the dependent variable, (3) selection and assignment of subjects, and (4) control over extraneous variables.[4]

Experimental treatments are alternative manipulations of the independent variable. Variations of advertising copy, graphic designs, and levels of prices charged are typical independent variables in marketing experiments.

Manipulation of the Independent Variable

independent variable
In an experimental design, the variable that can be manipulated, changed, or altered independently of any other variable.

experimental treatments
Alternative manipulations of the independent variable being investigated.

The experimenter has some degree of control over the **independent variable.** The variable is independent because its value can be manipulated by the experimenter to whatever he or she wishes it to be. Its value may be changed or altered independently of any other variable. The independent variable is hypothesized to be the causal influence.

Experimental treatments are the alternative manipulations of the independent variable being investigated. For example, prices of $1.29, $1.69, and $1.99 might be the treatments in a pricing experiment. Prices changes, advertising strategy changes, taste formulation, and so on are typical treatments.

TO THE POINT

You never know what is enough unless you know what is more than enough.

WILLIAM BLAKE

In marketing research the independent variable often is a *categorical* or *classificatory variable* that represents some classifiable or qualitative aspect of marketing strategy. To determine the effects of point-of-purchase displays, the experimental treatments that represent the independent variable are themselves the varying displays. Alternative advertising copy is another example of a categorical or classificatory variable. In other situations the independent variable is a *continuous variable*. The researcher must select the appropriate levels of that variable as experimental treatments. For example the number of dollars that can be spent on advertising may be any number of different values.

Experimental and Control Groups. In the simplest type of experiment, only two values of the independent variable are manipulated. For example, consider measuring the influence of advertising on sales. In the experimental condition (treatment administered to the **experimental group**), the advertising budget may be at $200,000. In the control condition (treatment administered to the **control group**), advertising may remain at zero or without change. By holding conditions constant in the control group, the researcher controls for potential sources of error in the experiment. Sales (the dependent variable) in the two treatment groups are compared at the end of the experiment to determine whether the level of advertising (the independent variable) had any effect.

experimental group
The group of subjects exposed to the experimental treatment.

control group
The group of individuals exposed to the control condition in an experiment, that is, not exposed to the experimental treatment.

Several Experimental Treatment Levels. The advertising/sales experiment with one experimental and one control group may not tell the advertiser everything he or she wishes to know about the advertising/sales relationship. If the advertiser wished to understand the functional nature of the relationship between sales and advertising at several treatment levels, additional experimental groups with advertising expenditures of $200,000, $500,000, and $1 million might be studied. This type of design would allow the experimenter to get a better idea of an optimal advertising budget.

More Than One Independent Variable. It is possible to assess the effects of more than one independent variable. For example, a restaurant chain might investigate the combined effects of increased advertising and a change in prices on sales volume. (More complex experimental designs are discussed in Chapter 12.) The purpose of most marketing research experimentation is to measure and compare the effects of experimental treatments on the dependent variable.

Selection and Measurement of the Dependent Variable

The **dependent variable** is so called because its value is expected to be dependent on the experimenter's manipulation; it is the criterion or standard by which the results are judged. Changes in the dependent variable are presumed to be a consequence of changes in the independent variable.

Selection of the dependent variable is a crucial decision in the design of an experiment. If we introduce a new pink grapefruit tea mix in a test market, sales volume is most likely to be the dependent variable. However, if we are experimenting with different forms of advertising copy appeals, defining the dependent variable may be more difficult. For example, measures of advertising awareness, recall, changes in brand preference, or sales might be used as the dependent variable depending on the purpose of the ads. In the unit pricing experiment the dependent variable was the average price paid per unit. However, the dependent variable might have been the preference for either format of pricing information (a cognitive variable), brand-switching behavior expressed as a percentage of consumers, or attitudes toward the store. Often the dependent variable selection

dependent variable
The criterion or standard by which the results of an experiment are judged; a variable expected to be dependent on the experimenter's manipulation.

process, like the problem definition process, is considered less carefully than it should be. The experimenter's choice of a dependent variable determines what type of answer is given to the research question.

In a test market the time period needed for the effects to become evident should be considered in choosing the dependent variable. Sales may be measured several months after the experiment to determine if there were any carryover effects. Changes that are relatively permanent or longer lasting than changes generated only during the period of the experiment should be considered; repeat purchase behavior may be important.

Consumers may try a "loser" once, but they may not rebuy. The introduction of the original Crystal Pepsi illustrates the need to think beyond consumers' initial reactions. When Crystal Pepsi was introduced, it received high initial trial, but experienced difficulty in repeat purchases. The brand never achieved high repeat sales within a sufficiently large market segment. Brand awareness, trial purchase, and repeat purchase are all possible dependent variables in an experiment. The dependent variable therefore should be considered carefully. Thorough problem definition will help the researcher select the most important dependent variable(s).

Selection and Assignment of Test Units

test units

Subjects (or entities) whose responses to experimental treatments are being observed or measured.

Test units are the subjects or entities whose responses to the experimental treatment are measured or observed. Individuals, organizational units, sales territories, or other entities may be the test units. People are the most common test units in most marketing and consumer behavior experiments. In our unit pricing example, supermarkets were the test units.

Sample Selection and Random Sampling Errors.

As in other forms of marketing research, random sampling errors and sample selection errors may occur in experimentation. For example, experiments sometimes go awry even when a geographic area is specially chosen for a particular investigation. A case in point was the experimental testing of a new lubricant for outboard motors by Dow Chemical Company. The lubricant was tested in Florida and Michigan. Florida was chosen because researchers thought that a warm-weather state, in which the product would have to stand up under continuous use, would prove the most demanding test. In Florida the lubricant was a success. However, the story was quite different in Michigan. Although the lubricant sold well and worked well during the summer, the following spring Dow discovered that in the colder northern climate it had congealed, allowing the outboard motors, idle all winter, to rust. The rusting problem never came to light in Florida where the motors were in year-round use. Thus, some *sample selection error* may occur because of the procedure used to assign subjects or test units to either the experimental or the control group.

random sampling error

An error that occurs because of chance; statistical fluctuations in which repetitions of the basic experiment sometimes favor one experimental condition and sometimes the other.

Random sampling error may occur if repetitions of the basic experiment sometimes favor one experimental condition and sometimes the other on a chance basis. An experiment dealing with charcoal briquets may require that the people in both the experimental and control groups be identical with regard to incidence of product usage and barbecuing habits. However, if subjects are randomly assigned to conditions without knowledge of their product usage, errors resulting from differences in that usage will be random sampling errors. Suppose a potato chip manufacturer who wishes to experiment with new advertising appeals wants to have the groups identical with respect to advertising awareness, media exposure, and so on. The experimenter must decide how to place subjects in each treatment group and which group should receive treatment. Researchers generally agree that the random assignment of participants to groups and experimental treatments to groups is the best procedure.

Randomization. Randomization—the random assignment of subject and treatments to groups—is one device for equally distributing or scattering the effects of extraneous variables to all conditions. Thus, the chance of unknown nuisance effects piling up in particular experimental groups can be identified. The effects of the nuisance variables will not be eliminated, but they will be controlled. Randomization assures the researcher that overall repetitions of the experiment under the same conditions will show the true effects, if those effects exist. Random assignment of conditions provides "control by chance."[5] Random assignment of subjects allows the researcher to assume that the groups are identical with respect to all variables except the experimental treatment.

randomization
A procedure in which the assignment of subjects and treatments to groups is based on chance.

Matching. Random assignment of subjects to the various experimental groups is the most common technique used to prevent test units from differing from one another on key variables; it assumes that all characteristics of the subjects have been likewise randomized. If the experimenter believes that certain extraneous variables may affect the dependent variable, he or she can make sure that the subjects in each group are matched on these characteristics. **Matching** the respondents on the basis of pertinent background information is another technique for controlling assignment errors. For example, in a taste test experiment for a dog food, it might be important to match the dogs into various experimental groups on the basis of age or breed. Similarly, if age is expected to influence savings behavior, a savings and loan conducting an experiment may have greater assurance that there are no differences among subjects if subjects in all experimental conditions are matched according to age.

matching
A procedure for the assignment of subjects to groups that ensures each group of respondents is matched on the basis of pertinent characteristics.

Although matching assures the researcher that the subjects in each group are similar on the matched characteristics, the researcher cannot be certain that subjects have been matched on all characteristics that could be important to the experiment.

Repeated Measures. In some experiments the same subjects are exposed to all experimental treatments. This eliminates any problems due to subject differences, but it causes some other problems that we will discuss later. When this occurs, the experiment is said to have **repeated measures.**

repeated measures
A situation that occurs when the same subjects are exposed to all experimental treatments to eliminate any problems due to subject differences.

Control over Extraneous Variables. The fourth decision about the basic elements of an experiment concerns control over extraneous variables. To understand this issue, we will examine the various types of experimental error.

In Chapter 8 we classified total survey error into two basic categories: random sampling error and systematic error. The same dichotomy applies to all research designs, but the terms *random (sampling) error and constant (systematic) error* are more frequently used when discussing experiments.

Constant Experimental Error. We have already discussed random error in the context of experimental selection and assignment of test units. **Constant error** (bias) occurs when the extraneous variables or the conditions of administering the experiment are allowed to influence the dependent variables every time the experiment is repeated. When this occurs the results will be confounded because the extraneous variables will not have been controlled or eliminated.

constant error
An error that occurs in the same experimental condition every time the basic experiment is repeated; a systematic bias.

For example, if subjects in an experimental group are always administered treatment in the morning and subjects in the control group always receive the treatment in the afternoon, a constant, systematic error will occur. In such a situation the time of day is a cause of constant error—an uncontrolled extraneous variable. In a training experiment the sources of constant error might be the persons who do the training (line or external specialists) or whether the training is on the employees' own time or on company time. These and other characteristics of the training may have an impact on the dependent variable and will have to be taken into account:

> The effect of a constant error is to distort the results in a particular direction, so that an erroneous difference masks the true state of affairs. The effect of a random error is not to distort the results in any particular direction, but to obscure them. Constant error is like a distorting mirror in a fun house; it produces a picture that is clear but incorrect. Random error is like a mirror that has become cloudy with age; it produces a picture that is essentially correct but unclear.[6]

Extraneous Variables. Most students of marketing realize that the marketing mix variables—price, product, promotion, and distribution—interact with uncontrollable forces in the market, such as competitors' activities, to influence consumer behavior and ultimately sales. The experiments discussed so far (indeed, most experiments) concern the identification of a single independent variable and the measurement of its effects on the dependent variable, thereby distorting the experiment.

The following illustration shows how extraneous variables may have an impact on results.[7] Suppose a television commercial for brand Z gasoline shows two automobiles on a highway. The announcer states that one car has used brand Z *without* the special additive and the other has used it *with* the additive. The car without the special additive comes to a stop first, and the car with it comes to a stop 10 to 15 yards further down the road. (We will assume that both cars used the same quantity of gasoline.) The implication of this commercial is that the special additive (the independent variable) results in extra mileage (the dependent variable). As experimenters who are concerned with extraneous variables that could affect the result, we can raise the following questions:

1. Were the *engines* of the same size and type? Were the conditions of the engines the same (tuning and so on)?

2. Were the *cars* of the same condition (gear ratios, fuel injector settings, weight, wear and tear, and so on)?

3. Were the *drivers* different? Were there differences in acceleration? Were there differences in the drivers' weights?

Because an experimenter does not want extraneous variables to affect the results, he or she must control or eliminate such variables.

demand characteristics

Experimental design procedures or situational aspects of an experiment that provide unintentional hints about the experimenter's hypothesis to subjects.

Demand Characteristics. The term **demand characteristics** refers to experimental design procedures that unintentionally hint to subjects about the experimenter's hypothesis. Demand characteristics are situational aspects of the experiment that demand that the participants respond in a particular way; hence, they are a source of constant error (see Exhibit 11.4). If participants recognize the experimenter's expectation or demand, they are likely to act in a manner consistent with the experimental treatment; even slight nonverbal cues may influence their reactions.

Exhibit 11.4 By Smiling or Looking Solemn, Experimenters Can Modify Subjects' Behavior

In most experiments the most prominent demand characteristic is the person who actually administers the experimental procedures. If an experimenter's presence, actions, or comments influence the subjects' behavior or sway the subjects to slant their answers to cooperate with the experimenter, the experiment has *experimenter bias*. When subjects slant their answers to cooperate with the experimenter, they in effect are acting as guinea pigs and tend to exhibit behaviors that might not represent their behavior in the marketplace. For example, if subjects in an advertising experiment understand that the experimenter is interested in whether they changed their attitudes in accord with a given advertisement, they may answer in the desired direction to please him or her. This attitude change reflects a **guinea pig effect** rather than a true experimental treatment effect.

guinea pig effect
An effect on the results of an experiment caused by subjects changing their normal behavior or attitudes in order to cooperate with an experimenter.

TO THE POINT

We are never deceived; we deceive ourselves.

JOHANN WOLFGANG VON GOETHE

A famous management experiment illustrates a common demand characteristic. Researchers were attempting to study the effects on productivity of various working conditions, such as hours of work, rest periods, lighting, and methods of pay, at the Western Electric Hawthorne plant in Cicero, Illinois. The researchers found that workers' productivity increased whether the work hours were lengthened or shortened, whether lighting was very bright or very dim, and so on. The surprised investigators realized that the workers' morale was higher because they were aware of being part of a special experimental group. This totally unintended effect is now known as the **Hawthorne effect** because researchers realize that people will perform differently when they know they are experimental subjects.[8]

If people in a laboratory experiment interact rather than being relatively isolated, their talk about subjects (for example, an advertised product) may produce joint decisions rather than a desired individual decision. For this reason, social interaction generally is restricted in laboratory experiments.

Hawthorne effect
An unintended effect on the results of a research experiment caused by the subjects knowing that they are participants.

To reduce demand characteristics, the researcher typically takes steps to make it difficult for subjects to know what he or she is trying to find out. Experiment training and experimental situations are designed to reduce cues that might serve as demand characteristics. For example the subjects may be told that the purpose of the experiment is one thing when it is actually something else. If the purpose of the experiment is disguised, the participant does not know how to be a "good" subject to help confirm the hypothesis. Of course, the use of deception (for example, telling a lie to the subject) presents an ethical question that must be resolved by the researcher (see page 319).

Establishing Control. The major difference between experimental research and other research is an experimenter's ability to hold conditions constant and to manipulate the treatment. To conclude that A causes B, a brewery experimenting with a new clear beer's influence on beer drinkers' taste perceptions must determine the possible extraneous variables other than the treatment that may affect the results and attempt to eliminate or control them. We know that brand image and packaging are important factors in beer drinkers' reactions, so the experimenter may wish to eliminate the effects associated with them. He or she may *eliminate* these two extraneous variables by packaging the test beers in plain packages without brand identification. When extraneous variables cannot be eliminated, experimenters may strive for **constancy of conditions,** that is, expose all subjects in each experimental group to situations that are exactly alike except for the differing conditions of the independent variable. For example, experiments to measure consumers' evaluations of tissue paper softness have indicated that variation in humidity influences reactions. In this situation holding extraneous variables constant might require that all experimental sessions be conducted in the same room at the same time of day.

A supermarket experiment involving four test products shows the care that must be taken to hold all factors constant. The experiment required that all factors other than shelf space be kept constant throughout the testing period. In all stores the same shelf level that had existed before the tests began was maintained throughout the rest period; only the amount of shelf space (shelf treatments) was changed. Another problem involved store personnel accidentally changing shelf spaces when stocking the test products. This distortion was minimized by auditing each store four times a week. In this way, any change could be detected in a minimum amount of time. The experimenter personally stocked as many of the products as possible, and the cooperation of stock clerks also helped reduce treatment deviations.

Another example involves the confounding effect of television program content on advertising copy effectiveness. A commercial that on one show produces a moderate brand recall may give a higher or lower recall result on another show of the same program type. To eliminate the confounding effects of program content, copy-testing experiments should be conducted in a constant environment. Some researchers believe that the only safe course is to test a commercial on several different shows and then focus on the average across all the shows used.

If the experimental method requires that the same subjects be exposed to two or more experimental treatments, an error may occur due to the *order of presentation*. If a soft-drink company plans to test consumers' comparison of a high-caffeine, extra-sugar version of its cola versus its regular cola, one of the drinks must be tasted before the other. Consumers might tend to prefer the first drink tasted if they cannot tell any difference between the drinks. Another example is an electronic games manufacturer who has subjects perform an experimental task requiring some skill (that is, playing a game). Subjects might perform better on the second task simply because they have had some experience with the first task. *Counterbalancing* attempts to eliminate the confounding effects of

constancy of conditions
A situation in which subjects in experimental groups and control groups are exposed to situations identical except for differing conditions of the independent variable.

order of presentation by requiring that half the subjects be exposed to treatment A first and then to treatment B while the other half receive treatment B first and then treatment A.

Blinding is used to control subjects' knowledge of whether or not they have been given a particular experimental treatment. The cola taste above might have used two groups of subjects, one exposed to the new formulation and the other exposed to the regular cola. If the subjects were blinded, all may have been told they had not been given the new formulation (or all may have been told they *had* been given the new formulation). This technique frequently is used in medical research when chemically inert pills *(placebos)* rather than medication are given to subjects. It may also be used in marketing experiments, for example, if the researchers themselves do not know which toothpastes are in the tubes marked with triangles, circles, or squares, they will not unconsciously influence the subjects. In these circumstances, neither the subjects nor the experimenter know which are the experimental and which are the controlled conditions. Both parties are blinded; hence, such experiments are called **double-blind designs.**

The random assignment of subjects and experimental treatments to groups is an attempt to control extraneous variations that result from chance. If certain extraneous variations cannot be controlled, the researcher must assume that the confounding effects will be present in all experimental conditions with approximately the same influence. (This assumption may not hold true if the assignments were not made on a random basis.) In many experiments, especially laboratory experiments, interpersonal contact between members of the various experimental groups and/or the control group must be eliminated or minimized. After the subjects have been assigned to groups, the various individuals should be kept separated so that discussion about what occurs in a given treatment situation will not become an extraneous variable that contaminates the experiment.

Problems with Extraneous Variables. In marketing experiments it is not always possible to control everything that would be desirable to have in the perfect experiment. For example, competitors may bring out a product during the course of an experiment. This form of competitive interference occurred in a Boston test market for Anheuser-Busch's import beer, Wurzburger Hofbrau, when Miller Brewing Company introduced its own brand, Munich Oktoberfest, and sent eight salespeople out to blitz the Boston market. A competitor who learns of a test market experiment may knowingly change its prices or increase advertising to confound the test results. This gives the competitor more time to investigate a similar new-product possibility.

Ethical Issues in Experimentation

Experimental researchers concern themselves with problems associates with privacy, confidentiality, deception, accuracy of reporting, and other ethical issues common to other research methods. The issues related to subjects' right to be informed, however, tend to be very prominent in experimentation. Research codes of conduct often suggest the experimental subject should be fully informed and receive accurate information. Yet experimental researchers who know that demand characteristics can invalidate an experiment may not give subjects complete information about the nature and purpose of the study. Simply put, experimenters often intentionally hide the true purposes of their experiments from the experiment. **Debriefing** is the process of providing subjects with all the

blinding
A technique used to control subjects' knowledge of whether or not they have been given a particular experimental treatment.

double-blind design
A technique in which neither the subjects nor the experimenter knows which are the experimental and which the controlled conditions.

debriefing
The process of providing subjects with all pertinent facts about the nature and purpose of the experiment after its completion.

EXPLORING RESEARCH ISSUES

An Extreme Example of Lack of Debriefing

IN AN EXPERIMENT CONDUCTED IN A NATURAL SET-ting, independent food merchants in a number of Dutch towns were brought together for group meetings, in the course of which they were informed that a large organization was planning to open up a series of supermarkets in the Netherlands. In the High Threat condition subjects were told that there was a high probability that their town would be selected as a site for such markets and that the advent of these markets would cause a considerable drop in their business. On the advice of the executives of the shopkeepers' organizations, who had helped to arrange the group meetings, the investigators did not reveal the experimental manipulations to their subjects.

I have been worried about these Dutch merchants ever since I heard about this study for the first time. Did some of them go out of business in anticipation of the heavy competition? Do some of them have an anxiety reaction every time they see a bulldozer?

Chances are that they soon forgot about this threat (unless, of course, supermarkets actually did move into town) and that it became just one of the many little moments of anxiety that must occur in every shopkeeper's life.

Do we have a right, however, to add to life's little anxieties and to risk the possibility of more extensive anxiety purely for the purposes of our experiments, particularly since deception deprives the subject of the opportunity to choose whether or not he wishes to expose himself to the risks that might be entailed?

pertinent facts about the nature and purpose of the experiment after the experiment has been completed.

Debriefing experimental subjects may relieve stress that results from deception or other questionable procedures. Communicating the purpose of the experiment and the researcher's hypotheses about the nature of consumer behavior is expected to counteract negative effects of deception and/or stress and to provide the educational experience for the subject.

> Proper debriefing allows the subject to save face by uncovering the truth for himself. The experimenter should begin by asking the subject if he has any questions or if he found any part of the experiment odd, confusing, or disturbing. This question provides a check on the subject's suspiciousness and effectiveness of manipulations. The experimenter continues to provide the subject cues to the deception until the subject states that he believes there was more to the experiment than met the eye. At this time the purpose and procedure of the experiment [are] revealed.[11]

When there is clear-cut deception or when the researcher perceives that there may be psychological harm in participating in an experiment (a rarity in marketing research), debriefing is often performed. However, if the researcher does not foresee potentially harmful consequences in participation, he or she may omit debriefing due to time and cost considerations.

Another issue that may—but typically does not—arise in marketing experiments is the subject's right to safety from physical and mental harm. Most researchers believe that if the subject's experience may be stressful or cause physical harm, the subject should receive adequate information about this aspect of the experiment before agreeing to participate.

Fundamental Questions in Experimentation

Basic versus Factorial Experimental Designs

In *basic experimental designs* a single independent variable is manipulated to observe its effect on another single dependent variable. However, we know that complex marketing-dependent variables such as sales, product usage, and preference are influenced by several factors. The simultaneous change in independent variables such as price and advertising may have a greater influence on sales than either variable changed alone. *Factorial experimental designs* are more sophisticated than basic experimental designs; they allow for an investigation of the interaction of two or more independent variables. Factorial experiments are discussed in the section on complex experimental designs in Chapter 12.

Field and Laboratory Experiments

A marketing experiment can be conducted in a natural setting (a field experiment) or in an artificial setting—one contrived for a specific purpose (a laboratory experiment). In a **laboratory experiment** the researcher has almost complete control over the research setting. For example, subjects are recruited and brought to an advertising agency's office, a research agency's office, or perhaps a mobil unit designed for research purposes. They are exposed to a television commercial within the context of a program that include competitors' ads, and they are not interrupted as they view the commercials. They are then allowed to make a purchase—the advertised product or one of several competing products—in a simulated store environment. Trial purchase measures are thus obtained. A few weeks later, subjects are contacted again to measure their satisfaction and determine repeat purchasing intention. This typical laboratory experiment gives the consumer an opportunity to "buy" and "invest." In a short time span, the marketer gets the chance to collect information on decision making.

Another variation of a simulated shopping experiment involves using a representative panel of homemakers who receive a weekly visit at home from a salesperson in a mobile shopping van. This allows the researcher to measure trial, repeat purchase, and buying rates. The visit is preceded by a mailed sales catalog and an order form that features the products being tested along with all the leading brands and any promotional support that is either current or being tested.

Other laboratory experiments may be more controlled or artificial. The **tachistoscope** allows the researcher to experiment with the visual impact of advertising, packaging, and so on by controlling the amount of time a visual image is exposed to a subject. Each stimulus (for example, package design) is projected from slides to the tachistoscope at varying exposure lengths (1/10 of a second, 3/10, and so). It simulates the split-second duration of a customer's attention in the same way a package might in a mass display.

Field experiments generally are used to fine-tune marketing strategies and to determine sales volume. For example, Betty Crocker's Squeezit (a 10 percent fruit juice drink in a squeeze-and-drink bottle) could not keep up with demand in test marketing. The research showed the product's national introduction needed to be postponed until production capacity could be increased.

AT&T used a field experiment to test an advertising concept considered an alternative to its Reach Out and Touch Someone theme. A cost-of-visit concept was developed because previous survey research had indicated that may light telephone users were demographically similar to heavy users with one exception:

laboratory experiment
An experiment conducted in a laboratory or other artificial setting to obtain almost complete control over the research setting.

tachistoscope
A device that controls the amount of time a visual image is exposed to a subject.

field experiment
An experiment conducted in a natural setting, where complete control of extraneous variables is not possible.

The light users had a psychological price barrier and felt that the meter kept running after the first 3 minutes of a long-distance call. In the experiment AT&T tested these cost-of-visit television commercials on a dual cable system that reached more than 14,000 households in a selected geographic area. One group of cable subscribers received the reach-out campaign, while the second group received the cost-of-visit commercials. All things were equal except for the ad copy. The results of the experiment showed that the cost-focused spots resulted in more long-distance calling during deep-discount periods than did the Reach-Out commercials.

McDonald's conducted a field experiment to test market Triple Ripple, a three-flavored ice cream product. The product was dropped because the experiment revealed distribution problems combined with limited customer acceptance. In the distribution system the product would freeze, defrost, and refreeze. Solving the problem would have required each McDonald's city to have a local ice cream plant with special equipment to roll the three flavors into one. A naturalistic setting for the experiment helped McDonald's executives realize the product was impractical.

These examples illustrated that experiments vary in their degree of artificiality. Exhibit 11.5 shows that as experiments increase in naturalism, they begin to approach the pure field experiment and as they become more artificial, they approach the laboratory type. The degree of artificiality in experiments refers to the amount of manipulation and control of the situation that the experimenter creates to ensure that the subjects will be exposed to the exact conditions desired.

In the field experiment, the researcher manipulates some variables but cannot control all the extraneous ones. An example is the National Broadcasting Company's research on new television programs. Viewers who subscribe to a cable television service are asked to view a cable preview on their home television sets at a certain time on a certain cable channel. While the program is being aired, telephone calls from the viewers' friends cannot be controlled but laboratory tests may show consumers the same program in a movie theater where the conditions are the same for all subjects, without the real-world interruptions of everyday life.

Generally subjects will be aware of their participation in laboratory experiments. Performance of certain tasks, responses to questions, or some other form of active involvement is characteristics of laboratory experiments. Subjects of laboratory experiments are commonly briefed to explain the purpose of the research. In some situations only field studies are usable because it is not feasible to simulate such things as reactions by a retailer's or a company's sales force to a new product.

controlled store test
A hybrid between a laboratory experiment and a test market; test products are sold in a small number of selected stores to actual customers.

One common hybrid between a laboratory experiment that simulates a controlled purchasing environment and a test market that provides a natural testing of consumers' reactions is the **controlled store test.** The products are put into stores in a number of small cities or into selected supermarket chains. Deliveries

---

Exhibit 11.5   The Artificiality of Laboratory versus Field Experiments

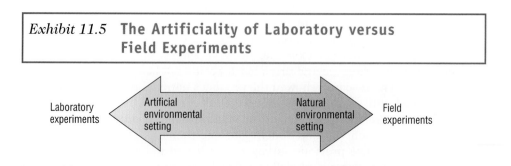

Laboratory experiments — Artificial environmental setting ⟷ Natural environmental setting — Field experiments

of the product are made not through the traditional warehouses, but by the research agency, so product information remains confidential. Swift's Soup Starter, for example, was sold in controlled store tests for six months before it was moved to a test market. The tests investigated more than one plan, including variations in price, promotion, spending levels, and advertising campaigns. Later a test market in a larger geographic area was used to confirm expectations and to fine-tune the marketing strategy. Controlled store tests offer secrecy, and sales movement and market share can be measured weekly, even daily if desired. However, national sales projections cannot be made; only benchmark sales data can be obtained because of the relatively small sample of stores and the limitations on the type of outlet where the product is tested.

Issues of Experimental Validity[9]

Internal Validity

Managers must address two fundamental problems when choosing or evaluating experimental research designs: *internal validity* and *external validity*. The first has to do with the interpretation of the cause-and-effect relationship in the experiment. **Internal validity** refers to the question of whether the experimental treatment was the sole cause of observed changes in the dependent variable. If the observed results were influenced or confounded by the extraneous factors previously discussed, the researcher will have problems making valid conclusions about the relationship between the experimental treatment and the dependent variable. If the observed results can be unhesitatingly attributed to the experimental treatment, the experiment will be internally valid.

It is helpful to classify several types of extraneous variables that may jeopardize internal validity. The six major ones are *history, maturation, testing, instrumentation, selection,* and *mortality.*

History. Suppose a before-and-after experiment is being conducted to test a new packaging strategy for an imported Chinese toy. If the Chinese engage in an anti-American political action that gets considerable media coverage, this action may jeopardize the validity of the experiment because many Americans may boycott this brand of toy. This is an example of a **history effect,** which refers to specific events in the external environment between the first and second measurements that are beyond the experimenter's control. A common history effect occurs when competitors change their marketing strategies during a test marketing experiment.

A special case of the history effect sometimes occurs. The **cohort effect** refers to a change in the dependent variable that occurs because members of one experimental group experienced different historical situations than members of other experimental groups. For example, two groups of managers used as subjects may be in different *cohorts* because one group experienced a different *history* and therefore might behave differently in a workplace experiment.

Maturation. People change over time; that is, they undergo a process of maturation. During the course of an experiment, subjects may *mature* or change in some way that will have an impact on the results. **Maturation effects** are changes within the respondents that operate as a function of time rather than of a specific event. During a daylong experiment subjects may grow hungry, tired, or bored. In

internal validity
The ability of an experiment to answer the question of whether an experimental treatment was the sole cause of changes in a dependent variable or whether the experimental manipulation did what it was supposed to do.

history effect
The loss of internal validity caused by specific events in the external environment occurring between the first and second measurements that are beyond the control of the experimenter.

cohort effect
A change in the dependent variable that occurs because members of one experimental group experienced different historical situations than members of other experimental groups.

maturation effect
An effect on the results of an experiment caused by experimental subjects maturing or changing over time.

an experiment over a longer time span, their maturation may influence internal validity because they grow older or more experienced or change in other ways that may influence the results. For example, suppose an experiment were designed to test the impact of a new compensation program on sales productivity. If this program were tested over a year's time, some of the salespeople probably would have matured due to increased selling experience or perhaps increased knowledge.

testing effect

The effect of pretesting in a before-and-after study, which may sensitize respondents or subjects when taking a test for the second time, thus affecting internal validity.

Testing. **Testing effects** are also called *pretesting effects* because the initial measurement or test alerts respondents to the nature of the experiment, and respondents may act differently than they would if no pretest measures were taken. In a before-and-after study, taking a pretest before the independent variable is manipulated may sensitize respondents when they are taking the test the second time. For example, students taking standardized achievement and intelligence tests for the second time usually do better than those taking the tests for the first time.[10] The effect of testing may increase awareness of socially approved answers, increase attention to experimental conditions (that is, the subject may watch closely), or make the subject more conscious than usual of the dimensions a problem.

Instrumentation. Measuring the dependent variable in an experiment requires the use of a questionnaire or other form of measuring instrument. If the identical instrument is used more than once, a testing effect may occur. To avoid the effects of testing, an alternate form of the measuring instrument (for example, a questionnaire or test) may be given during the postmeasurement. Although this may reduce the effect of testing because of a change in the measuring instrument, it may also result in an instrumentation effect.

instrumentation effect

An effect on the results of an experiment caused by a change in the wording of questions, interviewers, or other procedures used to measure the dependent variable.

A change in the wording of the questions, a change in the interviewers, or a change in other procedures used to measure the dependent variable causes an **instrumentation effect**, which may jeopardize internal validity. For example, if the same interviewers are used to ask questions for both before and after measurement, some problems may arise. With practice, interviewers may acquire increased skill in interviewing, or interviewer boredom may cause the instrument to be reworded in the interviewer's own terms. To avoid this problem, new interviewers are hired, but different individuals are a source of extraneous variation due to instrumentation variation. There are numerous sources of instrument decay or variation.

selection effect

A sampling bias that results from differential selection of respondents for the comparison groups.

Selection. The **selection effect** is a sample bias that results from differential selection of respondents for the comparison groups. This topic has already been addressed.

mortality (sample attrition) effect

A sample bias that results from the withdrawal of some subjects from the experiment before it is completed.

Mortality. If the experiment is conducted over a period of a few weeks or more, some sample bias may occur due to **mortality** or **sample attrition.** Sample attrition occurs when some subjects withdraw from the experiment before it is completed. Mortality effects may occur if many subjects drop from one experimental treatment group and not from other treatment or control groups. Consider a sales training experiment investigating the effects of close supervision (high pressure) versus low supervision (low pressure). The high-pressure condition may misleadingly appear superior if those subjects who completed the experiment did very well, but the high-pressure condition caused more subjects to drop out than other conditions. This apparent superiority may be due to a self-selection bias if only very determined and/or talented salespeople remain throughout the training period.

External Validity

The second validity problem concerns the researcher's ability to *generalize* the results from the experiment to the marketplace or the external environment. **External validity** is the ability of an experiment to generalize beyond the data of the experiment to other subjects or groups in the population under study. In essence it is a sampling question: To what extent can the results of a simulate shopping experiment be transferred to real-world supermarket shopping? Will a test market in Fort Wayne, Indiana, be representative of a nationwide introduction of the product under study? Can one extrapolate the results of a tachistoscope to an in-store shopping situation? Problems of external validity generally are related to the threat that a specific but limited set of experimental conditions will not deal with the interactions of untested variables in the real world. In other words the experimental situation may be artificial and may not represent the true setting and conditions in which the investigated behavior took place. If the study lacks external validity, the researcher will have difficulty repeating the experiment with different subjects, settings, or time intervals.

If subjects in a shopping mall view a videotape that simulates an actual television program with a test commercial inserted along with other commercials, will the subjects view the commercial just as they would if it were being shown on a regular program? There probably will be some contamination, but the experiment may still be externally valid if the researcher knows how to adjust results from an artificial setting to the marketplace. Comparative norms may be established based on similar, previous studies so that the results can be projected beyond the experiment. If an experiment lacks internal validity, projecting its result is not possible. Thus, the same threats to internal validity may jeopardize external validity.

external validity
The ability of an experiment to generalize beyond the experiment data to other subjects or groups in the population under study.

Student Surrogates.

One issue relating to external validity concerns the use of college students as experimental subjects. Time, money, and a host of other practical considerations often necessitate the use of student surrogates as research subjects. This practice is rather widespread in academic studies. Some evidence shows that students demonstrate considerable similarity to other household consumers, but other evidence indicates that they do not provide accurate predictions of other populations. This is particularly true when students are used as substitutes or surrogates for businesspeople. Any researcher who uses student surrogates should take care to ensure that the student subjects resemble the populations they are to portray. This may not be easy, unless the literacy, alertness, and rationality of the population under study parallel those of the student surrogates.

The issue of external validity should be seriously considered because the student population is likely to be atypical. Students are easily accessible, but they often are not representative of the total population.

Trade-Offs Between Internal and External Validity

Naturalistic field experiments tend to have greater external validity than artificial laboratory experiments. One of the problems that faces the marketing researcher is that internal validity generally is traded off for external validity because a laboratory experiment provides more control. A researcher who wishes to test advertising effectiveness via a split cable experiment has the assurance that the advertisement will be viewed in an externally valid situation, that is, in the respondent's home. However, the researcher has no assurance that some interruption (for example, a telephone call) will not have some influence that will reduce the internal validity of the experiment. Laboratory experiments with many controlled factors usually are high in internal validity, while field experiments generally have less internal validity, but greater external validity.

Classification of Experimental Designs

The design of an experiment may be compared to an architect's plans for a structure, whether a giant skyscraper or a modest home. The basic requirements for the structure are given to the architect by the prospective owner. It is the architect's task to fill these basic requirements; yet the architect has ample room for exercising his or her ingenuity. Several different plans may be drawn up to meet all the basic requirements. Some may be more costly than others; given two plans having the same cost, one may offer potential advantages that the second does not.

basic experimental design
An experimental design in which a single independent variable is manipulated to measure its effect on another single dependent variable.

There are various types of experimental designs. If only one variable is manipulated, the experiment is a **basic experimental design.** If the experimenter wishes to investigate several levels of the independent variables (for example, four price levels) or to investigate the interaction effects of two or more independent variables, the experiment requires a *complex,* or *statistical,* experimental design.

Symbolism for Diagramming Experimental Designs

The work of Campbell and Stanley has helped many students master the subject of basic experimental designs.[11] The following symbolism facilitates the description of the various experimental designs:

X = exposure of a group to an experimental treatment

O = observation or measurement of the dependent variable; if more than one observation or measurement is taken, subscripts (that is, O_1, O_2, etc.) indicate temporal order[12]

$\boxed{R}$ = random assignment of test units; $\boxed{R}$ symbolizes that individuals selected as subjects for the experiment will be randomly assigned to the experimental groups

As we diagram the experimental designs using these symbols, the reader should assume a time flow from left to right. Our first example will make this clearer.

Three Examples of Quasi-Experimental Designs

quasi-experimental design
A research design that cannot be classified as a true experiment because it lacks adequate control of extraneous variables.

Quasi-experimental designs do not qualify as true experimental designs because they do not adequately control for the problems associated with loss of external or internal validity.

one-shot design
An after-only design in which a single measure is recorded after the treatment is administered.

One-Shot Design. The **one-shot design,** or *after-only design,* is diagrammed as follows:

$$X \qquad O_1$$

Suppose that after a very cold winter an automobile dealer finds herself with a large inventory of cars. She decides to experiment with a promotional scheme offering a free trip to New Orleans with every car sold. She experiments with the promotion (X = experimental treatment) and measures sales (O_1 = measurement of sales after the treatment is administered). The dealer is not really conducting a formal experiment, she is just "trying something out."

This one-shot design is a case study of a research project fraught with problems. Subjects or test units participate because of voluntary self-selection of arbitrary assignment, not because of random assignment. The study lacks any kind of comparison or any means of controlling extraneous influences. We need a measure of what will happen when the test units have not been exposed to *X* to compare with the measures that result when subjects have been exposed to *X*. Nevertheless, under certain circumstances, even though this design lacks internal validity, it is the only viable choice.

The nature of taste tests or product usage tests may dictate the use of this design. In a taste test experiment consumers sampled Borden ice cream from boxes and cartons. When asked which was "creamier," they invariably chose the premium-shaped carton.

One-Group Pretest–Posttest Design. Suppose a real estate franchiser wishes to provide a training program for its franchisees. If it measures subjects' knowledge of real estate selling before (O_1) being exposed to the experimental treatment (*X*) and then measures real estate selling knowledge after (O_2) being exposed to the treatment, the design will be as follows:

$$O_1 \quad X \quad O_2$$

In this example the trainer is likely to conclude that the difference between O_2 and O_1 ($O_2 - O_1$) is the measure of the influence of the experimental treatment. This **one-group pretest-posttest design** offers a comparison of the same individuals before and after training. Although this is an improvement over the one-shot design, this research still has several weaknesses that may jeopardize internal validity. For example, if the time lapse between O_1 and O_2 was a period of several months, the trainees may have matured due to experience on the job (maturation effect). History effects may also influence this design. Perhaps some subjects dropped out of the training program (mortality effect). The effect of testing may also have confounded the experiment. For example, taking a test on real estate selling may have made subjects more aware of their lack of specific knowledge; either during the training sessions or on their own, they may have sought to learn subject material on which they realize they were ignorant.

If the second observation or measure (O_2) of salespersons' knowledge was not an identical test, the research may have the influence of instrument variation. If it gave an identical test but had different graders for the before and after measurements, the data may not be directly comparable.

Although this design has a number of weaknesses, it is used frequently in marketing research. Remember, the cost of the research is a consideration in most business situations. While there will be some problems of internal validity, the researcher must always take into account questions of time and cost.

one-group pretest–posttest design
A quasi-experimental design in which the subjects in the experimental group are measured before and after the treatment is administered, but there is no control group.

Static Group Design. In the **static group design** each subject is identified as a member of either an experimental group or a control group (for example, exposed or not exposed to a commercial). The experimental group is measured after being exposed to the experimental treatment, and the control group is measured without having been exposed to the experimental treatment

Experimental group: $X \quad O_1$
Control group: $\qquad O_2$

The results of the static group design are computed by subtracting the observed results in the control group from those in the experimental group ($O_1 - O_2$).

A major weakness of this design is its lack of assurance that the groups were equal on variables of interest before the experimental group received the treatment. If the groups were selected arbitrarily by the investigator, or if entry into either group was voluntary, systematic differences between the groups could invalidate the conclusions about the effect of the treatment. For example, suppose a company that manufactures trash compactors wishes to compare the attitudes

static group design
An after-only design in which subjects in the experimental group are measured after being exposed to the experimental treatment and the control group is measured without having been exposed to the experimental treatment; no premeasure is taken.

of subjects who have used a trash compactor for the first time with those who have not. If selection into the groups is voluntary, we might find that the group that receives the use of a trash compactor might have had some reason for choosing that option (for example, atypical amounts of garbage or poor garbage collectors). Sample attrition of experimental group members who do not like trash compactors might also be a source of error.

Random assignment of subjects may minimize problems with group differences. If groups can be determined by the experimenter rather than existing as a function of some other causation, the static group design is referred to as an *after-only design with control group.*

On many occasions, after-only designs are the only possible options. This is particularly true when conducting use tests for new products or brands. Cautious interpretation and recognition of the design's shortcomings may make this necessary evil quite valuable. For example, Airwick Industries conducted in-use tests with Carpet Fresh, a rug cleaner and room deodorizer. Experiments with Carpet Fresh, which originally was conceived as a granular product to be sprinkled on the floor before vacuuming, indicated that people were afraid the granules would lodge under furniture. This research led to changing the produce to have a powdery texture.

Three Better Experimental Designs

In a formal, scientific sense the three designs just discussed are not true experimental designs. Subjects for the experiments were not selected from a common pool of subjects and randomly assigned to one group or another. The three basic experimental designs discussed next will have the symbol $\boxed{R}$ to the left of the diagram to indicate that the first step in a true experimental design is the randomization of subject assignment.

Pretest–Posttest Control Group Design (Before–After with Control).

pretest–posttest control group design
A true experimental design in which the experimental group is tested before and after exposure to the treatment and the control group is tested at the same two times without being exposed to the experimental treatment.

The **pretest–posttest control group design,** or *before–after with control group design,* is the classic experimental design:

Experimental group: $\boxed{R}\ O_1 \quad X \quad O_2$

Control group: $\qquad \boxed{R}\ O_3 \qquad\quad O_4$

As the diagram indicates, the experimental group is tested before and after exposing these subjects to the treatment. The control group is tested at the same two times as the experimental group, but subjects are not exposed to the experimental treatment. This design has the advantages of the before–after design with the additional advantages gained by its having a control group. The effect of the experimental treatment equals:

$$(O_2 - O_1) - (O_4 - O_3)$$

If there is brand awareness among 20 percent of the subjects ($O_1 = 20$ percent, $O_3 = 20$ percent) before an advertising treatment, 35 percent awareness after in the experimental group ($O_2 = 35$ percent), and 22 percent awareness in the control group ($O_4 = 22$ percent), the treatment effect equals 13 percent:

$$(0.35 - 0.20) - (0.22 - 0.20)$$
$$(0.15) - (0.02) = 0.13 \text{ or } 13\%$$

The effect of all extraneous variables is assumed to be the same on both the experimental and the control groups. For instance, since both groups receive the pretest, no difference between them is expected for the pretest effect. This assumption is also made for effects of other events between the before-and-after measurement (history), changes within the subjects that occur with the passage of time (maturation), testing effects, instrument decay, and regression effects. In reality there will be some differences in the sources of extraneous variation. Nevertheless, in most cases assuming that the effect is approximately equal for both groups is a sound premise.

However, a *testing effect* is possible when subjects are sensitized to the subject of the research. This is analogous to what occurs when people learn a new vocabulary word. Soon they discover that they notice it much more frequently in their reading. In an experiment the combination of being interviewed on a subject and receiving the experimental treatment might be a potential source of error. For example, a subject exposed to a certain advertising message in a split cable experiment might say, "Ah, there is an ad about the product I was interviewed about yesterday!" The respondent may pay more attention than normal to the advertisement and be more prone to change his or her attitude than in a situation with no interactive testing effects. This weakness in the before–after with control group design can be corrected (see the next two designs).

Testing the effectiveness of television commercials in movie theaters provides an example of the before–after with control group design. Subjects are selected for the experiments by being told that they are going to preview several new television show pilots. When they enter the theater, they learn that a drawing for several types of products will be held, and they are asked to complete a product preference questionnaire (see Exhibit 11.6), then a first drawing is held. Next, the television commercials are shown. Finally, the emcee might indicate that there are some additional prizes and that a second drawing will be held, then the same questionnaire about prizes is filled out. The information from the first questionnaire is the before measurement, and that from the second questionnaire is the after measurement. The control group will receive similar treatment except that on the day they view the pilot television films, different (or no) television commercials will be substituted for the experimental commercials.

Posttest-Only Control Group Design (After-Only with Control).
In some situations pretest measurements are impossible. In others selection error is not anticipated to be a problem because the groups are known to be

---

Exhibit 11.6 Product Preference Measure in an Experiment

We are going to give away a series of prizes. If you are selected as one of the winners, which brand from each of the groups listed below would you truly want to win?

Special arrangements will be made for any product for which bulk, or one-time, delivery is not appropriate.

Indicate your answers by *filling* in the box like this: ■
Do not "X," check, or circle the boxes please.

COOKIES			ALLERGY RELIEF PRODUCTS		
(A three-months' supply, pick *ONE*.)			(A year's supply, pick *ONE*.)		
NABISCO OREO	☐	(1)	ALLEREST	☐	(1)
NABISCO OREO DOUBLE STUFF	☐	(2)	BENADRYL	☐	(2)
NABISCO NUTTER BUTTER	☐	(3)	CONTAC	☐	(3)
NABISCO VANILLA CREMES	☐	(4)	TAVIST–D	☐	(4)
HYDROX CHOCOLATE	☐	(5)	DRISTAN	☐	(5)
HYDROX DOUBLES	☐	(6)	SUDAFED	☐	(6)
NABISCO COOKIE BREAK	☐	(7)	CHLOR–TRIMETON	☐	(7)
NABISCO CHIPS AHOY	☐	(8)	OTHER (Please specify)	☐	(8)
KEEBLER E.L. FUDGE	☐	(9)			
KEEBLER FUDGE CREMES	☐	(10)			
KEEBLER FRENCH VANILLA CREMES	☐	(11)			

posttest-only control group design
An after-only design in which the experimental group is tested after exposure to the treatment and the control group is tested at the same time without having been exposed to the treatment; no premeasure is taken. Random assignment of subjects and treatment occurs.

equal. The **posttest-only control group design,** or *after-only with control group design,* is diagrammed as follows:

Experimental group: $\boxed{R}$ $\quad X \quad O_1$

Control group: $\boxed{R}$ $\qquad O_2$

The effect of the experimental treatment is equal to $O_1 - O_2$.

Suppose the manufacture of an athlete's-foot remedy wishes to demonstrate by experimentation that its product is better than the leading brand. No pretest measure about the effectiveness of the remedy is possible. The design is to randomly select subjects, perhaps students, who have contracted athlete's foot and randomly assign them to the experimental or control group. With only the posttest measurement, the effects of testing and instrument variation are eliminated. Furthermore, all of the same assumptions about extraneous variables are made; that is, they operate equally on both groups, as in the before–after with control group design.

Solomon Four-Group Design. By combining the pretest–posttest (before–after) with control group and the posttest-only) with control group designs, the **Solomon four-group design** provides a means for controlling the interactive testing effect as well as other sources of extraneous variation. In the following diagram the two *X*s symbolize the same experimental treatment given to each experimental group;

Solomon four-group design
A true experimental design that combines the pretest–posttest with control group and the posttest-only with control group designs, thereby providing a means for controlling the interactive testing effect and other sources of extraneous variation.

Experimental group 1 $\boxed{R}$ $\quad O_1 \quad X \quad O_2$

Control group 1 $\boxed{R}$ $\quad O_3 \qquad O_4$

Experimental group 2 $\boxed{R}$ $\qquad\quad X \quad O_5$

Control group 2 $\boxed{R}$ $\qquad\qquad O_6$

Although we will not go through the calculations, it is possible to isolate the effects of the experimental treatment and interactive testing in this design. Although this design allows for the isolation of the various effects, it is rarely used in marketing research because of the effort, time, and cost of implementing it. However, it points out that there are ways to isolate or control most sources of variation.

Compromise Designs. In many instances of marketing research, true experimentation is not possible; the best the researcher can do is *approximate* an experimental design. Such a **compromise design** may fall short of the requirements of assigning subjects or treatments randomly to groups.

Consider the situation in which the researcher wishes to implement a pretest–posttest control group design, but the subjects cannot be assigned randomly to the experimental versus the control group. Because the researcher cannot change a workplace situation, one department of an organization is used as the experimental group and another department is used as the control group. The researcher has no assurance that the groups are equivalent; he or she has compromised because of the nature of the situation.

compromise design
An approximation of an experimental design; may fall short of the requirements of random assignment of subjects or treatments to groups.

The alternative to the compromise design when random assignment of subjects is not possible is to conduct the experiment *without* a control group. Generally this is considered a greater weakness than using groups that have already been established.

When the experiment involves a longitudinal study, circumstances usually dictate a compromise with true experimentation.

Time Series Designs

Many marketing experiments may be conducted in a short period of time (a month or less than half a year). However, a marketing experiment to investigate long-term structural change may require a **time series design.** When experiments are conducted over long periods of time, they are most vulnerable to historical changes—in population, attitudes, economic patterns, and the like. Although seasonal patterns and other exogenous influences may be noted, when time is a major factor in design, the experimenter can do little to influence these factors. Hence, these designs are quasi-experimental because they generally do not allow the researcher full control over the treatment exposure or influence of extraneous variables.

Political pollsters provide an example. A pollster normally uses a series of surveys to track candidates' popularity. Consider the candidate who plans a major speech (the experimental treatment) to refocus the political campaign. The simple time series design can be diagrammed as follows:

$$O_1 \quad O_2 \quad O_3 \quad X \quad O_4 \quad O_5 \quad O_6$$

Several observations have been taken to identify trends before the treatment (X) is administered. After the treatment has been administered, several observations are made to determine if the patterns *after* the treatment are similar to those *before.* If the longitudinal pattern shifts after the political speech, the researcher may conclude that the treatment had a positive impact on the pattern. Of course, this time series design cannot give the researcher complete assurance that the treatment caused the change in the trend. Problems of internal validity are greater than in more tightly controlled before-and-after designs of shorter duration.

One unique advantage of the time series design is its ability to distinguish temporary from permanent changes. Exhibit 11.7 shows some possible outcomes in a time series experiment.

time series design

An experimental design used when experiments are conducted over long periods of time. It allows researchers to distinguish between temporary and permanent changes in dependent variables.

Exhibit 11.7 **Selected Time Series Outcomes**

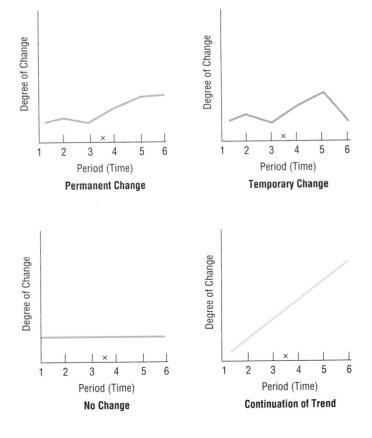

There is another problem in our political campaign example: A political conversion during August many affect the number of political conversions in September, which may influence what happens in October. In time series designs there may be carryover effects that cannot be controlled.

An improvement on the basic time series design is to use a *time series with control groups*. For example, many test markets use different geographic areas that are similar demographically as a basis for experimental control. Rarely will geographic areas be identical in any characteristic of interest; thus, control will be less than perfect.

Complex Experimental Designs

Complex experimental designs are statistical designs that isolate the effects of confounding extraneous variables or allow for manipulation of more than one independent variable in the experiment. *Factorial designs and Latin square designs, completely randomized designs,* and *randomized block designs,* as well as statistical discussions of these techniques, will be covered in Chapter 12, on complex experimental designs, and Chapter 22, on tests of differences.

Summary

Experimental research allows the investigator to control the research situation to evaluate causal relationships among variables. In an experiment, one variable (the independent variable) is manipulated to determine its effect on another (the dependent variable). The alternative manipulations of the independent variable are referred to as *experimental treatments.*

The choice of dependent variable is crucial because this determines the kind of answer given to the research problem. In some situations deciding on an appropriate operational measure of the dependent variable is difficult.

For experiments, random sampling error is especially associated with selection of subjects and their assignment to the treatments. The best way to overcome this problem is by random assignment of subjects to groups and of groups to treatments.

Other errors may arise from using nonrepresentative populations (for example, college students) as sources of samples or from sample mortality or attrition, in which subjects withdraw from the experiment before it is completed. In addition marketing experiments often involve extraneous variables that may affect dependent variables and obscure the effects of independent variables. Experiments may also be affected by demand characteristics when experimenters inadvertently give cues to the desired responses. Also, the guinea pig effect occurs when subjects modify their behavior because they wish to cooperate with an experiment.

Extraneous errors can be controlled by eliminating them or by holding them constant for all treatments. Some extraneous error may arise from the order of presentation. This can be controlled by counterbalancing the order. Blinding can be used, with subjects being kept ignorant of the treatment they are receiving. Sometimes the blinding is extended to the person who administers the test. Finally, random assignment is an attempt to control extraneous variables by chance.

Two main types of marketing experiments are filed experiments (such as test markets) conducted in natural environments and laboratory experiments conducted in artificial settings contrived for specific purposes.

Experiments are judged by two measures of validity. One is internal validity, the question of whether the independent variables was the sole cause of the change in the dependent variable. Six types of extraneous variables may jeopardize internal validity: history, maturation, testing, instrumentation, selection, and mortality. The second measure of validity is external validity, the extent to which the results are applicable to the real world. Field experiments are lower than laboratory experiments in internal validity, but higher on external validity.

Experimental designs fall into two groups. A basic design manipulates only one variable. A complex design isolates the effects of extraneous variables or uses more than one treatment or independent variable. Poor basic designs include the one-shot design, the one-group pretest–posttest design, and the static group design. Better basic designs include the pretest–posttest control group design, and the Solomon four-group design. Time series designs are used when experiments are conducted over long periods. They allow researchers to distinguish between temporary and permanent changes in dependent variables.

Key Terms and Concepts

Experiment	Hawthorne effect	Instrumentation effect
Independent variable	Constancy of conditions	Selection effect
Experimental treatments	Blinding	Mortality (sample attrition) effect
Experimental group	Double-blind design	External validity
Control group	Debriefing	Basic experimental design
Dependent variable	Laboratory experiment	Quasi-experimental design
Test units	Tachistoscope	One-shot design
Random sampling error	Field experiment	One-group pretest–posttest design
Randomization	Controlled store test	Static group design
Matching	Internal validity	Pretest–posttest control group design
Repeated measures	History effect	Posttest-only control group design
Constant error	Cohort effect	Solomon four-group design
Demand characteristics	Maturation effect	Compromise design
Guinea pig effect	Testing effect	Time series design

Questions for Review and Critical Thinking

1. Name some independent and dependent variables frequently studied in marketing.
2. A tissue manufacturer that has the fourth-largest share plans to experiment with a 50-cents-off coupon during November. It plans to measure sales volume by store scanners for November to determine effectiveness. What is the independent variable? The dependent variable? Do you see any problems with the dependent variable?
3. What purpose does the random assignment of subjects serve?
4. In a test of a new coffee, three styrofoam cups labeled A, B, and C are placed before subjects. The subjects are instructed to taste the coffee from each cup. What problems might arise in this situation?
5. What are demand characteristics? Give some examples.
6. Do you think the guinea pig effect is a common occurrence in experiments? Why or why not?
7. How may experimenters control for extraneous variation?
8. In the following situations name the type of experiment described. Evaluate the strengths and weaknesses of each design.
   a. A major petroleum corporation is considering phasing out its premium unleaded gasoline. It selects Nashville, Tennessee, as an experimental market in which the product might be eliminated and decides to watch product line sales results.
   b. A soft-drink manufacturer puts the same brand of orange drink into two different containers with different designs. Two groups are given a package and asked about the drink's taste. A third group is given the orange drink in an unlabeled package and asked the same question.
   c. An advertising agency pretested a television commercial with a portable television set, simulating an actual television program with the

test commercial inserted along with other commercials. This program was shown to a focus group and group discussion followed.

d. A manufacturer of a new brand of cat food tested product sampling with a trial-size package versus no sampling three price levels simultaneously to determine the best market penetration strategy.

9. Provide an example for each of the six major factors that influence internal validity.

10. Consider the following research project conducted by a company to investigate a self-contained heating and lighting source designed for use during power failures. The product was given to the experimental subjects and they were asked to wait until dark, then turn off their heat and lights and test the product. A few days later, they were telephoned and interviewed about their opinions of the product. Discuss the external and internal validity of this experiment.

11. In the following situations name the type of experiment described. Evaluate the strengths and weaknesses of each design.

a. A major fast-food corporation is considering a drug-testing program for its counter workers. It selects its largest outlet in Los Angeles, implements the program, and measures the impact on productivity.

b. A mass merchandiser conducts an experiment to determine whether a flexible work time program (allowing employees to choose their own work hours between 6 A.M. and 7 P.M.) is better than the traditional working hours (9 A.M. to 5 P.M.) for sales personnel. Each employee in the San José office is asked if employees in the La Jolla office remained on the traditional schedule.

12. Evaluate the ethical and research design implications of the following study.

Sixty-six willing Australian drinkers helped a Federal Court judge decide that Tooheys didn't engage in misleading or deceptive advertising for its 2.2 beer.

The volunteers were invited to a marathon drinking session after the Aboriginal Legal Service claimed Tooheys advertising implied beer drinkers could imbibe as much 2.2 as desired without becoming legally intoxicated. Drunken driving laws prohibit anyone with a blood-alcohol level above 0.05 from getting behind the wheel. The beer contains 2.2 percent alcohol, compared with 6 percent for other beers.

But the task wasn't easy; nor was it all fun. Some couldn't manage to drink in 1 hour the required 10 "middies," an Aussie term for a beer glass of 10 fluid ounces.

Thirty-six participants could manage only nine glasses. Four threw up and were excluded; another two couldn't manage the "minimum" nine glasses and had to be replaced.

Justice J. Beaumont observed that consuming enough 2.2 in an hour to reach the 0.05 level was "uncomfortable and therefore an unlikely process." Because none of the ads mentioned such extreme quantities, he ruled they couldn't be found misleading or deceptive.[13]

13. A nighttime cough relief formula contains alcohol. An alternative formulation contains no alcohol. During the experiment the subjects are asked to try the product in their homes. Alternative formulations are randomly assigned to subjects. No mention of alcohol is given in the instructions to subjects.

14. A consumer goods marketer conducts an experiment to determine if a new, more ecological package will sell more of its brand than the existing package, which has several layers of packaging. The old package does slightly better than the ecological package. Is it socially responsible to stay with the old package?

Exploring the Internet

1. Using the Yahoo search engine click on the Business and Economy option and continue clicking so that you follow this string: /Marketing/Marketing Research Companies. Find a company that conducts experimental research. Discuss the nature of its service.

2. Learn more about quasi-experimental designs at http://trochim.human.cornell.edu/kb/QUASIEXP.HTM.

Case 11.1 The I.G.A. Grocery Store

DAN KESSLER, THE MANAGER OF AN I.G.A. GROCERY store, had a brother-in-law who supervised a large number of keyboard operators at a public utility company. At a family gathering Kessler's brother-in-law mentioned that his company recently had begun programming background music into the keyboard operators' room. As a result productivity had increased and the number of errors had decreased.

Kessler though that music within a grocery store might have an impact on customers. Specifically, he thought that customers might stay in the store longer if slow, easy-to-listen-to music were played. After some serious thought, he considered whether he should hire a marketing researcher to design an experiment to test the influence of music tempo on shopper behavior.

QUESTIONS

1. Operationalize the independent variable.

2. What dependent variables do you think might be important in this study?

3. Develop a hypothesis for each of your dependent variables.

Case 11.2 Sandra Brown, D.D.S.

DENTISTS RECOMMEND TWICE-YEARLY CHECKUPS. Although the benefits of preventive health care have been promoted for several decades, some people visit dental services only when in pain.

One dentist, Sandra Brown, had read that sending out a recall card might increase participation in the 6-month dental checkup. She thought that having patients address a standard reminder card (See Case Exhibit 11.2-1) in their own handwriting would be more effective than the standard reminder card alone. She also thought that a promotional message appealing to an individual's aesthetic concern might be more appropriate than a reminder message.

She designed the following experiment for her dental clinic, located on the fringe of the downtown area. The clinic patients were primarily black and Mexican-Americans, and most were from blue-collar households. All patients were considered subjects for the experiment.

There were four experimental groups: (1) Patients who visited the dentist in May were given the standard recall card (to return in October) and asked to fill it out in their own handwriting; (2) patients who visited the dentist in June were given a promotional recall card (to return in November) and asked to fill it out in their own handwriting; (3) patients who visited the dentist in July received the standard recall card that was typed out (to return in December); (4) patients who visited the dentist in August received the promotional recall card that was typed out (to return in January).

QUESTIONS

1. Evaluate this experimental design.

2. What type of experimental design is this?

3. What improvements would you suggest for the experiment?

Case Exhibit 11.2-1   Standard Recall Card and One Experimental Version

---

> Dear Patient,
>   This is to remind you that it is time for a preventive dental examination.
>   Please call so that we may arrange a time that is convenient for you.
>
>   Sandra Brown, D.D.S.

> Dear Patient,
>   Preventive dental examinations keep you looking your best. Your teeth are part of your good looks.
>   Please call so that we may arrange a time that is convenient for you.
>   Let's keep your smile looking its best.
>
>   Sandra Brown, D.D.S.

Case 11.3   Family Circle

FAMILY CIRCLE MAGAZINE HAS A CIRCULATION OF 5 MILLION encompassing both single-copy and subscription sales. It is representative of the women's service field, which is composed of seven magazines similar in their mass market reach, demography, and range of editorial coverage.

In 1990 executives from *Family Circle,* Citicorp POS Information Services, and Simmons Market Research Bureau met regularly to brainstorm potential publishing applications of Citicorp's scanner-generated database. Citicorp's unique database tracked purchases, by household, of a larger number of households than any of its competitors.

The objective of this study was to measure the effectiveness of magazine advertising in generating increased sales. This study was different from past studies of print effectiveness in that it:

- Focused solely on the effectiveness of magazine advertising—it did not involve intermedia comparisons
- Measured actual behavior at the household level
- Isolated volume effects among households with known exposure to advertising
- Did not measure the effects of advertising on either attitude or recall
- Did not rely on consumer perceptions of either advertising exposure or product purchase

Citicorp—Measurement System

The Citicorp system allowed for capture of data at the household level. Citicorp provided the supermarket retailer with its own customer retention program in exchange for data access. The chain then recruited its customers to enroll in the program, giving them access to the program's benefits, which could take the form of check cashing or debit card privileges and cash savings through rebates or electronic couponing. For example, the program encouraged regular patronage at a single supermarket by offering electronic coupons that were automatically recorded to the customer account. All customer purchases were then entered into the Citicorp database.

Each participating household received one or more membership cards, much like credit cards, which were magnetically encoded with household identification numbers. The benefits were only obtained when the customer presented the membership card at the checkout counter, at which point transactional data could be tied back to the purchasing household.

Methodology

The study included only households enrolled in Citicorp programs since the beginning of 1990 and for whom measured chain purchases accounted for at least 70 percent of each household's total estimated grocery expenditures, based on its demographic characteristics. The data measured differences in purchase behavior between households known to have purchased *Family Circle's* April 24, 1990 issue (called *exposed household*) versus demographically similar households not known to have purchased that issue of that magazine (called *control households*).

Scanner data were used to identify households that had purchased the issue in the store, and *Family Circle's* subscriber file for the issue was matched against the universe of participating Citicorp households. Measurement took place in three markets: Chicago, where Dominick's and Jewel were the participating chains; Richmond, where Ukrop's was the first chain to participate in the Citicorp program; and Los Angeles, where Von's Pavilion stores were the most recent additions.

Within each market a control group of households was established that demographically matched those that purchased the April 24 issue of *Family Circle,* but that were not known to have purchased the issue. Matching was based on the age of the household head, household income, and household size. Aggregate data were collected from 299 stores, and Citicorp was able to capture a substantial proportion of the all commodity volume (ACV) within each of the chains represented.

PARTICIPATING CHAINS

MARKET	CHAIN	NUMBER OF STORES	ACV
Chicago	Jewel	146	69%
Chicago	Dominick's	101	38
Richmond	Ukrop's	21	89
Los Angeles	Von's Pavilion	31	41

Sales of advertised products to exposed versus control households were measured over a 28-week period. The measurement period consisted of three discrete intervals:

- 12 weeks prior to the appearance of the ad (the *base period*)
- 4 weeks immediately following the ad's release (the *observation period*)
- 12 weeks subsequent to the observation period (the *post period*)

The purchase behavior of nearly 100,000 households was measured. Of these, approximately 8,700 had purchased the April 24 issue of the magazine and over 90,000 served as control panelists.

HOUSEHOLD COUNTS

SEGMENT	TOTAL
Single-issue purchasers	4,940
Subscribers	3,743
Totals	
Exposed	8,683
Control	90,489

Brands Measured

Sales were measured for all brands that ran one or more four-color pages in the issue for which:

- Reliable data were available (a function of incidence of purchase and distribution)
- At least 70 percent of category sales occurred through supermarkets and grocery stores

Measured brands included beverages, dog biscuits, toilet paper, a cleaner, and food products.

Exposure to Other Media

Although the study controlled for demography, it did not control directly for exposure to other media. However, inferences on probable exposure to other media can be drawn from Simmons's information on the media consumption habits of *Family Circle* readers.

TV Viewing

Like the readers of other women's service magazines, *Family Circle* readers are fairly evenly spread across TV viewing quintiles, with a slight skew toward the heavier viewing end of the quintile distribution. In view of this distribution pattern and the demographic controls in place for the study, it is safe to conclude that there were no substantial differences in broadcast exposure for the exposed versus control groups. (See Case Exhibit 11.3-1.)

Magazine Readership

The picture is entirely different when magazine readership is examined. *Family Circle's* audience indexes at 253, in the heaviest magazine reading quintile. Exposure to *Family Circle* would, therefore, be expected to correlate highly with exposure to other magazine advertising. (See Case Exhibit 11.3-2).

Case Exhibit 11.3-1 **TV Quintiles**

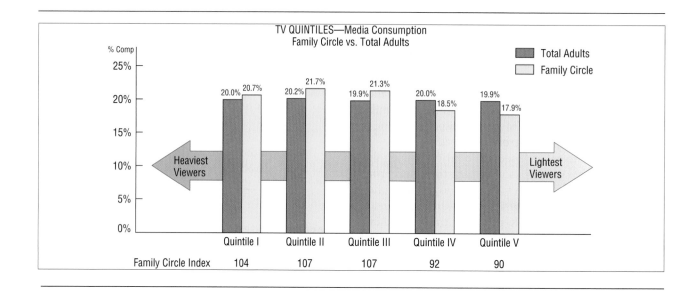

Case Exhibit 11.3-2 **Magazine Quintiles**

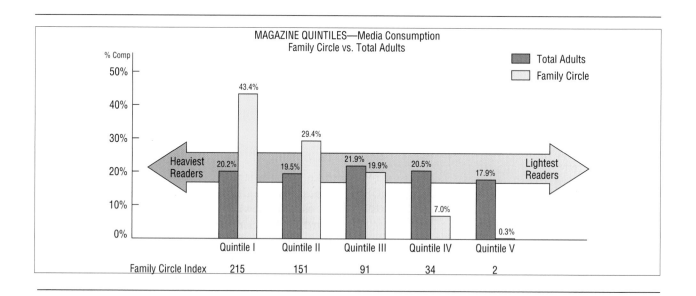

QUESTIONS

1. What type of experiment is described in the case?

2. What are the independent and dependent variables?

3. What efforts were attempted to control for extraneous variables?

4. Does the experiment have internal validity and external validity?

Case 11.4 Hamilton Power Tools (B)

HAMILTON POWER TOOLS, LIKE MANY ORGANIZATIONS, generated a large percentage of its profits from new products. In its chain saw division the company was increasingly focusing attention on the casual-user market segment's need for chain saws [see Case 6.1: Hamilton Power Tools (A)].

Bill Campagna, marketing manager, was now in a situation requiring a decision because of a competitor's actions. Recently a major competitor, Mc-Culloch, had introduced a 6-pound chain saw. Prior to this time, Hamilton's 9-pound chain saw was the world's lightest chain saw. Bill Campagna believed this competitive move took away a substantial promotional advantage because it eliminated Hamilton's ability to say that all other chain saws were heavier than its HL-9 model. Reacting to McCulloch's strategy, Hamilton's engineers produced a prototype of a 6-pound chain saw made of wood and existing chain saw parts. It looked almost exactly like a real chain saw.

A marketing research study was conducted to gain insights into whether consumers preferred the experimental 6-pound chain saw (hereafter referred as to HL-6) relative to Hamilton's existing HL-9 chain saw and relative to McCulloch's 6-pound chain saw. The basic research design was a personal interview asking consumers to compare the various models. (The McCulloch, originally painted yellow, was painted red and white to avoid any color bias. Thus, all three experimental chain saws were red and white.)

The basic assumptions underlying the research was that all these chain saws would be marketed to male homeowners and not to professional, institutional, or farm chain saw users. It was also assumed that the price of all three chain saws would be "about the same."

Hamilton's headquarters were in northern Illinois. To reduce costs, the same design used cluster sampling within Illinois and Wisconsin. Each county within these states had an equal chance of being selected as a cluster. Within each country selected as a cluster, the number of households selected was determined by investigating secondary data indicating the number of $50,000-plus households in each country, then a judgmental proportion

of all households in the county was selected. Where street maps of the counties were available, smaller areas were randomly selected and interviewing was conducted with every third house on every block within each area. In rural areas for which street maps were not available, individual towns were randomly selected and interviewing took place in every third house (outside of central city) until the quota was reached.

Personal interviews were used to collect the data at respondents' homes. As it was assumed that the researchers were concerned primarily with the opinions of men already familiar with chain saws, the first few questions of the survey asked information to qualify respondents either by ownership, previous use, or plans for future purchase. Only those men familiar with chain saws were interviewed.

In the remainder of the interview, each respondent was asked to choose between a pair of unidentified chain saws by stating his preference for one or the other. A total of three pairs of chain saws were shown to each respondent. Thus, after choosing one chain saw, indicating the respondent's preference from the first pair of chain saws, the respondent was asked to chose between the other chain saw (not previously shown) and the preferred chain saw identified in the previous comparison. Finally, the third pair of chain saws shown to the respondent was either (1) a comparison between the two "losing" chain saws if the same chain saw was preferred in both the first and second comparisons or (2) a comparison between the chain saw selected from the second comparison (if different from the first choice) and the losing chain saw of the first comparison. The chain saws shown in the first pair were randomly rotated to avoid any bias caused by the presentation of any pair of chain saws first.

QUESTIONS

1. Evaluate this research design.
2. Is this an experiment? Why or why not?

Chapter 12

Test Marketing and Complex Experiments

KATHY JO BRIHN IS LAUGHING IN THE CAR, BUT WHEN SHE walks into the supermarket in her hometown of Eau Claire, Wisconsin, her face goes blank.[1] As she strolls through the aisles to pick up a box of macaroni and cheese and a tube of toothpaste, she never drops her poker face. Kathy Jo is one of the few people in town, or in the whole country, who knows which products have been brought to Eau Claire for top-secret test marketing, but she never gives it away. She's an unassuming woman who looks more like the head of the PTA than the head of one of the country's most extensive product-testing operations, but her code of confidentiality would impress the CIA.

"It may seem like we're paranoid, but it's ingrained into us. What we see and hear at work stays at work," she said. "When I interview new employees, I always apologize that I can't tell them more about what the job really involves."

Ask to see the 30,000-square-foot warehouse and the staff breaks out in a sweat. Little wonder: It houses manufacturers' whole inventories, with as many as 100 SKUs in test at a time, all ordered, stocked, and policed by Information Resources Incorporated (IRI). Manufacturers get so skittish about keeping new products hush-hush, one even ran a test here without telling the local sales rep.

Eau Claire, a quiet town of 57,000 people about 90 miles east of Minneapolis, is where 4,000 families have been handpicked to be panel members. Those members show their "Shoppers' Hotline" card at checkout, and every purchase they make is tagged with their indi-

vidual shopper's six-digit number; every coupon is bagged for data entry back at IRI's inconspicuous office, tucked away in a residential neighborhood. IRI has retailer contracts to do about 100 tests a year in the seven groceries and five drugstores, and is negotiating with the Wal-Mart, Target, and two Shopkos in town.

Brihn and her 85-member crew have three goals as they put test products on shelves: Be normal, be normal, be normal. Anything that makes a

What you will learn in this chapter

To understand that test marketing provides an opportunity to experiment with new marketing strategies under realistic market conditions.

To define test marketing.

To discuss the useful functions that test marketing performs for marketing management.

To recognize that test marketing is a lengthy and costly procedure.

To determine how long a test market should last.

To understand what factors to consider in test market selection.

To discuss the problems associated with test marketing.

To outline the procedures for projecting test market results.

To distinguish between standard test marketing methods and control test marketing methods.

To understand the nature of electronic test markets, simulated test markets, and virtual-reality simulations.

To discuss the various complex experimental designs: completely randomized designs, randomized block designs, factorial designs, and Latin square designs.

To define the interaction effects and main effects in a factorial design.

product stand out, or changes the way consumer panelists shop, throws off the data.

Three retail test coordinators each oversee a grocery, drugstore, and mass merchandiser, acting as the retailers' main contact and maintaining each product on shelves. Each week they scan every product that's on display, using a hand-held computer to record Universal Product Codes and display location. They also collect data for customized reports, whatever variables a marketer wants to track: number of facings, size and type of display, shelf location for itself or competitors. "We don't give any more competitive data than anyone could get just walking in the store and looking at the shelf," Brihn said. But this is no casual stroll through the store.

The 50-person data-entry department keys in every packaged-good ad in newspapers for 17 markets in the Great Lakes and North Central regions, noting the ad's size, any coupon offers, and the most excruciating details on the product: flavors, sizes, type of discount. Data on product movement, displays, and ad features for every product in the market are transmitted daily to IRI's Chicago headquarters. Somewhere in that discreet little building there's 14 years' worth of data on every product that's moved through every store in town, and two years' worth of data on every ad that ever ran in the 17 markets the Eau Claire office tracks.

IRI maintains its own TV studio in each market, splicing in TV spots to target Shoppers' Hotline households. The system uses two cable TV channels to override regularly scheduled network, local, and cable TV spots with test TV spots. The system is so precise it can run a TV spot in one household and skip the next-door neighbor's.

IRI's efforts in Eau Claire illustrate the complexity and the detailed specifications in the test marketing process.

This chapter explores the nature of scientific test marketing. It also discusses more complex experimental designs that may be used in test markets or laboratory experiments.

The Nature of Test Marketing

Test marketing refers to scientific testing and controlled experimentation rather than merely "trying something out in the marketplace." Just because a businessperson introduced a product in a small marketing area before doing so on a national level does not mean a test market was conducted. Those who use this loose definition of test marketing may wonder why they succeeded in their test market, but failed in their national introduction.

test marketing
A scientific testing and controlled experimental procedure that provides an opportunity to measure sales or profit potential for a new product or to test a new marketing plan under realistic marketing conditions.

Test marketing is an experimental procedure that provides an opportunity for testing a new product or new marketing plan under realistic market conditions to measure sales or profit potential. Cities like Eau Claire or other small marketing areas where a new product is distributed and marketed usually provide a marketplace setting for field experiments.

The major advantage of test marketing is that no other form of research can beat the real world when it comes to testing actual purchasing behavior and consumer acceptance of a product. For example, Benefit, an innovative cereal that General Mills claimed would reduce cholesterol, was a health-oriented product that stirred up controversy and angered some consumer activists when it was test marketed. Although Benefit contained psyllium, a soluble fiber scientifically shown to reduce cholesterol, Procter & Gamble asked the Food and Drug

Administration to prevent General Mills from making health claims for Benefit and to rule that psyllium was a drug and not a food. In addition General Mills learned that Benefit, which didn't taste all that good, appealed to a much narrower market segment than what the marketing strategist had envisioned.

Functions of Test Marketing

Test marketing provides two useful functions for management. First, it offers the opportunity to estimate the outcomes of alternative courses of action. Estimates can be made about the optimal advertising expenditures, the need for product sampling, or how advertising and product sampling will interact. Researchers may be able to predict the sales effects of specific marketing variables, such as package design, price, or couponing and select the best alternative action. Test marketing permits evaluation of the proposed national marketing mix.

A marketing manager for Beech-Nut Life-Savers vividly portrays this function of experimentation in the marketplace:

> A market test may be likened to an orchestra rehearsal. The violinists have adjusted their strings, the trumpeters have tested their keys, the drummer has tightened his drums. Everything is ready to go. But all these instruments have not worked in unison. So a test market is like an orchestra rehearsal where you can practice with everything together before the big public performance.[2]

A researcher may not only evaluate the outcome by investigating the product's sales volume; he or she can also investigate the new product's impact on other items within the firm's product line. Test marketing allows a firm to determine whether a new product will cannibalize sales from already profitable company lines. For example, Nabisco's cracker business is mature. The company has many brands, and it may use test marketing to make sure that it is hitting the right consumer segment. A new cracker positioned at saltine users may be a tremendous sales success, but a test market may show that the people who are actually buying it are snack cracker users, and the new brand might take sales away from existing brands. In a similar situation H. J. Heinz Company was concerned that the introduction of Heinz Salsa ketchup would take sales away from Heinz regular ketchup. Test marketing provided the necessary information, and Heinz now markets both products. Test marketing is the best way to establish these market share relationships and to understand the problem of cannibalization.

The second useful function of test market experimentation is that it allows management to identify and correct any weaknesses in either the product or its marketing plan before making the commitment to a national sales launch, by which time it normally will be too late to incorporate product modifications and improvements. Thus, if test market results fall short of management's expectations, advertising weights, package sizes, and so on may be adjusted.

For example, McDonald's test marketed pizza for years. It learned competitors' reactions and the problems associated with small, individual-portion pizzas in its first test market experiment. The product strategy was repositioned, and the product testing shifted to marketing a 14-inch pizza that was not available until late afternoon. The research then focused on how consumers react to these pizzas sold in experimental restaurants remodeled to include "Pizza Shoppes" in which employees assemble ingredients on ready-made dough. Ultimately, McDonald's decided pizza should not be on its menu.

Chelsea, a soft drink, provides another illustration of this situation (see Chapter 3). In that case the barrage of criticism from some religious groups and the Virginia Nurses Association (accusing the manufacturer of encouraging children to become beer drinkers in adulthood) was a totally unanticipated problem. Information that shows marketing failures does not make the test market a failure; rather, it is a *research success*. Encountering these problems in a local testing situation enables management to make adjustments in marketing strategy before national introduction. The managerial experience gained in test marketing, therefore, can be invaluable.

TO THE POINT

You cannot create experience. You must undergo it.

ALBERT CAMUS

Test Marketing: A Lengthy and Costly Procedure

Test marketing is an expensive research procedure. Developing local distribution, arranging media coverage, and monitoring sales results take considerable effort. It should come as no surprise that this laborious process is costly. The testing of a packaged-goods product typically will cost several million dollars. As with other forms of marketing research, the value of the information must be compared with the costs of the research.

The expense of test marketing certainly is of great concern to marketing researchers. Making the decision would be easier if there were a guarantee that a product that was successful in test marketing would succeed nationally. Unfortunately, there are a great many uncertainties and risks even with test marketing.

The appropriate time period for a test market varies depending on the research objectives. Sometimes, as in Clorox's testing of its Wave detergent (renamed Clorox Super Detergent), the research takes several years. In other situations, as in Procter & Gamble's testing of Encaprin pain reliever (a product that ultimately failed in national distribution), the time period may be accelerated.

A marketing executive at Mattel says that his firm, although deeply committed to marketing research, does little test marketing for toys: "We telescope our market research and testing into a much shorter time. There's not time to put a new toy in a test market and attempt to learn about customer reaction."[3]

The marketing research manager in a firm that does no test marketing may say, "It takes too long. We have a good idea, we move fast with it." This attitude is not unique, and it illustrates another disadvantage of test marketing: It takes a long time to do it properly. The average test market requires approximately 9 to 12 months.

When a firm must commit a substantial amount of money to investments in plant and equipment, the cost of test marketing may appear minimal compared with that of a possible product failure. For example, Frito-Lay's McCracken's Apple Chips, a sliced baked apple chip, was test marketed because the manufacturing process (apples sliced like potatoes are used for chips) is both complex and expensive. However, in many cases, the decision to test market or not to test market is difficult. If the company chooses to avoid test marketing, it runs the risk of losing millions of dollars. Miller's Player's beer, a "superlight" beer, and Frito-Lay's Max Snax both failed in test markets. The mistake would have been even more costly had the brands been introduced nationally, though.

Test marketing is warranted only if it will save the company money in the long run. Because of time and money, test markets are used after other forms of research have been exhausted. Only products with a high probability of success are test marketed. Usually the go/no-go decision has already been made; the product has already gone through a screening process. Exploratory and other research suggest the product will produce an acceptable volume level. Thus, the test market will be used to refine the marketing mix or be designed to evaluate a given marketing plan relative to an existing or alternative plan.

The major advantage of test marketing is the opportunity to conduct a trial run in the marketplace. The benefits of this trial run, however, must be weighed against the probability of potential loss or failure inherent in a national introduction. Sometimes the wrong judgment is made. For instance, Unilever thought it had a winner with Persil Power, a concentrated laundry detergent, and the new product was nationally launched in the United Kingdom without a test market.[4] After the market launch, it was discovered that the powerful detergent was so strong it damaged clothes of many consumers. Competitor Proctor & Gamble discredited the product by demonstrating it caused clothes to tear and fade.

There is always some risk in decision making with or without test marketing. Risk may be minimized but never avoided.

Loss of Secrecy

If a firm delays national introduction by test marketing, a competitor may find out about the experiment and "read" the results of the test market. The firm, therefore, runs the risk of exposing a new product or its plans to competitors. If the competitor finds the product easy to imitate, it may beat the originating company to the national marketplace. While Clorox Super Detergent with Bleach remained in the test market stage, Procter & Gamble introduced Tide with Bleach nationally. Fab 1 Shot, a pouch laundry from Colgate-Palmolive, preempted Cheer Power Pouches by Procter & Gamble, but P&G wasn't sorry. Fab 1 Shot failed to be a commercial success. Although customers tried the new product, they stayed with the more traditional means of doing laundry over the long run.

When Not to Test Market

Not all product introductions are test marketed. Expensive durables, such as refrigerators, automobiles, and forklift trucks, rarely are test marketed because of the prohibitive cost of producing a test unit. Many line extensions and me-too products that do not change consumers' usage habits are considered relatively safe bets for national or regional introductions without test marketing. Many of these products, such as Swatch Olympic-themed watches, are introduced without test marketing. In other cases, test marketing is used as a last resort because a new concept might be easily imitated by competitors—secrecy is more important than research. Research studies conducted before making the decision to test market may present findings that leave no doubt in management's minds that everything is right. General Mills' Body Buddies cereal was not formally test marketed because the additional information the company could obtain from test marketing was not considered valuable enough to postpone introduction. Other considerations, such as the seasonality of the product, distribution strength, or experience with the product category, may also influence the test marketing decision.

Fit is a produce rinse from Procter & Gamble. It has been in a Denver test market for more than four years. An initial hurdle for the new product was overcoming resistance from produce marketers and grocery retailers who feared Fit's advertising would arouse fears about produce safety. Another reason for the long test market is that the research has shown that consumers require ample time to learn about the benefits of this unique product. Pringles, another P&G product, spent seven years in test market.

How Long Should a Test Market Last?

Pastry Shoppe Toast Spread, a spread that made toast taste like a sweet roll, had a high initial acceptance; after the initial trial purchase, the product was repurchased repeatedly. But then consumers abruptly lost interest. Tossables, a canned salad minus the lettuce, had a purchase interval different from those of salad dressing, canned vegetables, salad croutons, and other products that initially were thought to be similar. These examples illustrate that determining how long to test market is another decision that requires considerable deliberation.

In a discussion concerning the testing of packaged-goods products, a vice president of research for the J. Walter Thompson advertising agency made this statement:

> A new product's volume typically rises rapidly to a peak, then begins to decline. The product usually will peak out in three to four months and, about a year after introduction, volume will level out at between three-fourths and one-seventh of the peak.[5]

This suggests that a number of people try new products, but many do not repeat their purchases. Thus, test markets should be long enough for consumers to become aware of the product and to try it more than once. Test marketing for an adequate period of time minimizes potential biases due to abnormal buying patterns. For instance, a test market that is too short may overestimate sales, because typically the early triers are heavy users of the product:

> Time must be allowed for sales to settle down from their initial honeymoon level; in addition, the share and sales levels must be allowed to stabilize. After the introduction of a product, peaks and troughs will inevitably stem from initial customer interest and curiosity as well as from competitive product retaliation.[6]

The time required for test marketing also depends on the product; a package of chewing gum is consumed much sooner than a bottle of shampoo. The average time grocery and drug packaged goods are test marketed is 10 months.

After high initial penetration and when the novelty of the product has stabilized, the researcher may make an estimate of market share. When the product is to be removed from retail shelves, the marketer may inform customers that the item is no longer available.

Selecting Test Markets: A Sampling Problem

Selecting test markets is for the most part a sampling problem. The researcher wishes to choose a sample of markets that is representative of the population—of all cities and towns—throughout the United States. Thus, test market cities should represent the competitive situation, distribution channels, media usage patterns, product usage, and other relevant factors. Of course, there is no one ideal test market that is a perfect miniature of the entire United States. Nevertheless, the researcher must avoid cities that are not representative of the nation. Regional or city differences, atypical climates, unusual ethnic compositions, or different lifestyles may dramatically affect a marketing program.

Researchers who wish to select representative test markets have a more complex problem because use of three or four cities may be necessary. Cities are selected as experimental units, and one or more additional cities may be required as control markets. Thus, each of the experimental and control markets should be similar in population size, income, ethnic composition, and so on. Differences in these demographic factors and other characteristics among the experimental or control markets affect the test results. Because of the importance of having representative markets for comparisons, certain cities are used repeatedly for test market operations.

Exhibit 12.1 shows several popular test markets frequently used to test new products or elements of marketing plans.

Factors to Consider in Test Market Selection

Obtaining a representative test market requires considering many factors that may not be obvious to the inexperienced researcher. A vice president of ITT Continental Banking says:

> When I started in the business, I though people picked cities like Columbus, Ohio, because their populations were typical. But I found the main reasons were that they were isolated media markets and the distribution patterns were such that they didn't have to worry about the chain warehouse shipping outside of Columbus. It's difficult to translate information from a city which

represents 0.1 percent of the United States and multiply that to get 99.9 percent. I think it is much more important to get control of the distribution and the advertising message.[7]

As with all decisions, the objectives of the decision makers will influence the choice of alternative.

The following factors should be considered in the selection of a test market.

Population Size. The population should be large enough to provide reliable, projectable results, yet small enough to ensure that costs will not be prohibitive. New York City is not a popular test market; its size makes it unacceptable.

Demographic Composite and Lifestyle Considerations. Ethnic backgrounds, incomes, age distributions, lifestyles, and so on within the market should be representative of the nation. For example, test marketing on the West Coast may not be representative because people there tend to be quick to accept innovations that might not be adopted elsewhere.

Competitive Situation. Competitive market shares, competitive advertising, and distribution patterns should be typical so that test markets will represent other geographic regions. If they are not representative, projectability will be difficult.

Exhibit 12.1 Popular Test Markets

THE FOLLOWING IS A LIST OF AREAS IN WHICH MARKETERS FREQUENTLY TEST NEW PRODUCTS OR ELEMENTS OF their marketing plans. Standard markets are those in which the company sells the product through its regular distribution channels and monitors the results, usually by hiring an auditing service.

Albany–Schenectady–Troy	Lexington (Kentucky)
Boise	Little Rock
Buffalo	Louisville
Burlington (Vermont)	Midland (Texas)
Cedar Rapids–Waterloo	Milwaukee
Charlotte	Minneapolis–St. Paul
Chattanooga	Nashville
Cincinnati	Omaha
Colorado Springs–Pueblo	Orlando–Daytona Beach
Columbus (Ohio)	Pensacola (Florida)
Des Moines	Pittsburgh
Erie (Pennsylvania)	Portland (Oregon)
Evansville	Roanoke–Lynchburg
Fargo	Rochester (New York)
Fort Wayne	Sacramento–Stockton
Grand Rapids–Kalamazoo–Battle Creek	Salt Lake City
Green Bay	Seattle–Tacoma
Greensboro–Winston-Salem–High Point	South Bend–Elkhart
Greenville–Spartanburg–Asheville	Spokane
Indianapolis	Springfield (Illinois)
Jacksonville	St. Louis
Kansas City	Tulsa
Knoxville	Wichita–Hutchinson

Some companies test market outside the United States. Carewell Industries of Fairfield, New Jersey, tested its Dentax toothbrush in Singapore. While Singapore may not represent America's demographic profile, it offers extreme secrecy. It also offers a low-cost environment for launching a new product.

Consider the firm that test markets in one of its strongest markets. Its sales force has an easy time getting trade acceptance but might have difficulty in a market in which the firm is weak. That will influence the acceptance level, the cost of the sell-in (obtaining initial distribution), and the ultimate results of the test market. Hence, projecting the results of the test market into weaker markets becomes difficult.

Selecting an area with an unrepresentative market potential may cause innumerable problems. Firms probably should not test orange juice products in Florida, dairy products in Wisconsin, or antihistamines in Arizona.

Media Coverage and Efficiency. Local media (television spots, newspapers) will never exactly replicate national media. However, duplicating the national media plan or one similar to it is important. Newspapers' Sunday supplements used as a substitute for magazine advertising do not duplicate the national plan, but they may provide a rough estimate of the plan's impact. Ideally, a market should be represented by the three television networks, typical cable television programming, and newspaper coverage. Some magazines have regional editions or advertising inserts.

Media Isolation. Advertising from outside communities may contaminate the test market. Furthermore, advertising money is wasted when it reaches consumers who cannot buy the advertised product because they live outside the test area. Markets such as Tulsa, Oklahoma, and Green Bay, Wisconsin, are highly desirable because advertising does not spill over into other areas.

Self-Contained Trading Area. Distributors should sell primarily or exclusively in the test market area. Shipments in and out of markets from chain warehouses produce confusing shipping figures. Frito-Lay test marketed Olean-based versions of Ruffles, Lay's, Doritos, and Tostitos under the Max name in Cedar Rapids, Iowa. However, large amounts of the chips were purchased by droves of consumers in markets far from the test site.[8] Publicity about the no-fat chips had retailers fielding telephone orders from as far away as California, Texas, and New Jersey. Had the company relied solely on shipment information, it would have built plants for what became WOW! Chips and would have been much larger than needed.

Overused Test Markets. If consumers or retailers become aware of the tests, they will react in a manner different from their norm. Thus, one great test market should not be established. Tucson is one area now used less frequently than in the past because it has displayed an atypical reaction to new-product introductions. There always seemed to be a new display in the stores, and the public's reaction ceased to be average.

Availability of Scanner Data. Markets in which a high proportion of stores can supply scanner data are attractive to many test marketers. This topic is covered later in the chapter.

Estimating Sales Volume: Some Problems

The main reasons for conducting a test market are to estimate sales, attitude change, repeat-purchase behavior, and the like and to project the results on a national level. A number of methodological factors may cause problems in estimating the results on a national level. These are usually the results of mistakes in the design or execution of the test market.

Overattention

If too much attention is paid to testing a new product, the product may be more successful than it normally would be. The advertising agency may make sure that the test markets have excellent television coverage (which may or may not be representative of the national television coverage). If salespeople are aware that a test is being conducted in their territory, they may spend unusual amounts of time making the product more available or better displayed.

Unrealistic Store Conditions

Store conditions may be set at the level of the market leader rather than at the national level. For example, extra shelf facings, eye-level stocking, and other conditions resulting from artificial distribution may be obtained in the test market.

This situation may result from research design problems or overattention, as previously described. For example, if retailers are made aware that someone is paying more attention to their efforts with a given product, they may give it artificially high distribution and extra retail support.

Reading the Competitive Environment Incorrectly

Another common mistake is to assume that the competitive environment will be the same nationally as it was in the test market. If the competition is unaware of the test market, the results will not measure competitors' reactions to company strategy. Competitors' responses after a national introduction may differ substantially from what occurred in the test market. On the other side of the coin, competitors may react to a test market by attempting to undermine it. If they know that a firm is testing, they may attempt to disrupt test market results with increased promotions and lower prices for their own products. When Nestlé

WHAT WENT RIGHT?

The Monkey Attacks the Elephant

THE STRATEGY USED FOR FORMULA 409 LIQUID cleaner to interrupt Procter & Gamble's test market and subsequent national introduction of Cinch is rather unique. Although it occurred several years ago, it dramatically illustrates how a small company can influence the actions of a giant one by manipulating a test market. Formula 409 was a family effort and the company's only product. When the company's president learned that Procter & Gamble would be test marketing Cinch in Denver, he did not increase advertising or lower prices for Formula 409—indeed, he did just the opposite. The tactic was to unobtrusively withdraw distribution in the Denver area. Salespeople were discouraged from restocking

shelves. Thus, Procter & Gamble's test market success was overwhelming.

But wait—the marketers of Formula 409 had decided on a strategy that would discourage Procter & Gamble and other marketers in the long run. As Cinch was regionally rolling out, Formula 409's president decided to load up spray cleaner users with about a 6-month supply of the product; a giant-size bottle was attached to the regular-size one at a reduced price. Since most 409 users were thus stocked up when Cinch was introduced, they did not need to buy the new product. Hence, initial sales for the giant packaged-goods marketer were disastrous. Procter & Gamble pulled out of the market thinking that the volume of Formula 409 was extremely small and that Denver test market results were abnormal. The president of Formula 409 had bet that Procter & Gamble was too big to notice the subtle moves of small Formula 409—it was an elephant grown so large that the monkey (Formula 409) had heard it coming and darted out of the way.

Company introduced a line of diet products called New Cookery, most of its competitors engaged in an across-the-board price-cutting war.

Marketing researchers must also be aware that competitors will buy items to do chemical or technical analysis of the product. Researchers discovered that approximately one-fourth of Nestlé's sales volume for the New Cookery line was the result of competitors' purchasing the product in the test market.

Hartz Mountain and Sargent's pet care products became involved in legal proceedings due to disruption of the introduction of a new product.[11] Because the case concerned antitrust matters, the implications are not completely clear. However, it does suggest that abnormal advertising and price cutting may cause legal proceedings.

Incorrect Volume Forecasts

In the typical test market, unit sales volume or market share is the focus of attention. Shipments, warehouse withdrawals, or store scanner data may be the major base for projecting sales. Forecasted volume for test markets should be adjusted for test distribution levels, measurement problems with store data, and other differences between test markets and national markets.

Smooth and Easy sauce ("the gravy stick with all the gravy basics in one refrigerated bar") had a short product life. In the test markets, sales volume projections were inaccurate because the trade initially sold what turned out to be an eight-month supply. At one point in the test market, more bars were returned and discarded due to spoilage (372,000) than the total sold (207,000).

Frito-Lay test marketed several brands of WOW! Chips in Indianapolis before the product was launched nationally. These sales curves illustrate why test markets often last a year or more.[9] Initial trial purchases often do not reflect repeat-purchase rates. Marketers with many items in a line, for example, Frito-Lay's Baked Lays, must also look for possible cannibalization.

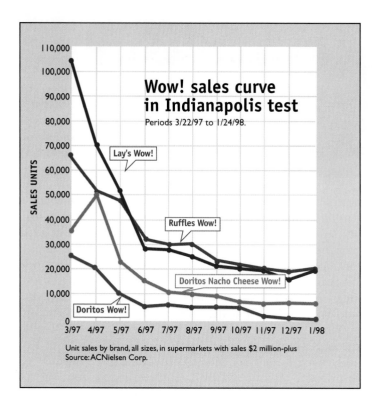

Wow! sales curve in Indianapolis test
Periods 3/22/97 to 1/24/98.

Unit sales by brand, all sizes, in supermarkets with sales $2 million-plus
Source: ACNielsen Corp.

Initial penetration, if projected directly, may overstate the situation. Many consumers who make a trial purchase may not repurchase the product. Researchers must be concerned with repurchase rates as well as with initial trial purchases. Supplementing retail store scanner data with purchase diaries and panel data will help indicate what sales volume will be over time.

Time Lapse

One relatively uncontrolled problem results from the time lapse between the test market experiment and the national introduction of the product. If the time period between the national introduction and the test market is a year or more (which is not unusual), the time difference can have an important effect on consumers' receptivity to the product.

Projecting Test Market Results

Consumer Surveys

In addition to actual sales data, most test marketers use consumer survey data. These help measure levels of change in consumer awareness of, consumer attitudes toward, and rates of purchasing and repeat purchasing of the product. Frequently this information is acquired via consumer panels. Sales-oriented measures, such as incidences of purchase and customer satisfaction ratings, are used to project sales volume nationwide.

Straight Trend Projections

Sales can be identified and the market share for the test area calculated. The simplest method of projecting test market results involves straight trend projections. Suppose the market share is 3-1/2 percent in the test market region. A straight-line projection assumes that the market share nationwide will be 3-1/2 percent. Rarely will every market be identical to the test market; yet this gross prediction may indicate whether the product has a viable marketing mix.

Ratio of Test Product Sales to Total Company Sales

A measure of the company's competitive strength in the test market region might be used as a basis for adjusting test market results. Calculating a ratio of test product sales to total company sales in the area may provide a benchmark for modifying projections into other markets.

Market Penetration x Repeat-Purchase Rate

To calculate market share for products where there will be repeat purchases, the following formula is used: Market penetration (trial buyers) × Repeat-purchase rate = Market share. For example, suppose a product is tried by 30 percent of the population and the repeat purchase rate is 25 percent. Market share will then be 7.5 percent (30 percent × 25 percent = 7.5 percent).

The **repeat-purchase rate** must be obtained from longitudinal research that establishes some form of historical record. Traditionally, the consumer panel has been necessary for recording purchases over time. Thus, panel data may indicate a cumulative product class buying rate, or **market penetration,** in the early weeks of the test market. As the test market continues, repeat purchases from these buyers can be recorded until the number of trial purchases has leveled off. Exhibit 12.2 indicates typical purchase and repurchase patterns for a new product in a test market.

repeat-purchase rate
The percentage of purchasers who make a second or repeat purchase.

market penetration
The percentage of potential customers who make at least one trial purchase.

Exhibit 12.2 **New-Product Trial Purchase Curve and Repeat-Purchase Curve**

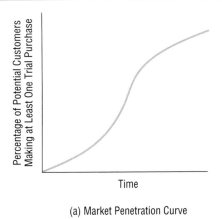

(a) Market Penetration Curve

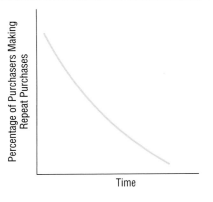

(b) Repeat Purchase Curve

Standard Method versus Control Method of Test Marketing

Our discussion so far has focused on the *standard method* to test marketing, which requires that the firm choose test markets and then obtain distribution using its own sales force. The major advantage of this method is that there is considerable external validity: Everything is just as it would be in a national introduction. However, as we already pointed out, there may be several problems (cost, lack of secrecy, and so on) with a standard test market.

In recent years, researchers have reduced test market costs and the probability of competitive interferences by using controlled store tests that simulate the retail conditions that would occur if the product were distributed nationally.

control method of test marketing

A "minimarket test" using forced distribution in a small city. Retailers are paid for shelf space so that the test marketer can be guaranteed distribution.

The **control method of test marketing** uses a "minimarket test" in a small city, using *control store distribution,* or forced distribution. A marketing research company that specializes in test marketing performs the entire test marketing task, including the initial sale to retailers (referred to as *sell-in*), warehousing, distribution, and shelving of the test product. The research company pays retailers for shelf space and therefore can guarantee distribution to stores that represent a predetermined percentage of the market's all-commodity volume (the total dollar sales for that product in a defined market). Thus, the firm is guaranteed distribution in stores that represent a predetermined percentage of the market.

The warehousing function and portions of the retailer's stocking function are performed by the research agency. Thus, the retailer is more willing to cooperate with the research because selling the product will be effortless. However, this raises the question of whether the retailer would react toward the product in the same fashion if the product were going through its normal distribution channels. With controlled store testing, out-of-stocks—a potential condition in the traditional channel of distribution—rarely occur. The research agency monitors the sales results without the use of an outside auditing firm.

For example, Market Facts, which operates controlled store testing in medium-sized metropolitan areas such as Orlando, Florida; Erie, Pennsylvania; Binghamton, New York; and Fort Wayne, Indiana, has auditors in test cities visit cooperating stores a minimum of two times each week during controlled store tests, minimizing out-of-stock conditions and ensuring maintenance of desired shelf conditions, location, facings, price, and so on. Thus, the experimental error that often interferes with sales tests is controlled.

The advantages of using the control method of test marketing are:

1. Reduced costs
2. Shorter time period needed for reading test market results
3. Increased secrecy from competitors
4. No distraction of company salespeople from regular product lines

Lower costs result from the smaller market test. Because distribution is guaranteed, no waiting period is necessary to obtain regular channels. Secrecy is increased, and monitoring the test product's movement is increasingly difficult for competitors.

One potential problem with the controlled store test is that distribution may be abnormally high. Also, retailers' complete cooperation with promotions, such as ensuring that the product is never out of stock, may result in higher-than-normal sales. This type of study becomes more like a laboratory study, in which factors are increasingly controlled. Thus, if a firm's objective is to see if it can obtain distribution for a product, a standard test market will be much more appropriate.

However, when the problem is to test a specific set of alternatives and determine which is the most appropriate marketing activity, controlled store testing may be superior to the standard test market.

High-Technology Systems Using Scanner Data

Several research suppliers offer test marketing systems that combine scanner-based consumer panels (discussed in Chapter 10) with high-technology broadcasting systems that allow experimentation with different advertising messages via split-cable broadcasts or other technology. These systems, sometimes called **electronic test markets,** enable researchers to measure the immediate impact of commercial television viewing of specific programs on unit sales volume.

A household's bar-coded identification number is entered into a store's computer when a purchase is made. The computer links the household's item-by-item purchases with television viewing data during extensive test marketing programs. For example, Information Resources Incorporated (IRI) has selected certain medium-sized cities, such as Pittsfield, Massachusetts, to serve as scanner-based test markets. The company installs an electronic device on every television in selected households that become scanner-based panel members. In these electronically wired households, the device measures television viewing habits in 5-second increments to determine whether a particular television commercial was viewed.

However, IRI's system also allows the researcher to manipulate what advertising the panel households see, a feature of greater significance to researchers interested in experimentation. The electronic device on the television set allows the researcher to cut into the regularly scheduled broadcasts and substitute a test commercial (introducing a new product, for example) for a regular commercial that is transmitted nationally over the television network. Furthermore, IRI has arranged with local newspapers and national magazines to print special editions for the test households. Thus, one household may get its morning paper with a cents-off coupon for a test product while the house next door receives a regular newspaper with no mention of the product at all. In this way experimental and control groups may be established and scanner-based sales data used as the dependent variable.

electronic test markets
A system of test marketing that measures results based on Universal Product Code data; often scanner-based consumer panels are combined with high-technology television broadcasting systems to allow experimentation with different advertising messages via split-cable broadcasts or other technology.

EXPLORING RESEARCH ISSUES

Simulated Test Markets in International Research

IN THE UNITED KINGDOM, TETLEY TEA BAGS IS THE number two brand in the tea market, but it was slowly losing market share to cheaper private-label brands. When Lyons Tetley Ltd. decided to take action to arrest this decline, it began researching potential physical product differentiation. This resulted in the identification of round bags as a concept worthy of development. In 1985 the round product was submitted to an unbranded, sequential, monadic product test among 200 frequent users of Tetley and competitors PG Tips, Quick Brew, and Typhoo. The overall preference for round bags over square bags was statistically significant at 55 percent to 34 percent.

Marketing research continued in two simulated test markets. These test markets involved housewives in England who attended a briefing session and were exposed to advertising for round bags. It was demonstrated that free sampling with significant amounts of product can enhance the quality of trial. The brand was relaunched into the southern half of Britain in July 1989 with great success.

Needless to say, the high-tech electronic test marketing systems increase the speed and accuracy of test marketing. But they also can be expensive; a full IRI test costs several million dollars per year.

Simulated Test Markets

simulated test market
A research laboratory in which the traditional shopping process is compressed into a short time span.

Marketing research program strategies often include plans for simulated test markets, because managers wish to minimize the number of products that go through the lengthy and costly process of full-scale marketing. **Simulated test markets** are research laboratories in which the traditional shopping process is compressed into a short time span. Consumers visit a research facility, where they are exposed to advertisements (usually within the context of a television program shown in a theater setting). They then shop in a room that resembles a supermarket aisle. Researchers estimate trial purchase rates and how frequently consumers will repurchase the product based on their simulated purchases in the experimental store.

Simulated test markets almost always use a computer model of sales to produce estimates of sales volume. For example, M/A/R/C Inc. offers the ASSESSOR modeling system. Simulated test markets cannot replace full-scale test marketing, but they allow researchers to make early predictions about the likelihood of success of a go/no-go decision. These results become significant information for determining which products ultimately will be introduced into real test markets.

A major problem with simulated test marketing occurs when the marketer does not execute the marketing plan the way it said it would (i.e., the one tested) during the simulated test. If the marketer changes the advertising copy, price, or another variable, the model used to measure product acceptance will no longer be accurate.

Virtual-Reality Simulations

virtual-reality simulated test market
An experiment that attempts to reproduce the atmosphere of an actual retail store with visually compelling images appearing on a computer screen.

Advances in computer graphics and three-dimensional modeling have led to the development of virtual-reality simulated test markets. A **virtual-reality simulated test market** attempts to reproduce the atmosphere of an actual retail store with visually compelling images appearing on a computer screen. The computer-simulated environment allows the research subject to "move" through a store, pause in front of a shelf or display, and inspect the various product offerings. The subject, acting as a shopper, can "pick up" a package displayed on the screen and, using mouse or trackball, turn the package to examine labels, list of ingredients, and other information printed on all sides of the package. Subjects can make a "purchase" by such methods as clicking on an icon (often a shopping cart) on the screen. During the shopping simulation, the computer can record the amount of time the subject spends shopping for each product category, the time the consumer spends inspecting information on the package, the number of items the subject purchases, and the order in which items are purchased.[10]

Virtual-reality simulated test markets have many potential uses. Of course, traditional experimental manipulations of price, package design, and advertising copy can be investigated with virtual-reality simulated test markets at a much lower cost than traditional test marketing. However, the real advantage of a virtual-reality test market is its ability to modify environments that would be extremely difficult or too expensive to modify in an actual test market. For example, a chain of fast-food restaurants notices that customers would stand at registers, staring at the menu board, and take a long time to place an order. Often this created long lines and customers waiting in these lines became frustrated and walked

Exhibit 12.3 **A Computer Screen from a Virtual-Reality Simulated Test Market**

away. Managers speculated that the menu boards were too extensive and confusing. A virtual-reality simulated test market with multiple virtual menu boards was easily designed on a computer. The research findings revealed that grouping products together into meals with a small discount increased ordering speed and total order size for a significant percentage of the research subjects. This research would have been very difficult to study with another research design.

Exhibit 12.3 shows a screen from a virtual-reality simulation that portrays a shopping center. The purpose of this virtual-reality simulation was to help design retail space that best fit with shoppers' behavior patterns.

Complex Experimental Designs

Test markets employ various complex experimental designs. Here we will discuss the structures of these designs; in Chapter 22 we will examine the statistical analysis of such experiments. These designs also have applications in areas other than test marketing.

Completely Randomized Design

The **completely randomized design** is an experimental design that uses a random process to assign experimental units to treatments. Randomization of experimental units is the researcher's attempt to control all extraneous variables while manipulating a single factor, the treatment variable. Several of the experiments discussed in previous chapters are completely randomized designs. As an example, consider a posttest-only with control group experiment to examine

completely randomized design
An experimental design that uses a random process to assign subjects (test units) and treatments to investigate the effects of only one independent variable.

Table 12.1   A Completely Randomized Design

	RESPONSE RATE EXPERIMENT		
GROUPS INCENTIVE	CONTROL: NO INCENTIVE	$1 PERSONAL INCENTIVE	$1 CHARITY
Response rate	23.3%	26.0%	41.3%
Number of observations (n)	150	150	150

Overall response rate 136/450 = 30.2%.

---

the effects of various incentives on increasing the response rate in a mail survey. Personal monetary payments versus monetary contributions to a charity selected by the respondents were the two experimental treatments (see Table 12.1). When a control group is used, there are three treatments: (1) no incentive to the control group, (2) one-dollar personal incentive, and (3) one-dollar charity incentive. Suppose the sample frame is divided into three groups of 150 each (n). Assigning treatments to groups is a simple random process. Table 12.1 shows how to compare response rates (the dependent variable) of each of the three treatment groups to determine which method of increasing response was the best. In our example the donation-to-charity incentive has the greatest influence on response rate.

A pretest–posttest design (before–after) with control group(s) that *replicates* or *repeats* the same treatment on different experimental units is another example of a completely randomized design. Analysis of variance (ANOVA) is a statistical technique that involves investigating the effects of one treatment variable on an interval-scaled dependent variable. In the completely randomized design ANOVA is the appropriate form of statistical analysis when the conditions of randomization and replication are met. This topic is discussed in Chapter 22.

Randomized Block Design

randomized block design
An extension of the completely randomized design in which a single extraneous variable that might affect test units' response to the treatment has been identified and the effects of this variable are isolated by blocking out its effects.

The **randomized block design** is an extension of the completely randomized design. A form of randomization is used to control for *most* extraneous variation; however, the researcher has identified a single extraneous variable that might affect test units' response to the treatment. The researcher will attempt to isolate the effects of this single variable by blocking out its effects.

The term *randomized block* originated in agricultural research that applied several levels of a treatment variable to each of several blocks of land. Systematic differences in agricultural yields due to the quality of the blocks of land may be controlled in the randomized block design. In marketing research the researcher may wish to isolate block effects, such as store size, territory location, market shares of the test brand or its major competition, per capita consumption levels for a product class, city size, and so on. Grouping test units into homogeneous blocks on the basis of some relevant characteristic allows researchers to separately account for one known source of extraneous variation.

Suppose that a manufacturer of Mexican food is considering two packaging alternatives. Marketers suspect that certain sections of the country might con-

Table 12.2 Randomized Block Design

		PERCENTAGE WHO PURCHASE PRODUCT		
TREATMENT	MOUNTAIN	NORTH CENTRAL WEST	NORTH CENTRAL EAST	MEAN FOR TREATMENTS
Package A	14.0% (Phoenix)	12.0% (St. Louis)	7.0% (Milwaukee)	11.0%
Package B	16.0 (Albuquerque)	15.0 (Kansas City)	10.0 (Indianapolis)	13.6
Mean for cities	15.0	13.5	8.5	

found the experiment. They have identified three regions where attitudes toward Mexican food may differ. Within each region they assume that the relevant attitudinal characteristics are relatively homogeneous. In a randomized block design each block must receive every treatment level. Assigning treatments to each block is a random process. In our example the two treatments will be randomly assigned to two cities within each region. Sales results such as those in Table 12.2 might occur. The logic behind the randomized block design is similar to that underlying the selection of a stratified sample rather than a simple random one. By isolating the block effects, one type of extraneous variation is partitioned out and a more efficient experimental design therefore results. This is because experimental error is reduced with a given sample size.

Factorial Designs

Suppose a brand manager believes that an experiment that manipulates a price factor only is too limited because price changes have to be communicated with increased promotional support. The brand manager suggests that more than one independent variable must be incorporated into the research design. Even though the single-factor experiments already considered may have one specific variable blocked and other confounding sources controlled, they are still limited. **Factorial designs** allow for the testing of the effects of two or more treatments (factors) at various levels.

factorial design
An experiment that investigates the interaction of two or more variables on a single dependent variable.

Consider the experimenter who wishes to answer the following questions:

1. What is the effect of varying the number of rows (facings) in a brand's shelf display?
2. What is the effect of varying its height from the floor?
3. Is the effect of varying the number of rows different if an item is near the floor as opposed to being near the top—is there an interaction between the effect of the rows and the level of the display?[11]

A factorial design might be used to answer these questions because it allows for the simultaneous manipulation of two or more independent variables at various levels. In this example the independent variables are the number of rows (facings) and shelf height. Increases in sales, the dependent variable, attributed to each of these variables considered separately are referred to as *main effects*. A **main effect** is the influence on the dependent variable of a single independent variable. Each individual variable has a separate main effect.

main effect
The influence of a single independent variable on a dependent variable.

Table 12.3 Factorial Design—Toy Robots

	PACKAGE DESIGN	
PRICE	RED	GOLD
$25	Cell 1	Cell 4
30	Cell 2	Cell 5
35	Cell 3	Cell 6

---

interaction effect

The influence on a dependent variable by combinations of two or more independent variables.

The effects of combinations of these two shelf policy variables is the **interaction effect**. A major advantage of the factorial design is its ability to measure interaction effects, which may be greater or smaller than the total of the main effects.

To further explain the terminology of experimental designs, let us use the example of a toy-robot manufacturer that wishes to measure the effect of different prices and packaging designs on consumers' perceptions of product quality. Table 12.3 indicates three experimental treatment levels of price ($25, $30, and $35) and two levels of packaging design (Red and Gold). The table shows that every combination of treatment levels requires a separate experimental group. In this experiment with three levels of price and two levels of packaging designs we have a 3 × 2 (read "three by two") factorial design, because the first factor (variable) is varied in three ways and the second factor is varied in two ways. A 3 × 2 design requires six cells, or six experimental groups (3 × 2 = 6).

The number of treatments (factors) and the number of levels of each treatment identify the factorial design. A 3 × 3 design incorporates two factors, each having three levels; a 2 × 2 × 2 design has three factors, each having two levels. The treatments need not have the same number of levels; for example, a 3 × 2 × 4 factorial design is possible. However, in the factorial experiment each treatment level is combined with every other treatment level. A 2 × 2 experiment requires four different subgroups or cells for the experiment; a 3 × 3 experiment requires nine combinations of subgroups or cells.

In addition to the advantage of investigating two or more independent variables simultaneously, factorial designs allow researchers to measure interaction effects. In a 2 × 2 experiment the interaction is the effect produced by treatments

---

Table 12.4 A 2×2 Factorial Design that Illustrates the Effects of Gender and Ad Content on Believability

	AD A	AD B		
Men	60	70	65	} Main effects of gender
Women	80	50	65	
	70	60		

Main effects of ad

Exhibit 12.4 **Graphic Illustration of Interaction between Gender and Advertising Copy**

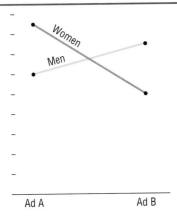

Ad A   Ad B

A and B simultaneously, which cannot be accounted for by either treatment alone. If the effect of one treatment differs at various levels of the other treatment, interaction occurs.

To illustrate the value of a factorial design, suppose a researcher is comparing two television commercials. The researcher is investigating the believability of the ads on a scale from 0 to 100 and wishes to consider the gender of the viewer as another factor. The experiment has two independent variables: gender × ads. This 2 × 2 factorial experiment permits the experimenter to test three hypotheses. Two hypotheses are about the main effects: which ad is more believable and which gender more consistently tends to believe magazine advertising. However, the primary research question deals with the interaction hypothesis. A high score indicates a highly believable ad. Table 12.4 shows that the mean believability score for both genders is 65.[12] This suggests that there is no main gender effect because men and women evaluate believability of the advertisements equally. The main effect for ads indicates that ad A is more believable than ad B (70 versus 60).

EXPLORING RESEARCH ISSUES

A Lethal Interaction

IN PHARMACOLOGY THE INTERACTION EFFECT IS USUally called a *synergistic effect*. An example is the lethal combination of barbiturate sleeping pills and alcoholic liquor. Each of these is a drug, and each reduces the number of heartbeats per minute.

Their combined effect, however, is a much more severe reduction than one would expect knowing their individual effects. This is actually a failure of the two treatments to be additive—their combined effect is much more than the sum of their individual effects. Another way of phrasing the synergistic effect is the following: The effect of one treatment differs depending on the level of the other treatment; that is, the reduction in pulse due to alcohol differs depending on whether or not barbiturates are in a person's system.

However, if we inspect the data and look within the levels of the factors, we find that men find ad B more believable and women find ad A more believable. This is an interaction effect because the believability score of the advertising factor differs at different values of the other independent variable, gender.

Graphic Interaction. Exhibit 12.4 graphs the results of the believability experiment. The line for men illustrates the two mean believability scores for the advertising copy for ads A and B; the other line represents the same relationship for women. When there is a difference between the slopes of the two lines, as in this case, the graph indicates interaction between the two treatment variables. The difference in the slopes means that the believability of the advertising copy depends on whether a man or a woman is viewing the advertisement.

Latin Square Design

Latin square design
A balanced, two-way classification scheme that attempts to control or block out the effect of two or more extraneous factors by restricting randomization with respect to the row and column effects.

The **Latin square design** attempts to control or block out the effect of two or more confounding extraneous factors. This design is so named because of the layout of the table that represents the design. A Latin square is a balanced, two-way classification scheme.[13] In the following 3×3 matrix each letter occurs only once in each row and in each column:

	ORDER OF USAGE		
Subject	1	2	3
1	A	B	C
2	B	C	A
3	C	A	B

The letters *A, B,* and *C* identify the three treatments; the rows and columns of the table identify the confounding factors. For example, a taste test might be confounded by the order of tasting; the first taste may seem better than the last. The taste test might also be confounded by individual taste preferences. To control for these factors, each subject is exposed to every treatment. If all the subjects receive three tastes and the order in which they taste are randomized, neither individual preference nor order effects may confound the experiment; thus, the order of treatment may be randomized under the restriction of balance required for the Latin square. The same type of balance is required for the second confounding factor. The end result of this design is that each treatment will be administered under conditions that involve all levels of both confounding factors. In summary the Latin square design manipulates one independent variable and controls for two additional sources of extraneous variation by restricting randomization with respect to the row and column effects.

A major assumption of the Latin square design is that interaction effects are expected to be minimal or nonexistent. Thus, it is assumed that the first subject does not have a strong preference for the first product used, and the third subject does not have a strong preference for the last product used.

A Latin square may have any number of treatments; for example, the arrangement for a five-treatment experiment is as follows:

5×5

A	B	C	D	E
B	C	D	E	A
C	D	E	A	B
D	E	A	B	C
E	A	B	C	D

Note that this 5×5 matrix requires 25 cells. It also indicates that the number of treatment levels for confounding both factors 1 and 2 must be equal. This may present certain problems. For example, suppose a retail grocery chain wishes to control for shelf space and city where the product is sold. The chain may be limited in its experiment because it markets in only three cities, but wishes to experiment with four shelf heights.

Having an unequal number of levels for each factor may be one drawback that will eliminate the Latin square design as a possibility. A second limitation is the assumption that there is no interaction effect. However, making this assumption allows the experiment to be conducted with fewer subjects than would be required for a comparable factorial design. Like most other forms of marketing research, this research design has its drawbacks, but in certain situations it has advantages.

Summary

Test marketing is an experimental procedure that provides an opportunity to test a new product or marketing plan under realistic conditions to obtain a measure of sales or profit potential. Its major advantage as a research tool is that it closely approximates reality. Test marketing provides the opportunity to estimate the outcomes of alternative courses of action. It also allows for identification and correction of weaknesses in the product or its marketing plan before a full-scale sales launch. Test market failures can be research successes by pointing out the need for this adjustment.

Test marketing is an expensive research procedure; the value of the information gained from test marketing must be compared with the cost. It can also expose the new product to competitive reaction before the product is introduced. Test marketing generally occurs late in the product development process when a high probability of success is predicted.

The test market should allow enough time for consumers to use up the product and make a repeat purchase if they choose to do so. Too short a test period may overstate potential sales because many initial buyers may not repeat their purchases.

Selecting test markets is a sampling problem. The researcher wishes to use sample markets that are representative of the whole population. Several factors are important in test market selection, including population size, demographics, lifestyles, competitive situation, media coverage and efficiency, media isolation, and a self-contained trading area. Researchers should also avoid overuse of particular markets, as people who are aware that a test is going on may alter their purchase behavior patterns.

One objective of test marketing is to estimate the sales that eventually may be expected. Several problems must be overcome. One is overattention to the product or test resulting in an overly high estimate of sales. A related problem is unrealistic store conditions. Also, competitive conditions in national introductions may be very different from those in a test market. Incorrect volume forecasts and time lapses between test and introduction may confound the results. Consumer surveys may be used along with the test market to supplement the work. Projections may be straight trends, adjusted for the company's competitive strength, or adjusted for market penetration and repeat-purchase rate.

An alternative to standard test marketing, which uses a company's own sales force and normal distribution channels, is the control method. Under this method, a marketing research service handles distribution to particular stores in a small city with controlled stocking and shelf facings. This test is more a laboratory situation than a real-world field experiment. Electronic test markets use scanner-based systems to immediately learn the impact of experimental manipulations. Simulated test markets are research laboratories that compress the shopping process into a short time span. Virtual-reality simulated test markets attempt to reproduce the atmosphere of an actual retail store with visually compelling images appearing on a computer screen.

Various complex experimental designs are commonly used in test marketing. These include the completely randomized design, the randomized block design, and various factorial designs. The factorial designs allow for interaction effects among variables. One variation is the Latin square, which attempts to block out confounding factors.

Key Terms and Concepts

Test marketing
Repeat-purchase rate
Market penetration
Control method of test marketing
Electronic test markets

Simulated test market
Virtual-reality simulated test market
Completely randomized design
Randomized block design
Factorial design

Main effect
Interaction effect
Latin square design

Questions for Review and Critical Thinking

1. What are the benefits of test marketing? When is test marketing likely? When is it unlikely?

2. Which of the following products or marketing strategies are likely to be test marketed? Why or why not?

   a. A computerized robot lawn mower

   b. A line of 8-ounce servings of vegetarian dishes for senior citizens

   c. A forklift truck

   d. A new brand of eye drops especially for brown-eyed people

   e. A new, heavy-duty KitchenAid mixer

   f. An advertising campaign to drink a cola drink in the morning

3. What measures should be used to project the results of test markets for the following products:
   a. a new candy bar

   b. a new solar-powered radio built into sunglasses

   c. a toothpaste's new advertising campaign?

4. How long should the test market periods last for the products in Question 3?

5. Name some geographical markets and corresponding products where there may be regional differences in product demand.

6. What is the difference between standard test marketing and controlled test marketing? What are the advantages and disadvantages of each?

7. How are the results of a test market projected to a national level? What problems exist? How can these problems be adjusted?

8. What factors are important in selecting test markets?

9. How does test marketing differ from limited introduction of a new product?

10. What service might be required from research suppliers to assist in (a) a standard market test and (b) a control store test?

11. What advantages does simulated test marketing have over traditional test marketing? What limitations does it have?

12. In a 2×2 factorial design, there are eight possible patterns of effects. Assume that independent variable A and independent variable B have significant main effects, but there is no interaction between them. Another combination might be no effects of variable A, but a significant effect of variable B with a significant interaction effect between them. Diagram each of these eight possible effects.

13. A mouthwash manufacturer learns that a competitor is test marketing a new lemon-flavored mouthwash in an Arizona city. The marketing research department of a competing firm is told to read the results of the test market, and the marketing manager is told to lower the price of its competing brand to disrupt the test market. Is this ethical?

 Exploring the Internet

American Demographics magazine rated Tulsa, Oklahoma, as America's most typical city with over 50,000 people.

Use the Internet to learn what would make Tulsa a good test market.

Case 12.1 Fortune Candy

ON DECEMBER 9 MIKE GAVAGAN AND TOM DALEY WERE discussing their test market plans for a new item, Fortune candy. The idea to include a fortune-telling message in a candy bar had struck Daley, manager of new product development, the day after he dined in a Chinese restaurant and enjoyed his fortune cookie message. He thought that the fortune cookie experience is a lot of fun, and adults should have it more often. Of course, working for a large grocery product firm had helped him direct his thinking toward Fortune candy. The product had passed the concept test stages and was now ready for the big step. Tom wanted a test either in the Quad Cities (Davenport and Bettendorf, Iowa, and Rock Island and Moline, Illinois) or in South Bend, Indiana.

Gavagan said, "Let's go to San Jose. The West Coast is on the cutting edge. If it goes over well there, it will go over anywhere. Our new candy is an indulgent, fun, lighthearted product, perfect for Californians. If we were testing a new soup, the Quad

Cities would be fine. The nation's eating habits change ever so slowly. A conservative market like that would be great for soup, but not for our new candy."

Daley said, "I know the West Coast would be great in February, but I think that Quad Cities are our best shot, or maybe South Bend."

QUESTIONS

1. Find demographic and retail sales information from *Sales and Marketing Management's Survey of Buying Power* on these locations.

2. Which test market should the company select? Why?

Case 12.2 The Laboratory Test Market

YANKELOVICH AND ASSOCIATES IS ONE OF THE COUNTRY'S largest marketing research firms. It provides a wide variety of research services. One of its standard research divisions is the laboratory test market (LTM). The laboratory test market is a method of compressing traditional test markets of new products into shorter time spans. It permits management to obtain early predictions as to how a new product will perform and to provide diagnostic data on the strengths and weaknesses of the brand relative to competition. The laboratory test market provides a means of understanding the attitudinal and behavioral factors that influence trial and repurchase decisions.

Laboratory test market facilities are available in all areas of the United States. They contain an experimental supermarket in which products are sold to consumers under controlled conditions, a theater-auditorium in which advertisements and other promotional materials can be exposed to consumers, rooms for interviewing consumers after they have made their purchases, and facilities for interviewing consumers by telephone after they have used the products purchased.

The following procedure is used in a laboratory test market designed to produce a sales level prediction.

First, a representative sample of consumers (the size and characteristics of the sample are contingent on the product category under investigation) participate in a series of experiments. The consumers are led, in groups of 30 to 35, into a theater, where they fill in a self-administered questionnaire with the aid of a moderator. This form furnishes data on age, family composition, living standard level (occupation of head of household, family income, and so on), practices and purchase behavior vis-à-vis the product category, and other pertinent background facts.

After the consumers have completed the questionnaire, an actual TV program is shown that contains a number of commercials for different existing brands in the product category as well as the brand/option being tested, along with communications for other product categories. (If finished commercials are not available, rougher presentations, in one form or another, can be used to communicate the product message for each brand.) It is not essential to the design that a commercial for every brand stocked in the laboratory store to be visited later be included in the program; in the real world, there are cases of products being marketed that are not supported by advertising. At the same time, it is desirable to include commercials for the leading, heavily advertised brands on the market.

After the consumers have seen the film, they are led in small groups to the store. The store is stocked with the brands that have been shown in the commercials and others that enjoy an important market share in the testing area. Upon entering the store, the consumers are provided with a fixed amount of money with which to simulate purchase. (This step has been found useful for maximizing the number of purchases. Experience has shown that an amount equivalent to about one-fourth of the average purchase price for the product class is a sufficient stimulus to encourage purchase.) The consumers are then asked to make a purchase or not, as they wish, knowing full well that the difference between the money they receive and the price of the product requires that they use their own money to make the purchase. The use of their own money is an important factor in the experiment. Only consumers who are interested in a particular product's benefit will spend their own money; furthermore, their assessment of the product after usage will be more realistic if their own money is invested.

After the consumers have made their purchases, data are collected both qualitatively (through group discussions) and quantitatively (through questionnaires) to determine their reactions to the product. The consumers then go home to use their various products as they normally would. They are not told, however, that they will be contacted for further interviewing. The purpose of this subsequent interview, usually made by telephone, is to measure the consumers' interest in repurchasing the brand and to identify their forecasted frequency of future product usage.

After a certain time period has elapsed (timing is contingent on product type), the consumers are reinterviewed by telephone to determine:

- Reactions to the product
- Reactions of other family members (for food entries)
- Degree of satisfaction or dissatisfaction
- Reasons for satisfaction or dissatisfaction
- Comparisons with previous products/brands used
- Usage data
- Repurchase data

If an extended usage test is to be incorporated into the research design, the consumers are given the opportunity to repurchase the product, which is then delivered to them. After a given time period, a follow-up interview takes place to obtain further product usage and assessment data.

The preceding data are collected and analyzed for *all* brands sold in the store. In this way, the data on the test product/option can be studied in relation to other brands to establish its relative strengths and weaknesses.

QUESTIONS

1. What advantages does the LTM offer over traditional test markets?

2. What limitations does the LTM have?

Chapter 13

Measurement

BBDO, AN ADVERTISING AGENCY, HAS DEVELOPED A measuring system to evaluate consumers' emotional responses to advertising.[1] Its Emotional Measurement System is a proprietary device that uses photographs of actors' faces to help consumers choose their reactions to commercials. Researchers at BBDO believe that the process virtually eliminates the inherent bias in traditional copy testing. With the conventional system, consumers often underestimate their emotional responses because they feel silly putting them into words, and words are subject to varying interpretations. Thus, traditional copy tests have tended to measure thoughts rather than feelings and, therefore, have failed to adequately measure emotional responses.

Rather than ask consumers to choose from a simple list or write in their own words, the agency has devised a deck of 53 photos—narrowed down from 1,800—representing what BBDO calls the "universe of emotions." Each features one of six actors with different expressions ranging from happy/playful to disgusted/revolted. A total of 26 categories of emotions is expressed.

Here's how the system works. As with most copy testing, participants are shown a single commercial or group of spots and then are given a questionnaire to test whether they remembered brand names and copy points. At any point during this process, the researchers hand out the photos. Each person is asked not to write or speak about the spot but to quickly sort through the photos, setting aside any or

all that reflect how he or she feels after viewing the commercial.

Innovative techniques such as the Emotional Measurement System have improved the measurement of marketing phenomena. This chapter discusses the basic measurement issues in marketing research.

What you will learn in this chapter

To know how a researcher might answer the question "What is to be measured?"

To define the term operational definition.

To distinguish among nominal, ordinal, interval, and ratio scales.

To understand the need for index or composite measures.

To define the three criteria for good measurement.

To discuss the various methods for determining reliability.

To discuss the various methods for assessing validity.

Exhibit 13.1 **A Two-Sided Ruler that Offers Alternative Scales of Measurement**

For Good Measure from the **National Bureau of Standards** Washington, D.C. 20234

What Is to Be Measured?

An object, such as the edge of your textbook, can be measured with either side of a ruler (see Exhibit 13.1). Note that one side has inches and the other has centimeters. However, the scale of measurement will vary depending on whether the metric side or the standard side is used. Many measurement problems in marketing research are similar to this ruler with its alternative scales of measurement. Unfortunately, unlike the two-sided ruler, many measurement scales used in marketing research are not directly comparable.

The first question the researcher must answer is "What is to be measured?" This is not as simple a question as it may at first seem. The definition of the problem, based on exploratory research or managerial judgment, indicates the concept to be investigated (for example, sales performance). However, a precise definition of the concept may require a description of how it will be measured—and frequently there is more than one way to measure a particular concept. For example, if we are conducting research to determine which factors influence a sales representative's performance, we might use a number of measures to indicate a salesperson's success, such as dollar or unit sales volume or share of accounts lost. Furthermore, true measurement of concepts requires a process of precisely assigning scores or numbers to the attributes of people or objects. The purpose of assigning numbers is to convey information about the variable being measured. Hence, the key question becomes "On what basis will numbers or scores be assigned to the concept?"

Suppose the task is to measure the height of a boy named Michael.

1. We can create five categories:

    (1) Quite tall for his age
    (2) Moderately tall for his age
    (3) About average for his age
    (4) Moderately short for his age
    (5) Quite short for his age

    Then we can measure Michael by saying that, because he is moderately tall for his age, his height measurement is 2.

2. We can compare Michael to 10 other neighborhood children. We give the

tallest child the rank of 1 and the shortest the rank of 11; Michael's height measurement using this procedure is 4 if he is fourth tallest among the 11 neighborhood children.

3. We can use some conventional measuring unit such as centimeters and, measuring to the nearest centimeter, designate Michael's height as 137.

4. We can define two categories:

   (1) A nice height

   (2) A not-so-nice height

   By our personal standard, Michael's height is a nice height, so his height measurement is 1.[2]

In each measuring situation, a score has been assigned for Michael's height (2, 4, 137, and 1). In scientific marketing research precision is the goal. The researcher must determine the best way to measure what is to be investigated.

On college campuses, girl or boy watching constitutes a measurement activity: What might be a 7 to one person may be a 9 to another. Precise measurement in marketing research requires a careful conceptual definition, an operational definition, and a system of consistent rules for assigning numbers or scores.

Concepts

Before the measurement process can occur, a marketing researcher must identify the concepts relevant to the problem. A **concept** (or construct) is a generalized idea about a class of objects, attributes, occurrences, or processes. Concepts such as *age, sex,* and *number of children* are relatively concrete properties, and they present few problems in definition or measurement. Other characteristics of individuals or properties of objects may be more abstract. Concepts such as *brand loyalty, personality, channel power,* and so on present greater problems in definition and measurement. For example, *brand loyalty* has been measured using the percentage of a person's purchases going to one brand in a given period of time, sequences of brand purchases, number of different brands purchased, amount of brand deliberation, and various cognitive measures, such as attitude toward a brand.

concept
A generalized idea about a class of objects, attributes, occurrences, or processes.

TO THE POINT

Not everything that can be counted counts, and not everything that counts can be counted.

ALBERT EINSTEIN

Operational Definitions

Concepts must be made operational in order to be measured. An **operational definition** gives meaning to a concept by specifying the activities or operations necessary to measure it.[3] For example, the concept of nutrition consciousness might be indicated when a shopper reads the nutritional information on a cereal package. Inspecting a nutritional label is not the same as nutrition consciousness, but it is a clue that a person may be nutrition conscious.

The operational definition specifies what the researcher must do to measure the concept under investigation. If we wish to measure consumer interest in a

operational definition
An explanation that gives meaning to a concept by specifying the activities or operations necessary to measure it.

Exhibit 13.2 Media Skepticism: An Operational Definition

CONCEPT	CONCEPTUAL DEFINITION	OPERATIONAL DEFINITION
Media skepticism	*Media skepticism* is the degree to which individuals are skeptical toward the reality presented in the mass media. Media skepticism varies across individuals, from those who are mildly skeptical and accept most of what they see and hear in the media to those who completely discount and disbelieve the facts, values, and portrayal of reality in the media.	Please tell me how true each statement is about the media. Is it very true, not very true, or not at all true? 1. The program was *not* very accurate in its portrayal of the problem. 2. Most of the story was staged for entertainment purposes. 3. The presentation was slanted and unfair. 4. I think the story was fair and unbiased. 5. I think important facts were purposely left out of the story. Individual items were scored on a 4-point scale with values from 1 to 4; higher scores represented greater skepticism. Media skepticism is defined as the sum of these five scores.

---

conceptual definition
A verbal explanation of the meaning of a concept. It defines what the concept is and what it is not.

specific advertisement, we may operationally define *interest* as a certain increase in pupil dilation. Another operational definition of interest might rely on direct responses: what people say they are interested in. Each operational definition has advantages and disadvantages.

An operational definition is like a manual of instructions or a recipe: Even the truth of a statement like "Gaston Gourmet likes key lime pie" depends on the recipe. Different instructions lead us to different results.[4]

An operational definition tells the investigator, "Do such-and-such in so-and-so manner."[5] Exhibit 13.2 presents a **conceptual definition** and an operational definition from a study on media skepticism.

Rules of Measurement

A *rule* is a guide that instructs us what to do. An example of a measurement rule might be: Assign the numerals 1 through 7 to individuals according to how brand loyal they are. If the individual is extremely brand loyal, assign a 7. If the individual is a total brand switcher with no brand loyalty, assign the numeral 1.

Operational definitions help the researcher specify the rules for assigning numbers. If the purpose of an advertising experiment is to increase the amount of time shoppers spend in a department store, for example, *shopping time* must be operationally defined. Once *shopping time* is defined as the interval between entering the door and receiving the receipt from the clerk, assignment of numbers via a stopwatch is facilitated. If a study on gasohol, a blend of ethyl alcohol and gasoline, is not concerned with a person's depth of experience, but defines people as users or nonusers, it could assign a 1 for *experience with gasohol* and a 0 for *no experience with gasohol*.

The values assigned in the measuring process can be manipulated according to certain mathematical rules. The properties of the scale of numbers may allow the researcher to add, subtract, or multiply answers. In other cases there may be problems with the simple addition of the numbers or other mathematical manipulations because this is not permissible within the mathematical system.

Types of Scales

A **scale** may be defined as "any series of items that is progressively arranged according to value or magnitude into which an item can be placed according to its quantification.[6] In other words, a scale is a continuous spectrum or series of categories. The purpose of scaling is to represent, usually quantitatively, an item's, person's, or event's place in the spectrum.

Marketing researchers use many scales or number systems. It is traditional to classify scales of measurement on the basis of the mathematical comparisons that are allowable with them. The four types of scale are the nominal, ordinal, interval, and ratio scales.

scale
Any series of items that are progressively arranged according to value or magnitude; a series into which an item can be placed according to its quantification.

Exhibit 13.3 **Nominal, Ordinal, Interval, and Ratio Scales Provide Different Information**

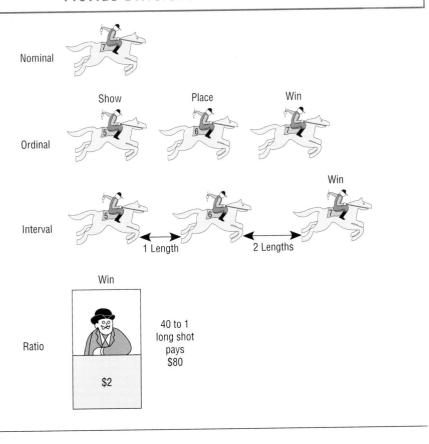

Nominal Scale

nominal scale

A scale in which the numbers or letters assigned to the object serve as labels for identification or classification.

Number 25 on the Saint Louis Cardinals is Mark McGuire. Sammy Sosa is number 21 on the Chicago Cubs. These numbers nominally identify these superstars. A **nominal scale** is the simplest type of scale. The numbers or letters assigned to objects serve as labels for identification or classification. These are scales in name only. Tulsa's census tract 25 and census tract 87 are merely labels. The number 87 does not imply that this area has more people or higher income than number 25. An example of a typical nominal scale in marketing research would be the coding of males as 1 and females as 2. As another example, the first drawing in Exhibit 13.3 depicts the number 7 on a horse's colors. This is merely a label for the bettors and racing enthusiasts.

Ordinal Scale

ordinal scale

A scale that arranges objects or alternatives according to their magnitude in an ordered relationship.

We know that when our horse comes in the "show" position at the racetrack, it has come in third behind the win and the place horses (see the second drawing in Exhibit 13.3). An **ordinal scale** arranges objects or alternatives according to their magnitude in an ordered relationship. When respondents are asked to *rank order* their shopping center preferences, ordinal values are assigned. In our racehorse example if we assign 1 to the win position, 2 to the place position, and 3 to the show position, we can say that 1 was before 2 and 2 was before 3. However, we cannot say anything about the degree of distance or the interval between the win and show horses or the show and place horses.

A typical ordinal scale in marketing asks respondents to rate brands, companies, and so on as excellent, good, fair, or poor. We know excellent is higher than good; but we do not know by how much.

Interval Scale

interval scale

A scale that both arranges objects according to their magnitudes and also distinguishes this ordered arrangement in units of equal intervals.

The third drawing in Exhibit 13.3 depicts a horse race in which the win horse was two lengths ahead of the place horse, which was one length ahead of the show horse. Not only is the order of finish known, but the distance between the horses is known.[7] **Interval scales** not only indicate order, but they also measure order (or distance) in units of equal intervals.

The location of the zero point is arbitrary. In the consumer price index if the base year is 1993, the price level during 1993 will be set at 100. Although this is an equal-interval measurement scale, the zero point is arbitrary. The classic example of an interval scale is the Fahrenheit temperature scale. If the temperature is 80°, it cannot be said that it is twice as hot as a 40° temperature, because 0° represents not the lack of temperature, but a relative point on the Fahrenheit scale. Due to the lack of an absolute zero point, the interval scale does not allow the conclusion that the number 36 is three times as great as the number 12, but only that the distance is three times as great. Likewise, when an interval scale is used to measure psychological attributes, the researcher can comment about the magnitude of differences or compare the average differences on the attributes that were measured, but cannot determine the actual strength of the attitude toward an object. However, the changes in concepts over time can be compared if the researcher continues to use the same scale in longitudinal research.

Ratio Scale

ratio scale

A scale that has absolute rather than relative quantities and an absolute zero where there is an absence of a given attribute.

To be able to say that winning tickets pay 40 to 1 for win bets or that racehorse number 7 is twice as heavy as racehorse number 5, we need a ratio scale (see the fourth drawing in Exhibit 13.3). **Ratio scales** assign absolute rather than relative

---

Exhibit 13.4 Descriptive Statistics for Types of Scales

Type of Scale[a]	Numerical Operation	Descriptive Statistics
Nominal	Counting	Frequency in each category Percentage in each category
Ordinal	Rank ordering	Median Range Percentile ranking
Interval	Arithmetic operations that preserve order and relative magnitudes	Mean Standard deviation Variance
Ratio	Arithmetic operations on actual quantities	Geometric mean Coefficient of variation

[a]All statistics appropriate for lower-order scales (nominal being the lowest) are appropriate for higher-order scales (ratio being the highest).

---

quantities. For example, both money and weight are ratio scales because they possess absolute zeros and interval properties. The absolute zero represents a point on the scale at which there is an absence of the given attribute. When one states that a person has zero ounces of gold, we understand the natural zero value for weight. In the measurement of temperature, the Kelvin scale (a ratio scale) begins at absolute zero, a point that corresponds to -273.16° on the Celsius scale (an interval scale). In distribution or logistical research it may be appropriate to think of physical attributes such as weight or distance as ratio scales in which the ratio of scale values are meaningful. For most behavioral marketing research, however, interval scales typically are the appropriate measurements. However, if a researcher wishes to construct ratios derived from the original scales, the scale of measurement must be ratio.

Mathematical and Statistical Analysis of Scales

The type of scale used in marketing research will determine the form of the statistical analysis. For example, a number of operations, such as calculation of a mean (mathematical average), can be conducted only if the scale is of an interval or ratio nature; they are not permissible with nominal or ordinal scales.

Exhibit 13.4 shows the appropriate descriptive statistics for each type of scale. The most sophisticated form of statistical analysis for nominal-scale data is counting. Because numbers are merely labels for classification purposes, they have no quantitative meaning. The researcher tallies the frequency in each category and identifies which category contains the highest number of observations (individuals, objects, etc.). An ordinal scale provides data that may be rank ordered from lowest to highest. Observations may be associated with percentile ranks such as the median. Because all statistical analyses appropriate for lower-order scales are suitable for higher-order scales, an interval scale may be used as a nominal scale to uniquely classify or as an ordinal scale to preserve order. In addition an interval scale's property of equal intervals allows researchers to compare differences among scale values and perform arithmetic operations such as addition and subtraction. Numbers may be changed, but the numerical operations must preserve order and relative magnitudes of differences. The mean and standard deviation may be calculated from true interval-scale data. A ratio scale has all the properties of nominal, ordinal, and interval scales. In addition it allows researchers to compare absolute magnitudes because the scale has an absolute zero point. Using the actual quantities for arithmetic operations is permissible. Thus, the ratios of scale values are meaningful.

Chapters 19 through 23 further explore the limitations of scalar data and appropriate mathematical analysis.

TO THE POINT

When you can measure what you are talking about and express it in numbers, you know something about it.

LORD KELVIN

Index Measures

So far we have focused on measuring a concept with a single question or observation. Measuring brand awareness, for example, might involve one question such as "Are you aware of ———?" However, measuring more complex concepts may require more than one question because the concept has several attributes. An **attribute** is a single characteristic or fundamental feature that pertains to an object, person, situation, or issue.

Multi-item instruments for measuring a single concept with several attributes are called **index measures,** or **composite measures.** One index of social class is based on three weighted variables: residence, occupation, and education. Measures of cognitive phenomena often are composite indexes of sets of variables or scales. Items are combined into composite measures. For example, a salesperson's morale may be measured by combining questions such as "How satisfied are you with your job? How satisfied are you with your territory? How satisfied are you in your personal life?" Measuring the same underlying concept using a variety of techniques is one method for increasing accuracy. Asking different questions to measure the same concept provides a more accurate cumulative measure than does a single-item estimate.

attribute
A single characteristic or fundamental feature that pertains to an object, person, or issue.

index (or composite) measure
A composite measure of several variables to measure a single concept; a multi-item instrument.

Three Criteria for Good Measurement

The three major criteria for evaluating measurements are reliability, validity, and sensitivity.

Reliability

A tailor measuring fabric with a tape measure obtains a "true" value of the fabric length. If the tailor repeatedly measures the fabric and each time estimates the same length, it is assumed that the tape measure is reliable. When the outcome of the measuring process is reproducible, the measuring instrument is reliable. **Reliability** applies to a measure when similar results are obtained over time and across situations. Broadly defined, reliability is the degree to which measures are free from random error and therefore yield consistent results. For example, ordinal level measures are reliable if they consistently rank order subjects in the same manner; reliable interval level measures consistently rank orders and maintain the distance between subjects. Imperfections in the measuring process that affect the assignment of scores or numbers different ways each time a measure is taken, such as a respondent misunderstanding a question, cause low reliability. The actual choice among plausible responses may be governed by such transitory factors as mood, whim, or the context set by surrounding questions; measures are not always error-free and stable over time.

There are two dimensions underlying the concept of reliability: *repeatability* and *internal consistency*. Assessing the *repeatability* of a measure is the first aspect of reliability. The **test-retest method** involves administering the same scale or measure to the same respondents at two separate times to test for stability. If the measure is stable over time, the reported test administered under conditions similar to the first test should obtain similar results. For example, suppose a researcher at one time attempts to measure buying intentions and finds that 12 percent of the population is willing to purchase the product. If the study is repeated a few weeks later under similar conditions and the researcher again finds that 12 percent of the population is willing to purchase the product, the measure appears to be reliable. The high stability correlation or consistency between the two measures at time 1 and time 2 indicates a high degree of reliability.

As an example at the individual rather than aggregate level, assume that a person does not change his or her attitude about bock beer. If repeated measurements of that individual's attitude toward bock beer are taken with the same attitude scale, a reliable instrument will produce the same results each time the attitude is measured. When a measuring instrument produces unpredictable results from one testing to the next, the results are said to be unreliable because of error in measurement.

As another example, consider the remarks a Gillette executive made about the reliability problems in measuring reactions to razor blades:

> There is a high degree of noise in our data, a considerable variability in results. It's a big mish mash, what we call the night sky in August. There are points all over the place. A man will give a blade a high score one day, but the next day he'll cut himself a lot and give the blade a terrible score. But on the third day, he'll give the same blade a good score. What you have to do is try to see some pattern in all this. There are some gaps in our knowledge.[8]

Measures of test-retest reliability pose two problems that are common to all longitudinal studies. First, the premeasure or first measure may sensitize the respondents to their participation in a research project and subsequently influence the results of the second measure. Furthermore, if the duration of the time period between measures is long, there may be an attitude change or other form of maturation of the subjects. Thus, a reliable measure can indicate a low or a moderate correlation between the first and second administration if this low correlation is due to an attitude change over time rather than to a lack of reliability.

The second underlying dimension of reliability concerns the homogeneity of the measure. An attempt to measure an attitude may require asking several similar (but not identical) questions or a battery of scale items. To measure the *internal consistency* of a multiple-item measure, scores on subsets of the items within the scale must be correlated.

reliability
The degree to which measures are free from random error and therefore yield consistent results.

test-retest method
Administering the same scale or measure to the same respondents at two separate points in time to test for stability.

split-half method
A method for assessing internal consistency by checking the results of one-half of a set of scaled items against the results from the other half.

equivalent-form method
A method that measures the correlation between alternative instruments, designed to be as equivalent as possible, administered to the same group of subjects.

The technique of splitting halves is the most basic method of checking internal consistency when a measure contains a large number of items. In the **split-half method** the researcher may take the results obtained from one-half of the scale items (for example, odd-numbered items) and check them against the results from the other half (even-numbered items).

The **equivalent-form method** is used when two alternative instruments are designed to be as equivalent as possible. The two measurement scales are administered to the same group of subjects. A high correlation between the two forms would suggest that the scale is reliable. However, a low correspondence between the two instruments creates a problem. The researcher will be uncertain as to whether the measure has intrinsically low reliability or whether the particular equivalent form has failed to be similar to the other form. Both the equivalent-form and split-half approaches to measuring reliability assume that the concept is unidimensional; they measure homogeneity or inter-item consistency rather than stability over time.

Reliability is a necessary condition for validity, but a reliable instrument may not be valid. For example, a purchase intention measurement technique may consistently indicate that 20 percent of the sample units are willing to purchase a new product. Whether the measure is valid depends on whether 20 percent of the U.S. population indeed purchases the product. A reliable but invalid instrument will yield consistently inaccurate results.

Validity

The purpose of measurement is to measure what we intend to measure. Achieving this obvious goal is not, however, as simple as it sounds. Consider the student who takes a test (measurement) in a statistics class and receives a poor grade. The student may say, "I really understood that material because I studied hard. The test measured my ability to do arithmetic and to memorize formulas rather than measuring my understanding of statistics." The student's complaint is that the test did not measure understanding of statistics, which was what the professor had intended to measure; it measured something else.

One method of measuring the intention to buy is the gift method. Respondents are told that a drawing will be held at some future period for a year's supply of a certain product. Respondents report which of several brands they would prefer to receive if they were to win. Do the respondents' reports of the brands they would prefer to win necessarily constitute a valid measure of the brands they will actually purchase in the marketplace if they do not win the contest? Could there be a systematic bias to identify brands they wish they could afford rather than the brands they would usually purchase? This is a question of **validity.**

validity
The ability of a scale to measure what was intended to be measured.

Another example of a validity question might involve a media researcher who wonders what it means when respondents indicate they have been *exposed* to a magazine. The researcher wants to know if the measure is valid. The question of validity expresses the researcher's concern with accurate measurement. Validity addresses the problem of whether a measure (for example, an attitude measure used in marketing) indeed measures what it is supposed to measure; if it does not, there will be problems.

Students should be able to empathize with the following validity problem. Consider the ongoing controversy about highway patrol officers using radar guns to clock speeders. A driver is clocked at 75 mph in a 55 mph zone, but the same radar gun aimed at a house registers 28 mph. The error occurred because the radar gun had picked up impulses from the electrical system of the squad car's idling engine. The house was not moving, and the test was not valid.

Airline travelers put "space," especially the distance between seat backs and leg room, high on their list. Space becomes extremely important if a flight is several hours long. Plog Travel Research found that when TWA gave people more leg room, they rated the meals higher, even though the meals did not change. In fact, a halo effect influenced the ratings of most other characteristics, not just the food.[9] Were the measures of food quality and airline characteristics other than leg room valid?

Establishing Validity.   Researchers have attempted to assess validity in many ways. Researchers attempt to provide some evidence of a measure's degree of validity by answering a variety of questions. Is there a consensus among my colleagues that my attitude scale measures what it is supposed to measure? Does my measure correlate with other measures of the same concept? Does the behavior expected from my measure predict actual observed behavior? The three basic approaches to establishing validity are face or content validity, criterion validity, and construct validity.

Face, or **content, validity** refers to the subjective agreement among professionals that a scale logically appears to accurately reflect what it purports to measure. The content of the scale appears to be adequate. When it appears evident to experts that the measure provides adequate coverage of the concept, that measure has face validity. Clear, understandable questions such as "How many children do you have?" generally are agreed to have face validity. In scientific studies, however, researchers generally prefer stronger evidence because of the elusive nature of attitudes and other marketing phenomena. For example, the A. C. Nielsen television rating system is based on a People Meter system that mechanically records whether a sample household's television is turned on and records the channel selection. If one of the viewers leaves the room or has fallen asleep, the measure is not a valid measure of *audience*

Criterion validity is an attempt to answer the question "Does my measure correlate with other measures of the same construct?" Consider the physical concept of *length*. Length can be measured with a tape measure, calipers, and odometer, and other variations of the ruler. If a new measure of length were developed (for example, through laser technology), finding that the new measure correlated with the other measures of length could provide some assurance that the new measure was valid. Criterion validity may be classified as either *concurrent validity* or *predictive validity* depending on the time sequence of associating the new measurement scale and the criterion measure. If the new measure is taken at the same time as the criterion measure, it assesses *concurrent validity. Predictive validity* is established when an attitude measure predicts a future event. The two measures differ only on the basis of a time dimension, that is, if the criterion is separated in time from the predictor measure.

A practical example of predictive validity is illustrated by a commercial research firm's test of the relationship between a rough commercial's effectiveness (for example, by recall scores) and a finished commercial's effectiveness (also by recall scores). Ad agencies often test animatic rough, photomatic rough, or live-action rough commercials before developing actual finished commercials. One marketing research consulting firm suggests that this testing has high pre-

face (or content) validity
Professional agreement that a scale's content logically appears to accurately reflect what was intended to be measured.

criterion validity
The ability of a measure to correlate with other standard measures of the same construct or established criterion.

Exhibit 13.5 Reliability and Validity on Target

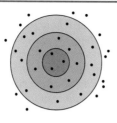
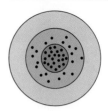
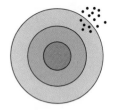

Old Rifle
Low Reliability
(Target A)

New Rifle
High Reliability
(Target B)

New Rifle Sunglare
Reliable but not Valid
(Target C)

---

construct validity

The ability of a measure to provide empirical evidence consistent with a theory based on the concepts.

dictive validity. Rough commercial recall scores provide correct estimates of the final finished commercial recall scores more than 80 percent of the time.[10] While face/content validity is a subjective evaluation, criterion-based validity provides a more rigorous empirical test.

Construct validity is established by the degree to which the measure confirms a network of related hypotheses generated from a theory based on the concepts. Establishing construct validity occurs during the statistical analysis of the data. With construct validity, the empirical evidence is consistent with the theoretical logic behind the concepts. In its simplest form, if the measure behaves the way it is supposed to in a pattern of intercorrelation with a variety of other variables, there is evidence of construct validity. For example, a consumer researcher developed a personality scale intended to measure several interpersonal response traits that management theorists previously had related to occupational preference. Testing the new scale against occupational preference would be evidence of construct validity. This is a complex method of establishing validity and of less concern to the applied researcher than to the basic researcher.

Reliability versus Validity

Let us compare the concepts of reliability and validity. A tailor using a ruler may obtain a reliable measurement of length over time with a bent ruler. A bent ruler cannot provide perfect accuracy, however, and it is not a valid measure. Thus, reliability, although necessary for validity, is not in itself sufficient. In marketing, a measure of a subject's physiological reaction to a package (for example, pupil dilation) may be highly reliable, but it will not necessarily constitute a valid measure of purchase intention.

The differences between reliability and validity can be illustrated using the rifle targets in Exhibit 13.5. An expert sharpshooter fires an equal number of rounds with a century-old rifle and a modern rifle.[11] The shots from the older gun are considerably scattered, but those from the new gun are closely clustered. The variability of the old rifle compared with that of the new one indicates it is less reliable. Target C illustrates the concept of a systematic bias influencing validity. The new rifle is reliable (little variance), but the sharpshooter's vision is hampered by glare from the sun; although consistent, the sharpshooter is unable to hit the bull's-eye.

Sensitivity

The sensitivity of a scale is an important measurement concept, particularly when *changes* in attitudes or other hypothetical constructs are under investigation. **Sensitivity** refers to an instrument's ability to accurately measure variability in stimuli or responses. A dichotomous response category, such as "agree or disagree," does not reflect subtle attitude changes. A more sensitive measure with numerous categories on the scale may be needed. For example, adding "strongly agree," "mildly agree," "neither agree nor disagree," "mildly disagree," and "strongly disagree" will increase the scale's sensitivity.

The sensitivity of a scale based on a single question or single item can also be increased by adding questions or items. In other words because index measures allow for a greater range of possible scores, they are more sensitive than single-item scales.

sensitivity
A measurement instrument's ability to accurately measure variability in stimuli or responses.

Summary

Many marketing research problems require the choice of an appropriate measuring system. The concept to be measured must be given an operational definition that specifies how it will be measured. There are four types of measuring scales. Nominal scales assign numbers or letters to objects only for identification or classification. Ordinal scales arrange objects or alternatives according to their magnitudes in an ordered relationship. Interval scales measure order (or distance) in units of equal intervals. Ratio scales are absolute scales, starting with absolute zeros at which there is a total absence of the attribute. The type of scale determines the form of statistical analysis to use.

Index or composite measures often are used to measure complex concepts with several attributes. Asking several questions may yield a more accurate measure than basing measurement on a single question.

Measuring instruments are evaluated by reliability, validity, and sensitivity. *Reliability* refers to the measuring instrument's ability to provide consistent results in repeated uses. *Validity* refers to the degree to which the instrument measures the concept the researcher wants to measure. *Sensitivity* is the instrument's ability to accurately measure variability in stimuli or responses.

Reliability may be tested using the test-retest method, the split-half method, or the equivalent-form method. The three basic approaches to dealing with issues of validity are to establish content validity, criterion validity, or construct validity. The sensitivity of a scale can be increased by allowing for a greater range of possible scores.

Key Terms and Concepts

Concept	Ratio scale	Validity
Operational definition	Attribute	Face (or content) validity
Conceptual definition	Index (or composite) measure	Criterion validity
Scale	Reliability	Construct validity
Nominal scale	Test-retest method	Sensitivity
Ordinal scale	Split-half method	
Interval scale	Equivalent-form method	

Questions for Review and Critical Thinking

1. What is the difference between a conceptual definition and an operational definition?
2. What descriptive statistics are allowable with nominal, ordinal, and interval scales?
3. Discuss the differences between validity and reliability.
4. What measurement problems might be associated with the People Meter method of audience ratings? Would any special problem arise in rating children's programs?
5. Why might a researcher wish to use more than one question to measure satisfaction with a particular aspect of retail shopping?
6. Comment on the validity and reliability of the following:
   a. A respondent's report of an intention to subscribe to *Consumer Reports* is highly reliable. A researcher believes this constitutes a valid measurement of dissatisfaction with the economic system and alienation from big business.
   b. A general-interest magazine advertised that the magazine was a better advertising medium than television programs with similar content. Research had indicated that for a soft drink and other test products, recall scores were higher for the magazine ads than for 30-second commercials.
   c. A respondent's report of frequency of magazine reading consistently indicates that she regularly reads Good Housekeeping and Gourmet and never reads Cosmopolitan.
7. Indicate whether the following measures are nominal, ordinal, interval, or ratio scales:

   a. Prices on the stock market
   b. Marital status, classified as "married" or "never married"
   c. Whether a respondent has ever been unemployed
   d. Professorial rank: assistant professor, associate professor, or professor
   e. Grades: A, B, C, D, or F
8. Go to the library and find out how Sales and Marketing Management magazine constructs its buying-power index.
9. Define the following concepts, then operationally define each one:
   a. A good bowler
   b. Television audience for the *Tonight Show*
   c. Purchasing intention for a palm-sized computer.
   d. Consumer involvement with cars
   e. Workaholic
   f. Fast-food restaurant
   g. The American Dream
10. Education often is used as an indicator of a person's socioeconomic status. Historically, the number of years of schooling completed has been recorded in the Census of Population as a measure of education. Critics say that this measure is no longer accurate as a measure of education. Comment.
11. Two academic researchers create a psychographic scale to measure travel behavior. Without measuring reliability or validity of the measuring instrument, they submit the article to a scholarly publication for review.

 Exploring the Internet

The Office of Scale Research (OSR) is located within the Department of Marketing at Southern Illinois University at Carbondale. The Office of Scale Research (OSR) Internet site provides a number of "technical reports" that deal with a wide variety of scaling issues. Go to
http://www.siu.edu/departments/mktg/OSR/
and select an article from the reading list. What types of scales are listed?

Case 13.1 Lieberman Research Inc.[12]

CAMPBELL'S SOUP COMPANY AND PEOPLE MAGAZINE hired Lieberman Research Incorporated to investigate the male food shopper. The following statement indicates the broad research objectives for the study:

While food shopping has been traditionally the responsibility of women, there is mounting evidence that food shopping is an activity in which men are becoming increasingly involved. Little is known about the characteristics of men who shop for food and men's food shopping habits. How large a role do men play in shopping for food? What are the characteristics that differentiate men who shop for food

items from men who do not shop for food? Are men's food shopping habits similar to or different from women's food shopping habits?

QUESTIONS

1. Suggest some conceptual definitions for the research variables to be studied.
2. Suggest some operational definitions for the research variables to be studied.

Case 13.2 FlyAway Airways[13]

WESLEY SHOCKER, RESEARCH ANALYST FOR FLYAWAY Airways, was asked by the director of research to make recommendations regarding the best approach for monitoring the quality of service provided by FlyAway Airways. FlyAway Airways is a national air carrier that has a comprehensive route structure consisting of long-haul, coast-to-coast routes and direct, nonstop routes between short-haul metropolitan areas. Current competitors include Midway and Alaska Airlines. FlyAway Airlines is poised to surpass the billion-dollar revenue level required to be designated as a major airline. This change in status brings a new set of competitors. To prepare for this move up in competitive status, Wesley was asked to review the options available for monitoring the quality of FlyAway Airways service and the service of its competitors. This involves better understanding the nature of service quality and the ways in which quality can be tracked for airlines.

After some investigation, Wesley discovered two basic approaches to measuring quality of airline service that can produce similar ranking results. His report must outline the important aspects to consider in measuring quality as well as the critical points of difference and similarity between the basic approaches to actually measuring quality.

Some Background on Quality

In today's competitive airline industry, it's crucial that an airline do all it can do to attract and retain customers. One of the best ways to do this is by offering a quality service to consumers. Perceptions of service quality vary from person to person, but an enduring element of service quality is the consistent achievement of customer satisfaction. For customers to perceive an airline as offering quality service, they must be satisfied, and that usually means receiving a service outcome that is equal to or greater than what was expected.

A consumer of airline services usually is concerned most with issues of schedule, destination, and price when choosing an airline. Given that most airlines have competition in each of these areas, other factors that relate to quality become important to the customer when making a choice between airlines. Both subjective (that is, food, pleasant employees) and objective (that is, on-time performance, safety, lost baggage) aspects of quality have real meaning to consumers beyond the basic areas of schedule, destination, and price. These secondary factors may not be equally critical, but they do impact quality judgments of the customer.

There are many possible combinations of subjective and objective aspects that could influence a customer's perception of quality at different times in the consumption process. Fortunately, since 1988 consumers of airline services have had access to objective information from the Department of Transportation regarding service performance in some basic categories. Unfortunately, the average consumer is most likely unaware of or uninterested in this detail of performance, and they rely on personal experience and subjective opinion to judge quality of service. Periodic surveys of subjective consumer opinion regarding airline service experience are available through several sources. These efforts rely on contact with a sample of consumers that may or may not have informed opinions regarding the quality of airline service for all airlines being compared.

A Consumer Survey Approach

In his research Wesley discovered a recently conducted study done to identify favorite airlines of frequent fliers. This study is typical of the survey-based, infrequent (usually only annually), subjective opinion efforts conducted to assess airline quality. A New York firm, Research & Forecasts, Inc., published results of a consumer survey of frequent fliers that used several criteria to rate domestic and international airlines. Criteria used to rate the airlines include comfort, service, reliability, quality of food, cost, delays, routes served, safety, and frequent flier plans. The questionnaire was sent to 25,000 frequent fliers.

The 4,462 people responding were characterized as predominantly male (59 percent), professional managers (66 percent) with an average age of 45 who traveled an average of at least 43 nights a year for both business and pleasure. This group indicated that the most important aspects in choosing an airline are (1) route structure (46 percent), (2) price (42 percent), (3) reliability (41 percent), (4) service (33 percent), (5) safety (33 percent), (6) frequent-flier plans (33 percent), and (7) food (12 percent). When asked to rate the airlines as to their overall favorite, the rankings in Case Exhibit 13.2–1 emerged.

A Weighted Average Approach

Wesley also discovered a newer, more objective approach to measuring airline quality. A study recently published by the National Institute for Aviation Research at the Wichita State University in Wichita, Kansas, takes a more quantitative approach

to identifying airline quality. The Airline Quality Rating (AQR) is a weighted average of 19 factors (see Case Exhibit 13.2–2) that have relevance when judging the quality of airline services. The AQR is based on data that are readily obtainable (most of the data are updated monthly) from published sources for each major airline operating in the United States. Regularly published data on such factors as consumer complaints, on-time performance, accidents, number of aircraft, and financial performance are available from the Department of Transportation, National Transportation Safety Board, Moody's Bond Record, industry trade publications, and annual reports of individual airlines.

In weighing the 19 factors a survey of expert opinion was conducted with a group of 65 experts in the aviation field. These experts included representatives of most major airlines, air travel experts, FAA representatives, academic researchers, airline manufacturing and support firms, and individual consumers. Each expert was asked to rate the importance that each individual factor might have to a consumer of airline services using a scale of 0 (no importance) to 10 (great importance). The average importance ratings for each of the 19 factors were then used as the weights for those factors in the AQR. Case Exhibit 13.2-2 shows the factors included in the Airline Quality Rating, the weights associated with each factor, and whether the factor has a positive or negative impact on quality from the consumer's perspective.

Using the Airline Quality Rating formula and recent data produces AQR scores and rankings for the 10 major U.S. airlines, as shown in Case Exhibit 13.2–3.

What Course to Chart?

Wesley has discovered what appear to be two different approaches to measuring quality of airlines. One relies on direct consumer opinion and is mostly subjective in its approach to quality and the elements

---

Case Exhibit 13.2-1 **Ranking of Major Airlines— Consumer Survey Approach**

1.	American	11.	Lufthansa
2.	United	12.	USAir
3.	Delta	13.	KLM
4.	TWA	14.	America West
5.	SwissAir	15.	JAL
6.	Singapore	16.	Alaska
7.	British Airways	17.	Qantas
8.	Continental	18.	Midway
9.	Air France	19.	Southwest
10.	Pan Am	20.	SAS

Case Exhibit 13.2-2 Factors Included in the Airline Quality Rating (AQR)[a]

FACTOR	WEIGHT
1. Average age of fleet	-5.85
2. Number of aircraft	+4.54
3. On-time performance	+8.63
4. Load factor	-6.98
5. Pilot deviations	-8.03
6. Number of accidents	-8.38
7. Frequent-flier awards	-7.35
8. Flight problems[b]	-8.05
9. Denied boardings[b]	-8.03
10. Mishandled baggage[b]	-7.92
11. Fares[b]	-7.60
12. Customer service[b]	-7.20
13. Refunds[b]	-7.32
14. Ticketing/boarding[b]	-7.08
15. Advertising[b]	-6.82
16. Credit[b]	-5.94
17. Other[b]	-7.34
18. Financial stability	+6.52
19. Average seat-mile cost	-4.49

$$AQR = \frac{w_1F1 - w_2F2 + w_3F3 + \ldots - w_{19}F19}{w_1 + w_2 + w_3 + \ldots + w_{19}}$$

[a] The 19-item rating has a reliability coefficient (Cronbach's Alpha) of 0.87.

[b] Data for these factors come from consumer complaints registered with the Department of Transportation.

considered. The other relies on performance data that are available through public sources and look to be more objective. Both approaches incorporate pertinent elements that could be used by consumers to judge the quality of an airline. The recommendation Wesley makes must consider the comprehensiveness and usefulness of the approach for FlyAway Airways as it moves into a more competitive environment. What course of action should Wesley recommend?

Case Exhibit 13.2-3 Airline Rankings

RANK	AIRLINE	AQR SCORE
1.	American	+0.328
2.	Southwest	+0.254
3.	Delta	+0.209
4.	United	+0.119
5.	USAir	+0.054
6.	Pan Am	+0.003
7.	Northwest	-0.063
8.	Continental	-0.346
9.	America West	-0.377
10.	TWA	-0.439

QUESTIONS

1. How comparable are the two different methods? In what ways are they similar? In what ways are they different?
2. What are the positive and negative aspects of each approach that Wesley should consider before recommending a course of action for FlyAway Airways?
3. What aspects of service quality does each approach address well and not so well?
4. Considering the two methods outlined, what types of validity would you consider to be demonstrated by the two approaches to measuring quality? Defend your position.
5. Which of the methods should Wesley recommend? Why?

Case 13.3 *Money Magazine:* The Best Places to Live in 1998[14]

IF YOU COULD LIVE ANYWHERE IN THE UNITED STATES, where would it be? San Francisco? New York City? Denver? Various surveys, such as *Rand McNally's Places Rated Almanac,* have attempted to identify the most livable metropolitan areas, but those previous lists have a serious flaw: They do not give extra weight to the key characteristics—such as safety, the weather, the local economy—that are most important to the public. Instead, they assume everyone cares equally about all factors.

In reality, of course, different factors do matter more or less to different people. With that in mind, *Money's* editors annually set out to determine what characteristics its readers prize. They then ranked 300 metropolitan areas by readers' preferences.

Specifically, *Money's* 1998 survey methodology involved hiring the research firm Roper/Starch Worldwide to ask a statistically valid sample of *Money's* subscribers what qualities they value in a place to live. In rating the importance of 41 factors on a scale of 1 to 10, respondents said their top priorities were clean water (9.0), low crime rate (8.9), clean air (8.8), and good public schools (8.5). Least essential were proximity to skiing (3.4), local symphony (4.0), and minor league sports.

Next, with assistance from Fast Forward, a Portland, Oregon, demographic consulting firm, *Money* collected the most timely data available on each of the 300 largest U.S. metropolitan statistical areas, as defined by the U.S. Office of Management and Budget. The data come from the government as well as from private firms (housing permits from the U.S. Housing Markets report; cost-of-living figures from the American Chamber of Commerce Researchers Association; hospitals with low mortality rates from the *Consumers' Guide to Hospitals;* environmental rankings from *The Green Index;* top restaurants from *The Mobil Guide;* and the abundance of orchestras from *Symphony* magazine).

Once the survey and data were together, *Money* crunched the numbers and gave each place a score based on how it fared on the quality-of-life factors. The things Americans consider most important, such as clean air and water, low crime, and good schools, received extra weight in this calculation; factors that didn't matter so much, such as nearby skiing facilities and symphony orchestras, had less of an impact on a place's total score.

In the 1998 survey, the best places were ranked by region of the country. Case Exhibit 13.3–1 lists the top places to live. Additional information may be found at http://pathfinder.com/money/bestplaces/.

QUESTIONS

1. Do you believe that this measure is reliable? What procedures might be used to test reliability?
2. Do you believe that this measure is valid? What procedures might be used to test validity?

Case Exhibit 13.3-1 The Top Places to Live

Midwest	Northeast
Minneapolis, MN (large)	**Washington, DC** (large)
Madison, WI (meduim)	**Trenton, NJ** (meduim)
Rochester, MN (small)	**Manchester, NH** (small)

West	South
Seattle, WA (large)	**Norfolk, VA** (large)
Boulder, CO (meduim)	**Richmond, VA** (meduim)
Fort Collins, CO (small)	**Charlottesville, VA** (small)

Chapter 14

Attitude Measurement

ATTITUDES OF NEWLY MARRIED WOMEN INDICATE THAT MARRIAGE is hot again. A *Redbook* magazine survey of young married women uncovers that the "new wife" is a woman who isn't surprised by the responsibilities of marriage (40 percent), believes she married at the right time (74 percent), and says the ideal age to marry is 26 years old.[1] Newly married women are going into marriage with a different approach and different expectations than their mothers. They take a proactive attitude and value flexibility in their marriage, all the while continuing to hold on to their own identity.

If her husband asks her to, she's willing to make even a major change for the sake of the marriage such as relocating—so long as it involves and affects both of them and their relationship (80 percent would go to a marriage counselor, 73 percent would relocate). But she won't change herself simply because he asked her to (just 36 percent would quit their jobs; only 35 percent would change the kinds of clothes they wear; and only 30 percent would try to gain or lose weight if they thought they looked fine).

Offered a job that entailed moving, 53 percent would "gladly" turn it down if their husbands didn't want to go. However, wives would leave the marriage if abused verbally (50 percent), abused physically (88 percent), cheated on (65 percent), and almost a quarter (22 percent) if they had serious differences in raising their children.

Almost half (47 percent) of the respondents see Jamie and Paul on television's *Mad About You* as the ideal couple. Paul Newman and Joanne Woodward take second (35 percent) with Tom Cruise and Nicole Kidman ranking third (31 percent).

Fifty-six percent say it's fine to flirt with other men (although slightly less [47 percent] would tell their

husbands they did it). And while 64 percent wouldn't cheat on their husbands with any man, 21 percent say they might if it were Mel Gibson, 18 percent would if it were Tom Cruise, and 14 percent would if it were Brad Pitt.

The most frequent arguments she has with her husband is about money (47 percent). The second most frequent argument is about his lack of communication (36 percent) followed by household chores (32 percent). She really doesn't like to put up with cigarette smoking (47 percent), cigar smoking (43 percent), or flirting (60 percent).

Understanding the attitudes of members of target markets, such as newly married women, is a vital aspect of marketing. Investigating how to measure attitudes—a common marketing activity—is the subject of this chapter.

Attitudes Defined

attitude
An enduring disposition to consistently respond in a given manner to various aspects of the world; composed of affective, cognitive, and behavioral components.

There are many definitions of *attitude*. **Attitude** usually is viewed as an enduring disposition to consistently respond in a given manner to various aspects of the world, including persons, events, and objects. One conception of attitude is reflected in this brief statement: "Sally loves shopping at Sam's. She believes it's clean, conveniently located, and has the lowest prices. She intends to shop there every Thursday." This short description has identified three components of attitudes: affective, cognitive, and behavioral. The affective component reflects an individual's general feelings of emotions toward an object. Statements such as "I love my Chevrolet Corvette," "I liked that book *A Corporate Bestiary*," or "I hate cranberry juice" reflect the emotional character of attitudes. The way one feels about a product, advertisement, or other object is usually tied to one's *beliefs* or *cognitions*. The cognitive component represents one's awareness of and knowledge about an object. One person might feel happy about the purchase of an automobile because she believes "it gets great gas mileage" or knows that the dealer is "the best in New Jersey." The behavioral component reflects buying intentions and behavioral expectations. This component reflects a predisposition to action.

Attitudes as Hypothetical Constructs

hypothetical construct
A variable that is not directly observable but is measurable by an indirect means, such as verbal expression or overt behavior.

Many variables that marketing researchers wish to investigate are psychological variables that cannot be directly observed. For example, someone may have an attitude toward a particular brand of shaving cream, but we cannot observe this attitude. To measure an attitude, we must infer from the way an individual responds (by a verbal expression or overt behavior) to some stimulus. The term **hypothetical construct** describes a variable that is not directly observable but is measurable by an indirect means such as verbal expression or overt behavior.

Measuring Attitudes Is Important to Managers

Most marketing managers hold the intuitive belief that changing consumers' or prospects' attitudes toward a product is a major marketing goal. At the individual level this is a complicated issue; however, aggregate attitude change has been shown to be related to aggregate sales volume changes. Because modifying attitudes plays a pervasive role in marketing strategies, the measurement of attitudes is an important task. For example, Whiskas brand cat food had been sold

EXPLORING RESEARCH ISSUES

A Hypothetical Construct Is Never Having to Say You're Sorry— Or, Love Is a Four-Letter Word

LOVE IS A FOUR-LETTER WORD. AND A HYPOTHETICAL construct, that is, a term that psychologists use to describe or explain consistent patterns of human behavior. Love, hate, thirst, learning, intelligence—all of these are hypothetical constructs. They are hypothetical in that they do not exist as physical entities; therefore, they cannot be seen, heard, felt, or measured directly. There is no love center in the brain that, if removed, would leave a person incapable of responding positively and affectionately toward other people and things. Love and hate are constructs in that we invent these terms to explain why, for instance, a young man spends all his time with one young woman while completely avoiding another. From a scientific point of view, we might be better off if we said that this young man's behavior suggested that he had a relatively enduring, positive-approach attitude toward the first woman, and a negative-avoidance attitude toward the second.

in Europe market by Mars' Pedigree Petfoods division for 30 years. Over time as the brand faced increased competition from new premium brands consumers had difficulty identifying with the brand. The company conducted attitude research to determine how people felt about their cats and their food alternatives. The study revealed that cat owners see their pets as both independent and dependent fragile being.[2] Cat owners held the attitude that cats wanted to enjoy their food but they needed nutrition. This attitude research was directly channeled into managerial action. Whiskas marketers begin positioning its product as having "Catisfaction" because of the owner's concern. Its advertisements feature a purring kitty, a silver tabby—a pedigreed cat—which symbolizes premium quality but also presents the image of a sweet cat. The message: "Give cats what they like with the nutrition they need. If you do, they'll be so happy for you that they'll purr for you." This effort reversed the sales decline the brand had been experiencing.

The Attitude-Measuring Process

A remarkable variety of techniques have been devised to measure attitudes. This stems in part from lack of consensus about the exact definition of the concept. Furthermore, the affective, cognitive, and behavioral components of an attitude may be measured by different means. For example, sympathetic nervous system responses may be recorded using physiological measures to quantify affect, but they are not good measures of behavioral intentions. Direct verbal statements concerning affect, belief, or behavior are used to measure behavioral intent. However, attitudes may also be measured indirectly using the qualitative exploratory techniques discussed in Chapter 6. Obtaining verbal statements from respondents generally requires that the respondents perform a task such as ranking, rating, sorting, or making choices.

A **ranking** task requires the respondent to rank order a small number of

ranking
A measurement task that requires respondents to rank order a small number of stores, brands, or objects in overall preference or on the basis of some characteristic of the stimulus.

rating
A measurement task that requires respondents to estimate the magnitude of a characteristic or quality that a brand, store, or object possesses.

sorting
A measurement task that presents a respondent with several objects or with information typed on cards and requires the respondent to arrange the objects or cards into a number of piles or otherwise classify the product concepts.

choice
A measurement task that identifies preferences by requiring respondents to choose between two or more alternatives.

stores, brands, or objects in overall preference or on the basis of some characteristic of the stimulus. **Rating** asks the respondent to estimate the magnitude of a characteristic or quality that an object possesses. A quantitative score, along a continuum that has been supplied to the respondent, is used to estimate the strength of the attitude or belief; in other words the respondent indicates the position on one or more scales at which he or she would rate the object. A **sorting** task might present the respondent with several product concepts printed on cards and require the respondent to arrange the cards into a number of piles or otherwise classify the product concepts. **Choice** between two or more alternatives is another type of attitude measurement. If a respondent chooses one object over another, the researcher can assume that the chosen object is preferred over the other. The following sections describe the most popular techniques for measuring attitudes.

Physiological Measures of Attitudes

Galvanic skin response, measures of blood pressure, pupil dilations, and other physiological measures may be used to assess the affective components of attitudes. These measures provide a means of measuring attitudes without verbally questioning the respondent. In general these measures can provide a gross measure of like or dislike, but they are not extremely sensitive measures for identifying the different gradients of an attitude. Each of these measures is discussed elsewhere in the text.

Attitude Rating Scales

Using rating scales to measure attitudes is perhaps the most common practice in marketing research. This section discusses many rating scales designed to enable respondents to report the intensity of their attitudes.

Simple Attitude Scaling

In its most basic form, attitude scaling requires that an individual agree with a statement or respond to a single question. For example, respondents in a political poll may be asked whether they agree or disagree with the statement "The president should run for re-election." An individual might indicate whether he or she likes or dislikes jalapeño bean dip. This type of self-rating scale merely classifies respondents into one of two categories; thus, it has only the properties of a nominal scale and limits the type of mathematical analysis that may be used with the simplified or basic scale.

Despite the disadvantages, simple attitude scaling may be used when questionnaires are extremely long, when respondents have little education, or for other specific reasons. A number of simplified scales are merely checklists: A respondent indicates past experience, preference, and the like merely by checking an item. In many cases the items are adjectives that describe a particular object.

Most attitude theorists believe that attitudes vary along continua. Early attitude researchers pioneered the view that the task of attitude scaling is to measure the distance between "good to bad," "low to high," "like to dislike," and so on. Thus, the purpose of an attitude scale is to find an individual's position on the continuum. If this is the case, these simple scales do not allow for fine distinctions between attitudes. Several other scales for making these more precise measurements have been developed.

Category Scales

The example just given is a rating scale that contains only two response categories: agree/disagree. Expanding the response categories provides the respondent with more flexibility in the rating task. Even more information is provided if the categories are ordered according to a particular descriptive or evaluative dimension. Consider the following question:

How often do you disagree with your spouse about how much to spend on various things?

☐ **Never**   ☐ **Rarely**   ☐ **Sometimes**   ☐ **Often**   ☐ **Very often**

This **category scale** is a more sensitive measure than a scale that has only two response categories; it provides more information.

Question wording is an extremely important factor in the usefulness of these scales. Exhibit 14.1 shows some common wordings for category scales. The issue of question wording is evaluated in Chapter 15 and its appendix, Question Wording and Measurement Scales for Commonly Researched Topics.

category scale
A rating scale that consists of several response categories, often providing respondents with alternatives to indicate positions on a continuum.

Method of Summated Ratings: The Likert Scale

Marketing researchers' adaptation of the method of summated ratings developed by Likert is an extremely popular means for measuring attitudes because it is simple to administer.[3] With the **Likert scale,** respondents indicate their attitudes by checking how strongly they agree or disagree with carefully constructed statements ranging from very positive to very negative attitudes toward some object. Individuals generally choose from approximately five response alternatives: strongly agree, agree, uncertain, disagree, and strongly disagree. The number of alternatives may range from three to nine.

Consider the following example from a study of food shopping behavior:

In buying food for my family, price is no object.

Strongly disagree	**Disagree**	**Uncertain**	**Agree**	**Strongly agree**
(1)	**(2)**	**(3)**	**(4)**	**(5)**

Likert scale
A measure of attitudes designed to allow respondents to rate how strongly they agree or disagree with carefully constructed statements; several scale items ranging from very positive to very negative toward an attitudinal object may be used to form a summated index.

To measure the attitude, researchers assign scores or weights to the alternative responses. In this example weights of 5, 4, 3, 2, and 1 are assigned. (The weights, shown in parentheses, would not be printed on the questionnaire.) Strong agreement indicates the most favorable attitudes on the statement, and a weight of 5 is assigned to this response. The statement used as an example is positive toward the attitude. If a negative statement toward the object (such as "I carefully budget my food expenditures") were given, the weights would be reversed, and "strongly disagree" would be assigned a weight of 5. A single scale item on a summated scale is an ordinal scale.

Exhibit 14.1 **Selected Category Scales**

QUALITY

| Excellent | Good | Fair | Poor | |
| Very good | Fairly good | Neither good nor bad | Not very good | Not good at all |

IMPORTANCE

| Very important | Fairly important | Neutral | Not so important | Not at all important |

INTEREST

| Very interested | | Somewhat interested | | Not very interested |

SATISFACTION

| Completely satisfied | Somewhat satisfied | Neither satisfied nor dissatisfied | Somewhat dissatisfied | Completely dissatisfied |
| Very satisfied | Quite satisfied | | Somewhat satisfied | Not at all satisfied |

FREQUENCY

All of the time	Very often	Often	Sometimes	Hardly ever
Very often	Often	Sometimes	Rarely	Never
All of the time	Most of the time		Some of the time	Just now and then

TRUTH

| Very true | Somewhat true | | Not very true | Not at all true |
| Definitely yes | Probably yes | | Probably no | Definitely no |

UNIQUENESS

| Very different | Somewhat different | | Slightly different | Not at all different |
| Extremely unique | Very unique | Somewhat unique | Slightly unique | Not at all unique |

A Likert scale may include several scale items to form an index. Each statement is assumed to represent an aspect of a common attitudinal domain. For example, Exhibit 14.2 shows the items in a Likert scale for measuring attitudes toward patients' interaction with a physician's service staff. The total score is the summation of the weights assigned to an individual's total responses. Here the maximum possible score for the index would be 20 if a 5 were assigned to "strongly agree" responses for each of the positively worded statements and a 5 to "strongly disagree" responses for the negative statement. (Item 3 is negatively worded and therefore is reverse coded.)

In Likert's original procedure, a large number of statements are generated and an *item analysis* is performed. The purpose of the item analysis is to ensure that final items evoke a wide response and discriminate among those with positive and negative attitudes. Items that are poor because they lack clarity or elicit mixed response patterns are eliminated from the final statement list. However,

---

Exhibit 14.2 Likert Scale Items for Measuring Attitudes Toward Patients'
Interaction with a Physician's Service Staff

1. My doctor's office staff takes a warm and personal interest in me.

2. My doctor's office staff is friendly and courteous.

3. My doctor's office staff is more interested in serving the doctor's needs than in serving my needs.

4. My doctor's office staff always acts in a professional manner.

---

many marketing researchers do not follow the exact procedure prescribed by Likert. Hence, a disadvantage of the Likert-type summated rating method is that it is difficult to know what a single summated score means. Many patterns of response to the various statements can produce the same total score. Thus, identical total scores may reflect different *attitudes* because of different combinations of statements endorsed.

Semantic Differential

The **semantic differential** is actually a series of attitude scales. This popular attitude measurement technique consists of the identification of a product, brand, store, or other concept followed by a series of 7-point bipolar rating scales. Bipolar adjectives, such as "good" and "bad," "modern" and "old-fashioned," or "clean" and "dirty," anchor the beginning and the end (or poles) of the scale. The subject makes repeated judgments of the concept under investigation on each of the scales. Exhibit 14.3 shows a series of scales to measure attitudes toward jazz saxophone recordings.

semantic differential
A measure of attitudes that consists of a series of 7-point rating scales that use bipolar adjectives to anchor the beginning and end of each scale.

The scoring of the semantic differential can be illustrated using the scale bounded by the anchors "modern" and "old-fashioned." Respondents are instructed to check the place that indicates the nearest appropriate adjective. From left to right, the scale intervals are interpreted as "extremely modern," "very modern," "slightly modern," "both modern and old-fashioned," "slightly old-fashioned," and "extremely old-fashioned":

Modern—:—:—:—:—:—:—Old-fashioned

The semantic differential technique originally was developed by Osgood and others as a method for measuring the meanings of objects or the "semantic

---

Exhibit 14.3 Semantic Differential Scales for Measuring
Attitude Toward Jazz Saxophone Recordings

Fast—:—:—:—:—:—:—Slow

Intellectual—:—:—:—:—:—:—Emotional

Contemporary—:—:—:—:—:—:—Traditional

Composed—:—:—:—:—:—:—Improvised

Flat—:—:—:—:—:—:—Sharp

Busy—:—:—:—:—:—:—Lazy

New—:—:—:—:—:—:—Old

Progressive—:—:—:—:—:—:—Regressive

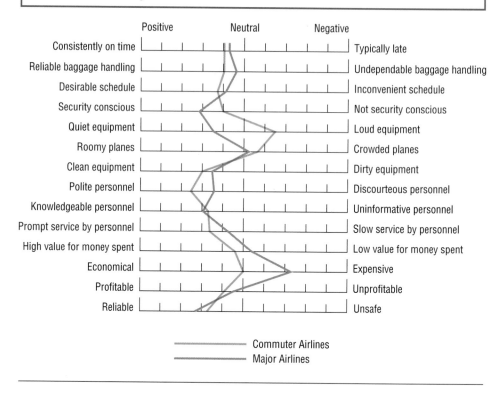

Exhibit 14.4 **Image Profile of Commuter Airlines versus Major Airlines**

	Positive	Neutral	Negative	
Consistently on time				Typically late
Reliable baggage handling				Undependable baggage handling
Desirable schedule				Inconvenient schedule
Security conscious				Not security conscious
Quiet equipment				Loud equipment
Roomy planes				Crowded planes
Clean equipment				Dirty equipment
Polite personnel				Discourteous personnel
Knowledgeable personnel				Uninformative personnel
Prompt service by personnel				Slow service by personnel
High value for money spent				Low value for money spent
Economical				Expensive
Profitable				Unprofitable
Reliable				Unsafe

——————— Commuter Airlines
——————— Major Airlines

space" of interpersonal experience.[4] Marketing researchers have found the semantic differential versatile and have modified its use for business applications. Replacing the bipolar adjectives with descriptive phrases is a frequent adaptation in image studies. The phrases "aged a long time," "not aged a long time," "not watery looking," and "watery looking" were used in a beer brand image study.

A savings and loan might use the phrases "low interest on savings" and "favorable interest on savings." These phrases are not polar opposites. Consumer researchers have found that respondents often are unwilling to use the extreme negative side of a scale. Research with industrial salespeople, for example, found that in rating their own performances, salespeople would not use the negative side of the scale. Hence, it was eliminated, and the anchor opposite the positive anchor showed "satisfactory" rather than "extremely poor" performance.

A weight is assigned to each position on the rating scale. Traditionally scores are 7, 6, 5, 4, 3, 2, 1, or +3, +2, + 1, 0, -1, -2, -3. Many marketing researchers find it desirable to assume that the semantic differential provides interval data. This assumption, although widely accepted, has its critics who argue that the data have only ordinal properties because the weights are arbitrary.

image profile

A graphic representation of semantic differential data for competing brands, products, or stores to highlight comparisons.

Exhibit 14.4 illustrates a typical **image profile** based on semantic differential data. Depending on whether the data are assumed to be interval or ordinal, the arithmetic mean or the median will be used to compare the profile of one product, brand, or store with that of a competing product, brand, or store.

Numerical Scales

Numerical scales have numbers as response options, rather than semantic space or verbal descriptions, to identify categories (response positions). For example, if the scale items have five response positions, the scale is called a 5-point numerical scale; with seven response positions, it is called a 7-point numerical scale; and so on.

Consider the following numerical scale:

> **Now that you've had your automobile for about 1 year, please tell us how satisfied you are with your Ford Taurus.**
>
> **Extremely satisfied 7 6 5 4 3 2 1 Extremely dissatisfied**

This numerical scale uses bipolar adjectives in the same manner as the semantic differential. In practice researchers have found that educated populations provide numerical labels for intermediate points on the scale that constitute as effective a measure as the true semantic differential.

numerical scale
An attitude rating scale similar to a semantic differential except that it uses numbers as response options instead of verbal descriptions to identify response positions.

Stapel Scale

The **Stapel scale** was originally developed in the 1950s to measure simultaneously the direction and intensity of an attitude. Modern versions of the scale use a single adjective as a substitute for the semantic differential when it is difficult to create pairs of bipolar adjectives. The modified Stapel scale places a single adjective in the center of an even number of numerical values (ranging, perhaps, from +3 to -3). It measures how close to or distant from the adjective a given stimulus is perceived to be. Exhibit 14.5 illustrates a Stapel scale item used in a measurement of a retailer's store image.

The advantages and disadvantages of the Stapel scale are very similar to those for the semantic differential. However, the Stapel scale is markedly easi-

Stapel scale
A measure of attitudes that consists of a single adjective in the center of an even-number range of numerical values.

Exhibit 14.5 A Stapel Scale for Measuring a Store's Image

Bloomingdale's
+3
+2
+1
Wide Selection
-1
-2
-3

Select a *plus* number for words that you think describe the store accurately. The more accurately you think the word describes the store, the larger the plus number you should choose. Select a *minus* number for words you think do not describe the store accurately. The less accurately you think the word describes the store, the larger the minus number you should choose; therefore, you can select any number from +3 for words that you think are very accurate all the way to -3 for words that you think are very inaccurate.

er to administer, especially over the telephone. Because the Stapel scale does not call for the construction of bipolar adjectives, as does the semantic differential, it is easier to construct. Research comparing the semantic differential with the Stapel scale indicates that results from the two techniques are largely the same.[5]

Constant-Sum Scale

Suppose United Parcel Service (UPS) wishes to determine the importance of the attributes of accurate invoicing, delivery as promised, and price to organizations that use its service in business-to-business marketing. Respondents might be asked to divide a constant sum to indicate the relative importance of the attributes. For example:

> **Divide 100 points among the following characteristics of a delivery service according to how important each characteristic is to you when selecting a delivery company.**
>
> **Accurate invoicing** _____
>
> **Delivery as promised** _____
>
> **Lower price** _____

constant-sum scale
A measure of attitudes in which respondents are asked to divide a constant sum to indicate the relative importance of attributes; respondents often sort cards, but this may also be a rating task.

This **constant-sum scale** works best with respondents who have higher educational levels. If respondents follow the instructions correctly, the results will approximate interval measures. As the number of stimuli increase, this technique becomes increasingly complex.

Brand preference may be measured using this technique in a manner similar to the paired-comparison method, as follows:

> **Divide 100 points among each of the following brands according to your preference for the brand:**
>
> **Brand A** _____
>
> **Brand B** _____
>
> **Brand C** _____

The constant-sum scale as described here is a rating technique. However, with minor modifications it can be classified as a sorting technique.

Graphic Rating Scales

graphic rating scale
A measure of attitude that allows respondents to rate an object by choosing any point along a graphic continuum.

A **graphic rating scale** presents respondents with a graphic continuum. The respondents are allowed to choose any point on the continuum to indicate their attitude. The scale illustrated in Exhibit 14.6 shows a traditional graphic scale, ranging from one extreme position to the opposite position. Typically a respondent's score is determined by measuring the length (in millimeters) from one end of the graphic continuum to the point marked by the respondent. Many researchers believe that scoring in this manner strengthens the assumption that graphic rating scales of this type are interval scales. Alternatively, the researcher may divide the line into predetermined scoring categories (lengths) and record respondents' marks accordingly. In other words the graphic rating scale has the advantage of allowing the researcher to choose any interval desired for scoring purposes. The disadvantage of the graphic rating scale is that there are no standard answers.

Exhibit 14.6 **Graphic Rating Scale**

Please evaluate each attribute in terms of how important it is to you by placing an X at the position on the horizontal line that most reflects your feelings.

Seating comfort	Not important	_____	Very important
In-flight meals	Not important	_____	Very important
Airfare	Not important	_____	Very important

Graphic rating scales are not limited to straight lines as sources of visual communication. The purpose of a graphic rating scale with picture response options or other type of graphic continuum is to enhance communication with respondents. A frequently used variation is the ladder scale, which also includes numerical options:

> Here is a ladder scale. [Respondent is shown Exhibit 14.7.] It represents the "ladder of life." As you see, it is a ladder with 11 rungs numbered 0 to 10. Let's suppose the top of the ladder represents the best possible life for you as you describe it, and the bottom rung represents the worst possible life for you as you describe it.
> **On which rung of the ladder do you feel your life is today?**

0 1 2 3 4 5 6 7 8 9 10

Exhibit 14.7 **A Ladder Scale**

Best Possible Life

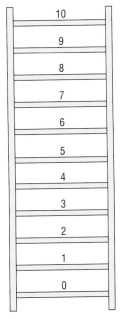

Worst Possible Life

Exhibit 14.8 Graphic Rating Scales with Picture Response Categories that Stress Visual Communication

Happy Face Scale

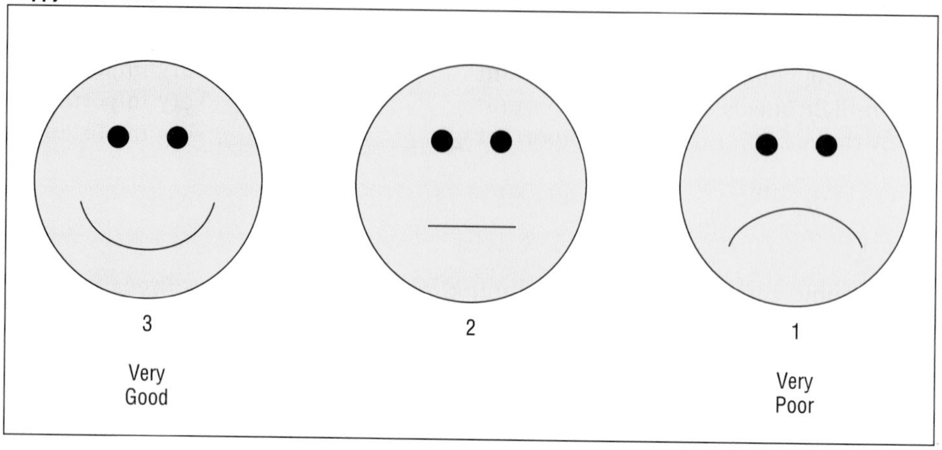

3	2	1
Very Good		Very Poor

Research to investigate children's attitudes has used happy face scales (see Exhibit 14.8). The children are asked to indicate which face shows how they feel about candy, a toy, or some other concept. Research with the happy face scale indicates that children tend to choose the faces at the ends of the scale. Although this may be because children's attitudes may fluctuate more widely than adults' or because they have stronger feelings both positively and negatively, it is a disadvantage of the scale.

Thurstone Interval Scale

Thurstone scale
An attitude scale in which judges assign scale values to the attitudinal statements and subjects are asked to respond to these statements.

In 1927 attitude research pioneer Louis Thurstone developed the concept that attitudes vary along continua and should be measured accordingly. The construction of the **Thurstone scale** is a rather complex process that requires two stages. The first stage is a ranking operation performed by judges who assign scale values to attitudinal statements. The second stage consists of asking subjects to respond to the attitudinal statements.

The Thurstone method is time consuming and costly. From a historical perspective it is very valuable, but its current popularity is low. It is rarely used in most applied marketing research and will not be discussed here.

Exhibit 14.9 summarizes the attitude-rating techniques discussed in this section.

Measuring Behavioral Intention

The behavioral component of an attitude involves the behavioral expectations of an individual toward an attitudinal object. Typically this represents a buying intention, a tendency to seek additional information, or plans to visit a show-

Exhibit 14.9 Summary of Advantages and Disadvantages of Rating Scales

RATING MEASURE	SUBJECT MUST	ADVANTAGES	DISADVANTAGES
Category scale	Indicate a response category	Flexible, easy to respond	Items may be ambiguous; with few categories, only gross distinctions can be made
Likert scale	Evaluate statements on a 5-point scale	Easiest scale to construct	Hard to judge what a single score means
Semantic differential and numerical scales	Choose points between bipolar adjectives on relevant dimensions	Easy to construct; norms exist for comparison, such as profile analysis	Bipolar adjectives must be found; data may be ordinal, not interval
Constant-sum scale	Divide a constant sum among response alternatives	Scale approximates an interval measure	Difficult for respondents with low education levels
Stapel scale	Choose points on a scale with a single adjective in the center	Easier to construct than semantic differential, easy to administer	Endpoints are numerical, not verbal, labels
Graphic scale	Choose a point on a continuum	Visual impact, unlimited scale points	No standard answers
Graphic scale— picture response	Choose a visual picture	Visual impact, easy for poor readers	Hard to attach a verbal explanation to a response

room. Category scales for measuring the behavioral component of an attitude ask about a respondent's likelihood of purchase or intention to perform some future action, such as:

How likely is it that you will purchase a MP3 player?

☐ **I definitely will buy**

☐ **I probably will buy**

☐ **I might buy**

☐ **I probably will not buy**

☐ **I definitely will not buy**

I would write a letter to my representative in Congress or other government official in support of this company if it were in a dispute with government.

☐ **Extremely likely**

☐ **Very likely**

☐ **Somewhat likely**

☐ **Likely, about a 50-50 chance**

☐ **Somewhat unlikely**

☐ **Very unlikely**

☐ **Extremely unlikely**

The wording of statements used in these scales often includes phrases such as "I would recommend," "I would write," or "I would buy" to indicate action tendencies.

A scale of subjective probabilities, ranging from 100 for "absolutely certain" to 0 for "absolutely no chance," may be used to measure expectations. Researchers have used the following subjective probability scale to estimate the chance that a job candidate will accept a sales position:

_____	100%	(Absolutely certain) I will accept
_____	90%	(Almost sure) I will accept
_____	80%	(Very big chance) I will accept
_____	70%	(Big chance) I will accept
_____	60%	(Not so big a chance) I will accept
_____	50%	(About even) I will accept
_____	40%	(Smaller chance) I will accept
_____	30%	(Small chance) I will accept
_____	20%	(Very small chance) I will accept
_____	10%	(Almost certainly not) I will accept
_____	0	(Certainly not) I will accept

Behavioral Differential

behavioral differential
A rating scale instrument similar to a semantic differential developed to measure the behavioral intentions of subjects toward future actions.

A general instrument, the **behavioral differential,** is used to measure the behavioral intentions of subjects toward any object or category of objects. As in the semantic differential, a description of the object to be judged is placed on the top of a sheet and the subjects indicate their behavioral intentions toward this object on a series of scales. For example, one item might be:

A 25-year-old female sales representative

Would—:—:—:—:—:—:—:—:Would not

Ask this person for advice.

Ranking

Consumers often rank order their preferences. An ordinal scale may be developed by asking respondents to rank order (from most preferred to least preferred) a set of objects or attributes. Respondents easily understand the task of *rank ordering* the importance of product attributes or arranging a set of brand names according to preference.

TO THE POINT

My tastes are very simple. I only want the best.

OSCAR WILDE

Paired Comparisons

Some time ago a chain saw manufacturer learned that a competitor had introduced a new lightweight (6-1/2-pound) chain saw. The manufacturer's lightest chain saw weighed 9-1/2 pounds. Executives wondered if they needed to introduce a 6-pound chain saw into the product line. The research design chosen was a **paired comparison**. A 6-pound chain saw was designed and a prototype built. To control for color preferences, the competitor's chain saw was painted the same color as the 9-1/2- and 6-pound chain saws. Respondents were presented with two chain saws at a time, then asked to pick the one they preferred. Three pairs of comparisons were required to determine the most preferred chain saw.

The following question illustrates the typical format for asking about paired comparisons.[6]

> I would like to know your overall opinion of two brands of adhesive bandages. They are Curad and Band-Aid. Overall, which of these two brands—Curad or Band-Aid—do you think is the better one? Or are both the same?
>
> Curad is better _____
>
> Band-Aid is better _____
>
> They are the same _____

If researchers wish to compare four brands of pens on the basis of attractiveness or writing quality, six comparisons $[(n)(n - 1)/2]$ will be necessary.

Ranking objects with respect to one attribute is not difficult if only a few products or advertisements are compared. As the number of items increases, the number of comparisons increases geometrically. If the number of comparisons is too large, respondents may fatigue and no longer carefully discriminate among them.

paired comparison
A measurement technique that consists of presenting the respondent with two objects and asking the respondent to pick the preferred object. Two or more objects may be presented, but comparisons are made in pairs.

Sorting

Sorting tasks require that respondents indicate their attitudes or beliefs by arranging items on the basis of perceived similarity or some other attribute. Researchers at the BBDO advertising agency have consumers sort photographs of people to measure their perceptions of a brand's typical user. R. H. Bruskin Associates uses a sorting technique called AIM (Association-Identification-Measurement), which consists of cards from a deck of 52. Each card reflects an element from advertising for the brand name being measured. This omnibus service measures how well customers associate and identify these elements with a particular product, company, or advertising campaign.[7] The following condensed interviewer instructions illustrate how sorting is used in the AIM survey:

> **Thoroughly shuffle deck.**
>
> **Hand respondent deck.**
>
> **Ask respondent to sort cards into two piles:**
>> *Definitely Not Seen or Heard.*
>>
>> *Definitely or Possibly Seen or Heard.*

Set aside Definitely Not Seen or Heard pile.

Hand respondent the Definitely or Possibly Seen or Heard pile.

Have respondent identify the item on each card in Definitely or Possibly Seen or Heard pile.

Record on questionnaire.

A variant of the constant-sum technique uses physical counters (for example, poker chips or coins) to be divided among the items being tested. In an airline study of customer preferences the following sorting technique could be used:

Here is a sheet that lists several airlines. Next to the name of each airline is a pocket. Here are 10 cards. I would like you to put these cards in the pockets next to the airlines you would prefer to fly on your next trip. Assume that all of the airlines fly to wherever you would choose to travel. You can put as many cards as you want in front of an airline, or you can put no cards in front of an airline.

	Cards
American Airlines	_____
Delta Airlines	_____
United Airlines	_____
Southwest Airlines	_____
TWA Airlines	_____

Randomized Response Questions

randomized response questions
For dealing with sensitive topics, a research procedure that uses a random procedure to determine which of two questions a respondent will be asked to answer.

In special cases such as when respondents are asked to provide sensitive or embarrassing information in a survey, the researcher may use **randomized response questions.** To understand this procedure, it is best to start by inspecting a portion of a questionnaire from an Internal Revenue Service Survey on income tax cheating:

In this section you will be asked some questions about different things you might have done when filling out your tax return. A flip of a coin will determine which questions you are to answer. All that we will know is your answer of either "yes" or "no"; we will not know which question you are answering. I'll show you how it works in a minute, but the important thing to know is that your answers are completely anonymous. Using special kinds of statistics we will *never* know what you do. So, we hope you will be completely honest with us. Only in this way will this survey be of help to us.

For example, let's flip the coin. (HAVE EXAMPLE CARD READY.) Let's say it comes up heads. Then you will respond to the "heads" statement: "I had scrambled eggs for breakfast this morning." If you did have scrambled eggs, you would say "yes." If you did not have scrambled eggs, you would say "no." Now, the coin could come up tails and you would respond to the "tails" question: "I had potatoes for dinner last night." You would say "yes" if you did and "no" if you didn't.

1. *Heads* Sometime in the past, I have failed to file a tax return when I think I should have.

Tails I have lived in this community for over 5 years.
   Yes...1
   No...2

2. *Heads* Sometime in the past, I purposely listed more deductions than I was entitled to.
   Tails I voted in the last presidential election.
   Yes...1
   No...2

3. *Heads* Sometime in the past, I purposely failed to report some income on my tax return—even just a minor amount.
   Tails I own a car.
   Yes...1
   No...2

4. *Heads* On at least one occasion, I have added a dependent that I wasn't entitled to.
   Tails I have been to a movie within the last year.
   Yes...1
   No...2

5. *Heads* To the best of my knowledge, my tax return for [year] was filled out with absolute honesty.
   Tails I have eaten out in a restaurant within the last 6 months.
   Yes...1
   No...2

6. *Heads* I stretched the truth just a little in order to pay fewer taxes for [year].
   Tails Generally, I watch one hour or more of television each day.
   Yes...1
   No...2

This Is the End of the Interview.
Thank You Very Much for Your Cooperation.

The coin flipping randomly determines which of the two questions the respondent answers. Thus, the interviewer does not know whether the sensitive question about income tax cheating or the meaningless question is being answered because the responses "yes" or "no" are identical for both questions.

The proportion of "yes" answers to the income tax question is calculated by a formula that includes previous estimates of the proportion of respondents who answer "yes" to the meaningless question and the probability (Pr) of the meaningless question being answered:

$$Pr(\text{"yes" answer}) = Pr(\text{"yes" on question A}) + Pr(\text{"yes" on question B})$$
$$= Pr(\text{question A is chosen}) \, \yen \, Pr(\text{"yes" question A})$$
$$+ Pr(\text{question B is chosen}) \, \yen \, Pr(\text{"yes" question B})$$

Although estimates are subject to error, the respondent remains anonymous, and response bias is thereby reduced.

The randomized response method originally was applied in personal interview surveys. However, randomized response questions in a slightly modified format have been successfully applied in other situations.

Other Methods of Attitude Measurement

Attitudes, as hypothetical constructs, are not measured directly. Therefore, measurement of attitudes is to an extent subject to the imagination of the researcher. The traditional methods used for attitude measurement have been presented here, but several other techniques are discussed in the published literature (for example, the Guttman scale) that can be used when a situation dictates. Advanced students will seek out these techniques when the traditional measures do not apply to their research problems. With the growth of computer technology, techniques such as *multidimensional scaling* and *conjoint analysis* are used more frequently. These complex techniques require knowledge of multivariate statistical analysis (see Chapter 24).

Selecting a Measurement Scale: Some Practical Decisions

Now that we have illustrated a number of attitude measurement scales, a natural question arises: "Which is most appropriate?" Like the selection of a basic research design, no single best answer applies to all research projects. The answer to this question is relative, and the choice of scale will depend on the nature of the attitudinal object to be measured, the manager's problem definition, and the backward and forward linkages to choices already made (for example, telephone survey versus mail survey). However, several questions will help focus the choice of a measurement scale:

1. Is a ranking, sorting, rating, or choice technique best?
2. Should a monadic or comparative scale be used?
3. What type of category labels, if any, will be used for the rating scale?
4. How many scale categories or response positions are needed to accurately measure an attitude?
5. Should a balanced or unbalanced rating scale be chosen?
6. Should a scale that forces a choice among predetermined options be used?
7. Should a single measure or an index measure be used?

We will now discuss each of these issues.

Is a Ranking, Sorting, Rating, or Choice Technique Best?

The answer to this question is determined largely by the problem definition and especially by the type of statistical analysis desired. For example, ranking provides only ordinal data, which limits the statistical techniques that may be used.

Should a Monadic or Comparative Scale Be Used?

If a scale is other than a ratio scale, the researcher must decide whether to use a standard of comparison in the verbal portion of the scale. Consider the following rating scale:

> **Now that you've had your automobile for about 1 year, please tell us how satisfied you are with its engine power and pickup.**
>
> | Completely satisfied | Very satisfied | Fairly well satisfied | Somewhat dissatisfied | Very dissatisfied |

This is a **monadic rating scale** because it asks about a single concept (the brand of automobile the individual actually purchased) in isolation. The respondent is not given a specific frame of reference. A **comparative rating scale** asks a respondent to rate a concept, such as a specific brand, in comparison with a benchmark—perhaps another, similar concept such as a competing brand—explicitly used as a frame of reference. In many cases the comparative rating scale presents an ideal situation as a reference point for comparison with the actual situation. For example:

> **Please indicate how the amount of authority in your present position compares with the amount of authority that would be ideal for this position.**
>
> **Too much   About right   Too little**

monadic rating scale
Any measure of attitudes that asks respondents about a single concept in isolation.

comparative rating scale
Any measure of attitudes that asks respondents to rate a concept in comparison with a benchmark explicitly used as a frame of reference.

What Type of Category Labels, if Any, Will Be Used for the Rating Scale?

We have discussed verbal labels, numerical labels, and unlisted choices. Many rating scales have verbal labels for response categories because researchers believe they help respondents better understand the response positions. The maturity and educational levels of the respondents will influence this decision. The semantic differential, with unlabeled response categories between two bipolar adjectives, and the numerical scale, with numbers to indicate scale positions, often are selected because the researcher wishes to assume interval-scale data.

How Many Scale Categories or Response Positions Are Needed to Accurately Measure an Attitude?

Should a category scale have four, five, or seven response positions or categories? Or should the researcher use a graphic scale with an infinite number of positions? The original developmental research on the semantic differential indicated an optimal size of five to eight points. However, the researcher must determine the number of meaningful positions that is best for the specific project. This issue of identifying how many meaningful distinctions respondents can practically make is the same issue as sensitivity, but at the operational rather than conceptual level.

Should a Balanced or Unbalanced Rating Scale Be Chosen?

The fixed-alternative format may be **balanced** or **unbalanced.** For example, the following question, which asks about parent-child decisions relating to television program watching, is balanced:

Who decides which television programs your children watch?

Child decides all of the time.

Child decides most of the time.

Child and parent decide together.

Parent decides most of the time.

Parent decides all of the time.

balanced rating scale
A fixed-alternative rating scale with an equal number of positive and negative categories; a neutral or indifferent point is at the center of the scale.

unbalanced rating scale
A fixed-alternative rating scale that has more response categories piled up at one end and an unequal number of positive and negative categories.

Researchers face a number of attitude scaling decisions. One choice they must make is whether a balanced or unbalanced scale should be used.

These answers are balanced because a neutral or indifference point is at the center of the scale.

Unbalanced scales may be used when responses are expected to be distributed at one end of the scale. Unbalanced scales, such as the following one, may eliminate this type of "end piling":

Satisfied

Neither satisfied nor dissatisfied

Quite dissatisfied

Very dissatisfied

The nature of the concept or knowledge about attitudes toward the stimulus to be measured generally will determine the answer to this question.

Should a Scale That Forces a Choice among Predetermined Options Be Used?

forced-choice rating scale
A fixed-alternative rating scale that requires respondents to choose one of the fixed alternatives.

nonforced-choice scale
A fixed-alternative rating scale that provides a "no opinion" category or that allows the respondents to indicate that they cannot say which alternative is their choice.

In many situations a respondent has not formed an attitude toward the concept being studied and simply cannot provide an answer. If a **forced-choice rating scale** compels the respondent to answer, the response is merely a function of the question. If answers are not forced, the midpoint of the scale may be used by the respondent to indicate unawareness as well as indifference. If many respondents in the sample are expected to be unaware of the attitudinal object under investigation, this problem may be eliminated by using a **nonforced-choice scale** that provides a "no opinion" category. For example:

How does the Bank of Commerce company compare with the First
National Bank?

Bank of Commerce is better than First National Bank.

Bank of Commerce is about the same as First National Bank.

Bank of Commerce is worse than First National Bank.

Can't say.

Asking this type of question allows the investigator to separate respondents who
cannot make an honest comparison from respondents who have had experience
with both banks. The argument for forced choice is that people really do have
attitudes, even if they are unfamiliar with the banks, and should be required to
answer the question. Higher incidences of "no answer" are associated with
forced-choice questions.

TO THE POINT

Refusing to have an opinion is a way of having one, isn't it?

LUIGI PIRANDELLO

Should a Single Measure or an Index Measure Be Used?

How complex is the issue to be investigated? How many dimensions does the
issue contain? Are individual attributes of the stimulus part of a holistic attitude,
or are they seen as separate items? The researcher's conceptual definition will
be helpful in making this choice.

The researcher has many scaling options. Generally, the choice is influenced
by plans for the later stages of the research project. Again, problem definition
becomes a determining factor influencing the research design.

Summary

Attitude measurement is particularly important in marketing research. Attitudes are
enduring dispositions to consistently respond in a given manner to various aspects of
the world, including persons, events, and objects. Three components are included:
the affective, or the emotions or feelings involved; the cognitive, or awareness or
knowledge; and the behavioral, or the predisposition to action. Attitudes are hypothetical constructs; that is, they are variables that are not directly observable, but are
measurable indirectly. Many methods for measuring attitudes have been developed,
such as ranking, rating, sorting, and choice techniques.

One class of rating scales, category scales, provides several response categories to allow respondents to indicate the intensity of their attitudes. The simplest is a "yes/no" or "agree/disagree" response to a single question. The Likert
scale uses a series of statements for which subjects indicate agreement or disagreement. The responses are assigned weights that are summed to indicate the
respondents' attitudes.

The semantic differential uses a series of attitude scales anchored by bipolar
adjectives. The respondent indicates where his or her attitude falls between the

polar attitudes. Variations on this method, such as numerical scales and the Stapel scale, are also used. The Stapel scale puts a single adjective in the center of a range of numerical values from +3 to -3.

Graphic rating scales use continua by which respondents indicate their attitudes. Constant-sum scales require the respondent to divide a constant sum into parts, indicating the weights to be given to various attributes of the item being studied.

Several scales, such as the behavioral differential, have been developed to measure the behavioral component of attitude.

People often rank order their preferences. Thus, ordinal scales that ask respondents to rank order a set of objects or attributes may be developed. In the paired-comparison technique two alternatives are paired and respondents are asked to pick the preferred one. Sorting requires respondents to indicate their attitudes by arranging items into piles or categories.

The accuracy of answers to sensitive questions may be enhanced by using randomized response questions and calculations based on probability theory.

The researcher can choose among a number of attitude scales. Choosing among the alternatives requires considering several questions, each of which is generally answered by comparing the advantages of each alternative to the problem definition.

A monadic rating scale asks about a single concept. A comparative rating scale asks a respondent to rate a concept in comparison with a benchmark used as a frame of reference.

Scales may be balanced or unbalanced. Unbalanced scales prevent responses from piling up at one end. Forced-choice scales require the respondent to select an alternative; nonforced-choice scales allow an option indicating the respondent's inability to select an alternative.

Key Terms and Concepts

Attitude
Hypothetical construct
Ranking
Rating
Sorting
Choice
Category scale
Likert scale

Semantic differential
Image profile
Numerical scale
Stapel scale
Constant-sum scale
Graphic rating scale
Thurstone scale
Behavioral differential

Paired comparison
Randomized response questions
Monadic rating scale
Comparative rating scale
Balanced/unbalanced rating scale
Forced-/nonforced-choice rating
  scale

Questions for Review and Critical Thinking

1. What is an attitude? Is there a consensus concerning its definition?
2. Distinguish between rating and ranking. Which is a better attitude measurement technique? Why?
3. In what type of situation would the choice technique be most appropriate?
4. In what type of situation would the sorting technique be most appropriate?
5. What advantages do numerical scales have over semantic differential scales?

6. Identify the issues a researcher should consider when choosing a measurement scale.
7. Name some situations in which a semantic differential might be useful.
8. Should a Likert scale ever be treated as though it had ordinal properties?
9. In each of the following indicate the type of scale and evaluate it:
   a. A U.S. representative's questionnaire sent to constituents:

Do you favor or oppose a constitutional amendment to balance the budget?

☐ **Favor** ☐ **Oppose** ☐ **Don't know**

b. In an academic study on consumer behavior:

Most people who are important to me think I

-3		+3
Definitely		**Definitely**
should not buy		**should buy**

[test brand] sometime during the next week.

c. Psychographic statement:

I shop a lot for specials.

Strongly agree	Moderately agree	Neutral	Moderately disagree	Strongly disagree
5	4	3	2	1

10. What problems might complicate an attempt to use attitude measures to predict specific behavior?

11. If a Likert summated scale has 10 scale items, do all 10 items have to be phrased as either positive or negative statements, or can positive and negative statements be mixed?

12. If a semantic differential has 10 scale items, should all the positive adjectives be on the right and all the negative adjectives be on the left?

13. A researcher wishes to compare two hotels on the following attributes:

Convenience of location

Friendly personnel

Value for money

a. Design a Likert scale to accomplish this task.

b. Design a semantic differential scale to accomplish this task.

c. Design a graphic rating scale to accomplish this task.

14. A researcher thinks many respondents will answer "don't know" or "can't say" if these options are printed along with agreement categories on the attitude scale. The researcher does not print either "don't know" or "can't say" on the questionnaire because the resulting data will be less complicated to analyze and report. Is this proper?

 Exploring the Internet

SRI International investigates U.S. consumers by asking questions about their attitudes and values. It has a Web site so people on the Internet can VALS-type themselves.

To find out your VALS-type go to http://future.sri.com:
and click on the VALS icon.

Case 14.1 HA-PAH-SHU-TSE

RAYMOND REDCORN IS AN OSAGE INDIAN. THE HA-PAH-Shu-Tse (Osage for "red corn") restaurant in Pawhuska, Oklahoma, is the only authentic Native American restaurant in the state and one of few in the country.

The Ha-Pah-Shu-Tse restaurant opened in 1972 with a seating capacity of 8; today, after expansion, crowds of up to 90 keep RedCorn and his wife busy. They are currently marketing an Indian fry bread mix, and they are planning on increased sales for their only packaged good. Indian fry bread mix has long been a staple of the Native American diet. The bread is sweet and contains basic ingredients such as flour, shortening, and sugar.

The Restaurant

Waltina RedCorn married into the Osage tribe 47 years ago and learned how to cook from two women named Grandma Baconrind and Grandma Lookout. They must have taught her well because customers of the Ha-Pah-Shu-Tse are not content just to eat there—they often have the RedCorns mail them fry bread mix. Raymond RedCorn finds that people who eat the unusual native dish usually request the recipe. He says, "I have not found anyone who does not like the bread." Customers aren't limited to local fans of Indian food. Because the fry bread is sold or served in restaurants and stores in Oklahoma as well as at one museum, people from as far away as Europe have tried it.

According to RedCorn, "About once a week, someone from England comes in." He serves these British customers fry bread or the restaurant's "best sellers, Indian Meat Pie or Navaho Taco," and tells them the story of fry bread and how it got him an invitation to the Buckingham Palace. When he was 18 years old, he was in London for a Boy Scout Jamboree. One evening he was frying the Indian bread when the British Boy Scout organizer approached with two young men. It was only after everyone had tasted RedCorn's culinary effort that the Prince of Wales was introduced. "The Indian delegation from Oklahoma was invited to set up their tents on the ground at the palace and spend the weekend being entertained by the young royalty," RedCorn tells.

The Product

The product as it is today took several years to perfect. The RedCorns wanted a mix that would need only the addition of water. Each batch was sent to relatives and friends for judgment on the taste until everyone was convinced it was the best it could be.

The mix, consisting of Indian flour, is already distributed in Tulsa, Bartlesville, and surrounding towns under the Ha-Pah-Shu-Tse brand name. It is packaged in 2- and 5-pound silver bags with Raymond RedCorn pictured in Osage tribal costume. Directions for making the fry bread are listed on the back of the package.

The Research Problem

When planning the marketing for the Indian fry bread mix, student consultants working with the Small Business Administration suggested some attitude research. They felt that the success of marketing the Ha-Pah-Shu-Tse product depended on knowing what consumer reactions to Indian foods would be. They believed that if the image of Indian foods and consumers' awareness of it were measured, RedCorn would have a better chance of marketing his product. In addition the student consultants felt that the name Ha-Pah-Shu-Tse violated many of the requirements for selecting a good brand name—it was not short, simple, or easy to recall and was difficult to pronounce and spell.

Questions

1. What marketing questions must be answered as Ha-Pah-Shu-Tse plans for expansion? How can marketing research help answer those questions?

2. What type of attitude scale would you recommend? How would you generate a set of items (attributes) to be measured?

3. Does an image profile seem appropriate in this case?

Case 14.2 Porsche

AFTER SELLING A RECORD 30,000 AUTOMOBILES IN THE United States in 1986, Porsche saw its sales begin to decline, reaching a low of approximately 4,000 in 1993. During the 1980s, the price of a Porsche 911 Carrera coupe was less than the average U.S. household's annual income. But in 1993, the price was about 25 percent more because of the strength of the deutsche mark and a luxury tax passed by Congress. However, after conducting marketing research to learn which market segments were prime customers, Porsche Cars North America found out that a higher price was not the only thing that had gone wrong.

The research showed that the demographics of Porsche owners were utterly predictable: a 40-year-old male college graduate with an income of over $200,000 a year. The psychographics, however, were another aspect of the company's marketing problem. The categories of Porsche owners appear in Case Exhibit 14.2-1.

Porsche's vice president of sales and marketing found the results astonishing. He said, "We were selling to people whose profiles were diametrically opposed. You wouldn't want to tell an elitist how good he looks in the car or how fast he could go.

As a result of the new insights from its marketing research, Porsche cut its prices, launched a new advertising campaign, and introduced a redesign of its classic rear-engine car, the 911.

QUESTIONS

1. What is the meaning of psychographics?

2. What role does attitude measurement play in a psychographic study?

3. If you had designed this study, what type of attitude scales would you have selected? Why?

Case Exhibit 14.2-1 Psychographic Profile of Porsche Buyers

TYPE	PERCENTAGE OF ALL OWNERS	DESCRIPTION
Top Guns	27%	Driven, ambitious types. Power and control matter. They expect to be noticed.
Elitists	24%	Old-money blue bloods. A car is just a car; no matter how expensive. It is not an extension of personality.
Proud Patrons	23%	Ownership is an end in itself. Their car is a trophy earned for hard work, and who cares if anyone sees them in it?
Bon Vivants	17%	Worldly jet setters and thrill seekers. Their car heightens the excitement in their already passionate lives.
Fantasists	9%	Walter Mitty types. Their car is an escape. Not only are they uninterested in impressing others with it, they also feel a little guilty about owning one.

Case 14.3 Attitudes toward Technology and Lifestyle

A MARKETING RESEARCH COMPANY SENT THE FOLLOWING attitude scales to members of its consumer panel.

Below is a list of statements that may or may not be used to describe your attitudes toward technology and your lifestyle. Please indicate to what extent each statement describes your attitudes by placing an "X" in a box from "1" to "10" where "10" means that statement "Describes your attitudes completely" and a "1" means that statement "Does not describe your attitudes at all." ("X" ONE BOX ACROSS FOR EACH STATEMENT.)

Other questions on the questionnaire were about ownership and/or use of computers, consumer electronic devices, satellite TV ownership, cellular phones, and Internet activity.

QUESTIONS

1. What type of attitude scale appears in the case study?

2. Evaluate the list of statements. Do the statements appear to measure a single concept?

3. What do they appear to be measuring?

Case Exhibit 14.2-1 Psychographic Profile of Porsche Buyers

	Does Not Describe Your Attitudes At All						Describes Your Attitudes at all Completely			
	1	2	3	4	5	6	7	8	9	10
I like to impress people with my lifestyle............	☐	☐	☐	☐	☐	☐	☐	☐	☐	☐
Technology is important to me	☐	☐	☐	☐	☐	☐	☐	☐	☐	☐
I am very competitive when it comes to my career	☐	☐	☐	☐	☐	☐	☐	☐	☐	☐
Having fun is the whole point of life	☐	☐	☐	☐	☐	☐	☐	☐	☐	☐
Family is important, but I have other interests that are just as important to me	☐	☐	☐	☐	☐	☐	☐	☐	☐	☐
I am constantly looking for new ways to entertain myself...	☐	☐	☐	☐	☐	☐	☐	☐	☐	☐
Making a lot of money is important to me...........	☐	☐	☐	☐	☐	☐	☐	☐	☐	☐
I spend most of my free time doing fun stuff with my friends	☐	☐	☐	☐	☐	☐	☐	☐	☐	☐
I like to spend time learning about new technology products...	☐	☐	☐	☐	☐	☐	☐	☐	☐	☐
I like to show off my taste and style	☐	☐	☐	☐	☐	☐	☐	☐	☐	☐
I like technology...	☐	☐	☐	☐	☐	☐	☐	☐	☐	☐
My family is by far the most important thing in my life	☐	☐	☐	☐	☐	☐	☐	☐	☐	☐
I put a lot of time and energy into my career	☐	☐	☐	☐	☐	☐	☐	☐	☐	☐
I am very likely to purchase new technology products or services..	☐	☐	☐	☐	☐	☐	☐	☐	☐	☐
I spend most of my free time working on improving myself..	☐	☐	☐	☐	☐	☐	☐	☐	☐	☐

Chapter 15

Questionnaire Design

A N EARLY GALLUP POLL ILLUSTRATES THAT THE ANSWER TO A question frequently is a function of the question's wording: "People were asked if they owned any stock. A surprisingly high degree of stock ownership turned up in interviews in the Southwest where respondents were naturally thinking of livestock. The question had to be reworded to make reference to 'securities listed on any stock exchange.'"[1]

Many experts in survey research generally believe that improving the wording of questions can contribute far more to accuracy than can improvements in sampling. Experiments have shown that the range of error due to vague questions or use of ambiguous words may be as high as 20 or 30 percentage points. Consider the following illustration of the critical consideration of selecting the word with the right meaning. The questions differ only in the use of the words *should*, *could*, and *might*:

> Do you think anything **should** be done to make it easier for people to pay doctor or hospital bills?

> Do you think anything **could** be done to make it easier for people to pay doctor or hospital bills?

> Do you think anything **might** be done to make it easier for people to pay doctor or hospital bills?[2]

The results from the matched examples: 82 percent replied that something *should* be done, 77 percent that something *could* be done, and 63 percent that something *might* be done. A 19-percentage-point difference separated the two extremes *should* and *might*. Ironically this is the same percentage point error as that in the *Literary Digest* poll, which is a frequently cited example of error associated with sampling.

What you will learn in this chapter

To recognize that questionnaire design is not a simple task and that proper wording of relevant questions can immensely improve the accuracy of a survey.

To recognize that the type of information needed to answer a manager's questions will substantially influence the structure and content of a questionnaire.

To recognize that decisions about the data collection methods (mail, telephone, or personal interviews) will influence question format and questionnaire layout.

To recognize the difference between open-ended response and fixed-alternative questions.

To understand the guidelines that help prevent the most common mistakes in questionnaire design.

To discuss how the proper sequence of questions may improve the questionnaire.

To understand how to plan and design a questionnaire layout.

To understand the importance of pretesting and revising a questionnaire.

To recognize how global markets may require a special effort.

This chapter outlines a procedure for questionnaire design and illustrates that a little bit of research knowledge can be a dangerous thing.

A Survey Is Only as Good as the Questions It Asks

Each stage is important in the interdependent marketing research process. However, a marketing research survey is only as good as the questions it asks. The importance of question wording is easily overlooked, but questionnaire design is one of the most critical stages in the survey research process.

Businesspeople who are inexperienced at marketing research frequently believe that constructing a questionnaire is a simple task. Amateur researchers find it quite easy to write short questionnaires in a matter of hours. Unfortunately, newcomers who naively believe that common sense and good grammar are all one needs to construct a questionnaire generally learn that their hasty efforts are inadequate.

Although common sense and good grammar are important in question writing, the art of questionnaire design requires far more. To assume that people will understand the questions is a common error. Respondents simply may not know what is being asked. They may be unaware of the product or topic of interest. They may confuse the subject with something else. The question may not mean the same thing to everyone interviewed. Finally, they may refuse to answer personal questions. Most of these problems can be minimized, however, if a skilled researcher composes the questionnaire.

TO THE POINT

How often misused words generate misleading thoughts.

HERBERT SPENCER

Questionnaire Design: An Overview of the Major Decisions

Relevance and *accuracy* are the two basic criteria to meet if a questionnaire is to fulfill a researcher's purposes. To achieve these ends a researcher who is systematically planning to design a questionnaire will be required to make several decisions, typically, but not necessarily, in the following order:

1.   What should be asked?
2.   How should questions be phrased?
3.   In what sequence should the questions be arranged?

4. What questionnaire layout will best serve the research objectives?

5. How should the questionnaire be pretested? Does the questionnaire need to be revised?

What Should Be Asked?

Certain decisions made during the early stages of the research process will influence the questionnaire design. The preceding chapters stressed the need to have a good problem definition and clear objectives for the study. The problem definition will indicate the type of information that must be collected to answer the manager's questions; different types of questions may be better at obtaining certain types of information than others. Furthermore, the communication medium of data collection—that is, telephone interview, personal interview, or self-administered questionnaire—will have been determined. This decision is another forward linkage that influences the structure and content of the questionnaire. The specific questions to be asked will be a function of the previous decisions.

The latter stages of the research process will have an important impact on questionnaire wording. The questions that should be asked will, of course, take the form of data analysis into account. When designing the questionnaire, the researcher should consider the types of statistical analysis that will be conducted.

Questionnaire Relevancy

A questionnaire is *relevant* if no unnecessary information is collected and only the information needed to solve the marketing problem is obtained. Asking the wrong question or an irrelevant question is a common pitfall. If the marketing task is to pinpoint store image problems, asking for general information about clothing style preferences will be irrelevant. To ensure information relevance, the researcher must be specific about data needs and have a rationale for each item of information.

Many researchers, after conducting surveys, find that they omitted some important questions. Therefore, when planning the questionnaire design, researchers must think about possible omissions. Is information on the relevant demographic and psychographic variables being collected? Are there any questions that might clarify the answers to other questions? Will the results of the study provide the answer to the marketing manager's problem?

Questionnaire Accuracy

Once the researcher has decided what should be asked, the criterion of accuracy becomes the primary concern. *Accuracy* means that the information is reliable and valid. While it is generally believed that one should use simple, understandable, unbiased, unambiguous, and nonirritating words, no step-by-step procedure for ensuring accuracy in question writing can be generalized across projects. Obtaining accurate answers from respondents depends strongly on the researcher's ability to design a questionnaire that will facilitate recall and motivate respondents to cooperate. Respondents tend to be more cooperative when the subject of the research interests them. When questions are not lengthy, difficult to answer, or ego threatening, there is a higher probability of unbiased answers. Question wording and sequence also substantially influence accuracy. We will address these topics in the chapter.

How Should Questions Be Phrased?

There are many ways to phrase questions, and many standard question formats have been developed in previous research studies. This section presents a classification of question types and provides some helpful guidelines for writing questions.

Open-Ended Response versus Fixed-Alternative Questions

Two basic types of questions can be identified based on the amount of freedom respondents have in answering.

Open-ended response questions pose some problem or topic and ask respondents to answer in their own words. If the question is asked in a personal interview, the interviewer may probe for more information. For example:

> **What names of local banks can you think of offhand?**
>
> **What comes to mind when you look at this advertisement?**
>
> **In what way, if any, could this product be changed or improved? I'd like you to tell me anything you can think of, no matter how minor it seems.**
>
> **What things do you like most about Federal Express' service?**
>
> **Why do you buy more of your clothing in Nordstrom's than in other stores?**
>
> **How can our stores better serve your needs?**
>
> **Please tell me anything at all that you remember about the BMW commercial you saw last night.**

Open-ended response questions are free-answer questions. They may be contrasted with fixed-alternative questions—sometimes called *closed* questions—which give respondents specific limited alternative responses and ask them to choose the one closest to their own viewpoints. For example:

> **Did you use any commercial feed or supplement for livestock or poultry in 1999?**
>
> ☐ Yes
>
> ☐ No

> **As compared with 10 years ago, would you say that the quality of most products made in Japan is higher, about the same, or not as good?**
>
> ☐ Higher
>
> ☐ About the same
>
> ☐ Not as good

open-ended response question
A question that poses some problem and asks the respondent to answer in his or her own words.

EXPLORING RESEARCH ISSUES

What a Difference Words Make

DOES ADVERTISING LOWER OR RAISE PRICES? The wording of the question influences the answer.

Consumer Attitude Toward Distribution:

The consumer must pay more for goods because of advertising.

No	33
Yes	39
Doubtful	17
No answer	11

Consumer Attitude Toward Distribution:

Advertising may cause the consumer to pay less for a product than if it were not advertised because it increases sales and makes it possible to cut the cost of production and marketing.

Yes	52
No	18
Doubtful	20
No answer	10

Do you think the Americans with Disabilities Act has affected your business?

☐ **Yes, for the better**

☐ **Yes, for the worse**

☐ **Not especially**

In which type of store is it easier for you to shop—a regular department store or a discount department store?

☐ **Regular department store**

☐ **Discount department store**

How much of your shopping for clothes and household items do you do in wholesale club stores?

☐ **All of it**

☐ **Most of it**

☐ **About one-half of it**

☐ **About one-quarter of it**

☐ **Less than one-quarter of it**

Open-ended response questions are most beneficial when the researcher is conducting exploratory research, especially when the range of responses is not known. Such questions can be used to learn which words and phrases people spontaneously give to the free-response question. Respondents are free to answer with whatever is uppermost in their minds. By obtaining free and unin-

A questionnaire for AMF Bowling Worldwide used an adjective checklist question. Here is how people who bowl saw themselves: attractive (38%), romantic (43%), competitive (41%), and sports enthusiasts (30%). Here is how all people saw themselves: attractive (28%), romantic (35%), competitive (33%), and sports enthusiasts (23%).[3]

hibited responses, the researcher may find some unanticipated reaction toward the product. Such responses will reflect the flavor of the language that people use in talking about products or services and thus may provide a source of new ideas for advertising copywriting. Also, open-ended response questions are valuable at the beginning of an interview. They are good first questions because they allow respondents to warm up to the questioning process.

The cost of administering open-ended response questions is substantially higher than that of fixed-alternative questions because the job of editing, coding, and analyzing the data is quite extensive. As each respondent's answer is somewhat unique, there is some difficulty in categorizing and summarizing the answers. This process requires that an editor go over a sample of questions to classify the responses into a given scheme, then all the answers must be reviewed and coded according to the classification scheme.

Another potential disadvantage of the open-ended response question is the possibility that interviewer bias will influence the answer. While most interviewer instructions state that answers are to be recorded verbatim, rarely does even the best interviewer get every word spoken by the respondent. Thus, an interviewer may have a tendency to take shortcuts in recording the answers. But even a few words different from the respondent's may substantially influence the results; the final answer thus may combine the respondent's and interviewer's ideas rather than the respondent's ideas alone. Also, when using open-ended response questions, articulate individuals tend to give longer answers. Such respondents often are better educated and from higher income groups and therefore may not be representative of the entire population.

fixed-alternative question
A question in which the respondent is given specific, limited-alternative responses and asked to choose the one closest to his or her own viewpoint.

In contrast, **fixed-alternative questions** require less interviewer skill, take less time, and are easier for the respondent to answer. This is because answers to closed questions must be classified into standardized groupings prior to data collection. Standardizing alternative responses to a question provides comparability of answers, which facilitates coding and tabulating, and ultimately interpreting the data.

Types of Fixed-Alternative Questions.

Earlier we saw a variety of fixed-alternative questions. We will now identify and categorize the various types.

The **simple-dichotomy,** or **dichotomous-alternative, question** requires the respondent to choose one of two alternatives. The answer can be a simple "yes" or "no" or a choice between "this" and "that." For example:

Did you make any long-distance calls last week?

☐ Yes   ☐ No

Several types of questions provide the respondent with *multiple-choice alternatives.* The **determinant-choice question** requires the respondent to choose one—and only one—response from among several possible alternatives. For example:

Please give us some information about your flight. In which section of the aircraft did you sit?

☐ First class

☐ Business class

☐ Coach class

The **frequency-determination question** is a determinant-choice question that asks for an answer about the general frequency of occurrence. For example:

How frequently do you watch the MTV television channel?

☐ Every day

☐ 5–6 times a week

☐ 2–4 times a week

☐ Once a week

☐ Less than once a week

☐ Never

Attitude rating scales, such as the Likert scale, semantic differential, Stapel scale, and so on, are also fixed-alternative questions. These were discussed in Chapter 14.

The **checklist question** allows the respondent to provide multiple answers to a single question. The respondent indicates past experience, preference, and the like merely by checking off items. In many cases the choices are adjectives that describe a particular object. A typical checklist question might ask:

Please check which of the following sources of information about investments you regularly use, if any.

☐ Personal advice of your broker(s)

☐ Brokerage newsletters

☐ Brokerage research reports

☐ Investment advisory service(s)

☐ Conversations with other investors

☐ Internet Web page

☐ None of these

☐ Other (please specify)———

simple-dichotomy (dichotomous-alternative) question
A fixed-alternative question that requires the respondent to choose one or two dichotomous alternatives.

determinant-choice question
A fixed-alternative question that requires a respondent to choose one—and only one—response from among multiple alternatives.

frequency-determination question
A fixed-alternative question that asks for an answer about the general frequency of occurrence.

checklist question
A fixed-alternative question that allows the respondent to provide multiple answers to a single question by checking off items.

A major problem in developing dichotomous or multiple-choice alternatives is the framing of the response alternatives. There should be no overlap among categories. Each alternative should be *mutually exclusive;* that is, only one dimension of an issue should be related to that alternative. The following listing of income groups illustrates a common error:

☐ **Under $15,000**
☐ **$15,000–30,000**
☐ **$30,000–55,000**
☐ **$55,000–70,000**
☐ **Over $70,000**

How many people with incomes of $30,000 will be in the second group, and how many will be in the third group? We would not know the answer. Alternatives grouped without forethought about analysis may diminish accuracy.
Few people relish being in the lowest category. Including a category lower than the lowest expected answers often helps to negate the potential bias caused by respondents avoiding an extreme category.

When the researcher is unaware of the potential response to a question, fixed-alternative questions obviously cannot be used. If the researcher assumes what the responses might be but is in fact wrong, he or she will have no way of knowing the extent to which the assumption was incorrect.

Unanticipated alternatives emerge when respondents feel that closed answers do not adequately reflect their feelings. They may make comments to the interviewer or write additional answers on the mail questionnaire indicating that the exploratory research did not yield a complete array of responses. After the fact, little can be done to correct a closed question with some alternatives missing; therefore, the research may benefit from time spent conducting exploratory research with open-ended response questions to identify the most likely alternatives before a descriptive questionnaire is written. The researcher should strive to ensure that there are sufficient response choices to include almost all possible answers.

Respondents may check off obvious alternatives, such as price or durability, it they do not see their individual choices to answer a question. Thus, a fixed-alternative question may tempt respondents to check an answer that is untrue, but perhaps more prestigious or socially acceptable. Rather than stating that they do not know why they choose a given product, they may select an alternative among those presented, or, as a matter of convenience, they may select a given alternative rather than think of the most correct response.

Most questionnaires mix open-ended and closed questions. As we have discussed, each form has unique benefits. In addition a change of pace can eliminate respondent boredom and fatigue.

Phrasing Questions for Mail, Telephone, and Personal Interview Surveys

The means of data collection (telephone, personal interviews, mail, or computer) will influence the question format and question phrasing. In general, mail and telephone questions must be less complex than those used in personal interviews. Questionnaires for telephone and personal interviews should be written in a conversational style. Exhibit 15.1 illustrates how a question may be revised for a different medium.

Exhibit 15.1 Reducing Complexity by Providing Fewer Responses

MAIL FORM:

How satisfied are you with your community?

1 Very satisfied
2 Quite satisfied
3 Somewhat satisfied
4 Slightly satisfied
5 Neither satisfied nor dissatisfied
6 Slightly dissatisfied
7 Somewhat dissatisfied
8 Quite dissatisfied
9 Very dissatisfied

REVISED FOR TELEPHONE:

How satisfied are you with your community? Would you say you are very satisfied, somewhat satisfied, neither satisfied nor dissatisfied, somewhat dissatisfied, or very dissatisfied?

Very satisfied	1
Somewhat satisfied	2
Neither satisfied nor dissatisfied	3
Somewhat dissatisfied	4
Very dissatisfied	5

Consider the following question from a personal interview:

Recently there has been a lot of discussion about the potential health to nonsmokers from tobacco smoke in public buildings, restaurants, and business offices. How serious a health threat to you personally is the inhaling of this secondhand smoke, often called *passive smoking:* Is it a very serious health threat, somewhat serious, not too serious, or not serious at all?

1.   **Very serious**

2.   **Somewhat serious**

3.   **Not too serious**

4.   **Not serious at all**

5.   **(Don't know)**

You probably noticed that the last portion of the question was a listing of the four alternatives that serve as answers. This listing at the end is often used in interviews to serve as a reminder of the alternatives to the respondent who has no visual material to portray the choices. The fifth alternative "Don't know" is in parentheses because, although it is known to the interviewer as an acceptable answer, it is not read because the researcher would prefer to "force" the respondent to choose from among the four listed alternatives.

The data collection technique also influences the layout of the questionnaire. This will be discussed later in the chapter.

I don't know the rules of grammar....If you're trying to persuade people to do something, or buy something, it seems to me you should use their language, the language they use every day, the language in which they think. We try to write in the vernacular.

DAVID OGILVY

The Art of Asking Questions[4]

No hard-and-fast rules determine how to develop a questionnaire. Fortunately, research experience has yielded some guidelines that help prevent the most common mistakes.

Avoid Complexity: Use Simple, Conversational Language

Words used in questionnaires should be readily understandable to all respondents. The researcher usually has the difficult task of using the conversational language of people from the lower education levels without talking down to the better-educated respondents. Remember, not all people have the vocabulary of a college student; a substantial number of Americans have never gone beyond high school.

Respondents may be able to tell an interviewer whether they are married, single, divorced, separated, or widowed, but providing their *marital status* may present a problem. The technical jargon of top corporate executives should be avoided when surveying retailers or industrial users. Brand image, positioning, marginal analysis, and corporate staff language will not have the same meaning for or be understood by the owner-operator in a retail survey. The vocabulary used in the following question from an attitude survey on social problems probably would confuse many respondents:

> **When effluents from a paper mill can be drunk and exhaust from factory smokestacks can be breathed, then man will have done a good job in saving the environment....What we want is zero toxicity; no effluents?**

Besides being too long, this question tends to be leading.

Avoid Leading and Loaded Questions

leading question
A question that suggests or implies certain answers.

Asking leading and loaded questions is a major source of bias in question wording. **Leading questions** suggest or imply certain answers. A study of the dry cleaning industry asked this question:

> **Many people are using dry cleaning less because of improved wash-and-wear clothes. How do you feel wash-and-wear clothes have affected your use of dry cleaning facilities in the past four years?**
>
> ☐ Use less ☐ No change ☐ Use more

The potential "bandwagon effect" implied in this question threatens the study's validity. *Partial mention of alternatives* is a variation of this phenomena:

WHAT WENT WRONG?

Too Good a Name!

THE ARM & HAMMER BRAND NAME HAS BEEN USED for a number of product line extensions, for example, heavy-duty laundry detergent, oven cleaner, and liquid detergent. Unfortunately, however, when the makers of Arm & Hammer baking soda launched Arm & Hammer underarm spray deodorant and Arm & Hammer spray disinfectant,

they did not fare well, even though marketing research studies indicated that consumers had expressed positive feelings about both products. What went wrong?

Researchers who investigated the product failures found that the Arm & Hammer name had such a strong consumer franchise that whenever it was associated with a new product or concept, consumer acceptance and buying intentions were always artificially high. When question wording included the socially desirable Arm & Hammer name, consumers were reluctant to reject it. The company had failed to realize how much response bias its name caused.

Do small imported cars, such as Toyotas, get better gas mileage than small U.S. cars?

How do you generally spend your free time, watching television or what?

Merely mentioning an alternative may have a dramatic effect. The following question was asked in a research study for a court case (*Universal City v. Nintendo,* 1984).[5]

To the best of your knowledge, was "Donkey Kong" made with the approval or under the authority of the people who produced the *King Kong* movies?

Eighteen percent of the respondents answered "yes." In contrast 0 percent correctly answered the question "As far as you know, who makes 'Donkey Kong'?"

Loaded questions suggest social desirability or are emotionally charged. Consider the following:

In light of today's farm crisis, it would be in the public's best interest to offer interest-free loans to farmers.

☐ **Strongly agree**   ☐ **Agree**   ☐ **Disagree**   ☐ **Strongly disagree**

A different answer might be given if the loaded portion of the statement, *farm crisis,* were worded to suggest a problem of less magnitude than a crisis.

A television station produced a 10-second spot to ask the following question:

loaded question
A question that suggests socially desirable answers or is emotionally charged.

> **We are happy when you like programs on Channel 7. We are sad when you dislike programs on Channel 7. Write us and let us know what you think of our programming.**

Few people wish to make others sad. This question invites only positive comments.

Answers to certain questions are more socially desirable than others. For example, a truthful answer to the following classification question might be painful:

Where did you rank academically in your high school graduating class?

☐ **Top quarter**

☐ **2nd quarter**

☐ **3rd quarter**

☐ **4th quarter**

When taking personality or psychographic tests, respondents frequently can interpret which answers are most socially acceptable even if the answers do not portray the respondents' true feelings. For example, which are the socially desirable answers for the following questions on a self-confidence scale?

I feel capable of handling myself in most social situations.

☐ **Agree**   ☐ **Disagree**

I seldom fear my actions will cause others to have low opinions of me.

☐ **Agree**   ☐ **Disagree**

Invoking the status quo is a form of loading that results in bias because most people tend to resist change.[6]

An experiment conducted in the early days of polling illustrates the unpopularity of change.[7] Comparable samples of respondents were simultaneously asked two questions about the presidential succession. One sample was asked: **"Would you favor or oppose adding a law to the Constitution preventing a president from succeeding himself more than once?"** The other sample was asked: **"Would you favor or oppose changing the Constitution in order to prevent a president from succeeding himself more than once?"** To the first question, 50 percent of the respondents answered in the negative; to the second question, 65 percent answered in the negative. Thus, the public would rather have added to than changed the Constitution.

Asking respondents "how often" they use a product or visit a store leads them to generalize about their habits because there usually is some variance in their behavior. In generalizing one is likely to portray one's *ideal* behavior rather than one's *average* behavior. For instance, brushing one's teeth after each meal may be ideal, but busy people may skip a brushing or two. An introductory **counterbiasing statement** or preamble to a question that reassures respondents that their "embarrassing" behavior is not abnormal may yield truthful responses:

counterbiasing statement
An introductory statement or preamble to a potentially embarrassing question that reduces a respondent's reluctance to answer by suggesting that certain behavior is not unusual.

> **Some people have the time to brush three times daily; others do not. How often did you brush your teeth yesterday?**

If a question embarrasses the respondent, it may elicit no answer or a biased response. This is particularly true with personal or classification data such as income or education. This problem may be mitigated by introducing the section of the questionnaire with a statement such as

To help classify your answers, we'd like to ask you a few questions. Again, your answers will be kept in strict confidence.

A question statement may be leading because it is phrased to reflect either the negative or the positive aspects of the issue. To control for this bias, the wording of attitudinal questions may be reversed for 50 percent of the sample. This **split-ballot technique** is used with the expectation that two alternative phrasings of the same question will yield a more accurate total response than will a single phrasing. For example, in a study on small-car buying behavior, one-half of the sample of imported-car purchasers received a questionnaire in which the statement read: **"Small U.S. cars are cheaper to maintain than small imported cars."** The other half of the import-car owners received a questionnaire in which the statement read: **"Small imported cars are cheaper to maintain than small U.S. cars."**

split-ballot technique
Using two alternative phrasings of the same questions for respective halves of the sample to yield a more accurate total response than will a single phrasing.

Avoid Ambiguity: Be as Specific as Possible

Items on questionnaires often are ambiguous because they are too general. Consider such indefinite words as *often, occasionally, regularly, frequently, many, good, fair,* and *poor.* Each of these words has many different meanings. For one person, *frequent* reading of *Fortune* magazine may be six or seven issues a year; for another, twice a year. A great variety of meanings are attributed to *fair.* The same is true for many other indefinite words.

Questions such as that used in a study of consumers to measure the reaction to a television boycott should be interpreted with care:

Please indicate the statement that best describes your family's television viewing during the boycott of Channel 7.

☐ We did *not* watch any television programs on Channel 7.

☐ We watched *hardly any* television programs on Channel 7.

☐ We *occasionally* watched television programs on Channel 7.

☐ We *frequently* watched television programs on Channel 7.

Some marketing scholars have suggested that the rate of diffusion of an innovation is related to the perception of the product attributes, such as *divisibility*,[8] which refers to the extent to which an innovation may be tried or tested on a limited scale. An empirical attempt to test this theory using semantic differentials was a disaster. Pretesting found that the bipolar adjectives *divisible–not divisible* were impossible for consumers to understand because they did not have the theory in mind as a frame of reference. A revision of the scale used these bipolar adjectives:

Testable —— : —— : —— : —— : —— : —— : —— *Not testable*
(sample use   **(sample use**
possible)   **not possible)**

However, the question remained ambiguous because the meaning was still unclear.

A brewing industry study on point-of-purchase advertising (store displays) asked:

What degree of durability do you prefer in your point-of-purchase advertising?

☐ **Permanent (lasting more than six months)**

☐ **Semipermanent (lasting from one to six months)**

☐ **Temporary (lasting less than one month)**

Here the researchers clarified the terms *permanent, semipermanent,* and *temporary* by defining them for the respondent. However, the question remained somewhat ambiguous. Beer marketers often use a variety of point-of-purchase devices to serve different purposes—but in this case, what purpose? Furthermore, a disadvantage in analysis existed because mere preference was given rather than a rating of the *degree* of preference. Thus, the meaning of a question may not be clear because it gives an inadequate frame of reference for interpreting the context of the question.

A student research group asked this question:

What media do you rely on most?
☐ **Television**
☐ **AM radio**
☐ **FM radio**
☐ **Newspapers**

This question is ambiguous because it does not ask about the content of the media. "Rely on most" for what—news, sports, entertainment?

Avoid Double-Barreled Items

double-barreled question
A question that may induce bias because it covers two issues at once.

A question covering several issues at once is referred to as a **double-barreled question** and should always be avoided. Making the mistake of asking two questions rather than one is easy, for example, **"Please indicate your degree of agreement with the following statement: 'Wholesalers and retailers are responsible for the high cost of meat.'"** Which intermediaries are responsible, the wholesalers or the retailers? When multiple questions are asked in one question, the results may be exceedingly difficult to interpret. For example, consider the following question from a *Redbook* survey entitled "How Do You Feel about Being a Woman?"

Between you and your husband, who does the housework (cleaning, cooking, dishwashing, laundry) over and above that done by any hired help?
☐ **I do all of it.**
☐ **I do almost all of it.**
☐ **I do over half of it.**
☐ **We split the work fifty-fifty.**
☐ **My husband does over half of it.**

The answers to this question do not tell us if the wife cooks and the husband washes the dishes.

Another survey by a consumer-oriented library asked:

Are you satisfied with the present system of handling "closed-reserve" and "open-reserve" readings? (Are enough copies available? Are the required materials ordered promptly? Are the borrowing regulations adequate for students' use of materials?)

☐ **Yes**   ☐ **No**

A respondent may feel torn between a "yes" to one part of the question and a "no" to another part. The answer to this question does not tell the researcher which problem or combination of problems concerns the library user.

Consider this comment about double-barreled questions:

Generally speaking, it is hard enough to get answers to one idea at a time without complicating the problem by asking what amounts to two questions at once. If two ideas are to be explored, they deserve at least two questions. Since question marks are not rationed, there is little excuse for the needless confusion that results [from] the double-barreled question.[9]

Avoid Making Assumptions

Consider the following question:

Should Macy's continue its excellent gift-wrapping program?

☐ **Yes**   ☐ **No**

This question has a built-in assumption: that people believe the gift-wrapping program is excellent. By answering "yes," the respondent implies that things are fine just as they are; by answering "no," he or she implies that the store should discontinue the gift wrapping. The researchers should not place the respondent in that sort of bind by including an implicit assumption in the question.

Another frequent mistake is assuming that the respondent had previously thought about an issue. For example, the following question appeared in a survey concerning Jack-in-the-Box: **"Do you think Jack-in-the-Box restaurants should consider changing their name?"** It is not at all likely that the respondent had thought about this question before being asked it. Nevertheless, most respondents answered the question even though they had no prior opinion concerning the name change. Research that induces people to express attitudes on subjects they do not ordinarily think about is meaningless.

Avoid Burdensome Questions That May Tax the Respondent's Memory

A simple fact of human life is that people forget. Researchers writing questions about past behavior or events should recognize that certain questions may make serious demands on the respondent's memory. Writing questions about prior events requires a conscientious attempt to minimize the problems associated with forgetting.

EXPLORING RESEARCH ISSUES

One or Two Questions?

A STUDY, PART OF AN ONGOING SERIES OF RESEARCH-on-research investigations conducted by Market Facts, Inc., was designed to establish an accurate means of measuring rate of purchase. As in other studies, it involved demographically matched samples of households with each sample receiving a different treatment. Self-administered questionnaires were mailed to female heads of households, and purchase data were obtained for the following products: all-purpose white glue, aspirin, replacement automobile tires, and record albums.

Two different ways of asking the purchase incidence questions were investigated. Alternative A was sent to one sample of 1,000 homes; Alternative B was sent to another sample of 1,000 homes. The samples were closely matched in terms of age, income, geography, and city size. Here is a sample pair of questions:

Alternative A

Below are listed several products. Please X each product you or anyone in your household *bought* in the *past three months*.

Alternative B

Below are listed several products. Please X each product you or anyone in your household *ever bought*. For each product ever bought, X the box that best describes when the product was *purchased most recently*:

Within the past 3 months

☐ **4–6 months ago**

☐ **7–12 months ago**

☐ **Over 12 months ago**

Following are the results:

PURCHASED WITHIN PAST 3 MONTHS

	A: ONE-STEP QUESTION (%)	B: TWO-STEP QUESTION (%)	PERCENTAGE POINT DIFFERENCE
White glue	46	32	+14
Aspirin	68	57	+11
Replacement auto tires	32	24	+8
Number of respondents	(800)	(800)	

In many situations respondents cannot recall the answer to a question. For example, a telephone survey conducted during the 24-hour period following the airing of the Super Bowl may establish whether the respondent watched the Super Bowl and then ask: **"Do you recall any commercials on that program?"** If the answer is positive, the interviewer might ask: **"What brands were advertised?"** These two questions measure *unaided recall,* because they give no clue as to the brand of interest to the respondent.

If the researcher suspects that the respondent may have forgotten the answer to a question, he or she may rewrite the question in an *aided-recall* format, that is, provide a clue to help jog the respondent's memory. For instance, the question about an advertised beer in an aided-recall format might be: **"Do you recall whether there was a brand of beer advertised on that program?"** or **"I am going to** read you a list of beer brand names. Can you pick out the name of the beer that was advertised on the program?" While aided recall is not as strong a test of attention or memory as unaided recall, it is less taxing to the respondent's memory.

Telescoping and squishing are two additional consequences of respondents' forgetting the exact details of their behavior. *Telescoping* occurs when respondents believe that past events happened more recently than they actually did. The opposite effect, *squishing,* occurs when respondents think that recent events took place longer ago than they really did. A solution to this problem may be to refer to a specific event that is memorable, for example, **"How often have you gone to a sporting event since the World Series?"** Because forgetting tends to increase over time, the question may concern a recent period: **"How often did you watch Home Box Office on cable television last week?"** (During the editing stage, the results can be transposed to the appropriate time period.)

In situations in which "I don't know" or "I can't recall" is a meaningful answer, simply including a "don't know" response category may solve the question writer's problem.

What Is the Best Question Sequence?

The order of questions, or the question sequence, may serve several functions for the researcher. If the opening questions are interesting, simple to comprehend, and easy to answer, respondents' cooperation and involvement can be maintained throughout the questionnaire. Asking easy-to-answer questions teaches respondents their role and allows them to build confidence; they know that this is a professional researcher and not another salesperson posing as one. If respondents' curiosity is not aroused at the outset, they can become disinterested and terminate their interviews.

A mail survey among department store buyers drew an extremely poor return rate. A substantial improvement in response rate occurred, however, when some introductory questions seeking opinions on pending legislation of great importance to these buyers were added. Respondents completed all the questions, not only those in the opening section.

In their attempt to "warm up" respondents toward the questionnaire, student researchers frequently ask demographic or classificatory questions at the beginning. This generally is not advisable because asking for personal information such as income level or education may be embarrassing or threatening to respondents. It usually is better to ask potentially embarrassing questions at the middle or end of the questionnaire, after a rapport has been established between respondent and interviewer.

Order Bias

Order bias results from an answer alternative's position in a set of answers or from the sequencing of questions. In political elections in which candidates lack high visibility, such as county commissioner and judgeship elections, the first name listed on the ballot often receives the highest percentage of votes. For this reason many election boards print several ballots so that each candidate's name appears in every possible position on the ballot.

order bias
Bias caused by the influence of earlier questions in a questionnaire or by an answer's position in a set of answers.

Order bias can also distort survey results. For example, a questionnaire's purpose is to measure level of awareness of several charitable organizations; Big Brothers and Big Sisters is always mentioned first, Red Cross second, and American Cancer Association third. Big Brothers and Big Sisters may receive an artificially higher awareness rating because respondents were more prone to yea-saying (by indicating awareness) for the first item in the list.

As another example, if questions about a specific clothing store are asked prior to those concerning the criteria for selecting a clothing store, respondents who state that they shop at a store where parking needs to be improved may also state that parking is less important a factor than they really believe it is to avoid appearing inconsistent. Specific questions may thus influence the more general ones. Therefore, it is advisable to ask general questions before specific questions to obtain the freest of open-ended responses. This procedure, known as the **funnel technique,** allows the researcher to understand the respondent's frame of reference before asking more specific questions about the respondent's particular level of information and intensity of opinions.

Consider the possibility that later answers may be biased by previous questions in this questionnaire on environmental pollution:

funnel technique
A procedure whereby general questions are asked before specific questions to obtain unbiased responses.

Circle the number on the following table that best expresses your feelings about the severity of each environmental problem:

PROBLEM	NOT A PROBLEM				VERY SEVERE PROBLEM
Air pollution from automobile exhausts	1	2	3	4	5
Air pollution from open burning	1	2	3	4	5
Air pollution from industrial smoke	1	2	3	4	5
Air pollution from foul odors	1	2	3	4	5
Noise pollution from airplanes	1	2	3	4	5
Noise pollution from cars, trucks, motorcycles	1	2	3	4	5
Noise pollution from industry	1	2	3	4	5

It is not surprising that researchers found that the responses to each air pollution question were highly correlated—in fact, almost identical.

When using attitude scales, there also may be an *anchoring effect.* The first concept measured tends to become a comparison point from which subsequent evaluations are made. Randomization of these items on a questionnaire of this type helps minimize order bias.

A related problem concerns the order of alternatives on closed questions. To avoid this problem, the order of these choices should be rotated if alternative forms of the questionnaire are possible. However, marketing researchers rarely print alternative questionnaires to eliminate problems resulting from order bias. A more common practice is to pencil in Xs or check marks on printed questionnaires to indicate that the interviewer should start a series of repetitive questions at a certain point. For example, the capitalized phrases in the following question provide instructions to the interviewer to "rotate" brands:

I would like to determine how likely you would be to buy certain brands of candy in the future. Let's start with (X'ED BRAND). (RECORD BELOW UNDER APPROPRIATE BRAND. REPEAT QUESTIONS FOR ALL REMAINING BRANDS.)

START HERE:	( ) MOUNDS	(x) ALMOND JOY	( ) SNICKERS
Definitely would buy	-1	-1	-1
Probably would buy	-2	-2	-2
Might or might not buy	-3	-3	-3
Probably would not buy	-4	-4	-4
Definitely would not buy	-5	-5	-5

Asking a question that does not apply to the respondent or that the respondent is not qualified to answer may be irritating or cause a biased response because the respondent wishes to please the interviewer or to avoid embarrassment. Including a **filter question** minimizes asking questions that may be inapplicable. Asking, "**Where do you generally have check-cashing problems in Springfield?**" may elicit a response even though the respondent has had no check-cashing problems; he or she may wish to please the interviewer with an answer. A filter question such as "**Do you ever have a problem cashing a check in Springfield? ——— Yes ——— No**" would screen out the people who are not qualified to answer.

Another form of filter question, the **pivot question,** is used to obtain income information and other data respondents may be reluctant to provide. For example,

> "**Is your total family income over or under $50,000?**" IF UNDER, ASK, "**Is it over or under $25,000?**" IF OVER, ASK, "**Is it over or under $75,000?**"
>
> Under $25,000 $50,001–$75,000
>
> $25,001–$50,000   Over $75,000

filter question

A question that screens out respondents who are not qualified to answer a second question.

pivot question

A filter question used to determine which version of a second question will be asked.

Exhibit 15.2 gives an example of a flowchart plan for a questionnaire. Structuring the order of the questions so that they are logical is another technique for ensuring the respondent's cooperation and eliminates any confusion or indecision. The researcher ensures maintaining legitimacy when the respondent can comprehend the relationship between a given question (or section of the questionnaire) and the overall purpose of the study. Furthermore, a logical order may also aid the individual's memory. Traditional comments to explain the logic of the questionnaire may ensure the respondent's continuation. Here are two examples:

> We have been talking so far about general shopping habits in this city. Now I'd like you to compare two types of grocery stores—regular supermarkets and grocery departments in wholesale club stores.

> So that I can combine your answers with other farmers who are similar to you, I need some personal information about you. Your answers to these questions—as all of the others you've answered—are confidential, and you will never be identified to anyone without your permission. Thanks for your help so far. If you'll answer the remaining questions, it will help me analyze all your answers.

Exhibit 15.2 **Flow of Questions to Illustrate the Level of Prompting Required to Stimulate Recall**

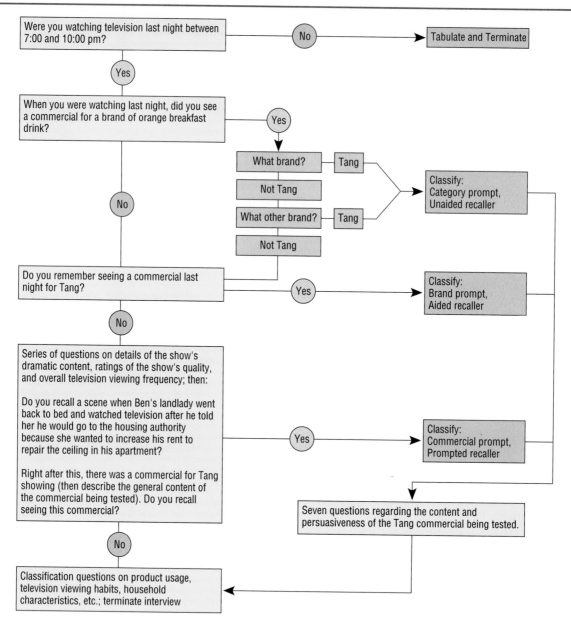

What Is the Best Layout?

The layout and physical attractiveness of the questionnaire are crucial in self-administered mail questionnaires. For different reasons it is also important to have a good layout in questionnaires designed for personal and telephone interviews. Exhibit 15.3 illustrates a warranty card that serves a dual purpose as a questionnaire. The layout is neat, attractive, and easy to follow.

Often the rate of return can be improved by adding the money that might have been spent on an incentive to improve the attractiveness and quality of the

---

Exhibit 15.3 A Dual-Purpose Warranty Registration Form

☐ Mr.
☐ Mrs.   **hartmann®**
☐ Ms. : _____ — Date of Purchase: _____

Street: _____ — Name of Store: _____

City: _____ — City: _____

State: _____ Zip: _____ — Have you owned Hartmann before? ☐ yes ☐ no

Please check applicable styles of Hartmann acquired this purchase:

Style of Hartmann	Any Color Belting Leather	Walnut Tweed	Mountain Blue Tweed	Coffee Packcloth/ Leather Trim	Black Packcloth/ Leather Trim	Coffee Packcloth/ Vinyl Trim
Framed Luggage						
Soft Pullman						
Hangbag						
Carry-on Luggage						

	Belting Leather			Walnut Tweed	Mountain Blue Tweed	Coffee Packcloth/ Leather Trim	Black Packcloth/ Leather Trim
	Black	Natural	Cordovan				
Framed Attaché							
Soft Briefcase							
Personal Accessory							

How did you acquire your Hartmann?
_____ Individual purchase (purchased for myself)
_____ Joint purchase
_____ Received as gift

Your Hartmann will be used primarily for:
_____ Business travel _____ Leisure travel

How did you become interested in Hartmann?
_____ Advertising
_____ Displayed in store
_____ Recommended by salesperson
_____ Recommended by friend/relative
_____ Other: _____
_____ Received as gift

Annual Household Income:
_____ Under $25,000   _____ $50,000-$69,999
_____ $25,000-$34,999   _____ $70,000-$89,999
_____ $35,000-$49,999   _____ $90,000 +

What influenced your choice of Hartmann?
_____ Style   _____ Unique features
_____ Guarantee   _____ Previous ownership
_____ Durability   _____ Hand craftsmanship
_____ Light weight   _____ Quality reputation
_____ Other: _____

Age:
_____ Under 18   _____ 45-54
_____ 18-24   _____ 55-64
_____ 25-34   _____ 65 and over
_____ 35-44

Occupation: _____
☐ full-time ☐ part-time ☐ retired

Comments about item purchased: _____

_____

Other comments: _____

If you'd like more information about Hartmann products, please contact our Customer Service Department toll-free at 1-800-331-0613.

please moisten to seal

---

questionnaire. An expert in mail surveys suggests that questionnaires should never be overcrowded, space should be provided to ensure decent margins, white space should be used to separate solidly printed blocks, and the unavoidable columns of multiple boxes should be kept to a minimum.[10]

A question should not begin on one page and end on another page. Splitting questions may cause a respondent to read only part of a question, to pay less attention to answers on one of the pages, or to be confused.

Questionnaires should be designed to appear as short as possible. Sometimes it is advisable to use a booklet form of questionnaire rather than stapling a large number of pages together. In situations in which it is necessary to conserve space on the questionnaire or to facilitate data entry or tabulation of the data, a multiple-grid layout may be used. The **multiple-grid question** asks several questions and instructs the respondent to answer the categories as they appear in a grid format. For example:

multiple-grid question
Several similar questions arranged in a grid format.

Exhibit 15.4 **Telephone Questionnaire**

1. Did you take the car you had checked to the Standard Auto Repair Center for repairs?
   -1 Yes   (SKIP TO Q. 3)   -2 No
2. (IF NO, ASK:) Did you have the repair work done?
   -1 Yes   -2 No
   ↓   ↓

   1. Where was the repair work   1. Why didn't you have the car
      done? _____   repaired? _____
                                                _____
   2. Why didn't you have the repair   _____
      work done at the Standard Auto Repair
      Center? _____

      _____
      _____
      _____

3. (IF YES TO Q. 1, ASK:) How satisfied were you with the repair work? Were you . . .
   -1 Very satisfied
   -2 Somewhat satisfied
   -3 Somewhat dissatisfied
   -4 Very dissatisfied
   (IF SOMEWHAT OR VERY DISSATISFIED:) In what way were you dissatisfied?

   _____
   _____
   _____

4. (ASK EVERYONE:) Do you every buy gas at the 95th Street Standard Center?
   -1 Yes   -2 No (SKIP TO Q. 6)
5. (IF YES, ASK:)   How often do you buy gas there?
   -1 Always
   -2 Almost always
   -3 Most of the time
   -4 Part of the time
   -5 Hardly ever
6. Have you ever had your car washed there?   -1 Yes   -2 No
7. Have you ever had an oil change or lubrication done there?   -1 Yes   -2 No

---

Airlines often offer special fare promotions. On a vacation trip would you take a connecting flight instead of a nonstop flight if the connecting flight were longer?

	Yes	No	Not sure
One hour longer?	☐	☐	☐
Two hours longer?	☐	☐	☐
Three hours longer?	☐	☐	☐

Experienced researchers have found that it pays to carefully phrase the title of the questionnaire. In self-administered and mail questionnaires a carefully constructed title may capture the respondent's interest, underline the importance of the research ("Nationwide Study of Blood Donors"), emphasize the interesting nature of the study ("Study of Internet Usage"), appeal to the respondent's ego ("Survey among Top Executives"), or emphasize the confidential nature of the study ("A Confidential Survey among. . . "). To avoid any negative influence from the wording of the title, the researcher should take steps to ensure that the title will not bias the respondent in the same way that a leading question may.

The researcher can design the questionnaire to facilitate the interviewer's job of following interconnected questions by using several forms, special instructions, and other tricks of the trade. Exhibits 15.4 and 15.5 illustrate portions of

---

Exhibit 15.5 **Personal Interview Questionnaire**

"Hello, my name is _____. I'm a Public Opinion Interviewer with Research Services, Inc. We're making an opinion survey about Banks and Banking, and I'd like to ask you . . ."

1. What are the names of local banks you can think of offhand? (INTERVIEWER: List names in order mentioned.)
    a. _____
    b. _____
    c. _____
    d. _____
    e. _____
    f. _____
    g. _____

2. Thinking now about the experiences you have had with the different Banks here in Boulder . . . have you ever talked to or done business with . . . (INTERVIEWER: Insert name of bank name red-checked below.)
    a. Are you personally acquainted with any of the employees or officers at _____?
    b. (If YES) Who is that?
    c. How long has it been since you have been inside _____?
        (INTERVIEWER: Now go back and repeat 2–2c for all other banks listed.)

	(2) Talked		(2a and 2b) Know Employee Or Officer		(2c) Been in Bank in:				
	Yes	No	No	Name	Last Year	1–5	5-Plus	No	DK
Arapahoe National Bank	1	2	1	_____	1	2	3	4	5
First National Bank	1	2	1	_____	1	2	3	4	5
Boulder National Bank	1	2	1	_____	1	2	3	4	5
Security Bank	1	2	1	_____	1	2	3	4	5
United Bank of Boulder	1	2	1	_____	1	2	3	4	5
National State Bank	1	2	1	_____	1	2	3	4	5

3. (HAND BANK RATING CARD) On this card there are a number of contrasting phrases or statements, for example, "Large" and "Small." We'd like to know how you rate (NAME OF BANK RED-CHECKED BELOW) in terms of these statements or phrases. Just for example: let's use the terms "fast service" and "slow service." If you were to rate Bank #1 on this scale it would mean you find their service "very fast." On the other hand, a 7 rating would indicate you feel their services is "very slow," whereas a 4 rating means you don't think of them as being either "very fast" or "very slow." Are you ready to go ahead? Good! Tell me then how you would rate (NAME OF BANK RED-CHECKED) in terms of each of the phrases or statements on that card.
    How about (READ NEXT BANK NAME)? . . . Continue on until Respondent has evaluated all six banks.

		Arapahoe National	First National	Boulder National	Security Bank	United Bank	National State
a.	Service	_____	_____	_____	_____	_____	_____
b.	Size	_____	_____	_____	_____	_____	_____
c.	Business vs. Family	_____	_____	_____	_____	_____	_____
d.	Friendliness	_____	_____	_____	_____	_____	_____
e.	Big/Small Business	_____	_____	_____	_____	_____	_____
f.	Rate of Growth	_____	_____	_____	_____	_____	_____
g.	Modernness	_____	_____	_____	_____	_____	_____
h.	Leadership	_____	_____	_____	_____	_____	_____
i.	Loan Ease	_____	_____	_____	_____	_____	_____
j.	Location	_____	_____	_____	_____	_____	_____
k.	Hours	_____	_____	_____	_____	_____	_____
l.	Ownership	_____	_____	_____	_____	_____	_____
m.	Community Involvement	_____	_____	_____	_____	_____	_____

(continued)

Exhibit 15.5 Personal Interview Questionnaire *(Continued)*

4. Suppose a friend of yours who has just moved to Boulder asked you to recommend a bank. Which local bank would you recommend? Why would you recommend that particular bank?

Arapahoe National	1
First National	2
Boulder National	3
Security Bank	4
United Bank of Boulder	5
National State Bank	6
Other (Specify)_____	
DK/Wouldn't	9

5. Which of the local banks do you think of as: (INTERVIEWER: Read red-checked item first, then read each of the other five.)
    the newcomer's bank? _____
    the student's bank? _____
    the Personal Banker bank? _____
    the bank where most C.U. faculty and staff bank? _____
    the bank most interested in this community? _____
    the most progressive bank? _____

6. Which of these financial institutions, if any, (HAND CARD 2) are you or any member of your immediate family who lives here in this home doing business with now?

    (IF NONE, Skip to 19.)

Bank	1
Credit Union	2
Finance Company	3
Savings and Loan	4
Industrial Bank	5
None of these	6
DK/Not sure	7

7. If a friend asked you to recommend a place where he or she could get a loan with which to buy a home, which financial institution would you probably recommend? (INTERVIEWER: Probe for specific name.) Why would you recommend (INSTITUTION NAMED IN 7)?

Would Recommend: _____	
Wouldn't	0
DK/Not Sure	9

---

telephone and personal interview questionnaires. Note how the layout and easy-to-follow instructions for interviewers in questions 1, 2, and 3 of Exhibit 15.4 help the interviewer follow the question sequence.

Instructions are often capitalized or in a boldface font to alert the interviewer that it may be necessary to proceed in a certain way. For example, if a particular answer is given, the interviewer or respondent may be instructed to skip certain questions or answer a special sequence of questions.

Note that Questions 3 and 6 in Exhibit 15.5 instruct the interviewer to hand the respondent a card bearing a list of alternatives. Cards may help respondents grasp the intended meaning of the question and remember all the brand names or other items. Also, Questions 2, 3, and 6 in Exhibit 15.5 instruct the interviewer that ratings of the banks will start with the bank that has been checked in red pencil on the printed questionnaire. The name of the red-checked bank is not

---

Exhibit 15.6 Example of a Skip Question

1. If you had to buy a set of tires for your family car tomorrow, which of the following three types of tires do you think you would buy?

    1   Biased (non-belted)—Go to Q. 3
    2   Biased-belted—Go to Q. 3
    3   Radial-belted

2. (If "Radial-belted" on Q. 1, ask): What brand of tires do you think you would buy?
3. What is your age?

the same on every questionnaire. By rotating the order of the check marks, the researchers attempted to reduce order bias caused by respondents reacting more favorably to the first set of questions. To facilitate coding, question responses should be precoded when possible, as in Exhibit 15.4.

The series of questions in Exhibit 15.6 may facilitate skip questions. Either skip instructions or an arrow drawn toward the next question is provided to inform the respondent which question comes next.

Layout is extremely important when questionnaires are long or require the respondent to fill in a large amount of information. In many circumstances headings or subtitles can indicate groups of questions to help the respondent grasp the scope or nature of the questions to be asked. Thus, at a glance, the respondent can follow the logic of the questionnaire.

Layout of questionnaires appearing on the Internet is also an important issue. For example, avoiding the problems associated with splitting questions and response categories may be difficult. On paper Likert scales are often shown in a multiple-grid format. Suppose a Likert scale consists of 15 statements and a grid-format layout places the response categories **strongly agree, agree, disagree,** and **strongly disagree** at the beginning of the question. Scrolling down beyond the first few statements may not allow the respondent to simultaneously see both the statements at the end of the list and the response categories at the top of the grid.

How Much Pretesting and Revising Are Necessary?

Many novelists write, rewrite, revise, and rewrite again certain chapters, paragraphs, or even sentences. The researcher works in a similar world. Rarely does he or she write only a first draft of a questionnaire. Usually the questionnaire is tried out on a group selected on a convenience basis and similar in makeup to the one that ultimately will be sampled. The researcher should not select a group too divergent from the target market (for example, selecting business students as surrogates for businesspeople), but pretesting does not require a statistical sample. The pretesting process allows the researcher to determine whether respondents have any difficulty understanding the questionnaire or if there are any ambiguous or biased questions. This process is exceedingly beneficial. Making a mistake with 25 or 50 subjects can save the potential disaster of administering an invalid questionnaire to several hundred individuals.

Tabulating the results of a pretest helps determine whether the questionnaire will meet the objectives of the research. A **preliminary tabulation** often illustrates that although a question is easily comprehended and answered by the respondent, it is inappropriate because it does not provide relevant information to help solve the marketing problem. Consider the following example from a survey among distributors of powder-actuated tools such as stud drivers concerning the percentage of sales to given industries:

preliminary tabulation
Tabulating the results of a pretest to help determine whether the questionnaire will meet the objectives of the research.

Please estimate what percentage of your fastener and load sales go to the following industries:

——% heating, plumbing, and air conditioning

——% carpentry

——% electrical

——% maintenance

——% other (please specify)——

Exhibit 15.7 **Mitigating a Response Problem with Questionnaire Design**

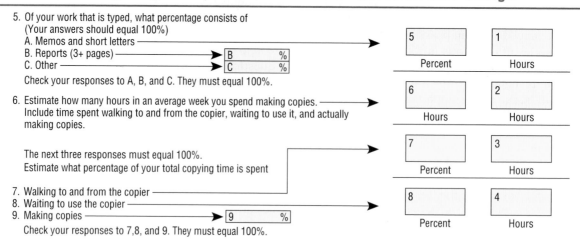

5. Of your work that is typed, what percentage consists of
   (Your answers should equal 100%)
   A. Memos and short letters ——————————→
   B. Reports (3+ pages) ————————→ B _____ %
   C. Other ————————————→ C _____ %
   Check your responses to A, B, and C. They must equal 100%.

5		1	
Percent		Hours	

6. Estimate how many hours in an average week you spend making copies. ——————→
   Include time spent walking to and from the copier, waiting to use it, and actually
   making copies.

6		2	
Hours		Hours	

   The next three responses must equal 100%.
   Estimate what percentage of your total copying time is spent

7		3	
Percent		Hours	

7. Walking to and from the copier ——————————
8. Waiting to use the copier —————————————
9. Making copies ——————————→ 9 _____ %
   Check your responses to 7, 8, and 9. They must equal 100%.

8		4	
Percent		Hours	

The researchers were fortunate to learn that asking the question in this manner made it virtually impossible to obtain the information actually desired. Most respondents' answers did not total 100 percent, and the question had to be revised.

Getting respondents to add everything correctly is a problem. Notice how the questions in Exhibit 15.7 from a survey on secretarial support mitigate this problem. Pretesting difficult questions such as these is essential.

What administrative procedures should be implemented to maximize the value of a pretest? Feedback on a questionnaire administered exactly as planned in the actual study often is not possible; for example, mailing out a questionnaire may require several weeks. Pretesting a questionnaire in this manner provides important information on response rate, but it may not point out why questions were skipped or why respondents found certain questions ambiguous or confusing. Personal interviewers can record requests for additional explanation or comments that indicate respondents' difficulty with question sequence or other factors. This is the primary reason why such individuals often are used for pretest work. Of course, self-administered questionnaires are not reworded to be personal interviews, but interviewers are instructed to observe respondents and ask for their comments after completing the questionnaire. When pretesting personal or telephone interviews, interviewers may test alternative wordings and question sequences to determine which format best suits the intended respondents.

No matter how the pretest is conducted, however, the researcher should remember that its purpose is to uncover any problems that the questionnaire may cause. Thus, pretests typically are conducted to answer questions about the questionnaire such as:

- Can the questionnaire format be followed by the interviewer?
- Does the questionnaire flow naturally and conversationally?
- Are the questions clear and easy to understand?
- Can respondents answer the questions easily?
- Which alternative forms of questions work best?

Pretests also provide means for testing the sampling procedure, for example, whether interviewers are following the sampling instructions properly and whether the procedure is efficient. Pretests also provide estimates for the response rates of mail surveys and the completion rates for telephone surveys.

Usually a questionnaire goes through several revisions. The exact number of revisions depends on the researcher's and client's judgment. Revising the questionnaire usually ends when both agree that the desired information is being collected in an unbiased manner.

Designing Questionnaires For Global Markets

Now that marketing research is being conducted around the globe, researchers must take cultural factors into account when designing questionnaires. The most common problem involves translation into another language. A questionnaire developed in one country may be difficult to translate because equivalent language concepts do not exist or because of differences in idiom and vernacular. For example, the concepts of uncles and aunts are not the same in the United States as in India. In India the words for *uncle* and *aunt* are different for the maternal and paternal sides of the family.[11] Although Spanish is spoken in both Mexico and Venezuela, one researcher found the Spanish translation of the English term *retail outlet* works in Mexico, but not in Venezuela. Venezuelans interpreted the translation to refer to an electrical outlet, an outlet of a river into an ocean, and the passageway into a patio.

International marketing researchers often have questionnaires back translated. **Back translation** is the process of translating the questionnaire from one language to another and then translating it back again by a second, independent translator. The back translator is often a person whose native tongue is the language that will be used for the questionnaire. This can reveal inconsistency between the English version and the translation, for correction if necessary. For example, when a soft-drink company translated its slogan "Baby, it's cold inside" into Cantonese for research in Hong Kong, the result read "Small Mosquito, on the inside, it is very cold." In Hong Kong *small mosquito* is a colloquial expression for a small child. Obviously the intended meaning of the advertising message had been lost in the translated questionnaire.[12] In another international marketing research project, "out of sight, out of mind" was back translated as "invisible things are insane."[13]

As indicated in Chapter 8, literacy influences the designs of self-administered questionnaires and interviews. Knowledge of the literacy rates in foreign countries, especially those that are just developing modern economies, is vital.

back translation
The process of translating a questionnaire into another language and then having a second, independent translator translate it back to the original language.

Summary

Good questionnaire design is a key to obtaining accurate survey results. The specific questions to be asked will be a function of the type of information needed to answer the manager's questions and the communication medium of data collection. Relevance and accuracy are the basic criteria for judging questionnaire results. *Relevance* means that no unnecessary information is collected and that the information needed for solving the marketing problem is obtained. *Accuracy* means that the information is reliable and valid.

Knowing how each question should be phrased requires some knowledge about the different types of questions available. Open-ended response questions pose some topic or problem and ask the respondent to answer in his or her own words. Fixed-alternative questions require less interviewer skill, take less time, and are easier to answer. Standardized responses are easier to code, tabulate, and interpret. Care must be taken to formulate the responses so that they do not overlap. Respondents whose answers do not fit any of the fixed alternatives may be forced to select alternatives that do not communicate what they really mean.

Open-ended response questions are especially useful in exploratory research or at the beginning of a questionnaire. They are more costly than fixed-alternative questions because of the uniqueness of the answers. Also, interviewer bias can influence the responses to such questions.

In fixed-alternative questions the respondent is given specific limited alternative responses and asked to choose the one closest to his or her own viewpoint.

Some guidelines for questionnaire construction have emerged from research experience. The language should be simple to allow for variations in education level. Leading or loaded questions suggest answers to the respondents. Other questions induce them to give socially desirable answers. Respondents have a bias against questions that suggest changes in the status quo. Their reluctance to answer personal questions can be reduced by explaining the need for them and by assuring the respondents of the confidentiality of their replies. The researcher should carefully avoid ambiguity in questions. Another common problem is the double-barreled question, which asks two questions at once.

Question sequence can be very important to the success of a survey. The opening questions should be designed to capture respondents' interest and keep them involved. Personal questions should be postponed to the middle or end of the questionnaire. General questions should precede specific ones. In a series of attitude scales the first response may be used as an anchor for comparison with the other responses. The order of alternatives on closed questions also can affect the results. Filter questions are useful for avoiding asking unnecessary questions that do not apply to a particular respondent. Such questions may be put into a flowchart for personal or telephone interviewing.

The layout of a mail or other self-administered questionnaire can affect its response rate. An attractive questionnaire encourages a response, as does a carefully phrased title. Finally, pretesting helps reveal errors while they can still be corrected easily. International marketing researchers must take cultural factors into account when designing questionnaires. The most widespread problem involves translation into another language. International questionnaires are often back translated.

Key Terms and Concepts

Open-ended response question
Fixed-alternative question
Simple-dichotomy (dichotomous-
    alternative) question
Determinant-choice question
Frequency-determination question
Checklist question

Leading question
Loaded question
Counterbiasing statement
Split-ballot technique
Double-barreled question
Order bias
Funnel technique

Filter question
Pivot question
Multiple-grid question
Preliminary tabulation
Back translation

1. Evaluate and comment on the following questions, taken from several questionnaires:

   a. A university computer center survey on SPSS usage:

   How often do you use SPSS statistical software? Please check one.

   ____Infrequently (once a semester)

   ____Occasionally (once a month)

   ____Frequently (once a week)

   ——All the time (daily)

   b. A survey of advertising agencies:

   Do you understand and like the Federal Trade Commission's new corrective advertising policy?

   ____Yes

   ____No

   c. A survey on a new, small electric car:

   Assuming 90 percent of your driving is in town, would you buy this type of car?

   ____Yes

   ____No

   If this type of *electric* car had the same initial cost as a current "Big 3" full-size, fully equipped car, but operated at one-half the cost over a five-year period, would you buy one?

   ____Yes

   ____No

   d. A student survey:

   Since the beginning of this semester, approximately what percentage of the time do you get to campus using each of the forms of transportation available to you per week?

   Walk ____ Bicycle ____

   Public transportation ____ Motor vehicle ____

   e. A survey of motorcycle dealers:

   Should the company continue its generous cooperative advertising program?

   f. A survey of farmer media behavior:

   Thinking about *yesterday*, put an X in the box below for *each* quarter-hour time period during which, so far as you can recall, you *personally* listened to *radio*. Do the same for *television*.

   6:00 to 10:00 a.m. by quarter-hours

	6:00–6:15	6:15–6:30	6:30–6:45	6:45–7:00	7:00–7:15	7:15–7:30	7:30–7:45	7:45–8:00
Radio →								
TV →								

	8:00–8:15	8:15–8:30	8:30–8:45	8:45–9:00	9:00–9:15	9:15–9:30	9:30–9:45	9:45–10:00
Radio →								
TV →								

   If you did not watch TV any time yesterday, X here ☐

   If you did not listen to radio any time yesterday, X here ☐

   g. A government survey of gasoline retailers:

   Suppose the full-service pump selling price for leaded regular gasoline is 132.8 cents per gallon on the first day of the month. Suppose on the 10th of the month the price is raised to 134.9 cents per gallon, and on the 25th of the month it is reduced to 130.9 cents per gallon. In order to provide the required data you should list the accumulator reading on the full-service leaded regular gasoline pump when the station opens on the 1st day, the 10th day, and the 25th day of the month and when the station closes on the last day of the month.

   h. An anti–gun control group's survey:

   Do you believe that private citizens have the right to own firearms to defend themselves, their families, and their property from violent criminal attack?

   ____Yes

   ____No

   i. A survey of the general public:

   In the next year, after accounting for inflation, do you think your real personal income will go up or down?

   1. Up

   2. (Stay the same)

   3. Down

   4. (Don't know)

   j. A survey of the general public:

   Some people say that companies should be required by law to label all chemicals and substances that the government states are potentially harmful. The label would tell what the chemical or substance is, what dangers it might pose, and what safety procedures should be used in handling the substance. Other people say that such laws would be too strict. They say the law should require labels on only those chemicals and substances that the companies themselves decide are potentially harmful. Such a law, they say, would be less costly for the companies and would permit them to exclude those chemicals and substances they consider to be trade secrets. Which of these views is closest to your own?

   1. Require labels on all chemicals and substances that the government states are potentially harmful.

   2. (Don't know)

   3. Require labels on only those chemicals and substances that companies decide are potentially harmful.

k.   A survey of voters:

Since agriculture is vital to our state's economy, how do you feel about the administration's farm policies?

Strongly favor

Somewhat favor

Somewhat oppose

Strongly oppose

Unsure

2.   When the Agency for Consumer Advocacy was under consideration, there was considerable debate regarding the validity of the poll. The Consumer Federation of America charged that the following question was loaded:

Those in favor of setting up an additional federal consumer protection agency on top of the other agencies say that current agencies are not getting the job done themselves. Those who oppose setting up the additional agency say we already have plenty of government agencies to protect consumers, and it's just a matter of making them work better. How do you feel?

The researchers felt otherwise. How do you feel about this disputed question?

3.   How might the wording of a question about income influence respondents' answers?

4.   What is the difference between a leading and a loaded question?

5.   Design an open-ended response question(s) to measure reactions to a magazine ad for a Xerox photocopier.

6.   Design a question(s) to measure how a person who has just been shown a television commercial might describe the commercial.

7.   Evaluate the questionnaire layout for the filter question that follows:

Are you employed either full time or part time?

Mark (x) one.   ☐ Yes   ☐ No

If yes: How many hours per week are you usually employed? *Mark (x) one.*

☐ Less than 35   ☐ 35 or more

What is the ZIP code at your usual place of work?

_____

8.   It has been said that surveys show that consumers hate advertising, but like specific ads. Comment.

9.   Design a complete questionnaire to evaluate a new fast-food fried chicken restaurant.

10.   Design a short, but complete questionnaire to measure consumer satisfaction with an airline.

11.   Develop a checklist of things to consider in questionnaire construction.

12.   Design a complete personal interview questionnaire for a zoo that wishes to determine who visits the zoo and how they evaluate it.

13.   Design a complete self-administered questionnaire for a bank to give to customers immediately after they open new accounts.

14.   Design a questionnaire for your local Big Brothers and Big Sisters organization to investigate awareness and willingness to volunteer time to this organization.

15.   Design a questionnaire for a bank located in a college town to investigate the potential for college students as checking account customers.

16.   The Apple Assistance Center is a hotline to solve problems for users of Macintosh computers and other Apple products. Design a short, postcard consumer satisfaction/ service quality questionnaire for the Apple Assistance Center.

17.   A client tells a researcher that she wants a questionnaire that evaluates the importance of 30 product characteristics and rates her brand and 10 competing brands on these characteristics. The researcher believes that this questionnaire will induce respondent fatigue because it will be far too long. Should the researcher do exactly what the client says or risk losing the business by suggesting a different approach?

18.   A lobbying organization designs a short questionnaire about its political position. It also includes a membership solicitation with the questionnaire. Is this right?

19.   A public figure who supports cost cutting in government asks the following question in a survey: "Do **you support a presidential line item veto to eliminate waste in government?**" Is this ethical?

 Exploring the Internet

1.   Visit Yahoo at http://www.yahoo.com Follow this string of links: Business/Corporations/Polls. What you find will depend on when you visit the site. However, you might find something such as a Movie Poll, where you pick your favorite film of the season. Evaluate the questions in the poll.

2.   Visit Google at http://www.google.com and search for the key phrase *questionnaire design.* How many Web sites contain this phrase? Find an interesting Web site and report on your findings.

Case 15.1   Canterbury Travels

HOMETOWN WAS LOCATED IN THE EAST-NORTH-CENTRAL United States and had a population of about 50,000. There were two travel agencies in Hometown before Canterbury Travels opened its doors.

Canterbury Travels was in its second month of operations. Owner Roxanne Freeman had expected to have more business than she actually had. She decided that she needed to conduct a survey to determine how much business Hometown offered. She also wanted to learn whether people were aware of Canterbury Travels. She thought that this survey would determine the effectiveness of her advertising.

The questionnaire that Roxanne Freeman designed is shown in Case Exhibit 15.1–1.

QUESTIONS

1. Critically evaluate the questionnaire.
2. Will Canterbury Travels gain the information it needs from this survey?

Case Exhibit 15.1-1   Travel Questionnaire

The following questionnaire pertains to a project being conducted by a local travel agency. The intent of the study is to better understand the needs and attitudes of Hometown residents toward travel agencies. The questionnaire will take only 10 to 15 minutes to fill out at your convenience. Your name will in no way be connected with the questionnaire.

1. Have you traveled out of state?   _____ Yes   _____ No
2. If yes, do you travel for:
    Business   Both
    Pleasure
3. How often do you travel for the above?

    0–1 times per month   0–1 times per year
    2–3 times per month   2–3 times per year
    4–5 times per month   4–5 times per year
    6 or more times per month   6 or more times per year
4. How do you make your travel arrangements?
    Airline   Travel agency
    Other (please specify) _____
5. Did you know that travel agencies do not charge the customer for their services?
    _____ Yes   _____ No
6. Please rate the following qualities that would be most important to you in the selection of a travel agency:

	Good				**Bad**
Free services (reservations, advice, and delivery of tickets and literature)	___	___	___	___	___
Convenient location	___	___	___	___	___
Knowledgeable personnel	___	___	___	___	___
Friendly personnel	___	___	___	___	___
Casual atmosphere	___	___	___	___	___
Revolving charge account	___	___	___	___	___
Reputation	___	___	___	___	___
Personal sales calls	___	___	___	___	___

7. Are you satisfied with your present travel agency?

	Very satisfied				**Very dissatisfied**
Holiday Travel	___	___	___	___	___
Leisure Tours	___	___	___	___	___
Canterbury Travel	___	___	___	___	___
Other _____	___	___	___	___	___

(continued)

Case Exhibit 15.1-1   Travel Questionnaire *(Continued)*

---

8. If not, what are you dissatisfied with about your travel agency?

	Good				Bad
Free services (reservations, advice, and delivery of tickets and literature)	___	___	___	___	___
Convenient location	___	___	___	___	___
Knowledgeable personnel	___	___	___	___	___
Friendly personnel	___	___	___	___	___
Casual atmosphere	___	___	___	___	___
Revolving charge account	___	___	___	___	___
Reputation	___	___	___	___	___
Personal sales calls	___	___	___	___	___

9. Did you know that there is a new travel agency in Hometown?

    _____ Yes   _____ No

10. Can you list the travel agencies in Hometown and their locations?

    _____

    _____

    _____

11. Do you use the same travel agency repeatedly?

	0–1 times per month	2–3 times per month	4–5 times per month	6 or more times per month	0–1 times per year	2–3 times per year	4–5 times per year	6 or more times per year
Holiday Travel								
Leisure Tours								
Canterbury Travel								
Other (please specify)								

12. Have you visited the new travel agency in Hometown?

    _____ Yes   _____ No

13. If yes, what is its name? _____

14. How do you pay for your travel expenses?

    Cash   Company charge

    Check   Personal charge

    Credit card   Other _____

15. Which of these have you seen advertising for?

    Holiday Travel

    Canterbury Travel

    Other _____

16. If yes, where have you seen or heard this advertisement?

17. Would you consider changing travel agencies?

    _____ Yes   _____ No

The following are some personal questions about you that will be used for statistical purposes only. Your answers will be held in the strictest confidence.

18. What is your age?

    19–25   46–55

    26–35   56–65

    36–45   Over 65

19. What is your sex?

    Male   Female

20. What is your marital status?

    Single   Divorced

    Married   Widowed

(continued)

Case Exhibit 15.1-1   Travel Questionnaire *(Continued)*

21. How long have you lived in Hometown?
   - 0–6 months
   - 7–12 months
   - 1–4 years
   - 5–10 years
   - 11–15 years
   - Over 15 years
22. What is your present occupation?
   - Business and professional
   - Salaried and semiprofessional
   - Skilled worker
   - Laborer
   - Student
23. What is the highest level of education you have completed?
   - Elementary school
   - Junior high school
   - Senior high school
   - Trade or vocational school
   - 1–2 years of college
   - 3–4 years of college
   - More than 4 years of college
24. What is your yearly household income?
   - $0–$5,000
   - $5,001–$10,000
   - $10,001–$15,000
   - $15,001–$25,000
   - $25,001–$40,000
   - $40,001–$60,000
   - $60,000 and above

Case 15.2   GTE Airfone[14]

THE QUESTIONNAIRE IN CASE EXHIBIT 15.2–1 was sent to a sample of frequent airline fliers.

QUESTION

1. Evaluate the questionnaire.

Case Exhibit 15.2–1   Airfone Questionnaire

If you have used the Airfone service please indicate your level of satisfaction with the Airfone service by circling the appropriate number below.

	Excellent 5	Good 4	Average 3	Fair 2	Poor 1
GTE Airfone service					
A1 Considering your Airfone usage, how would you rate your overall experience	5	4	3	2	1
A2 Availability of Airfone on flights on which you've traveled	5	4	3	2	1
A3 Availability of operating instructions	5	4	3	2	1
A4 Understandability of operating instructions	5	4	3	2	1
A5 Length of time to obtain dial tone	5	4	3	2	1
A6 Ability to complete a call on the first attempt	5	4	3	2	1
A7 Transmission quality (static)	5	4	3	2	1
A8 Level of telephone background noise	5	4	3	2	1
A9 Calls fading	5	4	3	2	1
A10 Hearing the called party clearly	5	4	3	2	1
A11 Called party hearing you clearly	5	4	3	2	1
A12 Frequency of calls disconnected	5	4	3	2	1
A13 Convenience of computer voice messages	5	4	3	2	1
A14 Current price structure	5	4	3	2	1
A15 Flight attendant helpfulness, assistance, and knowledge of the Airfone service	5	4	3	2	1

(continued)

Case Exhibit 15.2–1 `Airfone Questionnaire` *(Continued)*

Billing

B1	Accuracy of monthly charges	5	4	3	2	1
B2	Ease of understanding charges	5	4	3	2	1

The following questions concern your Airfone usage, airline travel, preferred charge method, and a comparison of the Airfone to cellular phones. Please answer as completely as possible.

1. In the past *year,* how often have you used the Airfone service?

(Enter # Times)

2. Have you used our Seatfone product?
    (Circle one answer)

    Yes   1
    No   2

3. Did you use the Airfone service to make urgent business calls, nonurgent business calls, or personal calls?
    (Circle all that apply)

    Urgent business calls   1
    Nonurgent business calls   2
    Personal calls   3

4. Approximately, how many airline round trips do you make annually?

    (Enter # Times)

5. Which airline do you most frequently travel on?

    (Enter Name of Airline)

6. Has the Airfone service made your travel time productive and more beneficial to your completing business while in flight?
    (Circle one answer)
    If yes, please explain how _____

    Yes   1
    No   2

7. Considering the value of the Airfone service, do you feel the cost of a call is comparable to the quality of service you've experienced?
    (Circle one answer)
    If no, please explain why _____

    Yes   1
    No   2

8. Given a choice of flights with the same schedule, destination, and cost, one with the Airfone service, the other without, which flight would you choose to travel on? *(Circle one answer)*

    With Airfone   1
    Without Airfone   2

9. Which credit cards do you own? *(Circle all that apply)*
1.	American Express	4.	Discover	7.	UATP
2.	Carte Blanche	5.	Enroute	8.	Visa
3.	Diners Club	6.	MasterCard	9.	AT&T

10. Which credit card have you used in the past to pay for the Airfone service? *(Circle all that apply)*
1.	American Express	4.	Discover	7.	UATP
2.	Carte Blanche	5.	Enroute	8.	Visa
3.	Diners Club	6.	MasterCard	9.	AT&T

11. Have you experienced problems activating the Airfone Service with your card(s)?
    (Circle one answer)

    Yes   1
    No   2

12. Which card would you prefer to use to pay for the Airfone service?
    (Circle all that apply)
1.	American Express	4.	Discover	7.	UATP
2.	Carte Blanche	5.	Enroute	8.	Visa
3.	Diners Club	6.	MasterCard	9.	AT&T

13. Do you own a cellular phone or use a company-paid cellular phone?
    (Circle one answer)

    Yes   1
    No   2

    If yes, how does the quality of the GTE Airfone compare to that of the cellular phone?
    (Circle one answer)

    Airfone is much higher quality than cellular   1
    Airfone is somewhat higher quality than cellular   2
    Airfone is about the same quality as cellular   3
    Airfone is somewhat lower quality than cellular   4
    Airfone is much lower than cellular   5

(continued)

Case Exhibit 15.2–1 Airfone Questionnaire *(Continued)*

14.	Have you ever seen any advertising for GTE Airfone?	Yes 1
	If yes, what did the advertising tell you about GTE Airfone?	No 2

_____

_____

If yes, where have you seen GTE Airfone advertising? *(Circle all that apply)*

In-flight airline magazines	1
Posters or billboards	2
TV at airport	3
Newspapers	4
Business publications	5
Card located in the seatback pocket	6
Other	7

15. Are you aware of our Service Guarantee that provides credit when you are not satisfied with the quality of an Airfone call?

If yes, how did you first become aware of it? *(Circle one only)*

Yes 1
No 2

In-flight airline magazines	1
Posters or billboards	2
TV at airport	3
Newspapers	4
Business publications	5
Card located in the seatback pocket	6
Flight attendant	7
Other	8

These next few questions are for classification purposes only.

_____

16. What is your job classification? *(Circle one answer)*

Professional	1
Executive	2
Managerial	3
Administrative	4
Technical	5
Other	6

17. What is your age? *(Circle one answer)*

18–24	1
25–34	2
35–44	3
45–54	4
55–64	5
65 or over	6

18. What is your sex? *(Circle one answer)*

Male	1
Female	2

19. What is your annual *individual* income? *(Circle one answer)*

Under $20,000	1
$20,000–$39,999	2
$40,000–$59,999	3
$60,000–$79,999	4
$80,000–$99,999	5
$100,000–$149,999	6
$150,000+	7

20. What is your level of education? *(Circle one answer)*

Attended high school	1
High school graduate	2
Some college	3
College graduate	4
Postgraduate degree	5

21. Finally, what changes/improvements would you like to see in our service?

_____

_____

Thanks again for your assistance! Please return this completed survey in the enclosed preaddressed, postage-paid envelope.

Case 15.3   Middlemist Precision Tool Company (B)

MIDDLEMIST PRECISION TOOL COMPANY WAS CONDUCT-ing research for its radial arm saw adjustment device (see Case 7.4). The company decided that it had two major markets for its product: professional wood-workers, such as carpenters, and do-it-yourself homeowners. It decided to concentrate on the do-it-yourself market and thought a survey would be appropriate.

QUESTIONS

1. What were Middlemist's primary information needs?

2. What type of survey should have been used in this study?

3. Design a questionnaire to satisfy Middlemist's information needs.

Case 15.4   McDonald's Spanish Language Questionnaire

THE FOLLOWING QUESTIONS ABOUT A VISIT TO McDonald's originally appeared in Spanish and were translated to English language questions.

QUESTIONS

1. What is the typical process for developing questionnaires for markets in which a different language is spoken?

2. Find someone who speaks Spanish and have him or her back translate the questions that appear in the case. Are these Spanish-language questions adequate?

AQUI SE EMPIEZA ➡ **1. En general, ¿qué tan satisfecho/a quedó con su visita a este McDonald's hoy?** .... 😦 NADA SATISFECHO/A ① ② ③ ④ ⑤ MUY SATISFECHO/A 😊

2. Su visita fue....... Adentro (**A**) o en el Drive-thru (**DT**) Ⓐ Adentro   Ⓓ Ⓣ Drive-thru

3. Su visita fue....... Durante el Desayuno (**D**), Almuerzo (**A**), Cena (**C**) Ⓓ Desayuno   Ⓐ Almuerzo   Ⓐ Cena

4. Su visita fue....... Entre semana (**E**) o Fin de semana (**F**) Ⓔ Entre semana   Ⓕ Fin de semana

COMIDA   **5.** ¿Quedó satisfecho/a con la comida que recibio hoy? Ⓢ Si   Ⓝ No
Si NO, ¿cuál fue el problema?
Favor de rellenar el(los) círculo(s) apropiado(s).

- Sandwich / platillo frío
- Apariencia desagradable
- Mal sabor de la comida
- Pocas papas en la bolsa / caja
- Papas / tortitas de papa frías
- Papas no bien saladas
- Bebida aguada / de mal sabor

Case 15.5   Schönbrunn Palace in Vienna

THE SCHÖNBRUNN PALACE IN VIENNA WAS CONSTRUCTED in the eighteenth century during the reign of the Hapsburgs. Today this former summer residence of the imperial family is one of Austria's top tourist attractions.

The following questions about a visit to the Schönbrunn in Vienna, Austria, originally appeared in German and were translated to English.

QUESTIONS

1. What is the typical process for developing questionnaires for markets in which different language is spoken?

2. Find someone who speaks German and have him or her back translate the questions that appear in the case. Are these German questions adequate?

Befragung der Besucher   **Schloß Schönbrunn**

Land/Staat _____   Bundesland (nur für Ö) _____

Alter _____ Jahre   Geschlecht □ männlich □ weiblich

Heutiges Datum ___ . ___ . 199__   Uhrzeit _____

• Waren Sie heute zum ersten Mal im Schloß Schönbrunn?
  □ ja   □ nein, zum ___. Mal

• Welche Tour haben Sie gemacht?
  □ *Grand Tour* (40 Räume)
  □ *Imperial Tour* (22 Räume)

• Welche Art von Führung haben Sie gewählt?
  □ *Schönbrunn Führung (Angebot des Schlosses)*
  □ *eigener Reiseführer (Reisegruppe, Fremdenführer)*
  □ *Tonbandführer (Audioguide)* in _____ *Sprache*
  □ *keinerlei Führung*

• Falls Sie an einer Führung teilgenommen haben:
  Wie finden Sie Ihren Führer bzw. Ihre Führerin?
  □ sehr freundlich   □ eher freundlich   □ eher unfreundlich   □ sehr unfreundlich
  weil ... _____

• Bei Verwendung eines Tonbandführers (Audioguide):
  Wie finden Sie die angebotenen Audioguides?
  □ sehr gut   □ eher gut   □ eher schlecht   □ sehr schlecht
  weil ... _____

• Wie ist Ihr Gesamteindruck vom Schloß Schönbrunn alles in allem?
  □ sehr gut   □ eher gut   □ eher schlecht   □ sehr schlecht

• Wie ist Ihr Eindruck vom Personal im Schloß?
  □ sehr gut   □ eher gut   □ eher schlecht   □ sehr schlecht
  weil ... _____

• Wie gut finden Sie sich im Schloß Schönbrunn/Park zurecht (Hinweisschilder, kennt man sich gut aus, findet man die Kassen, Toiletten, den Ausgang, etc.)?
  □ sehr gut   □ eher gut   □ eher schlecht   □ sehr schlecht
  weil ... _____

• Fühlten Sie sich nach dem Besuch gut informiert über das Schloß und seine Geschichte?
  □ sehr gut   □ eher gut   □ eher schlecht   □ sehr schlecht

• Wurden Sie bei der Besichtigung gestört?
  durch (andere) Gruppen:
  □ sehr stark   □ etwas   □ kaum   □ gar nicht
  durch Einzelbesucher:
  □ sehr stark   □ etwas   □ kaum   □ gar nicht

• Wie finden Sie die Art, wie die Räume dargestellt werden (Einrichtung, Möblierung, Beleuchtung, Dekoration, etc.)?
  □ sehr gut   □ eher gut   □ eher schlecht   □ sehr schlecht
  weil ... _____

• Haben Sie nach dem Besuch im Schloß Schönbrunn eine lebendige Vorstellung vom einstigen Leben bei Hof?
  □ ja   □ etwas   □ kaum   □ nein
  weil ... _____

• Was würden Sie noch gerne über das Schloß erfahren?

  _____

• Wie finden Sie die Eintrittspreise?
  □ viel zu teuer   □ etwas zu teuer   □ angemessen   □ günstig

• Wie finden Sie das Angebot im Museumshop?
  □ sehr gut   □ eher gut   □ eher schlecht   □ sehr schlecht
  weil ... _____

• Was könnte Ihrer Meinung nach noch verbessert werden?

  _____
  _____
  _____

Vielen Dank für Ihren Besuch und Ihre Anregungen!

Question Wording and Measurement Scales for Commonly Researched Topics

As Chapters 13, 14, and 15 explain, problem definitions and research objectives determine the nature of the questions to be asked. In most cases researchers will construct custom questions for their specific projects. However, in many instances different research projects share some common research objectives. This appendix compiles question wordings and measurement scales marketing researchers frequently use. It is by no means exhaustive. It does not repeat every question already discussed in the text. For example, it does not include the hundreds of possible semantic differential items or Likert scale items discussed in Chapter 14.

The purpose of this appendix is to provide a bank of questions and scales to provide an easy reference. It can be used when marketing research objectives dictate investigation of traditional issues.

Questions About Advertising

Awareness

Have you ever seen any advertising for (brand name)?

☐ Yes ☐ No

Are you aware of (brand name)?

☐ Yes ☐ No

If yes, how did you first become aware of (brand name)?

☐ In-flight airline magazine

☐ Poster or billboard at airport

☐ Television at airport

☐ Card in the seatback pocket

☐ Other (please specify)_____

Unaided Recall/Top of the Mind Recall

Can you tell me the names of any brands of (product category) for which you have seen or heard any advertising recently?

_____

_____

_____

(After reading a magazine or viewing a TV program with commercials) Please try to recall all the brands you saw advertised on/in (name of program or magazine). (DO NOT PROBE. WRITE BRAND NAMES IN ORDER MENTIONED BY RESPONDENT.)

(After establishing that the respondent watched a certain television program) Do you recall seeing a commercial for any (product category)?
(IF YES) What brand of (product category) was advertised?

Aided Recall

(After establishing that the respondent watched a certain television program or read a certain magazine) Now, I'm going to read you a list of brands. Some of them were advertised on/in (name of program or magazine); others were not. Please tell me which ones you remember seeing, even if you mentioned them before.

Brand A (Advertised)

Brand B (Not advertised)

Brand C (Advertised)

Do you remember seeing a commercial for (specific brand name)?
Yes   No

Recognition

(Show advertisement to respondent) Did you see or read any part of this advertisement?
☐ Yes   ☐ No

Message Communication/Playback (Sales Point Playback)

These questions require that the researcher first qualify awareness with a question such as: **Have you ever seen any advertising for (brand name)?** Message playback questions are then asked.

If yes, what did the advertising tell you about (brand name or product category)?

_____

_____

Other than trying to sell you the product, what do you think was the main idea in the description you just read (commercial you just saw)?

_____

_____

What was the main thing it was trying to communicate about the product?

What did the advertising for (brand name) say about the product?

_____

_____

What did you learn about (brand name) from this advertisement?

_____

_____

Attitude Toward the Advertisement

Please choose the statement below that best describes your feelings about the commercial you just saw.

☐ I liked it very much.

☐ I liked it.

☐ I neither liked nor disliked it.

☐ I disliked it.

☐ I disliked it very much.

Was there anything in the commercial you've just seen that you found hard to believe?

☐ Yes   ☐ No

What thoughts or feelings went through your mind as you went through the advertisement?

Attitude Toward Advertised Brand (Persuasion)

Several of the questions and measures about products or brands in the following section are also used for this purpose.

Based on what you've seen in this commercial, how interested would you be in trying the product?

☐ Extremely interested

☐ Very interested

☐ Somewhat interested

☐ Not very interested

☐ Not at all interested

The advertisement tried to increase your interest in (brand). How was your buying interest affected?

☐ Increased considerably

☐ Increased somewhat

☐ Not affected

☐ Decreased somewhat

☐ Decreased considerably

Based on what you've just seen in this commercial, how do you think (brand name) might compare to other brands you've seen or heard about?

☐ Better

☐ As good as

☐ Not as good as

Readership/Viewership

Have you ever read (seen) a copy of (advertising medium)?

☐ Yes ☐ No

How frequently do you (watch the evening news on channel *X*)?

☐ Every day

☐ 5–6 times a week

☐ 2–4 times a week

☐ Once a week

☐ Less than once a week

☐ Never

Questions About Ownership and Product Usage

Ownership

Do you own a (product category)?

☐ Yes ☐ No

Purchase Behavior

Have you ever purchased a (product category or brand name)?

☐ Yes ☐ No

Regular Usage

Which brands of (product category) do you regularly use?

☐ Brand A

☐ Brand B

☐ Brand C

☐ Do not use _____

Which brands of (product category) have you used in the past month?

☐ Brand A

☐ Brand B

☐ Brand C

☐ Do not use _____

In an average month, how often do you buy (product category or brand name)?

Record Number of Times per Month _____

How frequently do you buy (product category or brand name)?
- [ ] Every day
- [ ] 5–6 times a week
- [ ] 2–4 times a week
- [ ] Once a week
- [ ] Less than once a week
- [ ] Never

Would you say you purchase (product category or brand name) more often than you did a year ago, about the same as a year ago, or less than a year ago?
- [ ] More often than a year ago
- [ ] About the same as a year ago
- [ ] Less than a year ago

Questions About Goods and Services

Ease of Use

How easy do you find using (brand name)?
- [ ] Very easy
- [ ] Easy
- [ ] Neither easy nor difficult
- [ ] Difficult
- [ ] Very difficult

Uniqueness

How different is this brand from other brands of (product category)?
- [ ] Very different
- [ ] Somewhat different
- [ ] Slightly different
- [ ] Not at all different

How would you rate this product (brand name) on uniqueness?
- [ ] Extremely unique
- [ ] Very unique
- [ ] Somewhat unique
- [ ] Slightly unique
- [ ] Not at all unique

Please form several piles of cards so that statements that are similar to each other or say similar things are in the same pile. You may form as many piles as you like and you may put as many or as few cards as you want in a pile. You can set aside any statements that you feel are unique or different, and are not similar to any of the other statements.

Attribute Ratings/Importance of Characteristics

Measurement scales, such as the semantic differential and Likert scales, are frequently used for this purpose, especially measuring brand image or store image. See Chapter 15.

How important is (specific attribute), as far as you are concerned?

☐ Very important

☐ Of some importance

☐ Of little importance

☐ Of absolutely no importance

We would like you to rate (brand name or product category) on several different characteristics. (For concept tests, add: Since you may not have used this product before, please base your answers on your impressions from what you've just read.)

Characteristic A

☐ Excellent

☐ Good

☐ Fair

☐ Poor

Interest

In general how interested are you in trying a new brand of (product category)?

☐ Very interested

☐ Somewhat interested

☐ Not too interested

☐ Not at all interested

Like/Dislike

What do you like about (brand name)?

_____

_____

What do you dislike about (brand name)?

_____

_____

How do you like the taste of (brand name)?

☐ Like it very much

☐ Like it

☐ Neither like nor dislike it

☐ Dislike it

☐ Strongly dislike it

Preference

Which credit card do you prefer to use?

1. American Express
2. MasterCard
3. Visa
4. No preference

Expectations

How would you compare the way (company's) service was actually delivered with the way you had anticipated that (company) would provide the service?

☐ Much better than expected

☐ Somewhat better than expected

☐ About the same as expected

☐ Somewhat worse than expected

☐ Much worse than expected

Satisfaction

How satisfied were you with (brand name)?

☐ Very satisfied

☐ Somewhat satisfied

☐ Very dissatisfied

How satisfied were you with (brand name)?

☐ Very satisfied

☐ Very dissatisfied

☐ Somewhere in between

(If somewhere in between)

On balance would you describe yourself as leaning toward being more satisfied or more dissatisfied with (brand name) than the brand you normally use?

☐ Satisfied

☐ Dissatisfied

Now that you have owned (brand name) for 6 months, please tell us how satisfied you are with it.

☐ Completely satisfied

☐ Very satisfied

☐ Fairly well satisfied

☐ Somewhat dissatisfied

☐ Very dissatisfied

Quality

How would you rate the quality of (brand name)?

☐ Excellent

☐ Good

☐ Fair

☐ Poor

Please indicated how the quality of (Brand A) compares with the quality of (Brand B).

☐ Better

☐ About the same

☐ Worse

Problems

Have you experienced problems with (company's) service?

☐ Yes   ☐ No

When attempting to contact (company's) representative, how much of a problem, if any, was each of the following:

Phones busy

☐ No problem at all   ☐ Slight problem   ☐ Somewhat of a problem   ☐ Major problem

Put on hold too long or too often

☐ No problem at all   ☐ Slight problem   ☐ Somewhat of a problem   ☐ Major problem

What are the major shortcomings of (brand name)? (PROBE: What other shortcomings are there?)

Benefits

Do you think (product concept) would have major benefits, minor benefits, or no benefits at all?

☐ Major benefits

☐ Minor benefits

☐ No benefits at all

Improvements

In what ways, if any, could (brand name) be changed or improved? We would like you to tell us anything you can think of, no matter how minor it seems.

_____

_____

Buying Intentions for Existing Products

Do you intend to buy a (brand name or product category) in the next month (3 months, year, etc.)?

☐ Yes   ☐ No

If a free (product category) were offered to you, which would you select?

☐ Brand A

☐ Brand B

☐ Brand C

☐ Do not use

Buying Intentions Based on Product Concept

(Respondent is shown a prototype or asked to read a concept statement.) Now that you have read about (product concept), if this product were available at your local store, how likely would you be to buy it?

☐ Would definitely buy it

☐ Would probably buy it

☐ Might or might not buy it

☐ Would probably not buy it

☐ Would definitely not buy it

(Hand response card to respondent) Which phrase on this card indicates how likely you would be to buy this product the next time you go shopping for a product of this type?

☐ Would definitely buy it

☐ Would probably buy it

☐ Might or might not buy it

☐ Would probably not buy it

☐ Would definitely not buy it

Now that you have read about (product concept), if this product were available at your local store for (price), how likely would you be to buy it?

☐ Would definitely buy it

☐ Would probably buy it

☐ Might or might not buy it

☐ Would probably not buy it

☐ Would definitely not buy it

How often, if ever, would you buy (product concept)?

☐ Once a week or more

☐ Once every 2 to 3 weeks

☐ Once a month/every 4 weeks

☐ Once every 2 to 3 months

☐ Once every 4 to 6 months

☐ Less than once a year

☐ Never

Based on your experience, would you recommend (company) to a friend who wanted to purchase (product concept)?

☐ Recommend that the friend buy from (company)

☐ Recommend that the friend not buy from (company)

☐ Offer no opinion either way

Reason for Buying Intention

Why do you say that you would (would not) buy (brand name)? (Probe: What other reason do you have for feeling this way?)

Questions About Demographics

Age

What is your age please?

Education

What is your level of education?

☐ Some high school or less

☐ Completed high school

☐ Some college

☐ Completed college

☐ Some graduate school

☐ Completed graduate school

What is the highest level of education you have obtained?

☐ Some high school or less

☐ High school graduate

☐ Some college

☐ College graduate

☐ Postgraduate school

☐ Completed graduate school

Marital Status

What is your marital status?

☐ Married

☐ Divorced/separated

☐ Widowed

☐ Never married/single

Children

Are there any children under the age of 6 living in your household?

☐ Yes   ☐ No

If yes, how many?

Income

Which group describes your annual family income?

☐ Under $20,000

☐ $20,000–$39,000

☐ $40,000–$59,999

☐ $60,000–$79,999

☐ $80,000–$99,999

☐ $100,000–$149,999

☐ $150,000 or more

Please check the box that describes your total household income before taxes in (year). Include income for yourself as well as for all other persons who live in your household.

☐ Less than $10,000   ☐ $35,000–$39,999

☐ $10,000–$14,999   ☐ $40,000–$49,999

☐ $15,000–$19,999   ☐ $50,000–$59,999

☐ $20,000–$24,999   ☐ $60,000–$74,999

☐ $25,000–$29,999   ☐ $75,000 or more

☐ $30,000–$34,999

Occupation

What is your occupation?

☐ Professional   ☐ Technical

☐ Executive   ☐ Labor

☐ Managerial   ☐ Secretarial

☐ Administrative   ☐ Clerical

☐ Sales   ☐ Other

What is your occupation?

☐ Homemaker

☐ Professional/technical

☐ Upper management/executive

☐ Middle management

☐ Sales/marketing

☐ Clerical or service worker

☐ Tradesperson/machine operator

☐ Laborer

☐ Retired

☐ Student

Chapter 16

Sampling Designs and Sampling Procedures

WE KNOW THAT MAKING A GOOD FIRST IMPRESSION IS IMPOR-
tant because after a sample exposure to us people make
judgments about the types of people we are. Unless you
are a member of the Polar Bear swimming club, you will
test the early March waters of Lake Michigan with a toe before
diving in. Stand in a bookstore and observe the process of sampling.
Customers generally pick up a book, look at the cover, and then sample a few pages to get a feeling for the writing style and the content
before deciding whether to buy. The high school student who visits a
college classroom to listen to a professor's lecture is employing a sampling technique. Selecting a university on the basis of one classroom
visit may not be a scientific sample, but in a personal situation it may
be a practical sampling experience. These examples illustrate the
intuitive nature of sampling in everyday uses when it is impossible,
inconvenient, or too expensive to measure every item in the population.

Although sampling is commonplace in daily activities, most of
these familiar samples are not scientific. The concept of sampling
may seem simple and intuitive, but the actual process of sampling can
be quite complex. Sampling is a central aspect of marketing research,
and it requires in-depth examination.

This chapter explains the nature of sampling and how to determine the appropriate sample design.

What you will learn in this chapter

*To define the terms sample, popu-
lation, population element, and
census.*

*To explain why a sample rather
than a complete census may be
taken.*

*To discuss the issues concerning
the identification of the target population and the selection of a sampling frame.*

*To discuss common forms of sam-
pling frames and sampling frame
error.*

*To distinguish between random
sampling and systematic (nonsampling) errors.*

*To explain the various types of
systematic (nonsampling) errors
that result from sample selection.*

*To discuss the advantages and
disadvantages of the various types
of probability and nonprobability
samples.*

*To understand how to choose an
appropriate sample design.*

Sampling Terminology

sample
A subset or some part of a larger population.

population (universe)
Any complete group of entities that share some common set of characteristics.

population element
An individual member of a population.

census
An investigation of all the individual elements that make up a population.

The process of sampling involves using a small number of items or parts of the population to make conclusions about the whole population. A **sample** is a subset or some part of a larger population. The purpose of sampling is to enable one to estimate some unknown characteristic of the population.

We have defined sampling in terms of the population to be studied. A **population** or **universe** is any complete group—for example, of people, sales territories, stores, or college students—that share some common set of characteristics. When a distinction is made between population and universe, it is made on the basis of whether the group is finite (a population) or infinite (a universe). The term **population element** refers to an individual member of the population. A **census** is an investigation of all the individual elements that make up the population—a total enumeration rather than a sample.

Why Sample?

At a wine-tasting party guests all recognize the impossibility of anything but sampling. However, in a scientific study in which the objective is to estimate an unknown population value, why should a sample rather than a complete census be taken?

Pragmatic Reasons

Applied marketing research projects usually have budget and time constraints. If Ford Motor Corporation wished to take a census of past purchasers' reactions to the company's recalls of defective models, millions of automobile buyers would have to be contacted. Some of these would be inaccessible (for example, out of the country), and it would be impossible to contact all these people within a short time period.

A researcher who wants to investigate a population with an extremely small number of population elements may elect to conduct a census rather than a sample because the cost, labor, and time drawbacks would be relatively insignificant. Thus, a company concerned with salespersons' satisfaction with its computer networking system may have no pragmatic reason for avoiding in-house circulation of a questionnaire to all 25 of its employees. In most situations, however, there are many practical reasons for sampling. Sampling cuts costs, reduces labor requirements, and gathers vital information quickly. These advantages may be sufficient in themselves for using a sample rather than a census, but there are other reasons.

Accurate and Reliable Results

Another major reason for sampling is that most properly selected samples give sufficiently accurate results. If the elements of a population are quite similar, only a small sample is necessary to accurately portray the characteristic of interest. Most of us have had blood samples taken from the finger, the arm, or another part of the body. The assumption is that the blood is sufficiently similar

---

> **Exhibit 16.1   A Photographic Example of How Sampling Works**

Photograph 1
Commercial Actor–Ron Steelman

Photograph 2
2,000 dots

Photograph 3
1,000 dots

Photograph 4
250 dots

---

throughout the body to determine the characteristics of the blood on the basis of a sample. When the population elements are largely homogeneous, samples are highly representative of the population. Under these circumstances almost any sample is as good as another. Even when populations have considerable heterogeneity, however, large samples provide sufficiently precise data to make most decisions.

The well-known research firm A. C. Nielsen offers a simple demonstration of how sampling works (see Exhibit 16.1). Four photographs show how one can take different-sized samples and produce very generalizable conclusions. The first photograph is finely screened and, therefore, is printed with thousands of

William's Census Was Ahead of Its Time

AFTER WILLIAM THE CONQUEROR TOOK OVER England, he wanted to see what his conquest had netted him. Monarchs back then lacked basic information such as the number of estates or livestock in the kingdom. So in 1086, William ordered a unique survey. Every village and fief was counted to the last building, netting detailed data on how much land and wealth each person owned. He used the data to levy taxes. The result was "The Domesday Book," a corruption of "Doomsday," the Day of Judgment. The king's taxes were considered as inescapable as divine judgment. No other king of the Middle Ages conducted such a thorough inventory. Today, governments conduct censuses, keep our names and birthdates on file and zealously document everything that can be taxed. It's difficult to imagine an age when people were not an entry in the governmental books.

dots of ink. Because of the fineness of detail, one might say that this photograph contains nearly all of the detail, or information, that can be provided.

The other photographs provide less detail. Photograph 2 consists of approximately 2,000 dots. The face is still very clear, but less so than in the first photograph; some detail is missing, but the face is still recognizable. Photograph 3 is made up of only 1,000 dots, constituting a sample that is only half as large as that in photograph 2; the face can still be recognized. In photograph 4 the sample is down to 250 dots, yet if you look at the picture at a distance, you can still make out a face and identify it as the same one shown in photograph 1. The 250-dot sample is still useful even though it contains only a small fraction of the number of dots in the other photographs. *Precision* has suffered but *accuracy* has not.

Of course, samples are accurate only when researchers have taken care to properly draw representative samples. More will be said about this later in the chapter.

A sample may be more accurate than a census. A census of a large population introduces a greater likelihood of nonsampling errors. In a survey, mistakes may occur that are unrelated to the selection of people in the study; for example, a response may be coded incorrectly or entered into the wrong column. Interviewer mistakes, tabulation errors, and other nonsampling errors may increase during a census because of the increased volume of work. In a sample, however, increased accuracy is possible because the fieldwork and tabulation of the data can be more closely supervised than would be possible in a census. In a field survey, a small, well-trained, closely supervised group may do a more careful and accurate job of collecting information than a large group of nonprofessional interviewers who try to contact everyone. An interesting case in point is the use of samples by the Bureau of the Census to check the accuracy of the U.S. Census. If the sample indicates a possible source of error, the census is redone.

Destruction of Test Units

Many research projects, especially those in quality control testing, require the destruction of the items being tested. If a manufacturer of firecrackers wished to find out whether each unit met a specific production standard, there would be

---

Exhibit 16.2 Stages in the Selection of a Sample

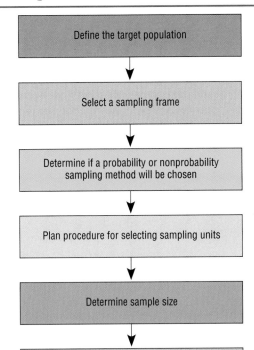

---

no product left after the testing. This is the exact situation in many marketing strategy experiments. For example, if an experimental sales presentation were presented to every potential customer, there would be no prospects left uncontacted after the experiment. In other words if there is a finite population and everyone in the population participates in the research and cannot be replaced, no population elements remain to be selected as sampling units. The test units have been destroyed or ruined for the purpose of the research project.

Practical Sampling Concepts

Researchers must make several decisions before taking a sample. Exhibit 16.2 overviews these decisions as a series of sequential stages even though the order of the decisions does not always follow this sequence. These decisions are highly interrelated. The issues associated with each of these stages, except for fieldwork, are discussed in this chapter and Chapter 17. Fieldwork is examined in Chapter 18.

WHAT WENT RIGHT?

You Can Learn a Lot from a Few: George Gallup's Nation of Numbers

IN THE SUMMER OF 1932 IOWA DEMOCRATS NOMINATED a 60-year-old widow named Ola Babcock Miller as the party's candidate for secretary of state. It was not a big deal. No Democrat had carried the state since the Civil War, but it was a nice thing to do, a gesture of respect for her late husband, a small-town newspaper publisher who had spent his life trying, vainly, to bring down Iowa Republicanism.

Mrs. Miller called in the family for help. Her son-in-law, a college professor who had just joined a New York advertising agency, had some ideas. Why not have some people go door to door, using this "scientific" plan he had, and ask voters what they wanted?

The son-in-law's name was George H. Gallup. Mrs. Miller won.

Young George—he was born in 1901—was a go-getter. His father had been a dreamer, a country schoolteacher who tried to develop what he called "a new logic of lateral thinking" and built an eight-sided house on the theory that it would offer better protection against plains windstorms.

George left the octagonal house and the hometown, Jefferson, as soon as he could find his way in a bigger world. The first step was Iowa City and the State University of Iowa. Then in 1922, between his junior and senior years, George answered an advertisement for summer employment in St. Louis. The *Post-Dispatch* hired 50 students to survey the city, questioning readers about what they liked and didn't like in the newspaper.

Each and every reader. The students were hired to go to every door in St. Louis—there were 55,000 homes in the city then—and ask the same questions. Gallup, one hot day, knocked on one door too many, got the same answers one time too many, and decided: There's got to be a better way.

"A New Technique for Objective Methods for Measuring Reader Interest in Newspapers" was the way, and the title of Gallup's Ph.D. thesis at Iowa. Working with the Des Moines *Register* and *Tribune* and the 200-year-old statistical theory probabilities of the Swiss mathematician Jakob Bernoulli, Gallup developed "sampling" techniques. You didn't have to talk to everybody, he said, as long as you randomly selected interviews according to a sampling plan that took into account whatever diversity was relevant in the universe of potential respondents—geographic, ethnic, economic.

Although not everybody understood or

Defining the Target Population

Once the decision to sample has been made, the first question concerns identifying the target population. What is the relevant population? In many cases this is not a difficult question. Registered voters may be clearly identifiable. Likewise, if a company's 106-person sales force is the population of concern, there are few definitional problems. In other cases the decision may be difficult. One survey concerning organizational buyer behavior incorrectly defined the population as purchasing agents whom sales representatives regularly contacted. Investigators discovered after the survey that industrial engineers within the customer companies had substantially affected buying decisions, but they rarely talked with the salespeople. Frequently the appropriate population element is the household rather than the individual member of the household. This presents some problems if household lists are not available.

At the outset of the sampling process, it is vital to carefully define the target believed then—or now—this intellectual invention was a big deal. "Guesswork eliminated in new method for determining reader interest" was the lead headline of the February 8, 1930, issue of the newspaper industry's trade journal, *Editor & Publisher*. There was a photograph of a big, stolid midwesterner above the caption: "George H. Gallup, instructor, U. of Iowa."

The instructor tried to explain what he was talking about and doing. "Suppose there are 7,000 white beans and 3,000 black beans well churned in a barrel," he said then, and again more than 52 years later as we walked together near his office in Princeton, New Jersey. "If you scoop out 100 of them, you'll get approximately 70 white beans and 30 black in your hand, and the range of your possible error can be computed mathematically. As long as the barrel contains many more beans than your handful, the proportion will remain within that margin of error 997 times out of 1,000."

Well, it seemed to work for newspapers, and George Gallup, instructor, was in great demand around the country. He became head of the journalism department at Drake University and then switched to a professorship at Northwestern—all the while doing readership surveys for papers in Chicago, Cleveland, Buffalo, and points east and west. He was hot, and in that summer of '32 a new

advertising agency, Young & Rubicam, invited him to New York to create a research department and procedures for evaluating the effectiveness of advertising. He did that, too. One of his first Y&R surveys, based on newspaper experience, indicated that the number of readers of advertisements was proportional to the length of the paragraphs in a piece of copy.

And, of course, by the end of that year, 1932, with his mother-in-law's election, Gallup was confident that his methodology was valid not only for beans and newspaper readers, but for voters, too. As long as you understood the sampling universe—white, black, male, female, rich, poor, urban, rural, Republican, Democratic—you could predict elections or calculate public attitudes on public questions by interviewing a relatively small number of people.

So Gallup went out and formed the grandly titled American Institute of Public Opinion. Keeping his job at Young & Rubicam, he began syndicating surveys to newspapers under the title: "America Speaks: The National Weekly Poll of Public Opinion." The first Gallup Poll, released in October 1935, focused on the question, asked of 3,000 Americans: "Do you think expenditures by the government for relief and recovery are: Too Little? Too Great? About Right?" Three out of five respondents said, "Too Great."

population so that the proper sources from which the data are to be collected can be identified. Answering questions about the crucial characteristics of the population is the usual technique for defining the target population. Does the term *comic book reader* include children under 6 years of age who do not actually read the words? Does *all persons west of the Mississippi* include people in east bank towns that border the river, such as East St. Louis, Illinois? The question "Whom do we want to talk to?" must be answered. It may be users, nonusers, recent adopters, or brand switchers. To implement the sample in the field, tangible characteristics should be used to define the population. A baby food manufacturer might define the population as all women still capable of bearing children. However, a more specific *operational definition* would be women between the ages of 12 and 50. While this definition by age may exclude a few women who are capable of childbearing and include some who are not, it is still more explicit and provides a manageable basis for the sample design.

The Sampling Frame

sampling frame
A list of elements from which a sample may be drawn; also called working population.

In practice, the sample will be drawn from a list of population elements that often differs somewhat from the defined target population. A **sampling frame** is a list of elements from which the sample may be drawn. A simple example of a sampling frame would be a list of all members of the American Medical Association. Generally it is not feasible to compile a list that does not exclude some members of the population. For example, if the student telephone directory is assumed to be a sampling frame of your university's student population, it may exclude those students who registered late, those without phones, or those who have their telephones listed only under their roommates' or pets' names. The sampling frame is also called the *working population* because it provides the list for operational work. If a complete list of population elements is not accessible, materials such as maps or aerial photographs may be used as a sampling frame. The discrepancy between the definition of the population and a sampling frame is the first potential source of error associated with sample selection. We will discuss such errors later in the chapter.

Mailing Lists.   Some firms, called *list brokers,* specialize in providing mailing lists that give the names, addresses, and phone numbers of specific populations. Exhibit 16.3 shows a page from a mailing list company's offerings. Companies such as this offer lists based on subscriptions to professional journals, ownership of credit cards, and a variety of other sources. One mailing list company obtained its listing of households with children from an ice cream retailer who gave away free ice cream cones on children's birthdays. (The children filled out cards with their names, addresses, and birthdays, which the retailer then sold to the mailing list company.)

A valuable source of information for names is R. L. Polk's series of city directories. A city directory records the name of each resident over 18 years of age and lists pertinent information about each household. A particularly valuable feature is the street directory pages. These pages are a **reverse directory** that provides, in a different format, the same information contained in a telephone directory. Listings may be found by city and street address and/or phone number rather than in alphabetical order of surnames. This is particularly useful when a retailer wishes to survey only a certain geographical area of the city or when census tracts are to be selected using income or another demographic criterion.

reverse directory
A directory similar to a telephone directory except that listings are by city and street address and/or phone number rather than by alphabetical order of surnames.

sampling frame error
An error that occurs when certain sample elements are not listed or are not accurately represented in the sampling frame.

A **sampling frame error** occurs when certain sample elements are excluded or when the entire population is not accurately represented in the sampling frame. One city's manager for community development, in preparation for an upcoming bond issue election, used randomly generated telephone numbers as the basis for a sample survey to gauge attitudes toward capital improvements. When the bond issue failed, consultants pointed out that the appropriate sampling frame would have been a list of registered voters, not any adult with a phone (since some might not have voted in this type of election). By including respondents who should not have been listed as members of the population, a sampling frame error occurred.

Population elements can also be overrepresented in a sampling frame. A savings and loan defined its population as all individuals who had savings accounts. However, when it drew a sample from a list of *accounts* rather than from the list of names of *individuals,* individuals who had multiple accounts were overrepresented in the sample.

Exhibit 16.3 Mailing List Directory Page

Lists Available - *Alphabetical*

S.I.C. Code	List Title	United States Total Count	State Count Page	Canadian Count
	A			
5122-02	Abdominal Supports	201	‡	28
8399-03	Abortion Alternatives Organizations	946	‡	*
8093-04	Abortion Information & Services	551	‡	277
5085-23	Abrasives	1811	‡	*
5169-04	Absorbents	145	‡	*
6541-03	Abstracters	4057	58	9
6411-06	Accident & Health Insurance	2113	‡	*
8748-52	Accident Reconstruction Service	125	‡	*
8721-01	Accountants	127392	64	6933
8721-02	Accounting & Bookkeeping General Svc	27996	64	2072
5044-08	Accounting & Bookkeeping Machines/Supls	889	‡	50
5044-01	Accounting & Bookkeeping Systems	624	‡	1230
8711-02	Acoustical Consultants	381	‡	91
1742-02	Acoustical Contractors	3063	47	433
1742-01	Acoustical Materials	878	‡	210
8999-10	Actuaries	1185	‡	*
8049-13	Acupuncture (Acupuncturists)	2921	62	493
5044-02	Adding & Calculating Machines/Supplies	5524	49	648
5044-09	Addressing Machines & Supplies	345	‡	29
5169-12	Adhesives & Glues	1187	‡	4
3579-02	Adhesives & Gluing Equipment	170	‡	204
6411-02	Adjusters	6164	57	8357
6411-01	Adjusters-Public	161	‡	*
8322-07	Adoption Agencies	1621	‡	32
8059-03	Adult Care Facilities	596	‡	*
8361-08	Adult Congregate Living Facilities	170	‡	*
7319-03	Advertising-Aerial	337	‡	26
7311-01	Advertising-Agencies & Counselors	27753	59	2552
7336-05	Advertising-Art Layout & Production Svc	457	‡	101
7331-05	Advertising-Direct Mail	6347	59	540
7311-03	Advertising-Directory & Guide	2465	‡	124
7319-01	Advertising-Displays	3441	59	571
7319-11	Advertising-Indoor	209	‡	63
7311-05	Advertising-Motion Picture	143	‡	11
7311-06	Advertising-Newspaper	4274	59	404
7312-01	Advertising-Outdoor	3052	59	297
7311-08	Advertising-Periodical	817	‡	78

S.I.C. Code	List Title	United States Total Count	State Count Page	Canadian Count
7313-03	Advertising-Radio	2866	59	247
7311-07	Advertising-Shoppers' Guides	392	‡	4
5199-17	Advertising-Specialties	12827	52	1648
7389-12	Advertising-Telephone	120	‡	*
7313-05	Advertising-Television	1746	‡	102
7319-02	Advertising-Transit & Transportation	179	‡	38
0721-03	Aerial Applicators (Service)	1479	‡	61
3999-01	Aerosols	158	‡	*
3812-01	Aerospace Industries	426	‡	*
	Affluent Americans		73	*
5191-04	Agricultural Chemicals	549	‡	210
8748-20	Agricultural Consultants	1047	‡	474
9999-32	Air Balancing	353	‡	*
5084-64	Air Brushes	219	48	*
4512-02	Air Cargo Service	6005	‡	342
5075-01	Air Cleaning & Purifying Equipment	2055	50	717
5084-02	Air Compressors	4358		
	(See Compressors Air & Gas)			
1711-17	Air Conditioning Contractors & Systems	50951	47	2667
	Available By Brands Sold			
	Airtemp (A)	187		
	Amana (B)	1450		
	Arco Aire (2)	673		
	Armstrong/Magic Chef (C)	395		
	Arvin (4)	106		
	Bryant (D)	2223		
	Carrier (E)	5927		
	Coleman (5)	1176		
	Comfortmaker/Singer (O)	989		
	Day & Night (Z)	749		
	Fedders (H)	318		
	Heli/Quaker (3)	1977		
	Janitrol (7)	587		
	Kero-Sun (W)	2		
	Lennox (K)	4390		
	Luxaire (L)	510		
	Payne (M)	553		

In countries with less well-developed economies such as Sri Lanka fewer than 5 percent of households may have telephones. Telephone directories cannot serve as sampling frames in such countries.

Sampling Frames for International Marketing Research. The availability of sampling frames around the globe varies dramatically. Not every country's government conducts a census of population, telephone directories are often incomplete, no voter registration lists exist, and accurate maps of urban areas are unobtainable.[1] However, in Taiwan, Japan, and other Asian countries a researcher can build a sampling frame relatively easily because those governments release some census information about individuals. If a family changes households, the change with updated census information must be reported to a centralized government agency before communal services (water, gas, electricity, education, etc.) are available.[2] This information is then easily accessible in the local *Inhabitants' Register*.

Sampling Units

sampling unit
A single element or group of elements subject to selection in the sample.

primary sampling unit (PSU)
A term used to designate a unit selected in the first stage of sampling.

secondary sampling unit
A term used to designate a unit selected in the second stage of sampling.

tertiary sampling unit
A term used to designate a unit selected in the third stage of sampling.

During the actual sampling process, the elements of the population must be selected according to a certain procedure. The **sampling unit** is a single element or group of elements subject to selection in the sample. For example, if an airline wishes to sample passengers, it may take every 25th name on a complete list of passengers. In this case the sampling unit would be the same as the element. Alternatively, the airline could first select certain flights as the sampling unit, then select certain passengers on each flight. In this case the sampling unit contains many elements.

If the target population has first been divided into units, such as airline flights, additional terminology must be used. The term **primary sampling units (PSU)** designates units selected in the first stage of sampling. Units selected in successive stages of sampling are called **secondary sampling units,** or **tertiary sampling units** (if three stages are necessary). When there is no list of population elements, the sampling unit generally is something other than the population element. In a random digit dialing study, for example, the sampling unit will be telephone numbers.

Random Sampling and Nonsampling Errors

Adgraphics sampled a small number of grocery stores that used its in-store advertising network, Shopper's Video, to test changes in brand awareness and buying intentions among shoppers. Investigators expected this sample to be representative of the grocery-shopping population. However, if there is a difference between the value of a sample statistic of interest (for example, the average-willingness-to-buy-the-advertised-brand score) and that of the corresponding value of the population parameter (again, willingness-to-buy score), a *statistical error* has occurred. Chapter 8 classified two basic causes of differences between statistics and parameters: random sampling errors and systematic (nonsampling) errors.

An estimation made from a sample is not exactly the same as a census count. **Random sampling error** is the difference between the sample result and the result of a census conducted using identical procedures. Of course, the result of a census is unknown unless one is taken, which is rarely done. Other sources of error also can be present. Random sampling error occurs because of chance variation in the scientific selection of sampling units. The sampling units, even if properly selected according to sampling theory, may not perfectly represent the population, but generally they are reliable estimates. Our discussion on the process of randomization (a procedure designed to give everyone in the population an equal chance of being selected as a sample member) will show that because random sampling errors follow chance variations they tend to cancel one another out when averaged. This means that properly selected samples generally are good approximations of the population. There is almost always a slight

random sampling error
The difference between the result of a sample and the result of a census conducted using identical procedures; a statistical fluctuation that occurs because of chance variations in the elements selected for a sample.

EXPLORING RESEARCH ISSUES

How Private Are Mailing Lists?

THE DIRECT MARKETING AND SURVEY RESEARCH industries require mailing lists to reach carefully targeted market segments. Survey research companies generally purchase mailing lists that they can use for sampling purposes or they hire the mailing list company to stuff envelopes and post surveys. Mailing list companies may use credit reports, driver's license information, and voter registration records as well as other databases to compile these lists. For example, TRW Target

Marketing Services, a company that had its origin as a service to approve individuals as creditworthy, sells mailing lists based on an individual's available credit or ownership of bank credit cards with nonzero balances.

Most credit agreements indicate that the consumer's name may be used for other purposes, and it has long been accepted practice to use credit information for purposes beyond establishing an individual's credit-worthiness.

The Direct Marketing Association's Mail Preference Service allows consumers to write to have their names taken off mailing lists. However, many consumers are unaware of this service. This raises the ethical question of how to balance the right of privacy against marketing researchers' need to know.

WHAT WENT WRONG?

Random Sequences That Don't Look Random

EVERY BASKETBALL PLAYER AND FAN KNOWS THAT players have hot and cold streaks. Players who have hot hands can't seem to miss while those who have cold ones can't find the center of the hoop. When psychologists interviewed team members of the Philadelphia 76ers, the players estimated they were about 25 percent more likely to make a shot after they had just made one than after a miss. Nine in ten basketball fans surveyed concurred that a player "has a better chance of making a shot after having just *made* his last two or three shots than he does after having just *missed* his last two or three shots." Believing in shooting streaks, players will feed a teammate who has just made two or three shots in a row, and many coaches will bench the player who misses three in a row. When you're hot you're hot.

The only trouble is, it isn't true. When the psychologists studied detailed individual shooting records, they found that the 76ers—and the Boston Celtics, the New Jersey Nets, the New York Knicks, and Cornell University's men's and women's basketball players—were equally likely to score after a miss as after a basket. Fifty percent shooters average 50 percent after just missing three shots, and 50 percent after just making three shots.

Why, then, do players and fans alike believe that players are more likely to score after scoring and miss after missing? In any series of 20 shots by a 50 percent shooter (or 20 flips of a coin), there is a 50-50 chance of four baskets (or heads) in a row, and it is quite possible that one person out of five will have a streak of five or six. Players and fans notice these random streaks and so form the myth that when you're hot you're hot.

The same type of thing happens with investors who believe that a fund is more likely to perform well after a string of good years than after a string of bad years. Past performances of mutual funds do not predict their future performances. When funds have streaks of several good or bad years, we may nevertheless be fooled into thinking that past success predicts future success.

The moral: Whether watching basketball, choosing stocks, flipping coins, or drawing a sample, remember the statistical principle that random sequences often don't look random. Even when the next outcome cannot be predicted from the preceding ones, streaks are to be expected.

difference between the true population value and the sample value, hence, a small random sampling error. Thus, every once in a while an unusual sample is selected because too many atypical people were included in the sample and a large random sampling error occurred. The theory behind this concept of sample reliability and other basic statistical concepts are reviewed in detail in Chapter 17. At this point, simply recognize that *random sampling error* is a technical term that refers *only* to statistical fluctuations that occur because of chance variations in the elements selected for the sample.

Random sampling error is a function of sample size. As sample size increases, random sampling error decreases. Of course, the resources available will influence how large a sample may be taken. (The topic of sample size is covered in Chapter 17.) It is possible to estimate the random sampling error that may be expected with various sample sizes. Suppose a survey of approximately 1,000 people has been taken in Fresno to determine the feasibility of a new soccer franchise. Assume that 30 percent of the respondents favor the idea of a new professional sport in town. The researcher will know, based on the laws of probability,

---

Exhibit 16.4   Errors Associated with Sampling

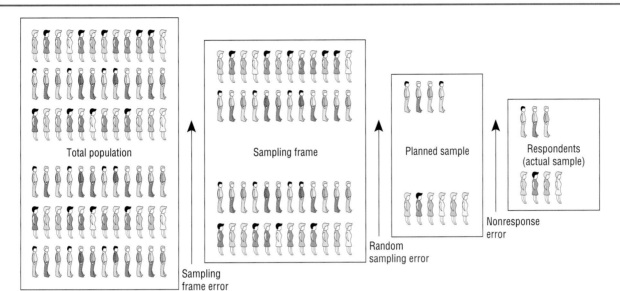

---

that 95 percent of the time a survey of slightly fewer than 900 people will produce results with an error of approximately plus or minus 3 percent. Had the survey been collected with only 325 people, the margin of error would increase to approximately plus or minus 5 percentage points. This example illustrates random sampling errors.

Systematic (nonsampling) errors result from nonsampling factors, primarily the nature of a study's design and the correctness of execution. These errors are *not* due to chance fluctuations. For example, highly educated respondents are more likely to cooperate with mail surveys than poorly educated ones, for whom filling out forms is a more difficult and intimidating task. Sample biases such as these account for a large portion of errors in marketing research. The term *sample bias* is somewhat unfortunate, because many forms of bias are not related to the selection of the sample.

We discussed nonsampling errors in Chapter 8. Errors due to sample selection problems, such as sampling frame errors, are systematic (nonsampling) errors and should not be classified as random sampling errors.

systematic (nonsampling) error
Error resulting from some imperfect aspect of the research design, such as mistakes in sample selection, sampling frame error, or nonresponses from persons not contacted or refusing to participate.

Less Than Perfectly Representative Samples

Random sampling errors and systematic errors associated with the sampling process may combine to yield a sample that is less than perfectly representative of the population. Exhibit 16.4 illustrates two nonsampling errors (sampling frame error and nonresponse error) related to sample design. The total population is represented by the area of the largest square. Sampling frame errors eliminate some potential respondents. Random sampling error (due exclusively to random, chance fluctuation) may cause an imbalance in the representativeness of the group. Additional errors will occur if individuals refuse to be interviewed or cannot be contacted. Such **nonresponse error** may also cause the sample to be less than perfectly representative. Thus, the actual sample is drawn from a population different (or smaller) than the ideal.

nonresponse error
The statistical differences between a survey that includes only those who responded and a perfect survey that would also include those who failed to respond.

Probability versus Nonprobability Sampling

There are several alternative ways to take a sample. The main alternative sampling plans may be grouped into two groups: probability techniques and nonprobability techniques.

In **probability sampling** every element in the population has a *known, nonzero probability* of selection. The simple random sample, in which each member of the population has an equal probability of being selected, is the best-known probability sample.

In **nonprobability sampling** the probability of any particular member of the population being chosen is unknown. The selection of sampling units in nonprobability sampling is quite arbitrary, as researchers rely heavily on personal judgment. *There are no appropriate statistical techniques for measuring random sampling error from a nonprobability sample. Thus, projecting the data beyond the sample is statistically inappropriate.* Nevertheless, there are occasions when nonprobability samples are best suited for the researcher's purpose.

We will now explore the various types of nonprobability and probability sampling. Although probability sampling is preferred, we will discuss nonprobability sampling first to illustrate some potential sources of error and other weaknesses in sampling.

probability sampling
A sampling technique in which every member of the population will have a known, nonzero probability of selection.

nonprobability sampling
A sampling technique in which units of the sample are selected on the basis of personal judgment or convenience; the probability of any particular member of the population being chosen is unknown.

Nonprobability Sampling

Convenience Sampling

convenience sampling
The sampling procedure of obtaining those people or units that are most conveniently available.

Convenience sampling (also called *haphazard* or *accidental sampling*) refers to the sampling procedure of obtaining the people or units that are most conveniently available. It may be convenient and economical to set up an interviewing booth from which to intercept consumers at a shopping center. During election times, television stations often present person-on-the-street interviews that are presumed to reflect public opinion. (Of course, the television station often warns that the survey was "unscientific and random" [*sic*].) The college professor who uses his or her students has a captive sample—convenient but perhaps unwilling and unrepresentative.

Researchers generally use convenience samples to obtain a large number of completed questionnaires quickly and economically. For example, it was supposedly a person-on-the-street straw poll, conducted by the *Chicago Sun Times,* that alerted former Senator Charles Percy to his problems in his first reelection campaign. The user of research based on a convenience sample should remember that projecting the results beyond the specific sample is inappropriate. Convenience samples are best used for exploratory research when additional research will subsequently be conducted with a probability sample.

In many cases, a research project using convenience sampling signals that the entire research project may lack objectivity. A supposedly "nationwide" poll in France was conducted with 1,000 Parisians—an example of how not to select a convenience sample. Not surprisingly, it was conducted by IFOP, a French opinion research firm that had been involved in tampering with survey results.

Internet Samples

Chapter 9 discussed Internet surveys that seek information from respondents who interact with software on an interact with software on an Internet Web set. At the present time, many of these surveys are conducted with volunteer respondents who, by intention or happenstance, visit an organization's Web site. These are clearly convenience samples. They may not be representative because of the haphazard manner by which many respondents arrive at a particular Web site or because of self-selection bias. Another complicating factor with Internet surveys is the lack of computer ownership and Internet access among all segments of the population. This is not to say that all Internet samples are unrepresentative of target populations. However, researchers should be keenly aware of potential sampling problems when using Internet surveys.

Judgment Sampling

Judgment, or **purposive, sampling** is a nonprobability sampling technique in which an experienced individual selects the sample based on his or her judgment about some appropriate characteristics required of the sample member. Researchers select samples to satisfy their specific purposes, even if it does not provide a fully representative sample. The consumer price index (CPI) is based on a judgment sample of market-basket items, housing costs, and other selected goods and services expected to reflect a representative sample of items consumed by most Americans. Test market cities often are selected because they are viewed as typical cities whose demographic profiles closely match the national profile. A fashion manufacturer regularly selects a sample of key accounts that it believes are capable of providing the information it needs to predict what will sell in the fall; the sample is selected to achieve a specific objective.

Judgment sampling often is used in attempts to forecast election results. People frequently wonder how a television network can predict the results of an election with only 2 percent of the votes reported. Political and sampling experts judge which small voting districts approximate overall state returns from previous election years, then these *bellwether precincts* are selected as the sampling units. Of course, the assumption is that the past voting records of these districts are still representative of the state's political behavior.

judgment (purposive) sampling
A nonprobability sampling technique in which an experienced researcher selects the sample based on personal judgment about some appropriate characteristic of the sample member.

Quota Sampling

Suppose a firm wishes to investigate consumers who currently own digital versatile disc (DVD) players. The researchers may wish to ensure that each brand of DVD player recorder is proportionately included in the sample. Strict probability sampling procedures would likely underrepresent certain brands and overrepresent other brands. If the selection process were left strictly to chance, some variation would be expected. The purpose of **quota sampling** is to ensure that the various subgroups in a population are represented on pertinent sample characteristics to the exact extent that the investigators desire. Stratified sampling, a probability sampling procedure, also has this objective, but it should not be confused with quota sampling. In quota sampling the interviewer has a quota to achieve. For example, an interviewer in a particular city may be assigned 100 interviews, 35 with owners of Sony DVD players, 30 with owners of Samsung DVD players, 18 with owners of Toshiba DVD players, and the rest with owners of other brands. The interviewer is responsible for finding enough people to meet the quota. Aggregating the various interview quotas yields a sample that represents the desired proportion of each subgroup.

quota sampling
A nonprobability sampling procedure that ensures that various subgroups of a population will be represented on pertinent characteristics to the exact extent that the investigator desires.

Possible Sources of Bias. The logic of classifying the population by pertinent subgroups is essentially sound. However, because respondents are selected according to a convenience sampling procedure rather than on a probability basis as in stratified sampling, the haphazard selection of subjects may introduce bias. For example, a college professor hired some of his students to conduct a quota sample based on age. When analyzing the data, the professor discovered that almost all the people in the "under 25 years" category were college educated. Interviewers, being human, tend to prefer to interview people who are similar to themselves. Quota samples tend to include people who are easily found, willing to be interviewed, and middle class. Field workers are given considerable leeway to exercise their judgment concerning selection of actual respondents. Interviewers often concentrate their interviewing in areas with heavy pedestrian traffic such as downtowns, shopping malls, and college campuses. Those who interview door-to-door learn quickly that quota requirements are difficult to meet by interviewing whoever happens to appear at the door; this tends to overrepresent less active people who are likely to stay at home. One interviewer related a story of working in an upper-middle-class neighborhood. After a few blocks, it changed into a neighborhood of mansions. Feeling that most of the would-be subjects were above his station, the interviewer skipped these houses because he felt uncomfortable knocking on doors that would be answered by servants.

Advantages of Quota Sampling. Speed of data collection, lower costs, and convenience are the major advantages of quota sampling over probability sampling. Although this method has many problems, careful supervision of the data collection may provide a representative sample for analyzing the various subgroups within a population. Quota sampling may be appropriate when the researcher knows that a certain demographic group is more likely to refuse to cooperate with a survey. For instance, if older men are more likely to refuse, a higher quota can be set for this group so that the proportions of each demographic category will be similar to the proportions in the population. A number of laboratory experiments also rely on quota sampling because it is difficult to find a sample of the general population who are willing to visit a laboratory to participate in an experiment.

Snowball Sampling

snowball sampling
A sampling procedure in which initial respondents are selected by probability methods and additional respondents are obtained from information provided by the initial respondents.

Snowball sampling refers to a variety of procedures in which initial respondents are selected by probability methods and additional respondents are obtained from information provided by the initial respondents. This technique is used to locate members of rare populations by referrals. Suppose a manufacturer of sports equipment is considering marketing a mahogany croquet set for serious adult players. This market is certainly small. An extremely large sample would be necessary to find 100 serious adult croquet players. It would be much more economical to survey, say, 300 people and find 15 croquet players and ask them for the names of other players. Reduced sample sizes and costs are a clear-cut advantage of snowball sampling. However, bias is likely to enter into the study because a person who is known to someone also in the sample has a higher probability of being similar to the first person. If there are major differences between those who are widely known by others and those who are not, this technique

TO THE POINT

A straw vote only shows which way the hot air blows.

O. HENRY

may present some serious problems. However, snowball sampling may be used to locate and recruit heavy users, such as consumers who buy more than 50 compact discs per year, for focus groups. As the focus group is not expected to be a generalized sample, snowball sampling may be very appropriate.

Probability Sampling

All probability sampling techniques are based on chance selection procedures. This eliminates the bias inherent in nonprobability sampling procedures because the probability sampling process is random. Note that the term *random* refers to the procedure for selecting the sample; it does not describe the data in the sample. *Randomness* refers to a procedure whose outcome cannot be predicted because it depends on chance. It should not be thought of as unplanned or unscientific—it is the basis of all probability sampling techniques. This section will examine the various probability sampling methods.

TO THE POINT

Make everything as simple as possible, but not simpler.

ALBERT EINSTEIN

Simple Random Sampling

Simple random sampling is a sampling procedure that ensures that each element in the population will have an equal chance of being included in the sample. Drawing names from a hat or selecting the winning raffle ticket from a large drum is a typical example of simple random sampling. If the names or raffle tickets are thoroughly stirred, each person or ticket should have an equal chance of being selected. This process is simple because it requires only one stage of sample selection, in contrast to other, more complex probability samples.

Although drawing names or numbers out of a fishbowl, using a spinner, rolling dice, or turning a roulette wheel may be used to draw a sample from small

simple random sampling
A sampling procedure that assures each element in the population of an equal chance of being included in the sample.

"Ah—Here comes a cross section of the public now!"

populations, when populations consist of large numbers of elements, tables of random numbers (see Table A.1 in the Appendix) or computer-generated random numbers are used for sample selection.

Selecting a Simple Random Sample.   Suppose a researcher is interested in selecting a simple random sample of all the Honda dealers in California, New Mexico, Arizona, and Nevada. Each dealer's name is assigned a number from 1 to 105, then each number is written on a separate piece of paper, and all the slips are placed in a large drum. After the slips of paper have been thoroughly mixed, one is selected for each sampling unit. Thus, if the sample size is 35, the selection procedure must be repeated 34 times after the first slip has been selected. Mixing the slips after each selection will ensure that those at the bottom of the bowl will continue to have an equal chance of being selected in the sample.

To use a table of random numbers, a serial number is assigned to each element of the population. Assuming a population of 99,999 or less, five-digit numbers are selected from the table of random numbers merely by reading the numbers in any column or row, by moving upward, downward, left, or right. A random starting point should be selected at the outset. For convenience, we will assume that we have randomly selected the first five digits in columns 1 through 5, row 1, of Table A.1 in the Appendix as our starting point. The first number in our sample would be 37751; moving downward, the following numbers would be 50915, 99142, and so on.

The random digit dialing technique of sample selection requires that the researcher identify the exchange or exchanges of interest (the first three numbers) and then use a table of numbers to select the next four numbers.

Systematic Sampling

systematic sampling
A sampling procedure in which a starting point is selected by a random process and then every nth number on the list is selected.

To illustrate **systematic sampling** suppose one wishes to take a sample of 1,000 from a list of 200,000 names. Using systematic selection, every 200th name from the list will be drawn.

The procedure is extremely simple. A starting point is selected by a random process; then every *n*th number on the list is selected. In a sample from a rural telephone directory that does not separate business from residential listings, every 23rd name might be selected as the *sampling interval*. In this sample of consumers, it is possible that Mike's Restaurant will be selected. This unit is inappropriate because it is a business listing rather than a consumer listing so the next eligible name is selected as the sampling unit and the systematic process continues.

While this procedure is not actually a random selection procedure, it does yield random results if the arrangement of the items in the list is random in character. The problem of *periodicity* occurs if a list has a systematic pattern, that is, is not random in character. Collecting retail sales information every seventh day would result in a distorted sample because there would be a systematic pattern of selecting sampling units. Sales for only one day of the week, perhaps Monday's sales, would be sampled. Another possible periodicity bias might occur in a list of contributors to a charity in which the first 50 are extremely large donors. If the sampling interval is every 200th name, a problem could result. Periodicity is rarely a problem for most sampling in marketing research, but researchers should be aware of the possibility.

Stratified Sampling

The usefulness of dividing the population into subgroups, or *strata,* that are more or less equal with respect to some characteristic was illustrated in our discussion of quota sampling. The first step of choosing strata on the basis of existing information, such as classifying retail outlets based on annual sales volume, is the same for both stratified and quota sampling. However, the process of selecting sampling units within the strata differs substantially. In **stratified sampling** a subsample is drawn using a simple random sample within each stratum. This is not true with quota sampling.

The reason for taking a stratified sample is to obtain a more efficient sample than would be possible with simple random sampling. Suppose, for example, that urban and rural groups have widely different attitudes toward energy conservation, but members within each group hold very similar attitudes. Random sampling error will be reduced because the groups are internally homogeneous, but comparatively different between groups. More technically, a smaller standard error may result from this stratified sample because the groups will be adequately represented when strata are combined.

Another reason for conducting a stratified sample is to ensure that the sample will accurately reflect the population on the basis of the criterion or criteria used for stratification. This is a concern because occasionally a simple random sample yields a disproportionate number of one group or another and the representativeness of the sample could be improved.

A researcher can select a stratified sample as follows. First, a variable (sometimes several variables) is identified as an efficient basis for stratification. A stratification variable must be a characteristic of the population elements known to be related to the dependent variable or other variables of interest. The variable chosen should increase homogeneity within each stratum and increase heterogeneity between strata. The stratification variable usually is a categorical variable or one easily converted into categories, that is, subgroups.

For example, a pharmaceutical company interested in measuring how often physicians prescribe a certain drug might choose physicians' training as a basis for stratification. In this example, the mutually exclusive strata are M.D.'s (medical doctors) and O.D.'s (osteopathic doctors).

Next, for each separate subgroup or stratum, a list of population elements must be obtained. If a complete listing is not available, a true stratified probability sample cannot be selected. Using a table of random numbers or some other device, a *separate* simple random sample is then taken within each stratum. If stratified lists are not available, they can be costly to prepare. Of course, the researcher must determine how large a sample to draw for each stratum. This issue is discussed in the following section.

Proportional versus Disproportional Sampling

If the number of sampling units drawn from each stratum is in proportion to the relative population size of the stratum, the sample is a **proportional stratified sample.** Sometimes, however, a disproportional stratified sample will be selected to ensure an adequate number of sampling units in every stratum. Sampling more heavily in a given stratum than its relative population size warrants is not a problem if the primary purpose of the research is to estimate some characteristic separately for each stratum, and if researchers are concerned about assessing the differences among strata. Consider, however, the percentage of retail drug outlets presented in Exhibit 16.5. There is a small percentage of large independent stores and a large percentage of other stores. The average store size, in dollar volume, for the chain store and large independent store strata varies substantially from the smaller independent stores' size. To avoid overrepresenting the medium-size and smaller stores in the sample, a disproportional sample is taken. In a **disproportional stratified sample** the sample size for each stratum is not allocated on a proportional basis with the population size, but it is dictated by analytical considerations. The logic behind this procedure relates to the general argument for sample size: As variability increases, sample size must increase to provide accurate estimates. Thus, the strata that exhibit the greatest variability are sampled more heavily to increase sample efficiency, that is, small-

stratified sampling
A probability sampling procedure in which simple random subsamples are drawn from within each stratum that are more or less equal on some characteristic.

proportional stratified sample
A stratified sample in which the number of sampling units drawn from each stratum is in proportion to the relative population size of that stratum.

disproportional stratified sample
A stratified sample in which the sample size for each stratum is allocated according to analytical considerations.

Exhibit 16.5 Demonstration of Disproportional Sampling Concept

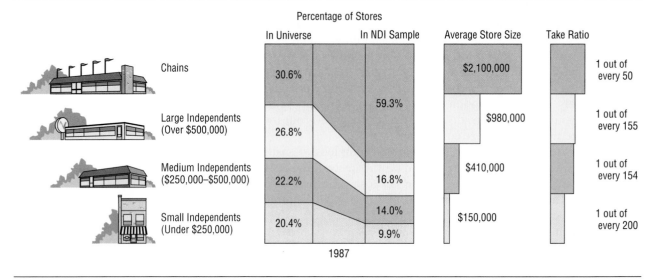

Percentage of Stores

	In Universe	In NDI Sample	Average Store Size	Take Ratio
Chains	30.6%	59.3%	$2,100,000	1 out of every 50
Large Independents (Over $500,000)	26.8%	16.8%	$980,000	1 out of every 155
Medium Independents ($250,000–$500,000)	22.2%	14.0%	$410,000	1 out of every 154
Small Independents (Under $250,000)	20.4%	9.9%	$150,000	1 out of every 200

1987

---

er random sampling error. In this example previous experience has shown differences among the strata on dollar volume (average store size). Actually, the example in Exhibit 16.5 illustrates an *optimal allocation stratified sample* that takes both *variation* and *size* of each stratum into consideration. Thus, the optimal sample size for each stratum may be determined. Complex formulas (beyond the scope of an introductory course in marketing research) have been developed to determine sample size for each stratum. A simplified rule of thumb for understanding the concept of optimal allocation is that the stratum sample size increases for strata of larger sizes with the greatest relative variability. Other complexities arise in determining population estimates. For example, when disproportional stratified sampling is used, the estimated mean for each stratum has to be weighed according to the number of elements in each stratum to calculate the total population mean.

Cluster Sampling

cluster sampling
An economically efficient sampling technique in which the primary sampling unit is not the individual element in the population but a large cluster of elements; clusters are selected randomly.

The purpose of **cluster sampling** is to sample economically while retaining the characteristics of a probability sample. Consider the researcher who must conduct 500 interviews with consumers scattered throughout the United States. Travel costs are likely to be enormous because the amount of time spent traveling will be substantially greater than the time spent in the interviewing process. If an aspirin marketer can assume the product will work as well in Phoenix as it does in Baltimore, or if a frozen pizza manufacturer assumes its product will taste the same in Texas as it does in Oregon, cluster sampling may be used. In a cluster sample the primary sampling unit is no longer the individual element in the population (for example, grocery stores) but a larger cluster of elements located in proximity to one another (for example, cities). The *area sample* is the most popular type of cluster sample. A grocery store researcher, for example, may randomly choose several geographic areas as primary sampling units and then interview all or a sample of grocery stores within the geographic clusters. Interviews are confined to these clusters only. No interviews occur in other clusters. Cluster sampling is classified as a probability sampling technique because of either the random selection of clusters or the random selection of elements within each cluster.

Exhibit 16.6   **Examples of Clusters**

POPULATION ELEMENT	POSSIBLE CLUSTERS IN THE UNITED STATES
U.S. adult population	States Counties Metropolitan Statistical Areas Census Tracts Blocks Households
College seniors	Colleges
Manufacturing firms	Counties Metropolitan Statistical Areas Localities Plants
Airline travelers	Airports Planes
Sports fans	Football Stadia Basketball Arenas Baseball Parks

Cluster samples frequently are used when lists of the sample population are not available. For example, in a downtown revitalization project to investigate employees and self-employed workers, a comprehensive list of these people was not available. A cluster sample was taken by selecting organizations (business and government) as the clusters. A sample of firms within the central business district was developed using a stratified probability sample to identify clusters. Next, individual workers within the firms (clusters) were randomly selected and interviewed concerning the central business district. Some examples of clusters appear in Exhibit 16.6.

Ideally a cluster should be as heterogeneous as the population itself—a mirror image of the population. A problem may arise with cluster sampling if the characteristics and attitudes of the elements within the cluster are too similar. For example, geographic neighborhoods tend to have residents of the same socioeconomic status. Students at a university tend to share similar beliefs. This problem may be mitigated by constructing clusters composed of diverse elements and by selecting a large number of sampled clusters.

Multistage Area Sampling

So far we have described two-stage cluster sampling. **Multistage area sampling** involves two or more steps that combine some of the probability techniques already described. Typically geographic areas are randomly selected in progressively smaller (lower-population) units. For example, a political pollster investigating an election in Arizona might first choose counties within the state to ensure that the different areas are represented in the sample. In the second step, precincts within the selected counties may be chosen. As a final step, the pollster may select blocks (or households) within the precincts, then interview all the blocks (or households) within the geographic area. Researchers may take as many steps as necessary to achieve a representative

multistage area sampling
Sampling that involves using a combination of two or more probability sampling techniques.

Exhibit 16.7 **An Illustration of Multistage Area Sampling**

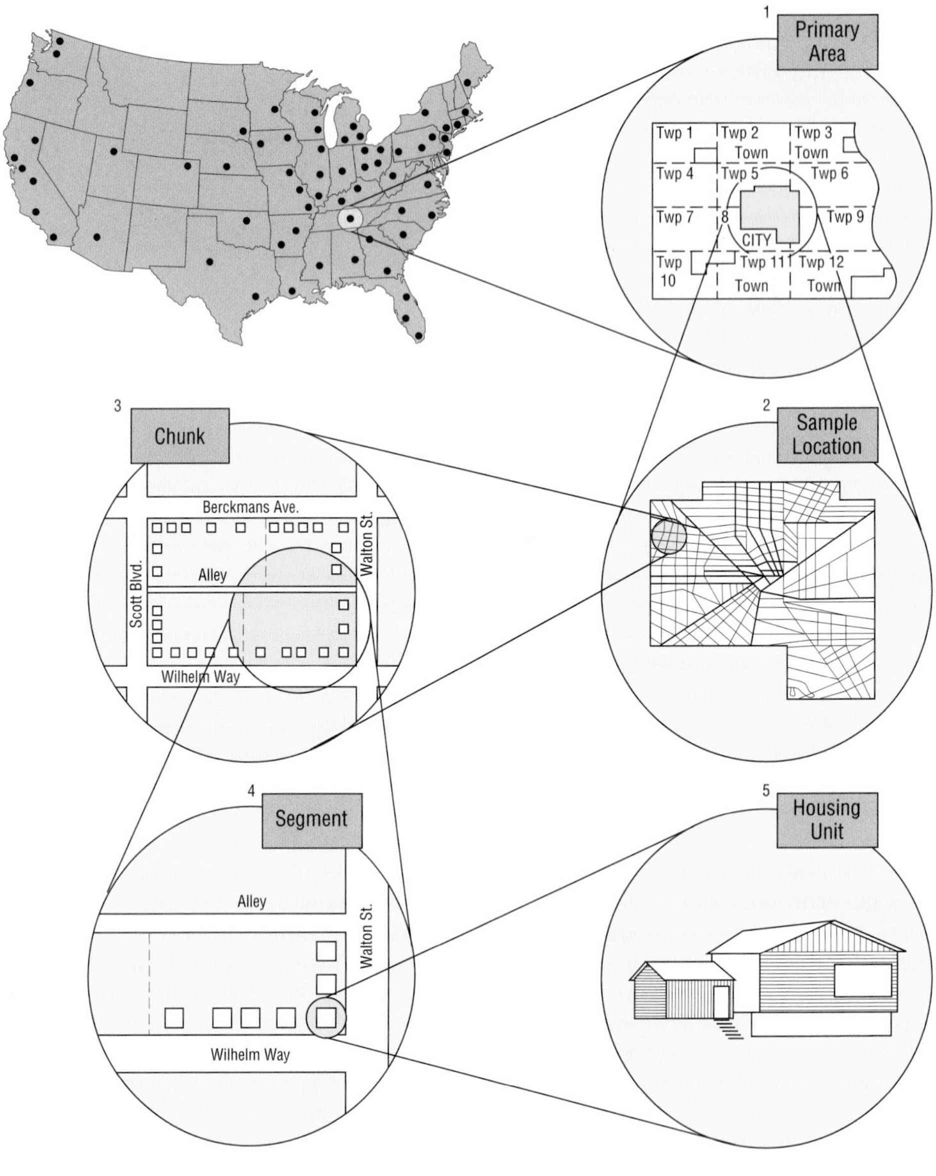

sample. Exhibit 16.7 graphically portrays a multistage area sampling process frequently used by a major academic research center. Progressively smaller geographic areas are chosen until a single housing unit is selected for interviewing.

The Bureau of the Census provides maps, population information, demographic characteristics for population statistics, and so on by several small geographical areas that may be useful in sampling. Census classifications of small geographic areas vary depending on the extent of urbanization within Metropolitan Statistical Areas (MSAs) or counties. Exhibit 16.8 illustrates the geographic hierarchy inside urbanized areas.

Exhibit 16.8   **Geographic Hierarchy Inside Urbanized Areas**

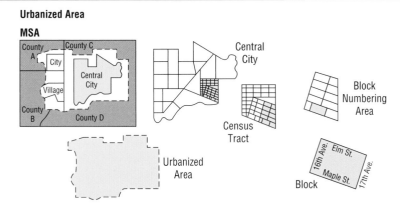

What Is the Appropriate Sample Design?

Exhibit 16.9 summarizes the advantages and disadvantages of each sampling technique. A researcher who must decide on the most appropriate sample design for a specific project will identify a number of sampling criteria and evaluate the relative importance of each criterion before selecting a sampling design. This section outlines and briefly discusses the most common criteria.

Degree of Accuracy

Selecting a representative sample is important to all researchers. However, the degree of accuracy required or the researcher's tolerance for sampling and nonsampling error may vary from project to project, especially when cost savings or another consideration may be a trade-off for a reduction in accuracy.

For example, when the sample is being selected for an exploratory research project, a high priority may not be placed on accuracy because a highly representative sample may not be necessary. For other, more conclusive projects, the sample result must precisely represent a population's characteristics, and the researcher must be willing to spend the time and money needed to achieve accuracy.

Resources

The cost associated with the different sampling techniques varies tremendously. If the researcher's financial and human resources are restricted, certain options will have to be eliminated. For a graduate student working on a master's thesis, conducting a national survey is almost always out of the question because of limited resources. Managers concerned with the cost of the research versus the value of the information often will opt for cost savings from a certain nonprobability sampling design rather than make the decision to conduct no research at all.

Exhibit 16.9 **Comparison of Sampling Techniques**

Nonprobability Samples

Description	Cost and Degree of Use	Advantages	Disadvantages
1. *Convenience:* The researcher uses the most convenient sample or economical sample units.	Very low cost, extensively used	No need for list of population	Unrepresented samples likely; random sampling error estimates cannot be measured; projecting data beyond sample inappropriate
2. *Judgment:* An expert or experienced researcher selects the sample to fulfill a purpose, such as ensuring that all members have a certain characteristic.	Moderate cost, average use	Useful for certain types of forecasting; sample guaranteed to meet a specific objective	Bias due to expert's beliefs may make sample unrepresentative; projecting data beyond sample inappropriate
3. *Quota:* The researcher classifies the population by pertinent properties, determines the desired proportion to sample from each class, and fixes quotas for each interviewer.	Moderate cost, very extensively used	Introduces some stratification of population; requires no list of population	Introduces bias in researcher's classification of subjects; non-random selection within classes means error from population cannot be estimated; projecting data beyond sample inappropriate
4. *Snowball:* Initial respondents are selected by probability samples; additional respondents are obtained by referral from initial respondents.	Low cost, used in special situations	Useful in locating members of rare populations	High bias because sample units not independent; projecting data beyond sample inappropriate

Probability Samples

Description	Cost and Degree of Use	Advantages	Disadvantages
1. *Simple random:* The researcher assigns each member of the sampling frame a number, then selects sample units by random method.	High cost, infrequently used in practice (except random digit dialing)	Only minimal advance knowledge of population needed; easy to analyze data and compute error	Requires sampling frame to work from; does not use knowledge of population that researcher may have; larger errors for same sampling size than in stratified sampling; respondents may be widely dispersed, hence higher cost
2. *Systematic:* The researcher uses natural ordering or the order of the sampling frame, selects an arbitrary starting point, then selects items at a preselected interval.	Moderate cost, moderately used	Simple to draw sample; easy to check	If sampling interval is related to periodic ordering of the population, may introduce increased variability
3. *Stratified:* The researcher divides the population into groups and randomly selects subsamples from each group. Variations include proportional, disproportional, or optimal allocation of subsample sizes.	High cost, moderately used	Ensures representation of all groups in sample; characteristics of each stratum can be estimated and comparisons made; reduces variability for same sample size	Requires accurate information on proportion in each stratum; if stratified lists are not already available, they can be costly to prepare

(continued)

> ## Exhibit 16.9 Comparison of Sampling Techniques *(Continued)*
>
> **Probability Samples**
>
> | Description | Cost and Degree of Use | Advantages | Disadvantages |
> | --- | --- | --- | --- |
> | 4. *Cluster:* The researcher selects sampling units at random, then does a complete observation of all units or draws a probability sample in the group. | Low cost, frequently used | If clusters geographically defined, yields lowest field cost; requires listing of all clusters, but of individuals only within clusters; can estimate characteristics of clusters as well as of population | Larger error for comparable size than with other probability samples; researcher must be able to assign population members to unique cluster, or duplication or omission of individuals will result |
> | 5. *Multistage:* Progressively smaller areas are selected in each stage by some combination of the first four techniques. | High cost, frequently used, especially in nationwide surveys | Depends on techniques combined | Depends on techniques combined |

Time

A researcher who needs to meet a deadline or complete a project quickly will be more likely to select a simple, less time-consuming sample design. A telephone survey using a sample based on random digit dialing takes considerably less time than a survey that uses an elaborate disproportional stratified sample.

Advance Knowledge of the Population

Advance knowledge of population characteristics, such as the availability of lists of population members, is an important criterion. In many cases, however, no list of population elements will be available to the researcher. This is especially true when the population element is defined by ownership of a particular product or brand, by experience in performing a specific job task, or on a qualitative dimension. A lack of adequate lists may automatically rule out systematic sampling, stratified sampling, or other sampling designs, or it may dictate that a preliminary study, such as a short telephone survey using random digit dialing, be conducted to generate information to build a sampling frame for the primary study. In many developing countries and in smaller American towns reverse directories are the exception rather than the rule; thus, researchers planning sample designs will have to work around this limitation.

National versus Local Project

Geographic proximity of population elements will influence sample design. When population elements are unequally distributed geographically, a cluster sample may become much more attractive.

Need for Statistical Analysis

The need for statistical projections based on the sample often is a criterion. Nonprobability sampling techniques do not allow researchers to use statistical analysis to project data beyond their samples.

Summary

Sampling is a procedure that uses a small number of units of a given population as a basis for conclusions about the whole population. Sampling often is necessary because it would be practically impossible to conduct a census to measure characteristics of all units of a population. Samples also are needed in cases where measurement involves destruction of the measured unit.

The first problem in sampling is to define the target population. Incorrect or vague definition of this population is likely to produce misleading results. A sampling frame is a list of elements, or individual members, of the overall population from which the sample is drawn. A sampling unit is a single element or group of elements subject to selection in the sample.

There are two sources of discrepancy between the sample results and the population parameters. One, random sampling error, arises from chance variations of the sample from the population. Random sampling error is a function of sample size and may be estimated using the central-limit theorem discussed in Chapter 17. Systematic, or nonsampling, error comes from sources such as sampling frame error, mistakes in recording responses, or nonresponses from persons not contacted or refusing to participate.

The two major classes of sampling methods are probability and nonprobability techniques. Nonprobability techniques include convenience sampling, quota sampling, and snowball sampling. They are convenient to use, but there are no statistical techniques with which to measure their random sampling error. Probability samples are based on chance selection procedures. These include simple random sampling, systematic sampling, stratified sampling, and cluster sampling. With these techniques, random sampling error can be accurately predicted.

A researcher who must determine the most appropriate sampling design for a specific project will identify a number of sampling criteria and evaluate the relative importance of each criterion before selecting a design. The most common criteria concern accuracy requirements, available resources, time constraints, knowledge availability, and analytical requirements.

Key Terms and Concepts

Sample	Secondary sampling unit	Quota sampling
Population (universe)	Tertiary sampling unit	Snowball sampling
Population element	Random sampling error	Simple random sampling
Census	Systematic (nonsampling) error	Systematic sampling
Sampling frame	Nonresponse error	Stratified sampling
Reverse directory	Probability sampling	Proportional stratified sample
Sampling frame error	Nonprobability sampling	Disproportional stratified sample
Sampling unit	Convenience sampling	Cluster sampling
Primary sampling unit (PSU)	Judgment (purposive) sampling	Multistage area sampling

Questions for Review and Critical Thinking

1. If we judge whether we want to see a new movie or television program on the basis of the "coming attractions" or television commercial previews, are we using a sampling technique? A scientific sampling technique?

2. Name some possible sampling frames for the following:
   a. Electrical contractors
   b. Tennis players
   c. Dog owners
   d. Foreign-car owners
   e. Wig and hair goods retailers
   f. Minority-owned businesses
   g. Men over 6 feet tall

3. Describe the difference between a probability sample and a nonprobability sample.

4. In what types of situations is conducting a census more appropriate than sampling? When is sampling more appropriate than taking a census?

5. Comment on the following sampling designs:
   a. A citizen's group interested in generating public and financial support for a new university basketball arena prints a questionnaire in area newspapers. Readers return the questionnaires by mail.
   b. A department store that wishes to examine whether it is losing or gaining customers draws a sample from its list of credit card holders by selecting every 10th name.
   c. A motorcycle manufacturer decides to research consumer characteristics by sending 100 questionnaires to each of its dealers. The dealers will then use their sales records to track down buyers of this brand of motorcycle and distribute the questionnaires.
   d. An advertising executive suggests that advertising effectiveness be tested in the real world. A one-page ad should be taken out in a magazine. One-half of the space is used for a half-page ad. On the other half, a short questionnaire requests that readers comment on the ad. An incentive will be given for the first 1,000 responses.
   e. In selecting its sample for a focus group, a research company obtains a sample through organized groups such as church groups, clubs, and schools. The organizations are paid for securing respondents; no individual is directly compensated.
   f. A researcher suggests replacing a consumer diary panel with a sample of customers who regularly shop at a supermarket that uses optical scanning equipment. The burden of recording purchases by humans will be replaced by computerized longitudinal data.

6. When would a researcher use a judgment, or purposive, sample?

7. A telephone interviewer asks, "I would like to ask you about race. Are you Native American, Hispanic, African American, Asian, or white?" After the respondent replies, the interviewer says, "We have conducted a large number of surveys with people of your background, and we do not need to question you further. Thank you for your cooperation." What type of sampling was used?

8. If researchers know that consumers in various geographic regions respond quite differently to a product category such as tomato sauce, is area sampling appropriate? Why or why not?

9. What are the benefits of stratified sampling?

10. What geographic units within a metropolitan area are useful for sampling?

11. Marketers often are particularly interested in the subset of a market that contributes most to sales (for example, heavy beer drinkers or large-volume retailers). What type of sampling might be best in this type of situation? Why?

12. Outline the step-by-step procedure you would use to select the following:
    a. A simple random sample of 150 students at your university
    b. A quota sample of 50 light users and 50 heavy users of beer in a shopping mall intercept sample
    c. A stratified sample of 50 mechanical engineers, 40 electrical engineers, and 40 civil engineers from the subscriber list of an engineering journal

13. Selection for jury duty is supposed to be a totally random process. Comment on the following computer selection procedures, and determine if they are indeed random processes:
    a. A program instructed the computer to scan the list of names and pluck names that were next to those from the last scan.
    b. Three-digit numbers were randomly generated to select jurors from a list of licensed drivers. If the weight information listed on the license matched the random number, the person was selected.
    c. The juror source list was obtained by merging a list of registered voters with a list of licensed drivers.

14. A company gathers focus group members from a list of articulate participants. It does not conduct a random sample, but selects its sample from this group to ensure a good session. The client did not inquire about sample selection when it accepted the proposal.

Exploring the Internet

1. Visit http://www.prb.org/edu/glossary.htm to find U.S. Census terms in a Glossary of Population Terms, Population Reference Bureau.

2. NYNEX Interactive Yellow Pages lists 16.5 million businesses. Go to http://www.niyp.com. Select the Business Type Option. Then select a state and bicycle. How many bicycle dealers are located in the state you chose? Select a systematic sample from this list.

3. Go to the U. S. Census Bureau's home page at
   http://www.census.gov
   If you want to view a complete list of metropolitan areas (MSAs), select the Population and Housing option and then select the Metropolitan Areas option.

4. The Institute of Museum Services' (IMS) 1992 National Needs Assessment survey of museums may be found at
   http://palimpsest.stanford.edu/byorg/ims/survey.
   The methodology and results of a study of U.S. museums can be found at this location. Visit this site to view the sampling methodology.

5. Use Lycos to search for ski resorts. At what URL address can you find a sampling frame of U.S. ski resorts?

Case 16.1 A. C. Nielsen—Can You Trust TV Ratings?[3]

A. C. NIELSEN, THE WORLD'S LARGEST MARKETING research company, runs a huge, continuous, partly automated survey of America's television viewing habits 24 hours a day, 365 days a year. Panel members allow a People Meter to be installed in their homes for 2 years. At any one time, approximately 4,000 American families are members of the Nielsen television panel, about one in every 23,000 television households.

Two statistics are used to evaluate television audiences. Rating is a measure of average audience and is expressed as a percentage of America's potential audience of 93.1 million households. Of course, not everyone is viewing television all the time; share is a measure of the percentage of households that are actually viewing televisions during a certain portion of the day. A typical standard deviation for the average program is 0.6. Thus a show with a rating of 15 has a 68 percent chance of having an actual rating between 14.4 and 15.6.

Nielsen has found that sampling is one of its most challenging operations. The sampling process begins with the creation every 10 years of a "sample frame," which is the population of households in America from which all Nielsen families are selected. First, using Census Bureau data, Nielsen's statistical department divides the country into successively smaller chunks of territory until it has a collection of 5,000 "block groups," or units of census geography comprising about 425 housing units each. Next, Nielsen sends squads of field agents into each block group to count every housing unit, both to account for any changes in the number of homes since the Census Bureau made its report and to note the addresses of potential Nielsen candidates. The crews merely count, until they reach a number selected at random by the company's media statisticians. Assume there are 425 homes in a block group. Nielsen picks a random number from 1 to 425. If the number is 125, the enumerator counts the first 124 homes without jotting down a single address. The next housing unit is the primary target household, a "Basic" in Nielsen-speak. This is the home Nielsen most dearly wants to recruit, and the one that sampling theory dictates Nielsen *must* recruit. If the address is vacant, or even if it is a vacant slab in a trailer park, Nielsen will keep coming back for 5 years in hopes that someone will have moved in.

In theory, every household has an equal shot at becoming a Nielsen family; in practice, however, the odds for some occupations are zero. Nielsen never

allows journalists to be members of its sample because they are "occupationally disqualified." Among the occupationally disqualified are television producers; advertising executives; marketing researchers; and, of course, every single employee of CBS, NBC, ABC, FOX, CNN, MTV, and local television stations. (Nielsen has good reason to worry. Station employees included by chance in diary panels have been known to load the diaries with their own station's programs.) Nielsen also builds in demographic safety values to avoid the unlikely but statistically possible selection of an aberrant sample—say, 4,000 black households.

Today's People Meter demands a lot from its hosts. Arthur Nielsen Sr. wrote in 1955 that one of the beauties of the Audimeter system was that it operated "entirely automatically and outside the collaborating family's day-to-day awareness." Today's People Meter is a nagging shrew consisting of three components: a computer the size of a compact-disc player known as the home unit; a smaller box with a numerical keypad and a faceplate of red and green lights which sits atop the TV set; and a remote control, typically with eight numbered buttons and an "OK" button. Nielsen assigns a button to everyone in a household, even children as young as 2. Everyone, even the 2-year-old, is expected to behave in appropriate Nielsen fashion—to press his or her button at the start of TV watching and at the end. Visitors use an unoccupied button, enter their sex and age on the numerical keypad, and then report their arrivals and departures. When a viewer punches in, the lights associated with that viewer's number change from red to green. Periodically the meter demands reassurance that someone is indeed watching and a single red bulb at the far right of the keypad box will blink. One press of the "OK" button calms the machine. The longer the prompt goes unanswered, however, the more adamant the meter becomes, blinking its bulbs in an increasingly frenzied manner until it is ablaze with flashing lights. Some meters finally emit a pained and disappointed beep.

Volunteers subject their homes to a lot of drilling and wiring. Nielsen requires that every single TV set, VCR, and cable converter be metered and connected to the home unit. Any satellite dish has to be metered separately with an "inclinometer" that records which way, and thus at which satellite, the dish is pointing. Nielsen even takes an inventory of unused TVs and the homeowner swears in an affidavit that the sets won't be used. A small plastic seal is attached to the plug prongs of the unused sets. On a return visit if the agent finds any seals broken, he or she will ask permission to meter the set; if not allowed to, the agent may eject the family from the sample.

Today's typical Nielsen home, says Larry Patterson, the company's director of field operations, has two TVs, one VCR, and one cable converter, requiring an array of equipment that takes 5 or 6 hours to install. The most complex house he has come across had six TVs, five VCRs, and cable access; installing the meters took 2 full days.

In return for all this equipping and pestering, each family picks gifts from a Nielsen catalog and gets cash payments of 2 dollars a month for each TV or VCR in the house. A household with one TV would get just $24 a year; the family with the complex system mentioned above would get $264.

The networks worry that the burden is too great, that Nielsen families experience "button fatigue" and begin engaging in such inappropriate behaviors as failing to log in or failing to require visitors to register their age and presence.

QUESTIONS

1. Evaluate the A. C. Nielsen sampling procedure.

2. Do you think there might by any problem recruiting households for the Nielsen panel?

3. Do you think button-pushing fatigue is a major problem? What groups might find regular button pushing the most difficult?

Case 16.2 Scientific Telephone Samples[4]

SCIENTIFIC TELEPHONE SAMPLES (STS), LOCATED IN Tustin, California, specializes in selling sampling frames for marketing research. The STS sampling frame is based on a database of all working residential telephone exchanges and working blocks in the United States. Thus, STS can draw from any part of the country—no matter how large or how small. The information is updated several times per year, and cross-checked against area code and assigned exchange lists furnished by the telephone companies. Exchange and/or working blocks designated for business or governmental telephones, car/boat/plane mobile units, and other commercial services are screened out.

STS can furnish almost any type of random digit sample desired, including:

- National samples (continental United States only, or with Alaska and Hawaii)
- Stratified national samples (by census region or division)
- Census regions or divisions
- State samples
- By ADI, DMA, CMSA, or MSA
- County samples
- By zip code
- City samples—selected by using zip codes assigned to that city

- Exchange samples—generated from your list of three digit exchanges
- Targeted RDD (including over 40 variables and special databases for high-income areas, Hispanics, African Americans, and Asians).

STS offers two different methodologies for pulling working blocks. Either type can be used regardless of the geographic sampling unit (for example, state, county, zip). The two versions are: Type A (EPSEM/pure/unweighted) and Type B (weighted/efficient).

Type A samples are pulled using a strict definition of randomness. They are called "unweighted" samples because each working block has an equal chance of being selected to generate a random digit number. Completed interviews from a Type A sample which has been dialed to exhaustion should be highly representative of the population under study.

Type B or "efficient" samples are preweighted so RDD numbers are created from telephone working blocks in proportion to the number of estimated household listings in each working block. Working blocks that are more filled with numbers will be more prevalent in your sample. For example, a working block which has 50 known numbers in existence would have twice the probability of being included as one which had just 25 numbers.

Type B samples are most useful when one is willing to overlook a strict definition of randomness in favor of slightly more calling efficiency because of fewer "disconnects." In theory, completed interviews from Type B samples may tend to overrepresent certain types of working blocks, but many researchers feel there is not much difference in representativeness.

QUESTIONS

1. Evaluate the geographic options offered by STS. Do they seem to cover all the bases?

2. Evaluate the STS method of random digit dialing.

Case 16.3 Action Federal Savings and Loan Corporation

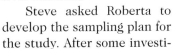

STEVE MILES MADE HIS BIG MOVE SIX MONTHS AGO. He quit his job as director of retail marketing at the largest bank in the state to become marketing manager for Action Federal Savings and Loan. It had been only 3-1/2 years since he received his bachelor's degree in marketing at the largest university in the state, but he was bright, personable, and ambitious. Now, after several months of orientation at Action Federal (Steve called it "Mickey Mouse"), he was beginning his own marketing operations, hiring Roberta Nimoy from City University as his marketing research assistant.

Steve wanted to do an image study of each of the 13 branches of Action Federal located throughout the state. The main branch and three others were located in the capital city and nearby suburbs; these were housed in tall office buildings in downtown locations. The other branches were located in rural areas, and their architecture was designed around the surroundings. One was located in a restored colonial home. Another, the Old Mill branch located next to a park with a historic windmill, was designed to be compatible with the nearby river and mill.

Steve asked Roberta to develop the sampling plan for the study. After some investigation, she learned that all the accounts were alphabetically listed in the main branch's computer. She thought that a list of names and addresses could be generated by taking a sample of 1,300. The computer would be programmed to randomly select every *n*th name. Since the savings and loan had approximately 112,000 customers, every 86th name would be selected.

QUESTIONS

1. Evaluate Action Federal's sampling plan.

2. What alternative sampling plans might be used?

Case 16.4 The Internal Revenue Service

THE INTERNAL REVENUE SERVICE WISHES TO CONDUCT A survey on income tax cheating. The objectives for this survey are:

1. To identify the extent to which taxpayers cheat on their returns, their reasons for doing so, and approaches the IRS can take to deter this kind of behavior

2. To determine taxpayers' experience and satisfaction with various IRS services

3. To determine what services taxpayers need

4. To develop an accurate profile of taxpayers' behavior as they prepare their income tax returns

5. To assess taxpayers' knowledge and opinions about various tax laws and procedures

The federal government always wishes to be extremely accurate in its survey research. A survey of approximately 5,000 individuals located throughout the country will provide the database for this study. The sample will be selected on a probability basis from all households in the continental United States.

Eligible respondents will be adults over age 18. Within each household, an effort will be made to interview the individual who is most familiar with completing federal tax forms. When there is more than one taxpayer in the household, a random process will be used to select the member to be interviewed.

QUESTION

1. Suppose you are a consultant hired to design the sample for a personal, in-home interview. Design a sample for the Internal Revenue Service survey.

Chapter 17

Determination of Sample Size

A Review of Statistical Theory

T HE DETERMINATION OF THE APPROPRIATE SAMPLE SIZE IS A crucial element of marketing research. To formally identify the proper sample size, statistical theory is necessary. Unfortunately, statistics has a bad image among students.

The fear of statistics is one of college students' most universal phobias. "Stat is too difficult—I'll never pass" is a lament often heard on campus. Students postpone their statistics classes until their last semester. Statistics students are frequently subject to mental blocks; they feel like Saint George trying to tame the raging statistical dragon, as the cartoon here illustrates. There is no need, however, for students to have this dread. Statistics can be easily mastered if one learns the tricks of the trade.

Why are there so many myths about statistics? Statisticians, much like lawyers, medical doctors, and computer scientists, have developed their own jargon. Laypeople do not understand professionals' technical terms. Cynics suspect this terminology is a ploy to impress others and, possibly, to justify charging higher fees. How many fishermen have you heard say, "Hand me the reticulated lattice joined at the interstices," when they simply want a *net?* Then again, when compared with professionals who use complex terminology, fishermen do not make much money.

The point is simple: If you do not understand the basics of the language, you will have problems in conversation. Statistics is the language of the marketing researcher. If administrators and marketing researchers do not speak the same language, communication will fail.

This chapter explains how to determine sample size and reviews some of the basic terminology of statistical analysis.

Taming the Statistical Beast

What you will learn in this chapter

To explain the difference between descriptive and inferential statistics.

To discuss the purpose of inferential statistics by explaining the difference between population parameters and sample statistics.

To make data usable by organizing and summarizing them into frequency distributions, proportions, and measurements of central tendency.

To identify and calculate the various measures of dispersion.

To explain why the standard deviation is an important measure of dispersion.

To identify the characteristics of the normal distribution.

To define standardized normal curve.

To compute the standardized value, Z, and to use the Z (standardized normal probability distribution) tables in the appendix of this book.

To distinguish among population, sample, and sampling distributions, and to identify the mean and standard deviation of each distribution.

To explain the central-limit theorem.

To compute confidence interval estimates.

To understand the three factors required for specifying sample size.

To estimate the sample size for a simple random sample when the characteristic of interest is a mean and when it is a proportion.

To understand which nonstatistical considerations influence the determination of sample size.

Table 17.1 **Frequency Distribution of Deposits**

AMOUNT	FREQUENCY (NUMBER OF PEOPLE WHO HOLD DEPOSITS IN EACH RANGE)
Under $3,000	499
$3,000–$4,999	530
$5,000–$9,999	562
$10,000–$14,999	718
$15,000 or more	811
	3,120

Reviewing Basic Terminology

The first five sections of this chapter summarize several key statistical concepts necessary for understanding the theory that underlies the derivation of sample size. These sections are intended for students who need to review many of the basic aspects of statistics theory. Many students, even those who received good grades in their elementary statistics classes, probably will benefit from a quick review of the basic statistical concepts. Some students will prefer to just skim this material and proceed to page 514, where the discussion of the actual determination of sample size begins. Others should study these sections carefully to acquire an understanding of statistics.

Descriptive and Inferential Statistics

The *Statistical Abstract of the United States* presents table after table of figures associated with the number of births, number of employees in each county of the United States, and other data that the average person calls "statistics." These are descriptive statistics. Another type of statistics, inferential statistics, is used to make inferences about a whole population from a sample. For example, when a firm test markets a new product in Sacramento and Birmingham, it wishes to make an inference from these sample markets to predict what will happen throughout the United States. Thus, there are two applications of statistics: (1) to describe characteristics of the population or sample and (2) to generalize from the sample to the population.

Sample Statistics and Population Parameters

The primary purpose of inferential statistics is to make a judgment about the population or the collection of all elements about which one seeks information. The sample is a subset or relatively small fraction of the total number of elements in the population. It is useful to distinguish between the data computed in the sample and the data or variables in the population. The term **sample statistics** designates variables in the sample or measures computed from the sample data. The term **population parameters** designates the variables or measured characteristics of the population. Sample statistics are used to make inferences about population parameters.[1] In our notation we will generally use Greek lowercase letters, for example, μ or σ, to denote population parameters and English letters to denote sample statistics, such as X or S.

sample statistics
Variables in a sample or measures computed from sample data.

population parameters
The variables in a population or measured characteristics of the population.

Table 17.2 Percentage Distribution of Deposits

Amount	Percent (Percentage of People Who Hold Deposits in Each Range)
Under $3,000	16
$3,000–$4,999	17
$5,000–$9,999	18
$10,000–$14,999	23
$15,000 or more	26
	100

Table 17.3 Probability Distribution of Deposits

Amount	Probability
Under $3,000	.16
$3,000–$4,999	.17
$5,000–$9,999	.18
$10,000–$14,999	.23
$15,000 or more	.26
	1.00

Making Data Usable

Frequency Distributions

Suppose a telephone survey has been conducted for a savings and loan association. The data have been recorded on a large number of questionnaires. To make the data usable, this information must be organized and summarized. Constructing a *frequency table* or **frequency distribution** is one of the most common means of summarizing a set of data. The process begins by recording the number of times a particular value of a variable occurs. This is the frequency of that value. In our survey example Table 17.1 represents a frequency distribution of respondents' answers to a question that asked how much customers had deposited in the savings and loan.

Constructing a distribution of relative frequency, or a **percentage distribution**, is also quite simple. In Table 17.2 the frequency of each value in Table 17.1 has been divided by the total number of observations. Multiplying the relative class frequencies by 100 converts them to percentages to give a frequency distribution of percentages.

Probability is the long-run relative frequency with which an event will occur. Inferential statistics uses the concept of a probability distribution, which is conceptually the same as percentage distribution except that the data are converted into probabilities (see Table 17.3).

frequency distribution
Organizing a set of data by summarizing the number of times a particular value of a variable occurs

percentage distribution
The organization of a frequency distribution into a table (or graph) that summarizes percentage values associated with particular values of a variable.

probability
The long-run relative frequency with which an event will occur.

Table 17.4 Number of Sales Calls per Day by Salespeople

SALESPERSON	NUMBER OF SALES CALLS
Mike	4
Patty	3
Billie	2
Bob	5
John	3
Frank	3
Chuck	1
Samantha	5
Total	26

Proportions

proportion

The percentage of elements that meet some criterion.

When a frequency distribution portrays only a single characteristic as a percentage of the total, it defines the **proportion** of occurrence. A proportion, such as the proportion of tenured professors at a university, indicates the percentage of population elements that successfully meet some standard concerning the particular characteristic. It may be expressed as a percentage, a fraction, or a decimal value.

Central Tendency

On a typical day, the sales manager counts the number of sales calls each sales representative makes. He or she wishes to inspect the data to see the center, or middle area, of the frequency distribution. Central tendency can be measured in three ways—the mean, median, or mode—each of which has a different meaning.

mean

A measure of central tendency; the arithmetic average.

The Mean We all have been exposed to the average known as the **mean.** The mean is simply the arithmetic average, and it is a common measure of central tendency. At this point it is appropriate to introduce the summation symbol, the capital Greek letter *sigma* (Σ). A typical use might look like this:

$$\sum_{i=1}^{n} X_i$$

This is a shorthand way to write the sum:

$$X_1 + X_2 + X_3 + X_4 + X_5 + \ldots + X_n$$

Suppose a sales manager supervises the eight salespeople listed in Table 17.4. Below the Σ is the initial value of an index, usually, i, j, or k, and above it is the final value, in this case n, the number of observations. The shorthand expression says to replace i in the formula with the values from 1 to 8 and total the observations obtained. The initial and final index values may be replaced by other values to indicate different starting or stopping points without changing the basic formula.

To express the sum of the salespeople's calls in Σ notation, we just number the salespeople (this is the index number) and associate subscripted variables with their numbers of calls:

INDEX		SALESPERSON	VARIABLE		NUMBER OF CALLS
1	=	Mike	X_1	=	4
2	=	Patty	X_2	=	3
3	=	Billie	X_3	=	2
4	=	Bob	X_4	=	5
5	=	John	X_5	=	3
6	=	Frank	X_6	=	3
7	=	Chuck	X_7	=	1
8	=	Samantha	X_8	=	5

We then write an appropriate S formula and evaluate it:

$$\sum_{i=1}^{8} X_i = X_1 + X_2 + X_3 + X_4 + X_5 + X_6 + X_7 + X_8$$
$$= 4 + 3 + 2 + 5 + 3 + 3 + 1 + 5$$
$$= 26$$

The formula for the arithmetic mean is:

$$\text{Mean} = \frac{\sum_{i=1}^{n} X}{n} = \frac{26}{8} = 3.25$$

The sum $\sum_{i=1}^{n}$ tells us to add all the Xs whose subscripts are between 1 and n inclusive, where n equals the number of observations. The mean number of sales calls in this example is 3.25.

Researchers generally wish to know the population mean, μ (lowercase Greek letter *mu*), which is calculated as follows:

$$\mu = \frac{\sum_{i=1}^{n} X}{N}$$

where

N = number of all observations in the population

Often we will not have enough data to calculate the population mean μ, so we will calculate a sample mean, (read as "X bar") with the following formula:

$$\overline{X} = \frac{\sum_{i=1}^{n} X}{n}$$

where

n = number of observations made in the sample

More likely than not, you already know how to calculate a mean. However, knowing how to distinguish among the symbols Σ, μ, and X is necessary to understand statistics.

EXPLORING RESEARCH ISSUES

The Well-Chosen Average

WHEN YOU READ AN ANNOUNCEMENT BY A CORPORA-tion executive or a business proprietor that the average pay of the people who work in his or her establishment is so much, the figure may mean something and it may not. If the average is a median, you can learn something significant from it: Half the employees make more than that; half make less. But if it is a mean (and believe me, it may be that if its nature is unspecified), you may

be getting nothing more revealing that the average of one $225,000 income—the proprietor's—and the salaries of a crew of underpaid workers. "Average annual pay of $28,500" may conceal both the $10,000 salaries and the owner's profits taken in the form of a whopping salary.

Let's take a longer look at that one. This table shows how many people get how much. The boss might like to express the situation as "average wage $28,500," using that deceptive mean. The mode, however, is more revealing: The most common rate of pay in this business is $10,000 a year. As usual, the median tells more about the situation than any other single figure does; half the people get more than $15,000 and half get less.

NUMBER OF PEOPLE	TITLE	SALARY	
1	Proprietor	$225,000	
1	President	75,000	
2	Vice presidents	50,000	
1	Controller	28,500	← Arithmetical average
3	Directors	25,000	
4	Managers	18,500	*(the one in the middle;*
1	Supervisor	15,000	← Median *12 above, 12 below)*
12	Workers	10,000	← Mode *(occurs most frequently)*

In our introductory discussion of the summation sign (Σ) we have used very detailed notation that included the subscript for the initial index value (i) and final index value (n). However, from this point on, references to Σ will not use the subscript for the initial index value (i) and final index value (n) unless there is a unique reason to highlight these index values.

median
A measure of central tendency that is the midpoint, the value below which half the values in a distribution fall.

The Median The next measure of central tendency, the **median,** is the midpoint of the distribution, or the 50th percentile. In other words, the median is the value below which half the values in the sample fall. In the sales manager example, 3 is the median because half the observations are greater than 3 and half are less than 3.

mode
A measure of central tendency; the value that occurs most often.

The Mode In apparel *mode* refers to the most popular fashion. In statistics the **mode** is the measure of central tendency that identifies the value that occurs most often. In our example Patty, John, and Frank make three sales calls per day. The value 3 occurs most often and thus, 3 is the mode. This is determined by listing each possible value and noting the number of times each value occurs.

Measures of Dispersion

The mean, median, and mode summarize the central tendency of frequency distributions. Knowing the tendency of observations to depart from the central tendency is also important. Calculating the dispersion of the data, or how the obser-

Table 17.5 Sales Levels for Products A and B (Both Average 200 Units)

	UNITS PRODUCT A	UNITS PRODUCT B
January	196	150
February	198	160
March	199	176
April	200	181
May	200	192
June	200	200
July	200	201
August	201	202
September	201	213
October	201	224
November	202	240
December	202	261

Exhibit 17.1 Low Dispersion versus High Dispersion

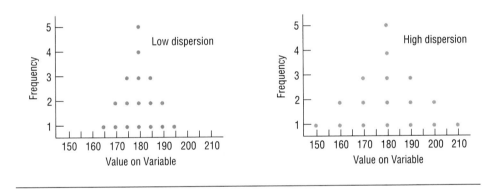

vations vary from the mean, is another way to summarize the data. Consider, for instance, the 12-month sales patterns of the two products shown in Table 17.5. Both have mean monthly sales volumes of 200 units, but the dispersion of observations for product B is much greater than that for product A. There are several measures of dispersion.

The Range The range is the simplest measure of dispersion. It is the distance between the smallest and the largest values of a frequency distribution. Thus, for product A the range is between 196 units and 202 units (6 units), whereas for product B the range is between 150 units and 261 units (111 units). The range does not take into account all the observations; it merely tells us about the extreme values of the distribution.

Just as people may be fat or skinny, distributions may be fat or skinny. For example, for product A the observations are close together and reasonably close to the mean. While we do not expect all observations to be exactly like the mean, in a skinny distribution they will lie a short distance from the mean, while in a fat distribution they will be spread out. Exhibit 17.1 illustrates this concept graphically with two frequency distributions that have identical modes, medians, and means but different degrees of dispersion.

The interquartile range is the range that encompasses the middle 50 percent of the observations—in other words, the range between the bottom quartile (lowest 25 percent) and the top quartile (highest 25 percent).

Deviation Scores. A method of calculating how far any observation is from the mean is to calculate individual deviation scores. To calculate a deviation from the mean, use the following formula:

$$d_i = (X_i - \overline{X})$$

If the value of 150 units for product B represents the month of January, we calculate its deviation score to be −50, that is, $150 - 200 = 50$. If the deviation scores are large, we will have a fat distribution because the distribution exhibits a broad spread.

Why Use the Standard Deviation? Statisticians have derived several quantitative indexes to reflect a distribution's spread or variability. The *standard deviation* is perhaps the most valuable index of spread or dispersion. Students often have difficulty understanding this concept. Learning about the standard deviation will be easier if we present several other measures of dispersion that may be used. Each of these has certain limitations that the standard deviation does not.

The first of these is the average deviation. We compute the average deviation by calculating the deviation score of each observation value—that is, its difference from the mean—and summing up each score, then dividing by the sample size (n):

$$\text{Average deviation} = \frac{\Sigma X(_i - \overline{X})}{n}$$

While this measure of spread seems interesting, it is never used. The positive deviation scores are always canceled out by the negative scores, leaving an average deviation value of zero. Hence, the average deviation is useless as a measure of spread.

One might correct for the disadvantage of the average deviation by computing the absolute values of the deviations. In other words, we would ignore all the positive and negative signs and use only the absolute values of each deviation. The formula for the mean absolute deviation is:

$$\text{Mean absolute deviation} = \frac{\Sigma |X_i - \overline{X}|}{n}$$

While this procedure eliminates the problem of always having a zero score for the deviation measure, there are some technical mathematical problems that make it less valuable than some other measures; it is mathematically intractable.

Variance Another means of eliminating the sign problem caused by the negative deviations canceling out the positive deviations is to square the deviation scores. The following formula gives the mean squared deviation:

$$\text{Mean squared deviation} = \frac{\Sigma (X_i - \overline{X})^2}{n}$$

This measure is useful to describe the sample variability. However, we typically wish to make an inference about a population from the sample. The divisor $n - 1$ is used rather than n in most pragmatic marketing research problems. This new measure of spread, called the variance, has the formula:

$$\text{Variance, } S^2 = \frac{\Sigma (X_i - \overline{X})^2}{n - 1}$$

Table 17.6 **Calculating a Standard Deviation: Number of Sales Calls per Day by Salespersons**

$n = 8$ $\overline{X} = 3.25$	X	$(X - \overline{X})$	$(X - \overline{X})^2$
	4	$(4 - 3.25) = 0.75$	0.5625
	3	$(3 - 3.25) = -0.25$	0.0625
	2	$(2 - 3.25) = -1.25$	1.5625
	5	$(5 - 3.25) = 1.75$	3.0625
	3	$(3 - 3.25) = -0.25$	0.0625
	3	$(3 - 3.25) = -0.25$	0.0625
	1	$(1 - 3.25) = -2.25$	5.0625
	5	$(5 - 3.25) = 1.75$	3.0625
	Σ a	a	13.5000

$$s = \sqrt{\frac{\Sigma(X = \overline{X})^2}{n - 1}} = \sqrt{\frac{13.5}{8 - 1}} = \sqrt{\frac{13.5}{7}} = \sqrt{1.9286} = 1.3887$$

aThe summation of this column is not used in the calculation of the standard deviation.

The variance is a very good index of the degree of dispersion. The variance, S^2, will equal zero if, and only if, each and every observation in the distribution is the same as the mean. The variance will grow larger as the observations tend to differ increasingly from one another and from the mean.

Standard Deviation. While the variance is frequently used in statistics, it has one major drawback. The variance reflects a unit of measurement that has been squared. For instance, if measures of sales in a territory are made in dollars, the mean number will be reflected in dollars, but the variance will be in squared dollars. Because of this, statisticians have taken the square root of the variance. The square root of the variance for a distribution, called the **standard deviation**, eliminates the drawback of having the measure of dispersion in squared units rather than in the original measurement units. The formula for the standard deviation is:

$$S = \sqrt{S^2} = \sqrt{\frac{\Sigma(X_i - \overline{X})^2}{n - 1}}$$

standard deviation
A quantitative index of a distribution's spread or variability; the square root of the variance for distribution.

Table 17.6 illustrates that the calculation of a standard deviation requires the researcher to first calculate the sample mean. In the example with eight salespeople's sales calls (Table 17.4), we calculated the sample mean as 3.25. Table 17.6 illustrates how to calculate the standard deviation for these data.

At this point the reader should think about the original purpose for measures of dispersion. We wanted to summarize the data from survey research and other forms of marketing research. Indexes of central tendencies, such as the mean, help us interpret the data. In addition we wish to calculate a measure of variability that will give us a quantitative index of the dispersion of the distribution. We have looked at several measures of dispersion to arrive at two very adequate means of measuring dispersion: the variance and the standard deviation. The formula given is for the sample standard deviation, S.

The formula for the population standard deviation, σ, which is conceptually very similar, has not been given. Nevertheless, the reader should understand that σ measures the dispersion in the population, and S measures the dispersion in the sample. These concepts are crucial to understanding statistics. Remember, the student of statistics must learn the language to use it in a research project. If you do not understand the concept at this point, review this material now.

The Normal Distribution

normal distribution
A symmetrical, bell-shaped distribution that describes the expected probability distribution of many chance occurrences.

One of the most useful probability distributions in statistics is the **normal distribution,** also called the *normal curve.* This mathematical and theoretical distribution describes the expected distribution of sample means and many other chance occurrences. The normal curve is bell shaped and almost all (99 percent) of its values are within ±3 standard deviations from its mean. An example of a normal curve, the distribution of IQ scores, appears in Exhibit 17.2. In our example, a standard deviation for IQ equals 15. We can identify the proportion of the curve by measuring a score's distance (in this case, standard deviation) from the mean (100).

Exhibit 17.2 The Normal Distribution: An Example of the Distribution of Intelligence Quotient (IQ) Scores

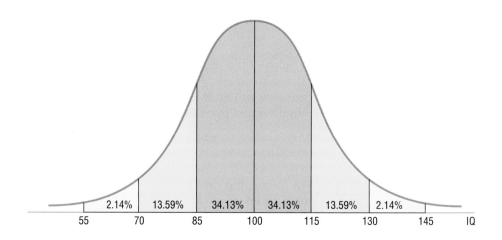

Exhibit 17.3 The Standardized Normal Distribution

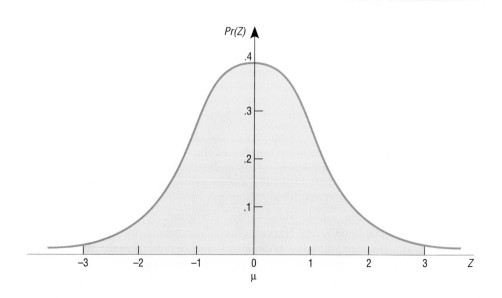

Table 17.7 The Standardized Normal Table

Z STANDARD DEVIATION FROM THE MEAN (UNITS)	Z STANDARD DEVIATIONS FROM THE MEAN (TENTHS OF UNITS)									
	0.0	0.1	0.2	0.3	0.4	0.5	0.6	0.7	0.8	0.9
	AREA UNDER ONE-HALF OF THE NORMAL CURVE[a]									
0.0	.000	.040	.080	.118	.155	.192	.226	.258	.288	.316
1.0	.341	.364	.385	.403	.419	.433	.445	.455	.464	.471
2.0	.477	.482	.486	.489	.492	.494	.495	.496	.497	.498
3.0	.499	.499	.499	.499	.499	.499	.499	.499	.499	.499

[a] Area under the normal curve over the segment measured in one direction from the mean to the distance indicated in each row-column combination. For example, the table shows that about 68 percent of normally distributed events can be expected to fall within 1.0 standard deviations on either side of the mean (0.341 times 2). An interval of almost 2.0 standard deviations around the mean will include 95 percent of all cases.

The **standardized normal distribution** is a specific normal curve that has several characteristics: (1) It is symmetrical about its mean; (2) the mean of the normal curve identifies its highest point (the mode) and the vertical line about which this normal curve is symmetrical; (3) the normal curve has an infinite number of cases (it is a continuous distribution), and the area under the curve has a probability density equal to 1.0; (4) the standardized normal distribution has a mean of 0 and a standard deviation of 1. Exhibit 17.3 illustrates these properties. Table 17.7 is a summary version of the typical standardized normal table found at the end of most statistics textbooks. A more complex table of areas under the standardized normal distribution appears in Table A.2 in the appendix.

standardized normal distribution
A purely theoretical probability distribution that reflects a specific normal curve for the standardized value, Z.

TO THE POINT

Order is heaven's law.

ALEXANDER POPE

The standardized normal distribution is a purely theoretical probability distribution, but it is the most useful distribution in inferential statistics. Statisticians have spent a great deal of time and effort making it convenient for researchers to find the probability of any portion of the area under the standardized normal distribution. All we must do is transform or convert the data from other observed normal distributions to the standardized normal curve. In other words, the standardized normal distribution is extremely valuable because we can translate or transform any normal variable, *X*, into the standardized value, *Z*. Exhibit 17.4 illustrates how to convert either a *skinny* distribution or a *fat* distribution into the standardized normal distribution. This has many pragmatic implications for the marketing researcher. The standardized normal table in the back of most statistics and marketing research books allows us to evaluate the probability of the occurrence of certain events without any difficulty.

The computation of the standardized value, *Z*, of any measurement expressed in original units is simple. It can be done by subtracting the mean from the value to be transformed and dividing by the standard deviation (all expressed in original units). The formula for this procedure and its verbal statement follow. In the formula note that σ, the population standard deviation, is used for calculation:[4]

$$Z = \frac{X - \mu}{\sigma}$$

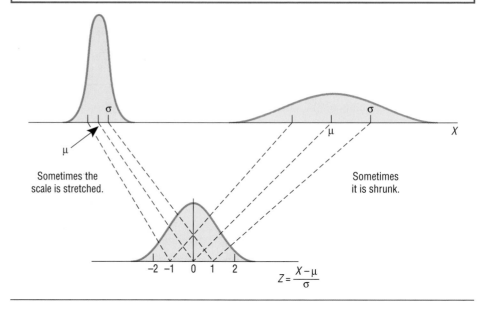

Exhibit 17.4 **Linear Transformation of Any Normal Variable into a Standardized Normal Variable**

Sometimes the scale is stretched.

Sometimes it is shrunk.

$$Z = \frac{X - \mu}{\sigma}$$

where

μ = the hypothesized or expected value of the mean

$$\text{Standardized value} = \frac{\text{Value to be transformed} - \text{Mean}}{\text{Standard deviation}}$$

Suppose that in the past a toy manufacturer has experienced mean sales, μ, of 9,000 units and a standard deviation, σ, of 500 units during September. The production manager wishes to know if wholesalers will demand between 7,500 and 9,625 units during September in the upcoming year. Because no tables in the back of the textbook show the distribution for a mean of 9,000 and a standard deviation of 500, we must transform our distribution of toy sales, *X*, into the standardized form using our simple formula. The following computation shows that the probability (*Pr*) of obtaining sales in this range is equal to .893:

$$Z = \frac{X - \mu}{\sigma} = \frac{7,500 - 9,000}{500} = 3.00$$

$$= \frac{9,625 - 9,000}{500} = 1.25$$

Using Table 17.7 (or Table A.2 in the appendix):

When $Z = -3.00$, the area under the curve (probability) equals .499.

When $Z = 1.25$, the area under the curve (probability) equals .394.

Thus, the total area under the curve is .499 + .394 = .893. The area under the curve that portrays this computation is the shaded area in Exhibit 17.5. The sales manager, therefore, knows there is a .893 probability that sales will be between 7,500 and 9,625.

At this point, it is appropriate to repeat that to understand statistics one must understand the language that statisticians use. Each concept discussed thus far is relatively simple, but a clear-cut command of these terminologies is essential for understanding what we will discuss later on.

Exhibit 17.5 **Standardized Distribution Curve**

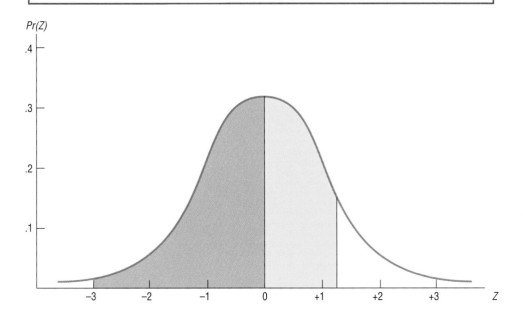

Now that we have covered certain basic terminology, we will outline the technique of statistical inference. However, before we do so, three additional types of distributions must be defined: population distribution, sample distribution, and sampling distribution.

Population Distribution, Sample Distribution, and Sampling Distribution

When conducting a research project or survey, the researcher's purpose is not to describe the sample of respondents, but to make an inference about the population. As we defined it previously, a population or universe is the total set or collection of potential units for observation. The sample is a smaller subset of this population.

A frequency distribution of the population elements is called a **population distribution.** The mean and standard deviation of the population distribution are represented by the Greek letters μ and σ. A frequency distribution of a sample is called a **sample distribution.** The sample mean is designated $\overline{X}$ and the sample standard deviation is designated S. The concepts of population distribution and sample distribution are relatively simple. However, we must now introduce another distribution: the *sampling distribution of the sample mean.*

Understanding the sampling distribution is the crux of understanding statistics. The sampling distribution is a theoretical probability distribution that in actual practice would never be calculated. Hence, practical, business-oriented students have difficulty understanding why the notion of the sampling distribution is important. Statisticians, with their mathematical curiosity, have asked themselves, "What would happen if we were to draw a large number of samples (say, 50,000), each having n elements, from a specified population?" Assuming that the samples are randomly selected, the sample means, $\overline{X}$s, could be arranged in a frequency distribution. Because different people or sample units will be selected in the different samples, the sample means will not be exactly equal. The shape of the sampling distribution is of considerable importance to

population distribution
A frequency distribution of the elements of a population.

sample distribution
A frequency distribution of a sample.

Exhibit 17.6 Schematic of the Three Fundamental Types of Distributions

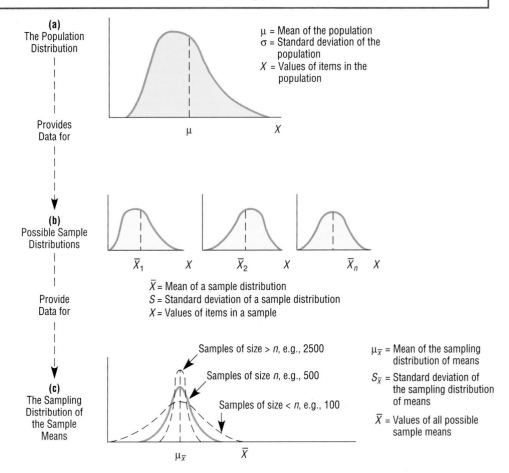

(a)
The Population Distribution

μ = Mean of the population
σ = Standard deviation of the population
X = Values of items in the population

μ X

Provides Data for

(b)
Possible Sample Distributions

$\overline{X}_1$ X $\overline{X}_2$ X $\overline{X}_n$ X

$\overline{X}$ = Mean of a sample distribution
S = Standard deviation of a sample distribution
X = Values of items in a sample

Provide Data for

Samples of size > n, e.g., 2500
Samples of size n, e.g., 500
Samples of size < n, e.g., 100

(c)
The Sampling Distribution of the Sample Means

$\mu_{\overline{X}}$ $\overline{X}$

$\mu_{\overline{X}}$ = Mean of the sampling distribution of means
$S_{\overline{X}}$ = Standard deviation of the sampling distribution of means
$\overline{X}$ = Values of all possible sample means

---

statisticians. If the sample size is sufficiently large and if the samples were randomly drawn, we know from the central-limit theorem that the sampling distribution of the mean will be approximately normally distributed.

A formal definition of the sampling distribution is as follows:

> A **sampling distribution** is a theoretical probability distribution that shows the functional relation between the possible values of some summary characteristic of n cases drawn at random and the probability (density) associated with each value over all possible samples of size n from a particular population.[5]

The sampling distribution's mean is called the *expected value* of the statistic. The expected value of the mean of the sampling distribution is equal to μ. The standard deviation of the sampling distribution is called the **standard error of the mean** ($S_{\overline{X}}$) and is approximately equal to

$$S_{\overline{X}} = \frac{\sigma}{\sqrt{n}}$$

To review, there are three important distributions that we must know about to make an inference about a population from a sample: the population distribution, the sample distribution, and the sampling distribution. They have the following characteristics:

sampling distribution
A theoretical probability distribution of sample means for all possible samples of a certain size drawn from a particular population.

standard error of the mean
The standard deviation of the sampling distribution.

DISTRIBUTION	MEAN	STANDARD DEVIATION
Population	μ	σ
Sample	$\overline{X}$	S
Sampling	$\mu_{\overline{X}} = \mu$	$S_{\overline{X}}$

We now have much of the information we need to understand the concept of statistical inference. To clarify why the sampling distribution has the characteristic just described, we will elaborate on two concepts: the standard error of the mean and the central-limit theorem. The reader may be wondering why the standard error of the mean, $S_{\overline{X}}$, is defined as $S_{\overline{X}} = \sigma/\sqrt{n}$. The reason is based on the notion that the variance or dispersion within the sampling distribution of the mean will be less if we have a larger sample size for independent samples. Most students will know intuitively that a larger sample size allows the researcher to be more confident that the sample mean is closer to the population mean. In actual practice the standard error of the mean is estimated using the sample's standard deviation. Thus, $S_{\overline{X}}$ is estimated using $S/\sqrt{n}$

Exhibit 17.6 shows the relationship among a population distribution, the sample distribution, and three sampling distributions for varying sample sizes. In part (a) the population distribution is not a normal distribution. In part (b) the sample distribution resembles the distribution of the population; however, there may be some differences. In part (c) each sampling distribution is normally distributed and the mean of each is the same. Note that as sample size increases, the spread of the sample means around μ decreases. Thus, with a larger sample size we will have a skinnier sampling distribution.

Central-Limit Theorem

Finding that the means of random samples of a sufficiently large size will be approximately normal in form and that the mean of the sampling distribution will approach the population mean is very useful. Mathematically, this is the assertion of the **central-limit theorem**, which states: As the sample size, n, increases, the distribution of the mean, $\overline{X}$, of a random sample taken from practically any population approaches a normal distribution (with a mean, μ, and a standard deviation, $\sigma\sqrt{n}$.).[6] The central-limit theorem works regardless of the shape of the original population distribution (see Exhibit 17.7).

A simple example will demonstrate the nature of the central-limit theorem. Assume that a consumer researcher is interested in the number of dollars children spend on toys each month. Assume further that the population the consumer researcher is investigating consists of 8-year-old children in a certain school. In this example the population consists of only six individuals. (This is a simple example and perhaps somewhat unrealistic; nevertheless, assume that the population size consists of only six elements.) Table 17.8 shows the frequency distribution of the six individuals. Alice, a relatively deprived child, has only $1 per month, whereas fat Freddy, the rich kid, has $6 to spend. The average expenditure on toys each month is $3.50, so the population mean, μ, equals 3.5 (see Table 17.9). Now assume that we do not know everything about the population, and we wish to take a sample size of two, to be drawn randomly from the population of the six individuals. How many possible samples are there? The answer is 15, as follows:

central-limit theorem
A theory that states that as a sample size increases the distribution of sample means of size n, randomly selected, approaches a normal distribution.

1, 2
1, 3   2, 3
1, 4   2, 4   3, 4
1, 5   2, 5   3, 5   4, 5
1, 6   2, 6   3, 6   4, 6   5, 6

Table 17.10 lists the sample mean of each of the possible 15 samples and the frequency distribution of these sample means with their appropriate probabilities. These sample means comprise a sampling distribution of the mean, and the distribution is *approximately* normal. If we increased the sample size to three, four, or more, the distribution of sample means would more closely approximate a normal distribution. While this simple example is not a proof of the central-limit theorem, it should give the reader a better understanding of the nature of the sampling distribution of the mean.

Exhibit 17.7 **Distribution of Sample Means for Samples of Various Sizes and Population Distributions**

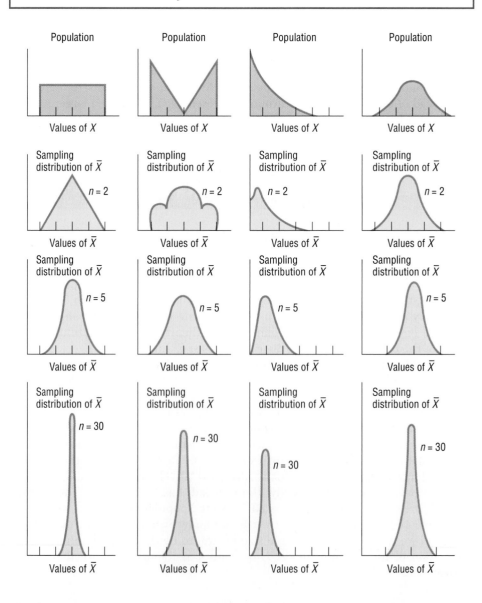

Table 17.8 Hypothetical Population Distribution of Toy Expenditures

Child	Toy Expenditures
Alice	$1.00
Becky	2.00
Noah	3.00
Tobin	4.00
George	5.00
Freddy	6.00

Table 17.9 Calculation of Population Mean

X
$ 1.00
2.00
3.00
4.00
5.00
6.00
Σ $21.00

Calculations:

$$\mu = \frac{\Sigma X}{N} = \frac{21}{6} = 3.5 = \mu$$

This theoretical knowledge about distributions can be used to solve two practical marketing research problems: estimating parameters and determining sample size.

Estimation of Parameters

A catalog retailer, such as Horchow, may rely on sampling and statistical estimation to prepare for Christmas orders. The company can expect that 28 days after mailing a catalog, it will have received X percent of the orders it will get. With this information, Horchow can tell within 5 percent how many ties it will sell by Christmas. Making a proper inference about population parameters is highly practical for a marketer that must have the inventory appropriate for a short selling season.

Suppose you are a product manager for Beatrice Foods and you recently conducted a taste test to measure intention to buy a reformulated Swiss Miss Lite Cocoa Mix. The results of the research indicate that when the product was placed in 800 homes and a callback was made two weeks later, 80 percent of the

Table 17.10 **Arithmetic Mean of Samples and Frequency Distribution of Sample Means**

SAMPLE MEANS

SAMPLE	ΣX	$\overline{X}$	PROBABILITY
$1, $2	$3.00	$1.50	1/15
1, 3	4.00	2.00	1/15
1, 4	5.00	2.50	1/15
1, 5	6.00	3.00	1/15
1, 6	7.00	3.50	1/15
2, 3	5.00	2.50	1/15
2, 4	6.00	3.00	1/15
2, 5	7.00	3.50	1/15
2, 6	8.00	4.00	1/15
3, 4	7.00	3.50	1/15
3, 5	8.00	4.00	1/15
3, 6	9.00	4.50	1/15
4, 5	9.00	4.50	1/15
4, 6	10.00	5.00	1/15
5, 6	11.00	5.50	1/15

FREQUENCY DISTRIBUTION

SAMPLE MEAN	FREQUENCY	PROBABILITY
$1.50	1	1/15
2.00	1	1/15
2.50	2	2/15
3.00	2	2/15
3.50	3	3/15
4.00	2	2/15
4.50	2	2/15
5.00	1	1/15
5.50	1	1/15

respondents said they would buy: 76 percent of those who did not previously use low-calorie cocoa and 84 percent of those who did. How can you be sure there were no statistical errors in your estimate? How confident can you be of these figures?

Students often wonder whether statistics are used in the business world. The two situations just described provide contemporary examples of the need for statistical estimation of parameters and the value of statistical techniques as managerial tools.

Our goal in using statistics is to make an estimate about the population parameters. The population mean, μ, and standard deviation, σ, are constants, but in most instances of marketing research they are unknown. To estimate the population values, we are required to sample. As we have discussed, $\overline{X}$ and S are random variables that will vary from sample to sample with a certain probability (sampling) distribution. A specific example of statistical inference would be a prospective racquetball entrepreneur who wishes to estimate the average number of days players participate in this sport each week. Our previous example was somewhat unrealistic because the population had only six individuals. When statistical inference is needed, the population mean, μ, is a constant but unknown parameter. To estimate the average number of playing days, we may take a sample of 300 racquetball players throughout the area where our entrepreneur is thinking of building club facilities. If the sample mean, $\overline{X}$, equals 2.6 days per week, we may use this figure as a **point estimate**. This single value, 2.6, is the best estimate of the population mean. However, we would be extremely lucky if the sample estimate were exactly the same as the population value. A less risky alternative would be to calculate a confidence interval.

point estimate
An estimate of the population mean using a single value, usually the sample mean.

Confidence Interval

If we specify a range of numbers or an interval within which the population mean should lie, we might be more confident that our inference is correct. A **confidence interval estimate** is based on the knowledge that $\mu = \overline{X} \pm$ a small sampling error. After calculating an interval estimate, we will be able to determine how probable it is that the population mean will fall within a range of statistical values. In the racquetball project the researcher, after setting up a confidence interval, would be able to make a statement such as "With 95 percent confidence, I think that the average number of days played per week is between 2.3 and 2.9." This information can be used to estimate market demand because the researcher has a certain confidence that the interval contains the value of the true population mean.

confidence interval estimate
A specified range of numbers within which a population mean should lie; an estimate of the population mean based on the knowledge that it will equate the sample mean plus or minus a small sampling error.

TO THE POINT

A little inaccuracy sometimes saves a ton of explanation.

H. H. HUNRO (SAKI)

The crux of the problem for the researcher is to determine how much random sampling error to tolerate. In other words, what should the *confidence interval* be? How much of a gamble should be taken that μ will be included in the range: 80 percent, 90 percent, 99 percent? The **confidence level** is a percentage that indicates the long-run probability that the results will be correct. Traditionally, researchers have used the 95 percent confidence level. While there is nothing magical about the 95 percent confidence level, it is useful to select this confidence level in our examples.

confidence level
A percentage or decimal value that tells how confident a researcher can be about being correct. It states the long-run percentage of confidence intervals that will include the true population mean.

Calculating a Confidence Interval. As mentioned, the point estimate gives no information about the possible magnitude of random sampling error. The confidence interval gives an estimate plus or minus the estimated value of the population parameter. We may express the idea of the confidence interval as follows:

$$\mu = \overline{X} \pm \text{a small sampling error}$$

More formally, assuming that the researchers select a large sample (more than 30 observations), the small sampling error is equal to:

$$\text{Small sampling error} = Z_{c.l.} S_{\overline{X}}$$

where

$\overline{X}$ = sample mean

$Z_{c.l.}$ = value of Z, or standardized normal variable, at a specified confidence level (*c.l.*)

$S_{\overline{X}}$ = standard error of the mean

The precision of our estimate is indicated by the value of $Z_{c.l.}S_{\overline{X}}$. It is useful to define the range of possible error, E, as follows:

$$E = Z_{c.l.}S_{\overline{X}}$$

where

$$E = \text{range of random sampling error}$$

Thus,

$$\mu = \overline{X} \pm E$$

or

$$\mu = \overline{X} \pm Z_{c.l.}S_{\overline{X}}$$

The confidence interval ($\pm E$) is always stated as one-half of the total interval.

The following step-by-step procedure allows researchers to calculate confidence intervals:

1. Calculate $\overline{X}$ from the sample.

2. Assuming σ is unknown, estimate the population standard deviation by finding S, the sample standard deviation.

3. Estimate the standard error of the mean, using the following formula: $S_X = S/\sqrt{n}$.

4. Determine the Z-values associated with the desired confidence level. The confidence level should be divided by 2 to determine what percentage of the area under the curve to include on each side of the mean.

5. Calculate the confidence interval.

The following example shows how calculation of a confidence interval can be used in a demographic profile, a useful tool for market segmentation. Suppose you plan to open a sporting goods store to cater to working women who golf. In a survey of your market area you find that the mean age ($\overline{X}$) of 100 women is 37.5 years, with a standard deviation (S) of 12.0 years. Knowing that it would be extremely coincidental if the point estimate from the sample were exactly the same as the population mean age (μ), you decide to construct a confidence interval around the sample mean using the steps just given:

1. $\overline{X} = 37.5$ years.

2. $S = 12.0$ years.

3. $S_{\overline{X}} = 12/\sqrt{100} = 1.2$.

4. Suppose you wish to be 95 percent confident, that is, assured that 95 times out of 100, the estimates from your sample will include the population parameter. Including 95 percent of the area requires that 47.5 percent (one-half of 95 percent) of the distribution on each side be included. From the Z-table (Table A.2 in the appendix), you will find that .475 corresponds to the Z-value 1.96.

5. Substitute the values for $Z_{c.l.}$ and $S_{\overline{X}}$ into the confidence interval formula:

$$\mu = 37.5 \pm (1.96)(1.2)$$
$$= 37.5 \pm 2.352.$$

You can thus expect that μ is contained in the range from 35.148 to 39.852 years. Intervals constructed in this manner will contain the true value of μ 95 percent of the time.

Step 3 can be eliminated by entering S and n directly in the confidence interval formula:

$$\mu = \overline{X} \pm Z_{c.l.} \frac{S}{\sqrt{n}}$$

Remember that $S/\sqrt{n}$ represents the standard error of the mean, $S_{\overline{X}}$. Its use is based on the central-limit theorem.

If the researcher wants to increase the probability that the population mean will lie within the confidence interval, he or she can use the 99 percent confidence level with a Z-value of 2.57. The reader may want to calculate the 99 percent confidence interval for the above example. The answer will be in the range between 34.416 and 40.584 years.

We have now examined the basic concepts of inferential statistics. You should understand the notion that the sample statistics, such as the sample means, $\overline{X}$s, can provide good estimates of population parameters such as μ. You should also realize that there is a certain probability of being in error when you make an estimate of the population parameter from sample statistics. In other words there will be a random sampling error, which is the difference between the survey results and the results of surveying the entire population. If you have a firm understanding of these basic terms and ideas, the remaining statistics concept will be relatively simple for you. The concepts already discussed are the essence of statistics. Several ramifications of the simple ideas presented so far will permit better decisions about populations based on surveys or experiments.

Sample Size

Random Error and Sample Size

When asked to evaluate a marketing research project, most people, even those with little marketing research training, begin by asking, "How big was the sample?" Intuitively we know that the larger the sample, the more accurate the research. This is in fact a statistical truth; random sampling error varies with samples of different sizes. In statistical terms increasing the sample size decreases the width of the confidence interval at a given confidence level. When the standard deviation of the population is unknown, a confidence interval is calculated using the following formula:

$$\overline{X} \pm Z \frac{S}{\sqrt{n}}$$

Observe that the equation for the plus or minus error factor in the confidence interval includes n, the sample size:

$$E = Z \frac{S}{\sqrt{n}}$$

If n increases, E is reduced. Exhibit 17.8 illustrates that the confidence interval (or magnitude of error) decreases as the sample size, n, increases.

We already noted that it is not necessary to take a census of all elements of the population to conduct an accurate study. The laws of probability give investigators sufficient confidence regarding the accuracy of collecting data from a sample. Knowledge of the theory concerning the sampling distribution helps researchers make reasonably precise estimates.

Exhibit 17.8 Relationship Between Sample Size and Error

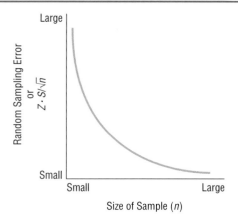

Students familiar with the law of diminishing returns in economics will easily grasp the concept that increases in sample size reduce sampling error at a *decreasing rate.* For example, doubling a sample of 1,000 will reduce random sampling error by 1 percentage point, but doubling the sample from 2,000 to 4,000 will reduce random sampling error by only another 1/2 percentage point. More technically, random sampling error is inversely proportional to the square root of *n.* (Exhibit 17.8 gives an approximation of the relationship between sample size and error.) Thus, the main issue becomes one of determining the optimal sample size.

Determining Sample Size

Questions that Involve Means

Three factors are required to specify sample size: (1) the variance, or heterogeneity, of the population; (2) the magnitude of acceptable error; and (3) the confidence level. Suppose a researcher wishes to find out whether 9-year-old boys are taller than 4-year-old boys. Even with a very small sample size, the correct information probably will be obtained. Intuitively we know this is logical based on the fact that the determination of sample size depends on the research question and the variability within the sample.

The *variance,* or *heterogeneity,* of the population is the first necessary bit of information. In statistical terms this refers to the *standard deviation* of the population. Only a small sample is required if the population is homogeneous. For example, predicting the average age of college students requires a smaller sample than predicting the average age of people who visit the zoo on a given Sunday afternoon. To test the effectiveness of an acne medicine, the sample must be large enough to cover the range of skin types because as *heterogeneity* increases, so must sample size.

The *magnitude of error,* or the confidence interval, is the second necessary bit of information. Defined in statistical terms as *E,* the magnitude of error indicates how precise the estimate must be. It indicates a certain precision level. From a managerial perspective, the importance of the decision in terms of profitability will influence the researcher's specifications of the range of error. If, for example, favorable results of a test market sample will result in the construction

---

Exhibit 17.9 Statistical Information Needed to Determine Sample Size for Questions That Involve Means

VARIABLE	SYMBOL	TYPICAL SOURCE OF INFORMATION
Standard deviation	S	Pilot study or rule of thumb
Magnitude of error	E	Managerial judgment or calculation $(ZS_{\overline{X}})$
Confidence level	$Z_{c.l.}$	Managerial judgment

---

of a new plant and unfavorable results will dictate not to market the product, the acceptable range of error probably will be small; the cost of an error would be too great to allow much room for random sampling errors. In other cases the estimate need not be extremely precise. Allowing an error of ±$1,000 in total family income instead of $E = \pm$ $50 may be acceptable in most market segmentation studies.

The third factor of concern is the *confidence level.* In our examples we will typically use the 95 percent confidence level. This, however, is an arbitrary decision based on convention; there is nothing sacred about the .05 chance level (that is, the probability of the true population parameter being incorrectly estimated). Exhibit 17.9 summarizes the information required about these factors to determine sample size.

Estimating the Sample Size

Once the preceding concepts are understood, determining the actual size for a simple random sample is quite easy. The researcher

1. Estimates the standard deviation of the population
2. Makes a judgment about the allowable magnitude of error
3. Determines a confidence level

The only problem is estimating the standard deviation of the population. Ideally, similar studies conducted in the past will give a basis for judging the standard deviation. In practice researchers who lack prior information conduct a pilot study to estimate the population parameters so that another, larger sample, with the appropriate sample size, may be drawn. This procedure is called a *sequential sampling* because researchers take an initial look at the pilot study results before deciding on a larger sample to provide more precise information.

A rule of thumb for estimating the value of the standard deviation is to expect it to be one-sixth of the range. If a study on television purchases expected the price paid to range from $100 to $700, a rule-of-thumb estimate for the standard deviation would be $100.

For the moment, assume that the standard deviation has been estimated in some preliminary work. If our concern is to estimate the mean of a particular population, the formula for sample size is:

$$n = \left(\frac{ZS}{E}\right)^2$$

where

Z = standardized value that corresponds to the confidence level
S = sample standard deviation or estimate of the population standard deviation
E = acceptable magnitude of error, plus or minus error factor (range is one-half of the total confidence interval)[7]

Suppose a survey researcher studying annual expenditures on lipstick wishes to have a 95 percent confidence level ($Z = 1.96$) and a range of error (E) of less than $2. The estimate of the standard deviation is $29.

$$n = \left(\frac{ZS}{E}\right)^2 = \left[\frac{(1.96)(29)}{2}\right]^2 = \left(\frac{56.84}{2}\right)^2 = 28.42^2 = 808$$

If the range of error (E) is acceptable at $4, sample size is reduced:

$$n = \left(\frac{ZS}{E}\right)^2 = \left[\frac{(1.96)(29)}{4}\right]^2 = \left(\frac{56.84}{4}\right)^2 = 14.21^2 = 202$$

Thus, doubling the range of acceptable error reduces sample size to approximately one-quarter of its original size—or, stated conversely in a general sense, doubling sample size will reduce error by only approximately one-quarter.

The Influence of Population Size on Sample Size

The A. C. Nielsen Company conducts television ratings. Throughout the years it has been plagued with questions about how it is possible to rate 98-plus million television homes with such a small sample (approximately 4,000 households). The answer to that question is that in most cases the size of the population does not have a major effect on the sample size. As we have indicated, the variance of the population has the largest effect on sample size. However, a finite correction factor may be needed to adjust a sample size that is more than 5 percent of a finite population. If the sample is large relative to the population, the foregoing procedures may overestimate sample size, and the researcher may need to adjust sample size.

The finite correction factor is $\sqrt{(N-n)/(N-1)}$, where N = population size and n = sample size.

Proportions: Sample Size Determination Requires Knowledge about Confidence Intervals

Researchers frequently are concerned with determining sample size for problems that involve estimating population proportions or percentages. When the sample size question involves the estimation of a proportion, the researcher requires some knowledge of the logic for determining a confidence interval around a sample proportion estimation (p) of the population proportion (π). For a confidence interval to be constructed around the sample proportion (p), an estimate of the standard error of the proportion (S_p) must be calculated and a confidence level specified.

The precision of our estimate is indicated by the value $Z_{c.l.}S_p$. Thus, our *plus* or *minus* estimate of the population proportion is:

$$\text{Confidence interval} = p \pm Z_{c.l.}S_p$$

If the researcher selects a 95 percent probability for the confidence interval, $Z_{c.l.}$ will equal 1.96 (see Table A.2 in the appendix).

The formula for S_p is:

$$S_p = \sqrt{\frac{pq}{n}} \qquad \text{or} \qquad \sqrt{\frac{p(1-p)}{n}}$$

where

S_p = estimate of the standard error of the proportion

p = proportion of successes

$q = (1 - p)$, or proportion of failures

Suppose that 20 percent of a sample of 1,200 recall seeing an advertisement. The proportion of success (p) equals .2 and the proportion of failures (q) equals .8. To estimate the 95 percent confidence interval,

$$\text{Confidence interval} = p \pm Z_{c.l} S_p$$

$$= .2 \pm 1.96 \, S_p$$

$$= .2 \pm 1.96 \, \sqrt{\frac{p(1 - p)}{n}}$$

$$= .2 \pm 1.96 \, \sqrt{\frac{(.2)(.8)}{1,200}}$$

$$= .2 \pm 1.96 \, (.0115)$$

$$= .2 \pm .022$$

Thus, the population proportion who see an advertisement is estimated to be included in the interval between .178 and .222, or roughly between 18 and 22 percent, with a 95 percent confidence coefficient.

To determine *sample size* for a proportion, the researcher must make a judgment about confidence level and the maximum allowance for random sampling error. Furthermore, the size of the proportion influences random sampling error; thus, an estimate of the expected proportion of successes must be made based on intuition or prior information. The formula is:

$$n = \frac{Z_{c.l}^2 \, pq}{E^2}$$

where

n = number of items in sample

$Z_{c.l}^2$ = square of the confidence level in standard error units

p = estimated proportion of successes

$q = (1 - p)$, or estimated proportion of failures

E^2 = square of the maximum allowance for error between the true proportion and sample proportion, or $Z_{c.l} S_p$ squared

To make this calculation, suppose a researcher believes that a simple random sample will show that 60 percent of the population (p) will recognize the name of an automobile dealership. The researcher wishes to estimate with 95 percent confidence ($Z_{c.l.} = 1.96$) that the allowance for sampling error will not be greater than 3.5 percentage points (E). Substituting these values into the formula,

$$n = \frac{(1.96)^2(.6)(.4)}{.035^2}$$

$$= \frac{(3.8416)(.24)}{.001225}$$

$$= \frac{.922}{.001225}$$

$$= 753$$

> ### Table 17.11 Selected Tables for Determining Sample Size When the Characteristic of Interest Is a Proportion

PARAMETER IN POPULATION ASSUMED TO BE OVER 70 PERCENT OR UNDER 30 PERCENT AND FOR 95 PERCENT CONFIDENCE LEVEL

SIZE OF POPULATION	SAMPLE SIZE FOR RELIABILITIES OF			
	±1% POINT	±2% POINTS	±3% POINTS	±5% POINTS
1,000	a	a	473	244
2,000	a	a	619	278
3,000	a	1,206	690	291
4,000	a	1,341	732	299
5,000	a	1,437	760	303
10,000	4,465	1,678	823	313
20,000	5,749	1,832	858	318
50,000	6,946	1,939	881	321
100,000	7,465	1,977	888	321
500,000 to ∞	7,939	2,009	895	322

PARAMETER IN POPULATION ASSUMED TO BE OVER 85 PERCENT OR UNDER 15 PERCENT AND FOR 95 PERCENT CONFIDENCE LEVEL

SIZE OF POPULATION	SAMPLE SIZE FOR RELIABILITIES OF			
	±1% POINT	±2% POINTS	±3% POINTS	±5% POINTS
1,000	a	a	353	235
2,000	a	760	428	266
3,000	a	890	461	278
4,000	a	938	479	284
5,000	a	984	491	289
10,000	3,288	1,091	516	297
20,000	3,935	1,154	530	302
50,000	4,461	1,195	538	304
100,000	4,669	1,210	541	305
500,000 to ∞	4,850	1,222	544	306

[a] In these cases, more than 50 percent of the population is required in the sample. Since the normal approximation of the hypergeometric distribution is a poor approximation in such instances, no sample value is given.

Actual Calculation of Sample Size for a Sample Proportion

In practice a number of tables have been constructed for determining sample size. Table 17.11 illustrates a sample size table for problems that involve sample proportions (p).

The theoretical principles for calculation of sample sizes of proportions are similar to the concepts discussed in this chapter. Suppose researchers wish to take samples in two large cities, New Orleans and Miami. They wish no more

Table 17.12 Allowance for Random Sampling Error (Plus and Minus Percentage Points) at 95 Percent Confidence Level

	SAMPLE SIZE						
RESPONSE	2,500	1,500	1,000	500	250	100	50
10(90)	1.2	1.5	2.0	3.0	4.0	6.0	8.0
20(80)	1.6	2.0	2.5	4.0	5.0	8.0	11.0
30(70)	1.8	2.5	3.0	4.0	6.0	9.0	13.0
40(60)	2.0	2.5	3.0	4.0	6.0	10.0	14.0
50(50)	2.0	2.5	3.0	4.0	6.0	10.0	14.0

than 2 percentage points of error, and they would be satisfied with a 95 percent confidence level (see Table 17.11). If we assume all other things are equal, in the New Orleans market, where 15 percent of the consumers favor our product and 85 percent prefer competitors' brands, we need a sample of 1,222 to get results with only 2 percentage points of error. In the Miami market, however, where 30 percent of the consumers favor our brand and 70 percent prefer other brands (a less heterogeneous market), we need a sample size of 2,009 to get the same sample reliability.

Table 17.12 shows a sampling error table typical of those that accompany research proposals or reports. Most studies will estimate more than one parameter. Thus, in a survey of 100 people in which 50 percent agree with one statement and 10 percent with another, the sampling error is expected to be 10 and 6 percentage points of error, respectively.

Determining Sample Size on the Basis of Judgment

Just as it is easy to select sample units to suit the convenience or judgment of the researcher, sample size may also be determined on the basis of managerial judgments. Using a sample size similar to those used in previous studies provides the inexperienced researcher with a comparison of other researchers' judgments.

Another judgmental factor that affects the determination of sample size concerns the selection of the appropriate item, question, or characteristic to be used for the sample size calculations. Several characteristics affect most studies and the desired degree of precision may vary for these items. The researcher must exercise some judgment to determine which item will be used. Often the item that will produce the largest sample size will be used to determine the ultimate sample size. However, the cost of data collection becomes a major consideration, and judgment must be exercised regarding the importance of such information.

Another sampling consideration stems from most researchers' need to analyze various subgroups within the sample. For example, suppose an analyst wishes to look at differences in retailers' attitudes by geographic region. The analyst will want to make sure to sample an adequate number of retailers in the New England, Mid-Atlantic, and South Atlantic regions to ensure that subgroup comparisons are reliable. There is a judgmental rule of thumb for selecting minimum subgroup sample size: Each subgroup to be separately analyzed should have a minimum of 100 or more units in each category of the major breakdowns. According to this procedure, the total sample size is computed by totaling the sample sizes necessary for these subgroups.

Determining Sample Size for Stratified and Other Probability Samples

Stratified sampling involves drawing separate probability samples within the subgroups to make the sample more efficient. With a stratified sample the sample variances are expected to differ by strata. This makes the determination of sample size more complex. Increased complexity may also characterize the determination of cluster sampling and other probability sampling methods. These formulas are beyond the scope of this book. Students interested in these advanced sampling techniques should investigate advanced sampling textbooks.

A Reminder about Statistics

The terms and symbols defined in this chapter provide the basics of the language of statisticians and researchers. To learn more about the pragmatic use of statistics in marketing research, one cannot forget these concepts. The speller who forgets that *i* comes before *e* except after *c* will have trouble every time he or she must tackle the spelling of a word with the *ie* or *ei* combination. The same is true for the student who forgets the basics of the "foreign language" of statistics.

Summary

Determination of sample size requires a knowledge of statistics. Statistics is the language of the researcher, and this chapter introduced its vocabulary. Descriptive statistics describe characteristics of a population or sample. Inferential statistics investigate samples to draw conclusions about entire populations.

A frequency distribution summarizes data by showing how frequently each response or classification occurs. A proportion indicates the percentage of a group that have a particular characteristic.

Three measures of central tendency are commonly used: the mean, or arithmetic average; the median, or halfway value; and the mode, or most frequently observed value. Each of these values may differ, and care must be taken to understand distortions that may arise from using the wrong measure of central tendency.

Measures of dispersion along with measures of central tendency can describe a distribution. The range is the difference between the largest and smallest values observed. The variance and standard deviation are the most useful measures of dispersion.

The normal distribution fits many observed distributions. It is symmetrical about its mean, with equal mean, median, and mode. Almost the entire area of the normal distribution lies within ±3 standard deviations of the mean. Any normal distribution can easily be compared with the standardized normal, or Z, distribution, whose mean is 0 and standard deviation is 1. This allows easy evaluation of the probabilities of many occurrences.

The techniques of statistical inference are based on the relationship among the population distribution, the sample distribution, and the sampling distribution. This relationship is expressed in the central-limit theorem.

Estimating a population mean with a single value gives a point estimate. A range of numbers within which the researcher is confident that the population mean will lie is a confidence interval estimate. The confidence level is a percentage that indicates the long-run probability that the confidence interval estimate will be correct.

The statistical determination of sample size requires knowledge of (1) the variance of the population, (2) the magnitude of acceptable error, and (3) the confidence level. Several computational formulas are available for determining sample size. Furthermore, a number of easy-to-use tables have been compiled to help calculate sample size. The main reason a large sample size is desirable is that sample size is related to random sampling error. A smaller sample makes a larger error in estimates more likely.

Many research problems involve the estimation of proportions. Statistical techniques may be used to determine a confidence interval around a sample proportion. Calculation of sample size for a sample proportion is not difficult. In fact, however, most researchers use tables that indicate predetermined sample sizes.

Key Terms and Concepts

Sample statistics
Population parameters
Frequency distribution
Percentage distribution
Probability
Proportion
Mean

Median
Mode
Standard deviation
Normal distribution
Standardized normal distribution
Population distribution
Sample distribution

Sampling distribution
Standard error of the mean
Central-limit theorem
Point estimate
Confidence interval estimate
Confidence level

Questions for Review and Critical Thinking

1. What is the difference between descriptive and inferential statistics?

2. The speed limits in 13 countries are:

COUNTRY	HIGHWAY MILES PER HOUR
Italy	87
France	81
Hungary	75
Belgium	75
Portugal	75
Britain	70
Spain	62
Denmark	62
Netherlands	62
Greece	62
Japan	62
Norway	56
Turkey	56

   Calculate the mean, median, and mode for these data.

3. Prepare a frequency distribution for the data in question 2.

4. Why is the standard deviation rather than the average deviation typically used?

5. Calculate the standard deviation for the data in question 2.

6. Draw three distributions that have the same mean value but different standard deviation values. Draw three distributions that have the same standard deviation value but different mean values.

7. A manufacturer of MP3 players surveyed 100 retail stores in each of the firm's sales regions. An analyst noticed that in the South Atlantic region the average retail price was $165 (mean) and the standard deviation $30. However, in the Mid-Atlantic region the mean price was $170, with a standard deviation of $15. What do these statistics tell us about these two sales regions?

8. What is the sampling distribution? How does it differ from the sample distribution?

9. What would happen to the sampling distribution of the mean if we increased sample size from 5 to 25?

10. Suppose a fast-food restaurant wishes to estimate average sales volume for a new menu item. The restaurant has analyzed the sales of the item at a similar outlet and observed the following results:
   $\overline{X} = 500$ (mean daily sales)
   $S = 100$ (standard deviation of sample)
   $n = 25$ (sample size)

The restaurant manager wants to know into what range the mean daily sales should fall 95 percent of the time. Perform this calculation.

11. In our example of research on lipstick, where $E = \$2$ and $S = \$29$, what sample size would we require if we desired a 99 percent confidence level?

12. Suppose you are planning a sample of cat owners to determine the monthly average number of cans of cat food they purchase. The following standards have been set: a confidence level of 99 percent and an error of less than 5 units. Past research has indicated that the standard deviation should be 6 units. What would be the required sample size?

13. In a survey of 500 people, 60 percent responded positively to an attitude question. Calculate a confidence interval at 95 percent to get an interval estimate for a proportion.

14. In a nationwide survey, a researcher expects that 30 percent of the population will agree with an attitude statement. She wishes to have less than 2 percentage points of error and to be 95 percent confident. What sample size does she need?

15. To understand how sample size is conceptually related to random sampling error, costs, and nonsampling errors, graph these relationships.

16. Suppose you are a political analyst and wish to be extremely confident that you can predict the outcome of an extremely close primary election. What should the sample size be for your poll? Are there any problems involved in determining the sample size for this election?

17. A researcher expects the population proportion of Cubs fans in Chicago to be 80 percent. The researcher wishes to have an error of less than 5 percent and to be 95 percent confident of an estimate to be made from a mail survey. What sample size is required?

18. An automobile dealership plans to conduct a survey to determine what proportion of new-car buyers continue to have their cars serviced at the dealership after the warranty period ends. It estimates that 30 percent of customers do so. It wants the results of its survey to be accurate within 5 percent, and it wants to be 95 percent confident of the results. What sample size is necessary?

19. City Opera, a local opera company, wishes to take a sample of its subscribers to learn the average number of years people have been subscribing. The researcher expects the average number of years to be 12 and believes the standard deviation would be about 2 years (approximately one-sixth of the range). He wishes to be 95 percent confident in his estimate. What is the appropriate sample size?

20. Using the formula discussed in this chapter, a researcher determines that at the 95 percent confidence level, a sample of 2,500 is required to satisfy a client's requirements. The sample the researcher actually uses is 1,200 because the client has specified a budget cap for the survey. What are the ethical considerations in this situation?

Exploring the Internet

1. Go to http://www.dartmouth.edu/~chance.html to visit the Chance database. The CHANCE course is an innovative program to creatively teach introductory materials about probability and statistics. The CHANCE course is designed to enhance quantitative literacy.

2. Go to Lycos at http://www.lycos.com. Enter "population sampling" into the query box and then hit the search icon. How extensive is the list of sources?

3. The IMS's 1992 National Needs Assessment survey of museums may be found at http://palimpsest.stanford.edu/byorg/ims/survey. Visit this site to view population estimates in a stratified sample. The results include the best and most recent estimates for number of U.S. museums and numerous other statistics on museums' demographics, activities, funding, and desired assistance.

4. The 1995 National Household Survey on drug abuse discusses sampling error and statistical significance in the context of its study. To investigate these estimates of sampling error from the survey data visit http://www.health.org/survey.htm.

5. The Platonic Realms Interactive Mathematics Encyclopedia is located at www.mathacademy.com. It provides many definitions of statistical and mathematical terms.

6. A Sample Size Calculator can be found at: http://www.researchinfo.com/calculators/sscalc.htm and at http://www.surveystem.com/sscalc.htm

Case 17.1 Coastal Star Sales Corporation (A)

COASTAL STAR SALES CORPORATION IS A WEST COAST wholesaler that markets leisure products from several manufacturers. Coastal Star has an 80-person sales force that sells to wholesalers in a six-state area divided into two sales regions. Case Exhibit 17.1-1 shows the names from a sample of 11 salespeople, some descriptive information about each person, and sales performance of each for the last two years.

QUESTIONS

1. Calculate a mean and a standard deviation for each variable.

2. Set a 95 percent confidence interval around the mean for each variable.

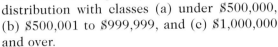

3. Calculate the median, mode, and range for each variable.

4. Organize the data for the current sales variable into a frequency distribution with classes (a) under $500,000, (b) $500,001 to $999,999, and (c) $1,000,000 and over.

5. Organize the data for years of selling experience into a frequency distribution with two classes, one less than five years and the other five or more years.

6. Convert the frequency distributions from question 5 to percentage distributions.

Case Exhibit 17.1–1 Coastal Star Sales Corporation: Salesperson Data

REGION	SALESPERSON	AGE	YEARS OF EXPERIENCE	SALES PREVIOUS YEAR	SALES CURRENT YEAR
Northern	Jackson	40	7	$ 412,744	$ 411,007
Northern	Gentry	60	12	1,491,024	1,726,630
Northern	La Forge	26	2	301,421	700,112
Northern	Miller	39	1	401,241	471,001
Northern	Mowen	64	5	448,160	449,261
Southern	Young	51	2	518,897	519,412
Southern	Fisk	34	1	846,222	713,333
Southern	Kincaid	62	10	1,527,124	2,009,041
Southern	Krieger	42	3	921,174	1,030,000
Southern	Manzer	64	5	463,399	422,798
Southern	Weiner	27	2	548,011	422,001

Case 17.2 The *New York Times*/CBS News Poll[8]

THE NEW YORK TIMES/CBS NEWS POLL OF AMERICAN business executives conducted telephone interviews with 499 senior executives at companies throughout the United States. The survey asked questions about their attitudes toward the political environment and its impact on business.

The sample of companies and executives was provided by Dun and Bradstreet Information Services and was randomly drawn from those listed in its nationwide database of private and publicly owned companies.

Companies with $5 million or more in annual revenues were eligible for the survey. Within each company one senior executive was interviewed. Titles eligible for the poll included owner, partner, chief executive, chairman, president, executive vice president, and senior vice president, with the first opportunity for an interview given to the most senior official.

The completed sample included 245 interviews in companies with $5 million to $99 million in annual revenue, 120 interviews in companies with $100 million to $499 million, and 134 interviews in companies with $500 million or more. The completed sample was then weighted by revenue size to reflect

the actual distribution of all listed companies in the country because small companies predominate.

In theory in 19 cases out of 20, results based on such samples will differ by no more than 6 percentage points in either direction from what would have been obtained by seeking out senior executives at all listed companies in the country with annual revenues of $5 million or more.

The potential sampling error for smaller subgroups is larger. For example, for the biggest companies, those with $500 million or more in annual revenue, it is plus or minus 9 percentage points.

QUESTIONS

1. What type of sampling method was utilized? What are the strengths and weaknesses of this procedure?

2. What confidence level was used to determine sample size?

3. Explain how to evaluate the random sampling error in the study.

Case 17.3 The Business Forms Industry

THE BUSINESS FORMS INDUSTRY IS HEAVILY DEPENDENT on personal selling. Case Exhibit 17.3–1 shows a sampling frame that lists 200 salespeople in the business forms industry.

The first column is an identification number associated with the salesperson listed in column 2. Column 3 indicates the salesperson's gender. Column 4 indicates the number of sales calls the salesperson has made during the last month. Column 5 gives the name of the company where the salesperson works. The last column is used for snowball sampling. During the snowball sampling procedure, the research must select a first-stage sample of nominators. The nominators then point out the salespeople whom they know, and these elements are also included in the sample. For example, T. Montz (I.D. number 14) knows four respondents—

I.D. number 1, A. Abbott; I.D. number 170, C. R. Gemelli; I.D. number 194, S. T. Siwula; and I.D. number 200, J. Zorilla.

A sales manager wishes to determine the mean number of sales calls per month.

QUESTIONS

1. Using a table of random numbers, draw a simple random sample (number of observations equal to 15). Discuss the step-by-step procedure that was implemented to draw the simple random sample. For the number of sales calls, calculate the sample mean and standard deviation for your sample. Calculate the proportion of women in the industry.

2. Using the results from question 1, determine how large a sample size would be necessary if the researcher wanted to be 95 percent confident and have a range of error no larger than two sales calls.

3. Draw a systematic sample of the sample size that you calculated in question 2. Calculate the sample mean and a 95 percent confidence interval for the mean.

4. Draw a snowball sample ($n = 20$) using a random-numbers table to determine the nominators.

5. Draw a two-stage cluster sample ($n = 20$) using each company as a single cluster. At the first stage, randomly select one of the clusters (or companies). At the second stage, use a random-numbers table to select four elements (or sales-people) from each of the five clusters selected at stage one. Calculate the sample mean in a 95 percent confidence interval.

Case Exhibit 17.3-1 Sampling Frame

IDENTIFICATION NUMBER	SALESPERSON NAME	GENDER	NUMBER OF SALES CALLS	COMPANY	SNOWBALL REFERRAL
1	Abbot, A.	M	42	Formcraft	14,34,47,48,154
2	Barton, R.	M	20	Formcraft	199,186,82
3	Brinson, C.	F	30	Formcraft	13,35,168
4	Bulter, D.	M	41	Formcraft	12
5	Chafin, J.	M	24	Formcraft	150,151,197,18
6	Ciliberti, R.	F	42	Formcraft	7,93,106,167
7	Dunn, P.	M	37	Formcraft	6,169,180,197
8	Gallin, F.	M	37	Formcraft	9,180,76,91,110
9	Hicks, G.	F	39	Formcraft	8,188,95,96,106
10	Howard, C.	M	42	Formcraft	108,116,119,130
11	Knoelel, D.	M	40	Formcraft	none
12	Leverick, D.	M	23	Formcraft	4,146
13	Mahon, J.	F	40	Formcraft	3,139,175
14	Montz, T.	M	40	Formcraft	1,170,194,200
15	Nelson, P.	M	40	Formcraft	17,29,44
16	Porras, F.	M	39	Formcraft	26,38,72,60
17	Riddell, G.	F	41	Formcraft	15,68,74,89
18	Stevens, W.	F	40	Formcraft	28,83,89,136
19	Traweek, S.	F	30	Formcraft	20,135,149,164,194
20	Young, B.	M	37	Formcraft	19,151
21	Aaron, A.	M	37	Western Business Forms	39,43,79
22	Abud, M.	M	39	Western Business Forms	none
23	Atkinson, O.R.	F	41	Western Business Forms	85
24	Barnett, J. J.	M	41	Western Business Forms	27,111
25	Battels, L.	M	38	Western Business Forms	38,59,134
26	Chen, S.	M	37	Western Business Forms	16,27,141
27	Craft, T.	M	38	Western Business Forms	24, 158, 161 179
28	Davis, A.	M	39	Western Business Forms	18,36,45
29	Floyd, P.	F	39	Western Business Forms	15, 181, 182
30	Gentry, D.	M	41	Western Business Forms	25,31,48,181
31	Holmes, S.	F	33	Western Business Forms	30,186
32	Jones, C.	F	39	Western Business Forms	42,43,198,49,58
33	Lee, K.	M	41	Western Business Forms	41,53,62,87
34	Lyon, D.	M	41	Western Business Forms	84
35	Olm, K.	M	38	Western Business Forms	3,40,90
36	Rawlings, D.	M	13	Western Business Forms	4,28,108,136
37	Salazar, A.	M	33	Western Business Forms	none
38	Ullman, L.	M	40	Western Business Forms	16,143,152,200
39	Wood, F.	M	33	Western Business Forms	21,44,138,145,149
40	Zapalac, J	M	40	Western Business Forms	38,158,161

(continued)

Case Exhibit 17.3-1 Sampling Frame *(Continued)*

Identification Number	Salesperson Name	Gender	Number of Sales Calls	Company	Snowball Referral
41	Allen, M.	M	41	McGregor Printing	33,57,70,71
42	Bell, R.	F	37	McGregor Printing	32,80,81
43	Branch, K.	F	34	McGregor Printing	21,32
44	Diaz, A.	M	38	McGregor Printing	15,39,98,165
45	Ellis, J.	M	31	McGregor Printing	28,47,56,65
46	Fagan, D.	F	34	McGregor Printing	none
47	Gonazalez, E.	M	40	McGregor Printing	1,45,195
48	Hestings, 0.	M	34	McGregor Printing	1,30,46,66
49	Lang, D.	F	40	McGregor Printing	50,51,52,53
50	Lorenz, K.	F	42	McGregor Printing	49,64,77,100,114,140,172
51	Meek, J.	M	28	McGregor Printing	52,49
52	Morris, N.	F	42	McGregor Printing	55,67,101,102
53	Newman, P.	M	25	McGregor Printing	33,49,54,71
54	Parker,L.	M	38	McGregor Printing	53,110
55	Potter, H.	M	38	McGregor Printing	52,56,109,111
56	Roy, M.	F	34	McGregor Printing	45,55,167
57	Scott, D.	F	31	McGregor Printing	41,195
58	Stone, M.	M	37	McGregor Printing	32,172,173
59	Trimble, L.	F	39	McGregor Printing	25,61,73,112
60	Williams, W.	F	25	McGregor Printing	16,63,69,108
61	Antill, J.	M	40	Controll Business Forms	59,118,183
62	Ashley, K.	F	41	Controll Business Forms	33,184
63	Berker,L.	F	41	Controll Business Forms	60,74,184,197
64	Burton, S.	M	41	Controll Business Forms	50,69,187
65	Carter, J.	M	40	Controll Business Forms	45,185
66	Edwards, K.	M	32	Controll Business Forms	48
67	Finger, T.	M	37	Controll Business Forms	52,189,190,191
68	Ganesh, G.	M	38	Controll Business Forms	17,193
69	Green, W.	F	38	Controll Business Forms	64,192,193,196
70	Ivey, T.	M	33	Controll Business Forms	41,78
71	Johnson, C.	F	34	Controll Business Forms	53,86,92,93
72	Jones, F,	M	31	Controll Business Forms	16,88,89,136,143
73	Landry, T.	M	36	Controll Business Forms	59,63,82
74	Lewis, C.	F	34	Controll Business Forms	17,89,90,104
75	Matthews, M.	M	38	Controll Business Forms	none
76	O'Neil, J.	F	41	Controll Business Forms	8,77,138
77	Rice, J.	F	38	Controll Business Forms	50,76,94,137
78	Sanchez, M.	F	38	Controll Business Forms	7,1,82
79	Welch, B.	M	33	Controll Business Forms	21
80	Zeff, S.	M	42	Controll Business Forms	42, 142, 143, 144, 145
81	Bishop, N.	F	39	Brunswick Press	42,115,140
82	Bryan, W.	M	37	Brunswick Press	2,73,144
83	Cloud, P.	M	40	Brunswick Press	18,7,117
84	Dyer, P.	F	36	Brunswick Press	34
85	Elliot, G.	M	36	Brunswick Press	23,11,147,155,156
86	Gray, J.	M	38	Brunswick Press	71,157,163,187
87	Hale, K.	M	41	Brunswick Press	33,38
88	Keller, J.	F	41	Brunswick Press	72787,89
89	Kramer, C.	F	38	Brunswick Press	18,74,90,91
90	Love, S.	M	32	Brunswick Press	35,89791
91	Morse, H.	M	41	Brunswick Press	8,89,90,196
92	Palmer, G.	M	36	Brunswick Press	71,104,105,120
93	Pyle, G.	M	39	Brunswick Press	6,71,121,133,147,148
94	Riley, T.	M	29	Brunswick Press	77,123

(continued)

Case Exhibit 17.3-1 Sampling Frame *(Continued)*

Identification Number	Salesperson Name	Gender	Nomber of Sales Calls	Company	Snowball Referral
95	Summer, V.	M	32	Brunswick Press	9,122,123,132,146
96	Thompson, L.	M	34	Brunswick Press	9,98,104
97	Trahan, J. R.	F	32	Brunswick Press	none
98	White, E.	M	37	Brunswick Press	44,96,106,9,104,195
99	Wison, F. A.	M	40	Brunswick Press	none
100	York, H.	F	39	Brunswick Press	50
101	Bizek, R.	M	32	Arnold Corporation	52,102
102	Blais, D. R.	M	40	Arnold Corporation	52,103,101
103	Harp, V.	M	41	Arnold Corporation	192
104	Hines, A.	M	40	Arnold Corporation	74,92,126,127
105	Moore, A. A.	F	38	Arnold Corporation	92,107,119
106	Payne, R. L.	M	36	Arnold Corporation	6,9,98,17,107
107	Payne, W.	M	30	Arnold Corporation	105,106,128,106
108	Peters, B.	M	37	Arnold Corporation	60,128,115,116
109	Peters, L. R.	M	33	Arnold Corporation	55,129
110	Raines, C.	M	24	Arnold Corporation	54,159,170
111	Richards, A. L.	M	39	Arnold Corporation	55,112
112	Rodgers, R.	M	36	Arnold Corporation	59,111
113	Samad, 1.	M	36	Arnold Corporation	24,174,176,184
114	Scruggs, J.	M	36	Arnold Corporation	50,117,130
115	Simmons, E. M.	F	41	Arnold Corporation	81,108,139,140
116	Smith, R. J.	M	36	Arnold Corporation	10,108
117	Starks, T. W.	M	36	Arnold Corporation	83,114,6,182
118	Tomey, E. L.	M	36	Arnold Corporation	61,131,142,142,184
119	Vail, M.	M	40	Arnold Corporation	10,105
120	Walker, K. L.	F	36	Arnold Corporation	92,121,134,191,
121	Abbott, J.	F	39	Moore Business Forms	93,120,134,191,192
122	Author, R. L.	F	36	Moore Business Forms	95,142,143
123	Bough, M.	F	36	Moore Business Forms	94,124,149,152,
124	Coleman, W.	M	35	Moore Business Forms	24,123,149,152,161
125	Collins, O. L.	F	35	Moore Business Forms	none
126	Eades, A.M.	M	35	Moore Business Forms	104,127
127	Enloe, S.D.	M	35	Moore Business Forms	104,126,128
128	Fisher, N.	M	41	Moore Business Forms	107,106,170
129	Holifield, W. B.	F	35	Moore Business Forms	109
130	Lott, M.	M	35	Moore Business Forms	10,114,176,131,118
131	Love, A.J.	M	35	Moore Business Forms	118,130,139,3
132	Lucas, D.	F	39	Moore Business Forms	95,80,118,141,122,133,93,17
133	Norris, L. A.	F	35	Moore Business Forms	93,132,122,118
134	Rouse, J.	F	38	Moore Business Forms	24,120,121,142,80
135	Rouwalk, C.	M	38	Moore Business Forms	19,142,148,151,152
136	Taynor, S. A.	M	38	Moore Business Forms	72,137,77,153
137	Teel, B.	M	38	Moore Business Forms	77,136,72,167,6,7,93
138	Waters, J.	M	42	Moore Business Forms	39,115,166,167
139	White, K.	M	42	Moore Business Forms	3,140,50
140	Willis, R.	M	40	Moore Business Forms	50,139,6,56,137
141	Argo, M.	F	42	Taylor-Made Forms	26,118,142,80,122
142	Aris, B.	M	42	Taylor-Made Forms	80, 118, 141, 122, 134, 135, 143
143	Baird, R. S.	M	42	Taylor-Made Forms	80,142,95,142
144	Balinski, J.	F	39	Taylor-Made Forms	82,142,146
145	Brancheau, C. C.	F	39	Taylor-Made Forms	80,169,147,148
146	Brown, S.	M	39	Taylor-Made Forms	4,95
147	Brugnoli, G. A.	M	34	Taylor-Made Forms	85,145
148	Brunt, R.	M	34	Taylor-Made Forms	93,145

(continued)

Case Exhibit 17.3-1 Sampling Frame *(Continued)*

IDENTIFICATION NUMBER	SALESPERSON NAME	GENDER	NUMBER OF SALES CALLS	COMPANY	SNOWBALL REFERRAL
149	Bybee, W. D.	F	42	Taylor-Made Forms	19,123,124,150
150	Cupps, T.	M	40	Taylor-Made Forms	5,149
151	Gurun, L.	F	14	Taylor-Made Forms	20
152	Kondelka, F.	F	15	Taylor-Made Forms	136
153	Kovalcik, A.	F	16	Taylor-Made Forms	136, 152, 159, 154, 1, 142
154	Kowis, M.	F	40	Taylor-Made Forms	1, 142,153, 155,
155	McZeal E.	F	42	Taylor-Made Forms	85, 145,153, 154,180
156	Meduris, C. A.	M	27	Taylor-Made Forms	85,145
157	Peters, W.	M	31	Taylor-Made Forms	86,163,189,190
158	Searl, S.	F	42	Taylor-Made Forms	27,35,40
159	Teziano, E.	M	39	Taylor-Made Forms	110, 54, 145, 153, 164, 174
160	Thiede, C.	M	42	Taylor-Made Forms	145
161	Avalos, H.	F	37	Key Printing	27,40,163,86
162	Awl, J. N.	F	37	Key Printing	145
163	Baird, D.	F	37	Key Printing	86,157,161,40
164	Balderas, O. L.	M	37	Key Printing	19,159,16,165
165	Bekins, J. B.	M	37	Key Printing	44,145,164,19
166	Bivin, W.	M	37	Key Printing	138,167,145,168
167	Breda, H.	M	42	Key Printing	6156,137
168	Freeman, J. F.	M	35	Key Printing	3,145,176
169	Gekeler, D.	M	35	Key Printing	7,145,176
170	Gemilli, C. R	M	42	Key Printing	14,110,193,68
171	Goss, E.	M	33	Key Printing	142
172	Gulick, R. W.	M	41	Key Printing	58,173
173	Hansen, C.	M	41	Key Printing	58,172,178
174	Kostelic, P. P.	M	33	Key Printing	113,180,181,88
175	Nowacki, D.	F	40	Key Printing	13,142
176	Pesi, J. V.	M	42	Key Printing	142,145,169,178,173
177	Smith, R. A.	M	42	Key Printing	none
178	Tomey, T. S.	M	42	Key Printing	173,145,176,142
179	Usrey, B.	M	42	Key Printing	27,145
180	Vader, L.	F	42	Key Printing	8,174,181,196
181	Blake, P.	M	19	Form Tech	29,174,180,182,117
182	Bretchel, W. J.	M	39	Form Tech	29,117,181,181,8,189
183	Burks, R.	M	35	Form Tech	61,145,184,62,113
184	Chirco, S. J.	M	35	Form Tech	62,113,183
185	Distefano, E.	M	36	Form Tech	none
186	Duong, C. V.	M	36	Form Tech	30,198,26
187	Dupka, A.	M	41	Form Tech	86,142,192,13
188	Fournier, P.	M	32	Form Tech	8,67,189
189	Gomez, J. G.	M	33	Form Tech	67,157,182,8
190	Harlar, C.	M	34	Form Tech	67,189,157,194
191	Lomax, J.	M	35	Form Tech	192, 134, 121, 142, 186, 187
192	Manos, E. P.	F	42	Form Tech	86,142,187
193	McAdoo, R. O.	F	37	Form Tech	68,145,170,14,110
194	Siwula, S. T.	F	38	Form Tech	14,145,190,67
195	Stanzel, J. Z.	M	39	Form Tech	41
196	Stubbs, D.	M	40	Form Tech	91,180,197,5,7
197	Wacpeng, L.	M	41	Form Tech	5,7,142
198	Wu, A.	F	42	Form Tech	32,145,187,199,2
199	Young, P. P.	M	39	Form Tech	2,145,189,32,186
200	Zorilla, J.	M	21	Form Tech	14,142

Chapter 18

Fieldwork

THEY STAND THERE, LOOKING FOR EYE CONTACT, SIZING UP THE crowd, looking for the right moment to go up and take a chance.[1] They know more times than not they will be rejected, yet they press on.

You've seen them. Chances are you have walked right past them, even given them the cold shoulder or at worst growled at them that you want to be left alone.

They are interviewers, usually women, who prowl outside the shops and restaurants looking for volunteers to participate in surveys, with questions ranging from how many beers you drink in a day to what you think of a certain line of clothing or your take on an advertising campaign by a large corporation.

In the business, it's called "mall intercept." It is, on the surface, a thankless task: going up to strangers, clipboard in hand, introducing yourself and trying to convince prospects that you aren't trying to sell them cheap long-distance service, aluminum siding or the latest debit card. It is a misperceived job. They aren't trying to disrupt a pleasant day of shopping with the family at the mall or stop a harried shopper from getting a last-minute gift. They are, quite simply, doing their job.

Quick Test Inc., has been asking questions at the Hawthorn Center in Vernon Hills, IL for 17 years. It is a business whose techniques have changed with the advent of computerized technology but whose image has remained standard for decades. Participants now are asked a few questions in the mall before they move to the Quick Test offices.

Ann Marie Hogan supervises about a dozen employees. They in-

clude an assistant manager, a questionnaire editor and 10 full- or part-time interviewers (recruiters). The interviewers are the people who try to persuade shoppers to give up anywhere from 5 to 90 minutes of their time to participate in field research.

What you will learn in this chapter

To recognize that fieldwork can be performed by many different parties.

To discuss the job requirements of fieldworkers.

To discuss in-house training for inexperienced interviewers.

To understand how fieldworkers secure interviews.

To define foot-in-the-door and door-in-the-face compliance techniques.

To understand the major principles of asking questions in the field.

To explain probing and give examples of different interviewers' probes.

To understand the appropriate procedure for recording responses in surveys.

To discuss the principles of good interviewing.

To discuss the activities involved in the management and supervision of fieldworkers.

It is a field crowded with but not restricted to women.

"We have a couple of males on staff, but a majority of the people in the field are women," Hogan said, explaining that companies that hire market research firms prefer having women recruiters to question female shoppers, who are presumed to be the primary shoppers in their households.

Hawthorn Center is an ideal hunting ground because shoppers coming from the surrounding area are basically young and have families, falling into the ideal 25–49 demographic age group. But that, of course, doesn't make them any more willing to give up their time for the sake of research.

The company seeking the information remains confidential, and in nearly every case when an interviewer seeks out a shopper, the person being surveyed is not told what company or product is involved.

In many cases, the recruiter won't even get far with a prospective interviewee. It is, in the words of Fern Levin, a market researcher for 30 years, a lesson in accepting rejection. "I got over it the first day I did it," said Levin. "You have to know that this is a job, and we're out there doing a job."

Ginny Conzelman of Waukegan is a relative rookie on the floor, having done recruiting for just a couple of months. She has found the negative reaction difficult to absorb.

"I just went up to someone to ask if they would be interested. They got so enraged they said they would file a harassment claim. Can you believe that?" Conzelman said.

Jim Hansen, general manager of the mall, tries to maintain a balance between his fact-finding tenants and the rest of the retail neighborhood, which doesn't want its customers chased away by survey takers.

"We make sure they don't have too many out there," Hansen said. "They tend to stay in that one area of the mall, which is heavily traveled. Once in a while, for different kinds of research, they will go to different places in the mall, but they tell us ahead of time. We can't have them right out in front of a particular store unless that store has contracted with them to do research. The important thing is that the shoppers aren't irritated."

Interviewers develop special skills to know which customers are more likely to give the coveted "yes." Eye contact is a key: if someone looks away, they aren't good candidates to even be approached.

Even in the 1980s, most companies seeking research data weren't willing to offer any inducements to lure shoppers into filling out forms, according to Hogan. Now some will offer product samples, a piece of candy or slice of ham, raffle tickets or cash payments as a means of persuading dubious participants to give up some of their time.

"It really depends on the client. It is their decision," Hogan said. "Sometimes it is a case of how much information they want. Sometimes the interviews are short and really don't take much time. Other times, it can take up to 90 minutes."

The advent of computers has, in a sense, made the task a bit easier. Before computers, interviewers would have to sit down, with clipboard in hand, and ask a consumer the questions in the middle of the mall with little privacy or comfort.

There are days and times of the week where interviewers will know that they face an uphill climb to get anyone to commit. Summer is slow unless it is around a holiday. A good month, Hogan explained, will have 1,200 to 1,300 people interviewed.

The cornerstone of the marketing research business is the interviewer. This chapter discusses the nature of an effective fieldwork operation and the practices fieldwork managers use to minimize errors.

The Nature of Fieldwork

A personal interviewer administering a questionnaire door to door, a telephone interviewer calling from a central location, an observer counting pedestrians in a shopping mall, and others involved in the collection of data and the supervision of that process are all **fieldworkers.** The activities they perform vary substantially. The supervision of data collection for a mail survey will differ from that for an observation study as much as the factory production process for a cereal will differ from that for a pair of ski boots. Nevertheless, just as quality control is basic to each production operation, there are some basic fieldwork issues. For ease of presentation, this chapter focuses on the interviewing process conducted by personal interviewers. However, many of the issues apply to all fieldworkers when translated into their specific settings.

fieldworker
An individual who is responsible for gathering data "in the field."

Who Conducts the Fieldwork?

The actual data collection process is rarely done by the person who designs the research. However, this stage is crucial because the marketing research project is no better than the data collected in the field. Therefore, the marketing research administrator must select capable people and trust them to gather the data. An irony of marketing research is that highly educated and trained individuals will design the research, but the people who gather the data typically have little research training or experience. Knowing that research is no better than the data collected in the field, research administrators must concentrate on carefully selecting field-workers.

Much fieldwork is conducted by research suppliers that specialize in data collection. When a second party is subcontracted, the job of the study designer at the parent firm is not only to hire a research supplier, but to build in supervisory controls over the field service. In some cases a third-party firm is employed. For example, a company may contact a marketing research firm that in turn subcontracts the fieldwork to a **field interviewing service.**

There are a number of field interviewing services and full-service marketing research agencies that perform door-to-door surveys, central location telephone interviewing, and other forms of fieldwork for a fee. These agencies typically employ field supervisors who supervise and train interviewers, edit completed questionnaires in the field, and telephone or recontact respondents to confirm that interviews have been conducted.

Whether the research administrator hires **in-house interviewers** or selects a field interviewing service, it is desirable that field-workers meet certain job requirements. Although the job requirements for different types of surveys will vary, normally interviewers should be healthy, outgoing, and of pleasing appearance, that is, well groomed and tailored. Fieldwork may be strenuous; the interviewer may be walking from house to house for 4 or more hours. Healthy individuals, generally between 18 and 55 years of age, seem to have the most stamina. People who enjoy talking with strangers usually make better interviewers. An essential part of the interviewing process is establishing a rapport with the respondent. Having interviewers who are outgoing helps ensure respondents' full cooperation. Interviewer bias may occur if the fieldworker's clothing or physical

field interviewing service
A research supplier that specializes in data gathering.

in-house interviewer
A fieldworker who is employed by the company conducting the research.

appearance is unattractive or unusual. Suppose that a male interviewer wearing a dirty T-shirt interviews subjects in an upper-income neighborhood. Respondents may consider him slovenly and be less cooperative than they would with a person who appeared to meet their standards.

TO THE POINT

The knowledge of the world is only to be acquired in the world and not in the closet.

LORD CHESTERFIELD

Interviewers and other field-workers generally are paid hourly rates or per-interview fees. Often interviewers are part-time workers from a variety of backgrounds. Although both men and women are employed as fieldworkers, the majority are women. Homemakers, graduate students, schoolteachers, and other people from diverse backgrounds frequently are hired as fieldworkers. Primary and secondary schoolteachers are an excellent source of temporary interviewers during the summer, especially when they work outside the school districts in which they teach. Their educational background and experience with the public make them excellent candidates.

In-House Training for Inexperienced Interviewers[2]

After personnel are recruited and selected, they must be trained. Suppose a woman who has just sent her youngest child off to first grade is hired by a marketing research interviewing firm. She has decided to become a working mother and a professional interviewer. The training she will receive after being hired may vary from virtually no training to an extensive, three-day program if she is selected by one of the larger marketing research agencies. Almost always there will be a **briefing session** on the particular project.

briefing session
A training session to ensure that each interviewer is provided with common information.

Although conducting surveys in Canada is much like research in the United States, there are some important differences. One of every four Canadians speaks only French. This means that telephone interviewers must speak both English and French. This is especially true if the research is conducted only in Quebec, where nine out of ten French-speaking Canadians reside.

WHAT WENT WRONG?

A Dress Rehearsal of the Census

THE GOVERNMENT MADE A SPECIAL EFFORT TO DO A better job of counting American Indians in the 2000 census.[3] In 1998, the Census Bureau conducted a "dress rehearsal" of the census methodology in Menominee County, Wisconsin, where the Menominee reservation is located and the 1990 population was 3,890 people, 90 percent of whom were Indian. The Census Bureau paid for radio, television, and newspaper advertisements and worked with tribal leaders to promote the dress rehearsal on the Wisconsin reservation.

According to the Census Bureau's Chicago regional director, there was a pretty intense campaign to educate people that the census was going on. The tribe held a powwow where tribal members were given free sodas, T-shirts, and trinkets, and the tribal chairman met with students at the school to encourage their families to cooperate with the census. What could go wrong?

As it turned out, plenty. Fewer than 41 percent of the residents returned questionnaires that had been hand delivered to them. By comparison, the response rate for similar tests at Columbia, South Carolina, and Sacramento, California, was 54 percent. The Census Bureau reported that 60 percent of the reservation households treated the questionnaire as "junk mail." So the Census Bureau had to spend extra money to send a second form.

The last time the government took the census, 12 of every 100 American Indians living on reservations were missed. Four percent of blacks and 5 percent of Hispanics weren't counted in 1990. In the dress rehearsal, Census Bureau officials say they eventually got questionnaires filled out for all 2,060 households in Menominee County, Wisconsin, but only after workers visited each residence that didn't return the form.

The objective of training is to ensure that the data collection instrument will be administered in a uniform fashion by all field-workers. The goal of these training sessions is to ensure that each respondent is provided with common information. If the data are collected in a uniform manner from all respondents, the training session will have been a success.

More extensive training programs are likely to cover the following topics:

1. How to make initial contact with the respondent and secure the interview
2. How to ask survey questions
3. How to probe
4. How to record responses
5. How to terminate the interview

Typically, the recruits will record answers on a practice questionnaire during a simulated training interview.

Making Initial Contact and Securing the Interview

Interviewers will be trained to make appropriate opening remarks that will convince the respondent that his or her cooperation is important; for example:

> **Good afternoon, my name is** _____ **from a national marketing research company. We are conducting a survey concerning** _____ **. I would like to get a few of your ideas.**

When making the initial contact in a telephone interview, the introduction might be:

> **Good evening, my name is** _____ **. I'm calling from Burke Marketing Research in Cincinnati, Ohio.**

By indicating that the telephone call is long distance, interviewers attempt to impress respondents because most people feel a long-distance call is something special, unusual, or important. Even though the call is normally a WATS-line call, it is still a subtle way to impress respondents.

Giving one's name personalizes the call. Personal interviewers may carry a letter of identification or an ID card to indicate that the study is a bona fide research project and not a sales call. Using the name of the research agency implies that the caller is trustworthy.

In its *Interviewer's Manual* the Survey Research Center at the University of Michigan recommends avoiding questions that ask permission for the interview, such as "May I come in?" and "Would you mind answering some questions?" Some people will refuse to participate or object to being interviewed. Interviewers should be instructed on handling objections. For example, if the respondent says, "I'm too busy right now," the interviewer might be instructed to respond, "Will you be in at 4 o'clock this afternoon? I would be happy to come back then." In other cases client companies will not wish to offend any individual; the interviewer will be instructed to merely say, "Thank you for your time." This might be the case with a telephone company or an oil company that is sensitive to its public image.

foot-in-the-door compliance technique
A technique to obtain a high response rate; compliance with a large or difficult task is induced by obtaining the respondent's compliance with an earlier, smaller request.

door-in-the-face compliance technique
A two-step process for securing a high response rate. In step 1 an initial request, so large that nearly everyone refuses it, is made. Next, a second request is made for a smaller favor; respondents are expected to comply with this more reasonable request.

Foot-in-the-Door/Door-in-the-Face Techniques. The **foot-in-the-door** and the **door-in-the-face compliance techniques** are useful in securing interviews. Foot-in-the-door theory attempts to explain compliance with a large or difficult task on the basis of respondents' earlier compliance with a smaller initial request. One experiment has shown that compliance with a minor telephone interview (that is, a small request that few people refuse) will lead to greater compliance with a second, larger request to fill out a long mail questionnaire. When the interviewer begins with an initial request so large that nearly everyone refuses it (that is, slams the door in his or her face), the interviewer then requests a small favor—to comply with a "short" survey. However, this research presents an ethical consideration if the respondent is deceived.

EXPLORING RESEARCH ETHICS

Polling the Desired Individual in Political Elections

To ACCURATELY PREDICT ELECTION OUTCOMES, political pollsters need to obtain representative samples. Typically, to avoid interviewing too many respondents of the same age or gender, the pollster should not always interview the first person who answers the phone because he or she is not always the individual who should be interviewed (disproportionately younger males answer the phone). When the designated respondent—usually the registered voter with the next birthday—is not home, the field-worker should schedule a callback—an expensive and time-consuming practice that few media pollsters conduct.

Asking the Questions

The purpose of the interview is, of course, to have the interviewer ask questions and record the respondent's answers. Considerable training in the art of asking questions can be extremely beneficial because interviewer bias can be a source of considerable error in survey research.

The major principles for asking questions are:

1. Ask the questions exactly as they are worded in the questionnaire.
2. Read each question very slowly.
3. Ask the questions in the order in which they are presented in the questionnaire.
4. Ask every question specified in the questionnaire.
5. Repeat questions that are misunderstood or misinterpreted.[4]

Although interviewers may be trained to know these rules, when working in the field many do not follow these procedures exactly. Inexperienced interviewers may not understand the importance of strict adherence to the instructions. Even professional interviewers take shortcuts when the task becomes monotonous. Interviewers may shorten questions or rephrase unconsciously when they rely on their memory of the question rather than reading the question as it is worded. Even the slightest change in wording can distort the meaning of the question and inject some bias into the study. By reading the question, the interviewer may be reminded to concentrate on avoiding slight variations in tone of voice on particular words or phrases.

If respondents do not understand a question, they usually will ask for some clarification. The recommended procedure is to repeat the question; or, if the person does not understand a word such as *nuclear* in the question "Do you feel nuclear energy is a safe energy alternative?" the interviewer should respond with "Just whatever it means to you." However, interviewers often supply their own personal definitions and ad lib clarifications, and these may include words that are not free from bias. One reason why interviewers do this is that field supervisors tend to reward people for submitting completed questionnaires and to be less tolerant of blanks due to alleged misunderstandings.

In a number of situations respondents volunteer information relevant to a question that is supposed to be asked at a later point in the interview. In this situation the response should be recorded under the question that deals specifically with that subject. However, rather than skipping the question that was answered out of sequence, the interviewer should be trained to say something like "We have briefly discussed this, but let me ask you..." By asking every question, complete answers are recorded. If the partial answer to a question answered out of sequence is recorded on the space reserved for the earlier question, and if the subsequent question is skipped, an omission error will occur when the data are tabulated.

Probing

General training of interviewers should include instructions on how to *probe*. Inexperienced interviewers must be trained to understand that respondents may give no answer, incomplete answers, or answers that require clarification. **Probing** may be needed for two types of situations. First, it is necessary when the respondent must be motivated to enlarge on, clarify, or explain his or her answers. It is the interviewer's job to probe for complete, unambiguous answers. The interviewer must encourage the respondent to clarify or expand on answers

probing
The verbal prompts made by a fieldworker when the respondent must be motivated to communicate his or her answer more fully. Probes are necessary so that respondents enlarge on, clarify, or explain answers.

by providing a stimulus that will not suggest the interviewer's own ideas or attitudes. The ability to probe with neutral stimuli is the mark of an experienced interviewer. Second, probing may be necessary when the respondent begins to ramble or lose track of the question. In such cases, the respondent must be led to focus on the specific content of the interview and avoid irrelevant and unnecessary information.

The interviewer will have several possible probing tactics to choose from, depending on the situation:

1. *Repeating the question.* When the respondent remains completely silent, he or she may not have understood the question or decided how to answer it. Mere repetition may encourage the respondent to answer in such cases. For example, if the question is "What is here that you do not like about this product?" and the respondent does not answer, the interviewer may probe: "Just to check, is there anything that you do not like about this product?"

2. *Using a silent probe.* If the interviewer believes that the respondent has more to say, a silent probe—that is, an expectant pause or look—may motivate the respondent to gather his or her thoughts and give a complete response. However, the interviewer must be careful that this technique does not lead to an embarrassing silence.

3. *Repeating the respondent's reply.* As the interviewer records the response, he or she may repeat the respondent's reply verbatim. This may stimulate the respondent to expand on the answer.

4. *Asking neutral questions or comments.* Asking a neutral question may specifically indicate the type of information that the interviewer is seeking. For example, if the interviewer believes that the respondent's motives should be clarified, he or she might ask, "Why do you feel that way?" If the interviewer feels that there is a need to clarify a word or phrase, he or she might say, "How do you mean _____?" Exhibit 18.1 lists some standard interview probes and the standard abbreviations that are recorded on the questionnaire with the respondent's answers.

The purpose of asking questions as probes is to encourage responses. Such probes should be neutral and not leading. Probes may be general (such as "anything else?") or they may be questions specifically designed by the interviewer to clarify a particular statement by the respondent.

Exhibit 18.1 Commonly Used Probes and Their Abbreviations

INTERVIEWER'S PROBE	STANDARD ABBREVIATION
Repeat question	(RQ)
Anything else?	(AE or Else?)
Any other reason?	(AO?)
Any others?	(Other?)
How do you mean?	(How mean?)
Could you tell me more about your thinking on that?	(Tell more)
Would you tell me what you have in mind?	(What in mind?)
What do you mean?	(What mean?)
Why do you feel that way?	(Why?)
Which would be closer to the way you feel?	(Which closer?)

Recording the Responses

The analyst who does not instruct fieldworkers in the techniques of recording during one study rarely forgets to do so in the next study. Although the concept of recording an answer seems extremely simple, mistakes can occur in this phase of the research. Each field worker should use the same mechanics of recording. For example, the interviewer may not understand the importance of using a pencil rather than a pen. To the editor who must erase and rewrite illegible words, however, use of a pencil is extremely important.

Exhibit 18.2   **Example of a Completed Questionnaire Page**

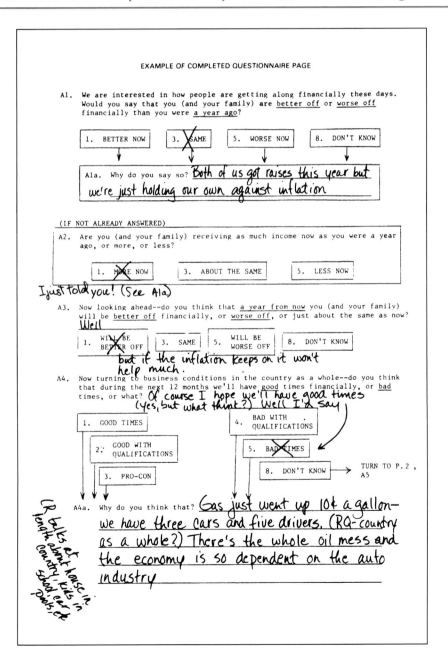

The rules for recording responses to fixed-alternative questions vary with the specific questionnaire. The general rule, however, is to place the check mark in the box that correctly reflects the respondent's answer. All too often interviewers skip recording the answer to a filter question because they believe the subsequent answer will make the answer to the filter question obvious. However, editors and coders do not know how the respondent was actually answering a question.

The general instruction for recording open-ended questions is to record the response verbatim, a task that is difficult for most people. Inexperienced interviewers should be given the opportunity to practice verbatim recording of answers before being sent into the field. The *Interviewer's Manual* of the Survey Research Center provides detailed instructions on recording interviews. Some of its suggestions for recording open-ended answers are:

1. Record responses during the interview.
2. Use the respondent's own words.
3. Do not summarize or paraphrase the respondent's answer.
4. Include everything that pertains to the question objectives.
5. Include all of your probes.[5]

Exhibit 18.2 shows an example of a completed questionnaire page. Note how the interviewer adds supplementary comments to the fixed-alternative questions and indicates probing questions by placing them in parentheses. The answers have been recorded without paraphrasing. The interviewer has resisted the temptation to conserve time and space by filtering comments. The RQ recorded in question A4a indicates a repeat question probe.

Terminating the Interview

The final aspect of training deals with instructing interviewers on how to close the interview and exit the household. Fieldworkers should not close the interview before they have secured all pertinent information. The interviewer who departs hastily may be unable to record the spontaneous comments respondents sometimes offer after all formal questions have been asked. Merely recording one of these comments may result in a new product idea or other creative marketing campaign. Avoiding hasty departures is also a matter of courtesy. The fieldworker should also answer any respondent questions concerning the nature and purpose of the study to the best of his or her ability.

The fieldworker may be required to reinterview the respondent at some future time. Thus, the respondent should be left with a positive feeling about having cooperated in a worthwhile operation. Finally, it is extremely important to thank the respondent for his or her time and cooperation.

Principles of Good Interviewing[6]

Yankelovich Partners is one of the nation's top marketing research organizations. One reason for its success is its careful attention to fieldwork. This section presents this organization's principles of good interviewing.

These principles apply no matter what the nature of the specific assignment; they are universal and represent the essence of sound data collection for marketing research purposes. For clarity, they have been divided into two categories: (1)

the basics—the interviewing point of view, and (2) *required practices*—standard inquiry premises and procedures.

The Basics

Interviewing is a skilled occupation; not everyone can do it, and even fewer can do it extremely well. The basic qualities of a good interviewer are these:

1. *Have integrity and be honest.* This is the cornerstone of all professional inquiry, regardless of its purpose.

2. *Have patience and tact.* Interviewers ask for information from people they have not previously known. Thus, all the rules of human relations that apply to inquiry situations—patience, tact, and courtesy—apply "in spades" to interviewing. Standard business conventions that control communications and contact are to be observed at all times.

3. *Pay attention to accuracy and detail.* Among the greatest interviewing "sins" are inaccuracy and superficiality, for the professional analyst can misunderstand, and in turn mislead, a client. A good rule to follow is not to record a response unless you fully understand it yourself. Probe for clarification and rich, full answers. Record responses verbatim: Never assume you know what a respondent is thinking or jump to conclusions as to what he or she might have said but did not.

4. *Exhibit a real interest in the inquiry at hand, but keep your own opinions to yourself.* Impartiality is imperative—if your opinions were wanted *you* would be asked, not your respondent. You are an asker and a recorder of other people's opinions, not a contributor to the study data.

5. *Be a good listener.* Too many interviewers talk too much, wasting time when respondents could be supplying more pertinent facts or opinions on the study topic.

6. *Keep inquiry and respondents' responses confidential.* Do not discuss the studies you are doing with relatives, friends, or associates; it is unacceptable to either the research agency or its clients. Above all, *never* quote one respondent's opinion to another—that is the greatest violation of privacy of all.

7. *Respect others' rights.* Marketing research depends on the goodwill of others to provide contributory information. There is a happy medium path to pursue in obtaining this information. On the one hand is failure to get it all; on the other is unnecessary coercion. The middle road is one of clear explanation, friendliness, and courtesy, carried out in an interested and persuasive way. Impress upon prospective respondents that their cooperation is important and valuable.

Required Practices

Here are the practical rules of marketing research inquiry, to be followed and used without exception:

1. *Complete the number of interviews according to the sampling plan assigned to you.* Both are calculated with the utmost precision so that when assignments are returned, the study will benefit from having available the amount and type of information originally specified.

2. *Follow directions provided.* Remember that there are many other interviewers working on the same study in other places. Lack of uniformity in proce-

dure can only spell disaster for later analysis. Each direction has a purpose, even though it may not be completely evident to you.

3. *Make every effort to keep schedules.* Schedules range from "hurry up" to "there should be plenty of time," but there is always a good reason, and you should be as responsive as possible. If you foresee problems, call and explain.

4. *Keep control of each interview you do.* It is up to you to determine the pace of a particular interview, keeping several points in mind:

    (a) There is an established *average* length of an interview from the time you start to talk to the respondent to the time you finish. It represents a *guideline,* but some interviews will be shorter and some longer.

    (b) Always get the whole story from the respondent and write it all down in the respondent's own words. Also, remember to keep the interview to the subject at hand and not let it wander off into unnecessary small talk.

    (c) Avoid offending the respondent by being too talkative yourself. Executives and other businesspeople have schedules to keep and are not impressed by small talk.

5. *Complete the questionnaires meticulously.* This means:

    (a) Follow exactly all instructions that appear directly on the questionnaire. Learn what these instructions direct you to do in advance.

    (b) Ask the questions from the first to the last in the exact numerical order (unless directed to do otherwise in some particular instances). Much thought and effort go into determining the order of the questioning to avoid bias or to set the stage for subsequent questions.

    (c) Ask each question exactly as it is written. There is never a justifiable reason for rephrasing a question. The cost would be lack of uniformity; the research agency would never know whether all respondents were replying to the same question or replying to 50 different interviewers' interpretations of the question.

    (d) Never leave a blank answer to a question. It will be difficult to tell whether you failed to ask it, whether the respondent could not answer due to lack of knowledge or certainty, or whether the respondent refused to answer it for personal reasons. If none of the answer categories provided prove suitable, write in what the respondent said, in his or her own words.

    (e) Use all the props provided to aid both interviewers and respondents: Show cards, pictures, descriptions, sheets of questions for the respondents to answer themselves, and so on. All have a specific interview purpose. Keys to when and how to use them appear on the questionnaire at the point at which they are to be used.

6. *Check over each questionnaire you have completed.* This is best done directly after it has been completed. If you find something you did wrong or omitted, correct it. Often you can call back a respondent, admit you missed something (or are unclear about a particular response), and then straighten out the difficulty.

7. *Compare your sample execution and quota assigned with the total number of questionnaires you have completed.* Do this before you consider your assignments finished.

8. *Clear up any questions with the research agency.* If questions arise either at the start or during an assignment for which you can find no explanatory instructions, call the agency to get the matter clarified (many agencies provide toll-free numbers so that there will be no expense to you).

Fieldwork Management

Marketing managers preparing for the fieldwork stage should consider the meaning of the following stanza from Robert Burns's poem "To a Mouse":

> *The best laid schemes o'mice and men*
> *Gang aft a—gley;*
> *An'lea'e us nought but grief and pain,*
> *For promis'd joy.*

The best plans of mice, men, and marketing researchers may go astray. An excellent research plan may go astray if the field operations are performed incorrectly. A proper research design will eliminate numerous sources of error, but careful execution of the fieldwork is necessary to produce results without substantial error. For these reasons fieldwork management is an essential part of the marketing research process.

Managers of field operations select, train, supervise, and control fieldworkers. Our discussion of fieldwork principles mentioned selection and training. This section investigates the tasks of the fieldwork managers in greater detail.

Briefing Session for Experienced Interviewers

Whether interviewers have just completed their training in fundamentals or are already experienced, there is always a need to inform them about the individual project. Both experienced and inexperienced fieldworkers must be briefed on the background of the sponsoring organization, sampling techniques, asking of questions, callback procedures, and other matters specific to the particular project.

If there are any special instructions, such as using show cards or videocassette equipment or restricted interviewing times, these should also be covered during the training session. Instructions for handling certain key questions are always important. For example, the following fieldworker instructions appeared in a survey of institutional investors who make buy-and-sell decisions about stocks for banks, pension funds, and so on:

Questions 13a, 13b

These questions will provide verbatim comments for the report to the client. Probe for more than one- or two-word answers and record verbatim. Particularly, probe for more information when respondent gives a general answer—e.g., "Poor management," "It's in a good industry." Ask: In what ways is management poor? What's good about the industry? And so on.

The training session for experienced interviewers might go something like this. All interviewers are called to the central office, where they receive a brief explanation of the firm's background and the general aims of the study. Interviewers are not provided with too much information about the purpose of the study, thus ensuring that they will not transmit any preconceived notions. For example, in a survey about the banks in a community, the interviewers should be told that the research is a banking study but not the name of the sponsoring bank. To train the interviewers about the questionnaire, a field supervisor conducts an interview with another field supervisor who acts as a respondent. The trainees observe the interviewing process and afterward are instructed to personally interview and record the responses of another field supervisor who acts as a respondent. After the interview, the trainees receive additional instructions.

Training to Avoid Procedural Errors in Sample Selection

The briefing session will also cover the sampling procedure. A number of research projects allow the interviewer to be at least partially responsible for selecting the sample. When this is the case, the potential for selection bias exists. This is obvious in the case of the quota sample, but less obvious in other cases. For example, in a probability sample in which every nth house is selected, the fieldworker uses his or her discretion in identifying housing units. Avoiding this error may not be as simple as it sounds. For example, in an old, exclusive neighborhood, a mansion's coach house or servants' quarters may have been converted into an apartment that should be identified as a housing unit. This type of dwelling and other unusual housing units (alley entrance only, lake cottages, or rooming houses) may be possible sources of selection errors. Errors in the selection of random digit dialing samples may also occur. Considerable effort in training and supervisory control should be expended to minimize these errors.

Another selection problem is the practice of contacting a respondent when and where it is convenient for both parties. Consider the following anecdote from an industrial marketing research interviewer:

> *Occasionally getting to the interview is half the challenge and tests the interviewer's ingenuity. Finding your way around a huge steel mill is not easy. Even worse, trying to find a correct turn-off to gravel pit D when it's snowing so hard that most direction signs are obliterated. In arranging an appointment with an executive at a rock quarry outside Kansas City, he told me his office was in "Cave Number 3." It was no joke. To my surprise, I found a luxurious executive office in a cave, which had long ago been hollowed by digging for raw material.*[7]

In that case finding the sample unit was half the battle.

Supervision of Fieldworkers

Although briefing and training interviewers will minimize the probability of interviewing the wrong households or asking biased questions, there is still considerable potential for errors in the field. Direct supervision of personal interviewers, telephone interviewers, and other fieldworkers is necessary to ensure that the technique communicated in the training sessions are implemented in the field.

The supervision of interviewers, like other forms of supervision, refers to controlling the efforts of workers. Field supervision of interviewers requires checking to see that field procedures are being properly followed. The supervisor checks field operations to ensure that the interviewing schedule is being met. Supervisors collect the questionnaires or other instruments daily and edit them for completeness and legibility. (See Chapter 19 for more detail on editing.) If there are any problems, supervisors discuss them with the field-workers, providing training when necessary.

In addition to quality control, continual training may be provided. For example, a telephone supervisor may notice that interviewers are allowing the phone to ring more than eight times before considering the call a "no answer." The supervisor can instruct interviewers that if a telephone is allowed to ring too long and then is answered, the respondent may be annoyed.

Sampling Verification

Another important job of the supervisor is to verify that the interviews are being conducted according to the sampling plan rather than to the selection of households most accessible to the interviewer. An interviewer might be tempted to go to the household next door for an interview rather than recording that the sampling unit was not at home, which would require a callback.

Careful recording of the number of completed interviews will help ensure that the sampling procedure is being properly conducted. It is the supervisor's function to motivate interviewers to carefully follow the sampling plan.

Closer supervision of the interviewing procedure occurs in central location telephone interviewing. The supervisor may be able to listen to the actual interview by switching onto the interviewer's line. Of course, this cannot be done if interviewers call from their homes.

Interviewing the Right Person.
Supervisors must make sure that the right people within the household or sampling unit are being contacted. One research project for a children's cereal required that several products be placed in the home. The children were expected to record their daily consumption and reactions to each cereal in a diary. A field supervisor observed that several mothers were filling out the diaries because their children had not done so. An investigation discovered that although the interviewers were supposed to contact the children to remind them to fill out the diaries, in almost half the cases the mothers were filling out the diaries after the children left for school. The novelty of the research project had worn off after a few days; the test of eating a specific cereal each day was no longer fun after the first few times, and the children had stopped keeping the diaries. Similar situations may occur with physicians, executives, and other busy people. The interviewer may find it easier to interview a nurse, secretary, or other assistant rather than wait to visit with the right person.

Interviewer Cheating

Interviewer cheating in its most blatant form occurs when an interviewer falsifies interviews, merely filling in fake answers rather than contacting respondents. Although this situation does occur, it is not common if the job of selection has been properly accomplished. However, less obvious forms of interviewer cheating occur with greater frequency. Quota samples often are seen as time consuming, and the interviewer may stretch the requirements a bit to obtain seemingly qualified respondents. In the interviewer's eyes a young-looking 36-year-old may be the same as a 30-year-old who fits the quota requirement; checking off the under-30 category thus isn't really cheating. Consider the field worker who must select only heavy users of a certain brand of hand lotion that the client says is used by 15 percent of the population, but the field worker is finding that only 3 percent

interviewer cheating
The practice of filling in fake answers or falsifying interviews by fieldworkers.

qualify as heavy users. The interviewer may be tempted to interview an occasional user to stretch the quota somewhat.

An interviewer may fake part of a questionnaire to make it acceptable to the field supervisor. In a survey on automobile stereo systems, an interviewer might be requested to ask for five reasons why consumers have purchased this product. If he or she finds that most people typically give one or two, or perhaps three, answers and even with extensive probing cannot think of five reasons, the interviewer might be tempted to cheat. Rather than have the supervisor think he or she was goofing off on the probing, the interviewer may fill in all five reasons based on past interviews. In other cases the interviewer may cut corners to save time and energy.

Interviewers may fake answers when they find questions embarrassing or troublesome to ask because of sensitive subjects. Thus, the interviewer may complete most of the questionnaire, but leave out a question or two because he or she found it troublesome or time consuming. For example, in a survey among physicians an interviewer might find questions about artificial insemination donor programs embarrassing, skip these questions, and fill in the gaps later.

What appears to be interviewer cheating often is caused by improper training or fieldworkers' inexperience. A fieldworker who does not understand the instructions may skip or miss a portion of the questionnaire.

Interviewers may be reluctant to interview sampling units who they feel may be difficult or undesirable to interview. Sometimes fieldworkers are instructed to say at the conclusion of each interview, "Thank you for your time—and by the way, my supervisor may call you to ask about my work. Please say whatever you wish." This or a similar statement not only increases the number of respondents willing to cooperate with the verification process, but improves the quality of fieldwork.

Verification by Reinterviewing

Supervision for quality control attempts to ensure that interviewers are following the sampling procedure and to detect falsification of interviews. Supervisors verify approximately 15 percent of the interviews by reinterviewing. Normally the interview is not repeated; rather, supervisors recontact respondents and ask about the length of the interviews and their reactions to the interviewer, then they collect basic demographic data to check for interviewer cheating. Such **verification** does not detect the more subtle form of cheating in which only portions of the interview have been falsified. A validation check may simply point out that an interviewer contacted the proper household, but interviewed the wrong individual in that household. This, of course, can be a serious error.

Fieldworkers should be aware of supervisory verification practices. Knowledge that there may be a telephone or postcard validation check often reminds interviewers to be conscientious in their work. The interviewer who is conducting a quota sample and needs an upper-income Hispanic male will be less tempted to interview a middle-income Hispanic man and falsify the income data in this situation.

Certain information may allow for partial verification without recontacting the respondent. For example, if a computer-assisted telephone interviewer does not know the phone number dialed by the computer or is unaware of other information about the respondent that may be available, questions added to the end of the telephone interview to identify a respondent's area code, phone number, city, zip code, and so on may help to verify the interview. The computer can also identify interviewers who cheat by recording every attempted call, the time intervals between calls, and the time required to conduct each completed interview.[8]

verification

The quality-control procedures in fieldwork to ensure that interviewers are following the sampling procedures and to determine whether interviewers are cheating.

Summary

The activities for collecting data in the field may be performed by the organization that needs the information, by research suppliers, or by third-party field service organizations. Proper execution of fieldwork is essential to produce research results without substantial error. Proper control of fieldwork begins with interviewer selection. Field workers generally should be healthy, outgoing, and well-groomed. New field workers must be trained in opening the interview, asking the questions, probing for additional information, recording the responses, and terminating the interview. Experienced fieldworkers are briefed for each new project to familiarize them with its specific requirements. A particular concern of the briefing session is close adherence to the prescribed sampling procedures.

Careful supervision of field workers also is necessary. Supervisors gather and edit questionnaires each day. They check to see that field procedures are being properly followed and that interviews are on schedule. They also check to ensure that the correct sampling units are being used and that the proper people are responding in the study. Finally, supervisors check for interviewer cheating and verify portions of the interviews by reinterviewing a certain percentage of each fieldworker's respondents.

Key Terms and Concepts

Field worker
Field interviewing service
In-house interviewer
Briefing session

Foot-in-the-door compliance
   technique
Door-in-the-face compliance
   technique

Probing
Interviewer cheating
Verification

Questions for Review and Critical Thinking

1. What qualities should field workers possess?
2. What impact have changes in women's lifestyles had on fieldwork in the last 25 years?
3. What is the proper method for asking questions? What should the interviewer do if a question is misunderstood? If a respondent answers a question before encountering it in the questionnaire?
4. When should interviewers probe? Give some examples of how probing should be done.
5. How should respondents' answers to open-ended questions be recorded?
6. How should the field worker terminate the interview?
7. Why is it important to ensure that field workers adhere to the sampling procedure specified for a project?
8. What forms does interviewer cheating take? How can such cheating be prevented or detected?
9. Contacting every individual in the United States is a major problem for the Bureau of the Census. List some other potential fieldwork problems that might arise in conducting the U.S. census. What might be done to mitigate these problems?
10. Comment on the following field situations.
    a. After conducting a survey with ten people, an interviewer noticed that many of the respondents were saying "Was I right?" after a particular question.
    b. A questionnaire asking about a new easy-opening can has the following instructions to interviewers: *"(Hand respondent can and matching instruction card.)* Would you please read the instructions on this card and then open this can for me? *(Interviewer: Note any comments respondent makes. Do not under any circumstances help him or her to open the can or offer any explanation as to how to open it. If respondent asks for help, tell him that the instructions are on the card. Do not discuss the can or its contents.)"*
    c. A researcher gives balloons to children of respondents to keep them occupied during the interview.
    d. An interviewer tells the supervisor, "With the price of gas, this job isn't paying as well as before!"

e.   When a respondent asks how much time the survey will take, the interviewer responds 15 to 20 minutes, then the respondent says, "I'm sorry, I have to refuse. I can't give you that much time right now."

11. Write some interviewer instructions for a telephone survey.

12. A field worker conducting a political poll is instructed to interview registered voters. The fieldworker interviews all willing participants who are eligible to vote (those who may register in the future) because allow-

ing their opinions to be recorded is part of her patriotic duty. Is she doing the right thing?

13. An interviewer finds that when potential respondents ask how much time the survey will take, most will refuse if they are told 15 minutes. The interviewer now says 10 minutes and finds that most respondents enjoy answering the questions. Is this the right thing to do?

14. A field worker asks respondents whether they will answer a few questions. However, the interviewer also observes the respondents' races and approximate age. Is this ethical?

Exploring the Internet

Go to Lycos at http://www.lycos.com. Enter "marketing research companies" into the query box and then hit the search icon. Based on the information supplied in this search, navigate the Internet to find the names of several companies that provide fieldwork services.

Case 18.1 Margaret Murphy O'Hara

MARGARET MURPHY O'HARA WAS FATIGUED. AS SHE wiped the perspiration from her brow, she felt that the Massachusetts summer sun was playing a trick on her. It was her first day at work, and the weather was hot. She had no idea that being a field interviewer required so much stamina. Even though she was tired, she was happy with her new job. She didn't yet have the knack of holding her purse, questionnaires, and clipboard while administering the show cards, but she knew she'd get the hang of it. The balancing act can be learned, she thought.

When she met Mary Zagorski, Margaret told Mary how her day went. Margaret said she thought the questionnaire was a bit too long. She laughed, saying that an elderly lady had fallen asleep after about 20 minutes of interviewing.

Margaret mentioned that a number of people had asked why they were selected. Margaret said she did not know exactly what to say when somebody asked, "Why did you pick me?"

She said that the nicest person she had interviewed was a man whose wife wasn't home to be surveyed. He was very friendly and didn't balk at being asked about his income and age like some of the other people she had interviewed.

She said she had one problem that she needed some help with. Four or five people refused to grant

the interview. Margaret explained that one woman answered the door and said she was too busy because her son, an army private, was leaving the country. The woman was throwing a little party for him before he went off to the airport. Margaret didn't want to spoil their fun with the survey. Another lady said that she was too busy and really didn't know anything about the subject anyway. However, she did suggest her next-door neighbor, who was very interested in the subject. Margaret was able to interview this person to make up for the lost interview. It actually went quite well.

Margaret said another woman wouldn't be interviewed because she didn't know anything about the Zagorski interviewing service, and Margaret didn't know quite what to tell her. Finally, she couldn't make one interview because she didn't understand the address: 9615 South Francisco Rear. Margaret told Mary it was quite a day, and she looked forward to tomorrow.

QUESTIONS

1. Is Margaret going to be a good professional interviewer?

2. What should Mary Zagorski tell Margaret?

Case 18.2   United States Census Bureau

EVERY 10 YEARS, THE CENSUS BUREAU TRIES TO COUNT everyone living in the United States by sending out questionnaires and going door to door, a method called a traditional head count.

In 1990, 65 percent of the mailed questionnaires were filled out and returned. Census counters went back to every household that didn't return a form. But the bureau was able to count only 98.4 percent of the population.

In 2000, the Census Bureau wants to use a method called statistical sampling.[9] Under this plan, the Census Bureau still would mail questionnaires and follow up in person. But it would stop door-to-door visits when it reached roughly 90 percent of the households in each neighborhood. Then the Census Bureau would estimate the number and types of people who were missed, based on a sample of households in each neighborhood.

After the initial count is finished, census counters would go back out to 750,000 randomly selected households across the country to determine whether those households were included in the initial count.

The results of the second interviews would be matched with the initial census returns from these households by number of people, age, sex, race, and whether the home is owned or rented by its occupants.

Using the results of these comparisons, the Census Bureau would determine the extent of the undercount or double count for different demographic groups, such as black males in a certain age category living in a specific geographic area. Then the Census Bureau would take those results and project them for each demographic group, block by block, across the country. The Census Bureau says this process will produce a more accurate count in less time than the current method and for less money.

This would be the first use of sampling in the decennial census. But sampling is used for many estimates and reports that the Census Bureau releases each month. It also was used to eliminate the undercount in 1990.

QUESTIONS

1. Can the sampling plan effectively achieve the Constitution's goal of enumeration, that is, to identify the number of people in each state?

2. What factors other than statistical factors might influence the Census Bureau's use of sampling?

Case 18.3   Tobin's Field Services (A)

TOBIN'S FIELD SERVICES IS A MARKETING RESEARCH company that specializes in surveys in which respondents must be recontacted. Case Exhibits 18.3-1, 18.3-2, and 18.3-3 are excerpts from three separate data collection forms designed for a single client.

Case Exhibit 18.3-1 indicates the first, a telephone survey for a retail store. It is a screening instrument for obtaining respondents who shop at the client's or competitors' stores. At the end of the interview, respondents are asked to provide their names, addresses, and telephone numbers so that they can be recontacted.

Case Exhibit 18.3-2 is a telephone recontact form to establish an appointment for a personal interview.

Case Exhibit 18.3-3 indicates the introductory remarks the personal interviewer will make to the respondent and shows the questionnaire.

QUESTIONS

1. Evaluate each of the exhibits from an interviewer's perspective. How much skill is required for each task? What type of interviewer would you hire?

2. What type of training would be required for interviewers working on the personal interview survey in Case Exhibit 18.3-3? Are there any questions that would be more difficult than others?

Case Exhibit 18.3-1   Retail Store Qualifying Study (Telephone Screening)

Study # _____

City:
- ❏ 1   Wichita
- ❏ 2   Oklahoma City
- ❏ 3   Shreveport
- ❏ 4   Kansas City
- ❏ 5   Mobile
- ❏ 6   Jackson

Retail Store Quantitative Study
(Telephone Screening)

Hello, I'm _____ from _____,
a national marketing research company. We are conducting a study and would like to ask you a few questions.

Screening

A.   Before we begin, do you, or any member of your family, work for . . .
- ❏ 1   A department, variety, or discount store
- ❏ 2   An advertising agency
- ❏ 3   A marketing research company

(If "yes" to any of the above, terminate and tally on contact sheet)

B.   By the way, have you been interviewed as part of a marketing research study within the past month?
- ❏ 1   Yes (Terminate and tally on contact sheet)
- ❏ 2   No (Continue)

1. I'm going to read you the names of a few stores. For each one, will you please tell me if you, or any member of your family, have *shopped* at this store with the *past year?* (Begin with checked store name and continue for remaining names. For each store mentioned above, ask:)

2. Have you, or any member of your family, shopped at _____(store name)_____ within the past *2 months?*

	Q.1 Shopped at in Past Year (8)	**Q.2** Shopped at in Past 2 Months (9)
Store A	❏ 1	❏ 1
Store B	❏ 2	❏ 2
Store C	❏ 3	❏ 3
Store D	❏ 4	❏ 4
Store E	❏ 5	❏ 5

Thank you very much for your cooperation. Your answers have been very helpful. As part of this marketing research study, we may be calling you back within the next few weeks to arrange for an additional interview in your home. If you are recontacted, the interview will be treated in the strictest confidence and no attempt will be made to sell you anything. Again, thank you, for your assistance.

(*Do not ask,* but check box if respondent refuses to be recontacted. ❏)

Name of Respondent: _____

Address: _____

City: _____ State: _____ Phone #: _____

Interviewer: _____ Date: _____

Case Exhibit 18.3-2 **Respondent Recontact Form**

For Office Use Only
Respondent # _____

Study # _____

City:
- ❏ 1   Wichita
- ❏ 2   Oklahoma City
- ❏ 3   Shreveport
- ❏ 4   Kansas City
- ❏ 5   Mobile
- ❏ 6   Jackson

(1–5)
(6)

Respondent Recontact Form

Hello, Mrs./Miss _____, I'm _____ from _____, a national marketing research company.

Earlier this month, we talked to you about some stores you may have shopped at. I'd like an opportunity to talk to you some more about this subject in your home. As we mentioned before, please let me assure you that your answers will be treated in the strictest confidence and that no one will try to sell you anything.

(Make Appointment:) Time: _____ Date: _____

Interviewer: _____ Date: _____

Respondent Quota #: ❏ 1   ❏ 2   ❏ 3

(7)

Case Exhibit 18.3-3 **Retail Store Quantitative Study (Personal Interview)**

Study # _____

City:
- ❏ 1   Wichita
- ❏ 2   Oklahoma City
- ❏ 3   Shreveport
- ❏ 4   Kansas City
- ❏ 5   Mobile
- ❏ 6   Jackson

(6)

Respondent Quota #:   ❏ 1   ❏ 2   ❏ 3   ❏ 4

(7)

Retail Store Quantitative Study
(Personal Interview)

Staple recontact sheet to front of this questionnaire

Hello, Mrs./Miss _____, I'm _____ from _____. We spoke to you about a week ago as

part of a marketing research study we are conducting on stores in our community. I'd like to ask you a few more questions about some stores you may have shopped at.

For the remainder of this interview I'd like to talk to you about these five stores.

(Hand card "A" to respondent. Rotate usage of cards A1–3)

Circle card used: A1   A2   A3

Now, I'm going to read you a number of different types of items you might buy at these stores. Will you please tell me the name of the *one* store you feel is the *best* for buying each type of item. Even though you may not have purchased the items at any of *these* stores, please tell me which *one of them* you feel is *best*.

(Begin with checked item and ask Q. 3a and Q. 3b. Repeat for remaining items.)

3a. In your opinion, which *one* store is *best* for buying *(Checked item)*? (Read names of all stores beginning with checked name. Accept only *one* answer.)

3b. In your opinion, which *one of the remaining* stores is the *next best* for buying *(Checked item)*? (Read names of all stores. Accept only *one* answer.)

(continued)

Case Exhibit 18.3-3 Retail Store Quantitative Study *(Continued)*

		Store A	Store B	Store C	Store D	Store E	
a. Kitchen accessories and equipment such as	(Q. 3a)	❏ 1	❏ 2	❏ 3	❏ 4	❏ 5	(10)
pots, pans, utensils, and serving pieces	(Q. 3b)	❏ 1	❏ 2	❏ 3	❏ 4	❏ 5	(11)
b. Clothing and shoes for children	(Q. 3a)	❏ 1	❏ 2	❏ 3	❏ 4	❏ 5	(14)
12 years old or less	(Q. 3b)	❏ 1	❏ 2	❏ 3	❏ 4	❏ 5	(15)
c. Household accessories and decorative items such as	(Q. 3a)	❏ 1	❏ 2	❏ 3	❏ 4	❏ 5	(16)
curtain rods, wall plaques, picture frames, and ashtrays	(Q. 3b)	❏ 1	❏ 2	❏ 3	❏ 4	❏ 5	(17)
d. Small electrical appliances such as	(Q. 3a)	❏ 1	❏ 2	❏ 3	❏ 4	❏ 5	(20)
toasters, mixers, can openers, and blenders	(Q. 3b)	❏ 1	❏ 2	❏ 3	❏ 4	❏ 5	(21)
e. Fabrics, yarns, notions, curtains,	(Q. 3a)	❏ 1	❏ 2	❏ 3	❏ 4	❏ 5	(22)
and draperies	(Q. 3b)	❏ 1	❏ 2	❏ 3	❏ 4	❏ 5	(23)
f. Everyday casual clothing and shoes	(Q. 3a)	❏ 1	❏ 2	❏ 3	❏ 4	❏ 5	(24)
for men and women	(Q. 3b)	❏ 1	❏ 2	❏ 3	❏ 4	❏ 5	(25)
g. Toys and games	(Q. 3a)	❏ 1	❏ 2	❏ 3	❏ 4	❏ 5	(26)
	(Q. 3b)	❏ 1	❏ 2	❏ 3	❏ 4	❏ 5	(27)

I'm going to read you a number of different types of items you might buy at these stores. Will you please tell me the names of the stores in which you, or members of your family, have purchased each type of item *within* the *past 2 months?*

(Begin with checked item)

4. *Within the past 2 months,* in which of the listed stores have you, or members of your family, purchased *(Checked item)?* Any others? Any others? (Record all answers) (Continue for remaining items)

	Store A	Store B	Store C	Store D	Store E	
a. Kitchen accessories and equipment such as pots, pans, utensils, and serving pieces	❏ 1	❏ 2	❏ 3	❏ 4	❏ 5	(8)
b. Sporting goods such as equipment for hunting, fishing, skiing, golf, tennis, backyard games, exercising, and camping	❏ 1	❏ 2	❏ 3	❏ 4	❏ 5	(9)
c. Clothing and shoes for children 12 years old or less	❏ 1	❏ 2	❏ 3	❏ 4	❏ 5	(10)
d. Household accessories and decorative items such as curtain rods, wall plaques, picture frames, and ashtrays	❏ 1	❏ 2	❏ 3	❏ 4	❏ 5	(11)
e. Home repair or improvement items such as tools, hardware, and other supplies	❏ 1	❏ 2	❏ 3	❏ 4	❏ 5	(12)
f. Small electrical appliances such as toasters, mixers, can openers, and blenders	❏ 1	❏ 2	❏ 3	❏ 4	❏ 5	(13)
g. Fabrics, yarns, notions, curtains, and draperies	❏ 1	❏ 2	❏ 3	❏ 4	❏ 5	(14)
h. Everyday casual clothing and shoes for men and women	❏ 1	❏ 2	❏ 3	❏ 4	❏ 5	(15)
i. Toys and games	❏ 1	❏ 2	❏ 3	❏ 4	❏ 5	(16)
j. Electronic equipment such as radios, stereo equipment, tape recorders, and televisions	❏ 1	❏ 2	❏ 3	❏ 4	❏ 5	(17)
k. Health, beauty aids, and toiletries	❏ 1	❏ 2	❏ 3	❏ 4	❏ 5	(18)

5. Which *one* of these stores do you, and members of your family, shop at *most often?* (Accept only one answer) (19)
   ❏ 1 Store A
   ❏ 2 Store B
   ❏ 3 Store C
   ❏ 4 Store D
   ❏ 5 Store E

   I'd like you to think about those particular stores that you and members of your family usually shop at.
   (Begin with checked store)

6. Approximately how long does it take you to drive to ___*(Checked store)*___ from your home?
   (Record in minutes)

(continued)

Case Exhibit 18.3-3 Retail Store Quantitative Study *(Continued)*

(Continue for remaining stores)

	Number of Minutes	
Store A	_____	(20)
Store B	_____	(21)
Store C	_____	(22)
Store D	_____	(23)
Store E	_____	(24)

Will you please tell me the names of the stores you feel are accurately described by each statement?

(Shuffle deck of cards)

7. Here is the first statement. (Hand top card to respondent) Which of the stores do you feel are accurately described by this statement? Any others? Any others? (Hand remaining cards to respondent one at a time)

	Store A	Store B	Store C	Store D	Store E	
a. Stands behind its merchandise	❑ 1	❑ 2	❑ 3	❑ 4	❑ 5	(25)
b. Has good parking facilities	❑ 1	❑ 2	❑ 3	❑ 4	❑ 5	(26)
c. You can save money there.	❑ 1	❑ 2	❑ 3	❑ 4	❑ 5	(27)
d. It's easy to return merchandise.	❑ 1	❑ 2	❑ 3	❑ 4	❑ 5	(28)
e. Has good-quality merchandise	❑ 1	❑ 2	❑ 3	❑ 4	❑ 5	(29)
f. Offers good value for the money	❑ 1	❑ 2	❑ 3	❑ 4	❑ 5	(30)
g. It's difficult to find a salesperson to help you.	❑ 1	❑ 2	❑ 3	❑ 4	❑ 5	(31)
h. Sales items are often sold out by the time you get there.	❑ 1	❑ 2	❑ 3	❑ 4	❑ 5	(32)
i. I would be embarrassed to tell my friends I bought something there.	❑ 1	❑ 2	❑ 3	N 4	N 5	(33)
j. The store has a warm, friendly atmosphere.	❑ 1	❑ 2	❑ 3	❑ 4	❑ 5	(34)
k. Overall, has prices lower than most other stores	❑ 1	❑ 2	❑ 3	❑ 4	❑ 5	(35)
l. You can always find a bargain when you shop there.	❑ 1	❑ 2	❑ 3	❑ 4	❑ 5	(36)
m. Has something for everyone in the family	❑ 1	❑ 2	❑ 3	❑ 4	❑ 5	(37)
n. Usually has enough checkout lines open	❑ 1	❑ 2	❑ 3	❑ 4	❑ 5	(38)
o. Advertised sales items are available in all store outlets.	❑ 1	❑ 2	❑ 3	❑ 4	❑ 5	(39)
p. Their store-branded merchandise is a good value.	❑ 1	❑ 2	❑ 3	❑ 4	❑ 5	(40)
q. Good place to shop for gifts	❑ 1	❑ 2	❑ 3	❑ 4	❑ 5	(41)
r. You can shop there quickly.	❑ 1	❑ 2	❑ 3	❑ 4	❑ 5	(42)
s. Has conveniently located stores	❑ 1	❑ 2	❑ 3	❑ 4	❑ 5	(43)
t. Accepts all types of credit cards	❑ 1	❑ 2	❑ 3	❑ 4	❑ 5	(44)
u. So crowded with people that it's hard to move around	❑ 1	❑ 2	❑ 3	❑ 4	❑ 5	(45)
v. Has knowledgeable salespeople	❑ 1	❑ 2	❑ 3	❑ 4	❑ 5	(46)
w. Has friendly, polite salespeople	❑ 1	❑ 2	❑ 3	❑ 4	❑ 5	(47)
x. You can shop there with confidence.	❑ 1	❑ 2	❑ 3	❑ 4	❑ 5	(48)
y. Provides a variety of helpful customer services	❑ 1	❑ 2	❑ 3	❑ 4	❑ 5	(49)
z. You can trust what they say in their advertisements.	❑ 1	❑ 2	❑ 3	❑ 4	❑ 5	(50)
aa. Merchandise is easy to find	❑ 1	❑ 2	❑ 3	❑ 4	❑ 5	(51)
bb. When I want a particular item, there are many brands to choose from.	❑ 1	❑ 2	❑ 3	❑ 4	❑ 5	(52)
cc. Usually one of the last stores to carry new products	❑ 1	❑ 2	❑ 3	❑ 4	❑ 5	(53)
dd. Sale merchandise shows both the original and sale price	❑ 1	❑ 2	❑ 3	❑ 4	❑ 5	(54)

8. Now I'm going to read you some statements that might be used to describe the type of people who might shop at these five stores. Will you please tell me the names of the stores that each type of person would likely to shop at? (Begin with checked item)

   Which of the stores do you feel that *(Checked item)* would be likely to shop at? Any others?

   Any others?

(Continue for remaining items) _____

Case Exhibit 18.3-3 Retail Store Quantitative Study (Continued)

	Store A	Store B	Store C	Store D	Store E	
a. Stands behind its merchandise	❏ 1	❏ 2	❏ 3	❏ 4	❏ 5	(25)
a. People who like to try new and different things	❏ 1	❏ 2	❏ 3	❏ 4	❏ 5	(8)
b. People who don't mind traveling some distance to shop	❏ 1	❏ 2	❏ 3	❏ 4	❏ 5	(9)
c. People in their 20s and 30s	❏ 1	❏ 2	❏ 3	❏ 4	❏ 5	(10)
d. Men	❏ 1	❏ 2	❏ 3	❏ 4	❏ 5	(11)
e. Families with growing children	❏ 1	❏ 2	❏ 3	❏ 4	❏ 5	(12)
f. People who *"shop around"* for the best price	❏ 1	❏ 2	❏ 3	❏ 4	❏ 5	(13)
g. People in their 40s and 50s	❏ 1	❏ 2	❏ 3	❏ 4	❏ 5	(14)
h. People who rely on advertising to help them shop	❏ 1	❏ 2	❏ 3	❏ 4	❏ 5	(15)
i. Doctors, lawyers, and other *professional* people	❏ 1	❏ 2	❏ 3	❏ 4	❏ 5	(16)
j. Women	❏ 1	❏ 2	❏ 3	❏ 4	❏ 5	(17)
k. People who believe that buying merchandise *on credit* is unwise	❏ 1	❏ 2	❏ 3	❏ 4	❏ 5	(18)
l. People who are do-it-yourselfers	❏ 1	❏ 2	❏ 3	❏ 4	❏ 5	(19)
m. People who rely on the advice of friends to help them shop	❏ 1	❏ 2	❏ 3	❏ 4	❏ 5	(20)

9a. Which of the stores we have been talking about would you say is most similar to Store C?

    ❏ 1 Store A   ❏ 2 Store B   ❏ 4 Store D   ❏ 5 Store E   (21)

(If respondent mentions one or more stores in Q. 9a, ask:)

9b. Why do you say that these stores are similar to Store C? Anything else? Anything else? (Probe for specifics) (Identify particular store discussed)

_____ (22)
_____ (23)
_____ (24)
_____ (25)

(If respondent does *not* mention any stores in Q. 9a, ask:)

9c. Why do you say that *none* of the other stores are similar to Store C? Anything else? Anything else? (Probe for specifics)

_____ (26)
_____ (27)
_____ (28)
_____ (29)

10a. What, if anything, do you particularly *dislike* about Store C?

_____ (30)
_____ (31)
_____ (32)
_____ (33)

10b. What, if anything, do you particularly *like* about Store C? Anything else? Anything else? (Probe for specifics)

_____ (34)
_____ (35)
_____ (36)
_____ (37)

11. Would you say that all Store C stores are similar in size and amount of merchandise carried, or are some different from the others?

    ❏ 1 Yes, similar in size (Skip to classification)   (38)

    ❏ 2 No, not similar in size . . . How are they different? Anything else? Anything else? (Probe for specifics)

_____ (39)
_____ (40)
_____ (41)
_____ (42)

(Now, for classification purposes only):   (43)

C. What is your approximate age?   (44)

    ❏ 1 Under 18   ❏ 2 18–24   ❏ 3 25–34   ❏ 4 35–44   ❏ 5 45–54   ❏ 6 55 and over

D. What is your current marital status?   (45)

    ❏ 1 Married   ❏ 2 Widowed   ❏ 3 Divorced   ❏ 4 Separated   ❏ 5 Single

---

(continued)

Case Exhibit 18.3-3 Retail Store Quantitative Study *(Continued)*

E. In total, how many people are currently living in your household? _____ (46)

F. How many of these are children? _____ (47)

G. How many of these children are . . . (48)

    a. 4 years old or less _____   c. 13–17 years old _____ (49)

    (50)

    b. 5–12 years old _____   d. 18 years old or more _____ (51)

H. Do you presently have a job outside your home?

    ❏ 1 Yes . . . . . .   Is it . . . ❏ 3 Full time   or   ❏ 4 Part time (52)

    ❏ 2 No

I. What is the last year of school completed by the head of your household?

    ❏ 1 Some grade school   ❏ 5 Some college

    ❏ 2 Completed grade school   ❏ 6 Completed college

    ❏ 3 Some high school   ❏ 7 Postgraduate work

    ❏ 4 Completed high school   ❏   Other (specify) _____ (53)

J. What is the occupation of the head of your household? In what industry is that?

    Occupation: _____ (54)

    Industry: _____

K. Finally, is your family's total income over or under $50,000?

    Under $50,000   *Over $50,000*

         Is it . . . Is it . . . (55)

          ❏ 1 Under $25,000   ❏ 5 Under $75,000

          ❏ 2 Exactly $25,000   ❏ 6 Exactly $75,000

    or ❏ 3 Over $25,000   ❏ 4 Exactly $50,000   ❏ 7 Over $75,000

Thank you very much for your cooperation . . .

Chapter 19

Editing and Coding

Transforming Raw Data into Information

N A MANAGERIAL SURVEY RESPONDENTS WERE ASKED:

Relative to other companies in the industry,
is your company:

One of the largest? ❑

About average in size? ❑

Small? ❑

One respondent checked both the category "one of the largest" and the category "about average in size." Next to the question the respondent wrote, "average in retailing, one of the largest in drugstore chains." The editor must decide whether the industry should be categorized as "retailing" or "drugstore chain industry" and then edit in the appropriate category. A numerical code is then assigned so that researchers, often with the aid of a computer, may analyze the data. This chapter discusses how editing and coding transform raw data into a format suitable for analysis.

This chapter discusses how managers make decisions about planning research strategies and tactics. It also overviews the types of research designs and briefly discusses the stages in the research process.

What you will learn in this chapter

To define and explain the terms editing and coding.

To discuss the purposes of field editing and in-house editing.

To describe the different tasks performed by the in-house editor.

To code fixed-alternative questions.

To code open-ended questions.

To define the terms code book and production coding.

To understand how computerized data processing influences the coding process.

Stages of Data Stages of Data Analysis

The process of analysis begins after the data have been collected. During the analysis stage several interrelated procedures are performed to summarize and rearrange the data. Exhibit 19.1 presents the research steps that follow data collection and are related to processing and analysis. We now turn our attention to this process of data reduction and analysis.

The goal of most research is to provide information. There is a difference between raw data and information. *Information* refers to a body of facts that are in a format suitable for decision making, whereas *data* are simply recorded measures of certain phenomena. The raw data collected in the field must be transformed into information that will answer the marketing manager's questions. The conversion of raw data into information requires that the data be edited and coded so that they may be transferred to a computer or other data storage media. If the database is large, a computer offers many advantages. In that case the data are entered into the computer following the coding procedure.

Editing

Occasionally a field-worker makes a mistake and records an improbable answer (for example, "birth year: 1843") or interviews an ineligible respondent (such as one too young to qualify). Some answers may be contradictory, such as *no* to automobile ownership, but *yes* to an expenditure on automobile insurance. These and other problems must be dealt with before the data can be coded. **Editing** is the process of checking and adjusting the data for omissions, legibility, and consistency and readying them for coding and storage.

Editing may be differentiated from **coding**, which is the assignment of categories or classifying symbols to previously edited data. Careful editing makes the coding job easier. The purpose of editing is to ensure completeness, consistency, and readability of the data to be transferred to storage. The editor's task is to check for errors and omissions on the questionnaires or other data collection forms. When the editor discovers a problem, he or she adjusts the data to make it more complete, consistent, or readable.

The editor may also have to reconstruct some data. For instance, a respondent may indicate weekly income rather than monthly income as requested on the questionnaire. The editor must convert the information to monthly data without adding any extraneous information. The process of editing has been compared to the process of restoring a work of art. The editor "should bring to light all the hidden values and extract all possible information from a questionnaire, while adding nothing extraneous."

Field Editing

Field supervisors often are responsible for conducting preliminary **field editing** on the same day as the interview. The purpose of field editing is to catch technical omissions, such as a blank page on the interview questionnaire, to check legibility of handwriting, and to clarify responses that are logically or conceptually inconsistent. If a field edit is conducted at the end of the day, supervisors who edit completed questionnaires will frequently be able to question interviewers, who may be able to remember the interviews and correct the problems. The

editing
The process of checking completeness, consistency, and legibility of data and making the data ready for coding and transfer to storage.

coding
The process of identifying and assigning a numerical score or other character symbol to previously edited data.

field editing
Preliminary editing by a field supervisor on the same day as the interview to catch technical omissions, check legibility of handwriting, and clarify responses that are logically or conceptually inconsistent.

Exhibit 19.1 **Overview of the Stages of Data Analysis**

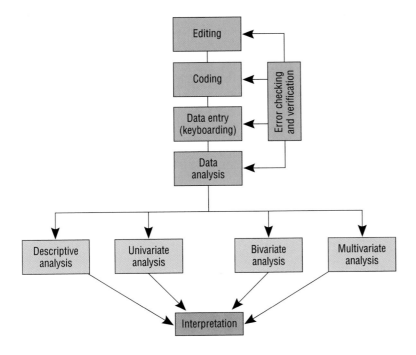

number of no answers or incomplete responses to some questions can be reduced with rapid follow-up stimulated by a field edit. The daily field edit also allows for possible recontacting of the respondent to fill in omissions before the situation has changed. It may also indicate the need for further interviewer training. For example, the field editor should check open-ended responses for completeness of probing or to see if the interviewers correctly follow skip patterns. When poor interviewing is reflected by lack of probing, additional interviewer training may be in order.

In-House Editing

Although simultaneous field editing is highly desirable, in many situations (particularly with mail questionnaires) early reviewing of the data is not always possible. **In-house editing** rigorously investigates the results of data collection. The research supplier or research department normally has a centralized office staff to perform the editing and coding function.

For example, Arbitron measures radio audiences by having respondents record their listening behavior—time, station, and place (home or car)—in diaries. After the diaries are returned by mail, in-house editors perform usability edits that check to ensure that the postmark is after the last day of the survey week, check the legibility of station call letters (station WXXX could look like WYYY), look for completeness of entries on each day of the week, and perform other editing activities. If the age or sex questions are not filled in, the respondent is called to ensure that this information is included.

in-house editing
A rigorous editing job performed by a centralized office staff.

TO THE POINT

Excellence is to do a common thing in an uncommon way.

BOOKER T. WASHINGTON

Editing for Consistency

The in-house editor's task is to adjust inconsistent or contradictory responses so that the answers will not be a problem for coders and keyboard operators. Suppose a telephone interviewer has been instructed to interview only registered voters in a state that requires voters to be at least 18 years old. The editor's review of a questionnaire may indicate that the respondent was only 17 years old. The editor's task here is to eliminate this obviously incorrect sampling unit. In this example the job is to ensure that the sampling unit is consistent with the objectives of the study. The editor checks for adherence to the data collection framework. For example, a survey on out-shopping behavior (shopping in towns other than the one in which the person resides) might have a question such as the following:

> **In which of the following towns do you shop for clothing? Please write in the clothing stores where you have shopped during the last month.**

A respondent might have accidentally listed a clothing store in town A, but checked the box next to town B. An error has resulted, and the answer must be changed to town A.

Editing requires checking for logically consistent responses. The in-house editor must determine if the answers a respondent gave to one question are consistent with those for other, related questions. Many surveys use filter questions or skip questions that direct the sequence of questions according to the respondent's answers. In some cases the respondent will have been asked a sequence of questions that should not have been asked. The editor should adjust these answers, usually to "no answer" or "inapplicable," so that the responses will be consistent. In other cases illogical answers will signal a recording error. For example, a respondent's housing value may be listed at $50,000. This may be inconsistent with the neighborhood in which the house is located and the 45-year-old respondent's occupational listing as a physician. The editor may find it highly unlikely that the answers to two questions could simultaneously be correct if both are true. The editor must use good judgment under these conditions.

Editing for Completeness

In some cases the respondent may have answered only the second portion of a two-part question. The following question indicates a situation in which an in-house editor may have to adjust the questionnaire for completeness:

> **Does your organization have more than one mainframe computer installation?**
> ❏ Yes ❏ No
> **If yes, how many?**

In this instance, it is possible that the respondent checked neither yes nor no, but indicated three computer installations. In this situation the editor may use a colored pencil to check the yes to ensure that this item is not missing from the questionnaire.

item nonresponse
The technical term for an unanswered question on an otherwise complete questionnaire.

Item nonresponse is the technical term for an unanswered question on an otherwise completed questionnaire. Specific decision rules for handling this problem should be meticulously outlined in the editor's instructions. In many situations the decision rule is to do nothing with the unanswered question. The editor merely indicates an item nonresponse by providing a message instructing the coder to record "missing value" or "blank" as the response. However, when the relationship between two questions is important, such as that of magazine readership to education level, it may be necessary for the editor to insert a **plug value.** The decision rule may be to plug in an average or neutral value in each instance of missing data. Another decision rule may be to alternate the choice of the response categories used as plug values (for example, yes the first time, no the second time, yes the third time). Still another decision rule might be to randomly select an answer. For example, suppose a respondent has indicated a first preference for brands of beers as Budweiser, but has given Stroh's and Miller the same ranking. The editor may randomly select the number two and three brands so that data analysis may be performed as planned. The editor must decide whether an entire questionnaire is usable. When a questionnaire has too many missing answers, it may not be suitable for the planned data analysis. In such a situation the editor can record that a particular incomplete questionnaire has been dropped from the sample.

plug value
An answer that an editor "plugs in" to replace blanks or missing values to permit completion of the data analysis; choice of value is based on a predetermined decision rule.

Editing Questions Answered Out of Order

Another task an editor may face is rearranging the answers given to an open-ended questionnaire. For example, the respondent may have provided the answer to a subsequent question in his or her comments to an earlier open-ended question. Because the respondent already had clearly identified the answer, the interviewer may have avoided asking the subsequent question, wishing to avoid hearing "I already answered that earlier" and to maintain interview rapport. To make the responses uniform with those on other questionnaires, the editor may move certain answers to the section related to the skipped question.

Facilitating the Coding Process

While all of the previously described editing activities will help coders, several editing procedures are designed specifically to simplify the coding process. For example, the editor checks to make sure every circled response is clearly definable; a response that overlaps two numbers and could be either 3 or 4 must be judged. The editor edits missing information and determines if the answer is "don't know (DK)" or "not ascertained (NA)." These and other decisions by the editor should not be arbitrary, but be based on a systematic procedure of fixed rules for making decisions.

Editing and Tabulating "Don't Know" Answers.

In many situations, the respondent answers "don't know." On the surface, this response seems to indicate that the respondent is not familiar with the brand, product, or situation or is uncertain and has not formulated a clear-cut opinion. This *legitimate* "don't know" means the same as "no opinion." Although the respondent may be unfamiliar with or uncommitted to the topic, there may be reasons other than the legitimate "don't know" answer. The *reluctant* "don't know" is given when the respondent simply does not want to answer the question and wishes to stop the interviewer from asking more. For example, asking about family income from an individual who is not the head of the household may elicit a "don't know" answer meaning "This is personal, and I really do not want to answer the question." If the individual does not understand the question, he or she may give a *confused* "I don't know" answer.

In some situations the editor can separate the legitimate "don't knows" ("no opinions") from the other "don't knows." The editor may try to identify the meaning of the "don't know" answer from other data provided on the questionnaire. For instance, the value of a home could be derived from a knowledge of the zip code and the average value of homes within that area.

The tabulation of "don't know" answers requires the editor to make a decision. One alternative is to record all "don't knows" as a separate category. This provides the actual response categories, but it may cause some problems with percentage calculation. Another alternative is to eliminate the "don't knows" from the percentage base. A third is to distribute the "don't know" answers among the other categories, usually proportionally. Although this is a simple procedure, it is criticized because it assumes that people who give "don't know" answers are the same as those who provide definite answers to a question on, say, income. In many situations this is not the case, and the "don't knows" are actually a highly homogeneous group.

Mechanics of Editing. Edited data frequently are written in with a colored pencil. When space on the questionnaire permits, the original data usually are left in to permit a subsequent edit to identify the original concepts. In the author's experience blue or green pencils have been used for editing and red pencils for coding.

Pretesting Edit

Editing the questionnaires during the pretest stage can prove very valuable. For example, if respondents' answers to the open-ended questions were longer than anticipated, the field-workers, respondents, and analysts would benefit from a change to larger spaces for the answers. Answers will be more legible because the writers have enough space, answers will be more complete, and answers will be verbatim rather than summarized. Examining answers to pretests may identify poor instructions or inappropriate question wording on the questionnaire.

Pitfalls of Editing. One possible problem in editing is subjectivity. To do a proper editing job, the editor must be intelligent, experienced, and *objective*. A *systematic procedure* for assessing the questionnaires should be developed by the research analyst so that the editor has clearly defined decision rules to follow.

Coding

codes
Rules for interpreting, classifying, and recording data in the coding process; the actual numerical or other character symbols.

field
A collection of characters that represent a single type of data.

record
A collection of related fields.

file
A collection of related records.

The process of identifying and classifying each answer with a numerical score or other character symbol is called *coding.* Assigning numerical symbols permits the transfer of data from the questionnaires to the computer. **Codes** generally are considered to be numbered symbols; however, they are more broadly defined as rules for interpreting, classifying, and recording the data.

Codes allow data to be processed in a computer. Researchers organize coded data into fields, records, and files. A **field** is a collection of characters (a *character* is a single number, letter, or special symbol such as a question mark) that represents a single type of data. A **record** is a collection of related fields, and a **file** is a collection of related records. Files, records, and fields are stored on tapes, disks, or hard drives. Each research study is recorded in a file, perhaps stored on a disk, of all completed questionnaires (see Exhibit 19.2). The file contains a record for each questionnaire. Each record has a field for various types of information about each respondent and for the respondents' coded answers to each question.

Exhibit 19.2   An Example of a File, Record, and Field

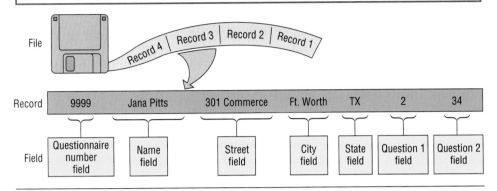

The Data Matrix. A **data matrix** is a rectangular arrangement of data into rows and columns. The accountant's spreadsheet, using traditional row and column accounting paper, is one example of a data matrix. Exhibit 19.3 illustrates a data matrix from a secondary data study investigating each state's population (in millions), average age, and automobile registrations (per 1,000 people). Each row in the matrix represents one state. In other words the rows represent records for individual cases reflecting the fundamental units of analysis.

Each column represents a particular field. In Exhibit 19.3 the columns represent variables that reflect data about each state. The first column contains an abbreviation of the state name. The second column shows the state's population in millions. The third column contains the average age in the state. The fourth column gives the number of automobile registrations per 1,000 residents for each state. The intersection of a row and column indicates where to enter a number or other code assigned to one state on a particular variable.

Years ago the data storage medium was the standard-sized 80-column punch card. Today an on-line computer terminal performing **direct data entry** is the most common input device for data storage, and punch cards are rarely used. Nevertheless, the terminology of direct data entry coding systems is based on that used in the traditional computer card system.

data matrix
A rectangular arrangement of data into rows and columns.

direct data entry
The use of an on-line computer terminal as an input device for data storage.

Exhibit 19.3   A Data Matrix

			Fields		
		State	Population (millions)	Average Age	Cars per 1,000
	Row	Column 1	Column 2	Column 3	Column 4
Alabama	Row 1	ALAB	4.0	29.3	543
Alaska	Row 2	ALAS	0.5	26.1	387
Arizona	Row 3	ARIZ	3.6	29.2	485
Arkansas	Row 4	ARK	2.4	30.6	442
	:	:	:	:	:
	:	:	:	:	:
	:	:	:	:	:
Wyoming	Row 50	WYO	0.5	27.1	609

Records (vertical label at left)

Exhibit 19.4 Coding for an Attitude Statement

Fixed-Alternative Question

In general self-regulation by business itself is preferable to stricter control of business by the government.

1. Strongly agree
2. Mildly agree
3. Mildly disagree

4. Strongly disagree
8. Don't know
9. No answer

Code Construction

Exhibit 19.4 portrays a typical survey question and its associated codes. When the question has a fixed-alternative (closed-ended) format, the number of categories that require codes is determined during the questionnaire design stage. The codes 8 and 9 conventionally are given to the respective "don't know" (DK) and "no answer" (NA) responses. However, many computer programs recognize that a blank field or a certain character symbol, such as a period (.), indicate a missing value (no answer). The choice of the computer program should be considered when selecting codes for "no answer" responses.

There are two basic rules for code construction. First, the coding categories should be *exhaustive;* that is, coding categories should be provided for all subjects, objects, or responses. With a categorical variable such as sex, the exhaustiveness of categories is not a problem. However, trouble may arise when the response represents a small number of subjects or when responses might be categorized into a class not typically found. For example, when questioned about automobile ownership, an antique car collector might mention that he drives a Packard Clipper. This may present a problem if separate categories are developed for all possible makes of cars. Solving this problem frequently requires inclusion of an "other" code category to ensure that the categories are all inclusive. For example, household size might be coded 1, 2, 3, 4, and 5 or more. The "5 or more" category assures all subjects of a place in a category.

Second, the coding categories should be *mutually exclusive* and *independent.* This means that there should be no overlap among the categories to ensure that a subject or response can be placed in only one category.

When a questionnaire is highly structured, the categories may be precoded before the data are collected. Exhibit 19.5 presents a questionnaire for which the precoded response categories were determined before the start of data collection.

In many cases, such as when researchers are using open-ended response questions to explore an unfamiliar topic, a framework for classifying responses to questions cannot be established before data collection. This situation requires some careful thought concerning the determination of categories after the editing process has been completed. This is called *postcoding,* or simply *coding.*

Precoding Fixed-Alternative Questions

Exhibit 19.5 shows the last page of a questionnaire that asks several demographic questions to classify individuals' scores. Question 29 has three possible answers, and they are precoded 1, 2, 3. Question 30 asks a person to respond yes (1) or no (2) to the question "Are you the male or female head of the household?" These

---

Exhibit 19.5 **Precoding Fixed-Alternative Responses**

---

29. Do you—or does anyone else in your immediate household—belong to a labor union?

¹☐ <u>Yes</u>, I personally belong to a labor union.
²☐ <u>Yes</u>, another member of my household belongs to a labor union.
³☐ <u>No</u>, no one in my household belongs to a labor union.

30. Are you the male or female head of the household—that is, <u>the person whose income is the chief source of support of the household?</u>

¹☐ Yes   ²☐ No

31. Would you please check the appropriate combined yearly income *before income taxes and any other payroll deductions)* from <u>all sources of all those</u> in your immediate household? *(Please include income from salaries, investments, dividends, rents, royalties, bonuses, commissions, etc.)* <u>Please remember that your individual answers will not be divulged.</u>

¹☐ Less than $4,000	⁷☐ $8,000–$8,999	¹³☐ $25,000–$29,999
²☐ $4,000–$4,999	⁸☐ $9,000–$9,999	¹⁴☐ $30,000–$39,999
³☐ $5,000–$5,999	⁹☐ $10,000–$12,499	¹⁵☐ $40,000–$49,999
⁴☐ $6,000–$6,999	¹⁰☐ $12,500–$14,999	¹⁶☐ $50,000–$74,999
⁵☐ $7,000–$7,499	¹¹☐ $15,000–$19,999	¹⁷☐ $75,000–$99,999
⁶☐ $7,500–$7,999	¹²☐ $20,000–$24,999	¹⁸☐ $100,000 or more

32a. Do you personally own corporate stocks? ¹☐ Yes   ²☐ No

**b. Do you own stocks in the corporation for which you work?
Do you own them in a corporation for which you do <u>not</u> work?
*(Please check as many as apply.)***

Own <u>STOCK</u> in:
¹☐ Company for which I work   ²☐ Other company

<u>THANK YOU VERY MUCH FOR YOUR COOPERATION</u>
If you would like to make any comments on any of the subjects covered in this study, please use the space below:

---

small numbers slightly raised to the left of the boxed areas indicate the codes for each response and will be used by the keyboard operator when entering the data into the computer. For example, for question 30 a field—perhaps column 32—in the data matrix may be assigned for the answer. If the respondent replies yes, a 1 will be entered. Question 31 will require a larger field because there are a large number of possible answers.

The Automarket Research questionnaire shown in Exhibit 19.6 illustrates another form of coding. Question 1a shows five possible answers: completely satisfied, coded 001; very satisfied, 002; fairly well satisfied, 003; somewhat dissatisfied, 004; and very dissatisfied, 005. It also shows the codes for question 1b, beginning with 006 and ending with 010. This questionnaire gives each possible answer in individual code number. This system of coding is used when the computer has been programmed to change these codes into traditional codes or categorical answers for each question.

The partial questionnaire in Exhibit 19.7 shows a precoded format for a telephone interview. In this situation the interviewer circles the coded numerical score as the answer to the question.

Precoding can be used if the researcher knows what the answer categories will be before data collection occurs. Thus, once the questionnaire has been designed and the structured (or closed-form) answers identified, coding becomes a routine process; in fact, in some cases the predetermined responses are based on standardized classification schemes. A coding framework that standardizes occupation follows:

Exhibit 19.6 A Precoded Fixed-Alternative Questionnaire

Automarket Research

This questionnaire should be completed by the **principal driver** of the vehicle indicated.
Thank you for taking time to answer these questions.

1. Now that you've had your vehicle for about one year, please tell us how satisfied you are in the following areas.

	Completely satisfied	Very satisfied	Fairly well satisfied	Somewhat dissatisfied	Very dissatisfied
a. Exterior quality of workmanship (fit and finish)?	001 ☐	002 ☐	003 ☐	004 ☐	005 ☐
b. Interior quality of workmanship (fit and finish)?	006 ☐	007 ☐	008 ☐	009 ☐	010 ☐
c. Engine power and pickup?	011 ☐	012 ☐	013 ☐	014 ☐	015 ☐
d. Smoothness of transmission?	016 ☐	017 ☐	018 ☐	019 ☐	020 ☐
e. Riding comfort?	021 ☐	022 ☐	023 ☐	024 ☐	025 ☐
f. Ease of handling?	026 ☐	027 ☐	028 ☐	029 ☐	030 ☐
g. Fuel economy?	031 ☐	032 ☐	033 ☐	034 ☐	035 ☐
h. Quietness?	036 ☐	037 ☐	038 ☐	039 ☐	040 ☐
i. Operation of the accessories (e.g., radio, air conditioner, heater, defroster, etc.)?	041 ☐	042 ☐	043 ☐	044 ☐	045 ☐
j. Overall satisfaction with the vehicle?	046 ☐	047 ☐	048 ☐	049 ☐	050 ☐

2a. Since the time of purchase, have you taken your Ford Motor Company vehicle to your selling dealer for any kind of service, including warranty work or repairs that you paid for? Yes 051 ☐ No 052 ☐ If no, please skip to question 5.

2b. If yes, what was the nature of the service? Check those that apply.

053 ☐ Paint/exterior moldings	056 ☐ Brakes/steering	059 ☐ Electrical system
054 ☐ Other body	057 ☐ Engine	060 ☐ Wheels/tires
055 ☐ Interior	058 ☐ Transmission	061 ☐ Maintenance service

062 ☐ Other (please describe) _____

	Completely satisfied	Very satisfied	Fairly well satisfied	Somewhat dissatisfied	Very dissatisfied
2c. How satisfied were you with the service you received?	063 ☐	064 ☐	065 ☐	066 ☐	067 ☐

3. Based on your visit(s) to your selling dealership for service, how satisfied would you say you are with each of the following? Mark one box across.

	Completely satisfied	Very satisfied	Fairly well satisfied	Somewhat dissatisfied	Very dissatisfied
a. The attitude of service department personnel (their interest in you and your problems)	068 ☐	069 ☐	070 ☐	071 ☐	072 ☐
b. Their overall treatment of you as a customer	073 ☐	074 ☐	075 ☐	076 ☐	077 ☐
c. Their promptness in writing up your order	078 ☐	079 ☐	080 ☐	081 ☐	082 ☐
d. Their politeness	083 ☐	084 ☐	085 ☐	086 ☐	087 ☐
e. Their understanding of your problem(s)	088 ☐	089 ☐	090 ☐	091 ☐	092 ☐
f. Convenience of scheduling the work	093 ☐	094 ☐	095 ☐	096 ☐	097 ☐
g. Convenience of service hours	098 ☐	099 ☐	100 ☐	101 ☐	102 ☐
h. Length of time to complete the work	103 ☐	104 ☐	105 ☐	106 ☐	107 ☐
i. Availability of needed parts	108 ☐	109 ☐	110 ☐	111 ☐	112 ☐
j. Their completing all the work you requested	113 ☐	114 ☐	115 ☐	116 ☐	117 ☐
k. The quality of work done (was it fixed right?)	118 ☐	119 ☐	120 ☐	121 ☐	122 ☐
l. Explanation of work and charges (if any)	123 ☐	124 ☐	125 ☐	126 ☐	127 ☐
m. Fairness of prices (if you were charged)	128 ☐	129 ☐	130 ☐	131 ☐	132 ☐
n. Appearance of service department	133 ☐	134 ☐	135 ☐	136 ☐	137 ☐

4. For the most recent service work

	Yes	No	
a. Was the vehicle ready when promised?	138 ☐	139 ☐	
b. Did anyone at the dealership follow up with you after your service visit to see if you were satisfied?	140 ☐	141 ☐	
c. Did the dealership do any repeat work on a problem which they themselves previously tried to but couldn't fix?	142 ☐	143 ☐	If no, please skip to question 5.

d. If yes, what was the nature of the service? Check those that apply.

144 ☐ Paint/exterior moldings	147 ☐ Brakes/steering	150 ☐ Electrical system
145 ☐ Other body	148 ☐ Engine	151 ☐ Wheels/tires
146 ☐ Interior	149 ☐ Transmission	152 ☐ Maintenance service

153 ☐ Other (please describe) _____

(over please)

> *Exhibit 19.7* **Precoded Format for Telephone Interview**

Study #45641   For office use only
Travel (Telephone Screening)   Respondent # _____
City:
Chicago
Gary
Ft. Wayne
Bloomington

Hello, I'm _____ from _____, a national survey research
company. We are conducting a study and would like to ask you a few questions.

A. Before we begin, do you, or any member of your family, work for . . .

  1 A travel agency   2 An advertising agency   3 A marketing research company

  (If "yes" to any of the above, terminate and tally on contact sheet)

B. By the way, have you been interviewed as part of a survey research study within the past month?
  1 Yes—(Terminate and tally on contact sheet)

  2 No—(Continue)

  1. Have you yourself made any trips of over 100 miles within the continental 48 states in the past
     3 months?

    1 Yes

    2 No—(Skip to Question 10)

  2. Was the trip for business reasons (paid for by your firm), vacation, or personal reasons?

	Last Trip	Second Last Trip	Other Trips
Business	1	1	1
Vacation	2	2	2
Personal (excluding a vacation)	3	3	3

What is your occupation? (PROBE: What kind of work is that?)

01	Professional, technical, and kindred workers	08	Service workers
02	Farmers	09	Laborers, except farm and mine
03	Managers, officials, and proprietors	10	Retired, widow, widower
04	Clerical and kindred workers	11	Student
05	Sales workers	12	Unemployed, on relief, laid off
06	Craftsmen, foremen, and kindred workers	13	Homemaker
07	Operatives and kindred workers	14	Other (specify)
		99	No occupation given

Computer-assisted telephone interviewing (CATI) and computer-interactive surveys require precoding. Changing the coding framework after the interviewing process has begun is extremely difficult because it requires changes in the computer programs.

Coding Open-Ended Questions

The usual reason for using open-ended questions is that the researcher has no clear hypotheses regarding the answers, which will be numerous and varied. The purpose of coding such questions is to reduce the large number of individual responses to a few general categories of answers that can be assigned numerical codes.

Exhibit 19.8 **Coding Open-Ended Questions About Chili**

You don't get that much meat in a can./
The beans are cooked just right./
It just (doesn't look) like any canned chili I've had.
I can see spices,/ I've never seen it in any canned chili.

It is not too spicy/ but it is tasty/—savory.
It's not (loaded with beans)—just enough beans./
It's moist/not too chewy./

Tastes (fresh)./ The canned stuff is too (soft).
Too overcooked usually./

It doesn't have a lot of filler/ and not too many beans./
It's not too spicy./

It's not too hot, it's mild./ Has enough spice/ to make it tas-tier. It seems to have a pretty good gravy. Some are watery./

1. Don't get that much meat in a can
2. Beans are cooked just right
3. I can see spices

4. It is tasty
5. Not too spicy/
6. Has just enough beans
7. Moist
8. Not too chewy

9. Fresh taste
10. Canned is usually overcooked

11. Not have a lot of filler
12. Not too many beans

13. Not too hot, it's mild
14. Has enough spice/
15. Gravy not watery

Similar answers should be placed in a general category and assigned the same code. For example, individuals asked why they were not purchasing a new microwaveable product might give the following answers:

- We don't buy frozen food very often.
- I like to prepare fresh food.
- Frozen foods are not as tasty as fresh foods.
- I don't like that freezer taste.

All of these answers could be categorized under "dislike frozen foods" and assigned the code 1. Code construction in these situations necessarily must reflect the judgment of the researcher.

A major objective in the code-building process is to accurately transfer the meanings from written responses to numeric codes. Experienced researchers recognize that the key idea in this process is that code building is based on thoughts, not just words. To ensure that coders convey respondents' thoughts, it is sometimes useful for them to see the test product or the mock-up of the test advertisement shown to respondents so that they will better understand the answers to open-ended questions. The end result of code building should be a list, in an abbreviated and orderly form, of all comments and thoughts given in answers to the questions.

TO THE POINT

Slow and steady wins the race.

AESOP

Differentiating categories of answers for the coding of open-ended questions is more difficult than with fixed-alternative questions. Developing an appropriate code from the respondent's exact comments is somewhat of an art. Researchers generally perform a test tabulation to identify verbatim responses from approximately 20 percent of the completed questionnaires and then establish coding categories that reflect the judgment of the person constructing the codes. The **test tabulation** is a small sample of the total number of replies to a particular question. Its purpose is preliminary identification of the stability and distribution of the answers that will determine how to set up a coding scheme. Exhibit 19.8 illustrates open-ended responses and preliminary open-ended codes generated for the question "Why does the chili you just tasted taste closer to homemade?" During the coding procedure, the respondent's opinions are divided into mutually exclusive thought patterns. These separate divisions may consist of a single word, a phrase, or a number of phrases, but in each case represent only one thought. Each separate thought is coded once. When a thought is composed of more than one word or phrase, only the most specific word or phrase is coded.

After tabulating the basic responses the researcher must determine how many answer categories will be acceptable. This will be influenced by the purpose of the study and the limitations of the computer program or plan for data entry. For example, if only one single-digit field is assigned to a particular survey question, the number of possible categories is limited. If an "other" or "miscellaneous" code category appears along with a "don't know/no answer" category, the code construction will be further limited.

test tabulation
During the coding process a small sample of the total number of replies to a particular question are tallied to construct coding categories.

Devising the Coding Scheme

The coding schemes should not be too elaborate. The coder's task is only to summarize the data. Table 19.1 shows a test tabulation for airport visitors' responses to a question that asked for comments about the Honolulu Airport. After the first cut at devising the coding scheme, the researcher must decide whether to revise it and whether the codes are appropriate for answering management's questions. A preliminary scheme with too many categories can always be collapsed or reduced at a later time in the analysis. If initial coding is too abstract and only a few categories are established, revising the codes to more concrete statements will be difficult unless the raw data are recorded.

In the Honolulu Airport example, the preliminary tabulation contained too many codes, but it could be reduced to a smaller number of categories. For example, the heading *Friendly/Attractive Personnel* could include the responses *Friendly staff/people, Polite VIP/Friendly/Helpful,* and *Cute VIP.* Experienced coders group answers under generalized headings that are pertinent to the research question. It is important to make the codes consistent. Individual coders should give the same code to similar responses. The categories should be sufficiently unambiguous so that coders will not classify items in different ways.

Coding open-ended questions is a very complex issue, and certain technical treatises concerning this subject may be referred to if complex problems develop.

Code Book

Up to this point we have assumed that each code's position in the data matrix already has been determined. However, this plan generally forms after the coding scheme has been designed for every question.

The **code book** identifies each variable in the study and its location on the floppy disk or other input medium. With the code book the researcher can identify any variable's description, code name, and field. Exhibit 19.9 illustrates a portion of a code book from the travel study illustrated in Exhibit 19.7. Notice that the first few fields record the study number, city, and other information used for identification purposes. Researchers commonly identify individual respondents by giving each an identification number or questionnaire number. When each interview is identified with a number entered into each computer record, errors discovered in the tabulation process can be checked on the questionnaire

code book
A book that identifies each variable in a study and a variable's description, code name, and position on the disk or tape.

Table 19.1 **Open-Ended Responses to a Survey about the Honolulu Airport**

	NUMBER
Prices high: restaurant/coffee shop/snack bar	90
Dirty—filthy—smelly restrooms/airport	65
Very good/good/excellent/great	59
Need air-conditioning	52
Nice/beautiful	45
Gift shops expensive	32
Too warm/too hot	31
Friendly staff/people	25
Airport is awful/bad	23
Long walk between terminal/gates	21
Clean airport	17
Employees rude/unfriendly/poor attitude	16
More signs/maps in lobby/streets	16
Like it	15
Love gardens	11
Need video games/arcade	10
More change machines/different locations	8
More padded benches/comfortable waiting area	8
More security personnel including HPD	8
Replace shuttle with moving walkways	8
Complaint: flight delay	7
Cool place	7
Crowded	7
Provide free carts for carry-on bags	7
Baggage storage inconvenient/need in different locations	6
Floor plan confusing	6
Mailbox locations not clear/more needed	6
More restaurants and coffee shops/more variety	6
Need a place to nap	6
Polite VIP/friendly/helpful	6
Poor help in gift shops/rude/unfriendly	6
Slow baggage delivery/service	6
Very efficient/organized	6
Excellent food	5
Install chilled water drinking fountains	5
Love Hawaii	5
More TV sets	5
Noisy	5
People at sundries/camera rude	5
Shuttle drivers rude	5
Something to do for passengers with long waits	5
Airport too spread out	4
Better information for departing/arriving flights	4
Better parking for employees	4
Better shuttle service needed	4
Cute VIP	4

> *Exhibit 19.9* **Portion of a Code Book from a Travel Study**

Study #45641
January 19 _____
N = 743

Question Number	Field or Column Number	Description and Meaning of Code Values
—	1–5	Study number (45641)
—	6	City
		1. Chicago
		2. Gary
		3. Ft. Wayne
		4. Bloomington
—	7–9	Interview number (3 digits on upper left-hand corner of questionnaire)
A	Not entered	Family, work for
		1. Travel agency
		2. Advertising agency
		3. Marketing research company
B	Not entered	Interviewed past month
		1. Yes
		2. No
1.	10	Traveled in past 3 months
		1. Yes
		2. No
2.	11	Purpose last trip
		1. Business
		2. Vacation
		3. Personal
	12	Purpose second last trip
		1. Business
		2. Vacation
		3. Personal
	13	Purpose other trips
		1. Business
		2. Vacation
		3. Personal

---

to verify the answer. When there are several answers to a single question, as in question 2b of Exhibit 19.6, the codes must be spread into several fields because of the possibility of multiple answers.

Production Coding

The actual process of transferring the data from the questionnaire or data collection form after the data have been collected is called **production coding.** Depending on the nature of the data collection form, codes may be written directly on the instrument or on a special **coding sheet,** which is on 80-column ruled paper that is a facsimile of the data matrix. The coding should be done in a central location so that a supervisor can help solve interpretation problems. The value of training coders should not be overlooked:

> The research staff should prepare one or two practice interviews-questionnaires made up by the research staff in duplicate so that all coders working on the study will be practice-coding the same interview. The few hours of time invested in training pay off highly in the reduction of coding errors. The objectives of coder training are to demonstrate the consistent and proper application of codes and to encourage the proper use of administrative procedures.[1]

production coding
The physical activity of transfering the data from the questionaire or data collection form after the data have been collected.

coding sheet
Ruled paper that is a facsimile of the data matrix; used to record codes.

Editing and Coding Combined. Frequently the person coding the questionnaire will perform certain editing functions. For example, the respondent may be asked to indicate an occupational title that subsequently may be coded for socioeconomic status. A question that asks for a description of the job or business often is used to ensure that there will be no problem in classifying the responses. For example, respondents who indicate "salesperson" could write their job description as "selling shoes in a shoe store" or "selling IBM supercomputers to the defense department." Generally, coders will perform this type of editing function. If questions arise, they can seek the help of a tabulation supervisor.

Computerized Data Processing. Most studies having large sample sizes use a computer for data processing. The process of transforming data from a research project, such as answers to a survey questionnaire, to computers is referred to as **data entry.** Several alternative means of entering data into the computer exist. A research system using computer-assisted telephone interviewing or with on-line direct data entry equipment automatically stores and tabulates responses as they are collected, which substantially reduces clerical errors that occur during the editing and coding process. Also for highly structured questionnaires **optical scanning systems** may be used to directly read material from *marked sense* questionnaires into the computer's memory. This type of system requires the mark sensing of "small circles" on a special sheet of paper devised for optical scanning (see Exhibit 19.10).

data entry
In data processing the activity of transforming data from a research project to computers.

optical scanning system
A data processing input device that directly reads material from mark sensed questionnaires.

Exhibit 19.10 An Optical Scanning Questionnaire

A8404 EP01-25394:321 NCS Trans-Optic®

PIRATES 1887 1987

PITTSBURGH PIRATES FAN SURVEY

In order to help us know you and serve you better, we would appreciate your completing this fan survey. If you wish to be eligible for today's special prize drawing (four club box seats to the game of your choice) please fill in your name and address. For other questions please darken the circle for the appropriate response.

1. GENDER: M F
2. AGE: 6-12 ○ 13-18 ○ 19-25 ○ 26-34 ○ 35-49 ○ 50+ ○

3. HOUSEHOLD INCOME: $0-9,999 ○ $10,000-19,999 ○ $20,000-34,999 ○ $35,000-49,999 ○ $50,000+ ○

4. HOUSEHOLD SIZE: I live alone ○ I live with 1 2 3 4 5 6+ other persons (including children)

5. Please check your highest level of education: Attended junior high or grade school ○ Attended high school ○ High school graduate ○ Attended college ○ College graduate ○ Post graduate ○

6. How many years have you been attending Pirate baseball? 1 2 3 4 5 6 7 8 9 10+

7. Please mark the number of Pirate games you attended last season: 0 1 2 3 4 5 6 7 8 9 10 11 12 13 14 15 16 17 18 19 20 21 22 23 24 25 26 27 28 29 30 31 32 33 34 35 36 37 38 39 40 41 42 43 44 45 46 47 48 49 50 51 52 53 54 55 56 57 58 59 60 61 62 63 64 65 66 67 68 69 70 71 72 73 74 75 76 77 78 79 80 81

8. Please mark the number of Pirate games you PLAN to attend this year: 1 2 3 4 5 6 7 8 9 10 11 12 13 14 15 16 17 18 19 20 21 22 23 24 25 26 27 28 29 30 31 32 33 34 35 36 37 38 39 40 41 42 43 44 45 46 47 48 49 50 51 52 53 54 55 56 57 58 59 60 61 62 63 64 65 66 67 68 69 70 71 72 73 74 75 76 77 78 79 80 81

9. Are you a season ticket holder? Yes ○ No ○ If you answered YES, what type of season ticket plan did you buy? Full Season ○ Night (Mon.-Thurs.) ○ Weekend Night (Fri & Sat) ○ Daylight ○ Fan Flex ○

10. What type of seat did you purchase for today's game? Club Box ○ Mezzanine Box ○ Terrace Box ○ Reserved ○ General Admission ○

11. With whom did you attend today's game? (You may select more than one.) Family ○ Spouse ○ Date ○ Friend(s) ○ Group ○ Business Associate ○ Alone ○ Other ○ If other, please specify ______

12. How many days in advance did you buy your tickets for today's game? 0 1 2 3 4 5 6 7 8 9 10 11 12 13 14 15 16 17 18 19 20 21 22 23 24 25 26 27 28 29 30 31 32 33 34 35 36 37 38 39 40 41 42 43 44 45 46 47 48 49 50 51 52 53 54 55 56 57 58 59 60 61 62 63 64 65 66 67 68 69 70 71 72 73 74 75 76 77 78 79 80 81+

13. Where did you travel from for today's game? Home ○ Work ○ Other ○ If other, please specify ______

14. LOCATION OF WORK: Downtown ○ North ○ South ○ East ○ West ○ Other ○ If other, please specify ______

15. What was your approximate travel time to today's game? (In minutes) 1 2 3 4 5 6 7 8 9 10 11 12 13 14 15 16 17 18 19 20 21 22 23 24 25 26 27 28 29 30 31 32 33 34 35 36 37 38 39 40 41 42 43 44 45 46 47 48 49 50 51 52 53 54 55 56 57 58 59 60 61+

16. Please indicate the game starting time you prefer.

WEEKDAY NIGHTS (Monday-Thursday)	6:35 p.m. ○	7:05 p.m. ○	7:35 p.m. ○
WEEKEND NIGHTS (Friday-Saturday)	6:35 p.m. ○	7:05 p.m. ○	7:35 p.m. ○

NAME ______
ADDRESS ______
CITY ______ **STATE** ______
ZIP ______
PHONE ______

17. Which TV stations do you watch and approximately how often? (You may mark more than one.)

	EVERY DAY	5-6 TIMES A WEEK	3-4 TIMES A WEEK	1-2 TIMES A WEEK	NEVER
KDKA	○	○	○	○	○
WPXI	○	○	○	○	○
WTAE	○	○	○	○	○
WPGH	○	○	○	○	○
WPTT	○	○	○	○	○
Others-please specify					
______	○	○	○	○	○
______	○	○	○	○	○

18. Which Radio stations do you listen to and approximately how often? (You may mark more than one.)

AM STATIONS	EVERY DAY	5-6 TIMES A WEEK	3-4 TIMES A WEEK	1-2 TIMES A WEEK	NEVER
KDKA	○	○	○	○	○
WTAE	○	○	○	○	○
KQV	○	○	○	○	○
WTKN	○	○	○	○	○
Others-please specify					
______	○	○	○	○	○
______	○	○	○	○	○
FM STATIONS					
B94	○	○	○	○	○
Y97	○	○	○	○	○
WHTX	○	○	○	○	○
WWSW	○	○	○	○	○
WDVE	○	○	○	○	○
Others-please specify					
______	○	○	○	○	○
______	○	○	○	○	○

19. What Newspapers do you read and approximately how often? (You may mark more than one.)

	EVERY DAY	SUN	MON	TUE	WED	THU	FRI	SAT
Pgh. Press	○	○	○	○	○	○	○	○
Pgh. Post Gazette	○		○	○	○	○	○	○
Others-please specify								
______	○	○	○	○	○	○	○	○
______	○	○	○	○	○	○	○	○

When data are not optically scanned or directly entered into the computer the moment they are collected, data processing begins with keyboarding. The keyboard equipment transfers coded data from the questionnaires or coding sheets onto a hard drive or floppy disk. As in every stage of the research process, there is some concern as to whether the data entry job has been done correctly. Keyboard operators, like anyone else, may make errors. To ensure 100 percent accuracy in transferring the codes to the tape, the job is *verified* by a second keyboard operator, who checks the accuracy of the data entered. If an error has been made, the verifier corrects the data entry. This process of verifying the data is never performed by the same person who entered the original data. A person who misread the coded questionnaire during the keyboarding operation might make the same mistake during the verifying process, and the mistake might go undetected.

Keyboard operators prefer to have the data on coding sheets so that they do not have to page through the questionnaire to enter the data. However, this usually increases the time and effort required for coding. Coding on the actual questionnaire eliminates the need to transfer the answers to coding paper. The particular resources of the project will dictate which source to use as input. Several of the questionnaires illustrated in this chapter indicate how coding may be placed on the questionnaire itself.

Recoding

In a number of situations it is easier to enter the raw data into the computer using the precoding on the questionnaire and then program the computer to **recode** certain raw data. This often occurs when a researcher measures attitudes with a series of both positive and negative statements. Reversing the order of the codes for the negative statements so that the statements' codes reflect the same order of magnitude as the positive statements requires only a simple data transformation. For instance, if a seven-point scale for variable 1 (VAR1) is to be recoded, the following programming statement might subtract the original code score from 8:

$$VAR1 = 8 - VAR1$$

Collapsing the number of categories or values of a variable or creating new variables also requires recoding. These topics, which are interrelated with data analysis, are discussed in Chapter 20.

recode
Using a computer to convert original codes used for raw data to codes that are more suitable for analysis.

Advanced scanner technology may be used as a form of data entry. With modern scanning devices, store audits can be conducted more quickly and accurately than in the past when data were recorded by hand.

Error Checking

The final stage in the coding process is error checking and verification, or data cleaning, to ensure that all codes are legitimate. For example, computer software can examine the entered data and identify coded values that lie outside the permissible range of acceptable answers. For example, if "sex" is coded 1 for "male" and 2 for "female" and a 3 code is found, a mistake obviously has occurred and an adjustment must be made.

Summary

Raw data must be edited and coded to be put into a form suitable for analysis. Editing involves checking and adjusting for errors or omissions on questionnaires or other data collection forms. Its purpose is to ensure completeness, consistency, and readability of the data. Field supervisors are responsible for preliminary editing. The daily field edit allows rapid follow-up on errors; interviewers may recall responses omitted or be able to recontact respondents. The in-house editor checks for consistency among answers and for completeness or may rearrange responses on an open-ended questionnaire. The editor's task includes readying material for coding.

Coding is the process of identifying and classifying each answer with a numerical score or other character symbol. It usually involves entering the data for computer storage. The coding categories should be exhaustive and provide for all possible responses. They should also be mutually exclusive and independent so that there is no overlap among categories. On highly structured questionnaires, the categories may be precoded. With open-ended questions, the answers are postcoded. This means that the categories are assigned after the data have been collected. The categories must be assigned according to the researcher's judgment. It is better to assign too many categories than too few, and it is easier to collapse several categories into one than to increase the number of categories. A code book identifies each variable and the codes for responses.

Production coding is the actual process of transferring the data from the questionnaire to the storage medium. Data are commonly keyboarded onto magnetic tape, disk, or hard drive. Other possibilities include computer systems for entering data directly into computer storage as they are collected. After the raw data are in the computer, programs may recode variables or check for errors.

Key Terms and Concepts

Editing	Field	Production coding
Coding	Record	Coding sheet
Field editing	File	Data entry
In-house editing	Data matrix	Optical scanning system
Item nonresponse	Direct data entry	Recode
Plug value	Test tabulation	
Codes	Code book	

Questions for Review and Critical Thinking

1. What is the purpose of editing? Provide some examples of questions that might need editing.
2. Suppose respondents in a political survey were asked if they favored or opposed the Agricultural Trade Act. Edit the following open-ended answers:
   a. I don't know what it is, so I'll oppose it.
   b. Favorable, though I don't really know what it is.
   c. You caught me on that. I don't know, but from the sound of it I favor it.
3. What are the potential meanings of "don't know" responses in a political poll to evaluate two candidates for city commissioner?
4. Comment on the coding scheme for the following question: "In which of these groups did your total *family* income, from all sources, fall last year—1995—before taxes? Just tell me the code number." (Refer to the table.)

Response	Code
Under $9,999	01
$10,000 to $14,999	02
$15,000 to $24,999	03
$25,000 to $39,999	04
$40,000 to $54,999	05
$55,000 to $69,999	06
$70,000 to $89,999	07
$90,000 to $99,999	08
$100,000 to $124,999	09
$125,000 or over	10
Refused to answer	11
Don't know	98
No answer	99

5. Suppose the following information had been gathered about the occupation of several respondents. How would you classify the following respondents' answers in the occupational coding scheme discussed in this chapter: plumber, butcher, retail sales, X-ray technician, and veterinarian?
6. A frequently asked question on campus is, "What is your major?" Suppose you wish to develop a coding scheme for this question. What would your scheme look like?
7. A researcher asks you to help build a coding scheme for types (not brands) of coffee found in supermarkets. These might be regular, instant, or decaffeinated. About how many codes might be needed?
8. A researcher asks, "What do you remember about advertising for Gillette Sensor Excell razors?" How should the code book for this question be structured? What problems does it present?
9. A sales manager records the number of days worked, the number of sales calls made, and actual sales volume for each of 15 sales representatives during October. Outline a data matrix for this database.
10. Design a short questionnaire with fewer than five fixed-alternative questions to measure student satisfaction with your college bookstore. Interview five classmates, then arrange the database into a data matrix.
11. A researcher investigated attitudes toward her company and noticed that one individual answered all image questions at one end of a bipolar scale. Should she decline to use this questionnaire in the data analysis?

 ## Exploring the Internet

1. The Research Triangle Institute (http://www.rti.org) has a Web page describing its coding of survey research data. Click on its Statistics, Health, and Social Policy page and surf to its coding factsheet (www.rti/units/shsp/factsheets/B015.htm).
2. The University of Michigan's the Institute for Social Research (http://www. isr.umich.edu/index.html) houses the The Survey Research Center where many business research projects (http://www.isr.umich.edu/src/projects. html) go to the Surveys of Consumers (http://athena.sca.isr.umich.edu scripts/contents.asp) and see how the questionnaire is coded.
3. Search the Internet to learn what companies offer optical scanning systems and services.

Case 19.1 U.S. Department of the Interior–Heritage Conservation and Recreation Service

SOME YEARS AGO THE U.S. DEPARTMENT OF THE INTE-rior conducted a telephone survey to help plan for future outdoor recreation. A nine-page question-naire concerning participation in outdoor recre-ational activities and satisfaction with local facilities was administered by the Opinion Research Corpora-tion of Princeton, New Jersey, to 4,029 respondents. The last two pages of the questionnaire appear in Case Exhibit 19.1-1. Assume the data will be entered onto floppy disks; each data entry should include the following information:

- Respondent number
- State code (all 50 states)

QUESTIONS

1. Design the coding for this portion of the questionnaire. Assume that previ-ous pages of the questionnaire will follow these data.

Case Exhibit 19.1-1 Sample Pages from Questionnaire

The following questions are for background purposes.

32. Do you live in an . . .
   - ☐ Urban location
   - ☐ Suburban location
   - ☐ Rural location

33. Counting yourself, how many members of your family live here? (If "1" on Q. 33, go to Q. 35) _____

34. How many family members are . . .

   Over 65 years _____
   40 to 65 years _____
   21 to 39 years _____
   12 to 20 years _____
   5 to 11 years _____
   Under 5 years _____

35. What is your age? (Years) _____

36. In school, what is the highest grade (or year) you have completed? (Circle response)

Elementary school	01	02	03	04	05	06
Junior high school	07	08			
High school	09	10	11	12	
College	13	14	15	16	
Graduate school	17	18	19	20	21

37. What is your occupation? What kind of work is that?
   - ☐ Professional, technical, and kindred workers
   - ☐ Farmers
   - ☐ Managers, officials, and proprietors
   - ☐ Clerical and kindred workers
   - ☐ Sales workers
   - ☐ Craftspersons, forepersons, and kindred workers
   - ☐ Operatives and kindred workers
   - ☐ Service workers
   - ☐ Laborers, except farm and mine

   - ☐ Retired, widow, widower
   - ☐ Student
   - ☐ Unemployed, on relief, laid off → Go to Q. 43
   - ☐ Housewife

   - ☐ Other (specify) _____

38. How many hours a week do you work at your place of employment? _____ (hours)

39. How many days of vacation do you get in a year? _____ (days)

40. Please tell me which of the following income categories most closely describe the total family income for the year before taxes, including wages and all other income. Is it . . .
   - ☐ Under $12,000
   - ☐ $12,000–$20,000
   - ☐ $20,001–$30,000
   - ☐ $30,001–$50,000
   - ☐ $50,001–$100,000
   - ☐ Over $100,001

41. Sex of respondent . . .
   - ☐ Male
   - ☐ Female

42. What is the ZIP code at your place of employment?

This concludes the interview; thank you very much for your cooperation and time.

Case 19.2 Shampoo 9–10

A SHAMPOO PRODUCT, CODE NAME "9—10," WAS GIVEN TO women for trial use. The respondents were asked their likes and dislikes about the product. Some sample codes are given in Case Exhibits 19.2-1 and 19.2-2.

The coding instructions were as follows. There were two separate sets of codes: The codes in Case Exhibit 19.2-1 were for coding the likes, and the codes in Case Exhibit 19.2-2 were for coding the dislikes. The headings identify fields in the data matrix and the different attributes of shampoo. The specific codes are listed under each attribute. If you had been coding, you would have first looked for the correct heading, then located the correct comment under that heading and used that number as the code.

For example, if under the "likes" questions a respondent had said, "The shampoo was gentle and mild," you would have looked in field 10, since this

was the "gentleness" field, and found the comment "Gentle/mild/not harsh"; you would then have written "11" next to the comment. If under "dislikes" someone had said, "I would rather have a shampoo with a creme rinse," you would have looked in field 16 for comparison to other shampoos and written in a "74" ("Prefer one with a creme rinse") besides that response.

The sample questionnaires appear in Case Exhibit 19.2-3.

QUESTIONS

1. Code each of the three questionnaires.
2. Evaluate this coding scheme.

Case Exhibit 19.2-1   Sample Codes for "Likes" Questions

Test No. _____ Shampoo _____

Question: Likes

Field 10	Gentleness	Field 11	Result on Hair
11	Gentle/mild/not harsh	21	Good for hair/helps hair
12	Wouldn't strip hair of natural oils	22	Leaves hair manageable/no tangles/ no need for creme rinse
13	Doesn't cause/helps flyaway hair	23	Gives hair body
14	Wouldn't dry out hair	24	Mends split ends
15	Wouldn't make skin/scalp break out	25	Leaves hair not flyaway
16	Organic/natural	26	Leaves hair silky/smooth
17		27	Leaves hair soft
18		28	Leaves hair shiny
19		29	Hair looks/feels/good/clean
10		20	
1–		2–	
1+	Other gentleness	2+	Other results on hair

Field 12	Cleaning	Field 13	Miscellaneous
31	Leaves no oil/keeps hair dry	41	Cheaper/economical/good price
32	It cleans well	42	Smells good/nice/clean
33	Lifts out oil/dirt/artifical conditioners	43	Hairdresser recommended
34	Don't have to scrub as much	44	Comes in different formulas
35	No need to wash as often/keeps hair cleaner longer	45	Concentrated/use only a small amount
36	Doesn't leave a residue on scalp	46	Good for whole family (unspecified)
37	Good lather	47	
38	Good for oily hair	48	
39		49	
30		40	
3–		4–	Other miscellaneous
3+	Other cleaninig	4+	Don't know/nothing

Case Exhibit 19.2-2   Sample Codes for "Dislikes" Questions

Test No. _____ Shampoo _____

Question: Dislikes

Field 14	Harshness	Field 15	Cleaning
51	Too strong	61	Doesn't clean well
52	Strips hair/takes too much oil out	62	Leaves a residue on scalp
53	Dries hair out	63	Poor lather
54	Skin reacts badly to it	64	Not good for oily hair
55		65	
56		66	
57		67	
58		68	
59		69	
50		60	
5–		6–	
5+	Other gentleness	6+	Other cleaning

Field 16	Comparison to Others	Field 17	Miscellaneous
71	Prefer herbal/organic shampoo	81	Don't like the name
72	Prefer medicated/dandruff shampoo	82	Too expensive
73	Same as other shampoos—doesn't work any differently	83	Not economical for long hair
74	Prefer one with a creme rinse	84	Use what hairdresser recommends
75	Prefer another brand (unspecified)	85	
76		86	
77		87	
78		88	
79		89	
70		80	
7–		8–	Other miscellaneous
7+	Other comparison to others	8+	Don't know what/disliked/nothing

Case Exhibit 19.2-3 **Sample Questionnaires for Shampoo 9-10 Survey**

1. What, if anything, did you particularly like about this shampoo?

    My hairdresser recommends it, so it must be good for your hair. It smells good too.

2. What, if anything, did you particularly dislike about this shampoo?

    It's too expensive. It doesn't have a cream rinse, so you still have to buy that too. It really doesn't work any better than other shampoos for the amount of money you pay for it.

---

1. What, if anything, did you particularly like about this shampoo?

    There are different kinds for different types of hair. I use the one for dry hair. It doesn't dry out my hair. It leaves it soft & shiny. It works so well I only have to use a little bit for each shampoo.

2. What, if anything, did you particularly dislike about this shampoo?

    Nothing. I liked it.

---

1. What, if anything, did you particularly like about this shampoo?

    I have limp, oily hair and have to wash it real often. With this shampoo I found it stayed cleaner longer, so I don't have to shampoo as often and my hair has more body.

2. What, if anything, did you particularly dislike about this shampoo?

    I like the shampoo but I don't think the name is very appealing.

Case 19.3 **Questionnaire Editing**

A MAIL QUESTIONNAIRE THAT INCLUDED A CONCEPT statement describing Nilla Wafer Sandwich Cookies, a proposed new product, was sent to members of a consumer panel. Exhibit 19.3-1 presents an excerpt from a questionnaire that a respondent filled out.

QUESTION

1. Does this questionnaire need editing? Please explain why or why not.

Case Exhibit 19.3-1 **Respondent Questionnaire (Completed)**

4a. Now that you have read the description for Nilla Wafer Sandwich Cookies, which statement best describes how likely you would be to buy Nilla Wafer Sandwich Cookies if it were being sold in the stores where you normally shop? ("X" ONE BOX)

36

Definitely would buy .... ❏ 1
Probably would buy .... ❏ 2
Might or might not buy .... ❏ 3
Probably would not buy .... ❏ 4
Definitely would not buy................... ☒ 5

4b. Why do you feel that way about buying this product? (PLEASE BE AS SPECIFIC AS POSSIBLE)

I don't normally buy cookies – I bake them myself. I feel Nilla Wafers are   (37)   (42)
pretty bland and have only used them in recipes that require them.   (38)   (43)
   (39)   (44)
   (40)   (45)
_____ (41)   (46)

47-51R

5. Now, thinking of each different variety of Nilla Wafer Sandwich Cookies, please indicate how likely you would be to buy each variety if it were available in the stores where you normally shop? ("X" ONE BOX FOR EACH VARIETY)

	Definitely Would Buy	Probably Would Buy	Might or Might Not Buy	Probably Would Not Buy	Definitely Would Not Buy	
Vanilla Creme	☒ 1	❏ 2	❏ 3	❏ 4	❏ 5	(52)
Chocolate Fudge	☒ 1	❏ 2	❏ 3	❏ 4	❏ 5	(53)
Peanut Butter.........................	☒ 1	❏ 2	❏ 3	❏ 4	❏ 5	(54)
Strawberry Jam.......................	☒ 1	❏ 2	❏ 3	❏ 4	❏ 5	(55)

56-62R

6. Compared to other products now on the market, would you expect this new product to be . . . ? ("X" ONE BOX)

Very different ..... ❏ 1   Somewhat different ..... ☒ 2   Not at all different ..... ❏ 3

7. Overall, how believable is the description of this product? ("X" ONE BOX)

Very believable ..... ☒ 1   Somewhat believable ..... ❏ 2   Not at all believable ..... ❏ 3

8. Considering the price of this product, do you think this product would be . . . ? ("X" ONE BOX)

65

A very good value for the money .... ❏ 1
A somewhat good value for the money......... ❏ 2
An average value for the money .... ❏ 3
A somewhat poor value for the money......... ❏ 4
A very poor value for the money .... ☒ 5

9. Considering the price of this product, do you think the price is . . . ? ("X" ONE BOX)

66

Very expensive .... ❏ 1
Somewhat expensive .... ☒ 2
About Average .... ❏ 3
Somewhat inexpensive.............. ❏ 4
Very Inexpensive .... ❏ 5

10. How often would you purchase this product? ("X" ONE BOX)

67

More than once a week .... ❏ 1	Once a month .... ❏ 5
Once a week........................ ❏ 2	Once every 2–3 months.................... ❏ 6
3 times a month .... ❏ 3	Less than once every 3 months......... ❏ 7
2 times a month .... ❏ 4	Would not purchase .... ☒ 8

Chapter 20

Basic Data Analysis

Descriptive Statistics

THE YANKELOVICH MONITOR CONDUCTS LONGITUDINAL SURVEYS to track social trends. According to a 1999 study by Yankelovich,[1] 92% of kids fix their own meals sometimes. While snacks and breakfast were prepared by children most frequently, 31% said they even fix their own dinners. Echoing the too-busy-to-cook trend that has led to grab-and-go dinners, the child chef phenom has grown over the past four years: While 48% said they make meals for themselves most of the time (vs. 40% in 1995), the percentage preparing meals for the entire family has increased even higher: More than one-quarter (26%) do so today, compared with 15% in 1995.

Furthermore, it doesn't seem as if most children consider cooking a grueling chore. 92% of those surveyed said they like or don't mind preparing meals. Reasons cited for enjoying this task included:

Can choose the food you like   67%
It's fun to cook 61%
Can eat what you want 57%
Can eat as little or as much as you want   51%
Can invent new/different food combos   47%

These interesting findings illustrate the results of a typical descriptive analysis. This chapter explains how to perform descriptive analysis.

The Nature of Descriptive Analysis

Marketing researchers edit and code data to provide input that will result in tabulated information for answering research questions. With this input, researchers statistically describe project results. Within this context the term *analysis* is difficult to define because it refers to a variety of activities and processes. One form of analysis consists of summarizing large quantities of raw data so that the results can be interpreted. Categorizing, or separating out the components or relevant parts of the whole data set, is also a form of analysis for comprehending patterns in the data. Rearranging, ordering, or manipulating data may provided descriptive information that will answer questions posed in the problem definition. All forms of analysis attempt to portray data so that the results may be studied and interpreted in concise and meaningful ways.

descriptive analysis
The transformation of raw data into a form that will make them easy to understand and interpret; rearranging, ordering, and manipulating data to generate descriptive information.

Descriptive analysis refers to the transformation of raw data into a form that will make them easy to understand and interpret. Describing responses or observations typically is the first stage of analysis. Calculation of averages, frequency distributions, and percentage distributions are the most common ways to summarize data.

Chapter 13 indicated that the type of measurement scale used in marketing research dictates the form of statistical analysis. Exhibit 20.1 shows how the level of scale measurement influences the choice of descriptive statistics. It is important to remember that all statistics appropriate for lower-order scales (nominal is the lowest) are suitable for higher-order scales (ratio is the highest).

Exhibit 20.1 **Descriptive Statistics Permissible with Different Types of Measurement**

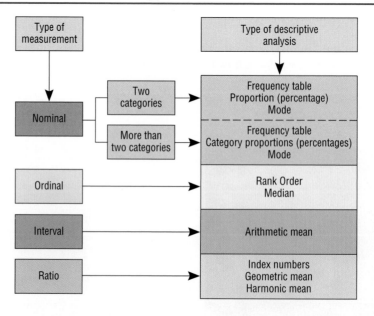

All statistics appropriate for lower-order scales (nominal is the lowest) are appropriate for higher-order scales (ratio is the highest).

Table 20.1   A Frequency Table for a Simple Tabulation

DO YOU SHOP AT IGA?

RESPONSE	FREQUENCY
Yes	330
No	120
Total	450

As the analysis progresses beyond the descriptive stage, researchers generally apply the tools of inferential statistics. Univariate analysis, covered in Chapter 21, allows researchers to assess the statistical significance of various hypotheses about a single variable.

Tabulation

Tabulation refers to the orderly arrangement of data in a table or other summary format. Counting the number of responses to a question and arranging them in a frequency distribution is a simple tabulation, or *marginal tabulation*. Simple tabulation of the responses or observations on a question-by-question or item-by-item basis provides the most basic—and in many cases the most useful—form of information for the researcher. It tells the researcher how frequently each response occurs. This starting point for analysis requires the researcher to count responses or observations for each category or code assigned to a variable. Table 20.1 illustrates a **frequency table**. When this tabulation process is done by hand, it is called *tallying*. Large sample sizes generally require computer tabulation of the data.

frequency table
The arrangement of statistical data in a row-and-column format that exhibits the count of responses or observations for each category assigned to a variable.

Coca-Cola's data analysis shows that the typical resident of Brooklyn, New York, drinks 105 Cokes annually. On Staten Island, however, the average number of Cokes consumed in a year is a whopping 429.[2] Descriptive analysis transforms raw data into a form that is easy to understand and interpret.

Percentages

Whether the data are tabulated by computer or by hand, percentage, cumulative percentages, and frequency distributions are useful. For example, most people find part B of Table 20.2 easier to interpret than part A because the percentages in part B are useful for comparing data for various time periods.

When a frequency distribution portrays only a single characteristic as a percentage of the total, the proportion of occurrence is defined. It may be expressed as a percentage, a fraction, or a decimal value.

Table 20.2 **Percentages Aid the Interpretation of Frequency Distributions and Cross-Tabulations**

(A) Number of People in Projected Population, 2000 to 2020[a]

	Population at End of Period	Population Change
2000 to 2010		
UNITED STATES.	300,431	24,118
Northeast	53,301	1,409
Midwest.	66,332	2,476
South	107,385	10,114
West	73,412	10,120
2010 to 2020		
UNITED STATES.	325,942	25,535
Northeast	53,352	2,057
Midwest.	68,984	2,657
South	117,498	10,116
West	84,109	10,703

(B) Number and Percentage of People in Projected Population, 2000 to 2020[a]

	Population Number	Percent of Population	Population Change	Percent Increase
2000 to 2010				
UNITED STATES.	300,431	100.0	24,118	8.0
Northeast	53,301	17.7	1,409	2.6
Midwest.	66,332	22.1	2,476	3.7
South	107,385	35.8	10,114	9.4
West	73,412	22.4	10,120	13.8
2010 to 2020				
UNITED STATES.	325,942	100.0	25,535	7.8
Northeast	53,352	16.4	2,057	3.9
Midwest.	68,984	21.7	2,657	3.9
South	117,498	36.1	10,116	8.6
West	84,109	25.8	10,703	12.7

[a] Population in thousands.

When discussing percentages, researchers must be precise in their language. For example, the difference between 40 percent and 60 percent is not 20 percent, but 20 *percentage points,* or an increase of 50 percent.

Measures of Central Tendency

According to American Demographics magazine, $435.41 is the average amount spent by college students (excluding transportation and hotel) on a spring break vacation to South Padre Island, Texas.[3] This is a measure of central tendency. Describing central tendencies of the distribution with the *mean, median,* or *mode* is another basic form of descriptive analysis. These measures are most useful when the purpose is to identify typical values of a variable or the most common characteristic of a group. If knowing the average or typical performance will satisfy the information need, these measures, described in Chapter 17, should be considered.

Cross-Tabulation

Mere tabulation of data may answer many research questions; in fact, many studies do not go beyond examining simple tabulations of question-by-question responses to a survey. Although frequency counts, percentage distributions, or averages summarize considerable information, stopping with simple tabulation may not yield the full value of the research. Most data can be further organized in

Table 20.3 Cross-Tabulation Tables from a Survey on Ethics in America

(A) REPORTED BEHAVIOR BY GENERAL PUBLIC (PERCENTAGE WHO HAVE EVER DONE EACH ACTIVITY)

GENERAL PUBLIC

| ACTIVITY | AGE | | GENDER | | EDUCATION | |
	UNDER 50 YEARS OLD	OVER 50 YEARS OLD	MEN	WOMEN	COLLEGE GRADUATE	HIGH SCHOOL GRADUATE
Taken home work supplies	50	26	47	33	58	21
Called in sick to work when not ill	40	18	Not reported		36	21

(B) REPORTED BEHAVIOR (PERCENTAGE WHO HAVE EVER DONE EACH ACTIVITY)

ACTIVITY PUBLIC	BUSINESS EXECUTIVES	GENERA
Taken home work supplies	74	40
Called in sick to work when not ill	14	31
Used company telephone for personal long-distance calls	78	15
Overstated deductions somewhat on tax forms	35	13
Driven while drunk	80	33
Saw a fellow employee steal something at work and did not report it	7	26

cross-tabulation

A technique for organizing data by groups, categories, or classes, thus facilitating comparisons; a joint frequency distribution of observations on two or more sets of variables.

a variety of ways. For example, in a survey that samples both men and women, the data commonly are analyzed by separating them into groups or categories based on sex. Analyzing results by groups, categories, or classes is the technique of **cross-tabulation.** The purpose of categorization and cross-tabulation is to allow the inspections and comparisons of differences among groups. This form of analysis also helps determine the type of relationship among variables. Since market segmentation is a major component of marketing strategy for many organizations, cross-tabulating the results of marketing research helps clarify the research findings as they pertain to market segments.

Table 20.3 summarizes several cross-tabulations from American citizens' responses to a questionnaire on ethical behavior in the United States. A researcher interested in the relative ethical perspectives of business executives and the general public can inspect this table and easily compare the two groups. The percentage table illustrates the added value of calculating percentages.

Another example of the usefulness of categorization and cross-tabulation can be found in most experiments. Obviously the data from the experimental and control groups should be separated or partitioned because researchers wish to compare the effects of a treatment.

Contingency Table

contingency table

The results of a cross-tabulation of two variables, such as survey questions.

Part a of Table 20.4 shows how the cross-tabulation of two survey questions (or variables) results in a **contingency table,** or data matrix. The frequency counts for the question "Do you shop at IGA?" are presented as column totals. The total number of men and women in the sample are presented as row totals. These row

---

Table 20.4 Possible Cross-Tabulations of One Question

(A) CROSS-TABULATION OF QUESTION "DO YOU SHOP AT IGA?" BY SEX OF RESPONDENT

	YES	No	TOTAL
Men	150	75	225
Women	180	48	225
Total	330	120	450

(B) PERCENTAGE CROSS-TABULATION OF QUESTION "DO YOU SHOP AT IGA?" BY SEX OF RESPONDENT, ROW PERCENTAGE

	YES	No	TOTAL (BASE)
Men	66.7%	33.3%	100% (225)
Women	80.0%	20.0%	100% (225)

(c) PERCENTAGE CROSS-TABULATION OF QUESTION "DO YOU SHOP AT IGA?" BY SEX OF RESPONDENT, COLUMN PERCENTAGE

	YES	No
Men	45.5%	62.5%
Women	54.5%	37.5%
Total (120)	100% (base)	100% (330)

and column totals often are called *marginals* because they appear in the table's margin. Each of four cells within part A represents a specific combination of the two variables. The cell that represents women who said they do not shop at IGA has a frequency count of 45.

The contingency table in part A is referred to as a *2 × 2 table* because it has two rows and two columns. Any cross-tabulation table may be classified according to the number of rows by the number of columns (*R* by *C*). Thus, a 3 × 4 table has three rows and four columns.

Percentage Cross-Tabulation

When cross-tabulating data from a survey, percentages help the researcher understand the nature of the relationship by allowing relative comparisons. The total number of respondents or observations may be used as a **base** for computing the percentage in each cell. When the objective of the research is to identify a relationship between the two questions (or variables), one of the questions is commonly chosen as a base for determining percentages. For example, look at the data in parts A, B, and C of Table 20.4. Compare part B with part C. Selecting either the row percentages or the column percentages will emphasize a particular comparison or distribution. The nature of the problem the researcher wishes to answer will determine which marginal total will serve as a base for computing percentages.

base
The number of respondents or observations (in a row or column) used as a basis for computing percentages.

Fortunately, a conventional rule determines the direction of percentages if the researcher has identified which variable is the independent variable and which is the dependent variable: The percentages should be computed *in the direction of the independent variable.* That is, the margin total of the independent variable should be used as the base for computing the percentages. Although survey research does not identify cause-and-effect relationships, one might argue that it is logical to assume that a variable such as gender might predict shopping behavior. Therefore, independent and dependent variables may be established to present the most useful information.

TO THE POINT

The more we study, the more we discover our ignorance.

PERCY BYSSHE SHELLEY

Elaboration and Refinement

The *Oxford Universal Dictionary* defines *analysis* as "the resolution of anything complex into its simplest elements." This suggests that once the researcher has examined the basic relationship between two variables, he or she may wish to investigate this relationship under a variety of different conditions. Typically a third variable is introduced into the analysis to elaborate and refine the researcher's understanding by specifying the conditions under which the relationship is strongest and weakest. In other words, a more elaborate analysis asks: "Will interpretation of the relationship be modified if other variables are simultaneously considered?"

Performing the basic cross-tabulation within various subgroups of the sample is a common form of **elaboration analysis.** The researcher breaks down the analysis for each level of another variable. For example, if the researcher has cross-tabulated shopping behavior by sex (see Table 20.4) and wishes to investi-

elaboration analysis
An analysis of the basic cross-tabulation for each level of another variable, such as subgroups of the sample.

		MARRIED		SINGLE	
		MEN	WOMEN	MEN	WOMEN
"Do you shop at IGA?"					
Yes		55%	80%	86%	80%
No		45%	20%	14%	20%

Table 20.5 Cross-Tabulation of Marital Status, Sex, and Responses to the Question "Do You Shop at IGA?"

gate another variable (say, marital status) that may modify the original relationship, a more elaborate analysis may be conducted. Table 20.5 breaks down the responses to the question "Do you shop at IGA?" by sex and marital status. The data show that marital status does not change the original cross-tabulation relationship among women, but it does change that relationship among men. The analysis suggests that we retain the original conclusion about the relationship between sex and shopping behavior for women; the data confirm our original interpretation. However, our refinements in analysis have pointed out a relationship among men that was not immediately discernible in the two-variable case: A higher percentage of single men shop at IGA than married men. The researcher can then conclude that marital status modifies the original relationship among men, that is, that there is an interaction effect.

moderator variable
A third variable that, when introduced into an analysis, alters or has a contingent effect on the relationship between an independent variable and a dependent variable.

spurious relationship
An apparent relationship between two variables that is not authentic.

In this situation marital status is a moderator variable. A **moderator variable** is a third variable that, when introduced into the analysis, alters or has a contingent effect on the relationship between an independent variable and a dependent variable.

In other situations the addition of a third variable to the analysis may lead us to reject the original conclusion about the relationship. When this occurs, the elaboration analysis will have indicted a **spurious relationship**—the relationship between the original two variables was not authentic. Our earlier example of high ice cream cone sales and drownings at the beach (Chapter 3) illustrated a spurious relationship. Additional discussion of this topic appears in Chapter 23, which deals with measures of association.

Elaborating on the basic cross-tabulation is a form of *multivariate analysis* because more than two variables are simultaneously analyzed to identify complex relationships. When a breakdown of the responses to three or more questions is required, the researcher may use multivariate statistical techniques to investigate the relationship. Such techniques are discussed in Chapter 24.

How Many Cross-Tabulations?

Surveys may ask dozens of questions. Computer-assisted marketing researchers often indulge in "fishing expeditions," cross-tabulating every question on a survey with every other question. Thus, every possible response becomes a possible explanatory variable. All too often this activity provides

---

> **Exhibit 20.2 Quadrant Analysis for a Microwave Meal**

		High Importance, Low Rating	High Importance, High Rating

I
m
p 7 | 7,1 (Easy to Prepare)
o
r 6 | 6,3 (Nutritious) | 6,6 (Good taste)
t 5 | 5,2 | 5,5 (Filling)
a 4 | (Family meal)
n
c
e 3 | 2,1 (Fancy meal) | 2,5 (Late night snack)

R 2 | Low Importance, Low Rating | Low Importance, High Rating
a
t 1
i   1   2   3   4   5   6   7
n
g

Ratings of Product Performance on Each Attribute

---

reams of extra computer output, but no additional insight to management. The number of cross-tabulations should be determined early, when research objectives are stated.

Quadrant Analysis

Quadrant analysis is a variation of cross-tabulation. It plots two rating scale questions in four quadrants of a two-dimensional table. Most research with quadrant analysis portrays or plots relationships between average responses about a product attribute's importance versus average ratings about a company's (or brand's) performance with respect to that product feature. Sometimes the term *importance-performance analysis* is used because consumers rate perceived importance of several attributes and rate how well the company's brand provides (and competitors' brands provide) the benefit associated with the attribute.

Exhibit 20.2 shows a quadrant analysis matrix for a gourmet microwave food product that was evaluated using two seven-point scales.[4] The upper-left quadrant with the combination high importance/low rating shows importance ratings above 4.0 and performance ratings at 4.0 or below.[5] The analysis shows that it is important for a microwave meal to be easy to prepare, but this new product rates low on this attribute. Consumers know what they want, but they are not getting it. The upper-right quadrant, high importance/high rating, shows importance ratings above 4.0 and performance ratings above 4.0. It is important for microwave meals to taste good and this product scores high on this attribute. Marketers often consider attributes in this quadrant to be "hot buttons" that will be useful in positioning the product. The lower quadrants show attributes of low importance to consumers with either low or high product ratings. This microwave product could be eaten as a late night snack, but this attribute is not important to consumers.

quadrant analysis
A variation of cross-tabulation that plots two rating scale questions in four quadrants of a two-dimensional table.

Data Transformation

Data transformation (also called *data conversion*) is the process of changing the original form of the data to a format suitable for performing a data analysis that will achieve research objectives. Researchers often modify the values of scalar data or create new variables. For example, many researchers believe that less response bias will result if interviewers ask respondents for their years of birth rather than their ages even though the objective of the data analysis is to investigate respondents' ages in years. This presents no problem for the research analyst because a simple data transformation is possible. The raw data coded as birth year can easily be transformed to age by subtracting the birth year from the current year.

TO THE POINT

All that we do is done with an eye to something else.

ARISTOTLE

Collapsing or combining adjacent categories of a variable is a common form of data transformation to reduce the number of categories. Exhibit 20.3 shows an example of a Likert scale item that has been collapsed. The "strongly agree" and "agree" response categories have been combined, as have the "strongly disagree" and "disagree" categories. The original five categories have been collapsed into three. In many cases, however, the establishment of categories requires careful thought. For example, how does one categorize women on their orientation toward the feminist movement? The first rule for identifying categories, as in other aspects of marketing research, is that the categories should be related to the research problem and purpose.

Creating new variables by respecifying the data with numeric or logical transformations is another common form of data transformation. For example, Likert summated scales reflect combinations of scores (raw data) from each attitude statement. The summative score for an attitude scale with three statements is calculated as follows:

$$\text{Summative score} = \text{Variable 1} + \text{Variable 2} + \text{Variable 3}$$

Exhibit 20.3 Collapsing a Five-Category Likert Scale

"The checkout lines at the student union bookstore are short."

Likert Scale as It Appeared on the Questionnaire

| Strongly agree | Agree | Neither agree or disagree | Disagree | Strongly disagree |

Tabulation of Responses in Original and Collapsed Versions

5-Point Scale	%	Collapsed Scale	%
Strongly agree	3		
		Strongly agree	15
Agree	12		
Neither agree or disagree	30	Neither agree or disagree	30
Disagree	45		
		Strongly disagree/disagree	55
Strongly disagree	10		

Table 20.6 **Hours of Television Usage per Week**	
HOUSEHOLD SIZE	HOURS:MINUTES
1	41:01
2	47:58
3+	60:49
Total U.S. average	52:36

This can be accomplished by simple arithmetic or by programming a computer with a data transformation equation that creates a new variable for the summative score.

Index Numbers

The consumer price index and the wholesale price index are secondary data sources that are frequently used by marketing researchers. These price indexes, like other **index numbers,** are the result of simple data transformations that allow researchers to compare a variable or set of variables over a given time period with another variable or set of variables over another time period. Scores or observations are recalibrated to relate them to a certain base period or base number.

Consider the information in Table 20.6, related to weekly television viewing (hours : minutes) by household size. Index numbers are computed in the following manner. First, a base number is selected, in this example the U.S. average of 52 hours and 36 minutes. The data transformation computes the index numbers by dividing the score for each category by the base number and multiplying by 100. The index shows percentage changes from the base number, for example:

index number
Score or observation recalibrated to indicate how it relates to a base number.

$$1 \text{ Person} \qquad \frac{41:01}{52:36} = 0.7832 \times 100 = 78.32$$

$$2 \text{ People} \qquad \frac{47:58}{52:36} = 0.9087 \times 100 = 90.87$$

$$3+ \text{ People} \qquad \frac{60:49}{52:36} = 1.1553 \times 100 = 115.53$$

$$\text{Total U.S. average} \qquad \frac{52:36}{52:36} = 1.0000 \times 100 = 100.00$$

If the data are time related, a base year is chosen. The index numbers are then computed by dividing each year's activity by the base-year activity and multiplying by 100. Index numbers require ratio measurement scales.

Calculating Rank Order

Respondents often rank order their brand preferences or other variables of interest to researchers. To summarize these data for all respondents, the analyst performs a data transformation by multiplying the frequency by the rank (score) to develop a new scale that represents the summarized rank orders.

For example, suppose a manager of a frequent-flier program had 10 executives rank their preferences for dream destinations that would be prizes in a sales promotion contest. Table 20.7 shows how the executives ranked each other of four locations: Hawaii, Greece, Paris, and Hong Kong. Table 20.8 tabulates the frequencies of these rankings. To calculate a summary rank ordering, the destination with the first (highest) preference was given the lowest number (1) and the least preferred destination was assigned the highest number (4). The summarized rank orderings were obtained with the following calculation:

Hawaii: $(3 \times 1) + (4 \times 2) + (2 \times 3) + (1 \times 4) = 21$

Paris: $(3 \times 1) + (1 \times 2) + (3 \times 3) + (3 \times 4) = 26$

Greece: $(2 \times 1) + (2 \times 2) + (4 \times 3) + (2 \times 4) = 26$

Hong Kong: $(2 \times 1) + (2 \times 2) + (2 \times 3) + (4 \times 4) = 28$

The lowest total score indicates the first (highest) preference ranking. The results show the following rank ordering: (1) Hawaii, (2) Paris, (3) Greece, and (4) Hong Kong.

Table 20.7 **Individual Rankings of Dream Destinations**				
EXECUTIVE	HAWAII	PARIS	GREECE	HONG KONG
1	1	2	4	3
2	1	3	4	2
3	2	1	3	4
4	3	4	3	1
5	2	1	3	4
6	3	4	1	2
7	2	3	1	4
8	1	4	2	3
9	4	3	2	1
10	2	1	3	4

Table 20.8 Frequency Table of Dream Destination Rankings

| | PREFERENCE RANKINGS | | | |
DESTINATION	1ST	2ND	3RD	4TH
Hawaii	3	4	2	1
Paris	3	1	3	3
Greece	2	2	4	2
Hong Kong	2	2	2	4

Tabular and Graphic Methods of Displaying Data

Tables and graphs (pictorial representations) may simplify and clarify research data. Tabular and graphic representations of the data may take a number of forms, ranging from a direct computer printout to an elaborate pictograph. The purpose of each table or graph, however, is to facilitate the summarization and communication of the data's meaning. For example, Table 20.9 illustrates the

Table 20.9 Regional Airline Usage for Vacation/Pleasure by Income and Education Class

	TOTAL	UNDER $20,000	$20,000– $39,000	$40,000– $59,000	$60,000 AND OVER
All consumers					
Expenditures (%)	100	10	7	16	67
Consumer units (%)	100	42	19	16	23
Index	100	26	36	100	291
Nonhigh school graduate					
Expenditures (%)	8	1	2	1	4
Consumer units (%)	35	21	6	4	4
Index	21	5	33	25	100
High school graduate					
Expenditures (%)	29	4	2	8	15
Consumer units (%)	30	11	6	6	7
Index	96	36	33	133	214
Attended/graduated college					
Expenditures (%)	63	5	3	7	48
Consumer units (%)	35	10	6	6	13
Index	180	50	50	116	369

Percentage population		Percentage expenditures
32	=	78

Exhibit 20.5   Visual Impact of Pie Charts and Bar Graphs

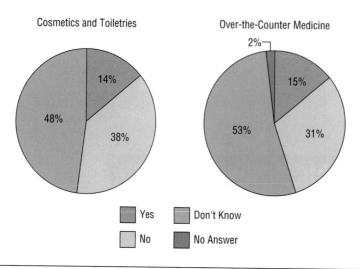

Are the Products That You Presently Use Tested on Animals?

Cosmetics and Toiletries

Over-the-Counter Medicine

| ■ Yes | ■ Don't Know |
| ■ No | ■ No Answer |

Note: 1,000 adults surveyed nationwide by telephone.

relationships among education, income, and regional airline usage expenditures for vacation/pleasure trips. The unshaded area emphasizes a key conclusion about market share. (Summarizing the information in the shaded box, 32 percent of the population makes 78 percent of the expenditures.) This form of presentation simplifies interpretation.

Although there are a number of standardized forms for presenting data in tables or graphs, the researcher may use his or her creativity to increase the effectiveness of a particular presentation. Bar charts, pie charts, curve diagrams, pictograms, and other graphic forms of presentation create strong visual impressions. Exhibit 20.4 shows how line graphs can show comparisons among groups over time.

Exhibit 20.5 shows how information from a survey on consumers' reactions to animal testing for consumer products can be enhanced by the use of a pie charts and bar graphs.

Chapter 25 discusses how these and other graphic aids may improve the communication value of a written report or oral presentation.

Computer Programs for Analysis

The proliferation of computer technology within businesses and universities has greatly facilitated tabulation and statistical analysis. Many collections, or packages, of programs for mainframe computers and workstations have been designed to tabulate and analyze numerous types of data. Such widely available computer program packages and statistical analysis systems as SAS, Statistical Package for the Social Sciences (SPSS), and MINI TAB eliminate the need to write a program every time you want to analyze data on the computer. There is also a wide variety of personal computer software for applications in marketing research.

WHAT WENT RIGHT?

Florence Nightingale: Inventor of the Pie Chart

FLORENCE NIGHTINGALE IS REMEMBERED AS A pioneering nurse and hospital reformer. Less well known is her equally pioneering use of statistics to persuade people. In advocating medical reform Nightingale also promoted statistical description; she developed a uniform procedure for hospitals to report statistical information. She invented the pie chart, in which proportions are represented as wedges of a circular diagram, and she struggled to get the study of statistics introduced into higher education.

One of Nightingale's analyses compared the peacetime death rates of British soldiers and civilians. She discovered and showed that the soldiers, who lived in barracks under unhealthy conditions, were twice as likely to die as civilians of the same age and sex. She then used the soldiers' 2 percent death rate to persuade the queen and the prime minister to establish a Royal Commission on the Health of the Army. It is just as criminal, she wrote, for the army to have a mortality of 20 per 1,000 "as it would be to take 1,100 men per annum out upon Salisbury Plain and shoot them."

Exhibit 20.4 Line Graphs to Highlight Comparisons over Time

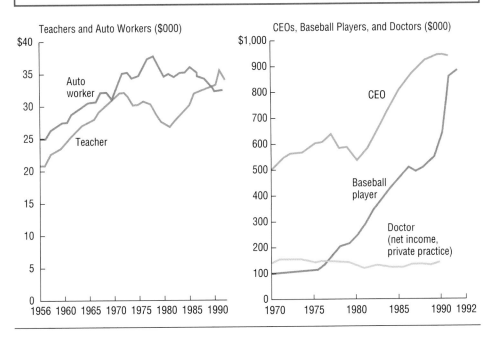

Exhibit 20.6   Selected Personal Computer Software Packages for Tabulation and Statistical Analysis

STATISTICAL PACKAGE

SAS SPSS STATPAK SYSTAT MINI TAB	These user-friendly packages emphasize statistical calculations. They also provide programs for entering and editing data, performing descriptive analysis, and performing hypothesis testing. Their output is easy to interpret.

SPREADSHEET PACKAGES

Microsoft Excel Lotus 1-2-3 QUATTRO PRO	These packages emphasize database management and allow for entering and editing data with minimal effort. They also incorporate some programs forde scriptive analysis, graphic analysis, and limited statistical analysis.

Exhibit 20.6 lists some of the more popular software products for statistical analysis and database management. Most of these packages contain sizable arrays of programs for descriptive analysis and univariate, bivariate, and multivariate statistical analysis. Several examples will be given to illustrate output from these statistical packages.

Exhibit 20.7 shows an SAS computer printout of descriptive statistics for two variables: **EMP** (number of employees working in an MSA, or Metropolitan Statistical Area) and **SALES** (sales volume in dollars in an MSA) for 10 MSAs. The number of data elements (N), mean, standard deviation, and other descriptive statistics are calculated.

Exhibit 20.8 presents output from the SPSS package that shows the results of a question on a survey about national problems in a frequency table. This SPSS output shows the absolute frequency of observations, the relative frequency as a percentage of all observations, and the adjusted frequency as a percentage of the number of respondents who provided a recorded answer rather than answering "don't know" or leaving the question blank.

A histogram is similar to a bar chart. Exhibit 20.9 shows an SPSS histogram plot of purchase price data from a survey. Each bar indicates the number of purchases.

Exhibit 20.7   SAS Output of Descriptive Statistics

STATE = NY

VARIABLE	N	MEAN	STANDARD DEVIATION	MINIMUM VALUE	MAXIMUM VALUE	STD ERROR OF MEAN	SUM	VARIANCE	C.V.
EMP	10	142.930	0232.665	12.800	788.800	73.575	1429.300	54133.0	162.782
SALES	10	5807.800	11905.127	307.000	39401.000	3764.732	58078.000	141732049.1	204.985N

Key: EMP = number of employees (000)
        SALES = Sales (000)

Exhibit 20.8   SPSS Computer Output Showing Frequencies

NATIONAL PROBLEMS MENTIONED

CATEGORY LABEL	CODE	COUNT	PERCENT OF RESPONSES	PERCENT OF CASES
Recession	1	119	12.0	26.5
Inflation	2	144	14.6	32.1
Lack of Religion	3	150	15.2	33.4
Political Corruption	4	129	13.1	28.7
Racial Conflict	5	92	9.3	20.5
Unions Too Strong	6	9	0.9	2.0
Big Business	7	141	14.3	31.4
Middle East Aggression	8	138	4.0	30.7
Weather	9	066	006.7	014.7
Total Responses		988	100.0	220.0

16 Missing Cases
449 Valid Cases

Exhibit 20.9   SPSS Histogram Output

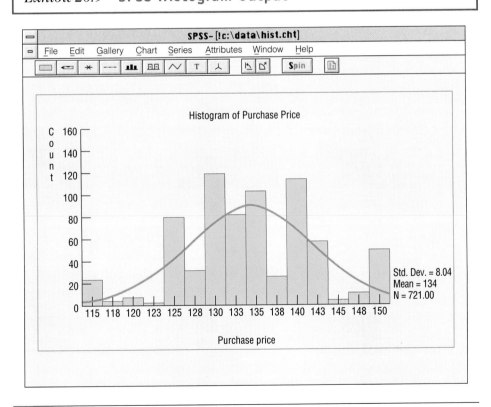

Exhibit 20.10 **SPSS Cross-Tabulation Output**

CROSS-TABULATION WITH ROW PERCENTS

SPSS/PC Release 1.0

Cross-tabulation: JOBCAT   Employment Category
By EDLEVEL   Education

EDLEVEL

	COUNT ROW PCT.	SOME HIGH SCHOOL 1	HIGH SCHOOL DIPLOMA 2	SOME COLLEGE 3	COLLEGE DEGREE 4	ADVANCED DEGREE 5	ROW TOTAL
JOBCAT Clerical	1	115 38.3	160 53.3	20 6.7	5 1.7		300 71.4
White Collar	2			70 63.6	25 22.7	15 13.6	110 26.2
Management	3				5 50.0	5 50.0	10 2.4
Column Total		115 27.4	160 38.1	90 21.4	35 8.3	20 4.8	420 100.0

Number of Missing Observations = 80

Exhibit 20.10 shows an SPSS cross-tabulation of two variables, education (EDLEVEL) and job category (JOBCAT), with the row total used as a basis for percentages. (Note: The program identifies the number of respondents for whom data were not provided for both variables as missing observations.)

As you can see, statistical software programs are quite versatile and they are extensively used in marketing research.

Computer Graphics/Computer Mapping

Graphic aids prepared by computers are rapidly replacing graphic aids drawn by artists. They are extremely useful for descriptive analysis. Computer-generated graphics and charts may be created inexpensively and quickly with easy-to-use computer software programs such as Lotus 1-2-3, Microsoft Exel and Astound. These software programs are both user friendly and versatile. Their versatility allows researchers to explore many alternative ways to communicate findings visually.

As we mentioned in Chapter 2, decision support systems can generate **computer maps** to portray data about sales, demographics, lifestyles, retail stores, and other features on two- or three-dimensional maps generated by computer.

computer map
The portrayal of demographic, sales, or other data on a two- or three-dimensional map generated by a computer.

Exhibit 20.11 Computer Graphic Illustrating Wiretap Surveillance Interception in 1997 by State6

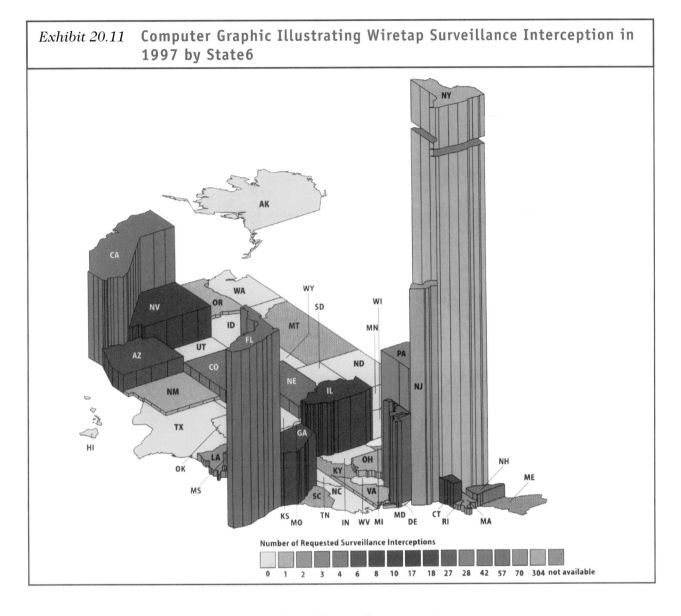

Number of Requested Surveillance Interceptions

0 1 2 3 4 6 8 10 17 18 27 28 42 57 70 304 not available

Exhibit 20.11 shows a computer map of the United States illustrating wiretap surveillance interception. The graphic illustration easily identifies states with large numbers of requests for surveillance interceptions. Many computer maps are used by marketers to show locations of high-quality customer segments. Competitors' locations are often overlaid for additional quick and easy visual reference. Scales that show miles, population densities, and other characteristics can be highlighted in color, with shading, and with symbols.

Many computer programs can draw **box and whisker plots,** which provide graphic representations of central tendencies, percentiles, variabilities, and the shapes of frequency distributions. Exhibit 20.12 shows a computer-drawn box and whisker plot for 100 responses to a question measured on a 10-point scale. The response categories are shown on the vertical axis. In the plot itself, the box represents 50 percent of the responses; it extends from the 25th to the 75th percentile. This gives a measure of variability called the **interquartile range,** but the term *midspread* is less complex and more descriptive. The location of the line within the box represents the median. The dashed lines that extend outside the

box and whisker plots
Graphic representations of central tendencies, percentiles, variabilities, and the shapes of frequency distributions.

interquartile range
A measure of variability.

Exhibit 20.12   **Computer-Drawn Box and Whisker Plot**

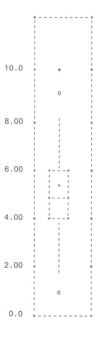

Mean	5.40
Median	5.00
75th percentile	6.00
25th percentile	4.00
Standard deviation	1.62

---

outlier

A value that lies outside the normal range of the data.

box are the whiskers. Each whisker extends either the length of the box (the mid-spread is 2 scale points in our example) or to the most extreme observation in that direction. An **outlier** is a value that lies outside the normal range of the data.

In Exhibit 20.12 outliers are indicated by either 0s or asterisks. Box and whisker plots are particularly useful for comparing group categories (e.g., men versus women) or several variables (e.g., relative importance of various product attributes).

Interpretation

interpretation

The process of making pertinent inferences and drawing conclusions concerning the meaning and implications of a research investigation.

An interpreter at the United Nations translates a foreign language into a native language to explain the meaning of a foreign diplomat's speech. In marketing research the interpretation process explains the meaning of the data. After the statistical analysis of the data, inferences and conclusions about their meaning are developed.

A distinction can be made between *analysis* and *interpretation*. **Interpretation** refers to making inferences pertinent to the meaning and implications of the research investigation and drawing conclusions about the managerial impli-

EXPLORING RESEARCH ISSUES

Body on Tap

A FEW YEARS AGO VIDAL SASSOON INC. TOOK LEGAL action against Bristol-Myers over a series of TV commercials and print ads for a shampoo named Body on Tap because of its beer content. The prototype commercial featured a well-known high fashion model saying:

"In shampoo tests with over 900 women like me, Body on Tap got higher ratings than Prell for body. Higher than Flex for conditioning. Higher than Sassoon for strong, healthy-looking hair."

The evidence showed that several groups of approximately 200 women each tested just one shampoo. They rated it on a six-step qualitative scale, from "outstanding" to "poor," for 27 separate attributes, such as body and conditioning. It became clear 900 women did not, after trying both shampoos, make product-to-product comparisons between Body on Tap and Sassoon or between Body on Tap and any of the other brands mentioned. In fact, no woman in the tests tried more than one shampoo.

The basis for the claim that the women preferred Body on Tap to Sassoon for "strong, healthy- looking hair" was to combine the data for the "outstanding" and "excellent" ratings and discard the lower four ratings on the scale. The figures then were 36 percent for Body on Tap and 24 percent (of a separate group of women) for Sassoon. When the "very good" and "good" ratings were combined with the "outstanding" and "excellent" ratings, however, there was only a statistically insignificant difference of 1 percent between the two products in the category of "strong, healthy- looking hair."

The research was conducted for Bristol-Myers by Marketing Information Systems Inc. (MISI), using a technique known as blind monadic testing. The president of MISI testified that this method typically is employed when what is wanted is an absolute response to a product "without reference to another specific product." Although he testified that blind monadic testing was used in connection with comparative advertising, that was not the purpose for which Bristol-Myers retained MISI. Rather, they wished to determine consumer reaction to the introduction of Body on Tap. And Sassoon's in-house research expert stated flatly that blind monadic testing cannot support comparative advertising claims.

cations of its variables. The logical interpretation of the data and statistical analysis are closely intertwined. Researchers interpret and analyze at the same time; that is, when a researcher calculates the means of each demographic category, he or she almost immediately infers group differences or the existence of a relationship. Almost automatically researchers seek out the significance of the statistical analysis for research problems as they order, break down, and manipulate the data.

TO THE POINT

The thing to do is to supply light.

WOODROW WILSON

From a management perspective, however, the qualitative meaning of the data and their managerial implications are an important aspect of the interpretation. Consider the crucial role played by interpretation of research results in investigating a new product—a lip stain that would color the lips a desired shade semipermanently, for time periods of about a month at a time:

The lip stain idea, among lipstick wearers, received very high scores on a rating scale ranging from "excellent" to "poor," presumably because it would not wear off. However, it appeared that even among routine wearers of lipstick the idea was being rated highly more for its interesting, even ingenious, nature than for its practical appeal to the consumer's personality. They liked the idea, but for someone else, not themselves....[Careful interpretation of the data] revealed that not being able to remove the stain for that length of time caused most women to consider the idea irrelevant in relation to their own personal needs and desires. Use of the product seems to represent more of a "permanent commitment" than is usually associated with the use of a particular cosmetic. In fact, women attached overtly negative meaning to the product concept, often comparing it with hair dyes instead of a long-lasting lipstick.[6]

This example shows that interpretation is crucial. However, this process is difficult to explain in a textbook because there is no one best way to interpret data. Many possible interpretations of data may be derived from a number of thought processes. Experience with selected cases will help students develop their own interpretative ability.

In all too many instances data are merely reported and not interpreted. Research firms may provide reams of computer output that do not state what the data mean. At the other extreme, some researchers tend to analyze every possible relationship between each and every variable in the study; they usually have not defined the problem during the earlier stages of research. Researchers who have a clear sense of the purpose of the research do not request statistical analysis of data that may have little or nothing to do with the primary purpose of the research.

Summary

Descriptive analysis refers to the transformation of raw data into an understandable form. Descriptive information is obtained by summarizing, categorizing, rearranging, and other forms of analysis. Tabulation refers to the orderly arrangement of data in a table or other summary format. Percentages, cumulative percentages, and frequency distributions are useful. The data may be described by measures of central tendency, such as the mean, median, or mode. Cross-tabulation shows how one variable relates to another to reveal differences between groups. Such cross-tabulations should be limited to categories related to the research problem and purpose. Putting the results into percentage form facilitates intergroup comparisons.

Performing the basic cross-tabulation within various subgroups of the sample is a common form of elaboration analysis. Elaboration analysis often identifies moderator variables or spurious relationships. A moderator variable is a third variable that, when introduced into the analysis, alters or has a contingent effect on the relationship between an independent variable and a dependent variable. A spurious relationship is indicated when adding a third variable to the analysis indicates that the relationship between the original two variables was not authentic.

Data transformation is the process of changing data's original form to a format that is more suitable to perform a data analysis. Index numbers relate data for a particular time period to that of a base year. To summarize rank order data, a data transformation is performed. Rank scores are multiplied by their frequency of occurrence to develop a new scale that represents summarized rank orderings.

Tables and graphs help to simplify and clarify the research data. Computer software greatly facilitates descriptive analysis. Many programs that enhance the construction of graphs and charts are available.

Computer mapping portrays demographic, sales, and other data on two- or three-dimensional maps that facilitate interpretation of descriptive data.

The interpretation of data uses the results of descriptive analysis. It involves making inferences about the real world and drawing conclusions about the data's managerial implications.

Key Terms and Concepts

Descriptive analysis
Frequency table
Cross-tabulation
Contingency table
Base

Elaboration analysis
Moderator variable
Spurious relationship
Quadrant analysis
Index number

Computer map
Box and whisker plots
Interquartile range
Outlier
Interpretation

Questions for Review and Critical Thinking

1. A survey asked respondents to respond to the statement "My work is interesting." Interpret the frequency distribution in the following SPSS output:

MY WORK IS INTERESTING.

CATEGORY LABEL	CODE	ABS. FREQ.	REL. FREQ. (PCT.)	ADJ. FREQ. (PCT.)	CUM. FREQ. (PCT.)
Very true	1.	650	23.9	62.4	62.4
Somewhat true	2.	303	11.2	29.1	91.5
Not very true	3.	61	2.2	5.9	97.3
Not at all true	4.	28	1.0	2.7	100.0
	0.	1,673	061.6	Missing	000.0
	Total	2,715	100.0	100.0	100.0

Valid Cases 1,042   Missing Cases   1,673

2. Using the data in the following table, perform the tasks that follow:

INDIVIDUAL	GENDER	AGE	COLA PREFERENCE	WEEKLY UNIT PURCHASES
John	M	19	Coke	2
Al	M	17	Pepsi	5
Bill	M	20	Pepsi	7
Mary	F	20	Coke	2
Jim	M	18	Coke	4
Karen	F	16	Coke	4
Tom	M	17	Pepsi	8
Dawn	F	19	Pepsi	1

(a) Prepare a frequency distribution of the respondents' ages.
(b) Cross-tabulate the respondents' genders with cola preference.

3. The following computer output shows a cross-tabulation of frequencies and provides frequency number (N) and row (R), column (C), and total (T) percentages. Interpret this output.

	ACROSS–E2	–HAVE HIGH SCHOOL DIPLOMA?			
	DOWN–G28	–HAVE YOU READ A BOOK IN PAST 3 MOS?			
	Yes	:NO			
N;R,C,T%	1.	2.		TOTAL	
1.	489	174	:	663	YES
	73.8	26.2	:		
	50.8	31.5	:		
	32.3	11.5	:	43.8	
2.	473	378	:	851	NO
	55.6	44.4	:		
	49.2	68.5	:		
	31.2	25.0	:	56.2	
	. . . . . .	. . . . . .		. . . . . .	
TOTAL	962	552	:	1514	
	63.5	36.5	:		

4. Interpret the following table:

ESTIMATE OF PERCENTAGE OF NET UNDERCOUNT OF THE POPULATION BY SEX, RACE, AND SELECTED BROAD AGE GROUP.

| | ALL RACES | | WHITE | | BLACK | |
AGE	MALE	FEMALE	MALE	FEMALE	MALE	FEMALE
All ages	3.3	1.8	2.5	1.4	9.9	5.5
20–24 years	3.3	1.4	2.5	1.1	12.1	5.2
25–34 years	5.7	2.8	4.3	2.4	18.5	6.7
35–44 years	5.3	0.9	3.6	0.5	17.7	4.0

5. Visit your local computer center and see if it has SPSS, SAS, SYSTAT, or MINI TAB computer packages.

6. What type of scalar data (that is, nominal, ordinal, interval, and ratio) typically are used in cross-tabulation analysis?

7. It has been argued that the analysis and interpretation of data are a managerial art. Comment.

8. The data in the following tables show some of the results of an Internal Revenue Service survey of taxpayers. Analyze and interpret the data.

The last year you filed an income tax return, did you get any suggestions or information that was especially helpful to you in filing?

	Absolute Frequency	Rel. Freq. (Pct.)	Adj. Freq. (Pct.)
Yes	156	29.5	29.8
No	368	69.7	70.2
Don't know	1	0.2 Missing	
Not ascertained	1	0.2 Missing	
Blank	002	000.4	Missing
	528	100.0	100.0

What kind of information was it?

	Absolute Frequency	Rel. Freq. (Pct.)	Adj. Freq. (Pct.)
Learned about energy credit	8	1.5	5.4
Learned about another deduction	46	8.7	31.3
Obtained info. about forms to use	9	1.7	6.1
Received pamphlets/forms	40	7.6	27.2
Other	44	8.3	29.9
Don't know	6	1.1	Missing
Not ascertained	2	0.4	Missing
Blank	373	070.6	Missing
	528	100.0	100.0

9. A data processing analyst for a research supplier finds that preliminary computer runs of survey results show that consumers love a client's new product. The employee buys a large block of the client's stock. Is this ethical?

10. A researcher finds that in a survey of 100 people, 15 of the respondents answer "don't know" to a question that has "yes" and "no" as alternatives. The researcher uses 85 as a base for calculating the percentage of respondents who answer "yes" or "no." Is this the right thing to do?

 Exploring the Internet

1. Go to http://www.spss.com and click on "SPSS market research" and then "Analysis". What services are provided?

2. Go to http://www.sas.com to learn about the statistical software programs the SAS Institute offers.

3. The IMS's 1992 National Needs Assessment survey of museums may be found at http://palimpsest.stanford.edu/byorg/ims/survey. Visit this site to review how descriptive statistics can be reported.

4. To see descriptive data analysis in a report on smokeless tobacco go to the Federal Trade Commission's Bureau of Consumer Protection at http://www.ftc.gov.bcp/reports/smokeless97.htm.

5. Economic Chart Dispenser provides links to charts and data for over 68,000 series http://bos.business.uab.edu/charts/.

6. Go to the Census Bureau's home page (http://www.census.gov) to see how census data are reported.

Case 20.1 TULSA'S CENTRAL BUSINESS DISTRICT (B)

THE METROPOLITAN TULSA CHAMBER OF COMMERCE was involved in revitalizing the downtown area. Its research department tried to supply local businesses with all the pertinent information they needed for growth planning. It believed that one particular piece of information needed concerned the Central Business District's (CBD) daytime population, which was expected to consist primarily of employees. The chamber wished to learn work habits, shopping behavior, and attitudes toward the Central Business District. Also of interest, although of a lesser priority, were the quantity and quality of the nighttime population.

The research director of the Chamber of Commerce commissioned four interrelated studies. The objective of one of these research projects was to determine how female consumers in the Tulsa community at large felt about shopping in downtown Tulsa and to identify their shopping patterns. Furthermore, the study was conducted to measure demographics with which to identify the key target market for downtown shoppers.

Methodolgy

Exploratory research to identify the prime areas for research was conducted using a very open-ended personal interview. The findings from this preliminary research were incorporated into a mail survey questionnaire. A total of 770 questionnaires were mailed out, 9 of which were not delivered. Of the 761 questionnaires distributed 356 were returned, yielding a 47 percent response rate.

The questionnaires were mailed to "the Mrs." of a sample of households listed in the Tulsa telephone directory. As anticipated, 90 percent of the respondents were female. The other 10 percent presumably were households without female shoppers or in which the male head of the household was the primary shopper. Selected results from the study appear in the following paragraphs.

Results: Downtown as a Place To Shop

Shopping Conditions. To evaluate general shopping conditions in the Tulsa community and downtown Tulsa, two separate questions were asked. Consumers' overall ratings of shopping conditions in both areas are given in Case Table 20.1-1. The differences in the ratings of the Tulsa community at large versus the downtown were rather dramatic—90 percent of the respondents felt that shopping conditions in the Tulsa community at large were either excellent or good, whereas only 18.5 percent perceived this to be true of downtown Tulsa. Almost 40 percent of the respondents considered shopping conditions in downtown Tulsa poor.

Respondents were asked how often they shopped at each of six shopping centers located in the Tulsa area. Case Table 20.1-2 shows the frequency of shopping at each. Almost 65 percent of the respondents indicated they never shopped in downtown Tulsa; only 7.8 percent shopped there once a month or more frequently. The Southroads/Southland shopping centers appeared to be the most popular, with a substantial percentage of regular shoppers. The Northland shopping center appeared to have a problem, as 84.4 percent of the respondents never shopped there, and hardly any regularly.

Respondents were asked to rank five shopping centers according to their preferences. Case Table 20.1-3 indicates which shopping centers consumers preferred: of the five, downtown Tulsa was the least preferred. Southroads/ Southland rated high again and appeared to be the most preferred.

Case Table 20.1-1 Overall Ratings of Shopping Conditions in the Tulsa Community versus Downtown Tulsa

	TULSA COMMUNITY		DOWNTOWN	
	FREQUENCY	%	FREQUENCY	%
Excellent	174	51.3	7	2.2
Good	132	38.9	53	16.3
Fair	27	8.0	136	41.8
Poor	6	1.8	129	39.7
Base	(339)	(100.0)	(325)	(100.0)

Case Table 20.1-2 **Frequency of Shopping at Tulsa Shopping Centers**

	Downtown		Southroads/ Southland		Utica Square		Woodland Hills		Fontana		Northland	
	No.	%	No.	%	No.	%	No.	%	No.	%	No.	%
Never	214	64.5	4	1.1	56	16.1	72	21.5	149	45.6	276	84.4
About once a year	60	18.1	15	4.3	87	25.0	45	13.4	61	18.7	18	5.5
Several times a year	32	9.6	102	29.2	102	29.3	106	31.6	75	22.9	15	4.6
About once a month	8	2.4	94	26.9	41	11.8	56	16.7	28	8.6	7	2.1
Two or three times a month	6	1.8	82	23.5	24	6.9	26	7.8	10	3.0	9	2.8
Nearly every week or every other week	12	3.6	52	14.9	38	10.9	30	9.0	4	1.2	2	0.6
Base	(332)	(100.0)	(349)	(100.0)	(348)	(100.0)	(335)	(100.0)	(327)	(100.0)	(327)	(100.0)

Case Table 20.1-3 **Shopping Center Preferences**

Preference	Downtown Tulsa (%)	Southroads/ Southland (%)	Utica Square (%)	Woodland Hills (%)	Fontana (%)
First	4.7	59.3	18.0	20.6	0.4
Second	4.7	32.1	31.6	30.8	4.6
Third	10.2	7.5	31.6	30.1	21.3
Fourth	12.4	1.1	17.1	9.5	57.3
Fifth	68.0	0.0	1.8	8.9	16.4

Demographic Analysis Of The Downtown Shopper

To obtain a profile of the downtown shopper, frequency of shopping downtown was cross-classified with demographic variables. The question "How often do you shop at the following shopping centers (downtown Tulsa)?" received the answers given in Case Table 20.1-2. As relatively few respondents were frequent shoppers in the downtown area, the responses "about once a month," "two or three times a month," and "nearly every week or every other week" were combined into one category. Con-

sumers who responded in one of these categories were labeled regular downtown shoppers; those who responded "about once a year" or "several times a year" were categorized as infrequent shoppers; those who responded "never" were labeled nonshoppers. The demographic characteristics of the sample are given in Case Table 20.1-4.

QUESTIONS

1. What hypotheses have been implicitly used in the tabulation of the data for Case Tables 20.1-1 through 20.1-4?

Case Table 20.1-4 Demographic Analysis of Downtown Shoppers

Demographics		Nonshoppers (%)	Infrequent Shoppers (%)	Regular Shoppers (%)
Sex	Female	92.0	85.6	76.9
	Male	8.0	14.5	23.1
Marital Status	Now married	77.5	72.2	65.4
	Never married	8.0	5.6	19.2
	Divorced	8.4	8.9	3.9
	Widowed	6.1	13.3	7.7
	Separated	0.0	0.0	3.9
Number of Children (under 18)	None	52.1	55.1	68.0
	1	18.0	15.8	20.0
	2	21.8	19.1	8.0
	3	6.7	6.7	4.0
	4	1.0	2.2	0.0
	5 or more	0.4	1.1	0.0
Education	Grammar school	1.9	1.1	3.9
	Attended high school	6.1	7.8	11.5
	High school graduate or equivalent	31.5	34.5	34.6
	Attended college	34.3	28.9	26.9
	College graduate	16.9	13.3	7.7
	Postgraduate college	9.4	14.4	15.4
Age	Under 25	9.9	7.8	3.8
	25–34	29.1	18.9	19.2
	35–44	16.9	24.5	7.7
	45–54	19.2	17.7	19.2
	55–64	11.2	14.4	26.9
	65 and over	13.6	16.6	23.0
Family Income	Under $5,000	4.5	9.0	13.6
	$5,000–$9,999	13.9	14.0	27.3
	$10,000–$24,999	17.8	22.0	18.2
	$25,000–$29,999	19.3	11.6	13.6
	$30,000–$44,999	12.9	16.3	22.7
	$45,000–$59,999	12.4	12.8	0.0
	$60,000 and over	19.3	14.0	4.6

2. Analyze and interpret the data. Prepare a summary report for the Chamber of Commerce to indicate a profile of the downtown consumer.

   Answering questions 3 and 4 will require knowledge of material presented in Chapters 21 and 22.

ADVANCED QUESTIONS

3. What statistical technique would be most appropriate for analyzing the data in Case Table 20.1-4? Is there enough information in the table to make this test?

4. Suppose you wished to compare the means of the three shopping groups to test the hypothesis that there were no differences on the demographic statements. What would be the appropriate statistical technique?

Case 20.2 Tulsa's Central Business District (C): Investigating Computer Output

During the course of the data analysis of one of the studies mentioned in Case 20.1, several computer programs were run. Some of the questions asked during a survey of business executives measured attitudes toward the downtown area.

An SPSS program was used to calculate descriptive statistics related to two of the attitudinal statements: "Off-street parking in Tulsa's downtown is inadequate" (PARKINAD) and "Tulsa's downtown is an active retail center" (RETAIL). The variables were coded "strongly agree" = 5. This appears in Case Exhibit 20.2-1, along with some alphabetical labels (in boldface).

Furthermore, one question on the questionnaire asked, "Is downtown Tulsa a better or worse place to work than a year ago, or is it about the same?" WORKPLAC was the label for this question. The SPSS computer output is given in Case Exhibit 20.2-2.

The coding guide indicates that responses were coded 1 = "better," 2 = "worse," and 3 = "about the same."

QUESTIONS

1. Is the data analysis in Case Exhibit 20.2-1 appropriate?

2. What do the statements and numbers next to the labels A through W mean in Case Exhibit 20.2-1?

3. Is the data analysis in Case Exhibit 20.2-2 appropriate?

4. What do the statements and numbers next to the labels A through P mean in Case Exhibit 20.2-2?

Case Exhibit 20.2-1 SPSS Output for Mean and Other Descriptive Statistics for Two Variables

A Tulsa Employees
B File   Tulsa
C Variable PARKINAD

D Mean	2.114	**E**	**V** Standard Error	0.059	**W**	**R** Standard Deviation	1.217	**S**
T Variance	1.480	**U**	Kurtosis	−0.399		Skewness	0.860	
P Range	4.000	**Q**	**L** Minimum	1.000	**M**	**N** Maximum	5.000	**O**
F Sum	907.000	**G**						
H Valid Observations-	429	**I**	**J** Missing Observations-	6	**K**			

Variable RETAIL

Mean	1.834	Standard Error	0.049	Standard Deviation	1.021
Variance	1.042	Kurtosis	0.563	Skewness	1.178
Range	4.000	Minimum	1.000	Maximum	5.000
Sum	794.000				
Valid Observations-	433	Missing Observations-	2		

Case Exhibit 20.2-2   SPSS Output for Frequency Distribution for a Survey Question

Tulsa Employees
File   Tulsa
A WORKPLAC

Category Label	Code	Absolute Frequency	Relative Frequency (%)	Adjusted Frequency (%)	Cumulative Adjusted Frequency (%)
	1	103 **B**	23.7 **F**	24.9 **H**	24.9 **J**
	2	75	17.2	18.1	43.0 **K**
	3	236	54.3	57.0	100.0
C Out of Range		21 **D**	4.8	Missing	100.0
	Total	435 **E**	100.0 **G**	100.0 **I**	

Mean	2.321	Standard Error	0.042	Median	2.623
Mode	3.000	Standard Deviation	0.847	Variance	0.717
Kurtosis	−1.280	Skewness	−0.666	Range	2.000
Minimum	1.000	Maximum	3.000		
M Valid Cases	414 **N O**	Missing Cases	21	**P**	

Case 20.3   Downy-Q Quilt

THE RESEARCH FOR DOWNY-Q IS AN EXAMPLE OF A commercial test that was conducted when an advertising campaign for an established brand had run its course. The revised campaign, "Fighting the Cold," emphasized that Downy was an "extra-warm quilt"; previous research had demonstrated this to be an important and deliverable product quality. The commercial test was requested to measure the campaign's ability to generate purchase interest.

The marketing department had recommended this revised advertising campaign and was now anxious to know how effectively this commercial would perform. The test concluded that "Fighting the Cold" was a persuasive commercial. It also demonstrated that the new campaign would have greater appeal to specific market segments.

Method

Brand choices for the same individuals were obtained before and after viewing the commercial. The commercial was tested in 30-second, color-moving, storyboard form in a theater test. Invited viewers were shown programming with commercial inserts. Qualified respondents were women who had bought quilts in outlets that carried Downy-Q. The results are shown in Case Tables 20.3-1 through 20.3-4.

QUESTION

1. Interpret the data in these tables. What recommendations and conclusions would you offer to Downy-Q management?

Case Table 20.3-1 **Shifts in Choice of Downy-Q Quilt before and after Showing of Commercial**

BRAND CHOICE AFTER COMMERCIAL	BRAND CHOICE BEFORE COMMERCIAL	
	DOWNY-Q ($n = 23$)	OTHER BRAND ($n = 237$)
Downy-Q	78	19
Other brand	22	81

Question: We are going to give away a series of prizes. If you are selected as one of the winners, which of the following would you truly want to win?

Case Table 20.3-2 **Prepost Increment in Choice of Downy-Q**

DEMOGRAPHIC GROUP	"FIGHTING THE COLD"		NORM: ALL QUILT COMMERCIALS	
	BASE	SCORE	AVERAGE	RANGE
Total audience	(260)	+15	+10	6–19
By marital status				
Married	(130)	+17		
Not married	(130)	+12		
By age				
Under 35	(130)	+14		
35 and over	(130)	+15		
By employment status				
Not employed	(180)	+13		
Employed	(170)	+18		

Question: We are going to give away a series of prizes. If you are selected as one of the winners, which of the following would you truly want to win? (Check list.)

Case Table 20.3-3 Adjective Checklist for Downy-Q Quilt Commercial

Adjective	"Fighting the Cold" (%)	Norm: All Quilt Commercials (%)
Positive		
Appealing	18	24
Clever	11	40
Convincing	20	14
Effective	19	23
Entertaining	5	24
Fast moving	12	21
Genuine	7	4
Imaginative	7	21
Informative	24	18
Interesting	13	17
Original	7	20
Realistic	8	3
Unusual	3	8
Negative/amateurish	9	11
Dull	33	20
Bad Taste	4	4
Repetitious	17	16
Silly	8	19
Slow	8	7
Unbelievable	3	5
Unclear	3	2
Unimportant	14	14
Uninteresting	32	19

Question: Which of these words do you feel come closest to describing the commercial you've just seen? (Check list.)

Case Table 20.3-4 Product Attribute Checklist for Downy-Q

Attributes	"Fighting the Cold" (%)
Extra warm	56
Lightweight	48
Pretty designs	45
Durable fabrics	28
Nice fabrics	27
Good construction	27

Question: Which of the following statements do you feel apply to Downy-Q? (Mark as many or as few as you feel apply.)

Chapter 21
Univariate Statistical Analysis

I N Chapter 20 we saw that, the average amount a college student spends during a spring break vacation to South Padre Island, Texas is $435.41. This figure is a finding of descriptive analysis, but how reliable is this estimate? Suppose the local chamber of commerce has assumed that the average amount spent is less than $300. Would this assumption be untenable? Is it reasonable to accept that figure from descriptive analysis? Is it possible to go beyond the simple tabulation of frequencies and the calculation of averages to find some sort of criterion for answering questions about differences between what one expected to find and the actual results of research? This chapter attempts to provide answers to questions like these.

As we already discussed, for most projects, analysis begins with some form of descriptive analysis to reduce the raw data into summary formats. Often researchers will wish to go beyond the simple tabulation of frequency distributions and the calculation of averages. In these cases, they may conduct *univariate tests of statistical significance*. The foundation of univariate statistical estimation of parameters involves hypothesis testing when the research focuses on *one variable at a time*.

Stating a Hypothesis

What Is a Hypothesis?

hypothesis
An unproven proposition or supposition that tentatively explains certain facts or phenomena; a proposition that is empirically testable.

In marketing theory a **hypothesis** is an unproven proposition or supposition that tentatively explains certain facts or phenomena; it is a statement of assumption about the nature of the world. In its simplest form a hypothesis is a guess. A sales manager may hypothesize that salespeople who are highest in product knowledge will be the most productive. An advertising manager may hypothesize that if consumers' attitudes toward a product change in a positive direction, there will an increase in consumption of the product. Statistical techniques allow us to decide whether or not our theoretical hypothesis is confirmed by the empirical evidence.

Null and Alternative Hypotheses

null hypothesis
A statement about a status quo that asserts that any change from what has been thought to be true will be due entirely to random sampling error.

Because scientists should be bold in conjecturing, but extremely cautious in testing, statistical hypotheses generally are stated in a null form. A **null hypothesis** is a statement about a status quo. It is a conservative statement that communicates the notion that any change from what has been thought to be true or observed in the past will be due entirely to random error. In fact, the true purpose of setting up the null hypothesis is to provide an opportunity for nullifying it. For example, the academic researcher may expect that highly dogmatic (that is, closed-minded) consumers will be less likely to try a new product than will less dogmatic consumers. The researchers would generally formulate a conservative null hypothesis. The null hypothesis in this case would be that there is *no difference* between high dogmatics and low dogmatics in their willingness to try an innovation. The **alternative hypothesis** is that there *is* a difference between high dogmatics and low dogmatics. It states the opposite of the null hypothesis.

alternative hypothesis
A statement that indicates the opposite of the null hypothesis.

Hypothesis Testing

Generally we assign the symbol H_0 to the null hypothesis and the symbol H_1 to the alternative hypothesis. The purpose of hypothesis testing is to determine which of the two hypotheses is correct. The process of hypothesis testing is slightly more complicated than that of estimating parameters because the decision maker must choose between the two hypotheses. However, the student need not worry because the mathematical calculations are no more difficult than those we have already made.

The Hypothesis-Testing Procedure

The process of hypothesis testing goes as follows. First, we determine a statistical hypothesis. We then imagine what the sampling distribution of the mean would be if this hypothesis were a true statement of the nature of the population. Next, we take an actual sample and calculate the sample mean (or appropriate statistic, if we are not concerned about the mean). We know from our previous discussions of the sampling distribution of the mean that obtaining a sample value that is exactly the same as the population parameter would be highly unlikely; we expect some small difference (although it may be large) between the sample mean and

STATISTICAL TUTOR

Typical Hypothesis Test

A HARDWARE FRANCHISE HAS ALMOST 1,000 RETAIL outlets. Monthly sales of a particular tool have averaged 612 units for each franchise. The sales manager believes a competitor's new price on a similar item may have an impact on sales. Using a random sample of 64 franchises, the sales manager wishes to test whether the observed sample mean differs from the benchmark figure.

QUESTIONS

1. Is the difference between the benchmark and observed value statistically significant?
2. Does the magnitude of the increase (or decrease) in market behavior justify a change in marketing strategy?

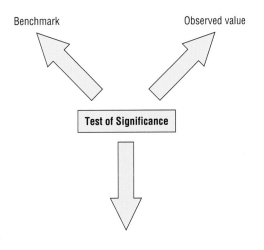

Evidence of consumer or market behavior (awareness, usage, and sales)

Benchmark   Observed value

Test of Significance

the population mean. We then must determine if the deviation between the obtained value of the sample mean and its expected value (based on the statistical hypothesis) would have occurred by chance alone—say, 5 times out of 100—if in fact the statistical hypothesis had been true. To repeat, we ask this question: "Has the sample mean deviated substantially from the mean of the hypothesized sampling distribution by a value large enough for us to conclude that this large a deviation would be somewhat rare if the statistical hypothesis were true?" Suppose we observe that the sample value differs from the expected value. Before we can conclude that these results are improbable (or even probable), we must have some standard or decision rule for determining if in fact we should reject the null hypothesis and accept the alternative hypothesis. Statisticians define this decision criterion as the *significance level*.

The **significance level** is a critical probability in choosing between the null hypothesis and the alternative hypothesis. The level of significance determines the probability level—say, .05 or .01—that is to be considered too low to warrant support of the null hypothesis. Assuming the hypothesis being tested is true, if the probability of occurrence of the observed data is smaller than the significance level, then the data suggest that the null hypothesis should be rejected. In other

significance level
The critical probability in choosing between the null and alternative hypothesis; the probability level that is too low to warrant support of a null hypothesis.

words, there has been evidence to support contradiction of the null hypothesis, which is equivalent to supporting the alternative hypothesis.

The terminology used in discussing confidence intervals identifies what we call the *confidence level,* or a *confidence coefficient.* The confidence interval may be regarded as the set of acceptable hypotheses or the level of probability associated with an interval estimate. However, when discussing hypothesis testing, statisticians change their terminology and call this the *significance level,* α (the Greek letter *alpha*).

An Example of Hypothesis Testing

An example should clarify the nature of hypothesis testing. Suppose the Red Lion restaurant is concerned about its store image, one aspect being the friendliness of the service. In a personal interview customers are asked to indicate their perceptions of services on a 5-point scale, where 1 indicates "very unfriendly" service and 5 indicates "very friendly" service. The scale is assumed to be an interval scale, and experience has shown that previous distribution of this attitudinal measurement assessing the service dimensions was approximately normal.

Now, suppose the researcher entertains the hypothesis that customers feel the restaurant has neither friendly nor unfriendly service. The researcher formulates the null hypothesis that the mean is equal to 3.0:

$$H_0 : \mu = 3.0$$

The alternative hypothesis is that the mean does not equal 3.0:

$$H_1 : \mu \neq 3.0$$

Next, the researcher must decide on a region of rejection. Exhibit 21.1 shows a sampling distribution of the mean assuming the null hypothesis, that is, assuming $\mu = 3.0$. The shaded area shows the region of rejection when $\alpha = .025$ in each tail of the curve. In other words, the *region of rejection* shows those values that

---

Exhibit 21.1 **A Sampling Distribution of the Mean Assuming μ = 3.0**

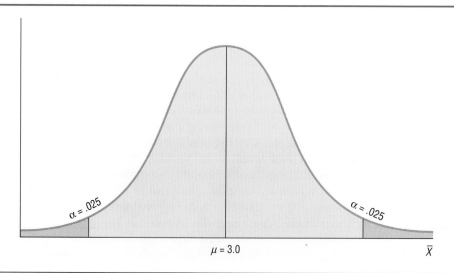

$\alpha = .025$ $\alpha = .025$

$\mu = 3.0$ $\overline{X}$

are very unlikely to occur if the null hypothesis is true, but relatively probable if the alternative hypothesis is true. The values within the unshaded area are called acceptable at the 95 percent confidence level (or 5 percent significance level, or .05 alpha level), and if we find that our sample mean lies within this region of acceptance, we conclude that the null hypothesis is true. More precisely, we fail to reject the null hypothesis. In other words, the range of acceptance (1) identifies those acceptable values that show a difference between the hypothesized mean in the null hypothesis and (2) shows that difference of any sample values in this range to be so minuscule that we would conclude that this difference was due to random sampling error rather than to a false null hypothesis.

In our example, the Red Lion restaurant hired research consultants who collected a sample of 225 interviews. The mean score on the 5-point scale equaled 3.78. If σ is known, this is used in the analysis; however, this is rarely true and was not true in this case.[1] The sample standard deviation was $S = 1.5$. Now we have enough information to test the hypothesis.

The researcher has decided that the decision rule will be to set the significance level at the .05 level. This means that in the long run the probability of making an erroneous decision when H_0 is true will be fewer than 5 times in 100 (.05). From the table of the standardized normal distribution, the researcher finds that the Z score of 1.96 represents a probability of .025 that a sample mean will lie above 1.96 standard errors from μ. Likewise, the tables show that about .025 of all sample means will fall below -1.96 standard errors from μ.

The values that lie exactly on the boundary of the region of rejection are called the **critical values** of μ. Theoretically, the critical values are $Z = -1.96$ and $+1.96$. Now we must transform these critical Z-values to the sampling distribution of the mean for this image study. The critical values are:

critical values
The values that lie exactly on the boundary of the region of rejection.

$$\text{Critical value—lower limit} = \mu - ZS_{\overline{X}} \text{ or } \mu - Z\frac{S}{\sqrt{n}}$$

$$= 3.0 - 1.96\left(\frac{1.5}{\sqrt{225}}\right)$$
$$= 3.0 - 1.96(.1)$$
$$= 3.0 - 1.96$$
$$= 2.804$$

$$\text{Critical value—upper limit} = \mu + ZS_{\overline{X}} \text{ or } \mu + Z\frac{S}{\sqrt{n}}$$

$$= 3.0 + 1.96\left(\frac{1.5}{\sqrt{225}}\right)$$
$$= 3.0 + 1.96(.1)$$
$$= 3.0 + 1.96$$
$$= 3.196$$

Based on the survey, $\overline{X} = 3.78$. In this case, the sample mean is contained in the region of rejection (see Exhibit 21.2). Thus, since the sample mean is greater than the critical value, 3.196, the researcher says that the sample result is statistically significant beyond the .05 level. In other words, fewer than 5 of each 100 samples will show results that deviate this much from the hypothesized null hypothesis, when in fact the H_0 is actually true.

What does this mean to the management of the Red Lion? The results indicate that customers believe the service is friendly. It is unlikely (less than 5 in 100) that this result would occur because of random sampling error. It means that the restaurant should worry about factors other than the friendliness of the service personnel.

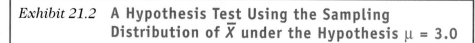

Exhibit 21.2 A Hypothesis Test Using the Sampling Distribution of $\overline{X}$ under the Hypothesis $\mu = 3.0$

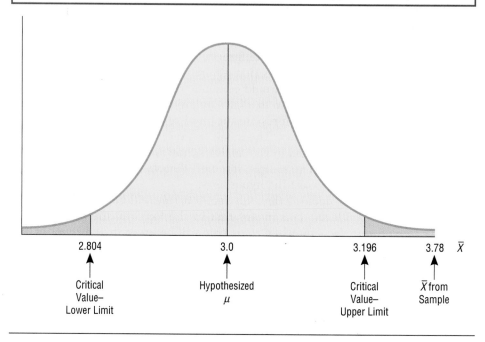

An alternative way to test the hypothesis is to formulate the decision rule in terms of the Z-statistic. Using the following formula, we can calculate the observed value of the Z-statistic given a certain sample mean, $\overline{X}$:

$$Z_{\text{obs}} = \frac{\overline{X} - \mu}{S_{\overline{X}}}$$
$$= \frac{3.78 - \mu}{S_{\overline{X}}}$$
$$= \frac{3.78 - 3.0}{.1}$$
$$= \frac{.78}{.1} = 7.8$$

In this case, the Z-value is 7.8 and we find that we have met the criterion of statistical significance at the .05 level. This is statistically significant at the .000001 level.

Type I and Type II Errors

Hypothesis testing, as we previously stated, is based on probability theory. Because we cannot make any statement about a sample with complete certainty, there is always the chance that an error can be made. In fact, the researcher runs the risk of committing two types of errors. Exhibit 21.3 summarizes the state of affairs in the population and the nature of Type I and Type II errors. The four possible situations in the exhibit result because the null hypothesis can be either true or false, and the statistical decision will be to either accept the null hypothesis or reject it.

EXPLORING RESEARCH ISSUES

Type I and Type II Errors in the Legal Profession

ALTHOUGH MOST ATTORNEYS AND JUDGES DO NOT concern themselves with the statistical terminology of Type I and Type II errors, they do follow this logic. For example, our legal system is based on the concept that a person is innocent until proven guilty. Assume that the null hypothesis is that the individual is innocent. If we make a Type I error, we will send an innocent person to prison. Our legal system takes many precautions to avoid Type I errors. A Type II error would occur if a guilty party were set free (the null hypothesis would have been accepted). Our society places such a high value on avoiding Type I errors that Type II errors are more likely to occur.

If the decision has been made to reject the null hypothesis and the null hypothesis is in fact true, we will have made what is called a **Type I error.** A Type I error has the probability of alpha (α), the level of statistical significance that we have set up. Simply put, a Type I error occurs when the researcher concludes there is a statistical difference, when in reality one does not exist. If the alternative hypothesis is in fact true and the null hypothesis is false, but we conclude that we should not reject the null hypothesis, we will have made what is called a **Type II error.** The probability of making this incorrect decision is called beta (β). No error will occur if the null hypothesis is true and we make the decision to accept it. We will also make a correct decision if the null hypothesis is false and the decision is made to reject the null hypothesis.

Type I error
An error with the probability of alpha; an error caused by rejecting the null hypothesis when it is true.

Type II error
An error with the probability of beta; an error caused by failing to reject the null hypothesis when the alternative hypothesis is true.

TO THE POINT

It is terrible to speak well and be wrong.

SOPHOCLES

Unfortunately, without increasing sample size the researcher cannot simultaneously reduce Type I and Type II errors because there is an inverse relationship between the two. Thus, reducing the probability of a Type II error increases the probability of a Type I error. In marketing problems, Type I errors generally are more serious than Type II errors and there is greater concern with determining the significance level, alpha, than with determining beta.[2]

Exhibit 21.3 **Type I and Type II Errors in Hypothesis Testing**

STATE OF NULL HYPOTHESIS IN THE POPULATION	DECISION	
	ACCEPT H_0	REJECT H_0
H_0 is true	Correct—no error	Type I error
H_0 is false	Type II error	Correct—no error

Choosing the Appropriate Statistical Technique

Now that one statistical technique for hypothesis testing has been illustrated, it should be noted that a number of appropriate statistical techniques are available to assist the researcher in interpreting data. The choice of the method of statistical analysis depends on (1) the type of question to be answered, (2) the number of variables, and (3) the scale of measurement.

Type of Question to Be Answered

The type of question the researcher is attempting to answer is a consideration in the choice of statistical technique. For example, a researcher may be concerned simply with the central value of a variable or the distribution of that variable. Comparison of two salespeople's monthly average sales will require a *t*-test of two means, whereas a comparison of quarterly sales distributions will require a chi-square test.

The researcher should anticipate the method of statistical analysis before the choice of research design and before determining the type of data to collect. Once the data are collected, the initial orientation toward analysis of the problem will be reflected in the research design.

Number of Variables

univariate statistical analysis
Analysis that assesses the statistical significance of a hypothesis about a single variable.

The number of variables that will be simultaneously investigated is a primary consideration in the choice of statistical technique. A researcher who is interested only in the average number of times a prospective home buyer visits financial institutions to shop for interest rates concentrates on investigating only one variable at a time. The researcher conducts **univariate statistical analysis** when wishing to generalize from a sample about one variable at a time. Statistically describing the relationship between two variables at one time, such as the relationship between advertising expenditures and sales volume, requires bivariate statistical analysis. Tests of differences and measuring the association among variables are discussed in Chapters 22 and 23. Multivariate statistical analysis, discussed in Chapter 24, is the simultaneous investigation of more than two variables. For example, predicting sales volumes on the basis of advertising expenditure and other variables, such as gross national product (GNP) and number of people in the sales area, is an example of multivariate analysis.

Scale of Measurement

The scale of measurement on which the data are based or the type of measurement reflected in the data determines the permissible statistical techniques and appropriate empirical operations that may be performed. Testing a hypothesis about a mean, as we have just discussed, requires interval scaled or ratio scaled data. Suppose a researcher is concerned with a nominal scale that identifies users versus nonusers of bank credit cards. The researcher may use only the mode as a measure of central tendency because of the type of scale. In other situations the median may be used as the average or a percentile may be used as a measure of dispersion if the data are measured on an ordinal scale. For example, the ranking of brand preferences generally employs an ordinal scale.

Exhibit 21.4 **Examples of Selecting the Appropriate Univariate Statistical Method**

SAMPLE MARKETING PROBLEM	STATISTICAL QUESTION TO BE ASKED	POSSIBLE TEST OF STATISTICAL SIGNIFICANCE
Interval or Ratio Scales		
Compare actual vs. hypothetical values of average salary	Is the sample mean significantly different from the hypothesized population mean?	Z-test (if sample is large) t-test (If sample is small)
Ordinal Scales		
Compare actual evaluations and expected evaluations	Does the distribution of scores for a scale with the categories excellent, good, fair, and poor differ from the expected distribution?	Chi-square test
Determine ordered preferences for all brands in a product class	Does a set of rank orderings in a sample differ from an expected or hypothetical rank ordering?	Kolmogorov-Smirnov test
Nominal Scales		
Identify sex of key executives	Is the number of female executives equal to the number of male executives?	Chi-square test
Indicate percentage of key executives who are male	Is the proportion of male executives the same as the hypothesized proportion?	t-test of a proportion

Parametric versus Nonparametric Hypothesis Tests

The terms *parametric statistics* and *nonparametric statistics* refer to the two major groupings of statistical procedures. The major distinction between them lies in the underlying assumptions about the data to be analyzed. When the data are interval or ratio scaled and the sample size is large, parametric statistical procedures are appropriate. These procedures are based on the assumption that the data in the study are drawn from a population with a normal (bell-shaped) distribution and/or normal sampling distribution. When researchers do not make this assumption about the population, nonparametric methods are used. Making the assumption that the population distribution or sampling distribution is normal generally is inappropriate when data are either ordinal or nominal. Thus, nonparametric statistics are referred to as *distribution free.*[3]

Data analysis of both nominal and ordinal scales typically uses nonparametric statistical tests. If an investigator has two interval-scaled measures, such as gross national product (GNP) and industry sales volume, parametric tests to make a comparison of the intervals are appropriate. Possible statistical tests might include product-moment correlation analysis, analysis of variance, or a Z-test for a hypothesis about a mean.

Exhibit 21.4 provides guidelines for selecting the appropriate univariate statistical method. Although you may be unfamiliar with most of them, the exhibit is meant to illustrate that there is a variety of statistical techniques that vary according to the properties of the scale. Furthermore, similar tables that show examples of the selection of appropriate bivariate and multivariate statistical techniques will appear in Chapters 22, 23, and 24. The appropriate technique will vary both by the

STATISTICAL TUTOR

The Statistical Dragon Meets the Internet

THE WORLD WIDE WEB PROVIDES A NEW EDUCATIONAL medium for teaching statistics. The following sites are some of the best sites providing materials and interactive exercises so students can learn how to use statistics properly.

STATLIB

StatLib is a system for distributing statistical software, datasets, and information by electronic mail, FTP, and the World Wide Web at http://lib.stat.cmu.edu/.

SURFSTAT.AUSTRALIA

SurfStat.australia is an on-line text in introductory statistics from the University of Newcastle at http://surfstat.newcastle.edu.au/surfstat/.

DATA AND STORY LIBRARY

The Data and Story Library is an on-line library of datafiles and stories that illustrate the use of basic statistics methods at http://lib.stat.cmu.edu/DASL/.

GLOBALLY ACCESSIBLE STATISTICAL PROCEDURES

The Globally Accessible Statistical Procedures initiative is designed to make statistical routines easily available via the World Wide Web at http://www.stat.sc.edu/rsrch/gasp/.

ELECTRONIC ENCYCLOPEDIA OF STATISTICAL EXAMPLES AND EXERCISES

Electronic Encyclopedia of Statistical Examples and Exercises is a resource for the study of statistics that includes real-world examples of the uses and abuses of statistics and statistical inference. Web address is http://stat.mps.ohio-state.edu/projects/eesee/index.html.

THE RICE VIRTUAL LAB IN STATISTICS

The Rice Virtual Lab in Statistics provides hypertext materials such as HyperStat Online at http://www.ruf.rice.edu/~lane/rvls.html and http://www.ruf.rice.edu/~lane/hyperstat/contents.html.

GUIDE TO BASIC LABORATORY STATISTICS

Guide to Basic Laboratory Statistics is an informal guide to elementary inferential statistical methods used in the analysis of data from experiments. The Web address is http://nimitz.mcs.kent.edu/~blewis/stat/scon.html.

WEBSTAT

WebStat is a statistical software package created at the University of South Carolina for statistical analysis via the World Wide Web at http://www.stat.sc.edu/~west/webstat/.

---

properties of the scale and by the number of variables investigated. The actual selection of a univariate statistical test involves many potential choices because there are more alternatives than those illustrated in Exhibit 21.4. A complete discussion of all the relevant techniques is beyond the scope of this discussion at this point.

The *t*-Distribution

In a number of situations researchers wish to test hypotheses that concern population means with sample sizes that are not large enough to be approximated by

Exhibit 21.5 **The *t*-Distribution for Various Degrees of Freedom**

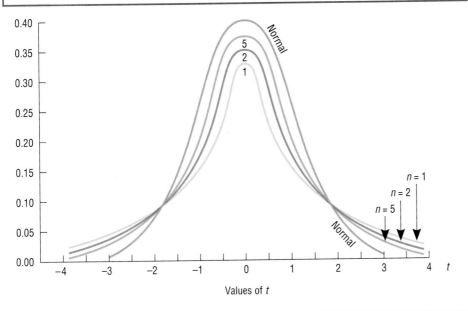

Values of *t*

the normal distribution. When the sample size is small ($n \leq 30$) and the population standard deviation is unknown, we use the *t*-distribution. The **t-distribution,** like the standardized normal curve, is a symmetrical, bell-shaped distribution with a mean of zero and a unit standard deviation. When sample size (n) is larger than 30, the *t*-distribution and *Z*-distribution may be considered almost identical. Since the *t*-distribution is contingent on sample size, there is a family of *t*-distributions. More specifically, the shape of the *t*-distribution is influenced by its **degrees of freedom.**

Exhibit 21.5 illustrates *t*-distributions for 1, 2, 5, and an infinite number of degrees of freedom. The number of degrees of freedom (*d.f.*) is equal to the number of observations minus the number of constraints or assumptions needed to calculate a statistical term. Another way to look at degrees of freedom is to think of adding four numbers together when you know their sum, for example,

$$
\begin{array}{r}
4 \\
2 \\
1 \\
\underline{X} \\
10
\end{array}
$$

The value of the fourth number has to be 3. In other words, there is a freedom of choice for the first three digits, but the fourth value is not free to vary. In this example there are three degrees of freedom.

The calculation of *t* closely resembles the calculation of the *Z*-value. To calculate *t*, use the formula

$$
t = \frac{\overline{X} - \mu}{S_{\overline{X}}}
$$

with $n - 1$ degrees of freedom.

t-distribution
A symmetrical, bell-shaped distribution that is contingent on sample size. It has a mean of zero and a standard deviation equal to 1.

degrees of freedom
The number of degrees of freedom is equal to the number of observations minus the number of constraints or assumptions needed to calculate a statistical term.

The researcher asks two questions to determine whether the Z-distribution or the t-distribution is more appropriate for calculating a confidence interval or conducting a test of statistical significance. The first question is: "Is the population standard deviation (σ) known?" If the answer is yes, the Z-distribution is appropriate. A second question is also asked when σ is unknown (the situation in most marketing research studies); it is: "Is the sample size greater than 30?" If the answer is no, the t-distribution should be used; if it is yes, the Z-distribution may be used because as sample size increases, the t-distribution becomes increasingly similar to the Z-distribution.

Calculating a Confidence Interval Estimate Using the t-Distribution

Suppose a business organization is interested in how long newly hired MBA graduates remain on their first jobs. On the basis of a small sample of employees with MBAs, the researcher wishes to estimate the population mean with 95 percent confidence. The data from the sample are presented in Table 21.1, which indicates sample mean $\overline{X} = 3.7$ years with a sample standard deviation $S = 2.66$.

To find the confidence interval estimates of the population mean for this small sample,

$$\mu = \overline{X} \pm t_{c.l.} S_{\overline{X}}$$

or

$$\text{Upper limit} = \overline{X} + t_{c.l.} S/\sqrt{n}$$
$$\text{Lower limit} = \overline{X} - t_{c.l.} S/\sqrt{n}$$

where

μ = population mean
$\overline{X}$ = sample mean
$t_{c.l.}$ = critical value of t at a specified confidence level
$S_{\overline{X}}$ = standard error of the mean
S = sample standard deviation
n = sample size

More specifically, the step-by-step procedure for calculating the confidence interval is as follows:

1. Calculate $\overline{X}$ from the sample.
2. Since σ is unknown, estimate the population standard deviation by finding S, the sample standard deviation.
3. Estimate the standard error of the mean using the following formula: $S_{\overline{X}} = S/\sqrt{n}$.
4. Determine the t-values associated with the desired confidence level. To do this, go to Table A.3 in the appendix. Although the t-table provides information similar to that in the Z-table, it is somewhat different. The t-table format emphasizes the chance of error or significance level (α) rather than the 95 percent chance of including the population mean in the estimate. Our example is a two-tailed test. Thus, since a 95 percent confidence level has been selected, the significance level equals .05 (1.00 − .95 = .05). Once this has been determined, all one has to do to find the t-value is look under the .05 column for *two-tailed tests* at the row in which degrees of freedom (*d.f.*) equal the appropriate value ($n − 1$).
5. Calculate the confidence interval.

Table 21.1 **Length of Initial Employment for a Sample of 17 MBA Graduates**

NUMBER OF YEARS ON FIRST JOB
3
5
7
1
12
1
2
2
5
4
2
3
1
3
4
2
6

$\Sigma X = 63$ $\overline{X} = 3.7$ $S = 2.66$ $S_{\overline{X}} = .645$

In the example about the MBA students, we know that $\overline{X} = 3.7$, $S = 2.66$, and $n = 17$.

To calculate the confidence interval, we must go to Table A.3 in the appendix and look under 16 degrees of freedom ($n - 1$, $17 - 1 = 16$) for the t-value at the 95 percent confidence level (.05 level of significance), in this case $t = 2.12$. Thus,

$$\text{Upper limit} = 3.7 + 2.12\ (2.66/\sqrt{17}) = 5.07$$
$$\text{Lower limit} = 3.7 - 2.12\ (2.66/\sqrt{17}) = 2.33$$

In our hypothetical example it may be concluded with 95 percent confidence that the population mean for the number of years spent on the first job by MBAs is between 5.07 and 2.33.

Univariate Hypothesis Test Using the t-Distribution

The step-by-step procedure for a *t-test* is conceptually similar to that for hypothesis testing with the Z-distribution. To illustrate, suppose a department store manager believes that the average number of customers who return or exchange merchandise each day is 20. The store records the number of returns and exchanges for each of the 25 days it was open during a given month. The researcher calculates a sample mean, $\overline{X} = 22$, and a sample standard deviation, $S = 5$.

The first step is to state the null hypothesis and the alternative hypothesis:

$$H_0{:}\mu = 20$$
$$H_1{:}\mu \neq 20$$

t-test
A hypothesis test that uses the t-distribution rather than the Z-distribution. It is used when testing a hypothesis with a small sample size and unknown σ.

Next, the researcher calculates $\overline{X}$ and S and estimates the standard error of the mean ($S_{\overline{X}}$):

$$S_{\overline{X}} = S/\sqrt{n}$$
$$= 5/\sqrt{25}$$
$$= 1$$

The researcher then finds the t-value associated with the desired level of statistical significance. If a 95 percent confidence level is desired, the significance level is .05.

Next, the researcher must formulate a decision rule to specify the critical values by computing the upper and lower limits of the confidence interval to define the regions of rejection. This requires determining the value of t. For 24 degrees of freedom ($n - 1$, $25 - 1$), the t-value is 2.064. These critical values are:

$$\text{Lower limit: } \mu - t_{c.l.} S_{\overline{X}} = 20 - 2.064 \, (5/\sqrt{25})$$
$$= 20 - 2.064 \, (1)$$
$$= 17.936$$
$$\text{Upper limit: } \mu + t_{c.l.} S_{\overline{X}} = 20 + 2.064 \, (5/\sqrt{25})$$
$$= 20 + 2.064 \, (1)$$
$$= 22.064$$

Finally, the researcher makes the statistical decision by determining if the sample mean falls between the critical limits. Based on the department store sample, $\overline{X} = 22$. In this case the sample mean is *not* included in the region of rejection. Even though the sample result is only slightly less than the critical value at the upper limit, the null hypothesis cannot be rejected. In other words, the department store manager's assumption appears to be correct.

As with the Z-test, there is an alternative way to test a hypothesis with the t-statistic. This is by using the formula

$$t_{\text{obs}} = \frac{\overline{X} - \mu}{S_{\overline{X}}}$$
$$t_{\text{obs}} = \frac{22 - 20}{1} = \frac{2}{1} = 2$$

We can see that the observed t-value is less than the critical t-value of 2.064 at the .05 level when there are 24 ($25 - 1$) degrees of freedom.

The Chi-Square Test for Goodness of Fit

Table 21.2 shows the responses to a survey to investigate awareness of a particular brand of automobile tire. This frequency distribution, or one-dimensional table from a sample of 100, suggests that the majority of the population (60 percent) is aware of the brand.

chi-square (χ^2) test
A hypothesis test that allows for investigation of statistical significance in the analysis of a frequency distribution.

The **chi-square (χ^2) test** allows us to test for significance in the analysis of frequency distributions. Thus, categorical data on variables such as sex, education, or dichotomous answers may be statistically analyzed. Suppose, for example, that we wish to test the null hypothesis that the number of consumers aware of a certain tire brand equals the number unaware of the brand. The logic inherent in the

χ^2 test allows us to compare the observed frequencies (O_i) with the expected frequencies (E_i) based on our theoretical ideas about the population distribution or our presupposed proportions. In other words, the technique tests whether the data come from a certain probability distribution. It tests the "goodness of fit" of the observed distribution with the expected distribution.

Calculation of the Univariate χ^2

Calculation of the chi-square statistic allows us to determine whether the difference between the observed frequency distribution and the expected frequency distribution can be attributed to sampling variation. The steps in this process are as follows:

1. Formulate the null hypothesis, and determine the expected frequency of each answer.
2. Determine the appropriate significance level.
3. Calculate the χ^2 value using the observed frequencies from the sample and the expected frequencies.
4. Make the statistical decision by comparing the calculated χ^2 value with the critical χ^2 value. (It will soon be explained how to find this value in Table A.4 in the appendix.)

To analyze the brand awareness data in Table 21.2, start with a null hypothesis that suggests that the number of respondents aware of the brand will equal the number of respondents unaware of it. Thus, the expected probability of each answer (aware or unaware) is .5; in a sample of 100, 50 people would be expected to respond yes, or aware, and 50 would be expected to respond no, or unaware. After the researcher has determined that the chi-square test is appropriate at the .05 level of significance (or some other probability level), the chi-square statistic may be calculated.

To calculate the chi-square statistic, use the following formula:

$$\chi^2 = \sum \frac{(O_i - E_i)^2}{E_i}$$

where

χ^2 = chi-square statistic
O_i = observed frequency in the ith cell
E_i = expected frequency in the ith cell

Table 21.2 **One-Way Frequency Table for Brand Awareness**

AWARENESS OF TIRE MANUFACTURER'S BRAND	FREQUENCY
Aware	60
Unaware	40
	100

STATISTICAL TUTOR

Chi-Square Test

THE SITUATION:

A PRIVATE ART MUSEUM THAT SPONSORS A PROGRAM OF summer art classes for children expects an equal number of boys and girls to enroll in its classes. A random sample from its list of students shows more girls than boys.

QUESTIONS TO BE ANSWERED:

1. Is the difference between the expected (hypothetical) distribution and the observed distribution statistically significant?

2. If statistically significant, is the nature of the difference in distribution of any managerial value?

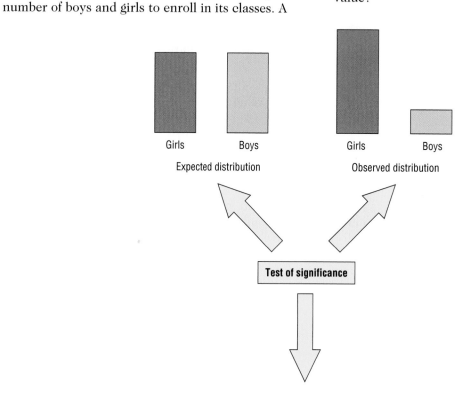

Sum the squared differences:

$$\chi^2 = \frac{(O_1 - E_1)^2}{E_i} + \frac{(O_2 - E_2)^2}{E_2}$$

Thus, we determine that the chi-square value equals 4:

$$\chi^2 = \frac{(60 - 50)^2}{50} + \frac{(40 - 50)^2}{50}$$
$$= 4$$

Table 21.3 shows the detailed calculation for this problem.

Table 21.3 **Calculating the Chi-Square Statistic**

Brand Awareness	Observed Frequency (O_i)	Expected Probability	Expected Frequency (E_i)	$(O_i - E_i)$	$\dfrac{(O_i - E_i)^2}{E_i}$
Aware	60	.5	50	10	$\dfrac{100}{50} = 2.0$
Unaware	40	.5	50	−10	$\dfrac{100}{50} = 2.0$
Total	100	1.0	100	0	$\chi^2 = 4.0$

Like many other probability distributions, the χ^2 distribution is not a single probability curve, but a family of curves. These curves, although similar, vary according to the number of degrees of freedom $(k - 1)$. Thus, we must calculate the number of degrees of freedom. (Remember, *degrees of freedom* refers to the number of observations that can be varied without changing the constraints or assumptions associated with a numerical system.) Do this as follows:

$$d.f. = k - 1$$

where

k = number of cells associated with column or row data.[4]

In the brand awareness problem there are only two categorical responses. Thus, its degrees of freedom equal 1 ($d.f. = 2 - 1 = 1$).

Now the computed chi-square value needs to be compared with the critical chi-square values associated with the .05 probability level with 1 degree of freedom. In Table A.4 of the appendix the critical chi-square value is 3.84. Thus, the calculated chi-square is larger than the tabular chi-square, and the null hypothesis—that the observed values are comparable to the expected values—is rejected.[5]

We discuss the chi-square test further in Chapter 22, as it is also frequently used to analyze contingency tables.

Hypothesis Test of a Proportion

The population proportion (π) can be estimated on the basis of the sample proportion (p). Researchers often test univariate statistical hypotheses about population proportions. The method of conducting a **hypothesis test of a proportion** is conceptually similar to hypothesis testing when the mean is the characteristic of interest. Mathematically, however, the formulation of the standard error of the proportion differs.

Consider the following example. A state legislature is considering a proposed right-to-work law. One legislator has hypothesized that 50 percent of the state's labor force is unionized. In other words, the null hypothesis to be tested is that the proportion of union workers in the state is .5.

hypothesis test of a proportion
Conceptually similar to hypothesis testing when the mean is the characteristic of interest but, mathematically, the formulation of the standard error of the proportion differs.

The researcher formulates the statistical null hypothesis that the population proportion (π) equal 50 percent (.5):

$$H_0 : \pi = .5$$

The alternative hypothesis is that π does not equal .5:

$$H_1 : \pi \neq .5$$

Suppose the researcher conducts a survey with a sample of 100 workers and calculates $p = .6$. Even though the population proportion is unknown, a large sample allows the use of the Z-test (rather than the t-test). If the researcher decides that the decision rule will be set at the .01 level of significance, the critical Z-value of 2.57 is used for the hypothesis test. Using the following formula, we can calculate the observed value of Z given a certain sample proportion:

$$Z_{obs} = \frac{p - \pi}{S_p}$$

where

p = sample proportion
π = hypothesized population proportion
S_p = estimate of the standard error of the proportion

The formula for S_p is:

$$S_p = \sqrt{\frac{pq}{n}} \quad \text{or} \quad \sqrt{\frac{p(1-p)}{n}},$$

where

S_p = estimate of the standard error of the proportion
p = proportion of successes
$q = (1 - p)$, proportion of failure

In our example,

$$S_p = \sqrt{\frac{(.6)(.4)}{100}}$$
$$= \sqrt{\frac{.24}{100}}$$
$$= \sqrt{.0024}$$
$$= .04899$$

The Z_{obs} can now be calculated:

$$Z_{obs} = \frac{p - \pi}{S_p}$$
$$= \frac{.6 - .5}{.04899}$$
$$= \frac{.1}{.04899}$$
$$= 2.04$$

The Z_{obs} value of 2.04 is less than the critical value of 2.57, so the null hypothesis cannot be rejected.

In our example the researcher drew a large sample and had to estimate the standard error of the proportion. When the sample size is small, the Z-test is not appropriate and the t-test should be used. The standard rule of thumb for determining whether the sample size is too small is to (1) multiply n by π and (2) multiply n by $(1 - \pi)$. If either product is 5 or below, the sample size is considered too small to permit the Z-test.

Additional Applications of Hypothesis Testing

The discussion of statistical inference in this chapter has been restricted to setting up a confidence interval around the sample mean to estimate the population mean, to chi-square tests of significance in the analysis of frequency distributions, and to Z-tests to test hypotheses about sample proportions when sample sizes are large. As our discussion of the population proportion suggests, there are other hypothesis tests concerning population parameters estimated from sample statistics that are not mentioned here. Many of these tests are no different conceptually in their methods of hypothesis testing. However, the formulas for conducting statistical tests are mathematically different. While these formulations may be important to the reader, the purpose of this chapter has been to discuss basic statistical concepts. The reader has learned the basic terminology in this chapter and should have no problem generalizing to other statistical problems.

As we emphasized in Chapter 17, the key to understanding statistics is learning the basics of the language. This chapter has presented verbs, nouns, and some of the rules of the grammar of statistics. It is hoped that some of the myths about statistics have been shattered.

Summary

This chapter discussed univariate statistical procedures for hypothesis testing when the research focuses on one variable. A hypothesis is a statement of assumption about the nature of the world. A null hypothesis is a statement about the status quo. The alternative hypothesis is a statement that indicates the opposite of the null hypothesis.

In hypothesis testing, a researcher states a null hypothesis about a population mean and then attempts to disprove it. The Z-test defines a region of rejection based on a significance level on the standardized normal distribution beyond which it is unlikely that the null hypothesis is true.

If a sample mean is contained in the region of rejection, the null hypothesis is rejected.

There are two possible types of error in statistical tests: Type I, rejecting a true null hypothesis, and Type II, accepting a false null hypothesis.

A number of appropriate statistical techniques are available to assist the researcher in interpreting data. The choice of statistical analysis method depends on (1) the type of question to be answered, (2) the number of variables, and (3) the scale of measurement.

Univariate statistical analysis allows the researcher to assess the statistical significance of various hypotheses about a single variable. Bivariate or multivariate analysis is used when two or more variables are to be analyzed. Nonparametric statistical tests are used on nominal and ordinal data, and parametric tests are used for interval or ratio scales. However, if a researcher cannot reasonably assume a normal population or sampling distribution, nonparametric tests may be used.

This chapter presents the technique for using *t*-distributions to estimate confidence intervals for the mean. Calculation of the confidence interval uses the central-limit theorem to estimate a range around the sample mean, which should contain the population mean.

The *t*-distribution is used for hypothesis testing with small samples when the population standard deviation is unknown. The hypothesis test is analogous to the *Z*-test. The chi-square test allows testing of statistical significance in the analysis of frequency distributions: An observed distribution of categorical data from a sample may be compared with an expected distribution for goodness of fit. Conceptually, the hypothesis test of a proportion follows a method similar to the *Z*-test for a mean.

Key Terms and Concepts

Hypothesis	Type I error	*t*-test
Null hypothesis	Type II error	Chi-square (χ^2) test
Alternative hypothesis	Univariate statistical analysis	Hypothesis test of a proportion
Significance level	*t*-distribution	
Critical values	Degrees of freedom	

Questions for Review and Critical Thinking

1. What is the purpose of a statistical hypothesis?
2. What is the significance level? How does a researcher choose a significance level?
3. List the steps in the hypothesis-testing procedure.
4. Distinguish between a Type I and Type II error.
5. What are the factors that determine the choice of the appropriate statistical technique?
6. After a bumper crop, a mushroom grower hypothesizes that mushrooms will remain at the wholesale average price of $1 per pound. State the null hypothesis and the alternative hypothesis.
7. Assume you have the following data: $H_0{:}\mu = 200$, $S = 30$, $n = 64$, and $\overline{X} = 218$. Conduct a two-tailed hypothesis test at the .05 significance level.
8. Assume you have the following data: $H_0{:}\mu = 2{,}450$, $S = 400$, $n = 100$, and $\overline{X} = 2{,}300$. Conduct a hypothesis test at the .01 significance level.
9. If the data in question 8 had been generated with a sample of 25 ($n = 25$), what statistical test would be appropriate?
10. How does the *t*-distribution differ from the *Z*-distribution?

11. The answers to a researcher's question will be nominally scaled. What statistical test is appropriate to compare the sample data with hypothesized population data?
12. A researcher plans to ask employees whether they favor, oppose, or are indifferent about a change in the company retirement program. Formulate a null hypothesis for a chi-square test, and determine the expected frequencies for each answer.
13. Give an example in which a Type I error may be more serious than a Type II error.
14. Refer to the brand awareness χ^2 data on pages 625–627. What statistical decisions could be made if the .01 significance level were selected rather than the .05 level?
15. Determine a statistical hypothesis and perform a chi-square test on the following survey data.
    a.   Star Trek: Voyager should be broadcast before 9 P.M.

Agree	40
Neutral	35
Disagree	25
	100

b. Demographic characteristics of a group indicate:

Republicans	100
Democrats	100
	200

16. A researcher hypothesizes that 15 percent of the people in a test market will recall seeing a particu- lar advertisement. In a sample of 1,200 people, 20 percent say they recall the ad. Perform a hy- pothesis test.

17. A client asks a researcher to conduct a univariate hy- pothesis test (a *Z*-test) on a single Likert-scaled item. The researcher conducts the analysis even though many researchers say these types of scales are ordi- nal, not interval. Is this the right thing to do?

Exploring the Internet

1. The Data and Story Library is an on-line library of datafiles and stories that illustrate the use of basic statistics methods. Web address is http://lib.stat.cmu. edu/DASL/.

2. StatLib is a system for distributing statistical software, datasets, and information by electronic mail, FTP, and the World Wide Web at http://lib.stat.cmu.edu/.

3. The Federal Reserve Bank of St. Louis maintains a database called FRED (Federal Reserve Economic Data). Use a search engine to navigate to the FRED database. Then select the "U.S. Employment in Retail Trade" option. Calculate a mean for the last five-year period. Then set up a hypothesis for the next five- year period.

Case 21.1 Quality Motors

QUALITY MOTORS IS AN AUTOMOBILE DEALERSHIP THAT regularly advertises in its local market area. It has claimed that a certain make and model of car averages 30 miles to a gallon of gas and mentions that this figure may vary with driving conditions. A local consumer group wishes to verify the advertising claim. To do so, it selects a sample of recent purchasers of this make and model of automobile. It asks them to drive their cars until two tanks of gasoline are used up and to record the mileage. The group then calculates and records the miles per gallon for each year. The data in Case Exhibit 21.1-1 portray the results of the tests.

QUESTIONS

1. Formulate a statistical hypothesis to test the consumer group's purpose.

2. Calculate the mean average miles per gallon. Compute the sample variance and sample standard deviation.

3. According to your hypothesis, construct the appropriate statistical test using a .05 significance level.

Case Exhibit 21.1-1 Miles per Gallon Information

Purchaser	Miles per Gallon	Purchaser	Miles per Gallon
1	30.9	13	24.2
2	24.5	14	27.0
3	31.2	15	26.7
4	28.7	16	31.0
5	35.1	17	23.5
6	29.0	18	29.4
7	28.8	19	26.3
8	23.1	20	27.5
9	31.0	21	28.2
10	30.2	22	28.4
11	28.4	23	29.1
12	29.3	24	21.9
		25	30.9

Case 21.2 Coastal Star Sales Corporation (B)

SEE COASTAL STAR SALES CORPORATION (A), CASE 17.1, for a description of the data.

QUESTIONS

1. Develop a hypothesis concerning the average age of the sales force at Coastal Star and test the hypothesis.

2. Calculate the mean for the previous year's sales, and use this as the basis to form a hypothesis concerning the current year's sales. Test the hypothesis concerning the current year's sales.

Chapter 22

Bivariate Statistical Analysis

Tests of Differences

D DB Needham Worldwide, an international advertising agency, conducts an annual Lifestyle Study to track the psychographic character of the American public. After it ran an abridged version of the lifestyle questionnaire in its in-house magazine, it decided to include an article with the title, "I Have Met the Customer and He Ain't Me," for a subsequent issue. Comparisons between the group of people who worked at the advertising agency and the average Americans who participated in the survey were dramatic and statistically significant. For example, only 52 percent of the advertising agency staff members responded that job security was more important than money versus 75 percent of the general public.

Some of the findings are especially surprising. For example, 46 percent of agency respondents said they had gone bowling in the previous year, versus 30 percent of the public. And 75 percent of agency respondents said they had bought a lottery ticket in the previous year, versus 61 percent of the public. Other striking differences:

- *I want to look different from others*—agency 82 percent, public 62 percent.
- *There's too much sex on prime-time TV*—agency 50 percent, public 78 percent.
- *TV is my primary form of entertainment*—agency 28 percent, public 53 percent.

- *I went to a bar or tavern in the past year*—agency 91 percent, public 50 percent.
- *I like the feeling of speed*—agency 66 percent, public 35 percent.
- *There should be a gun in every home*—agency 9 percent, public 32 percent.

What you will learn in this chapter

To understand that bivariate statistics deal with the simultaneous investigation of two variables.

To discuss reasons for conducting tests of differences.

To understand how the type of measurement scale influences the selection of a bivariate test of difference.

To calculate a chi-square test for a contingency table.

To understand the difference between observed versus expected frequencies and how to calculate the expected frequencies for a chi-square test.

To calculate a t-test for two independent samples for differences of means.

To calculate a Z-test for two independent samples to compare differences between two proportions.

To understand the concept of analysis of variance (ANOVA).

To state a null hypothesis in a test of differences among three or four group means.

To interpret analysis of variance summary tables.

● *I hate to lose even friendly competition*—agency 58 percent, public 44 percent.

● *My favorite music is classic rock*—agency 64 percent, public 35 percent.

● *My favorite music is easy listening*—agency 27 percent, public 51 percent.

● *Couples should live together before getting married*—agency 50 percent, public 33 percent.

● *My greatest achievements are still ahead of me*—agency 89 percent, public 65 percent.

The upshot for ad people is clear. Agency personnel who assume that the target customers are themselves just may end up with advertising that talks to no one—other than themselves.

Making comparisons such as this involves bivariate analysis, the topic of this chapter. The purpose of descriptive analysis is to summarize data. After accomplishing this, the researcher may wish to measure the association between variables or test the differences between groups of objects. This chapter goes beyond univariate statistics, in which the analysis focuses on one variable at a time. Tests of differences are in the realm of bivariate statistics, in which the researcher is concerned with scores on two variables.[1]

What Is the Appropriate Test of Difference?

One of the most frequently tested hypotheses states that two groups differ with respect to some behavior, characteristic, or attitude. For example, in the classical experimental design, the researcher tests differences between subjects assigned to the experimental group and subjects assigned to the control group. The researcher may be interested in whether male and female consumers purchase a product with equal frequency. These are bivariate **tests of differences.**

Exhibit 22.1 illustrates that both the type of measurement and the number of groups to be compared influence the type of **bivariate statistical analysis.** Often researchers are interested in testing differences in mean scores between groups or in comparing how two groups' scores are distributed across possible response categories. We will focus our attention on these issues.[2] Construction of contingency tables for chi-square analysis gives a procedure for comparing the distribution of one group with that of another group. This is a good starting point from which to discuss testing of differences.

tests of differences
An investigation of a hypothesis that states that two (or more) groups differ with respect to measures on a variable.

bivariate statistical analysis
Data analysis and hypothesis testing when the investigation concerns simultaneous investigation of two variables.

TO THE POINT

You got to be careful if you don't know where you're going, because you might not get there.

YOGI BERRA

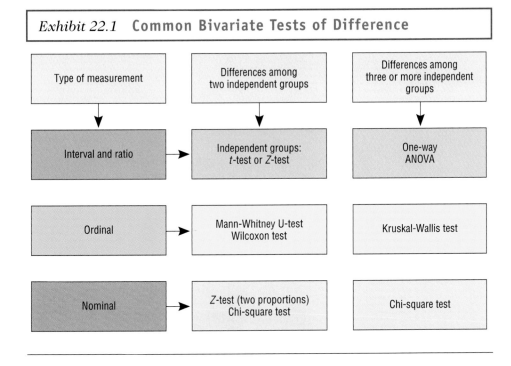

Exhibit 22.1 Common Bivariate Tests of Difference

Cross-Tabulation Tables: Using the Chi-Square Test for Goodness of Fit

One of the simplest techniques for describing sets of relationships is the cross-tabulation. A cross-tabulation, or contingency table, is a joint frequency distribution of observations on two or more sets of variables. This generally means that tabulation of subgroups will be conducted for purposes of comparison. The chi-square distribution provides a means for testing the statistical significance of contingency tables. This allows us to test for differences in two groups' distributions across categories. (Another reason for concern is whether two or more variables are interrelated or associated; this will be discussed in Chapter 23.)

As mentioned in Chapter 21, the statistical logic involved in the **chi-square test for a contingency table** is that of comparing the observed frequencies (O_i) with the expected frequencies (E_i). It tests the goodness of fit of the observed distribution with the expected distribution.

Table 22.1 reproduces Table 21.2. This one-dimensional table suggests that the majority of the population (60 percent) is aware of the brand. However, if we analyze the data by subgroups based on sex of respondents, as in Table 22.2, we

chi-square test for a contingency table
A test that statistically analyzes significance in a joint frequency distribution.

Table 22.1 **One-Way Frequency Table for Brand Awareness**

AWARENESS OF TIRE MANUFACTURER'S BRAND	FREQUENCY
Aware	60
Unaware	40
Total	100

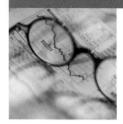

STATISTICAL TUTOR

Chi-Square Test: A Test of Differences Among Groups

QUESTIONS

1. Is the difference between the distribution statistically significant?

2. If statistically significant, is the nature of the difference in distributions of any managerial value?

A SURVEY AMONG DEMOCRATS, REPUBLICANS, AND INdependents asked: "How often do you contribute money to candidates of an opposition party?"

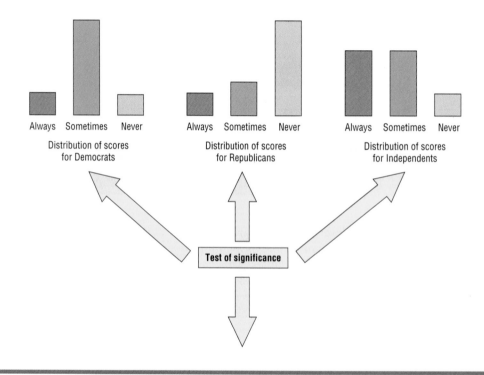

Always Sometimes Never

Distribution of scores for Democrats

Always Sometimes Never

Distribution of scores for Republicans

Always Sometimes Never

Distribution of scores for Independents

Test of significance

can see the logic of cross-classification procedures. Inspection of Table 22.2 suggests that most men are aware of the brand of tires, but most women are not. Thus, in our simple analysis we conclude that there is a difference in brand awareness between men and women. (It might also be stated that brand awareness may be associated with sex of respondent.)

So far we discussed the notion of statistical significance. Is the observed difference between men and women the result of chance variation due to random sampling? Is the discrepancy more than sampling variation? The chi-square test allows us to conduct tests for significance in the analysis of the $R \times C$ contingency table (where R = row and C = column). The formula for the chi-square statistic is the same as that for one-way frequency tables (see Chapter 21):

$$\chi^2 = \sum \frac{(O_i - E_i)^2}{E_i}$$

> ### *Table 22.2* Contingency Table (Cross-Tabulation) for Brand Awareness by Sex

AWARENESS OF TIRE MANUFACTURER'S BRAND	MEN	WOMEN	TOTAL
Aware	50	10	60
Unaware	$\frac{15}{65}$	$\frac{25}{35}$	$\frac{40}{100}$

where

$$\chi^2 = \text{chi-square statistic}$$
$$O_i = \text{observed frequency in the } i\text{th cell}$$
$$E_i = \text{expected frequency in the } i\text{th cell}$$

Again, as in the univariate chi-square test, a frequency count of data that nominally identify or categorically rank groups is acceptable for the chi-square test for a contingency table. Both variables in the contingency table will be categorical variables rather than interval- or ratio-scaled continuous variables.

We begin, as in all hypothesis-testing procedures, by formulating the null hypothesis and selecting the level of statistical significance for the particular problem. Suppose, for example, that we wish to test the null hypothesis that an equal number of men and women are aware of the brand in the preceding example and that the hypothesis test will be made at the .05 level of statistical significance.

In managerial terms the researchers asks whether men and women have different levels of brand awareness, and the problem is translated into a statistical question: "Is brand awareness independent of the respondent's sex?" Table 22.2 is a 2×2 ($R \times C$) contingency table that cross-classifies answers to the awareness question (rows) and the respondent's sex (columns).

To compute the chi-square value for the 2×2 contingency table (Table 22.2), the researcher must first identify an expected distribution for that table. Under the null hypothesis that men and women would be equally aware of the tire brand, the same proportion of positive answers (60 percent) should come from both groups. In other words, the proportion of men aware of the brand would be the same as the proportion of women aware of it. Likewise, the proportion of men unaware of the brand would equal the proportion of women unaware.

There is an easy way to calculate the expected frequencies for the cells in a cross-tabulation. To compute an expected number for each cell, use the formula

$$E_{ij} = \frac{R_i C_j}{n}$$

where

$$R_i = \text{total observed frequency in the } i\text{th row}$$
$$C_j = \text{total observed frequency in the } j\text{th column}$$
$$n = \text{sample size}$$

A calculation of the expected values does not utilize the actual observed numbers of respondents in each individual cell; only the total column and total row values are used in this calculation. The expected cell frequencies are calculated as shown in Table 22.3.

Table 22.3 **Calculation of Observed versus Expected Frequencies for Brand Awareness Problem**

Awareness of Tire Manufacturer's Brand	Men	Women	Total
Aware	50(39)*	10(21)	60
Unaware	15(26)	25(14)	40
	65	35	100

---

*Expected frequencies are in parentheses. They were calculated as follows:

$$E_{11} = \frac{(60)(65)}{100} = 39$$

$$E_{12} = \frac{(60)(35)}{100} = 21$$

$$E_{21} = \frac{(40)(65)}{100} = 26$$

$$E_{22} = \frac{(40)(35)}{100} = 14$$

To compute a chi-square statistic, use the same formula as before, but calculate degrees of freedom as the number of rows minus one $(R - 1)$ times the number of columns minus one $(C - 1)$:

$$\chi^2 = \sum \frac{(O_i - E_i)^2}{E_i}$$

with $(R - 1)(C - 1)$ degrees of freedom.

Table 22.3 shows the observed versus the expected frequencies for the brand awareness question. Using the data in Table 22.3, the chi-square statistic is calculated as follows:

$$\chi^2 = \frac{(50 - 39)^2}{39} + \frac{(10 - 21)^2}{21} + \frac{(15 - 26)^2}{26} + \frac{(25 - 14)^2}{14}$$
$$= 3.102. + 5.762 + 4.654 + 8.643$$
$$= 22.161$$

The number of degrees of freedom equal 1:

$$(R - 1)(C - 1) = (2 - 1)(2 - 1) = 1$$

From Table A.4 in the Appendix, we see that the critical value at the .05 probability level with 1 *d.f.* is 3.84. Thus, the null hypothesis is rejected. Brand awareness does not appear to be independent of the respondent's sex—in fact, the tabular value for the .001 level is 10.8, and the calculated value of 22.1 far exceeds this tabular value.

Proper use of the chi-square test requires that each expected cell frequency (E_{ij}) have a value of at least 5. If this sample size requirement is not met, the researcher may take a larger sample or combine (collapse) response categories.

The *t*-Test for Comparing Two Means

The *t*-test may be used to test a hypothesis stating that the mean scores on some interval- or ratio-scaled variable will be significantly different for two independent samples or groups. It is used when the number of observations (sample size) in either group is small (less than 30) and the population standard deviation is unknown. To use the **t-test for difference of means,** we assume the two samples are drawn from normal distributions and the variances of the two populations or groups are equal (homoscedasticity). Further, we assume interval data.

The null hypothesis about differences between groups is normally stated as follows:

$$\mu_1 = \mu_2 \quad \text{or} \quad \mu_1 - \mu_2 = 0$$

In most cases comparisons are between two sample means $(\overline{X}_1 - \overline{X}_2)$.

A verbal expression of the formula for *t* is:

$$t = \frac{\text{Mean 1} - \text{Mean 2}}{\text{Variability of random means}}$$

Thus, the *t*-value is a ratio of the information about the difference between means (provided by the sample) and the standard error in the denominator. The question is whether the observed differences have occurred by chance alone. To calculate *t,* we use the following formula:

$$t = \frac{\overline{X}_1 - \overline{X}_2}{S_{\overline{X}_1 - \overline{x}_2}}$$

where

$\overline{X}_1$ = mean for group 1
$\overline{X}_2$ = mean for group 2
$S_{\overline{X}_1 - \overline{x}_2}$ = pooled or combined standard error of difference between means

A **pooled estimate of the standard error** is a better estimate of the standard error than one based on the variance from either sample. This requires an assumption that the variances of both groups (populations) are equal. To calculate the pooled standard error of the difference between means of independent samples, we use the following formula:

$$S_{\overline{X}_1 - \overline{x}_2} = \sqrt{\left(\frac{(n_1 - 1)S_1^2 + (n_2 - 1)S_2^2}{n_1 + n_2 - 2} \right)\left(\frac{1}{n_1} + \frac{1}{n_2} \right)}$$

where

S_1^2 = variance of group 1
S_2^2 = variance of group 2
n_1 = sample size of group 1
n_2 = sample size of group 2

t-test for difference of means
A technique used to test the hypothesis that the mean scores on some interval- or ratio-scaled variables will be significantly different for two independent samples or groups.

pooled estimate of the standard error
An estimate of the standard error for a t-test of independent means that assumes the variances of both groups are equal.

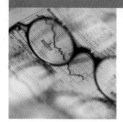

STATISTICAL TUTOR

t-Test for Difference of Means

A BANK TAKES A SAMPLE TO COMPARE THE ANNUAL salaries (in dollars) of its professional female employees with its professional male employees.

QUESTIONS

1. Is the difference between the means of men and women *statistically significant?*
2. Is the magnitude of difference large enough to justify a differential treatment strategy?

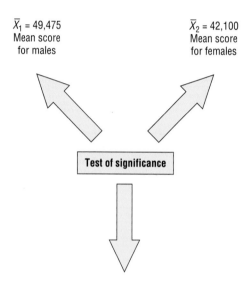

$\bar{X}_1 = 49{,}475$
Mean score
for males

$\bar{X}_2 = 42{,}100$
Mean score
for females

Test of significance

An illustration of the *t*-test would be to test the difference between sociology majors and business majors on scores on a scale to measure attitudes toward business. We will assume that the attitude scale is an interval scale. The result of the simple random sample of these two groups of college students is presented in Table 22.4. A high score indicates a favorable attitude toward business. The null hypothesis is that there is no difference in attitudes toward business (as indicated by mean scores) between the two groups. The relevant data computation is:

$$S_{\bar{X}_1 - \bar{X}_2} = \sqrt{\left(\frac{(n_1 - 1)S_1^2 + (n_2 - 1)S_2^2}{n_1 + n_2 - 2}\right)\left(\frac{1}{n_1} + \frac{1}{n_2}\right)}$$

$$= \sqrt{\left(\frac{(20)(2.1)^2 + (13)(2.6)^2}{33}\right)\left(\frac{1}{21} + \frac{1}{14}\right)}$$

$$= .797$$

Table 22.4 Comparison of Student Attitudes Toward Business

BUSINESS STUDENTS	SOCIOLOGY STUDENTS
$\overline{X}_1 = 16.5$	$\overline{X}_2 = 12.2$
$S_1 = 2.1$	$S_2 = 2.6$
$n_1 = 21$	$n_2 = 14$

The calculation of the *t*-statistic is:

$$t = \frac{\overline{X}_1 - \overline{X}_2}{S_{\overline{X}_1 - \overline{X}_2}}$$

$$= \frac{16.5 - 12.2}{.797}$$

$$= \frac{4.3}{.797}$$

$$= 5.395$$

In a test of two means, degrees of freedom are calculated as follows:

$$d.f. = n - k$$

where

$$n = n_1 - n_2$$
$$k = \text{number of groups}$$

In our example *d.f.* equals 33. If the .01 level of significance is selected, reference to Table A.3 in the appendix yields the critical *t*-value. The *t*-value of 2.75 must be surpassed by the observed *t*-value if the hypothesis test is to be statistically significant at the .01 level. The calculated value of *t*, 5.39, far exceeds the critical value of *t* for statistical significance, so it is significant at $\alpha = .01$. In other words, this research shows that business students have significantly more positive attitudes toward business than sociology students.

As another example, 11 sales representatives are categorized as either young (1) or old (2) on the basis of their ages in years, as shown in Exhibit 22.2. The exhibit presents an SAS computer output that compares the mean sales volume for these two groups.

Exhibit 22.2 SAS *t*-Test Output

t-TEST PROCEDURE VARIABLE: CR SALES

AGE	*n*	MEAN	STANDARD DEVIATION	STANDARD ERROR	MINIMUM	MAXIMUM	VARIANCES	*t*	DF	PROB > |*T*|
1	6	61879.33333	22356.20845	9126.88388	41152.00000	103059.0000	Unequal	−0.9758	5.2	0.3729
2	5	86961.80000	53734.45098	24030.77702	42775.00000	172530.0000	Equal	−1.0484	9.0	0.3218

For *HO*: Variances are equal, *F* = 5.78 with 4 and 5 *DF* Prob > *F* = 0.0815.

If σ is known, or if σ is unknown but the number of observations in both groups is large, the appropriate test of mean differences between two groups is a Z-test rather than a t-test. The procedure is conceptually identical to the one just discussed.

The Z-Test for Comparing Two Proportions

What type of statistical comparison can be made when the observed statistics are proportions? Suppose a researcher wishes to test a hypothesis that wholesalers in the northern and southern United States differ in the proportion of sales they make to discount retailers. Testing the null hypothesis that the population proportion for group 1 (π_1) equals the population proportion for group 2 (π_2) is conceptually the same as the t-test of two means. Again, sample size is the appropriate criterion for selecting either a t-test or a Z-test. This section illustrates a **Z-test for differences of proportions**, which requires a sample size greater than 30.

Z-test for differences of proportions
When the observed statistic is a proportion, this technique is used to test the hypothesis that the two proportions will be significantly different for two independent samples or groups.

The hypothesis, which is

$$H_0: \pi_1 = \pi_2$$

may be restated as

$$H_0: \pi_1 - \pi_2 = 0$$

The comparison between the observed sample proportions p_1 and p_2 allows the researcher to ask whether the differences from two *large* random samples occurred due to chance alone. To test a Z-test statistic, use the following formula:

$$Z = \frac{(p_1 - p_2) - (\pi_1 - \pi_2)}{S_{p_1 - p_2}}$$

where

p_1 = sample proportion of successes in group 1
p_2 = sample proportion of successes in group 2
$\pi_1 - \pi_2$ = hypothesized population proportion 1 minus hypothesized population proportion 2
$S_{p_1 - p_2}$ = pooled estimate of the standard error of differences in proportions

Normally the value of $\pi_1 - \pi_2$ is expected to be zero, so this formula is actually much simpler than it looks at first inspection.

To calculate the standard error of the differences in proportions, use the formula:

$$S_{p_1 - p_2} = \sqrt{\bar{p}\bar{q}\left(\frac{1}{n_1} + \frac{1}{n_2}\right)}$$

STATISTICAL TUTOR

Z-Test for Difference in Proportions

IN A SURVEY OF 400 SAILBOAT OWNERS, THE PROPORTION of respondents with annual incomes over $100,000 was 10 percent. A follow-up check of nonrespondents indicated that the proportions of nonrespondents with incomes over $100,000 was 21 percent.

QUESTIONS

1. Is the difference in proportion of those with incomes over $100,000 between survey respondents and nonrespondents statistically significant?

2. If the difference is statistically significant, is the magnitude of the difference large enough to distort the representatives of the survey?

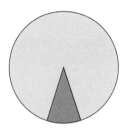

10% Proportion of survey respondents

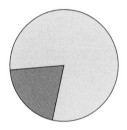

21% Proportion of nonsurvey respondents

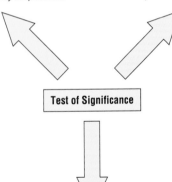

Test of Significance

where

$\bar{p}$ = pooled estimate of proportion of successes in a sample
$\bar{q}$ = $(1 - \bar{p})$, or a pooled estimate of proportion of failures in a sample
n_1 = sample size for group 1
n_2 = sample size for group 2

Because under the null hypothesis π is unknown, a weighted average of the sample proportion is calculated. To calculate the pooled estimator, $\bar{p}$, use the formula:

$$\bar{p} = \frac{n_1 p_1 + n_2 p_2}{n_1 + n_2}$$

Suppose the survey data were as follows:

	Northern Wholesalers	Southern Wholesalers
	$p_1 = .35$	$p_2 = .40$
	$n_1 = 100$	$n_2 = 100$

First, the standard error of the difference in proportions is

$$S_{p_1-p_2} = \sqrt{\bar{p}\,\bar{q}\left(\frac{1}{n_1} + \frac{1}{n_2}\right)}$$

$$= \sqrt{(.375)(.625)\left(\frac{1}{100} + \frac{1}{100}\right)} = .068$$

where

$$\bar{p} = \frac{(100)(.35) + (100)(.40)}{100 + 100} = .375$$

If we wish to test the two-tailed hypothesis of no difference, we must calculate an observed Z-value. Thus,

$$Z = \frac{(p_1 - p_2) - (\pi_1 - \pi_2)}{S_{p_1-p_2}}$$

$$= \frac{(.35 - .40) - (0)}{.068}$$

$$= -.73$$

In this example we accept the null hypothesis of no difference at the .05 level because the calculated Z-value is less than the critical Z-value of 1.96.

Analysis of Variance (ANOVA)

analysis of variance (ANOVA)
Analysis involving the investigation of the effects of one treatment variable on an interval-scaled dependent variable; a hypothesis-testing technique to determine whether statistcally significant differences on means occur between two or more groups.

When the means of more than two groups or populations are to be compared, one-way **analysis of variance (ANOVA)** is the appropriate statistical tool. This bivariate statistical technique is referred to as *one-way* because there is only one independent variable (even though there may be several levels of that variable).[3] An example of an ANOVA problem might be to compare women who are working full time outside the home, working part time outside the home, or working full time inside the home on their willingness to purchase life insurance. Here there is *one* independent variable—working status. This variable is said to have three levels: full-time employment, part-time work, and employment only within the home. Because there are three groups (levels), a *t*-test cannot be used to test for statistical significance.

If we have three groups or levels of the independent variable, the null hypothesis is stated as follows:

$$\mu_1 = \mu_2 = \mu_3$$

The null hypothesis is that all the means are equal. In the life insurance example, we are concerned with the average purchasing intention of three different types of women. As the term *analysis of variance* suggests, the problem requires comparing variances to make inferences about the means. The logic of this technique goes as follows: The variance of the means of the three groups will be large if these women differ from one another in terms of purchasing intentions. If we calculate this variance within groups and compare it with the variance of the group means about a grand mean, we can determine if the means are significantly different. This will become clearer as we investigate the *F*-test.

The F-Test

The **F-test** is a procedure for comparing one sample variance with another sample variance. (The principle is similar to the chi-square test, in which a sample variance is compared with a population variance.) The *F*-test determines whether there is more variability in the scores of one sample than in scores of another sample. The key question is whether the two sample variances are different from each other or whether they are from the same population.

The *F*-test utilizes measures of sample variance rather than the sample standard deviation because standard deviations cannot be summed and summation *is* allowable with the sample variance.

To obtain the *F*-statistic (or *F*-ratio), the larger sample variance is divided by the smaller sample variance. To test the null hypothesis of no difference between the sample variances, a table of the *F*-distribution is necessary. Using Table A.5 or A.6 in the Appendix is much like using the tables of the *Z*- and *t*-distributions that we have previously examined. These tables portray the *F*-distribution, which is a probability distribution of the ratios of sample variances. These tables indicate that the distribution of *F* is actually a family of distributions that changes quite drastically with changes in sample sizes. Thus, degrees of freedom must be specified. Inspection of an *F*-table allows the researcher to determine the probability of finding an *F* as large as the calculated *F*.

> **F-test**
> *A procedure used to determine whether there is more variability in the scores of one sample than in the scores of another sample.*

Identifying and Partitioning the Total Amount of Variation

In an analysis of variance, the basic consideration for the *F*-test is identifying the total amount of variation. There will be two forms of variation: (1) variation of scores due to random error or within-group variation due to individual differences and (2) systematic variation of scores between the groups as the result of the manipulation of an independent variable or due to characteristics of the independent variable. Thus, we can partition **total variance** into *within-group variance* and *between-group variance*.

The *F*-distribution is the ratio of these two sources of variances; that is,

> **total variance**
> *The sum of within-group variance and between-group variance.*

$$F = \frac{\text{Variance between groups}}{\text{Variance within groups}}$$

A larger ratio of variance between groups to variance within groups implies a greater value of *F*. If the *F*-value is large, the results are likely to be statistically significant.

Table 22.5   A Test Market Experiment on Pricing

	Sales in Units (thousands)		
	Regular Price, $.99	Reduced Price, $.89	Cents-Off Coupon, Regular Price
Test Market A, B, or C	130	145	153
Test Market D, E, or F	118	143	129
Test Market G, H, or I	87	120	96
Test Market J, K, or L	84	131	99
Mean	$\bar{X}_1 = 104.75$	$\bar{X}_2 = 134.75$	$\bar{X}_3 = 119.25$
Grand mean	$\bar{\bar{X}} = 119.58$		

Calculation of the F-Ratio

The data in Table 22.5 represent a hypothetical packaged-goods company's test market experiment on pricing. Three pricing treatments are administered in four separate areas (12 test areas, *A–L,* were required). These data will be used to illustrate ANOVA.

Terminology for variance estimates is derived from the calculation procedures. An explanation of the terms used to calculate the *F*-ratio should clarify the meaning of the analysis of variance technique. The calculation of the *F*-ratio requires that we partition the total variation into two parts:

$$\text{Total sum of squares} = \text{Within-group sum of squares} + \text{Between-group sum of squares}$$

or

$$SS_{\text{total}} = SS_{\text{within}} + SS_{\text{between}}$$

The total sum of squares, or SS_{total}, is computed by squaring the deviation of each score from the grand mean and summing these squares:[4]

$$SS_{\text{total}} = \sum_{i=1}^{n} \sum_{j=1}^{c} (X_{ij} - \bar{\bar{X}})^2$$

where

X_{ij} = individual score, that is, the *i*th observation or test unit in the *j*th group

$\bar{\bar{X}}$ = grand mean

n = number of all observations or test units in a group

c = number of *j*th groups (or columns)

In our example,

$$
\begin{aligned}
SS_{\text{total}} = &(130 - 119.58)^2 + (118 - 119.58)^2 + (87 - 119.58)^2 \\
&+ (84 - 119.58)^2 + (145 - 119.58)^2 + (143 - 119.58)^2 \\
&+ (120 - 119.58)^2 + (131 - 119.58)^2 + (153 - 119.58)^2 \\
&+ (129 - 119.58)^2 + (96 - 119.58)^2 + (99 - 119.58)^2 \\
= &\ 5,948.93
\end{aligned}
$$

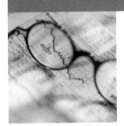

STATISTICAL TUTOR

Analysis of Variance

AN EXPERIMENT IS CONDUCTED WITH FOUR GROUPS. Each group receives a different written instruc- tion for performing a warehousing task, and the average productivity for each group is recorded.

QUESTIONS

1. Are the differences among the four groups statistically significant?

2. Is the magnitude of difference between group 1 and group 4 large enough to justify a differ- ential strategy?

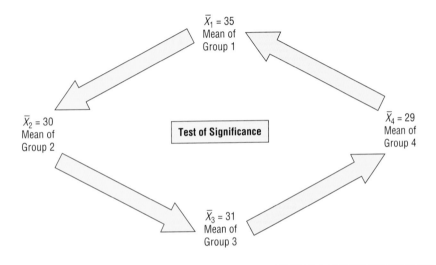

$\bar{X}_1 = 35$
Mean of Group 1

$\bar{X}_2 = 30$
Mean of Group 2

Test of Significance

$\bar{X}_4 = 29$
Mean of Group 4

$\bar{X}_3 = 31$
Mean of Group 3

SS_{within}, the variability that we observe within each group, is calculated by squar- ing the deviation of each score from its group mean and summing these scores:

$$SS_{\text{within}} = \sum_{i=1}^{n} \sum_{j=1}^{c} (X_{ij} - \bar{X}_j)^2$$

where

X_{ij} = individual score
$\bar{X}_j$ = group mean for the jth group
n = number of observations in a group
c = number of jth groups

In our example,

$$
\begin{aligned}
SS_{\text{within}} = \ & (130 - 104.75)^2 + (118 - 104.75)^2 + (87 - 104.75)^2 \\
& + (84 - 104.75)^2 + (145 - 134.75)^2 + (143 - 134.75)^2 \\
& + (120 - 134.75)^2 + (131 - 134.75)^2 + (153 - 119.25)^2 \\
& + (129 - 119.25)^2 + (96 - 119.25)^2 + (99 - 119.25)^2 \\
= \ & 4{,}148.25
\end{aligned}
$$

$SS_{between}$, which is the variability of the group means about a grand mean, is calculated by squaring the deviation of each group mean from the grand mean, multiplying by the number of items in the group, and summing these scores:

$$SS_{between} = \sum_{j=1}^{c} n_j(\overline{X}_j - \overline{\overline{X}})^2$$

where

$\overline{X}_j$ = group mean for the jth group
$\overline{\overline{X}}$ = grand mean
n_j = number of items in the jth group

In our example,

$$SS_{between} = 4(104.75 - 119.58)^2 + 4(134.75 - 119.58)^2$$
$$+ 4(119.25 - 119.58)^2$$
$$= 1,800.68$$

The next calculation requires dividing the various sums of squares by their appropriate degrees of freedom. The results of these divisions produce the variances, or *mean squares*. To obtain the mean square between groups, $SS_{between}$ is divided by $c - 1$ degrees of freedom:

$$MS_{between} = \frac{SS_{between}}{c - 1}$$

In our example,

$$MS_{between} = \frac{1,800.68}{3 - 1} = \frac{1,800.68}{2} = 900.34$$

To obtain the mean square within groups, SS_{within} is divided by $cn - c$ degrees of freedom:

$$MS_{within} = \frac{SS_{within}}{cn - c}$$

In our example,

$$MS_{within} = \frac{4,148.25}{12 - 3} = \frac{4,148.25}{9} = 460.91$$

Finally, the F-ratio is calculated by taking the ratio of the mean square between groups to the mean square within groups. The between-groups mean square is the numerator and the within-groups mean square is the denominator:

$$F = \frac{MS_{between}}{MS_{within}}$$

In our example,

$$F = \frac{900.34}{460.91} = 1.95$$

Table 22.6 ANOVA Summary Table

SOURCE OF VARIATION	SUM OF SQUARES	DEGREES OF FREEDOM	MEAN SQUARE	F-RATIO
Between groups	$SS_{between}$ or $\sum\limits_{i=1}^{c} n_j(\overline{X}_j - \overline{\overline{X}})^2$	$c - 1$	$MS_{between}$ or $\dfrac{SS_{between}}{c-1}$	—
Within groups	SS_{within} or $\sum\limits_{i=1}^{n}\sum\limits_{j=1}^{c} (X_{ij} - \overline{X}_j)^2$	$cn - c$	MS_{within} or $\dfrac{SS_{within}}{cn-c}$	$F = \dfrac{MS_{between}}{MS_{within}}$
Total	SS_{total} or $\sum\limits_{i=1}^{n}\sum\limits_{j=1}^{c} (X_{ij} - \overline{\overline{X}})^2$	$cn - 1$	—	—

Where c = number of groups
n = number of observations in a group

Table 22.7 Pricing Experiment ANOVA Table

SOURCE OF VARIATION	SUM OF SQUARES	DEGREES OF FREEDOM	MEAN SQUARE	F-RATIO
Between groups	1,800.68	2	900.34	—
Within group	4,148.25	9	460.91	1.953
Total	5,948.93	11	—	—

There will be $c - 1$ degrees of freedom in the numerator and $cn - c$ degrees of freedom in the denominator:

$$\frac{c-1}{cn-c} = \frac{3-1}{3(4)-3} = \frac{2}{9}$$

In Table A.5 in the appendix the critical value of F at the .05 level for 2 and 9 degrees of freedom indicates that an F of 4.26 would be required to reject the null hypothesis.

In our example we conclude that we cannot reject the null hypothesis. It appears that all the price treatments produce approximately the same sales volume.

The information produced from an analysis of variance is traditionally summarized in table form. Tables 22.6 and 22.7 summarize the formulas and data from our example.

Summary

Bivariate statistical techniques analyze scores on two variables at a time. Tests of difference investigate hypotheses stating that two (or more) groups differ with respect to a certain behavior, characteristic, or attitude. Both the type of measurement and the number of groups to be compared influence researchers' choice of the type of statistical test of differences.

The chi-square statistic allows one to test whether an observed sample distribution fits some given distribution. It can be used to analyze contingency, or cross-tabulation, tables. In this case the test allows one to determine whether two groups are independent. If they are not, then the variables are interrelated. For example, a marketing researcher may wish to determine whether the respondent's sex makes a difference for some observed variable. The *t*-test for two independent samples is used to determine if the means of two independent samples are significantly different. An example would be the comparison of two populations' characteristics using the same measure of an attribute on samples from each population.

The *t*-test is appropriate when the population standard deviation is unknown. The *t*-test should be chosen over the *Z*-test if the sample size is small. A *Z*-test for two independent samples typically is used if a large sample has been drawn from each group, because the *t*-distribution approximates the *Z*-distribution when the sample is large. A *Z*-test for two independent samples may be used to determine if two proportions are significantly different.

One-way analysis of variance (ANOVA) compares the means of samples from more than two populations to determine whether their differences are statistically significant. The technique is one-way because it deals with only one independent variable, although several levels of that variable may be used. The total variance in the observations is partitioned into two parts, that from within-group variation and that from between-group variation. The ratio of the variance between groups to the variance within groups gives an *F*-statistic. The *F*-distribution is a measure used to determine whether the variability of two samples differ significantly. In ANOVA if the observed statistic is greater than the test value for some level of significance, the hypothesis that there is no significant difference in the means of the sample groups may be rejected.

Key Terms and Concepts

Test of differences
Bivariate statistical analysis
Chi-square test for a contingency
  table

t-test for difference of means
Pooled estimate of the standard error
Z-test for differences of proportions
Analysis of variance (ANOVA)

F-test
Total variance
Within-group variance
Between-group variance

Questions for Review and Critical Thinking

1. What tests of difference are appropriate in the following situations?
   a. Average campaign contributions of Democrats, Republicans, and independents are to be compared.
   b. Advertising managers and brand managers respond "yes," "no," or "not sure" to an attitude question. Their answers are to be compared.
   c. One-half of a sample received an incentive in a mail survey; the other half did not. A comparison of response rate is desired.
   d. A researcher believes that married men will push the grocery cart when grocery shopping with their wives.

2. Perform a chi-square test on the following data:

A. REGULATION IS THE BEST WAY TO ENSURE SAFE PRODUCTS	MANAGERS	BLUE-COLLAR WORKERS
Agree	58	66
Disagree	34	24
No opinion	8	10
Totals	100	100

B. OWNERSHIP OF RESIDENCE	MALE	FEMALE
Yes	25	16
No	7	8
Totals	32	24

C. AGE OF SHOPPER	STORE A	STORE B
20–34	27	73
35–54	31	82
55 and over	11	93
Totals	69	248

3. Collapse the response categories in the following table so that it meets the assumption of the chi-square test, then perform the test.

	OWNERSHIP	
EDUCATION	OWNERS	NONOWNERS
Less than grade 8	0	8
Some high school	5	9
High school graduate	30	25
Some college	10	11
College graduate	12	15
Master's degree	3	6
Ph.D. degree	2	1

4. Interpret the SPSS computer output for the following chi-square test. Variable $F7$ is "How did you get to work last week?" Variable $E6$ is "Do you have a college degree?"

SPSS Test Run on State Data File State Survey Cross-Tabulation of How Did You Get to Work Last Week? by *E6*. Have College Degree

COUNT ROW PERCENT COLUMN PERCENT TOTAL PERCENT		*E6* YES 1.	No 2.	Row TOTAL
F7 Driver	1.	159 39.1 74.0 30.7	248 60.9 81.8 47.9	407 78.6
Passenger	2.	15 44.1 7.0 2.9	19 55.9 6.3 3.7	34 6.6
Bus	3.	5 55.6 2.3 1.0	4 44.4 1.3 0.8	9 1.7
Walked	6.	13 68.4 6.0 2.5	6 31.6 2.0 1.2	19 3.7
At home	7.	9 32.1 4.2 1.7	19 67.9 6.3 3.7	28 5.4
Other	8.	14 66.7 6.5 2.7	7 33.3 2.3 1.4	21 4.1
Column Total		215 41.5	303 58.5	518 100.0

Chi-square = 13.98101 with 5 degrees of freedom significance = 0.0157
Number of missing observations = 2,197

5. A store manager's computer-generated list of all retail sales employees indicates that 70 percent are full-time employees, 20 percent are part-time employees, and 10 percent are furloughed or laid-off employees. A sample of 50 employees from the list indicates that there are 40 full-time employees, 6 part-time employees, and 4 furlough/laid-off employees. Conduct a statistical test to determine whether the sample is representative of the population.

6. Test the hypothesis of no differences between savings and loans and other financial institutions for average payback period (years) for loans for residential solar systems.

SAVINGS AND LOANS	OTHER FINANCIAL INSTITUTIONS
$\overline{X}_1 = 8.7$	$\overline{X}_2 = 7.7$
$S_1^2 = 0.5$	$S_2^2 = 0.6$
$n_1 = 100$	$n_2 = 64$

7. The territories in a company's eastern and western regions were rated for sales potential based on the company's evaluation system. A sales manager wishes to conduct a *t*-test of means to determine if there is a difference between the two regions. Perform this calculation based on the following data:

REGION	TERRITORY	RATING
West	1	74
West	2	88
West	3	78
West	4	85
West	5	100
West	6	114
West	7	98
East	1	81
East	2	63
East	3	56
East	4	68
East	5	80
East	6	79
East	7	69

8. Given the following data, is there a difference between means?

	SAMPLE 1	SAMPLE 2
Sample mean	324	301
Sample variance	166.41	81
Sample size	44	56

9. A sales force ($n = 67$) received some management-by-objectives training. Are the before/after mean scores for salespeople's job performance statistically significant at the .05 level?

SKILL	BEFORE	AFTER	T
Planning ability	4.84	5.43	4.88
Territory coverage	5.24	5.51	1.89
Activity reporting	5.37	5.42	0.27

10. The incomes of owners of trash compactors were compared with those of nonowners. The average income was as follows:

	OWNERS	NONOWNERS
$\overline{X}$	4.6	3.5

Higher values represent higher levels of income. (Actual scaled average: less than $7,500 = 1, $7,501–$15,000 = 2, $15,001–$25,000 = 3, $25,001–$40,000 = 4, $40,001–$60,000 = 5, over $60,000 = 6.) Is a *t*-test appropriate?

11. Test the hypotheses of no difference for the following two groups on bubble bath usage:

Women under 35	Women 35–54
$p_1 = 13\%$	$p_2 = 23\%$
$S_{p1} = .04$	$S_{p2} = .04$
$n_1 = 144$	$n_2 = 169$

12. Conduct a *Z*-test to determine whether the following two samples indicate that the population proportions are significantly different at the .05 level:

	Sample 1	Sample 2
Sample proportion	.77	.68
Sample size	55	46

13. Interpret the following *t*-test results. Are they statistically significant?

GROUP 1: E2 EQ 1.00
GROUP 2: E2 NE 1.00

VARIABLE	GRP	N	MEAN	STD DEV	STD ERR
D2	1	935	2.282	1.406	.046
	2	529	2.297	1.525	.06

SEPARATE VARIANCE

VARIABLE	MEAN	DIFFERENCE TD ERR	T	DF	PROB
D2	−.014	.081	−.18	1024	.858

POOLED VARIANCE

VARIABLE	MEAN	DIFFERENCE STD ERR	T	DF	PROB
D2	−.014	.079	−.18	1462	.855

14. Suppose a researcher has one nominal-scaled variable and one interval-scaled variable. The researcher wishes to use a chi-square test. What can be done?

15. A researcher conducts an experiment with wholesalers to manipulate perception of task difficulty and to measure level of aspiration for performing the task a second time. Group 1 was told the task was very difficult, group 2 was told the task was somewhat difficult but attainable, and group 3 was told the task was easy. Perform an ANOVA on the following data:

	SUBJECTS' LEVEL OF ASPIRATION (10-POINT SCALE)		
SUBJECTS	GROUP 1	GROUP 2	GROUP 3
1	6	5	5
2	7	4	6
3	5	7	5
4	8	6	4
5	8	7	2
6	6	7	3
Cases	6	6	6

16. A researcher finds that 122 respondents have checking accounts at banks, 131 at savings and loans, and 4 at credit unions. The researcher groups the 4 respondents who answered "credit union" in with the savings and loans group so a bivariate comparison between banks and S&Ls can be made. Is this ethical?

 ## Exploring the Internet

1. Go to the SPSS home page at http://www.spss.com. Navigate to "Statistical Coach" to learn what procedure is best to perform the statistical tests mentioned in this chapter.
2. The Federal Reserve Bank of St. Louis maintains a database called FRED (Federal Reserve Economic Data). Use a search engine to navigate to the FRED database. Randomly select a five-year period between 1970 and 1995 and then compare average figures for U.S. employment in retail trade with those for U.S. employment in wholesale trade. What statistical tests are appropriate?

Case 22.1 Hard Rock Cafe

THE ORIGINAL HARD ROCK CAFE WAS ESTABLISHED IN London in 1971. Since then other locations featuring collections of musical memorabilia have opened in major cities in Europe and America.

A researcher was concerned with the characteristics of the clientele at a Hard Rock Cafe at lunchtime and in the evenings. On a Saturday during July, the researcher collected the age data in Case Exhibit 22.1-1 by randomly sampling table numbers at the cafe and then obtaining the ages of everyone sitting at each table.

QUESTIONS

1. How would you analyze the differences between the evening and the luncheon clientele?
2. Perform the statistical analysis that you conclude is the best.

Case Exhibit 22.1-1   Age Data

	LUNCH		EVENING
Table 1	11	Table 1	26
	9		26
	43		27
	39		28
Table 2	40	Table 2	21
	42		23
	13		21
	9		
Table 3	12	Table 3	24
	13		24
	44		23
	47		
Table 4	44	Table 4	24
	10		22
	12		21
	11		24
Table 5	9	Table 5	22
	39		23
	46		27
	11		
Table 6	32	Table 6	22
	9		18
Table 7	39	Table 7	22
	13		19
	11		
Table 8	43	Table 8	23
	5		24
	12		24
			21
Total number of people	28		25

Case 22.2   Tulsa's Central Business District (D)

THE RESEARCH DIRECTOR MENTIONED IN CASE 20.1 RAN A cross-tabulation using the SPSS computer program to relate the sex of the respondent (SEX) with the question "About how often during the workweek do you shop downtown?" (CBDSHOP). Sex was coded women (0) and men (1).

The variable CBDSHOP had six possible answers. However, the answers were collapsed into three categories: frequent shopper (1), occasional shopper (4), and nonshopper/infrequent shopper (6).

The SPSS output appears in Case Exhibit 22.2-1.

QUESTIONS

1. Is this form of analysis appropriate?

2. Interpret the computer output.

Case Exhibit 22.2-1   Cross-Tabulation of CBDSHOP by Sex

A	K	COUNT ROW PERCENT COLUMN PERCENT TOTAL PERCENT	SEX C		Row TOTAL	
			WOMEN 0	MEN 1		
B CBDSHOP						
			66	21	87	**I**
			75.9	24.1	20.3	**J**
Frequent	1		29.9	10.1		
shopper			15.4	4.9		
			72	85	157	
			45.9	54.1	36.6	
Occasional	4		32.6	40.9		
shopper			16.8	19.8		
			83	102	185	
Nonshopper/			44.9	55.1	43.1	
infrequent	6		37.6	49.0		
shopper			19.3	23.8		
Column			221 **G**	208	429	**E**
Total			51.5 **H**	48.5	100.0	**F**

Raw chi-square = 25.93349 with 2 degrees of freedom. Significance = 0.0000

D   Number of missing observations = 6

Case 22.3   Tobin's Field Services (B)

TOBIN'S FIELD SERVICES CONDUCTED A SURVEY FOR A RETAIL store. (See Case 18.2 for additional details.) The questionnaire in Case Exhibit 18.2-3 was designed with four purposes in mind: (1) to determine retail purchasing behavior, (2) to determine the image of the stores within the region, (3) to provide an indication of the market segmentation strategy that might be utilized, and (4) to find out consumers' specific likes and dislikes about the various retail stores.

The researchers were quite pleased with the questionnaire. However, they had not decided how to analyze the data beyond descriptive analysis.

QUESTIONS

1. What hypotheses could have been made concerning market segmentation?

2. What test of differences would seem most appropriate to test your hypotheses?

3. What would be the appropriate statistical techniques?

Case 22.4   Solo Sugar Substitute[5]

SOLO IS A SUGAR SUBSTITUTE. THE CREATIVE DEPARTMENT OF the manufacturer's advertising agency had developed two versions of an advertising theme that emphasized the theme "less calories than sugar with the same taste." The manufacturer of Solo did not have its own marketing research department, and therefore its advertising agency commissioned research to determine which of these two versions would create stronger purchase interest. Agency researchers conferred with company marketing personnel over basic brand strategies. The company helped specify what should be measured and how the information should be interpreted.

The researcher concluded that the shorter copy line would have greater impact in stimulating purchase interest. Neither version successfully communicated one of the product's attributes, however, and the researcher recommended that this issue be explored further.

Objective

The purpose of this study was to determine the impact of the two voice-over copy lines read by an announcer for a Solo TV commercial. Both lines conveyed the theme of fewer calories than sugar but the same taste. The two copy lines, designated "shorter copy" and "longer copy," were these:

Shorter copy: "Solo. Less than half the calories

of sugar, and tastes like the real thing. Solo, for regular use."

Longer copy: "Solo. Results you can't possibly get with sugar. Solo, less than half the calories of sugar, and tastes like the real thing—no bitter aftertaste."

Method

Each copy line was exposed to a different group of women who used sugar substitutes. The shorter copy line was exposed to 149 women; the longer one was exposed to 127 women. The basic criterion for evaluating each copy line was the percentage who preferred the Solo product to its retail cash equivalent, that is, a product versus a cash offer. These data are presented in the following exhibits.

QUESTIONS

1. What type of statistical test should be used for Case Exhibit 22.4-1? For Case Exhibit 22.4-2? Perform these tests if the data shown allow you to do so.

2. Interpret the data in Case Exhibit 22.4-1 and Case Exhibit 22.4-2.

Case Exhibit 22.4-1   Preference Between Solo and Cash for Two Copy Lines

RESPONSE	SHORTER COPY (PERCENT)	LONGER COPY (PERCENT)
Preference:	(n = 149)	(n = 127)
Solo	58	41
Cash	42	59

Question: Suppose you have the choice of taking either this product or _____ in cash. Which would you rather have—the product or the cash?

Case Exhibit 22.4-2   Ratings of Solo on Three Product Attributes (by Copy Line)

	SHORTER COPY (MEAN)	LONGER COPY (MEAN)
Gives you the right number of calories	6.12	5.26
Gives fewer calories than other brands	5.71	4.63
Tastes like real sugar	4.29	4.12
Base	(149)	(127)

Appendix 22A

Nonparametric Statistics for Tests of Differences

For many of the statistical tests you have learned to use, it has been necessary to assume that the population (or sampling distribution) is normally distributed.[6] If it is normal, the error made in making inferences about the population from sample data can be estimated. If it is not normal, however, the error may be large and cannot be estimated. It is therefore valuable to know some tests in which a strong assumption such as normality does not need to be made about the population distribution; these are called *nonparametric* tests. You have already studied one of them: the χ^2 test. There are many others, but only three of them are included here.

The term *nonparametric* is confusing. It was originally applied when no assumption needed to be made about the population distribution (as in the χ^2 tests) and when there was no estimate of a population parameter. Almost always, however, some assumption needs to be made. So *nonparametric* is now used to mean that a less stringent requirement than normality is made for the population distribution. Also, the meaning of the phrase *nonparametric test* has been extended to include any test that uses nominal-scaled or ordinal-scaled data. Thus, a comparison of the heights of two samples of women is made with a nonparametric test if, instead of measuring each person's height, all the women are simply arranged in order of height in a row (the two tallest come from sample 1, the third tallest comes from sample 2, and so on). Because the data are ranked and not ratio or interval scaled, a nonparametric test is used, even if it is known that the heights in both populations from which the samples were chosen are normally distributed.

Nonparametric tests have many advantages: They avoid the error caused by assuming a population is normally distributed when it is not, the computations that need to be made are often very simple, and the data may be easier to collect (almost certainly so when nominal or ordinal-ranked data are used rather than ratio- or interval-scaled data). Why are nonparametric tests not always used, then? The answer is that you do not get something for nothing. If the population distribution is normal so that, say, a *t*-test or a nonparametric test may be chosen, the former generally will give a smaller value of β *Type II* error (i.e., a smaller error) than the latter for a given, fixed level of *Type I* error (value of α). If this is the case, sample size will have to be larger for the nonparametric test if the same limits on an α and β are to be attained as with a *t*-test. For the same sample size, then, the *t*-test results usually will be more reliable. Also, the null hypotheses are sometimes more general; rejection may imply that two population distributions are different, but it is not known whether they have different means, different variances, or differently shaped distributions (e.g., one normal and the other not).

Wilcoxon Matched-Pairs Signed-Ranks Test

The *Wilcoxon matched-pairs signed-ranks test* is a good measure of differences when the researcher wishes to test the hypothesis $\mu_1 = \mu_2$ and the researcher knows that the samples are not independent, or when the researcher wishes to compare magnitude of differences in ordinal rankings, such as preference ratings between two alternatives. A common situation is the "before/after" experiment, where the same subjects are measured twice.

Suppose an executive wishes to know whether a training program will have a positive impact on attitude toward achievement within the organization. Table 22A.1 shows attitude ratings before and after a training program for 11 sales managers. The Wilcoxon matched-pairs signed-ranks test begins by calculating the signed difference for each matched-pair of observations. If the two observations in a pair of observations are the same, this pair is dropped from the analysis. Next, these differences are rank ordered according to their absolute size. If there are two (or more) pairs with identical absolute-difference values, such as for manager 2 and manager 9, an average rank score is given to each of the pairs. Finally, the positive or negative sign is assigned to the rank scores, and the scores for the positive and negative groups are separately totaled. The symbol Tp is the summed ranks for the positive differences, and the symbol Tn is the summed ranks for the negative differences.[7] T represents the smaller of Tp or Tn, and for small samples T is the test statistic.

In our example T_n has the smaller value. Thus the calculated value of T is 17. In the Wilcoxon matched-pairs signed-ranks test, the null hypothesis is rejected if the calculated value of T is *equal to or less than* the critical T-value that can be found in Table A.8 in the Appendix of Statistical Tables at the end of the book. In that table N represents the number of pairs. At $N = 10$ (because the tied pair is discarded from the analysis) the critical T-value is 8 at the .05 level of statistical significance. Because the calculated value of T (17) is greater than 8, we cannot reject the null hypothesis. When the sample size is large, the sampling distribu-

---

Table 22A.1 **Training Program Example**

Manager	"Before" Score	"After" Score	Sign of Difference	Absolute Difference	Signed Rank Rank	Signed Rank Positive	Signed Rank Negative
1	56	71	+	15	10	10	
2	46	49	+	3	3.5	3.5	
3	74	73	−	1	1		1
4	66	72	+	6	8	8	
5	59	55	−	4	5.5		5.5
6	45	40	−	5	7		7
7	85	87	+	2	2	2	
8	63	67	+	4	5.5	5.5	
9	67	64	−	3	3.5		3.5
10	79	79		0	—	—	—
11	70	78	+	8	9	9	
						$T_p = 38$	$T_n = 17$

tion is approximately normal, and the *Z*-value may be calculated using the following formula:

$$Z = \frac{T - \dfrac{N(N+1)}{4}}{\sqrt{\dfrac{N(N+1)\,(2N+1)}{24}}}$$

Mann-Whitney Test

Many tests of group differences concern the comparison of two sample means to determine whether there is a statistically significant difference between two population means. The *Mann-Whitney* (or *ranked-sum*) *test* allows for testing group differences when the populations are not normally distributed or when it cannot be assumed that the samples are from populations equal in variability. It is an alternative to the *t*-test for two independent samples.

To see how this test is used, consider the following data on the number of minutes needed by two groups of workers to learn how to repair a chain saw.[8] Group A received classroom training, whereas group B received only on-the-job training.

		Average
Group A	35, 39, 51, 63, 48, 31, 29, 41, 55	43.46
Group B	85, 28, 42, 37, 61, 54, 36, 57	50

The means of these two samples are 43.56 and 50. In this case we wish to decide whether the difference between the means is significant.

The two samples are arranged jointly as if they were one sample, in order of increasing time, and we get the ranked-sum test:

Time	Group	Rank
28	B	1
29	A	2
31	A	3
35	A	4
36	B	5
37	B	6
39	A	7
41	A	8
42	B	9
48	A	10
51	A	11
54	B	12
55	A	13
57	B	14
61	B	15
63	A	16
85	B	17

We assign each value to group A or to group B, then we assign the ranks, 1, 2, 3, 4,…, 17 to the scores, in this order, as the table shows.

The group A scores occupy the ranks of 2, 3, 4, 7, 8, 10, 11, 13, and 16. The group B scores occupy the ranks of 1, 5, 6, 9, 12, 14, 15, and 17. Now we sum the ranks of the group with the smaller sample size, in this case group B, and get:

$$1 + 5 + 6 + 9 + 12 + 14 + 15 + 17 = 79$$

The sum of the ranks is denoted by R. In this case $R = 79$.

We always let n_1 and n_2 denote the sizes of the two samples, where n_1 represents the smaller of the two. Thus, R represents the sum of the ranks of this smaller group. If both groups are of equal size, either one is called n and R represents the sum of the ranks of this group. Statistical theory tells us that if both n_1 and n_2 are large enough, each equal to 8 or more, then the distribution of R can be approximated by a normal distribution. The test statistic is given by the formula

$$Z = \frac{R - \mu_R}{\sigma_R}$$

where

$$\mu_R = \frac{n_1(n_1 + n_2 + 1)}{2}$$

$$\sigma_R = \sqrt{\frac{n_1 n_2(n_1 + n_2 + 1)}{12}}$$

Using a .05 level of significance, we reject the null hypothesis of equal means if $Z > 1.96$ or $Z < -1.96$.

In our case $R = 79$, $n_1 = 8$, and $n_2 = 9$, so that

$$\mu_R = \frac{n_1(n_1 + n_2 + 1)}{2}$$

$$= \frac{8(8 + 9 + 1)}{2}$$

$$= 72$$

and

$$\sigma_R = \sqrt{\frac{n_1 n_2(n_1 + n_2 + 1)}{12}}$$

$$= \sqrt{\frac{8(9)(8 + 9 + 1)}{12}}$$

$$= \sqrt{108}$$

$$= 10.39$$

The test statistic then becomes

$$Z = \frac{R - \mu_R}{\sigma_R} = \frac{79 - 72}{10.39} = 0.67$$

Since the value $Z = 0.67$ falls in the acceptance region, we do not reject the null hypothesis. There is no significant difference between the means of these two groups.

Comment

The method we have just described is called the *Mann-Whitney test*. Statisticians have constructed tables that give the appropriate critical values when both sample sizes, n_1 and n_2, are smaller than 8. The interested reader can find such tables in many books on nonparametric statistics. The corresponding exact statistic is called the *Mann-Whitney U test*.

Kruskal-Wallis Test for Several Independent Samples

When a researcher wishes to compare three or more groups or populations and the data are ordinal, the *Kruskal-Wallis test* is the appropriate statistical technique. This test may be thought of as a nonparametric equivalent of analysis of variance. However, as with all nonparametric tests, the assumptions are less restricting: The researcher does not have to assume that the underlined populations are normally distributed or that equal variances are shared by each group. If there are three groups, the null hypothesis is that population 1 equals population 2, which equals population 3. In other words, the Kruskal-Wallis test is a technique to determine whether the three populations have the same distribution shape and dispersion.

The test requires that the data be ranked from lowest to highest or that the original data be converted so that a numerical rank may be assigned to every observation. If two observations are ranked the same (i.e., when ties occur), the mean rank score is assigned to both observations. To illustrate the calculation of the *H*-statistic, consider the following example. An advertising agency employs three different film production companies to produce its television commercials. The advertising agency has taken a sample of five commercials from each of the production houses, and agency executives have ranked the production quality of the commercials from highest quality (1) to lowest quality (15). These ranks are shown in Table 22A.2. The advertising agency considered two commercials to be ranked of equal quality. Hence, rather than being ranked a 3 and a 4, each commercial is ranked 3.5.

Table 22A.2 **Quality Rankings of Television Commercials**

	RANKS	
PRODUCTION COMPANY 1	PRODUCTION COMPANY 2	PRODUCTION COMPANY 3
9.0	6.0	1.0
5.0	13.0	7.0
3.5	10.0	15.0
14.0	2.0	12.0
8.0	3.5	11.0
$R_1 = 39.5$	$R_2 = 34.5$	$R_3 = 46$

The Kruskal-Wallis test statistic, the *H*-statistic, is calculated as follows:

$$H = \frac{12}{n(n+1)} \left[\sum \frac{R_i^2}{n_i} \right] - 3(n+1)$$

where

R_i = sum of the ranks of the *i*th group
n_i = sample size of the *i*th group
n = combined sample sizes of all groups

$$H = \frac{12}{n(n+1)} \left(\frac{R_1^2}{n_1} + \frac{R_2^2}{n_2} + \frac{R_3^2}{n_3} \right) - 3(n+1)$$

$$= \frac{12}{15(15+1)} \left[\frac{(39.5)^2}{5} + \frac{(34.5)^2}{5} + \frac{(46)^2}{5} \right] - 3(15+1)$$

$$= \frac{12}{240} \left(\frac{1,560.25}{5} + \frac{1,190.25}{5} + \frac{2,116}{5} \right) - 48$$

$$= 0.05(973.3) - 48$$

$$= 48.665 - 48$$

$$= 0.665$$

When the sample size (n_i) from each group or population exceeds four observations, the *H* is approximately the same as the χ^2, with degrees of freedom equal to $K - 1$, where K equals the number of groups.

In our example, degrees of freedom equals 2 $(3 - 1)$. Table A.4 in the appendix shows that the critical value at the .05 level with 2 degrees of freedom is 5.991. Because the calculated *H* value is 0.665, we cannot reject the null hypothesis.

ANOVA for Complex Experimental Designs

ANOVA for a Randomized Block Design

To test for statistical significance in a randomized block design, or RBD (see Chapter 12), another version of analysis of variance is utilized. The linear model for the RBD for an individual observation is:[9]

$$Y_{ij} = \mu + \alpha_j + \beta_i + \epsilon_{ij}$$

where

Y_{ij} = individual observation on the dependent variable
μ = grand mean
α_j = jth treatment effect
β_i = ith block effect
ϵ_{ij} = random error or residual

The statistical objective is to determine whether significant differences among treatment means and block means exist. This will be done by calculating an F-ratio for each source of effects.

The same logic and assumptions that apply in single-factor ANOVA—to use variance estimates to test for differences among means—apply in ANOVA for randomized block designs (see Chapter 22). Thus, to conduct the ANOVA, the total sum of squares (SS_{total}) is partitioned into nonoverlapping components.[10]

$$SS_{total} = S_{treatments} + SS_{blocks} + SS_{error}$$

The sources of variance are defined as follows:

Total sum of squares:

$$SS_{total} = \sum_{i=1}^{r} \sum_{j=1}^{c} (Y_{ij} - \overline{\overline{Y}})^2$$

where

$$Y_{ij} = \text{individual observation}$$
$$\bar{\bar{Y}} = \text{grand mean}$$
$$r = \text{number of blocks (rows)}$$
$$c = \text{number of treatments (columns)}$$

Treatment sum of squares:

$$SS_{\text{treatments}} = \sum_{i=1}^{r} \sum_{j=1}^{c} (\bar{Y}_j - \bar{\bar{Y}})^2$$

where

$$\bar{Y}_j = j\text{th treatment mean}$$
$$\bar{\bar{Y}} = \text{grand mean}$$

Block sum of squares:

$$SS_{\text{blocks}} = \sum_{i=1}^{r} \sum_{j=1}^{c} (\bar{Y}_i - \bar{\bar{Y}})^2$$

where

$$\bar{Y}_j = i\text{th block mean}$$
$$\bar{\bar{Y}} = \text{grand mean}$$

Sum of squares error:

$$SS_{\text{error}} = \sum_{i=1}^{r} \sum_{j=1}^{c} (Y_{ij} - \bar{Y}_i - \bar{Y}_j - \bar{\bar{Y}})^2$$

The SS_{error} may also be calculated in the following manner:

$$SS_{\text{error}} = SS_{\text{total}} - SS_{\text{treatments}} - SS_{\text{blocks}}$$

The degrees of freedom for $SS_{\text{treatments}}$ is equal to $c - 1$ because $SS_{\text{treatments}}$ reflects the dispersion of treatment means from the grand mean, which is fixed. Degrees of freedom for blocks is $r - 1$ for similar reasons. SS_{error} reflects variations from both treatment and block means; thus, $d.f. = (r - 1)(c - 1)$.

Mean squares are calculated by dividing the appropriate sum of squares by the corresponding degrees of freedom.

Table 22B.1 is an ANOVA table for the randomized block design. It summarizes what has been discussed and illustrates the calculation of mean squares.

F-ratios for treatment and block effects are calculated as follows:

$$F_{\text{treatment}} = \frac{\text{Mean square treatment}}{\text{Mean square error}}$$

$$F_{\text{blocks}} = \frac{\text{Mean square blocks}}{\text{Mean square error}}$$

SOURCE OF VARIATION	SUM OF SQUARES	DEGREES OF FREEDOM	MEAN SQUARES
Between blocks	SSblocks	r - 1	$\dfrac{SS_{\text{blocks}}}{r-1}$
Between treatments	SStreatments	c - 1	$\dfrac{SS_{\text{treatments}}}{c-1}$
Error	SSerror	(r - 1)(c - 1)	$\dfrac{SS_{\text{error}}}{(r-1)(c-1)}$
Total	SStotal	rc - 1	—

Table 22B.1 **ANOVA Table for Randomized Block Designs**

Factorial Designs

There is considerable similarity between the factorial design (see Chapter 12) and the one-way analysis of variance. The sum of squares for each of the treatment factors (rows and columns) is similar to the between-groups sum of squares in the single-factor ANOVA model; that is, each treatment sum of squares is calculated by taking the deviation of the treatment means from the grand mean. Determining the sum of squares for the interaction is a new calculation because this source of variance is not attributable to the treatments as sum of squares or the error sum of squares.

ANOVA for a Factorial Experiment

In a two-factor experimental design the linear model for an individual observation is:

$$Y_{ijk} = \mu + \beta_i + \alpha_j + I_{ij} + \epsilon_{ijk}$$

where

Y_{ijk} = individual observation on the dependent variable
μ = grand mean
β_i = ith effect of factor B—row treatment
α_j = jth effect of factor A—column treatment
I_{ij} = interaction effect of factors A and B
ϵ_{ijk} = random error or residual

Partitioning the Sum of Squares for a Two-Way ANOVA

Table 22B.2 gives the symbolic notation for a two-way ANOVA. Again, the total sum of squares can be allocated into distinct and overlapping portions:

Sum of squares total	=	Sum of square rows (treatment B)	+	Sum of squares columns (treatment A)	+	Sum of squares interaction	+	Sum of squares error

> ## Table 22B.2 Symbol Notation for Two-Factor ANOVA
>
> Y_{ijk} = individual observation on the dependent variable
> $\overline{\overline{Y}}$ = grand mean
> $\overline{Y}_i$ = mean of ith treatment—factor B
> $\overline{Y}_j$ = mean of jth treatment—factor A
> $\overline{Y}_{ij}$ = mean of the interaction effect
> j = level of factor A
> i = level of factor B
> k = number of an observation in a particular cell
> r = total number of levels of factor B (rows)
> c = total number of levels for factor A (columns)
> n = total number of observations in the sample

or

$$SS_{\text{total}} = SSR_{\text{treatment B}} + SSC_{\text{treatment A}} + SS_{\text{interaction}} + SS_{\text{error}}$$

Sum of squares total:

$$SS_{\text{total}} = \sum_{i=1}^{r} \sum_{j=1}^{c} \sum_{k=1}^{n} (Y_{ijk} - \overline{\overline{Y}})^2$$

Sum of squares rows (treatment B):

$$SSR_{\text{treatment B}} \sum_{i=1}^{r} (\overline{Y}_i - \overline{\overline{Y}})^2$$

Sum of squares columns (treatment A):

$$SSC_{\text{treatment A}} \sum_{j=1}^{c} (\overline{Y}_j - \overline{\overline{Y}})^2$$

Sum of squares interaction:

$$SS_{\text{interaction}} \sum_{i=1}^{r} \sum_{j=1}^{c} \sum_{k=1}^{n} (Y_{ij} - \overline{Y}_i - \overline{Y}_j - \overline{\overline{Y}})^2$$

The above is one form of calculation. However, $SS_{\text{interaction}}$ generally is indirectly computed in the following manner:

$$SS_{\text{interaction}} = SS_{\text{total}} - SSR_{\text{treatment B}} - SSC_{\text{treatment A}} - SS_{\text{error}}$$

Sum of squares error:

$$SS_{\text{error}} \sum_{i=1}^{r} \sum_{j=1}^{c} \sum_{k=1}^{n} (Y_{ijk} - \overline{Y}_{ij})^2$$

These sums of squares, along with their respective degrees of freedom and mean squares, are summarized in Table 22B.3.

Table 22B.3   ANOVA Table for Two-Factor Design

Source of Variation	Sum of Squares	Degrees of Freedom	Mean Square	F-Ratio
Treatment B	$SSR_{\text{treatment B}}$	$(r-1)$	$MSR_{\text{treatment B}} = \dfrac{SSR_{\text{treatment B}}}{r-1}$	$\dfrac{MRS_{\text{treatment B}}}{MS_{\text{error}}}$
Treatment A	$SSC_{\text{treatment A}}$	$(c-1)$	$MSC_{\text{treatment A}} = \dfrac{SSC_{\text{treatment A}}}{c-1}$	$\dfrac{MSC_{\text{treatment A}}}{MS_{\text{error}}}$
Interaction	$SS_{\text{interaction}}$	$(r-1)(c-1)$	$MS_{\text{interaction}} = \dfrac{SS_{\text{interaction}}}{(r-1)(c-1)}$	$\dfrac{MS_{\text{interaction}}}{MS_{\text{error}}}$
Error	SS_{error}	$rc(n-1)$	$MS_{\text{error}} = \dfrac{SS_{\text{error}}}{rc(n-1)}$	
Total	SS_{total}	$rcn-1$		

Bivariate Statistical Analysis

Measures of Association

IF YOU FOUND A VARIABLE THAT FORECASTED THE NEXT YEAR'S direction of the stock market with an accuracy of better than 95 percent, would you be interested in its prediction? If so, watch the Super Bowl. In the 31 Super Bowls from 1967 to 1997, 28 out of 31 times the market rose by year's end when a team from the original NFL won the championship or fell by year's end when a team from the old American Football League (now the NFL's American Football Conference) won. The value of stock market indexes is associated with the football league winning the Super Bowl. Most likely this is mere coincidence, but many investors still root for teams from the original NFL.

Many marketing questions deal with the association between two (or more) variables. Questions such as "Is sales productivity associated with pay incentives?" or "Is socioeconomic status associated with the likelihood of purchasing a recreational vehicle?" or "Does work status relate to attitudes toward the role of women in society?" can be answered by statistically investigating the relationships between the two variables in question. This chapter investigates how to analyze questions such as these.

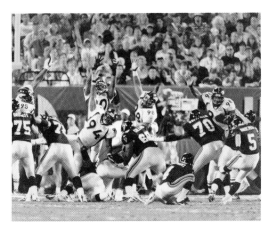

What you will learn in this chapter

To give examples of the types of marketing questions that may be answered by analyzing the association between two variables.

To list the common procedures for measuring association and to discuss how the measurement scale will influence the selection of statistical tests.

To discuss the concept of the simple correlation coefficient.

To calculate a simple correlation coefficient and a coefficient of determination.

To understand that correlation does not mean causation.

To interpret a correlation matrix.

To explain the concept of bivariate linear regression.

To identify the intercept and slope coefficients.

To discuss the least-squares method of regression analysis.

To draw a regression line.

To test the statistical significance of a least-squares regression.

To calculate the intercept and slope coefficients in a bivariate linear regression.

To interpret the analysis of variance summary tables for linear regression.

The Basics

In marketing, sales is often the dependent variable we wish to predict. The independent variables that we may find associated with the dependent variable *sales* may be aspects of the marketing mix, such as price, number of salespeople, or amount of advertising, and/or uncontrollable variables, such as population or gross national product. For example, most managers would not be surprised that the sale of baby strollers is associated with the number of babies born a few months prior to the sales period. In this case the dependent variable is the sales volume of baby strollers, and the independent variable is the number of babies born. The mathematical symbol X is commonly used for the independent variable, and Y typically denotes the dependent variable. It is appropriate to label dependent and independent variables only when it is assumed that the independent variable caused the dependent variable.

In many situations, measures of differences, such as the chi-square test, provide information about whether two or more variables are interrelated or associated. For example, a chi-square test between a measure of price consciousness and a measure of brand awareness provides some information about the independence or interrelationship of the two variables. Although measures such as the chi-square are useful sources of information about association, statisticians have developed several techniques with which to estimate the strength of association.

Exhibit 23.1 shows that the type of measure used will influence the choice of the proper statistical **measure of association.** This chapter describes simple cor-

measure of association
A general term that refers to a number of bivariate statistical techniques used to measure the strength of a relationship between two variables.

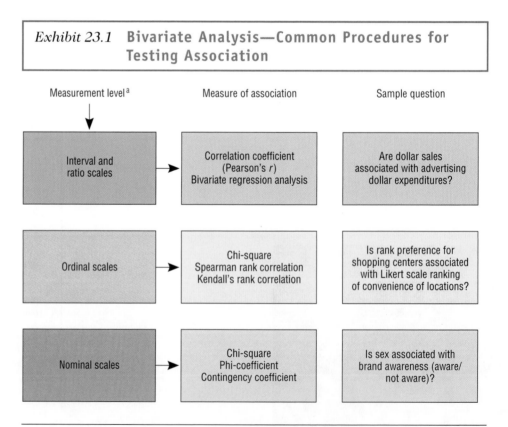

Exhibit 23.1 **Bivariate Analysis—Common Procedures for Testing Association**

Measurement level[a]	Measure of association	Sample question
Interval and ratio scales	Correlation coefficient (Pearson's *r*) Bivariate regression analysis	Are dollar sales associated with advertising dollar expenditures?
Ordinal scales	Chi-square Spearman rank correlation Kendall's rank correlation	Is rank preference for shopping centers associated with Likert scale ranking of convenience of locations?
Nominal scales	Chi-square Phi-coefficient Contingency coefficient	Is sex associated with brand awareness (aware/ not aware)?

[a]If at least one of the two variables has a given level of measurement, the appropriate procedure is to use the one with the fewest assumptions about the data.

relation (Pearson's product-moment correlation coefficient—r) and bivariate regression. Both techniques require interval-scaled or ratio-scaled data. The other techniques mentioned are for advanced students who have specific requirements for these tests.[2]

Simple Correlation Coefficient

The most popular technique for indicating the relationship of one variable to another is simple correlation analysis. The **correlation coefficient** is a statistical measure of the covariation or association between two variables. The correlation coefficient (r) ranges from +1.0 to −1.0. If the value of r equals +1.0, there is a perfect positive linear (straight-line) relationship. If the value of r equals −1.0, a perfect negative linear relationship, or a perfect inverse relationship, is indicated. No correlation is indicated if r equals 0. A correlation coefficient indicates both the magnitude of the linear relationship and the direction of that relationship. For example, if we find that the value $r = -.92$, we know we have a relatively strong inverse relationship—that is, the greater the value measured by variable X, the lower the value measured by variable Y.

correlation coefficient
A statistical measure of the covariation or association between two variables.

The formula for calculating the correlation coefficient for two variables, X and Y, is as follows:

$$r_{xy} = r_{yx} = \frac{\Sigma(X_i - \overline{X})(Y_i - \overline{Y})}{\sqrt{\Sigma(X_i - \overline{X})^2 \Sigma(Y_i - \overline{Y})^2}}$$

where the symbols $\overline{X}$ and $\overline{Y}$ represent the sample averages of X and Y, respectively.

An alternative way to express the correlation formula is:

$$r_{xy} = r_{yx} = \frac{\sigma_{xy}}{\sqrt{\sigma_x^2 \sigma_y^2}},$$

where

$$\sigma_x^2 = \text{variance of } X$$
$$\sigma_y^2 = \text{variance of } Y$$
$$\sigma_{xy} = \text{covariance of } X \text{ and } Y$$

with

$$\sigma_{xy} = \frac{\Sigma(X_i - \overline{X})(Y_i - \overline{Y})}{N}$$

If associated values of X_i and Y_i differ from their means in the same direction, their covariance will be positive. The covariance will be negative if the values of X_i and Y_i tend to deviate in opposite directions.

The simple correlation coefficient actually is a standardized measure of covariance. In the formula the numerator represents covariance and the denominator is the square root of the product of the sample variances. Researchers find the correlation coefficient useful because they can compare two correlations without regard for the amount of variance exhibited by each variable separately.

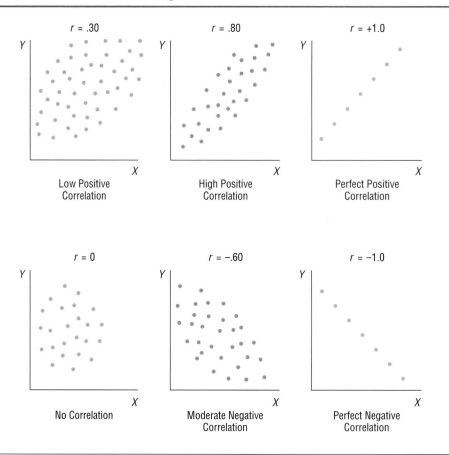

Exhibit 23.2 **Scatter Diagram to Illustrate Correlation Patterns**

Exhibit 23.2 illustrates the correlation coefficients and scatter diagrams for several sets of data.

An Example

To illustrate the calculation of the correlation coefficient, an investigation is made to determine whether the average number of hours worked in manufacturing industries is related to unemployment. A correlation analysis of the data in Table 23.1 is used to determine whether the two variables are associated.

The correlation between two variables is −.635, which indicates an inverse relationship. Thus, when the number of hours worked is high, unemployment is low. This makes intuitive sense. If factories are increasing output, regular workers typically work more overtime and new employees are hired (reducing the unemployment rate). Both variables are probably related to overall economic conditions.

Correlation and Causation

It is important to remember that correlation does not mean causation. No matter how highly correlated the rooster's crow is to the rising of the sun, the rooster does not cause the sun to rise. A high correlation exists between teachers' salaries and the consumption of liquor over a period of years. The approximate correlation coefficient is $r = .9$. This high correlation does not indicate how much teachers drink, nor does it indicate that the sale of liquor increases teachers'

Table 23.1 Correlation Analysis of Number of Hours Worked in Manufacturing Industries with Unemployment Rate

Unemployment Rate (X_i)	Number of Hours Worked (Y_i)	$X_i - \bar{X}$	$(X_i - \bar{X})^2$	$Y_i - \bar{Y}$	$(Y_i - \bar{Y})^2$	$(X_i - \bar{X})(Y_i - \bar{Y})$
5.5	39.6	0.51	0.2601	−0.71	0.5041	−0.3621
4.4	40.7	−0.59	0.3481	0.39	0.1521	−0.2301
4.1	40.4	−0.89	0.7921	0.09	0.0081	−0.0801
4.3	39.8	−0.69	0.4761	−0.51	0.2601	0.3519
6.8	39.2	1.81	3.2761	−1.11	1.2321	−2.0091
5.5	40.3	0.51	0.2601	−0.01	0.0001	−0.0051
5.5	39.7	0.51	0.2601	−0.61	0.3721	−0.3111
6.7	39.8	1.71	2.9241	−0.51	0.2601	−0.8721
5.5	40.4	0.51	0.2601	0.09	0.0081	0.0459
5.7	40.5	0.71	0.5041	0.19	0.0361	0.1349
5.2	40.7	0.21	0.0441	0.39	0.1521	0.0819
4.5	41.2	−0.49	0.2401	0.89	0.7921	−0.4361
3.8	41.3	−1.19	1.4161	0.99	0.9801	−1.1781
3.8	40.6	−1.19	1.4161	0.29	0.0841	−0.3451
3.6	40.7	−1.39	1.9321	0.39	0.1521	−0.5421
3.5	40.6	−1.49	2.2201	0.29	0.0841	−0.4321
4.9	39.8	−0.09	0.0081	−0.51	0.2601	0.0459
5.9	39.9	0.91	0.8281	−0.41	0.1681	−0.3731
5.6	40.6	0.61	0.3721	0.29	0.0841	0.1769

$$\bar{X} = 4.99$$
$$\bar{Y} = 40.31$$
$$\Sigma(X_i - \bar{X})^2 = 17.8379$$
$$\Sigma(Y_i - \bar{Y})^2 = 5.5899$$
$$\Sigma(X_i - \bar{X})(Y_i - \bar{Y}) = -6.3389$$

$$r = \frac{\Sigma(X_i - \bar{X})(Y_i - \bar{Y})}{\sqrt{\Sigma(X_i - \bar{X})^2 \Sigma(Y_i - \bar{Y})^2}}$$

$$= \frac{-6.3389}{\sqrt{(17.837)(5.589)}}$$

$$= \frac{-6.3389}{\sqrt{99.712}}$$

$$= -.635$$

salaries. It is more likely that teachers' salaries and liquor sales covary because they are both influenced by a third variable, such as long-run growth in national income and/or population.

In this example the relationship between the two variables is apparent, but not real. Even though the variables are not causally related, they can be statistically related. This can occur because both are caused by a third or more other factors. When this is so, the variables are said to be *spuriously related*.

TO THE POINT

Statistics are like a bikini. What they reveal is suggestive, but what they conceal is vital.

AARON LEVENSTEIN

EXPLORING RESEARCH ISSUES

Causality

YEARS AGO THE *NEW YORK HERALD TRIBUNE* QUOTED Sir Ronald Fisher, the father of experimental design, on the subject of cigarette smoking and cancer. Fisher pointed out that the only way to establish a causal connection between the two would be to randomly assign a large sample of newborn babies to two groups, those from whom cigarettes would be withheld and those who would be forced to smoke them. Some 70 or 80 years later we might have conclusive evidence of the true effects of smoking on death by various causes.

Sir Ronald was simply repeating a lesson that many of us learned in school: To observe a consistent relationship between two variables over time, or over cases at one point in time, does not prove

that one causes the other. This is stated in the simple slogan: "Correlation is not causation" or "correlation is not necessarily causation." As the statistician said when he quit smoking, "I know that correlation is not causation, but in this case I'm willing to take a chance."

He put in a nutshell exactly what we do whenever we put a causal interpretation on *any* result, experimental or nonexperimental: We take a chance. Sometimes we express that chance precisely, as in the confidence level at which we reject a hypothesis in a designed experiment; but usually even then, and virtually always in practical business situations, we really have only a subjective estimate of that chance. We have failed to consider sources of error other than sampling; these must be absent if that confidence level is to be meaningful. Statistics teaches to the contrary, sampling is not always the main source of error in testing hypotheses, and in many marketing situations it can be unimportant relative to errors due to bias in sample selection.

Coefficient of Determination

coefficient of determination (r^2)
A measure obtained by squaring the correlation coefficient; that proportion of the total variance of a variable that is accounted for by knowing the value of another variable.

If we wish to know the proportion of *variance* in Y that is explained by X (or vice versa), we can calculate the **coefficient of determination** by squaring the correlation coefficient (r^2):

$$r^2 = \frac{\text{Explained variance}}{\text{Total variance}}$$

The coefficient of determination, r^2, measures that part of the total variance of Y that is accounted for by knowing the value of X. In the example between unemployment and hours worked $r = -.635$; therefore, $r^2 = .403$. About 40 percent of the variance in unemployment can be explained by the variance in hours worked, and vice versa.

Correlation Matrix

correlation matrix
The standard form for reporting correlational results.

The **correlation matrix** is the standard form for reporting correlational results. It may be compared to a between-city mileage table, except that the research variables are substituted for cities and a coefficient of correlation is substituted for mileage. Table 23.2 shows a correlation matrix that includes some measures of sales force performance and job satisfaction as they relate to characteristics of the sales force, job attitudes from the Role Orientation Index, and territory work load.[3] The student will encounter this type of matrix on many occasions. Note that the main diagonal consists of correlations of 1.00. This will always be the case

Table 23.2 Pearson Product-Moment Correlation Matrix for Salesperson Example[a]

	VARIABLES	S	JS	GE	SE	OD	VI	JT	RA	TP	WL
S	Performance	1.00									
JS	Job satisfaction	.45[b]	1.00								
GE	Generalized self-esteem	.31[b]	.10	1.00							
SE	Specific self-esteem	.61[b]	. 28[b]	.36[b]	1.00						
OD	Other-directedness	.05	−.03	−.44[b]	−.24[c]	1.00					
VI	Verbal intelligence	−.36[b]	−.13	−.14	−.11	−.18[d]	1.00				
JT	Job-related tension	−.48[b]	−.56[b]	−.32[b]	−.34[b]	.26[b]	−.02	1.00			
RA	Role ambiguity	−.26[c]	−.24[c]	−.32[b]	−.39[b]	.38[b]	−.05	.44[b]	1.00		
TP	Territory potential	.49[b]	.31[b]	.04	.29[b]	.09	−.09	−.38[b]	−.26[b]	1.00	
WL	Work load	.45[b]	.11	.29[c]	.29[c]	−.04	−.12	−.27[c]	−.22[d]	.49[b]	1.00

[a] Numbers below the diagonal are for the sample; those above the diagonal are omitted.
[b] $p < .001$.
[c] $p < .01$.
[d] $p < .05$.

when a variable is correlated with itself. The data in this example are from a survey of industrial salespeople selling steel and plastic strapping and seals used in shipping. Performance (*S*) was measured by identifying the salesperson's actual annual sales volume in dollars. Notice that the performance variable has a .45 correlation with the work-load variable, which was measured by recording the number of accounts in the sales territory. Notice also that the salesperson's perception of job-related tension (*JT*) as measured on an attitude scale has a −.48 correlation with performance (*S*). Thus, when perceived job tension is high, performance is low. Of course, the correlation coefficients in these examples are moderate.

Another question researchers ask concerns statistical significance. The procedure for determining statistical significance is the *t*-test of the significance of a correlation coefficient. Typically, it is hypothesized that $r = 0$, and then a *t*-test is performed. The logic behind the test is similar to that for the significance tests already considered. In a large correlation matrix such as Table 23.2, it is customary to footnote each statistically significant coefficient.[4]

Regression Analysis

Regression is another technique for measuring the linear association between a dependent and an independent variable. Although regression and correlation are mathematically related, regression assumes the dependent (or criterion) variable, *Y*, is predictively or "causally" linked to the independent (or predictor) variable, *X*. Regression analysis attempts to predict the values of a continuous, interval-scaled dependent variable from the specific values of the independent variable. Although regression analysis has numerous applications, forecasting sales is by far the most common.

The discussion here concerns **bivariate linear regression.** This form of regression investigates a *straight-line relationship* of the type $Y = \alpha + \beta X$, where *Y* is the dependent variable, *X* is the independent variable, and α and β are two constants to be estimated. The symbol α represents the *Y* intercept, and β is the slope coefficient. The slope β is the change in *Y* due to a corresponding change in one unit of *X*.

bivariate linear regression
A measure of linear association that investigates a straight-line relationship of the type Y = α + βX, where Y is the dependent variable, X is the independent variable, and α and β are two constants to be estimated.

The slope may also be thought of as rise over run (the rise in units on the *Y*-axis divided by the run in units along the *X*-axis). (The Δ is the notation for "a change in.")

Suppose a researcher is interested in forecasting sales for a construction distributor (wholesaler) in Florida. Furthermore, the distributor believes a reasonable association exists between sales and building permits issued by counties. Using bivariate linear regression on the data in Table 23.3, the researcher will be able to estimate sales potential (*Y*) in various counties based on the number of building permits (*X*). To better illustrate the data in Table 23.3, we have plotted them on a scatter diagram (Exhibit 23.3). In the diagram the vertical axis indicates the value of the dependent variable, *Y*, and the horizontal axis indicates the value of the independent variable, *X*. Each single point in the diagram represents an observation of *X* and *Y* at a given point in time, that is, a paired value of *X* and *Y*. The relationship between *X* and *Y* could be "eyeballed"; that is, a straight line could be drawn through the points in the figure. However, this procedure is subject to human error: Two researchers might draw different lines to describe the same data.

Least-Squares Method of Regression Analysis

The task of the researcher is to find the best means for fitting a straight line to the data. The least-squares method is a relatively simple mathematical technique that ensures that the straight line will most closely represent the relationship between *X* and *Y*. The logic behind the least-squares technique goes as follows: No straight line can completely represent every dot in the scatter diagram; there will be a discrepancy between most of the actual scores (each dot) and the predicted score based on the regression line. Simply stated, any straight line drawn will generate errors. The least-squares method uses the criterion of attempting to make the least amount of total error in prediction of *Y* from *X*. More technically, the procedure used in the least-squares method generates a straight line that minimizes the sum of squared deviations of the actual values from this predicted regression line. Using the symbol *e* to represent the deviations of the dots from the line, the least-squares criterion is as follows:

$$\sum_{i=1}^{n} e_i^2 \text{ is minimum}$$

where

$e_i = Y_i - \hat{Y}_i$ (the residual)

Y_i = actual value of the dependent variable

$\hat{Y}_i$ = estimated value of the dependent ("Y hat")

n = number of observations

i = number of the particular observation

The general equation for a straight line is $Y = \alpha + \beta X$, where a more appropriate estimating equation includes an allowance for error:

$$Y = \hat{a} + \hat{\beta}X + e$$

The symbols $\hat{a}$ and $\hat{\beta}$ are used when the equation is a regression estimate of the line. Thus, to compute the estimated values of a and β, we use the following formulas:

$$\hat{\beta} = \frac{n(\Sigma XY) - (\Sigma X)(\Sigma Y)}{(\Sigma X^2) - (\Sigma X)^2}$$

Table 23.3 Relationship of Sales Potential to Building Permits Issued

Dealer	Y Dealer's Sales Volume (Thousands)	X Building Permits
1	77	86
2	79	93
3	80	95
4	83	104
5	101	139
6	117	180
7	129	165
8	120	147
9	97	119
10	106	132
11	99	126
12	121	156
13	103	129
14	86	96
15	99	108

Exhibit 23.3 Scatter Diagram and Eyeball Forecast

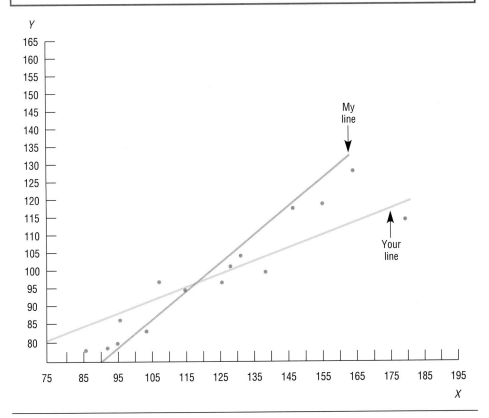

EXPLORING RESEARCH ISSUES

Walkup's First Laws of Statistics

Law No. 1

Everything correlates with everything, especially when the same individual defines the variables to be correlated.

Law No. 2

It won't help very much to find a good correlation between the variable you are interested in and some other variable that you don't understand any better.

Law No. 3

Unless you can think of a logical reason why two variables should be connected as cause and effect, it doesn't help much to find a correlation between them. In Columbus, Ohio, the mean monthly rainfall correlates very nicely with the number of letters in the names of the months!

and

$$\hat{a} = \overline{Y} - \hat{\beta}\,\overline{X}$$

where

$\hat{\beta}$ = estimated slope of the line (the regression coefficient)
$\hat{a}$ = estimated intercept of the Y-axis
Y = dependent variable
$\overline{Y}$ = mean of the dependent variable
X = independent variable
$\overline{X}$ = mean of the independent variable
n = number of observations

We can solve these equations with simple arithmetic (see Table 23.4). To estimate the relationship between the distributor's sales to a dealer and the number of building permits, we perform the following manipulations:

$$\hat{\beta} = \frac{n(\Sigma XY) - (\Sigma X)(\Sigma Y)}{n(\Sigma X^2) - (\Sigma X)^2}$$

$$= \frac{15(193,345) - 2,806,875}{15(245,759) - 3,515,625}$$

$$= \frac{2,900,175 - 2,806,875}{3,686,385 - 3,515,625}$$

$$= \frac{93,300}{170,760} = .54638$$

$$\hat{a} = \overline{Y} - \hat{\beta}\overline{X}$$

$$= 99.8 - .54638(125)$$

$$= 99.8 - 68.3$$

$$= 31.5$$

The formula $\hat{Y} = 31.5 + 0.546X$ is the regression equation used for the prediction of the dependent variable. Suppose the wholesaler considers a new

Table 23.4 Least-Squares Computation

	Y	Y^2	X	X^2	XY
1	77	5,929	86	7,396	6,622
2	79	6,241	93	8,649	7,347
3	80	6,400	95	9,025	7,600
4	83	6,889	104	10,816	8,632
5	101	10,201	139	19,321	14,039
6	117	13,689	180	32,400	21,060
7	129	16,641	165	27,225	21,285
8	120	14,400	147	21,609	17,640
9	97	9,409	119	14,161	11,543
10	106	11,236	132	17,424	13,992
11	99	9,801	126	15,876	12,474
12	121	14,641	156	24,336	18,876
13	103	10,609	129	16,641	13,287
14	86	7,396	96	9,216	8,256
15	99	9,801	108	11,664	10,692
Σ	$\Sigma Y = 1,497$ $\overline{Y} = 99.8$	$\Sigma Y^2 = 153,283$	$\Sigma X = 1,875$ $\overline{X} = 125$	$\Sigma X^2 = 245,759$	$\Sigma XY = 193,345$

dealership in an area where the number of building permits equals 89. Sales may be forecasted in this area as:

$$\hat{Y} = 31.5 + .546(X)$$
$$= 31.5 + .546(89)$$
$$= 31.5 + 48.6$$
$$= 80.1$$

Thus, the distributor may expect sales of 80.1 ($80,100) in this new area.[5]

Calculation of the correlation coefficient gives an indication of how accurate the predictions may be. In this example the correlation coefficient is $r = .9356$ and the coefficient of determination is $r^2 = .8754$.

Drawing a Regression Line

To draw a regression line on the scatter diagram, only two predicted values of Y need plotting. Using data for dealer 7 and dealer 3, a straight line connecting the points 121.6 and 83.4 can be drawn.

$$\text{Dealer 7 (actual } Y \text{ value} = 129): \hat{Y}_7 = 31.5 + .546(165)$$
$$= 121.6$$
$$\text{Dealer 3 (actual } Y \text{ value} = 80): \hat{Y}_3 = 31.5 + .546(95)$$
$$= 83.4$$

Exhibit 23.4 shows the regression line.

To determine the error (residual) of any observation, the predicted value of Y is calculated first. The predicted value is then subtracted from the actual value.

> *Exhibit 23.4* **Least-Squares Regression Line**

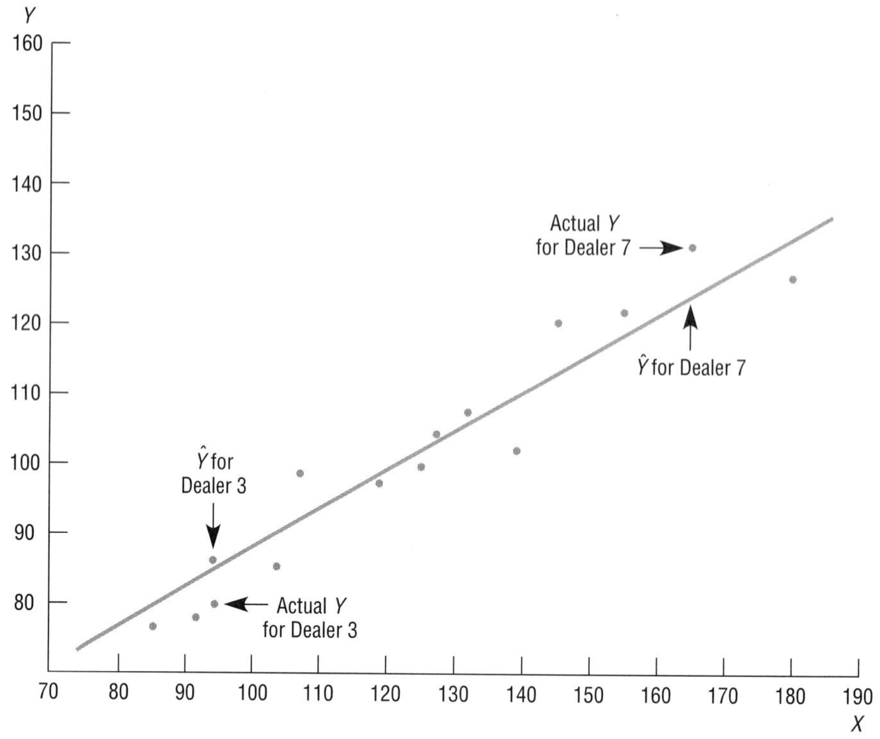

For example, the actual observation for dealer 9 is 97, and the predicted value is 96.5; thus, only a small margin of error, $e = .5$, is involved in this regression line:

$$
\begin{aligned}
e_i &= Y_9 - \hat{Y}_9 \\
&= 97 - 96.5 \\
&= 0.5
\end{aligned}
$$

where

$$\hat{Y}_9 = 31.5 + .546(119)$$

Test of Statistical Significance

Now that we have illustrated the error term, a more detailed look at explained and unexplained variation is possible. Exhibit 23.5 explains the fitted regression line. If a researcher wishes to predict any dealer's sales volume (Y) without knowing the number of building permits (X), the best prediction will be the average sales volume ($\overline{Y}$) of all dealers. Suppose, for example, that a researcher wishes to predict dealer 8's sales without knowing the value of X. The best estimate would be 99.8 ($\overline{Y} = 99.8$). Exhibit 23.5 shows that this would be a large error, because dealer 8's actual sales were 120. After the regression line has been fitted, this error can be reduced. With the regression equation, dealer 8's sales are predicted to be 111.8, thus reducing the error to only 8.2 (120 − 111.8) rather than 20.2 (120 − 99.8)—that is, error is reduced by using $Y_i - \hat{Y}_i$ rather than $Y_i - \overline{Y}$. This is the explained deviation due to the regression. The smaller number, 8.2, is the deviation not explained by the regression.

Exhibit 23.5 **Scatter Diagram of Explained and Unexplained Variation**

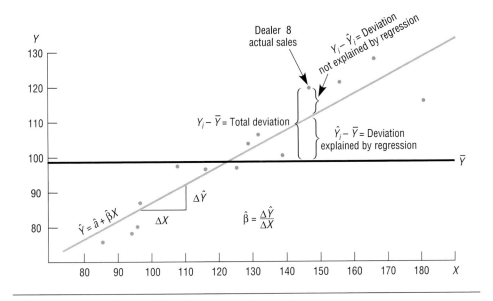

Thus, the total deviation can be partitioned into two parts:

$$(Y_i - \bar{Y}) = (\hat{Y}_i - \bar{Y}) + (Y_i - \hat{Y}_i)$$

$$\begin{array}{ccc} \text{Total} \\ \text{deviation} \end{array} = \begin{array}{c} \text{Deviation} \\ \text{explained by} \\ \text{the regression} \end{array} + \begin{array}{c} \text{Deviation} \\ \text{unexplained by} \\ \text{the regression} \\ \text{(residual error)} \end{array}$$

where

$\bar{Y}$ = mean of the total group
$\hat{Y}_i$ = value predicted with regression equation
Y_i = actual value

For dealer 8 the total deviation would be $120 - 99.8 = 20.2$, the deviation explained by the regression would be $111.8 - 99.8 = 12$, and the deviation unexplained by the regression would be $120 - 111.8 = 8.2$. If these values are summed over all values of Y_i (that is, all observations) and squared, these deviations will provide an estimate of the variation of Y explained by the regression and that unexplained by the regression:

$$\Sigma(Y_i - \bar{Y})^2 = \Sigma(\hat{Y}_i - \bar{Y})^2 + \Sigma(Y_i - \hat{Y}_i)^2$$

$$\begin{array}{c} \text{Total} \\ \text{variation} \\ \text{explained} \end{array} = \begin{array}{c} \text{Explained} \\ \text{variation} \end{array} + \begin{array}{c} \text{Unexplained} \\ \text{variation} \\ \text{(residual)} \end{array}$$

We have thus partitioned the total sum of squares, SS_t, into two parts: the regression sum of squares, SS_r, and the error sum of squares, SS_e:

$$SS_t = SS_r + SS_e$$

Table 23.5 Analysis of Variance Table for Bivariate Regression

Source of Variation	Degrees of Freedom	Sum of Squares	Mean Square (Variance)
Explained by regression	$k-1$	$SS_r = \sum(\hat{Y}_i - \overline{Y})^2$	$SS_r/k-1$
Unexplained by regression (error)	$n-k$	$SS_e = \sum(Y_i - \hat{Y}_i)^2$	$SS_e/n-k$

where k = number of estimated constants (variables)

n = number of observations

F-test (regression)

A procedure to determine whether there is more variability explained by the regression or unexplained by the regression.

An **F-test,** or an *analysis of variance,* applied to a regression can be used to test the relative magnitude of the SS_r and SS_e with their appropriate degrees of freedom. Table 23.5 indicates the technique for conducting the *F*-test.

For the example on sales forecasting, the analysis of variance summary table, which shows relative magnitudes of the mean square, is presented in Table 23.6. From Table A.6 in the appendix, we find that the *F*-value 91.3, with 1 degree of freedom in the numerator and 13 degrees of freedom in the denominator, exceeds the probability level of .01. The *coefficient of determination, r^2,* reflects the proportion of variance explained by the regression line. To calculate r^2:

$$r^2 = \frac{SS_r}{SS_t} = 1 - \frac{SS_e}{SS_t}$$

EXPLORING RESEARCH ISSUES

A Note of Caution about Forecasting

THE NONSTATISTICAL DEFINITION OF REGRESSION involves moving backward or going back to an earlier form—this emphasizes the historical nature of the data. This suggests forecasting with statistical regression analysis, which may reflect the past but not necessarily future trends, should be approached with caution. In *Life on the Mississippi,* Mark Twain illustrated this concern about forecasting rather well:

> In the space of one hundred and seventy-six years the Lower Mississippi has shortened itself two hundred and forty-two miles. This is an average of a trifle over one mile and a third per year. Therefore, any calm person, who is not blind or idiotic, can see that in the Old Oölitic Silurian Period, just a million years ago next November, the Lower Mississippi River was upward of one million three hundred thousand miles long, and stuck out over the Gulf of Mexico like a fishing-rod. And by the same token any person can see that seven hundred and forty-two years from now the Lower Mississippi will be only a mile and three-quarters long, and Cairo and New Orleans will have joined their streets together, and be plodding comfortably along under a single mayor and a mutual board of aldermen. There is something fascinating about science. One gets such wholesale returns of conjecture out of such a trifling investment of fact.

		DEGREES OF		
SOURCE OF VARIATION	SUM OF SQUARES	FREEDOM	MEAN SQUARE	F-VALUE
Explained by regression	3,389.49	1	3,398.49	91.30
Unexplained by regression (error)	483.91	13	37.22	
Total	3,882.40	14		

Table 23.6 Analysis of Variance Summary Table for Regression of Sales on Building Permits

---

TO THE POINT

Forecasting is like trying to drive a car blindfolded and following directions given by a person who is looking out the back window.

ANONYMOUS

In our example r^2 is calculated as .875:

$$r^2 = \frac{3,398.49}{3,882.4} = .875$$

The coefficient of determination may be interpreted to mean that 87 percent of the variation in sales was explained by associating the variable with building permits.

Summary

In many situations two variables are interrelated or associated. Many bivariate statistical techniques can be used to measure this association. Researchers select the appropriate technique based on each variable's scales of measurement.

Simple correlation is the measure of the relationship of one variable to another. The correlation coefficient (r) indicates the strength of the association of two variables and the direction of that association. Correlation does not prove causation, as variables other than those being measured may be involved. The coefficient of determination (r^2) measures the amount of the total variance in the dependent variable that is accounted for by knowing the value of the independent variable. The results of a correlation computation often are presented in a correlation matrix.

Bivariate linear regression investigates a straight-line relationship between one dependent variable and one independent variable. The regression can be done intuitively by plotting a scatter diagram of the X and Y points and drawing a line to fit the observed relationship. The least-squares method mathematically determines the best-fitting regression line for the observed data. The line determined by this method may be used to forecast values of the dependent variable, given a value for the independent variable. The goodness of the line's fit may be evaluated with a variant of the ANOVA (analysis of variance) technique or by calculating the coefficient of determination.

Key Terms and Concepts

Measure of association
Correlation coefficient

Coefficient of determination (r^2)
Correlation matrix

Bivariate linear regression
F-test (regression)

Questions for Review and Critical Thinking

1. The discussion in this chapter is limited to linear relationships. Try to diagram some nonlinear relationships that show r values of zero using the test methods shown in the text.

2. Comment on the following:
   a. Suppose Abraham Lincoln answered a survey questionnaire and indicated he had not received a grade-school diploma. The researcher found that Lincoln's educational score did not correlate highly with the expected variables. What was wrong?
   b. An international marketer has said, "When political instability increases, the price of quality increases." Is this a testable hypothesis?
   c. In 8 of 11 years when a racehorse won the Triple Crown (Kentucky Derby, Preakness, and Belmont Stakes), the stock market dropped.

3. The management of a regional bus line thought the company's price of gas might be correlated with its passenger/mile ratio. The data and a correlation matrix follow. Comment. (Note that r is called *rho*.)

	BUS LINE	
YEAR	AVERAGE WHOLESALE PRICE OF GAS	PASSENGERS/MILES
1	56.5	8.37
2	59.4	8.93
3	63.0	9.15
4	65.6	9.79
5	89.0	11.20

Correlation Coefficients/Probability > $|R|$ under HO: $RHO = O/N = 5$

	YEAR	PRICE	MILE
Year	1.00000	0.87016	0.95127
	0.00000	0.05510	0.01280
Price	0.87016	1.00000	0.97309
	0.05510	0.00000	0.00530
Mile	0.95127	0.97309	1.00000
	0.01280	0.00530	0.00000

4. A correlation matrix (correlation coefficients and probability level under the hypothesis *rho* = 0) for a company's sales force (age, years of service, and current sales) is given below. Comment.

	AGE	YEARS OF SERVICE	CURRENT SALES
Age	1.00000	0.68185	0.21652
	0.00000	0.02080	0.52250
Years of service	0.68185	1.00000	0.64499
	0.02080	0.00000	0.03210
Current sales	0.21652	0.64499	1.00000
	0.52250	0.03210	0.00000

5. Interpret the following data:
   a. $\hat{Y} = \hat{a} + \hat{\beta}X$, $\hat{Y} = 3.5 + .7X$, where Y = the likelihood of buying a new car and X = total family income.
   b. $\hat{Y} = \hat{a} + \hat{\beta} X$, $\hat{Y} = 3.5 + .4X$, where Y = the likelihood of buying tickets to a rock concert and X = age.

6. The following ANOVA summary table is the result of a regression of sales on year of sales. Is the relationship statistically significant at the .05 level? Comment.

SOURCE OF VARIATION	SUM OF SQUARES	DEGREES OF FREEDOM	MEAN SQUARE	F-VALUE
Explained by regression	605,370,750	1	605,370,750	3.12
Unexplained by regression	1,551,381,712	8	193,922,714	
Total		9		

7. A metropolitan economist is attempting to predict the average total budget of Phoenix retired couples based on U.S. urban average retired couples' total budgets. An r^2 of .7824 is obtained. Will the regression be a good predictive model?

8. The following table gives a football team's sales, percentage of games won, and number of active alumni:

YEAR	SEASON-TICKET SALES	PERCENTAGE OF GAMES WON	NUMBER OF ACTIVE ALUMNI
1990	4,995	40	NA
1991	8,599	54	NA
1992	8,479	55	NA
1993	8,419	58	NA
1994	10,253	63	NA
1995	12,457	75	6,315
1996	13,285	36	6,860
1997	14,177	27	8,423
1998	15,730	63	9,000

   a. Interpret the correlation between each set of variables.
   b. Calculate: Regression sales = Percentage of games won.
   c. Calculate: Regression sales = Number of active alumni.

9. Are the different forms of consumer installment credit in the following table highly correlated?

		CREDIT CARD DEBT OUTSTANDING (MILLIONS OF DOLLARS)				
YEAR	GAS CARDS	TRAVEL AND ENTERTAINMENT CARDS	BANK CREDIT CARDS	RETAIL CARDS	TOTAL CREDIT CARDS	TOTAL INSTALLMENT CREDIT
1	$ 939	$ 61	$ 828	$ 9,400	$11,228	$ 79,428
2	1,119	76	1,312	10,200	12,707	87,745
3	1,298	110	2,639	10,900	14,947	98,105
4	1,650	122	3,792	11,500	17,064	102,064
5	1,804	132	4,490	13,925	20,351	111,295
6	1,762	164	5,408	14,763	22,097	127,332
7	1,832	191	6,838	16,395	25,256	147,437
8	1,823	238	8,281	17,933	28,275	156,124
9	1,893	273	9,501	18,002	29,669	164,955
10	1,981	238	11,351	19,052	32,622	185,489
11	2,074	284	14,262	21,082	37,702	216,572

10. A manufacturer of disposable washcloths/wipes told a retailer that sales for this product category closely correlated with sales of disposable diapers. The retailer thought he would check this out for his own sales-forecasting purposes. The researcher says, "Disposable washcloth/wipes sales can be predicted with knowledge of disposable diaper sales." Is this the right thing to say?

Exploring the Internet

1. Go to the SPSS home page at http://www.spss.com. Navigate to "statistical coach." What SPSS statistical programs can be used to perform the statistical tests mentioned in this chapter?

2. The Federal Reserve Bank of St. Louis maintains a database called FRED (Federal Reserve Economic Data). Use a search engine to navigate to the FRED database. Randomly select a five-year period between 1970 and 1995 and then find the correlation between average U.S. employment in retail trade and U.S. employment in wholesale trade. What statistical test is appropriate?

Case 23.1 Springfield Electric Company

THE SPRINGFIELD ELECTRIC COMPANY MANUFACTURED electric pencil sharpeners. The company had always operated in New York and New Jersey and decided to expand beyond that region. The company president thought a new plant needed to be constructed. The president felt no need for contiguous expansion and favored a West Coast plant.

The marketing manager believed that sales were correlated with the number of workers employed in the geographic areas; in fact, she felt that electric pencil sharpener sales were correlated with the number of white-collar workers in an area. However, all she could get were the statistics for total employees. Case Exhibit 23.1–1 shows Springfield's sales of electric pencil sharpeners and the total number of employees in 17 Metropolitan Statistical Areas (MSAs) in New York and New Jersey. Case Exhibit 23.1–2 shows the

number of employees in the MSAs in Washington, Oregon, and California. The marketing manager thought she could forecast sales for the western expansion with these data.

QUESTIONS

1. Calculate and interpret the correlation coefficient data in Case Exhibit 23.1–1.

2. Estimate the regression equation coefficient for the data (assuming sales as the independent variable).

3. Forecast sales in the states of California, Washington, and Oregon based on the data in Case Exhibit 23.1–2.

Case Exhibit 23.1-1	Data on Total Employees and Springfield Sales in New York and New Jersey MSAs

METROPOLITAN STATISTICAL AREA	NUMBER OF EMPLOYEES (THOUSANDS)	SALES
New York		
Albany–Schenectady–Troy	58.3	3,749
Binghamton	37.0	2,695
Buffalo	135.6	4,926
Elmira	12.8	2,808
Nassau–Suffolk	149.0	7,423
New York	788.8	43,401
Poughkeepsie	24.3	3,254
Rochester	139.1	8,924
Syracuse	53.6	13,119
Utica–Rome	30.8	3,151
New Jersey		
Allentown–Bethlehem–Easton	110.7	6,123
Atlantic City	8.7	2,666
Jersey City	74.2	3,210
Long Branch–Asbury Park	22.8	2,078
New Brunswick–Perth Amboy–Sayreville	78.9	2,894
Newark	252.1	14,989
Paterson–Clifton–Passaic	60.1	3,806

Case Exhibit 23.1-2	Number of Employees in Selected MSAs

METROPOLITAN STATISTICAL AREA	NUMBER OF EMPLOYEES (THOUSANDS)
Washington	
Richland–Kennewick	7.8
Seattle–Everett	123.6
Spokane	11.1
Tacoma	18.7
Yakima	8.8
Oregon	
Eugene–Springfield	18.2
Portland	90.5
Salem	12.5
California	
Anaheim–Santa Ana–Garden Grove	149.0
Bakersfield	7.1
Fresno	20.5
Los Angeles–Long Beach	750.3
Modesto	18.7
Oxnard–Simi Valley–Ventura	14.9
Riverside–San Bernardino–Ontario	51.8
Sacramento	20.5
Salinas–Seaside–Monterey	8.0
San Diego	71.4
San Francisco–Oakland	172.7
San Jose	151.1
Santa Barbara–Santa Maria–Lompoc	14.0
Santa Cruz	5.7
Santa Rosa	8.6
Stockton	20.0
Vallejo–Fairfield–Napa	7.4

Case 23.2   Center for American Enterprise: A Study of Psychological and Demographic Contributors to Consumerism[6]

A FEW YEARS AGO THE CENTER FOR AMERICAN ENTERprise commissioned a study to determine the causes of consumerism. This was done in an effort to stem the tide of growing disenchantment with American business and its practices among a wide number of consumers.

The center, located in Dallas, Texas, was a private foundation funded by a large number of corporations to spread the ideal of the free enterprise system. It conducted a number of projects to better understand what Americans knew about business and published numerous brochures that were sent to high schools and elementary schools throughout the United States. The center believed consumerism, that is, consumer discontent, was a major problem facing business and wished to pursue it as an area of study.

Since the center did not have the expertise to properly formulate the research problem and its accompanying theory, it decided to seek outside assistance for this project. Commissioned to do the study were three professors, Thomas, Rogers, and Michaels, at Southern Methodist University, who had done considerable research on the topic. The report they generated follows.

Report on Psychological and Demographic Correlates of Consumer Discontent

The study of consumerism and the allied psychological state of consumer discontent has been theoretically and empirically examined within the confines of the economic system. Although these market interfaces provide discrete areas for analyzing consumerism or consumer discontent, they may be only symptomatic of broader psychological states currently existing in society. With the exception of one study relating consumer alienation to marketing activities, little research has actively explored potential relationships between psychological states and discontent with the market system. Identification of those psychological states and demographic characteristics associated with consumer discontent would provide valuable insight into the dynamics of this phenomenon and assist in the development of constructive approaches for dealing with it from a public policy perspective.

Study Purpose

The purpose of this study is to examine the relationships among selected psychological states, demo-

graphic variables, and consumer discontent. Specific objectives of this study are threefold:

1. To determine if consumer discontent with the marketplace is rooted in more basic conceptions of an individual's life-space.

2. To determine the appropriateness of psychological constructs as potential contributors and explanatory states for investigating consumer discontent.

3. To identify demographic correlates of consumer discontent.

Method

A two-stage area sampling procedure was used to select 228 individuals from the Dallas, Texas, metropolitan area. A subsequent analysis of demographic data indicated that the sample represented a cross section of the area. Individuals were personally contacted in their homes by trained interviewers.

Respondents were given a self-administered questionnaire containing a list of 145 statements designed to measure life satisfaction, powerlessness, anomie, alienation, normlessness, social isolation, aggression, and consumer discontent. All statements were scored on a five-point Likert-type scale except for the six-point Likert-type scale of consumer discontent. Demographic data on the respondents were also collected.

Results

Results of the study are shown in Case Exhibits 23.2–1 and 23.2–2. Case Exhibit 23.2–1 presents the correlation matrix between the measures of psychological states and the consumer discontent scale. The correlations indicate that consumer discontent is indeed related to basic psychological states.

Case Exhibit 23.2–2 presents the correlation matrix between demographic variables and the consumer discontent scale. Examination of demographic variables also reveals that discontent is related to certain characteristics of the populace.

Together, the psychological and demographic correlates of consumer discontent provide a profile of the discontented consumer. Consumer discontent may be an outgrowth of more basic psychological states that reflect disassociation with society in general and specifically with the marketplace. One may speculate that dislocation in society will produce consumer discontent. Given the growing complexity of business and society, it appears that this may become an even more pervasive problem in the future and thus warrants further research at this time.

QUESTIONS

1. Interpret the results of the correlation matrix.

2. Develop a profile of the discontented consumer and the contented consumer.

3. What policy implications would you suggest based on these results?

Case Exhibit 23.2-1 Correlation Matrix of Scale Responses

(*N* = 228)	*CD*	*LS*	*AN*	*AL*	*PO*	*NO*	*SI*	*AG*
Consumer discontent (*CD*)	1.00	−.11[b]	.37[a]	.42[a]	.37[a]	.28[a]	.34[a]	.21[a]
Life satisfaction (*LS*)		1.00	−.44[a]	−.44[a]	−.33[a]	−.25[a]	−.44[a]	−.27[a]
Anomie (*AN*)			1.00	.66[a]	.56[a]	.47[a]	.54[a]	.25[a]
Alienation (*AL*)				1.00	.80[a]	.77[a]	.79[a]	.31[a]
Powerlessness (*PO*)					1.00	.46[a]	.42[a]	.15[b]
Normlessness (*NO*)						1.00	.42[a]	.32[a]
Social isolation (*SI*)							1.00	.28[a]
Aggression (*AG*)								1.00

[a] $p < .01$.

[b] $p < .05$; Pearson product-moment correlation coefficients.

Case Exhibit 23.2-2 Correlation of Scale Responses with Demographic Characteristics

(*N* = 228)	*CD*	*LS*	*AN*	*AL*	*PO*	*NO*	*SI*	*AG*
Age	.13[b]	.14[b]	.10	.31[a]	.07	.29[a]	.37[a]	.13[b]
Sex[1]	−.13[b]	−.05	.02	−.15[b]	−.11	−.06	−.18[b]	.11
Race[2]	−.06	.08	.04	−.15[b]	−.13[b]	−.21[a]	−.03	−.06
Family Size	.02	−.16[a]	.21[a]	.24[a]	.11[b]	.17[b]	.27[a]	.09
Income	.31[a]	−.29[a]	.22[a]	.37[a]	.30[a]	.31[a]	.30[a]	.17[b]
Occupation[3]	−.26[a]	.08	−.20[a]	−.26[a]	−.23[a]	−.15[b]	−.23[a]	.01
Education	.15[b]	−.03	−.11	.20[a]	.27[a]	.16[b]	.06	.11

[a] $p < .01$.

[b] $p < .05$.

[1] Scored: male = 1, female = 2.

[2] Scored: Caucasian = 1, Black = 2, Mexican American = 3, other = 4.

[3] Scored: professional = 1, skilled worker = 2, unskilled worker = 3, unemployed = 4, retired = 5.

Nonparametric Measures
of Association

In a number of situations the assumption that a researcher's data are metric (interval or ratio scaled) cannot be met.[7] A nonparametric correlation technique may be substituted for the Pearson correlation technique.

A group of correlation measures deals with rank-order data. Two groups of consumers might be asked to rank, in order of preference, the brands of a product class. The researcher then wishes to determine the agreement or correlation between the two groups. Two possible statistics can be computed to accomplish this purpose: the Spearman rank-order correlation coefficient (r_s) and the Kendall rank correlation coefficient, τ *(tau)*.

The *Spearman rank coefficient* is computed by:

$$r_s = 1 - \frac{6 \sum\limits_{i=1}^{n} d_i^2}{n^3 - n}$$

where d_i is the difference between the ranks given to the ith brand by each group. Thus, if brand B were ranked first by group 1 and sixth by group 2, d_b^2 would be equal to $(1 - 6)^2$, or 25. In some cases two brands may be given equal scores by a group or be tied for a certain rank. If the number of ties is not large, their effect is small, and we simply assign the average of the ranks that would have been assigned had no ties occurred. We then calculate r_s as before. If the number of ties is large, however, we can introduce a correction factor to offset their effect on r_s.

Consider the relationship between a sales manger's ratings of employees' sales aptitude and their years of service with the organization. The data are portrayed in Table 23A.1, which illustrates how r_s *(rho)* is calculated. The highest rating is given the highest ranking (10).

$$
\begin{aligned}
r_s &= 1 - \frac{6 \sum\limits_{i=1}^{n} d_i^2}{n^3 - n} \\[6pt]
&= 1 - \frac{6(68)}{(10)^3 - 10} \\[6pt]
&= 1 - .412 = .588
\end{aligned}
$$

The answer $r_s = .588$ is interpreted in a manner similar to that for the Pearson correlation coefficient.

Table 23A.1 Example of Spearman Rank Correlation

| | RAW DATA | | RANKING VALUES | | DIFFERENCES | |
| | SALES APTITUDE RATING | YEARS OF SERVICE | RANK OF X | RANK OF Y | D_I | |
EMPLOYEE	(X)	(Y)	(X_R)	(Y_R)	$(X_R - Y_R)$	D_I^2
1	3	5	3.5	4.5	−1.0	1.00
2	5	11	6.5	9.0	−2.5	6.25
3	1	1	1.0	1.0	0.0	0.00
4	4	3	5.0	2.0	3.0	9.00
5	8	5	10.0	4.5	5.5	30.25
6	3	4	3.5	3.0	0.5	0.25
7	6	13	8.0	10.0	−2.0	4.00
8	2	6	2.0	6.0	4.0	16.00
9	5	9	6.5	7.0	0.5	0.25
10	7	10	9.0	8.0	1.0	1.00
						$\Sigma d^2 = 68$

Kendall's rank correlation coefficient, tau, is useful for the same type of situation as is appropriate for the Spearman coefficient, but its computation is not quite as straightforward and may best be explained by an example. Suppose two groups have ranked brands A, B, C, and D in the following way:

BRAND	A	B	C	D
Group I	3	4	2	1
Group II	3	1	4	2

Rearranging the items so that groups I's ranks appear in order, we see the following:

BRAND	D	C	A	B
Group I	1	2	3	4
Group II	2	4	3	1

To determine the degree of consistency between the two rankings, we examine group II's rankings to see how many are in the correct order vis-á-vis one another. The first pair, D and C, are in natural order—that is, 2(D) comes before 4(C)— and we assign a score of +1 to this pair. We proceed to compare the rank for brand D with the ranks of the other brands. The second pair, D and A, is assigned a score of +1, while the pair D and B is assigned a score of -1 because groups I and II do not agree. The total so far is +1. Each rank in turn is compared similarly, and the final total is −2. (Rank of C versus A = −1, C versus B = −1, A versus B = −1, yielding a final real value of −2.) The next step is to compare this actual total with the maximum possible total. A maximum value would occur if group II rankings were identical to those of group I, which is found by taking four things, two at a time, or

$$\binom{N}{2} = \binom{4}{2} = \frac{4!}{2!(4-2)!} = 6$$

Tau is, therefore, equal to the ratio of the actual total over the maximum possible total, or

$$\tau = \frac{\begin{array}{c} \text{Actual} \\ \text{total} \\ \text{score} \end{array}}{\binom{N}{2}} = \frac{-2}{6} = -0.33$$

This is the measure of correlation between the two ranks. Tied observations are treated in the same way as for the Spearman coefficient. Values obtained for r_s and τ from the same data will not be equal and are not comparable to one another.

These means of correlation can be subjected to tests of significance to determine whether the correlations are sufficiently different from change expectations and thus are not due to random sampling error alone. However, those tests and the rules governing their use exceed the scope of this appendix. The reader should refer to specialized statistical texts for the appropriate tests.[8]

The *contingency coefficient* is intended to measure association of nominal data recorded in bivariate contingency tables.[9] It is the only correlation coefficient appropriate for use with nominal data, with the possible exceptions of the phi coefficient, which is limited to 2×2 tables. There is no restriction on the number of categories, provided the number of measures is quite large.

The magnitude of a chi-square statistic calculated from a contingency table is a function of the relationship between the row and column variables. This fact is used to develop a formula for the calculation of the contingency coefficient:

$$C = \frac{\chi^2}{n + \chi^2}$$

where

      C = contingency coefficient
    χ^2 = calculated chi-square value
      n = sample size or total number of observations

The test for statistical significance is the same as in the chi-square test of independence.

Unfortunately, the size of the contingency coefficient is a function of the number of cells in the table, and under no circumstances is it possible for the coefficient to be unity, even though a perfect relationship may exist. The maximum value of the contingency coefficient for a 2×2 table is .707, for a 3×3 table .816, and for a 4×4 table .866.

Chapter 24

Multivariate Statistical Analysis

BUSINESS EXECUTIVES ARE A GREAT VACATION MARKET.[1] EACH year, they average four vacations of at least three days and two nights. Shorter vacations do not mean that they spend less money—three in four executives agree that they would rather take a shorter vacation at a luxury hotel than a longer vacation at a budget hotel. However, are all executive vacationers alike? Do they have the same attitudes toward vacations? Are there demographic variables that help differentiate between market segments?

Attitude surveys are often utilized as a basis for market segmentation. Marketing researchers for Hyatt Hotels measured executives' attitudes toward vacations and used multivariate analysis to identify five distinct segments.

The largest segment called fugitives (25 percent) are overstressed and looking for an escape. Once on vacation, they forget their diets, drink more, and are less sexually inhibited. They do not, however, stop worrying about their jobs, the cost of the vacation, and the homes, children, and pets they leave behind. Fugitives are predominantly women baby boomers (60 percent) with 57 percent of the fugitives being between the ages of 25 and 44.

Power players and stress fighters each represents 21 percent of executive vacations. Stress fighters make it their mission to relax on vacation. Because of their extreme health orientation, they aggressively pursue athletics and refrain from eating and drinking excessively. Fifty-three percent of stress fighters are baby boomers with half being women. Eighty-four percent are married and 77 percent have children.

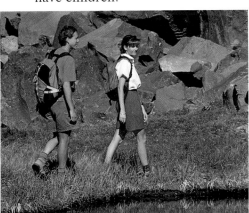

Power players know how to mix business with pleasure. They stay in touch with the office, but say that it does not interfere with their vacations. Their habits do not change significantly while they are away from the office, which may be why they do not experience a significant improvement in job performance when they get back. Power players are calm, cool, and confident people who are likely to be seen at the poolside talking on a cellular telephone. They are older and more male dominated than the other segments—74 percent are aged 45 or older, and 68 percent are men.

Nineteen percent of vacationing executives are schedulers who have as much fun planning their vacations as actually taking them. Schedulers are quintessential tourists. They enjoy sightseeing and absorbing the local culture. They do not keep in touch with the office and feel that their job performance improves when they return. Fifty-eight percent of schedulers are 45 or older, and half are women.

Thirteen percent of executive vacationers are fun worshipers. Nearly 70 percent are women, 60 percent are aged 25 to 44, and only 40 percent have children. They concentrate on leaving their worries behind and having a good time. While on vacation, fun worshipers become more athletic, outgoing, and romantic. They return to their jobs reinvigorated.

Marketers need demographics, but a demographic profile can be enhanced. Attitudinal studies allow marketers to think of segments as being composed of real people with real concerns and real attitudes about products. Using multivariate analysis with attitudes and demographic variables helps marketers visualize target markets as real people.

The computer has influenced the rapid diffusion of multivariate analysis in marketing research. A number of computer software packages have changed techniques that once were expensive and exotic into affordable and regular forms of analysis. With the multivariate statistical revolution, students need to understand these powerful tools of analysis. This chapter presents a nontechnical description of some multivariate methods; it does not include computation formulas.

The Nature of Multivariate Analysis

Most business problems are inherently multidimensional. Corporations can be described along a wide variety of dimensions. The price of domestic automobiles can be simultaneously influenced by rate of inflation, advertising expenditures, and the balance of payments. Consumers can evaluate various shopping centers on the basis of many attributes. As researchers become increasingly aware of the multidimensional nature of their problems, they will use multivariate analysis more and more to help them solve complex problems.

TO THE POINT

The essence of mathematics is not to make simple things complicated, but to make complicated things simple.

S. GUDDER

multivariate statistical analysis
Statistical methods that allow the simultaneous investigation of more than two variables.

The investigation of one variable at a time is referred to as *univariate analysis,* which we discussed in Chapter 21. Investigation of the relationship between two variables is *bivariate analysis,* discussed in Chapters 22 and 23. When problems are multidimensional and involve three or more variables, we use **multivariate statistical analysis.** Multivariate statistical methods allow us to consider the effects of more than one variable at the same time. For example, suppose a forecaster wishes to estimate oil consumption for the next five years. While consumption might be predicted by past oil consumption records alone, adding additional variables such as average number of miles driven per year, coal production, and nuclear plants under construction might give greater insight into the determinants of oil consumption. Consumers who are evaluating grocery stores may be concerned with distance to each store, perceived cleanliness, price levels, and many other store attributes. To understand problems such as these, researchers need multivariate analysis.

Classifying Multivariate Techniques

Exhibit 24.1 presents a useful classification of most multivariate statistical techniques. Two basic groups of multivariate techniques are classified: *dependence methods* and *interdependence methods*.

The Analysis of Dependence

If we use a multivariate technique to explain or predict the dependent variable(s) on the basis of two or more independent variables, we are attempting to analyze dependence. An instance in which a researcher is interested in specifying a relationship between one dependent variable and several independent variables is illustrated by a common judgment: Is a person a good or a poor credit risk based on age, income, and marital status? Forecasting the dependent variable, sales, on the basis of numerous independent variables is a frequently investigated problem in the analysis of dependence. *Multiple regression analysis, multiple discriminant*

Exhibit 24.1   A Classification of Selected Multivariate Methods

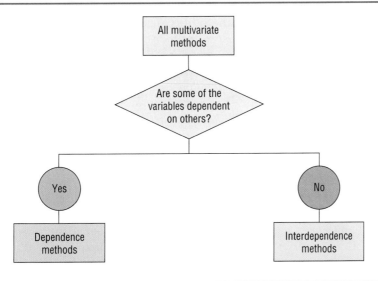

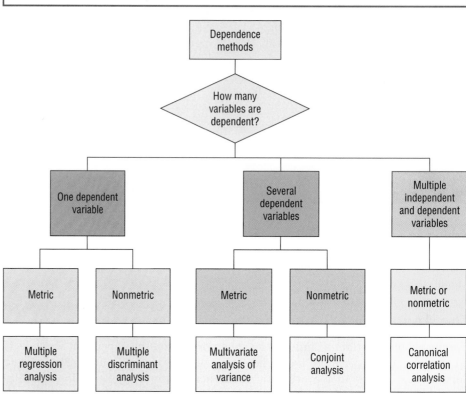

Exhibit 24.2 **Multivariate Analysis: Classification of Dependence Methods**

dependence methods
A category of multivariate statistical techniques; dependence methods explain or predict a dependent variable(s) on the basis of two or more independent variables.

interdependence methods
A category of multivariate statistical techniques; interdependence methods give meaning to a set of variables or seek to group things together.

analysis, multivariate analysis of variance, and *canonical correlation analysis* are all **dependence methods.**

The Analysis of Interdependence

The goal of **interdependence methods** of analysis is to give meaning to a set of variables or to seek to group things together. No one variable or variable subset is to be predicted from or explained by the others. The most common interdependence methods are *factor analysis, cluster analysis,* and *multidimensional scaling.* A marketing manager who wants to identify profitable market segments or clusters might utilize these techniques. Another example is the identification and classification of cities that are similar in population size, income distribution, race and ethnic distribution, and consumption of a manufacturer's product for the selection of comparable test markets.

Influence of Measurement Scales

As in other forms of data analysis, the nature of the measurement scales will determine which multivariate technique is appropriate for the data. Exhibits 24.2 and 24.3 show that selection of a multivariate technique requires consideration of the types of measures used for both independent and dependent sets of variables. For ease of diagramming, Exhibits 24.2 and 24.3 refer to nominal and ordinal scales as *nonmetric* and interval and ratio scales as *metric.* Exhibit 24.2 assumes the independent variable is metric.

> **Exhibit 24.3   Multivariate Analysis: Classification of Interdependence Methods**

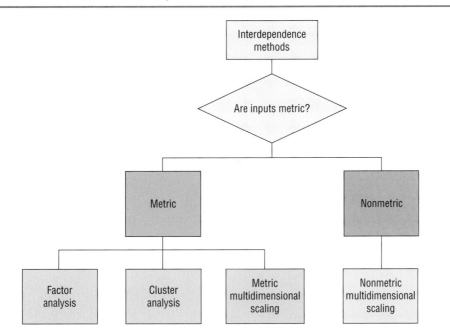

Analysis of Dependence

Multiple Regression Analysis

Multiple regression analysis is an extension of bivariate regression analysis that allows for simultaneous investigation of the effect of two or more independent variables on a single, interval-scaled dependent variable. In Chapter 23 we illustrated bivariate linear regression analysis with an example concerning a construction dealer's sales volume. In this example, variations in the dependent variable were attributed to changes in a single independent variable. Yet reality suggests that several factors are likely to affect such a dependent variable. For example, sales volume might be hypothesized to depend not only on the number of building permits, but also on price levels, amount of advertising, and income of consumers in the area. Thus, the problem requires identification of a linear relationship with multiple regression analysis. The multiple regression equation is:

$$Y = a + \beta_1 X_1 + \beta_2 X_2 + \beta_3 X_3 \ldots + \beta_n X_n$$

Another forecasting example is useful for illustrating multiple regression. Assume that a toy manufacturer wishes to forecast sales by sales territory. It is thought that retail sales, the presence or absence of a company salesperson in the territory (a binary variable), and grammar school enrollment are the independent variables that might explain the variation in sales. The data appear in Table 24.1. Table 24.2 shows the statistical results from multiple regression after mathematical computations have been made. The regression equation

$$Y = 102.18 + .387X_1 + 115.2X_2 + 6.73X_3$$

multiple regression analysis
An analysis of association that simultaneously investigates the effect of two or more independent variables on a single, interval-scaled dependent variable.

Table 24.1 **Data for a Multiple Regression Problem**

Y SALES (000)	X_1 RETAIL SALES (000)	X_2 SALESPERSON (1) OR AGENT (000)	X_3 GRAMMAR SCHOOL ENROLLMENT (000)
222	106	0	23
304	213	0	18
218	201	0	22
501	378	1	20
542	488	0	21
790	509	1	31
523	644	0	17
667	888	1	25
700	941	1	32
869	1,066	1	36
444	307	0	30
479	312	1	22

indicates that sales are positively related to X_1, X_2, and X_3. The coefficients (βs) show the effect on the dependent variables of a 1-unit increase in any of the independent variables. The value $\beta_2 = 115.2$ indicates that an increase of $115,200 (000 included) in toy sales is expected with each addition unit of X_2. Thus, it appears that adding a company salesperson will have a very positive effect on sales. Grammar school enrollments also may help predict sales. An increase of 1 unit of enrollment (1,000 students) indicates a sales increase of $6,730 (000 included). Retail sales volume (X_1) in the territory adds little to the predictive power of the equation ($387).

In multiple regression the terminology for β_1, β_2, and so on changes. These coefficients are now called *coefficients of partial regression*. Each independent variable is usually correlated with the other independent variables. Thus, the correlation between Y and X_1 with the correlation that X_1 and X_2 have in common with Y held constant is the *partial correlation*. Because the partial correlation between sales and X_1 has been adjusted for the effect produced by variation in X_2 (and other independent variables), the correlation coefficient obtained from the bivariate regression will not be the same as the partial coefficient in the multiple regression. In other words, the original value of β is the simple bivariate regression coefficient. In multiple regression, the coefficient β_1 is defined as the partial regression coefficient for which the effects of other independent variables are held constant.

The *coefficient of multiple determination*, or multiple index of determination, is shown in Table 24.2. As in bivariate regression, the coefficient of multiple

Table 24.2 **Statistical Results of a Multiple Regression Analysis**

$$Y = 102.18 + .387X_1 + 115.2X_2 + 6.73X_3$$

Coefficient of multiple determination (R^2)	.845
F-value	14.6

determination indicates the percentage of variation in Y explained by the variation in the independent variables. $R^2 = .845$ tells the researcher that the variation in the independent variables accounted for 84.5 percent of the variance in the dependent variable. Typically, introducing additional independent variables into the regression equation explains more of the variation in Y than is possible with fewer variables. In other words, the amount of variation explained by two independent variables in the same equation usually explains more variation in Y than either one explains separately.

To test for statistical significance, an F-test is necessary to compare the different sources of variation. The F-test allows for testing of the relative magnitudes of the sum of squares due to the regression (SS_r) and the error sum of squares (SS_e), with their appropriate degrees of freedom:

$$F = \frac{(SS_r)/k}{(SS_e)/(n - k - 1)}$$

where

$$k = \text{number of independent variables}$$
$$n = \text{number of respondents}$$

Table A.5 in the appendix shows the F-distributions for hypothesis testing at the .05 significance level. In the preceding example the F-ratio equals 14.6. Degrees of freedom ($d.f.$) are calculated as follows:

$$d.f. \text{ for the numerator} = k$$
$$d.f. \text{ for the denominator} = n - k - 1$$

In this example,

$$d.f. \text{ (numerator)} = 3$$
$$d.f. \text{ (denominator)} = 12 - 3 - 1 = 8$$

Table A.5 indicates that an F-value of 4.07 or more is necessary to reject the null hypothesis at the .05 level of statistical significance. Thus, it can be concluded that the estimated functional relationship is not due to chance or random variation; there does appear to be an association between the dependent and independent variables other than random variation in the data.

A continuous, interval-scaled dependent variable is required in multiple regression as in bivariate regression. Interval scaling is also required for the independent variables; however, dummy variables, such as the binary variable in our example, may be used. A *dummy variable* is a variable that has two (or more) distinct levels that are coded as 0 and 1.

There are several other assumptions for multiple regression (and other multivariate techniques), all of which require advanced study. Several excellent technical books deal with this topic.[2] The growing use of commercially available computer programs allows the researcher to compute multiple regressions without a great deal of effort. Managers should be aware of the appropriateness of this technique in using their databases.

Discriminant Analysis

In a myriad of situations the researcher's purpose is to classify objects, by a set of independent variables, into two or more mutually exclusive categories. A physician can record a person's blood pressure, weight, and blood cholesterol level and then categorize that person as having a high or low probability of a heart attack. A researcher interested in retailing failures may be able to group firms as to whether they eventually failed or did not fail on the basis of independent variables such as location, financial ratios, or management changes. A bank may want to discriminate between potentially successful and unsuccessful sites for electronic fund transfer system machines. A sales manager may want to distinguish between applicants to hire and those not to hire. The challenge is to find the discriminating variables to use in a predictive equation that will produce better than chance assignment of the individuals to the two groups.

discriminant analysis

A statistical technique for predicting the probability of objects belonging in two or more mutually exclusive categories (dependent variable) based on several independent variables.

The prediction of a categorical variable (rather than a continuous, interval-scaled variable as in multiple regression) is the purpose of **discriminant analysis.** In each of the above problems, the researcher must determine which variables are associated with the probability that an object will fall into one of several groups or categories. In a statistical context the problem of studying the direction of group differences is one of finding a linear combination of independent variables, the discriminant function, that shows large differences in group means. Discriminant analysis is a statistical tool for determining such linear combinations. The researcher's task is to derive the coefficients of the discriminant function (a straight line).

The example we will use concentrates on the two-group discriminant analysis problem where the dependent variable, Y, is measured on a nominal scale. (Although n-way discriminant analysis is possible, it is beyond the scope of this discussion.) Suppose a personnel manager for an electrical wholesaler has been keeping records on successful versus unsuccessful sales employees. The personnel manager believes it is possible to predict whether an applicant will succeed on the basis of age, sales aptitude test scores, and mechanical ability scores. As stated at the outset, the problem is to find a linear function of the independent variables that shows large differences in group means. The first task is to estimate the coefficients of the applicant's discriminant functions. To calculate the individual's discriminant scores, the following linear functions is used:

$$Z_i = b_1 X_{1i} + b_2 X_{2i} + \ldots + b_n X_{ni}$$

where

Z_i = ith applicant's discriminant score
b_n = discriminant coefficient for the nth variable
X_{ni} = applicant's value on the nth independent variable

Using all the individuals in the sample, a discriminant function is determined based on the criteria that the groups be maximally differentiated on the set of independent variables.

Returning to the example with three independent variables, suppose the personnel manager finds the standardized weights in the equation to be:

$$Z = b_1 X_1 + b_2 X_2 + b_3 X_3$$
$$= .069 X_1 + .013 X_2 + .0007 X_3$$

This means that age (X_1) is much more important than sales aptitude test scores (X_2). Mechanical ability (X_3) has relatively minor discriminating power.

In the computation of the linear discriminant function, weights are assigned to the variables to maximize the ratio of the difference between the means of the two groups to the standard deviation within groups. The standardized discriminant coefficients or weights provide information about the relative importance of each of these variables in discriminating between the two groups.

Table 24.3 Confusion Matrix

	Predicted Group		
Actual Group	Successful	Unsuccessful	
Successful	34	6	40
Unsuccessful	7	38	45

A major purpose of discriminant analysis is to perform a classification function. The purpose of classification in our example is to predict which applicants will be successful and which will be unsuccessful and to group them accordingly. To determine whether the discriminant analysis can be used as a good predictor of applicant success, information provided in the "confusion matrix" is used. Suppose the personnel manager has 40 successful and 45 unsuccessful employees in the sample. The confusion matrix in Table 24.3 shows that the number of correctly classified employees (76 percent) is much higher than would be expected by chance. Tests can be performed to determine whether the rate of correct classification is statistically significant.

Canonical Correlation Analysis

Canonical correlation is a very complex statistical technique that is seldom used, but we will examine it here briefly. When the research analyst has two criterion variables (dependent variables) and multiple predictor variables (independent variables), **canonical correlation analysis** is an appropriate statistical technique. Multiple regression analysis investigates the linear relationship between a single dependent or criterion variable and multiple independent variables. Canonical correlation is an extension of multiple regression. It focuses on the relationship between two sets of interval-scaled variables.

To illustrate canonical correlation, suppose a researcher wishes to specify the correlation between a set of shopping behavior variables (the criterion set) and some personality variables (the predictor set). The researcher wants to know how several personality traits influence grocery shopping behavior, such as list preparation, use of store coupons, number of stores visited, and number of trips per week. The researcher is attempting to find personality profiles that tend to be associated with various shopping patterns.

Calculation of the canonical correlation maximizes the correlation between two linear combinations. For example, the linear combination for shopping behavior might be as follows:

$$Z = a_1X_1 + a_2X_2 + \ldots + a_nX_n$$

The linear combination for the personality variables might be:

$$W = b_1Y_1 + b_2Y_2 + \ldots + b_nY_n$$

As in regression analysis, a set of canonical coefficients or weights is identified for the predictor set of variables.

Furthermore, a set of canonical coefficients or weights is identified for the criterion set. To interpret the canonical analysis, the researcher examines the relative magnitude and the signs of the several weights that define each equation to look for a meaningful interpretation.

canonical correlation analysis
A statistical technique used to determine the degree of linear association between two sets of variables, each consisting of several variables.

Exhibit 24.4   Summary of Multivariate Techniques for Analysis of Dependence

TECHNIQUE	PURPOSE	NUMBER OF DEPENDENT VARIABLES	NUMBER OF INDEPENDENT VARIABLES	TYPE OF MEASUREMENT	
				DEPENDENT	INDEPENDENT
Multiple regression	To investigate simultaneously the effect of several independent variables on a dependent variable	1	2 or more	Interval	Interval
Discriminant analysis	To predict the probability of objects or individuals belonging in two or more mutually exclusive categories based on several independent variables	1	2 or more	Nominal	Interval
Canonical correlation	To determine the degree of linear association between two sets of several variables	2 or more	2 or more	Interval	Interval
MANOVA	To determine whether statistically significant differences on means of several variables occur simultaneously between two levels of a variable	2 or more	1	Interval	Nominal

Multivariate Analysis of Variance (MANOVA)

multivariate analysis of variance (MANOVA)
A statistical technique that provides a simultaneous significance test of mean difference between groups for two or more dependent variables.

Like canonical correlation, **multivariate analysis of variance (MANOVA)** is useful when there are multiple interval- or ratio-scaled dependent variables. There may be one or more nominally scaled independent variables. By manipulating the sales compensation system in an experimental situation and holding the compensation system constant in a controlled situation, the experimental researcher may wish to identify the effect of the compensation system on sales volume as well as job satisfaction and turnover. With MANOVA a significance test of mean difference between groups can be made simultaneously for two or more dependent variables.

Exhibit 24.4 summarizes the multivariate techniques for analysis of dependence.

Analysis of Interdependence

We now turn our attention to the analysis of interdependence. Rather than attempting to predict a variable or set of variables from a set of independent variables, we can use techniques like *factor analysis, cluster analysis,* and *multidimensional scaling* to better understand the structure of a set of variables or objects.

Exhibit 24.5 **Factor Analysis Example**

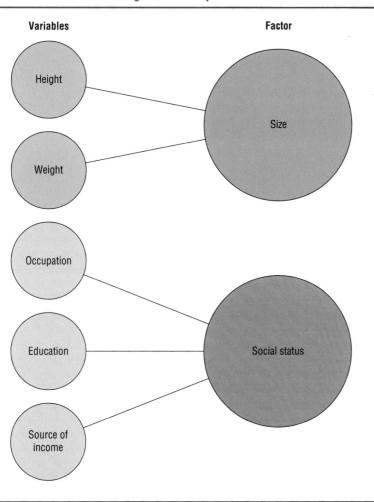

Factor Analysis

Suppose we measure the heights, weights, occupations, educations, and sources of income for 50 men. The results of a **factor analysis** might indicate that height and weight may be summarized by the underlying dimension of size. The variables occupation, education, and source of income may be summarized by the underlying concept of social status. In this example, two new variables, or *factors,* explain the five variables at a more generalized level (see Exhibit 24.5).

The general purpose of factor analysis is to summarize the information contained in a large number of variables into a smaller number of factors. Factor analysis refers to a number of diverse techniques used to discern the underlying dimensions or regularity in phenomena.[3]

If a researcher has a set of variables and suspects that they are interrelated in a complex fashion, he or she may use factor analysis to untangle the linear relationships into separate patterns. The statistical purpose of factor analysis is to determine linear combinations of variables that will aid in investigating the interrelationships.

For example, suppose a researcher collects a variety of data on intermediaries' attitudes toward their working relationships with a manufacturer. Questions might concern delivery, pricing arrangements, discounts, sales personnel,

factor analysis
A type of analysis used to discern the underlying dimensions or regularity in phenomena. Its general purpose is to summarize the information contained in a large number of variables into a smaller number of factors.

repair service, and other relevant issues. However, the researcher may want to reduce the large number of variables to certain underlying constructs or dimensions that will summarize the important information contained in the variables. Thus, the researcher's purpose is to discover the basic structure of a domain and add substantive interpretation to the underlying dimensions. Factor analysis accomplishes this by combining these questions to create new, more abstract variables called *factors*. In general, the goal of factor analysis is parsimony: to reduce a large number of variables to as few dimensions or constructs as possible.

Interpreting Factor Results

The use of factor analysis to reduce a large number of variables to a few interpretable dimensions is illustrated in the following consumer behavior example in a health care setting.[4] With advances in medical science, the demand has increased for nonregenerative body parts, such as kidneys, and regenerative body parts, such as blood. Researchers were attempting to investigate whether willingness to donate body parts was a unidimensional domain. Based on factor analysis (see Table 24.4), they uncovered three separate under-lying dimensions of willingness to donate: factor 1—blood, skin, and marrow donations; factor 2—death (cadaver) donation; and factor 3—kidney donation.

Factor Loadings. The factor loadings in Table 24.4 are roughly analogous to the correlation (or set of correlations) of the original variables with the factor. Each factor loading is a measure of the importance of the variable in measuring each factor. In the example, the statement "If needed, I am willing to give blood to a relative or close friend" has a high factor loading (.6339) on factor 1 and a relatively low loading on factors 2 and 3. Inspection of the table indicates that for each of the variables loading on the blood-skin-marrow factor (factor 1), the loadings are much higher on factor 1 than on factors 2 and 3. Factor loadings provide a means for interpreting and labeling the factors.

Total Variance Explained. Along with the factor loadings, Table 24.4 portrays a percentage of total variance of the original variable as explained by each factor. Factor 1 summarizes 36.9 percent of the variance and factor 2 summarizes 12.2 percent of the variance. Together the two factors summarize 49.1 percent of the total variance. This explanation of variance is equivalent to the R^2 in multiple regression.

Factor Score. Each individual observation has a score or value associated with each original variable. Factor analysis procedures derive factor scores, which represent each observation's calculated value, or score on each factor. The factor score will represent an individual's combined response to the several variables that represent the factor.

The factor scores may be used in subsequent analysis. When the factors are to represent a new set of variables that may predict or be dependent on some phenomenon, the new input may be factor scores.

In addition to reducing a large number of variables to a manageable number of dimensions, factor analysis may reduce the problem of multicollinearity in multiple regression.[5] If several independent variables are highly correlated, a factor analysis as a preliminary step prior to regression analysis and use of factor scores may reduce the problem of having several intercorrelated independent variables. Thus, factor analysis may be used to meet the statistical assumptions of various models.

Communality. A researcher may wish to know how much a variable has in common with all factors. Communality is a measure of the percentage of a variable's variation that is explained by the factors. A relatively high communality indicates that a variable has much in common with the other variables taken as a group.

Table 24.4 Factor Analysis with Varimax Rotation— Ten Willingness-to-Donate Variables[a]

		FACTOR LOADINGS		
	VARIABLE AND FACTOR DESCRIPTION	FACTOR 1	FACTOR 2	FACTOR 3
Blood, Skin, Marrow	If needed, I am willing to give *blood* to a relative or close friend.	[.6339][b]	.0988	.0517
	I would be willing to donate *blood* at least once every two months.	[.3807]	.1646	.2009
	If I witnessed a traffic accident, I would not be willing to donate *blood* to a victim.	[−.4244]	−.0304	−.1503
	I would give a piece of my *skin* to a relative who has been seriously burnt.	[.4556]	.1405	.1356
	If necessary, I would donate some *bone marrow* to be extracted from my breastbone to a relative.	[.5337]	.3440	.2681
Death Donation	I am willing to donate both my eyes to a stranger upon my *death*.	.1412	[.7944]	.2946
	I am willing to arrange an agreement to donate my heart or any other vital organ for use after my *death*.	.2410	[.7582]	.1664
Kidney Donation	I would never donate one of my *kidneys* to someone outside of my family, not even to a close friend.	−.1669	−.2544	[−.6770]
	If needed, I would donate one of my *kidneys* to a stranger at this very moment.	.1641	.1486	[.6584]
	If at this moment I learned that a relative desperately needed a *kidney* to survive, I would not donate one of mine.	−.3814	−.1596	[−.5272]
	Explained variance per factor	36.9%	12.2%	10.2%
	Cumulative	36.9%	49.1%	59.3%

[a]377 respondents
[b][ ] indicates the highest loading in each row.

How Many Factors?

This discussion has concentrated on summarizing the patterns in the variables with a reduced number of factors. The question arises: "How many factors will be in the problem's solution?" This question requires a lengthy answer. It is complex because there can be more than one possible solution to any factor analysis problem, depending on factor rotation. A discussion of the technical aspects of the concept of factor rotation is beyond the scope of this book. However, the term rotation is important in factor analysis and should be explained briefly. Solutions to factor analysis problems may be portrayed by geometrically plotting the values of each variable for all respondents or observations. Geometric axes may be drawn to represent each factor. New solutions are represented geometrically by rotation of these axes. Hence, a new solution with fewer or more factors is called a *rotation.*

While the concept of factor analysis is relatively easy to grasp, the technical vocabulary of factor analysis includes a number of unusual terms, such as *eigenvalues, rotated matrix,* and *orthogonal.* Because this is a simplified introduction to the topic of multivariate statistics, we will not define each of these terms. Competent statisticians should be consulted when working on problems that involve factor analysis.

Cluster Analysis

cluster analysis

A body of techniques with the purpose of classifying individuals or objects into a small number of mutually exclusive groups, ensuring that there will be as much likeness within groups and as much difference among groups as possible.

Cluster analysis refers to a body of techniques used to identify objects or individuals that are similar with respect to one criterion or several criteria. The purpose of cluster analysis is to classify individuals or objects into a small number of mutually exclusive and exhaustive groups. The researcher seeks to determine how objects or individuals should be assigned to groups to ensure that there will be as much likeness within groups and as much difference among groups as possible. The cluster should have high internal (within-cluster) homogeneity and external (between-cluster) heterogeneity.

A typical use of cluster analysis is to facilitate market segmentation by identifying subjects or individuals who have similar needs, lifestyles, or responses to marketing strategies. Clusters or subgroups of recreational vehicle owners may be identified on the basis of their similarity with respect to recreational vehicle usage and the benefits they want from recreational vehicles. Alternatively, the researcher might use demographic or lifestyle variables to group individuals into clusters identified as market segments.

We will illustrate cluster analysis with a hypothetical example of the type of vacations taken by 12 individuals. Vacation behavior is represented on two dimensions: number of vacation days and dollar expenditures on vacations during a given year. Exhibit 24.6 is a scatter diagram that represents the geometric distance between each individual in two-dimensional space. The diagram portrays three clear-cut clusters. The first subgroup, consisting of individuals L, H, and B, suggests a group of individuals who have many vacation days but do not spend much money on their vacations. The second cluster, represented by individuals A, I, K, G, and F, represents intermediate values on both variables, average amounts of vacation days and average dollar expenditures on vacations. The third group, individuals C, J, E, and D, consists of individuals who have relatively few vacation days but spend large amounts on vacations.

In this example, individuals are grouped on the basis of their similarity or proximity to one another. The logic of cluster analysis is to group individuals or

---

Exhibit 24.6 **Clusters of Individuals on Two Dimensions**

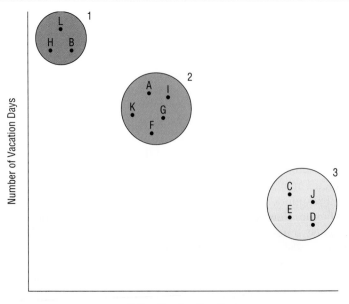

Table 24.5   Cluster Analysis of Test Market Cities

Cluster Number	City	Cluster Number	City	Cluster Number	City
1	Omaha	7	Sacramento	13	Allentown
	Oklahoma City		San Bernardino		Providence
	Dayton		San Jose		Jersey City
	Columbus		Phoenix		York
	Fort Worth		Tucson		Louisville
2	Peoria	8	Gary	14	Paterson
	Davenport		Nashville		Milwaukee
	Binghamton		Jacksonville		Cincinnati
	Harrisburg		San Antonio		Miami
	Worcester		Knoxville		Seattle
3	Canton	9	Indianapolis	15	San Diego
	Youngstown		Kansas City		Tacoma
	Toledo		Dallas		Norfolk
	Springfield		Atlanta		Charleston
	Albany		Houston		Fort Lauderdale
4	Bridgeport	10	Mobile	16	New Orleans
	Rochester		Shreveport		Richmond
	Hartford		Birmingham		Tampa
	New Haven		Memphis		Lancaster
	Syracuse		Chattanooga		Minneapolis
5	Wilmington	11	Newark	17	San Francisco
	Orlando		Cleveland		Detroit
	Tulsa		Pittsburgh		Boston
	Wichita		Buffalo		Philadelphia
	Grand Rapids		Baltimore	18	Washington
6	Bakersfield	12	Albuquerque		St. Louis
	Fresno		Salt Lake City		
	Flint		Denver		
	El Paso		Charlotte		
	Beaumont		Portland		

Note: Points not in a cluster—Honolulu, Wilkes-Barre.

objects by their similarity or distance from each other. The mathematical procedures for deriving clusters will not be dealt with here, as our purpose is only to introduce the technique.

A classic study provides a very pragmatic example of the use of cluster analysis.[6] Marketing managers frequently are interested in finding test market cities that are very similar so that no extraneous variation will cause differences between the experimental and control markets. In that study, the objects to be clustered were cities. The characteristics of the cities, such as population, retail sales, number of retail outlets, and percentage of nonwhites, were used to identify the groups. Cities such as Omaha, Oklahoma City, Dayton, Columbus, and Fort Worth were similar and cities such as Newark, Cleveland, Pittsburgh, Buffalo, and Baltimore were similar, but individual cities within each group were dissimilar to those within other groups or clusters. (See Table 24.5 for additional details.)

This example should clarify the difference between factor analysis and cluster analysis. In factor analysis the researcher might search for constructs that

EXPLORING RESEARCH ISSUES

Seven Commandments for Users of Multivariate Methods

DO NOT BE TECHNIQUE ORIENTED. FOCUS ON management's needs, then choose an appropriate analytical tool.

Consider multivariate models as information for management. Multivariate models (equations or perceptual maps) are an aid to, not a substitute for, managerial judgment.

Do not substitute multivariate methods for researcher skill and imagination. Statistics do not ensure causality and are not substitutes for common sense.

Develop a communication skill. Management seldom accepts findings based on methods it doesn't understand.

Avoid making statistical inferences about the parameters of multivariate models. We are seldom certain of the distribution of a market population due to nonsampling and measurement errors.

Guard against the danger of making inferences about the market realities when such inferences may be due to the peculiarities of the method. Be sure the statistical findings are consistent with sound theory and common sense.

Exploit the complementary relationship between functional and structural methods. Use one method to support another.

---

underlie the variables (population, retail sales, number of retail outlets); in cluster analysis, the researcher would seek constructs that underlie the objects (cities).

Cluster analysis differs from multiple discriminant analysis in that the groups are not predefined. The purpose of cluster analysis is to determine how many groups really exist and to define their composition. It describes a sample of objects by examining only a sample; it does not predict relationships.

Multidimensional Scaling

multidimensional scaling
A statistical technique that measures objects in multidimensional space on the basis of respondents' judgments of the similarity of objects.

Multidimensional scaling provides a means for measuring objects in multidimensional space on the basis of respondents' judgments of the similarity of objects. The perceptual difference among objects is reflected in the relative distance among objects in the multi-dimensional space.

Traditionally, attitudes have been measured using a scale for each component of an attitude and then combining the individual scores into an aggregate score. In the most common form of multidimensional scaling, subjects are asked to evaluate an object's similarity to other objects. For example, a sports car study may ask respondents to rate the similarity of a BMW convertible to a Corvette. The analyst then attempts to explain the difference in objects on the basis of the components of attitudes. The unfolding of the attitude components helps explain why objects are judged to be similar or dissimilar.

In another example, MBA students were asked to provide their perceptions of relative similarities among six graduate schools. Next, the overall similarity scores for all possible pairs of objects were aggregated for all individual respondents and arranged in a matrix. With the aid of a complex computer program, the judgments about similarity were statistically transformed into distances by placing the graduate schools into a specified multi-dimensional space. The distance between similar objects on the perceptual map was small for similar objects; dissimilar objects were farther apart.

Exhibit 24.7 Perceptual Map of Six Graduate Business Schools: Simple Space

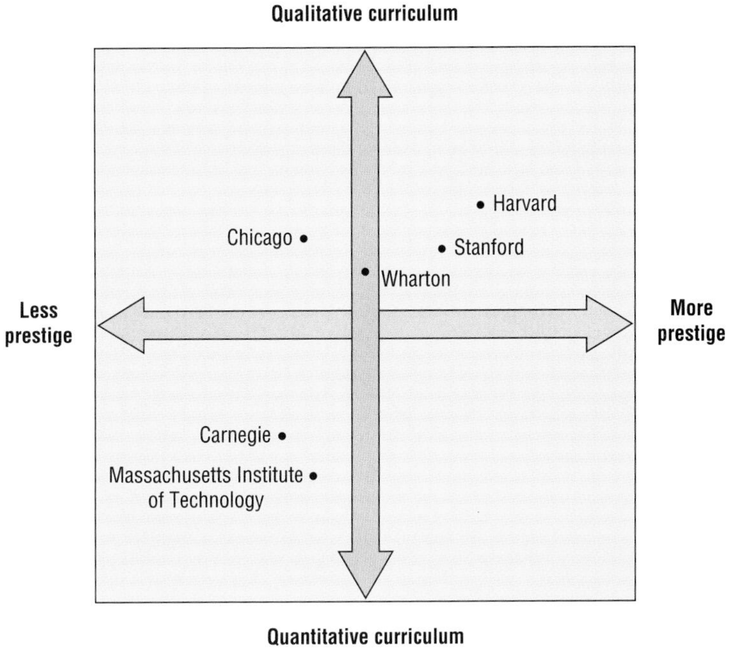

Exhibit 24.7 shows a perceptual map in two-dimensional space. Inspection of the map illustrates that Harvard and Stanford were perceived as quite similar to each other. MIT and the Carnegie Institute were perceived as very similar; however, MIT and Chicago were perceived as dissimilar. The researchers identified the two axes as "quantitative versus qualitative curriculum" and "less versus more prestige." The labeling of the dimension axes is a task of interpretation for the researcher and is not statistically determined. As with other multivariate techniques in the analysis of interdependence, there are several alternative mathematical techniques for multidimensional scaling.

Exhibit 24.8 summarizes the multivariate techniques for analysis of interdependence.

Exhibit 24.8 Summary of Multivariate Techniques for Analysis of Interdependence

TECHNIQUE	PURPOSE	TYPE OF MEASUREMENT
Factor analysis	To summarize the information contained in a large number of variables into a reduced number of factors	Interval
Cluster analysis	To classify individuals or objects into a smaller number of mutually exclusive and exhaustive groups to ensure that there will be as much likeness within groups and as much difference among groups as possible	Interval
Multidimensional scaling	To measure objects in multidimensional space on the basis of respondents' judgments of the similarity of objects	Varies depending on technique

Summary

Multivariate statistical analysis is used in problems that involve three or more variables. The availability of computer software designed to process multivariate statistics has made such usage more practical in recent years. Dependence methods use two or more independent variables to predict a dependent variable(s). Interdependence methods group subsets of variables.

A common dependence method is multiple regression. It is an extension of bivariate linear regression that uses more than one independent variable. The coefficients of partial regression obtained in multiple regression hold all other independent variables constant and thus are not identical to the corresponding simple regression coefficients. The coefficient of multiple determination (R^2) represents the portion of the variance in the dependent variable accounted for by the model. An *F*-test can be used to determine statistical significance.

Another dependence technique is discriminant analysis. It uses independent variables to classify observations into one set of mutually exclusive categories.

Canonical correlation and multivariate analysis of variance are more complex dependence techniques. Canonical correlation uses multiple criterion (dependent) variables and multiple predictor (independent) variables. Multivariate analysis of variance, or MANOVA, allows significance tests of mean differences between groups for two or more dependent variables.

The first interdependence method is factor analysis. It is used to summarize the information contained in a large number of variables into a smaller number of factors. A second method, cluster analysis, classifies observations into a small number of mutually exclusive and exhaustive groups; these should have as much similarity within groups and as much difference between groups as possible. In cluster analysis the groups are not predefined. A third interdependence method is multidimensional scaling. It measures objects in a multidimensional space based on respondents' judgments about similarity. The procedure explains the perceived relationships by unfolding the attitude components of the judgments.

Key Terms and Concepts

Multivariate statistical analysis
Dependence methods
Interdependence methods
Multiple regression analysis

Discriminant analysis
Canonical correlation analysis
Multivariate analysis of variance
   (MANOVA)

Factor analysis
Cluster analysis
Multidimensional scaling

Questions for Review and Critical Thinking

1. How do multivariate statistical analysis methods differ from univariate and bivariate methods?
2. What is the distinction between dependence methods and interdependence methods?
3. What is the aim of multiple linear regression? Discriminant analysis? Canonical correlation? Multivariate analysis of variance?
4. Give an example of a situation for which each of the techniques mentioned in question 3 might be used.
5. What is the aim of factor analysis? Cluster analysis? Multidimensional scaling?
6. Give an example of a situation for which each of the techniques mentioned in question 5 might be used.

7. Why have computer software packages increased the use of multivariate analysis?

8. Why might a researcher want to use multivariate rather than univariate or bivariate analysis?

 9. A researcher uses multiple regression to predict a client's sales volume using gross domestic product, personal income, disposable personal income, unemployment, and the consumer price index. What should the researcher be obligated to tell the client about this multiple regression model?

Exploring the Internet

1. The American Statistical Association home page is located at http://www.amstat.org/. Select the careers in the statistics option and learn what a career in statistics might have to offer.

2. Go to the SPSS home page at http://www.spss.com. What SPSS statistical programs can be used to perform the statistical tests mentioned in this chapter?

3. The Federal Reserve Bank of St. Louis maintains a database called FRED (Federal Reserve Economic Data). Use a search engine to navigate to the FRED database. Select a variable to be the dependent variable in a multiple regression analysis. What variables might be utilized in a multiple regression to predict this variable?

Case 24.1 The Utah Jazz[7]

THE MANAGEMENT OF THE UTAH JAZZ READ AN ARTICLE dealing with market segmentation in the professional basketball market. Descriptions of the data collection method and the results follow.

Data Collection

Data came from a survey of adult residents of a large western metropolitan area. Respondents were selected in accordance with a quota sample of the area that was based on the age and sex characteristics reported in the most recent census. Six age categories for both males and females were used to gain representation of these characteristics in the market. In addition, interviewers were assigned to various parts of the area to ensure representation of the market with respect to socioeconomic characteristics. A total of 225 respondents age 18 and over provided data for the study.

Interviews were conducted by trained interviewers using a self-completion questionnaire. The presence of the interviewers served to answer any questions that might arise as well as to ensure compliance with the instructions.

Measures for the variables in the three categories of AIO (attitudes, interest, and opinions) were obtained using six-point rating scales. For example, the item for price proneness asked: "When you are buying a product such as food, clothing, and personal care items, how important is it to get the lowest price?" This item was anchored with "Not at all important" and "Extremely important."

The broadly defined category of demographics included standard socioeconomic characteristics as well as media preferences and attendance at professional hockey matches and university basketball games. Demographics were obtained using a variety of forced-choice and free-response measures, the nature of which are indicated in the variable information presented in Case Exhibit 24.1-1. The categorical measures of type of dwelling and preferred type of radio programming were coded as dummy variables for analysis. The criterion measure of patronage came from an open-ended question asking how many NBA games the respondent had attended during the past season.

Data Analysis

The distribution of responses to the attendance item was skewed, as might be expected. Thus, 57.3 percent

of the respondents reported having attended none of the 41 possible games. Those who attended at least one game were recorded in accordance with specification of the light half and the heavy half of the market. This category of patrons was split as nearly as possible at the median, *giving 20.9 percent who attended one or two games and 21.8 percent who attended three or more*. The three patronage categories thus used for analysis were subsequently termed the *none, low,* and *high* segments.

Given the categorical nature of the criterion measure and the continuous nature of the predictor variables, both univariate analysis of variance and discriminant analysis were employed for the survey. Each of the four categories of predictor variables was subjected to a *separate discriminant* analysis to test the multivariate hypothesis of relationship between patronage and the predictor set in question. The univariate ANOVAs were used to provide complementary information about the nature of the segments.

Results

Case Exhibit 24.1-1 gives the results of the analyses conducted on the four sets of predictor variables. Each set produced at least one variable that was significant in univariate analysis. Three of the four discriminant analyses were significant.

The first predictor set involving AIOs, "marketing orientation," provided only a single variable that ANOVA showed to differentiate among the members of the three patronage segments. The discriminant analysis was nonsignificant.

"Interests in leisure pursuits" emerged as more predictive. By univariate ANOVA, four variables were found significant at the .05 level. The discriminant analysis was significant at $p = .004$.

"Opinions about professional sports" provided significant prediction of patronage. Seven of the nine variables reached significance at the .05 level in univariate analysis. The discriminant analysis was significant beyond $p = .001$, and it produced two significant functions. The first significant function provided 79.8 percent of the explained variance, and the second function provided 20.2 percent.

Finally, the set "demographics" was also found to be related to patronage. Counting the four dummy-coded measures of dwelling type and the five similar preferences for radio programming as separate variables, 7 of the 22 demographics reached significance in univariate analysis. The discriminant analysis was significant at $p = .004$.

QUESTION

1. Interpret the managerial significance of the ANOVA and multiple discriminant analysis results.

Case Exhibit 24.1-1   Characteristics of the Market for Professional Basketball

	MEANS					LOADING	
VARIABLES	NONE ($n = 129$)	LOW ($n = 47$)	HIGH ($n = 49$)	F-RATIO	p	I	II
Market Orientation[a]							
Price proneness	3.99	4.04	3.63	1.31	.271		
Quality proneness	4.95	4.74	4.82	0.74	.480		
Product awareness	4.45	4.02	4.00	3.71	.026		
Product involvement	4.34	4.43	4.14	0.66	.517		
Prepurchase planning	4.21	3.85	3.82	2.03	.134		
Brand loyalty	3.95	4.39	3.92	0.96	.384		
Information search	3.83	3.55	3.96	1.06	.347		
Interests in Leisure Pursuits[b]							
Need for change from work routine	4.11	4.34	4.55	1.92	.150	.34	
Need for independence in leisure choice	4.88	4.94	4.96	0.09	.911	.08	
Need for companionship during leisure	4.85	5.13	4.88	1.16	.317	.10	
Preference for passive versus active pursuits	3.64	4.15	4.57	7.28	.001	.70	
Self-image as athletic	3.67	4.38	4.47	5.89	.003	.60	
Childhood attendance at sporting events	3.38	3.89	4.18	5.41	.005	.60	
Pleasure from sporting events	3.14	3.66	4.27	10.62	.000	.84	
Opinions about Professional Sports[c]							
Athletes as a reference group	3.51	3.64	4.18	3.90	.022	.30	−.19
Excitement from enthusiastic crowd	4.27	4.72	4.73	2.70	.069	.24	.20
Excitement from animosity between teams	3.29	3.28	4.27	6.94	.001	.36	−.41
Acceptance of alcoholic beverages at games	2.60	3.64	3.39	6.88	.001	.34	.46
Enjoyment from large crowds	3.91	3.85	4.49	3.22	.042	.23	−.32
Enjoyment when standing at games	3.37	3.44	3.90	2.25	.108	.22	−.17
Excitement of professional basketball	4.09	3.91	4.67	5.34	.005	.27	−.49
Satisfaction from professional basketball	3.17	3.70	4.80	24.98	.000	.78	−.26
Importance of a winning team	4.26	4.69	5.07	6.12	.003	.39	.02
Demographics[d]							
Years in local area (number of years)	24.47	23.51	19.04	2.02	.135	−.24	
Sex (0 = female, 1 = male)	0.40	0.55	0.65	5.45	.006	.39	
Marital status (0 = single, 1 = married)	0.60	0.62	0.45	2.00	.138	−.21	
Household size (number of persons)	3.13	3.27	3.14	0.11	.896	.01	
Rents apartment (0 = no, 1 = yes)	0.18	0.32	0.35	3.70	.026	.30	
Rents a house (0/1)	0.09	0.09	0.08	0.03	.967	−.03	
Owns a house (0/1)	0.60	0.49	0.41	3.08	.048	−.29	

(continued)

Case Exhibit 24.1-1 Characteristics of the Market for Professional Basketball *(Continued)*

| | MEANS | | | | | LOADING | |
VARIABLES	NONE (n = 129)	LOW (n = 47)	HIGH (n = 49)	F-RATIO	p	I	II
Owns a condominium (0/1)	0.05	0.02	0.06	0.50	.607	.01	
Head of household (0/1)	0.52	0.64	0.67	2.19	.115	.24	
Occupational prestige of self (NORC scale)	68.05	69.36	70.63	1.27	.284	.19	
Job leaves evenings free for entertainment (0/1)	0.87	0.85	0.92	0.57	.567	.10	
Prefers easy-listening music radio programming (0/1)	0.39	0.34	0.29	0.83	.438	−.15	
Prefers contemporary popular music radio (0/1)	0.16	0.28	0.27	1.96	.143	.20	
Prefers rock music radio (0/1)	0.14	0.11	0.27	2.76	.066	.23	
Prefers country-western music radio (0/1)	0.15	0.19	0.08	1.22	.299	−.12	
Prefers talk and news radio programming (0/1)	0.09	0.04	0.06	0.52	.597	−.08	
Education (years of schooling)	13.08	13.66	13.56	5.11	.007	.38	
Age (years)	41.51	39.79	33.59	4.21	.016	−.34	
Annual household income (7-point scale)	4.88	5.11	5.16	0.65	.523	.13	
Monthly personal expenditures on entertainment for household (dollars)	85.10	112.45	101.29	1.38	.254	.13	
Attendance at university basketball (games last year)	0.92	1.89	4.14	15.29	.000	.66	
Attendance at professional hockey (matches last year)	0.69	2.28	2.78	5.33	.006	.37	

[a]Canonical discriminant analysis not significant at $p = .189$; therefore, no loadings are given.
[b]Canonical discriminant analysis significant at $p = .004$, first function significant. Centroids for the market segment groups are: none, −.29; low, .19; high, .59.
[c]Canonical discriminant analysis significant at $p = .000$, both functions significant. Centroids for the market segment groups on the first function are: none, −.47; low, .26; high, 1.00. Centroids on the second function are: none, −.10; low, .57; high, −.27.
[d]Canonical discriminant analysis significant at $p = .004$, first function significant. Centroids for the market segment groups are: none, −.41; low, .14; high, .97.

Case 24.2 Coastal Star Sales Corporation (C)

USE THE DATA IN CASE EXHIBIT 17.1-1 OF CASE 17.1 for the following questions.

QUESTIONS

1. Calculate all bivariate regression equations that will predict current sales. Which is the best one?

2. Using multiple regression, find a model that will help explain current sales.

3. Conduct a multiple discriminant analysis to see if you can predict the region in which a salesperson works.

4. Use cluster analysis to see if there are any natural groupings among the salespeople.

ADDITIONAL CASE MATERIAL

The comprehension cases in Part 7 include certain questions that may be used in conjunction with the Edu-Stat databases to discuss issues in this chapter.

Chapter 25

Communicating Research Results:

Research Report, Oral Presentation, and Research Follow-Up[1]

AFTER SPENDING DAYS, WEEKS, OR EVEN MONTHS WORKING ON A project, the researcher is likely to feel that preparation of the report is just an anticlimactic formality. After all, it seems that all the real work has been done; it just has to be put on paper. This attitude can be disastrous, however. The project may have been well designed, the data carefully obtained and analyzed by sophisticated statistical methods, and important conclusions reached, but if the project is not effectively reported, all of the preceding efforts will have been wasted. Often the research report is the only part of the project that others will ever see. Users of the report cannot separate the content of the project from the *form* in which it is presented. If people who need to use the research results have to wade through a disorganized presentation, are detoured by technical jargon they do not understand, or find sloppiness of language or thought, they will probably discount the report and make decisions without it, just as if the project had never been done. Thus, the research report is a crucial means for communicating the whole project—the medium by which the project makes its impact on decisions.

This chapter explains how research reports, oral presentations, and follow-up conversations help communicate research results.

What you will learn in this chapter

To explain how the research report is the crucial means for communicating the whole research project.

To discuss the research report from a communications model perspective.

To define research report.

To outline the research report format and its parts.

To discuss the importance of using graphics in research reporting.

To explain how tables and charts are useful for presenting numerical information and how to interpret their various components.

To identify the various types of research charts.

To discuss how the oral presentation may be the most efficient means of supplementing the written report.

To understand the importance of research follow-up.

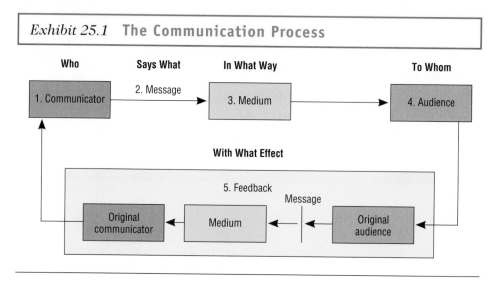

Exhibit 25.1 **The Communication Process**

Communications Model Insights

communication process
The process by which one person or source sends a message to an audience or receiver and then receives feedback about the message.

Some insights from the theory of communications help to clarify the importance of the research report. Exhibit 25.1 illustrates one view of the **communication process.** Several elements influence successful communication.

1. The *communicator*—the source or sender of the message (the writer of the report)
2. The *message*—the set of meanings being sent to or received by the audience (the *findings* of the research project)
3. The *medium*—the way in which the message is delivered to the audience (the oral or written report itself)
4. The *audience*—the receiver or destination of the message (the manager who will make a decision based—we hope—on the report finding)
5. *Feedback*—a reverse flow of communication also involving a message and channel, from the audience to the original communicator, that may be used to modify subsequent communications (the manager's response to the report)

This model of communication oversimplifies the case, though. It implies that the message flows smoothly from the writer to the reader, who in turn promptly provides the writer with feedback. Actually, things are more complex, and Exhibit 25.2 emphasizes one of the difficulties.

TO THE POINT

It is a luxury to be understood.

RALPH WALDO EMERSON

Both the communicators and the audience each have fields of experience. These overlap to some extent; otherwise no communication would be possible. Nevertheless, there is much experience that is not common to both parties. As the communicators send a message, they encode it in terms that make sense to

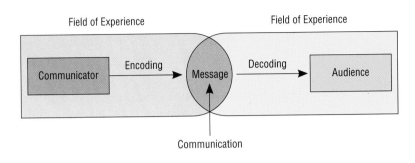

Exhibit 25.2 **The Communicator and the Audience Must Share Some Common Field of Experience**

them based on their fields of experience. As the individuals in the audience receive the message, they decode it based on their own fields of experience. The message is successfully communicated only if the parties share enough common experience for it to be encoded, transmitted, and decoded with roughly the same meaning.

In the research setting, there is a communicator (the researcher) who has spent a great deal of time studying a problem. The researcher has looked at secondary sources, gathered primary data, used statistical techniques to analyze the data, and reached conclusions. When the report on the project is written, all this baggage will affect its contents. The researcher may assume that the reader has a lot of background information on the project and produce pages and pages of unexplained tables, assuming the reader will unearth from them the same patterns the researcher has observed. The report may contain technical terms such as *parameter, F-distribution, hypothesis test, correlations,* or *eigen-value,* assuming that the reader will understand. Another researcher may assume the reader does not have a lot of background information and may go overboard by explaining everything in the report in sixth-grade terms. Although the researcher's intent is to ensure that the reader will not get lost, he or she may insult the reader in the process.

Usually when readers receive a report, they have not thought much about the project. They may not know anything about statistics and may have many other responsibilities. If the report cannot be understood quickly, they may put it on the stack of things to do someday.

For a report to get attention, delivering it to its audience is not sufficient. It needs to be written to hit the common experience of the researcher and the

WHAT WENT WRONG?

Golden Rule for Report Writing

NEVER USE A LONG WORD WHERE A DIMINUTIVE ONE will do.

reader. The effort to hit that zone is the writer's responsibility, not the reader's. Unless a report is really crucial, a busy reader will not spend time and effort struggling through an inadequate and difficult document.

The Report in Context

research report

An oral presentation or written statement of research results, strategic recommendations, and/or other conclusions to a specific audience.

A **research report** is an oral presentation and/or written statement whose purpose is to communicate research results, strategic recommendations, and/or other conclusions to management and/or other specific audiences. This chapter deals primarily with the final *written* report that an extensive research project requires. While one can easily adapt the chapter's suggestions for a shorter, less formal report, one should remember that the final report may not be the only kind prepared. For a small project, a short oral or written report on the results may be all that is needed. In extensive projects, many written documents, interim reports, a long, final, written report, and several oral presentations may be involved. In addition technical materials may be posted on the organizations intranet.

The emphasis on the final report should not be taken to mean that other communications, such as progress reports during the course of the project, are any less important to its eventual success.

Report Format

report format

The makeup or arrangement of parts that are necessary to a good research report.

Although every research report is custom-made for the project it represents, some conventions of **report format** are universal. They represent a consensus about the parts necessary for a good research report and how they should be ordered. This consensus is not a law, however. Every book on report writing suggests its own unique format, and every report writer has to pick and choose the parts and order that will work best for the project at hand. Many companies and universities also have in-house report formats or writing guides for writers to follow. The format presented in this chapter serves as a starting point from which a writer can shape his or her own appropriate format. This format is as follows:

1. Title page (sometimes preceded by a title fly page)
2. Letter of transmittal
3. Letter of authorization
4. Table of contents (and lists of figures and tables)
5. Summary
   (a) Objectives
   (b) Results
   (c) Conclusions
   (d) Recommendations
6. Body
   (a) Introduction
       (1) Background
       (2) Objectives
   (b) Methodology

    (c) Results

    (d) Limitations

    (e) Conclusions and recommendations

7. Appendix

    (a) Data collection forms

    (b) Detailed calculations

    (c) General tables

    (d) Bibliography

    (e) Other support material

This format is illustrated graphically in Exhibit 25.3.

Tailoring the Format to the Project

The format may need adjustment for two reasons: (1) to obtain the proper level of formality and (2) to decrease the complexity of the report. The format given here is for the most formal type of report, such as that for a large project done within an organization or that from a research agency to a client company. This type of report probably would be bound with a fancy cover and could be hundreds of pages long.

For less formal reports, each part would be shorter and some parts would be omitted. Exhibit 25.4 illustrates how the format is adapted to shorter, less formal reports. The change may be compared to variations in clothing according to the formality of the occasion. The most formal report is dressed, so to speak, in a tuxedo or long evening gown. It includes the full assortment of prefatory parts—title fly page, title page, and letters of transmittal and authorization.

The next level of formality would be like an everyday business suit, dropping parts of the prefatory material that are not needed in this situation and reducing the complexity of the report body. In general, as the report goes down through the sport coat, slacks, and blue jeans stages, the prefatory parts are dropped and the complexity and length of the report body are reduced.

Exhibit 25.3 **Report Format**

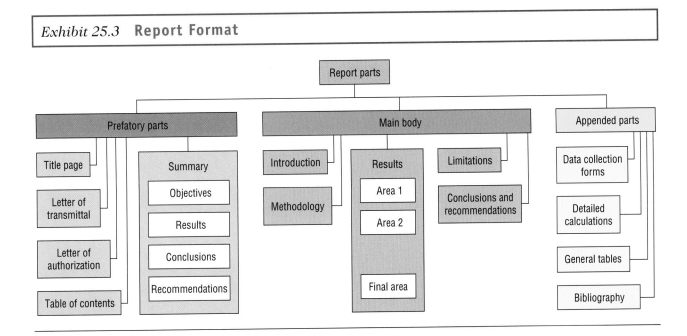

Exhibit 25.4   Adapting Format to Level of Formality

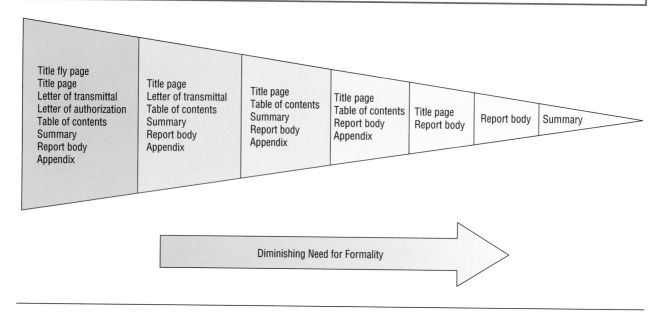

| Title fly page |
| Title page |
| Letter of transmittal |
| Letter of authorization |
| Table of contents |
| Summary |
| Report body |
| Appendix |

Title page
Letter of transmittal
Table of contents
Summary
Report body
Appendix

Title page
Table of contents
Summary
Report body
Appendix

Title page
Table of contents
Report body
Appendix

Title page
Report body

Report body

Summary

Diminishing Need for Formality

How does the researcher decide on the appropriate level of formality? The general rule is to include all the parts needed for effective communication in the particular circumstances—and no more. This factor relates to how far up in management the report is expected to go and on how routine the matter is. A researcher's immediate supervisor does not need a 100-page, "full-dress" report on a routine project. However, the board of directors does not want a one-page, "blue jeans" report on a big project that backs a major expansion program. The full-dress report to top management may later be stripped of some of the prefatory parts (and thus reduced in formality) for wider circulation within the company.

TO THE POINT

The covers of this book are too far apart.

AMBROSE BIERCE

The Parts of the Report

Title Page. The *title page* should state the title of the report, for whom the report was prepared, by whom it was prepared, and the date of release or presentation. The title should give a brief but complete indication of the purpose of the research project. Addresses and titles of the preparer and recipient may also be included. On confidential reports, a list of the people to whom the report should be circulated may be supplied. For the most formal reports, a title fly page should precede the title page; on this page, only the title appears.

Letter of Transmittal. The *letter of transmittal* is included in relatively formal to very formal reports. Its purpose is to release or deliver the report to the recipient. It also serves to establish some rapport between the reader and the writer. This is the one part of the formal report in which a personal or even slightly informal tone should be used. The transmittal should not dive into the report findings except in the broadest terms.

Exhibit 25.5 **Sample Letter of Transmittal**

SOFTPROOF LEATHER PRODUCTS COMPANY, INC.
KENT, OHIO 44240

December 1, 19XX

Mr. Carl M. Wheeler
Vice President for Marketing
Home Office

Subject: Presentation of Report on Study of Small-Volume Customers

Dear Mr. Wheeler:

Here is my report on the study of small-volume customers. This report, the
subject of our conference today, was prepared according to your authorization
memorandum dated April 21, 19XX.

As we suspected would be the case when we started the study, the report
recommends that we take a very careful new look at our present attitude toward
serving customers whose volumes are less than $20,000 per year. Some of the
experienced salesmen whom we contacted in personal interviews gave us some
excellent suggestions about what our new attitude should be.

The returns from our mail survey of small-volume customers were not as high
as we wanted them to be. We do believe, though, that the questionnaires
returned are representative of the customers involved in the study. The
follow-up survey of a sample of customers who did not return the first
questionnaire was most reassuring on this point.

As is perhaps typical of a research department, we discovered during this
study another problem area which might bear investigation. This area is
that of redefining the boundaries of our sales territories. We are now doing
some preliminary thinking about this problem. Should we decide research is
warranted, we later will make our recommendations to you.

We are grateful to you, Mr. Wheeler, for your cooperation in this important
study. Your keeping the president informally up to date on our progress
should pave the way toward his accepting the recommendations made in the
report.

                                    Sincerely,

                                    Harold M. Johnson

                                    Harold M. Johnson
Approved: Associate Analyst
December 1, 19XX   Sales Analysis Section

T. T. Landham
Director and Senior Analyst
Sales Analysis Section

Exhibit 25.5 presents a sample letter of transmittal. Note that the opening releases the report and briefly identifies the factors of authorization. The letter comments generally on findings and matters of interest regarding the research. The closing section expresses the writer's personal interest in the project just completed and in doing additional, related work.

Letter of Authorization. The *letter of authorization* is a letter to the researcher approving the project, detailing who has responsibility for it, and describing the resources available to support it. Because the researcher would not write this personally, writing guidelines will not be discussed here. In many situations simply referring to the authorization in the letter of transmittal is sufficient. If so, the letter of authorization need not be included in the report. In some cases, though, the reader may be unfamiliar with the authorization or may need detailed information about it. In such cases the letter should be included, preferably in an exact reproduction of the original.

Table of Contents. The *table of contents* is essential to any report more than a few pages long. It should list the divisions and subdivisions of the report with page references. The table of contents is based on the final outline of the report, but it should include only the first-level subdivisions. In short reports inclusions of only the main divisions will be sufficient. If the report includes many figures or tables, a list of these should also be included, immediately following the table of contents.

Summary. The *summary* briefly explains why the research project was conducted, what aspects of the problem were considered, what the outcome was, and what should be done. It is a vital part of the report. Studies have indicated that nearly all managers read a report's summary while only a minority read the rest of the report. Thus, the writer's only chance to produce an impact may be in the summary.

The summary should be written only after the rest of the report has been completed. It represents the essence of the report. Its length should be one page (or, at most, two), so the writer must carefully sort out what is important enough to include in it. Several pages of the full report may have to be condensed into one summarizing sentence. Different parts of the report may be condensed more than others; the number of words in the summary need not be in proportion to the length of the section being discussed. The summary should be written to be self-sufficient; in fact, the summary is often detached from the report and circulated by itself.

The summary contains four elements. First, it states the objectives of the report, including the most important background information and the specific purposes of the project. Second, it presents the methodology and the major results. Next come the conclusions. These are opinions based on the results and constitute an interpretation of the results. Finally come recommendations, or suggestions for action, based on the conclusions. In many cases managers prefer not to have recommendations included in the report or summary. Whether or not recommendations are to be included should be clear from the particular context of the report.

introduction section
The part of the body of the report that discusses background information and the specific objectives of the research.

The Body. The *body* constitutes the bulk of the report. It begins with an **introduction** that sets out the background factors that made the project necessary as well as the objectives of the report. It continues with discussions of the methodology, results, and limitations of the study and finishes with conclusions and recommendations based on the results.

The introduction explains why the project was done and what it aimed to discover; it should include the basic authorization and submittal data. The relevant background comes next. Enough background should be included to explain why the project was worth doing, but unessential historical factors should be omitted. The question of how much is enough should be answered by referring to the needs of the audience. A government report that will be widely circulated requires more background than a company's internal report on customer satisfaction. The last part of the introduction explains exactly what the project tried to discover. It discusses the statement of the problem and research questions in a manner similar to the way they were stated in the research proposal. Each purpose presented here should have a corresponding section on results later in the report.

research methodology section
The part of the body of the report that presents the findings of the project. It includes tables, charts, and an organized narrative.

The second division of the body explains the **research methodology.** This part is a challenge to write because it must explain technical procedures in a manner appropriate for the audience. The material in this section may be supplemented with more detailed explanations in the appendix or a glossary of technical terms. This division should address four areas:

Information technology is changing how marketing research knowledge is communicated. Many organizations post research reports on their private intranets so the information is available to executives around the world.

1. *Research design.* Was the study exploratory, descriptive, or causal? Did the data come from primary or secondary sources? Were results collected by survey, observation, or experiment? A copy of the survey questionnaire or observation form should be included in the appendix. Why was this particular design suited to the study?

2. *Sample design.* What was the target population? What sampling frame was used? What sample units were used? How were they selected? How large was the sample? What was the response rate? Detailed computations to support these explanations should be saved for the appendix.

3. *Data collection and fieldwork.* How many and what types of field-workers were used? What training and supervision did they receive? Was the work verified? This section is important for establishing the degree of accuracy of the results.

4. *Analysis.* This section should outline the general statistical methods used in the study but should not overlap with the results.

The **results section** should occupy the bulk of the report with the presentation of those findings of the project that bear on the objectives in some logical order. The results should be organized as a continuous narrative, designed to be convincing but not to oversell the project. Summary tables and charts should be used to aid the discussion. These may serve as points of reference to the data being discussed and free the prose from excessive facts and figures. Comprehensive or detailed charts, however, should be saved for the appendix.

results section
The part of the body of the report that presents the findings of the project. It includes tables, charts, and an organized narrative.

Because no research is perfect, its limitations should be indicated. If problems arose with nonresponse error or sampling procedures, these should be discussed. However, the discussion of limitations should avoid overemphasizing the weaknesses; its aim should be to provide a realistic basis for assessing the results.

The last division of the body is the **conclusions and recommendations section.** As mentioned earlier, conclusions are opinions based on the results, and recommendations are suggestions for action. The conclusions and recommendations should be presented here in more detail than in the summary and include justification as needed.

conclusions and recommendations section
The part of the body of the report that provides opinions based on the results and suggestions for action.

Appendix. The *appendix* presents the "too" material. Any material that is too technical or too detailed to go in the body should appear in the appendix. This includes materials of interest only to some readers or subsidiary materials not directly related to the objectives. Some examples of appendix materials are data collection forms, detailed calculations, discussions of highly technical questions, detailed or comprehensive tables of results, and a bibliography (if appropriate). Since the advent of company Intranets, much appendix material is posted on internal web pages.

Effective Use of Graphic Aids

graphic aids
Pictures or diagrams used to clarify complex points or emphasize a message.

The person who first said, "A picture is worth a thousand words" probably had graphic aids in mind. Used properly, **graphic aids** can clarify complex points or emphasize a message. Used improperly or sloppily, however, they can distract or even mislead. The key to effective use of graphic aids is to make them an integral part of the text. The graphics should always be interpreted in the text. This does not mean the writer should exhaustively explain an obvious chart or table, but it *does* mean that the key points should be pointed out and related to the discussion in progress.

Several types of graphic aids may be useful in research reports; these include tables, charts, maps, and diagrams. The following discussion briefly covers the most common ones, tables and charts. The reader interested in other types should consult more specialized sources.

Tables

Tables are most useful for presenting numerical information, especially when several pieces of information have been gathered about each item discussed. For example, consider how hard it would be to follow all the information in Table 25.1 if it were presented in narrative form. Using figures allows the writers to point out the significant features without getting bogged down in detail. The body of the report should include only relatively short summary tables; comprehensive tables should be reserved for an appendix.

Each table should include the following:

1. *Table number.* This allows for simple reference from the text to the table. If the text includes many tables, a list of tables should be included just after the table of contents.

2. *Title.* The title should indicate the contents of the table and be complete enough to be intelligible without referring to the text. The table number and title are generally placed at the top because the table is read from the top down.

Table 25.1 Parts of a Table

Table number — Title

No. 745. Consumer Price Indexes (CPI-U), by Major Groups: 1939 to 1995

[1982-84 = 100. Represents annual averages of monthly figures. Reflects buying patterns of all urban consumers. See text section 15. See *Historical Statistics, Colonial Times to 1970,* series E 135-173 for similar data]

YEAR	ALL ITEMS	COM- MODITIES	ENERGY	FOOD	SHELTER	APPAREL AND UPKEEP	TRANS- PORTATION	MED- ICAL CARE	FUEL OIL	ELEC- TRICITY	UTILITY (PIPED GAS)	TELE- PHONE SERV- ICES
1939	13.9	14.8	(NA)	11.8	(NA)	21.6	14.3	10.3	5.8	28.9	12.9	36.1
1940	14.0	14.9	(NA)	12.0	(NA)	21.8	14.2	10.4	6.1	28.6	12.8	36.1
1941	14.7	15.9	(NA)	13.1	(NA)	22.8	14.7	10.4	6.3	28.4	12.7	36.3
1942	16.3	18.2	(NA)	15.4	(NA)	26.7	16.0	10.7	7.2	28.3	12.6	38.3
1943	17.3	19.9	(NA)	17.1	(NA)	27.8	15.9	11.2	7.8	28.2	12.5	39.5
1944	17.6	20.1	(NA)	16.9	(NA)	29.8	15.9	11.6	7.9	28.2	12.4	40.7
1945	18.0	20.7	(NA)	17.3	(NA)	31.4	15.9	11.9	7.5	28.0	12.3	41.3
1946	19.5	22.9	(NA)	19.8	(NA)	34.4	16.7	12.5	7.6	26.9	12.1	41.3
1947	22.3	27.6	(NA)	24.1	(NA)	39.9	18.5	13.5	9.0	26.6	12.2	42.0
1948	24.1	29.6	(NA)	26.1	(NA)	42.5	20.6	14.4	11.5	26.8	12.6	44.1
1949	23.8	28.8	(NA)	25.0	(NA)	40.8	22.1	14.8	10.9	27.1	13.1	46.0
1950	24.1	29.0	(NA)	25.4	(NA)	40.3	22.7	15.1	11.0	27.2	13.2	49.5
1951	26.0	31.6	(NA)	28.2	(NA)	43.9	24.1	15.9	11.6	27.4	13.1	50.6
1952	26.5	32.0	(NA)	28.7	(NA)	43.5	25.7	16.7	11.9	27.6	13.4	52.5
1953	26.7	31.9	(NA)	28.3	22.0	43.1	26.5	17.3	12.5	28.0	13.8	54.3
1954	26.9	31.6	(NA)	28.2	22.5	43.1	26.1	17.8	12.6	28.1	14.1	53.4
1955	26.8	31.3	(NA)	27.8	22.7	42.9	25.8	18.2	13.0	28.5	14.6	52.9
1956	27.2	31.6	(NA)	28.0	23.1	43.7	26.2	18.9	13.6	28.6	14.9	53.5
1957	28.1	32.6	21.5	28.9	24.0	44.5	27.7	19.7	14.3	28.7	15.1	54.5
1958	28.9	33.3	21.5	30.2	24.5	44.6	28.6	20.6	13.5	29.1	16.0	56.1
1959	29.1	33.3	21.9	29.7	24.7	45.0	29.8	21.5	13.7	29.5	16.5	57.4
1960	29.6	33.6	22.4	30.0	25.2	45.7	29.8	22.3	13.5	29.9	17.6	58.3
1961	29.9	33.8	22.5	30.4	25.4	46.1	30.1	22.9	14.0	29.9	17.9	58.5
1962	30.2	34.1	22.6	30.6	25.8	46.3	30.8	23.5	14.0	29.9	17.9	58.5
1963	30.6	34.4	22.6	31.1	26.1	46.9	30.9	24.1	14.3	29.9	17.9	58.6
1964	31.0	34.8	22.5	31.5	26.5	47.3	31.4	24.6	14.0	29.8	17.9	58.6
1965	31.5	35.2	22.9	32.2	27.0	47.8	31.9	25.2	14.3	29.7	18.0	57.7
1966	32.4	36.1	23.3	33.8	27.8	49.0	32.3	26.3	14.7	29.7	18.1	56.5
1967	33.4	36.8	23.8	34.1	28.8	51.0	33.3	28.2	15.1	29.9	18.1	57.3
1968	34.8	38.1	24.2	35.3	30.1	53.7	34.3	29.9	15.6	30.2	18.2	57.3
1969	36.7	39.9	24.8	37.1	32.6	56.8	35.7	31.9	15.9	30.8	18.6	58.0
1970	38.8	41.7	25.5	39.2	35.5	59.2	37.5	34.0	16.5	31.8	19.6	58.7
1971	40.5	43.2	26.5	40.4	37.0	61.1	39.5	36.1	17.6	33.9	21.0	61.6
1972	41.8	44.5	27.2	42.1	38.7	62.3	39.9	37.3	17.6	35.6	22.1	65.0
1973	44.4	47.8	29.4	48.2	40.5	64.6	41.2	38.8	20.4	37.4	23.1	66.7
1974	49.3	53.5	38.1	55.1	44.4	69.4	45.8	42.4	32.2	44.1	26.0	69.5
1975	53.8	58.2	42.1	59.8	48.8	72.5	50.1	47.5	34.9	50.0	31.1	71.7
1976	56.9	60.7	45.1	61.6	51.5	75.2	55.1	52.0	37.4	53.1	36.3	74.3
1977	60.6	64.2	49.4	65.5	54.9	78.6	59.0	57.0	42.4	56.6	43.2	75.2
1978	65.2	68.8	52.5	72.0	60.5	81.4	61.7	61.8	44.9	60.9	47.5	76.0
1979	72.6	76.6	65.7	79.9	68.9	84.9	70.5	67.5	63.1	65.6	55.1	75.8
1980	82.4	86.0	86.0	86.8	81.0	90.9	83.1	74.9	87.7	75.8	65.7	77.7
1981	90.9	93.2	97.7	93.6	90.5	95.3	93.2	82.9	107.3	87.2	74.9	84.6
1982	96.5	97.0	99.2	97.4	96.9	97.8	97.0	92.5	105.0	95.8	89.8	93.2
1983	99.6	99.8	99.9	99.4	99.1	100.2	99.3	100.6	96.5	98.9	104.7	99.2
1984	103.9	103.2	100.9	103.2	104.0	102.1	103.7	106.8	98.5	105.3	105.5	107.5
1985	107.6	105.4	101.6	105.6	109.8	105.0	106.4	113.5	94.6	108.9	104.8	111.7
1986	109.6	104.4	88.2	109.0	115.8	105.9	102.3	122.0	74.1	110.4	99.7	117.2
1987	113.6	107.7	88.6	113.5	121.3	110.6	105.4	130.1	75.8	110.0	95.1	116.5
1988	118.3	111.5	89.3	118.2	127.1	115.4	108.7	138.6	75.8	111.5	94.5	116.0
1989	124.0	116.7	94.3	125.1	132.8	118.6	114.1	149.3	80.3	114.7	97.1	117.2
1990	130.7	122.8	102.1	132.4	140.0	124.1	120.5	162.8	98.6	117.4	97.3	117.7
1991	136.2	126.6	102.5	136.3	146.3	128.7	123.8	177.0	92.4	121.8	98.5	119.7
1992	140.3	129.1	103.0	137.9	151.2	131.9	126.5	190.1	88.0	124.2	100.3	120.4
1993	144.5	131.5	104.2	140.9	155.7	133.7	130.4	201.4	87.2	126.7	106.5	121.2
1994	148.2	133.8	104.6	144.3	160.5	133.4	134.3	211.0	85.6	126.7	108.5	123.1
1995	152.4	136.4	105.2	148.4	165.7	132.0	139.1	220.5	84.8	129.6	102.9	124.0

NA Not available

Source: U.S. Bureau of Labor Statistics, *Monthly Labor Review* and *Handbook of Labor Statistics,* periodic.

Table 25.2 **Reporting Format for a Typical Cross-Tabulation from a Survey**

Which subjects did your household argue about in the past 12 months?

	AGE			
	UNDER 35 YEARS	35–49 YEARS	50–64 YEARS	65 YEARS OR MORE
Argued about something	79%	80%	58%	37%
Money	54	45	25	12
Children	33	43	24	6
Household chores	35	35	17	8
Diets/health	22	25	21	16
Job decisions	28	20	8	3
In-laws	24	15	10	4
Sex	20	19	7	4
Where to live	24	9	9	7
Vacations	12	12	10	6
Politics	8	6	7	4
Religion	10	6	4	3
Did not aruge about anything	21	20	42	63

---

3. *Stubhead and bannerhead.* The stubhead contains the captions for the rows of the table, and the bannerhead (or boxhead) contains those for the columns.

4. *Footnotes.* Any explanations or qualifications for particular figures or sections should be given in footnotes.

5. *Source notes.* If a table is based on material from one or more secondary sources rather than on new data generated by the project, the sources should be acknowledged, usually below the table.

Table 25.2 illustrates a typical table from a survey research report; it cross-tabulates demographics with survey responses. Table 25.3 shows how data from a statistical test might be reported in table form.

Table 25.3 **Reporting a Typical Statistical Test**

Will investors be more cautious about buying stock in companies with questionable advertising?

	BUSINESS	ADVERTISING MANAGEMENT
Yes	57%	46%
No	27	35
Not sure	16	19
	$n = 177$	$n = 154$

$\chi^2 = 4.933$ $d.f. = 2$ $p < .08$

Table 25.4	A Stubhead Format Allowing Several Cross-Tabulations to Be Included in a Single Table

Confidence in Church/Organized Religion

Question: I am going to read you a list of institutions in American society. Would you tell me how much confidence you, yourself, have in each one—a great deal, quite a lot, some, or very little?

The Church or Organized Religion

	Great Deal	Quite a Lot	Some	Very Little	None	No Opinion	Number of Interviews
National	42%	24%	21%	11%	1%	1%	1,528
Sex							
Men	36	27	22	13	1	1	755
Women	48	21	20	9	1	1	773
Age							
Total under 30	39	26	24	10	1	*	320
18–24 years	38	28	24	9	1	*	138
25–29 years	40	23	23	13	1	*	182
30–49 years	38	25	23	12	1	1	593
Total 50 & older	50	21	18	10	*	1	608
50–64 years	48	23	18	10	*	1	302
65 and older	52	18	18	10	1	1	306
Region							
East	33	24	28	13	1	1	388
Midwest	44	26	20	9	*	1	398
South	51	24	14	9	1	1	444
West	39	20	25	15	1	*	298
Race							
Whites	42	23	22	11	1	1	1,334
Nonwhites	45	27	18	8	1	1	184
Blacks	47	26	18	7	*	2	151
Hispanics	42	25	21	10	1	1	104

*Less than 1 percent.

Bannerheads and Stubheads for Tables. Suppose an airline asks a question about customers' satisfaction with its baggage-handling service. In addition to a table showing the simple frequency for each category, most research analysts would cross-tabulate answers to the baggage-handling questions with several demographic variables such as gender, income, education, and age. To present multiple cross-tabulations individually in a separate table requires considerable space. Thus, many research reports use a space-saving format with either stubheads for rows or bannerheads for columns to allow the reader to view several cross-tabulations at the same time.

Table 25.4 presents several cross-tabulations in a single table with stubheads.

Charts

Charts translate numerical information into visual form so that relationships may be easily grasped. The accuracy of the numbers is reduced to gain this advantage. Each chart should include the following:

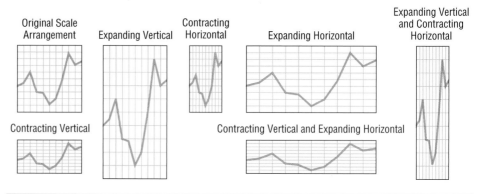

Exhibit 25.6 **Distortion by Alternating Scales**

Changing the Visual Image
Contracting or expanding vertical (amount) scale or horizontal
(time) scale tends to change the visual picture

1. *Figure number.* Charts (and other illustrative material) should be numbered in a separate series from tables. The numbers allow for easy reference from the text. If there are many charts, a list of them should be included after the table of contents.

2. *Title.* The title should describe the contents of the chart and be independent of the text explanation. The number and title are usually placed at the bottom of the chart.

3. *Explanatory legends.* Enough explanation should be put on the chart to spare the reader a need to look at the accompanying text. Such explanations should include labels for axes, scale numbers, and a key to the various quantities being graphed.

Exhibit 25.7 **Distortion from Treating Unequal Time Intervals as Equal**

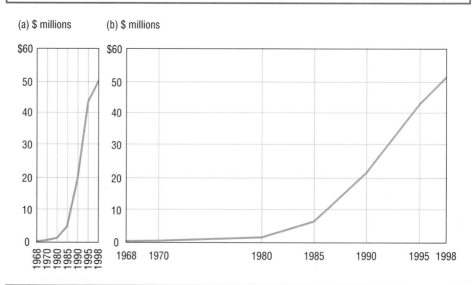

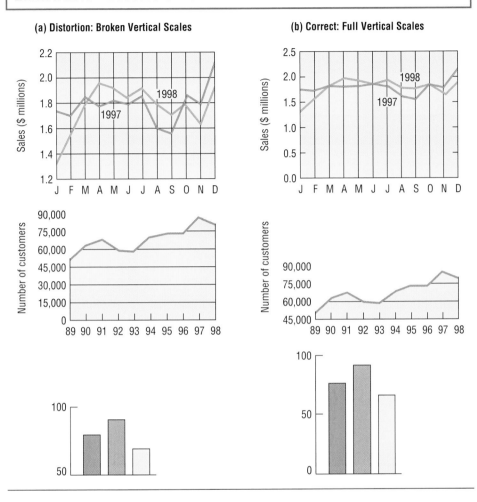

Exhibit 25.8 Distortion of Chart from Broken Vertical Scales

(a) Distortion: Broken Vertical Scales

(b) Correct: Full Vertical Scales

4. *Source and footnotes.* Any secondary sources for the data should be acknowledged. Footnotes may be used to explain items, although they are less common for charts than for tables.

Charts are also subject to distortion, whether unintentional or deliberate. Exhibit 25.6 shows how altering the scale changes the impression of the data. A particularly severe kind of distortion comes from treating unequal intervals as if they were equal; this generally results from a deliberate attempt to distort data. Exhibit 25.7 shows this type of distortion, in which someone has attempted to make the rise on the chart more dramatic by compressing the portion in which the data show little real change.

Another common distortion is to begin the vertical scale at some value larger than zero. Exhibit 25.8 shows how this exaggerates the amount of change in the period covered. This kind of broken scale is often used in published reports of stock price movements. In this case it is assumed that the reader is interested mostly in the changes and is aware of the exaggeration. For most research reports, however, this will not be the case. Graphs should start at zero on the vertical axis.

Pie Charts. One of the most useful kinds of charts is the pie chart. It shows the composition of some total quantity at a particular time. As Exhibit 25.9 shows, each angle, or "slice," is proportioned to its percentage of the whole and should be labeled with its description and percentage. The writer should not try to in-

---

Exhibit 25.9 Series of Pie Charts

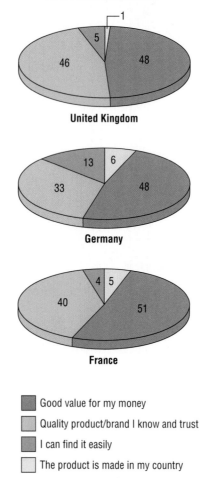

"Which of the following do you think is the single most important consideration when considering the purchase of a product?"

United Kingdom

Germany

France

- Good value for my money
- Quality product/brand I know and trust
- I can find it easily
- The product is made in my country

---

clude too many small slices; about six slices is a typical maximum. Pie charts are commonly used by companies to show how their revenues were used or the composition of their sales.

Line Graphs. Line graphs are useful for showing the relationship of one variable to another. The dependent variable generally is shown on the vertical axis and the independent variable on the horizontal axis. The most common independent variable for such charts is time, but it is by no means the only one. Exhibit 25.10 depicts a *simple line graph*. Other variations are also useful. The *multiple line graph* (Exhibit 25.11) shows the relationship of more than one "dependent" variable to the independent variable. The lines for each dependent variable need to be in contrasting colors or patterns and should be clearly labeled. The writer should not try to squeeze in too many variables; this can quickly lead to confusion rather than clarification. A second variation is the *stratum chart* (Exhibit 25.12), which shows the composition of a total quantity and its changes as the independent variable changes. It requires the same caution as the multiple line graph.

Exhibit 25.10   Simple Line Graph

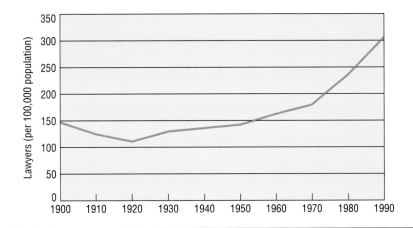

Exhibit 25.11   Multiple Line Graph

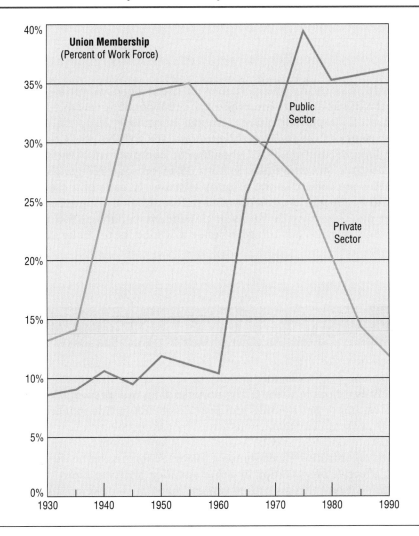

Exhibit 25.12 **Stratum Chart**

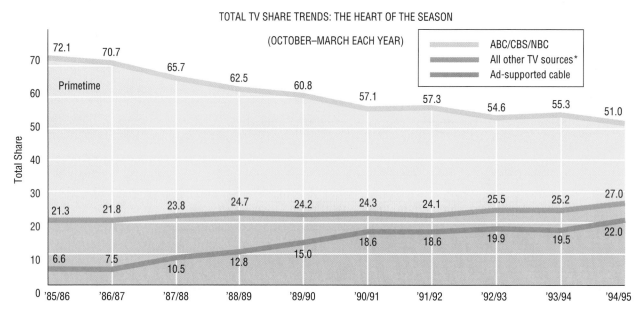

TOTAL TV SHARE TRENDS: THE HEART OF THE SEASON

(OCTOBER–MARCH EACH YEAR)

Legend:
- ABC/CBS/NBC
- All other TV sources*
- Ad-supported cable

Total Share (vertical axis): 0, 10, 20, 30, 40, 50, 60, 70

ABC/CBS/NBC (Primetime): 72.1, 70.7, 65.7, 62.5, 60.8, 57.1, 57.3, 54.6, 55.3, 51.0

All other TV sources*: 21.3, 21.8, 23.8, 24.7, 24.2, 24.3, 24.1, 25.5, 25.2, 27.0

Ad-supported cable: 6.6, 7.5, 10.5, 12.8, 15.0, 18.6, 18.6, 19.9, 19.5, 22.0

Years (horizontal axis): '85/86, '86/87, '87/88, '88/89, '89/90, '90/91, '91/92, '92/93, '93/94, '94/95

*All other TV includes independents, pay cable, Fox affiliates, and PBS. Note: All shares are based on the sum of total U.S. HH delivery (not HUT). Source: Nielsen NCAR 4th-1st quarters. Courtesy of CAB.

Bar Charts Bar charts show changes in the dependent variable (again on the vertical axis) at discrete intervals of the independent variable (on the horizontal axis). A simple bar chart is shown in Exhibit 25.13 on page 735. A common variant is the *subdivided bar chart* (see Exhibit 25.14 on page 736). It is much like the stratum chart, showing the composition of the whole quantity. The *multiple bar chart* (see Exhibit 25.15 on page 737) shows how multiple variables are related to the primary variable. In each of these cases, each bar needs to be clearly identified with a different color or pattern. The writer should not use too many divisions or dependent variables. Too much detail obscures the essential advantage of charts, which is to make relationships easy to grasp.

The Oral Presentation

oral presentation

A verbal summary of the major findings, conclusions, and recommendations given to clients or line managers to provide them with the opportunity to clarify any ambiguous issues by asking questions.

The conclusions and recommendations of most research reports will be presented orally as well as in writing. The purpose of an **oral presentation** is to highlight the most important findings and provide clients or line managers with the opportunity to clarify any ambiguous issues by asking questions.

The oral presentation may be as simple as a short conference with a manager at the client organization's location or a formal report to the board of directors. The key to effective presentation in either situation is preparation.

Communication specialists often suggest that a person preparing an oral presentation should begin at the end.[2] In other words, while preparing a presentation, a researcher should think about what he or she wants the client to know when it has been completed.

Exhibit 25.13 **Simple Bar Chart**

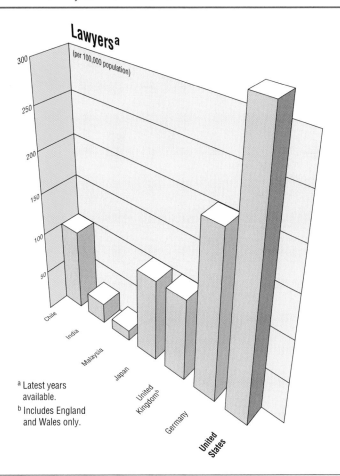

Lawyers[a]
(per 100,000 population)

300
250
200
150
100
50

Chile
India
Malaysia
Japan
United Kingdom[b]
Germany
United States

[a] Latest years available.
[b] Includes England and Wales only.

The researcher should select the three or four most important findings for emphasis and rely on the written report for a full summary. The researcher needs to be ready to defend the results. This is not the same as being defensive; rather, it means being prepared to deal in a confident, competent manner with the questions that will arise. Remember that even the most reliable and valid research project is worthless if the managers who must act on its results are not convinced of its importance.

As with written reports, a key to effective oral presentation is adaptation to the audience. Delivering an hour-long formal speech when a 10-minute discussion is called for (or vice versa) will reflect poorly on both the presenter and the report.

The principles of good speechmaking apply to a research presentation. Lecturing or reading to the audience is sure to impede communication at any level of formality. The presenter should refrain from reading prepared text word for word. By relying on brief notes, familiarity with the subject, and as much rehearsal as the occasion calls for, the presenter will foster better communication. He or she should avoid research jargon and use short, familiar words. The presenter should maintain eye contact with the audience and repeat the main points. Because the audience cannot go back and replay what the speaker has said, the presentation often is organized around a standard format: "Tell them what you are going to tell them, tell them, and tell them what you just told them."

Graphic and other visual aids can be as useful in an oral presentation as in a written one. Presenters can choose from a variety of media. Slides, overhead projector acetates, and on-screen computerized presentations are useful for larger audiences. For smaller audiences, the researcher may put the visual aids on posters

Exhibit 25.14 **Subdivided Bar Chart**

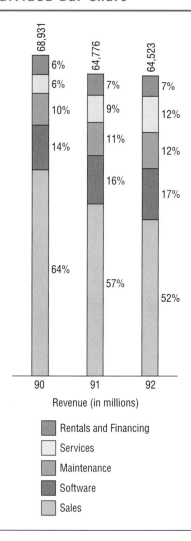

or flip charts. Another possibility is to duplicate copies of the charts for each participant, possibly supplemented by one of the other forms of presentation.

Whatever medium is chosen, each visual aid should be designed to convey a simple, attention-getting message that supports a point on which the audience should focus its thinking. As they do with written presentations, presenters should interpret the graphics for the audience. The best slides are easy to read and interpret. Large typeface, multiple colors, bullets that highlight, and other artistic devices can enhance the readability of charts.

The use of gestures during presentations can also help convey the message and make them more interesting to watch. Here are some tips on how to gesture:[3]

- Open up your arms to embrace your audience. Keep your arms between your waist and shoulders.
- Drop your arms to your sides when not using them.
- Avoid quick and jerky gestures; they make you appear nervous. Hold gestures longer than you would in normal conversation.
- Vary gestures. Switch from hand to hand and at other times use both hands or no hands.
- Don't overuse gestures.

Exhibit 25.15 **Multiple Bar Chart**

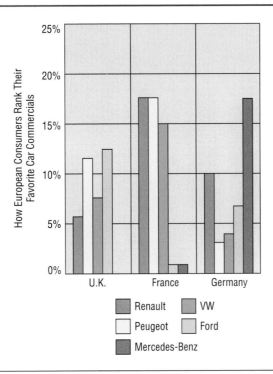

EXPLORING RESEARCH ISSUES

Noah's Law of Overhead Transparencies

DURING MANY ORAL RESEARCH REPORTS, THE PRESENTER uses transparencies that viewers in the back row cannot read. In fact, some presenters use transparencies that viewers in the front row cannot read.

All viewers would be much happier if all presenters were to follow Noah's Law of Overhead Transparencies. Noah's Law says: Never, ever, under any circumstances whatsoever, put more than 40 words on a transparency. A number counts as a word. Noah's Law is called Noah's Law

because when God made it rain for 40 days and 40 nights, He flooded the whole world, and no presenter should attempt that with one overhead.

Note that, in Noah's Law, 40 is the absolute upper limit. Twenty is a good average. Seven is even better. If seven words look lonely, presenters can always MAKE THE LETTERS BIGGER.

Advertising legendary David Ogilvy was a devout follower of Noah's Law. He thought so highly of it that he invented and enforced Ogilvy's Corollary. Ogilvy's Corollary says: Never put anything on a transparency (or a slide or a chart) that you don't intend to read out loud to your audience word for word. He reasoned that when one message comes in on the visual channel while another comes in on the auditory channel, the audience will probably neglect one message or the other.

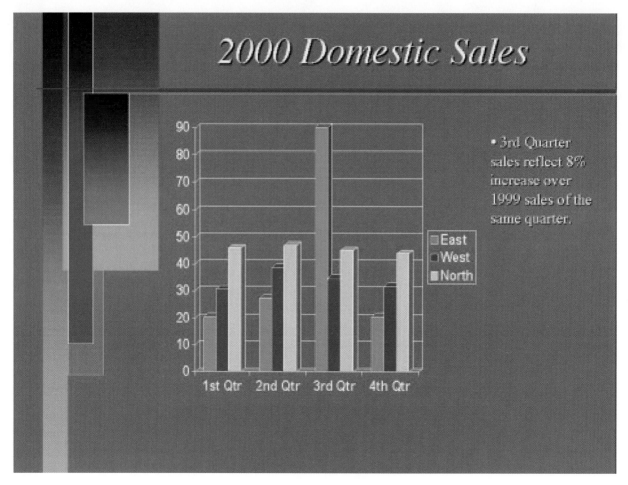

Oral presentations can be enhanced with on-screen computerized graphics. Presentation software, such as Microsoft's PowerPoint, allows the researcher to select background design, color, bullets that highlight, and other graphic effects that make communication of the message more effective. It is a good idea to use simple attractive graphics and avoid overwhelming the audience with flashiness.

The Research Follow-up

research follow-up
Recontacting decision makers and/or clients after they have had a chance to read over the research report to determine whether the researchers need to provide additional information or clarify some issues that may concern management.

Research reports and oral presentations should communicate research findings so that managers can make business decisions. In many cases the manager who receives the research report is unable to interpret the information and draw conclusions relevant to managerial decisions. For this reason, effective researchers do not treat the report as the end of the research process. They conduct a **research follow-up,** in which they recontact decision makers and/or clients after the latter have had a chance to read over the report. The purpose is to determine whether the researchers need to provide additional information or clarify some issues that may concern management. Just as marketing research may help an organization learn about its customers' satisfaction, the research follow-up can help marketing research staffers ensure the satisfaction of their customers, marketing management.

Summary

Report preparation is the final stage of the research project. It is an important stage because the project can guide management decisions only if it is effectively communicated. The theory of communication emphasizes that the writer (communicator) must tailor the report (message) so that it will be understood by the manager (audience), who has a different field of experience. The research report is defined as the presentation of the research findings directed to a specific audience to accomplish a particular purpose.

The consensus on the format for research reports includes certain prefatory parts, the body of the report, and appended parts. The report format should be varied to suit the level of formality of the particular situation.

The prefatory parts of a formal report include a title page, letters of transmittal and authorization, a table of contents, and a summary. The summary is the most often read part of a report and should include a brief statement of the objectives, results, conclusions, and recommendations. The report body includes an introduction that gives the background and objectives, a statement of methodology, and discussion of the results, their limitations, and appropriate conclusions and recommendations. The appendix includes various material that is too specialized to appear in the body of the report.

Effective use of graphic aids enhances the presentation. Tables present large amounts of numerical information in a concise manner. Charts present numerical data in a way that highlights their relationships. Pie charts, line graphs, and bar charts are useful forms of charts, and all have variants for special purposes.

Most research projects will be reported orally as well as in writing, so the researcher needs to prepare an oral presentation. The presentation should defend the results without being defensive. The presentation must be tailored to the situation and the audience. Here, too, graphic aids are useful supplements.

The research follow-up involves recontacting decision makers after the report has been submitted to determine whether the researchers need to provide further information or clarify any issues of concern to management.

Key Terms and Concepts

Communication process	Research methodology section	Graphic aids
Research report	Results section	Oral presentation
Report format	Conclusions and recommendations section	Research follow-up
Introduction section		

Questions for Review and Critical Thinking

1. Why is it important to think of the research report from a communications perspective?

2. As a manager, what degree of formality would you want from your research department?

3. What types of tables might be used to describe some of the various statistical tests discussed in previous chapters?

4. Do you believe that computer graphics will have an impact on the research report writing format?

5. Go to your library and try to find some research reports. How do they meet the standards set forth in this chapter?

6. How does the oral presentation of research differ from the written research report?

7. What rules should be followed when preparing slides or on-screen computerized presentations?

8. What ethical concerns arise when you prepare (or read) a report?

Exploring the Internet

1. Georgia Institute of Technology's Graphics, Visualization, and Usability Center (http://www.gvu.gatech.edu) reports results of its WWW surveys. Click on one of its surveys to see an entire research report.

2. For a summary report, see eTRUST Internet Privacy Study. This report prepared by the Boston Consulting Group for the FCC can be found at http://www.ftc.gov/bcp/privacy2/comments1/etrust/index.htm.

3. Go to American Demographics magazine's home page at http://www.marketingtools.com.
   a. Browse a back issue of *American Demographics*. Find a story that appears to be a summary of research reports.
   b. What research reports are available in its Marketing and Research catalog?

Case 25.1 American Pharmaceutical Industries [4]

AMERICAN PHARMACEUTICAL INDUSTRIES IS A RELATIVELY well-established firm whose major source of revenue is derived from physician-prescribed drugs. Until recently most of its significant marketing research activities were contracted out with agencies that specialized in this type of research. However, a major decision has been made to establish its own marketing research department under the direction of Franklin Link. Link is responsible directly to the vice president for marketing, who holds a Ph.D. in marketing. Link himself has several years of research experience with a major manufacturer of hospital and medical office supplies.

Virtually all the research American Pharmaceutical Industries has conducted in the past, and most of that expected in the future, closely relates to very specific questions. However, at Link's suggestion, senior corporate management has approved a relatively extensive study on physician decision making with regard to the selection of drugs. Part of the data-gathering process involves personal as well as telephone interviews in which the interviewer represents himself or herself as an employee of a fictitious marketing research agency. Since some of the questions involve having physicians make evaluative statements about specific brands or drug companies, it is believed that a response bias might be introduced if American Pharmaceutical Industries were identified. Moreover, the interviewers were instructed to tell physicians that the research agency was conducting the research for its own general purposes and not for a specific client. This procedure was not discussed with George Hempel, vice president for marketing.

Physician cooperation was relatively good, and Link felt the data to be of high quality and considerable practical value. The project was completed at the end of Link's seventh month with American Pharmaceutical Industries, and he was anxious to make an extensive report to senior management. Link felt that they would share his feeling about the merits of the study. Link asked Hempel if a meeting with senior management could be arranged. Hempel asked for a written report first and was provided with an extensive document. To the vice president's dismay, the report contained considerable information that directly and indirectly seriously challenged the wisdom of much of American Pharmaceutical Industries' marketing strategy for introducing new products while supporting the general strategy for well-established products. Hempel directed Link to write up a brief summary of the research results pertaining to well-established products and to make only passing reference to the implications of the research for new product marketing. This report was to serve as a substitute for the meeting Link had requested.

QUESTIONS

1. What ethical questions about data collection and reporting of results face American Pharmaceutical?

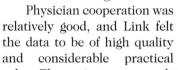

A Final Note on Marketing Research

MARKETING RESEARCH IS NOT A PANACEA OR A SUBSTITUTE FOR judgment; it is only a tool. Yet marketing research, properly conducted and relied on by management, can play an indispensable role in better marketing decision making. It is hoped that the student has gained a greater appreciation of the diverse nature of marketing research from reading this textbook. Marketing research is not a black-and-white area in which there is always a correct technique for solving a given problem. It is a gray area that in many cases requires considerable experience, a bit of skill, and the touch of an artist. It is also hoped that the reader will be interested in further exploration of more complex aspects of marketing research now that he or she has mastered the basics.

Case 1

Sunbelt Energy Corporation

Sunbelt Energy Corporation is a diversified petroleum company engaged in producing and marketing gasoline, motor oil, petrochemicals, and a number of other energy-related activities such as coal mining, uranium extraction, and atomic power generation. Sunbelt markets its petroleum products through its own retail outlets and independent suppliers in a 25-state area within the continental United States. Sunbelt's company-owned service stations feature the latest in station design and automation. Sunbelt's retail marketing strategy emphasizes modern station designs, and the firm continually works to improve the appearance of both its company-owned and independent retail outlets. A research study to investigate consumers' reaction to a new method of payment was conducted in a single town in which the company owns all stations. The company investigated the use of automated payment machines (using the same technology as automated teller machines used by banks) and gasoline credit cards for payment of gasoline services.

The specific objectives of the research were to determine the following:

1. The overall percentage of customers who use the automatic payment machines
2. What machine features people who use the automatic payment machines like
3. What improvements to the machines could be made to assist their current users
4. What improvements to the automatic payment machines could be made to induce nonusers to use the machines
5. The percentage of people who not only purchase gasoline but also purchase something else at the station
6. The percentage of people who pay using cash, a Sunbelt credit card, or a bank credit card

The research was conducted in a southwestern city where the company owns all retail outlets and each station has automatic payment machines. Respondents were interviewed as they filled their cars with gasoline. The personal interview lasted only a few minutes because most people wish to purchase gasoline and then leave as quickly as possible. This time frame restricted the number of questions that could be asked. All questions were short and to the point.

Four stations in the town had automatic teller machines. Fifty interviews were conducted at each station for a total of 200 personal interviews. The stations were

- Station Number 1—Limestone
- Station Number 2—Boulevard
- Station Number 3—Performance Plaza
- Station Number 4—Madison Convenient Store

Sampling

Every automobile that entered the service station in the self-service lanes was considered a member of the sampling frame. After a car arrived, the interviewer waited until the customer got out of his or her car and made a selection at the pump. As the gasoline was being pumped into the tank, interviewers introduced themselves and conducted the interviews. Only one individual refused to grant an interview. The questionnaire is shown in Case Exhibit 1.1.

Case Exhibit 1.1   Personal Interview Questionnaire

"Hello, my name is _____. In cooperation with Sunbelt, I am conducting a survey on how Sunbelt can better serve you. I'd like to ask you a few short questions."

Question 1

To start off, did you know that this station has an automated teller machine?

Yes __   No __

Question 2

In addition to a gasoline purchase, are you planning to purchase anything else, such as a soft drink, motor oil, or cigarettes?

Yes __   No __

Question 3

For today's purchase, are you planning to pay using the automated teller machine, or are you planning to go inside and pay the station attendant?

Go inside and pay attendant __   Use the automated teller machine __
(Skip to Question 9)   (Proceed to Questions 4, 5, 6, 7, and 8)

Question 4

Have you ever used the automated teller machine to pay for your gasoline purchase?

Yes __   No __
(Proceed to next question)   (Go to question 8)

Question 5

What features of the automated teller machine do you like?

_____
_____
_____
_____
_____

Question 6

What features of the automated teller machine do you dislike?

_____
_____
_____
_____

Question 7

From your viewpoint are there any improvements that could be made to make it easier to use the automated teller machine?

_____
_____
_____
_____

(continued)

Case Exhibit 1.1 Personal Interview Questionnaire (Continued)

Question 8

Up to today, what features of the automated teller machine have caused you not to use it?

_____
_____
_____
_____
_____

(Skip to the observation section)

Question 9

Will you be paying for your purchase in cash, or will you be using a credit card?

Pay with cash __   Pay with a credit card __
(Skip to observation part)   (Proceed to Question 10)

Question 10

Will you use a Sunbelt Credit Card, or will you use a Visa or MasterCard for payment?

   Sunbelt card __   Use other type __
   (Proceed to Question 11)   (Skip to observation section)

Question 11

Have you ever used the automated teller machine for your purchase?

   Yes __   No __
   (Proceed to Questions 12, 13, and 14)   (Proceed to Question 15)

Question 12

What features of the automated teller machine do you like?

_____
_____
_____
_____
_____

Question 13

What features of the automated letter machine do you dislike?

_____
_____
_____
_____

Question 14

From your viewpoint are there any improvements that could be made to make it easier to use the automated teller machine?

_____
_____
_____
_____
_____

(Skip to observation section)

(continued)

Case Exhibit 1.1 **Personal Interview Questionnaire** *(Continued)*

Question 15
What features of the automated teller machine have caused you not to use it?

_____

_____

_____

_____

(Skip to the observation section)

Observation Section

On behalf of Sunbelt, I thank you for your time and comments.

Is the driver of the vehicle male or female?	Male __	Female __
Is the driver under or over 40?	Under __	Over __
Are there any passengers in the vehicle?	Yes __	No __
Does the vehicle have Washington County tags?	Yes __	No __

Additional Information

Several of the questions will require the use of a computerized database. Your instructor will provide information about the floppy disk if this material is part of the case assignment. See Case Exhibit 1.2 for a listing of variable names for the Sunbelt database.

QUESTIONS

1. Evaluate the research objectives.

2. Evaluate the research design in light of the stated research objectives.

3. Using the computerized database, obtain simple frequencies for the answers to each question (the answers to the open-ended questions are not included in the database).

4. Perform the appropriate cross-tabulations.

5. Perform the appropriate univariate and bivariate statistical tests after you develop hypotheses for these particular tests.

Case Exhibit 1.2 **Variable Names in the Sunbelt Data Set**

VARIABLE NAME	LABEL
ATM	Auto Teller Knowledge
ELSE	Purchase Anything Else
USE	Use ATM to Pay
USEGAS	Use ATM to Pay for Gas
CASH	Pay with Cash or Credit Card
SUNBELT	Use Sunbelt Credit Card
EVER	Ever Use ATM for Purchase
SEX	Male or Female
AGE	Under or Over 40
PASS	Passengers: Yes or No
TAGS	Washington County Tags

Case 2

Employees Federal Credit Union

Employees Federal Credit Union is the credit union for a Fortune 500 firm. Any employee of the organization is eligible for membership in the employees' credit union.

Over the past few years, the Employees Federal Credit Union (EFCU) has accumulated a large amount of surplus cash funds, which have been invested in certificates of deposit. It has also experienced a lower loan/share ratio than other credit unions of similar size. Because of these factors, the credit union's average earnings on its investments have slowly declined and its profit margins are being squeezed. As a result, the EFCU Board of Directors decided that a research project should be conducted to determine why its members are not borrowing money from the credit union. More specifically, the research project was mandated to answer the question of why the members are borrowing money from other alternative sources instead of the credit union.

In addition to the above, the EFCU Board of Directors expressed its desire to determine what the membership's attitudes were toward the overall management and operations of the credit union. It was determined that the following questions should be addressed, as well:

- How informed is the membership about the services provided by the credit union?
- Do any differences in opinion toward borrowing funds and the services provided by the credit union exist between headquarters-based and nonheadquarters-based members?

Research Objectives

To respond to the questions raised by the board, the following objectives were developed. The research design was formulated to address each of the objectives stated below:

- To determine the reasons why people join the credit union
- To determine the reasons why members use other financial institutions when they need to borrow funds
- To measure member attitudes and beliefs about the proficiencies of the credit union employees
- To determine whether there are any perceived differences between headquarters-based and nonheadquarters-based members

- To determine member awareness of the services offered by the credit union
- To measure member attitudes and beliefs about how effectively the credit union is operated

Research Design and Data Collection Method

The research data were collected by a mail questionnaire survey. This technique was determined to be the best method for collecting the research data for the following reasons:

- The wide geographical dispersion of the credit union membership
- The minimization of the cost of conducting the research
- The sensitivity of several of the questions asked in the questionnaire
- The flexibility of being able to wait for the survey results before taking any action

A copy of the questionnaire used to gather the research data is provided in Case Exhibit 2.1. Most of the questions were designed as structured questions because of the variation in the educational backgrounds, job functions, and interests of the members surveyed. However, the respondents were given the flexibility to answer several key questions in an unstructured format. The Likert scale was principally used where attitude measurements were requested.

Case Exhibit 2.1 **EFCU Member Opinion Survey**

---

1. Are you currently a member of the Employees Federal Credit Union (EFCU)?
   Yes ( )   No ( )
   If no, please have the member of your household who is a member of the EFCU complete the questionnaire. If no one in your household is a member, please return the questionnaire in the enclosed prepaid envelope.
2. Why did you join the credit union? (Check as many answers as are applicable.)
   —Convenience
   —Higher interest rates on my savings than other financial institutions pay
   —More personal than other facilities
   —Wanted a readily available source for borrowing money
   —Advertisements prompted me to join
   —Other—please explain: _____

Statements 3 through 6 ask for your opinion of the credit union employees. Check the response that best describes your rating of the credit union employees in each category. Please check only one response for each statement.

3. The credit union employees are courteous.

Strongly disagree	Disagree	Uncertain	Agree	Strongly agree
( )	( )	( )	( )	( )

4. The credit union employees are helpful.

Strongly disagree	Disagree	Uncertain	Agree	Strongly agree
( )	( )	( )	( )	( )

(continued)

Case Exhibit 2.1   EFCU Member Opinion Survey (Continued)

---

5. The credit union employees are professional.

Strongly disagree	Disagree	Uncertain	Agree	Strongly agree
( )	( )	( )	( )	( )

6. The credit union employees are always available.

Strongly disagree	Disagree	Uncertain	Agree	Strongly agree
( )	( )	( )	( )	( )

7. What is your opinion about the rates the credit union is paying on its share (members/savings) accounts?
   A. Very high —   B. High —   C. Average —
   D. Low —   E. Very low —   F. No opinion —

8. What is your opinion about the rates the credit union is charging its members to borrow funds?
   A. Very high —   B. High —   C. Average —
   D. Low —   E. Very low —   F. No opinion —

9. How often do you receive a financial statement of your account activity?

Too often	Very often	About right	Not often enough	Never
( )	( )	( )	( )	( )

10. How would you rate the accuracy of your statements?

Excellent	Good	Fair	Poor
( )	( )	( )	( )

11. Are they easy to understand?
    Yes ( ) No ( )

12. Do you feel that the credit union maintains your account information in a confidential manner?
    Yes ( )   No ( )

The next set of questions are important in determining how effective the credit union has been in communicating its different services to the members. Please answer each question honestly—remember, there are no right or wrong answers.

Circle the response that best describes your awareness of the services offered by the credit union.

   Circle 1—If you were aware of the service and have used it.
   Circle 2—If you were aware of the service but have not used it.
   Circle 3—If you did not know this service was offered by the credit union.

	Aware and Have Used	Aware But Have Not Used	Unaware of Service
13. Regular share accounts	1	2	3
14. Special subaccounts	1	2	3
15. Christmas club accounts	1	2	3
16. Individual retirement accounts	1	2	3
17. MasterCard credit cards	1	2	3
18. Signature loans	1	2	3
19. New-car loans	1	1	3
20. Late model car loans	1	2	3
21. Older model car loans	1	2	3
22. Household goods/appliance loans	1	2	3
23. Recreational loans	1	2	3
24. Share collateralized loans	1	2	3
25. IRA loans	1	2	3
26. Line of credit loans	1	2	3

(continued)

Case Exhibit 2.1   EFCU Member Opinion Survey *(Continued)*

---

27. Do you currently have a loan with the credit union?
    Yes ( )   No ( )
28. During the past year, have you borrowed money from a bank or other lending source other than the credit union?
    Yes ( )   No ( )
    If no, go to question 30.
29. Why did you go to a source other than the credit union?
    —My loan application at the credit union was not approved.
    —The credit union did not offer this type of credit.
    —I found better loan rates elsewhere.
    —I have an established credit line elsewhere.
    —I prefer to use a local financial institution.
    —Other: _____

For statements 30 through 34, check the response that best describes your feelings about the statements. Check only one response for each statement given.

30. The credit union's loan rates are lower than those offered by other institutions.

Strongly disagree	Disagree	Uncertain	Agree	Strongly agree
( )	( )	( )	( )	( )

31. The credit union personnel will keep my personal financial information confidential.

Strongly disagree	Disagree	Uncertain	Agree	Strongly agree
( )	( )	( )	( )	( )

32. The credit union is prompt in processing loan applications.

Strongly disagree	Disagree	Uncertain	Agree	Strongly agree
( )	( )	( )	( )	( )

33. The current financial services provided by the credit union meet the needs of its members.

Strongly disagree	Disagree	Uncertain	Agree	Strongly agree
( )	( )	( )	( )	( )

34. The loan applications used by the credit union are simple and easy to complete.

Strongly disagree	Disagree	Uncertain	Agree	Strongly agree
( )	( )	( )	( )	( )

35. Which of the services provided by the credit union do you like best?
36. Which of the services provided by the credit union do you like least?
37. Overall, how do you feel the credit union is being managed and operated?
    A. Excellent—   B. Good—   C. Average—
    D. Poor—   E. Very poor—   F. No opinion—
38. Do you live in the headquarters area?
    Yes ( )   No ( )
    If yes, go to question 40.
39. Do you feel the credit union meets your needs as well as those members who live in the headquarters area?
    Yes ( )   No ( )
    If no, please explain:_____

(continued)

Case Exhibit 2.1 **EFCU Member Opinion Survey** *(Continued)*

40. If you were managing the credit union, what changes would you make and what additional services, if any, would you provide?

_____

_____

_____

_____

_____

I sincerely appreciate the time and effort you made in completing this questionnaire. Thank you for your help.

Sampling Procedures

The population of the EFCU is well-defined; consequently, a simple random sample of the membership was selected. A sample size of 300 was calculated using the estimated population standard deviation based on the responses from 15 members to question 37 of the questionnaire. Question 37 was used because it capsulized the essence of the research project.

The random numbers used in making the selection of the sampling units were generated with the help of a personal computer. The sampling frame used was the January 31, 1992, trial balance listing of the EFCU membership. According to the sampling frame, EFCU had 3,531 members on that date. As a result, the 300 random numbers were generated within the range of 1 to 3,531. The random numbers were matched to a corresponding number in the sampling frame, and those individuals were selected to receive copies of the survey questionnaire.

Fieldwork

Most of the fieldwork for the research project, including all of the editing and coding of the survey data, was performed by the Supervisory Committee Chairperson. The following is a list of the (much-appreciated) assistance received during the field procedures:

- Bob Perkins obtained a copy of the most currently available listing of the membership of the EFCU.
- The payroll department prepared mailing labels for all the members in the sample who were having withholding for the credit union made out of their payroll checks.
- The credit union clerks obtained the addresses and prepared mailing labels for all the remaining individuals selected in the sample.
- Administrative assistants helped in copying and collating the survey questionnaires and preparing them for mailing.
- Ron Walker mailed all of the survey questionnaires.

The survey data from the structured questions were coded based on classifications established by the researcher. The codes were input into a series of databases using an IBM personal computer and a statistical software package.

Of the 125 returned questionnaires, two were not included in the survey results. One of the questionnaires was returned without the first two pages attached, and the other questionnaire appeared to be deliberately falsified. Not only were all the responses of the falsified questionnaire at the extremes, but a number of noted contradictions existed, as well.

Additional Information

Several of the questions will require the use of a computerized database. Each variable name is represented by its question number. Q1 is the variable name for question 1, "Are you a member of the Employees Federal Credit Union?" Q2 is the variable name for question 2, etc. Your instructor will provide information about the floppy disk containing the EFCU's data set if this material is part of the case assignment.

QUESTIONS

1. Evaluate the research objectives.
2. Evaluate the research design in light of the stated research objectives.
3. Using the computerized database, obtain simple frequencies for the answers to each question (the answers to the open-ended questions are not included in the database).
4. Perform the appropriate cross-tabulations.
5. Perform the appropriate univariate and bivariate statistical tests after you develop hypotheses for these particular tests.

Case 3

University Van Pool

Oklahoma State University is a major university. Its main campus in Stillwater is located an equal distance (approximately 75 miles) from Oklahoma City and Tulsa, the state's two largest metropolitan areas. Almost 20,000 students are enrolled in classes on the Stillwater campus.

It was suggested that because many OSU students commuted from Oklahoma City (approximately 500) or Tulsa (approximately 700), a van pooling system could be a viable operation. The basic concept was to have central locations in both Tulsa and Oklahoma City where students could board vans (or buses) and ride to the university campus. Students would be dropped off at the same location on the return trip. A commuter student would be the driver of the van, which would substantially reduce the cost of operating the service. Case Exhibit 3.1 provides additional information about the cost associated with operating this service.

Case Exhibit 3.1   Cost Associated with Van Pooling

An example of a cost analysis on a per-trip basis for vans is presented below. This analysis assumes that a van can carry 15 people but on the average will be carrying 10 people ($\frac{2}{3}$ load factor) plus the driver. We also assume that we don't have to pay for the driver, i.e., he or she is a student and will drive instead of paying for the ride.

Using the per-trip cost of the van, we figure that we would need to charge each person $4.50 per trip to break even.

Cost of van	$12,000.00		
Less trade in	$ 4,000.00		
Net cost of van	$ 8,000.00		
Useful life of van		80,000 miles	
Net cost of van per mile			$ 0.10
Gasoline cost	$1.25/gal		
Fuel efficiency of van		12.5 mpg	
Net cost of gasoline per mile			$ 0.10
Insurance and maintenance per mile			$ 0.10
Total cost of van per mile			$ 0.30
Number of miles per van per trip		150 miles	
Cost per van per trip			$45.00
Load factor estimate		10 people/van	
Cost per person per trip			$ 4.50

The Survey Research Project

A telephone survey was conducted to determine how many OSU students were regular commuters and to estimate the demand for the commuting service. The questionnaire used in the study appears in Case Exhibit 3.2. The student directory served as a sampling frame. Initially pages from the directory were randomly selected. For each page selected as a primary sampling unit, an interviewer was instructed to call every name that listed Tulsa or Oklahoma City as the student's address. The first question on the questionnaire determined whether the student was actually commuting. This resulted in a sample size of 224 commuting students.

The data from the survey were edited and coded to be analyzed using the SPSS computer program. The variables from the data set entitled "Commuter" are listed in Case Exhibit 3.3. A missing value is represented by a period. (The data are also available in Microsoft Excel.)

Case Exhibit 3.2 Marketing Research Questionnaire: Commuting Service to Stillwater, Oklahoma

---

Hello, I'm _____your name_____. We are conducting a survey to find out if it would be feasible for OSU to establish a van or bus commuting service for students commuting to school in Stillwater.

1. Do you commute to OSU to attend classes? ____Yes ____No

    If yes, continue with the interview.

    If no, terminate and try again.

2. How many times a week do you travel to Stillwater to attend classes?

    ____times per week.

3. How do you get to Stillwater—drive your own car, pool with other students, or some other method?

    __1_ Drives own car
    __2_ Rides in pool
    __3_ Other

    If student rides in a pool

4. What percentage of the time are you the driver in your car pool? ____%

5. What mileage does your car get on the road? ____mpg

6. What do you think is your total cost per month to commute to OSU? $____

Two alternative methods available for providing a commuting service to OSU are providing a van or a bus. A bus would be similar to riding commercially in that it would depart early in the morning to be at school by 8:00 a.m. and return after 12:00 noon. A second bus would depart so as to arrive by 12:30 p.m. and would return after 5:00 p.m. A licensed driver would be hired to drive the bus by the university. A van would have similar departure times, but arrangements would be made so that the commuters would do the driving on a rotating basis.

I am going to make a number of statements about these possible methods of commuting and would like you to indicate your agreement or disagreement with each of the statements. When I give you the statement, I would like you to either strongly agree, agree, slightly agree, indicate no feeling, slightly disagree, disagree, or strongly disagree.

Go over this with the respondent to be sure he or she understands what you are trying to do.

7. The inconvenience of commuting by bus or van outweighs the advantages.

    __7_ SA __6_ A __5_ SA __4_ N __3_ SD __2_ D __1_ SD

8. I could use the time riding over to Stillwater to study.

    __7_ SA __6_ A __5_ SA __4_ N __3_ SD __2_ D __1_ SD

(continued)

Case Exhibit 3.2   **Marketing Research Questionnaire: Commuting Service to Stillwater, Oklahoma** *(Continued)*

---

9. I would rather be able to come and go as I please.

    _7_ SA   _6_ A   _5_ SA   _4_ N   _3_ SD   _2_ D   _1_ SD

10. Having to wait for the van or bus coming home would take too much time.

    _7_ SA   _6_ A   _5_ SA   _4_ N   _3_ SD   _2_ D   _1_ SD

11. I don't like riding buses because they are so uncomfortable.

    _7_ SA   _6_ A   _5_ SA   _4_ N   _3_ SD   _2_ D   _1_ SD

12. Riding a van would be better than riding a bus.

    _7_ SA   _6_ A   _5_ SA   _4_ N   _3_ SD   _2_ D   _1_ SD

13. If I were in a van pool, I would be willing to do some of the driving.

    _7_ SA   _6_ A   _5_ SA   _4_ N   _3_ SD   _2_ D   _1_ SD

14. Having to drive to the pickup point is too much of a bother.

    _7_ SA   _6_ A   _5_ SA   _4_ N   _3_ SD   _2_ D   _1_ SD

15. Driving myself is getting too expensive.

    _7_ SA   _6_ A   _5_ SA   _4_ N   _3_ SD   _2_ D   _1_ SD

16. I would worry too much about the dependability of a van or bus.

    _7_ SA   _6_ A   _5_ SA   _4_ N   _3_ SD   _2_ D   _1_ SD

17. I could save money by taking a van or bus.

    _7_ SA   _6_ A   _5_ SA   _4_ N   _3_ SD   _2_ D   _1_ SD

18. If a bus were available, I would use it.

    _7_ SA   _6_ A   _5_ SA   _4_ N   _3_ SD   _2_ D   _1_ SD

19. If a van were available, I would use it.

    _7_ SA   _6_ A   _5_ SA   _4_ N   _3_ SD   _2_ D   _1_ SD

20. I don't like riding a van because they are so uncomfortable.

    _7_ SA   _6_ A   _5_ SA   _4_ N   _3_ SD   _2_ D   _1_ SD

21. I would be concerned about the driving by others in a van.

    _7_ SA   _6_ A   _5_ SA   _4_ N   _3_ SD   _2_ D   _1_ SD

22. Taking a van or bus is too much of a hassle.

    _7_ SA   _6_ A   _5_ SA   _4_ N   _3_ SD   _2_ D   _1_ SD

Finally, I have some questions about you as a student. This survey is strictly confidential, and your name will never be used in any results.

23. What is your class status?   _1_ Fresh   _2_ Soph   _3_ Jr   _4_ Sr   _5_ Grad
24. Do you consider yourself full or part time?   _1_ Full   _2_ Part
25. Are you also employed?   _1_ Yes   _2_ No
    If yes,
26. Full or part time?   _1_ Full   _2_ Part
27. Your age?
28. Sex   _1_ Male   _2_ Female (You should be able to figure that out.)
29. Are you married?   _1_ Yes   _2_ No
30. How are you financing your education?
    _1_ Own funds   _2_ Parents   _3_ Scholarship   _4_ GI Bill   _5_ Other
31. What percentage savings would you need to realize before you would be interested in riding a bus?   ___ %   ___ Wouldn't ride a bus.
32. What percentage savings would you need to realize before you would be interested in riding a van?   ___ %   ___ Wouldn't ride a van.

Thank you very much for your time in answering this survey.

Case Exhibit 3.3 **Commuter Data Set Variables**

ID	Identification number	HASSLE	Van or bus too much hassle
CITY	1 = Tulsa, 2 = OKC	STATUS	1 = freshman, 5 = grad student
—	Question 1 not coded	FULLTIME	1 = full time, 2 = part time
FREQ	Frequency per week (Question 2)	EMPLOYED	1 = yes, 2 = no
METHOD	1 = own car, 2 = pool, 3 = other	EMPFULL	1 = full, 2 = part-time employed
PDRIVE	% drive own car	AGE	Age
MILEAGE	Car mileage, mpg	SEX	1 = male, 2 = female
ESTCOST	Estimated cost per month	MARRIED	1 = yes, 2 = no
INCONV	Inconvenience	FINANCE	1 = own, 2 = parents, 3 = school, 4 = GI bill, 5 = other
STUDY	I could study	PSAVBUS	% savings bus
COMEGO	Come and go	RBUS	1 = wouldn't ride bus at all
TIME	Too much time	PSAVVAN	% savings van
BUSCOMF	Bus is uncomfortable	RVAN	1 = wouldn't ride van at all
VANBUS	Van better than bus	ASAVBUS*	Amount bus savings needed
DRIVEV	Would drive van	ASAVVAN	Amount van savings needed
PICKUP	Pickup is a bother	GASCOST	Computed gas cost
EXPENSE	Driving is expensive	DIFF	Estimate—computed gas cost
DEPEND	Worry about dependability	COSTT	Cost per trip
SAVE	I could save money	BUSSAVT	Bus savings needed per trip
USEBUS	I would use a bus	VANSAVT	Van savings needed per trip
USEVAN	I would use a van	MAXBUS	Maximum price for bus
VANCOMF	Van is uncomfortable	MAXVAN	Maximum price for van
CONCERN	Concern about drivers	VRIDER	Van rider; 1 = yes, 2 = no

*Variables through RVAN are directly from the raw data taken from the questionnaire. The rest of the variables were calculated from the original variables as follows:

ASAVBUS	= PSAVBUS × ESTCOST
ASAVVAN	= ASAVVAN × ESTCOST
GASCOST	= FREQ × PDRIVE/100 × 52/12 × 150 × 1.25/MILEAGE
DIFF	= ESTCOST − GASCOST
COSTT	= ESTCOST/(FREQ × 52/12)
BUSSAVT	= ASAVBUS/(FREQ × 52/12)
VANSAVT	= ASAVVAN/(FREQ × 52/12)
MAXBUS	= COSTT − BUSSAVT
MAXVAN	= COSTT − VANSAVT

IF MAXVAN>4.5 THEN VRIDER = 1, ELSE IF MAXVAN ≠ 1 THEN VRIDER = 2

GASCOST is an estimate of what the marginal cost of the trip to and from Stillwater to Tulsa or Oklahoma City would be for gasoline alone. It assumes a gasoline price of $1.25 per gallon and a 150-mile round trip (75 miles to the pick-up location in the heart of each city).

QUESTIONS

1. Evaluate the research design.

2. What variables in the available data set will be most important to solve the problem? Identify which of these are dependent variables and which are independent variables.

3. Using the computerized data base called Commuter, demonstrate that you can perform descriptive analyses such as calculation of frequency distributions and calculation of means.

4. Using cross-tabulation analysis determine which market segment is most likely to use the van pool.

5. Is the van pool economically feasible in Tulsa? In Oklahoma City?

Case 4

Wichita Clinic

The Wichita Clinic is a multispecialty health care clinic jointly owned and operated by 102 physicians. The physicians maintain their practices in the facility, which is located near a large hospital. Like many service organizations that have recently adopted the marketing concept, the Wichita Clinic was concerned with delivering a quality service. As part of its effort to provide patient satisfaction, the Wichita Clinic decided to use a consultant to measure the quality of health care provided by the clinic. He developed a measure that was an adaptation of the service quality (SERVQUAL) scale.

Measurement

The adapted scale to measure service quality by medical care providers utilizes 7-point Likert scales to gather consumer attitudes regarding perceived service quality. The adaptation of the SERVQUAL scale closely followed the 22-item format of the original scale except the scale language was adapted to the medical services setting.

Expectations/Perceptions Scales

The theory behind perceived service quality is based on the discrepancy approach, which states that *service quality* equals *perceptions* minus *expectations*. In this research a difference between preencounter expectations (before the patient visited the clinic for medical care) and postencounter perceptions of the service outcome (after treatment) was measured using matched-pair statements. Expectation statements sought to establish initial levels of general attitudes regarding medical care services. Outcome perceptions were measured in a second questionnaire administered after each respondent's specific service encounter.

For example, expectation statement 1 (E1) had respondents indicate agreement or disagreement that providers of medical care services should possess "physical facilities that are pleasant and visually appealing."

The corresponding outcomes perception statement (P14) had respondents indicate agreement or disagreement with the statement "The appearance of the physical facilities of Wichita Clinic is in keeping with the medical services provided."

Service quality (Q1) for "facilities should be appealing" was computed by subtracting E1 from P14. (See Case Exhibit 4.1 for a listing of the quality variables.)

Case Exhibit 4.1   Quality Rating Variables

VARIABLE NAME	LABEL	EQUATION[a]
Q1	Appealing facilities	Q1 = P14 – E1
Q2	Up-to-date equipment	Q2 = P18 – E14
Q3	Employees well-dressed	Q3 = P10 – E19
Q4	In keeping with service	Q4 = P1 – E9
Q5	Promise and do it	Q5 = P22 – E21
Q6	Provider is sympathetic	Q6 = P19 – E2
Q7	Dependable	Q7 = P15 – E13
Q8	At time promised	Q8 = P6 – E18
Q9	Records kept	Q9 = P2 – E8
Q10	Tell when services provided	Q10 = P20 – E17
Q11	Expect prompt service	Q11 = P11 – E3
Q12	Employees helpful	Q12 = P7 – E12
Q13	Employees too busy	Q13 = P3 – E7
Q14	Can't trust	Q14 = P16 – E16
Q15	Feel safe	Q15 = P12 – E4
Q16	Polite	Q16 = P8 – E11
Q17	Get organizational support	Q17 = P4 – E6
Q18	Individual attention	Q18 = P21 – E22
Q19	Employees—personal attention	Q19 = P17 – E5
Q20	Employees know needs	Q20 = P13 – E20
Q21	Best interests at heart	Q21 = P9 – E15
Q22	Operating hours	Q22 = P5 – E10
SQ	Summated service quality score	SQ = Q1 + Q2 + ... + Q22

[a]Service quality variables transformed by subtracting expectation score from perception score.

Overall Quality Scale

The postencounter questionnaire asked respondents to give an overall rating (excellent, good, fair, poor) of service quality regarding their recent medical care service encounter. This variable, P23, coded "excellent" as 4 and "poor" as 1.

Behavioral Intent on Items

The postencounter questionnaire also asked the consumers of the medical services about a broad range of behavioral intentions. Respondents were asked to express the likelihood of several future behaviors using a 7-point Likert-type scale ranging from "definitely would" to "definitely would not." For example, respondents indicated whether they would complain to the local medical society. The other behavioral actions measured were the variables for intentions to recommend, to complain, to seek similar care elsewhere, and so on; these are listed in Case Exhibit 4.2.

Physicians' Suggestions as Reported by Patients

The postencounter questionnaire asked each respondent what the physician had recommended. Four variables resulted from this self-report data: routine follow-up, another appointment for the same problem, suggested appointment with specialists, and scheduled hospital stay.

Case Exhibit 4.2 Overall Quality and Behavioral Intention Variables

VARIABLE NAME	LABEL
OVERALLQ	Overall quality
RETURN	Intention to return to see same doctor
RTOFAM	Intention to recommend to family and friends
CTOFAM	Intention to complain to family and friends
CMNTCCIN	Intention to compliment management
CPLAINL	Intention to complain to local medical society
CPLAINC	Intention to complain to clinic management
SEEKELSE	Intention to seek similar care elsewhere
USENONE	Intention not to use any provider
DISCUSS	Actually discussed visit with _____

Case Exhibit 4.3 Demographic Variables

VARIABLE NAME	LABEL
AGE	Age
INSURED	Insurance coverage
EDUC	Education level
MARITAL	Marital status
EMPLOYED	Employed outside home
EMPSTAT	Full-time/part-time employment
OCCUP	Occupation
UNEMP	Unemployed
SPEMP	Spouse employed outside the home
FAMILY	Number in family
UNDER 18	Number of children under 18
SEX	Sex (gender)
INCOME	Annual household income
HEALTH	Health status

Demographics

Several demographic variables were included in the preencounter questionnaire. Data on age, sex, income level, marital status, employment status and occupation, size of household, insurance coverage, education level, and health status were reported. Case Exhibit 4.3 lists the variables that were investigated.

Methodology

Sample units (patients) were drawn randomly from the pool of regular daytime appointment lists for 11 primary-care (internal medicine) physicians on the staff of the Wichita Clinic. Appointments targeted were scheduled between June 12 and July 28.

A total of 967 preencounter questionnaires were mailed to the sample. The accompanying cover letter from the clinic's medical director asked the patient to complete the questionnaire, seal it in an envelope provided, and return the completed questionnaire to the clinic at the time of a scheduled appointment. Preencounter questionnaires were not return mailed due to the need for matching with postencounter questionnaires. Patients received preencounter questionnaires from 3 to 10 days prior to their scheduled appointments. For those patients who completed and returned the preencounter questionnaire, a post-encounter questionnaire and a postage-paid return envelope were supplied after the appointment was completed. A unique code number was assigned to each preencounter questionnaire as it was returned, and that same number was assigned to the postencounter questionnaire given to the patient to facilitate matching. The necessity of code numbers was explained to patients to avoid feelings of lost confidentiality.

Of the 967 questionnaires mailed to the sample, a total of 244 preencounter questionnaires were returned. Of these, 34 were unmatchable due to miscues in the return process for the preencounter questionnaire, 10 were unusable due to incomplete responses or lack of identifying code labels on either the pre- or postencounter survey, and 41 were unusable due to nonreturn of a postencounter questionnaire. This left a total of 159 usable paired survey responses for a net return rate of 16.4 percent. A portion of the nonresponse rate, amounting to 14.0 percent, can be attributed to canceled appointments during the study period.

Additional Information

Several of the questions will require the use of a computerized database. Your instructor will provide information about the floppy disk that contains the Wichita clinic data set if the material is part of the case assignment.

QUESTIONS

1. Evaluate the research design in light of the stated research objectives.
2. Does the new measurement scale appear to be valid and reliable?
3. Using the computerized database, obtain simple frequencies for the answers to each question.
4. Perform the appropriate cross-tabulations.
5. Perform the appropriate univariate and bivariate statistical tests after you develop hypotheses for these particular tests.

Case 5

Values and the Automobile Market

During the 1990s, the luxury car segment became one of the most competitive in the automobile market. Many American consumers who have purchased luxury cars prefer imports from Germany and Japan.

A marketing vice president with General Motors once commented, "Import committed buyers have been frustrating to us." This type of thinking lead industry analysts to argue that to successfully compete in the luxury car segment, U.S. carmakers need to develop a better understanding of the consumers so they can better segment the market and consequently better position their products via more effective advertising. Insight into the foreign–domestic luxury car choice may result from examining owners' personal values in addition to their evaluations of car attributes; because luxury cars, like many other conspicuously consumed luxury products, may be mainly purchased for value expressive reasons.

Industry analysts believe it would be important to assess the viability of using personal values as a basis for explaining ownership of American, German, and Japanese luxury cars. Further they believed they should also assess whether knowledge of owners' personal values provides any additional information in explaining ownership of American, German, and Japanese luxury cars beyond that obtained from their evaluations of the car attributes.

Personal values are likely to provide us insights into reasons for ownership of luxury cars for at least two reasons. First, Americans have always had a very personal relationship with their cars and have used them as symbols of their self concept. For instance, people who value a *sense of accomplishment* are quite likely to desire a luxury car that they feel is an appropriate symbol of their achievement, whereas people who value *fun, enjoyment, and excitement* are likely to desire a luxury car that they perceive as fun and exciting to drive. An advertiser trying to persuade the former segment to purchase a luxury car should position it as a status symbol that will help its owners demonstrate their accomplishments to others. Similarly, an advertiser trying to persuade the latter segment to purchase a luxury car should position it as a fun and exciting car to drive. In other words, effective advertising shows consumers how purchasing a given product will help them achieve their valued state because brands tied to values will be experienced more favorably than brands that deliver more mundane benefits.

Second, when a market is overcrowded with competing brands offering very similar options—as is the case with the luxury car market—consumers are quite likely to choose between brands on the basis of value-expressive considerations.

Method

Data were collected via a mail survey sent to 498 consumers chosen at random from a list obtained from a syndicated research company located in an affluent county in a southern state. The list contained names of those people who had purchased either a luxury American car (Cadillac or Lincoln Mercury), a luxury German car (Mercedes or BMW), or a luxury Japanese car (Infiniti or Lexus) within the last year. A cover letter explained that this was part of an academic research project. People were asked to return the questionnaires anonymously to a university address (a postage-paid envelope was provided with each survey). Beyond an appeal to help the researchers, respondents were not offered any other incentive to complete the surveys. Of the 498 questionnaires originally sent, 17 were returned by the post office as undeliverable. One-hundred fifty-five completed surveys were received, for a response rate of 32.2 percent.

The Survey Instrument

The survey included questions on (1) various issues that people consider when purchasing new cars, (2) importance of car attributes, (3) importance of different values, and (4) demographics (sex, age, education, and family income). Questions relating to the issues that people consider when purchasing new cars were developed through initial interviews with consumers and were measured with a 7-point Likert scale with end anchors as "strongly agree" and "strongly disagree." (See Case Exhibit 5.1.) A list of 12 car attributes was developed from the initial interviews with consumers and by consulting *Consumer Reports*. (See Case Exhibit 5.2.) The importance of each attribute was measured with a 7-point numerical scale with end points labeled as "very important" and "very unimportant."

Case Exhibit 5.1 **Issues That Consumers Consider When Buying Luxury Automobiles**

Having a luxury car is a major part of my fun and excitement.[a] (Issue 1)

Owning a luxury car is a part of "being good to myself." (Issue 2)

When I was able to buy my first luxury car, I felt a sense of accomplishment. (Issue 3)

I enjoy giving my friends advice about luxury cars. (Issue 4)

Getting a good deal when I buy a luxury car makes me feel better about myself. (Issue 5)

I seek novelty and I am willing to try new innovations in cars. (Issue 6)

I tend to buy the same brand of the car several times in a row. (Issue 7)

I tend to buy from the same dealer several times in a row. (Issue 8)

I usually use sources of information such as *Consumer Reports* in deciding on a car. (Issue 9)

I usually visit three or more dealerships before I buy a car. (Issue 10)

I would read a brochure or watch a video about defensive driving. (Issue 11)

When buying a new luxury car, my family's opinion is very important to me. (Issue 12)

My family usually accompanies me when I am shopping for a new luxury car. (Issue 13)

I usually rely upon ads and salespersons for information on cars. (Issue 14)

I usually rely upon friends and acquaintances for information on cars. (Issue 15)

When shopping for a car, it is important that the car dealer make me feel at ease. (Issue 16)

Most of my friends drive luxury import cars. (Issue 17)

Most of my friends drive luxury domestic cars. (Issue 18)

I think celebrity endorsers in ads influence people's choices of luxury cars. (Issue 19)

I would not buy a luxury car if I felt that my debt level is higher than usual. (Issue 20)

[a]Note: Subjects responses were measured with 1 as "strongly agree" and 7 as "strongly disagree."

Case Exhibit 5.2 Car Attributes

ATTRIBUTE	CODE	ATTRIBUTE	CODE
Comfort	Comfort	Low maintenance cost	Lomc
Safety	Safety	Reliability	Rely
Power	Power	Warranty	Warrant
Speed	Speed	Nonpolluting	Nonpol
Styling	Styling	High gas mileage	Gasmle
Durability	Durabil	Speed of repairs	Repairs

Case Exhibit 5.3 List of Values

ATTRIBUTE	CODE	ATTRIBUTE	CODE
Fun-Enjoyment-Excitement	Fun	Sense of accomplishment	Accomp
Sense of belonging	Belong	Warm relationship	Warm
Being well respected	Respect	Security	Security
Self-fulfillment	Selfful	Self-respect	Selfres

For measuring the importance of values, the List of Values (LOV) scale in Case Exhibit 5.3 was used. Respondents were asked to rate each of the eight values (we combined fun-enjoyment and excitement into one value) on a 7-point numerical scale with end points labeled as "very important" and "very unimportant."

The Sample

Of the 155 respondents in our sample, 58 (37.4 percent) owned an American luxury car, 38 (24.5 percent) owned a European luxury car, and 59 (38.1 percent) owned a Japanese luxury car. The majority of our sample consisted of older (85 percent were 35 years of age or above), more educated (64 percent were college graduates), and economically well-off (87.2 percent earned $65,000 or more) consumers.

The Code Book

Case Exhibit 5.4 lists the SPSS variable names and identifies codes for these variables. (Note this data set is also available in Microsoft Excel.)

Additional Information

Several of the questions will require the use of a computerized database. Your instructor will provide information about the floppy disk that contains the VALUES data set if the material is part of the case assignment.

Case Exhibit 5.4   List of Variables and Computer Codes

ID—Identification number

AGE—Age (categories are 2 = 35 years and under, 3 = 36–45 yrs, 4 = 46–55 yrs, 5 = 56–65 yrs, 6 = 65+ yrs)

SEX—Sex (1 = male, 0 = female)

EDUC—Education (1 = less than high school, 2 = high school grad, 3 = Some college, 4 = College grad, 5 = College degree)

ISSUES—Income (1 = less than $35,000, 2 = $35–50,000, 3 = $50–65,000, 4 = $65,000+)

CAR—Type of luxury car (American car, European car, Japanese car)

Issue—The sequence of issues listed in Case Exhibit 5.1. (Strongly agree = 1; strongly disagree = 7)

ATTRIBUTES—The sequence of car attributes listed in Case Exhibit 5.2. (Very important to you = 1; very unimportant to you = 7)

VALUES—The sequence of values listed in Case Exhibit 5.3. (Very important = 1; very unimportant = 7)

QUESTIONS

1. Is the sampling method adequate? Is the attitude measuring scale sound? Explain.

2. Using the computerized database with a statistical software package, calculate the means of the three automotive groups for the values variables. Are any of the value differences between American, Japanese, and European car owners significantly different?

3. Are there any significant differences on importance of attributes?

4. Write a short statement to interpret the results of this research.

ADVANCED QUESTIONS

5. Are any of the value scale items highly correlated?

6. Should multivariate analysis be used to understand the data?

Case 6

LastDance
Health Care Systems

Senior citizens have different health care needs than the rest of the population. Today there are more seniors living in the United States than ever before. As baby boomers grow older, it is anticipated that the baby boomer generation will have higher standards of quality and higher customer service level expectations. LastDance is a managed care provider in the North Central Region of the country. LastDance wants to be prepared for any changes in expectations so they can increase their customer service levels and retain their image as a top quality managed care provider. They conducted a survey of consumer service level expectations of seniors age 65 and over and current LastDance customers under the age of 65. The major survey objectives were:

- To identify health care delivery and service expectations of consumers aged 55 and older

- Compare the expectations of consumers aged 55–64 with those of consumers aged 65 and older

Methodology

One thousand questionnaires were mailed to each group, under 65 and over 65. The mailing list for the 65 and over group was purchased from a commercial mailing list provider; the mailing list for the 55–64 group was from LastDance's internal decision support system. Each envelope contained a cover letter, a questionnaire, and a return envelope. No monetary incentive was included. The questionnaire consisted of 35 questions, with four classification questions and thirty-one questions regarding consumer expectation levels. See Case Exhibit 6.1 for the questionnaire and the associated codes. A list of variables appears in Case Exhibit 6.2.

QUESTIONS

1. Evaluate the survey's methodology. Are the study's objective clear? Is the research design sound?

2. Use the data disk to profile the respondents to the survey.

3. Identify three questions from the survey and prepare three hypotheses for research investigation.

4. Use the data disk to prepare a descriptive research report.

Case Exhibit 6.1 **Last Dance Health Care Systems**

Health Care Services Improvement

Thank you very much for participating in our research study. Please read each question thoroughly and answer to the best of your knowledge. Simply mark an "X" in the box next to your response.

A. Appointments *The first few questions are about your appointments with your Primary Care Physician.*

1. How long is reasonable to wait for an appointment to see your primary care doctor for a minor illness (such as a cold or the flu)?

☐ Same day (1) ☐ 1–3 days (2) ☐ 4–7 days (3)
☐ 8-14 days (4) ☐ 15–30 days (5) ☐ 31–60 days (6) ☐ more than 60 days (7)

B. Physician Specialist *A specialist is a doctor who focuses on a certain field of medicine (e.g. a heart specialist).*

2. How long is reasonable for you to wait for a referral from your primary care doctor to see a specialist for non-emergency care?

☐ Same day (1) ☐ 1–3 days (2) ☐ 4–7 days (3)
☐ 8-14 days (4) ☐ 15–30 days (5) ☐ 31–60 days (6) ☐ more than 60 days (7)

C. Doctor's Office and Waiting Room

3. How much time do you consider acceptable to drive to your primary care doctor's office from your home?

☐ Less than 10 minutes (1) ☐ 10 to 15 minutes (2) ☐ 16 to 30 minutes (3)
☐ 31 to 45 minutes (4) ☐ 46 minutes to 1 hour (5) ☐ more than 1 hour (6)

4. How long would you expect to wait from the time you arrive at a physician's office until you are taken to the exam room?

☐ Less than 10 minutes (1) ☐ 10 to 15 minutes (2) ☐ 16 to 30 minutes (3)
☐ 31 to 45 minutes (4) ☐ 46 minutes to 1 hour (5) ☐ more than 1 hour (6)

5. I believe a comfortable waiting room is important during a visit to the doctor's office.

☐ Strongly agree (1) ☐ Agree (2) ☐ Uncertain (3)
☐ Disagree (4) ☐ Strongly disagree (5) ☐ Don't know (6)

D. Exam Room

6. How long would you expect to be in the exam room until the doctor sees you?

☐ Less than 10 minutes (1) ☐ 10 to 15 minutes (2) ☐ 16 to 30 minutes (3)
☐ 31 to 45 minutes (4) ☐ 46 minutes to 1 hour (5) ☐ more than 1 hour (6)

E. Doctors

The following questions are designed to measure your expectations of your doctor. Please check one box for each question..

7. I expect to be able to select my primary care doctor from a large number of choices.

☐ Strongly agree (1) ☐ Agree (2) ☐ Uncertain (3)
☐ Disagree (4) ☐ Strongly disagree (5) ☐ Don't know (6)

(continued)

Case Exhibit 6.1 Survey Instrument (*Continued*)

---

8. I expect to see a doctor rather than a physician's assistant during my visit.

☐ Strongly agree (1) ☐ Agree (2) ☐ Uncertain (3)
☐ Disagree (4) ☐ Strongly disagree (5) ☐ Don't know (6)

9. I expect to see the same doctor every visit.

☐ Strongly agree (1) ☐ Agree (2) ☐ Uncertain (3)
☐ Disagree (4) ☐ Strongly disagree (5) ☐ Don't know (6)

10. I expect to know my doctor's background (education, training, etc.) before my first visit.

☐ Strongly agree (1) ☐ Agree (2) ☐ Uncertain (3)
☐ Disagree (4) ☐ Strongly disagree (5) ☐ Don't know (6)

11. I expect my doctor to be board certified in his/her specialty.

☐ Strongly agree (1) ☐ Agree (2) ☐ Uncertain (3)
☐ Disagree (4) ☐ Strongly disagree (5) ☐ Don't know (6)

12. It is important that my doctor listen carefully to me.

☐ Strongly agree (1) ☐ Agree (2) ☐ Uncertain (3)
☐ Disagree (4) ☐ Strongly disagree (5) ☐ Don't know (6)

13. It is important that my doctor answer all my questions in terms that I can understand.

☐ Strongly agree (1) ☐ Agree (2) ☐ Uncertain (3)
☐ Disagree (4) ☐ Strongly disagree (5) ☐ Don't know (6)

14. I expect my doctor to call me at home after my office appointment to follow up on treatment.

☐ Strongly agree (1) ☐ Agree (2) ☐ Uncertain (3)
☐ Disagree (4) ☐ Strongly disagree (5) ☐ Don't know (6)

15. If my doctor left the health plan that I currently belong, to, I would try to follow him/her.

☐ Strongly agree (1) ☐ Agree (2) ☐ Uncertain (3)
☐ Disagree (4) ☐ Strongly disagree (5) ☐ Don't know (6)

F. Doctor's Office

16. I expect a polite receptionist in the doctor's office.

☐ Strongly agree (1) ☐ Agree (2) ☐ Uncertain (3)
☐ Disagree (4) ☐ Strongly disagree (5) ☐ Don't know (6)

17. I expect the phones in my doctor's office to be answered by a person rather than an automated voice system.

☐ Strongly agree (1) ☐ Agree (2) ☐ Uncertain (3)
☐ Disagree (4) ☐ Strongly disagree(5) ☐ Don't know (6)

18. I expect the phones in my doctor's office to be answered within three rings.

☐ Strongly agree (1) ☐ Agree (2) ☐ Uncertain (3)
☐ Disagree (4) ☐ Strongly disagree (5) ☐ Don't know (6)

19. I expect a medically knowledgeable receptionist in the doctor's office.

☐ Strongly agree (1) ☐ Agree (2) ☐ Uncertain (3)
☐ Disagree (4) ☐ Strongly disagree (5) ☐ Don't know (6)

G. Managed Care

20. Which best describes your type of health plan (check one).

☐ A. **Traditional Insurance:** You receive care from physicians in their private offices. You may seek care from any physician. You must submit claim forms and the insurance company or Medicare pays the doctor. You may be responsible for a percentage of the doctor's bill.

☐ B. **HMO:** You can only go to a clinic or healthcare center for the physician care you receive. You may have to pay a copay ($5–$10), but you do not have to submit claim forms for payment. X-ray, laboratory and pharmacy services are provided in the clinic. You may be referred to other physicians if needed.

(continued)

Case Exhibit 6.1   Survey Instrument (*Continued*)

☐ C. **PPO:** You receive care from physicians in their private offices. You may seek care from any physicians but the plan has an approved list of physicians who provide you care at less expense. You must generally go elsewhere for X-ray, laboratory and pharmacy services.

☐ D. **IPA:** You receive care only from physicians on the plan's approved list in their private practice offices. You may seek care from any hospital or doctor not on the list, but you are fully responsible to pay for your care. You must generally go elsewhere for X-ray, laboratory and pharmacy services.

☐ E. **OTHER:** please specify _____

_____

21. If you checked plan type A in question 20 above, go to question 27, otherwise please continue with question 22.

    ☐ Strongly agree (1)   ☐ Agree (2)   ☐ Uncertain (3)
    ☐ Disagree (4)   ☐ Strongly disagree (5)   ☐ Don't know (6)

22. I understand how to use my managed care health plan to receive care.

    ☐ Strongly agree (1)   ☐ Agree (2)   ☐ Uncertain (3)
    ☐ Disagree (4)   ☐ Strongly disagree (5)   ☐ Don't know (6)

23. The quality of care provided by managed care is at least as good as that provided in other health insurance arrangements.

    ☐ Strongly agree (1)   ☐ Agree (2)   ☐ Uncertain (3)
    ☐ Disagree (4)   ☐ Strongly disagree (5)   ☐ Don't know (6)

24. I believe that all managed care organizations are similar in terms of the benefits that they provide.

    ☐ Strongly agree (1)   ☐ Agree (2)   ☐ Uncertain (3)
    ☐ Disagree (4)   ☐ Strongly disagree (5)   ☐ Don't know (6)

25. I believe that all managed care organizations are similar in terms of the quality of doctors that they provide.

    ☐ Strongly agree (1)   ☐ Agree (2)   ☐ Uncertain (3)
    ☐ Disagree (4)   ☐ Strongly disagree (5)   ☐ Don't know (6)

26. I believe that all managed care organizations provide the same level of customer services to members.

    ☐ Strongly agree (1)   ☐ Agree (2)   ☐ Uncertain (3)
    ☐ Disagree (4)   ☐ Strongly disagree (5)   ☐ Don't know (6)

27. I am satisfied with my current health care plan.

    ☐ Strongly agree (1)   ☐ Agree (2)   ☐ Uncertain (3)
    ☐ Disagree (4)   ☐ Strongly disagree (5)   ☐ Don't know (6)

28. In a managed care plan, I would expect to have free membership to a health club.

    ☐ Strongly agree (1)   ☐ Agree (2)   ☐ Uncertain (3)
    ☐ Disagree (4)   ☐ Strongly disagree (5)   ☐ Don't know (6)

29. In a managed care plan, I would expect to have free transportation to my doctor's office.

    ☐ Strongly agree (1)   ☐ Agree (2)   ☐ Uncertain (3)
    ☐ Disagree (4)   ☐ Strongly disagree (5)   ☐ Don't know (6)

30. In a managed care plan, I would expect my primary care doctor's office to be within 15 minutes driving time of my home.

    ☐ Strongly agree (1)   ☐ Agree (2)   ☐ Uncertain (3)
    ☐ Disagree (4)   ☐ Strongly disagree (5)   ☐ Don't know (6)

31. In a managed care plan, I would expect to be offered health awareness classes provided by my managed care organization.

    ☐ Strongly agree (1)   ☐ Agree (2)   ☐ Uncertain (3)
    ☐ Disagree (4)   ☐ Strongly disagree (5)   ☐ Don't know (6)

(continued)

Case Exhibit 6.1 Survey Instrument (*Continued*)

32. I expect a managed care plan to help me live a healthier lifestyle.

☐ Strongly agree (1)   ☐ Agree (2)   ☐ Uncertain (3)
☐ Disagree (4)   ☐ Strongly disagree (5)   ☐ Don't know (6)

I. Demographics

The last few questions are for classification purposes only.

33. What is your age?

☐ under 55 (1)   ☐ 55–59 (2)   ☐ 60–64 (3)   ☐ 65-69 (4)
☐ 70–74 (5)   ☐ 75–79 (6)   ☐ 80-84 (7)   ☐ 85 or older (8)

34. What is your gender?

☐ Male (1)   ☐ Female (2)

35. Which of the following best describes your ethnic background?

☐ Hispanic (1)   ☐ Native American (5)
☐ Black or African-American (2)   ☐ Other (6)
☐ Asian (3)   ☐ Refused (7)
☐ White or Caucasian (4)

Thank you for taking the time to complete this survey.

Case Exhibit 6.2 Variable Names

ID
Q1–Q32 Questions in the order they appear on the questionnaire in Exhibit 1
Age
Gender
Race

Thorndike Sports Equipment

Introduction

Thorndike Sports Equipment dramatically portrays marketing and business research in a real-world setting. This innovative educational drama consists of five video units especially created for this textbook. Each unit focuses on a particular aspect of a racquetball racquet manufacturer's need for and utilization of marketing research and data analysis.

Each project unit allows students to put themselves into a problem-solving situation and then experience what personal encounters could occur in an actual company. Although the units focus on distinctive projects, they are interrelated. The drama is actually a serial with marketing research needs evolving as the situation progresses throughout each segment.

Company Background

The Thorndike Sports Equipment company was founded 34 years ago. The company began as a sporting goods wholesaler, but Luke Thorndike, founder and current president, moved the company into manufacturing when large-sized tennis racquets were new to the market. A neighbor, who was an engineer and Luke's tennis partner, had suggested an innovative new product feature for oversize racquets. Luke bought the idea and success-fully introduced the company's first tennis racquet. Since then the company's engineering know-how has provided Thorndike with competitive advantages for many of its products. For example, its engineering staff designed a new golf ball that will go 10 percent farther than conventional balls. Thorndike is in an industry in which technical developments strongly affect success.

Today the company manufactures and markets many sporting goods products. Its product mix includes composite bicycle wheels, aerodynamic golf balls, and high technology tennis racquets. Its racquetball racquet product line has recently been in trouble. Sales revenues are down and the division is losing money.

Project Unit One

Characters

- Luke Thorndike, founder and current president of Thorndike
- Ted Thorndike, Luke's grandson
- Joyce Hernandez, manager of customer service

The Setting

Luke Thorndike, age 64, has asked his grandson to consider working for the company. Ted, who just graduated from college, received his bachelor's degree in marketing and is anxious to work in marketing research. Luke suspects his company has not kept up with the latest academic ideas. He is looking forward to new ideas from Ted.

Putting Yourself in the Picture

1. Suppose you were in Ted's place. It's your first day on the job. What would you be thinking about before going to work?

2. Suppose you were introduced to Joyce Hernandez, manager of customer service. What would you ask her about her job and her perspective on Thorndike's customers?

Project Unit Two

Characters

- Luke Thorndike, founder and current president of Thorndike
- Ted Thorndike, executive vice president
- Sally Smith, production/engineering

The Setting

Ted needs to familiarize himself with the racquetball racquet market. He goes to the library, and he talks with Sally Smith about product quality and production activity.

Putting Yourself in the Picture

1. Suppose you were at the library trying to learn as much as you could about the racquetball racquet market. Where would you start? What else would you do?

2. What production information about racquetball racquets could Sally provide that would be important to the development of a marketing strategy?

Project Unit Three

Characters

- Luke Thorndike, founder and current president of Thorndike
- Ted Thorndike, executive vice president
- Sally Smith, production/engineering
- Samantha Dawson, plant representative, International Racquet Workers Union
- Racquetball players

The Setting

Talking with production engineers, Ted learned that the racquets coming off the line do not all weigh the same. According to Sally the racquet weights "vary all over the lot." Ted and Sally found that there is a great deal of production variation for Thorndike's racquetball racquets. Luke wants to avoid purchasing a $700,000 molding machine—a quick but expensive fix for production problems. Ted thinks marketing research will help. He needs to know more about racquetball and racquetball players.

Putting Yourself in the Picture

1. Suppose you were planning the marketing research. Is exploratory research necessary? What purpose would it serve? What form should it take if you were to do exploratory research? Should a survey be conducted? What exactly would you do?

Project Unit Four

Characters

- Luke Thorndike, founder and current president of Thorndike
- Ted Thorndike, executive vice president
- Brad Striker, a professional New York bargaining agent

The Setting

Statistical analysis is important in manufacturing companies. Use of probability sampling and confidence interval estimates are frequently necessary to prove advertising claims. Negotiations with unions involve marketing skill as well as analytical skill, such as the analysis of statistical trends.

Major Issue 1

Seeing a fishing pole in his grandfather's office, Ted Thorndike's first thought is that old Luke is going to go fishing again and leave him to manage the store. He is quite surprised to learn the fishing pole is actually an inspiration for a new series of advertisements that Luke has in mind.

The elder Thorndike explains, "Ted, this fishing pole is made of graphite, the same stuff that goes into our Graph-Pro racquetball racquet. It's so flexible and strong that it can be bent so the two ends actually touch each other. They even show this in the ads." Although Luke realizes that you can't do exactly the same thing with a racquetball racquet, he'd like to put some of his racquets into a horizontal mounting device, then see how much weight they'll take before they break.

If the amount of weight is impressive enough, Luke plans to include this kind of test in the television advertisements he's planning for the firm's racquetball racquet. However, he wants to be careful not to brag about the racquet being able to hold *too* much weight, since the firm could get into trouble with the government and other truth-in-advertising advocates.

He asks Ted to set up a test in which racquets are mounted horizontally, then the weight of the ends is gradually increased until they break. Based on the test results, a weight value could be selected such that the average racquet would almost certainly be able to withstand this amount. Although accuracy is important, Ted has been instructed not to break more than 15 or 20 racquets in coming up with an average for all the racquets.

For 20 racquets subjected to this severe test, the weight (in pounds) at which each one failed was as follows:

221	228	223	218	218
208	220	217	224	225
224	222	229	215	221
217	230	236	222	234

Putting Yourself in the Picture

1. Ted believes it's reasonable to assume the population of breaking strengths is approximately normally distributed. Because of Luke's concern about being able to support the advertising claim, he wants to be very conservative in estimating the population mean for these breaking strengths. Ted needs some help in deciding how conservative he would like to be and in coming up with a number that can be promoted in the ads.

Major Issue 2

Negotiations are taking place for a new labor agreement between Thorndike Sports Equipment and its manufacturing employees. The company and the union have agreed to consider linking hourly wages to the predicted Consumer Price Index (CPI) for each of the four years of the new contract. The latest proposal would specify an hourly wage that is 10 percent of the estimated CPI (e.g., if the estimated CPI for a given year were 132.5, the hourly wage for that contract year would be $13.25).

Table 1.1 shows the CPI for 1960 through 1988, along with the year and the year code. The base period for the CPI figures is 1982 through 1984, for which the average is 100.

Putting Yourself in the Picture

1. Suppose you were Ted working with the union. How would you use your knowledge of the statistical techniques used in marketing research to help explain the nature of this problem?

2. Assuming that the new contract will be in force from 1990 through 1993, use a computer statistical package to help determine the hourly wage that would be paid in each year of the contract if the estimated CPI is an extrapolation based on a bivariate linear regression fitted to the 1960 to 1988 data.

Project Unit Five

Characters

- Ted Thorndike, vice president
- Kermit Clawson, an outstanding young professional player

The Setting

Ted and Luke Thorndike have been approached by several local racquetball players, each of whom would like to be sponsored by Thorndike Sports Equipment during regional tournaments to be held during the next calendar year. In the past, Luke has resisted the sponsorship possibility. His philosophy has been, "Our rac-

> ### Table 1.1   Values of the Consumer Price Index (CPI) for 1960 Through 1988 (The base period is 1982–84 = 100)

Year	Year Code	CPI	Year	Year Code	CPI
1960	0	29.6	1975	15	53.8
1961	1	29.9	1976	16	56.9
1962	2	30.2	1977	17	60.6
1963	3	30.6	1978	18	65.2
1964	4	31.0	1979	19	72.6
1965	5	31.5	1980	20	82.4
1966	6	32.4	1981	21	90.9
1967	7	33.4	1982	22	96.5
1968	8	34.8	1983	23	99.6
1969	9	36.7	1984	24	103.9
1970	10	38.8	1985	25	107.6
1971	11	40.5	1986	26	109.6
1972	12	41.8	1987	27	113.6
1973	13	44.4	1988	28	118.3
1974	14	49.3			

quets are the best in the business. If they're smart, they'll use a Thorndike racquet; and if we're smart, we won't give it to them for free."

It wasn't easy, but Ted finally convinced Luke of the benefits to be gained by exposing racquet club members and tournament spectators to high-caliber players who rely on Thorndike racquets and related sports equipment.

The Thorndikes compromise between Luke's original idea of sponsoring no one and Ted's proposal to sponsor at least three players. Their eventual selection is Kermit Clawson, an outstanding young player who finished third in the regional championship tournament last year. Kermit and the Thorndikes have reached agreement on all of the details of the sponsorship arrangement but must decide on which combination of racquet and string would be best.

Kermit is a power player who relies heavily on the speed of his serves and return shots. The Thorndike line currently includes four "power" racquets, each of which can be strung with one of the three types of string most often used by strong hitters like Kermit. Ted sets up a test in which Kermit will hit *two* "power serves" with each combination of racquet and string. The 24 serves will be made in a random order, and each will be clocked with a radar gun. Besides helping Kermit select the combination he likes best, the test will also help the Thorndikes study what Ted has referred to as the "main" and "interactive" effects of the racquet and strings. The miles per hour (MPH) data from the 3 × 4 design with two trials for each racquet/string combination are shown below.

	Racquet 1	Racquet 2	Racquet 3	Racquet 4
String 1	105, 108	113, 109	114, 112	109, 108
String 2	110, 108	109, 107	118, 114	113, 113
String 3	113, 112	114, 109	114, 114	110, 107

Putting Yourself in the Picture

1. From these data, which combination of racquet and string would you recommend that Kermit use? Also, employ the appropriate ANOVA procedure in helping Ted respond to Luke's statement that "the racquets are all the same, the strings are all the same, and it doesn't matter which string goes into which racquet."

Appendix A

Statistical Tables

Table A.1   Random Digits

37751	04998	66038	63480	98442	22245	83538	62351	74514	90497
50915	64152	82981	15796	27102	71635	34470	13608	26360	76285
99142	35021	01032	57907	80545	54112	15150	36856	03247	40392
70720	10033	25191	62358	03784	74377	88150	25567	87457	49512
18460	64947	32958	08752	96366	89092	23597	74308	00881	88976
65763	41133	60950	35372	06782	81451	78764	52645	19841	50083
83769	52570	60133	25211	87384	90182	84990	26400	39128	97043
58900	78420	98579	33665	10718	39342	46346	14401	13503	46525
54746	71115	78219	64314	11227	41702	54517	87676	14078	45317
56819	27340	07200	52663	57864	85159	15460	97564	29637	27742
34990	62122	38223	28526	37006	22774	46026	15981	87291	56946
02269	22795	87593	81830	95383	67823	20196	54850	46779	64519
43042	53600	45738	00261	31100	67239	02004	70698	53597	62617
92565	12211	06868	87786	59576	61382	33972	13161	47208	96604
67424	32620	60841	86848	85000	04835	48576	33884	10101	84129
04015	77148	09535	10743	97871	55919	45274	38304	93125	91847
85226	19763	46105	25289	26714	73253	85922	21785	42624	92741
03360	07457	75131	41209	50451	23472	07438	08375	29312	62264
72460	99682	27970	25632	34096	17656	12736	27476	21938	67305
66960	55780	71778	52629	51692	71442	36130	70425	39874	62035
14824	95631	00697	65462	24815	13930	02938	54619	28909	53950
34001	05618	41900	23303	19928	60755	61404	56947	91441	19299
77718	83830	29781	72917	10840	74182	08293	62588	99625	22088
60930	05091	35726	07414	49211	69586	20226	08274	28167	65279
94180	62151	08112	26646	07617	42954	22521	09395	43561	45692
81073	85543	47650	93830	07377	87995	35084	39386	93141	88309
18467	39689	60801	46828	38670	88243	89042	78452	08032	72566
60643	59399	79740	17295	50094	66436	92677	68345	24025	36489
73372	61697	85728	90779	13235	83114	70728	32093	74306	08325
18395	18482	83245	54942	51905	09534	70839	91073	42193	81199
07261	28720	71244	05064	84873	68020	39037	68981	00670	86291
61679	81529	83725	33269	45958	74265	87460	60525	42539	25605
11815	48679	00556	96871	39835	83055	84949	11681	51687	55896
99007	35050	86440	44280	20320	97527	28138	01088	49037	85430
06446	65608	79291	16624	06135	30622	56133	33998	32308	29434

Table A.2 Area under the Normal Curve

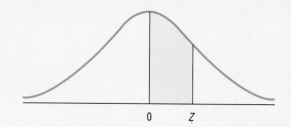

z	.00	.01	.02	.03	.04	.05	.06	.07	.08	.09
0.0	.0000	.0040	.0080	.0120	.0160	.0199	.0239	.0279	.0319	.0359
0.1	.0398	.0438	.0478	.0517	.0557	.0596	.0636	.0675	.0714	.0753
0.2	.0793	.0832	.0871	.0910	.0948	.0987	.1026	.1064	.1103	.1141
0.3	.1179	.1217	.1255	.1293	.1331	.1368	.1406	.1443	.1480	.1517
0.4	.1554	.1591	.1628	.1664	.1700	.1736	.1772	.1808	.1844	.1879
0.5	.1915	.1950	.1985	.2019	.2054	.2088	.2123	.2157	.2190	.2224
0.6	.2257	.2291	.2324	.2357	.2389	.2422	.2454	.2486	.2518	.2549
0.7	.2580	.2612	.2642	.2673	.2704	.2734	.2764	.2794	.2823	.2852
0.8	.2881	.2910	.2939	.2967	.2995	.3023	.3051	.3078	.3106	.3133
0.9	.3159	.3186	.3212	.3238	.3264	.3289	.3315	.3340	.3365	.3389
1.0	.3413	.3438	.3461	.3485	.3508	.3531	.3554	.3577	.3599	.3621
1.1	.3643	.3665	.3686	.3708	.3729	.3749	.3770	.3790	.3810	.3830
1.2	.3849	.3869	.3888	.3907	.3925	.3944	.3962	.3980	.3997	.4015
1.3	.4032	.4049	.4066	.4082	.4099	.4115	.4131	.4147	.4162	.4177
1.4	.4192	.4207	.4222	.4236	.4251	.4265	.4279	.4292	.4306	.4319
1.5	.4332	.4345	.4357	.4370	.4382	.4394	.4406	.4418	.4429	.4441
1.6	.4452	.4463	.4474	.4484	.4495	.4505	.4515	.4525	.4535	.4545
1.7	.4554	.4564	.4573	.4582	.4591	.4599	.4608	.4616	.4625	.4633
1.8	.4641	.4649	.4656	.4664	.4671	.4678	.4686	.4693	.4699	.4706
1.9	.4713	.4719	.4726	.4732	.4738	.4744	.4750	.4756	.4761	.4767
2.0	.4772	.4778	.4783	.4788	.4793	.4798	.4803	.4808	.4812	.4817
2.1	.4821	.4826	.4830	.4834	.4838	.4842	.4846	.4850	.4854	.4857
2.2	.4861	.4864	.4868	.4871	.4875	.4878	.4881	.4884	.4887	.4890
2.3	.4893	.4896	.4898	.4901	.4904	.4906	.4909	.4911	.4913	.4916
2.4	.4918	.4920	.4922	.4925	.4927	.4929	.4931	.4932	.4934	.4936
2.5	.4938	.4940	.4941	.4943	.4945	.4946	.4948	.4949	.4951	.4952
2.6	.4953	.4955	.4956	.4957	.4959	.4960	.4961	.4962	.4963	.4964
2.7	.4965	.4966	.4967	.4968	.4969	.4970	.4971	.4972	.4973	.4974
2.8	.4974	.4975	.4976	.4977	.4977	.4978	.4979	.4979	.4980	.4981
2.9	.4981	.4982	.4982	.4983	.4984	.4984	.4985	.4985	.4986	.4986
3.0	.49865	.4987	.4987	.4988	.4988	.4989	.4989	.4989	.4990	.4990
4.0	.49997									

Table A.3 Distribution of *t* for Given Probability Levels

d.f.	LEVEL OF SIGNIFICANCE FOR ONE-TAILED TEST					
	.10	.05	.025	.01	.005	.0005
	LEVEL OF SIGNIFICANCE FOR TWO-TAILED TEST					
	.20	.10	.05	.02	.01	.001
1	3.078	6.314	12.706	31.821	63.657	636.619
2	1.886	2.920	4.303	6.965	9.925	31.598
3	1.638	2.353	3.182	4.541	5.841	12.941
4	1.533	2.132	2.776	3.747	4.604	8.610
5	1.476	2.015	2.571	3.365	4.032	6.859
6	1.440	1.943	2.447	3.143	3.707	5.959
7	1.415	1.895	2.365	2.998	3.499	5.405
8	1.397	1.860	2.306	2.896	3.355	5.041
9	1.383	1.833	2.262	2.821	3.250	4.781
10	1.372	1.812	2.228	2.764	3.169	4.587
11	1.363	1.796	2.201	2.718	3.106	4.437
12	1.356	1.782	2.179	2.681	3.055	4.318
13	1.350	1.771	2.160	2.650	3.012	4.221
14	1.345	1.761	2.145	2.624	2.977	4.140
15	1.341	1.753	2.131	2.602	2.947	4.073
16	1.337	1.746	2.120	2.583	2.921	4.015
17	1.333	1.740	2.110	2.567	2.898	3.965
18	1.330	1.734	2.101	2.552	2.878	3.992
19	1.328	1.729	2.093	2.539	2.861	3.883
20	1.325	1.725	2.086	2.528	2.845	3.850
21	1.323	1.721	2.080	2.518	2.831	3.819
22	1.321	1.717	2.074	2.508	2.819	3.792
23	1.319	1.714	2.069	2.500	2.807	3.767
24	1.318	1.711	2.064	2.492	2.797	3.745
25	1.316	1.708	2.060	2.485	2.787	3.725
26	1.315	1.706	2.056	2.479	2.779	3.707
27	1.314	1.703	2.052	2.473	2.771	3.690
28	1.313	1.701	2.048	2.467	2.763	3.674
29	1.311	1.699	2.045	2.462	2.756	3.659
30	1.310	1.697	2.042	2.457	2.750	3.646
40	1.303	1.684	2.021	2.423	2.704	3.551
60	1.296	1.671	2.000	2.390	2.660	3.460
120	1.289	1.658	1.980	2.358	2.617	3.373
∞	1.282	1.645	1.960	2.326	2.576	3.291

Table A.4 Chi-Square Distribution

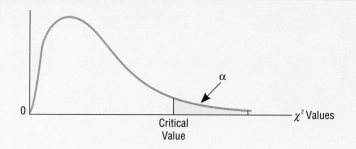

Degrees of Freedom (d.f.)	Area in Shaded Right Tail (α)		
	.10	.05	.01
1	2.706	3.841	6.635
2	4.605	5.991	9.210
3	6.251	7.815	11.345
4	7.779	9.488	13.277
5	9.236	11.070	15.086
6	10.645	12.592	16.812
7	12.017	14.067	18.475
8	13.362	15.507	20.090
9	14.684	16.919	21.666
10	15.987	18.307	23.209
11	17.275	19.675	24.725
12	18.549	21.026	26.217
13	19.812	22.362	27.688
14	21.064	23.685	29.141
15	22.307	24.996	30.578
16	23.542	26.296	32.000
17	24.769	27.587	33.409
18	25.989	28.869	34.805
19	27.204	30.144	36.191
20	28.412	31.410	37.566
21	29.615	32.671	38.932
22	30.813	33.924	40.289
23	32.007	35.172	41.638
24	33.196	36.415	42.980
25	34.382	37.652	44.314
26	35.563	38.885	45.642
27	36.741	40.113	46.963
28	37.916	41.337	48.278
29	39.087	42.557	49.588
30	40.256	43.773	50.892

Example of how to use this table: In a chi-square distribution with 6 degrees of freedom (d.f.), the area to the right of a critical value of 12.592—i.e., the α area—is .05.

Table A.5 Critical Values of $F_{v_1 v_2}$ for $\alpha = .05$

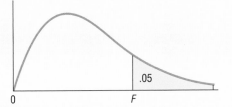

v_1 = DEGREES OF FREEDOM FOR NUMERATOR

		1	2	3	4	5	6	7	8	9	10	12	15	20	24	30	40	60	120	∞
	1	161	200	216	225	230	234	237	239	241	242	244	246	248	249	250	251	252	253	254
	2	18.5	19.0	19.2	19.2	19.3	19.3	19.4	19.4	19.4	19.4	19.4	19.4	19.5	19.5	19.5	19.5	19.5	19.5	19.5
	3	10.1	9.55	9.28	9.12	9.01	8.94	8.89	8.85	8.81	8.79	8.74	8.70	8.66	8.64	8.62	8.59	8.57	8.55	8.53
	4	7.71	6.94	6.59	6.39	6.26	6.16	6.09	6.04	6.00	5.96	5.91	5.86	5.80	5.77	5.75	5.72	5.69	5.66	5.63
	5	6.61	5.79	5.41	5.19	5.05	4.95	4.88	4.82	4.77	4.74	4.68	4.62	4.56	4.53	4.50	4.46	4.43	4.40	4.37
	6	5.99	5.14	4.76	4.53	4.39	4.28	4.21	4.15	4.10	4.06	4.00	3.94	3.87	3.84	3.81	3.77	3.74	3.70	3.67
	7	5.59	4.74	4.35	4.12	3.97	3.87	3.79	3.73	3.68	3.64	3.57	3.51	3.44	3.41	3.38	3.34	3.30	3.27	3.23
	8	5.32	4.46	4.07	3.84	3.69	3.58	3.50	3.44	3.39	3.35	3.28	3.22	3.15	3.12	3.08	3.04	3.01	2.97	2.93
	9	5.12	4.26	3.86	3.63	3.48	3.37	3.29	3.23	3.18	3.14	3.07	3.01	2.94	2.90	2.86	2.83	2.79	2.75	2.71
	10	4.96	4.10	3.71	3.48	3.33	3.22	3.14	3.07	3.02	2.98	2.91	2.85	2.77	2.74	2.70	2.66	2.62	2.58	2.54
	11	4.84	3.98	3.59	3.36	3.20	3.09	3.01	2.95	2.90	2.85	2.79	2.72	2.65	2.61	2.57	2.53	2.49	2.45	2.40
	12	4.75	3.89	3.49	3.26	3.11	3.00	2.91	2.85	2.80	2.75	2.69	2.62	2.54	2.51	2.47	2.43	2.38	2.34	2.30
	13	4.67	3.81	3.41	3.18	3.03	2.92	2.83	2.77	2.71	2.67	2.60	2.53	2.46	2.42	2.38	2.34	2.30	2.25	2.21
	14	4.60	3.74	3.34	3.11	2.96	2.85	2.76	2.70	2.65	2.60	2.53	2.46	2.39	2.35	2.31	2.27	2.22	2.18	2.13
	15	4.54	3.68	3.29	3.06	2.90	2.79	2.71	2.64	2.59	2.54	2.48	2.40	2.33	2.29	2.25	2.20	2.16	2.11	2.07
	16	4.49	3.63	3.24	3.01	2.85	2.74	2.66	2.59	2.54	2.49	2.42	2.35	2.28	2.24	2.19	2.15	2.11	2.06	2.01
	17	4.45	3.59	3.20	2.96	2.81	2.70	2.61	2.55	2.49	2.45	2.38	2.31	2.23	2.19	2.15	2.10	2.06	2.01	1.96
	18	4.41	3.55	3.16	2.93	2.77	2.66	2.58	2.51	2.46	2.41	2.34	2.27	2.19	2.15	2.11	2.06	2.02	1.97	1.92
	19	4.38	3.52	3.13	2.90	2.74	2.63	2.54	2.48	2.42	2.38	2.31	2.23	2.16	2.11	2.07	2.03	1.98	1.93	1.88
	20	4.35	3.49	3.10	2.87	2.71	2.60	2.51	2.45	2.39	2.35	2.28	2.20	2.12	2.08	2.04	1.99	1.95	1.90	1.84
	21	4.32	3.47	3.07	2.84	2.68	2.57	2.49	2.42	2.37	2.32	2.25	2.18	2.10	2.05	2.01	1.96	1.92	1.87	1.81
	22	4.30	3.44	3.05	2.82	2.66	2.55	2.46	2.40	2.34	2.30	2.23	2.15	2.07	2.03	1.98	1.94	1.89	1.84	1.78
	23	4.28	3.42	3.03	2.80	2.64	2.53	2.44	2.37	2.32	2.27	2.20	2.13	2.05	2.01	1.96	1.91	1.86	1.81	1.76
	24	4.26	3.40	3.01	2.78	2.62	2.51	2.42	2.36	2.30	2.25	2.18	2.11	2.03	1.98	1.94	1.89	1.84	1.79	1.73
	25	4.24	3.39	2.99	2.76	2.60	2.49	2.40	2.34	2.28	2.24	2.16	2.09	2.01	1.96	1.92	1.87	1.82	1.77	1.71
	30	4.17	3.32	2.92	2.69	2.53	2.42	2.33	2.27	2.21	2.16	2.09	2.01	1.93	1.89	1.84	1.79	1.74	1.68	1.62
	40	4.08	3.23	2.84	2.61	2.45	2.34	2.25	2.18	2.12	2.08	2.00	1.92	1.84	1.79	1.74	1.69	1.64	1.58	1.51
	60	4.00	3.15	2.76	2.53	2.37	2.25	2.17	2.10	2.04	1.99	1.92	1.84	1.75	1.70	1.65	1.59	1.53	1.47	1.39
	120	3.92	3.07	2.68	2.45	2.29	2.18	2.09	2.02	1.96	1.91	1.83	1.75	1.66	1.61	1.55	1.50	1.43	1.35	1.25
	∞	3.84	3.00	2.60	2.37	2.21	2.10	2.01	1.94	1.88	1.83	1.75	1.67	1.57	1.52	1.46	1.39	1.32	1.22	1.00

v_2 = DEGREES OF FREEDOM FOR DENOMINATOR

Table A.6 Critical Values of $F_{v_1 v_2}$ for $\alpha = .01$

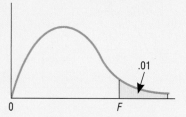

v_1 = Degrees of Freedom for Numerator

v_2 = Degrees of Freedom for Denominator

	1	2	3	4	5	6	7	8	9	10	12	15	20	24	30	40	60	120	∞
1	4,052	5,000	5,403	5,625	5,764	5,859	5,928	5,982	6,023	6,056	6,106	6,157	6,209	6,235	6,261	6,287	6,313	6,339	6,366
2	98.5	99.0	99.2	99.2	99.3	99.3	99.4	99.4	99.4	99.4	99.4	99.4	99.4	99.5	99.5	99.5	99.5	99.5	99.5
3	34.1	30.8	29.5	28.7	28.2	27.9	27.7	27.5	27.3	27.2	27.1	26.9	26.7	26.6	26.5	26.4	26.3	26.2	26.1
4	21.2	18.0	16.7	16.0	15.5	15.2	15.0	14.8	14.7	14.5	14.4	14.2	14.0	13.9	13.8	13.7	13.7	13.6	13.5
5	16.3	13.3	12.1	11.4	11.0	10.7	10.5	10.3	10.2	10.1	9.89	9.72	9.55	9.47	9.38	9.29	9.20	9.11	9.02
6	13.7	10.9	9.78	9.15	8.75	8.47	8.26	8.10	7.98	7.87	7.72	7.56	7.40	7.31	7.23	7.14	7.06	6.97	6.88
7	12.2	9.55	8.45	7.85	7.46	7.19	6.99	6.84	6.72	6.62	6.47	6.31	6.16	6.07	5.99	5.91	5.82	5.74	5.65
8	11.3	8.65	7.59	7.01	6.63	6.37	6.18	6.03	5.91	5.81	5.67	5.52	5.36	5.28	5.20	5.12	5.03	4.95	4.86
9	10.6	8.02	6.99	6.42	6.06	5.80	5.61	5.47	5.35	5.26	5.11	4.96	4.81	4.73	4.65	4.57	4.48	4.40	4.31
10	10.0	7.56	6.55	5.99	5.64	5.39	5.20	5.06	4.94	4.85	4.71	4.56	4.41	4.33	4.25	4.17	4.08	4.00	3.91
11	9.65	7.21	6.22	5.67	5.32	5.07	4.89	4.74	4.63	4.54	4.40	4.25	4.10	4.02	3.94	3.86	3.78	3.69	3.60
12	9.33	6.93	5.95	5.41	5.06	4.82	4.64	4.50	4.39	4.30	4.16	4.01	3.86	3.78	3.70	3.62	3.54	3.45	3.36
13	9.07	6.70	5.74	5.21	4.86	4.62	4.44	4.30	4.19	4.10	3.96	3.82	3.66	3.59	3.51	3.43	3.34	3.25	3.17
14	8.86	6.51	5.56	5.04	4.70	4.46	4.28	4.14	4.03	3.94	3.80	3.66	3.51	3.43	3.35	3.27	3.18	3.09	3.00
15	8.68	6.36	5.42	4.89	4.56	4.32	4.14	4.00	3.89	3.80	3.67	3.52	3.37	3.29	3.21	3.13	3.05	2.96	2.87
16	8.53	6.23	5.29	4.77	4.44	4.20	4.03	3.89	3.78	3.69	3.55	3.41	3.26	3.18	3.10	3.02	2.93	2.84	2.75
17	8.40	6.11	5.19	4.67	4.34	4.10	3.93	3.79	3.68	3.59	3.46	3.31	3.16	3.08	3.00	2.92	2.83	2.75	2.65
18	8.29	6.01	5.09	4.58	4.25	4.01	3.84	3.71	3.60	3.51	3.37	3.23	3.08	3.00	2.92	2.84	2.75	2.66	2.57
19	8.19	5.93	5.01	4.50	4.17	3.94	3.77	3.63	3.52	3.43	3.30	3.15	3.00	2.92	2.84	2.76	2.67	2.58	2.49
20	8.10	5.85	4.94	4.43	4.10	3.87	3.70	3.56	3.46	3.37	3.23	3.09	2.94	2.86	2.78	2.69	2.61	2.52	2.42
21	8.02	5.78	4.87	4.37	4.04	3.81	3.64	3.51	3.40	3.31	3.17	3.03	2.88	2.80	2.72	2.64	2.55	2.46	2.36
22	7.96	5.72	4.82	4.31	3.99	3.76	3.59	3.45	3.35	3.26	3.12	2.98	2.83	2.75	2.67	2.58	2.50	2.40	2.31
23	7.88	5.66	4.76	4.26	3.94	3.71	3.54	3.41	3.30	3.21	3.07	2.93	2.78	2.70	2.62	2.54	2.45	2.35	2.26
24	7.82	5.61	4.72	4.22	3.90	3.67	3.50	3.36	3.26	3.17	3.03	2.89	2.74	2.66	2.58	2.49	2.40	2.31	2.21
25	7.77	5.57	4.68	4.18	3.86	3.63	3.46	3.32	3.22	3.13	2.99	2.85	2.70	2.62	2.53	2.45	2.36	2.27	2.17
30	7.58	5.39	4.51	4.02	3.70	3.47	3.30	3.17	3.07	2.98	2.84	2.70	2.55	2.47	2.39	2.30	2.21	2.11	2.01
40	7.31	5.18	4.31	3.83	3.51	3.29	3.12	2.99	2.89	2.80	2.66	2.52	2.37	2.29	2.20	2.11	2.02	1.92	1.80
60	7.08	4.98	4.13	3.65	3.34	3.12	2.95	2.82	2.72	2.63	2.50	2.35	2.20	2.12	2.03	1.94	1.84	1.73	1.60
120	6.85	4.79	3.95	3.48	3.17	2.96	2.79	2.66	2.56	2.47	2.34	2.19	2.03	1.95	1.86	1.76	1.66	1.53	1.38
∞	6.63	4.61	3.78	3.32	3.02	2.80	2.64	2.51	2.41	2.32	2.18	2.04	1.88	1.79	1.70	1.59	1.47	1.32	1.00

Table A.7 Critical Values of the Pearson Correlation Coefficient

	LEVEL OF SIGNIFICANCE FOR ONE-TAILED TEST			
	.05	.025	.01	.005
	LEVEL OF SIGNIFICANCE FOR TWO-TAILED TEST			
d.f.	.10	.05	.02	.01
1	.988	.997	.9995	.9999
2	.900	.950	.980	.990
3	.805	.878	.934	.959
4	.729	.811	.882	.917
5	.669	.754	.833	.874
6	.622	.707	.789	.834
7	.582	.666	.750	.798
8	.549	.632	.716	.765
9	.521	.602	.685	.735
10	.497	.576	.658	.708
11	.576	.553	.634	.684
12	.458	.532	.612	.661
13	.441	.514	.592	.641
14	.426	.497	.574	.623
15	.412	.482	.558	.606
16	.400	.468	.542	.590
17	.389	.456	.528	.575
18	.378	.444	.516	.561
19	.369	.433	.503	.549
20	.360	.423	.492	.537
21	.352	.413	.482	.526
22	.344	.404	.472	.515
23	.337	.396	.462	.505
24	.330	.388	.453	.496
25	.323	.381	.445	.487
26	.317	.374	.437	.479
27	.311	.367	.430	.471
28	.306	.361	.423	.463
29	.301	.355	.416	.486
30	.296	.349	.409	.449
35	.275	.325	.381	.418
40	.257	.304	.358	.393
45	.243	.288	.338	.372
50	.231	.273	.322	.354
60	.211	.250	.295	.325
70	.195	.232	.274	.303
80	.183	.217	.256	.283
90	.173	.205	.242	.267
100	.164	.195	.230	.254

Table A.8 Critical Values of *T* in the Wilcoxon Matched-Pairs, Signed Ranks Test

| N | LEVEL OF SIGNIFICANCE FOR TWO-TAILED TEST | | |
	.05	.02	.01
6	1	—	—
7	2	0	—
8	4	2	0
9	6	3	2
10	8	5	3
11	11	7	5
12	14	10	7
13	17	13	10
14	21	16	13
15	25	20	16
16	30	24	19
17	35	28	23
18	40	33	28
19	46	38	32
20	52	43	37
21	59	49	43
22	66	56	49
23	73	62	55
24	81	69	61
25	90	77	68

Glossary of Frequently Used Symbols

Greek Letters

α (alpha)	level of significance or probability of a Type I error
β (beta)	probability of a type II error or slope of the regression line
μ (mu)	population mean
ρ (rho)	population Pearson correlation coefficient
Σ (summation)	take the sum of
π (pi)	population proportion
σ (sigma)	population standard deviation
χ^2	chi-square statistic

English Letters

$d.f.$	number of degrees of freedom
F	F-statistic
n	sample size
p	sample proportion
Pr ( )	probability of the outcome in the parentheses
r	sample Pearson correlation coefficient
r^2	coefficient of determination (squared correlation coefficient)
R^2	coefficient of determination (multiple regression)
S	sample standard deviation (inferential statistics)
$S_{\bar{X}}$	estimated standard error of the mean
S_p	estimated standard error of the proportion
S^2	sample variance (inferential statistics)
t	t-statistic
X	variable or any unspecified observation
$\bar{X}$	sample mean
Y	any unspecified observation on a second variable, usually the dependent variable
$\hat{Y}$	predicted score
Z	standardized score (descriptive statistics) or Z-statisti

Glossary of Terms

a   The Y-intercept.

Acquiescence bias   A category of response bias that results because some individuals tend to agree with all questions or to concur with a particular position.

Administrative error   An error caused by the improper administration or flawed execution of a research task.

Advocacy research   Research undertaken to support a specific claim in a legal action.

Affective component   The component of attitude that reflects an individual's general feelings or emotions toward an object.

Alternative hypothesis   A statement that indicates the opposite of the null hypothesis.

Analysis of variance (ANOVA)   Analysis involving the investigation of the effects of one treatment variable on an interval-scaled dependent variable; a hypothesis testing technique to determine whether statistically significant differences on means occur between two or more groups.

Analysis of variance summary table   A table that shows the results of an analysis of variance, such as the relative magnitudes of a mean square.

Analytical models   Statistical software systems, spreadsheet software, and decision model banks that combine and restructure databases, diagnose relationships, estimate variables, and otherwise analyze the data within the system.

Applied research   Research undertaken to answer questions about specific problems or to make decisions about particular courses of action.

Area sample   A type of cluster sample based on geographical area.

At-home scanning system   A system whereby consumer panelists perform their own scanning after taking home the products using hand-held wands that read UPC symbols.

Attitude   An enduring disposition to consistently respond in a given manner to various aspects of the world; composed of affective, cognitive, and behavioral components.

Attribute   A single characteristic or fundamental feature pertaining to an object, person, situation, or issue.

Auspices bias   Bias in the responses of subjects caused by the respondents being influenced by the organization conducting the study.

Average deviation   A measure of dispersion derived by calculating the deviation score of each observation value, summing up each score, and dividing the total by the sample size (n).

Back translation   In international marketing research it is necessary to translate questionnaires into foreign languages. To avoid language problems, a questionnaire is first translated from one language to another. It is then translated back again by a second, independent translator. The entire process is back translation.

Backward linkage   A term implying that the later stages of the research process will influence the early stages.

Balanced rating scale   A fixed-alternative rating scale with an equal number of positive and negative categories; a neutral or indifferent point is at the center of the scale.

Bar chart   A graphic aid that shows changes in a variable at discrete intervals.

Base (base number)   The number of respondents or observations used as a basis for computing percentages.

Basic experimental design   An experimental design in which a single independent variable is manipulated to measure its effect on another single dependent variable.

Basic (pure) research   Research conducted to expand the boundaries of knowledge itself; conducted to verify the acceptability of a given theory.

Behavioral component   The component of attitude that reflects buying intentions and behavioral expectations; reflects a predisposition to action.

Behavioral differential   A rating scale instrument similar to a semantic differential developed to measure the behavioral intentions of subjects toward future actions.

Beta (b)   The slope, or rise over run.

Bivariate linear regression   A measure of linear association that investigates a straight-line relationship of the type $Y = a + bX$, where Y is the dependent variable, X is the independent variable, and a and b are two constants to be estimated.

Bivariate statistical analysis   Data analysis and hypothesis testing when the investigation concerns simultaneous investigation of two variables; test of differences or measures of association between two variables at a time.

Blinding   A technique used to control subjects' knowledge of whether or not they have been given a particular experimental treatment.

Box and whisker plots   Graphic representation of central tendencies, percentiles, variables, and the shapes of frequency distributions.

Briefing session   A training session to ensure that each interviewer is provided with common information.

Callback   An attempt to recontact an individual selected for the sample.

Canonical correlation analysis   A statistical technique used to determine the degree of linear association between two sets of variables, each consisting of several variables.

Case study method   The exploratory research technique that intensively investigates one or a few situations similar to the problem situation.

Categorical (classificatory) variable   A variable that has a limited number of distinct values.

Category scale   A rating scale that consists of several response categories, often providing respondents with alternatives to indicate positions on a continuum.

Causal research   Research conducted to identify cause-and-effect relationships among variables.

Cell   Section of a table representing a specific combination of two variables or a specific value of a variable.

Census   An investigation of all the individual elements that make up a population.

Central-limit theorem   A theory that states that as a sample size increases the distribution of sample means of size n, randomly selected, approaches a normal distribution.

Central location interviewing Telephone interviews conducted from a central location; it allows more effective supervision and control of the quality of interviewing.

Chart A graphic aid that translates numerical information into visual form so that relationships may be easily grasped.

Checklist question A fixed-alternative question that allows the respondent to provide multiple answers to a single question by checking off items.

Chi-square (χ_2) test A hypothesis test that allows for investigation of statistical significance in the analysis of a frequency distribution.

Chi-square test for a contingency table A test that statistically analyzes significance in a joint frequency distribution.

Choice A measurement task that identifies preferences by requiring respondents to choose between two or more alternatives.

Classificatory variable An independent variable that represents some classifiable or qualitative aspect of business strategy, respondents, or attributes.

Client Term often used by the research department to refer to line management for whom services are being performed.

Cluster analysis A body of techniques with the purpose of classifying individuals or objects into a small number of mutually exclusive groups, ensuring that there will be as much likeness within groups and as much difference among groups as possible.

Cluster sampling An economically efficient sampling technique in which the primary sampling unit is not the individual element in the population but a large cluster of elements; clusters are selected randomly.

Code book A book that identifies each variable in a study and a variable's description, code name, and position on the disk or tape.

Code of ethics A set of guidelines that states the standards and operating procedures for ethical practices by researchers.

Codes The rules for interpreting, classifying, and recording data in the coding process; the actual numerical or other character symbols.

Coding The process of identifying and assigning a numerical score or other character symbol to previously edited data.

Coding sheet Ruled paper that is a facsimile of the data matrix; used to record codes.

Coefficient of correlation A statistical measure of the covariation or association between two variables. There are several correlation techniques that may provide information on whether two or more variables are interrelated or associated.

Coefficient of determination (r^2) A measure obtained by squaring the correlation coefficient; that proportion of the total variance of a variable that is accounted for by knowing the value of another variable.

Cognitive component The component of attitude that represents one's awareness of and knowledge about an object.

Cohort effect A change in the dependent variable that occurs because members of one experimental group experienced different historical situations than members of other experimental groups.

Communality In factor analysis, a measure of the percentage of a variable's variation that is explained by the factors.

Communication process The process by which one person or source sends a message to an audience or receiver and then receives feedback about the message.

Comparative rating scale Any measure of attitudes that asks respondents to rate a concept in comparison with a benchmark explicitly used as a frame of reference.

Completely randomized design An experimental design that uses a random process to assign subjects (test units) and treatments to investigate the effects of only one independent variable.

Compromise design An approximation of an experimental design; may fall short of the requirements of random assignment of subjects or treatments to groups.

Computer-assisted telephone interview A type of telephone interview in which the interviewer enters the respondent's answers directly into the computer.

Computer-interactive survey A survey in which the respondent completes a self-administered questionnaire displayed on the monitor of a computer. Respondents interact directly with a computer programmed to ask questions in a sequence determined by respondents' previous answers.

Computer map The portrayal of demographic, sales, or other data on a two- or three-dimensional map generated by a computer.

Concept A generalized idea about a class of objects, attributes, occurrences, or processes; an abstraction of reality that is the basic unit for theory development.

Concept testing Any exploratory research procedure that tests some sort of stimulus as a proxy for an idea about a new, revised, or repositioned product, service, or strategy.

Conceptual definition A verbal explanation of the meaning of a concept. It defines what the concept is and what it is not.

Conclusions and recommendations section The part of the body of the report that provides opinions based on the results and suggestions for action.

Conclusions and report preparation stage The stage in the marketing research process in which the researcher interprets information and draws conclusions so they can be communicated to the decision makers.

Concomitant variation The way in which two phenomena or events vary together.

Concurrent validity A classification of criterion validity whereby a new measure correlates with a criterion measure taken at the same time.

Confidence interval estimate A specified range of numbers within which a population mean should lie; an estimate of the population mean based on the knowledge that it will equate the sample mean plus or minus a small sampling error.

Confidence level A percentage or decimal value that tells how confident a researcher can be about being correct. It states the long-run percentage of confidence intervals that will include the true population mean.

Constancy of conditions A situation in which subjects in experimental groups and control groups are exposed to situations identical except for differing conditions of the independent variable.

Constant error An error that occurs in the same experimental condition every time the basic experiment is repeated; a systematic bias.

Constant-sum scale A measure of attitudes in which respondents are asked to divide a constant sum to indicate the relative importance of attributes; respondents often sort cards, but this may also be a rating task.

Construct validity The ability of a measure to provide empirical evidence consistent with a theory based on the concepts.

Consumer panel A longitudinal survey of the same sample of individuals or households to record (in a diary) their attitudes, behavior, or purchasing habits over time.

Content analysis The systematic observation and quantitative description of the manifest content of communication.

Contingency table The results of a cross-tabulation of two variables, such as two survey questions.

Continuous variable A variable that has an infinite number of values.

Contrived observation Observation in which the investigator creates an artificial environment in order to test a hypothesis.

Control group The group of individuals exposed to the control condition in an experiment, that is, not exposed to the experimental treatment.

Control method of test marketing A "minimarket test" using forced distribution in a small city. Retailers are paid for shelf space so that the test marketer can be guaranteed distribution.

Controlled store test A hybrid between a laboratory experiment and a test market; test products are sold in a small number of selected stores to actual customers.

Convenience sampling The sampling procedure of obtaining those people or units that are most conveniently available.

Correlation coefficient A statistical measure of the covariation or association between two variables.

Correlation matrix The standard form of reporting correlational results.

Counterbiasing statement An introductory statement or preamble to a potentially embarrassing question that reduces a respondent's reluctance to answer by suggesting that certain behavior is not unusual.

Cover letter The letter that accompanies the questionnaire in a mail survey. It generally has the purpose of inducing the reader to complete and return the questionnaire.

Criterion validity The ability of a measure to correlate with other standard measures of the same construct or established criterion.

Critical values The values that lie exactly on the boundary of the region of rejection.

Cross-checks The comparison of the data from one source with data from another source to determine the similarity of independent projects.

Cross-functional teams Teams composed of individuals from various organizational departments such as engineering, production, finance, and marketing who share a common purpose.

Cross-sectional study A study in which various segments of a population are sampled and data are collected at a single moment in time.

Cross-tabulation A technique for organizing data by groups, categories, or classes, thus facilitating comparisons; a joint frequency distribution of observations on two or more sets of variables.

Cumulative percentage A percentage that results from addition of successive percentages.

Custom research A marketing research study designed for an individual client and tailored to the client's unique needs.

Data Facts or recorded measures of certain phenomena.

Data collection system The system that includes the internal records and reports system, the marketing intelligence system, and the marketing research system.

Data conversion (1) The process of changing the original form of the data to a format suitable to achieve the research objective (2) in data processing, the activity of transforming data from a research project to computers. Also called *data transformation*.

Data entry In data processing the activity of transforming data from a research project to computers.

Data gathering stage The stage of the marketing research process in which the researcher collects the data.

Data matrix A rectangular arrangement of data into rows and columns.

Data processing and analysis stage The stage of the marketing research process in which the researcher performs several interrelated procedures to convert the data into a format that will answer management's questions.

Data processing error A category of administrative error that occurs because of incorrect data entry, computer programming, or other procedural errors during the analysis stage.

Data transformation See Data conversion.

Database A collection of raw data or information arranged in a logical manner and organized in a form that can be stored and processed by a computer.

Data mining The use of massively parallel computers to dig through volumes of data to discover patterns about an organization's customers and products. It is a broad term that applies to many different forms of analysis.

Database search and retrieval system Any computerized system that allows an investigator to make queries about the existence of certain data and to retrieve the data if they exist.

Debriefing The process of providing subjects with all pertinent facts about the nature and purpose of the experiment after its completion.

Database marketing The practice of maintaining customer databases with customers' names, addresses, phone numbers, past purchases, responses to past promotional offers, and other relevant data, such as demographic and financial data.

Decision makers' objectives Managerial goals expressed in measurable terms.

Decision support system A computer-based system that helps decision makers confront problems through direct interaction with databases and analytical models.

Degrees of freedom The number of degrees of freedom is equal to the number of observations minus the number of constraints or assumptions needed to calculate a statistical term.

Demand characteristics Experimental design procedures or situational aspects of an experiment that provide unintentional hints about the experimenter's hypothesis to subjects; situational aspects of an experiment that demand that participants respond in a particular way.

Dependence methods A category of multivariate statistical techniques; dependence methods explain or predict a dependent variable(s) on the basis of two or more independent variables.

Dependent variable A criterion or variable expected to be predicted or explained. The criterion or standard by which the results of an experiment are judged; a variable expected to be dependent on the experimenter's manipulation.

Depth interview A relatively unstructured, extensive interview in which the interviewer asks many questions and probes for in-depth answers.

Descriptive analysis The transformation of raw data into a form that will make them easy to understand and interpret; rearranging, ordering, and manipulating data to generate descriptive information.

Descriptive research Research designed to describe characteristics of a population or a phenomenon.

Descriptive statistics Statistics used to describe or summarize information about a population or sample.

Determinant-choice question A fixed alternative question that requires a respondent to choose one—and only one—response from among multiple alternatives.

Dichotomous-alternative question See Simple-dichotomy question.

Direct data entry The use of an online computer terminal as an input device for data storage.

Direct observation A straightforward attempt to observe and record what naturally occurs; the investigator does not create an artificial situation.

Director of marketing information systems See Director of marketing research.

Director of marketing research The person who provides leadership and integrates staff-level activities by planning, executing, and controlling the marketing research function; sometimes called *director of marketing information systems.*

Discriminant analysis A statistical technique for determining linear combinations of independent variables that show large differences in group means. The intent is to predict the probability of objects belonging in two or more mutually exclusive categories based on several independent variables.

Disguised question An indirect question that assumes the purpose of the study must be hidden from the respondent.

Disproportional stratified sample A stratified sample in which the sample size for each stratum is allocated according to analytical considerations.

Door-in-the-face compliance technique A two-step process for securing a high response rate. In step 1 an initial request, so large that nearly everyone refuses it, is made. Next, a second request is made for a smaller favor; respondents are expected to comply with this more reasonable request.

Door-to-door interview A personal interview conducted at the respondent's household or place of business.

Double-barreled question A question that may induce bias because it covers two issues at once.

Double-blind design A technique in which neither the subjects nor the experimenter know which are the experimental and which the controlled conditions.

Drop-off method A method of distributing self-administered questionnaires whereby an interviewer drops off the questionnaire and picks it up at a later time.

Dummy tables Representations of the actual tables that will be in the findings section of the final report; used to gain a better understanding of what the actual outcomes of the research will be.

Editing The process of checking completeness, consistency, and legibility of data and making the data ready for coding and transfer to storage.

Elaboration analysis An analysis of the basic cross-tabulation for each level of another variable, such as subgroups of the sample.

Electronic data interchange Occurs when one company's computer system is integrated with another company's system.

Electronic test markets A system of test marketing that measures results based on universal product code scanner data; often UPC consumer panels are combined with high-technology television broadcasting systems to allow experimentation with different advertising messages via split-cable broadcasts or other technology.

Environmental scanning Information gathering and fact-finding that is designed to detect indications of environmental changes in their initial stages of development.

Equation A formal statement that shows the equality between two variables.

Equivalent-form method A method to establish reliability that measures the correlation between alternative instruments, designed to be as equivalent as possible, administered to the same group of subjects.

Experience survey An exploratory research technique in which individuals who are knowledgeable about a particular research problem are questioned.

Experiment A research investigation in which conditions are controlled so that an independent variable(s) can be manipulated to test a hypothesis about a dependent variable; allows evaluation of causal relationships among variables while all other variables are eliminated or controlled.

Experimental group The group of subjects exposed to the experimental treatment.

Experimental treatments Alternative manipulations of the independent variable being investigated.

Exploratory research Initial research conducted to clarify and define the nature of a problem.

External data Data created, recorded, or generated by an entity other than the researcher's organization.

External sources Sources of secondary data that are found outside the organization.

External validity The ability of an experiment to generalize beyond the experiment data to other subjects or groups in the population under study.

Extremity bias A category of response bias that results because response styles vary from person to person; some individuals tend to use extremes when responding to questions.

Eye camera See Eye-tracking monitor.

Eye-tracking monitor A mechanical device used to observe eye movements; also called an *eye camera.* Some eye monitors use infrared light beams to measure unconscious eye movements.

Expressive behavior A type of behavior that can be scientifically observed, such as tone of voice or facial expression.

F-statistic A test statistic that measures the ratio of one sample variance to an-other sample variance, such as the variance between groups to the variance within groups.

***F*-test (analysis of variance)** A procedure to determine whether there is more variability in the scores of one sample than in the scores of another sample.

***F*-test (regression)** A procedure to determine whether there is more variability explained by the regression or unexplained by the regression.

Face validity Professional agreement that a scale's content logically appears to accurately reflect what was intended to be measured.

Factor analysis A type of analysis used to discern the underlying dimensions or regularity in phenomena. Its general purpose is to summarize the information contained in a large number of variables into a smaller number of factors.

Factorial design An experiment that investigates the interaction of two or more independent variables on a single dependent variable.

Factor loading In factor analysis, a measure of the importance of each variable in measuring each factor.

Factor score In factor analysis, a score that represents each observation's calculated value on each factor.

Fax survey Uses fax machines as a way for respondents to receive and return questionnaires.

Feedback A reverse flow of communication that may be used to modify subsequent communication.

Field A collection of characters that represent a single type of data.

Field editing Preliminary editing by a field supervisor on the same day as the interview to catch technical omissions, check legibility of handwriting, and clarify responses that are logically or conceptually inconsistent.

Field experiment An experiment conducted in a natural setting, where complete control of extraneous variables is not possible.

Field interviewing service A research supplier that specializes in data gathering.

Field worker An individual who is responsible for gathering data "in the field."

File A collection of related records.

Filter question A question that screens out respondents who are not qualified to answer a second question.

Fixed-alternative question A question in which the respondent is given specific, limited-alternative responses and asked to choose the one closest to his or her own viewpoint.

Focus group interview An unstructured, free-flowing interview with a small group of people.

Follow-up A letter or postcard reminder requesting that the respondent return the questionnaire.

Foot-in-the-door compliance technique A technique to obtain a high response rate; compliance with a large or difficult task is induced by obtaining the respondent's compliance with an earlier, smaller request.

Forced-choice rating scale A fixed-alternative rating scale that requires respondents to choose one of the fixed alternatives.

Forecast analyst The person who provides technical assistance such as running a computer analysis to forecast sales.

Forward linkage A term implying that the early stages of the research process will influence the design of the later stages.

Frequency-determination question A fixed-alternative question that asks for an answer about the general frequency of occurrence.

Frequency distribution Organizing a set of data by summarizing the number of times a particular value of a variable occurs.

Frequency table The arrangement of statistical data in a row-and-column format that exhibits the count of responses or observations for each category assigned to a variable.

Funnel technique A procedure whereby general questions are asked before specific questions to obtain unbiased responses.

Global Information System An organized collection of computer hardware, software, data, and personnel designed to capture, store, update, manipulate, analyze, and immediately display information about worldwide business activity.

Graphic aids Pictures or diagrams used to clarify complex points or emphasize a message.

Graphic rating scale A measure of attitude that allows respondents to rate an object by choosing any point along a graphic continuum.

Guinea pig effect An effect on the results of an experiment caused by subjects changing their normal behavior or attitudes in order to cooperate with an experimenter.

Hawthorne effect An unintended effect on the results of a research experiment caused by the subjects knowing that they are participants.

Hidden observation A situation in which the subject is unaware that observation is taking place.

History effect The loss of internal validity caused by specific events in the external environment occurring between the first and second measurements that are beyond the control of the experimenter.

Hypothesis An unproven proposition or supposition that tentatively explains certain facts or phenomena; a proposition that is empirically testable, a probable answer to a research question.

Hypothesis test of a proportion Conceptually similar to hypothesis testing when the mean is the characteristic of interest but, mathematically, the formulation of the standard error of the proportion differs.

Hypothetical construct A variable that is not directly observable but is measured by an indirect means, such as verbal expression or overt behavior.

Iceberg principle The principle indicating that the dangerous part of many marketing problems is neither visible to nor understood by marketing managers.

Image profile A graphic representation of semantic differential data for competing brands, products, or stores to highlight comparisons.

Independent variable (1) A variable that is expected to influence a dependent variable. (2) In an experimental design, the variable that can be manipulated, changed, or altered independently of any other variable.

Index measure A composite measure of several variables to measure a single concept; a multi-item instrument.

Index number Score or observation recalibrated to indicate how it relates to a base number.

Index of retail saturation A calculation that describes the relationship between retail demand and supply.

Inferential statistics Statistics used to make inferences or judgments about a population on the basis of a sample.

Information A body of facts that are in a format suitable for decision making or in a context that defines the relationship between two pieces of data.

Informed consent Notion that suggests the individual understands the reason for the research and waives his or her right to privacy when he or she agrees to participate in the research study.

In-house editing A rigorous editing job performed by a centralized office staff.

In-house interviewer A field-worker who is employed by the company conducting the research.

Instrument A data collection form, such as a questionnaire, or other measuring device.

Instrumentation effect An effect on the results of an experiment caused by a change in the wording of questions, interviewers, or other procedures to measure the dependent variable.

Interaction effect The influence on a dependent variable by combinations of two or more independent variables.

Intercept An intercepted segment of a line. The point at which a regression line intersects the *Y*-axis.

Interdependence methods A category of multivariate statistical techniques; interdependence methods give meaning to a set of variables or seek to group things together.

Internal consistency A dimension of reliability that concerns the degree of consistency among items in a multiple-item measure.

Internal and proprietary data Secondary data that originate inside the organization.

Internal records and reports system A data collection and retrieval system that establishes orderly procedures to ensure that recurrent data are routinely collected, entered, and stored in the computer.

Internal validity The ability of an experiment to answer the question of whether an experimental treatment was the sole cause of changes in a dependent variable or whether the experimental manipulation did what it was supposed to do.

Internet survey Survey in which a computer user navigates to a particular Web site where questions are displayed.

Interpretation The process of making pertinent inferences and drawing conclusions concerning the meaning and implications of a research investigation.

Interquartile range The range that encompasses the middle 50 percent of the observations.

Interval scale A scale that both arranges objects according to their magnitudes and also distinguishes this ordered arrangement in units of equal intervals.

Interviewer bias A response bias that occurs because the presence of the interviewer influences answers.

Interviewer cheating The practice of filling in fake answers or falsifying interviews by field-workers.

Interviewer error Mistakes made by interviewers when performing their tasks.

Introduction section The part of the body of the report that discusses background information and the specific objectives of the research.

Item nonresponse The technical term for an unanswered question on an otherwise complete questionnaire.

Judgment (purposive) sampling A nonprobability sampling technique in which an experienced researcher selects the sample based on personal judgment about some appropriate characteristic of the sample member.

Laboratory experiment An experiment conducted in a laboratory or other artificial setting to obtain almost complete control over the research setting.

Latin square design A balanced, two-way classification scheme that attempts to control or block out the effect of two or more extraneous factors by restricting randomization with respect to the row and column effects.

Leading question A question that suggests or implies certain answers.

Least-squares method A method of regression analysis that attempts to ensure that a straight line will be the most representative of the relationship between two variables; the line generated minimizes the sum of squared deviations of actual values from the predicted regression line.

Likert scale A measure of attitudes designed to allow respondents to rate how strongly they agree or disagree with carefully constructed statements; several scale items ranging from very positive to very negative toward an attitudinal object may be used to form a summated index.

Line graph A graphic aid that shows the relationship of one variable to another. The dependent variable generally is shown on the vertical axis and the independent variable on the horizontal axis.

Loaded question A question that suggests socially desirable answers or is emotionally charged.

Longitudinal study A survey of respondents at different points in time, thus allowing analysis of changes over time.

Mailing list A list giving the names, addresses, and phone numbers of specific populations.

Mail survey A self-administered questionnaire sent to respondents through the mail.

Main effect The influence of a single independent variable on a dependent variable.

Mall intercept interview A personal interview conducted in a shopping mall or other high-traffic area.

Managerial action standard A statement about an objective in measurable terms, such as level of performance.

Manager of customer quality research The person who specializes in conducting surveys to measure consumers' satisfaction and their perceptions of product quality.

Manager of decision support systems The person who supervises the collection and analysis of sales data.

Marginals Row and column totals in a contingency table.

Market penetration The percentage of potential customers who make at least one trial purchase.

Market tracking The observation and analysis of trends in industry volume and brand share over time.

Marketing concept The marketing philosophy that stresses consumer orientation, emphasizes long-range profitability, and suggests the integration of marketing and other organizational functions.

Marketing information system (MIS) An organized set of procedures and methods to continually gather, sort, analyze, evaluate, store, and distribute pertinent, timely, and accurate information for decision making. *See also* Decision support system.

Marketing intelligence system A data collection system that consists of a network of sources and regular procedures to obtain everyday information about developments in the external marketing environment.

Marketing research (1) The systematic and objective process of generating information to aid in making marketing decisions. (2) The function that links the consumer, customer, and public to the marketer through information—information used to identify and define marketing opportunities and problems; generate, refine, and evaluate marketing actions; monitor marketing performance; and improve understanding of marketing as a process. Marketing research specifies the information required to address these issues; designs the method for collecting the information; manages and implements the data collection process; analyzes the results; and communicates the findings and their implications.

Matching A procedure for the assignment of subjects to groups that ensures each group of respondents is matched on the basis of pertinent characteristics.

Maturation effect An effect on the results of an experiment caused by experimental subjects maturing or changing over time.

Mean A measure of central tendency; the arithmetic average.

Measure A quantitative result; an estimate of the dimensions, extent, or capacity of something.

Measures of association A general term that refers to a number of bivariate statistical techniques used to measure the strength of a relationship between two variables.

Median A measure of central tendency that is the midpoint, the value below which half the values in a distribution fall.

Mixed-mode survey A survey that combines two different survey modes, such as telephone and mail, to collect data.

Mode A measure of central tendency; the value that occurs most often.

Model A representation of a system or process. A decision-making aid that represents or copies a behavior or process and draws actionable knowledge from sets of data.

Model building Involves using secondary data to help specify relationships between two or more variables. Model building can involve the development of descriptive or predictive equations.

Moderator The person who leads a focus group discussion.

Moderator variable A third variable that, when introduced into an analysis, alters or has a contingent effect on the relationship between an independent variable and a dependent variable.

Monadic rating scale Any measure of attitudes that asks respondents about a single concept in isolation.

Mortality (sample attrition) effect A sample bias that results from the withdrawal of some subjects from the experiment before it is completed.

Multidimensional scaling A statistical technique that measures objects in multidimensional space on the basis of respondents' similarity judgments of objects.

Multiple-grid question Several similar questions arranged in a grid format.

Multiple regression analysis An analysis of association that simultaneously investigates the effect of two or more independent variables on a single, interval-scaled dependent variable.

Multistage area sampling Sampling that involves using a combination of two or more probability sampling techniques.

Multivariate analysis of variance (MANOVA) A statistical technique that provides a simultaneous significance test of mean difference between groups for two or more dependent variables.

Multivariate statistical analysis Statistical methods that allow the simultaneous investigation of more than two variables.

Nominal scale A scale in which the numbers or letters assigned to the object serve as labels for identification or classification.

Nonforced-choice rating scale A fixed-alternative rating scale that provides a "no opinion" category or that allows the respondents to indicate that they cannot say which alternative is their choice.

Nonparametric statistics Statistical procedures that utilize nominal- or ordinal-scaled data and make no assumptions about the distribution of the population.

Nonprobability sampling A sampling technique in which units of the sample are selected on the basis of personal judgment or convenience; the probability of any particular member of the population being chosen is unknown.

Nonrespondent A person who is not contacted or who refuses to cooperate in the research.

Nonresponse error The statistical differences between a survey that includes only those who responded and a perfect survey that would also include those who failed to respond.

Nonsampling error. See Systematic error.

Normal distribution A symmetrical, bell-shaped distribution that describes the expected probability distribution of many chance occurrences.

Not-at-home A person who is not at home on the first or second attempt at contact.

Null hypothesis A statement about a status quo that .asserts that any change from what has been thought to be true will be due entirely to random sampling error.

Numerical scale An attitude rating scale similar to a semantic differential except that it uses numbers as response options instead of verbal descriptions to identify response positions.

Observation The systematic process of recording the behavioral patterns of people, objects, and occurrences without questioning or otherwise communicating with them.

Observer bias A distortion of measurement resulting from the cognitive behavior or actions of the witnessing observer.

One-group pretest–posttest design A quasi-experimental design in which the subjects in the experimental group are measured before and after the treatment is administered, but there is no control group.

One-shot design An after-only design in which a single measure is recorded after the treatment is administered.

Open-ended response question A question that poses some problem and asks the respondent to answer in his or her own words.

Operational definition An explanation that gives meaning to a concept by specifying the activities or operations necessary to measure it.

Optical scanning system A data processing input device that directly reads material from mark sensed questionnaires.

Optimal allocation (stratified sampling) A stratified sampling procedure in which both the size and the variation of each stratum are considered.

Oral presentation A verbal summary of the major findings, conclusions, and recommendations given to clients or line managers to provide them with the opportunity to clarify any ambiguous issues by asking questions.

Order bias Bias caused by the influence of earlier questions in a questionnaire or by an answer's position in a set of alternative answers.

Ordinal scale A scale that arranges objects or alternatives according to their magnitude in an ordered relationship.

Outlier A value that lies outside the normal range of a set of data.

Paired comparison   A measurement technique that consists of presenting the respondent with two objects and asking the respondent to pick the preferred object. Two or more objects may be presented, but comparisons are made in pairs.

Panel study   A longitudinal study that involves collecting data from the same sample of individuals over time.

Parameter   A variable or measured characteristic of a population.

Parametric statistics   Statistical procedures that utilize interval- or ratio-scaled data and assume population or sampling distributions with normal distributions.

Percentage   A part of a whole expressed in hundreds; a proportion.

Percentage distribution   The organization of a frequency distribution into a table (or graph) that summarizes percentage values associated with particular values of a variable.

Performance-monitoring research   Research that regularly, sometimes routinely, provides feedback for evaluation and control of marketing activity.

Periodicity   A problem that occurs in systematic sampling when the original list has a systematic pattern.

Personal interview   A survey that gathers information through face-to-face contact with individuals.

Physical actions   A type of behavior that can be scientifically observed, such as shopping patterns or television viewing.

Physical-trace evidence   A visible mark of some past occurrence.

Picture frustration   A version of the TAT that uses a cartoon drawing in which the respondent suggests dialogue in which the characters might engage.

Pie chart   A graphic aid that shows the composition of some total quantity at a particular time; each angle, or "slice," is proportional to its percentage of the whole.

Pilot study   A collective term for any small-scale exploratory research technique that uses sampling but does not apply rigorous standards.

Pivot question   A filter question used to determine which version of a second question will be asked.

Plug value   An answer to an item non-response that an editor "plugs in" to permit completion of the data analysis;

choice of value is based on a predetermined decision rule.

Point estimate   An estimate of the population mean using a single value, usually the sample mean.

Pooled estimate of the standard error   An estimate of the standard error for a *t*-test of independent means that assumes the variances of both groups are equal.

Population (universe)   Any complete group of entities that share some common set of characteristics.

Population distribution   A frequency distribution of the elements of a population.

Population element   An individual member of a population.

Population parameters   The variables in a population or measured characteristics of the population.

Posttest-only control group design   An after-only design in which the experimental group is tested after exposure to the treatment and the control group is tested at the same time without having been exposed to the treatment; no pre-measure is taken.

Predictive validity   A classification of criterion validity whereby a new measure predicts a future event or correlates with a criterion measure administered at a later time.

Preliminary tabulation   Tabulating the results of a pretest to help determine whether the questionnaire will meet the objectives of the research.

Pretesting   Administering a questionnaire to a small group of respondents to detect ambiguity or bias in the questions or to iron out fundamental problems in the instructions or administrative procedures.

Pretest–posttest control group design   A true experimental design in which the experimental group is tested before and after exposure to the treatment and the control group is tested at the same two times without being exposed to the experimental treatment.

Primary sampling unit (PSU)   A term used to designate a unit selected in the first stage of sampling.

Probability   The long-run relative frequency with which an event will occur.

Probability distribution   A distribution, that is a complete listing, of all possible outcomes and their probabilities.

Probability sampling   A sampling technique in which every member of the population will have a known, nonzero probability of selection.

Probing   The verbal prompts made by an interviewer when the respondent must be motivated to communicate his or her answer more fully. Probes are necessary to get respondents to enlarge on, clarify, or explain answers.

Problem definition   The indication of a specific marketing decision area that will be clarified by answering some research questions.

Problem definition stage   The stage of the marketing research process in which management seeks to identify a clear-cut statement of the problem or opportunity.

Production coding   The physical activity of transferring the data from the questionnaire or data collection form after the data have been collected.

Program strategy   The overall plan to conduct a series of marketing research projects; a planning activity that places each marketing project into the company's marketing plan.

Projective technique   An indirect means of questioning that enables a respondent to project beliefs and feelings onto a third party, onto an inanimate object, or into a task situation.

Proportion   The percentage of elements that successfully meet some criterion.

Proportional stratified sample   A stratified sample in which the number of sampling units drawn from each stratum is in proportion to the relative population size of that stratum.

Proposition   A theoretical statement that is concerned with the relationships among concepts; asserts a universal connection between events that have certain properties.

Proprietary marketing research   A data collection system that gathers new data to investigate specific problems.

Pseudo-research   Activities that appear to be research but are conducted for the purposes of organizational politics rather than objective gathering of information.

Psychogalvanometer   A device that measures galvanic skin response, a measure of involuntary changes in the electrical resistance of the skin.

Pupilometer   A mechanical device used to observe and record changes in the diameter of a subject's pupils.

Push technology A term referring to an Internet information technology that automatically delivers content to the researchers or manager's desktop.

Quasi-experimental design A research design that cannot be classified as a true experiment because it lacks adequate control of extraneous variables.

Quota sampling A nonprobability sampling procedure that ensures that various subgroups of a population will be represented on pertinent characteristics to the exact extent that the investigator desires.

Random digit dialing A method of obtaining a representative sample in a telephone interview by using random numbers to generate telephone numbers.

Random error An error that occurs because of chance statistical fluctuation in which repetitions of the basic experiment sometimes favor one experimental condition and sometimes the other. *See also* Random sampling error.

Randomization A procedure in which the assignment of subjects and treatments to groups is based on chance.

Randomized block design An extension of the completely randomized design in which a single extraneous variable that might affect test units' response to the treatment has been identified and the effects of this variable are isolated by blocking out its effects.

Randomized response questions A research procedure for dealing with sensitive topics that uses a random procedure to determine which of two questions a respondent will be asked to answer.

Random sampling error The difference between the result of a sample and the result of a census conducted using identical procedures; a statistical fluctuation that occurs because of chance variations in the elements selected for a sample.

Range The distance between the smallest and largest values of a frequency distribution.

Ranking A measurement task that requires respondents to rank order a small number of stores, brands, or objects in overall preference or on the basis of some characteristic of the stimulus. Also called *rank ordering*.

Rank ordering See Ranking.

Rating A measurement task that requires respondents to estimate the magnitude of a characteristic or quality that a brand, store, or object possesses.

Ratio scale A scale that has absolute rather than relative quantities and an absolute zero where there is an absence of a given attribute.

Recoding Using a computer to convert original codes used for raw data to codes that are more suitable for analysis.

Record A collection of related fields.

Refusal A person who is unwilling to participate in the research.

Region of rejection An area under a curve with values that are very unlikely to occur if the null hypothesis is true, but relatively probable if the alternative hypothesis is true.

Regression (bivariate) analysis A technique that attempts to predict the values of a continuous, interval-scaled dependent variable from the specific values of the independent variable.

Reliability The degree to which measures are free from random error and therefore yield consistent results.

Repeatability A dimension of reliability that concerns whether a test conducted under conditions similar to a previous administration yields similar results.

Repeated measures A situation that occurs when the same subjects are exposed to all experimental treatments to eliminate any problems due to subject differences.

Repeat-purchase rate The percentage of purchasers who make a second or repeat purchase.

Report format The makeup or arrangement of parts that are necessary to a good research report.

Research analyst The person responsible for client contact, project design, preparation of proposals, selection of research suppliers, and supervision of data collection, analysis, and reporting activities.

Research assistant The person who provides technical assistance with questionnaire design, analysis of data, and so on.

Research design A master plan that specifies the methods and procedures for collecting and analyzing needed information.

Research design stage The stage in the marketing research process in which the researcher determines a framework for the research plan of action by selecting a basic research method.

Research follow-up Recontacting decision makers and/or clients after they have had a chance to read over the research report to determine whether the researchers need to provide additional information or clarify some issues that may concern management.

Research generalist The person who serves effectively as a communication link between management and the research specialist because he or she understands the needs of both parties.

Research methodology section The part of the body of the report that explains the research design, sampling procedures, and other technical procedures used for collecting the data.

Research objective The researcher's version of the marketing problem; it explains the purpose of the research in measurable terms and defines standards for what the research should accomplish.

Research proposal A written statement of the research design that includes a statement explaining the purpose of the study and a detailed, systematic outline of procedures associated with a particular research methodology.

Research report An oral presentation or written statement of research results, strategic recommendations, and/or other conclusions to a specific audience.

Research report summary A summary of a research report that contains (1) objectives of the research, (2) results, (3) conclusions, and (4) recommendations.

Research sophistication A stage in which managers have considerable experience in the proper use of research techniques.

Research supplier A commercial marketing research service that conducts marketing research activity for clients. The marketing research supplier may be thought of as a marketing research consulting company.

Residual The difference between the actual value of the dependent variable and the estimated value of the dependent variable in the regression equation.

Respondent The person who verbally answers an interviewer's questions or provides answers to written questions.

Respondent error A classification of sample biases resulting from some respondent action or inaction such as nonresponse or response bias.

Response bias A bias that occurs when respondents tend to answer questions in a certain direction that consciously or unconsciously misrepresents the truth.

Response latency The amount of time necessary to make a choice between two alternatives; used as a measure of the strength of preference.

Response rate The number of questionnaires returned or completed divided by the total number of eligible people who were contacted or requested to participate in the survey.

Results section The part of the body of the report that presents the findings of the project. It includes tables, charts, and an organized narrative.

Reverse directory A directory similar to a telephone directory except that listings are by city and street address and/or phone number rather than by alphabetical order of surnames.

Role-playing technique A projective technique that requires the subject to act out someone else's behavior in a particular setting.

Rotation In factor analysis, a new solution with more or fewer factors obtained by rotating the axes representing the factors.

Sample A subset or some part of a longer population.

Sample attrition See Mortality effect.

Sample bias A persistent tendency for the results of a sample to deviate in one direction from the true value of the population parameter.

Sample distribution A frequency distribution of a sample.

Sample selection error An administrative error caused by improper sample design or sampling procedure execution.

Sample size The number of sampling units in a study. The size of a sample specified by (1) the estimated variance of the population, (2) the magnitude of acceptable error, and (3) the confidence level.

Sample statistics Variables in a sample or measures computed from sample data.

Sample survey See Survey.

Sampling The process of using a small number of items or parts of a larger population to make conclusions about the whole population.

Sampling distribution See Sampling distribution of the mean.

Sampling distribution of the mean A theoretical probability distribution of sample means for all possible samples of a certain size drawn from a particular population.

Sampling error See random sampling error.

Sampling frame A list of elements from which a sample may be drawn; also called *working population.*

Sampling frame error An error that occurs when certain sample elements are not listed or are not accurately represented in the sampling frame.

Sampling interval In systematic sampling, the number of names on the sampling frame between sampling units.

Sampling stage The stage in the marketing research process in which the researcher determines who is to be sampled, how large a sample is needed, and how sampling units will be selected. *See also* data gathering stage.

Sampling unit A single element or group of elements subject to selection in the sample.

Scale Any series of items that are progressively arranged according to value or magnitude; a series into which an item can be placed according to its quantification.

Scanner-based consumer panel A type of consumer panel in which the participants' purchasing habits are recorded with a laser scanner rather than a purchase diary.

Scanner data Product and brand sales data obtained by using optical character recognition scanners in retail stores.

Scientific method Systematic techniques or procedures used to analyze empirical evidence in an unbiased attempt to confirm or disprove prior conceptions.

Secondary data Data that have been previously collected for a project other than the one at hand.

Secondary sampling unit A term used to designate a unit selected in the second stage of sampling.

Selection effect A sample bias that results from differential selection of respondents for the comparison groups.

Self-administered questionnaire A questionnaire, such as a mail questionnaire, that is read and filled in by the respondent rather than by the interviewer.

Self-selection bias A bias that occurs because people who feel strongly about a subject are more likely to respond than people who feel indifferent about it.

Semantic differential A measure of attitudes that consists of a series of 7-point rating scales that use bipolar adjectives to anchor the beginning and end of each scale.

Sensitivity A measurement instrument's ability to accurately measure variability in stimuli or responses.

Sentence completion method A projective technique in which respondents are required to complete a number of partial sentences with the first word or phrase that comes to mind.

Significance level The critical probability in choosing between the null and alternative hypotheses; the probability level that is too low to warrant support of a null hypothesis.

Simple-dichotomy question A fixed-alternative question that requires the respondent to choose one of two dichotomous alternatives. Also called a *dichotomous-alternative question.*

Simple random sampling A sampling procedure that assures each element in the population of an equal chance of being included in the sample.

Simulated test market A research laboratory in which the traditional shopping process is compressed into a short time span. Computer models are used to predict sales.

Single source data Diverse types of data offered by a single company. The data is usually integrated by a common variable such as geographic area or store.

Site analysis techniques Involves use of secondary data to select the best location for retail or wholesale operations.

Situation analysis The informal gathering of background information to familiarize researchers or managers with the decision area.

Slope The inclination of a regression line as compared to a base line. Rise (vertical distance) over run (horizontal distance).

Snowball sampling A sampling procedure in which initial respondents are selected by probability methods and additional respondents are obtained from information provided by the initial respondents.

Social desirability bias Bias in responses caused by respondents' desire, either conscious or unconscious, to gain prestige or appear in a different social role.

Societal norms Codes of behavior adopted by a group that suggest what a member of a group ought to do under given circumstances.

Solomon four-group design A true experimental design that combines the pretest–posttest with control group and the posttest-only with control group designs, thereby providing a means for controlling the interactive testing effect and other sources of extraneous variation.

Sorting A measurement task that presents a respondent with several objects or with information typed on cards and requires the respondent to arrange the objects or cards into a number of piles or otherwise classify the product concepts.

Spatial relations and locations Physical distance or other physical patterns studied in scientific observation, such as traffic counts.

Split-ballot technique Using two alternative phrasings of the same question for respective halves of the sample to yield a more accurate total response than will a single phrasing.

Split-half method A method for assessing reliability that measures the degree of internal consistency by checking the results of one-half of a set of scaled items against the results from the other half.

Spurious relationship An apparent relationship between two variables that is not authentic.

Standard deviation A quantitative index of a distribution's spread or variability; the square root of the variance for distribution.

Standard error of the mean The standard deviation of the sampling distribution.

Standardized normal curve See Standardized normal distribution.

Standardized normal distribution A purely theoretical probability distribution that reflects a specific normal curve for the standardized value, Z. A normal curve with a mean of 0 and a standard deviation of 1.

Standardized research service A research organization that has developed a unique methodology for investigating a specialty area, such as advertising effectiveness.

Stapel scale A measure of attitudes that consists of a single adjective in the center of an even-number range of numerical values.

Static group design An after-only design in which subjects in the experimental group are measured after being exposed to the experimental treatment; no premeasure is taken.

Stratified sampling A probability sampling procedure in which simple random subsamples are drawn from within each stratum that are more or less equal on some characteristic.

Structured question A question that imposes a limit on the number of allowable responses.

Survey A method of primary data collection in which information is gathered by communicating with a representative sample of people.

Syndicated service A marketing research supplier that provides standardized information for many clients.

Systematic (nonsampling) error Error resulting from some imperfect aspect of the research design, such as mistakes in sample selection, sampling frame error, or nonresponses from persons not contacted or refusing to participate.

Systematic sampling A sampling procedure in which a starting point is selected by a random process and then every nth number on the list is selected.

***t*-distribution** A symmetrical, bell-shaped distribution that is contingent on sample size. It has a mean of zero and a standard deviation equal to one.

***t*-test** A univariate hypothesis test that uses the *t*-distribution rather than the Z-distribution. It is used when the population standard deviation is unknown and the sample size is small.

***t*-test for difference of means** A technique used to test the hypothesis that the mean scores on some interval- or ratio-scaled variable will be significantly different for two independent samples or groups.

Table A graphic aid generally used for presenting numerical information, especially when several pieces of information can be systematically arranged in rows and columns.

Tabulation The orderly arrangement of data in a table or other summary format.

Tachistoscope A device that controls the amount of time a visual image is exposed to a subject.

Telephone interview A survey that gathers information through telephone contact with individuals.

Telephone survey The data collection method that utilizes telephone interviewing to collect the data.

Television monitoring Computerized mechanical observation used to obtain television ratings.

Temporal patterns In scientific observation, the length of time for an act or event to occur, such as amount of time spent shopping or driving.

Tertiary sampling unit A term used to designate a unit selected in the third stage of sampling.

Testing effect The effect of pretesting in a before-and-after study, which may sensitize respondents or subjects when taking a test for the second time, thus affecting internal validity.

Test marketing A scientific testing and controlled experimental procedure that provides an opportunity to measure sales or profit potential for a new product or to test a new marketing plan under realistic marketing conditions.

Test-retest method A method to measure reliability, administering the same scale or measure to the same respondents at two separate points in time to test for stability.

Test of difference An investigation of a hypothesis that states that two (or more) groups differ with respect to measures on a variable.

Test tabulation During the coding process a small sample of the total number of replies to a particular question are tallied to construct coding categories.

Test unit A subject (or entity) whose responses to experimental treatments are being observed or measured.

Thematic apperception test (TAT) A projective technique that presents a series of pictures to research subjects and asks them to provide a description of or a story about the pictures.

Theory A coherent set of general propositions used to explain the apparent relationships among certain observed phenomena. Theories allow generalizations *beyond* individual facts or situations.

Third-person technique A projective technique in which the respondent is asked why a third person does what he or she does or what a third person thinks about a product. The respondent is expected to transfer his or her attitudes to the third person.

Thurstone scale An attitude measure in which judges assign scale values to the attitudinal statements and subjects are asked to respond to these statements.

Time series design An experimental design used when experiments are conducted over long periods of time. It allows researchers to distinguish between temporary and permanent changes in dependent variables.

Total quality management A business philosophy stressing that management must focus on implementing customer-driven quality throughout the organization. It stresses continuous quality improvement.

Total variance The sum of within-group variance and between-group variance.

Tracking study A type of longitudinal study that uses successive samples to compare trends and identify changes in variables such as consumer satisfaction, brand image, or advertising awareness.

Type I error An error with the probability of alpha; an error caused by rejecting the null hypothesis when it is true.

Type II error An error with the probability of beta; an error caused by failing to reject the null hypothesis when the alternative hypothesis is true.

Unbalanced rating scale A fixed-alternative rating scale that has more response categories piled up at one end and an unequal number of positive and negative categories.

Undisguised question A straight-forward question that assumes the respondent is willing to answer.

Univariate statistical analysis Analysis that assesses the statistical significance of a hypothesis about a single variable.

Unstructured question A question that does not restrict the respondents' answers.

User interaction system Computer software written to manage the interface between the user and the system.

Validity The ability of a scale to measure what was intended to be measured.

Variable Anything that may assume different numerical values.

Variance A measure of dispersion; the sum of squared deviation scores divided by sample size minus one.

Verbal behavior A type of behavior that can be scientifically observed, such as sales conversations.

Verbal records Records used in scientific observation, such as content of advertisements.

Verification The quality control procedures in fieldwork to ensure that interviewers are following the sampling procedures and to determine whether interviewers are cheating.

Virtual-reality simulated test market An experiment that attempts to reproduce the atmosphere of an actual retail store with visually compelling images appearing on a computer screen.

Visible observation A situation in which the observer's presence is known to the subject.

Voice-pitch analysis A physiological measurement technique that records abnormal frequencies in the voice that are supposed to reflect emotional reactions to various stimuli.

Word association test A projective technique in which the subject is presented with a list of words, one at a time, and asked to respond with the first word that comes to mind.

Z-test A univariate hypothesis test using the standardized normal distribution, which is the distribution of Z.

Z-test for differences of proportions When the observed statistic is a proportion, this technique is used to test the hypothesis that the two proportions will be significantly different for two independent samples or groups.

Endnotes

Chapter 1

[1]Louise Kramer, "On the Run" *Advertising Age,* August 24, 1998, pp. 1, 35.

[2]Judann Ollack, "Sara Lee Urges Daily Indulgence in $15 Mil Effort," *Advertising Age,* October 19, 1998, pp. 1, 6.

[3]Carol Vogel, "Dear Museumgoer: What Do You Think?" *New York Times,* December 20, 1992, pp. 1-H, 32-H.

[4]Michelle Keyo, "Web Site of the Week: Jelly Belly: Using Sampling to Build a Customer Database," Inc. Online, December 9, 1996.

[5]Stephanie Thompson, "Food for What Ails You," *Brandweek,* May 4, 1998, p. 38.

[6]Louise Kramer, "Pepsi Moves New Storm into Broad Battfield," *Advertising Age,* July 13, 1998, pp. 1, 40.

[7]John C. Maxwell Jr., "Specialty Coffee Brews Gain as Total Sales Fall," *Advertising Age,* June 5, 1995, p. 45.

[8]"Sunday," *The New York Times Magazine,* April 23, 1995, p. 16.

[9]Adapted from Elena Bowes, "From Cookies to Appliances, PanEuro Efforts Build," *Advertising Age,* June 22, 1992, p. I–29.

[10]American Marketing Association, Report of the Committee on Definitions of Marketing Research, 1987.

[11]Adapted from the definition of research in American Marketing Association, Committee on Definitions, *Marketing Definition: A Glossary of Marketing Terms* (Chicago: American Marketing Association, 1960), p. 17; American Marketing Association, Report of the Committee on Definitions of Marketing Research, 1987. the official AMA definition is as follows: "Marketing research is the function which links the consumer, customer, and public to the marketer through information—informati on used to identify and define marketing opportunities and problems; generate, refine, and evaluate marketing actions; monitor marketing performance; and improve understanding of marketing as a process. Marketing research specifies the information required to address these issues; designs the method for collecting the information; manages and implements the data collection process; analyze the results; and communicates the findings and their implications."

[12]For discussions on this issue, see George Day, "The Capabilities of Market-Driven Organizations," *Journal of Marketing,* October 1994, pp. 37–52; John C. Narver and Stanley F. Slater, "The Effect of Marketing Orientation on Business Profitability," *Journal of Marketing,* October 1990, pp. 20–35; A. K. Kohli and B. J. Jaworski, "Marketing Orientation: The Construct, Research Proposition, and Managerial Implications," *Journal of Market ing,* 1990 (2), 1–18; Bernard J. Jaworski and Ajay K. Koli, "Market Orientation: Antecedents and Consequences," *Journal of Marketing,* July 1993, pp. 53–70; and Stanley F. Slater and John C. Narver, "Does Competitive Environment Moderate the Market Orientation-Performance Relationship?" *Journal of Marketing,* January 1994, pp. 46–55; Gary L. Frankwick, James C. WArd, Michael D. Hutt, and Peter H. Reingen, "Evolving Patterns of Organizational Beliefs in the Formation of Strategy," *Journal of Marketing,* April 1994, pp. 96–110; and James M. Sinkula, William E. Baker, and Thomas Noordewier, "A Framework for Market-Based Organizational Learning: Linking Values, Knowledge, and Behavior," *Journal of the Academy of Marketing Science,"* Fall 1997, pp. 305–318.

[13]Mary Kuhn and Kitty Devin, "The 1995 New Product Hit Parade," *Food Processing,* November 1, 1995.

[14]"Palmolive for Pots and Pans, *Advertising Age,* June 29, 1998 p. s14.

[15]For a more extensive discussion of this issue, see William G. Zikmund and Michael d'Amico, *Marketing* (Cincinnati: SouthWestern, 1999).

[16]"Burger King Opens Customer Hot Line," *Marketing News,* May 28, 1990, p. 7.

[17]Betsy D. Gelb and Gabriel M. Gelb, "What Research Inside the Organization Can Accomplish," *Marketing Research,* December 1991, p. 44.

[18]Adapted from Jon Berry, "The Art of Rubbermaid," *Adweek,* March 16, 1992, p. 24.

[19]G. K. Sharman, "Sessions Challenge Status Quo," *Marketing News,* November 10, 1997, p. 18.

[20]For a detailed discussion of marketing strategy and tactics, see Zikmund and d'Amico, *Marketing,* Chapter 2.

21David Schwartz, *Concept Testing: How to Test Product Ideas before You Go to Market* (New York: AMACOM, 1987), p. 91.

[22]Thomas C. Kinnear and Ann R. Root, eds, *1994 Survey of Marketing Research* (Chicago: American Marketing Association, 1995), p. 43.

[23]Aimee L. Stern, "Courting Consumer Loyalty, with Feel-Good Bond," *New York Times,* January 17, 1993, p. F–10.

[24]Adapted with permission from David Churchill, "Cabin Pressures," *Management Today,* October 1, 1994, p. 96. COPYRIGHT 1994, Management Publications Ltd. (U.K.)

[25]Karen Benezra, "Fritos Around the World," *Brandweek,* March 27, 1995, p. 32; "Chinese Chee-tos," *New York Times,* November 27, 1994, p. 31; "Chee-tos Make Debut in China But Lose Cheese in Translation," *USA Today,* September 2, 1994, p. B–1.

[26]N. Carroll Mohn, "Pricing Research for Decision Making," *Marketing Research,* Winter 1995, pp. 11–12.

[27]"Ford Tests Low-Mileage Lease," *Marketing News<I> March 27, 1995, p. 1.*

[28]Adapted with permission from Ian P. Murphy, "Ameritech Test Towns Market Innovation," *Marketing News,* November 18, 1996, p.2.

[29]A photo of Smilkster, cartoon spokesperson for Smilk, appears in Paul Lukas, "Would You Buy Milk from a Bull?" *Fortune,* April 14, 1997, p. 40.

[30]"Revised Pillsbury Spot in the Pink," *Advertising Age,* February 13, 1986, p. 15.

[31]"You Say Tomato, I Say Tomahto," *Express Magazine,* Spring 1992, p. 19.

[32]Kenneth Wylie, "100 Leading Research Companies," *Advertising Age,* May 20, 1996, p. 44.

[33]Adapted with permission from Louis E. Broone and David L. Kurtz, *Contemporary Marketing* (Ft. Worth: Dryden Press, 1995), pp.42–43.

34Adapted with permission from Jill Lieber, "Braves Bank on Future, Converted Olympic Stadium Incorporates Latest Technology," *USA Today,* April 3, 1997, p. 3c.

Chapter 2

[1]Adapted with permission from Jennifer deJony, "View from the Top," *Inc.* Technology #1, 1995, downloaded from the Internet July 3, 1998.

[2]Anne Stuart, "Five Uneasy Pieces, Part 2," *CIO Magazine,* June 1, 1996.

[3]Thomas H. Davenport and Lawrence Prusak, *Working Knowledge of How Organizations Manage What They Know* (Boston: Harvard Business School Press, 1998).

[4]Ellen M. Knapp, "Knowledge Management," *Business and Economic Review, Columbia*; July–September, 1998, pp. 3–6.

[5]http://www.cio.com/forums/knowledge.

[6]See Thomas G. Exter, "The Next Step Is Called GIS," *American Demographics Desk Reference,* May 1992.

[7]This quote appeared in H. G. Wells, *The Brain: Organization of the Modern World,* 1940.

[8]Steven Crofts, "Business Intelligence," special advertising

section, *Fortune*, October 27, 1997, p. 54.

[9]The following is a more detailed explanation of data warehousing. "Bill Inmon is often quoted and referenced for his ideas on data warehouses. . . . In Inmon's eyes a warehouse has a multi-tiered structure of data/information . . . which includes examples from employee data. Snapshots of current, detailed data from operational systems are extracted, reformatted, and loaded to the warehouse tables. These detailed data form the basis, the foundation for other layers. Then, from the detailed data can be developed one or more layers of summarized data tables (which he would call lightly summarized and highly summarized). Also, as detailed data are historically accrued in the warehouse, the older snapshots can be archived to a historical layer. Inmon also adds a supporting element of metadata—descriptions of the data and of the data transformation rules—to the mix. This descriptive/help information enables much greater understanding of the data by all warehouse users." Source: Michael Bosworth, "Rolling Out a Data Warehouse Quickly at Umass: A Simple Start to a Complex Task," *CAUSE/EFFECT* 18, no. 1, Spring 1995. See also Bill Inmon, "The Structure of the Information Warehouse," *Data Management Review*, August 1993, pp. 5–8.

[10]Adapted from "Special K Drops Thin Motels," *AP*, February 6, 1998 from the Internet.

[11]Excerpt reprinted with permission from Regis, *Real Time* (Boston: Harvard Business School Press, 1997), p. 3–4.

[12]John Markoff, "Building the Electronic Superhighway," *New York Times*, January 24, 1993, p. F-6.

[13]For an extensive listing of databases, see the annual *Gale Directory of Databases* (Detroit: Gale Research, Inc., two volumes).

[14]Patrick Thibodeau, "Online Population Estimates Differ," *Computerworld*, 1998, downloaded July 3, 1998.

[15]Thomas A. Stewart, "The Netplex: It's a New Silicon Valley," *Fortune*, March 7, 1994, p. 98.

[16]Patrick A. Moore and Ronald E. Milliman, Western Kentucky University, "Application of the Internet in Marketing Education," (paper presented to the Southwest Marketing Association, Houston, Texas, 1995).

[17]Rick Tetzeli, "The Internet and Your Business," *Fortune*, March 7, 1994, p. 92.

[18]Moore and Milliman, "Application of the Internet."

[19]Adapted with permission from Miryam Williams, "Getting to Know You," *WebMaster Magazine*, September 1996.

[20]Charles S. Parker, *Understanding Computers Today and Tomorrow* (Fort Worth, TX: Dryden Press, 1998), p. 69.

[21]Matthew Grimm, "Ford Connects," *Brandweek*, January 4, 1999, p. 19.

[22]Lee Fleming, "Digital Delivery: Pushing Content to the Desktop," downloaded from the Digital Information Group, 1997.

[23]Nicholas Negroponte, *Being Digital* (New York: Knopf, 1995), p. 6.

[24]Joshua Quittner, "Invasion of Privacy," *Time*, August 25, 1997, p. x.

[25]"Three Visions of an Electronic Future," *New York Times*, March 24, 1966, p. F-22.

[26]Paul Schneider, "Behind Company Walls: It's the Internet," *Arizona Business Gazette*, March 7, 1996.

[27]"Technology: Sun Microsystems Planning to Unveil 'Intranet' Products," *Wall Street Journal*, March 26, 1996.

[28]Donald E. L. Johnson, "Knowledge Management Is New Competitive Edge," *Health Care Strategic Management*, Chicago: July 1998, pp. 2–3.

[29]Ibid.

[30]"Three Visions of an Electronic Future," *New York Times*, March 24, 1996, p. F22.

[31]Paul Schneider, "Behind Company Walls: It's the Intranet," *Arizona Business Gazette*, March 7, 1996.

[32]Adapted with permission from Julia King, "Decision-Support Software Cuts Loan Processing Time," *ComputerWorld*, February 1996.

[33]Adapted with permission from Louis E. Boone and David L. Kurtz, *Contemporary Business*, 9th ed. (Fort Worth, TX: Dryden Press, 1999), p. 407.

Chapter 3

[1]This section is based on Richard Draft, *Management* (Hinsdale, Ill.: Dryden Press, 1994), pp. 252–255; and John R. Schermerhorn Jr., James G. Hunt, and Richard N. Osborn, *Managing Organizational Behavior* (New York: John Wiley and Sons, 1991), pp. 364–366.

[2]Jack Neff, "Kids Take Longer to Train, Diaper Business Swells," *Advertising Age*, July 20, 1998, p. 3.

[3]Adam Bryant, "Zen and the Art of Buying a Car," *The New York Times*, September 8, 1992, p. F-10.

[4]"Those Precocious 13-Year-Old Girls," *Brandweek*, January 25, 1993, p. 13.

[5]Paul E. Green, Donald S. Tull, and Gerald Albaum, *Research for Marketing Decisions* (Upper Saddle River, NJ: Prentice-Hall, 1988), pp. 105–107.

[6]Each topic is discussed in greater depth in later chapters.

[7]A. Einstein and L. Infeld, *The Evolution of Physics* (New York: Simon and Schuster, 1942), p. 95.

[8]Pretests of full-blown surveys and experiments also are considered pilot studies. These smaller versions of the formal studies generally are used to refine techniques rather than for problem definition and hypothesis clarification.

[9]Carol Vogel, "Dear Museumgoer: What Do You Think?" *The New York Times*, December 20, 1992, pp. H-1 and H-32.

[10]Adapted from Willard I. Zangwill, "Manager's Journal: When Customer Research Is a Lousy Idea," *The Wall Street Journal*, March 8, 1993, p. A12.

[11]Adapted with permission from Gerry Khermouch, "Sticking Their Neck Out," *Brandweek*, November 9, 1998, pp. 25–34.

Chapter 4

[1]Lee Adler and Charles S. Mayer, *Managing the Marketing Research Function* (Chicago: American Marketing Association, 1977), p. 18.

[2]James B. Stuart, R. J. Reynolds Tobacco Company, personal communication.

[3]Vincent P. Barabba, "Market Research Technique—What, Why, Who, Where, When, and How?" *Harvard Business Review*, June 14, 1989.

[4]Thomas C. Kinnear and Ann Root, eds., *1994 Survey of Marketing Research* (Chicago: American Marketing Association, 1995).

[5]Stuart, personal communication.

[6]John Aulino, "Will the Real Market Research Manager Stand Up?" *Marketing Review* (April 1975), p. 12. American Marketing Association, New York Chapter.

[7]Adler and Mayer, "Managing the Marketing Research Function," p. 32. Also, Steward Smith, "Research and Pseudo-research in Marketing," *Harvard Business Review* (March–April 1974), p. 76.

[8]"Push Polling Imparts Negative Spin," *Tulsa World*, May 30, 1995, p. 6.

[9]Exhibit 4.6 is based on John G. Keane, "Some Observations on Marketing Research in Top Management Decision Making," *Journal of Marketing* (October 1969), p. 14. Some other desirable skills are discussed in Joby John and Mark Needel, "Entry-Level Marketing Research Recruits: What Do Recruiters Need?" *Journal of Marketing Education* (spring 1989), pp. 68–73.

[10]Excerpts reprinted with permission from "Honomichi Global Top 25," *Marketing News*, August 17, 1998.

[11]For an alternative perspective, see Kenneth C. Schneider's excellent article "Marketing Research Industry Isn't Moving toward Professionalism," *Marketing Educator* (Winter 1984), pp. 1, 6; Steven J. Skinner, O. C. Ferrell, and Alan J. Dubinsky, "Organizational Dimensions of Marketing-Research Ethics," *Journal of Business Research* 16 (1988), pp. 209–223; Patrick E. Murphy and Gene R. Laczniak, "Traditional Ethical Issues Facing Marketing Researchers," *Marketing Research*, March 1992, pp. 8–21.

[12]Leo Bogart, "The Researcher's Dilemma," *Journal of Marketing* (January 1962), pp. 6–11.

[13]H. Keith Hunt, "The Ethics of Research in the Consumer Interests: Panel Summary," ed. by Norleen M. Ackerman, Proceedings of the American Council of Consumer Interests Conference, 1979, p. 152.

[14]Fred W. Morgan Jr., "Judicial Standards for Survey Research: An Update and Guidelines," *Journal of Marketing* (January 1990), pp. 59–70.

[15]"Consumer Demand, Not New Laws Will Protect Web Privacy," *USA Today*, July 7, 1998, p. 12A.

[16]Ibid.

[17]Adapted with permission from Bruce Horovitz, "Privacy Flap Sinks AmEx Database Deal," *USA Today*, July 15, 1998, p. b1.

[18]Kim H. Bayne, "Privacy Still a Business Web Issue," *Advertising Age*, June 29, 1998, p. 37.

[19]Rick Bruner, "eTRUST Patches Its Seal of Approval," *Advertising Age*, June 9, 1997.

[20]Reprinted with permission of Epicurious Food.

Chapter 5

[1]From *Preparing Instructional Objectives* by Robert F. Mager. Copyright © 1984 by David S. Lake Publishers, Belmont, CA 94002. Reprinted with permission.

[2]Exploring Research Issues: Adapted from Charles Ramond, *The Art of Using Science in Marketing*, p. 17. Copyright © 1974 by Charles Ramond. Reprinted by permission of Harper & Row Publishers, Inc.

[3]Russell L. Ackoff, *Scientific Method* (New York: John Wiley and Sons, 1962), p. 71.

[4]Randall G. Chapman, "Problem-Definition in Marketing Research Studies," *Journal of Marketing Research* (spring 1989), pp. 51–59. Also, Yoo S. Yang, Robert P. Leone, and Dala L. Alden, "A Market Expansion Ability Approach to Identify Potential Exporters," *Journal of Marketing* (January 1992), p. 88.

[5]Martin Weinberger, "Seven Perspectives on Consumer Research," *Marketing Research: A Magazine of Management and Applications* (December 1989), pp. 9–17.

[6]Neil Bruce Holbert, "Research: The Ways of Academe and Business," *Business Horizons* (February 1976), p. 38.

[7]Based on *A General Taxpayer Opinion Survey*, Office of Planning and Research, Internal Revenue Service, March 1980.

[8]Space restrictions do not permit us to present complete research proposals. Often entire questionnaires appear as exhibits in proposals. Students interested in additional information on writing research proposals should review Chapter 25 on writing the research report.

[9]Excerpt reprinted with permission from Paul E. Green, Abba M. Krieger and Terry G. Varra, "Evaluating New Products," *Marketing Research: A Magazine of Management and Applications* (Winter 1997), pp. 17–18.

Chapter 6

[1]Excerpt reprinted with permission from Marshall Sella, "Will a Flying Doll . . . FLY?" *The New York Times*, December 25, 1994, pp. 20–25, 40–43.

[2]Bruce Rayner, "Product Development: Now Hear This!" *Electronic Business*, August 1997.

[3]Dave Fusaro, "Food Products of the New Millennium," *Prepared Foods*, January 1, 1996.

[4]David Schwartz, *Concept Testing How to Test New Product Ideas before You Go to Market* (New York: AMA-COM, 1987), p. 57

[5]Gary Hamel and C.K. Prahalad, "Corporate Imagination and Expeditionary Marketing," *Harvard Business Review*, (July–August 1991), p. 85

[6]Excerpt reprinted with permission from Ray Burch, "Marketing Research: Why It Works, Why It Doesn't Work," speech to the Chicago American Marketing Association Chapter, 1973. Reprinted with the permission of Chicago Chapter of the American Marketing Association.

[7]*1990 Winners: The Effie Gold Awards* (New York: Amercian Marketing Association of New York/American Association of Advertising Agencies, 1990), pp. 47-48.

[8]Edward M. Tauber, "Research to Increase Sales of Existing Brands," *Business Hoizons* (April 1977), p.31.

[9]John M. Hess, "Group Interviewing," in *New Science of Planning*, ed. R.L. King (Chicago: American Marketing Association, 1968), p.194

[10]Carol Vogel, "Dear Museumgoer: What Do You Think?" *The New York Times*, December 20, 1992, p. H-1.

[11]Steve Rabin, "How to Sell across Cultures," *American Demographics*, March 1, 1994, p. 56.

[12]Excerpt reprinted with permission from Betsy D. Gelb and Michael P. Eriksen, "Market Research May Help Prevent Cancer," *Marketing Research* (September 1991), pp. 41–42.

[13]Rebecca Piirto Heather, "Future Focus Groups," *American Demographics*, January 1, 1994, p. 6.

[14]Adapted from Tibbett Speer, "Nickelodeon Puts Kids Online," *American Demographics*, January 1, 1994, p. 16.

[15]Nicholas Negroponte, "Being Anonymous," *Wired*, October 1998, p. 216.

[16]Kate Maddox, "Virtual Panels Add Real Insights for Marketers," *Advertising Age*, June 29, 1998, p. 34.

[17]The Iowa Poll, August 1977. Also, Mason Haire, "Projective Techniques in Marketing Research," *Journal of Marketing* (April 1950), pp. 649–652.

[18]Philip Kotler, "Behavioral Models for Analyzing Buyers," *Journal of Marketing* (October 1965), pp. 37–45.

[19]Liz Laurie, "Play Techniques Probe Kids' Real Feelings, Opinions of New Products," *Marketing News*, January 28, 1977, p. 2. Also, Ronald Alsop, "Advertisers Put Consumers on the Couch," *The Wall Street Journal*, May 13, 1998, p. 19.

[20]Adapted with permission from Mike Hoffman, "Hocus Pocus Focus," *INC*, July, 1998, p. 90.

[21]Excerpt reprinted from Louis E. Boone and David L. Kurtz, *Contemporary Marketing* (Fort Worth: Dryden Press, 1995), p. 279.

Chapter 7

[1]The idea for Exhibit 7.1 came from Robert W. Joselyn, *Designing the Marketing Research Project* (New York: Petrocelli/Charter, 1977).

[2]John L. Manzell, *Opportunity in Mexico: A Small Business Guide* (Buffalo: Free Trade/Small Business Association, 1992), p. 12.

[3]"Datawatch," *Advertising Age*, January 18, 1993, p. I-12.

[4]"NBA Year in Review," *Tulsa World*, October 29, 1995, p. 13.

[5]This section is based on Michael Levy and Barton Weitz, *Retail Management* (Homewood: IL, Richard D. Irwin © 1992), pp. 357–358.

[6]Lorna M. Daniells, *Business Information Sources, 3rd ed.* (Berkeley, Cal.: University of California Press, 1993); H. Webster Johnson, Anthony J. Faria, and Ernest L. Maier, "How to Use the Business Library: With Sources of Business Information" (Cincinnati: South-Western, 1984), p. 29.

[7]Please note that the Internet changes daily, and any particular URL address or instruction may not apply after the passage of time.

[8]"Going with the Grain," *Advertising Age*, September 11, 1995, p. 3.

[9]The description of the data bank is reprinted from information that can be accessed from the NTDB home page.

Chapter 8

[1]Adapted with permission from Temma Ehrenfeld, "More Power to J. D. Power," *Fortune*. © 1992, Time, Inc. All rights reserved.

[2]Farrar, Straus and Giroux, Inc. Excerpts from Michael J. Arlen,

Thirty Seconds, pp. 185–186, 1979, 1980. This material first appeared in *The New Yorker*.

[3]The popularity of marketing research has affected the willingness of respondents to participate in surveys. People are increasingly refusing to participate in surveys. Studies on survey research show that approximately three in four adult Americans have participated in some form of survey in their lives. See Walker Marketing Research, Industry Image Study: Research on Research, 1988.

[4]Sheree R. Curry, "Lunch Ain't What It Used to Be," *Fortune*, November 10, 1997, p. 286.

[5]Sheatsley, "Survey Design," in *Handbook of Marketing Research*, ed. Robert Ferber (New York: McGraw-Hill, 1974), pp. 2–66.

[6]The Literary Digest study is cited in Chapter 3.

[7]Douglas Aircraft, *Consumer Research*, p. 13.

[8]Jennifer Lawrence, "Gender-Specific Works for Diapers—Almost Too Well," *Advertising Age*, February 8, 1993, pp. S-1–S-11.

[9]See Robert J. Lavidge, "Seven Tested Ways to Abuse and Misuse Strategic Advertising Research," *Marketing Research: A Magazine of Management and Applications* (March 1990), p. 43; "VCR/VDP Market Products and Important Research Questions," *Marketing News*, January 6, 1984, p. 7. Lavidge says: "Suppose a researcher asks purchasing intention questions for an inexpensive nondurable product using answer categories as follows: 'Definitely will buy,' 'Probably will buy,' 'May or may not buy,' 'Probably will not buy,' and 'Definitely will not buy.' Based on past experience the researchers may estimate that about 80 percent of the 'definitely will buy' respondents plus 30 percent of the 'probably will buy' category will actually buy the product if it becomes available on the market."

[10]The term questionnaire technically refers only to mail and self-administered surveys, and the term *interview schedule* is used for interviews by telephone or face-to-face. However, *questionnaire* refers to all three forms of communications in this book.

[11]*Americans and the Arts: Highlights from a Survey of Public Opinion*, Research Center of the Arts, p. 14.

[12]Becky Ebencamp, "Scotchgard Will Talk to Consumers," *Brandweek*, September 21, 1998, p. 9.

[13]"Ethnic Marketing: Surveys Point to Group Differences," *Brandweek*, July 18, 1994, p. 32.

[14]Janice Castro, "Making It Better," *Time*, November 13, 1989, pp. 78–81; and David A. Gavin, "Competing on the Eight Dimensions of Quality," *Harvard Business Review* (November–December 1987), pp. 101–108.

[15]Janice Castro, pp. 78–81.

[16]*Profiles in Quality: Blueprints for Action from 50 Leading Companies* (Boston: Allyn and Bacon, 1991), p. 113.

[17]This section is based on material in Profiles in Quality, pp. 97–98.

[18]This section is based on material in Profiles in Quality, pp. 97–98.

[19]Gavin, "Eight Dimensions."

Chapter 9

[1]Donald T. Warwick and Charles A. Lininger, *The Sample Survey: Theory and Practice* (New York: McGraw-Hill, 1975), p. 2.

[2]L. C. Lockley, "Notes on the History of Marketing Research," *Journal of Marketing* (April 1950), p. 733.

[3]For a complete discussion of conducting surveys in Hispanic barrios, see Sigfredo A. Hernandes and Carol J. Kaufman, "Marketing Research in Hispanic Barrios: A Guide to Survey Research," *Marketing Research: A Magazine of Management and Applications* (March 1990), pp. 11–27.

[4]Estimate Calculating from Information in Vincent P. Barabba, "The Marketing Encyclopedia," *Harvard Business Review* (January–February 1999).

[5]Peter Tuckel and Trish Shukers, "The Answering Machine Dilemma," *Marketing Research* (Fall 1997), pp. 5–9.

[6]P. S. Tuckel and B. M. Finberg, "The Answering Machine Poses Many Questions for Telephone Survey Research," *Public Opinion Quarterly* (Summer 1991).

[7]Adapted with permission from Sally Beattie, "Ameritech's New Phone Service Aims to Keep Telemarketers at Bay," *Wall Street Journal*, September 23, 1998, p. 10.

[8]*Your Opinion counts, 1986 Refusal Rate Study* (Indianapolis, IN: Walker Marketing Research, 1986), p. 14. See also Julene M. Struebbe, B. Kernan and Thomas J. Georgan, "The Refusal Problem in Telephone Survey," *Journal of Advertising Research* (June–July 1986), pp. 29–37.

[9]Philip Meyer, "Pollsters Switch Tactics," *USA Today*, November 2, 1998, p. 19A.

[10]"Sacramento Is Top Unlisted Market," *The Frame* (February 1995) and "Sacramento Is Most Unlisted," *The Frame* (March 1997). This information can also be found at http://www.worldopinion.com.

[11]"Some Things We've Learned About Global Research," *Research International*, Advertisement from Research International, New York.

[12]For various response rate calculations, see Frederick Wiseman and Maryann Billington, "Comment on a Standard Definition of Response Rates," *Journal of Marketing Research* (August 1984), pp. 336–338. Also, the researcher may wish to take into account the possibility of respondents registering opinions twice. See Thomas J. Steele, Warren L. Schwendig, and Nina M. Ray, "Do Multi-Wave Mailings Lead to Multi-Response in Mail Surveys?" *Applied Marketing Research: A Journal for Practitioners* (Spring 1989), pp. 15–20, and Thomas J. Steele, W. Lee Schwendig, and John A. Kilpatrick, "Duplicate Responses to Multiple Survey Mailings: A Problem," *Journal of Advertising Research*, (March, 1989).

[13]Valentine Appel and Julian Baim, "Correcting Response Rate Problems," paper presented to the Advertising Research Foundation, April 1991; and "Who Slammed the Door on Research," *American Demographics* (September 1991), p. 14.

[14]For an interesting article dealing with this issue, see Michael Geurts and David Whitlark, "A Little Inducement Goes a Long Way," *Marketing Research: A Magazine of Management and Applications*, (Summer 1994), pp. 13–15.

[15]Based on the press release "PepsiCo Foods International to Introduce Lay's Potato Chips to Consumers Worldwide," *PRNewsire*, November 30, 1995.

[16]Lewis C. Winters, "International Psychographics," *Marketing Research: A Magazine of Management and Application* (September 1992), p. 48.

[17]For a complete discussion of fox surveys, see the excellent article by John P. Dickson and Douglas L. Maclachlan, "Fax Surveys: Return Patterns and Comparison with Mail Surveys," *Journal of Marketing Research* (February 1996), pp. 108–113.

[18]Bill MacElroy and Bill Geissler, "Interactive Surveys Can Be More Fun Than Traditional," *Marketing News*, October 24, 1994, pp. 4–5.

[19]Aileen Crowley, "E-Mail Surveys Elicit Fast Response, Cut Costs," *PCWeek*, January 30, 1995.

[20]Neil Postman, *Technopoly: The Surrender of Culture to Technology* (New York: Vintage Books, 1993), pp. 6–15.

[21]James P. Ronda, "Thomas Moran and the Eastern Railroads," *The Gilcrease Journal* (Spring/Summer) 1997, p. 38.

[22]Neil Postman, *Technopoly: The Surrender of Culture to Technology*. (New York: Vintage Books, 1993), pp. 6–15.

[23]For an interesting empirical study, see Ishmael P. Akaah and Edward A. Riordan, "The Incidence of Unethical Practices in Marketing Research: An Empirical Investigation," *Journal of the Academy of Marketing Sciences* (Spring 1990), pp. 143–152.

[24]Excerpts reprinted from Joe Schwartz, "Marketing the Verdict (Advantages of Jury Research)," *American Demographics*, February 1, 1993, p. 52.

Chapter 10

[1]Claire Selltiz, Lawrence S. Wrightsman, and Stuart W. Cook, *Research Methods in Social Relations* (New York: Holt, Rinehart and Winston, 1976), p. 251.

[2]Joshua Macht, "The New Market Research," *Inc.* (July 1998), pp. 92–93.

[3]Adapted with permission from the April 30, 1980 issue of *Advertising Age,* Copyright © 1980 by Crain Communications, Inc.

[4]Angus Campbell, Philip E. Converse, and Willard L. Rodgers, *The Quality of American Life* (New York: Russell Sage Foundation, 1976), p. 112. Although weather conditions did not correlate with perceived quality of life, the comfort variable did show a relationship with the index of well-being. This association might be confounded by the fact that ventilation and/or airconditioning equipment is less common in less affluent homes. Income was previously found to correlate with quality of life. Also, William Rathje and Cullen Murphy, "Garbage Demographics," *American Demographics* (May 1992) pp. 50–53.

[5]Witold Rybczynski, "We Are What We Throw Away," *New York Times Book Review,* July 5, 1992, pp. 5–6.

[6]Justin Martin, "Ignore Your Customer," *Fortune,* May 1, 1995, p. 126.

[7]"Live, Simultaneous Study of Stimulus, Response Is Physiological Measurement's Great Virtue, *Marketing News,* May 15, 1981, pp. 1, 20.

[8]"View from Research," *Advertising Age,* January 23, 1984, p. m 29. Perception Research Services, Inc.

[9]Herbert B. Krugman's statement as quoted in "Live, Simultaneous Study of Stimulus, Response Is Physiological Measurement's Greatest Virtue," *Marketing News,* May 15, 1981, p. 1.

[10]For an expanded discussion of the physiological research, see James A. Muncy, "Physiological Responses of Consumer Emotions: Theory, Methods, and Implications for Consumer Research," paper presented at the American Marketing Association Marketing Educators' Conference, 1987.

[11]Adapted with permission from Bruce Rayner, "Product development Now Hear This!" *Electronic Business,* August 1997, p. x.

[12]Edmund L. Andrews, "Delving into the Consumer Unconscious," *New York Times," July 22, 1990, p. F-9. copyright © 1990 by the New York Times Company. Reprinted by permission.*

Chapter 11

[1]Adapted with permission from Brian Wansink, "How and Why a Package's Size Influences Usage Volume," Trace Discussion Paper TI 95-1, Timgergen Instituet, Amsterdam-Rotterdam, The Netherlands. The author is a visiting professor at Wharton School, University of Pennsylvania.

[2]Anne G. Perkins, "Package Size: When Bigger Is Better," *Harvard Business Review* (March–April 1995), p. 14.

[3]See J. Edward Russo, "The Value of Unit Price Information," *Journal of Marketing Research* (May 1977), pp. 93–201; J. Edward Russo, Gene Krieser, and Sally Miyashita, "An Effective Display of Unit Price Information," *Journal of Marketing* (April 1975), pp. 11–19. The example provided in this section is a hypothetical one based on the experiments and material presented in these two articles.

[4]Vernon Ellingstad and Norman W. Heimstra, *Methods in the Study of Human Behavior* (Monterey, CA: Brooks-Cole, 1974), pp. 61–62.

[5]Barry F. Anderson, *The Psychological Experiment: An Introduction to the Scientific Method* (Belmont, CA: Brooks-Cole, 1971), p. 28.

[6]Anderson, *The Psychological Experiment*, pp. 42–44.

[7]M. Venkatesan and Robert J. Holloway, *An Introduction to Marketing Experimentation: Methods, Applications and Problems* (New York: Free Press, 1971), p. 14.

[8]See F. J. Roethlisberger and W. J. Dickson, Management and the Worker (Cambridge, MA: Harvard University Press, 1939).

[9]This section is based on Donald T. Campbell and Julian C. Stanley, *Experimental and Quasi-Experimental Designs for Research* (Chicago: Rand McNally, 1963), pp. 5–9.

[10]Based on Campbell and Stanley, p. 9.

[11]Alice M. Tybout and Gerald Zaltman, "Ethics in Marketing Research: Their Practical Relevance," *Journal of Marketing Research* (November 1974), pp. 357–368. Also, Campbell and Stanley, *Experimental and Quasi-Experimental Designs*, pp. 13–25.

[12]The term *observation* is used in the most general way. Although most marketing experiments will use some other form of measurement rather than direct observation of some dependent variable, the terminology used by Campbell and Stanley is used here because of its traditional nature.

[13]Geoffrey Lee Martin, "Drinkers Get Court Call." Reprinted with permission from the May 20, 1991, issue of *Advertising Age.* Copyright, Crain Communications, Inc., 1991.

Chapter 12

[1]Adapted with permission from Betsy Spethmann, "Test Market USA," *Brandweek*, May 8, 1995, pp. 40–41.

[2]*Market Testing Consumer Products* (New York: National Industrial Conference Board, 1967), p. 13.

[3]Timothy Harris, "Marketing Research Passes Toy Marketer Test," *Advertising Age*, August 24, 1987, p. s-8.

[4]Juliana Koranteng, "Unilever Rolls Out Persil Tablets in Europe Soup Derby," *Advertising Age*, May 4, 1998, p. 52.

[5]"Not All Products Deserve Market Testing: Barry Hull," *Marketing News*, April 20, 1979, p. 8.

[6]N. D. Cadbury, "When, Where, and How to Test Market," *Harvard Business Review* (May–June 1975), pp. 96–105.

[7]Sally Scanlon, "The True Test," *Sales and Marketing Management* (March 1979), p. 57.

[8]Judann Pollack, "Price Issues Dog Frito Olean Tests," *Advertising Age*, November 25, 1996, p. 4.

[9]Judann Pollack, "Frito Claims Success . . . ," *Advertising Age*, July 20, 1998, p. 30.

[10]This section is based on materials presented in Raymond R. Burke, "New Technology Helps Managers Envision the Future," *Harvard Business Review* (March–April 1996), pp. 120–131.

[11]Ronald E. Frank and William F. Massy, "Shelf Positions in Space Effects on Sales," *Journal of Marketing Research* (February 1970), pp. 59–66.

[12]The sample size for the experiment is intentionally small and the data are hypothetical for ease of presentation.

[13]B. J. Winer, *Statistical Principles in Experimental Design*, 2d ed. (New York: McGraw-Hill, 1971), p. 685.

Chapter 13

[1]Adapted with permission from *Advertising Age,* January 29, 1990, p. 12, Gary Levin, "Emotion Guides BBDO's Ad Tests." Copyright 1990 Crain Communications, Inc. All rights reserved.

[2]Sarah M. Dinham, *Exploring Statistics: An Introduction for Psychology and Education* (Monterey, CA: Brooks/Cole, 1976), p. 3.

[3]This definition is adapted from Fred N. Kerlinger, *Foundations of Behavioral Research* (New York: Holt, Rinehart and Winston, 1973), p. 31.

[4]Barry F. Anderson, *The Psychology Experiment* (Monterey, CA: Brooks/Cole, 1971), p. 26.

[5]Fred N. Kerlinger, *Behavioral Research: A Conceptual Approach* (New York: Holt, Rinehart and Winston, 1979), p. 41.

[6]Benjamin B. Wolman, ed., *Dictionary of Behavioral Science* (New York: Van Nostrand-Reinhold, 1973), p. 333.

[7]This example assumes a standard measure for the term *length.*

[8]Chris Wells, "The War of the Razors," *Esquire* (February 1980), p. 3.

[9]Cathy Lynn Grossman, "Passenger-Jet Designers Ponder Pie-in-the-Sky Idea," *USA Today,* April 18, 1995, p. 3D.

[10]Burke Marketing Research, *Rough Commercial Recall Testing.*

[11]Keith K. Cox and Ben M. Enis, *The Marketing Research Process* (Pacific Palisades, CA: Goodyear, 1972), pp. 353–355. Also see

Fred N. Kerlinger, *Foundations of Behavioral Research,* 3rd ed. (Fort Worth: Holt, Rinehart and Winston, 1986).

[12]Based on Lieberman Research Incorporated, *The Male Food Shopper: How Men Are Changing Food Shopping in America,* sponsored by Campbell's Soup Company and *People* magazine.

[13]Dean E. Headley, Brent D. Bowen, and Jacqueline R. Liedtke. This case, originally titled "Navigating through Airline Quality," was reviewed and accepted for publication by the Society for Case Research.

[14]Materials in this case are based on information the September 1992 issue of *Money Magazine* and from http://pathfinder.com/money/bestplaces/. Used with special permission; copyright Time, Inc.

Chapter 14

[1]Adapted with permission from "*Redbook* Survey Uncovers 'New Wife' in Ranks of Young Married Women," PointCost Network, August 21, 1996.

[2]Karen Nickel Anhalt, "Whiskas Campaign Recruits a Tiny Tiger," *Advertising Age International,* October 19, 1998, p. 41.

[3]Rensis Likert," A Technique for the Measurement of Attitudes," *Archives of Psychology* 19 (1931), pp. 44–53.

[4]Charles Osgood, George Suci, and Percy Tannenbaum, *The Measurement of Meaning* (Urbana, Ill.: University of Illinois Press, 1957). Seven-point scales were used in the original work; however, subsequent researchers have modified the scale to have five points, nine points, and so on.

[5]Dennis Menezes and Norbert F. Elbert, "Alternative Semantic Scaling Formats for Measuring Store Image: An Evaluation," *Journal of Marketing Research* (February 1979), pp. 80–87.

[6]Yoram Wind, Joseph Denny, and Arthur Cunningham, "A Comparison of Three Brand Evaluation Procedures," Public Opinion Quarterly (summer 1979), p. 263.

[7]R. H. Bruskin Associates, 303 George Street, New Brunswick, N.J. Used by permission.

Chapter 15

[1]Charles W. Roll Jr. and Albert H. Cantril, *Polls: Their Use and Misuse in Politics* (New York: Basic Books, 1972), p. 106.

[2]Stanley L. Payne, *The Art of Asking Questions* (Princeton, N.J.: Princeton University Press, 1951), pp. 8–9. The reader who wants a more detailed account of question wording is referred to this classic book on that topic.

[3]"USA Snapshots," *USA Today,* February 26, 1998, p. C1.

[4]This heading is borrowed from Payne, *The Art of Asking Questions.*

[5]Fred W. Morgan, "Judicial Standards for Survey Research: An Update and Guidelines," *Journal of Marketing* (January 1990), pp. 59–70.

[6]Payne, *The Art of Asking Questions,* p. 185.

[7]Roll and Cantril, *Polls: Use and Misuse,* pp. 106–107.

[8]The others are *relative advantage, compatibility, complexity,* and *communicability.*

[9]Payne, *The Art of Asking Questions,* pp. 102–103.

[10]This section relies heavily on Paul L. Erdos, *Professional Mail Surveys* (New York: McGraw-Hill, 1970).

[11]Philip R. Cateora, *International Marketing* (Homewood, Ill.: Richard D. Irwin, 1990), pp. 387–389.

[12]Ibid., pp. 387–389.

[13]Subhash C. Jain, *International Marketing* (Boston: PWS Kent, 1990), p. 338.

[14]Authorization for limited use granted by GTE Airfone, Incorporated.

Chapter 16

[1]Phillip R. Cateora, *International Marketing* (Homewood, Ill.: Irwin, 1990), pp. 384–385.

[2]Sabra E. Brock, "Marketing Research in Asia: Problems, Opportunities, and Lessons," *Marketing Research* (September 1989), p. 47.

[3]Excerpts adapted with permission from "Watching Americans Watch TV," *Atlantic Monthly* (March 1992), pp. 73–77.

[4]Material for this case is used with permission from Scientific Telephone Samples' *User's Manual,* Scientific Telephone Samples, Griffin Towers, 6 Hutton Center Drive, Suite 1245, Santa Ana, CA 92707.

Chapter 17

[1]Most of the statistical material in this book assumes that the population parameters are unknown, which is the typical situation in most applied research projects.

[2]Ibid.

[3]Ibid.

[4]In practice, most survey researchers will not use this exact formula. A modification of the formula, Z = ***OUTSET EQUATION MSP. 42***, using the sample standard deviation in an adjusted form, is frequently used.

[5]William L. Hayes, *Statistics* (New York: Holt, Rinehart and Winston, 1963), p. 193.

[6]Thomas H. Wonnacott and Ronald J. Wonnacott, *Introductory Statistics, 2d ed.* (New York: John Wiley & Sons, 1972), p. 125.

[7]Note that the derivation of this formula is
(1) $E = ZS$; (2) E ***OUTSET EQUATIONS MSP. 43***

[8]"How the Poll Was Conducted," *The New York Times,* December 13, 1992, p. y-19. Copyright © 1992 by The New York Times Company. Reprinted by permission.

Chapter 18

[1]Adapted with permission from Randy Minkoff, "Matters of Opinion Foot Soldiers of Marketing Research Battle for a Moment of Your Time on the Mall," *Chicago Tribune,* July 5, 1998.

[2]This section relies heavily on *Interviewer's Manual,* rev. ed. (Ann Arbor: Survey Research Center, Institute for Social Research, University of Michigan, 1976).

[3]"Census to Target American Indians," *The Associated Press,* August 6, 1998, p. xx.

[4]*Interviewer's Manual,* p. 11.

[5]*Interviewer's Manual,* pp. 11–13.

[6]This section is adapted from Yankelovich, Skelly and White, Inc., *Interviewing Handbook for Senior Council Interviewers.*

[7]G. Birch Ripley, "Confessions of an Industrial Marketing Research Executive Interviewer," Marketing News, September 10, 1976, p. 20.

[8]Alan Dutka, AMA Handbook for Customer Satisfaction (Lincolnwood, IL: NTC Business Books, 1993), p. 108.

[9]Adapted with permission from Hoya El Nasser, "The Nation's Homepage: How Sampling Would Work," *USA Today,* November 29, 1998.

Chapter 19

[1]John A. Sonquist and William C. Dunkelberg, Survey and Opinion Research: Procedures for Processing and Analysis (Englewood Cliffs, N.J.: Prentice-Hall, 1977), pp. 41–72. This is an excellent source of information about processing survey data.

Chapter 20

[1]Excerpt reprinted with permission from Judith Waldrop, "Most Restaurant Meals Are Bought on Impulse," *American Demographics,* February 1, 1994, p. 16.

[2]Bruce Horovitz, "Coke's New Marketing Chief Really Knows the Business," *USA Today,* July 13, 1998, p. 7B.

[3]Lynn Woods, "Where the Breakers Are," *American Demographics*, March 1999, p. 50.
[4]Adapted from David Schwartz, *Concept Testing* (New York: AMACOM, 1987), pp. 80–81.
[5]Alternative methods may be used to determine the quadrants. They will not be discussed here.
[6]Todd Lapin, "Wiretap Nation," *Wired* (August 1998), p. 88. Also, Bill Iuso, "Concept Testing: An Appropriate Approach," *Journal of Marketing Research* (May 1975), p. 230. Published by the American Marketing Association.
[7]Adapted with permission from Melvin Prince, Consumer Research for Management Decisions (New York: John Wiley and Sons, 1982), pp. 163–166.

Chapter 21

[1]Technically the t-distribution should be used when the population variance is unknown and the standard deviation is estimated from sample data. However, with large samples it is convenient to use the Z-distribution, because the t-distribution approximates the Z-distribution.
[2]A complete discussion of this topic is beyond the scope of this book. See almost any statistics textbook for a more detailed discussion of Type I and Type II errors.
[3]A more complex discussion of the differences between parametric and nonparametric statistics appears in Appendix 22A.
[4]The reader with an extensive statistics background will recognize that there are a few rare cases in which the degrees of freedom do not equal k - 1. However, these cases will rarely be encountered by readers of this level of book, and to present them would only confuse the discussion here.
[5]An example of how to use the chi-square table is given in Table A.4 of the Appendix.

Chapter 22

[1]Joseph M. Winski, "Study: The Customer Ain't Me." Reprinted with permission from the January 20, 1992, issue of Advertising Age. © Crain Communications, Inc., 1992.
[2]Three nonparametric tests—the Wilcoxon matched-pairs signed-ranks test, the Kruskal-Wallis test, and the Mann-Whitney U test—and ANOVA for complex experimental designs are covered in appendixes to this chapter.
[3]A one-way analysis of variance may also be referred to as a single-factor analysis of variance, because only one variable (factor) is manipulated.
[4]At first, the appearance of and looks complicated. Our example shows that the procedure is not difficult, but it does require that each observation for within a group (n) be summed up and then these totals summed for all groups (c). Sum of squares is an abbreviated term for "sum of the squared deviation scores."
[5]Adapted with the permission of Melvin Prince, Consumer Research for Management Decisions (New York: John Wiley and Sons, 1982), pp. 161–162.
[6]This section is reprinted with minor adaptations from Norma Gilbert, Statistics (Philadelphia: Saunders College Publishing, 1931), pp. 380–381.
[7]If a completely random relationship between the observations in each pair exists, the values of Tp and Tn are expected to be equal.
[8]This example is modified from Joseph Newmark, *Statistics and Probability in Modern Life* (New York: Holt, Rinehart and Winston, 1977), pp. 434–436.
[9]We assume no interaction effect between treatments and blocks.
[10]In the ANOVA table, it is conventional to place the treatments in the columns and the blocks in the rows. Because of this, SStreatments may be referred to as SScolumns and SSblocks or SSrows in some research reports.

Chapter 23

[2]For a discussion of the other measures of association, see the appendix to this chapter and Jean Dickinson Gibbons, *Nonparametric Methods for Quantitative Analysis* (New York: Holt, Rinehart and Winston, 1976).
[3]See Richard P. Bagozzi, "Salesforce Performance and Satisfaction as a Function of Individual Difference, Interpersonal and Situational Factors," *Journal of Marketing Research* (November 1978), pp. 517–531.
[4]To calculate a *t*-test under the null hypothesis *rho* = 0, *t* is distributed with *d.f. n - 2*:
$t = r/s$, where $s_r = ???\sqrt{1 - r^2/n - 2}$
Table A.7 of the appendix provides the critical value of *r* for the Pearson correlation coefficient to test the null hypothesis that *rho* equals zero.
[5]This is a point estimate. A confidence interval can be calculated for this sales estimate; however, the topic is beyond the scope of this book.
[6]Copyright © 1981, Dr. William J. Lundstrom, reprinted with permission.
[7]Portions of this section are reprinted, with adaptations, from Gerald Zaltman and Philip Burger, *Marketing Research* (Hinsdale, IL.: Dryden Press, 1976), pp. 448–449.
[8]For more detail, see A. M. Mood and F. A. Graybill, *Introduction to the Theory of Statistics*, 2nd ed. (New York: McGraw-Hill, 1963); and Jean Dickinson Gibbons, *Nonparametric Methods of Quantitative Analysis* (New York: Holt, Rinehart and Winston, 1976).
[9]This material is based on John T. Roscoe, *Fundamental Research for Behavioral Science* (New York: Holt, Rinehart and Winston, 1975), pp. 260–261.

Chapter 24

[1]Adapted with permission from Judith Waldrop, "Executive Downtime," American Demographics, August 1, 1993, p. 4.
[2]For excellent discussions of multivariate analysis, see Joseph F. Hair Jr., Rolph E. Anderson, Ronald L. Tatham, and Bernie J. Grablowsky, *Multivariate Data Analysis with Readings*, 3d ed. (New York: Macmillan, 1994).
[3]The purpose of this section is to discuss factor analysis techniques at an intuitive level. The discussion is not complicated by the various mathematically complex differences among the techniques. An excellent discussion of the mathematical aspects of factor analysis appears in R. J. Rummel, "Understanding Factor Analysis," *Journal of Conflict Resolution*, XI, no. 4, pp. 444–480.
[4]Edgar A. Pessemier, Albert C. Bemmaor, and Dominique M. Hanssens, "Willingness to Supply Human Body Parts: Some Empirical Results," Journal of Consumer Research 4 (December 1977), pp. 131–140.
[5]The multiple regression model assumes that the independent variables are independent of one another. Multicollinearity is the technical term used when some of the predictor variables are correlated with one another. For example, the consumer price index and the federal mortgage rate both show a similar historical trend. Thus, it would be difficult to appraise each one's distinct influence on a dependent variable, rather than their joint influence.
[6]See Ronald E. Frank and Paul E. Green, "Numerical Taxonomy in Marketing Analysis: A Review Article," *Journal of Marketing Research* (February 1968), pp. 83–98.
[7]Adapted from Kent L. Granzin and Donald M. Jensen, "Market Segmentation and the Professional Basketball Market." (Paper presented at the American Marketing Association Conference, Chicago, August 1984). Reprinted with permission. Published by American Marketing Association.

Chapter 25

[1]This chapter was written by John Bush, Oklahoma State University. It originally appeared in William G. Zikmund, *Business Research Methods* (Hinsdale, IL: Dryden Press, 1984) and is adapted with permission.

[2]"A Speech Tip," *Communication Briefings,* 14(2), p. 3.

[3]Adapted with permission from Marjorie Brody, president, Brody Communications, 1200 Melrose Ave., Melrose Park, PA 19126, as it appeared in "How to Gesture When Speaking," *Communication Briefings* 14(11), p. 4.

[4]Randall L. Schultz, Gerald Zaltman, and Philip C. Burger, *Cases in Marketing Research,* pp. 229–230, published in 1975 by The Dryden Press, a division of Harcourt Brace College Publishers.

Credits

Chapter 1

Exhibit 1.2: Courtesy of General Electric Corporation; P. 16: WHAT WENT RIGHT? adapted with permission from Ian P. Murphy, "Ameritech Test Towns Market Innovation," *Marketing News*, November 18, 1996, p. 2; P. 19: WHAT WENT WRONG? from "Revised Pillsbury Spot in the Pink," *Advertising Age*, February 13, 1986, p. 15; Video Case 1.1: Hard Candy, adapted with permission from Louis E. Boone and David L. Kurtz, *Contemporary Business*, 9th edition, (Fort Worth, TX: Dryden Press, 1999) pp. 719-720.

Photo Credits: P. 1: © 1999 Don Couch Photography; P. 5: Courtesy of Partnership for a Drug-Free America; P. 7: © 1999 Don Couch Photography; P. 9: © Michael Newman/PhotoEdit/PNI; P. 21: Photo courtesy of Colgate Palmolive Company.

Chapter 2

Chapter 2 opening vignette adapted with permission from Jennifer deJone, "View From the Top," *Inc. Technology*, #1, 1995, downloaded from the Internet July 3, 1998; P. 33: © 1998 *Wired*, Condé Nast Publications; P. 35: WHAT WENT WRONG? adapted from "Special K Drops Thin Models," *Associated Press*, February 6, 1998; P. 36: RESEARCH INSIGHT excerpt reprinted with permission from Regis McKenna, *Real Time* (Boston: Harvard Business School Press, 1997), pp. 3-4; P. 42: WHAT WENT RIGHT? adapted with permission from Miryam Williams, "Getting to Know You," *WebMaster Magazine*, September 1996; Case 2.1: Bank Montreal, adapted with permission from Julia King, "Decision-support Software Cuts Loan Processing Time," *ComputerWorld*, February 19, 1996; Video Case 2.1: Fossil, adapted with permission from Louis E. Boone and David L. Kurtz, *Contemporary Business*, 9th edition, (Fort Worth, TX Dryden Press, 1999), p. 407.

Photo Credits: P. 27: © Bill Horsman/Stock, Boston/PNI; P. 28: © 1999 Don Couch Photography; P. 30: © Michael St. Maur Shiell/Black Star/PNI; P. 33: Screen shot courtesy of Environmental Systems Research Institute; P. 40: Screen shot courtesy of NetLingo. Copyright © 1999 NetLingo; P. 44 (top three): Screen shots courtesy of YAHOO! Copyright © 1999 YAHOO!; P. 44 (bottom): Screen shot courtesy of Merriam-Webster, Inc. Copyright © 1999 Merriam-Webster, Inc.; P. 45: Screen shots courtesy of WebCrawler. Copyright © 1999 WebCrawler ; P. 47 Screen shot courtesy of PointCast. Copyright © 1999 PointCast.

Chapter 3

P. 57: EXPLORING RESEARCH ETHICS "The Elephant's Child," from Rudyard Kipling, *Just So Stories*; P. 66 WHAT WENT WRONG? adapted from Willard I. Zangwill, "Manager's Journal: When Customer Research is a Lousy Idea," *The Wall Street Journal*, March 8, 1993, p. A12; P. 68: WHAT WENT RIGHT? adapted with permission from Gerry Khermouch, "Sticking Their Neck Out," *Brandweek*, November 9, 1998, pp. 225-234; Video Case 3.1: Paradigm Entertainment, from Louis E. Boone and David L. Kurtz, *Contemporary Business*, 9th edition, (Fort Worth, TX Dryden Press, 1999), p. 38; Case 3.3: Frito Lay, reprinted with permission from Jennifer Lach, "From Bland to Brand: Frito-Lay Adds Some Spice to Win Over Hispanics," *American Demographics*, March 1999, P. 57.

Photo Credits: P. 53: © AP/Wide World Photos; P. 56 Copyright © 1999 Kimberly-Clark Corporation; P. 63: Focus Suites of Philadelphia; P. 64: © 1999 Don Couch Photography.

Chapter 4

Exhibit 4.1: Courtesy of General Foods; P. 84: WHAT WENT WRONG? Dudley M. Ruch, "Getting the Lowdown on the Role of Marketing Research in the Corporation," *Advertising Age*, October 18, 1982, M25. Used with permission. Copyright 1982 © Crain Communications; Exhibit 4.7: Excerpt reprinted with permission from "Honomichi Global Top 25," *Marketing News*, August 17, 1998; P. 92: Courtesy of A.C. Nielsen; Exhibit 4.9: "AMA Adopts New Code of Ethics," *Marketing News*, September 11, 1987, pp. 1, 10. Reprinted with permission. Published by American Marketing Association; Exhibit 4.10: Reprinted with permission of the Marketing Research Association, Inc., Chicago, Illinois; P. 102: WHAT WENT WRONG? excerpt reprinted with permission from Cynthia Crossen, *Tainted Truth* (New York: Simon and Schuster, 1994), p. 95; P. 103: WHAT WENT WRONG? adapted with permission from Bruce Horovitz, "Privacy Flap Sinks AmEx Database Deal," *USA Today*, July 15, 1998, p. B1; Case 4.2 Epicurious Food: Privacy Policy reprinted with permission of Epicurious Food.

Photo Credits: P. 77: © Peter Van Rhijn/Superstock; P. 104 Screen shot courtesy of TRUSTe. Copyright © 1999 TRUSTe.

Chapter 5

P. 114: EXPLORING RESEARCH ISSUES adapted from Charles Ramond, *The Art of Using Science in Marketing*, p. 17, © 1974 Harper & Row Publishers, Inc. Reprinted with permission; P. 119: WHAT WENT RIGHT? from Patrick Coyne, "The ACD Conference on Interactive Media," *Communication Arts*, January/February 1995, pp. 135-140. Excerpted with permission from Coyne & Blanchard, Inc.; P. 122: WHAT WENT WRONG? from Martin Weinberger, "Seven Perspectives on Consumer Research," *Marketing Research: A Magazine of Management and Applications*, December 1989, pp. 9-17; Exhibit 5.7: based on *A General Taxpayer Opinion Survey*, Office of Planning and Research, Internal Revenue Service, March 1980; Case 5.1 EZPass: excerpt reprinted with permission from Paul E. Green, Abba M. Krieger, and Terry G. Varra, "Evaluating New Products," *Marketing Research: A Magazine of Management and Applications*, Winter 1997, pp. 17-18.

Photo Credits: P. 113: © Amos Nachooum/The Image Bank; P.121: © PhotoDisc.

Chapter 6

Exhibit 6.1: Glen L. Urban and John R. Hauser, *Design and Marketing of New Products*, © 1980 Prentice-Hall, Inc. Reprinted by permission; P. 147: WHAT WENT RIGHT? adapted from David Walker, "Rubbermaid Tries Its Hand at Bristles and Wood," ADWEEK'S *Marketing Week*, March 5, 1990, pp. 20-21. Adapted with permission of ADWEEK'S *Marketing Week*, Ad Source: Courtesy Rubbermaid Incorporated, Wooster, Ohio. Agency: DDB Needham Worldwide, Inc.; Exhibit 6.2: "Charlie Haas on Advertising," *New West Magazine*, November 5, 1979, pp. 32-39; Exhibit 6.3: Betsy D. Gelb and Michael P. Eriksen, "Market Research May Help Prevent Cancer," *Marketing Research*, September 1991, p. 46. Published by American Marketing Association. Reprinted by permission.; Exhibit 6.5: from Donald F. Cox, Ed., *Risk Taking and Information Handling in Consumer Behavior*, (Boston: Division of Research, Harvard Business School) © 1967, pp. 65-66. Reprinted by permission; Case Exhibit 6.1-1: William G. Zikmund and William J. Lundstrom, *A Collection of Outstanding Cases in Marketing Management* (St. Paul, MN: West Publishing, 1979). All rights reserved; Case 6.2 Today's Man, adapted with permission from Mike Hoffman, "Hocus-Pocus Focus," *Inc.*, July 1998, p. 90.

Photo Credits: P. 135: Harcourt Photo/Annette Coolidge; P. 137: © Bob Daemmrich Photography; P. 141: © Joseph Devenney/The Image Bank; P. 145: © Jed Jacobsohn/AllSport USA; P. 146: ©Alexander Vertikoff/J. Paul Getty Museum; P. 155: © Tony Freeman/PhotoEdit.

Chapter 7

Chapter 7 opening vignette reprinted with permission with minor adaptation from Tom Maguire, "Gettin' in the Swing of Things," *American Demographics*, January 1999; P. 178 WHAT WENT WRONG? adapted with permission from Dan Fost, "How to Think About the Future," *American Demographics*, February 1998; P. 181 WHAT WENT RIGHT? excerpt reprinted with permission from Bill Gates, *The Road Ahead* (New York: Viking Penguin, 1995), p. 138; P. 184 WHAT WENT RIGHT? excerpt reprinted with permission from Janet Novack, "The Data Miners," *Forbes*, February 12, 1996.

Appendix 7B

PP. 213-214: ProQuest screen shots courtesy of ProQuest Direct © Bell & Howell Information and Learning.

Photo Credits: P. 169: © Leonard Ignelzi/AP Wide World Photos; P. 176: ©James Marshall/Corbis Images; P. 182: Copyright © TIBCO.

Chapter 8

P. 224: EXPLORING RESEARCH ISSUES excerpt adapted with permission from Carole Sugarman, *Washington Post* Staff Writer, "Eating Right: Americans Ask, 'Why Not Beef?' Increase in Consumption Seems More a Matter of Price Than Nutrition," *Washington Post*, January 17, 1995; P. 226: WHAT WENT WRONG? Christy Marshall, "Here's the Word on Surveys About Burger Favorites," adapted with permission from the March 21, 1983 issue of *Advertising Age*. Copyright © 1983 by Crain Communications, Inc.; P. 232: WHAT WENT RIGHT? Becky Ebenkamp, "Scotchgard Will Talk to Consumers," *Brand Week*, September 21, 1998, p. 9; Exhibit 8.4: Adapted from David A. Aaker, *Managing Brand Equity* (New York: Macmillan, 1991), pp. 90-95.

Photo Credits: P. 217: © 1999 Don Couch Photography; P. 219: © PhotoDisc; P. 220: © 1999 Don Couch Photography; P. 221: Jeff Zaruba, courtesy of Marriott International; P. 223: © David Hiser/Tony Stone Images; P. 225: © 1999 Don Couch Photography; P. 227: © Charles Gupton/Tony Stone Images.

Chapter 9

PP. 250-251: EXPLORING RESEARCH ISSUES: Adapted from *A General Taxpayer Opinion Survey*, "Office of Planning and Research, Internal Revenue Service, 1980; P. 257: EXPLORING RESEARCH ISSUES adapted with permission from Sally Beatty, Ameritech's New Phone Service Aims to Keep Telemarketers at Bay," *The Wall Street Journal*, September 23, 1998, p. B10.; Exhibit 9.1 Courtesy of Washington State University and Don A. Dillman, *Mail and Telephone Surveys: The Total Design Method* (New York: John Wiley & Sons, 1978), p. 169; Case 9.3: PC Ratings, reprinted with permission from the Home Testing Institute.

Photo Credits: P. 252 © Dave G. Houser/Corbis Images; P. 260: © 1999 Don Couch Photography; P. 269 (left): © C. Bruce Forster/AllStock/PNI; P. 269 (center) © 1999 Don Couch Photography; P. 269 (right): © 1999 Don Couch Photography; P. 270: © Greenfield Online.

Chapter 10

PP. 288-289: WHAT WENT RIGHT? adapted with permission from Erik Larson's "Attention Shoppers: Don't Look Now, but You Are Being Tailed." Copyright © 1993 by Erik Larson. First appeared in *Smithsonian* magazine. Reprinted by permission of Georges Borchardt, Inc. for the author; Exhibit 10.2: Excerpted from Nancy M. Henley, *Body Politics: Power, Sex, and Nonverbal Communication* (New York: Simon & Schuster, 1977), p. 181; P. 292: WHAT WENT WRONG? Howard B. Waitzkin, "Information Giving and Medical Care," *Journal of Health and Social Behavior* 26 (1985), pp. 81-101; Case 10.1: Texas Instruments and E-Lab, adapted with permission from Bruce Rayner, "Product Development, Now Hear This!" *Electronic Business*, August 1997; Case Exhibit 10.3.1: U.S. Bureau of the Census.

Photo Credits: P. 285: © Superstock; P. 286: © 1999 Don Couch Photography; P. 289: Iowa Field Research, Ankeny, Iowa, a division of the Grapentine Company; P. 291: Courtesy of International Business Machines Corporation; P. 296: Illustration of Personal Harbor office systems module courtesy of Steelcase, Inc.

Chapter 11

Exhibit 11.1: Reprinted by permission from the *Journal of Marketing*, published by the American Marketing Association, J. Edward Russo, Gene Krieser, and Sally Miyashita, "An Effective Display of Unit Price Information," April 1975, p. 14; P. 320: EXPLORING RESEARCH ISSUES Hervert Kelman, "Human Use of Human Subjects: The Problem of Deception in Social Psychological Experiments," *Psychological Bulletin* (January 1967), pp. 1-11; Case 11.3: Family Circle, from Rebecca McPheters, *The Family Circle Study of Print Advertising Effectiveness* (New York: The New York Times Magazine Group—Women's Publishing Division, 1991).

Photo Credits: P. 307 © Harcourt photo/Annette Coolidge.

Chapter 12

Chapter 12 opening vignette adapted with permission from Betsy Spethmann, "Test Market USA," *Brandweek*, May 8, 1995, pp. 40-41 ; P. 351 WHAT WENT RIGHT? based on National Public Radio, "All Things Considered," February 8, 1983; and Paul Soloman and Thomas Friedman, *Life and Death on the Corporate Battlefield* (New York: Simon & Schuster, 1983), pp. 26-27; P. 352: Wow! Sales Curve from Judann Pollack, "Frito Claims Success, *Advertising Age*, July 20, 1998, p. 30; Exhibit 12.3: Reprinted by permission of *Harvard Business Review*, "New Technology Helps Managers Envision the Future," Raymond R. Burke, March-April 1996, p. 130. Copyright © 1996 by the President and Fellows of Harvard College. All rights reserved; P. 361: EXPLORING RESEARCH ISSUES "A Lethal Interaction," Ya-Lun Chou, *Statistical Analysis with Business and Economics Applications* (Fort Worth: Holt, Rinehart and Winston, 1975), p. 365.

Photo Credits: P. 341: © PhotoDisc; P. 346: © 1999 Don Couch Photography; P. 349 © Tony Stone Images.

Chapter 13

Chapter 13 opening vignette adapted with permission from "Gary Levin, "Emotion Guides BBDO's Ad Tests," *Advertising Age*, January 29, 1990, p. 12. Copyright © 1990 Crain Communications, Inc. Exhibit 13.1: National Bureau of Standards, Washington, DC; Exhibit 13.2: Modified from materials in Michael D. Cozzens and Noshir S. Contractor, "The Effect of Conflicting Information on Media Skepticism," *Communications Research*, August 1987, pp. 437-451; Exhibit 13.5: From Keith K. Cox and Ben M. Enis, *The Marketing Research Process* (Pacific Palisades, CA: Goodyear, 1972), pp. 353-355. Adapted with permission from Scott, Foresman and Company. See also *Foundations of Behavioral Research*, 3rd Edition, by Fred N. Kerlinger (Fort Worth: Holt, Rinehart and Winston, Inc., 1986); CASE 13.1 Lieberman Research, Inc., based on Lieberman Research, Inc. *The Male Food Shopper: How Men are Changing Food Shopping in America*, sponsored by Campbell's Soup Company and People magazine; Case Exhibit 13.3-2 and Case Exhibit 13.3-3: Reprinted with permission from Margaret Sheryl Nance-Nash, "The Places to Live in Today," *Money*, September, 1995, pp. 126, 130.

Photo Credits: P. 368: Courtesy of BBDO, Chicago.

Chapter 14

Chapter 14 opening vignette adapted with permission from "Redbook Survey Uncovers 'New Wife' in Ranks of Young Married Women," PointCast Network, August 21, 1996; P. 387: EXPLORING RESEARCH ISSUES *Psychology Today: An Introduction* (Del Mar, CA: CRM Books, 1970), p. 613; Exhibit 14.2: Stephen W. Brown and Teresa A. Swarts, "A Gap Analysis of Professional Service Quality," *Journal of Marketing*, April 1989, p. 95. Reprinted with permission; Exhibit 14.3: Joel Huber and

Morris B. Holbrook, "Using Attribute Ratings for Product Positioning: Some Distinctions Among Compositional Approaches," *Journal of Marketing Research*, November 1979, p. 510. Reprinted with permission of American Marketing Association; Exhibit 14.4: J. Richard Jones and Sheila I. Cocke, "A Performance Evaluation of Commuter Airlines: The Passengers' View," *Proceedings*, Transportation Research Forum, Vol. 22 (1981), p. 524. Reprinted with permission; Exhibit 14.5: Dennis Menezes and Norbert F. Elbert, "Alternate Semantic Scaling Formats for Measuring Store Image: An Evaluation," *Journal of Marketing Research*, (February 1979), pp. 80-87. Reprinted by permission of American Marketing Association; Case 14.1: Ha-Pah-Shu-Tse, adapted with permission from Roger D. Blackwell and W. Wayne Talarzyk, *Consumer Attitudes Toward Health Care and Medical Malpractice* (Columbus, OH: Grid, 1977). The research reported in this case was conducted under a grant from the Malpractice Research Fund of the Ohio State Medical Association. From W. Wayne Talarzyk, Contemporary Cases in Marketing, 2nd edition, published in 1979 by The Dryden Press.

Photo Credits: P. 385 © Bob Thomas/Tony Stone Images; P. 404 © 1999 Don Couch Photography.

Chapter 15

Chapter 15 opening vignette from Charles W. Roll, Jr. and Albert H. Cantril, *Polls: Their Use and Misuse in Politics* (New York: Basic Books, 1972), p. 106; P. 415: EXPLORING RESEARCH ISSUES "What a Difference Words Make," Stephen A. Greyser and Raymond A. Bauer, "Americans and Advertising," *Public Opinion Quarterly*, 30, Spring 1966, pp. 69-78. Reprinted by permission of Elsevier Science Publishing Co., Inc.; Exhibit 15.1: Don A. Dillman, *Mail and Telephone Surveys: The Total Design Method* (New York: John Wiley & Sons, 1978), p. 209. Reprinted with permission; P. 426: EXPLORING RESEARCH ISSUES From Omar J. Bendikas, "One-step Questionnaire May Overstate Response: Two-step Questionnaires Hike Involvement, Accuracy," *Marketing News*, May 18, 1979, p. 9. Reprinted with permission; Exhibit 15.2: "General Foods Corporation: Tang Instant Breakfast Drink (B)," © 1978 F. Stewart DeBruicker and Harvey N. Singer, The Wharton School, University of Pennsylvania, Reprinted with permission; Exhibit 15.5: Reprinted by permission from Research Services, Inc. of Denver, CO and the United Bank of Boulder, CO; Exhibit 15.7: from IBM Management Staff Booklet for Systems Design, 1975. (Z140-3008-2 U/M 001); Case 15.2: GTE Airfone, authorization for limited use granted by GTE Airfone, Inc.

Photo Credits: P. 411: © C.T. Tracy/FPG International; P. 416: © 1999 Don Couch Photography.

Chapter 16

Exhibit 16.1: Adapted with permission from A.D. Fletcher and T.A. Bowers, *Fundamentals of Advertising Research* (Columbus, OH: Grid Publishing, 1983), pp. 60-61; P. 464: EXPLORING RESEARCH ISSUES Reprinted with permission from "Millennium Milestones: William's census was ahead of its time," *Tulsa World*, March 27, 1999, p. A-3. © Gannett News Service; P. 466: WHAT WENT RIGHT? From "George Gallup's Nation of Numbers," *Esquire*, December 1983, pp. 91-92; P. 471: EXPLORING RESEARCH ETHICS "The Privacy Debate," *Advertising Age*, October 17, 1988, pp. 12-13 and Diane K. Bowers, "The Privacy Challenger," *Marketing Researcher*, September 1991, p. 61; P. 472: WHAT WENT WRONG? From David G. Meyers, *Exploring Psychology* (New York: Worth Publishers, 1990), p. 471; Exhibit 16.4: Adapted with permission from Scott, Foresman and Company, from Keith K. Cox and Ben M. Enis, *The Marketing Research Process*, (Pacific Palisades, CA: Goodyear, 1972) and Danny N. Bellenger and Barnet A. Greenberg, *Marketing Research: A Management Information Approach* (Homewood, IL: Richard D. Irwin, 1978), pp. 154-155; Exhibit 16.5: Courtesy of Nielsen Marketing Research, Northbrook, IL; Exhibit 16.7: From *Interviewer's Manual*, Revised Edition (Ann Arbor, MI: Survey Research Center, Institute for Social Research, University of Michigan, 1976) p. 36. Reprinted by permission; Exhibit 16.8:

From "Geography—Concepts and Products," *U.S. Bureau of the Census—Factfinder for the Nation*, August 1985, p. 3.; Case 16.1: A.C. Nielsen—Can You Trust TV Ratings? excerpts adapted with permission from "Watching Americans Watch TV," *Atlantic Monthly*, March 1992; Case 16.2: Scientific Telephone Samples. Material for this case is used with permission from Scientific Telephone Samples' User's Manual, Scientific Telephone Samples, Griffin Towers, 6 Hutton Center Drive, Suite 1245, Santa Ana, CA 92707.

Photo Credits: Cartoon P. 461 by Charles Saxon, New Canaan, CT, Reprinted with permission; P. 470 © Hugh Sitton/Tony Stone Images; Cartoon P. 477: Reprinted with permission from *Advertising Age*, June 12, 1979, p. 12. Copyright © Crain Communications, Inc.

Chapter 17

P. 498: EXPLORING RESEARCH ISSUES From Darrell Huff and Irving Geis, *How to Lie with Statistics* (New York: W.W. Norton, 1954), p. 33. Adapted with permission; Exhibit 17.4: Thomas H. Wonnacott and Ronal J. Wonnacott, *Introductory Statistics* (New York: John Wiley & Sons, 1969), p. 70. Reprinted with permission; Exhibit 17.6: Adapted from D.H. Sanders , A.F. Murphy, and R.J. Eng, *Statistics: A Fresh Approach*, (McGraw-Hill, 1980), p. 123. Used with permission of McGraw-Hill Book Co.; Exhibit 17.7: Ernest Kurnow, Gerald J. Glasser, and Frederick R. Ottman, *Statistics for Business Decisions* (Homewood, IL: Richard D. Irwin, 1959), pp. 182-183. Used with permission; Exhibit 17.8: From Fred N. Kerlinger, *Foundations of Behavioral Research*, (Holt, Rinehart & Winston, 1986), p. 117. Adapted with permission; Table 17.11: From Nan Lin, *Foundations of Social Research*, p. 447. Copyright © 1976 by Nan Lin. Used with permission; Table 17.12: From Nan Lin, *Foundations of Social Research*, p. 447. Copyright © 1976 by Nan Lin. Used with permission; Case 17.2: The New York Times/CBS News Poll from "How the Poll Was Conducted," *The New York Times*, December 13, 1992, p. Y19. Copyright © 1992 by The New York Times Company. Reprinted with permission.

Photo Credits: Cartoon P. 493 by Tony Hall, from Sarah M. Dinham, *Exploring Statistics: An Introduction for Psychology and Education* (Pacific Grove, CA: Brooks/Cole Publishing, 1976), title page. Reprinted by permission.

Chapter 18

Chapter 18 opening vignette reprinted with permission from Randy Minkoff, "Matters of Opinion: Foot Soldiers of Marketing Research Battle for a Moment of Your Time in the Mall," *Chicago Tribune*, July 5, 1998. P. 533: WHAT WENT WRONG? from "Census to Target American Indians," *The Associated Press*, August 6, 1998; P. 534: EXPLORING RESEARCH ETHICS "Horse Race: All Polls Are Not Created Equal," Outlook, *U.S. News & World Report*, September 28, 1992; Exhibit 18.1: *Interviewer's Manual*, Revised Edition (Ann Arbor, MI: Survey Research Center, Institute for Social Research, University of Michigan, 1976), p. 16. Reprinted by permission; Exhibit 18.2: *Interviewer's Manual*, Revised Edition (Ann Arbor, MI: Survey Research Center, Institute for Social Research, University of Michigan, 1976), p. 26. Reprinted by permission; Case 18.2: United States Census Bureau, reprinted with permission from Haya El Nasser, "The Nation's Homepage: How Sampling Would Work," *USA Today*, November 29, 1998.

Photo Credits: P. 529 © Stuart Cohen/The Stock Market; P. 532 © Ann Purcell/Corbis Photos.

Chapter 19

Exhibit 19.1: John A. Sonquist and William C. Dunkelberg, *Survey and Opinion Research: Procedures for Processing and Analysis* (Englewood Cliffs, NJ: Prentice-Hall, 1977), p. 8. Adapted with permission; Exhibit 19.5: Reprinted from the 1976 U.S. *News & World Report Study of American Opinion*, published by U.S. News & World Report, Inc.; Exhibit 19.6: From A.R. Automarket Research, P.O. Box 5021, Southfield, Michigan 48086-

5021; Exhibit 19.8: Walker Research, "Coding Open Ends Based on Thoughts," *The Marketing Researcher*, December 1979, pp. 1-3. Used by permission; Table 19.1: Reprinted with permission of the State of Hawaii, Department of Transportation; Exhibit 19.10: Pittsburgh Pirates Fan Survey; Case 19.2: Shampoo 9-10 (The name of this product is fictitious.) adapted with permission from Jeffrey L. Pope, *Practical Marketing Research*, (New York: AMA-COM, 1981), pp. 90-92. Copyright © 1981 by AMA-COM, a division of American Management Associates. All rights reserved.

Photo Credits: P. 555 © Mark E. Gibson; P. 571 © Jeff Zaruba.

Chapter 20

Chapter 20 opening vignette excerpt reprinted with permission from Judith Waldrop, "Most Restaurant Meals are Bought on Impulse," *American Demographics*, February 1, 1994, p. 16; Table 20.2: Calculated from Census Bureau, "Population Projections for Stats for Age, Sex, Race, and Hispanic Origin: 1993 to 2020," as reported in "Three Guesses," *American Demographics*, October 1994, p. 41; Table 20.3: From Roger Ricklefs, "Ethics in America," *The Wall Street Journal*, October 31, 1983, pp. 33, 42; November 1, 1983, p. 33; November 2, 1983, p. 33; and November 3, 1983, pp. 33, 37; Table 20.6: Adapted from 1987 Nielsen Television Report; P. 593: WHAT WENT RIGHT? Adapted with permission from David G. Meyers, *Exploring Psychology*, (New York: Worth Publishers, 1990), p. 464; Exhibit 20.4: "Salaries (Constant 1992 Dollars)," *Forbes*, September 14, 1992, p. 282. Reprinted with permission of *Forbes* magazine. Copyright © 1992 Forbes, Inc.; Exhibit 20.5: From *Advertising Age*, February 25, 1990, p. S-2. Reprinted with permission. Copyright © 1990 by Crain Communications, Inc.; Exhibit 20.8: From *SPSSX User's Guide*, 3rd Ed. (Chicago: SPSS, Inc.), p. 667; Exhibit 20.9: From *Real Stats Real Easy, SPSS for Windows*, Copyright © 1992, SPSS, Inc. Reprinted with permission of SPSS, Inc.; Exhibit 20.10: From *Making STAT Magic*, Copyright © 1984, SPSS, Inc. Reprinted with permission of SPSS, Inc.; Exhibit 20.12: From "Graphic Displays of Data: Box and Whisker Plots," *Market Facts*, Inc.; P. 599: EXPLORING RESEARCH ETHICS Sidney Diamond, "Market Research Latest Target in Ad Claim," *Advertising Age*, January 25, 1982, p. 52. Reprinted with permission. Copyright ©1982 by Crain Communications, Inc.; Case 20.3: Downy-Q Quilt, adapted with permission from Melvin Prince, Consumer Research for Management Decisions (New York: John Wiley and Sons, 1982), pp. 163-166.

Photo Credits: P. 579 © Peter L. Chapman/Stock, Boston/PNI; P. 581 © AP Photo/Coca-Cola Company; P. 593 © Mercury Archives/The Image Bank.

Chapter 21

Photo Credits: P. 612 © Bob Daemmrich/Stock, Boston/PNI.

Chapter 22

Chapter 22 opening vignette reprinted with permission from Joseph M. Winski, "Study: The Customer Ain't Me," *Advertising Age*, January 20, 1992. Copyright © 1992 by Crain Communications, Inc.

Photo Credits: P. 633 © PhotoDisc.

Chapter 23

P. 676: EXPLORING RESEARCH ISSUES "Causality," Charles Ramond, *The Art of Using Science in Marketing* (New York: Harper & Row, 1979), pp. 20-21; P. 680: EXPLORING RESEARCH ISSUES reprinted with permission from Lewis E. Walkup, "Walkup's First Five Laws of Statistics," *The Bent*, a publication of Tau Beta Pi, Summer, 1974, p. 43, as quoted in Robert W. Joselyn, *Designing the Marketing Research Project* (New York: Petrocelli/Charter, 1977), p. 175. Copyright © 1977 by Petrocelli/Charter Co. Reprinted by permission of Van Nostrand Reinhold; P. 684: EXPLORING RESEARCH ISSUES "A Note of Caution about Forecasting," quoted passage from *Life on the*

Mississippi, by Mark Twain. Originally copyrighted in 1874; Case 23.2: Center for American Enterprise: *A Study of Psychological and Demographic Contributors to Consumerism*, reprinted with permission of Dr. William J. Lundstrom. Copyright © 1981.

Photo Credits: P. 671 © Pierre DuCharme/Reuters/Archive Photos.

Chapter 24

Chapter 24 opening vignette adapted with permission from Judith Waldrop, "Executive Downtime," *American Demographics*, August 1, 1993, p. 4; Exhibit 24.4: The idea for this table was generated from information from D.S. Tull and G. Albaum, *Survey Research: A Decisional Approach*, p. 218. Copyright © 1973 by Intext Educational Publishers. Reprinted by permission of Harper and Row Publishers, Inc.; Table 24.4: Reprinted from Edgar A. Pessemier, Albert C. Bemmaor, and Dominique Hanssenns, "Willingness to Supply Human Body Parts: Some Empirical Results," *Journal of Consumer Research*, 4, December 1977, Table 2, p. 134; Table 24.5: Reprinted with permission from Paul E. Green, Ronald E. Frank, and Patrick J. Robinson, "Cluster Analysis in Text Market Selection," *Management Science*, 13, April 1967, p. B393 (Table 2). Copyright © 1967 by The Institute of Management Sciences; P. 710: EXPLORING RESEARCH ISSUES Jagdish N. Sheth, "Seven Commandments for Users of Multivariate Methods," in Multivariate Methods, Jagdish N. Sheth, Ed., 1977, pp. 333-335. Published by American Marketing Association. Reprinted with permission; Exhibit 24.7: P.E. Green, F.J. Carmone, and P.J. Robertson, "Nonmetric Scaling Methods: An Exposition and Overview," *The Wharton Quarterly*, 2, 1968, pp. 159-173; Case 24.1: The Utah Jazz, reprinted with permission of Kent L. Granzin and Donald M. Jensen, "Market Segmentation and the Professional Basketball Market." Paper presented at the American Marketing Association Conference, Chicago, 1984. Published by American Marketing Association.

Photo Credits: P. 695: © Bob Woodward/Mountain Stock.

Chapter 25

Exhibit 25.5: Adapted from David M. Robinson, *Writing Reports for Management Decisions* (Columbus, OH: Merrill, 1969), p. 340. Reprinted with permission; Table 25.2: "Americans and Their Money," The fourth national survey from *Money* magazine, 1986, p. 49; Table 25.3: *Report to the Federal Trade Commission on the Effects of the STP "Public Notice" Advertising Campaign*, June 1979; Table 25.4: Reprinted from "Confidence in Church/Organized Religion," *The Gallup Report*, 238, July 1985; Exhibit 25.6: Adapted from Mary Eleanor Spear, *Practical Charting Techniques* (New York: McGraw-Hill, 1969), p. 56. Reprinted with permission; Exhibit 25.7: Adapted from Mary Eleanor Spear, *Practical Charting Techniques* (New York: McGraw-Hill, 1969), p. 57. Reprinted with permission; Exhibit 25.9: "A Series of Pie Charts," *Advertising Age International*, April 27, 1992, pp. 1-26/ Reprinted with permission. Copyright © 1992 Crain Communications, Inc.; Exhibit 25.10: From "The Lawsuit Industry," *Forbes*, September 14, 1992, p. 304. Reprinted with permission. Copyright © 1992 Forbes, Inc.; Exhibit 25.11: From *1987 Nielsen Report: Television*, p. 5. Reprinted with permission; Exhibit 25.12: From *Brandweek*, June 12, 1995, p. 31. Reprinted with permission; P. 737: EXPLORING RESEARCH ISSUES Adapted from William D. Wells, University of Minnesota, "Noah's Law of Overhead Transparencies," *ACR Newsletter*, June 1993, p. 10. Published by the Association for Consumer Research, Peter Bloch, 222 Middlebush Hall, University of Missouri, Columbia, MO 65211. Adapted with permission; Exhibit 25.13: "The Lawsuit Industry," *Forbes*, September 14, 1992, p. 304. Reprinted with permission. Copyright © 1992 Forbes, Inc.; Exhibit 25.14: IBM 1992 Annual Report, p. 34; Exhibit 25.15: *Advertising Age International*, April 27, 1992, pp. 1-26. Reprinted with permission. Copyright © 1992 Crain Communications, Inc.; Case 25.1: American Pharmaceutical Industries, from Randall L. Schultz, Gerald Zaltman, and Philip C. Burger, *Cases in Marketing Research*, published in 1975 by The Dryden Press, a division of Harcourt Brace College Publishers, pp. 229-230.

Index

http://www.att.com – AT&T
http://www.marriott.com – Marriott International
http://www.arbitron.com – The Arbitron Company
http://www.restaurant.org – National Restaurant
   Association
http://www.burgerking.com – Burger King Corp.
http://www.mcdonalds.com – McDonald's
   Corporation
http://www.colgate.com – Colgate-Palmolive Co.
http://www.nra.org – National Rifle Association
http://www.pampers.com – Proctor & Gamble
http://www.acnielsen.com – ACNielsen Corporation
http://www.dnb.com – Dun & Bradstreet, Inc.
http://www.commerce.net – CommerceNet
http://www.aol.com – America Online
http://www.3m.com – 3M
http://www.ikea.com – Ikea Systems
http://www.xerox.com – Xerox Corporation
http://www.ricoh-usa.com – Ricoh Corporation
http://www.canon.com – Canon Inc.
http://www.arborinc.com – Arbor, Inc.
http://www.bankone.com – Bank One Corporation
http://www.ropercenter.uconn.edu – Roper Center
http://www.asiresearch.com – ASI Research
http://www.msc.unisa.edu.au – Marketing Science
   Centre
http://www.thewalkergroup.com – The Walker
   Group, Inc.
http://www.yankelovich.com – Yankelovich
   Partners, Inc.

Chapter 9

http://www.ford.com – Ford Motor Company
http://www.chrysler.com – DaimlerChrysler
http://www.ameritech.com – Ameritech Corp.
http://www.acnielsen.com – ACNielsen Corporation
http://www.sotech.com – Socratic Technologies
http://www.americanresearchco.com – American
   Research Company, Inc.
http://www.surveyonline.com – SurveyOnline
http://www.aol.com – America Online
http://www.ama.org – American Marketing
   Association
http://www.cartalk.com – Car Talk
http://www.asiresearch.com – ASI Research
http://www.npd.com – NPD Group
http://www.customersat.com – CustomerSat.Com
http://www.walkerinfo.com – Walker Information

Chapter 10

http://www.envirosell.com – Envirosell Inc.
http://www.quakeroats.com – The Quaker Oats
   Company
http://www.revlon.com – Revlon
http://www.hallmark.com – Hallmark
http://www.bloomingdales.com – Bloomingdales
http://www.nrf.com – National Retail Federation
http://www.att.com – AT&T
http://www.fisher-price.com – Mattel, Inc.

http://www.msichicago.org – Chicago Museum of
   Science and Industry
http://www.ftc.gov – Federal Trade Commission
http://www.acnielsen.com – ACNielsen Corporation
http://www.steelcase.com – Steelcase Inc.
http://www.aol.com – America Online
http://www.toyota.com – Toyota

Chapter 11

http://www.crisco.com – Proctor & Gamble
http://www.wired.com – Wired Digital Inc.
http://www.pepsico.com – PepsiCo, Inc.
http://www.dow.com – The Dow Chemical
   Company
http://www.anheuser-busch.com – Anheuser-Busch
   Companies, Inc.
http://www.millerbrewing.com – Miller Brewing
   Company
http://www.bettycrocker.com – General Mills, Inc.
http://www.att.com – AT&T
http://www.mcdonalds.com – McDonald's
   Corporation
http://www.nbc.com – National Broadcasting
   Company
http://www.yahoo.com – Yahoo! Inc.

Chapter 12

http://www.wal-mart.com – Wal-Mart Stores, Inc.
http://www.target.com – Dayton-Husdon
   Brands, Inc.
http://www.pg.com – Proctor & Gamble
http://www.generalmills.com – General Mills, Inc.
http://www.nabisco.com – Nabisco
http://www.heinz.com – H.J. Heinz Company
http://www.mcdonalds.com – McDonald's
   Corporation
http://www.clorox.com – The Clorox Company
http://www.mattel.com – Mattel Inc.
http://www.fritolay.com – Recot, Inc.
http://www.millerbrewing.com – Miller Brewing
   Company
http://www.unilever.com – Unilever Corporation
http://www.colgate.com – Colgate-Palmolive Co.
http://www.jwtworks.com – J. Walter Thompson
http://www.nestle.com – Nestlè SA
http://www.demographics.com – American
   Demographics, Intertec Publishing Corporation

Chapter 13

http://www.bbdo.com – BBDO Worldwide
http://www.gillette.com – The Gillette Company
http://www.twa.com – Trans World Airlines
http://www.siu.edu/departments/mktg/OSR/ - Office
   of Scale Research

Chapter 14

http://redbook.women.com/rb/ - Redbook Magazine
   part of Women.com
http://www.chevy.com – General Motors Corp.